D0753141

WITHDRAWN

# DATE DUE

*The Interpretation of*

# St. Matthew's Gospel

By

## R. C. H. LENSKI

AUGSBURG PUBLISHING HOUSE

Minneapolis, Minnesota

TO
THE AMERICAN LUTHERAN
CONFERENCE

# ABBREVIATIONS

R. = A Grammar of the Greek New Testament in the Light of Historical Research, by A. T. Robertson, fourth edition.

B.-D. = Friedrich Blass' Grammatik des neutestamentlichen Griechisch, vierte, voellig neugearbeitete Auflage besorgt von Albert Debrunner

C.-K. = Biblisch-theologisches Woerterbuch der Neutestamentlichen Graezitaet von Dr. Hermann Cremer, zehnte, etc., Auflage, herausgegeben von D. Dr. Julius Koegel.

B.-P. = Griechisch-Deutsches Woerterbuch zu den Schriften des Neuen Testaments, etc., von D. Walter Bauer, zweite, etc., Auflage zu Erwin Preuschens Vollstaendigem Griechisch-Deutschen Handworterbuch, etc.

M.-M. = The Vocabulary of the Greek Testament, Illustrated from the Papyri and other Non-Literary Sources, by James Hope Moulton and George Milligan.

*Concordia Triglotta* = Triglot Concordia. The Symbolical Books of the Ev. Lutheran Church.

*Note.* — The translation is intended only as an aid in understanding the Greek.

# INTRODUCTION

## The Caption

The captions κατὰ Μαθθαῖον, κατὰ Μάρκον, etc., are traced back from the oldest of our manuscripts, the Vaticanus, 1209, (B), to Irenæus in 185, and to the earliest collections of apostolic writings in the incipient formation of a New Testament canon. The Latins had the translation *secundum Matthaeum*, etc., in their ancient versions, and the Egyptians likewise. The Syrians did not have it, because the written gospel first came to them in the composite work of their countryman Tatian, the so-called Diatessaron, in which the four records of the evangelists were combined.

In these elliptical κατά captions the only word we can supply is εὐαγγέλιον. In fact, this was soon added in some of the copies, sometimes with the addition of the adjective ἅγιον: "The Gospel (or the Holy Gospel) according to Matthew," etc. But εὐαγγέλιον, either when supplied or when added in these captions, was understood in its original sense: the substance or content of "the glad news" that in Jesus, God had fulfilled his Old Testament promises of a Savior and salvation. Paul used the verb εὐαγγελίζεσθαι in this sense in Pisidian Antioch: "we bring you glad tidings," how that the promise, which was made unto the fathers, God hath fulfilled, etc., Acts 13:32, etc. Likewise, when Mark begins his record with the caption: ἀρχὴ τοῦ εὐαγγελίου Ἰησοῦ Χριστοῦ, he intends to recount historically how this "glad news" began in the person and the work of Jesus Christ, thereafter to be proclaimed in all the world. This broad meaning of the term was accepted for many

(5)

years, so that we must understand the ancient captions in the sense: "as Matthew presents the gospel or glad news of our salvation"; "as Mark presents it"; etc. The only narrowing that occurred, and that quite naturally, was that εὐαγγέλιον came to mean also "the glad news" as presented historically in a written record. The word was used as a designation for one of the four books written by the evangelists. It thus came to be applied also to similar books in the pseudo-literature of the New Testament apocrypha, for instance, "The Gospel according to Peter."

In the old captions the preposition κατά retained its ordinary meaning: "according to," in the Latin, *secundum*. It did not directly indicate authorship, so that we cannot translate κατά "by": "By Matthew," "By Mark," etc. And yet authorship is most certainly included in this broad preposition. In these captions the sense of κατά is never that the records in question are compilations, made by others than Matthew, Mark, etc., and are only in a general way derived from the teachings of these men. We see this with all clearness in the case of Mark and of Luke. Mark drew all his material from Peter, yet his book is never called: "The Gospel according to Peter," but always: "The Gospel according to Mark," or simply: "According to Mark." Why? Because this historical version of "the glad news" was written by Mark himself; never because only the sources go back to Mark, while some writer, who drew from Mark and used his material, wrote the book. Back of Luke are Paul and the sources to which Luke himself points in 1:1-4; yet his Gospel was always designated "According to Luke." It was regarded as Luke's version of "the glad news" as written by Luke himself, not by another who only drew on materials furnished by Luke. These simple facts are decisive for the other two Gospels. "According to Matthew" and "According to John" are "the glad news," not merely

as derived from these two apostles by pupils of theirs
or by men who (innocently or otherwise) imperson-
ated them but as actually being written by them. It is
impossible to regard, either "critically" or otherwise,
the four identical captions, originally affixed to our
four Gospels by the church:

"According to Matthew,"
"According to Mark,"
"According to Luke,"
"According to John,"

in any but the identical sense: the version of each as
written by each. Whatever men are pleased to maintain today, the church never regarded one or two of
these κατά as meaning one thing, and the others something far different. If the versions of "the glad news"
ascribed to Mark and to Luke were penned by these
two men, then the other two versions were likewise
penned by the other two men.

This most ancient proof is quite decisive for determining the fact that the authorship of the First Gospel
can be ascribed to none other than to Matthew himself.
Reaching farther back than the patristic and the traditional statements, the testimony of the captions exceeds
theirs in weight and value. Only in one way could it
be invalidated, namely by direct evidence that the four
κατά were not understood in the same sense by the first
church. The critics do not admit the evidence of this κατά
phrase and deny that any of the four Gospels were written by the men to whom they have been attributed by the
ancient church. But their views do not affect the
cogency of our argument.

### The Earliest Use of Matthew

As far back as evidence goes, Matthew was regarded as the writer of the First Gospel, and his book

was also accepted as authoritative Holy Scripture, written under divine inspiration. We may point to the *Epistle of Barnabas* (130 A. D.) which regards Matt. 22:14, "Many are called, but few are chosen," as Holy Scripture, and which indicates by a combination of Matt. 9, verses 13 and 9, that Barnabas always considered this Gospel as having been composed by Matthew. We may note that in the year 120, in Rome and elsewhere, Matt. 2 was discussed in scholarly fashion with reference to the coming of the Magi to Bethlehem. We may examine the letters of Ignatius and of Polycarp, the friend of Papias, about 110 A. D. These letters give evidence that the congregations to whom they were addressed were entirely conversant with Matthew's Gospel. In his letter to the Ephesians the former refers to Matt. 2:1-12, and in other letters to Matt. 3:15 and 10:16. Polycarp proceeds in the same way. And we may add Clement of Alexandria and his namesake of Rome. A glance at the *Didache* or "Teaching of the Twelve Apostles" (also about 110 A. D.) shows that Matt. 6:9, etc., is used in admonishing Christians not to pray like hypocrites but to use the Lord's Prayer. This is quoted from Matthew with only minor liturgical changes and adds even the doxology, found in Matthew in abbreviated form. The *Didache* mentions "the Lord's yoke," Matthew 11:29, etc., quotes Matt. 7:6, shows knowledge of Matt. 28:19, etc., and in various ways reveals its intimacy with the Sermon on the Mount and with the First Gospel in general. All this is done in the way which one would expect at this early date. This early use of our Gospel makes the impression that Matthew, like the other three evangelists, was considered as one of the sacred writings, known and established as authoritative throughout the church for many years.

## John and Matthew

We come down to the end of the first century when John was still living and when he wrote his Gospel. John's Gospel interlocks with the other three and presupposes a knowledge of them on the part of his readers to such an extent that the final Gospel cannot be understood without them. Again and again John omits what his readers ought to be told but what they already know from Matthew, Mark, and Luke. Take John 1:6, 15 regarding the Baptist. John takes for granted that his readers are acquainted with Matt. 3:1, etc., and with the other Gospel accounts, which tell the Baptist's story in full. John's Gospel is nothing less than a multifarious attestation of the other three Gospels, including that of Matthew. In particular we must note that John assumes throughout, not only the existence of Matthew's Gospel, as well as that of Mark and of Luke, but also the full authority of all three in all the churches and the completest knowledge of their very words on the part of the members of the churches. Right in Ephesus where John wrote the other Gospels must have been used for years both in public worship and in constant instruction.

This superlative evidence from John's Gospel is often overlooked when the authorship, the authenticity, etc., of the other Gospels are examined. Yet it remains of supreme value. These other three Gospels really have a double apostolic attestation: that embodied in their own composition and that derived from the final Gospel. John's attestation remains, at least in part, even when critics let him contradict or correct the other Gospel writers. Only by denying John's authorship of the Fourth Gospel is his attestation to the other Gospels destroyed.

### The Hebrew Composition of Matthew

While the ancient church is absolutely unanimous in ascribing the First Gospel to Matthew, the man who occupies the seventh or the eighth place in the New Testament lists of the apostles, a number of ancient writers report that Matthew wrote something in Hebrew. The first word to this effect was written by Papias (125 A. D.) : Ματθαῖος μὲν οὖν ἑβραΐδι διαλέκτῳ τὰ λόγια συνετάξατο. "Now Matthew compiled the logia in the Hebrew dialect." Papias adds that each person translated these Hebrew logia as best he could. The main question is as to just what Papias understood by these logia. He does not say that he ever saw them or found them in use. He uses the aorist ἡρμήνευσε when he tells about the use to which they were put. This means that he is reporting an interesting historical fact, and that in his time these logia were no longer used and probably were not even any longer known. We next hear of Irenæus in the second half of the first century, who writes that Matthew issued "a gospel" in Hebrew at the time when Peter and Paul were preaching and founding the church in Rome (about 64-65 A. D.). Yet the church in Rome had been founded long before this time, and not by an apostle but by the Christian converts who had moved to Rome and brought their faith with them. Aside from this error, the question here is whether Irenæus has in mind the same writing as Papias, only calling the logia a Gospel, or whether he has in mind a different writing, an actual Gospel written in Hebrew by Matthew. Few would be willing to believe that Matthew wrote two different books in Hebrew.

Pantænus (about 180 A. D.) claims to have seen a Hebrew Gospel by Matthew in southern Arabia, which was brought there by Bartholomew. This report, however, has never had much influence. Next is the statement of Origen (born about 185 A. D.) which he makes on the basis of a tradition, that Matthew was the first to write and that he composed and issued a Gospel in Hebrew for the Jewish believers. Eusebius himself, who collected these opinions for his church history, expresses himself to the same effect. We may add that Jerome·(second half of the fourth century) thought that he had discovered Matthew's Hebrew Gospel in the Aramaic "Gospel of the Nazarenes," or "Gospel of the Hebrews," a Jewish Christian sect, but he himself later discovered his mistake.

## *The Hypothesis of an Original Hebrew Matthew*

Various forms of this hypothesis have been offered. One is that the logia of Papias were a collection of sayings by Jesus, which Matthew collected and published in Hebrew. In course of time, in the hands of the church, this nucleus received many additions, but these were not made by Matthew. Eventually this expanded Hebrew or Aramaic original was translated into Greek by some unknown writer and was at once accepted by the church without a single dissenting or questioning voice as "the Gospel according to Matthew," on a par with the Gospels according to Mark, Luke, and John. The translation into Greek may be dated as early as the year 65. Another prominent form of this hypothesis is that the logia of Papias really formed an entire Hebrew Gospel, originating from Matthew's pen in the years 64-67 and being translated into Greek by an unknown writer in the year 90 or thereabout. In some forms of this hypothesis Matthew furnishes but a small part of the Gospel which always bore his name. To overcome this obviously unpalatable view the logia of Papias are converted into a complete Hebrew Gospel with only the translation into Greek ascribed to the unknown writer. To support this view the effort is made to show that our present Greek Matthew in various places betrays the fact that it is not a Greek original but is written in translation Greek. In these hypotheses the idea of divine inspiration is openly or quietly set aside. In fact, these hypotheses are thought to offer freedom of interpretation. We may now emancipate ourselves from the task of harmonizing the four Gospel accounts. We may allow contradictions between Matthew and the other Gospels, especially John, or, if not open contradictions, then at least corrections. The field for this freedom is widened or narrowed according to what is made of the translator. He may be conceived as more than a translator, as a man who used his Hebrew sources in his own free way, or as a man who worked strictly according to his original.

A new hypothesis for the so-called synoptic problem is thus also produced. If Matthew wrote his Hebrew Gospel a little before Mark wrote his Greek Gospel, Mark could have used this Hebrew Gospel of Matthew's; and afterward, when the unknown translator rendered Matthew into Greek, he could have used Mark's Greek Gospel. The synoptic problem thus receives a new turn. And with these hypotheses to start from, the Gospels are re-examined to see what traces can be discovered in support of the hypotheses. Yet this method never leads to satisfactory results.

*The Hypothesis of a Hebrew Matthew Breaks Down*

Whatever Matthew wrote in Hebrew was so ephemeral that it disappeared completely at a date so early that even the earliest fathers never obtained sight of the writing. Nor can this undeniable fact be reduced by the remark that when Matthew was translated into Greek, this Greek at once superseded the Hebrew. Anything written in any language by one of the Twelve must have been highly prized and treasured accordingly. The translation could not have been made as late as the year 90. Then the Hebrew original would have been at hand at this late date. But Mark and Luke were available in Greek for a score of years prior to 90. Why, then, did the Hebrew Matthew continue in use to such an extent that finally a translation into Greek was deemed necessary? Again, if besides the Greek Mark and Luke the Hebrew of Matthew held its place until a translation was made in the year 90, it cannot be assumed that the original Hebrew should have disappeared completely so soon. However generally the Greek translation was used in the churches, it would be only a translation. The original of Matthew's Gospel would have been retained as being hallowed by the apostle's name and as being highly valuable for comparison with the translation. Even if the translation be dated much earlier, the value of the original would have led to its preservation. The conclusion is inevitable, Matthew himself never wrote an entire Gospel in Hebrew. The ephemeral nature of what he wrote and the early complete disappearance of his writing attest this fact. To assume the contrary is to surrender this decisive fact.

If Matthew's Hebrew composition consisted only of a small collection of the Lord's sayings, called logia by Papias, these could never have grown into the complete Gospel we now have, for the present Gospel is a literary work built on an excellent plan. A work that grows by slow accretions would by its very nature be entirely different. Besides, too much is asked of us when we are requested to believe that this slowly growing work was able to retain the significant title "According to Matthew" only on the strength of its original nucleus of logia from Matthew's pen. This holds equally for the variant hypothesis that an unknown writer took Matthew's Hebrew logia and worked them into the present complete Greek Gospel. This clashes with what we note in the case of the Second Gospel. Mark drew his material from Peter; Papias himself tells us this, as Eusebius 3, 39 reports. Yet the Second Gospel was never named "According to Peter," but from the start "According to Mark," the actual writer. In the face of this incontestable fact it is unwarranted to assume that, with far less of original material from Matthew, and that only in Hebrew, the First Gospel should have been called "According to Matthew" and not "according to its actual writer" who composed the entire work in Greek. Moreover, this writer was unknown, hence not a man of standing in the church as Mark was. Is it likely that a work from his hand, even if it contained certain Hebrew material from Matthew, would at once be ranked on a par with the other Gospels? We know that the authorship of other New Testament writings was questioned by some, so that these writings were called the antilegomena. Was the entire church satisfied regarding this unknown writer of the Greek Matthew? Did no one ever raise a question about him and his qualifications? And this the more, since his work never bore his own name but that of one of the apostles?

These hypotheses are sometimes modified. The Hebrew Gospel of Matthew, we are told, was translated into Greek with Matthew's consent and under Matthew's eyes. Or, his logia were expanded into our present Greek Gospel by some pupil of Matthew's under the apostle's supervision. But this view, too, breaks down. Was Matthew so lordly or so lazy that he was not willing to do this work himself? Or was he not quite competent and in need of help? The assumption of an amanuensis, resting on the interpretation of two passages, is also untenable. The various hypotheses melt under the flame of undeniable facts. Matthew himself wrote his Gospel, and he wrote it as we have it now, in Greek.

In this connection let us add, what has long been noted, that the tax collector Matthew, as a *portitor* or gatherer of port dues in Capernaum, must have been conversant with the Greek, otherwise he could not have held a position of this kind. His knowledge of this language must have advanced as time went on. It is well to note the influx of Hellenists into the church, beginning at Pentecost; proselytes followed in increasing numbers. Acts 10 reports the conversion of the entire connection of Cornelius by Peter; and Gal. 2:1-3 indicates the presence of a Greek like Titus, the companion of Paul, among the brethren at Jerusalem. It is altogether in order that Matthew should have written a Greek Gospel.

## *Is the Greek Matthew a Translation?*

Papias says that the Hebrew logia of Matthew were interpreted or expounded (ἡρμήνευσε) by each person as best he knew how. This refers to oral exposition by individuals here and there. Papias speaks of no written Greek translation, nor has he ever seen one. The others, who speak of a Hebrew "Gospel," say nothing about a translation. This is strange if the Greek Matthew in the hands of these fathers was a translation of the Hebrew Gospel of which they make mention. Not until we come to Jerome in the fourth century are we told that he does not know who the translator was: *quod quis postea in Graecum transtulerit non satis certum est.* We see that even he only supposes that a translation had been made. Yet it is still asserted that our Greek Matthew is a translation. If our Greek Matthew is a translation, it ought to be easy to demonstrate this linguistically. A book the size of Matthew's would afford all manner of evidence that it was translated into Greek from a Hebrew original if this were the case. Yet it has often been remarked that the

Greek Matthew reads like an original. Moulton calls the language "colorless Hellenistic of the average type," and R. 119 adds that "the book is not intensely Hebraistic" even though it was evidently intended for former Jews. All that R. ventures to say is that Matthew has an instinct for Hebrew parallelism and Hebrew elaboration, his thought and outlook being Hebraistic.

The attempt to prove that Matthew's Gospel is a translation on linguistic evidence has been unsuccessful. Thus 1:21 is said to be "simply unintelligible" because "Jesus" is elucidated by means of σώζειν, although English readers have always found the English verb "save" quite intelligible in this connection and are not perplexed because "Savior" or "the Lord's salvation" is not added as an interpretation of the name "Jesus." In 10:25 "Beelzebub" is without a Greek equivalent; likewise κορβανᾶς in 27:6, for which 15:5 has the Greek δῶρον, "gift"; and again ῥακά in 5:22 has no elucidation. But all these are original Aramaic terms, used as such in the discourses of Jesus, and are altogether intelligible to Jewish Christians. A late translator, writing for Gentile Christians, would have rendered them in Greek (as Matthew did in 15:5 with regard to δῶρον) or would have added an explanation in Greek. These terms prove the opposite of a translation. The obscurity found in Ναζωραῖος in 2:23 no more proves that this Gospel is a translation than any other obscurity in writing would. To call πέραν τοῦ Ἰορδάνου, when used as a noun in 4:25, and Γαλιλαίας and Ἰουδαίας, genitives after ἀπό in 4:25, 15, evidence of translation is to place undue emphasis upon trifles. In 16:19 and 18:18 δέειν and λύειν, "to bind" and "to loose," are said to be unintelligible to Greek readers on the supposition that these verbs are intended to reproduce the rabbinic "declare forbidden" and "declare permitted," and that they have nothing to do with John 20:23. This rabbinic exegesis may be challenged and, even if it were correct, would not prove that these expressions are a translation. To call Bar-Jonah in Matt. 16:17 a translator's mistake on the claim that Peter's father was named Jochanan, is to play one reading against another and proves nothing. And why object to the Aramaic *bar* in Matthew when John 18:40 has "Barabbas"? The same is true regarding Καναναῖος and Χαναναία in 10:4 and 15:22, which are correct transcriptions.

This exhausts the list of linguistic proofs for a translation. We are told that these are "modest conjectures" which might be multiplied if the original Hebrew Matthew were available. But these few instances are scarcely sufficient to convince the thoughtful reader that Matthew's Gospel as we now have it is a translation and not an original production.

If the Greek Matthew was a late translation by an unknown writer, or if it was an outgrowth of certain logia written by Matthew, it is difficult to explain how it was received as authoritative in the church. But the fact stands that Matthew held a higher place in the regard of the church than Mark, although the authority of Peter stood back of the latter. When the pagan Celsus made his attack on the Biblical books in the second century he chose Matthew's Gospel not Mark's because he considered Matthew the more prominent citadel. Nor did he assail its authority in the church as being a translation, or its authorship as not being that of an apostle.

The heretic Marcion, in the middle of the second century, called all the apostles pseudo-apostles, but neither he nor any other critic ventured the conjecture that the Greek Matthew was not written by Matthew. What a telling blow could have been struck by these early opponents of Christianity if they had had a suspicion that the First Gospel in its current form was not written by the apostle whose name it bore! When

Tatian compiled his *Diatessaron*, the very title of his book shows that he considered the Greek Matthew on a par with the other three Gospels. The attempt to show that this Gospel is a translation from the way in which the LXX and the Hebrew original are utilized in the quotations from them found in Matthew needs no refutation until it produces more tangible results.

## The Old Tradition

We may accept the statement of Papias that Matthew compiled certain logia in Hebrew and that these were used for a time and then disappeared without leaving a trace. Just what these logia contained will always be open to question. If they consisted of sayings of Jesus, Matthew may have embodied them in his Greek Gospel. This would argue for the view that he wrote his Gospel at a comparatively early date, so that the older logia soon disappeared. When others after the time of Papias speak of a Hebrew "Gospel" written by Matthew they may have in mind the logia of which Papias spoke, of which they, too, had heard either from Papias or from others. These others could hardly have in mind the sectarian "Gospel of the Hebrews" or the volume that Pantænus may have seen in Arabia. No one has ventured to assert that in addition to the Hebrew logia Matthew also composed a complete Hebrew Gospel. The fathers, from Papias to Eusebius, who perpetuated the old tradition regarding the Hebrew Gospel, themselves rest their assertion on tradition, i. e., on reports that they had heard. And none of these fathers, not even Papias himself, was able to name a single person who had seen — not to say handled — this alleged Hebrew Matthew. The reports of the fathers regarding a Hebrew "Gospel" must be considered as hearsay, unsupported by a tangible fact and contradicted by all the probabilities involved as well as by several uncontested facts.

## The Date of Matthew

Origen accepted the tradition that Matthew was the first evangelist to write a Gospel. This agrees with the listing of the Gospels, evidently intended to indicate their chronological order, given by both Irenæus and the Muratorian canon. When Clement of Alexandria states that the Gospels containing chronologies were the first to be written, basing this on the statements of his old teachers, hé grants the very first place to Matthew and raises the question of priority only regarding Mark and Luke. We may thus accept the finding that Matthew's Gospel was the first to be composed. Some have referred to Irenæus when fixing the date of writing at about the year 65. But this church father's remark about Peter and Paul "founding" the church at Rome and about Matthew writing a Hebrew "Gospel" at this time makes his statement rather doubtful. The date of Matthew is really a matter of conjecture. At the latest Matthew could not have written after the year 65, probably even five years earlier; some, however, have dated his writing about twenty years earlier. The place of writing is unknown, and not even a guess can be hazarded.

This settles the question as to Matthew's position in the so-called synoptical problem. Matthew wrote before Mark and Luke and thus drew on neither of these two. Since Matthew wrote in person he was his own source. The hypothesis of a *Quelle* or written source or sources from which the First Gospel drew breaks down the moment the authorship of Matthew is established. Only an unknown writer, composing a Gospel of his own from such material as he might be able to collect, could use sources. And no writer, known or unknown, could produce at a late date anything as grand, as true, and as authoritative as the Matthew we now have. Nor would the church have received his late work without a question, to say nothing of affixing to it the title "According to Matthew."

## Matthew's Plan and His Readers

"In grandness of conception and in the power with which a mass of material is subordinated to great ideas no writing in either Testament, dealing with a historical theme, is to be compared with Matthew. In this respect the present writer would be at a loss to find its equal also in the other literature of antiquity." — Zahn. This estimate is correct, save that it omits a comparison with John on the plea that John does not deal with a historical theme. He certainly does and in general follows Matthew's method. Both utilize their historical material as radiations from a glorious center. In John this center is the God-man Jesus, in Matthew it is the Messiah promised to the Jews. Matthew is second only to John.

Matthew's theme is *Jesus Christ, David's son, Abraham's son* (1:1), i. e., the Christ or Messiah who came in the person of Jesus as promised to David and before him to Abraham. This theme Matthew carries through with a mass of detail. All his material is historical, including the discourses, for they were actually uttered. In fact, the greater part of Matthew consists of discourses and in this respect resembles John. Matthew handles this material with complete mastery. He is not fettered by chronological considerations, as an ordinary historian is. While he follows the general chronological order as given by the life of Jesus he, nevertheless, groups some details according to their character and their significance.

Matthew writes from the Jewish standpoint for Jewish readers. Jewish terms and Jewish matters, therefore, receive little or no elucidation — his readers are expected to understand.

This Gospel has been called an apology, and its purpose has been conceived as being chiefly apologetic. But this is hardly correct, save in so far as any historical and objective presentation carries with it its own convincing power, especially for those for whom it is intended. The great number of Old Testament quotations introduced by Matthew are strictly in line with his theme. They are bound to impress all readers and especially such as have been trained in the Old Testament religion. Matthew's Gospel thus connects the New Testament with the Old in the grandest way. From its beginning, including the chronology, Matthew presents the Jewish nation in its true colors as manifesting the unbelief that rejected the Messiah, so that the Gentiles superseded the Jews, who failed to take their proper place in the New Testament kingdom. When this feature of the Gospel is regarded as narrowing down the readers whom Matthew had in mind, namely already converted Jews, the fact is overlooked that unconverted Jews must likewise be shown this sad fact of national unbelief; for only by breaking away from it in true repentance can any Jew really enter the kingdom. This break, too, must be decisive and complete. Matthew leaves no illusions on this point. His Gospel is not Jewish in the sense of Judaizing, mingling Jewish notions with the true gospel. If the so-called "Gospel of the Hebrews" appropriated anything from Matthew, foreign Judaistic elements were inserted by the sects which used this document and rejected the genuine Gospels.

It has been said that Matthew does not write as an eyewitness, does not weave into his narrative sections small, intimate details, does not note time, place, and circumstances in detail. Mark is compared, who preserves such details obtained from an eyewitness, Peter. John, too, is full of these touches. It is not true, however, that Matthew is devoid of all details that indicate the eyewitness. The reason he has less than Mark may well be due to the type and the character of the man. His eye and his ear did not catch so many of the little details that we love to see retained. To the present day eyewitnesses differ very markedly in this respect. Then, also, the plan which Matthew followed in his Gospel, the mass of material which he set himself to write into a whole, did not favor the amplitude of narration, found for instance in John 4. In many places we see that he was concerned with giving the main data to his readers and thus omitted the slighter details.

Back of all the evangelists, and thus also of Matthew and his Gospel, is the Lord with his promise given in John 14:26; 16:14. All naturalistic explanations of the Gospel are doomed to failure in the premises. No four witnesses could possibly remember and recount years later with exactitude what they saw and heard during the years they were with Jesus. This is especially true of the discourses. We ourselves are unable to report discourses which we have heard only a few years, yea, a few weeks ago. Omit the inspiration of the Holy Spirit, and the four Gospels together, and each by itself, stand as inexplicable phenomena. They simply could not have been produced. But they were produced and stand before us majestically in eloquent silence. The Spirit used each of these writers, taking each as he was, and enabled them to write, each in his own way, so that the writing was what the Spirit wanted for the church of the coming ages. No wonder that all inspired writing thus stands in a class by itself, supreme over all other writing and stamped forever as divine.

Some have outlined Matthew's Gospel in a broad way, making from four to seven parts. When fewer parts are made, the reason for making only so few is not apparent. For our purpose the following outline will suffice:

*The Book of the History of Jesus Christ, Son of David, Son of Abraham*

1. Christ born as David's and Abraham's son, ch. 1.
2. Christ's experience as a child, ch. 2.
3. Christ's forerunner and anointing, ch. 3.
4. Christ begins his Messianic work, ch. 4.
5. Christ's Sermon on the Mount, ch. 5-7.
6. Christ works many miracles, ch. 8-9.
7. Christ appoints his apostles, ch. 10.
8. Christ's answer to the Baptist and his further words of judgment and of grace, ch. 11.
9. Christ's clash with the Pharisees, ch. 12.
10. Christ speaks many parables, ch. 13.
11. Christ hears of the Baptist's murder and begins to withdraw, ch. 14.
12. Christ again clashes with the Pharisees and withdraws and warns the Pharisees and the Sadducees and his disciples, ch. 15-16:12.
13. Christ at Cæsarea Philippi, preparing the disciples for his death, ch. 16:13 - 17:23.
14. Christ at Capernaum, instructing his disciples, ch. 17:24-18.
15. Christ beyond Jordan, ch. 19-20:16.
16. Christ on his way to Jerusalem, ch. 20:17-34.
17. Christ enters Jerusalem, his last teaching, ending with the woes upon the Pharisees, ch. 21-23.
18. Christ's discourse on the destruction of Jerusalem and on his Parousia, ch. 24-25.
19. Christ's Passion, ch. 26-27.
20. Christ's Resurrection, ch. 28.

# CHAPTER I

I

## Christ Born as David's and Abraham's Son, Chapter 1

*The Genealogy 1:1-17*

Matthew writes for Jewish Christians in order to establish them in their faith that Jesus is the Christ promised in the Old Testament. Unconverted Jews who may read his book will be drawn to this faith when they see the full evidence here presented that Jesus is, indeed, the Christ. Although written with these readers especially in mind, Gentile Christians and unconverted Gentiles will be equally benefited, for they, too, are to hold or to be brought to this faith. It is a mistake to think that Matthew disregarded the latter two classes of people. To this day we must be sure that Jesus Christ properly bears the latter name, which designates his Messianic office. It is absolutely vital, then, that we should know that Jesus Christ is the direct and true descendant of Abraham through David. For if he were not, he could not possibly be the Messiah.

For this reason Matthew begins his Gospel with the genealogy of Jesus. **The book of the generation of Jesus Christ, son of David, son of Abraham.** This is evidently a caption, and this raises the question whether this caption is intended for the first seventeen verses alone or for the entire Gospel. The alternative lies between these two and not, as some have supposed, between the entire first chapter and the Gospel as such. We gain nothing decisive from the word βίβλος, which means only a scroll of papyrus; nor from the combination βίβλος γενέσεως, for everything depends on what γένεσις includes. We regard this genitive as the LXX translation of *misheppachah* in Exod. 6:24, etc., Num. 1:18, and thus might translate "family roll." See C.-K. 233. The point to be noted is that this meaning makes the term as here used face backward, as is plain also from the use of the Hebrew equivalent in the Pentateuch. The person named is described and identified by a reference to his ancestors. So also here the title used by Matthew already states the family line of Jesus Christ: "son of David, son of Abraham." Verses 2-17 furnish only the detailed family line, the generations reaching back to David and from him back to Abraham. These two are the essential ancestors that Jesus Christ had to have, for the Messiah was to be of the seed of David and of the seed of Abraham. We thus regard verse 1 as the comprehensive heading or summary of the next sixteen verses.

Others refer γένεσις to the Hebrew *toledoth*, the singular being used in Gen. 2:4; 5:1, elsewhere the plural: "this is the generation," "these are the generations." Accordingly γένεσις is taken to mean "the history": "The book of the history of Jesus Christ, son of David, son of Abraham." This caption is then regarded as a title for the entire Gospel. But this view is open to serious objection. In no case in Genesis does toledoth usher in the history of an individual but always the history of the individual and his descendants. Kautzsch, therefore, properly translates toledoth "family history." But Jesus has no family. When, nevertheless, γένεσις is regarded as "the history" of Jesus Christ, it is strange that a genealogy at once follows. We should have a statement to the effect that this history is to begin with a tracing of the ancestry of Jesus, and then the line should be carried back from Jesus to Abraham.

It will not do to reply that the two appositions in the title of this Gospel: "son of David, son of Abraham," are appended as an intimation that a genealogy is now to follow. These appositions are not appended for such a purpose. For then part of the title of the entire Gospel (the appositions) would refer only to the next sixteen verses. Finally, in Genesis toledoth never includes a list of ancestors in the family history; naturally, because it never faces backward. Matthew's γένεσις does this very thing. So also the name he appends: "Jesus Christ, son of David, son of Abraham"; for these appositions are integral parts of the name. This βίβλος or scroll shows this ancestry. The γένεσις of v. 1 has the same force as the γένεσις in v. 18; both mean "origin."

Words used in a title need not have the article, R. 793, hence βίβλος γενέσεως. "Jesus" is the Savior's personal name (1:21), *Yehoshu'a*, or *Yeshu'a*, "*Yahweh* is help or salvation," meaning "the one through whom Jehovah brings salvation." The addition Χριστός, a verbal from χρίω, the Hebrew "Messiah," "the Anointed," is here not an appellative, "the Christ," but a second personal name denoting office, "Christ." He became Jesus at the time of his birth (1:25) and Christ at the time of his anointing with the Spirit (3:16). Both of the following appositions belong to "Jesus Christ."

2) The designation in v. 1: "Jesus Christ, David's son, Abraham's son," marks Jesus as the one in whom the Messianic promises made to David and to Abraham were fulfilled. Hence the line of descent begins with Abraham. This line is traced in the Hebrew manner, as in Gen. 5:6, etc.; 11:10, etc., naming the father who "begot" the son. In the case of the first two fathers, however, the line is single and exclusive: Isaac, not Ishmael; Jacob, not Esau. In the case of the third father, Jacob, the line broadens to "Judah and his

brothers"; for, although Judah represents the actual
line of descent of Jesus, all the twelve patriarchs were
the direct heirs of the Messianic promise. The twelve
together produced the chosen nation from which the
Messiah sprang.

3)   As the mention of the brothers of Judah in
v. 2. already indicates, Matthew furnishes more than
a mere list of names; in the names he epitomizes the
history of the chosen nation.  This explains the next
link in the line:  **Judah begat Perez and Zerah
of Tamar.**   In this case the mother is named, Judah's
own daughter-in-law, to recall Gen. 38 with all its
shame.  In the bloodline of the Messiah there appear
such grave blemishes.  Matthew draws the attention of
his readers to several of them.  We must not generalize
and speak of sin and wickedness without restriction,
for then Matthew would have marked the evil character
and the deeds of some of the kings of the Messianic
line.  These blemishes deal with women:  Tamar,
Rahab, Ruth, and her of Uriah.  They all reflect on
the bloodline as such.  From a line so stained the
Messiah finally was born.  God condescended to use
such ancestors for his Son.  Matthew, however, has
more in mind than merely again to reveal the stains of
this ancestral line.  Some have thought that his purpose was to humble Jewish pride, but his aim is more
specific.  When he recounts how the Messiah was born
he brings out a feature that Luke does not mention,
namely that before Joseph took Mary to himself she
was found to be withchild, which fact at first in
Joseph's eyes and in afteryears in the eyes of Jewish
slanderers laid her open to the gravest accusation of
unfaithfulness to Joseph.  These Jews claimed that
the father of Jesus was Pandira or Pantheras, and for
this reason rejected him.  These base slanderers are
reminded by Matthew of what they might well call real
blemishes in the Messiah's Abrahamitic and Davidic

bloodline.   Let them occupy themselves with these real stains, attested in the Old Testament history itself, and not slander the pure maiden whom God chose to be the mother of his Son.   Of the twins born to Tamar God allowed Perez to continue to live.

4)   From Perez to David the descent is traced according to Ruth 4:18-22.   Whether any links are omitted we cannot say, nor does Matthew intimate anything on this point.

5)   **Of Rahab** (Hebrew "Rachab") draws attention to this woman, a Canaanite (Jos. 6:25) and a harlot at that, and yet an ancestress of the Messiah! One tradition makes Rahab the wife of Joshua who married her after the destruction of Jericho.   While Matthew's source for making her the wife of Salmon has not been discovered, no reason exists for doubting the evangelist's record.   The addition, **of Ruth,** introduces another woman proselyte, a Moabitess, whose story is well known although we should not forget to add that she was descended from an ancestor conceived in incest, Gen. 19:30, etc.

6)   Thus we reach **David, the king.**   The apposition marks the first break: the ancestral line had reached royalty.   Although it had risen to this great height, the very first king introduces another grave blemish into the line as the phrase shows: **of her of Uriah,** namely Bathsheba, to whom Solomon was born.   The simple way in which Matthew connects Israel's two greatest kings is telling to the highest degree.   Behind the little phrase lies adultery and murder and the death of the first child.   And this woman, though unnamed, was a queen; rightfully she belonged to Uriah.

7)   With Solomon begins the second group of fourteen, all of whom are kings, the list being drawn from I Chron. 3: 10-14.

8) As regards 'Οζίας, transliterated "Ozias" in the A. V., really "Uzziah" as in the R. V., this name has the same meaning as "Azariah," which is given to him in I Chron. 3:12. Matthew uses Uzziah, because the readers of the Old Testament were more familiar with this name of the king from their reading of the prophets (Isa. 1:1; 6:1; 7:1; Hos. 1:1; Amos 1:1; Zech. 14:5).

9) When Matthew proceeds from Uzziah to Jotham he omits three kings: Ahaziah who reigned one year (II Kings 8:26); Joash, forty years (12:2); and Amaziah, twenty-one years (14:2). Their length of reign cannot be the reason for their excision from Matthew's list. Nor can Matthew be charged with an oversight in transcribing the names from Chronicles. The wickedness of these kings is not the reason why they are here dropped, because other kings that were more wicked are retained in the list: Manasseh and Amon. Matthew's aim by no means is to present a line resplendent in holiness. The old explanation, that Ahaziah was a grandson of Jezebel on his mother's side, and that the curse of Ahab and Jezebel extended to the third generation, is inadequate, for women of actual heathen origin became direct ancestors of the Messiah. These three successive kings are purposely dropped by Matthew for the simple reason that he intends to make the three groups of ancestors comprise the same number of names, namely fourteen. He very likely shortened also the third group, v. 12-16, in order to have it contain only fourteen names. See v. 17.

10) No comment is needed on this verse.

11) A great deal has been said on Josiah and his grandson Jechoniah. While the latter would make up the number 14 in the second group, the third group, if it is counted so that each name is used but once, would show only 13 links. Yet in v. 17 Matthew himself invites us to make the count and to note that each

group contains exactly 14 names. Few will think that
he counted Jechoniah, the unhappy man who reigned
only three months and was then carried into exile,
twice, once as number 14 in the second group, and
again as number 1 in the third group, when no other
name in the entire genealogy is counted twice. Few
also will count Mary as a separate link in addition to
Joseph in order thus to obtain 14 links for the third
group. A simple answer to the problem is to assume a
translator from a Hebrew Matthew and then to say
that this translator wrote "Jechoniah" in v. 11, where
Matthew's Hebrew had "Jehoiakim," the father of
Jechoniah. This would, indeed, furnish us the additional name, so that we could count 42 different names
in three groups of 14, never using one twice. Yet this
error in translation would have us assume that in this
one case, between the father Jehoiakim and the son
Jechoniah, Matthew omitted the verb "begot." Since
elsewhere "begot" is invariably inserted, it could not
have been omitted here. Both in v. 11 and in v. 12,
Matthew wrote "Jechoniah" and he wrote in Greek —
the "unknown translator" did not exist.

The matter becomes plain when one reads II Kings
23:30 — 25:7. When Josiah perished at Megiddo, his
oldest son came to the throne but was carried to Egypt
where he died. In his place Pharaoh appointed Jehoiakim king in Jerusalem. In this way this second son
of Josiah came to the throne. After a reign of eleven
years he perished at the hand of the king of Babylon,
and his oldest son Jehoiachin, Matthew's Jechoniah,
came to the throne. After three months' reign he was
carried to Babylon, where he spent long years in exile.
Then his uncle, Josiah's third son Zedekiah (*Zidkiyahu*,
to be distinguished from Jechoniah's brother Zedekiah,
*Zidkiyah*, I Chron. 3:15, 16) became king and soon was
blinded and also carried into exile. Matthew is not
writing a mere list of names; all the names are bound

up with Israel's history. The royal line of David perished with Josiah's grandson Jechoniah. That is why the grandson is named in v. 11 and not Jechoniah's father Jehoiakim. The historical complications involved are pointed out by Matthew when he writes: "Josiah begot Jechoniah καὶ τοὺς ἀδελφούς at the deportation to Babylon." Here ἀδελφοί cannot mean "brothers," for Jechoniah had only one brother of whom we hear nothing more. These are Jechoniah's relatives, including the uncle who occupied the throne after him. Instead of following Josiah with the mere name Jehoiakim in v. 11, and then in v. 12 going on with another mere name Jechoniah, Matthew brings in the entire tangled and tragic history. All Jewish readers would at once understand that καὶ τοὺς ἀδελφούς referred to a generation between Josiah and Jechoniah, two sons of Josiah who reigned before Jechoniah and one who reigned after him. Any one of these three brothers might have continued the line; it was the second who did although he was deported with the first group of exiles. Though the third of the three brothers, Zedekiah, came to the throne and might have continued the line, it did not pass through him.

The word μετοικεσία refers to the deportation which was carried out in two great acts; it does not include the entire period of the seventy years of exile. The genitive Βαβυλῶνος is objective: "to Babylon," R. 501, really "the Babylon-removal," R. 494; so also in v. 12.

12) **After the Babylon-removal** mentions the deportation a second time and thus emphasizes this tragic historical fact and its weighty significance, the loss of the throne on the part of the house of David. The reign of Zedekiah after the deportation of Jechoniah proved abortive. Shealtiel was born in exile as the μετά phrase states. Hence we need not figure his father's age at the time of deportation as though anything depended on that. As regards the line Jechon-

iah — Shealtiel — Zerubbabel note Ezra 3:2; Neh.
12:1; Hag. 1:1, 12, 14; 2:2, 23. Yet in I Chron. 3:19
Zerubbabel is the son of Pedaiah: and in Luke 3:27
Shealtiel is the son of Neri, a descendant of David
through David's son Nathan and not through Solomon.
These are not contradictions and have not been considered as such. Jechoniah's son Assir (I Chron. 3:17)
left only a daughter, who, according to the law relative
to heiresses (Num. 27:8; 36:8, 9), married a man of
her paternal tribe, viz., Neri of David's line through
Nathan. Thus we have the step from Jechoniah to
Shealtiel. Matthew gives us the legal line on which
all Jewish descendants lay stress as we shall see in the
case of Joseph, the legal father of Jesus; Luke gives
the natural line of descent, not that of Joseph, but of
Mary; her descent from David, etc., being vital for
Gentile descendants. So in the case of Zerubbabel: he
is the legal son and heir of Shealtiel, the natural son of
Pedaiah. When Shealtiel died without leaving children, his brother Pedaiah married the widow in accordance with the Levirate law (Deut. 25:5-10; Matt.
22:24-28), raising up seed to his brother.

13-15)   Abiud is not named in I Chron. 3; nor are
any of the following names found in the Scriptures.
The line was traced in the priests' records, which were
cherished with great care because of the promise that
the Messiah would come from the house of David. But
the scepter had departed from Judah — all the names
are those of unknown descendants.

16)   **And Jacob begot Joseph, the husband of
Mary, of whom was born Jesus, the one called
Christ.** Through the entire line runs the verb
"begot — begot — begot." Significantly it makes a
halt when it reaches Joseph. He, the husband of Mary,
did *not* beget Jesus, the Messiah. In marked contrast
with this regular begetting of one ancestor by another
we are told by Matthew that the last thus begotten was

Joseph, "the husband (ἀνήρ) of Mary, and that Jesus "was born," ἐγεννήθη (γεννάω, used also regarding the mother alone, as here) of her. How this happened follows at once. Since "Jesus" was a name frequently found among the Jews, the participial statement is added: ὁ λεγόμενος Χριστός, which means that Jesus rightfully bore this second official name "Christ"; on which see v. 1. Thus Matthew's genealogy presents Joseph as the legal father of Jesus, which makes Jesus legally the heir of David and of Abraham. If Jesus had been born without a legal father, of Mary without a legal husband, his legal right to the inheritance from Abraham and David by virtue of the divine promise would have been void. In addition to the legal standing of Jesus as the rightful, legal son of Joseph we may note the protection this standing secured for his mother and for himself. The two records of Matthew (v. 18, etc.) and Luke (2:4, etc.) vividly bring out this point.

The record of Matthew is questioned in two ways. First, by an appeal to an old Syriac version, and secondly, by the claim that Matthew's whole genealogy is "meaningless if it does not contemplate Joseph as the actual father of Jesus." Here we meet a typical example of "critical" methods. Of all the ancient texts in existence, including all the ancient versions, one (usually identified by the symbol Ss) is singled out as containing a reading which the "critics" use to rid themselves of the virgin birth. All Greek texts and all other versions are set aside, for this one Syriac translation, the codex Ss and its reading, is made "the original reading," and all other texts are regarded as "an accommodation to the doctrine of the Virgin Birth." For the critically assured text of v. 16 Moffatt substitutes his translation of this one Syrian translation: "and Joseph (to whom the virgin Mary was betrothed), the father of Jesus, who is called 'Christ.'" In the *Moffat Commentary* Th. R. Robinson lends this his unqualified support. And this is done in the face of all the information long available in Zahn, *Introduction to the New Testament,* II, 565, etc. We quote the following: "The zeal with which many have seized upon the reading of Ss as a bit of the primitive Gospel, without looking to right or left, is explained by the old prejudice that the genealogy of Jesus, leading as it does to Joseph, could have been prepared only by one who took him to be the actual father of Jesus. But the alleged contradiction between the genealogy and the following narrative is found equally in Luke — and so in both of the only old Christian writings extant which trace the Davidic descent of Jesus in a genealogy. That his Davidic descent was ever understood in the Christian community in any other sense is a hypothesis without support in existing literature. . . . The hope of finding indications in old MSS. and versions that the authors of lost gospels or brief writings which may have been worked over in our Matthew and Luke regarded Joseph as the physical father of Jesus, should at last be dismissed. An author who knew how to make even the dry material of a genealogy down to its last detail contribute to the purpose of his thought regarding the slandered miracle of the Messiah's birth, cannot at the same time have taken over statements from a genealogy of Joseph or Jesus used by him which directly contradicted his conception of this fact. Any text of Matthew which contained such statements would be condemned in advance as one altered against the author's intent."

A study of this one text (Ss), by which the modernist would replace all others, even in popular English translation, reveals that this highly inferior text does not say or intend to say what the critics would have it say. Like some Greek texts which reveal alteration, Ss also introduces "the virgin" and "was betrothed," both terms intended, as in all the texts that

have them, fully to safeguard the virgin birth — the
very thing the critics would remove. This Ss changes
the verb ἐγεννήθη to ἐγέννησεν, the verb used throughout
the genealogy. But this was done by Ss, not to make
Joseph the physical father of Jesus, but to make the
final verb read like all the verbs that precede. Its
subject would be Mary, and we should translate: "to
whom the virgin Mary, betrothed to him, *bore* Jesus,"
etc. But even if, as the critics claim, the subject of
this last ἐγέννησεν is Joseph, this verb, as Zahn states,
"in no sense expresses *physical* fatherhood" but intends to "designate Jesus as Joseph's son only in the
same way as in 1:1 he was called David's son." "His
(the Syrian translator's) intention cannot have been
to represent Joseph as the physical father of Jesus,
for it is impossible that one who had this purpose
should at the same time and in the same sentence speak
even more clearly than the A text (i. e., the assured
Greek text) of Mary's virginity; exclude the existence
of marital relations between her and Joseph; and in
1:18-25 emphasize as strongly as the catholic text that
Jesus was begotten through the agency of the Holy
Spirit." Thus even Ss answers the contention of these
critics that the virgin birth is not in "the original
text" of Matthew.

17) **All the generations, therefore, from Abraham to David are fourteen generations; and from
David to the deportation to Babylon fourteen generations; and from the deportation to Babylon to
the Christ fourteen generations.** We have seen
that Matthew himself made the second group of ancestors number fourteen by dropping three kings of
Israel. He very likely secured the number fourteen
in the third group in the same way. But why did he
want the three groups to be equal? The answer is
that he wanted us to understand that all three groups
had equal weight and importance as far as the Messiah

is concerned. The second contained the names of kings, but it was no more important than the third. The first began with Abraham, and the second with David, but neither exceeded the third, which began with a wretched exile — Jechoniah wore prison clothes for 36 years. For, after all, "the house of David did not produce the Christ but received him as a gift; he did not come from the natural soil of David's house but was planted into David's house," Delitzsch. Since $14 = 7 \times 2$, some would find symbolism in these three fourteens. Yet what the symbolism would symbolize, no one has yet made plain. It seems most likely that Matthew found 14 names in the first group and then arranged the rest in two more groups of 14. Twice already we have had mention of the deportation (v. 11, 12); now it is again mentioned twice. This shows intent on the part of the author. The lower the house of David sank, the nearer the day of the Messiah came. Back of the course of this history in its three great stages is God himself who sent his Son in the fulness of time and not until then.

The word πᾶσαι cannot mean "all" the generations that actually lived from Abraham to Jesus; this "all" refers to those enumerated by Matthew. Where did Matthew find these lists of names? We see that Luke found his much longer list without trouble. In the case of Matthew, however, we see that he did not merely copy the list as he found it; he adapted it in a highly intelligent and purposeful way, dividing the names into groups, omitting some, adding the names of each of four women in a significant manner, and marking the groups by historical references. The effort is made to show from the forms of the names, their spelling, and the supposed errors in transcription, that the Greek list as we have it today shows that it is a translation from the original Hebrew of Matthew. But the names were all recorded in Hebrew when Matthew

first found them.   He himself transliterated them into
Greek.   When later scribes multiplied the copies of
his Gospel, these may easily have tried to "improve"
on the original.   We need no Hebrew Matthew with a
late tranlator into Greek to explain the peculiarities
now found in this genealogical list.

### The Virgin Birth, 1:18-25

18) What the genealogy leads us to expect, and
what its conclusion in v. 16 all but states outright,
is now fully presented, namely the actual historical
facts of just how Jesus Christ was conceived and born.
Luke presents the same facts but from the angle of
Mary; Matthew, after giving us Joseph's ancestry,
presents the virgin birth from the angle of Joseph.
He thus brings in Joseph's situation when Mary was
discovered to be pregnant, squarely meeting the hostile
Jewish slander about the illegitimate birth of Jesus.
The value of Matthew's record of the miraculous facts
connected with the birth of Jesus is thus inestimable.
Matthew 1:18, etc., like Luke 2 and John 1:13 (correctly interpreted), constitutes one of the great *sedes
doctrinae* for the virgin birth, voiced in all ecumenical
confessions of the church, beginning with the Apostles'
Creed:   "Who was conceived by the Holy Ghost, born
of the Virgin Mary."   The facts presented in full
detail by these evangelists are denied by modernism.
But all these denials are mere echoes of the same
denials made in the age of rationalism.   They are
subjective dogmatical opinions without historical facts
on which to stand.   The facts and their inspired
record remain unaltered and unalterable as they have
been from the moment when they occurred.   Their
denial places those who make it outside the pale of
Christianity.   The Christ who was not conceived and
born as the evangelists record is no Christ in any

true sense, is nothing but a figment of men's brains. Any religion based upon this sort of Christ is as vacuous as the Christ upon which it is based.*

**Now the generation of the Christ was as follows. His mother Mary having been betrothed to Joseph, before they came together she was found withchild of the Holy Ghost.** The continuative δέ links the new account with the preceding genealogy, R. 1184; it merely ushers in the new section and is not adversative. The name τοῦ Χριστοῦ heads the paragraph; the addition "Jesus" is not textually assured. This official name links the new section with both v. 16 and v. 17. The genitive, placed forward as it is, has the emphasis: *Christ's* genesis is here recorded. Already this emphasis prepares for the miraculous manner of his entry into the world. He who would be *the Christ,* the culmination of the entire history of divine promise, would in his very genesis exceed all his human ancestors. The assured reading is γένεσις, "generation" in the sense of "origin"; not γέννησις, "engendering," a narrower term with but minor textual authority. It is the same word as that used in 1:1, where it is found as a genitive with βίβλος and is thus applied to the human ancestry of Jesus, while here it is the main noun and designates the conception and the birth of Christ.

This is evident from the predicate οὕτως ἦν, "was thus" as is now to be described. It is *the manner* of the origin which Matthew sets out to describe. No other person had an origin "on this wise." The origin of Adam was wonderful, indeed, that of the second Adam is still more so. When Matthew sets out to describe the manner of Christ's genesis, the fact as such is already taken for granted. We see from the way in which Matthew begins that he is not writing for readers to whom the matters he here relates are altogether new. He mentions neither time nor place. The latter is indicated only incidentally in 2:1, in a different connection. The persons, too, are not formally introduced to the readers; their mention in v. 16 is quite sufficient for Matthew's purpose. All we need is to be placed at the moment when the miracle involved in the human generation of the Messiah became apparent to human eyes.

The genitive absolute, "his mother Mary having been betrothed to Joseph," is made to stand out prominently by the very fact that this participial clause is placed forward and even refers to the subject of the main sentence, R. 514, 1132. The aorist passive participle designates the historical fact of the betrothal which had occurred at a previous time. The Jewish betrothal was a solemn promise before witnesses (Ezra. 16:8; Mal. 2:14), embodying the essentials of the marriage vow. No further promises followed. In later times it was ratified in writing. By virtue of the betrothal the bridegroom and the bride became husband and wife as is also shown in the next verse where Joseph is called Mary's husband, and in v. 20 where she is called his wife (Deut. 22:24). It is a mistake to regard "husband" and "wife" as proleptic terms denoting the husband and his wife to be. This is reading into the Jewish procedure our modern conception of an engagement. The Jewish betrothal was the marriage itself. But the Jewish custom placed an interval, longer or shorter, between the betrothal and the bringing home of the bride to her husband's house. No religious ceremony and no vows of any kind accompanied this home-bringing although it was made a festive occasion with a procession and a feast following (Matt. 25:1, etc.). These Jewish procedures were only national and Oriental customs, not laws enjoined by God; and however socially and morally binding upon Jews they were while in vogue, they cannot now be imposed upon us as being of divine right.

Into this interval between the betrothal and the home-bringing Matthew places his readers when he adds, "before they came together," πρὶν ἤ with the infinitive, the main verb being affirmative. We are, of course, unable to say how long after the betrothal or how soon' before the expected coming together Joseph made the discovery of Mary's pregnancy. The point is immaterial for Matthew's narrative. The aorist συνελθεῖν denotes nothing but the home-bringing which followed the Jewish espousal. It is not identical with *coire* or with "he knew her not" in v. 25, although the home-bringing naturally included the sexual union of the couple. Happily Joseph looked forward to the festive day when with his friends he would go and bring home his wife to his own home. Then occurred what struck him as a calamity: his wife "was found withchild." The aorist εὑρέθη simply states the fact; this verb is used instead of the more usual δῆλος or φανερὸς εἶναι, R. 1121, and ἔχουσα (ἔμβρυον) ἐν γαστρί, "having (an embryo) in the womb," is the conventional Greek for "being withchild."

We are not told that Joseph alone made the discovery of his wife's condition. Yet neither Matthew nor Luke refer to any other person. It is evident from the evangelist's statement that Mary had revealed nothing to Joseph of the angel's message given to her and of her submission to the will of God. The angel had directed her to her relative Elisabeth in the hill country, and she had gone to commune with this friend, but as far as Joseph was concerned, having no intimation as to what God's will might be, she left all in God's hands. This was an act of absolute reliance upon God, the more admirable the more we realize her situation as it must have been. An espoused woman, if found unfaithful, could be punished with death, Deut. 22:23, 24. To what extent this law was observed at this time we have no means of knowing. Mary had absolutely no means of proving her spotlessness to Joseph or to any other person in Nazareth. Misgivings and doubts of various kinds, we may well assume, assailed her. Her one refuge was to place herself altogether into the hands of God. And this was well.

When describing Mary's condition Matthew at once adds the phrase: ἐκ Πνεύματος Ἁγίου, "of the Holy Ghost." This at once sheds the full light of divine truth upon the fact here recorded. Matthew has the thought of his readers in mind. Not for one instant are we left in doubt; every unworthy thought is completely forestalled. In this brief phrase Matthew records what is popularly called the virgin birth, and on this phrase hangs the entire paragraph, yea, all else that the New Testament reports concerning the Word made flesh. Either the eternal Son of God entered our race as Matthew here declares, or he did not. If he did not, if Jesus was an ordinary human bastard, or Joseph's natural son by an act of forbidden cohabitation, then they who will may call him their Savior — their lascivious fancy cannot raise him from the mire into which they have cast him.

19) **And Joseph, her husband, being righteous and not willing to make her a public example resolved to divorce her privately.** We may also translate, "as her husband"; for what Joseph resolved to do was the right of a husband, which he was by virtue of his betrothal. We must not bring in the idea of "breaking off the engagement," which is out of line with this Jewish situation. The two motives which influenced Joseph are indicated by the two present participles. "Being righteous" marks Joseph as a truly religious Jew, puts him in the same class with Zacharias and Elisabeth who were "righteous before God, walking in all the commandments and ordinances of the Lord blameless," makes him like Simeon who was "righteous and devout." The word

refers to the heart as well to the conduct. As a truly religious Jew, Joseph could not think of consummating his marriage with Mary under the present circumstances.

But we hear nothing about a burst of anger on his part; quite the contrary. "And not willing to make her a public example" shows us the second motive for the resolve he reached. He truly loved his betrothed wife and was torn with grief because of what his eyes saw in this gentle maiden whom he had always found a model of purity and who still bore this character. Two courses were open to Joseph: the one harsher, to charge Mary with adultery and thus to make her a public example (παραδειγματίσαι), letting such Jewish law as was in force at that time take its course; the other course, far more gentle, was to make use of the lax divorce laws of the Jews and without charging her with any crime give Mary a letter of divorcement, stating the cause in a veiled way or stating none at all. Joseph resolved on the milder course; ἐβουλήθη (aorist) means that he came to this decision, while the durative θέλων denotes only the desire that prompted him. The verb ἀπολῦσαι is the regular term for divorcing one from the marriage tie, Matt. 5:31, etc.; 19:3-9; Mark 10:2-12. Already this answers the contention that making her a public example signifies giving her a letter of divorce, and that λάθρα ἀπολῦσαι means merely to separate from her by a mutual agreement. The latter would be as little "secret" as the former, as far as that point is concerned. Moreover, it would still leave Joseph Mary's legal husband. In addition, it would not satisfy the law as then in vogue and thus could not satisfy Joseph's sense of right. Letters of divorce were both private and legal, needing no publication before a court.

20) Joseph had not yet carried out the resolution at which he had arrived when God intervened.

**But when he had thought on these things,** i. e., had
turned them over in his mind and reached his decision, **lo, an angel of the Lord appeared to him during a dream saying to him:    Joseph, son of David,
fear not to take possession of Mary, thy wife; for
what was conceived in her is of the Holy Spirit.
And she shall give birth to a son, and thou shalt
call his name Jesus, for it is he that shall save his
people from their sins.** The deponent, ἐνθυμηθέντος,
here the aorist passive form, is transitive, R. 817.    At
the proper moment God intervenes.    His hand is made
visible to us in the earthly story of Jesus in a most remarkable way.    As he guided the events pertaining to
his Son, so he still guides all things for his sons even
though his hand is now invisible.    The angels of
heaven are his servants and messengers, and it has
been well said that we think of them too little amid
the changing circumstances of our lives and look only
for natural laws and natural causes, whereas God's
help is often extended through supernatural hands.

The interjection ἰδού, "lo" draws attention to the
astounding thing that occurred at this critical moment.
Behold the gracious guidance of God, his watchful care,
the wondrous way in which he works, and the certainty
with which he attains the necessary result!    We have
no article with ἄγγελος Κυρίου, and thus this is one of
Yahweh's angels, "that do his commandments, hearkening unto the voice of his word," Ps. 103:20; and not
the *Maleach Yahweh* who so frequently appears in the
Old Testament and is Yahweh himself.    We may well
assume that this angel is Gabriel, the same one who
appeared to Mary, "the Mighty One of Jehovah," or,
"Hero of Jehovah," to whom it was especially given
to assist in ushering the Son into the world.    He
appears to Joseph "during a dream," κατά to indicate
extent and ὄναρ found only in the nominative and the
accusative.    The time for the fulfillment of Joel's

prophecy had come, "your old men shall dream dreams, your young men shall see visions," 2:28. Heaven had approached earth, therefore angels drew nigh, and the veil that hid their presence was pierced now and again.

We have no reason to think that this appearance of an angel was different from the one described in 2:13, where evidently the vision came at night while Joseph was asleep. We may well imagine Joseph lying on his bed, thinking on these things while sleep for a time fled his eyes until at last he sank into unconsciousness. Then the wondrous dream came to him. Yet Joseph did not dream about this angel. It was not like the unreal images, some lovely, some horrible, some silly and senseless that come to a sleeper in a dream. The angel of Joseph's dream was real, ἐφάνη, "he appeared." God is able to use man's waking and his sleeping condition for making him see and hear his angel messengers. And when God sends an angel messenger to a sleeper he never has the least difficulty in demonstrating that the appearance in the dream is actual and not like the mere images that at other times come to our consciousness during sleep. Joseph knew that this angel had been at his bedside that night. He regarded this dream and the one in 2:13 exactly as did Zacharias and Mary the angel vision they beheld with open eyes. Among the forms of revelation employed by God, dreams, such as this of Joseph, occupy the lowest rank. See Delitzsch, *Biblische Psychologie.* God himself chooses the form of revelation, adapting it to the person concerned. How did Matthew know about Joseph's dreams? Exactly in the way in which Luke knew the events which he recorded about Jesus' nativity. He who sent the angel to Joseph knew how to have this and other events preserved truthfully for the church of future days.

The angel addresses Joseph as "son of David," υἱός a nominative, usual in appositions to vocatives,

R. 464. Matthew's genealogy has shown Joseph to
be a descendant of the royal house of David; so also
was Mary. This fact is here made the basis of an
appeal to him on this most important occasion to prove
himself a true son of David, a man who has the Messianic faith of David, since the promise to David was
now in course of fulfillment. "Son of David" regards
Joseph as a prince, and princely things were expected
of him, to be a protector of the very Prince of heaven
itself. Men love great names but so often fail to live
up to them.

The fears and the misgivings of Joseph are removed
because they have no foundation in reality; μὴ φοβηθῇς
is the subjunctive in an aorist negative command as in
the classics. Joseph would in no way compromise himself, condone a crime, risk his happiness, or do anything hurtful or doubtful in taking possession of his
wife, παραλαβεῖν, which is much like συνελθεῖν in v. 18,
save that it indicates Joseph's activity, while the latter
indicates that of Joseph and Mary. On the contrary,
by taking possession of his wife, bringing her to his
own home, Joseph would do God's will, serve God's Son,
shield and protect the mother of his Lord, himself
receive a thousand blessings, and show himself a true
prince of David's line. "It is an honor for the wedded
state that our Lord Jesus Christ, God's Son, was not
born of a simple unmarried maid but of Mary who was
espoused as a true wife to Joseph, her husband. . . . .
Thus also our Lord Christ was born of his mother
according to the law in wedlock and honored it with
his birth." Luther.

The real point which had induced Joseph's decision
to divorce Mary is met most decisively by the γάρ clause
in the angel's statement: "for what is conceived of her
is of the Holy Spirit." "Conceived of the Holy Ghost,"
Apostolic Creed. "And was incarnate by the Holy
Ghost of the Virgin Mary and was made man," Nicene

Creed. Thus all other Christian creeds, voicing the
united faith of all ages of the Christian Church. In
the Latin draft the Smalcald Articles add to "of the
pure, holy Virgin Mary," *semper virgine* (*Concordia
Triglotta*, 460), a conviction held in Reformation times
but devoid of actual Bible proof. "In Holy Scripture
the word *born* does not always signify the outward
birth as when the child comes from the mother's body;
but the Scriptures, when speaking of our humanity,
also call that *born* when the child is made alive in the
mother's body as is here clearly stated, 'born of the
Holy Spirit,' as was Christ." Luther. Jesus had not
yet left the womb, hence τὸ γεννηθέν refers to the embryo
and its conception: "that which was conceived," the
aorist pointing to the past act of conception; and thus
also the neuter article is used, leaving the sex unnamed.

In the phrase ἐκ Πνεύματος Ἁγίου no article is needed
in the Greek, R. 761 and 795. This point has been
settled. This is true also with regard to Θεός and Κύριος.
These terms are really proper names and thus may or
may not have the article. Modernistic unitarian views
deny the plain grammatical fact in order to convert the
Third Person of the Godhead into the impersonal power
of God. Yet this assault is unable to abolish the virgin
birth. In the angel's statement Ἁγίου is placed after
the Greek copula, lending an emphasis which the English cannot reproduce. If the angel had said "Spirit of
God," the critics could more easily have found room
for their view; but "Holy Spirit" blocks every critical
effort. From this word of the angel Matthew borrowed the phrase he uses in v. 18. The Third Person
of the Godhead was so fully known to all Jews that no
word of explanation is added, either here in the case
of Joseph or in the case of Mary (Luke 1:35), or in
the case of the crowds who listened to the Baptist
(John 1:32-34). Examine the evidence in detail in
all the Gospels and note that it includes the knowledge

of the Son as the Second Person. It is a critical claim
that the Trinity was not revealed to the Jews in the
Old Testament. The Jewish assaults against the deity
of Jesus never operated with the claim that no Son of
God and no Spirit of God existed but only with the idea
that this man Jesus should call himself God's Son.

The ineffable mystery of the incarnation is expressed
by the angel in the simplest words yet in the most
adequate way. The same feature is evident in all
the evangelists when they speak of this mystery.
Here is one of the clear marks of divine inspiration;
facts and realities that the human mind will never
comprehend are expressed in words of utter simplicity
yet of perfect adequacy. In every case the fact is
placed beyond question as a fact, but the profundity of
the manner of the fact, *how* this or that is or can be,
is left unrevealed. The reason for the latter is plain:
the *how* lies beyond human comprehension. Who can
understand how the conception took place ἐκ Πνεύματος
Ἁγίου when no man has yet understood just how a common human being with his personality and all his
physical and mental peculiarities is conceived in the
usual act of procreation? What ἐκ contains is voiced
confessionally: "The most blessed Virgin bore not a
mere man but, as the angel testifies, such a man as is
truly the Son of the most high God, who showed his
divine majesty even in his mother's womb, inasmuch
as he was born of a virgin, with her virginity inviolate.
Therefore she is truly the mother of God and, nevertheless, remained a virgin." *Concordia Triglotta*, 1023.

21) Still more completely are Joseph's fears
dispelled: "And she shall give birth to a son," etc.
Bengel remarks: "Not, *to thee*," as the angel said to
Zacharias, Luke 1:13, when announcing the birth of the
Baptist; compare Gen. 17:19, where Abraham is told,
Sarah "shall bear *thee* a son." Though similar, the
angel's statement to Joseph is vastly different. Note

how categorically it and also the next statement are expressed: "she shall give birth to a son . . . he shall save," etc. No *if* or *and* about it. The determinate counsel and the foreknowledge of God never fail. And now Joseph's part in this counsel is revealed to him: "and thou shalt call his name Jesus," καλέσεις, a volitive future of command, differing from the simple futuristic or predictive futures τέξεται and σώσει. God is instating Joseph as the legal father and as the foster-father of the unborn child. What was already indicated in the bidding to "take possession of Mary, thy wife," is here stated in so many words. Joseph's course is made entirely clear. Only the choice of the child's name is not left to Joseph, for he is under a far higher Father who himself attends to this important task. God named his Son, Ἰησοῦς, "Yahweh is helper," "Yahweh saves"; see 1:1. The name is descriptive, embracing the entire saving work of God's Son; and because of the divine character of this work it by implication describes also the person of the Son.

The reason for this name is clearly stated: "for it is he that shall save his people from their sins." We must translate somewhat in this fashion in order to bring out the fact that αὐτός emphasizes "he" in the verb: "it is *he* — *he* alone" who shall save, etc. The verb "to save," σώζειν, like σωτήρ and σωτηρία, always denotes rescue and deliverance from danger and, when it is used soteriologically, rescue from the worst of mortal dangers, that of sin, death, and hell. But coupled with the act of rescue is the idea of keeping those rescued safe and secure, preserving them so that the danger shall not again involve them. Thus "to save" is one of the cardinal terms of the Scriptures. Compare σωτήρ in Mary's hymn, Luke 1:47, and σωτηρία in that of Zacharias, Luke 1:69.

"His people," λαὸς αὐτοῦ, denotes the Jews but in the sense in which Jesus said that he was sent to the lost sheep of the house of Israel. "His people" is not restrictive: the Jews alone. The term is in place here, for Joseph is to understand that Mary's child is to bring the deliverance long promised to the chosen nation. By delivering the Jews he would deliver all nations. It is impossible to give a double meaning to "his people": first the people of Israel, and secondly the spiritual Israel or all believers. The two fail to harmonize. If faith and the actual appropriation of salvation is to be the mark of λαὸς αὐτοῦ, then only a small part of the Jewish nation is included in the second meaning.

The view that a paronomasia between the name "Jesus" and the verb "to save," ought to be employed, and that this paronomasia is lost by the use of σώσει in the Greek, since the verb root is not identical with the root of the name, is untenable. If a play on these words might have been made in the Hebrew or the Aramaic, this is no reason for insisting that it was thus made and that it was lost in the Greek because the Greek translator of Matthew's Hebrew failed to reproduce it. This sort of proof will never establish the fact that Matthew wrote his Gospel in Hebrew, and that some unknown person later translated it into Greek. See the introduction. Matthew wrote in Greek. He properly explains "Jesus" by using σώζειν. What more is needed? What more could Matthew do in the Greek, assuming that he thought of a paronomasia in the Hebrew? He did as we do when we think of a play on words which we might make in one language but find we cannot easily make in another — he did not make it. It would be only an embellishment. Matthew wrote for Jewish readers who understood what "Jesus" means; when, nevertheless, he adds the explanation in the Greek, this has a far higher purpose than to make plain an etymology. He aims to show the kind of "Jesus" this child would be.

Jesus shall save his people "from their sins." With one stroke all political ideas are swept away for Joseph, such as deliverance from the Roman yoke, or from the ills this yoke had brought on the nation. The real evils under which the Jews suffered were "their sins." Sometimes the collective ἁμαρτία, "sin," is used, heaping all together into one vast unit mass; again, as here, this collective is spread out in the great plural "sins," all varieties and kinds, yea, each and every individual thought, word, and deed by which men miss the mark set by God's law — ἁμαρτάνειν, "to miss the mark." These sins destroy us, body and soul, in time and in eternity. To save from these sins is salvation indeed. Who is mighty enough to effect such a salvation? Only he who was conceived of the Holy Spirit in the womb of Mary, God's Son. For to save from sins is to separate the sinner from his sins so that these sins can no longer reach him or inflict their deadly, damning power upon him. But what man ever separated himself or another from even a single sin? Every sin clings closer than a shadow and will cling thus forever unless God's own Son frees, rescues, saves us.

22) **And the whole of this has occurred in order that it be fulfilled what was spoken by the Lord through the prophet saying,**

**Lo, the virgin shall be withchild and shall give birth to a son,**
**And they shall call his name Immanuel; which is, when interpreted, With us God.**

Several considerations lead to the conclusion that these are still the words of the angel spoken to Joseph, all except the clause which translates "Immanuel." If Matthew were here writing an observation of his own he would be interrupting the narrative and should have written these two verses after v. 25, where they

would have been in place.    In v. 18 he set out to tell
the γένεσις of Christ, which means both his conception
and his birth; but at the end of v. 21 we have heard
only of the conception, the birth not being mentioned
until v. 25.    Weightier still is the consideration that
until the end of v. 21 the angel gave no support to
Joseph's faith save only his word; but if v. 22, 23 are
words of the angel, he would give Joseph the strongest
kind of support by citing to him the very promise now
being fulfilled.

"The whole of this" is singular, hence not ταῦτα
πάντα but τοῦτο ὅλον, this with all its features and parts.
The formula here used: "in order that it be fulfilled
what was spoken by the Lord (Κύριος for Yahweh)
through the prophet," is used almost constantly by
Matthew throughout his Gospel with only occasional
variation.    He adopted this formula from the angel's
lips.    In every case the veracity of God is substantiated, the greatness, power, wisdom, and grace of God
who stands behind both the prophecy itself and its
eventual fulfillment.    When the fulfillment is an act
of God such as the miraculous conception and birth of
his Son, God's foreknowledge is due to his purpose,
his πρόθεσις is first and his πρόγνωσις dependent thereon;
when the act foretold is one regarding man, the foreknowledge or πρόγνωσις is enough, infallibly recording in
advance what man will do.    The verb πληρωθῇ pictures
the promise or the prophecy as an empty vessel which
is at last filled when the event occurs.    The preposition
ὑπό introduces the direct agent with the passive verb,
and διά the mediate agent, R. 820.    The actual speaker
thus is Yahweh, and the prophet the medium or mouthpiece through (διά) which he speaks.    This describes
exactly the miracle of prophecy and of divine inspiration.    These prepositions, running, as they do, through
Scripture, are clear and convincing evidence of inspiration.    God is the *causa efficiens* (ὑπό), God's agents or

instruments the *causae instrumentales* (διά). The angel did not need to name the prophet to Joseph who would know that Isa. 7:14 was referred to; and Matthew's readers would also know.

23) King Ahaz of Judah turned from Jehovah and sought help from the heathen king of Assyria. When he was told to ask a sign of God, either in the depth or in the height above, with a pious phrase he declined to do so. With strong rebuke Isaiah told Ahaz that God himself would give him a sign, namely this sign, that a virgin shall conceive and bear a son whose name she would call Immanuel. This sign meant to Ahaz that no helper would arise from the perverted house of David as represented in the wicked male descendants; that all the following wicked generations would perish; and that finally from this unnamed virgin the great divine Helper, Immanuel, would be born. "Lo" or "behold" draws attention to the wonder.

In their denials of the virgin birth the critics say that the Greek παρθένος, "virgin" or "maiden," is misleading and declare: "The Hebrew has no thought of a miraculous birth, for the term rendered *maiden* simply means an adult woman, still young enough to become a mother, and is by no means confined to virgins." It is true that *'almah* does not etymologically, like *bethulah*, denote a virgin but in general a young woman, as *'elem'* denotes a young man. They are like the German *Jungfrau* and *Juengling*. But this is only part of the story. The LXX translated *'almah* ἡ παρθένος, "the virgin." Zahn reports that since the time of Jerome it has been noted that in all the Old Testament passages where *'almah* occurs it is always used for "virgin," and that also in Isa. 54:4 *'alumim,* coupled as it is with *'almanuth* (widowhood), means only maidenhood. Moreover, the Hebrew, the LXX, and Matthew have the article. The sign is not that *a* virgin, some young woman, shall conceive in a natural way, but *"the* virgin," the specific virgin to whom also Micah 5:3 refers. "It is the virgin, whom the Spirit of prophecy reveals to the prophet, and who, although he cannot name her, stands before his soul as one chosen for extraordinary things. How exalted she appears to him is indicated by her giving the name to her son, and this the name Immanuel." Delitzsch (see his fine comment on this passage). The force of this comment is perceived when we compare Isa. 8:8; 9:5, 6; 11:1-10. No married woman conceiving in the ordinary manner, and no girl allowing herself to be seduced, could give birth to a son as great as the one Isaiah describes in these passages.

Isaiah's sign was that the virgin would conceive and bear a son whom she would rightfully call Immanuel, namely the Immanuel described by Isaiah himself: to be born, Isa. 7:14; actually born, Isa. 9:6; in his glorious reign, Isa. 11. The fulfillment of this promised sign is the incarnation and virgin conception and birth of God's own Son, who by this wondrous birth became "Immanuel," "With us God." Matthew adds the Greek translation: Μεθ' ἡμῶν ὁ Θεός, not so much because his Jewish readers would not understand "Immanuel" but in order to have them all and any others dwell on the full significance of this name. The same angel told Mary that her virgin-born son would be called "the Son of God," Luke 1:35. "He is God in bodily presentation, therefore a miracle in the form of a superhuman person. We would not dare to say this, because it transcends the Old Testament plane of knowledge, but the prophet himself says so, Isa. 9:6; 10:21; his statement is as clear as possible, we dare not darken it in the interest of a preconceived construction of history. The incarnation is, indeed, a veiled mystery in the Old Testament, but the veil is not so dense that it admits of no rays striking through. A ray of this kind, cast by the Spirit of prophecy into the spirit of the prophet, is this prophecy concerning Immanuel. But if the Messiah is Immanuel in the sense that, as the prophet explicitly says, he is himself *El* (God), then his birth also must be a miraculous one. The prophet, indeed, does not say that 'the virgin' who had not known a man would bear a son without this, so that the son would be born, not out of the house of David, but as a gift of heaven into it; but this 'virgin' was and remained a riddle in the Old Testament, mightily stirring up the inquiry and search (I Pet. 1:10-12), and awaiting a solution in historic fulfillment." Delitzsch. This solution the New Testament records.

24) **And Joseph, having arisen from his sleep, did as the angel of the Lord ordered him and took possession of his wife and did not know her until she gave birth to a son; and he called his name Jesus.** What Joseph thought is left to our imagination. Matthew tells what he did. He obeyed the angel's order as one coming from Yahweh by bringing his wife to his home and thus consummating the marriage entered into at the time of the betrothal.

25) Normally this would include marital. sexual intercourse. But the angel's revelation to Joseph concerning the divine nature of the child Mary had conceived, to which was undoubtedly added Mary's communication about Gabriel's appearance and revelation to her, caused Joseph to forego this marital right. The euphemism οὐκ ἐγίνωσκεν αὐτήν is frequently found in the Greek, also in the Hebrew and the Latin. The idea is "to know intimately," i. e., sexually, the verb being intensified. The imperfect tense intends to take the reader to the point marked by "until." Yet this clause, like all similar clauses in the New Testament, neither states nor implies what occurred afterward. That the writer must indicate otherwise. Luther's *semper virgine* in the Smalcald Articles can neither be substantiated nor denied on the basis of this "until" clause.

The reason for assuming the full marital relation after the birth of Jesus rests on other grounds, namely on the marriage bond itself. What Mary and Joseph revealed about their relation before the birth is what Matthew reports. If this relation continued afterward, we have a right to expect that it, too, would have been revealed and thus recorded by Matthew. The ordinary reader must take it that Matthew was altogether unconcerned about the intimacy after the birth, and that thus this normal intimacy followed.

The matter cannot be decided by pointing to πρωτότοκον in Luke 2:7, as though "firstborn" implies that other children were born later; see Exod. 13:2. The question whether Joseph and Mary had other children still remains an open question since no decisive statement occurs in the Gospels or elsewhere. Other children are named, but whether they were born to Mary cannot be established. To resort to general principles or considerations leads to no certainty.

We need not trouble about Isa. 7:14 where "the virgin" is the one who calls her son Immanuel, and Luke 1:31, where she is to give her son the name Jesus, while in Matthew 1:23 the angel uses the plural "they shall call," and in v. 25 Joseph bestows the name as commanded by the angel in v. 21. Joseph and Mary acted in perfect harmony as to the name "Jesus." "Immanuel" was not a given name but was descriptive of the divine nature of Jesus and of his incarnation.

## II

### Christ's Experience as a Child, Chapter 2

*The Adoration of the Magi, 2:1-12*

From the childhood of Jesus Matthew selects two highly contrasting and highly significant incidents: Gentiles adore him as the King of the Jews, and the king of the Jews attempts to murder him. While Matthew does not state this, both incidents are prophetic for the Messianic King and for his kingdom.

1) **Now after Jesus was born in Bethlehem of Judea in the days of Herod, the king, lo, magi from eastern parts arrived at Jerusalem.** Here, as in 1:25, the birth of Jesus is mentioned only in a minor clause, intimating that it is not Matthew's intention to furnish only history. He selects the historical events for a pragmatic purpose, so that each in its place and all combined may convey what lies back of the events themselves. Matthew thus reminds us of John, although each proceeds in his own way. The place and the time of the birth are not afterthoughts but pertain directly to the account now in hand. The readers will understand what follows when they are told that Jesus was born in Bethlehem, close to Jerusalem, and "of Judea" is added, not to distinguish this Bethlehem from another in Galilee, but to draw attention to the fact that Jesus, a descendant of Judah, was born in this country that was at one time allotted to the tribe of Judah; and also to bring this country into contrast with Egypt and then with Galilee, to which Joseph

finally retired, again living in Nazareth. Herod the
Great still ruled the land, bearing the royal title of king
which had been granted him by the Romans. His
introduction into the account is not intended to date
the birth of Jesus but to prepare for the action which
follows. Luke records the date of the birth more
exactly.

The surprising event now to be recorded is introduced by the interjection "lo." The surprise is so
great that the critics find the account concerning the
magi incredible and reduce it to legend and myth.
They indicate this when they translate μάγοι "magicians," which to modern readers suggests charlatans.
Matthew's account pictures these men as being of an
entirely different type. They were not sorcerers, con-
jurors, soothsayers, or the like. Their popular designation as "wise men" well defines what μάγοι really
signifies. The narrative presents them as astronomers, and this helps to indicate the part of the east
from which they came. This cannot have been Arabia.
Medo-Persia is also excluded, because the magi caste of
this territory was not noted for its study of the stars.
These magi hailed from Babylon, where since the most
ancient times and far down into the Christian Era
astronomy and astrology were sedulously pursued.
The fact that these magi undertook the long journey to
Jerusalem in order to discover the newborn "King of
the Jews," whose star they had seen, indicates that
they were not Jews, but also that the great Messianic
hope of the Jews, a hope in which they as Gentiles had
place and part, had been communicated to them by
Jews and had fascinated their hearts. This tallies
with what we know of Daniel, who 600 years prior to
this was made "chief of the governors over all the wise
men of Babylon," Dan. 2:48, "master of the magicians,
astrologers, Chaldeans, and soothsayers," Dan. 5:11.
Those who think of later Jewish contacts may add

them to what in Daniel's case is history. We must
next add the remarkable conversion to Judaism of
Helena, the queen of Adeabene, and of her son Izates,
about 40-50 after the birth of Jesus. The queen supplied Jerusalem with grain during a great famine,
Josephus, *Antiquities*, XX, 2, 1-5; 4, 3. The Mishna
reports that the king and his mother sent costly gold
vessels to the Temple in Jerusalem. The bones of both
these royal persons were sent to Jerusalem for burial.
To Matthew's first readers it did not seem so incredible
that a commission of magi should come to Jerusalem
from Babylon.

In later times many fancies arose regarding these
magi. We do not know whether they were three in
number, which conclusion rests only on the three kinds
of gifts they brought; and they were certainly not
kings, a fancy which was satisfied only with the thought
that kings should do homage to the King of the Jews.
Their names, too, are only inventions. The verb
παρεγένετο marks only their arrival in Jerusalem.

**2) Saying, Where is he that was born king of
the Jews? For we saw his star in the east and came
to worship him.** The question assumes as fact that
the birth has taken place; ὁ τεχθείς, the aorist passive
participle, denotes the past fact. The Greek is content
with this, not indicating that the fact occurred quite
recently. "King of the Jews" may recall to us the
superscription on the cross, also Nathanael's exclamation, "King of Israel," John 1:49. "King" is one of
the Old Testament Messianic titles, and the fact that
the Messiah would reign was every Jew's expectation.
"King of the Jews" marks these Chaldeans or "wise
men" as being Gentiles, though it indicates nothing
regarding the source from which they drew this title.
Rawlinson, *The Cuneiform Inscriptions*, 3, 51-64, reports regarding astrological tablets with formulas:
when this or that occurs, a great king will arise in the

west; then justice and righteousness, peace and joy
will rule in all lands and bless all nations; and other
similar expressions. Most naturally these men came
to the Jewish capital to find this King or at least to
learn of his whereabouts.

The ground on which the magi base their question
is their observation of "his star" (αὐτοῦ forward for
emphasis). They call this star "his" because they
deem its appearance a sign that the expected King has
also appeared. The singular in the phrase ἐν τῇ
ἀνατολῇ cannot be identical with the plural in v. 1 and
denote the eastern country of Babylon whence the magi
came. This phrase must denote the eastern heavens
where the star was first observed by these astronomers.
Effort has been made by searching ancient records,
even Chinese astronomical tables, and noted astronomers like Kepler have joined it in order to determine
something about this star. Some have thought of a
comet, some of a constellation, some of a meteor, etc.,
but all to no purpose. Nothing definite has been determined beyond what Matthew reports the magi themselves as saying. We must note what is said in v.
9, 10. It ought to be plain that this was not a star
such as others that our astronomers observe and study.
It appeared and then vanished; finally it reappeared,
moved on before the magi, and then stood above where
the child was in Bethlehem. No star such as we note
in the distant skies could behave in this manner. What
these magi saw was a startling phenomenon, shining
brightly like a star but so low in the heavens that it
could stand above a house and indicate it in distinction
from other houses. How high it stood when first seen,
and how low it sank when it guided the magi to
Joseph's home is not stated. No wonder astronomers
have been puzzled. This star is a miraculous phenomenon, vouchsafed to these magi by God in order
to lead them to Jesus. First its mission is to start

them on their journey; next its mission is to guide them
to the very house where Jesus was to be found.
These men read the purpose of the star aright.
How they connected it with the Messiah we shall never
know. That they did so they themselves say. "We
came," they say, "to worship him," προσκυνῆσαι, to
prostrate ourselves before him in the Oriental manner
of deepest obeisance as befits the humble subjects of
a great Oriental monarch or the humble worshippers
of God.

3) **Now when Herod, the king, heard it he was
troubled, and all Jerusalem with him.** This reads as
though the magi did not at once go to Herod; in v. 7 he
calls them to himself secretly. The news of the search
of the magi became known in the city, and word was
brought to Herod. He was troubled, ἐταράχθη, inwardly
shaken and upset. "And all Jerusalem with him," in
company with him. Ἱεροσόλυμα is here considered a feminine singular like the indeclinable transliterated form,
R. 253; see also 3:5. The reason why the city was
troubled cannot have been the same as that which upset
the king. To say that the city was devoted to the king
and feared that its interests would suffer with those
of the king is to misconceive the situation. Herod
understood well enough that the King referred to by
the magi was the promised Messiah of the Jews. What
he feared was a grand Jewish movement in favor of
this royal Messiah, dethroning the alien house of
Herod which had usurped the throne of David. The
city readily guessed the true reason of Herod's agitation and on its part feared the violent measures the
bloody old despot might take in putting down any
movement that might arise in favor of the Messiah
King. The contrast is highly dramatic and significant:
the Gentile magi come from distant lands to worship
the newborn King, Herod and the Jewish capital are
upset at the thought of such a King.

4) Herod's first move is to find out where the
Messiah is to be born.  Superstitious fear of the truth
of the sign the magi have seen is combined with confidence in Scripture prophecies; and yet the wickedness in his heart imagines that he will be able to
destroy this royal Babe.  **And having gathered all
the high priests and scribes of the people, he inquired of them where the Christ is born.**  He calls a
plenary session of the Sanhedrin.  While this body
was composed of three sets of members: the high
priests, the scribes, and the elders, all three are not
always mentioned when designating this body.  "Of
the people" may be construed with both preceding
nouns.  The scribes were the professional students of
the law and the experts in its exposition; only the most
prominent of them held membership in the Sanhedrin.
The plural "high priests" refers to the family of the
ruling high priest.  The office was no longer held for
life but was transferred from one to another for
political reasons.  Former high priests still retained
the title, which seems to have been accorded also to
other relatives of the high priest who were members
of the Sanhedrin.  Either in person or through a
representative the king demanded to know "where the
Christ is born."  The question clearly indicates that
Herod knows who is referred to by "the King of the
Jews"; ὁ Χριστός is, of course, appellative.  The present
tense may be considered a futuristic prophetic present,
R. 866, or the timeless present in an abstract statement.

5)  **But they said to him, In Bethlehem of Judea;
for thus it has been written through the prophet:**

**And thou, Bethlehem, land of Judah,
By no means art least among the leaders of
    Judah;
For out of thee shall come forth one that leads,
Who shall shepherd my people Israel.**

Herod may have known the answer to his question, for the Jews generally knew it as John 7:42 plainly shows. What Herod wanted was an official, authoritative declaration from the highest authority available. His wicked motive must not blind us to the good sense he showed by demanding an answer from the Sanhedrin. Yet we note the hand of God in the providence which has put the Sanhedrin of the Jews, its highest religious authority, back of the Scriptural finding that the Messiah must be born in Bethlehem, and that the Old Testament so declares in Micah 5:2. The very great value of this providence Matthew felt when he wrote this Gospel for Jewish readers. Every Jew down to this day is faced by Micah 5:2 and the Sanhedrin's answer to Herod. The Messiah is an individual not the Jewish nation itself. His birth must occur in Bethlehem and nowhere else. If Jesus is not this Messiah, then let the Jew tell us what Micah 5:2 means and let him contradict both this prophet and his own Sanhedrin if he will.

Very properly the Sanhedrin quotes the Scripture passage from which its answer is drawn. From what other source could any true answer be drawn? Moreover, to this day all men are able to examine the answer and to see for themselves whether it is correct according to Micah's word. It most certainly is. "In Bethlehem of Judea" must stand even as the Sanhedrin pronounced. The only alternative is to reject Micah and together with him the Old Testament as such. When this is done, all divine religious grounds have been removed. The perfect tense γέγραπται must be noted as the constant formula for the written Word: once thus written, it stands forever. Note also διά, as in 1:22, "through the prophet," he being the instrument, God the real agent; compare 1:22 on this mark of inspiration. Matthew's Gospel is full of Old Testament quotations; but it is surely noteworthy that the first two quotations recorded by Matthew are adduced, not by him, but by others, by an angel and by the Sanhedrin. When, then, Matthew himself quotes the Old Testament, we see that he only follows these notable examples.

6) The fact that the quotation is made by the Sanhedrin itself and not by Matthew is as clear as that the first quotation is made by the angel in 1:23. It is an unwarranted assumption, underlying so much of the comment on quotations, that all quotations must be exactly literal and reproduce the *ipsissima verba* of the original. The New Testament writers use the same freedom in quoting that we ourselves and others use. We dare not misquote, which means that we dare not change the true meaning of the original. Beyond that we are free. Part of this liberty is that we may quote interpretatively, which means that we may make such changes in the original as will bring out its true meaning for the situation or the case we may just have in hand. The one point for which the Sanhedrin quotes Micah 5:2 is the name of the place of the birth of the Messiah. The deviations from the original intend to make the prophet's meaning fully clear as to this point. Thus the ancient name "Ephratah" ("fruitful") was not needed in addition to the current name "Bethlehem" ("house of bread") ; and the Sanhedrists substituted "land of Judah" from I Sam. 17:12: "Beth-lehem-judah," since the comparison of the prophet dealt with the section in which Bethlehem lay and the other sections of Judah.

The change from, "too little to be among the thousands of Judah" (thus literally), to, "by no means least," etc., states the thought only in a little different way. Too little to have a place when the thousands were counted by no means puts this section down as the least among all the sections. This is really a fine litotes, for it means to say that this little section is really the greatest of all because it would be the birth-place of the Messiah. An *'eleph* is a thousand, count-ing families and family heads, and *'alluph* is *Gau-haeuptling*, the head or chief of a section having at least a thousand families. When the Sanhedrin thus used the plural of the latter instead of that of the former, so that Matthew wrote in Greek, ἐν τοῖς ἡγεμόσιν, it is altogether unnecessary to assume that the San-hedrists had a Hebrew text that was different from ours, or that the supposed translator of Matthew's Hebrew Gospel mistranslated; for each section in Judah naturally had a ἡγεμών, a leader or chief. In-stead of naming "the thousands" (population) the Sanhedrists merely named "the leaders or chiefs" of the thousands. They thus also secure a play on words between ἐν τοῖς ἡγεμόσιν and ἡγούμενος: "among the lead-ers" and "one that leads" (the Messiah). The many lead only their respective thousand, but this One leads all Israel. The wording of the Sanhedrists is thus decidedly to the point.

"Shall come forth" translates Micah's verb quite exactly, as also the question to be answered deals with the birthplace of the Christ. The Sanhedrin so under-stood the prophet's word. Their final words, "who shall shepherd my people Israel," are nothing but an expansion of Micah's words, "he that is to be ruler in Israel," adapting II Sam. 5:2. Micah's fourth line is omitted as not being pertinent to the answer desired by Herod. The figure of shepherding a people, ruling them with the wise and tender care of a shepherd, thus recalls the rule of David and brings in an expression often found in both Testaments.

7) The wily king now knew the place; he needed to know another point: the time of the birth. In ὁ τεχθείς (v. 2) the magi had stated only that the King "was born." **Then Herod, after secretly calling the magi, ascertained from them the time of the shining**

**star.** The inquiry addressed to the Sanhedrin was
public and stated exactly and openly what Herod
desired to know. His question had a natural air as
being one prompted by the curiosity aroused by the
arrival of the magi and as meeting their inquiry:
*where* is this King? The meeting with the magi is
secret for the reason that Herod wants to hide his
interest in the matter of this King, lest Jerusalem
become suspicious regarding this interest, and the
populace be still more disturbed. In this secret audience the king also hides his intent. He really wants
to find out just *when* this King was born. But he says
nothing about this King or his birth. He is curious
only about the star, in particular about "the time" of
the star, i. e., the length of time it shone. His real
object is to find out just when it first appeared, for he
thinks that will mark the date of this King's conception
or of his birth.

The present participle φαινομένου is generally regarded as an imperfect, since the imperfect has no
participle and thus uses the present: "the time of the
star that shone or appeared," i. e., how long it shone.
But it may also be used irrespective of time, since the
point Herod was after was τὸν χρόνον, the extent of the
time. The implication is that the star was now not
visible. The magi could not point to it in Jerusalem;
they did not again see it until the night they left for
Bethlehem (v. 9). While it may be true that the first
appearance of the star in Babylonia was coincident
with the conception or with the birth of Jesus, just as
Herod probably assumed, we do not know how long it
shone, how soon after its appearance the magi realized
what it signified, or when at last they started for
Jerusalem. The two years and under in v. 16 only
indicate that Herod meant to make sure that Jesus
would be caught in the slaughter; in other words, he
allowed his minions an ample margin. The exact date

of Jesus' birth cannot be determined from the present narrative.

8) Herod learned what he wanted to know for his purpose without raising suspicion in the magi. In fact, he pretended the same religious interest in this King as that which animated the magi. **And he sent them to Bethlehem and said, When you have gone, carefully search out about the young child. And when you find, report to me in order that I, too, may come and worship him.** A lie such as this could hope to impress the magi, who knew neither Herod nor Jerusalem, only when it was offered to them in a secret conference. Unwittingly these Oriental admirers of the Messianic King are to become Herod's tools for that king's destruction. The hellish net is most cunningly spread. The aorist participle πέμψας here expresses time that is simultaneous with that of the aorist main verb εἶπεν. We must use two finite verbs and thus lose the point that the sending is the minor action. Πορευθέντες, however, indicates action previous to that of ἐξετάσατε, hence: "when you have gone, search out," etc. The same is true regarding the purpose clause: "that I, too, having come, may worship him."

9) Elated over the valuable information they had received and over the king's holy sentiments, so perfectly in accord with their own, the magi left the audience and that very night departed for Bethlehem. **And they, after hearing the king, went. And, lo, the star which they saw in the east was going before them until, having come, it stood above where the young child was.** After the audience with the king the magi promptly left for Bethlehem. The aorist merely reports the fact. Significantly they left alone. No numerous delegation from Herod's palace accompanied them to help in discovering the Child and to join in worship of the Messiah King. Were the magi

struck by this significant circumstance? They went on alone.

The road to Bethlehem, a journey of only two hours, was direct and most easy to find; the magi needed no guide. Hence the surprise marked by "lo" at the appearance of the star. The tense in the expression "which they saw in the east" (see v. 2), implies: and not since then. At that time they saw it "in the east," i. e., in that direction; now it "was going before them," προῆγεν, the descriptive imperfect. But this imperfect, picturing the movement as going on, requires that we be told how it ended. So the clause with the aorist follows: "until, having come, it stood," etc. The star moved as a guide; the star arrived (ἐλθών); the star stood (ἐστάθη). It is all perfectly plain, absolutely miraculous, unlike any star that ever existed.

We are, however, told that the star did not move, that the magi went only in the general direction of the star; it was "no guiding star"; the whole thing was merely an optical illusion and the star appeared to stand still only when the magi stood still. We are also told about stars in the heart, which act like the magnet pointing toward the pole. Finally, we are told that the star did not do what Matthew writes because this was impossible. All these views operate with a star high in the heavens like the other stars and forget that on a clear night literally hundreds of stars will twinkle above Bethlehem, and no new star among them could direct any man either on the way or to a certain house in the town, or, for that matter, in the open country. Unless Matthew is telling a fictional child's story, this star hung so low, with a light brilliant to the eye, that it did just what he reports: move just above the road, move from north to south, and finally stand above the very house where the Child was, so low that it designated that house and no other. The idea that the magi inquired for a house where a boy had recently been born is not indicated in the text. God pointed out the house by means of his star.

**10) Now when they saw the star they rejoiced with joy exceedingly great.** Evidently this took place when they again beheld the star after leaving Jerusalem. The participle, though used with a verb of emotion, is circumstantial, R. 1122, indicating the cause of the joy. Already the cognate accusative ἐχάρησαν χαράν, "they rejoiced with joy," means that they rejoiced greatly; but Matthew adds both an adjective and an adverb: "rejoiced with joy very great," σφόδρα, one of Matthew's favorite words. Luther thinks the magi felt sad before this, yet they seem to have been happy enough. But when the star appeared and moved as it did, their joy knew no bounds; for not only was God directing them miraculously, they also knew they would soon be in the presence of the King. That star has left a radiance of "joy exceedingly great" which has never grown dim.

**11) And having come into the house, they saw the young child together with Mary, his mother; and having fallen down, they worshipped him; and having opened their treasures, they offered him gifts: gold and frankincense and myrrh.** Three circumstantial aorist participles to indicate the preliminary and minor actions, three aorist finite verbs to express the main actions, the three sentences constructed alike, and the whole most graphically told. "The house" = "where the young child was," the house indicated by the star. This by no means has Matthew say that Jesus was born in this house. It is now some time after the birth. Joseph undoubtedly secured a house for his little family at the earliest possible moment after the birth. The mention of only Mary with the child is probably due to the fact that they found the child in her arms. No significance is to be attached to the omission of the mention of Joseph who must have admitted the magi at the door.

The great fact must ever be noted that the magi fell down and worshipped this child, born in this little village and not in Jerusalem; living in a house and in surroundings of the poorest kind; lying in the arms of a mother who was ranked among the lowliest of the land.   And these were men who were often in the presence of the king of Babylon, themselves high, mighty, and wealthy.   From the capital and King Herod they had come to this poor house.   They treat it as the grandest of palaces and this little child as the most glorious king.   How could they do this? Their hearts must have beheld what their eyes did not see.

The little pronoun αὐτῷ is noteworthy.   Not to the child and to Mary but to the child alone they offer their worship and their gifts.   What could the little child know about prostration and offerings?   The only others present were Mary and Joseph, and surely the magi could not desire to impress two such humble people.   The question is therefore rightly asked whether these magi thought only of an earthly king. Everything about them and their arrival in the presence of this Babe points to a religious understanding on their part.   God would not lead men as he had led them if this child were only exceptional in this regard, that through some future providence Herod's throne or some earthly realm like Babylon should become its possession.   The verb προσήνεγκαν befits offerings made to God.

Their "treasures" are the receptacles in which their valuable gifts were kept.   We do not read that they brought gifts to Herod even when they had their audience with them.   The gifts they had carried many a mile from Babylon are for this little Child who is able to receive them only through his parents.   And

they are certainly royal gifts. To call them products
of their land is probably a mistake. We know of no
gold native to the territory of Babylon, and frankincense and myrrh of the finest quality came from India
and, undoubtedly, were imported. That gold should
be an offering seems natural. If jewels and fine
apparel had been added, these, too, would have been
in order. But what was this child to do with the
fine odor of frankincense which was burnt on altars,
or with myrrh, an aromatic gum, or the perfume
drawn from it? If these offerings, so lavishly prof-
fered, have a religious motive they are more readily
intelligible. If these magi see before them a divine
child they are right in offering not only the gold with
the thought of relieving his poverty but in carrying
out their original intention and now not holding back
the frankincense and the myrrh.

The moderns esteem these gifts too lightly when
they call them merely royal. They often ask what this
or that person had in mind when he said or did this or
that, but such an inquiry does not seem to come to
their minds when they read about the magi making
these gifts. The ancients did better: gold, they
thought, was intended for the child as being the King;
frankincense for him as being God; and myrrh for
him as destined to die. This interpretation is both
the oldest and the most widely accepted. Devout
minds of later times content themselves with allegorizing for devotional and homiletical purposes: the gold
of faith, the frankincense of prayer, and the myrrh
of patient suffering. This allegorizing is typically
modern by letting the gifts reflect, not what the Child
is (King, God, Sacrifice), but what we do (believe,
pray, suffer). The ancients were nearer the truth.
The thought that the price these gifts brought
assisted in the flight to Egypt is foreign to Matthew's
narrative.

12) **And having been divinely warned in a dream not to turn back to Herod, they withdrew by another road to their country.** The verb χρηματίζω is used with regard to any divine communication; the idea that here it was in the form of a warning is derived from the situation alone. The verb does not always imply that God is first asked and then makes a reply. Just as God sent the star so he sent this communication. The entire journey of the magi thus appears as being under God's immediate direction. On the phrase "in a dream," and on the use of dreams in giving revelations, see 1:20. The magi are not innocently and unwittingly to play into Herod's murderous hands. God is guarding the holy Child. In ἀναχωρεῖν lies the idea of withdrawal from danger; the magi slipped away by taking the road to Jericho and across the Jordan and thus were beyond the power of Herod.

Matthew himself does not say that the coming of these Gentiles was a fulfillment of prophecy. Probably, when Matthew wrote his Gospel, this incident had not yet been made the subject of Jewish attack and thus for Jewish readers did not need to be fortified by references to prophecy. Yet Ps. 72:10; Isa. 60:6, and other prophecies are certainly in line with the present remarkable incident. Matthew, it seems, regards the adoration of the magi as itself being a factual prophecy of the future reception of the King of the Jews in the great Gentile world, even as he closes his Gospel with the commissioning of the church and the apostles to all nations. The great contrast between Jerusalem and the magi is significant to the highest degree. The magi come all the way from Babylon, Jerusalem has Bethlehem right at its door. God condescends to use a strange star, a means adapted to the magi, for bringing them to the revelation in the Word (Micah) and thus to the Messiah, and these magi respond wholeheartedly; Jerusalem has had the Word for ages and, when it learns of Bethlehem through the magi, responds not at all. From Jerusalem comes only an attempt to murder the Messiah. The cold facts as here recorded are certainly damaging to the Jews. The news that their highest and holiest hopes are being realized leaves them under the dominance of the lowest motives. It has been well said: the apologist becomes a prosecutor.

The Sanhedrists are frequently represented as being orthodox, correct in doctrine but spiritually dead. Flings at teachers of sound theology are then based on this view. But the high priests were rank liberalists in doctrine, and the entire question in the present case was one of mere location with which doctrine is even now not concerned. Graver is the assault on Matthew's use of the narrative concerning the magi, making history reflect an underlying idea. Zahn's reply is to the point. "Is it, therefore, not to be history? Or is this name merited only by the brutal facts which torture the thoughtful and the godly observer of history because they leave his mind empty?"

### The Slaughter of the Innocents, 2:13-25

13) **Now when they had withdrawn, lo, an angel of the Lord appears to Joseph in a dream, saying: Arise, take the young child and his mother and be fleeing into Egypt and be there until I shall tell thee. For Herod is about to seek the young child in order to destroy it.** Matthew frequently uses the genitive absolute as a temporal clause: "they having withdrawn," the participle being drawn from the verb used in v. 12, ἀναχωρεῖν, here "to evade danger." Matthew's entire account reads as though Joseph intended to

remain in Bethlehem indefinitely had it not been for the intention of Herod. The Child must have been weeks old by the time the magi arrived. The impression their surprising visit made is at once followed by another with a surprise of the very opposite kind. If the magi left Jerusalem toward evening and arrived in Bethlehem an hour or so after dark, they, as well as Joseph, received the divine warning that same night, and both the magi and Joseph must have left Bethlehem that very night. On "an angel of the Lord" and on the matter of divine communications in a dream, as well on κατά in the phrase employed, see 1:20. The interjection "lo" has its own peculiar significance in this instance because of the startling nature of the message. God honors Joseph as the legal father and also the foster-father of Jesus. The care of the Child is in his hands, and so the angel comes to him with directions.

The angel's command is literally, "Having arisen, take possession of the young child," etc. The accessory action is expressed by the aorist participle, the passive form with the active meaning. The main verb παράλαβε is identical with the one used in 1:20, the aorist tenses to indicate single acts. Joseph is to arise at once, bundle up the Child and Mary, and hurry from Bethlehem with them. The present imperative φεῦγε is durative to indicate the flight that will require days of travel. "To Egypt" Joseph is to move his little family, to a distant, foreign land, to which he had never expected to go. Yet many Jews lived also in Egypt; Joseph would find many countrymen and friends there. The magi are warned in only the briefest way, just "not to turn back to Herod"; but Joseph, as in 1:20, etc., receives both full directions and adequate explanation. He is to stay in Egypt until the angel himself tells him when to come back, thus promising him another appearance at a future day. And now the reason for these astonishing directions is stated with great clearness. On their brief visit the magi may well have told how they had seen the star in Babylonia, and how Herod had directed them to Bethlehem, and how by the aid of the star they had found the very house in which the holy family lived. Now the perfidy of Herod is revealed to Joseph: "Herod is about to seek the young child in order to destroy it," μέλλει with the present infinitive with τοῦ is constantly used to express purpose, and the aorist ἀπολέσαι indicates a brief, momentary act.

So close to adoration and offerings murder stalked. We may well imagine the consternation that followed when, shortly after the dream, Joseph awoke and also awakened Mary. Yet they felt safe under Jehovah's protection, whose angel had brought them warning. We may ask just why Jehovah chose flight for the Child instead of using some other means to thwart Herod's plans. Later we shall see Jesus repeatedly evading his murderous enemies. God knows how to use both supernatural and natural means, and in the present case both are combined.

14) **And he, having arisen, took the young child and his mother at night and withdrew to Egypt.** The genitive νυκτός expresses time within which, "at night," at some hour during the night. When morning came, the family had disappeared, and the magi had also disappeared. If a few people in Bethlehem had seen them the evening before, they must have been greatly perplexed the next morning when they as well as Joseph's little family were gone. Observe the verb "withdrew," the same verb used in verses 12 and 13. While Bethlehem was deep in sleep, Joseph and his charges fled. We cannot think that they told a soul that they were leaving or whither they were going, lest Herod should find out and overtake them; for, surely, they could not travel rapidly.

The way in which Matthew narrates these events is characteristic of him. He has details enough, but all his details are quite essential to his aim and purpose. Many details that we should like to have inserted in order to picture the events as they actually occurred are sternly omitted. Matthew's eye is directed toward the Old Testament, where God drew the outlines of the coming Messiah, and these outlines Matthew fills in with the actual history of the Messiah who had come. This greater purpose is enough for him, and all that is less he leaves aside. We should like to know whether Joseph and Mary went afoot, or whether for Mary at least an ass was provided, as the painters love to picture the Flight. But Matthew has no answer to such questions. They fled at night — that is all.

15) **And he was there until the death of Herod, that it might be fulfilled what was spoken by the Lord through the prophet, saying, Out of Egypt did I call my son.** Nothing is as yet said about the return, only the duration of the stay in Egypt is stressed. And with this stay Matthew connects the second line of Hos. 11:1. The same formula of quotation is used as was used in 1:22, which see. "What was spoken by the Lord," τὸ ῥηθέν, is what we now possess in writing. The neuter aorist participle states only the past fact of God's speaking, while in the other regularly employed formula (v. 5) the perfect γέγραπται adds to the past fact of writing the present existence of that writing. By referring to the written Word as "what was spoken by the Lord," Matthew marks each written statement of the Word as something that was spoken by the Lord. How this formula expresses inspiration, and that in the true Biblical sense, we have pointed out in 1:22.

Matthew naturally discards the LXX with its plural τὰ τέκνα, which is well enough for general purposes but not nearly exact enough for what the prophet really says and what Matthew intends to use. So he himself translates the Hebrew: "Out of Egypt did I call my son." In this first Old Testament quotation which Matthew introduces of his own accord he cites only the words he intends to use. And this is the real difference between the present quotation and that made by the Sanhedrin in v. 6, where the essential point was only the name of the birthplace, and all other words were of minor importance and could thus be rendered with any desired freedom if only their general sense remained. See the remarks on v. 6. Now Hos. 11:1 is really only a historical statement although it is made by Jehovah himself. The first line of the passage, "When Israel was a child, then I loved him," shows that Jehovah is speaking of the childhood period of Israel when the young nation grew up in Egypt. Matthew reads Hos. 11:1 in exactly that sense and changes nothing. And yet he says that this statement of the prophet found its fulfillment when the child Jesus dwelt in Egypt. In what sense does Matthew understand: "that it might be fulfilled"?

He certainly intends more than a mere coincident resemblance between the childhood of Israel as Jehovah's son or chosen nation and the childhood of Jesus, the divine Son, both spending their early days in Egypt and thus both being called back from Egypt into the Holy Land. Mere accidental coincidences amount to little. Matthew sees far more here. Mere escape from Herod was not nearly all that God had in mind for Jesus. Then he might have arranged for the transfer of the holy family to Babylon by the aid of the magi. Abstractly considered it would have made no difference from what foreign land God would recall Jesus. What Matthew points out is an inner and divinely intended connection between the two sojourns in Egypt. God brought about the first sojourn and made that first sojourn a factual prophecy of the second, which he also brought about. The first is thus a divinely intended type of the second. It is *not* accidental that the angel sent Joseph to Egypt and to no other land. In addition to the word-prophecies we must recognize the fact-prophecies. It is the nature of the latter that they can be recognized only by and through their fulfilment. It is always the antitype which reveals the type as what it really is in God's original intention. So here we see how the wickedness of Jacob's sons brought Joseph to Egypt, and Herod's wickedness did the same in the case of Jesus. Again, God caused this wickedness to lead to a refuge for the youthful people Israel in the shelter of Egypt, and then sheltered Jesus in Egypt in the same way. His wisdom and his love arranged it all.

But God did more. Into the type he laid the key for the future recognition of the antitype. Matthew does not refer merely to the fact of Israel's early sojourn in Egypt. The fact itself contains no key. He takes Hosea's inspired statement of the fact in which the child Israel is by Jehovah himself called "my son." Read apart from the antitype, this designation had only its ordinary meaning, but read in conjunction with the antitype Jesus, "my son" becomes highly significant. Deut. 32:18 states that Israel was begotten as Jehovah's son, and this is a fatherhood which exceeds that of Abraham and of Jacob (Isa. 63:16) and thus points to the miraculous begetting of the Son Jesus "of the Holy Spirit" (1:20; Luke 1:35). We now see how Matthew connects "my son" in Hosea and Israel's early sojourn in Egypt as a true type and a divinely intended prophecy of "my Son," the Messiah, who likewise must sojourn in Egypt. Both had to leave the Holy Land, and all

the Messianic hopes connected with them seemed to
be utterly lost in far-off Egypt. Yet "did call out of
Egypt" places the sure hand of God behind all these
hopes. Israel returned from Egypt for its mission,
and so did this greater Son, Jesus.

We have seen that Matthew connects Hosea's word
with the stay of Jesus in Egypt and not with the
return from Egypt, which is not reported until v. 21.
This rightly leads to the conclusion that something
is connected with that stay. Back into the first century the Jewish slanders have been traced (Zahn,
*Matthaeus*, 108) which prolonged the stay of Jesus in
Egypt and made him there learn the magical arts, the
formulas of which he etched into his skin and afterward
practiced as miracles in the Holy Land. Matthew
meets these slanders effectively. Israel itself lived in
this same Egypt for a long time; only as a small child
was Jesus in Egypt, for three years and six or seven
months; and it was the Jewish king's intent of murder
that necessitated the stay in Egypt. The true facts
remove the slanderous allegations.

16) Now the narrative proceeds. **Then Herod,
when he saw that he was made a fool by the magi,
was highly enraged, and, having sent, slew all the
boys in Bethlehem and in all the borders thereof
from two years old and under, according to the time
which he ascertained from the magi.** The magi had
not come back as they had very likely promised to do
when Herod gave them their directions. Since Bethlehem was only two hours distant, Herod must have
looked for them the next day, at least the second day.
Then, becoming suspicious, it was a matter of a few
hours to discover that the magi had vanished. The rest
follows blow upon blow. Matthew has all the dramatic
essentials, though, of course, as is his method, these
alone. Herod saw "that he was made a fool by the
magi," ἐμπαίζω, *einen zum Narren haben.* The con-

viction flashed into this deceiver's mind that the magi
had seen through his cunning scheme and had left him
waiting like a fool while they slipped away. He
judged them by his own standard. At once he burst
into violent rage, θυμόω, used only here, and passive, like
our "was enraged." This blinded his good sense; for
if the magi had sensed his treachery, he might well
conclude that they had warned the parents. In his
blind rage Herod orders the killing of the baby boys
in the whole neighborhood. The subsidiary actions
are neatly expressed by participles, so here ἀποστείλας,
"having sent," i. e., having given commission to some
officers to have the bloody deed done; ἀνεῖλε (ἀναιρέω),
"he made away with," i. e., he murdered. The deed
is Herod's. How it was done Matthew does not record
as being immaterial for his purpose. We may
imagine that bands of soldiers were rushed into Bethlehem (others think of assassins with daggers) and
searched every house.

We do not think that any secrecy was attempted
or any cunning trick devised to get hold of the victims.
The whole account presents brutal, ruthless action.
The babes were snatched from their mothers and
slashed to death before their eyes. Terror reigned.
The age of the boys is specified: "from two years old
and under," and διετοῦς is an adjective in the genitive
singular, construed *ad sensum* with no noun to be
supplied; κατωτέρω, a comparative adverb, literally
"more downward." This age limit Herod arrived at
on the basis of what he had quietly ascertained from
the magi regarding the time of the star's appearance
in Babylon (see v. 7). We may take it that Herod
set the limit sufficiently high so as to be sure to include Jesus. "From two years old" includes all
that were not yet three years old and all below that
age. The number killed is not given and is estimated
from the probable population and from the average

number of baby boys in such a population. Yet statistical averages are not followed by all commentators. Some of them allow themselves to be influenced by the circumstance that Josephus, who records the great, bloody crimes of Herod, omits mention of this crime. Why he does so has not been ascertained although various hypotheses are offered. Some critics cite the silence of Josephus as proof for the unhistorical character of Matthew's account, although the *argumentum e silentio* is never proof. In order to make the crime small enough so that Josephus neglected to record it, the number of boys is placed at six to eight; others go up to thirty.

These little babes are really the first Christian martyrs.

17) **Then was fulfilled what was spoken through Jeremiah, the prophet, saying:**

**A voice in Ramah was heard,**
**Weeping and mourning great,**
**Rachel sobbing for her children**
**And would not be comforted because they are not.**

Here Matthew shows us how he wants us to regard Herod's frightful act of murder. It was part of the calamities that Israel brought upon itself by its unbelief and wickedness; we may say that in the case of some it was the last of these calamities before the revelation of the Messiah. The idea is not merely superficial likeness: inconsolable weeping in Bethlehem. The inner cause of the two weepings is identical, and thus the one is poured into the other to make the vessel full. Israel's sin caused the Assyrians to carry the ten tribes of the northern kingdom into an exile where they entirely disappeared: "they are not." It is the same sin that placed a foreign monster, the Idumean Herod, on the Jewish throne at the time of the birth of the Messiah and thus enabled him to slay the children of Bethlehem, so that of them, too, it was true: "they were not."

Yet Matthew does not write ἵνα as he does in the quotations in 1:22 and 2:15. In these latter two cases God's intention and purpose ruled, not so in Herod's act, for which he personally bears the sole responsibility. The fact that Matthew omits the phrase "by the Lord" is of no moment, since in Jer. 31:15 these words are introduced by, "thus saith the Lord." The fact that Matthew mentions the name of the prophet whom he quotes may in this instance be due to the circumstance that Jeremiah is the prophet of sorrow and weeping. On the further points involved in the formulas of quotation see 1:22; 2:5, 15. There has been much discussion on Ramah and on a possible personal connection of Rachel with this town. Ramah is a town north of Jerusalem, and in Jeremiah it is mentioned by the Lord because the people who were carried into exile were assembled at Ramah. Other places that have this name are out of the question; and the suppositions that Rachel was buried at Ramah, or that Matthew confused Ramah with Bethlehem, or mystically identified the two, or forgot that the Bethlehemites were descended from Lea through Judah and not from Rachel through Ephraim and Joseph — deserve little mention. Rachel is intended to represent the nation just as "the daughter of Zion" does. In her, as the favorite wife of Jacob who so greatly longed for children, "the voice of weeping and mourning great" for the exiles who are carried away is made concrete and realistically individual. Poetically she is pictured as still being alive and watching the deportation, not as being dead and weeping in her grave.

Matthew himself translates the Hebrew with very minor changes. "Rachel" is in apposition to "a voice

in Ramah." Of course, the voice referred to is that
of Rachel; it is not some unknown voice sounding
into Ramah from the outside. Ramah lies on the
heights at the border of the two kingdoms; the voice
of weeping could thus be heard in both lands. The
imperfect ἤθελε describes the continuance of Rachel's
inconsolable condition, and yet this open tense points
to an outcome of her sorrow, namely to the comfort
pronounced by Jehovah in Jer. 31:16, 17. This comfort is not included in Matthew's quotation; .still we
may here add that, when she is told by Jehovah that
her children "shall come again from the land of the
enemy," this does not refer to a physical return of
the lost ten tribes to Palestine during some millennium, but to the future conversion of the Gentiles, by
whom the ten tribes were absorbed.

19) **Now when Herod was dead, lo, an angel of
the Lord appears to Joseph in a dream in Egypt, saying: Arise, take the young child and his mother, and
be going into Israel's land; for they have died who
were seeking the life of the young child.** As in v. 1
and v. 13 a genitive absolute again marks the time,
the aorist τελευτήσαντος merely noting the fact that
Herod had come to his end. That is all that Matthew
says about Herod, but read Josephus, *Antiquities*,
17, 6, 5, regarding that horrible end: entrails rotting,
privy member putrified and producing worms, unbear-
able stench, convulsions, etc., prolonged, useless
attempts at cures, bloody, murderous thoughts — the
death of a moral monster. Matthew has the Hebrew
style which repeats a chosen way of saying a thing,
introducing scarcely any variation. So here compare
1:20 and 2:13: each after a genitive absolute has:
"lo, an angel of the Lord appeared (appears) to him
(to Joseph) in a dream, saying." See the exposition
of 1:20. As promised in 2:13, the angel returns to

direct the further course of Joseph. In what locality of Egypt the family dwelt is unknown.

20) The directions of the angel begin exactly as those in v. 13. But now the imperative is πορεύου, "be going," befitting a leisurely return. And only the Holy Land in general is indicated in the phrase "to Israel's land," a designation used only in these closing verses, the genitive, however, using the ancient honorable and religious name "Israel" to designate the nation. As the phrase "to Egypt" in v. 13 leaves the choice of a specific locality to Joseph, so now again Joseph may choose just where in Israel's land he would dwell.

Once more we note that the Lord adds the full explanation for the sake of Joseph: "for they have died," etc., the perfect tense with the strong present connotation, "and now are dead." The plural subject perplexes the commentators. Some point to Exod. 4:19, but there the plural is altogether informal and is even made emphatic by the addition of "all," while in the present case only Herod has been mentioned as seeking the life of the Child, and only his death has been mentioned in the genitive absolute at the head of the verse. This induces some to regard οἱ ζητοῦντες (a timeless present, R. 1111) as a plural of category, which is used when an individual is referred to, in order to make the thought general, that no danger of any kind now threatens the Child's life, thus: "Herod and in him the entire class of mortal foes," B.-D. 141. The majestic plural cannot be considered. R. 392, 406 thinks the plural is intended to conceal identity. Since ψυχή is commonly used as a designation for "life," it is not necessary to refer to the "soul" and its connection with the blood shed by a violent death. To seek the life means to seek to kill.

21) **And he, having arisen, took the young child and his mother** (the same wording as in v. 14) **and went into Israel's land.** This reads as though, just as the angel had left the location open for future decision, so also Joseph left it open until something more would determine the choice.

22) **But after hearing that Archelaus was reigning over Judea in place of his father Herod, he feared to go there; and having been divinely directed in a dream, withdrew into the parts of Galilee, and, having come, settled in a town called Nazareth, in order that what was spoken through the prophets might be fulfilled, for he shall be called a Nazarene.** Not until Joseph reached the Holy Land did he hear of the accession of Archelaus to the throne of Judea. This son of Herod the Great received Judea, Samaria, and Idumea but had received only the title "ethnarch" and not "king" from Caesar Augustus. By a final change in his father's will the oldest son Antipas (Antipater) received only Galilee and Perea. Philip I (whose wife Herodias and daughter Salome left him) received nothing. Philip II obtained Batanæa, Trachonitis, etc. Josephus records the details, among them the bloody act with which Archelaus began his reign. One of Herod's last acts was the slaying of Judas and Matthias for instigating the pulling down of the golden eagle Herod had placed above the Temple gate. At the time of the following Passover Archelaus, though not as yet confirmed as ruler by Caesar, found several people commiserating the martyrs. He ordered his calvary to surround the Tempel and slew 3,000. The rest fled to the mountains, and everybody abandoned the Passover, "lest something worse should ensue." This was the news that greeted Joseph in "Israel's land" and filled him with dread.

From Luke we learn that at first Joseph and Mary lived in Nazareth in Galilee and how it came about that they moved to Bethlehem. Matthew writes as though they intended to stay in Bethlehem indefinitely and were driven away only by Herod's plot. And now that Herod was dead, all the implications of Matthew's narrative are to the effect that Joseph would like to have settled in Bethlehem. The reason is not difficult to find. Galilee was despised by Jerusalem as "Galilee of the Gentiles," inhabited by a mixed population, Matt. 4:15; Isa. 9:1; I Macc. 5:15. Whatever was done in Galilee was done, as it were, "in secret," and only what was done in Jerusalem was considered as being done "to the world," on the real Jewish world stage, John 7:3, 4. In Jerusalem the Temple stood, and here was the vital center of the theocracy. According to Joseph's thought the proper place for the young Messiah to grow up was the neighborhood of the Holy City and certainly not the half-Gentile Galilee. A comparison of Matthew and of Luke does not reveal a discrepancy or contradiction but only adds to our information. But Joseph found his fears too great to risk residence in Bethlehem or anywhere in Judea. The present tense βασιλεύει is due to indirect discourse; after a past tense the Greek does not need to change the tense. It is like the English "was reigning." The verb does not necessarily mean, "to be king"; it is used generally with reference to rulers, "to reign" or govern.

In v. 12 χρηματίζω has the idea of warning because of the context. The verb itself in the passive means only to receive a divine communication, and this is the thought here. There is no implication in the verb that Joseph prayed to God and thus received an answer from above. The opposite is the case. In the midst of his fears God directed him as he had done twice before. The expression is exactly like that

used in v. 12 regarding the divine directions given
to the magi "in a dream." In neither case is "an
angel of the Lord" mentioned, and thus none should
be introduced by us. How these two communications
were made we are not told. The scruples of Joseph
about returning to Galilee were overcome. By taking
Jesus to this country he would not be acting contrary
to Jehovah's will. With "the parts of Galilee" open
to him, Joseph quite naturally selected Nazareth and
settled in his former home where he and Mary had
many friends.

23) While God thus left the choice of the town
to Joseph, and Joseph alone selected this place, the
hand of providence was, nevertheless, in the selection
thus made. This is made evident by the purpose
clause: "in order that what was spoken through the
prophets might be fulfilled, for he shall be called a
Nazarene." It is needless to go through the history
of the exegesis of this passage which has certainly
perplexed many. The use of ὅπως instead of ἵνα is
immaterial, for both have the same meaning. But
the plural "through the prophets" is important. It
cannot refer to *one* prophet speaking for all. This
plural evidently refers either to the prophetic books
in general or to the entire Old Testament. It also
shows that no quotation is to follow which will introduce some word that was uttered by several prophets.
This means that ὅτι is not *recitativum*, like our quotation marks, pointing to a direct quotation. No λέγων
precedes ὅτι, which shuts out not only a direct quotation but also an indirect prophetic utterance. The
prophets nowhere said even in substance "that he shall
be called Ναζωραῖος."

Two views are thus removed, both of which are
based on a play on words. The first is that, growing
up in Nazareth, Jesus would be called a Nazarite, one
separated and dedicated by a special vow and thus

living an ascetic life. But even the etymology is wrong, to say nothing of the fact that Jesus never lived the ascetic life nor bore the name of a Nazarite. The second is that his growing up in Nazareth tallies with Isa. 11:1, where the Messiah is called *netzēr*, "a shoot" or "branch." This combination, which Jerome says he learned from Jewish Christians, has satisfied the more critical and has been entered in books of reference. Yet *netzēr* is only a figurative term, used only once by one prophet, and is only one of similar figures: *choter*, "reed" or sapling, also in Isa. 11:1 *tzemach*, "sprout," in Jer. 23:5; 33:15. It is very well to point to the likeness: Nazareth, an insignificant place from which no one expected anything; Jesus, outwardly just as insignificant-looking. But *"Netzēr,"* whatever its etymological connection with "Nazareth," is not the name applied to the Messiah by the prophets; in order to have more than the one prophet, the synonymous terms from entirely different roots cannot be brought in; and Jesus never bore the name *"Netzēr"* or "Nazarene" in the sense of "Shoot," "Sprout," or "Branch."

This ὅτι means "for" or "because." Jesus lived in Nazareth in order to fulfill the prophets; and the evidential reason, by which we ourselves can see that his living in Nazareth fulfilled the prophets, is that afterward, due to his having lived there, he was called "the Nazarene." We may add that even his followers were called "Nazarenes." Matthew writes nothing occult or difficult. A Nazarene is one who hails from Nazareth. Matthew counts on the ordinary intelligence of his readers, who will certainly know that the enemies of Jesus branded him the "Nazarene," that this was the name that marked his Jewish rejection and would continue to do so among Jews. They put into it all the hate and odium possible, extending it, as stated, to his followers. And this is "what was spoken through the prophets." One and all told how the Jews would despise the Messiah, Ps. 22:6; Isa. 49:7; 53:3; Dan. 9:26; every prophecy of the suffering Messiah, and every reference to those who would not hear him, like Deut. 18:18. The Talmud calls Jesus *Yeshu Hannotzri* (the Nazarene); Jerome reports the synagogue prayer in which the Christians are cursed as Nazarenes: "and the Notrim and the Minim may suddenly be destroyed; may they be blotted out of the book of life and not be written with the just." Compare Acts 24:5, "sect of the Nazarene," and Paul's characterization. If Jesus had been reared in Jerusalem, he could not have been vilified as the Nazarene. It was God who let him grow up in Nazareth and thus furnished the title of reproach to the Jews in fulfillment of all the reproach God had prophesied for the Messiah through the prophets.

# CHAPTER III

## III

### Christ's Forerunner and Anointing, Chapter 3

*Christ's Forerunner and His Work, 3:1-12*

The reason that Matthew proceeds from the childhood of Jesus to John the Baptist and the opening of Jesus' ministry is the fact that the intervening time offered nothing for Matthew's purpose: to present Jesus to Jewish readers as the Messiah. All that this span of years affords is covered by the brief record in Luke 2:41-52. No tradition regarding this period was in existence. In spite of all his searching Luke found nothing to report save the incident that occurred when Jesus was twelve years old, and, much like Matthew, he at once passes on to the work of the Baptist.

**1)** **Now in these days comes forward John the Baptist, acting as a herald in the wilderness of Judea, saying, Be repenting! for the kingdom of the heavens has come near.** The critics find some strange things in the phrase "in those days," which need not be refuted here. Matthew writes in Old Testament style (Exod. 2:11) and by "those" connects our thoughts with his previous narratives and their remarkable character. The view that Matthew copied the phrase from Mark 1:9 is answered by the difference in the connections. Matthew is content with this broad reference, whereas· Luke specifies the time as being the fifteenth year of the reign of Tiberius, thus when Jesus was about twenty-nine years old. The historical present παραγίνεται (R. 868) lends a touch of vividness: "comes forth," *tritt auf*, in order to begin his great work. Matthew's interest is centered in the preaching and the work of the Baptist, so he omits the details regarding his parentage and his early days. This "John" ("Yahweh has been gracious") is identified by his usual appellation, "the Baptist," even Josephus, writing, "John, called the Baptizer."

His work of baptizing is already brought out in his name and is then mentioned in its proper connection in v. 6. While baptizing was distinctive of John and thus gave him the added name, his work in general was that of a prophet, more specifically of a herald, sent by God to the nation. That is why Matthew at once adds κηρύσσων, "acting as a κῆρυξ or a herald," as one who with a loud voice announces what his superior has ordered him to announce. When we translate this Greek word "preaching," the original meaning of the verb must be retained. Preaching, in the Biblical sense, is merely to announce clearly and distinctly exactly what God orders us to announce in his Word. We dare not change that message by alteration, by omission, or by addition. The preacher is not to utter his own eloquent wisdom but is to confine himself to the foolishness and the *skandalon* of the gospel. The announcement the Baptist was to make was quite specific and limited as we shall see; and he attempted no more than this. "In the wilderness of Judea" only in a general way indicates the locality of the Baptist's activity, in this respect resembling the opening phrase "in those days." From v. 6 we see that the valley of the Jordan is referred to and specifically its lower end which borders on Judea. The Fourth Gospel states that the Baptist's first work was done "in Bethabara beyond Jordan" (i. e., "in Bethany," the correct reading.) The most probable site is the northern ford near Succoth, the same by which Jacob crossed over from Mahanaim. This region is called desert because it has never been inhabited, except later by ascetics like the Essenes and the hermits who sought seclusion there. With the feminine adjective τῇ ἐρήμῳ supply χώρᾳ, "the desert place."

John worked in obedience to an immediate call from God; in this respect he was like the prophets of old; compare Luke 3:2, "the word of God came" to him. His preaching and his work were divinely directed by immediate revelation. Moreover, John was born as a member of the Jewish tribe to whom priestly functions belonged, and thus no Jew questioned his authority to perform such functions, i. e., to teach and to administer religious rites. He did not choose this desert country on his own accord but was directed by God. The *Ghor* or ravine through which the Jordan flows is dense with wild growth but because of the excessive heat unfit for ordinary habitation; and the adjacent upland, whether level or rugged, is also undesirable "wilderness." This wild region was chosen for the Baptist's work by God because it symbolized and pictured the spiritual state of the nation now being called to repentance in such an unusual and dramatic way. It called to mind the desert wanderings of Israel for forty years when their unbelief had shut them out of the promised land for so long a time.

2) Matthew presents only the essentials which the Baptist announced. In μετανοεῖτε, "be repenting," we are introduced to one of the most important words in the New Testament, the Hebrew *nicham*, "repent by changing the mind," and *schub*, "to turn" or to be converted. Μετανοεῖν originally means: "to perceive or see afterward" (μετά), i. e., when it is too late; "to change one's mind" and thus "to regret" and "to repent." The Scriptural use of the term added a spiritual depth that is far beyond the thought of secular writers. The word at once signified that religious change of the heart which turns from sin and guilt to cleansing and

forgiveness by God's grace. The linguistic difference between μετανοεῖν and its synonym ἐπιστρέφειν is that the former looks both backward toward the regretted sin and forward to the accepted pardon, while the latter looks rather to the grace received. The present tense, "be repenting," indicates a state or condition, one befitting the day of the Messiah, thus a life lived in repentance.

The assertion that on the Baptist's lips the call to repent meant less than it later signified on the lips of the apostles, in particular that it did not include faith in the Messiah, is answered by John 1:8: "The same came for a witness to the Light, that all men through him might *believe*"; by Luke 3:18, where the Baptist's preaching is called εὐαγγελίζεσθαι, "to preach the gospel"; and by the fruits of this repentance, which are such as only faith in the Redeemer and forgiveness of sins can produce.

The Baptist has been regarded as belonging to the Old Testament prophets. But Mark 1:1, etc., characterizes his work as belonging to the ἀρχὴ τοῦ εὐαγγελίου, "the beginning of the gospel of Jesus Christ." In the Smalcald Articles Luther calls the Baptist "the fiery angel St. John, the true preacher of repentance," *Concordia Triglotta*, 487, 30. At times "repentance" and "to repent" are used with reference to contrition alone, and again with reference to contrition plus faith, i. e., conversion in its entirety. For the latter use compare Mark 1:15; Acts 20:21; Luke 24:46, 47, where the wider sense of the term is indicated; and for the former, Luke 13:5; 15:7; and our present passage, where the narrower sense is in place. The latter is well described in *Concordia Triglotta*, 259, 29 and 35.

The reason for repentance is: "for the kingdom of the heavens has come near," the perfect tense ἤγγικεν (ἐγγίζω) is durative-punctiliar (R. 895): has been drawing near and is thus now at hand. Matthew alone writes ἡ βασιλεία τῶν οὐρανῶν, and he does so at least

32 times; the others write ἡ βασιλεία τοῦ Θεοῦ, which is found only a few times in Matthew's Gospel. The distinction is merely formal; one and the same kingdom is referred to. Both genitives may be considered genitives of possession: the kingdom which belongs to the heavens, belongs to God. But it is difficult to keep the qualitative idea out of the former: the kingdom whose very nature is that of heaven; and the subjective idea out of the latter: the kingdom that God rules. The plural "of the heavens" is a translation of the Hebrew *schamayim,* a usage that is natural for Matthew. It is used both in the Greek and in the English besides the singular: "the heavens" — "heaven." There is no need to bring in the seven heavens to explain this plural. We may very well think of Daniel 2:44, and 7:14, to gain a proper conception of what the Baptist had in mind.

This grand Biblical concept cannot be defined by generalizing from conditions obtaining in the kingdoms of the earth. These are only imperfect shadows of God's kingdom. God makes his own kingdom, and only where he is with his power and his grace his kingdom is found; earthly kingdoms, which are many and various, make their kings, often also unmake them, and their kings are nothing apart from what their kingdoms may make them. So also we are not really subjects in God's kingdom but partakers of it, i. e., of God's rule and kingship; earthly kingdoms have only subjects. In God's kingdom we already now bear the title "kings unto God," and eventually the kingdom, raised to the nth degree, shall consist of nothing but kings in glorious array, each with his crown, and Christ thus "the King of kings," a kingdom made up entirely of kings with no subjects at all.

This divine kingdom goes back to the beginning and **rules** the world and shall so rule until the consummation at the end of time. All that is in the world, even every hostile force, is subservient to the plans of God. The children and sons of God, as heirs of the kingdom, in whom God's grace is displayed, constitute the kingdom in its specific sense. The kingdom is in them. This kingdom is divided by the coming of Christ, the King, in the flesh to effect the redemption of grace by which this specific kingdom is really established among men. Hence we have the kingdom before Christ, looking toward his coming, and the kingdom after Christ, looking back to his coming — the promise and the fulfillment to be followed by the consummation — the kingdom as it was in Israel, as it now is in the Christian Church, the *Una Sancta* in all the world, and as it will be at the end forever.

With this understanding of the kingdom, that where the King is and rules with his power and his grace there the kingdom is to be found, we see what the Baptist means when he says, "the kingdom has come near." Jesus was approaching, and by the revelation of himself with power and grace as the Messiah and by the completion of his redemptive work he would stand forth as the King of salvation from heaven and would by faith enter into the hearts of men, making them partakers of his kingdom. Thus γάρ is justified. Since the kingdom is so near in Christ, the King, all men should long to receive this kingdom. The one and only way to do this is to repent, to turn from sin, self-righteousness, and worldly security by the power of grace in the Baptist's Word and Sacrament to the King and his kingdom with its pardon, peace, and joy.

3)  **For this is the one spoken of through Isaiah, the prophet, saying,**

**A voice of one shouting in the desert,**
**Make ready the way of the Lord,**
**Make straight his paths!**

"For" explains the presence of the Baptist at this time and his message concerning the kingdom and his call to repentance. God sent him with this message and call in fulfillment of the prophecy spoken by God "through Isaiah, the prophet," some 700 years earlier. "The voice" spoken of in Isa. 40:3-5 is not only a type of the Baptist. Matthew says that it is more; so does the Baptist himself in John 1:19-24, "I am the voice of one crying in the wilderness," etc.; so does Jesus in Matt. 11:10, "This is he of whom it is written," etc. The restoration of their homeland to the Jews after the Babylonian captivity was only a minor part of God's grace to them; the fullest measure of that grace did not appear until the Messiah came, and with that full measure Isaiah comforted his people long in advance of the arrival of the blessed day. That day had now at last come. Οὗτος takes up all that Matthew says about the Baptist in the two verses preceding. The passive ὁ ῥηθείς points to Yahweh as the speaker, and διά to the prophet as the human instrument he used. Here is the Biblical doctrine of divine inspiration in a nutshell: see the exposition of 1:22.

Matthew's quotation agrees with both the Hebrew and the LXX, except that in the former the parallelism of the poetic lines requires that we construe, "in the wilderness prepare," while Matthew has, "one shouting in the desert" or wilderness. Since both the voice and the preparation are found in the desert, the difference is immaterial. The poetic lines are highly dramatic, they are like a tableau: "Voice of a crier!" *qol qore'* (*status constructus*) ; the two words in the Hebrew, as well as in Matthew. are like an exclamation. Delitzsch writes: "The person disappears in the glory of his calling, receding before the contents of his cry. The cry sounds like the long drawn-out trumpet blast of a herald." In the same dramatic way we are placed out "in the wilderness." When commentators on

Isaiah explain the imagery here used as being derived
from the Lord's coming to Egypt through the Arabian
(southern) desert to bring his people into Canaan, they
do what is unnecessary; for there was also a great
stretch of desert between Babylon, where Israel was
held in exile, and their homeland, Palestine. This
desert, however, is used figuratively by Isaiah; it
denotes the hindrances and obstacles which separate
the people from Jehovah. Hence a road must be prepared through them on which Jehovah may come to his
people to deliver them. Though Babylon is inhabited,
it is a heathen land and is thus pictured as a desert or
wilderness in which Jehovah's people were lost. All
this was symbolized by the Baptist who was ordered to
shout in the literal wilderness near the Jordan.

Once the moral and the spiritual import of the
prophet's imagery is perceived, the shouting of the
voice, namely the Baptist's call to prepare the Lord's
way, will also be understood. The wilderness with its
obstructions is found in the hearts of the people; here
the Lord's way is to be prepared. In Isa. 40:3, 4
mountains and hills are to be levelled, etc. To make a
way through them is a task that is utterly beyond
human power. That is exactly the impression to be
made on the readers and hearers. Strictly speaking,
only the Lord himself can construct a way through such
obstacles. When, nevertheless, he orders us to build
this way, the obvious sense is that we can do it only by
the power of grace which the Lord himself bestows.
That is why the Baptist cried, "Repent!" Impenitence
raises the mountains of obstruction; repentance opens
the way for the Lord. And true repentance is wrought
by the Lord's own law and gospel in which his power
and grace are active. "Make ready the way of the
Lord!" Luther writes: "Such preparation is spiritual, it consists in the deep conviction and confession
that you are unfit, a sinner, poor, damned, and miser-

able with all the works you are able to do. Where this conviction is wrought, the heart will be opened for the Lord's entrance with his forgiveness and gifts."

4) The man thus described with his message and with his prophetic connection is now presented in his personal appearance and mode of life. **Now this John had his garment of camel's hair, and a leather girdle around his waist; and his nourishment was locusts and wild honey.** We must regard αὐτός as being merely demonstrative: "this John" (R. 686), pointing to all that has already been said about him; and not as being intensive: "John himself," since no contrast is apparent. Living and working in the wilderness, he dressed and ate accordingly. The two imperfect tenses picture the man. His very appearance was a stern sermon. It was a call to all those who made food and drink, house and raiment their chief concern in life to turn from such vanity and to provide far more essential things. He was a living illustration of how little man really needs here below — something we are prone to forget. And by drawing people out into the wilderness John made them share a bit of his own austere life. Men left their mansions, offices, shops, their usual round of life, and for a time at least gave their thoughts to higher things. Yet we need not overdraw as artists do when they picture the Baptist clothed in a camel's skin; he had an ἔνδυμα, a long, loose garment, woven, as the ἀπό phrase shows, out of "camel's hair," and thus coarse and rough in texture like the garments of the very poor. With this rough robe there naturally went a girdle to hold it at the waist, ὀσφύς, for which Greek word we use the plural "loins." The girdle kept the robe from flapping open and made it possible to tuck it up when walking. Made of leather, it, too, was cheap. We may take it that this *enduma* was John's only garment. No sandals are mentioned.

From Zech. 13:4 we see that "a rough garment" or "a garment of hair" was the customary dress of a prophet and was used even by false prophets in order to deceive. In II Kings 1:8 King Ahaziah recognizes Elijah when this prophet is described to him as "an hairy man and girt with a girdle of leather about his loins." Since Elijah prefigured the Baptist in his stern preaching of repentance (Mal. 4:5; Matt. 11:4; Mark 9:11, 12; Luke 1:17), this similarity of dress cannot be accidental. In this very wilderness Elijah made his last appearance.

Four varieties of locusts were allowed as food, Lev. 11:22. They are still eaten by the poor and in times of famine, being abundant in the spring and often coming in great swarms. The wings and the legs were torn off, the bodies were dried, or roasted, or ground up and baked, seasoned with salt, and could be kept for some time. Palestine was famed for its wild bees and honey, which are found especially in the wilder regions. The adjective ἄγριον with μέλι prevents us from thinking of some sweet substance prepared by men, or of sweet exudations from leaves. The abundant natural wild honey is referred to.

The Baptist's mode of life marks him as a Nazarite (Luke 1:15), and until the time of his preaching he must have lived like a hermit (Luke 1:80). In this respect he was the antithesis of Jesus (Matt. 11:18).

5) To the preaching, the prophecy, and the person Matthew adds the actual work. **Then there kept going out to him Jerusalem and all Judea and the surrounding country of the Jordan and were being baptized by him in the river Jordan, confessing their sins.** "Then" means when the Baptist came forward (v. 1) to execute his divinely appointed task. One crowd after another arrived in the desert from the proud capital Jerusalem, the very center of Jewish life. No wonder others followed from everywhere in

Judea and the Jordan region, including Transjordania. Matthew stops with mention of this; he might have added Galilee, where Jesus spoke 11:7, etc., concerning the Baptist (compare also the first disciples of the Baptist who came from Galilee). The two imperfects, ἐξεπορεύετο and ἐβαπτίζοντο, are used in descriptive narrative, compared by R. 883 to a "moving-picture show." The feminine adjective ἡ περίχωρος is due to the noun γῇ that must be supplied.

6) Matthew's ἐβαπτίζοντο says absolutely nothing regarding the mode of baptism which the Baptist employed. Nothing regarding the mode can be obtained from the added preposition ἐν, "in the river Jordan," for which Mark 1:9 uses εἰς, with no difference in meaning, R. 525. This ἐν is locative (R. 524), stating where the baptism took place; it denotes place (R. 586) and nothing more. The readiness with which the multitudes submitted to baptism is explained by the fact that purificatory rites by the application of water were not new nor strange to the Jews; and these rites were not administered by immersion, Lev. 14:7, 27; Num. 8:7; 19:13; Heb. 9:13; also Exod. 19:10; Lev. 15, entire chapter; 16:26; 28; 17:15; 22:6: Deut. 23:10. These were washings, rinsings, and bathings and *not* immersions. The Jews expected that, when the Messiah came, he would use a purificatory rite such as this; see the question on this point put to the Baptist by the Pharisees in John 1:25. Instead, therefore, of seeking to explain Matthew's verb "were being baptized" by some later fixed practice obtaining in the Christian Church at the time when Matthew wrote, the Christian practice must be explained by the purificatory rites used by the Jews since the days of Moses. Since none of these were immersions, immersion was not the mode of either the Baptist's or Jesus' baptism.

The verb βαπτίζω, as all lexicons agree, refers to any mode of applying water. It is linguistically unwar-

ranted to restrict it to one mode to the exclusion of all
other modes, and that a mode for which Jewish practice
furnishes no evidence. How could immersions be
administered on the desert journey and in a city like
Jerusalem, where water was never abundant? But did
not the Baptist labor near the river Jordan? If his
baptism was administered by immersion, then, since
the estimated number he baptized during the brief
period of a little over a year in which he labored was
between 200,000 and 500,000, he must have lived an
aquatic life. We have no evidence that he used his
disciples as his assistants when baptizing. Moreover,
he also baptized at Ænon (John 3:23), the very name
of which means "Springs." The πολλὰ ὕδατα, literally
"many waters," rivulets flowing from these springs,
made the place suitable for his work, not by furnishing
water for immersions, but by providing water for
drinking, a great necessity where many people were
gathered. Of course, he could use these "waters" also
to pour or to sprinkle when baptizing.

Yet the idea prevails that the Baptist immersed.
This is plainly traditionalism. It is well illustrated in
the case of Zahn, who admits that there are no indications of the mode of baptism in Matthew's words and
yet, when he tries to imagine how the Baptist baptized,
speaks of a *Vollbad.* Some refer to the baptism of
Jewish proselytes, but they fail of proof regarding two
points. This rite is not mentioned until the second
century, and no one can show that it was practiced at
the time of the Baptist; still more vital, no evidence is
at hand that the baptism of proselytes was more than
a washing, it was like similar Jewish rites. We may
add that nowhere does it appear that the Baptist
thought that he was making proselytes of the Jews
whom he baptized.

John "preached (and what he preached he, of
course, practiced) the baptism of repentance unto

remission of sins," Mark 1:4; Luke 3:3. This cannot refer to a future forgiveness, but as surely as the repentance led to the baptism, so surely the baptism bestowed the forgiveness then and there. The similar expression found in Acts 2:38, "to be baptized for the remission of sins," certainly refers to forgiveness bestowed by baptism. When Jesus speaks to Nicodemus about being born again by baptism he refers to the sacrament of the Baptist. To be born again of water and the Spirit defines the nature of this baptism as containing the Spirit and as working regeneration. None of Christ's apostles received a baptism that differed from that of the Baptist, yet I Pet. 3:21 states that baptism "saves." Acts 19:1-7 reports that certain believers who had received John's baptism were rebaptized by Paul. But these people did not even know that there was a Holy Spirit. The Baptist himself could not have baptized them; this must have been done by some former disciple of the Baptist who refused to follow Christ, and whose baptisms were thus no real baptisms. We today regard no baptism as real and valid that has been administered apart from the Trinity, which includes the Holy Spirit.

The Baptist's sacrament merged into that of Jesus (John 3:26; 4:1, 2). In essence and in efficacy both were the same. The Baptist's was on the level of the revelation given at that time; that of Jesus on the level of his completed work. That of the Baptist made followers of the Christ about to come; that of Jesus followers of the Christ who had come. Both bestowed forgiveness: the one the forgiveness about to be wrought, the other the forgiveness that had been wrought. Thus the baptism of John was preparatory for Israel alone, Christ's permanent for all nations. And only in this way the one made ready for and then gave way to the other.

Those who translate ἐβαπτίζοντο "got themselves baptized," and do this because "the Aramaic verb is active," base their view on an Aramaic Matthew which no one has seen. Since ὑπό regularly names the agent after the passive, Matthew's Greek verb is passive. The effort to make it active has a purpose behind it, namely that "the rite was not intended to have any definite effects on the new recruits" (note this designation); "baptism was not something that was done to them, it was something that they did; they professed themselves to be fit and proper members of the new order." This inverts Matthew's statement. Baptism is no mere profession. In the case of every baptism of a repentant Jew forgiveness was bestowed by this sacrament. Therefore Matthew adds, "they were being baptized, confessing their sins." True repentance always leads to confession. All that the present participle says is that the confession of sins accompanied the baptism. And the claim is specious that, if the confession was a requisite for the baptism, we should have the aorist participle. Since the main verb is durative, the added participle would also be durative; for both forms here used intend to describe customary actions. The Baptist preached repentance, and then all who were moved to repentance confessed and were baptized, and this went on from day to day.

7) It v. 7-12 Matthew furnishes us a sample of the preaching of the Baptist. It displays the full power of his preaching, striking the conscience of his hearers with fullest force. Matthew's sample, however, consists of an address made on a special occasion to a special set of people. **Now when he saw many Pharisees and Sadducees coming to his baptism he said to them: Offsprings of vipers, who did warn you to flee from the coming wrath? Do, therefore, fruit worthy of repentance. And think not to say in your-**

**selves, As father we have Abraham; for I say to you, that God is able of these stones to raise up children for Abraham.** The aorist ἰδών points to a day when the Baptist saw a crowd of Pharisees and Sadducees coming to be baptized. They must have come together from Jerusalem. The Baptist's work was at its height as we see from the fact that it drew so many of this type of men from the very capital itself. It should not be denied that they intended to be baptized, for ἐπί expresses aim or purpose (R. 602), and the Baptist's entire address has this their intention as its basis. Comparing John 1:19, etc., and v. 24, etc., we may conclude that the scene here described by Matthew occurred first, and some time later the two delegations of which John writes arrived to demand an official answer from the Baptist concerning himself and his work.

The Pharisees formed the Jewish sect or party which laid the utmost stress on the strictest outward observance of the law, including the rabbinical traditions and regulations which professed to build a formidable protecting hedge about the law. They were utterly self-righteous, and cultivated a hollow formalism that was ostentatious to a degree, especially in observing ceremonies, fastings, almsgiving, long prayers, tithes, etc. Christ portrays them as thorough hypocrites. The Sadducees rejected the rabbinical traditions, also the doctrine of the resurrection, of the angels and of spirits, of immortality and the judgment to come. They were freethinkers and skeptics, with a corresponding laxness in morals, yet included in their number many of the richest and most influential Jews such as the family of the high priest. While in general they were in opposition to the Pharisees, the Sadducees occasionally joined with them when their interests coincided. See Josephus, *Antiquities*, 18, 1-4.

The two nouns have but one Greek article, which shows that the Baptist regarded them as constituting one class, addressing the same words to both parties. He treats them as insincere, hypocritical, impenitent persons and as such unfit to be baptized. "When he saw them coming for his baptism" means that after the Baptist had concluded his preaching and was ready to baptize the penitent sinners, he saw these Pharisees and Sadducees coming with the others in order to receive the sacrament. Then it was that the Baptist stopped them. When imagining the scene, the writer's personal opinion is that the Baptist baptized the thousands who made confession by dipping a branch of hyssop, or some other branch, into the water and thereby sprinkling one convenient group after another. Very likely these Pharisees and Sadducees did not mix with the common people, whom we know they despised, but came forward as a separate group, the common people respectfully making way for them and not attempting to join their group. This leaves the natural question as to why these haughty people wished to be baptized. The only answer that can be given is drawn from the general situation: the movement that had assumed immense proportions; the fear that, unless they joined it, they would lose their influence; the desire to grasp the leadership in this new movement. A change of heart failed to enter into the step these Pharisees and Sadducees resolved to take. From Luke 3:7, etc., we see that others also failed to repent, for the Baptist's words were addressed not only to these two leading classes but "to the multitudes."

The situation thus is dramatic in the highest degree. The very address is like a blow in the face. These proud sons of Abraham, these honored leaders of the nation the Baptist addresses as "offsprings of vipers," exposing in one expression the great and fatal sin that marked their character. The form γεννήματα designates living creatures (from γεννάω), while γενήματα (from γίνομαι) refers to fruits of the earth, R. 213. The ἔχιδνα, "viper," is a small, very poisonous serpent, such as the one that fastened its deadly fangs in Paul's hand at Melita, Acts 28:3. The Baptist does not say "viper" but "offsprings of vipers," for others had preceded them, and they had entered into the sin of their fathers. What trait of character the figure of the viper means to express is evident: deadly hypocrisy, base treachery, and the fatal deceptions which they practiced and in which they lived (Matt. 12:2, 24; 15:2; 16:1; 22:15). Their original progenitor is the serpent which deceived Eve; hence Christ called them "the children of the wicked one," 13:38; John 8:44; Acts 13:10. When it comes to dealing with these deadly sins no words are minced by the Baptist or by Jesus or by the apostles. The conscience is struck with a directness that almost takes away the breath.

The stunning address opens a dismaying question: "Who did warn you to try to flee from the coming wrath?" Somebody, John says, secretly and in an underhanded way (ὑποδείκνυμι) whispered this to them and did it in order to deceive them. John leaves this somebody unnamed, since only the devil prompts a man to try to flee from God's wrath by mere outwardly religious acts. Note the aorist φυγεῖν. The devil suggested that these hypocrites could actually escape God's wrath by a hypocritical religious act. By means of this tense John exposes the devil's trick, who makes these men think that they will really escape when by such actions as theirs they will only run the more directly into the coming wrath. By this exposure of the devil's trick John truly warns these men, not by underhanded whispers, but by open words. There are two points in John's question: first, that nobody can escape by insincere, outward use of the means of grace; secondly, that the way of escape is

still open, even for hypocrites such as the Pharisees
and the Sadducees, if by God's grace they allow themselves to be turned from hypocrisy to true, sincere
repentance and the honest use of the divine means
of grace.

The "wrath" of God, while it is an anthropopathic
expression, is no figure of speech but a terrible reality;
it is mentioned over 300 times in the Old Testament
and many times in the New. It is the necessary reaction of God's holiness and righteousness to sin as
the persistent rejection of his love and his grace. It
is always active, not merely at the end of the world
but in constant acts of judgment from day to day,
although these are now often withheld by God's longsuffering. "The coming wrath," ἡ μέλλουσα ὀργή, is a
pregnant expression for the final manifestation of
God's wrath at the end of the world (see v. 12). The
connection of this wrath, in point of punishment and
judgment, with the coming of the Messiah may be seen
in Zeph, 1:15 (*dies irae, dies illa*) ; 2:2; Mal. 3:2, etc.,
18; 4:1, 5. When the Jews thought that the Messianic wrath would be turned upon the Gentiles alone,
in particular upon their Roman oppressors, they were
sadly mistaken.

8) Over against the false way, suggested by the
devil, which deceives men into thinking they have
escaped when they have not, the Baptist sets the one
and only true way: οὖν, purely illative, R. 1192. The
expression "do fruit" is one of the many in the
Scriptures in which figure and interpretation are
combined: the fruit consists of acts that are done;
and the aorist imperative demands actual doing,
R. 835. The verb ποιεῖν is a Greek rendering of the
Hebrew 'asah, *schaffen*, produce by work and effort.
Luke, as well as Matthew, uses it repeatedly in connection with "fruit." Thus what is here called fruit is
termed "works meet for repentance" in Acts 26:20;

and Luke 3:8 has the plural "fruits," dividing what
may be viewed as a whole into its component parts,
the various acts which show a changed heart. The
genitive "of repentance" cannot be appositional because it depends on the adjective "worthy"; hence
repentance cannot itself be the fruit. Examples of
this fruit the Baptist himself mentions to certain
classes of people in Luke 3:11-14. "Fruit" indicates
an organic connection between the works and the
repentance, just as a tree brings the fruit peculiar
to its nature. The adjective ἄξιος, "of equal weight,"
requires works of a type and character that is sufficient to show the actual presence of repentance in
the heart. The latter is invisible; hence we judge its
presence by the former, which are visible. We dare
judge in no other way. We often note a superficial
repentance; it brings fruit different from that
demanded by the Baptist, namely a passing regret, a
few tears, perhaps, a transient emotion, a few sighs,
an excuse or two, a wish to be different, a resolve
to change by our own efforts, a brief outward bet-
terment, and the like. The Baptist demands the repentance which is true conversion, wrought by God
himself through the very preaching of the Baptist, and
thus easily and clearly attested by the resultant life.
These Pharisees could not remain Pharisees, nor these
Sadducees, Sadducees. Though baptized a hundred
times, they could not escape the coming wrath. The
Baptist is not demanding something peculiar and
extravagant from these upper-class Jews; he merely
insists that his original requirement be met without
deception or evasion. What he said to these men was
intended for the ears of all who were there and heard
him.

9)  Matthew chose to record this address of the
Baptist because it especially brought out so strikingly
the Baptist's spiritual conception of the kingdom, and

this in direct opposition to the prevalent external' and false conception of the Jews, especially of the upper classes. In this connection, compare what Christ said regarding Abraham in John 8:33, etc. "And think not to say in yourselves, As father we have Abraham." The ingressive aorist μὴ δόξητε (R. 834) is the subjunctive in a negative command, hence peremptory: "Do not start to think when I tell you this." "In yourselves" is added because these hypocritical Jews would be inclined secretly to cherish this thought. The predicate object "as father" is placed first, and the direct object "Abraham" last, making both emphatic. The old Jewish conviction was that all the physical descendants of Abraham, through Jacob, were safe from God's wrath because of their father Abraham; they were sure that this connection with Abraham guaranteed to them all the blessings of the Messianic kingdom to the exclusion of the Gentile world. See how Jesus shatters this conviction in John 8:39, 40. The rich man in hell also had Abraham for his "father" and heard from him the word "son," but it availed him nothing.

"For I say unto you" meets this false Jewish assumption squarely by giving the reason that the Jews should not hold this false thought. In "I say to you" the full authority of the Baptist confronts these Jews; he speaks as God's own prophet. He tells them the decisive truth "that God is able of these stones to raise up children unto Abraham," i. e., to fill the places these Jews leave vacant by being false children of Abraham. The figure has tremendous force: to turn common, lifeless stones, such as were lying there in the wilderness, into true spiritual children of Abraham! The figure describes most drastically the creative power of God's grace. If these Jews turn their hearts into flinty stones by resisting God's converting grace, God will by that same grace turn other men, whom these Jews regard as nothing but dead, useless stones, into truly repentant sinners. But the contrast is not merely between men and stones, replacing impenitent men by such as seem to us incapable of spiritual impressions. If this were all, then the thought might be a contrast only between Jews, the proud upper class as represented in the Pharisees and the Sadducees, and the despised lowest class, open sinners, harlots, publicans, etc. But the contrast is between the Jews of any and of all classes as descendants of Abraham and common stones that have no descent at all. These stones represent Gentiles. The Baptist is not using an abstract comparison, he is uttering prophecy. Matthew reports this prophecy for his specific purpose. His Gospel is written for Jews, all of whom need the Baptist's word. From chapter two onward, the record of the Gentile magi, through the pertinent parts of the Gospel and finally its significant conclusion this thought of the repentance and conversion of the Gentiles recurs. See, for instance, 8:10-12.

10) As the kingdom with its call to repentance is at hand, so of necessity also the judgment of wrath upon the impenitent. Everything about this kingdom is spiritual, wholly unlike the formalism of the work-righteous Pharisees, or the rationalistic worldliness of the skeptic Sadducees. Repentance saves, impenitence damns. **And already the ax lies at the root of the trees. Therefore, every tree not doing excellent fruit is hewn out and is thrown into fire.** Time is pressing, judgment is fast drawing near. How true the Baptist's words are we see from the destruction of Jerusalem forty years later. Jesus repeated the Baptist's warnings in the parable of the barren fig tree, in the call to "walk whilé ye have the light" (John 12:35), and in other passages; see also Isa. 55:6; Mal. 4:5. This is, indeed, operating with fear as a

religious motive. After love and grace fail to appeal, the threat and the terror of judgment alone are left. Because man still has a conscience, the *terrores con-scientiae*, which the law intends to produce, will have their rightful place, no matter what rationalistic minds may predicate of God and of his law.

The figure of "doing fruit" is expanded in the most telling way. In addition to the fruit we have the tree, the root, the ax, the hewing out, and the consuming fire. "Already" is placed first and is the more emphatic because of its distant position from the verb, R. 418, 423. Judgment is ready to descend. The article in the expression "the ax" points to the one divine judgment, pictured as an ax, together with fire, to match "the trees." This plural refers to all the impenitent Jews. The present tenses are timeless, picturing the thought as such, as is done in general propositions. This is true especially of the verbs "is hewn out" and "is thrown." The ax lies "at the root," πρός, facing it with dire intent. While κεῖται is present, its root is perfect and has the sense of completion; it does not express linear action but condition or state. The ax "lies," having been placed at the root, R. 881. As an instrument it connotes the hand that shall swing the ax. The figure is overdrawn when it is thought to mean that the ax is already being swung by the hand, and its blade is about to cut into the root. The ax merely lies; the trees designated for being felled have already been selected, and the ax has already been deposited beneath them. Only one ax, yet many trees. The figure is of necessity strained since one and the same judgment strikes many individuals. Hence also the singular "root" is used for all the trees. In the divine imagery we often find that the figure seems to exert itself to convey the full reality; human pictures are too weak to convey all that should be conveyed. So the reality at times protrudes through the figure. When the divine speakers use the figures they always have the full reality in mind and are never, like other speakers or writers, fettered by mere figures.

"To the root," not to the twigs, or to the branches. Not even a stump will be left; judgment will be complete. The plural "trees" is dissolved into the singular "every tree," which yet omits none; πᾶν without the article following = "every." Judgment is discriminatingly just: none but the fruitless, yet every one of these. The characterization μὴ ποιοῦν καρπὸν καλόν takes up the thought of v. 8, the present participle characterizing the tree as one whose nature it is not to "do" anything in the way of "excellent fruit," bringing only καρπὸν κακόν, good-for-nothing fruit. Repentance is here again not viewed as good fruit but as belonging to the tree and marking its nature. Only by the inward change of repentance (contrition and faith, v. 2), through grace and the Word is a man made a good tree, and being such, the "excellent fruit" follows as a matter of course, evidencing the spiritual nature of the tree at whose root no ax will ever lie.

The verb ἐκκόπτεται = "is hewn out" from among the good trees, hewn at the very root. And then it "is thrown into fire," the phrase being placed forward for the sake of emphasis. The very timelessness of these present tenses lends them additional power. This is what is done. *When* it is done makes no difference. Keep your mind on these terrible acts while the day of grace still lasts. The Scriptures frequently speak of fire when describing the judgment. Mal. 4:1, "The day cometh, that shall burn as an oven"; the branches cut from the Vine are burned, John 15:6; the tares are gathered and burned, Matt. 13:40. All God's judgments are like fire, especially the final one; for the wicked shall go "into hell, into the fire that never shall be quenched."

Mark 9:43, "into everlasting fire," "into hell fire," Matt. 18:8, 9. The Sadducees of all ages have tried to quench this fire by making sport of it, thereby preparing themselves the more for it and hastening its coming to themselves.

11) To the word regarding the impending judgment the Baptist adds the word concerning the still present grace (v. 11) and closes by combining the final outcome of both (v. 12). The connection is confused by some when they misunderstand the final phrase in v. 11 and take "fire" in this phrase to denote judgment. **I on my part am baptizing you in water for repentance; but the one coming after me is stronger than I, whose sandals I am not fit to carry. He shall baptize you in connection with the Holy Spirit and fire.** Here John performs his main function, to point to "the Coming One," ὁ ἐρχόμενος (11:3; Luke 7:19), a well-known designation for the Messiah, derived from Old Testament statements such as Gen. 49:10, "until Shiloh come." It is notable that, like Jesus, the Baptist avoids the title "Messiah," evidently because of the political tinge the Jews had come to connect with this term. Against all such political and allied ideas the spiritual character of the Baptist's work contended. He mentions "the One Coming" as though he has referred to him quite often in his preaching. For this Coming One he is endeavoring to make all his auditors ready. The other thought here indicated is that no one shall for a moment think that the Baptist himself is the Messiah. This comes out very clearly in Luke 3:15, etc., where the words of our verse and the following one are repeated with the preamble: "And as the people were in expectation, and all men mused in their hearts of John, whether he were the Christ, or not; John answered, saying to all, I indeed baptize you," etc. The Baptist again denied this expectation in John 1:26, 27.

First the tremendous difference existing between the two persons is made prominent. John is a prophet, divinely commissioned, and made such an impression on the people that they thought he might himself be the Messiah. But John tells them, "the One Coming after me is stronger than I." The phrase ὀπίσω μου, really, "behind me," is to be understood temporally, "after me." John says: "I am only his humble forerunner. If you think I am great, he who will be here presently is infinitely greater." How much greater is strikingly brought out: "whose sandals I am not fit to carry." It was the humblest slave's task to remove and to carry away his master's sandals; in Luke 3:16 note: "the latchet of whose shoes I am not worthy to unloose." Mark and Luke add the detail of the untying, Matthew mentions only the carrying away. How great, then, is this Coming One if this prophet of God is not fit to carry his sandals which only his feet have touched? The answer is: the Coming One is God's own Son. John's words are not self-abasement, no Oriental extravagance; as a prophet filled with the Spirit he speaks absolute truth. Note that ἰσχυρότερος, from the noun ἰσχύς, refers to the personal possession of power. John implies that he, too, is ἰσχυρός, "strong," the divine strength of the Word having been given to him. This is not false humility. Who, then, could be stronger? Only he who is himself "the Word" (the Logos).

With this difference between the persons corresponds the difference of their work. John makes this plain by another comparison. Since he is appointed to baptize he places beside his baptizing that act of the Coming One which can also be called a baptizing. John baptizes with the ordinary sacrament which employs water; God's Son will crown his great redemptive work by baptizing in connection with the Holy Spirit and fire. A divinely appointed man may use water in the sacrament; only the Son of God can pour out the Holy Spirit, and even he only after completing his redemptive work and then ascending to heaven.

When John describes his own strength he says, "I on my part (emphatic ἐγώ) am baptizing you with water for repentance." This was the power put into his hands by God. It marked him as the forerunner of Christ. We have no right to stress εἰς μετάνοιαν so as to make repentance only the result of baptism, as something that only followed baptism as its aim and purpose. This is contrary to the durative imperative μετανοεῖτε in v. 2, "be repenting," i. e., live in repentance. "For repentance" refers to the repentance manifested by all those who came to be baptized by John.

The expression ἐν ὕδατι does not mean, "with water only," so that John's baptism becomes nothing but a symbolical sprinkling with water or an immersion in water. To claim that, because Jesus baptized with the Holy Ghost, John's baptism was devoid of the Holy Ghost, is to draw an untenable conclusion. As the Holy Ghost wrought all spiritual effects throughout the Old Testament, so he wrought in both John's preaching and in his baptism and in all gospel preaching until the day of Pentecost, from which day onward his presence, power, and gifts flow out in wholly unrestrained measure and over all the earth. The distinction is not: before Pentecost *no* Spirit; after Pentecost the Spirit. If this were true, no soul could have been saved before Pentecost. The distinction is: before the actually completed work of redemption the limited preparatory work of the Spirit; after that the superabounding fullness of the Spirit. The idea that even our present baptism is only water, a mere sign and symbol without the Spirit, only a confessional act and work of obedience on our part; and that the only baptism that gives us the Spirit is the so-called "Baptism of the Spirit" by which the Spirit is thought to seize a man suddenly without the use of divine means (converting him by this seizure and later suddenly and totally sanctifying him), is a fanatical view which casts aspersions upon the very means of grace by which the Spirit does come to us and substitutes for these means human emotions, imaginings, and dreams by which the Spirit never comes.

The Coming One, John says, "shall baptize you with the Holy Ghost and fire." Here we have Jesus' own commentary: "John truly baptized with water; but ye shall be baptized with the Holy Ghost not many days hence," Acts 1:5. And v. 8: "Ye shall receive power, after that the Holy Ghost is come upon you," etc. Also Peter reports how the Holy Spirit fell upon Cornelius and the Gentiles with him "as on us at the beginning," i. e., Pentecost. He adds: "Then remembered I the word of the Lord, how that he said, John indeed baptized with water, but ye shall be baptized with the Holy Ghost," Acts 11:16. The miraculous outpouring of the Holy Ghost at the time of Pentecost is the supreme work and thus the final great mark of the Messiah. None but the Son who had gone to the Father (John 16:7) after completing redemption could thus send the Comforter. This Mightier One, who was to show his might by thus miraculously sending the Spirit, was also miraculously pointed out to the Baptist and by no less a sign than the descent of the Spirit upon him "in a bodily shape like a dove," Luke 3:22. Compare John 1:32-34.

It ought to be evident that in the parallel phrases ἐν ὕδατι and ἐν Πνεύματι the preposition must have the same meaning. One may admire the courage of those who, after taking "in water" in the sense of immersion in water, do not shrink from letting "in Spirit and fire" likewise mean immersion in Spirit and fire. But

no immersion took place on Pentecost, and ἐν does not
suggest this idea. R. 586 regards ἐν ὕδατι as locative; but this cannot be its force in the parallel
phrase. Others prefer the instrumental idea, usually
expressed by "with"; but the Spirit is not an instrument or a means such as water and fire. The ἐν has
its ordinary meaning, "in connection with." John baptized "in connection with water" as everybody saw;
Christ would perform a baptizing "in connection
with the Holy Spirit and fire" as everybody would also
see. The nature of the two connections indicated by
ἐν lies in the nouns that follow.

One ἐν combines the Spirit and fire: ἐν Πνεύματι
Ἁγίῳ καὶ πυρί, and thus regards them as one concept
which is also placed over against the one water. Even
where this is recognized, it is nearly always misapplied; for "in the Holy Spirit" is referred to a work
of grace (not, however, Pentecost, but a peculiar
immediate bestowal) and, separated from this by
the interval of the whole New Testament era, "in fire"
is regarded as the final work of judgment. The reason
for this is the fact that in v. 10 "fire" is used figuratively in connection with judgment. This view inserts a second "in" which is not there. This view
misunderstands v. 11, which speaks only of grace
and leaves the reference to judgment to v. 12. This
view overlooks the fact that judgment is never conceived as a baptism with fire or with another element;
baptism and baptizing always imply cleansing and
not destruction. This view assumes that "fire" is
always a symbol of judgment and destruction. But
see the refiner's fire in Mal. 3:2, 3, fire as an image
of purification in Zech. 13:9; Isa. 6:6, 7; I Pet. 1:7,
and the "spirit of burning" taking away filth in
Isa. 4:4. Pentecost, the fulfillment of John's prophecy, has the two combined in the clearest manner:
the Spirit and cloven tongues of fire as the visible

manifestation of the Spirit. Thus the church, too, has never had the least trouble with this fire. She sings:

> "Come as the fire and purge our hearts
> Like sacrificial flame."
>
> *Reed.*

> "Come, Holy Spirit, from above
> With Thy celestial fire;
> Come and with flames of zeal and love
> Our hearts and tongues inspire."
>
> *Cotterill.*

> "And each believing soul inspire
> With Thine own pure and holy fire."
> *Luther*, translated by Massie.

Finally note the contrast between fire and water: the latter in the case of John, the former in the case of Christ; but both in grace.

12) It is one of the features of Old Testament prophecy that it views the two comings of the Messiah, that for the purpose of redemption and that for the purpose of final judgment, without regard to the great interval existing between them. The prophets see the future, but without the perspective of time. The Baptist does the same: the Coming One pours out the Spirit with all his grace (v. 11) and also separates the grain from the chaff. The great length of time lying between these two occurrences remains unrevealed. To assume that these prophecies are to have no interval, i. e., that the final judgment would soon follow Pentecost, is to misunderstand the prophecies, all of which intend to hide from us the time of the end, as they do to this day. Understanding this feature, we see why the Baptist joins the description of the Messiah's final work to that of Pentecost by a mere relative clause: **Whose winnowing shovel is in his hand, and he will thoroughly clean**

**his threshing floor; and he will collect his grain into
the garner, but the chaff he will burn up with fire
unquenchable.** From the figure of the trees, and
the fruit they bear the Baptist passes to the allied
figure of the grain and the chaff and all the imagery
connected with these. The idea of the Coming One
is retained. The idea of a mere man, though he
be as great as the Baptist, doing what is here described
is unimaginable. The deity of the Messiah looms
behind the two works described (v. 11 and 12) ; both
demand that the Messiah be the Son of God and nothing less.

The work is divided into two natural parts: 1)
separation as in 25:32; 2) disposal of the separated
parts: in 25:34, "Come," etc., and in 25:41, "Depart,"
etc. This separation begins already in this life. The
grain and the chaff, believers and unbelievers, are
utterly distinct from each other. And so we see "the
congregation of the saints" (Ps. 89:5; 149:1) drawing
together, on the one hand, and "the congregation of
evildoers" (Ps. 26:5), on the other, and blessed is he
who keeps away from the latter (Ps. 1:1). But in
this life, even in the organization of the church (v. 7),
this separation is not fully effected, nor can it be
made fully visible to men as long as we live in a
world in which "it doth not yet appear what we
shall be: but we know that, when he shall appear,
we shall be like him; for we shall see him as he
is," I John 3:2.

The word "fan" denotes a large wooden shovel
designed for tossing up grain after it is threshed out
on a smooth, elevated "threshing floor" and the loose
straw has been raked away. The remaining mass of
mingled "grain" and "chaff," when tossed up, is
separated by the wind, the heavy grain falling in a
heap, the loose, light chaff being blown to one side.
Nor shall the two ever be again mixed — their separa-

tion is now final. "Whose winnowing shovel is in his hand" pictures the mighty Messiah as being ready at any moment to begin this task of separation. In Luke 3:17, where this word is also recorded, two infinitives follow, both effective aorists. Matthew uses future tenses. A fine distinction results: Matthew simply records the future facts concerning the grain and concerning the chaff; Luke inserts the idea of divine purpose regarding the grain and omits this regarding the chaff, stating only the fact concerning it. The form διακαθαριεῖ is future, and διά in the verb is perfective: will clean "clear through," "throughly" (A. V.), an old form for "thoroughly." To clean the threshing floor means to remove all the straw and chaff and to leave a great heap of grain. Both wheat and barley are called σῖτος, "grain." Both were extensively grown in Palestine, where, as in Syria, the old way of threshing may still be seen.

After the separation has been effected and the threshing floor completely cleaned as stated, both the grain and the refuse find disposal. The former is collected in the ἀποθήκη (ἀπό and τίθημι), the place for "putting it away," the granary or storehouse. It is valuable and treasured accordingly. In fact, the one great object of tilling the field was to obtain this grain. The "chaff" is just waste; hence the Messiah "will burn it up," κατακαύσει, the κατά again being perfective but with the thought of "down": burn it completely. This alone would be sufficient. But this might be understood as denoting annihilation of the wicked. The Baptist shuts out this idea by adding: "with fire unquenchable." The remarkable thing is that the final adjective "unquenchable" departs from the figure and adds the reality after the manner of Biblical allegory (on which see Trench, *Parables*, p. 9). As noted in v. 10, the figure is too weak to bring out all that ought to be stated, so the reality is added. If the wicked were to be annihilated, the fire would burn itself out; instead, it will never be quenched, its burning will go on eternally, as an eternal punishment for the wicked. Many views have been advanced to show that "eternal" as applied to the fate of the wicked in the Scriptures signifies only a long age of time; but then "eternal" as referring to the blessedness of the saints in heaven would also have to be a blessedness that finally ends. "Unquenchable" answers such views. It shuts out both annihilation and final restitution. Speculations as to the nature of this unquenchable fire are valueless. God will provide a fire that is fully adequate; and those who burn in it will not in the least question its peculiar nature.

The imagery of the Baptist is wholly transparent, especially to Jews who know this imagery from the Old Testament. Only the godly who repent and accept the Coming One in faith are "grain," true children of the kingdom, true children of Abraham. Only they will enter heaven. All the rest are chaff which the wind blows away, Ps. 1:4. How valueless is chaff compared with grain? Who ever planted a field in order to garner nothing but chaff? All the proud works of men — what do they make of men when the judgment comes? Light as chaff will all those be who bring nothing else on that great day. Christ alone, held to by faith, makes us grain.

### Christ's Baptism and Anointing, 3:13-17

13) Matthew's account is much fuller than Mark's and Luke's. Mark is often praised for introducing touches and details into his account; and here we notice this feature also in Matthew's Gospel. We shall note similar instances as they occur. In each of the preceding chapters two closely related sections are presented: in the first the genealogy and the birth, in the

second the magi and the murder of the innocents. So
in this third chapter we have the Baptist and Jesus'
baptism. **Then comes forward Jesus from Galilee
to the Jordan unto John to be baptized by him.**
"Then" points to the time just described when the
Baptist was at the full height of his activity. The
verb παραγίνεται is identical with that used in v. 1 concerning the Baptist, and it is used in the same sense.
As the Baptist stepped out of retirement into his great
public mission, so Jesus now does the same. He leaves
Galilee (Nazareth) where he had lived all these years
and appears at the Jordan. "To John," with πρός,
denotes contact and communication with John. The
infinitive with τοῦ regularly denotes purpose: Jesus
came to be baptized by John. There seems to be a
good deal of misunderstanding regarding this act of
Jesus, further explanation of which the evangelists
withhold. We may say only that, since his Messianic
calling was clear to Jesus already at the age of twelve,
it certainly was now fully clear to him. That implies
that he certainly also understood the mission of his
forerunner John. The hour had come and Jesus
acts.

14) The implication of the infinitive is that Jesus
requested John to baptize him. **But John would
have hindered him, saying, I have need to be baptized by thee, and comest thou to me?** Διακωλύω,
used only here in the New Testament, is a choice
term: "to hinder earnestly." The conative imperfect
indicates action begun but interrupted: attempted to
hinder. This was not opposition but reluctance due
to scruples. The question in John's words must not
be overlooked. John's treatment of Jesus is the very
opposite of that accorded the Pharisees and the Sadducees (v. 7). These he refused to baptize on account
of their sins and their impenitence, Jesus he refuses
to baptize because of his sinlessness and because of

his own sinfulness. He who towered above the Pharisees and the Sadducees bows in deepest humility before Jesus.

"I have need to be baptized of thee, and comest thou to me?" voices John's surprise and perplexity. We see that he knows a good deal about Jesus. He himself, indeed, tells us, "I knew him not," John 1:31, 33; but this implies only that at first the divine assurance had not been given him that Jesus was the Messiah and by no means excludes the thought that on other grounds he felt sure that Jesus was the Messiah. God had promised to reveal the Messiah to John in a special manner, and until this revelation came, however certain John felt about the person who would be designated thus he could not with absolute and divine certainty declare, "This is he." John was a kinsman of Jesus. It is altogether likely that from his own parents he had heard the wonderful story of Jesus' conception and birth and the subsequent events. The lives of the two, however, differed widely. John spent the years of his youth at Juttah, far south in Judah, near Hebron; Jesus grew up in the carpenter's shop in Galilee. We do not know whether the two ever saw each other until they met here at the Jordan. All the more remarkable is the word of John by which he makes a complete exception of Jesus.

The surprise lies in the comparison which John makes between Jesus and himself. By saying that Jesus has no need of being baptized by him, God's prophet though he was, John virtually declares that Jesus is no sinner, for John's baptism was for sinners only. By saying that he has need of being baptized by Jesus, John confesses his own sinfulness and places himself in the same class with the sinful people whom he baptized daily. By acknowledging the right of Jesus to baptize, yea, to baptize even him whom God had commissioned to baptize the Jewish people as he

was now doing, John places Jesus, not on the same
plane with himself, a prophet divinely sent, but far
above himself, in an office far above his own. "I have
need to be baptized by thee" is often taken to mean,
"baptized with the Holy Spirit." But this rests on
the misunderstanding that John's baptism was only
a water rite, a mere symbol, while that of Jesus would
be, not the miracle of Pentecost, but a sudden seizure
by the Spirit, such as it is assumed still takes place.

15) **But answering, Jesus said to him, Permit it
now; for thus it is proper for us to fulfill all righteousness. Then he permitted him.** This is the first
recorded word of Jesus since he spoke to his mother
when he was twelve years old. The formula: "answering, he said," the participle being added pleonastically, or the use of two finite verbs: "he answered and
said," always marks the importance of the statement
thus introduced. The passive forms are used in the
active sense. A serene, certain, comprehensive mastery pervades this word of Jesus. The scruples of
John are allayed. He who was sent to lead the people
as the first great prophet of the New Testament is
here himself led. In fact, he here proves himself to
be a true prophet, for he recognizes and obeys his
heavenly Master when that Master cômes to him.
"Permit it now," *lasse es,* ἄφες (second aorist from
ἀφίημι), is idiomatic. We perceive the majesty of this
word when we note that by it Jesus fully concurs in
what John has just said concerning their relative
purity and greatness. The sense is: "It is even as
thou sayest, John; yet this is the very reason why
you may permit what I ask." The "now" implies that
at another time, instead of John serving Jesus, John
may well expect and ask to be served by Jesus.

Another thought lies in ἄφες ἄρτι: the baptism of
Jesus is not such that Jesus could say, "I have need
to be baptized by thee," as John rightly and truly

says this concerning himself. All Jesus can say is, "Permit it now." The exceptional character of the baptism requested is thus implied in Jesus' case. The word "now" refers to this moment when Jesus is about to assume his office. Sufficient reason for the baptism of Jesus exists only "now" and could not exist at any other time in his life or in connection with his work.

The connective γάρ brings the explanation: "for thus it is proper," etc. Whereas John said, "I have need," Jesus says only, "It is proper," πρέπον ἐστίν, it is fit and in place, the present neuter participle with the copula, a periphrastic present tense, R. 81, 1119. In the case of sinners a need exists, namely to wash away their sins. On the nature and the efficacy of John's baptism see v. 6. In the case of Jesus, who has no sin, no such need exists. The words πρέπον ἐστίν show that in the case of Jesus' baptism there was an inner purpose that was entirely different from that obtaining in the case of the others baptized by John or of John's own baptism, if one could have been administered to him. What this purpose was we begin to see when we consider that, although Jesus did not *need* the baptism, he, nevertheless, asked for it. If he, being sinless, needed not the sacrament that washed sinners clean, why did he ask for it? Could he not have gone on in his sinlessness as heretofore and remained thus to the end? He certainly could have as far as his own person was concerned. The fact that Jesus, nevertheless, asks for the baptism and says that it is proper for him to receive it and for John to administer it (note ἡμῖν, "for us") indicates that Jesus thinks, not of himself alone, apart from sinful men and concerned only about his own person, but as being concerned with men, as being sent to assume the great office and work of saving them. Simply as a perfectly holy person it would not have become Jesus to ask for, or John to grant him, baptism; but as the holy person sent to save all the unholy ones, now that the great work was to be begun, it, indeed, became Jesus and John to observe this baptism.

The point that made it so proper is stated: "it is proper for us to fulfill all righteousness." "For us" = John and Jesus. The matter pertains to them alone. This, then, is neither the moral nor the ceremonial law. By associating himself with John in this matter of the baptism Jesus is thinking of their respective offices. It was proper that they should carry out whatever their respective positions required. It is thus that Jesus views his baptism. The view that it is an act of "righteousness" only in so far as it marks the willing obedience of Jesus, God having ordered John to baptize and Jesus (though not needing the baptism) submitting to it, makes the baptism a formality and misunderstands what John's baptism was. It was not law but gospel, not a demand to obey but a gift of grace to be received and accepted as such. By accepting John's baptism Jesus is in no sense obeying a law, a useless law in his case; and in no sense accepting grace and pardon, since he is, indeed, sinless. Jesus is choosing baptism by John as the right way by which to enter upon his great office, and he is doing this with a fine sense of propriety including John as well as himself. He, the Sinless One, the very Son of God, chooses to put himself alongside of all the sinful ones for whom John's sacrament was ordained. He thus connects himself with all instances of John's baptism; for it is his mediation that makes these truly efficacious for sinners. By thus joining himself to all these instances of John's baptism he signifies that he is now ready to take upon himself the load of all these sinners, i. e., to assume his redemptive office.

It was thus also proper and right that Jesus should come and, as it were, offer himself voluntarily for this great office and not wait until he would be called or until it would be laid upon him. For this office, especially in so far as it involved the sacrifice upon the cross, had to be assumed voluntarily. Shortly after this baptism John calls Jesus *the Lamb* of God, referring directly to the sacrifice. Jesus himself calls his suffering a baptism, Luke 12:50 and elsewhere. These are rays which illuminate the character of this act when John baptized Jesus.

Luther presents the view (Erlangen edition, 19, 2, 482, etc.; 20, 457; and elsewhere) that in this baptism Jesus acted as our substitute. Loaded with the world's sin, he buried it in the waters of Jordan. When following Luther some go so far as to say that what Christ obtained for us in his baptism is now conveyed to us by the means of grace (Word and Sacraments) as though salvation was fully secured for us by Christ's baptism. Luther's view strains the words by attempting to give the same significance to Christ's baptism as is given to that of the sinners who flocked to the Jordan, Christ coming with the sins of others and having them washed away, the others having their own sins removed. This produces a double removal of the same sins.

The idea that the law required of priests and of teachers that they be thirty years old and be consecrated by a religious washing and anointing can be substantiated only in the case of the Levites (Num. 4:3) and would make the whole transaction with regard to Christ, including the anointing with the Spirit, nothing but a legal ceremonial observance. It is far more than that. The modernistic view has Jesus come to John just as others did, to enroll himself among the servants of the new kingdom and to submit to the same ritual as the rest. This makes

the King himself one of the servants. Some other
views should be forgotten. We cull two minor
thoughts that should be preserved. One is that Jesus
honored John's baptism, which he certainly did, but
only incidentally, for he uses John's ministration for
a far higher purpose. The other is that Jesus intended to sanctify the water of this sacrament which
he himself would afterward send out to all the world.
*Concordia Triglotta,* 736, 21; Mueller, *Die symboli-
schen Buecher,* 770, 14.

"Then he permitted him" — that is all; no description of the mode, no details of any kind concerning
the baptismal act, not even the verb "to baptize."
Luke has only the participle βαπτισθέντος, "having
been baptized"; Mark has the finite verb ἐβαπτίσθη,
"and was baptized by John in the Jordan." The Holy
Spirit seems purposely to withhold a mention of the
mode. If the mode were such a vital thing, we may
certainly conclude that the Holy Spirit would in this
most important case have indicated it for us with sufficient clearness; but he does nothing of the kind. All
the ancient pictorial representations of the baptism of
Jesus, as well as of other baptisms, show other modes,
never immersion, Clement F. Rogers, *Baptism and
Christian Archæology,* Oxford, Clarendon Press. This
layman collected all the ancient pictorial representations, starting with the prevalent assumption that he
would find immersion there presented. When he
found the opposite, he changed his view. Even the
ruins of ancient baptisteries show that these were
too shallow to have permitted immersion. We are not
told of witnesses to Jesus' baptism, but it would be
unsafe to conclude that none were present.

16) **And having been baptized, Jesus went up
immediately from the water. And lo, the heavens
were opened, and he saw the Spirit of God descending as a dove and coming upon him. And lo, a voice**

**out of the heavens, saying, This is my Son, the Beloved, in whom I was well pleased.** The aorist participle preceding an aorist finite verb ordinarily denotes action prior to the verb; and only when the nature of the actions demands it, do the two express simultaneous action. The former is the case here: Jesus was baptized, and after the baptism was finished, he went up from the water, going up the riverbank. The modifiers attached to the main verb make this doubly certain: "he went up immediately from, or away from, the water." Matthew does not say that Jesus came up out of, or from under, the water. What he does say is that, after the baptism was finished ($\beta a\pi\tau\iota\sigma\theta\epsilon\acute{\iota}s$), whatever may have been the mode of administration, Jesus without delay ($\epsilon\mathring{\upsilon}\theta\acute{\upsilon}s$) walked away from the water of the river, so that his anointing with the Spirit of God did not take place, as many artists picture it, while he was being baptized or while he stood knee-deep in the water but on the bank of the river, a little distance from the water. There is no implication that Jesus was *under* the water. In Mark 1:9, 10 the baptism is related in one sentence, the movement away from the water in another. Matthew's $\mathring{a}\pi\acute{o}$ should be considered together with Mark's $\mathring{\epsilon}\kappa$ (1:10): neither refers to the baptismal act as such; neither puts Jesus under the water; both speak of what followed the baptismal act. Jesus stepped out of the water ($\mathring{\epsilon}\kappa$) onto the bank and walked from the water ($\mathring{a}\pi\acute{o}$) onto the bank. This would be the sense even if $\beta a\pi\tau\iota\sigma\theta\epsilon\acute{\iota}s$ indicated immersion. Neither of these prepositions can be used to prove that immersion was the mode employed for Jesus' baptism.

When Matthew writes, "Immediately he walked up from the water, and lo, the heavens were opened," the impression is made that Jesus acted intentionally. By the baptism Jesus gives himself to the work of sin-bearing; by the anointing and the voice from heaven

the Father accepts him for this work. The two acts
constitute a grand whole. We must not separate
them although they are distinct and not to be mingled
or confounded. Some are inclined to do this when
they speak of the Spirit's descent upon Jesus as though
this were a feature of his baptism, which it was not.
The application of this fact to our baptism, namely
that in the same way, through baptism and in it, the
Spirit comes to us with his regenerating grace, is
incorrect. He, indeed, does so come, but upon Jesus
he came, not in and through baptism, but *after* the
baptism.

"Lo" marks the miracle. "The heavens were
opened," with its aorist, states an actual fact. This
was not a mere vision and certainly not a mere impression (*Eindruck*) in the mind of Jesus. The
evident fact should not be weakened by talking about
a new relation of Jesus to the Father. The supposition regarding the occurring of something in the
heart of Jesus, *die innere Erregung seines Geistes-
lebens,* though it be coupled with the outward
phenomenon, like all other human speculations only
obscures the facts. The views that the heavens just
happend to brighten above Jesus, or that a thunder-
storm brought on flashes of lightning, are rationalistic
theories. Ezekiel (1:1) saw the heavens opened;
Stephen likewise (Acts 7:56) ; compare also Rev. 4:1;
Isa. 64:1. "Heaven opens itself, which hitherto was
closed, and now becomes at Christ's baptism a door
and a window, so that one can see into it; and henceforth there is no difference any more between God
and us; for God the Father himself is present and
says, This is my beloved Son." Luther. The additional αὐτῷ is textually questionable, nor would it add
to the sense the thought that what occurred pertained
to Jesus. The heavens did not remain open, and it
is an insertion into the text to say that now a new,

mysterious intercourse was opened between Jesus and
the heavenly world. We are not told what became
visible when the heavens were suddenly opened as we
are told in the case of Ezekiel and of Stephen. Yet
we may well say that the heavenly glory was visible
and that John and any others present beheld its
radiance. Matthew, however, focuses everything
upon Jesus.

The subject of εἶδεν, "he saw," is the same as that
of ἀνέβη, "he walked up," namely Jesus. John 1:32, 33
makes it certain that John, too, saw the Spirit's descent
upon Jesus; in fact, his seeing this was the divinely
appointed proof for him that Jesus was, indeed, the
Messiah. Matthew's concern is not with John but
with Jesus. What he saw is graphically described
(more fully than by Mark): "the Spirit of God
descending as a dove and coming upon him." Πνεῦμα
Θεοῦ, without the articles, seems to be the correct reading; with these proper nouns the articles may or may
not be used; the sense would be the same. When we
see from John 1:29-34 with what clarity the Baptist
spoke of what his eyes, too, saw here beside the Jordan,
the mistake of those appears who deny that the Old
Testament revealed the Trinity to the Jews or revealed the Trinity only dimly and imperfectly. All
of the Baptist's hearers understood him. Later on
the Jews object only to the claim that the man Jesus
should call himself God's Son; they never once raise
the issue that God is only one person and not three.
It is specious to raise the question as to how fully
the Baptist and the Jews themselves grasped the
reality of the three divine Persons and then to rate
their knowledge as low as possible.

Because of his very nature the Spirit is invisible,
but God never had difficulty when he wished to appear
to the fathers. Why the Spirit chose the form of a
dove has often been asked. Luther thinks that it

was done because of the Spirit's friendliness, because
it is without wrath and bitterness, the Spirit desiring
to show that he has no anger towards us but is ready
to help us to become godly and to be saved. Others
point to purity, innocence, and meekness as being
symbolized by the dove. Gen. 1:2 is the only place
in which a somewhat analogous expression occurs concerning the Spirit. We may content ourselves by
saying that the dovelike form intended to convey
the idea of the graciousness of the Spirit. The two
present participles καταβαῖνον and ἐρχόμενον picture how
the dovelike form came down upon Jesus, and
ἐπ᾽ αὐτόν is elucidated by John 1:32, 33: he "remained
upon him," did not return whence he came. The
Spirit was a permanent gift to Jesus. As his conception "of the Spirit," so this coming of the Spirit
was a gift. It pertained to the human nature of
Jesus. In his deity the Son was of the identical
essence with both the Father and the Spirit, nor could
the Spirit be given to him. But in his human nature,
which he had assumed in order by it to work out our
redemption, he could receive the Spirit as a gift; and
he did receive the Spirit when the great work was
now to begin.

The coming down of the Spirit upon Jesus is the
anointing prophesied in Ps. 45:7: "God, thy God,
hath anointed thee with the oil of gladness above
thy fellows." Isa. 61:1: "The Spirit of the Lord
God is upon me; because the Lord hath anointed me
to preach," etc. (Luke 4:18). See also Acts 10:38:
"God anointed Jesus of Nazareth with the Holy Ghost
and with power." The prophets received some of the
gifts of the Spirit; Jesus, lifted far above them, with
an infinitely greater task to perform, received the
Spirit as such. What power thus filled him we see
when he is now led up of the Spirit to be tempted,
Matt. 4:1, and when he returns in the power of the

Spirit into Galilee to teach there in his wonderful way and to work miracles. Luther writes: "Here he begins rightly to be Christ," namely the Anointed One, "and was thus inaugurated into his entire Messianic office as our Prophet, High Priest, and King."

Rationalism thinks that a common dove fluttered over Jesus. Some resort to figurative interpretations or assume a twofold vision, namely that what Jesus and the Baptist beheld in the spirit was also symbolized for their eyes and their ears, so that they thought they actually saw and heard. But the shepherds actually saw and heard the angels, so Jesus and John saw and heard what occurred when the Spirit came down and the Father spoke from above.

17) A second "lo" calls attention to the next manifestation: "a voice out of the heavens," ἐκ with the strict idea "from within," i. e., the opened heavens, R. 597. The nominative stands alone, needing no verb. The words spoken by this voice reveal that it is the Father's. This voice and what it declares are as real to the ears as is the form of a dove to the eyes. The fact that the Baptist, too, heard it, he evidences when in John 1:34 he says of Jesus, "this is the Son of God."

Mark and Luke record the words as being addressed to Jesus, "Thou art my Son, the Beloved," etc., which we regard as the actual form in which they were spoken. Matthew writes, "This is my Son, the Beloved," etc., and intends the words for us. While being addressed to Jesus, they are also intended for all others as we plainly see from John 1:34. Some make a distinction between "my beloved Son" as referring to the eternal Godhead of the Son before the incarnation, and "in whom I was well pleased" as referring to Christ in his flesh: but the reason for this is too obscure. Οὗτος refers to the God-man as he stood on the riverbank. In what sense this voice

intended ὁ υἱός μου to be understood cannot be in doubt
after the preceding chapters in Matthew, to say nothing of all the rest of the Scriptures. This Son is the
Second Person of the Godhead. Those who deny the
deity of this Son must settle their accounts with the
Father. "My Son, the Beloved," ὁ ἀγαπητός, adds the
verbal adjective, which, like most verbals, has a
passive meaning: the Father loves him. The verb
ἀγαπᾶν denotes the highest type of love, that which is
coupled with full comprehension and understanding
and is accompanied with corresponding purpose.
When it is used, as here, regarding one who is worthy
of that love, ἀγαπᾶν includes the completest and highest
manifestations of this love; this is impossible when
the sinful world, enemies, and unworthy persons are
the objects. The verb φιλεῖν expresses the love of
affection, and while it is also fitting when it is referred to the relation existing between the Father and
the Son, it expresses far less.

Unless we see the God-man in Jesus we shall fail
to see why God should here call from heaven that this
is his Son, the Beloved. This announcement has to
do with the work on which Jesus is entering. It predicates far more than that the Son ἄσαρκος is the Son
and as such from eternity the Beloved. That fact
would evidently need no announcement, nor would
it be connected with this baptism by such an announcement. The announcement deals with the Son ἔνσαρκος,
with the Son as incarnate in Jesus, and with him as
now entering on his Messianic work. It thus proclaims who Jesus really is: "my Son," and voices the
Father's love for him as he now proceeds to do the
Father's will in this great work. Some regard
ἀγαπητός as equivalent to μονογενής, "the Only-begotten,"
and assert that this is the fixed meaning of the term.
The evidence adduced, however, amounts only to this
that an only son was at times also called "the beloved"

(son), thus in Gen. 22:2, 12, 16, which is the chief proof offered. The main objection to this interpretation lies in the sense attributed to μονογενής, namely that in John 1:14, 18; 3:16, 18; I John 4:9 this term refers only to the human birth of Jesus, that thus only he was "the Only-begotten," and not to the *generatio aeterna* of the Son in his divine nature. From all eternity the Son was the Only-begotten; and when that Son came of his own volition to carry out his Father's redemptive will, the Father called him "the Beloved."

And to this the Father added: "in whom I was well pleased." This clause is not an exposition of "the Beloved," saying only about the same thing. Our versions convey this idea by disregarding the aorist tense εὐδόκησα, by translating, "in whom *I am well pleased.*" This tense *"was pleased"* becomes clear when we understand that the verb εὐδοκεῖν, when it is employed regarding persons, often has an intensive sense and is equal to ἐκλέγεσθαι and αἱρετίζειν, "to select or choose for oneself." The good pleasure expresses itself in the choice. See C.-K., 253. Thus "in whom I was well pleased" really says, "I was well pleased in choosing him." The clause goes back to the moment when God selected his Son for the redemptive work, and when that Son accepted that work. The aorist is historical and nothing more. The mighty fact of the heavenly selection of the Son who now stands incarnate at the Jordan is thus announced. That is why the Spirit is now sent upon him.

The eternal Son is the Father's Elect for the great task. This Son, now incarnate and now presenting himself for the task, is thus the Beloved. Upon the human nature of this Elect and Beloved One the Spirit himself is bestowed for the great task. All this Jesus knew without the Father's words. All this is announced for the Baptist and for all of us to know.

And thus in what transpires here at the Jordan we have one of the clearest and completest revelations of the Trinity: the Father speaking from heaven — the Son standing incarnate at the Jordan — the Spirit as a dove descending out of heaven. Yet here, too, we have this revelation only in a limited degree, only in so far as these three divine Persons are engaged in our redemption and salvation. The deeper mysteries of the Holy Trinity remain hidden from us. God, as it were, is compelled to reveal so much in order that we may know how our salvation is wrought. Even so much of the Trinity is beyond mortal comprehension. Its revelation has only the one purpose indicated and was never intended to answer the curious questions which rationalistic intellects (not hearts) may raise. The church has called this the economic Trinity, the revelation concerned with the economy of our salvation.

# CHAPTER IV

## IV

### Christ Begins His Messianic Work, Chapter 4

*Christ's Temptation in the Wilderness, 4:1-11*

We have three accounts of this event. That of
Luke alone is a real parallel, and that of Mark only
a brief summary. Matthew could not have drawn
on Luke, or Luke drawn on Matthew, judging from
the two narratives. As far as Matthew is concerned,
he wrote in advance of both Luke and Mark. The
idea that Mark presents the original tradition on
which the accounts of Matthew and Luke were based
is cancelled by the other idea of the critics that Mark
is the writer who introduces the detailed touches which
Matthew is thought to lack. Mark simply abbreviated
what Matthew had already narrated at length, adding
something from oral tradition. The further questions
about the nature of the Temptation and how it must be
conceived are answered after the text of the narrative
itself has been examined.

1) **Then Jesus was led up into the wilderness
by the Spirit to be tried by the devil.** Both the adverb
"then" and the facts now related show the close connection of this section with the anointing just recorded.
There is no reason why ἀνήχθη cannot mean, "was led
up," namely from the Ghor or depression through
which the Jordan flows to a lonely spot on the neigh-
boring mountains. If the observation is correct that
in the LXX ἡ ἔρημος is used to designate the wilderness
beyond the Jordan in distinction from ἡ ἔρημος τῆς
Ἰουδαίας, we may assume that the temptation occurred

in that locality although the traditional sites should
not be taken too seriously.   In view of 3:16, 17, "by
the Spirit," cannot mean "by Jesus' own spirit" but
must mean by the Holy Spirit who had come upon
Jesus and remained upon him permanently for his
ministry.   This passive verb, however, in no way
expresses a reluctance on the part of Jesus to meet
the tempter.   It intends to bring out the very opposite: the willingness of Jesus to do the divine will.   It
does even more: it wards off the idea that Jesus
entered into this temptation of his own accord when
at this very beginning of his ministry it might have
been wise to avoid such a decisive test.   We often
rashly subject ourselves to temptation.   Jesus was
led into his ordeal by his Father's own Spirit.   And
this means that the temptation had to occur, and at
this very time.   It was God's own will that this mighty
battle should be fought now.

The remarkable combination ought to be noted:
God's Spirit and the devil, ὑπὸ τοῦ Πνεύματος — ὑπὸ τοῦ
διαβόλου.  The one bestows all his power upon the
human nature of Jesus, the other at once puts this
power to a supreme test.   In a strange way God's
will and the devil's will meet in a tremendous clash.
We may take it that Satan knew all about this man
Jesus, miraculously conceived and born by Mary and
then living so long and so quietly in Nazareth.   As an
invisible spectator he beheld what transpired after the
baptism at the Jordan.   So this was God's Messiah,
come to crush Satan, destroy his works, and to erect
the kingdom of God among men.   At once the devil
resolved to break this divine champion.   He had
conquered the first Adam, he would conquer the
second, and that at once.   Before this Jesus got
under way with his work, Satan would lay him
low with his old cunning.   God willed that it should
be so.

The infinitive πειρασθῆναι denotes purpose, and the aorist denotes completeness: to be tested to the finish. The devil was to exert the full extent of his power, God offering no restraint. The verb itself is really a *vox media,* "to try," "to test," "to put to the proof." It obtains its sinister sense from the context, and because this is often evil, πειράζω has its dark connotation "to tempt," and ὁ πειράζων means "the tempter." "By the devil" was Jesus to be tempted in a mortal test. Satan would strike in person and would not entrust the issue to a lesser agent. As regards ὁ διάβολος, really an adjective used as a noun, "the slanderer," "the adversary," we need not waste time by bringing in the volume of Biblical evidence which reveals "the devil" as the fallen angel Satan, the author of sin, the head of the hellish kingdom, forever opposed to God and devoted to man's eternal ruin because of this opposition. Consult the details in C.-K., 187, etc. If no devil exists as he is described in the Bible, the whole Bible is false, and man himself is converted into his own devil.

2) **And after fasting for forty days and for forty nights he finally was hungry.** This statement is the preamble to the temptation that now begins and helps to explain Satan's first onset. By fasting for so long a time Jesus did not weaken himself for the final battle as some have suggested. It is useless to refer to the two periods of forty days spent by Moses on Sinai without food or drink (Exod. 34:28; Deut. 9:9, 18), or to the forty foodless days of Elijah while traveling to Horeb (I Kings 19:8), or to other long fasts of ordinary men. Since the body of Jesus was wholly unaffected by sin, its power of enduring abstinence from food by far exceeds ours. An idea of partial fasting, living without ordinary food due to wandering in the desert, is wholly shut out by Luke 4:2: "he did eat nothing in those days." Mat-

thew writes: "afterward (ὕστερον) he was hungry";
and Luke: "and when they were completed (the days),
he hungered."

This long fast should not be regarded as a preparation for the coming temptation. We nowhere read
that Jesus fasted and *prayed*. This is not a retirement
of Jesus such as he at other times sought for communion with God. Jesus did not spend these forty days in
the happy enjoyment of the good pleasure of his Father
and thus forgot all about food. He was led up into
the mountainous wilderness for quite a different purpose, namely, "to be tempted by the devil." Mark uses
ἐκβάλλει, "he is thrown out into the desert," and then
adds that he was there πειραζόμενος ὑπὸ τοῦ Σατανᾶ, "being
tempted by Satan," namely during the entire time
which he spent in the desert. This durative participle
after ἦν does not indicate purpose: "in order to be
tempted," and thus the temptation should not be restricted to the three attacks at the end of the forty
days. Luke also has this present participle: πειραζόμενος
ὑπὸ τοῦ διαβόλου. Since Luke has it after ἤγετο, if he had
purpose in mind and thus only the three fully recorded
temptations, he would have employed the infinitive or a
purpose clause. During the entire forty days Jesus
endured the temptation of the devil, and this experience
caused him to forget all about food. He gained no
breathing spell whatever to allow his mind to turn to
the wants of his body. It is not necessary to assume
that Jesus did not sleep during these forty nights; that
would surely have been mentioned if it had been a fact.

We have no revelation regarding the continuous
temptation. The supposition that it was so severe and
of such a nature that human language is unable to
convey what it was, is untenable, for then we should
have a description of only the minor temptations,
which is certainly not the case.

When thinking about the long days full of temptation the ὑπό phrase used by all three evangelists must
be kept in mind.  This is *the* preposition used for the
personal agent with passives.  Satan alone caused
this long temptation.  None of it arose from the
thoughts and the desires in Jesus' heart concerning
either his Sonship or his Messiahship.  Deductions
from temptations arising in our sinful thoughts and
desires are inadequate for giving us the inwardness of
the temptation endured by the sinless Son of God.  The
fact that the hunger was not felt for just forty days,
no more and no less, cannot be considered accidental.
We read about other periods of precisely forty days in
the Scriptures, so that it seems as though some mysterious law underlies this number.

3)  **And when the tempter had come he said to
him, If thou art a son of God, say that these stones
shall become bread.**  The circumstantial participle
is temporal.  Not until this time did the tempter
appear in person.  How he launched his previous
assaults is not indicated.  The fact that Satan now
appeared in some tangible form is generally admitted.
But the supposition that all angels possess an etherial
form of some kind and by this are able to appear, is
unbiblical speculation, usually also ending in ascribing
some tangible form even to God.  As πνεύματα angels
differ from men in having no bodily form of any kind.
Yet good angels freely appear to men when they are
sent by God; men see them and hear them speak.  God
appears in the same way (3:16, 17).  Apart even from
II Cor. 11:14, Satan too, who is an angel, must have the
power to appear.  The supposition that, because he
here quotes the Scriptures, he must have come as a
Jewish scribe, or, if that is too specific, as a man of
authority, is answered by the last two temptations.  He
came as what he was, Satan; and Jesus knew with

whom he was dealing and that Satan had come to put him to the supreme test.

Exactly as he did in Gen. 3:1 and in Job 1:9; 2:4, 5, Satan starts the temptation by raising a cloud of doubt. While he uses a condition of reality: "if thou art a son of God," the "if" really questions the fact, for Satan demands that Jesus furnish the proof. We see that Satan questions the very word of the Father spoken from the opened heavens. When doing so, he cunningly modifies the Father's word. He does not say, "*the* Son of God," *the* one and only eternal Son, but, "*a* son of God," one of a class, related to God only by the divine favor (ἀγαπητός, "beloved," 3:17) and chosen only thus to be the Messiah. Our versions translate (also Luke), "the Son of God," and it must be admitted that the unarticulated υἱὸς τοῦ Θεοῦ may be so rendered; it is like a title. As far as Satan's demand of proof is concerned, no real difference would obtain. Satan says, "a son," because Jesus is man, a fact strongly emphasized by his present hunger for food. "Only such a son art thou," he suggests. And even that, Satan implies, needs proof. The thought that, if Jesus would furnish this proof, Satan himself would also accept this sonship of Jesus plus his Messiahship, is out of line; for this is a temptation for Jesus by submitting the proof to prove even this kind of sonship. Note that all who today deny the deity of Jesus or his eternal Sonship agree with the devil in calling Jesus only "a son of God" and are better than the devil only in this regard that they regard him to be such "a son" whereas the devil implies that he doubts it.

How is Jesus to prove that he is "a son of God"? "Say that these stones shall become bread." The ἵνα clause is the object of εἰπέ; it states what Jesus is to say, R. 993. The temptation lies in this bidding on the part of Satan. The tempter did not really doubt that a word spoken by Jesus could turn the stones lying

there into bread. Satan knew that as the Messiah
Jesus could perform this and other miracles, for even
the Jews expected miracles of the Messiah. Like the
tempter, the Jews asked for peculiar miracles, which,
if they had been wrought by Jesus, would have plunged
him into sin. In this respect the Jews were simply
tools of the devil, continuing the temptations here advanced by Satan in person. Ordinary Christians have
the right idea when they say: "If Jesus would have
done what Satan said he would have obeyed Satan
instead of God." So, by acceding to the Jews' request
he would have done their wrong and wicked will and
not the Father's. But this involves much more. We
cannot say that it would have been wrong for Jesus to
supply himself with bread by means of a miracle. Most
likely Jesus himself ate of the bread gathered after the
feeding of the 5,000 and of the 4,000, the bread he had
himself miraculously produced. Why should he on
those occasions have remained hungry when all the rest
were fully fed? But here all is different. The Greek
has no word for "loaves" but merely uses the plural
of "bread" when it wants to indicate a number of the
flat cakes into which bread was baked (*contra* R. V.
margin and others).

By the very act of miraculously transforming these
stones into bread to prove himself "a son of God" Jesus
would prove himself a false "son." That act would
imply *distrust of his Father.* By the Father's own
Spirit Jesus was here to undergo the severest temptation. The Father's own will had brought him to this
hunger. For forty days the Father had supported the
body of Jesus so that it did not even feel the hunger
resulting from the fasting. Now Jesus is no longer to
look up to his Father with a true son's trust but is to
look down to these stones, to use them for evading this
hunger? Does it seem strange that the Father should
leave a son of his to hunger thus, or unworthy for a

son of this Father to be in such a state of hunger; so that, in order to make sure he is a son, the son must provide food for himself? Was not this son, who is even the eternal Son, to suffer infinitely greater agony than the present hunger?

The judgment that this first temptation is one that does not directly concern the Messianic mission of Jesus overlooks the essential point which appears in the conditional clause: "if thou art a son of God." Both the hunger and the making of bread out of stones are connected with the devil's method of proving sonship, and sonship in this case involves Messiahship; for as the Son Beloved, Jesus was the one chosen (see 3:17).

4) Jesus conquers the tempter by acting as a true "son" should act, to say nothing about "the Son." The devil's suggestion is not for one moment entertained by Jesus' mind. The implied distrust the devil wants Jesus to show toward his Father is at once met by *the most perfect trust and reliance on the Father.* **But he answering said** (compare 3:15), **It has been written, Not on bread alone shall a man live, but on every utterance going forth through God's mouth.** The sum and substance of this reply is trust: the trust of any true son of God, the trust of the incarnate Son. This trust rose in its might and crushed the very suggestion of distrust or mistrust and thus overcame the temptation.

The importance of the reply is indicated by the preamble: "he answering said." The remarkable thing is that Jesus meets every assault with a word of Scripture: γέγραπται, "it has been written," the perfect tense with the implication: "and once written, now stands forever." Hence we may translate, "it is written." Jesus smites the devil with "the sword of the Spirit, which is the Word of God," Eph. 6:17. He who could himself say, "Verily, verily, I say to you!" and could speak with divine authority in every utterance of his

own, turns to the Word already written and uses that
and only that.   The quotation from Deut. 8:3 stamps
the Pentateuch as the Word of God; for the formula
"it has been written" is used only with reference to the
divine Word.   What God wanted Israel to learn during
the forty years in the desert when he humbled Israel,
suffered it to hunger, and fed it with manna, that Jesus
did not need to learn, that he knew perfectly even now
when he was distressed with hunger.   Israel was a
type of the Messiah in many phases of its history, and
that is the case here with regard to these forty days of
fasting in the desert.   Israel often murmured and
sinned when it was hungry or thirsty, not so Jesus,
God's true Son.   The word Moses spoke for God rings
out from the lips of Jesus as the innermost conviction
of his heart and voices his absolute trust in God.   By
this word and this act this "son" in the true way proved
that he was "a son."

Note the gradation: "the Son" (thus the Father in
3:17) — "a son" (thus the devil) — "a man" (thus
Jesus in the quotation).   Does the devil lower Jesus
and refer to him only as "a son," one of a class?   Jesus
does not reply, "I am *the* Son."   He is not debating
with the devil and has no call to enlighten the fiend of
darkness.   He is here to conquer Satan.   So Jesus
meets the insult, which questions even his sonship, by
a reply which pertains to all men merely as men.   This
actually makes the devil ridiculous.   Did he himself
really imagine that it was bread that kept a man alive;
or did he really think that Jesus could be fooled by such
a false notion?   That is true with regard to all lies and
lying assumptions: when they are exposed by the light
of truth they appear as what they actually are, ridiculous, preposterous, the notions of fools.   The devil's
bidding that Jesus hurry and appease his hunger with
stones made into bread, wants Jesus to believe the silly
notion that a man's life, to say nothing about the life

of "a son of God," rests "on bread alone," ἐπ' ἄρτῳ μόνῳ,
on this ground or basis (R. 604) "alone" and thus apart
from God, the Creator of both the man and the bread.
In his blind folly the devil may think so, Moses knew
better, Israel learned better, every "son of God" knows
better, only fools blinded by the devil do not know
better. The future "shall live" is probably volitive,
the tense expressing the divine will; not merely futuristic regarding what shall occur (R. 889).

"On the contrary," ἀλλά (after a negative statement), whether a man knows it or not, he lives only
"on every utterance going forth (ἐκ in the participle)
through God's mouth" (a Hebraistic turn, R. 649).
The sense is beclouded when the question is put as to
whether ῥῆμα refers to merely the uttered word or to the
thing uttered. None of the utterances of God are just
words and thus mere sounds. The Hebrew term *motsa'*,
when it is used in connection with lips or mouth, means
*Ausgehendes* (Ed. Koenig, *Woerterbuch,* on Deut. 8:3)
and could thus be expressed by the neuter participle
ἐκπορευόμενον without the addition of ῥῆμα. We may thus
lay no stress on the latter word; the real sense lies in
the participle: "what goes forth through God's mouth,"
on that the life of a man rests. The addition "every"
thus also becomes clear. What goes forth through
God's mouth is what God orders, and his orders for
maintaining a man's life may be varied. See the orders
by which Israel was kept alive in the desert, Moses
without food on Sinai, Elijah while travelling forty
days and nights on one meal, and again when being
fed by ravens, and again when making the widow's
meal and oil abound for many days (I Kings 17:1-16;
19:4-8); Jesus when fed by angels, v. 11. No amount
of bread or other food will keep a man alive without a
word and an order from God's mouth.

The first temptation resembles the one that occurred in Eden. It deals with food and uses food to

awaken distrust of God and of God's Word. What succeeded in Eden, in the land of plenty, failed in the destitute wilderness. What succeeded in the case of Adam and Eve who were well-fed, failed in the case of Jesus who was in great hunger. The temptation assailed Jesus from his human side; he resisted it, not by means of his divinity, but as man, with his trust in God and in God's Word. By doing it in this way he enables us today to follow his example. All true sons may follow this "son."

5) The second attack reverses the first. Failing on one flank, the devil turns swiftly against the other. The first two temptations thus form counterparts; the two are halves which form a whole. **Then the devil takes him with himself into the holy city and placed him on the wing of the Temple and says to him, If thou art a son of God, throw thyself down. For it has been written,**

> **To his angels he will give injunction concerning thee;**
> **And on their hands will they bear thee up**
> **Lest ever thou strike thy foot against a stone.**

We have noted παραλαμβάνειν in 1:20 and in 2:13, 20; here it has the same sense: "to take possession of and thus also to take along." The present tense pictures the devil taking Jesus with him in this manner. The aorist, "and placed," or "stood him," simply states the fact. "The holy city," the Temple, and then the quotation of the Holy Scriptures to Jesus, the Holy One of God, certainly are in strong contrast to "the devil," to whom nothing is holy when prosecuting his unholy work. There are interpreters who deny the actuality of what Matthew describes as facts. Since the devil is a spirit, we are told that what is here stated must have taken place "in the spirit." The devil's power did not actually place Jesus on the wing of the Temple but only controlled his senses so that Jesus "felt himself" standing on the wing of the Temple. It is also added that this included dizziness because Josephus, *Antiquities*, 15, 11, 5, mentions this feeling in describing the height above the rocks below. But is Jesus only mentally to throw himself down from this height? And if the second temptation occurred only in the mind, are the other two different?

Like Job, Jesus was placed into Satan's power so that the latter might tempt him to the uttermost. The transfer of Jesus to the Temple was a physical transfer. There is no difficulty as to willingness on Jesus' part; he consented to the Father's will to be tempted as the devil might will to tempt him. We need not say that Jesus transferred himself to the Temple; παραλαμβάνει and ἔστησε indicate that the devil provided the motive power. Throughout, Jesus only submits to the tempter's operations. The devil was permitted to take Jesus where he desired for the purpose of temptation.

The ἱερόν is not the ναός or Sanctuary (the building housing the Holy and the Holy of Holies) but the entire Temple area with all its buildings and courts. The πτερύγιον is "the wing of the Temple"; note the article: not some wing but the one specifically so called. The diminutive has lost its force in the Greek. This "wing" was most likely the one from which James was thrown down, Acts 12:2; Eusebius 2, 23. This was a part of the outer wall that encircled the entire Temple area. The most acceptable location is the στοὰ βασιλική or royal porch on the south wall, a deep ravine lying between it and the opposite suburbs; others think of the east wall along Solomon's Porch where the drop is 400 cubits or 600 feet. Josephus describes both locations in *Ant.* 15, 11, 5, and the latter also in 20, 9, 7. Not a word is said about people in the Temple courts, before whom Jesus was to make a display by throwing himself from a great height and remaining unharmed.

This idea, which is wholly foreign to the text and contrary to the very nature of the second temptation, has led some to think of the roof parapet or of the roof gable of the Sanctuary.

6) The conditional clause in the tempter's bidding is the same in form and in thought as in v. 3. But the temptation runs in the opposite direction. As a true son Jesus had just demonstrated his absolute trust in God regarding his bodily needs. And as a true son he has just pointed to the Word of God on which his trust rested. At both points the new assault is aimed. If Jesus is such a true and trustful son of God, let him demonstrate the fact by something more decisive than continued patient hunger. That, the devil implies, is a cheap way of showing real trust. And yet, like the liar that he is, this cheap method was the very one he assailed but a moment ago when he sought to entice Jesus to distrust God by not waiting for bread from God but by rushing himself to provide it. The heroic way to display trust, Satan says, is to test some promise of God to the limit and on the instant. Let Jesus throw himself down from this great Temple height and prove that God's promise in Ps. 91:11, 12 is true. If Jesus has real filial trust, the devil intimates, he will not hesitate a moment; and, of course, if God fails to keep his Word, that Word is nothing, and Jesus might as well be dead as to live and to rely on empty promises.

The cunning of the temptation is doubled by the devil's use of Scripture. By himself quoting Scripture the devil would block any further resort of Jesus to Scripture; he would wrest the sword of the Spirit from Jesus' hand. The devil here shows himself an expert in handling Scripture. Luther well calls him a *doctor non promotus sed expertus.* The passage he quotes seems to fit the proposal he makes in the most perfect way. Read the entire Psalm and see how all of it fits quite exactly. All that Satan has done is to invent an act to match the two verses quoted, one in which God's angels can bear a man up and prevent him from crashing his feet on the stones beneath. They will catch him under the arms and let him light on the rocks below as gently as feather down. The devil's art of quoting Scripture has been spread far and wide in the devil's school, and some of his pupils and graduates are doctors that are quite as expert as he is.

In this case the deception does not lie in misapplying to Jesus what really does not apply to him. Psalm 91 applies to any son of God and certainly also to this Son. Satan abbreviates by omitting the line, "to keep thee in all thy ways." Some find the deception in this omission as though the promise of God were conditional: to protect us only when we walk in the path of divine duty. But then the words should read, "to keep thee in all *his ways.*" If the deception lay in omitting this line, it would have been rather easy to overthrow Satan. A misquotation is removed by the corrected quotation. Jesus, however, makes no correction, does not point to the omitted line but accepts the quotation as being substantially correct. The deception in the use of this quotation by Satan lies in setting one Scripture against another. One statement is stressed, and others that should go with it are quietly disregarded. The trick is constantly practiced, often on a large scale, when a mass of passages are combined in such a way that it makes the Bible say what it most certainly does not say, in fact, openly contradicts elsewhere in the plainest language. This type of deception easily catches the unwary, especially the devout who regard the Scriptures highly; it is also the delight of those who love to harass devout believers while they think they are fortifying themselves behind impregnable walls.

7) **Jesus said to him, Again it has been written, Thou shalt not test out the Lord, thy God.** The temptation is overcome with a single word. A true

son knows what his father says and means; so Jesus knows that all the great promises of his Father's protection are intended for our humble trust in him and never once for our presumption. It would be a caricature of humble trust to take a gracious promise of God and by some foolhardy act to challenge God to see whether he will, indeed, do what he has said, or, still worse, simply to presume that he must do what his words say. As the first temptation, under the plea of acting like a true son, tries to lead to *distrust* of the Father, so the second temptation, under the same plea, tries to lead to *a false trust* of the Father. What such false trust really is the Father himself has declared in plainest language, and as a true son, who knows all that his Father has said, Jesus sets at the side of the word quoted by the devil another word that must be considered together with it.

On the use of ἔφη as an aorist see R. 311. The adverb πάλιν never has the sense of *contra* or opposition. Jesus does not set one Scripture against another. The adverb means "again," *rursus*. Jesus places one Scripture beside another and thus establishes the great principle of all true interpretation: *Scriptura ex Scriptura explicanda est*, Scripture is explained and must be explained by Scripture. Any false conclusions or deductions from one passage are eliminated by comparing other pertinent passages. No man dare press into a passage a thought that contradicts another passage. Here all exegesis that operates with contradictions in the Scripture has its answer. It is generally the easy way out where the real solution of what looks like a contradiction is not readily found. In the present case all is clear: Ps. 91:11, 12 dare not be pressed to clash with Deut. 6:16: "Thou shalt not test out the Lord, thy God."

This word of God rests on the incident recorded in Exod. 17:7 when the people demanded that God furnish them water with the challenging cry, "Is the Lord among us or not?" Their sin was the fact that they tested out God, tried or tempted him. Instead of praying and trustfully relying on God, leaving the fulfillment of his promises of help in need to his abounding grace, the people chided and challenged God. They did it in the bad situation in which they found themselves. They did it by presumptuous lack of trust. They virtually said: "If God does not do what we demand, then there is no God among us, then his promises amount to nothing." In this negative way they tempted or tried him out. And this was their sin.

The devil wants Jesus to commit this sin in the opposite or positive way, which is far worse. Jesus is in no danger but is deliberately to throw himself into mortal danger. And he is to do this for no reason whatever save to try out God regarding his promise — as though God had not proved often enough that he helps his own and keeps his Word. Without necessity plunging into mortal danger may look like supreme, heroic trust in God and thus as supreme proof of truly being a son of God. That is the lure of this temptation. In reality this is false trust and thus, as Jesus points out, nothing but tempting God, of which no true son of God would ever be guilty as little as he would be guilty of lack of trust. All lack of trust and all false trust are closely akin. Both tempt and challenge God with their presumptions as to what he must do to keep his promises. If Jesus were to throw himself down from the Temple height he would presumptuously go beyond God's promise and thus tempt God and sin against him and his promise. By pointing out that truth from the written Word itself the tempter and his temptation are vanquished.

8) **Again the devil takes him with himself to a very high mountain and shows him all the kingdoms of the world and the glory of them; and he said to**

**him, These all will I give to thee if thou, by falling down, wilt worship me.** Luther says that he who in the first temptation showed himself as a black devil, and in the second as a light, white devil, using even God's own Word, now displays himself as a divine, majestic devil, who comes right out as though he were God himself. Satan drops his mask and appears as the prince and ruler of this world. He no longer operates with the appeal, "if thou art a son of God," suggesting some ungodly way by which Jesus is to prove that he is such a son. Cunningly he accepts the fact that Jesus is a son, even the one chosen to be the Messiah, and on this Satan rests the final temptation.

Those who regard the transfer of Jesus to the Temple wing as a mental act, thrust into the mind and thought of Jesus by Satan, think of the transfer "to a very high mountain" in the same way. Jesus feels himself to be on such a mountain; in reality he never left the wilderness. Seeing the kingdoms of the world, we are told, was only a mental act; so why not also the being on a mountain? For no physical mountain affords a view of all the kingdoms of the world. One answer to this is that, if the showing of the kingdoms was mental only, no mental mountain was necessary, it would be wholly superfluous. The second is that the plain verbs of both Matthew and Luke shut out this hypothesis. The third is that, if by his mere volition Satan could project thoughts and feelings into the mind of Jesus and could make Jesus think he was where he actually was not, the mind of Jesus would be utterly helpless under the will of Satan. The statement that Jesus "still remained master of his thinking and willing" is the assertion of the commentator who would harmonize his view with the Gospel accounts. Only by means of the words which Satan spoke could he present thoughts to the mind of Jesus; and these lying thoughts Jesus promptly rejected.

The verb δείκνυσιν (Luke, ἔδειξεν) can scarcely mean that Satan flashes the thought of all the kingdoms of the world and of their glory into the mind of Jesus. "And shows" means "shows to the eyes of Jesus." Luke adds that this was done ἐν στιγμῇ χρόνου, "in an instant of time." This phrase does not refer symbolically to the transient nature of all these kingdoms and their glory, flashing brightly for an instant and then being as quickly gone. This στιγμή is an actual instant. Before the very eyes of Jesus as he looked out over the world from that mountaintop the prince of this world, by his occult power, flashed in an instant a view of the mighty realm he ruled. "And the glory of them" brings out the feature that made "all the kingdoms of the world" so desirable and attractive to Jesus who was to be the true king of this vast realm but only by achieving the kingship through suffering and death. How this showing was performed, especially how the glory was made to appear, and that all in an instant, is beyond us.

9) We need not trouble about the neuter plural ταῦτα πάντα which refers to "all the kingdoms of the world and the glory of them." Luke has: "all this authority and the glory of them." The devil offers Jesus the rule of this grand domain and the glory that would go with this rule. Luke adds the devil's explanation as to how he is able to make this grand offer: "for to me it has been delivered, and to whom I will I give it." He speaks as though he were the rightful ruler of all these kingdoms, and as though God himself had given him this rule. This, of course, is a lie, for he is an illegitimate ruler who has usurped his authority and will be brought to book for his usurpation. Also his presumption that he is so supreme in his rulership that he is able to make a gift of it to whomever he may will is a lie. A usurper's gift is spurious, and whoever would accept his gift makes himself a party to his usurpation. All

the arrogant pride of the devil who first fell away from God through pride comes out in his offer: "These all will I give thee."

The boldest stroke, however, lies in the little condition attached to the offer: "if thou, by falling down, wilt worship me." The circumstantial aorist participle πεσών enhances the act of worship and, like the aorist subjunctive προσκυνήσῃς, signifies a single act. The verb is used with reference to Oriental prostration before great human lords but especially also with reference to prostration before God in the deepest religious reverence and adoration (2:2, 8, 11, the latter also with the participle). The reply of Jesus shows that the latter meaning is in the devil's mind. Satan's proposition is this: God has turned all these kingdoms over to him, and he is willing to turn them over to Jesus if, as Satan is under God, Jesus will place himself under Satan. Satan offers to make Jesus the Messiah-King just as God wants him to be this King. It can all be done by means of one little act of prostration before Satan. Instead of a long, bitter road to the throne one short step will reach the crown.

The whole proposition intends to appeal to the human nature of Jesus. Like a god Jesus can rule at once. There is no need to face shame, agony, and ignominious death. Instead of the bitter cup only a single obeisance. Satan would place himself in harmony with God by making Jesus the King. Yet the whole proposition is false from beginning to end. Satan does not bow before God in worship as Jesus is to bow before Satan. Satan has not received the kingdoms from God, he rules them as the enemy of God, as a rebel against God, as a usurper whom God is dethroning through Jesus. By the one act of worship Jesus would also become a rebel against God and at the same time a tool of Satan. The kingdoms and their glory, promised to Jesus by Satan, would remain Satan's. The transfer would be an illusion. Instead of being a King, Jesus would be a slave of Satan. The way in which Satan tried to buy Jesus is the way in which he bought Eve: "Ye shall be as gods." Thus he bought Judas, but the price was the trivial thirty pieces of silver. Ever he still buys men in this way, but never at a price so great as the offered Jesus. It may seem foolish on Satan's part to offer such a temptation to Jesus and to think that Jesus might be caught thus. But after succeeding with his proffers to other men in thousands of instances, Satan felt that this man Jesus would certainly succumb to an offer that was more magnificent than any he had ever made. The author of all evil lies most completely under the blinding power of evil. As men, when they are submerged in sin, lose all moral judgment, so by his fall Satan lost all sense of righteousness and truth and moves only in absolute, moral darkness.

10) **Then Jesus says to him, Begone, Satan! For it has been written, The Lord, thy God, shalt thou worship, and him alone shalt thou serve.** The holy indignation of Jesus is apparent. Not until this time does Jesus add a word of his own to the Scriptures with which he smote the tempter, and this word is the command to Satan to begone. He calls him "Satan," because this is the fiend's personal name. Certainly, its significance, "adversary," receives its full weight in the exclamation of Jesus. The supposition that until this time Jesus did not know that he was dealing with Satan, and that, if he had known, he would have ordered him away at once, is untenable. Jesus was to be tempted by the devil and knew this from the start. The first two temptations fully reveal Satan. The reason why Jesus delayed until this time to order away Satan is not the fact that Satan had

now thrown off his mask; as far as Jesus was concerned, Satan was never masked.  The plain reason
is the fact that Satan has exhausted his temptations.
Jesus was by the Spirit of God exposed to all the
tempting power Satan possessed.  By ordering away
Satan Jesus did not withdraw himself from further
and more severe assaults.  When Satan made his third
effort he had no temptation that could possibly prove
stronger.  The ordeal was finished.  The command to
Satan to begone is the announcement of victory on
the part of Jesus.  Satan is ordered to begone because
he has been utterly vanquished.

The blow of final victory is another word of Scripture.  Even now the last stroke is delivered by the
sword of the Spirit.  We are to know that the written
Word is the one and only shield and weapon by which
to overthrow the evil one.  If Jesus had at the last
used a word of his own, we might think that the written Word is after all not enough.  The quotation is
taken from Deut. 6:13; but "thou shalt fear" in the
Hebrew and in the LXX is rendered by "thou shalt
worship," conforming to the tempter's word.  Yet
*yare'* denotes the fear of reverence which is expressed by the humble and reverent act of worship.
The Hebrew has: "and serve him," to which the LXX
adds: "him alone."  Since this is the true sense of
the original, Jesus retains it.  The service of λατρεία
or worship (often with offerings) belongs to deity
alone.  Rendered to others, it becomes the abomination of idolatry.  Satan attempted to lure Jesus into
a flagrant transgression of the First Commandment,
the most fundamental of all, in which the whole law
centers.  Since no greater commandment exists, and
no more essential part of this greatest commandment
than the act of reverent worship, Satan is at an end.

As he had done in the other two temptations, so
also in this third Jesus speaks only as "a son," a

true Israelite.  As man, Jesus, too, was under God, under the law of God and hence honored and worshipped God and kept all his commandments as all men ought to keep them.  In the battle with Satan, Jesus made no use of his divine prerogatives and powers.  He vanquished Satan as man.  And thus "we have not an High Priest which cannot be touched with the feeling of our infirmities; but was in all points tempted like as we are, yet without sin," Heb. 4:15.

11)  **Then the devil leaves him.  And lo! angels came to him and engaged in serving him.**  "Leaves him," ἀφίησιν αὐτόν, means more than that the devil departed; he desisted from further attacks upon Jesus, "stood away from him," as Luke writes with the significant addition: "for a season," literally, "until a suitable season."  Utterly routed in this set and formal attack, the devil afterward tried to dissuade Jesus from his holy course and finally brought about his death through Judas' betrayal.  In one form or in another the third temptation was repeated (Matt. 16:22, 23; John 6:15; 14:30).

Matthew leaves Jesus, as far as we know, on the mountain whither Satan had carried him.  Whether the angels, who now came to him and "were engaged in serving him" (διηκόνουν, the durative imperfect), bore him back into the wilderness, where the devil first attacked him, or to some other place, who can say?  The verb signifies service freely rendered for the benefit of the person concerned.  We may be quite sure that this service included furnishing food for the hungry body of Jesus.  Others include *solatium*, augmenting the victory of Jesus, and helping him to celebrate the triumph.

Matthew presents the three temptations in their historical order; Luke arranges the places in a climax: desert — mountain — Jerusalem and the Temple.  The fact that Matthew's order is the historical one is evident from the command at the end of the third temptation, ordering Satan to leave.

The account of Christ's temptation is not a parable, or a myth, or a legend. Either of the latter two would make this portion of Scripture a human invention. Then other portions may be of the same empty nature, and we should be at sea regarding any and all portions. Some think of a dream or a vision. There is no report that Christ ever had dreams or visions, and where such means are used in the case of others Matthew and the Scriptures say so. A victory over Satan in a dream or a vision would not be an actual victory. Communications are received by men in dreams, though not from Satan, but battles are not fought in dreams or in visions.

Some regard the entire occurrence as a mental one. Jesus fought out the battle with the spurious and perverted Messianic ideal of the Judaism of his day in a long inner, mental struggle. One version of this makes everything mental: the wilderness, the devil, the wing of the Temple, the mountain, the angels, etc. Instead of dreaming it all or having it come to him in a vision, Jesus thought it all. If this is true, then the entire temptation rose out of the mind and the heart of Jesus himself and took such a hold on him that he wrestled with it for forty days. Ethically this is incredible. The pure and holy heart of Jesus is incapable of producing Satanic thoughts, incapable, too, of dallying with them for an instant, to say nothing of forty days. If the entire temptation was only mental, the evangelists did not present it thus. A less radical view compromises. The devil and the wilderness are real but not the wing of the Temple or the mountain. The stones are real, and Jesus is to change them into real bread, but he is not really to leap from the wing of the Temple to real rocks below — he is to do this only mentally. He does not see real kingdoms, actual glory, although he is to snatch at these unreal gifts by a real act of worship. The evangelists describe realities throughout. They also seem to have a proper conception of what the devil is able to do. Even their psychology is sane and sensible. Satan is able to present thoughts to the mind of Jesus and to suggest acts to his will only by means of words, Jesus instantly rejecting both the thoughts and the acts. He is not able to invade the mind of Jesus without the use of words, making Jesus think things by mere volitions of Satan's will. The latter assumption lays Jesus' mind open to Satan, and such a view cannot be accepted by believing commentators.

It is often also assumed that the temptation of Jesus must have been like ours also in this respect that Jesus might have succumbed to it. It is usually presented in this form; if Jesus could not have fallen, his temptation was not a real temptation (meaning: like ours) ; it is presented in the Scriptures as having been real, hence Jesus might have fallen. These conclusions would be sound if Jesus could be placed on the same level with us believers in our present state, or with Adam and Eve in Eden, or with the angels prior to Satan's fall in heaven. But the Scriptures attest that Jesus was not merely "a son of God" (v. 3 and 6) but *the* Son of God, the incarnate second Person of the Godhead. God cannot fall into sin. This is absolutely true regarding all three Persons. Only by the theory of a *kenosis* which empties Jesus of the Godhead and leaves him nothing but man could a fall into sin under temptation be possible for him.

Neither the Father nor the Spirit could be tempted by Satan because both are only God. The Son could be tempted because he became man. He alone of the three persons, by assuming our human nature, could suffer human hunger and could be asked to appease that hunger in a sinful way. He alone, by his human nature, was made dependent on his Father and could thus be asked to abuse his dependence by a false trust in his Father. He alone, in his human nature, faced the cross and could thus be asked to evade it and follow an easier course. Temptation was possible to Jesus only on the side of his humanity.

The verb πειράζω means to try or test. The greatness of the strength tested changes nothing regarding the reality of the test to which it is subjected. The strain applied is just as real when the strength endures it as when the strength is too weak to endure it. Jesus, the Stronger, remained unmoved under all the force Satan, the strong one, brought against him. Thus the test or temptation was real in every way and not an illusion. We see this more readily when we think of the test made, not by immoral solicitation, but by suffering and death for the world's sin. When the test was made, the outcome was not for a moment in doubt. Yet the agony and the death were real although Jesus bore them triumphantly.

*Christ's Work in Galilee — a Summary, 4:12-25*

The baptism of Jesus was followed by his temptation. From this Jesus returned to the Jordan, won six disciples (John 1:35-51), and returned to Galilee. The Baptist continued his work, Jesus attended the festivals at Jerusalem (John 2:13, etc., 5:1). Matthew is not concerned with these events. He is not writing a chronological history; his method is pragmatic: to present a great life-picture of Jesus as the Messiah. At this point he presents a summary survey of the ministry of Jesus in Galilee when the work was at its height.

12) **Now when he heard that John was delivered up he withdrew into Galilee and left Naza-**

**reth and came and dwelt in Capernaum by the sea, in the regions of Zebulun and Naphtali.** Matthew offers no connection in time between the temptation and the present account. Yet the temporal participle marks a point of time that lay far beyond the temptation. This gap covers the rest of the Baptist's work, for he is now in prison, and the tragic news has reached Jesus. By this participial clause Matthew also indicates that he is acquainted with all the preceding events although in following the plan of his Gospel he passes them by without mention. We cannot say that this is due to the fact that he was called later and consequently had no personal knowledge of these events, for he narrates both the baptism and the temptation. Still less can we assume a contradiction with John's Gospel which reports some of the events omitted by Matthew. It is taken for granted that the readers know the story of the Baptist and his tragic end. Later in his Gospel Matthew utilizes some of the details of the Baptist's later life (11:2; 14:3). Here only the fact of the arrest is introduced to mark the general point of time; even the name of Herod Antipas who ordered the arrest is omitted.

The Baptist's arrest indicates the time when Jesus resolved to do his main work in Galilee. The verb ἀναχωρεῖν, "to withdraw," often implies fear of danger as a motive for the withdrawal, but not always, and not here; for Jesus did not flee to Galilee in order to escape a fate similar to that which had come to the Baptist. Herod Antipas was the tetrarch of Galilee and Perea and certainly had full power in his own dominion. In this instance to withdraw means to retire. Instead of seeking the fullest publicity in Jerusalem, the great center of the Jewish world, Jesus transferred his main activity to Galilee, the Jewish province that was farthest removed from the capital and quite generally looked down upon by the proud inhabitants of that center. Wisdom and prudence dictated this decision on the part of Jesus; it conserved best the interest of the work which he had come to do.

13) John 2:12 reports that Jesus transferred his home from Nazareth to Capernaum shortly after he first returned to Galilee from the Jordan. When Matthew writes, "and having left Nazareth, having come, he dwelt in Capernaum," these aorists merely mark facts without particular reference to the exact past moment of time. We are simply to know that, when the Baptist was imprisoned, Jesus no longer lived in Nazareth but in Capernaum. Both cities are regarded as feminine nouns with πόλις understood, R. 759. It seems as though Jesus had planned his extensive Galilean ministry long before the arrest of the Baptist and had moved his home to Capernaum quite early; then, when the arrest occurred, the plan was put into operation.

Capernaum (εἰς is static, R. 593) was far more suitable for the purpose of Jesus than Nazareth could be, since it was situated on the populous shores of the Sea of Galilee and on the great trade route, the *via maris*, which extended from Damascus and the East to the Mediterranean coast. It was easy to radiate out to all parts of Galilee from this center. The adjective παραθαλασσίαν, "beside the sea," R. 613, points to the shipping; Jesus himself often crossed this sea in boats. Yet to Matthew the transfer of residence to Capernaum is important only as being connected with the selection of Galilee for Christ's extensive Messianic ministry. To Jewish minds this is really astounding, and Matthew writes for just such minds. In Jewish eyes the only fitting place for the Messiah's work was Judea and in particular Jerusalem; a Galilean Messiah seemed an impossibility to them. The addition, "in the regions of Zebulun and

Naphtali," points to the Galilean land in general and is drawn from the prophecy which Matthew at once appends. But the phrase ἐν ὁρίοις is not intended to point to the two tribes Zebulun and Naphtali, as though Capernaum lay near or upon this line. These old boundary lines had long ceased to divide the country. Capernaum lay in Naphtali with the old boundary line being to the south. The phrase means "in the regions"(*fines*) and is added to indicate that this territory of the two tribes could easily be reached from Capernaum as a center in fulfillment of Isaiah's prophecy. Zebulun and Naphtali are combined as one territory in which Capernaum lay.

14)    All Jews who were perplexed because of the Messiah's working so extensively in Galilee are pointed to Isa. 9:1, 2: **in order that it might be fulfilled what was spoken through Isaiah, the prophet, saying:**

**The land of Zebulun and the land of Naphtali,**
**Along the way of the sea, beyond the Jordan,**
**Galilee of the Gentiles,**
**The people sitting in darkness**
**Saw a great light,**
**And to them sitting in death's region and shadow,**
**Light rose up for them.**

On Matthew's formula of quotation see 1:22 and 2:17. In the present instance a direct prophecy concerning the Messiah is fulfilled by Christ. The passive τὸ ῥηθέν implies Yahweh as the speaker, and διά marks the prophet as his mouthpiece; the reference is to a word that was first spoken and then written by Isaiah. This presents divine inspiration exactly as it occurred.

15)    We need not concern ourselves with the difficulties encountered in the Hebrew of Isa. 9:1, for all that Matthew quotes from this verse are the territorial

designations: "the land of Zebulun and the land of Naphtali, the way of the sea, beyond Jordan, Galilee of the Gentiles"; and these he adds as appositions to the subject of v. 2, not in the least altering the substance of the prophet's words. R. 469 regards these nouns as vocatives, but they may also be regarded as simple nominatives in apposition with ὁ λαός, or simply as nominative absolutes. And there are five: 1) land of Zebulun, 2) land of Naphtali, 3) along the way to the sea, 4) beyond the Jordan, 5) Galilee of the Gentiles. All five denote stretches of territory. The ὁδὸν θαλάσσης, Isaiah's *derek hayyam*, is not the road that leads to the Mediterranean but the stretch of country to which this great ancient road, the *via maris*, led. The accusative ὁδόν is adverbial to denote extent, and this adverbial with a genitive is used as a nominative or as an independent expression. The same is true regarding the phrase: πέραν τοῦ Ἰορδάνου, "beyond the Jordan," i. e., Perea, which lies at the extreme east, while "along the way of the sea" lies at the extreme west. The fifth term: "Galilee of the Gentiles," is not Galilee as such but the northern stretch of Palestine beyond Naphtali. All this territory Jesus covered during his ministry, radiating out from Capernaum as the general center.

This entire region had suffered severely during past ages. Delitzsch writes: "Since the days of the Judges all these stretches of country were by reason of their proximity exposed to corruption by heathen influences and by subjugation through heathen enemies. The northern tribes on the other side suffered most by reason of the almost constant wars with the Syrians and the later war with the Assyrians, and the deportation of the inhabitants gradually increased under Phul, Tiglatpileser, Salmanassar until a total depopulation resulted." While in Christ's time this region was populous enough, the people of Galilee were to a large extent a mixed race, and their spiritual condition, in spite of their connection with the central sanctuary at Jerusalem, was deplorable in every way, especially also since that sanctuary had long ceased to represent the true worship of Jehovah.

16) Isaiah's description is entirely correct: "the people sitting in darkness." They are still called ὁ λαός, a term frequently used to designate Israel as the chosen "people" in distinction from τὰ ἔθνη, "the nations" or "the Gentiles." Isaiah has "walked in darkness," which the LXX retain, but which Matthew renders freely "sitting." "Darkness," however, is more than the absence of the light, the divine truth of salvation; the Scriptures use the term with reference to the power of evil, especially as represented in delusion and religious falsehood. The true gospel light had gone out under the power of Jewish formalism and work-righteousness. Now the astounding fact is that this most benighted portion of the entire Jewish land should be chosen to receive the light through the extended ministry of Christ. Isaiah foretold this event: they "see a great light," which the evangelist, since the prophecy was now fulfilled, replaces with the past tense: they "saw a great light." This is the Messianic salvation embodied in Christ and proclaimed by him.

In the parallelism of Hebrew poetry a second synonymous couplet repeats this wonderful thought with variation. The description of the people is intensified. "Darkness" is not enough to express their sad condition: they sit (Isaiah has "dwell") "in death's region and shadow," from which they are unable to escape. Matthew translates *beerets tsalmaveih*, "in the land of the black shadow," ἐν χώρᾳ καὶ σκιᾷ θανατοῦ, "in the region and shadow of death." Compare *tsalmaveth*, "valley of the shadow of death"

(black shadow) in Ps. 23:4. The genitive is evidently to be construed with both datives, and the datives
constitute a hendiadys: "death's black shadowland,"
which is a fine rendering of the Hebrew construct
chain (LXX: ἐν χώρᾳ σκιᾷ θανάτου). Delitzsch: "We
must conceive the apostate mass of the people as having been destroyed, for if death has cast its shadow
over a land, it is a desert. In this situation those who
remain in the land see a great light breaking through
the black-bordered sky. The people who looked up
vainly with cursing, Isa. 8:21, are no more; it is the
remnant of Israel which sees the light of spiritual
and bodily redemption above its head." In the
prophet's description of this light in the following
verses (6, 7) note: "For unto us a child is born, unto
us a son is given," etc. Matthew again has the aorist:
"light rose up for them." In this way "they saw a
great light": God let it rise for them. The redundant
αὐτοῖς helps to emphasize the dative "to them sitting."
The figure is that of a glorious sunrise after a black
and deadly night. In both the prophecy and its fulfillment we must not miss the strong note of unde-
served grace. The people were at their lowest ebb,
all spiritual light was gone, there was absolutely no
hope or help in themselves: then God stepped in and
in pure grace sent them a heavenly gift, the help of
salvation in Christ Jesus.

17) **From then on began Jesus to herald and
say, Be repenting! for the kingdom of the heavens
has come near.** Prepositions may be used with
adverbs, R. 576; so here: "from then on." The aorist
"began" marks the point of beginning, and the following present infinitives, "to herald and say," indicate
the continuous work thus set in motion. Matthew has
the same verb which he used to describe the Baptist's
work: κηρύσσειν, "to herald," generally rendered, "to
preach," but always signifying to announce publicly

as a herald, to proclaim. The point to be noted is that to preach is not to argue, reason, dispute, or convince by intellectual proof, against all of which a keen intellect may bring counterargument. We simply state in public or testify to all men the truth which God bids us state. No argument can assail the truth presented in this announcement or testimony. Men either believe the truth as all sane men should, or refuse to believe it as only fools venture to do.

It is evident that Matthew wants us to understand that Jesus took up the work of the Baptist's heralding, now extending it throughout Galilee, whither the Baptist had not been sent. Many Galileans had heard the Baptist (11:7-9), but to many regions of Galilee the Baptist's message had not come, save perhaps through more or less reliable reports. Now Jesus himself sounds the great announcement to them. On the announcement itself see the exposition in 3:2.

18) The account which now follows is merely incidental in the summary description of the Galilean ministry of Jesus. The readers are to picture Jesus as being accompanied by a number of disciples who were not merely attached to him personally but were under his training for the great future work awaiting them. The insertion of the present incident into this summary section is, therefore, without a mark of time. All we are able to gather is that the disciples named were called to follow Jesus when his Galilean ministry got well under way.

**Now, when walking along by the Sea of Galilee, he saw two brothers, Simon, called Peter, and Andrew, his brother, throwing a casting net into the sea; for they were fishermen.** This scene is entirely distinct from the one described in Luke 5:1, 2. No multitude is here pressing upon Jesus, he is alone. He is walking along not standing. The fishermen are in the boat, busy throwing out their casting net, and have not disembarked to wash their nets. Already these differences show that Matthew does not want to record the same incident as Luke. Simon and Andrew are introduced in the simplest manner. They are brothers, and their profession is that of fishermen. We see them in the midst of their work. This could not have been the place where they usually kept their boats and prepared their nets as was the case in Luke 5:2; but they were somewhere along the shore where successful fishing could be done. In v. 21 Jesus walks forward a distance to the place where the boats were kept. Simon and Andrew, however, are introduced as Matthew's readers have always known them: the former as the one "called Peter," and the latter as "his brother." In this way Matthew intimates that both men had already become followers of Jesus as John 1:35, etc., reports, who also informs us that Simon had been given the name Peter.

The attachment first formed at the Jordan associated these men with Jesus as his disciples who followed him as the Messiah (John 1:41), of whom Moses and the prophets wrote (v. 45), the Son of God and King of Israel (v. 49). This following did not preclude a return to their old occupation as fishermen especially when Jesus remained at Capernaum and in the neighborhood. What Matthew now records is an advance upon this discipleship, a call to apostleship, to be followed eventually by a formal instatement as apostles, 10:1, etc. It is thus that we now find these men βάλλοντας, "throwing," the present participle marking their act as regular work, even also as they were professional fishermen. The ἀμφίβληστρον is a net that can be thrown from either side of the boat, while a σαγήνη is a dragnet, and a δίκτυον a net of any kind.

19) **And he says to them, This way, after me! and I will make you fishers of men!** The adverb

δεῦτε is used as the plural of the adverb δεῦρο in calling
someone hither; it has the force of an imperative,
R. 1023, and "after me" means that Jesus intends to
go on.  But the imperative, hortative, subjunctive, or,
as here, future indicative, which follows, states the
purpose for which one is called hither.  This purpose
is the chief point.  Hence we should not regard this
expression as a command to follow Jesus and a
promise as to what Jesus will do.  R. 949 misconceives the force of the adverb when he makes it
equivalent to a conditional clause with ἐάν: "if you
come after me, I will make," etc.  The entire call is
a gracious expression of Jesus' will, and the adverb
"hither" or "this way" is merely incidental.  The
call is stated in transparent figurative language and
is adapted to these fishermen who were even now busy
with their task.  "I will make you fishers of men"
means that Jesus will train them for the great work
of winning men for the gospel and salvation.  This
call does not imply that they are to join Jesus for
their own sakes as was the case with reference to the
call which John 1:35, etc., reports.  This call presupposes that these men had already followed that other
call, were already disciples and believers, already knew
the gospel and the work of spreading its salvation.  This
call is for the sake of others, ἄνθρωποι, "men," human
beings.  The term is universal and not restricted to
Jews.

A grand prospect is opened to these two brothers.
Their previous attachment to Jesus had prepared them
so that they would be ready when this call came.  Not
yet were they ready to go and to catch men.  They
would need further intensive training, and this Jesus
would now begin with them.  Because of the wording
of this call it has often been identified with Luke 5:10:
"from henceforth thou shalt catch men."  But only the
imagery of the two calls is similar.  The call recorded

in Luke comes later, follows a miracle after preaching to a multitude from Peter's boat, and is addressed to Peter alone. The call recorded in Matthew and in Mark is preliminary; that in Luke has the distinct addition, that, by the miracle of the great catch of fish, tremendous success is promised to the fishers of men.

20) **And they immediately, having left the nets, followed him.** Peter and Andrew at once obeyed the call. They dropped their ordinary profession, left "the nets" on the shore, no doubt in the hands of their helpers, and followed Jesus for the schooling they were now to receive for a far greater calling.

Those who identify Luke's account with that of Matthew and of Mark state in support of their view that the disciples could not have twice left all; and they add that if the disciples returned to their former work after the first call they would have been apostates. But Matthew and Mark do not say that the disciples left all or left their old work for good and all. What they did was to follow Jesus and thus to signify their acceptance of his great call. Jesus certainly did not want them to throw away their property. And while Jesus remained at Capernaum they could certainly, without prejudice to the call they had accepted on the first invitation, occasionally earn a little at their old work. Even after the resurrection of Jesus seven of the disciples worked a night long at fishing, John 21:1, etc.

21) **And, having walked forward from there, he saw other two brothers: James, the son of Zebedee, and John, his brother, in the boat with Zebedee, their father, engaged in repairing their nets; and he called them.** The two pairs of brothers are some distance apart, for the participial clause draws attention to the separation. As Jesus "saw" the first two, so he "saw" the second two. The first two are called

away from their actual fishing, the second from their repairing the nets. All this is quite distinct from the scene presented in Luke. What we know about Peter and about Andrew in their relation to Jesus applies equally to James and to John, who are identified as the sons of Zebedee for Matthew's readers. The call to these sons is, of course, the same as that extended to the other pair of brothers.

22) **And they, having left the boat and their father, followed him.** They respond with the same alacrity. Since their father was mentioned as being with them, Matthew remarks that they left him. Zebedee was not called to the ministry. But he consents to the call of his sons and remains behind alone. So he, too, believed in Jesus and rejoiced in the great work for which Jesus chose his sons.

23) Matthew now completes his general description of Jesus' Galilean ministry. In these last three verses he surveys the entire work as it constantly increased throughout the regions already named, with reports of it reaching Syria, the great territory to the north. The survey thus presented takes us to 21:1, etc., when Jesus entered Jerusalem for his passion. Nothing is said about Judea and Samaria or about Jerusalem in particular. The fact that Jesus taught and wrought also in the capital was not remarkable, but it certainly was noteworthy that he covered all of Galilee. The fact that Jesus called men for the ministry at the beginning of his activity in Galilee prepares us for 10:1, etc., where we are told that he sent all twelve of the men so called to have their first taste of this work by assisting Jesus in Galilee.

**And Jesus kept going about in all Galilee, continuing to teach in their synagogues and to herald the gospel of the kingdom and to heal every disease and every weakness among the people.** The Baptist

chose one spot, then another; Jesus travelled over all
of Galilee, and the imperfect περιῆγεν pictures him
doing so. The three present participles do the same.
Only in v. 17, where Jesus takes up the Baptist's
work, is the unmodified κηρύσσειν used regarding the
preaching of Jesus. In the case of the Baptist only
this verb is used to describe his activity, on which
see 3:1. Ordinarily the activity of Jesus is characterized by the word διδάσκειν, "to teach," which is never
used with reference to the Baptist. The latter always
preached out-of-doors, Jesus very frequently in the
synagogues before the audiences which gathered regularly every Sabbath day and probably at this time
already on the second and the fifth day of the week
to hear the reading of the Scriptures and to engage
in public prayers. Since the days of the Babylonian
captivity synagogues, i. e., assemblies, had become a
fixed institution among the Jews. In addition to the
service indicated, whenever competent persons were
present, addresses connected with the Word were
delivered to the people.

The second participle, "continuing to herald the
gospel of the kingdom," recalls the Baptist's heralding and intimates that this continued throughout the
ministry of Jesus. The content of this heralding was
τὸ εὐαγγέλιον, "the glad news," since the burden of the
proclamation was salvation and life everlasting. The
glad news dealt with "the kingdom," and we may
recall all the parables, in which Jesus revealed now
this now that feature of the kingdom. The genitive
may be objective; on the kingdom compare the exposition in 3:2.

The Baptist wrought no miracles, but Jesus
wrought them in great numbers: "continuing to heal
every disease and every weakness among the people."
The tangible evidence was thus presented that in Jesus
the kingdom with all its heavenly blessedness was

actually present. The object is not only doubled for the sake of emphasis, but "every" is repeated for the same purpose. The word νόσος refers to disease, and μαλακία to the soft, weakened condition resulting from disease. No type or kind of disease, and no case, whatever its stage of development, did Jesus leave unhealed. And this healing was always perfect restoration to health in an instant by word or by touch or by both. It is true, λαός is used extensively with reference to the Jewish people. Yet we are not ready to state that "among the people" here means that the healings were restricted to Jews. We cannot think that any among the mixed population of Galilee were turned away; note, for instance, 8:1-13.

24) **And the report of him went forth into the whole of Syria; and they brought to him all that were ill, seized with all kinds of diseases and tortures, demoniacs and moon-struck and paralytics; and he healed them.** The imperfect tense used in v. 23, with its accompanying present participles, is now followed by aorists which state so many facts. "The report of him," ἡ ἀκοὴ αὐτοῦ has the objective genitive. The whole of Syria heard about Jesus. This does not refer to Galilee as being included in the general term "Syria," but to Syria proper, the region north of Galilee toward Damascus, Antioch, etc. In these cities many Jews were living who kept in close touch with their native land. Besides, intercourse for commercial purposes was constant and lively.

Beginning with v. 23, Matthew links his sentences with the simple paratactic καί, R. 428. He adds that all the sick were brought to Jesus. This does not mean that the whole of Syria brought the sick but that, wherever Jesus went, the people did not wait for him to discover some sick person or other but at once brought them to him. "All that were ill," τοὺς κακῶς ἔχοντας, is general, and with an adverb ἔχειν means "to be." In v. 23 the diseases are stressed, here the persons suffering from them. To the first participle a second is added predicatively: "seized with all kinds of diseases and tortures," i. e., grave cases, many of them in severe pain. Appositionally three classes are added, those of the very worst type: "demoniacs, moon-struck, paralytics."

There is a strong tendency among modern commentators to deny the reality of demoniacal possession as recorded in the Scriptures. The demoniacs are thought to have been people who were afflicted with some mania, an unbalanced condition of mind, perhaps were lunatics or epileptics. But what is gained? The great miracles remain even when such a view is taken. These views, however, may lead to serious results. Either Jesus knew or did not know that these were demoniacs. If he did not know their real condition, we have a Savior who was as ignorant as the people of his own day. If he did know that these people were not devil-possessed, then he acted as if they were, and we have a Savior who could act a lie. To say that Jesus "accomodated himself" to the popular opinion leaves his case under a fatal, moral stigma. The fact is that he never descended to any falsehood, however widely and strongly held.

The Scriptures distinguish clearly between all ordinary forms of disease and the peculiar affliction of demoniacal possession. Jesus, for instance, addressed the demons, and these replied to him and often did so in statements which the human sufferers themselves could not have made. "It is in vain to clear away from these Gospel narratives the devil and his demons. Such an exegesis is opposed to the whole faith of the world at that time. If we are now to make these statements mean just what we please, why did not a single man of the ancient world understand them

so? Are we becoming wiser? Then let us congratu-
late ourselves on our good fortune; but we cannot on
that account compel these venerable writers to say
what in their own time they neither could nor would
say." Horst, *Zauber-Bibliothek*, Matson, *The Adversary*, 177, etc., settles the question as to present-
day cases; some still occur in heathen lands. "A certain abnormal state of mind exists, which is not
insanity according to the legal definition of the term.
It is a state unaffected, so far as science can prove,
by any physical condition of the body; on which medicine appears to have no effect, and on which religion
alone seems to exercise a beneficial control." Christ
gave his apostles power to drive out possessing spirits.
The supposition that Christ accomodated himself to
the views of the people in order to help these sufferers denies his omnipotent power as the Son of God
and reduces him to the level of modern "healers."
Nor can anyone show why he did not enlighten at
least his chosen disciples but permitted them to remain under the old delusion. What Jesus told the
seventy when they returned to him after driving out
devils also more than establishes the reality of such
terrible possession, Luke 10:18, etc.

Some regard the "moon-struck," σεληνιαζόμενοι, as
being epileptics (R. V., for instance), others as being
lunatics (A. V.), and these latter are correct. Those
who think of epileptics suppose that their ailment
fluctuated with the phases of the moon; but this view
cannot be substantiated. The old word "lunatic," one
affected by the moon, corresponds exactly to the Greek
term, but neither word has anything to do with the
moon's phases. The "paralytics" are those who have
suffered paralysis, which may be due to a number of
causes and produces many incurable cases. "And he
healed them," i. e., without the least difficulty and
without a single exception. The aorist states the his-

torical fact. In this simple way, without an effort to excite the reader over the tremendousness of the fact here presented, inspiration records the miracles of Jesus. These healings (the verb occurs twice) are acts of grace and mercy, performed as such, and thus they distinguish the character of Jesus as the Messiah and of the message he brought. These miracles still stand as the divine seals attesting the message to which they were appended. And this attestation, once made and forever fixed in a divinely inspired record, needs no repetition and, therefore, has none.

25) Matthew completes the summary of Jesus' wonderful Galilean ministry by adding one more feature. **And great multitudes followed him from Galilee and Decapolis and Jerusalem and Judea and beyond the Jordan.** Of course, this occurred when the ministry of Jesus was at its height. Naturally, crowds were drawn from Galilee, flocking to him from every corner. But Galilee became the magnet for other lands. Decapolis is the region northeast of Samaria beyond the Jordan, so named after the ten cities which formed a kind of federation. Most of the inhabitants were Gentiles. Among these cities were Scythopolis, Gadara, Hippo, and Pella. Samaria is omitted, for the Samaritans hated the Jews to such an extent that they would not respond. Syria has already been named, and evidently sent its contingent. But even Jerusalem was stirred together with Judea in general so that many were attracted to despised Galilee. "Beyond the Jordan" (v. 15) is regarded as a noun in the genitive and designates Perea, the territory south of Decapolis, east of the river, toward the Dead Sea. These crowds followed Jesus about in many places, at times gathering by thousands, so that Jesus often found little time for rest and privacy. Before this great audience Jesus spoke and wrought his miracles.

In this section, v. 12-25, Matthew presents the general program of the main body of his Gospel. We see the type of book he intends to write. It is not a mere chronological account of the life of Jesus but a presentation of the great facts which reveal Jesus as the Messiah, yet all are recorded in due chronological order. The chronology only serves, it does not govern. In this respect Matthew resembles John. The entire conception of his Gospel is masterful and grand.

# CHAPTER V

## V

### Christ's Sermon on the Mount, Chapters 5-7

In the Sermon on the Mount, Matthew, of course, presents an example of Christ's teaching. For that matter, he presents various other examples in the course of his Gospel. This sermon is more. It presents the entire life in the kingdom, from the first entrance into the kingdom here on earth to the final consummation of the kingdom in the last judgment. Only when this comprehensive nature of the sermon is perceived will its true greatness be perceived and the propriety of Matthew's placing this sermon in the forefront of his Gospel.

The Sermon on the Mount could not have been preached at the opening of Christ's ministry in Galilee. Its entire contents, as well as the account of the circumstances connected with its delivery, point to the height of Christ's ministry as the time of the delivery. Those who call this sermon Christ's "inaugural," "his introductory address," "the revelation of his Messianic plans," are led to this view by the prominent place given to this sermon by Matthew's Gospel but do not take into account the entire plan of Matthew's composition. When this sermon was preached, the Twelve had already been appointed apostles, and many others had become Jesus' disciples. The sermon is addressed to them. The multitudes who also heard it are secondary. These crowds were to hear and to know what the true disciples of Christ really possessed and what their lives in the kingdom would henceforth be.  In this way, and only in this way, the sermon opened the door of the kingdom to the crowds, showed them what was inside, and bade them to enter and to join those already inside.

The Sermon on the Mount has often been regarded as law and not as gospel.  Jesus is thought of as expounding the true sense of the law over against the shallow and perverted exposition of the Jewish scribes and rabbis, doing again the work of Moses because the Jews had lost the true understanding of Moses. But it would be an astounding thing for Christ to do this, and it would be equally astounding for Matthew to place three chapters of law in the forefront of his Gospel.  This conception is due to the fact that the theme of the sermon and the hearers to whom it is addressed are not properly understood.  The Beatitudes are pure gospel; the hearers particularly addressed in 5:11-16 are by Jesus himself characterized as true disciples of his, and the entire sermon is directed to them.  The body of the sermon deals with the life of these true disciples and employs the law only as the *Regel* or rule by which they live and prove themselves to be true disciples.  The Sermon on the Mount is the counterpart to the address on the last judgment, 25:31-46, in which works are decisive both for those on the right and those on the left: works as evidence for the presence of faith, and other works as evidence for its absence.  The sermon speaks of the works the disciples are to do in the power of the gospel and of faith, and the discourse on the judgment of the works the disciples have done and the ungodly have not done.  In the sermon gospel and law are properly combined, and the gospel is the fundamental content.

Although it would be exegetically quite essential to outline the structure of the sermon, few attempt to do so.  The following outline may serve:

Introduction (5:3-16) : The blessed children of the kingdom — who they are — how they are blessed of God, despised of men, invaluable as salt and light to the world.

The theme lies in verses 17-20.

### The Children of the Kingdom in the Righteousness that is theirs

I.   *The law is in their hearts and thus controls their conduct* (5:21-48). This is developed concretely by examples from the law and personally from the disciples as followers of Christ.

II.  *The Father is before their eyes, and thus they are freed from hypocrisy* (6:1-34). This is developed by examples from the religious life of the disciples in the same concrete and personal way (observe how "Father" runs through the chapter).

III. *The judgment is their warning, and thus they attain the kingdom above* (7:1-23). The development is by personal admonitions with the judgment as the background.

Conclusion: The transparent figure of the wise and the foolish builder, applying to the entire sermon and to all its hearers.

1) **Now when he saw the multitudes he went up into the mountain; and when he sat down, his disciples came to him. And he opened his mouth and began to teach them, saying, etc.** Neither time nor place are specified. While we may be interested in both, Matthew's Jewish readers should have their whole attention centered on the substance of the sermon. So the preliminaries are brief: only a transitional δέ, the multitudes, the disciples, and what we

may gather from the sermon. From Luke 6:12, etc., we learn that Jesus had chosen the Twelve as apostles, that other disciples were present in addition to a great concourse of people. The sermon itself presupposes a degree of advancement on the part of the disciples. Only in v. 20 does it refer to entering the kingdom, a word that was evidently intended for those who had not yet entered. In v. 12 it refers to the Twelve, associating them with the prophets of old; and in v. 19 it distinguishes between the teachers who shall be least and those that shall be great in the kingdom. According to Luke, Jesus went up into the mountain the night before and retired for prayer. It was in the morning, just after the Twelve had been chosen, that Jesus chose a spot where all could see and hear him, a large level place between the heights or along the mountainside, and there began his teaching, ἐδίδασκεν, the ingressive imperfect, R. 885.

"The mountain," with its Greek article, is best taken to refer to the one right at hand, R. 756. The expression is similar to our "into the woods," "into the field," when we have no special woods or field in mind. Yet some stress the article: "the New Testament Sinai," "the mount of sacred history," but this stress refers to what the sermon now to be preached made of this mountain. The locality seems to have been near Capernaum; late tradition takes it to be the Horns of Hattin.

"The multitudes," with its Greek article, points back to 4:25, and thus strengthens the inference that the sermon was spoken at the height of Jesus' ministry in Galilee. It was customary for teachers, and for preachers to sit cross-legged while speaking, the hearers assuming the same position. The writer saw a speaker sitting thus on a raised platform in a mosque in Damascus in 1925, another in the mosque of the dervishes in Constantinople, the hearers in each

case sitting on the floor. The word μαθηταί means more
than pupils or learners, namely those who have learned,
who have imbibed their master's spirit. They may
still learn, but what they have already learned is what
makes them "disciples."

2) "Having opened his mouth" is the common
Hebrew expression *pithach peh* and is here added to
mark the impressiveness of the occasion. The imperfect "began to teach" invites us, too, as we read, to follow this teaching.

### The Introduction and the Theme

3) **Blessed the beggarly in spirit; for theirs is
the kingdom of the heavens.** The Beatitudes read
like a Psalm; μακάριοι at once recalls the *'ashre* of
Ps. 1:1. "Blessed!" intoned again and again, sounds
like bells of heaven, ringing down into this unblessed
world from the cathedral spires of the kingdom inviting
all men to enter. The word, like its opposite οὐαί,
"woe," is neither a wish regarding a coming condition, nor a description of a present condition, but a
judgment pronounced upon the persons indicated, stating that they must be considered fortunate. The form
is almost exclamatory: "O the blessedness of those
who," etc.! And it is Jesus who renders this judgment, which is, therefore, absolutely true although
all the world may disagree. Each of the eight judgments is at once established by revealing in what the
blessedness actually consists; and the eighth judgment
is even doubled, and its blessedness is unveiled in two
strong statements. All this blessedness is spiritual,
each part of it coming from the great Messianic kingdom, true soul-blessedness, a rich possession now but
with a glorious promise of still greater riches — the
very opposite of the word's happiness which is poi-
soned already in the bud and soon blasted forever.
"Blessed" means joy for those concerned. But this is

the heavenly way: the great gifts of the kingdom are ours, insuring a constant flow of joy, so that, even if for a moment we be sad and sorrowful, the joy will again well up in our hearts.    John 15:11.

The word πτωχός is derived from a verb which signifies cringing, crouching like a beggar. (M.-M. 559). It is stronger than "poor," it is "cringingly, beggarly poor." We do not regard the added dative as a locative, R. 523, as naming the place where this crouching takes place; nor is it instrumental as R. 523 maintains against B.-D.; but as B.-D. 197 says, a dative of relation: "beggarly poor with respect to the spirit," or, imitating Luther's rendering in v. 8: *die armen Geistes sind* (Zahn); like ʻani unᵉkeh ruach in Isa. 66:2: "But to this man will I look, even to him that is poor, and of a contrite spirit, and trembleth at my word." The poverty here referred to is not one against which the will rebels but one under which the will bows in deep submission. It is more than a state or condition, it is also an attitude of the soul over against God. It is the attitude that grows out of the profound realization of utter helpnessness and beggary as far as any ability or possession of self are concerned. These wretched beggars bring absolutely nothing to God but their complete emptiness and need and stoop in the dust for pure grace and mercy only. This is the condition and attitude of *true repentance* preached by the Baptist and by Jesus as basic for all who would come to God and to his kingdom. The disciples had attained it, and the Twelve gave the special evidence in that they forsook all and followed Jesus, looking to him and receiving from him alone.

The astonishing thing is that Jesus should pronounce people such as this "blessed," fortunate in the highest degree. Pharisees, Sadducees, and the world generally would do the very opposite. But the coin of all such is counterfeit, never passes with God, who ac-

cepts no coin from men but only beggars' empty hearts
and hands. And thus it is not at all astonishing that
such beggars, stooping before God, are "blessed."
"For theirs is the kingdom of the heavens," "theirs" in
the sense of "theirs alone," barring out all others who
come before God with a different attitude.

The text reads: "is" = is *now*; yet some interpreters would tell us that this refers to a *future* possession because the following verses have future
tenses. But how about v. 10? Others make the
copula timeless and refer to the Aramaic where the
copula is omitted, and they consider "the kingdom"
eschatologic: "the world as it will be when it has
again become God's in the regenerated world of the
future." But this is contrary to all that the gospel
reveals concerning God. He feeds and satisfies the
poor, Luke 1:53; he does it the instant they come to
him and does not only promise future bread; we are
to eat now, and we do eat the Bread of Life, possess
the treasures of the kingdom. For the kingdom which
the Baptist and Jesus proclaimed as being at hand is
"within you," Luke 17:21, an actual *present possession*. Christ's kingdom is one of grace and glory combined; the grace is now here, the glory has not yet
been revealed, I John 3:2.

"Kingdom" (compare the exposition in 3:2) must
not be taken in the sense of an outward realm as we
speak of earthly kingdoms, thinking of land and of
people. This "kingdom of the heavens" centers in the
King, Jesus Christ, and in the powers of grace, might,
and glory that go out from him. Where he is, there
the kingdom is because there he exercises grace and
power. The rich and proud in spirit resist that
exercise as it would work in and over them for salvation. The poor in spirit cry out for that exercise of
saving grace and help. It is impossible that the King
should let them go on crying — he at once fills their

hands and their hearts. Whatever he may have in
store for them in the future, already now he has a
vast abundance. Thus the *poor* in spirit become *rich*
toward God, Luke 12:21. Their royal riches consist
in Christ's grace, pardon, adoption, sanctification, "all
spiritual blessings in heavenly places in Christ,"
Eph. 1:3. Not that these gifts now end the attitude
of the beggarly in spirit, so that this term no longer
describes them. The case is this: as long as we live
in this world of sin and in spite of all grace "sin
daily," so long our poor hands are stretched out to
God's grace in Christ, daily receiving grace for grace.
And the flow of God's rich grace goes out and can go
out to us only as long as we keep that attitude to
which God himself has brought us and in which his
grace works to keep us. Thus the kingdom is ours
*now*, and, being ours, in its progress it will bring us
all that God still has laid up for us.

4) **Blessed they that are mourning; for just
they shall be consoled.** This second pronouncement
is as paradoxical as the first. The verb denotes loud
mourning such as the lament for the dead  or for a
severe, painful loss. The sorrow for our sins in true
contrition should not be excluded from this mourning.
Do our sins inflict no loss upon us? Do they not rob
us of what is dearer than relatives, money, or other
goods? Instead of excluding sorrow for sin, this is
the chief part of the lament. But, of course, we must
include all other grief and sorrow due to the power
of sin in the world as this inflicts blows, losses, and
pain upon the godly. It includes every wrong done
us, as well as every painful consequence of our own
wrongdoing. It is almost self-evident that this mourning is not like that of the world which howls loud
enough when its sins find it out: "but the sorrow of the
world worketh death," II Cor. 7:10.

Behind this sorrow of the godly lies the recognition of the merciless power of sin and of our helplessness to ward it off and to escape. Hence this mourning is a constant cry to God in their distress. The substantivized participle is the present tense and thus characterizes the godly as mourning constantly. As far as contrition is concerned, let us keep in mind the first of Luther's famous 95 Theses, that our entire life must be a continuous contrition and repentance. As far as other sorrows are concerned, "we must through much tribulation enter into the kingdom of God," Acts 14:22; in fact, all the passages that speak of tribulation belong here. God's people are, indeed, a mournful lot!

But how can they be called blessed, emphatic αὐτοί, "they, just they," "they alone"? Because they are the only ones who "shall be consoled." The passive implies that God is their consoler. And this *is* a future tense. Chiliasts interpret: "shall be consoled in the glorious earthly Messianic Millennium, when all the forces of evil are crushed, when all the Christians shall at last be triumphant." Until that time these mourners must remain comfortless save for the prospect of that distant comfort. But Christ says, "I will not leave you comfortless: I will come to you," John 14:18; and when he came, we read, "Then were the disciples glad, when they saw the Lord," John 20:20. No; this chiliastic comfort kingdom is but a mirage. The future tense is future to the mourning: the comfort always at once follows the mourning. Remember the "little while" in John 16:16. The greatest of all comfort is the absolution pronounced upon every contrite mourning sinner. Without this all other comfort is vain. And in tribulation God's Word, God's deliverance and help, God's support, cheer and uplift us as nothing else could so. Finally, God's promises of

future deliverance from all evil in the heavenly kingdom of glory fill us with abounding comfort.  As our
mourning rises unto God in this vale of sin and tears,
so his constant comfort flows down to us.  Thus we
who mourn are of all men most blessed, for we, indeed,
are comforted.

5)  **Blessed the meek; for just they shall inherit
the earth.**  The best commentary is Ps. 37; note v. 11.
"The meek" are the mild, gentle, patient.  The word
refers to an inward virtue exercised toward persons.
When they are wronged or abused they show no resentment and do not threaten or avenge themselves.  The
opposite are the vehement, bitter, wild, and violent.
Jesus is the greatest example of meekness.

The paradox is again startling, the fact that people
of this kind "shall inherit the earth."  Jesus does not
say, "the *new* earth," yet many regard his word as a
reference to the millennial earth or to Rev. 21:1.  And
Jesus says "shall inherit," namely with Christ, the heir
of all the earth.  This lot is theirs in accordance with
their Lord's will and testament.  Read Ps. 37: the
wicked shall soon be cut down like the grass and wither
as the green herb — evildoers shall be cut off — yet a
little while and the wicked shall not be; yea, thou shalt
diligently consider his place, and it shall not be — and
so the story of the wicked goes on.  There is not much
inheriting of *this earth* according to the Psalm.  But
look at the *'anavim* (also in Isa. 61:1), "the meek."
Jesus is merely repeating Ps. 37:11, 22.  They are
cautioned not to vex themselves when the wicked grow
haughty and appear mighty and great.  They may
suffer, but the divine blessing constantly follows them
also in *this* life and on *this* earth.  It will not do to say
that the temporal blessings promised to Israel in the
old covenant are not to be regarded as being promised
also to those living in the new covenant.  The Christian Church has fared even better than Israel fared.

The idea that in the Psalm "earth" signifies Canaan and thus the heavenly Canaan in Jesus' beatitude, is specious; for Jesus indicates no difference of this kind. It will always be true (v. 16) : "A little that a righteous man hath is better than the riches of many wicked," for his little has God's blessing, and their much God's curse. Our meekness, however, often shines by its absence; our covetousness, pride, and other faults necessitate God's discipline, who always follows higher aims that reach beyond temporalities. Chemnitz writes that God lets his children find a little nest on the house that is intended entirely for them. Luther agrees that this beatitude adds the promise of "temporal life and goods on earth."

6) **Blessed those hungering and thirsting for righteousness; for they shall be filled.** In verses 5, 6 the order is the same as in the Lord's Prayer: first the Fourth Petition for bread, then the Fifth for forgiveness of sins. Hunger and thirst are very commonly used to express strong spiritual desires and needs. Both participles are durative present tenses, for this hungering and thirsting continues and, in fact, increases in the very act of being satisfied. Daily we cry for forgiveness, and daily God satisfies us. We are blessed just because our hunger and our thirst continue. If they should cease, Jesus could no longer pronounce us blessed because he could no longer satisfy us. Perfectionism finds no support here.

"Righteousness," δικαιοσύνη, is one of the cardinal terms of the gospel, fundamental for the entire Scriptures. It is the quality of one who is pronounced "righteous" by the eternal Judge according to his norm of right. The term is always forensic. Always back of it stands the divine Judge and his judgment bar; always it embodies his judicial verdict of acquittal. No man, however wise and powerful, has ever discovered a way to turn a guilty, sinful soul into a right-

eous one.  Men justify and declare themselves righteous, but this amounts to no more than the criminal's
denial of his crime and never stands before the court
which has the full evidence of his guilt.  But what is
beyond all human ability is brought about by Christ
who by his holy life and sacrificial death met the demands of God's norm of right, met them in our stead
and now transfers his perfect righteousness to us
through faith and thus wins our pardon and acquittal
before the divine judgment bar.  "Righteousness" cannot here mean the power of right in human affairs in
the world of men generally; for the passive "shall be
filled" denotes a gift of God to certain persons, rendering them "righteous" in his sight.  It cannot denote a
virtue, the so-called acquired righteousness, when men
live righteously and do what is right.  The passive
verb shuts out also this.  This word cannot be translated "goodness." Δικαιοσύνη is never ἀγαθωσύνη.  On
δίκαιος, δικαιοσύνη, and δικαιόω see C.-K. 296, 311, 317, and
learn once for all that these terms and other derivatives
in both Testaments and elsewhere, in both secular and
religious uses, are never anything but forensic, a verdict pronouncing righteous.

"Shall be filled" is again future, the verb matching
the figure of hunger and thirst.  But this is not a distant future in a supposed millennium or in heaven but
one that at once feeds the hungry and gives drink to
the thirsty.  The moment faith in Christ is wrought, at
that moment righteousness is declared without even the
interval of a second.  And ever and ever as we yearn
to be righteous in God's judgment, his Word in a thousand places declares us so.  With these declarations,
all of them advance pronouncements of the final verdict at the last day, every contrite and believing sinner
can satisfy and fill his soul.  The verb χορτάζω is strong.
It is used to express the feeding and fattening of cattle with fodder and grain and men with abundance of

food. He who is daily fed with Christ's righteousness
is blessed indeed!

7) **Blessed the merciful; for just they shall be
treated mercifully.** The first four beatitudes look
toward God, the next three toward men. These treat
of three virtues which mark the godly as blessed. "The
merciful" are, of course, the same persons as those
referred to in the previous beatitudes. Luther well
says that in all the beatitudes faith is presupposed as
the tree on which all the fruit of blessedness grows.
This, then, is not mere natural mercy as it is occasionally found among men generally but the mercy growing
out of our personal experience of the mercy of God.
God's mercy toward us always makes us likewise merciful, 18:21, etc. The noun ἔλεος and its derivatives
always deal with what we see of pain, misery, and distress, these results of sin; and χάρις, "grace," always
deals with the sin and guilt itself. The one extends
relief, the other pardon; the one cures, heals, helps, the
other cleanses and reinstates. With God χάρις is always
first and ἔλεος second.

The agent back of the passive "shall be treated mercifully" is again God, and again the future means at
once as we show mercy. In this future tense we ought
to see the impossibility of a reference to the hereafter.
There will be no misery there and thus no possibility
of merciful treatment on the part of God. God first
makes us merciful and then even blesses us for being
merciful. This beatitude has stimulated God's people
to do all manner of eleemosynary work. It is well
known how absolutely bare of even the idea of mercy
many heathen religions are. The mercy of unchristian
men about us, such as it is, disjoined from Christ, relieving only physical distress, is one of the indirect
results of Christianity, never an outgrowth of the natural heart as such. The fearful cruelty which slumbers
in the unregenerate heart, when occasion brings it out,

is often appalling, and its worst feature is "man's cruelty to man."

8) **Blessed the pure in heart; for just they shall see God.** Some regard "the pure in heart" as a reference to sanctification, either in the wider sense (pardon plus good works) or in the narrower (good works) ; although only perfectionists think of complete sinlessness or "total sanctification." The Beatitudes are a perfect chain not a loose aggregation. Placed between mercy to our fellow-men and peacemaking, purity in heart must denote a single virtue. A glance into the Old Testament shows us the *bar lebab,* the exact counterpart to καθαρὸς τῇ καρδία in Ps. 24:4; compare 73:1; Gen. 20:5, 6; and then I Tim. 1:5; II Tim. 2:22; I Pet. 1:22, and Zahn's conclusion is evident: "pure in heart" = *sinceritas,* singleness of heart, the honesty which has no hidden motive, no selfish interest, and is true and open in all things. Nothing is lost by thus specifying this virtue, for it is possible only in a heart that is justified and sanctified by God.

As the virtue, so the reward of grace: "just they shall see God." Whatever may be said regarding seeing God in his Word by faith and regarding seeing him spiritually in communion with him in this life, "shall see God" must here be the *visio Dei* in the other world, promised to the glorified saints, I Cor. 13:12; I John 3:2, 3. Between God who is pure and the pure in heart (the dative as in v. 3) an affinity exists, the consummation of which is reached in heaven. The greatest joy of heaven will be the vision of God. We need not think of looking into the unfathomable essence of God; for as God's presence delights the angel hosts and fills them with ineffable blessedness, so his presence will be made manifest to the pure in heart. Blessedness will flood them like light in the beatific vision of the All-pure.

9) **Blessed the peacemakers; for just they shall be called God's sons.** Compare Eph. 4:3; Rom. 14:19; I Cor. 14:33; Heb. 12:14; etc. At peace with God and thus themselves filled with sweet peace, they. live in peace, if possible, with all men and work to keep and to make peace wherever peace is threatened or lost. Theirs is the work of true Christians who follow in the footsteps of the Prince of Peace. Nor is this "peace at any price," which ignores confessional principles and is unwilling to contend for the faith once delivered to the saints (Jude 3). These are not unionistic peacemakers who combine contrary doctrines by agreeing to disagree. Truth of God comes first, peace with men second. Friends are dear, the Word of our greatest Friend dearest. No "blessed" was spoken by Jesus upon the disrupters of the church who insist on their false views, nor upon those who regard the peace and the fellowship of their brother-confessors as being of slight value, so that they may run after other fellowships. The true peace of the church is a blessed possession, we cannot guard it too closely. Contentious, stubborn, obstreperous church members — this beatitude ought to make them impossible. Also in the world, wherever strife arises, the followers of Christ work for peace in the spirit of their Master.

The passive "shall be called" implies "by God," for he alone can bestow the title "God's sons" in truth and in reality. Here, too, the future tense means that God shall call them his sons now when they prove their relation to him by their peacemaking. Chiliasts again think of their future mirage kingdom, and others of the world to come. "God's sons, *υἱοί*, shall they be called; the title is not *τέκνα*, "children." The latter carries rather the connotation of tender affection, the former that of dignity and high standing. Hence also "they shall be called" God's sons; this high dis-

194     *The Interpretation of Matthew*

tinction shall be accorded to them, and by God himself.
God himself shall own them as sons of his.  He who
sent his Son to make peace between God and man will
acknowledge as his sons those who in the spirit of his
Son also make peace.

10)  Strange to say and a general paradox to all
the designations of the godly thus far used, in particular also of the last, peacemakers, these people,
loving and working for peace, shall themselves be
accorded the opposite of peace in this warring world.
**Blessed they that have allowed themselves to be per-
secuted for the sake of righteousness; for theirs is
the kingdom of the heavens.  Blessed are you whenever they shall revile you and persecute and say
everything wicked against you by lying, for my sake.
Rejoice and exult; for your reward is great in the
heavens; for thus they did persecute the prophets
before you.**

In this final beatitude "blessed" occurs twice, but
the second is evidently only a repetition and thus marks
an emphatic conclusion of the entire line of the beatitudes.  This full elaboration of the final beatitude
casts a special glamour over it, making one welcome
persecution when it comes.  Come it will as the Lord
here intimates.  In the previous beatitudes present
participles are used, only here we have a perfect participle and that passive.  It cannot here be equal to a
present: "are persecuted" (A. V.), and it seems to be
more than just the ordinary perfect passive: "have
been persecuted."  In all the previous beatitudes the
designations indicate more than just inflictions, they
show an inner attitude.  This seems to be the case with
regard to δεδιωγμένοι.  This passive perfect may be regarded as permissive: "who have allowed themselves to
be persecuted," or: "have endured persecution."  The
idea is that they did not flee from it but willingly submitted to it when it came to them.  Thus the perfect

tense is explained; they held out under persecution and are now people of this kind, martyrs who have stood firm in just trials.

They endured "for the sake of righteousness," ἕνεκεν δικαιοσύνης, the same term that was used in v. 6, and it has the same forensic sense. It is God who as the great Judge pronounces his verdict upon them and thus accords them the quality of righteousness. These are true believers and as such righteous in God's eyes. They confess their faith and live up to it in their lives and thus prove obnoxious to the world which visits persecution upon them. "For the sake of righteousness" thus means more than that they suffered innocently, although this, too, is included. They suffered because of what they were in their character and their lives, for the divine approval that rested upon them. God adjudged them righteous, the world, in flagrant opposition to God, adjudged them abominable. Because their whole character and their life, as approved of God, constituted a standing rebuke to the world, indicating God's judicial disapproval of the character and the life of the world, the world turned against them and thus persecuted them.

Having stood firm under the test of persecution in the righteousness they attained by God's grace, their great blessedness is that "theirs is the kingdom of the heavens," all the grace, gifts, and glory that go with the rule of the Messiah and King. See the exposition of 3:2. Whatever the world may take from them is more than made up by this heavenly possession which no one can take from them. To have Christ and all that Christ bestows by his kingdom and rule is more than life, liberty, or earthly goods.

11) The fact that this is still the same beatitude although "blessed" is repeated is evident from the applicatory second person which is now used and from the description of the persecution just mentioned.

"Blessed are you" shows how the disciples are to apply all these beatitudes, although they are couched in the third person, to themselves, including in particular the last. The intimation in ὅταν, "whenever," is that many cases of the kind now specified will occur. The three plural verbs have indefinite subjects: "whenever they shall revile you," etc. No need to say who is referred to. They are the enemies of Jesus and his disciples who oppose the kingdom. The three aorists express actuality. Men will actually "revile" the disciples, upbraid them with violent language; "persecute" or inflict injury upon them; and ever afterward "will say everything wicked against you" whenever they mention you. These certainly are painful inflictions. Two important modifiers are added: ψευδόμενοι "by lying," for which we should use an adverb: "falsely," and ἕνεκεν ἐμοῦ, "for my sake." These two modifiers expand what the phrase "for the sake of righteousness" contains, namely the innocence of the disciples and the real cause of this persecution, their adherence to Jesus and to his teaching. On this subject Jesus spoke fully to his disciples at various times and especially on the night before his death, John 15:18, etc. Jesus never held out any false prospects to his followers.

12) Instead of grieving and lamenting in view of this persecution or under the distress it inflicts, Jesus tells his disciples to "rejoice and exult." The two imperatives are durative: their gladness is never to leave them, no matter what they are called on to endure. An example of how the Twelve lived up to this injunction is found in Acts 5:41: "rejoicing that they were accounted worthy to suffer shame (v. 40, beating) for his name"; add all the painful experiences of Paul and the martyrdom of so many. "Rejoice" is not enough, "exult" or "skip and shout for joy," ἀγαλλιᾶσθε, is added.

At once the adequate reason for the rejoicing under such circumstances is added: "for your reward is great in the heavens." This μισθός is "pay," but never in the sense of something earned by works or sufferings of ours but as something unearned and freely bestowed by grace by the generous hand of God (19:29). For he is ever a God who will let no man do a thing for him and for his Son unless he reward it with an abundance that comports with his own greatness and glory. This "pay" is "great," not according to our merit, which does not exist, but according to him who bestows it beyond any merit of ours. It is "in the heavens," laid up for us there like a wonderful capital drawing interest, to be paid out to us in due time. It consists, not in salvation, which becomes ours by faith before we ever do or suffer anything for Christ's sake, but in the greater glory that shall be ours in heaven.

With γάρ an explanation is added: "for thus they did persecute the prophets before you," namely in the old dispensation. Here Jesus points to the most illustrious martyrs of the past (23:34, etc.), so many of whom gave up even their lives for God. He ranges the Twelve and his other disciples alongside of these prophets. In one and in only one way may we join this most illustrious company in heaven: by joyfully suffering persecution for Christ's sake. Beyond question the highest glory in heaven belongs to the martyred prophets, and next to them stand in due order all others who in their various stations suffered for Christ. Not in spite of our persecutions are we to rejoice, but because of our persecutions. The wounds and hurts are medals of honor. They attest that we belong to Christ not to the world. In war promotion is rapid, and the war for Christ never ceases. II Tim. 4:7, 8. Yet, so many are afraid of a few scars for his sake.

The Beatitudes are not a string but a circle or circlet, for the last, like the first, bestows the whole kingdom. All are paradoxical but strikingly true. Together they cover the whole life of the Christian, the first four in regard to God, the second four in regard to men. The main features of life are selected and combined in a grand whole. From the second to the seventh pertinent parts of the kingdom are assured, but no disciple who has such a part can have it without having the whole. Yet, whatever our experience in the disciple life — for that experience the kingdom has a corresponding blessing.

13)     The Beatitudes (v. 3-10) are objective. Only the two applicatory verses 11, 12 are subjective. But when Jesus now turns from our relation to God (the Beatitudes) to our relation to the world (v. 13-16), his words are subjective. The transition to this second relation is made in the last beatitude, which, therefore, also received a subjective turn in v. 11, 12. First God's blessing to us (v. 3-12), now through and by us blessing for the world (v. 13-16). **You alone are the salt of the earth. But if the salt become insipid, with what shall it again be turned into salt? For nothing is it good any longer except, thrown outside, to be trodden under foot by men.** The strong emphasis on ὑμεῖς, which is placed forward for that reason, has the force of "you — you alone," i. e., Christ's disciples. The predicate, too, has the article, τὸ ἅλας, which implies that subject and predicate are identical and convertible, so that we may say, "The salt of the earth are you." R. 768. The effort is made to limit "you" to the apostles and in connection with them to the called pastors of the church, but neither the text nor the circumstances nor the nature of the subject justify such a limitation. All believers who possess what the Beatitudes bestow by that bestowal are made the salt of the earth.

"Are" states a fact, which justifies those editors who accent ἐστέ. In preaching this is often made an admonition, "ought to be." But the admonition would be far stronger if the incontrovertible fact were stressed that all believers *are salt;* their very faith makes them salt, and if they are not salt they are not believers. Much has been said regarding "salt," its use in Jewish sacrifices, Lev. 2:13; Ezek. 43:24; Mark 9:49; in binding covenants, Num. 18:19; II Chron. 13:5; Elisha purifying the water of Jericho with salt, II Kings 2:21; a pinch of salt placed into the child's mouth in connection with baptism; the Arab holding inviolate him with whom he had eaten salt. Commentators waver between the single use of salt in counteracting corruption or the double use of doing this and also rendering food palatable. In Christ's word the *tertium comparationis* is a unit idea not a duality. The thought of making the world palatable to God is quite impossible. All that Christ has in mind with the figure of salt is that his disciples check the moral corruption of the world, so that it does not quickly perish in its own moral rottenness. This figure by no means exhausts our function in the world, even also as other figures at once follow. The world would prefer that we were honey instead of salt (Besser). The caution is needed that salt is *not* a food.

"The salt of the earth," like, "the light of the world," has a universal sweep, it extends far beyond mere Judaism. *All* the earth is referred to, and "earth" because earth is correlated with corruption as in the funeral liturgy: "earth to earth." "World" suggests darkness. The thought is tremendous that *we* believers should be such salt. This is due to the fact that Christ and the kingdom dwell in us, changing our inward nature and working not only in us but also through us in blessing for the whole earth.

"If the salt becomes insipid," with ἐάν, contemplates expected cases, so that salt may actually lose its saltness, μωρανθῇ, becoming μωρόν or tasteless, ἄναλον, unsalty, Mark 9:50. Remote cases are often cited to show that in olden times natural salt, when procured in an impure state, mixed with other chemicals, might thus actually lose its power and become unsalty. This sort of proof is deemed necessary on the assumption that Jesus would not use a figure taken from anything that does not actually occur in nature. But the assumption is untenable: Jesus does use such figures. Who lights a lamp and then sets it under a bushel? What father would send his son as did the one mentioned in 21:37? Where is the lord who would reward his servants as did the one in the parable of the Talents and in that of the Pounds? These impossible figures serve to bring out most strikingly the reality Jesus intends to picture. Let us acknowledge the fact that Jesus used figures with a mastery that goes beyond all "good writers." The very idea of salt losing its saltness! But that is what happens in the case of Christians, the spiritual salt of the earth. The fact that Jesus is using as a figure something that is impossible in nature is shown by the question: "With what shall it again be turned into salt?" "There is no salt of salt," Jansen. Once the saltiness is gone out of salt, nothing can again restore the saltness to that salt. Both ideas are beyond nature — salt losing its saltiness and having it restored. Yet Jesus here speaks of both as though men had actually found the former and tried the latter. The Christian who loses his faith and thus his wholesome effect upon the world is worse than the man who never had faith.

All that can be done with saltless salt is to throw it out of the house into the road, for men to tread it under foot. The εἰ μή clause has no verb, this being supplied from ἰσχύει. There is something contemptuous in both the passive aorist participle βληθέν, the worthless stuff "thrown outside," and in the present infinitive καταπατεῖσθαι, "to be constantly trodden down" by the men who walk the street. The figure is that of judgment which begins now. As bad as it is never to enter the kingdom, to be thrown out of it is still worse. "Think of the solemn fulfillment of this word in the case of dead churches of the Orient which have literally been trodden under the foot of the servants of the crescent; think of the terrible judgments that have come upon European Christian nations." Pank. There is bitter truth also in the fact that a saltless and powerless Christianity makes more unbelievers than all the books of infidels that were ever written. "Have salt in yourselves!" Mark 9:50.

14) **You alone are the light of the world. A city lying on top of a mountain cannot be hidden.** Ὑμεῖς as in v. 13: "you alone of all men." In the supreme sense Christ is the light of the world, John 8:12; 9:5; 12:35; Isa. 49:6; 60:1. The antithesis of light is darkness, John 1:5; Eph. 6:12; Isa. 9:2, etc. In a secondary sense Christians are the light of the world; Christ immediately, they mediately; he the original, they the derived; he the sun, they the moon reflecting light. See this relation in John 8:12; 12:36; I Thess. 5:5. We have the same derivation of light from Christ in the figure of the lamp, which does not light itself.

Salt is for corruption, light is for darkness. Substantially both are the same, but formally one points to foulness (I John 5:19; Gal. 5:19-21; Rom. 1:23-32), the other to ignorance, blindness, and folly (Eph. 4:18; II Thess. 2:10; Matt. 24:11) As the Christians oppose and overcome the foulness around them, so they oppose and drive out the falseness. All this they do through the Christ who is in them through Word and Sacrament.

"A city lying on top of a mountain" is the first auxiliary illustration, bringing out fully the point that a light must shine out afar. But the figure is now broadened. The plural ὑμεῖς does not refer merely to so many individuals, each operating for himself. They all form a grand, united whole, like a city, which at once calls to mind Ps. 48:2; 87:3: "Mount Zion, the city of the great King," "O city of God." The figure is concise but it pictures a safe place which, with its protecting towers and walls, is visible for many miles around, to which men may flee from the dangerous wilderness round about. Everybody can see it on top of its mountain; all can find refuge there.

15) **Neither do they light a lamp and set it under the peck measure but on the lampstand, and it shines for all in the house.** The plurals are indefinite; "they," anybody. "The lamp," "the measure," "the lampstand" are definite and denote these articles as they are found in the house. The figure of the lamp is the second auxiliary figure to that of the light. It emphasizes the point that a light is intended to light for somebody. The Christians as a body cannot be hid; they are like a city on top of a high hill. An individual Christian, however, may think of hiding his light and, in fact, may do so. Hence this figure of the lamp and the peck measure. The former is a small receptacle for oil which is metal or earthenware, is provided with a wick and has a handle so that it may be carried from place to place. The λύχνος was regularly set upon the λυχνία provided for it, a slender stand, made of metal. Some old references have been hunted up which state that a μόδιον, a little smaller than our peck measure, *was* at times placed over a lighted lamp. But who lights a lamp in order to cover that lighted lamp? That would be ridiculous. If the light is not wanted, the lamp is not lit, or the light is blown out. If the light is wanted, the lamp is lit and placed upon its stand. For what do you suppose Christ lighted us? To have us hidden from sight? No, but to act as a lamp (λάμπει) to all in the house.

16) **Thus let your light shine before men that they may see your excellent works and may glorify**

**your Father in the heavens.** Note the correlatives οὕτως . . . ὅπως (R. 710), which introduce the conclusion and the application. All the figures are now made plain by the introduction of the reality. If our faith is the light, our works of faith are the rays that radiate from that light. We ourselves *are* the light even as the Baptist *"was* a burning and a shining light"; and yet, because our light is derived, we *have* the light: "he that followeth me shall not walk in darkness but shall *have* the light of life." Luther reminds us especially of the confessional works of the first table of the law, "the three high commandments which refer to God's honor, name, and Word," not, of course, omitting the second table, the love to our neighbor with its many works. In our day of humanitarian works and "charity" and "a moral life" without Christ the chief works by which the faith of Christ's disciples shines out and must shine out deserve especial attention: the acts of true Christian worship, the support of gospel preaching and teaching at home and afar, the stand against error and all anti-Christian and unchristian religious forces, the fearless confession of the divine truth, the loyalty to the principles of this truth under all circumstances, the readiness to bear ridicule, slander, loss, and persecution of all kinds for the sake of the faith and the truth of the Word. We all need the peremptory aorist command: λαμψάτω.

What lies in "the light *of the world"* is now brought out. In all these "excellent works" (τὰ καλὰ ἔργα) there dare never be self-glory, which would at once vitiate them all, but that men "may see" these works, whether they believe because of them or not, and "may glorify your Father in the heavens," i. e., if possible, may be brought to that. The works wrought by the Word shine with a heavenly brightness in this dark world of sinful works; and this light will draw many to Christ, so that they, too, believe and thus give praise and glory

to God, the Father, who sent Christ, and on their part
join us in the same radiant works.

17)    After Jesus has described the blessed relation
of his disciples to God in the Messianic kingdom, and,
connecting with that (v. 11, 12), their great task of
letting their blessedness shine out into the world in
good works for God's glorification, he is ready to
announce the great theme of his sermon.    This is nothing other than *the Righteousness* which the disciples
must possess and display in the kingdom for the saving
of the world.    In presenting this great theme Jesus
states most emphatically that all it contains is in absolute harmony with the entire Old Testament Scriptures
but is likewise in glaring disharmony with the righteousness advocated and built up by the scribes and the
Pharisees.    It was highly necessary for Jesus to present
his theme in this manner.    The scribes and the Pharisees professed to be the genuine exponents of the Old
Testament.    When Jesus now contradicted them so
completely in principle and in detail, the disciples were
in danger of concluding that Jesus intended to abolish
or at least to modify the Old Testament.    The exactly
contrary was true.    The righteousness Jesus sets forth
as the essential of the kingdom contradicts that of the
Pharisees just because it fulfills the Old Testament in
reality and truth.

THEME:    *The Children of the Kingdom in the
Righteousness that is theirs*

**Do not think that I came to abrogate the Law or
the Prophets; I did not come to abrogate but to fulfill.**    The aorist imperative does not imply that the
disciples had such a thought, but it does emphatically
forbid such a thought.    R. 833 considers ἦλθον constative; it may be thus regarded "came" or "did come,"
including Jesus' entire mission.    One of the common
ways in which the Jews designated the Old Testament

was, "The Law and the Prophets," to which at times was added, "and the other Books." Here the adversative "or" divides the Old Testament into two parts: "the Law" or Pentateuch; "the Prophets" or all the rest of the Old Testament. Jesus did not come to disturb or to set aside either of the two. All Jews knew that the Samaritans accepted only the Five Books of Moses and rejected the rest of the Old Testament. Occasionally the opponents of Jesus had slanderously called him "a Samaritan." Jesus, therefore, most emphatically proclaims his full adherence to the whole Old Testament canon. Let those note it well who think lightly of the Old Testament or question any part of the canon. Compare the Gospels and note the use which Jesus made of various utterances and portions of the Old Testament. It is one grand unit, all in perfect harmony, and the prophetic books substantiate and expound the Torah or Pentateuch.

The work and mission of Jesus is not "to abrogate," καταλῦσαι (an effective aorist, R. 857), annul, or destroy, any part of the Old Testament because it is now useless and no longer to be respected by the disciples. The very contrary is true: Jesus came "not to abrogate but to fullfill." No object is mentioned in the second statement although, of course, the Law and the Prophets are referred to. The whole stress is concentrated on the verbs; and "not to abrogate," a negative, enhances the force of the positive "to fulfill," πληρῶσαι, again an effective aorist, R. 834, and both infinitives denote purpose.

The verb "to fulfill" suggests the image of a vessel which is filled to the top. The vessel here referred to is the written Word, the Law and the Prophets; and this vessel is filled when what the Word records occurs. The mission of Jesus is to fulfill the Law and the Prophets, not partially, but *in toto*. His entire mission is embraced in the one word, πληρῶσαι, which, therefore, is used in the second statement without an object, in the absolute sense. When Jesus is through working, the whole Old Testament will be fulfilled. The meaning of the verb is altered when it is thought to signify "to complete," as though by his teaching or his work Jesus is to finish what the Old Testament began. The Old Testament is already complete, for it describes all that the Messiah and his kingdom will be. It needs no addition and should suffer no subtraction. The vessel needs no enlargement or alteration; all it awaits is to be filled full by what Jesus is and does. "To fulfill" does not mean "to develop," as though the Old Testament contains only the germs or rudiments. In view of the exposition of various commandments (v. 21, etc.) "fulfill" cannot mean that the work of Jesus consists in adding the true spiritual exposition to the Old Testament commandments or teachings in general. For Jesus adds nothing new; he shows only what the Old Testament itself contains, and does this only because of the rabbinical perversions.

"To fulfill" cannot, as Luther and others think, be restricted to Christ's teaching, just because Christ teaches in this sermon. It includes all for which Christ "did come," even as the infinitive is wholly without a modifier. Another restriction is inserted when the prophecies concerning Christ are excluded from the fulfillment and only the requirements and the demands of the Old Testament are considered as the vessel that is to be filled. This restriction is based on the view that this sermon sets forth the righteousness required *of us* for membership in the kingdom. Christ is thought to teach us the good works (v. 16) that *we* must have. But this restriction of "to fulfill" is doubly specious. In v. 17 Christ is not speaking of us but of himself. Twice he says ἦλθον, "I did come," and all three infinitives have him as their subject. Any righteousness of ours, including all true good works, rests on him alone and on him as first having fulfilled all the Law and the Prophets. Every blessing of the Beatitudes flows from Christ and from what he did for us by his fulfillment. The moment this is overlooked the very heart of the sermon is lost; it then becomes nothing but a moral lecture, a new version of the old Pharisaic work-righteousness. Rationalism and modernism so regard the sermon, but their view cannot be accepted.

Our old dogmatical writers and the commentators who have learned from them are the ones who have really understood this sermon. They have seen that "to fulfill the Law and the Prophets" refers to the fulfillment of the Old Testament prophecies, including the entire *satisfactio* with both the *obedientia activa* and *passiva*, Christ's entire vicarious atonement, and in addition all that Christ will still do until the consummation of the kingdom is reached (I Cor. 15:24; see the author's exposition of this and the following verse in his commentary). Part of this grand fulfillment is Christ's teaching regarding his own work, including that of his apostles, by his teaching and his Word enabling us to apprehend all that he has done for us, so that we may, indeed, appear righteous before God.

18) **For, amen, I say to you, until the heaven and the earth passes away, one iota or one particle of a letter shall in no wise pass away from the Law until all shall come to be.** With γάρ Christ establishes the object of his mission to fulfill the Old Testament. Not one particle of the written Word will pass away without receiving its fulfillment. This statement Christ seals with "amen" and then with, "I say to you." In the formula: "amen, I say to you," "amen" is the seal of *verity*, "I say to you" the stamp of *authority*. "Amen" is the transliterated Hebrew word for "truth," "verity," an adverbial accusative in the Greek, ἀληθῶς, "verily." In Hebrew it appears only at the end of. a statement or an obligation like our liturgical Amen. "All

search in Jewish literature has not brought to light a
real analogy for the idiomatic use of the single or the
double ἀμήν on the part of Jesus." Zahn. This means
the use at the beginning of the statement. The best
one can say is that Jesus used the double "amen" when
he spoke Aramaic just as John reports, and that when
transcribing this into Greek, the synoptists deemed
the single ἀμήν sufficient for their readers. The supposition that John's double amen is intended to reproduce
the sound of the Aramaic words for "I say" is unlikely
and leaves unexplained why John still adds to the
double amen the words: "I say to you." The entire
formula is always solemn and introduces only statements of great weight.

"Until the heaven and the earth passes away"
means until the end of time. The verb in the singular
regards "the heaven and the earth" as a totality, R. 405.
The present sky and earth are referred to, but not an
annihilation of both but rather a complete change, the
heaven of God and the angels being joined to the heaven
and the earth of man, Rev. 21:1-3. The subjunctive
παρέλθῃ is the verb of the main clause, and οὐ μή with a
subjunctive or a future indicative is the strongest form
of negation. Here the negation is a weighty litotes
for the assertion: "shall most certainly stand." The
"iota" is the Hebrew "yod," the tiniest letter, a mere
little hook; the κεραία is a tiny projection which distinguishes a larger Hebrew letter from another that is
otherwise quite similar. The expression that not a
single iota or piece of a letter shall pass away is proverbial: not the smallest part of the written Old Testament shall fall away and be lost (ἰῶτα κτλ., R. 933, expressing God's will). "The Law" refers to the Torah
in the broader sense, namely, the entire Old Testament,
for which the fuller term, "the Law and the Prophets,"
was used in v. 17. It is unwarranted to regard "the
Law" as referring only to the legal requirements of the

Old Testament, to something found in the Old Testament, a part of it. Every part of that old written Word shall stand, prophecy as well as command.

The first protasis with ἕως ἄν indicates only the time: "until the heaven and the earth passes away"; parallel with this, the second protasis with ἕως ἄν advances from the time to what shall occur during this time: "until all shall come to be" exactly as stated in the Old Testament, fulfilled by Christ in every detail. To the very end of time Christ's work of fulfillment will extend, and when that end is reached, πάντα, "all things," i. e., all that the Old Testament states, will have occurred. The kingdom will then have reached its consummation. There will be no need to ask about the written Word after that. The thought is not that it will then pass away. In the blessed hereafter no written Word will be needed. And yet all that *was* written and that we *now* have in God's writing will stand forever down to the last letter and portion of a letter. All of it will stand in the fulfillment Christ will have wrought: every prophecy concerning Christ down to the last judgment and the final glory of his kingdom; every divine requirement concerning us, wrought out by Christ in our final glorification down to our eternal glorification in his kingdom; even the letter of the Word concerning the wicked in their consignment to hell. This is what it means that Christ came "to fulfill."

Any number of human plans, promises, resolutions, laws, and regulations prove abortive. Failing in their purpose, they are cast aside. Not so even the slightest word of God. It will attain whereunto it was spoken and written by God. Some of God's words *have* already reached their complete purpose and fulfillment and now stand thus in both Testaments, for instance, all that was written about Christ's redemptive work. Other words of God *are* still in process of fulfillment,

for instance, what he has said about the church. Still
other words have *not yet* been fulfilled, for instance,
those concerning the consummation. These still stand
like empty vessels waiting for their contents to be
poured into them. But eventually every written word
of God will stand like a vessel that is filled to the brim.
"Until all things come to be" will then be attained.
Compare 1:22; 2:23; 3:3; 4:14, etc., showing how
certain Old Testament words were fulfilled, these vessels receiving their contents. This answers the question regarding the ceremonial and ritual laws of the
Jews. Their purpose was fully attained when Jesus
came. Then, like vessels that were filled, they were
set aside to stand thus forever. Nothing more could
be put into them. The Old Testament, however, contains any number of words concerning the new covenant. These vessels are now being filled, and at the
last day they, too, will be full to the brim and will stand
thus forever.

19) From himself and his own task of fulfillment
Jesus now turns to his disciples and to their treatment
of the words of God. **Who, therefore, shall set aside
one of the least of these requirements and shall
teach men thus shall be called least in the kingdom
of the heavens; but who shall do and teach them,
he alone shall be called great in the kingdom of the
heavens.** When speaking of the disciples Jesus cannot duplicate what he says regarding himself. He
must of necessity limit the application to the ἐντολαί,
"the requirements," which God makes of us. This
term, however, is more than the Mosaic or legal commandments contained in the Old Testament; it includes
all that God asks of us as disciples, in particular also
repentance (3:2; 4:17) and faith in the Messiah, and
then, of course, also newness of life. Through his
Word and his Spirit God enables us to meet "these
requirements," yet they are his ἐντολαί nonetheless.

Through his power and his grace we meet them in a double way: do them and teach others to do them; in our own hearts and lives and in our teaching of others.

The two possibilities which Jesus contrasts are not the extremes: complete rejection of the requirements and full acceptance of them. This would apply only to non-disciples and disciples; to exclusion from the kingdom and inclusion. The contrast is far less, it is one so frequently found among those who are disciples. A disciple may "set aside one of the least of these requirements," and here Jesus uses λύειν whereas in v. 17, when speaking of himself, he has the far stronger καταλύειν. We may "set aside" a word of God by our own ignorance, wrong interpretation, manipulation for selfish or other ulterior reasons, even by teaching others "thus," i. e., to do the same, yet that fact would not in the least alter that word. In v. 17 the thought is expressed that Jesus as the Messiah might actually "abrogate" the Old Testament or part of it and do this in accord with God's own will. It is unwarranted to reduce what Jesus says regarding himself in v. 17, 18 to the level of what he says of the disciples in v. 19. Jesus is not considering our setting aside any of God's requirements, for most of these are so vital that any disciple who did set them aside would cease to be a disciple and would forfeit the kingdom. He contemplates the setting aside "of one of the least of these requirements" contained in the Word. This means "least" in the objective and not merely in the subjective sense, i. e., least in our opinion. The idea that all the divine requirements are of the same importance, and that this is substantiated by what Jesus says about the iota and the part of a letter is untenable. Some requirements are supreme and essential; others, secondary; and still others, least. To be sure, they all belong together and form a grand unit, and whoever sets aside even the least may progress in his wrong course and soon set aside some essential part; yet, for all that, "least" means "least" just as Jesus says.

Just as Jesus came to fulfill the entire Old Testament, so his true disciples will cling to its entire contents and to their fulfillment by Jesus, setting aside not even the least part. But if the wrong thing be done, nevertheless, the individual doing it "shall be called least in the kingdom of the heavens" over against the one who does and teaches all the requirements and is therefore "called great in the kingdom of the heavens." Back of the two passive κληθήσεται stands God himself. Men may applaud and call him great who in his foolish wisdom, by his practice and his teaching, sets aside one of these least requirements; they admire even those who set aside some of the essentials; but not so God. On the kingdom, etc., see 3:2; for already this passage shows that Jesus has in mind the kingdom as it is now present with us not merely eschatologically the kingdom of glory as it shall be at the end of the world. On this subject see I Cor. 3:11-15. Right here in the Christian Church God regards him great who does and teaches all that his will and his Word require and him least who sets aside even one of the least of the requirements of his will and his Word.

There is a warning in the word "least" and in the word "one." For, if already he is least who cancels just "one of the least" requirements, how, then, does God rate him who tampers with several of these least requirements or with one or more that are higher? Those who regard "the kingdom" eschatologically think that "least" and "great" refer to the degrees of glory which shall be portioned out to us in heaven. Since Jesus has in mind the church on earth, "least" and "great" now apply to us. Yet it is true, in heaven the glory will be apportioned accordingly. Already here God calls us exactly what we are in relation to his will, Word, and kingdom, and will certainly do the same in heaven. Some deny the degrees of glory in heaven, but such degrees exist, even as hell also has its few and many stripes and even a nethermost part.

20) The thought expressed in v. 20 should prevent us from letting γάρ prove or establish the ranking which God accords the different disciples in his kingdom. This γάρ merely elucidates and explains. Among the Jews the scribes and the Pharisees were regarded as those who most perfectly and completely taught and lived up to the will and the ἐντολαί of God as embodied in the Old Testament. The people looked up to them as being the very greatest in the kingdom, and they held the same high estimate concerning themselves. These estimates were, of course, wholly false, as Jesus will also show in detail in his sermon. The scribes and the Pharisees were the opposite of models for the disciples in meeting the will of God. Hence the explanation: to be great, or to be even the least in the kingdom Christ's disciples will have to surpass the scribes and the Pharisees by far. **For I say to you,** as the very King of this kingdom of the heavens, **that unless your righteousness shall surpass by far that of the scribes and Pharisees, in no wise shall you enter into the kingdom of the heavens.** There is but one article in the expression "the scribes and Pharisees" (see 2:4; 3:7). While it is true that the former were the acknowledged expounders and teachers of the Old Testament, and the latter the great Jewish party which professed to live up to the legal regulations of the Torah in the most scrupulous manner, here this distinction is not stressed. The two are regarded as one body, for the vital point in which they utterly failed was the attainment of the righteousness which in God's judgment admits to the kingdom. The scribes retarded this attainment by their learning and their official teaching, and the Pharisees by the empty formalism with which they practiced this teaching.

The negation οὐ μή with the subjunctive εἰσέλθητε (cf. v. 18) in the most decisive way bars out of the kingdom all whose righteousness is of the same nature as that of the scribes and the Pharisees. Some wish to make exceptions of men like Nicodemus and Gamaliel, but neither of these was in the kingdom. Jesus told the former that he had to be reborn before he could see the kingdom. The idea that the scribes and the Pharisees will be the least in the kingdom is mistaken; because of their type of righteousness they are and will remain outside of the kingdom. Δικαιοσύνη here has the same force that it has in v. 6; see the full exposition of that verse. The only difference lies in the genitive "*your* righteousness" in comparison with that of the scribes and Pharisees. Christ admits that the latter have a certain kind of righteousness; he tells the disciples that their righteousness must be of an entirely different kind if they expect to enter the kingdom. It must "surpass" or be more abundant than that of the scribes and Pharisees. The adverb πλεῖον adds the idea of comparison: "by far," *magis quam*, "more than." In what respect the righteousness of the disciples must excel that of these Jews is not stated; the body of the sermon will fully show that. Luke 16:15 brings out the difference: "Ye are they which justify yourselves before men; but God knoweth your hearts: for that which is highly esteemed among men is abomination in the sight of God." The formal, outward righteousness of the scribes and Pharisees was adjudged righteousness by these men themselves but before the heavenly Judge it was the very opposite of genuine righteousness. The excess of the righteousness of the disciples, therefore, lay in this that it would be pronounced true righteousness by the one and only Judge, God himself, and would thus admit to the kingdom.

The question is asked whether Christ here speaks of the righteousness of faith or of the righteousness of life, and the usual answer is that he speaks only of the latter. This is thought to be the case because in the body of the sermon Christ contrasts the true fulfillment of the law with the sham fulfillment practiced by the scribes and Pharisees. But this fact already should give us pause that no fulfillment of the law which even the best of Christ's disciples may attain admits them to the kingdom. The kingdom is not acquired by our good works. Luther writes: "What now is the better righteousness? This, that work and heart together are pious and directed according to God's Word. The law will have not only the work but the pure heart which throughout comports with the Word of God and the law. Yes, you say, where will one find such a heart? I do not find it in me; thou, too, not in thee. What, then, shall we do about it? We have no high righteousness and yet we hear the judgment that, unless our righteousness is better than that of the scribes and Pharisees, we shall not enter the kingdom of heaven. This is what we are to do: besides all the good we are able to do we are to humble ourselves before God and say, Dear Lord, I am a poor sinner, be gracious to me and judge me not according to my works but according to thy grace and mercy, which thou hast promised and prepared in Christ. Thus this doctrine leads to this, that the Lord would warn us against spiritual pride and would bring us to the knowledge of our unclean, wicked hearts and sinful nature and thus lead us to the hope of his grace." This, then, is the true righteousness.

Still more should be said. We cannot separate v. 20 from v. 17-19, especially from v. 17. Our entire discipleship rests on Christ's fulfillment of the Law and the Prophets. Only our faith in his redemptive fulfillment makes us disciples. Thus alone are we the salt of the earth and the light of the world, and as such alone can we show forth "excellent works," v. 16. As

such alone can we be good trees bringing forth good
fruit (7:16-23).   Without Christ's redemptive fulfillment we shall never surpass the righteousness of the
scribes and Pharisees which Christ rejects (7:21-23).
The righteousness of which Christ speaks is not the
righteousness of life over against the righteousness of
faith but the righteousness of life as manifesting the
righteousness of faith.   Read about the works enumerated in 25:34-39, and then the verdict in v. 40:   "Ye
have done it *unto me*" (faith) over against v. 45:   "Ye
did it *not unto me*" (no faith).   The Sermon on the
Mount sets forth the genuine works of faith in Christ
in contrast with all other so-called works.

Here, then, we have the theme of the sermon:
Righteousness.   It is not treated abstractly but concretely: the Righteousness which marks Christ's true
disciples.   We venture the formulation:   The Children
of the Kingdom in the Righteousness That Is Theirs.

### The Elaboration of the First Part of the Sermon

### The Law is in the Hearts of the Disciples and thus Controls their Conduct, 5:21-48

21)    This is true with regard to the Fifth Commandment.   **You heard that it was said to the
ancients, Thou shalt not murder! and whoever murders shall be held to the judgment.**   Jesus begins
with the Fifth Commandment as *a praecepto apertis-
simo* (Bengel), the one of whose fulfillment the scribes
and Pharisees most likely boasted especially.   "You
heard" means: from your teachers, the scribes and
Pharisees, on whom you were entirely dependent for
your instruction; ἠκούσατε, aorist, whereas we prefer
"have heard," R. 844.   They told you that "it was
said," of course, by Moses, "to the ancients," to whom
he first brought the law:   "Thou shalt not murder!

and whoever murders shall be held to the judgment."
This is all the scribes and Pharisees told you regarding
this commandment, and, of course, you believed them,
holding that what Moses told the ancients now binds
also you.   The scribes and Pharisees apparently expounded this commandment correctly by adding, what
Moses did not add, that the murderer "shall be held
to the judgment."   That, indeed, sounded very severe.
Accordingly, also you brought the murderers before
your courts of law and had them sentenced to the
proper punishment.

But this was all that you heard: nothing but a civil
law to be applied to an actual murderer by a civil court.
Just so you did not commit murder and run foul of the
court!   Not a word about God and what by this commandment he requires of the heart!   Not a word about
the lusts and the passions that lead to actual murder
and, though they produce no murder, are just as wicked
as murder!   The ἡ κρίσις refers to "the judgment" rendered by any Jewish court of law.   The common local
courts, arranged according to Deut. 16:18, consisted of
seven judges and two *shoterim* or assistant Levites
(Josephus, *Ant.* 4, 8, 14).   The Talmud reports that
there were courts of twenty-three judges in larger towns
and of only three in villages.   On the senate of the elders
see Deut. 21:18, etc.; 22:13, etc., also 19:12.

22)   **But I say to you that everyone angry at his
brother shall be held to the judgment; and whoever
says to his brother, Blamed bonehead! shall be held
to the Sanhedrin; and whoever says, Blamed fool!
shall be held for the Gehenna of the fire.**   "I say to
you" is opposed to "you have heard."   What the disciples now hear Jesus saying is vastly different from
what they heard the scribes and Pharisees pronounce.
The opposition does not lie in "it was said."   Jesus is
not contradicting or correcting Moses; for he came to
fulfill the very law given and written by Moses (v. 17).

Right here he is expounding what Moses meant by "Thou shalt not murder," i. e., that he never had in mind merely a civil law for a civil court but the heart of every Jew, yea, of every human being.

Thus Jesus takes up the sins of the heart against the Fifth Commandment, namely anger and its most common manifestation of calling ugly epithets. I John 3:15 shows us what Jesus has in mind: "Whosoever hateth his brother is a murderer; and ye know that no murderer hath eternal life abiding in him." The usual exegesis regards this word of Jesus as a presentation of three sins and three penalties, the second being graver than the first, and the third graver than the second: for anger alone, the judgment of the court; for calling an ugly name in anger ("Raca!"), the court of the Sanhedrin; and for an angry curse ("Thou fool!"), hell-fire. But Jesus cannot have either such distinctions in the sins or in the penalties in mind. What about other sins such as to strike a person in anger, to wound him, finally also to kill him? What greater penalty could be inflicted beyond hell-fire? In v. 21 "the judgment" is evidently that of a civil court, remanding the murderer for execution. To what graver penalty could the Sanhedrin remand? What court of law could possibly try a case of anger, to which no expression had been given, and order execution for anger? And who would think that the great Sanhedrin would try a man for angrily calling an ugly name? The first two mentioned are civil courts, yet Jesus is evidently not repeating the folly of the scribes and Pharisees by making this commandment a mere civil law. What court could send a man to hell? These questions are not answered by the usual exegesis. No mention is made of the fact that in God's sight anger is equal to murder and makes us worthy of hell.

Zahn is correct. Jesus is satirizing the casuistic method of the scribes and Pharisees. They would

make such distinctions in transgressions, and these
distinctions would turn out a farce when it came to
designating the penalties. Since anger is equal to
murder in God's sight, the angry man would have to
be executed by a civil court — if this commandment is
to be considered in the superficial manner of the scribes
and Pharisees. Well, then the man who uttered the
angry epithet would have to be taken to a still higher
court, say the Sanhedrin, which, however, could do no
more than the lower court. If the angry epithet should
be a trifle different, well, then hell-fire might be decreed. But by whom? There was no court higher than
the Sanhedrin. According to this casuistry, what
would be left for the crimes of striking, wounding, and
actual killing? The purpose of this satire is to de-
molish the entire Jewish treatment of this commandment as a mere civil law. Civil courts cannot possibly
consider the infractions that start in the heart and
break out in ugly names. That is why the scribes and
Pharisees omitted all these infractions and never instructed the people regarding them. They even taught
as though Moses himself did no more for the ancients
to whom, at God's command, he gave the law. Against
this gross perversion Jesus hurls his satire. By saying
that anger is equal to murder and worthy of the death
penalty and an angry epithet likewise Jesus shows how
God judges these sins; and when for a similar epithet
he decrees hell-fire, he shows that in the judgment of
God hell is the penalty for all these sins, beginning
with anger and on through to murder.

The usual exegesis makes a distinction between
ρακά and μωρέ. The former is probably derived from
*req*, through the Syrian *raqa*, and thus means an empty
one who acts as a numskull. Uttered in anger, it would
be something like our "Blamed bonehead!" See Zahn;
M.-M. 562 is insufficient. The latter sounds like a
genuine Greek word, μωρός, "stupid," "foolish," although

in the Greek it is not used for calling names. But this Greek word was adopted by the Jews and was used by them as a vile epithet, somewhat like our "Blamed fool!" Matthew, therefore, really leaves both epithets untranslated, for his Jewish readers would understand the words without a translation. The two epithets are in reality synonymous, one referring to an empty mind, and the other to a slow mind. The second is sometimes made far graver than the first by regarding μωρός as a Greek translation of the Hebrew *nabal,* "fool," and referring to Ps. 14:1; 53:2, where "fool" is equivalent to atheist. But in the Psalm passages the LXX translates *nabal* ἄφρων, and in no language does the simple word "fool" mean atheist. Some fools, it is true, show their folly by talking atheistically. Or μωρέ is regarded as a Hebrew word that is derived from *marah,* "to rebel," i. e., against God. Either of these explanations would make the word a kind of curse, but neither is tenable. Both are efforts to put enough gravity into μωρέ to warrant being sent to hell.

South of the walls of Jerusalem lay the valley that was desecrated by Moloch worship, in which children were burned (Jer. 2:23; 7:31; II Chron. 28:3; 33:6), Josiah declared the place unclean (II Kings 23:10), and it was then used as a place for the disposal of offal (Jer. 7:32, etc.; 31:40). Thus *ge ben-Hinnom,* "the valley of the son of Hinnom," became γέεννα or Gehenna, a designation for hell, the place of the damned. The addition "of the fire" refers to the fire of hell. The eleven passages in which Gehenna occurs cannot refer to the valley near Jerusalem. We have no evidence that the Jews ever burned criminals alive, or that the bodies of dead criminals were dragged out to this valley, or that constant fires were kept going there. Hell cannot be abolished by such interpretations of Gehenna.

23) From what God thus requires of the heart Jesus draws a conclusion as to a specific instance which may illustrate a true disciple's conduct. **If, therefore, thou art offering thy gift at the altar and there rememberest that thy brother has something against thee, leave there thy gift in front of the altar, go first, be reconciled with thy brother, and then, having come, be offering thy gift.** With ἐάν Jesus presents a supposed case, he puts it into the second person singular, thus making it highly personal and effective. The case is one that appears in endless variations in actual life. Of course, it is derived from the Jewish forms of worship which Jesus himself followed; in due time these forms were superseded. But the example still applies. If not before, then in God's presence, in our public worship any sin lying upon our conscience ought to come to remembrance. The present tense προσφέρῃς is descriptive: "engaged in bringing," while the punctiliar aorist μνησθῇς marks the sudden remembrance. "That thy brother has something against thee," means rightfully against thee. By word or by deed, by omission or by commission, before God and thy conscience thou hast wronged thy brother, no matter whether he holds it against thee or not. Thy memory and thy conscience hold it against thee, and that is enough. In these affairs each person must be his own honest judge. A brother may be wrongfully offended, without cause, charging thee where he has no right to do so. Then the guilt is on him not on thee.

24) God looks at the heart, and no act of worship is acceptable to him that comes from a heart which is guilty of unconfessed wrong to another. Burdened with such guilt, thou thyself art not acceptable, either now in his house of worship or afterward at his judgment bar. Though the scribes and Pharisees may decree that no act of offering may be interrupted, lay-

ing the emphasis on the offering instead of on the heart, Jesus commands to leave the offering right there before the screen which separates the court of the men in the Temple from the court of the priests and to go first (read ὕπαγε πρῶτον together) and be reconciled to thy brother. The passive of διαλλάσσω means that thou art to become wholly ἄλλος or "other" to thy brother. Go, confess thy wrong, and ask thy brother's pardon. When this is rightly done, that ends whatever he rightly holds or may hold against thee. Of course, he should be glad to have thee come, be satisfied with thy honest confession, demand no more, and cheerfully forgive. This would be the desired reconciliation for both persons concerned. But if he should be unreasonable and refuse to forgive, thou for thy part art, nontheless, reconciled; the guilt would now rest only on him. With the wrong thus removed from thee, come back (ἐλθών) and go on with thy offering (πρόσφερε, the present imperative to indicate all that pertains to the act, although R. 882 would make this present punctiliar).

This example is perfect in every way. Here is a simple case of fulfilling the Fifth Commandment with the heart. Here we have no perfectionism, for wrong is done a brother, yet the wrong is removed, and by this removal the commandment is truly kept. This is done by God's grace, for his grace, favor, forgiveness, blessings we desire and implore by our offerings and our worship. The old covenant, requiring sacrifices in the Temple, pointed to the Messiah whose coming mediation bestowed grace and pardon on all repentant Jewish believers; and the new covenant, now without those sacrifices, points to Christ and his accomplished mediation and thus bestows grace and pardon on all repentant Christian believers. Thus the righteousness of faith brings forth the righteousness of life through grace.

25) The specific example given in v. 23, 24 is now broadened by an admonition couched in figurative or parabolic language. **Be disposed to come to terms quickly with thy opponent at law while thou art in his company on the way, lest, perhaps, the opponent at law hand thee over to the judge, and the judge hand thee over to the officer, and thou be thrown into prison. Amen, I say to thee, in no way shalt thou come out thence until thou hand over the last penny.** The imagery is borrowed from the old legal method of dealing with debtors who could be remanded to prison until they paid the last cent of their debt. The parable is narrowed unduly when the application is limited to disputes about money. Jesus is expounding the Fifth Commandment not the Seventh. He has just given an illustration of a man who has in some way wronged his brother and should go and be reconciled to him. The parable about the debtor carries this illustration to its conclusion.

The term ἀντίδικος is neutral, any opponent at law; to the plaintiff it would be the defendant, and to the defendant the plaintiff. In the parable, however, Jesus addresses the defendant; he owes the debt. The sensible thing for him to do is to make a settlement with the creditor before his case is brought to the judge. It is plain, of course, that in the parable the debtor is the man who has wronged his brother according to the previous example. Many are content to stop with that. But it would be strange if Jesus had no word of admonition and warning for the brother who has been wronged. He, too, owes a debt to the brother who has wronged him: he owes that brother forgiveness. He owes that debt the moment he is wronged and certainly ought to pay it most joyfully when his brother comes to him for reconciliation. Otherwise the roles will be reversed. The brother who did the wrong will have paid his debt by confessing and asking for forgiveness, and the other will remain in his debt by withholding his forgiveness.

The periphrastic present imperative ἴσθι εὐνοῶν, "be well-minded," here has the meaning, "be disposed to come to terms." When all ill will has been dropped, this will be easy; the whole matter can at once be settled in the right way, without further damage to either party. So again, at bottom, this commandment deals with the heart. This is the real teaching of Moses and the law; this the scribes and Pharisees had lost because their hearts were alienated from God and from his Messiah; this Christ restores in the hearts of all his true disciples. "Quickly" is explained by the clause: "while thou art in his company (μετ' αὐτοῦ) on the way," i. e., before it is too late. While we are still together in this life we may easily settle our misdeeds against each other. But, significantly, debtor and creditor are depicted as being on the way to the judge. For while earthly judges sit only in cases that are formally brought before their courts, every infraction against God's law, when it is without repentance, confession, etc., must finally reach his court. Just as an ordinary creditor finally turns a refractory debtor over to an earthly judge, so, if death separates the wrongdoer from the wronged, the case between them goes to the divine Judge, and just as an ordinary judge makes short shrift of an ordinary refractory debtor, so will the divine Judge do with him who has wronged his brother and refused to confess and to seek forgiveness. As the ordinary debtor is turned over to the judge and by him is turned over to the court officer (τῷ ὑπερέτῃ, who carries out the orders of the judge) and is by the latter thrown into prison, so the divine Judge will dispose of the man who has wronged his brother and remained obdurate. The *tertium comparationis* lies in the action of the two judges. Hence we need not seek to fill in the details of the picture.

26) Only the prison is emphasized when Jesus warns the wrongdoer that he will never be able to leave it. The φυλακή, therefore, pictures hell, "the Gehenna of the fire," v. 22. Roman Catholicism centers on the clause: "until thou hand over the last penny," and refers φυλακή to purgatory and thus finds ways of paying off our guilt in this imagined place. The Catholic contention that ἕως ἄν always introduces something that is expected to happen and often does happen should not be contested, not even on the basis of 18:30, 34, which are like the present clause. It is true, many an ordinary debtor who has been thrown into prison has somehow managed to pay his debt even to the last κοδράντης, *quadrans*, ¼ cent, the Greek term being left untranslated by the Jews. But this possibility pertains only to the figurative language of Jesus. It presents no possibility for a sinner after death and judgment because the Scriptures know of no such possibility. Ἕως ἄν may raise the question: "But how will he pay at all in the φυλακή to which God will remand him, to say nothing about paying the last *quadrans?*" The only answer the Scriptures give is: "Payment there is impossible."

27) That the law must be in the hearts of the disciples is shown from the correct exposition of the Sixth Commandment. **You heard that it was said, Thou shalt not commit adultery!** From the scribes and the Pharisees you heard this, heard it as the old law of Moses (Exod. 20:14; Deut. 5:18), as a piece of civil legislation, and that is all. "To the ancients," though here omitted, is understood. But neither Moses nor God intended that this commandment should be only a civil law or an outward rule of life. What this commandment includes Jesus now states.

28) **But I say to you that every man looking at a woman to lust after her did already commit adultery with her in his heart.** So far the prohibition of

this commandment extends. Even the Decalog shows
this when in its final commandment it forbids lust,
Exod. 20:17; Deut. 5:18. Πᾶς ὁ (see R. 773) is masculine, hence "every man." The present participle βλέπων
characterizes the man by his act of continued looking.
The construction πρὸς τό with the infinitive denotes purpose (not result), it is somewhat like our phrase, "with
a view to," etc.    (R. 1003, 1075); the aorist infinitive
is effective, referring to accomplished lusting; verbs of
desire govern the genitive.    Jesus does not say that by
the accomplished lusting or by and during the act of
looking at the woman the man in question commits
adultery.    The aorist ἐμοίχευσεν, with ἤδη emphasizing
the feature of the time, precedes these acts.    The man
who casts lustful looks is an adulterer to begin with.
The sin is already "in his heart" and only comes out in
his lustful look. If the heart were pure, without
adultery, no lustful look would be possible. Hence
Jesus does not state how the guilty man can free himself of the sin as did the man mentioned in v. 23, 24.
The man's very heart and nature must be so changed by
divine grace that lustful looks will become impossible
for him.

It ought to be understood that what is thus said of
a man (πᾶς ὁ, masculine) is equally true of a woman.
Likewise, "every man" is general and cannot be restricted to married men; and γυναῖκα cannot refer only
to a married woman who belongs to another man.    A
bachelor's lustful look upon a maid is certainly as
adulterous as the lustful look of a married man upon
another man's wife.    To introduce a man's look upon
his own wife is specious, for adultery between these
two is excluded, I Cor 7:9. Jesus uses ἐμοίχευσεν to
match the μοιχεύσεις of the commandment, and both are
to be understood in the broad sense, adultery including
the more specific fornication.    What the Sixth Commandment calls for is a pure heart which keeps even

the eyes pure.  On this the scribes and Pharisees had
no instruction to offer.  Such a pure heart is the
product of regenerating and sanctifying grace alone.

29)  **But if thy right eye entraps thee, pluck it
out and throw it from thee; for it is better for thee
that one of thy members perish and not thy entire
body be thrown into Gehenna.**  Here Jesus meets
an excuse offered by the man with a lustful eye who
blames the sin he commits onto the eye.  He would
shield his heart by a reference to his eye.  He receives
the sound, sensible, natural answer, "Get rid, then, of
the eye!"  The saneness of the answer is established
by γάρ which presents the universal rule in the strong
form here applicable.  No man hesitates to have a
virulently diseased part of his body amputated by the
surgeon in order that he may not lose his life.  It is
the only thing to do; otherwise the man dies.  If,
indeed, your right eye is so diseased with sin, as you
assert, that this eye cannot look on a beautiful woman
without trapping you into lust, then, on your own
assertion about your eye, only one thing will save you
from hell, to pluck it out and cast it away from you.
For on your own admission the only alternative would
be that the dangerous eye continue to inflame your
whole body with lust and thus send it down to hell.

This case is not like that mentioned in v. 23, 24.
There the conscience is aroused, and Jesus tells the
man how to quiet it aright; but here a specious excuse
is offered.  This man claims that he cannot help it that
his eye inflames him to lust, and Jesus draws from the
fallacious excuse the equally fallacious conclusion as to
the remedy.  He tells the man that what he really pro-
poses by such an excuse is the excision of his own
wicked eye.  Hence v. 29 has δέ, while v. 23 has οὖν.
This also explains εἰ with the indicative: Jesus takes
a real case and treats it as such.  Mark 9:43-47 has ἐάν
with the subjunctive instead of the εἰ used in Matt.

18:8, 9 in an identical saying of Jesus.   Whereas εἰ has
in mind a present reality, ἐάν contemplates a future
possibility, R. 1018-1019.   The force of the conclusion
drawn by Jesus is the same in both cases.

The fallacy lying in the excuse is thus exposed.   The
seat of the sin is not in the eye but, as Jesus has already
indicated in v. 28, in the heart.   To make this clearer
he mentions only the right eye and in v 30 only the
right hand.   Remove either, and the left eye, the left
hand will produce the same sin if, as the excuse asserts,
the devil is in the member not in the heart.   In fact, a
blind man and even a eunuch may be lascivious.   All
excuses which blame the body and man's bodily nature as though these creations of God make lust and
other sins inevitable, a mere function of our bodily
being, just the course of nature, end in the absurdities
of successive amputations until the whole body is
thrown away.   This, of course, is foolish, and that
means that the premise which involves so foolish a conclusion is false.   The seat of lust and sin is in the
heart, mind, and soul, which abuse the eye and the
other members.   The commandment is intended first
and essentially for the heart.   The alternatives are not
at all: either a mere outward, civil law against criminal acts or plucking out the eye, cutting off the hand
to make the body behave.   A new heart must be created in us, and this will rejoice to run the way of God's
commandments and will succeed in attaining the better
righteousness.

Neither the older allegorical or the newer symbolical interpretation which make eye and hand unreal are
tenable.   The literalism which deals with the actual
removal of eyes, hands, etc., is entirely too wooden.
How many of Christ's disciples maimed themselves
thus?   The verb σκανδαλίζειν always means actually to
entrap, while σκάνδαλον (σκανδάληθρον), the crooked stick
to which the bait was affixed and by which the trap was

sprung, refers to the enticement which may or may not lure to sin. The figure in the verb is not that of stumbling over an object that lies in one's path. M.-M. 576. Ἔξελε is from ἐξαιρέω. The subject of the impersonal συμφέρει is the ἵνα clause, R. 992.

30) **And if thy right hand entrap thee, etc.,** merely extends the refutation of the shallow excuse (18:8 and Mark 9:45 add also the foot). To think of spiritual amputations misses the very point of the refutation Jesus offers. This idea is somewhat ludicrous, for certainly none of us is to have only one spiritual eye, one spiritual hand or foot. What Jesus urges is the spiritualization of the heart; its renewal through grace makes all our members the instruments and the servants of righteousness. Rom. 12:1.

31) The scribes and Pharisees not only disregarded the application of the Sixth Commandment to the heart and thus failed to see the sinfulness of lust, they extended this disregard to the outward conduct by regarding the law as actually permitting all manner of divorce and as insisting only on the outward formality of handing over a certificate of divorce. Thus Jesus adds the statement that the commandment which forbids the lust most certainly also forbids divorce. **Moreover** (δέ), **it was said, Whoever shall release his wife, let him give her a divorce-certificate,** ἀποστάσιον, the same as βιβλίον ἀποστασίου in 19:7 and in Mark 10:4. Here the simple ἐρρέθη is sufficient to mark the fact that Jesus refers to the word of Moses written in Deut. 24:1 etc., which was used by the scribes and Pharisees to justify their lax divorce practice. Therefore, too, Jesus summarizes Deut. 24:1 as the Jews did when they assumed that this passage allowed their divorces and demanded only that a divorce-certificate be handed to the wife. In 19:7 Jesus explains how it came about that divorce was allowed by Moses; here Jesus refers to Deut. 24

only as the false Jewish justification for their evil practice in order to place over against this practice the true intent of God's commandment. The school of Rabbi Shammai interpreted "the shame of nakedness" (Hebrew), "some uncleanness in her" (A. V.) in Deut. 24:1 as denoting approaches to adultery (actual adultery being punished by death in Moses' time) ; the laxer school of Hillel, whom the Jewish practice followed, interpreted the expression as a reference to anything displeasing to the husband; Akiba permitted divorce when the husband found a more desirable wife.

**32)    But I say to you that every man releasing his wife without cause of fornication brings about that she is stigmatized as adulterous; and he who shall marry her that has been released is stigmatized as adulterous.**    What Jesus declares as being the force of the Sixth Commandment regarding marriage is summarized in 19:6: "What God hath joined together, let not man put asunder."    God alone severs the bond by death, Rom. 7:2, 3.    Every other severance is excluded by the Sixth Commandment and takes place only when this commandment is violated.    Once this is understood, the words of Jesus become clearer, and several wrong interpretations are removed.    Jesus is not expounding Deut. 24:1, but Exod 20:14 as quoted in v. 27.    He is not setting up *one* cause for divorce over against the idea of *many* causes, but is forbidding *all* divorce and *all causes* for divorce as being against God's intent as expressed in Exod. 20:14.    Speaking to an audience of Jews who knew nothing of a woman divorcing her husband, he naturally specifies only the case of a husband divorcing his wife.    The fact that among us where also wives divorce their husbands his words apply to them equally, needs hardly to be added; see Mark 10:12, who writes for Gentiles.

Those who say that Jesus here makes a wife's fornication a *legal* cause for which a husband may

secure a legal divorce make the word of Jesus a mere
legal verdict whereas, in reality, it is something far
more fundamental, namely the true moral exposition
of the Sixth Commandment. Fornication as such violates the commandment in the grossest fashion; and
fornication on the part of a wife adds to this violation
another that is equally gross: by this act the wife
severs her marital bond. By it she then and there
destroys her own marriage; and she does this apart
from anything her husband may do in consequence,
apart also from any law that he may invoke. Of
course, the same effect is produced upon the marriage
by the fornication of a husband. The reason that
Jesus exemplifies by reference to the wife only has
already been stated. Fornication on the part of either
spouse breaks the Sixth Commandment in a double
way: it also al.vays destroys the marriage bond. That
is why Jesus virtually says that the offended husband
may dismiss a fornicating wife; ἀπολύειν refers to the
Jewish situation. He may rid himself of her; vice
versa, if he be the fornicator, she may rid herself of
him (not, indeed, according to Jewish law but morally
before God). And she may do this without breaking
the Sixth Commandment. For it is the fornicator that
destroyed the marriage and left the spouse with a disrupted marriage. Jesus is not discussing the legal
steps that may or may not be taken. Jesus does not
legislate.

The term λόγος here used is not "report" or rumor
of fornication but is like αἰτία, *ratio*, "cause of fornication," the sin being a fact. It is true, the ancient legal
practice stoned the fornicatress and thus ended the
matter of the marriage; but she was stoned as one who
had broken her marriage. At the time of Jesus this
old law was not carried out; the legal practice was now
that the husband might drive out the wife.

But here is a wife "without cause of fornication," and yet for some reason or other her husband proceeds to destroy her marriage with him, ὁ ἀπολύων κτλ., "he that releases his wife" by making use of the lax law of the Jews (Jesus is speaking of them). It is now the *husband* who destroys the marriage. The guilt of breaking the commandment rests on him. The innocent wife is by this man's action forced into a position similar to that of the innocent husband whose wife broke his marriage by her fornication. Jesus says that by his act the husband forces the wife into a position that is contrary to the Sixth Commandment: "he brings about that she is stigmatized as adulterous." The form μοιχευθῆναι is passive, and the agent of this passive is the husband. Jesus makes this emphatic by using ποιεῖ, "he, the husband, makes or brings about," and adding the passive infinitive. This is an aorist passive: by his ποιεῖν he once for all forces his wife out of the marriage. She who according to the commandment, οὐ μοιχεύσεις, ought to be in her marriage, is now, contrary to the commandment, outside of it through the wicked action of her husband.

Dictionaries, commentators, and translators regard μοιχευθῆναι and also μοιχᾶται as active, and they do this in the face of v. 27, 28 where we have the actives: first the future μοιχεύσεις, then the aorist ἐμοίχευσεν. No attempt is made to prove that the passive forms of this verb have the same sense as the active. Yet the passive μοιχευθῆναι is translated "to commit adultery" (active). This is done by adding in parenthesis: "he makes her to commit adultery (in case she marries again)." But this parenthesis is untenable. When is this woman made what Jesus says? The moment her husband drives her out whether she marries again or not. Even when women such as this eventually married again, they were made μοιχευθῆναι the very moment they were driven out. It ought also to be

plain that Jesus here scores the husband who drives
out his wife. Of what is the woman guilty? Jesus
has no indictment against her. She is the one that
is wronged; that is what the passive states, and doubly
so with ποιεῖ before it. Jesus here shows against whom
this wicked husband sins: first against his innocent
and helpless wife, and secondly against any man who
may later on consent to marry her (hence the second
passive μοιχᾶται). Zahn alone sees that the infinitive
is passive, for which he deserves full credit; but under
the influence of the traditional exegesis he fails to see
that the agent of this passive must be the subject of
ποιεῖ, namely, "everyone who dismisses his wife." So
he falls back into the old error: he makes the agent
of μοιχευθῆναι the man mentioned in the next sentence
who later on may marry this wronged woman. This
is grammatically untenable. The agent of a passive
infinitive or of an active infinitive cannot be introduced from a sentence that follows.

A further complication is due to our helplessness
in translating this passive infinitive (also the passive
μοιχᾶται) into English. We have no passive corresponding to the active "to commit adultery." But
this is no justification for translating these two passives as though they were actives like the two actives
in v. 27, 28. Since our English fails us here, we must
express the two passive forms as best we can to bring
out the passive sense of the Greek forms. We attempt
this by translating the infinitive, "he brings about
that she is stigmatized as adulterous," and the finite
verb, "he is stigmatized as adulterous." We are ready
to accept a better translation but only one that keeps
the passive sense of the verbs.

Nothing in the words of Jesus forbids such a
woman (or, if the case is the reverse, such a man)
to marry again. Such a prohibition is often assumed
but is without warrant in Jesus' own words. It is

this assumption that led to the current mistranslations. All that the passive μοιχευθῆναι states is that this woman has been forced into a position that appears to men as though she, too, had violated the commandment, οὐ μοιχεύσεις. She is an unfortunate woman whose marriage has been disrupted without guilt on her part. Her wicked husband has fastened this stigma upon her. It is impossible for her to publish to all the world just how she comes to be in the position forced upon her It ought to be apparent that here we have essentially the same case that Paul treats in I Cor. 7:15. The Jewish husband drives out his wife and thus disrupts the marriage; the Gentile husband leaves his wife and thus disrupts his marriage. Both sunder the marriage. Paul says, "the sister (or if the case be the reverse: the brother) is not under bondage," i. e., is free from the marriage which the ungodly spouse disrupted Exactly the same is true of the Jewish wife who is driven out by her husband. These two are one case not two as is quite generally assumed. But we must stop talking about "one" or "two causes of divorce." Neither Jesus nor Paul is stating causes for divorce; neither is legislating or speaking of legal steps. Both are dealing with the sinful acts which disrupt a marriage in violation of the divine commandment. It ought to be a great satisfaction to see that Paul and Jesus agree in every respect, and that Paul does not add anything to what Jesus stated.

But the effect of the husband's evil act of driving out his wife affects not only the wife but also any man who may eventually marry her. Note the passive τὴν ἀπολελυμένην, "her that has been released or dismissed," restating what Jesus said about the wicked act of this husband; he is the agent back of this passive participle. The man who marries this wronged woman, he, too, μοιχᾶται, "is stigmatized as

adulterous." The verb μοιχάω is in sense identical with
μοιχεύω. But here again the passive should not be
overlooked. This man as little "commits adultery"
as the woman "commits adultery." Neither "commits" anything, both have had something committed
upon them. The man who marries this woman thereby shares her position. Hence also the present durative tense μοιχᾶται: he constantly bears this stigma; he
is joined to a woman whose marriage has been
destroyed by her former husband. As long as both
live, this shadow will follow them. It is thus that
Jesus unfolds to his Jewish hearers in the Jewish
environment in which they live the vicious effects
upon the innocent when the Sixth Commandment
is wickedly transgressed by rending the marriage tie.

33) Another perversion of the law on the part
of the scribes and Pharisees, who always leave out
the heart and thus attain no real righteousness, pertains to oaths and the Second Commandment. **Again
you heard that it was said to the ancients** (on this
formula compare the exposition of v. 21), **Thou
shalt not make oath falsely; moreover, thou shalt
perform unto the Lord thine oaths.** This sums up
Lev. 19:12 and Deut. 23:21, etc.; compare Num. 30:3,
etc. Jesus finds no fault with this brief restatement
used by the scribes and Pharisees in their teaching.
Their great fault was the fact that in both of these
words of Moses they saw nothing but a general permission to use all sorts of oaths and then spent all
their casuistic ingenuity on determining the degree
of binding force of the different forms of oaths, concluding that those which did not directly name God
had no binding force. They argued that if one is
not to swear falsely he certainly may swear truly;
and that if he is duly to hand over (ἀποδίδωμι) what
he has promised with an oath, the use of the oath
must be free to all. Jesus points out that the true

deductions from these words of Moses run in the very
opposite direction.  They pertain to the heart as does
every law of God.

34)     **But I say to you not to swear at all; neither
by the heaven because it is God's throne; nor by the
earth because it is his feet's footstool; nor by** (εἰς,
R. 594; ἐν, 588) **Jerusalem because it is the great
King's city; nor shalt thou swear by thy head because thou art not able to make one hair white or
black.  But let your statement** (λόγος, what you
say) **be, Yea, yea; Nay, nay; and what is more than
these is due to the wicked one** (ἐκ, originates from
him).  This is what Jesus presents as the correct
deduction from the words of Moses concerning perjury and all oaths — the root of the matter which
goes down into the heart.  Why this prohibition of
perjury?  Because men not only lied but even swore
to lies, both originating from the devil (ἐκ τοῦ
πονηροῦ)  Why this injunction to keep a promise
sealed with an oath?  Because men would break even
such promises, acting on a motive prompted by the
devil.  Do this prohibition and this injunction then
open wide the door to the promiscuous use of oaths?
They do the very opposite; they really say "not to
swear at all."  Just as the permission to send away
a wife for the reason of fornication does not open the
door for all manner of divorces, so the regulations
about oaths do not justify oaths.  The law about
divorce really implies no divorce, and the law about
oaths no oaths at all.

35)     The fact that true oaths are here referred
to goes without saying.  In fact, Jesus declared that
all the minor oaths, which the Jews used with the
understanding that they were not binding, are also
true oaths.  For though God is not directly mentioned in each oath he is most certainly involved.  The
four μήτε merely add four further negatives after

μὴ ὀμόσαι; in the case of only the last μήτε is the verb repeated.

"By heaven!" means, "By *God's* throne!" The omission of the article before "throne," "footstool," and "city" places the emphasis on the added genitives, which are, therefore, also placed at the end. "By the earth!" means, "By *his* feet's footstool!" "By Jerusalem!" means, "By the Great King's (God's) city!" Only shallow formalists would argue that Moses' regulation about oaths justified the widest use of oaths, and that avoidance of the direct mention of the divine name, especially the name Yahweh (which all Jews avoided as being too sacred to be pronounced) justified the freest use of these oaths which were then really not binding save in some cases. For the cunning Jewish distinctions see 23:16-22. Jesus' condemnation of all these oaths in spite of Jewish casuistry makes it certain that "not to swear at all" means exactly what he says, "Use no oaths whatever!"

36) The elucidation about swearing by one's head, an oath so frequently used by both Jews and pagans, follows a different line because the head is not directly connected with God. Jesus does not say that a man's head really does not belong to the man but, like his whole body, unto God, the Creator. Here the reference to God is by way of man's powerlessness in regard to his head. It is, indeed, *his* head and yet so little his to offer in pawn by way of an oath that he is unable to make one hair of his head white or black, i. e., to grow with this or that color according to his will. The skeptic may say that nature attends to that. Jesus means that God's power is exercised over every man's head even to the extent of controlling the color with which each tiny hair grows (compare 10:30). Only he who disregards God in his heart can swear by his head.

37) The man whose heart is true to God utters every statement he makes (λόγος) as though it were made in the very presence of God before whom even his heart with its inmost thought lies bare. With a heart thus pledged to truth, his lips will find no need to add anything to his "yea" and "nay." The doubling: "Yea, yea; Nay, nay" in Christ's command merely indicates the positive nature of the assertions and the denials. Like other duplications, these two are made for the sake of emphasis. In other words, a disciple may repeat his statement. Jesus often uses such repetitions, often making the second statement fuller than the first. From John's Gospel we see that he used the double "amen" or "verily." A question may often induce us to reaffirm what we have already said. We cannot make the first "yea" the subject and the second its predicate; this is likewise true regarding the two "nay." In James 5:12 the wording is different; no tenable reasons are advanced for the assertion that James has the original form of Jesus' words, and that the Greek of Matthew is an imperfect translation of the Aramaic original of Matthew. James is not giving the words of Jesus as they were uttered by him; Matthew, however, does. Thus for a disciple who always speaks the truth as though being in God's presence all oaths are ruled out.

What is more than these simple, truthful "yeas" and "nays" is due to, originates from, the wicked one. The positive τὸ περισσόν is a popular substitute for the comparative πλέον. "What is more" = equals any oath added to our truthful statements. By inserting oaths we imply that our statements are not truthful, that we really cannot be believed except under oath. If this implication is true, then we are, indeed, liars, children of the devil, the father of lies and of liars (John 8:44), if the implication is not true, we are liars when making it and thus relate ourselves to the devil. The thought requires that ἐκ τοῦ πονηροῦ be masculine: "due to the wicked one," not neuter: "due to the wickedness." Why weaken the power of the thought by substituting the impersonal power of evil for the personal author of evil? And is there any wickedness that is not due to the devil?

This final statement of Jesus' shows why oaths are still necessary. The prince of this world rules so many men that the state, which has to deal with the ungodly as well as with the godly, is compelled to require oaths in order to establish truth and to confirm promises. Since the world is so full of liars, the state cannot trust a simple "yea" or "nay." Hence the Scriptures permit necessary oaths, Heb. 6:16. Jesus himself took an oath before the Jewish legal authorities, but Pilate did not put him under oath. Because in a lying world even God's people become doubtful and inclined to mistrust, God, too, uses the oath, swearing by himself, Heb. 6:17. It is invalid reasoning to claim that oaths as such are "of the wicked one," and that, therefore, every oath is a sin. It is the necessity for the oath, a necessity due to the world full of lies, that is produced by Satan and his influence upon men. The church has no room for oaths because everything said and done in the church is done in God's own presence. In their intercourse with men Christians will make no use of oaths, for they speak and act as being in God's presence. This leaves the oath to the state alone, and also state penalties for perjury. When certain associations demand oaths of those who join them, their demand brands them as being ungodly; and when they exact oaths regarding promises, the contents of which are still unknown to the person concerned, they show themselves as doubly ungodly. To promise what one does not yet know is to forswear oneself, Lev. 5:4, 5. Every oath of this kind has no binding power, should be repudiated and confessed as sin so that God's pardon may be secured.

38) Jesus now turns to the perversion of the penal law against crime. **You heard that it was said, An eye for an eye, a tooth for a tooth,** i. e., shall the criminal give. Thus your courts shall exact their penalties, making them equal to the crimes committed; Exod. 21:24, 25, "burning for burning, wound for wound, stripe for stripe"; Lev. 24:20, "breach for breach"; Deut. 19:21, "life for life,            hand for hand, foot for foot." Thus the scribes and Pharisees deduced that in his dealings with others every man should likewise retaliate in kind and should in every case insist on his full rights. The fact that Moses also said: "Thou shalt not avenge, nor bear any grudge against the children of thy people, but shalt love thy neighbor as thyself," Lev. 19:18; and that Solomon, who as king administered the penal laws, nevertheless wrote: "Say not, I will do so to him as he hath done to me, I will render to the man according to his work," Prov. 24:29: this went for naught. The worst feature of this perversion was the fact that those who insisted on their rights adorned their revengeful and base actions with the very Word of God as though God himself bade them act as they did.

39) Again Jesus does not abrogate or change the penal laws as being too harsh, as not being humanitarian enough, or as needing reform in other respects. He has not come to abrogate but to fulfill. **But I say to you not to resist the wicked man; but whoever smites thee on thy right cheek, turn to him also the other; and to him bent on going to law with thee and on taking thy tunic, leave to him also thy robe; and whoever shall impress thee for one mile, go with him two.** The severity with which the courts are compelled to deal with proved criminals is

certainly not the norm and pattern of life for the disciples whose hearts are filled with the love of God. What the judge in a court must under criminal law exact as the demand of justice (exemplified by Jesus' reference to the Jewish criminal code) constitutes only the last step to which the governmental authorities are compelled to resort against criminals (Rom. 13:4). Instead of furnishing the general pattern for our conduct toward our fellow-men these final penal measures do the very opposite. The law is not placed into our hands but is taken out of them. The very God who placed that law and its execution where it belongs, into the hands of the government, places another law and its execution, the law of love, into the hearts of Christ's disciples. This is our law of action when we are wronged. And this law requires of us patience, forbearance, willingness to forego our rights and to suffer wrong in order to overcome the evil with good, so that the courts may not need to step in. By obeying this law of love from the heart the better righteousness will be ours in the verdict of the divine Judge.

First the general principle: "not to resist the wicked man"; then several specifications. The τῷ πονηρῷ cannot refer to the devil although in v. 37 τοῦ πονηροῦ signifies the devil; for we must always resist the devil, James 4:7; Eph. 6:13. This is equally true regarding the neuter, "wickedness." Since all the exemplifications cited mention men as wronging us, τῷ πονηρῷ is the man who treats us wickedly. "Not to resist the wicked man" is set over against the penal law of an eye for an eye, etc. This law is intended for the government alone which is to administer it after due process of law and is not to be applied by the individual himself when he is wronged. The best commentary is the action of Jesus himself as recorded in John 18:22, 23, also I Pet. 2:23. "If a neighbor knocks out your eye, are you justified in knocking out his eye to get even with him? It is getting even with him in sin." Loy. And the worst feature of this sin is the anger, resentment, and passion which fill the heart when such resistance is offered. Christ's word is intended to keep our hearts clean of all such carnal propensities. Those misunderstand its meaning who demand a "non-resistance" which would ignore or overthrow all righteousness. The law of love is not intended to throw open the floodgates to unrestrained cruelty and crime.

39) This explains also the three illustrations of the non-resistance that is due to love. Rather than to give way to anger when struck unjustly on the right cheek, or in anger even to strike back on the principle of an eye for an eye, etc., the disciple who has Christ's love in his heart will turn the other cheek for a second blow that otherwise would not be struck.

40) Rather than resentfully to contest a lawsuit which threatens to attach his χιτών, the tunic worn next to the body, as payment for an alleged debt, the disciple of love will of his own accord turn over to his unjust opponent also his ἱμάτιον, the outer robe, which was considered so indispensable that, when it was taken as a pledge, it had to be returned by sundown (Exod. 22:26) since the poor man would need it as a covering for the night (Deut. 24:12, 13).

41) The verb ἀγγαρεύειν is derived from ἄγγαρος, the Persian postal courier, and was taken over from the Persian by both the Aramaic and the Greek. The courier was authorized to requisition animals and anything else he might need to expedite him on his trip. Thus the verb came to mean "to press into service," as Simon of Cyrene, for instance, was compelled to bear Christ's cross. Jesus supposes the case that one is thus unjustly forced to travel, perhaps as a porter with a load, one thousand paces, 1,680 yards, a Roman

mile. Rather than rebelliously to resist the imposition
with a heart full of bitterness the true disciple will of
his own accord, in perfect cheerfulness of heart, add a
second Roman mile.

The striking feature about these three illustrations
is the doubling, and each time the second half of the
deed that accepts injustice and wrong is wholly voluntary on the disciple's part.  In this way Jesus graphically despicts the disciple's mastery over his own heart
and will in keeping himself free from the natural bitter passions to which sin makes us prone.  In this
regard the three examples resemble the injunction
given in v. 29, 30: rather to suffer anything than to
lose the love that insures us the better righteousness
in God's judgment.  All three examples, however, are
intended only for the spiritual interest of the disciple
and never for a moment for those who inflict injustice
upon him, never to abet them or to encourage them in
their baseness.

42) The fourth illustration differs from the
others in that it presents no doubling.  **To him that
asks thee give; and from him that wants to borrow
of thee turn not away.**  Jesus does not say, "Give
double what is asked."  This example is in contrast
with the one preceding, for here we have request
instead of compulsion.  Instead of harboring bitterness the heart might be inclined to hardness, lack
of pity, etc.  The text does not intimate that this
is importunate begging or insistance on borrowing.
The reading δός, aorist imperative, is preferable since
it harmonizes with the aorist ἀποστραφῇς; in Luke 6:30
the present imperative is in place both on account
of the idea of repeated requests lying in παντί and on
account of the second durative imperative, ἀπαίτει.  The
old law inculcated the duty of giving and of lending
in Lev. 25:35, and forbade the selfishness of turning
these acts to personal advantage as might be done by

usury, Exod. 22:25; Lev. 25:36, 37. The loving desire to help is to prompt these deeds.

For the sake of the disciple Jesus speaks and not for the encouragement of the wicked man. With the latter God will deal and for his punishment God has authorized penal laws. When this is borne in mind, no extravagant interpretation will be put upon the four examples which are introduced by Jesus. "If a ruffian strikes me in wilful wickedness, or in conscious violation of all law takes away my property to gratify his greed or spite, or in bare malice to inflict an injury upon me, asks me to give or lend him my money or goods without any claim of suffering or need on his part, shall I understand Christ's words to mean that the love which the Holy Spirit has given me will find its appropriate expression in yielding to his Satanic assaults and demands, and even doubling my loving compliance with his ungodly desires? I think not" — and Loy is right. Christ's injunctions are not intended to be applied mechanically, just formally, or with foolish blindness which loses sight of the true purposes of love. Love is not to foster crime in others or to expose our loved ones to disaster and perhaps to death. Coupled with selfish love is the wisdom which applies love. Christ never told me not to restrain the murderer's hand, not to check the thief and robber, not to oppose the tyrant, or by my gifts to foster shiftlessness, dishonesty, and greed.

43) To the illustrations of the better righteousness as exemplified by single commandments of the law Jesus now adds the final one taken from the summary of the entire second table of the law, the commandment of love to our neighbor. **You heard that it was said** (on this formula compare v. 21), **Thou wilt love thy neighbor and wilt hate thine enemy.** This is the way in which the scribes and Pharisees taught the people the great sum of the second table.

They mutilated even the words they quoted from
Lev. 19:18 by omitting "as thyself." The scribe
mentioned in Mark 12:33, and the lawyer in
Luke 10:27 are exceptions. This omission in the
usual rabbinical teaching was no innocent abbreviation. For the original command was not intended to
state *whom* we are to love so as to raise the question
as to who this neighbor is, Luke 10:29, as the scribes
and the Pharisees actually did; but to state *what* we
are to do, namely, to love, even placing ἀγαπήσεις forward for the sake of emphasis, and *how much* we
are to do, namely, to love, even placing ἀγαπήσεις for-
contrast is not at all between the persons but between
the actions: we are to love, "not hate thy brother
in thine heart," Lev. 19:17; not wrong him, v. 19, or
stand against his blood, v. 16. By shifting the
emphasis these false teachers brought in the question
as to who our neighbor is and then limited the word
so that those not included in "neighbor" were not to
be loved but hated. This was a flagrant perversion
of the law which included all the members of the
Jewish nation down to the lowest and extended even
to the stranger, Exod. 12:43-49. "One law shall be
to him that is homeborn, and unto the stranger that
sojourneth among you." The question regarding the
enemies of Jehovah, who are to be treated as such,
does not enter here; compare Ps. 139:21. Jehovah's
enemies who reject all his love and are thus finally
destroyed are not to be confounded with our personal
enemies, nor are conclusions to be drawn from the
former with reference to the latter. The future
ἀγαπήσεις is a common substitute for the imperative
(R. 330) and is volitive (R. 943).

How bold the perversion was appears in the corollary which the scribes and Pharisees drew: "thou wilt
hate thine enemy," τὸν ἐχθρόν σου, thy personal enemy.
It is often supposed that love for our enemies is

unknown in the ancient Jewish code and came about
as the product of a moral evolution; but Lev. 19:18
ushers in the commandment of love by the prohibition
against taking vengeance or bearing any grudge
"against the children of thy people," and vengeance
and grudges could be directed only against those who
have injured us, i. e., our personal enemies. If, according to Leviticus, we are to love our neighbor as ourselves instead of taking vengeance and bearing a
grudge we have exactly what Jesus here commands
his disciples. So this is not a new commandment
but nothing but the old commandment brought forth
again. With their vicious corollary about hating our
enemies the scribes and Pharisees had only fallen from
the ancient moral height.

44) **But I say to you, Love your enemies and
pray for those persecuting you in order that you
may be sons of your Father in the heavens, seeing
that he makes his sun rise on wicked and good and
sends rain on righteous and unrighteous.** Once more
as God's own Son and the Lord of the law, with the
emphatic ἐγώ and the voice of authority, Jesus crushes
the rabbinical perversion and restates what Moses and
the prophets (v. 17) really commanded God's people.
He uses the plural to include all his hearers, and the
present imperative ἀγαπᾶτε means, "love constantly."
"Your enemies" are personal enemies who are defined
in the parallel command as "those persecuting you,"
hating and trying to do you injury. On their part
they are flagrantly transgressing the law. But their
doing so is not to induce us to follow their evil example; compare Lev. 19:18. Our enemies will have
a fearful account to render to God; we are to be preserved from having such an account to meet. In spite
of all their enmity we are to go on in love.

Ἀγαπᾶν deserves careful attention. It signifies something that is altogether higher than φιλεῖν, the love of

mere affection and liking. This latter kind of love
would be impossible in the case of an enemy: he would
not accept our affection, would strike us if we tried
to embrace him. Nor would we be able to like our
enemies, even as we nowhere read that Jesus liked
the wicked Jews, his enemies. The verb ἀγαπᾶν denotes the love of intelligence, comprehension, and corresponding purpose. It, indeed, sees all the hateful-
ness and the wickedness of the enemy, feels his stabs
and his blows, may even have something to do toward
warding them off; but all this fills the loving heart
with the one desire and aim, to free its enemy from
his hate, to rescue him from his sin, and thus
to save his soul. Mere affection is often blind, but
even then it thinks that it sees something attractive
in the one toward whom it goes out; the higher love
may see nothing attractive in the one so loved, nor
is this love called out by anything that is attractive;
its inner motive is simply to bestow true blessings
upon the one loved, to do him the highest good. I
cannot like a filthy, vicious beggar and make him my
personal friend; I cannot like a low, mean criminal
who may have robbed me and threatened my life; I
cannot like a false, lying, slanderous fellow who, perhaps, has vilified me again and again; but I can by
the grace of Jesus Christ love them all, see what is
wrong with them, desire and work to do them only
good, most of all to free them from their vicious
ways. On God's ἀγάπη see the author's commentary
on John 3:16.

The A. V. follows the less critical text which inserts
two clauses from Luke 6:27, 28, and only reverses
them. Matthew merely abbreviates. The true ἀγάπη
does all it itself can and then enlists also the aid of
God. Both the imperative προσεύχεσθε and the substantivized participle διωκόντων are present tenses and
durative; our enemies may go on persecuting us, we

are to go on praying for them.    The root idea of ὑπέρ, "over," easily becomes the notion "in behalf of," "for the benefit of," R. 630.    The best commentary on such praying is Jesus' prayer on Calvary for his executioners.    Our prayer will be that God's grace may bring our enemies to see their sins and their wrong, to repent and thus to obtain God's pardon.    Only the ἀγάπη which Jesus puts into our hearts as his disciples is able to produce such prayer.

45)    How this love is to come into our hearts and completely control them Jesus has already indicated in the Beatitudes (see especially v. 6) and in the figures of the salt and the light in v. 13-16.    In the added purpose clause this is again brought out.    We are "sons of our Father in the heavens" when we are reborn by grace through faith in the Son and as such "sons" we will, indeed, be able to love our enemies even as our heavenly Father loves them.    The emphasis is on γένησθε, which, however, does not mean that by loving our enemies we shall "become" sons of God, a thought that is wholly foreign to the Scriptures even if it be thought to mean: become his sons in the future glorious Messianic kingdom.    By faith we are now sons of God.    This aorist punctiliar subjunctive refers to the establishing of a fact.    That we are, indeed, sons of God will become a settled fact when our likeness to our Father in loving our enemies as he loves his furnishes the open evidence.    "Your Father in the heavens" brings out the full idea of our sonship.    So great is our Father whose sons we are, and such is his character, namely heavenly, which is far different from all that is merely earthly.    And we are related to him as sons.    His grace has put us sinners into this wonderful and blessed relation through the great Son himself who came to make us sons.    What a motive, then, for us to love as he does and as he

bids us love through his Son and thus to show that we
are his sons!

"Seeing that," ὅτι (compare John 2:18; 8:22, 43),
brings out the thought as to why loving our enemies
would make it plain that we are sons of this Father.
Here is "his sun"; he made it and he controls it. Yet
he lets it rise on the "wicked" who by their vicious
deeds show that they are his open enemies as well as
on the "good" who by their good deeds show that they
are his friends. The active ἀνατέλλει is causative:
"cause to rise," R. 801; B.-D. 309, 1. God does the
same with reference to the rain. The impersonal
βρέχει has the implied subject God, R. 392; B.-D. 309, 1.
God rains on "righteous and unrighteous." The absence of the article in the case of these four adjectives
used as nouns emphasizes the quality each expresses.
The arrangement of these adjectives is chiastic:
wicked — good: righteous — unrighteous. This
chiasm helps to express the thought that when bestowing sunshine and rain to produce the crops men need
for their support neither the one class nor the other
is first as far as God is concerned. "Good" and
"wicked" express moral character as evidenced in
good and in wicked lives. But these "good" are
"righteous," and these "wicked" "unrighteous," and
these added designations, both of which are forensic,
point to God's judgment. Already now and eventually in the last judgment (see 25:46, where the two
classes again appear) God pronounces the one class
good and righteous and the other class wicked and
unrighteous. The good deeds of the former reveal
their faith, regeneration, and sonship; the evil deeds
of the latter their lack of faith, of spiritual life, and
of divine childhood. The world's judgment of good
and wicked counts for nought. The scribes and
Pharisees and many who today are praised as

"good" will not appear as such when God judges them.

The fact that God makes no difference in sending sunshine and rain and many other earthly blessings on his sons and on his enemies we must remember is due to his ἀγάπη with its blessed purpose. "Or despisest thou the riches of his goodness and forbearance and longsuffering; not knowing that the goodness of God leadeth thee to repentance?" Rom. 2:4. Let us not think that it costs God nothing to send sunshine and rain on the unrighteous. It is his mighty ἀγάπη that restrains him from sending only destruction upon them. By his benefactions he would lead the wicked to repentance. With this loving purpose of his our action toward our enemies is to accord, demonstrating that we are, indeed, his sons. This disposes of the statement that what Jesus here says does not stand the test of truth, since by the same acts of nature God also destroys both the wicked and the good. The fallacy of such reasoning is apparent: the sunshine and the rain are, of course, one and the same for the wicked and the good, just as it is one storm, flood, or fire that kills the wicked and the good. But the purpose behind these acts of nature is not the same for the wicked and for the good. All things work together for good to them that love God, but men who will not repent despite God's goodness must go to their doom through God's judgment.

46) The double statement introduced by γάρ elucidates by a double *argumentum e contrario* how the disciples as sons of the heavenly Father could not maintain their position if they should refuse to show love such as that of their Father. If they withheld their love from their enemies they would remain on the old, low level of open sinners and of heathen people. **For if you love only those who love you, what credit have you? Are not the tax collectors doing the**

**same thing?    And if you salute your brethren alone,
what especial are you doing?    Are not the Gentiles
doing the same thing?    You shall, therefore, be perfect as your heavenly Father is perfect.** These
questions are highly dramatic, containing, as they
do, their own answers. They completely shatter the
rabbinical teaching on love. To love only those who
love us raises us not a whit above the moral level of
tax collectors, the despised, renegade Jews who for
their own profit bought up the taxes assessed by the
Romans in some locality, paid over the assessed
amount, and then collected from the people as much
more as they could. Even these men, untrue to their
own nation, known as extortioners, loved those who
loved them. Here, too, although it is used in a base
sense, ἀγαπᾶν has the idea of intelligence and purpose.
They well knew what they were doing, and their purpose was plain. Does Lev. 19:18 mean no more
than this?

The term μισθός is used in a wide sense, it is not "pay"
or "reward" for our love but recognition on God's
part. Can he in any way acknowledge, recognize,
give us "credit" for such love? Then he would have
to own and credit also the love of these base tax
collectors.

47) But the teaching of the scribes and Pharisees
is worse. They centered upon the expression: "the
children of thy people" in Lev. 19:18, and disregarded
all the additions the law itself made. They drew a
sharp line between Jews and Gentiles, despising the
latter as *goyim*, as utterly unworthy of a Jew's attention. They taught that Jew needed to salute only Jew
and regarded a Gentile as being no better than a dog.
To be sure, the pagan Gentile retaliated in kind and
gave the arrogant Jew no more greeting than the Jew
gave him. Both Jew and Gentile saluted only his own
"brethren" or fellow-nationals. It is to this that

Jesus refers, citing the common friendly salutations as the cheapest form of love. The word for "salute" is more than Luther's *freundlich tun*; it signifies to welcome, to greet on arrival, to bid farewell at departure, and to do this in the Oriental manner by an affectionate embrace. By saluting only their Jewish brethren the scribes and Pharisees brought their morality down to the pagan level. What did they more, περισσόν (see v. 37), than these dogs of pagans? Can the disciples be satisfied with anything as low as that?

48) So the conclusion follows (οὖν): as sons of God the disciples must be like their Father. Verse 45 is restated in the form: "You shall be perfect as your heavenly Father is perfect." Starke writes: "The little word 'as' (ὡς) shows that we are to make God our model in all his perfections and follow him in spirit and in truth; not, however, that complete equality is demanded. For God's attribues are infinite while our virtues are finite and, compared with God's, a mere shadow." The future ἔσεσθε is equal to an imperative as in so many legal formulas. In Greek ὑμεῖς is emphatic even by its position after the verb: "you on your part" over against the scribes and Pharisees. They mutilated and perverted the law and tried to subtract as much as possible even from the outward acts that were commanded, haggling with God even on these points. Thus there was nothing perfect about their obedience, it consisted of useless outward scraps. The disciples of Jesus are to be totally different, τέλειοι, "wholly devoted to the will of God revealed to every sincere Israelite in the Word of the divine law and in the model of the divine conduct," Zahn.

The thought and the expression are drawn from Deut. 18:13: "Thou shalt be perfect (upright, sincere) with the Lord thy God." But Jesus adds that

God himself is perfect in this sense, namely true and upright in his dealings with us and therefore the model for all his sons. He is τέλειος who has reached the τέλος or goal, i. e., the one indicated in the context. Here it is a translation of the Hebrew *tham*, "complete," like the whole number, the full time, an animal without blemish or deformity. The sense is that he is τέλειος who gives himself to the law of love without holding back on any point, including even his enemies in genuine ἀγάπη as God does in his love. The English translation "perfect" is largely responsible for the idea of absolute sinlessness often given as the meaning of τέλειος; and it is unfortunate that we have no derivative from "goal" adequately to render the Greek. The fact that absolute sinlessness is not the thought expressed here we see from v. 6, where the blessed disciples still hunger for righteousness, and from v. 7, where they still need mercy and are blessed by constantly obtaining it.

It is incorrect, then, to think that the goal of loving our enemies is too high for us. This goal we must reach by the grace of God, otherwise God cannot regard us as his sons. But even then our love toward both our friends and our enemies will show many a flaw which we will confess and for which we will day by day ask and receive pardon. Perfectionism may imagine that it is able to attain sinlessness in this life; this goal we shall not reach until we enter glory. Equally incorrect is the idea that in these expositions of the law Jesus offers only "counsels for the perfect" which are unattainable on the part of lesser Christians. Christ has no double standard. His greatest saints are found among the common believers who by grace have become pure in heart (v. 8).

# CHAPTER VI

### Christ's Sermon on the Mount.    Part II, Chapter 6

*The Children of the Kingdom in the Righteousness that Is theirs.*

*The Father is before their eyes, and thus they are freed from hypocrisy.*

This is developed in a concrete and personal presentation by examples from the religious life.    The word *Father* runs through the chapter.

1)    Chapter 5 deals with the *false teaching* of the scribes and Pharisees and the wrong conduct that resulted; chapter 6 deals with their *false piety* apart from any special teaching.    The first three examples of this false piety are cases of hypocrisy, and the fourth is similar, pretending to trust God and yet trusting Mammon.

**Take heed not to do your righteousness in fron: of men with a view to be observed by them, else you have no reward with your Father in the heavens.** This is the opening statement for the first three examples of hypocrisy, v. 2-18.    With προσέχετε supply νοῦν: literally "hold your mind toward this," etc., do it constantly.    Instead of δικαιοσύνην some inferior texts have ἐλεημοσύνην, "alms," in the A. V.    The Hebrew *tsedaqah* as well as the Aramaic equivalent were used to denote mercy, kindness toward the poor, as appears from the LXX and from other translations.    Thus it was easy to take "righteousness" in the sense of "alms," especially since Jesus deals with almsgiving in his first illustration.    But here "to do righteousness" refers to the entire range of good works; v. 1 introduces not only v. 2-4, but v. 2-18.    "Righteousness" is here not a quality in us from which our acts flow but something righteous that we ourselves do, something that we expect God to pronounce righteousness in distinction from the imputed righteousness. The righteousness we do is to be better than that of the scribes and Pharisees (5:20); it must grow out of faith and a regenerate heart and thus be done unto God and not as a display before men.

This is the point to which we must give heed. While men are, indeed, "to see" our good works (5:16), these works are to be seen in such a way that men will "glorify your Father in heaven." The danger is that we may do them "in front of men, with a view to be observed by them," so that we "may have glory of men" (v. 2). In πρὸς τό with the infinitive we have purpose, R. 1075, and this purpose is the secret motive for doing the righteousness. And θεαθῆναι is used for viewing a spectacle, the dative αὐτοῖς, as with some passives, indicating the agent. It may flatter us when men praise *us* for our good deeds instead of giving all praise to God for them. Under this stimulus we may do even great and wonderful deeds (7:22, 23) the more to turn men's eyes upon us. But where this motive prevails, no matter how great the deeds may be, in God's sight they are completely ruined; in his judgment they cease to be "righteousness."

The formula εἰ δὲ μήγε is stereotyped and never has a verb; the sense is: "but if you do not take heed." "Else you have no reward with your Father" implies that true works of righteousness do receive a reward at the hands of the Father. The phrase παρὰ τῷ πατρὶ ἱμῶν points to a reward laid up at the Father's side to be given us in due time. We need hardly say that this is wholly a reward (μισθός as in 5:46) of grace, yet as such promised to us and fully assured. This makes the matter altogether clear and simple. He who performs his good works to be seen of men has in this seeing of theirs the reward he is after. His own purpose of these good works is thus fulfilled. Works done as a display before men are, of course, not done for God, to please his eye. They could not be done for him for he abominates duplicity: pretending that we are seeking his praise when we are secretly seeking only our own. Why should he reward such works? The matter is really a choice between two rewards: the transient, empty praise of men; the praise and the blessing of the Father "in the heavens." Only a fool would snatch at the former, thereby losing the latter. Augustine calls the love of honor the deadly bane of true piety; other vices bring forth evil works, this vice seeks to do good works and destroys them.

2) **Whenever, therefore, thou doest alms, trumpet not in front of thee like the hypocrites do in the synagogues and in the streets in order that they may be glorified by men. Amen, I say to you, they have their reward in full.** On the principle just laid down "therefore" builds the first specification. Ὅταν with the present subjunctive shows that Jesus expects us to do alms regularly. Μή with the aorist subjunctive is the regular form for a negative command with the aorist; and the aorist means: "do not begin to trumpet," R. 853. Note the force of ὑπό in ὑποκριταί, giving us the idea of an actor under a mask (R. 633); also of ἀπό in ἀπέχουσι: the hypocrites have, as it were, their money down as soon as their trumpet has sounded, R. 577, 866. The aoristic present with the perfective ἀπό makes this realistic. In ποιοῦσιν we have a gnomic present (R. 866), which denotes actions done at any time. Diligent search fails to verify the view that the Pharisees used trumpets to call the poor together and to assemble a crowd to witness their almsgiving. Nor would trumpets be used in a synagogue. This indicates that "do not start trumpeting"

is figurative; we should say, "do not advertise." Yet
"in the synagogues and in the streets" is quite literal;
the Pharisees chose public places to show off
their charities. Their delight was "to be glorified
by men"; that God might be glorified was not their
concern.

The example of the Pharisees is bold and strong,
yet as such it includes every hypocrisy of this kind
down to the secret desire to have our good deeds
praised by men for our own sakes. Luther points out
that but few respond when we say that God and his
angels will be pleased and that God will reward a
hundredfold; and that many grow slack when men
ignore and show ingratitude.

"Amen" (see 5:18) puts the seal of verity, and "I
say to you" the seal of authority on Christ's judgment:
"they have their reward in full." They are already
paid off in the very coin they are after. Desiring
only the glory from men, they have it. If any man's
duplicity goes so far as to think that he will also
receive glory from God, he certainly fools himself
(25:45: "ye did it not to me"). How much of Christian giving is of this Pharisaic kind we need not say.
Church papers and the secular press often serve as
trumpets.

3) **But when thou art doing alms, let not thy
left realize what thy right is doing in order that
thine alms may be in secret; and thy Father, seeing
in secret, will give thee what is due.** According to
Besser the Temple provided a place where bashful
benefactors might place their gifts to be distributed
to the bashful poor, and the place was named "Silence."
Many explanations about the left not knowing what
the right is doing are unsatisfactory. The added purpose clause makes the matter clear; what the right
hand does when giving alms is to be done so secretly
that even the left hand may not find it out. The

hands are usually so close together that, if they could
see, each would be fully aware of what the other
is doing. When one hand does what even the other
fails to see, that is doing a thing "in secret" indeed.
In the third person the aorist imperative is retained
in prohibitions; the second person would have the subjunctive; hence γνώτω, R. 943, and repeatedly.

4) "In secret" is, of course, not in conflict with
5:16. Luther has the key: "Thus I do not see it
though other people may see it." The left hand does
not represent men who are, indeed, to glorify God on
seeing my good works. The left hand represents myself just as the right does: the right, me with my good
deed; the left, me with my good opinion about my deed.
If, then, the left does not even know what the right is
doing, I shall be absolutely free of desiring any praise
or credit from men. This is the secrecy Christ wants
even when all the church knows my deeds. The whole
matter is in the heart, it is not a mechanical rule about
hiding our gifts. For one might hide all his giving in
the secret hope of eventually being discovered and then
being praised for the saintly secrecy of his gifts.

We must drop ἐν τῷ φανερῷ from the text. The contrast is between the two phrases ἐν τῷ κρυπτῷ, "in secret."
All our good works are to be done for God alone so that
they may please him. In this sense they are to be done
"in secret," for him who "sees in secret," and whose
seeing penetrates to the inmost motive underneath our
deeds. Done thus, with a motive that does not need to
fear God's eyes, we shall look to him alone for a reward
of grace and not to men and to their praise when our
works bid them glorify God. God is pleased to bestow
his reward of grace on us. In ἀποδώσει we again have
ἀπό (v. 2): "will give what is due," i. e., according to
his grace and promise of grace, of course, not according
to any merit we might claim. He will reward even a
cup of water given in his name. As vicious as is the

secret desire for the praise of men, so vicious is the
secret mercenary desire to trade our good works for
far greater rewards from him.

5) **And whenever you are praying you shall
not be as the hypocrites, seeing that they love to
be praying, standing in the synagogues and on the
corners of the wide streets in order to make a display to men. Amen, I say to you, that they have
their reward in full.** "And" parallels the exercise
of prayer with that of almsgiving; the need of others
whom we may be able to relieve with our own need
which God is to relieve. Ὅταν with the present subjunctive expects us to be praying regularly. Jesus
takes our necessity of prayer for granted. This time
he uses the volitive future in his command: "you shall
not be," etc., R. 874, 942, so often used imperatively.

Generally, ὅτι is regarded as being causal (R. 963),
yet it hardly states *why* we are not to be "as the hypocrites" (see v. 2) but *in what respect* we are not to be
like them: "seeing that," etc. The emphasis is not on
the "standing," for this was a regular attitude in Jewish prayer, but on the places in which they loved to
stand. These were as public as possible, "in the synagogues" where many worshippers would see these
scribes and Pharisees and "on the corners of the wide
streets," the πλατεῖαι (supply ὁδοί; the ῥύμη mentioned in
v. 2 is an ordinary narrow street), where many people
passed in four directions. These devout Pharisees
pretended that they were accidentally caught at such
a frequented corner by the hour of prayer and then
would not let the public place deter them but turned
toward Jerusalem or toward the Temple and made their
prayers. Their pretense must have been transparent
enough, but hypocrisy was not ashamed to go to this
length.

Their purpose was: "in order to make a display to
men," φανῶσι (φαίνω), "to shine" to men. In all prayer

the inner motive and the attitude of the heart are the decisive things. Only worldly superficiality will let the outward act pass as being of full value and will disregard the motive and the purpose. These hypocrites did not really pray, they only imitated prayer. Wuttke rightly says that only gold is imitated because it is so precious. Instead of finding fault with Christianity because hypocrites imitate its forms of worship, Christianity deserves the highest honors because men imitate it. A nation is at a low ebb when it has no real and true religion in its midst that attracts imitators. As regards true piety, this is always connected with a certain reticence and shrinks from public advertisement. The full-blown rose loses its petals and is gone; let your heart be a half-open rose, its chalice turned toward the sun, but its heart still hidden. Because prayer is so high and holy, the devil likes to ruin it in many ways, and he certainly succeeds in the case of all hypocrites.

Here again Jesus adds: "Amen," etc., as in v. 2, which see. "How should God not be absent from such prayers, when we ourselves are not present with them?"

6) The turn to the singular makes the admonition more personal. **But thou, whenever thou art praying, enter into thy room and, having shut the door, pray to thy Father who is in secret; and the Father who sees in secret will give thee what is due.** The subject σύ is placed forward for the sake of emphasis: "but thou" in contrast with the hypocrites. "Whenever thou art praying" expects each of us to do this regularly. The ταμεῖον, or the older ταμιεῖον, originally a storeroom that could be locked, is a person's own room, not, however, the "upper room" on the roof of the building, although this latter might serve as a place for solitary prayer. The contrast is here not with regard to public prayer in the congregation, but only with regard to personal prayer made for the purpose of

display before men. Jesus himself called the Temple the house of prayer where public prayer was made. He took part with all the people in the worship in the synagogue. The disciples saw and heard him pray. In fact, a special promise is added when two or three unite in prayer.

To shut the door of one's own room means to pray in complete privacy. All intrusion is barred out, the worshipper is alone with God. True praying must start in secret since its very nature is personal communion of the soul with God, and an attitude of prayer and any words of prayer that are not intended for God but to impress men are the worst possible prostitution of prayer. Hence to shut out men and any extraneous influences is an aid to prayer. He who has learned to pray thus in secret will know, too, how to commune with God when other worshippers join him in prayer. Therefore, right praying in secret will aid participation in public worship.

The aorists εἴσελθε, etc., refer to a single act of private prayer. The middle aorist imperative πρόσευξαι is distinguished from the active aorist infinitive προσεῦξαι only by the accent. This word for "to pray" is used only regarding worship and prayer that is addressed to God, while other terms which express petition, request, etc., may also be used when men are addressed. The emphasis is on τῷ πατρί σου τῷ ἐν τῷ κρυπτῷ. R. 776, etc., points out that the repetition of the article makes the modifier "in secret" emphatic, adding it as a sort of climax in apposition with "to thy Father." There is a correspondence between praying "in secret" and the Father who is in secret. This correspondence is emphasized: "and the Father who sees in secret," i. e., in the secret room, even in the secret heart of the one praying. Here again "openly" is not in the best texts. Ἀποδώσει is explained in v. 4. Jesus speaks of prayer as a good work and thus says that for this good work,

truly good in his sight, he "will give what is due," just
as he will for any other good work. Jesus says nothing
about God's answer to the prayer that is thus acceptable to him. God's answer to every acceptable prayer
is assured and is here taken for granted. Of course,
the answer may also be the reward for the work that
God accepts.

7) The hypocrisy which makes a display of prayers
is also inclined toward wordiness in prayer, trying to
impress men or even God himself by piling up many
words. **Moreover, while praying, do not babble
like the Gentiles, for they think that they shall be
heard for their loquacity. Do not, therefore, become like them, for your Father knows of what you
have need before you ask him.** The derivation of
βατταλογεῖν is still in doubt, C.-K. 683, etc. The word is
found only here in Matthew and once in the sixth century. It has nothing to do with stammering. Its
meaning seems to be "to babble," *schwatzen,* Luther;
*plappern,* to utter a lot of useless and superfluous
words. "Like the Gentiles" is more than a reference
to the custom of the pagans in their praying, for the
Jews often prayed in the same way. The heathen tried
to tire out their gods with such endless prayers. Mere
formulas were repeated over and over again; the Jews
had such prayer formulas, Catholics also have them in
the form of their rosary. It is heathen folly to measure prayer by the yard. The aorist imperative is
peremptory.

The folly of this procedure is the fact that such
people "think that they shall be heard for their loquacity," πολυλογία, the great volume of their words, even if
they are not mere thoughtless babble. Even undue
length vitiates prayers, a truth which many to this day
fail to understand, thinking that long prayers spoken
with an unctuous tone mark true spirituality.

8) "Do not, therefore, become like them," again a peremptory aorist imperative, doubles the prohibition for the disciples as though Jesus felt that there was a danger in this direction. Instead of letting the wrong example of others mislead us, such an example should serve as a warning to us. Another consideration is brought in: God knows our needs even before we ask. To talk and to act as though we had to inform him of everything and as though by omitting some detail he would be left in ignorance, is to debase God and thus to insult him. Why forget that he is omniscient? The opposite error is that, since God knows all our needs and is ever ready to help, prayer is unnecessary save in its reaction on us, relieving our hearts and making us more comfortable. Prayer is more than autosuggestion with a mere psychological effect. "Ye have not, because ye ask not, or because ye ask amiss," James 4:2. Not to pray and ask is to reject both the commands and the promises of God and to throw away the means which God himself has appointed for us to secure his blessings and to secure them so that they will, indeed, be blessings. On πρὸ τοῦ with the infinitive see R. 1075; the aorist αἰτῆσαι is not constative (R. 857) but effective, indicating actual asking.

9) **In this manner, therefore, be praying,** προσεύ-χεσθε, present imperative, whenever you pray. Jesus adds an illustration of the right manner of prayer, that is right in form, content, and spirit. Not a word of it is superfluous, and that not as to style but as to the substance here put into words. *The Lord's Prayer* is perfect in every respect; no human prayer has ever equalled it. Both οὕτως and ὑμεῖς are emphatic: "*thus . . . you*," i. e., as my disciples. Both words place the disciples in contrast with all others who may pray. It is incorrect to assert that any Jew could today use this prayer. "Thus" and "you" require faith in the

God who sent Jesus as the Messiah. In the old covenant any Jew who believed in the coming Messiah could have prayed this prayer; and in the new covenant only those Jews (and Gentiles) can pray it who believe in Jesus, the Messiah. In Luke 11:1, etc., we have the same prayer with some changes. The contexts are so decidedly different that we are compelled to conclude that, as was true with regard to other sayings of Jesus, this prayer, too, was repeated by him. The claim that Luke gives the real occasion and that Matthew inserted the prayer in this sermon has never been made plausible.

**Father of ours who art in the heavens, Hallowed be thy name.** In the Greek πάτερ is placed first, and many translations follow that word order. Our English idiom prefers, "Our Father." Only a true child of God can address him as "Father," and only faith in Christ makes one a child of God. Only true disciples and believers can truly pray this prayer; all others find advice in John 8:42, 43. They may try to call him "Father" as the Jews did in the *Sch<sup>e</sup>mone esre* (prayer of 18 verses), or as the Unitarian, the modernist, and the deist of today do, but God's only answer will be, "I never knew you." "Our" presupposes the possession of faith, it is like the Old Testament "the Lord, *our God.*" We on our part appropriate him, and he on his part endorses that appropriation. "Our" is plural so that, whether one prays this prayer by himself or in union with others, the intercession for all the other children of God is always included. Thus *love* is joined to *faith* in "our Father." But must we not include also the world? No (John 17:9), we are not to combine God's children with those of the world. And yet, as in Christ's Great Intercession (John 17) where he says, "that the world may believe," we do pray for the world, namely in the first three petitions. As for us,

so for the world, the one avenue to the Father and to
his blessings is through faith in Christ.

"Our Father" draws him down to us, but the apposition "who art in the heavens" (in the Greek appositions to vocatives are in the nominative) reveals the
greatness of him who is thus drawn down. The thought
is not that he is *only* in heaven, yet heaven is his
glorious abode. The plural "heavens" is frequently
used by Matthew as a rendering of the Hebrew *hasha-
mayim*. This prayer is intended for the disciples on
earth who raise their hearts and their eyes to heaven,
their future home. Our guarantee for this hope is the
fact that our Father is in heaven. Thus in this address *hope* is added to *faith* and to *love*.

Loehe points to the first three petitions as parallels
to the first three Commandments. Each of these three
refers to God above, then the petitions that follow, like
the Commandments that follow, descend to our earthly
affairs. The pronoun "thy" binds the three petitions
together and separates them from the rest which have
the pronouns "us" and "our." God's "name" is more
than any individual term by which we refer to him,
more than all these terms taken together. His name
is that by which he makes himself known to us, his
revelation. God's Word is his ὄνομα, his complete name,
made known to us so that we may know God and enter
into communion with him. In every passage of Scripture God looks toward us, and we must see *him* there.
But for us Christ is the heart of this name, John 14:9.
It is presumptuous on our part to invent any name for
God such as "the great architect of the universe."
This is a deviation from his Word and from Christ or
the result of perverted piety.

The three aorist imperatives of the first three petitions are striking because all three are the third person; the other four are the second person. These first
three have a mandatory sound; what they say *must* be

done. God could not consent to the opposite, nor could
God's children. The aorist tense helps to emphasize
this: God will certainly do what he is in this striking
way asked to do. For back of these imperatives is
God himself. The name, the kingdom, and the will are
his. His name is not a mere sound, concept, thought
revealed to us; it is God himself revealed to us. His
kingdom is not the mass of his subjects merely but his
kingly authority, dominion, power, and rule as revealed
in all his subjects. His will is not a mere statement of
what he wants but he himself in his action of willing
and accomplishing his will. The ἁγιασθήτω does not suggest the thought that an increase of holiness could be
given to God or to his name. He and his revelation
are what they are irrespective of us. The imperative
has men in mind, namely the thought that many do not
receive God's revelation of himself and revere and
honor it as they should. Even God's children fall short
in many respects. "To hallow," "to sanctify" means
to set apart from everything common and profane, to
esteem, prize, honor, reverence, and adore as divine
and infinitely blessed. The opposite is "to profane," to
treat the Word as not being divine, to neglect, change,
or contradict it by word or by deed. The passive "be
hallowed" calls on God to make his Word and revelation in Christ Jesus supreme in the hearts of men. By
placing the verb forward it receives great emphasis.

10) **Thy kingdom come.** On "kingdom" see
3:2. This kingdom is the heavenly reign and rule of
God through Christ in the gospel of grace. Where
Christ is, there this kingdom and rule is, and, of course,
also those who through him participate in the blessings
of this rule and kingdom, the kings and priests unto
God. "Let it come" means by its own inherent power,
and the aorist is effective (R. 855): "let it come actually and completely." This aorist is not a reason for
thinking only of the consummation, the kingdom of

glory. This consummation includes all that precedes
it in the rule of grace, which finally shall become the
rule of glory (I Cor. 15:24-28). It also includes the
defeat of the kingdom of that wicked old Pharaoh,
Satan, pictured in the escape of Israel from the Red Sea
and in the drowning of the pursuing hosts. Note that
again the verb is placed forward.

This is also true with regard to the next petition.
**Thy will be done, as in heaven, just so on earth.**
This is God's good and gracious will, Luther (John
6:40). The thought is not that he has more than one
will but that the highest aims and purposes of his one
will regarding us center in his grace. That will centers in Christ who came to do his Father's will and
will carry it to its goal. If no opposition interfered
with God's will, a prayer such as this would not be
needed; but here the same undercurrent of hostility in
"the devil, the world, and our flesh" is implied. In this
petition God's children put their own wills into complete
harmony with their Father's will and thus into opposition to the will of all his foes. Let us realize this when
we pray thus. Let us also realize that our lives are
placed wholly under our Father's will, and that we
accept what his blessed will sends us, also crosses,
trials, sufferings, etc. "As in heaven," etc., applies only
to the third petition; for in the second we cannot say
that the kingdom can "come *in heaven*"; it has always
been there. Ps. 103:21 shows how God's will is done
in heaven. In this way it is to be done also on earth —
perfectly, with every creature being an agent of that
will; καί, "just so," R. 1181.

Note the climax: first, the Father's revelation;
secondly, his authority and rule; thirdly, his own personal will which exercises this rule and, therefore, also
has given this revelation. These impressive aorists
imply more than that these petitions are to be realized
only to a certain degree, say as much as possible. They

call for a complete hallowing, coming, and doing and thus look forward to the great consummation when every opposition will be abolished forever, and God will be all in all (I Cor. 15:28; Rev. 21:1-4).

11) The *three* petitions that pertain to God are symbolic of the Trinity; the *four* pertaining to us symbolize the world; and the *seven* symbolize God in connection with the world. Even in such points this prayer is perfect. Yet Luke has only six petitions (twice three), showing that the real perfection lies in the substance. The variation between Matthew and Luke is no reason for altering the fixed form of the Lord's Prayer which the church employs in its liturgy, catechism, etc. Now the imperatives are the second person, and we feel the difference. The objects mentioned in these four petitions cannot be identified with God himself as were his name, kingdom, and will; they are only gifts and acts of God for our various needs. The aorist imperatives are still strong because all four petitions harmonize with God's will. The four again rise to a climax, and their perfect order permits no transposition.

**Our needful bread give us this day.** The emphasis is now not on the verb but on the "bread." Jesus begins with our least but often most troublesome need and with one stroke takes the bread out of the way, leaving our hearts free for the more vital needs. "Bread" is a concrete and compact term for what we need to sustain our bodily life, and no finer exposition of it than that found in Luther's Smaller Catechism has ever been given. In the whole Greek language ἐπιούσιος appears only here and in Luke 11:3, and linguists are still not agreed on its derivation and its precise meaning. The Vulgate and Jerome translate *supersubstantialis*, and the Catholic Douai version, "our supersubstantial bread" — which but few will understand — meaning the bread above (ἐπί) all nature (οὐσία), "the Bread of Life." The best efforts to date regard οὐσία as the root in the sense: *was zum Dasein gehoert*, what belongs to our existence; hence: "our needful bread," Am. Com., R. V., and the exhaustive discussion in C.-K. 407, etc. This adjective which is appended by a second article (R. 776, see v. 6) makes the adjective a kind of climax to the emphatic noun. The disciples, as God's children, receive all their bread as a gift from their Father's hand. "Give us this day" is interpreted by Luke, "go on giving us (δίδου, present imperative) day by day." We are to be satisfied with having enough for the day. Thus we are to renew our petition daily, always depending wholly on our Father. God often and generally gives us far more than enough for the day; but even in the midst of great plenty (which may be swept away in an instant) our real safety lies in the Father alone. Jesus excludes greed and worry. Ps. 37:25.

**12) And dismiss for us our debts as we, too, did dismiss our debtors.** Here the verb is placed first and thus is emphatic: "dismiss," "send away," "as far as the east is from the west," so that they will never be found. The ὀφειλήματα, "debts" or "obligations" which we must justly meet Luke defines as our "sins," ἁμαρτίαι. It goes without saying that this dismissal is effected by grace alone, through Christ, by contrition and faith — justification by faith alone. On debts and on our debtors see Matt. 18:23, etc. So great are our debts to God that we can never hope to pay them, and our only help is that God will remit them gratis, by way of gift, for Christ's sake. The aorist expresses definite, final remission. This tense does not say that God is to remit daily; this is not needed since our prayer is renewed daily. Justification is continuous: "richly and daily forgives all sins to me and all believers," Luther.

The ὡς is not causal (R. 963, 967) ; it does not state the reason why God should treat us likewise but the necessary *requisitium subjecti* (Calov) without which no believer would dare to appear before God to ask for his remission. In view of the remission we think of asking for, our hearts must be cleansed of all resentment against others. The aorist ἀφήκαμεν designates an act that just happened (R. 967), i. e., that we have now remitted although we may not at once have done so when we were sinned against. "To dismiss our debtors" means that we no longer consider them as debtors. Their debts to us are as nothing compared with what we owe God. Our forgiving others is the evidence that God's grace has really wrought faith in us and made us his children.

13) **And bring us not into temptation but deliver us from the evil.** From past sins the prayer turns to possible future sins and dangers. James 1:13 settles the matter as far as the tempter is concerned. James 1:2-4, 12; I Pet. 4:12, 13 settle the point that we are bound to be tempted and tried in this life. I Cor. 10:13 indicates how God answers this sixth petition. "Temptation" is here used in the pregnant sense, referring not only to the act of tempting or of being tempted but to any situation in which, because of our own weakness and Satan's cunning, we should succumb to sin. The realm of attractive things where our lusts may carry us away and the realm of direful things, pain, shame, etc., where fright and cowardice may bring us to fall are included. Our petition, then, is the opposite of false security, temerity, and presumption. We ask our Father to take providential charge of us and thus not to bring us into temptation in the effective sense; hence, to keep us out of some situations because our faith could not endure them (example, Peter) and in other situations so to strengthen us that we may be victorious. Two things stand out in this

petition: the faith which dreads the fall and the assurance that in his own way God will not let us fall.

The adversative ἀλλά does not combine the sixth and the seventh petitions into one. The two are too diverse to form two halves of a whole, one being the negative side, the other the positive. Even such repetition is avoided in this prayer. "But" is due merely to the negative form of the sixth petition. The aorist ῥῦσαι implies effective and thus also complete and final deliverance. The newer commentators as well as Luther and the A. V. regard ἀπὸ τοῦ πονηροῦ as neuter: "from the evil," not as masculine: "from the evil one," the devil. All moral wickedness is referred to, and pain and distress only in so far as they may injure our souls. While the abstract term "temptation" might connote the devil, the sixth petition speaks of providential leadings and thus avoids this connotation and its implication in the seventh petition. Thus the deliverance we ask, while it includes rescue from wickedness throughout our lives, really asks for deliverance from the entire wicked world by a blessed death. In the nature of the case this is the final petition — we need nothing more when it is at last granted. Thus these seven petitions form a complete circle. The seventh links into the first. God's name and revelation bring us the grace by which we shall be delivered from this wicked world. In this respect the Lord's Prayer resembles the Ten Commandments: the fear and love of God is to free us from all coveting and lust.

The textual authority for the genuineness of the doxology with the amen is rather greater than one is led to think by commentators who sometimes refer to II Tim. 4:18 as the source. It seems that the doxology was added when the prayer came to be used in the church and thus was inserted with some variations into copies of Matthew's Gospel. The doxology with its ascription of praise eminently fits the prayer although it is hardly derived from Second Timothy. We have no reason to eliminate it when we now use the prayer.

14) To the prayer Jesus adds an explanation regarding the way in which to pray it aright. **For if you dismiss for men their missteps, your heavenly Father will dismiss them also for you; but if you do not dismiss for men their missteps, neither will your Father dismiss your missteps.** This explanation (γάρ), added to the prayer, does not refer only to the fifth petition, as is supposed, nor only to the last three petitions, but refers to the entire prayer. Luther sees the connection when he says that here Christ throws a band around all Christians. Remember, *we* are to pray, and this *we* is plural, and that means not only for each other but also in union with each other. From the first "our" to the last "us" we pray as brethren. The one thing that makes us the Father's children and thus brethren who can pray as such, is the fact that our sins are forgiven. If they are not forgiven, we are out of the sacred circle, and all our praying is vain. Now one of the plain marks by which we can judge where we stand, is our own forgiveness of others. For, if we forgive, God forgives us, and then we can pray this prayer; if we do not forgive, God does not forgive us, and we are out of the prayer. Of course, all this refers to v. 12, yet not as explaining that petition but as something that is wider and greater.

In τοῖς ἀνθρώποις Jesus includes all men, even non-disciples. The παράπτωμα is any act by which one falls to the side (παρά), off the right path, thus "a misstep," "a blunder." This word is used extensively as a designation of sin. We cannot call it a mild term, as some do; for it indicates only one side of sin, a fatal misstep, just as ἁμαρτία denotes another, a missing of the mark. Jesus uses παραπτώματα for the same reason that he used ὀφειλήματα in v. 12: he selects a term which fits both men's offenses against us and our offenses against God. In v. 14 the contrast is between the persons: "for men," "also for you."

15) But in v. 15 the contrast is between the missteps, hence this term is repeated, and the second dative ὑμῖν is omitted.

16) **Moreover, whenever you are fasting be not as the hypocrites, melancholy; for they make unsightly their faces in order to make a sight to men as fasting. Amen, I say to you, that they have their reward in full.** Fasting often accompanied prayer. In this, too, "the hypocrites" (see v. 2) should be a warning to the disciples for they make themselves look "melancholy" and woebegone. The law required fasting only on the Day of Atonement (Lev. 23:27, etc.). The Jews fasted also on anniversaries of national calamities and in cases of great drought. Here, however, Jesus refers to private fasting such as was practiced by the Pharisees on every Thursday (when Moses ascended Mt. Sinai) and on Monday (when he came down again). Fasting and sorrow went together. It had its place in Judaism not as an ascetic practice but as an accompaniment of prayer when expressing deep sorrow for sin and asking God to turn his penalties away. But the Pharisees practiced private fasting as a means to secure the reputation of great holiness among the people. The wordplay in ἀφανίζουσι and φανῶσι we endeavor to imitate by the translation, "make unsightly," "to make a sight." They disfigured their faces with ashes so that they became "unseen" and thus made "a sight" of them for men. On "amen," etc., see v. 2. Since they were seeking the applause of men alone, when they got it, they had the coin they wanted, paid down at once and in full.

17, 18) **But thou, when fasting, oil thy head and wash thy face in order that thou make no display to men as fasting but to thy Father in secret;**

**and thy Father, who sees in secret, will give thee
what is due.** Jesus offers no new law in regard to
fasting and does not interfere with the voluntary custom of fasting. But all hypocrisy in fasting is abominable to him. He forbids any and all display of this
religious practice before men. "Oil thy head and wash
thy face" is in opposition to making the face unsightly,
hence is not figurative but a concrete way of expressing
the thought for Jewish hearers: "in order that thou
make no display (φανῶσι as in v. 5) to men as fasting."
Do your fasting in secret to the Father who sees in
secret, and when it is done thus in purity of heart, he
will reward you (see the conclusion of v. 6).

19) Hypocrisy deceives others, yet it deceives the
person guilty of it most of all. From the deception of
others Jesus now turns to the deception of self; and
the example he uses is the seeking of perishable treasures instead of the imperishable. The cure for this
folly is the same as the cure for all deception: the disciples must keep the Father before their eyes. Note
how "Father" is thus repeated in v. 26 and 32; even
the reference to what "the Gentiles do" is renewed in
v. 32. This answers the assertion that v. 19-29 are
not original in the Sermon on the Mount, and that the
true place for them is Luke 12:22, etc.

**Do not treasure for yourselves treasures on the
earth where moth and eating make things disappear,
and where thieves break through and steal; but
treasure for yourselves treasures in heaven where
neither moth nor eating makes things disappear, and
where thieves do not break through nor steal; for
where your treasure is, there will be also your heart.**
Jesus might have continued with another ὅταν clause
followed by a negative command (as in v. 2, 5, 16):
"Whenever you treasure treasures do not be like those
who deceive themselves." Since from the hypocrites
(v. 3, 5, 16) he turns to self-deception he varies the

form and starts with the negative command, "do not
treasure." Here the present imperative may mean,
"stop treasuring," forbidding something the disciples
were already doing, R. 853. "To treasure treasure"
(cognate object) makes the thought highly emphatic,
especially by the repetition in v. 20.

Graphically Jesus brings out the self-deception.
To treasure treasures that take wings and disappear,
ἀφανίζειν (as in v. 16), "to make to vanish," "to take
from sight," is to deceive and cheat oneself. You think
you have treasures and in reality you do not have them.
Instead of describing the perishable nature of these
treasures by a relative clause, "which disappear," Jesus
names the place "where" these treasures are stored:
"on the earth, where," etc. This is no place to store
treasures, for here on earth any treasures we may seek
to keep for ourselves (ὑμῖν here has the force of a reflexive) are subject to all manner of destructive forces.
Three of these Jesus names, and the first two are combined. Because σής and βρῶσις are named together, the
latter is thought to have a meaning that is similar to the
former. Yet βρῶσις means simply "eating," either the
act of eating as distinguished from βρῶμα, the food eaten,
or *das Essen,* the food and the act of eating combined.
In order to get a mate to "moth" βρῶσις is taken to mean
"Fresser" and thus "rust" or "corrosion." The Hebrew
is referred to in order to secure such a meaning, but it
would have this meaning in this passage only. The
simple fact is that βρῶσις means "eating" and nothing
else. In v. 25, etc., clothing and food are again mentioned as a treasure about which men worry. So here
"moth and eating" are the two that make clothes and
human food disappear. A moth-eaten garment, however fine, is unsightly and is thrown away, and our
food disappears by being eaten either by ourselves or
by vermin. The only alternative worthy of consideration is that "moth and eating" are a hendiadys, the

moth's eating; but this would make the first ὅπου clause refer only to clothes.

The third way in which earthly treasures of all kinds disappear is by the work of thieves who "dig through and steal." The two "where" clauses are, of course, not exhaustive. Clothes wear out, food spoils, and we lose valuables in other ways than by theft. But these three specifications are sufficient to indicate how foolish it is to lay up treasures on earth. Though we succeed in keeping the moth and the thieves away, all earthly treasures are transient because they are subject to destructive forces.

20) Just as the negative present imperative may mean, "stop treasuring," so the positive may mean, "start treasuring." "In heaven" is the direct opposite of "on the earth." The places mark and characterize the respective treasures. Those we lay up "in heaven" are neither fine garments, rich and abundant bodily food, nor earthly valuables of any kind; hence "where neither moth nor eating," etc. What these heavenly treasures are we are told in v. 33: "the kingdom and his righteousness."

21) The γάρ clause states why the place is so important in the matter of treasures and of treasuring. What really makes a treasure valuable is the affection of the heart. He whose treasures are on earth has his heart anchored to the earth; he whose treasures are in heaven has his heart anchored there. The earth and all its treasures must pass away; what, then, about the heart that loses all its treasures? Heaven alone abides forever; the heart whose treasures are there will never lose them.

22) Since by setting its affection upon something the heart makes a treasure of it, everything depends upon the eye. **The lamp of the body is the eye.** The predicate is placed forward for the sake of emphasis, and the article used with it shows that the predi-

cate is identical with the subject, R. 768. The proposition is self-evident. The eye is the one member of the body which acts as a lamp by which a man sees. The context, however, limits the application to *the treasures* which the earth offers to the body. These seek to captivate the eye and thus to win the heart and the body and their affection. The thought that the eye furnishes the necessary light for all *bodily actions* is quite foreign to the connection.

Everything thus depends on the spiritual quality of the eye. **If, therefore, thy eye be single, the entire body will be full of light; but if thy eye be wicked, thy entire body will be full of darkness.** When he speaks of the eye with reference to *the body,* Jesus has in mind the earthly treasures which captivate the eye. These are *bodily* treasures, such as rich clothing, wealth of food, money, and other valuables. How these treasures will be viewed by the eye in regard to the body will depend upon whether the eye is "single" or "wicked." The fact that ἁπλοῦς and πονηρός are opposite conditions goes without saying. But some think that here these adjectives are part of the figure and thus describe the natural eye. Because πονηρός was used by Plato with reference to a diseased eye (in the expression πονηρία ὀφθαλμῶν), it is assumed that the adjective here means a "diseased" eye, and that ἁπλοῦς, therefore, must mean a sound or "healthy" eye, although not a single instance of this meaning has been found. This disease is thought to have been ophthalmia. But this view loses sight of the connection.

Both ἁπλοῦς and πονηρός are spiritual qualities. The eye that is "single" looks to the one thing alone that is named in v. 33. It sees this and this alone as its true treasure. And thus the entire body will be φωτεινόν, "full of light," never for a moment deceiving itself in regard to bodily and earthly treasures as though these were genuine.

23) But the eye that is πονηρός (a term that is far stronger than κακός), "wicked," godless, idolatrous, looks at earthly treasures in a corresponding way. It places these ahead of God and his kingdom. Hence the entire body is σκοτεινόν, "full of darkness," full of the self-deception which places bodily and earthly treasures ahead of all others and sees them as the only possessions that are worth-while. Jesus, therefore, exclaims: **If, therefore, the light in thee is darkness, how great that darkness!** The two preceding ἐάν clauses speak of expected cases; the εἰ clause contemplates an actual case. This is described by a striking paradox: if *the light* is *darkness*. The idea is not that the eye is blind. In this case the natural eye sees just as perfectly as the natural eye of the true disciple. But instead of being a light to the person concerned it is in reality darkness. Seeing, it does not see what is so plainly to be seen and thus it deceives. The addition of ἐν σοί with a second article makes the phrase equally emphatic with the noun it modifies: "the light, the one in thee," R. 776, etc.; see v. 6. Here we have the commentary on the eye that is not "single" but "wicked." The repetition of τὸ σκότος makes the term decidedly emphatic. The very organ that ought to furnish "light" furnishes nothing but "darkness." In drastic language the light is darkness. "That darkness (the article of previous reference) how great!"

24) Thus far the contrasts are exclusive: either treasures on earth or treasures in heaven. The self-deception thus lies in choosing the one kind in place of the other. Now Jesus turns to the self-deception which would grasp at both. **No one can be a slave to two masters.** The proposition is again self-evident. The emphasis is on δουλεύειν with which, as a matter of course, goes the idea of having a master. The matter is viewed exclusively from the standpoint of the slave; hence οὐδείς is the subject. How two masters would act

in such a case is not touched upon. A slave's person
and his work belong wholly to his master. This
excludes the possibility of devoting himself and his
work to a second master. Two masters or even more
might own a slave jointly and might even share in his
service; but this would make the two one, and this
thought is thus not a contradiction of the proposition.
The thought that underlies this word of Jesus is the
fact that no man is his own master; it is ingrained in
our very nature that our heart, will, and work be governed by another. The only question is who this other
shall be.

With γάρ Jesus elucidates the impossibility from the
standpoint of the slave. Suppose he did try to be a
slave to two masters. The two masters would surely
not consent to such a thing, and the slave would only
make a fool of himself to make such an attempt.
**For either he will hate the one and will love the
other or he will hold to one and will despise the
other;** and thus the slave himself will demonstrate
that he cannot be a slave to two masters. Hate and
love refer to the slave's inner, personal motive, while
hold to and despise refer to the nature of his actions.
After all, the slave makes one of the two his real master.
It is mere self-delusion to think that he is really a slave
to both masters. In ἀγαπᾶν, although the word is here
used with reference to a mere slave, we have the love
that involves a certain intelligence plus the corresponding purpose; more is intended than simple φιλεῖν or
liking. Note the contrast between ἀντί and κατά in the
compound verbs: "to hold oneself face to face with"
— "to think down or against someone," R. 573. Here
ἕτερος is proper, not ἄλλος, because the two masters Jesus
has in mind are opposites, R. 749.

Since all this is so plain and self-evident, Jesus
makes the application: **You cannot be slaves to
God and to mamon** (all the uncials and most of the

minuscules have μαμωνᾷ, with one *m*). The cunning which would try to divide its devotion and its service between these two masters cannot possibly succeed; it only deceives itself. While the derivation of μαμωνᾶς has not been determined (C.-K. 712), its meaning is plain. It is not the name of an idol but a designation for valuable possessions, was probably of Aramaic origin and yet current among the ancient Greek Christians and needed no translation, so that even Luke 16:13 retains the word much as we do today. This word enables Jesus to name the second master as though he, too, were a kind of god, the opposite of the true God to whom alone the disciples should be attached.

25) On the principle thus laid down and elucidated Jesus rests the admonitions and the illustrations which ought to keep us undivided slaves of God and free us from all attachment to mamon. **For this reason I say to you, Stop worrying for your life, what you shall eat or what you shall drink; nor yet for your body, what you shall put on.** The present imperative implies that the disciples had worried, and that this is to cease, R. 853. The word ψυχή refers to the immaterial part of man as this animates the material (the body), hence in this connection the meaning is "your life," and the dative is the ordinary dative of advantage, "for your life," R. 538. The first two questions form a pair. The worry about drink refers to the hot climate of Palestine and to the lack of water in that rugged land. Food and drink we need daily, clothes last longer, hence they are placed last. The subjunctives of deliberation are retained in the indirect discourse which changes the first person (v. 31) to the second, R. 1028, 1044. Compare the treasures indicated in v. 19. Worry about earthly and bodily needs turns the heart from God.

**Is not the life more than the nourishment, and the body more than the thing put on?** This question uses the argument from the greater to the less. Will he who gave us our life and the body fail to give us the little food we need and the few garments we require? The most elementary logic ought to place every disciple above worry.

26) A simple illustration drives this truth home. **Look at the birds of the heaven, that they do not sow nor reap nor gather into storehouses; and your heavenly Father nourishes them. Are you not far superior to them?** Luther pictures the little birds as "live saints" who sing their praises to God without the least worry and are fed by him day by day. They are even without our advantages, for we can sow, reap, and store up supplies whereas they live from hand to mouth. Yet see how God feeds them! What old fools are we who cannot learn from them! The argument is now reversed, from the less to the greater. The verb διαφέρω, literally "to bear apart," means "to differ" (R. 581), i. e., advantageously. We are "by far" (μᾶλλον) different, i. e., superior to them. Will God nourish birds and forget his own children? Here again the keyword "your heavenly Father" appears. The cure for all hypocrisy (v. 2-18) and for all self-deception is this that we keep our eyes upon this Father. Though he made the birds and feeds them, he is in the relation of a "Father" only to us who are his children in Christ Jesus. To us he is far more than he is to the birds.

27) The question about the length of life completes the thought connected with the birds and their food. **Moreover, who of you, by worrying, is able to add to his lifetime a single half yard?** While ἡλικία is used with reference to stature, it is also used with reference to length of life. Here we have no

reason to think of stature, which produces a ridiculous thought. Who except a dwarf or a child would
want to be a half yard taller? Nor does πῆχυς, the
length of a forearm, about 18 inches, compel us to
think of bodily height. Ps. 39:5 speaks of the length
of life as "a handbreadth," a few inches. Other examples have been found where linear measures are
used when speaking of time. Worry does not lengthen
life, it usually shortens life. The participle indicates
means: "by worryng," R. 1128.

28) From food Jesus turns to dress and uses another example from nature. **And concerning something to put on** (ἔνδυμα, as in v. 25), **why are you
worrying?** when it is equally useless, foolish, and
hurtful? **Consider well the lilies of the field, how
they grow. They do not toil nor do they spin. Yet
I say to you, that even Solomon in all his glory did
not robe himself like one of these.** The aorist imperative implies actual learning, and κατά makes the
verb perfective: "learn well or thoroughly" the lilies.
As "the birds of the heaven" in v. 26 are those that fly
freely, so "the lilies of the field" are those that grow
wild, without human care. The point to be noted
regarding them is "how they grow." Without labor
of any kind and without spinning a thread they come
to wear garments so exquisite that Jesus exclaims:

29) "I tell you" their garment exceeds all that
Solomon at the height of his royal glory ever wore,
περιεβάλετο, "threw around himself" (middle, R. 807)
in the way of a regal robe. And he certainly was
Israel's most magnificent king. "Like one of these"
bids us pause and marvel at even one of the lovely
flowers. Jesus spoke these words in the open, which
makes the reference to the birds and the lilies the more
effective. Just what flower κρίνον designates no one
really knows. Some have thought of the iris, others of
more than one variety of flower.

30) Again the application employs the argument from the less to the greater and with overwhelming effect. **But if the grass of the field which today exists and tomorrow is thrown into an oven God thus enrobes, how much more not you, men of little faith!** The flowers that Jesus refers to have a grasslike foliage and are thus called χόρτος as are all plants of this type. Some think that actual grass is referred to, the lilies growing in the grassy field and thus decorating the grass. But this view is shut out by the verb ἀμφιέννυσι, "to clothe round about," which refers to the flowers and not to ordinary grass. Both the designation "grass" for the little lily plants and the description of their brief life and beauty heighten the contrast with the disciples who are destined for eternal life. In a country where fuel was scarce dried grass and stalks of all kinds were used to heat ovens for baking. Combined with the appeal from the less to the greater is a second appeal that is just the reverse, from the greater to the less. If God enrobes the lowly and ephemeral lilies so *gorgeously,* he surely will give *common* garments to his far higher creatures. In v. 26 "your Father" rested the appeal on the special relation of children to their heavenly Parent. Now Jesus adds that already as "God," our Creator, under whose benign providence all his children live, he will provide us with the needful clothing.

The apodosis needs no verb and is thus the more incisive: "how much more not you!" The negative οὐ implies an affirmative reply. Ὀλιγόπιστοι is a distinctive New Testament term. It is found four times in Matthew, once in Luke: "men of little trust." This address, placed effectively at the end, shows that Jesus is still speaking of the disciples although he uses "God" and not "your Father." While the term admits the trust of the disciples it reproves the littleness of this trust as this is evidenced by the worry that still persists. Our trust ought to shut out every bit of worry.

31) Hence (οὖν) the admonition: **Do not, therefore, worry, saying, What shall we eat? or, What shall we drink? or, With what shall we enrobe ourselves?** In v. 25 the present imperative forbids the worrying already begun: "stop worrying"; now the aorist follows (a subjunctive because negative commands use this mode in the aorist) forbidding all worrying as such: "do not worry at all." The order is quite peremptory because it is an aorist. In the three questions the subjunctives are deliberative, all in direct discourse, and all disjunctively parallel; in v. 25 they are in indirect discourse, and the first two are drawn together. No question such as these three — and many more might be added — is ever to worry our hearts.

32) The two γάρ add two connected reasons. **For all these things the Gentiles seek after; for your heavenly Father knows that you have need of these things all.** To the first negative reason the second positive reason is added as its counterpart. In v. 7 the ἐθνικοί are the Gentiles as pagan individuals; here τὰ ἔθνη are all the pagan nations. Worry is like heathen unbelief. The pagan world knows nothing about God who is "our Father" (6:9) in Christ Jesus. Their moral life is according. In v. 7 Jesus has pointed to Gentile men as a horrible example. Do the disciples want to descend to this abominable level? Since Jesus is speaking to Jews, this reference to the Gentiles is highly effective. Note that in πάντα ταῦτα, "*all* these things," and then in τούτων ἁπάντων, "*these* things all," the first words have the emphasis, R. 705. Pagan people imagine that they themselves must provide for their needs, hence their seeking is bent upon (ἐπί in the verb) all these things.

The disciples live in a higher world, they have a Father in heaven. And "he knows that you have need

of these things all." Compare v. 8: "even before you
ask him." Being, indeed, "your Father," of a heavenly
character, almighty and full of love especially for his
children, he will act accordingly. Leave all your worries to him.

33) The disciples, too, will seek; but they will
seek something that is far beyond the thought of the
heathen world. **But be seeking first the kingdom
and the righteousness that are his, and these things
all will be added unto you.** This supreme seeking,
described as hunger and thirst in 5:6, is the distinctive
mark of all true disciples. We may translate the present imperative, "go on seeking." The desire for the
kingdom and the righteousness is constantly satisfied,
for what we seek is ours by grace; and yet the seeking
is always to continue, for the object of our desire can
be ever more fully attained. This seeking is, of course,
in no sense synergistic but the desire of the regenerate
and believing heart to enter ever more fully into union
with God. Grace kindles the desire and keeps it ever
active in this life.

On "the kingdom" compare 5:3; also 3:2 and 6:10;
on "the righteousness," 5:6. Here the two are combined, for αὐτοῦ belongs to both. To seek "his kingdom"
is to desire more and more participation in the rule of
the Father's grace in Christ, enjoying more and more
the blessings (5:3, etc.) of that rule of grace which
eventually becomes a rule of glory. Only the righteous
participate in the kingdom, hence all seeking of the
kingdom is at the same time a seeking after "his righteousness," that which he has prepared for us in Christ,
bestows upon us by faith, and ever acknowledges as
righteousness in his judgment. "To seek" means on
our part "to seek to obtain and enjoy." The pronoun
"his" makes the treasures sought stand out as objective; they are God's, as C.-K. 317 states: God's royal
rule and his righteousness, i. e., "that he himself in his

absolute majesty receive his rights." For by pronouncing us righteous and thereby making us partakers of his kingdom God is vindicated both in his royal rule, as the "only Potentate, the King of kings, and Lord of lords" (I Tim. 6:15)), and in his own perfect righteousness.

The adverb πρῶτον does not imply that we may make earthly treasures the object of our seeking as long as we put them in second place. This would contradict all that Jesus has said. In the very next clause he tells us that "these things all shall be added unto us," thrown in, as it were, for good measure. On the other hand, "first" or "in the first place" does not imply that he who seeks the kingdom first will seek nothing more. After the second petition of the Lord's Prayer comes the fourth. The promises given to prayer are entirely general, covering every need. He who seeks the kingdom, etc., first will seek all other things from the Father in the right way, by humble and submissive prayer, without worry, and without a false estimate of these other things. Thus Christ's promise will be fulfilled: "these all" will be supplied to you, I Kings 3:11, etc.; I Tim. 4:8.

34) In conclusion the command of v. 31 is repeated but with a new and final modification. **Do not, therefore, worry into the morrow, for the morrow will worry for itself. Sufficient for the day is the trouble thereof.** We translate, "into the morrow," for εἰς indicates either the limit (as in this case) or the duration ("until"), R. 594. We are not to go from today into tomorrow with worry. "For the morrow" in the sense of "about tomorrow" would require a genitive (as in the last clause) or an accusative or a different preposition. The idea that we may worry about today but not about tomorrow is shut out. Of course, ἡ αὔριον (supply ἡμέρα) refers to any morrow, thus reaching into the indefinite future.

The morrow "will worry for itself" is a striking personification which bids us throw all our worries onto the morrow and thus go on without worry day after day. If the morrow is to do the worrying, we are free; and as the morrow is always in the future and just beyond us, our worries are also always to be beyond our reach. The idea is not, "Let God worry!" for he never worries. Nor, "Wait until the morrow comes and then worry!" for the morrow always moves on, and the idea that it becomes today is far from the thought of this striking statement. Nor can we change the meaning of μεριμνήσει into something good such as, "will take care of itself"; for the verb runs through this entire section and should not be given a new and even opposite meaning in this final statement. No; the morrow is never here, it does not exist today. If, then, the morrow is to do the worrying, no worrying will ever be done. And that is what Jesus desires.

Why not be satisfied with today as though it did not have enough κακία, and we had to go into the future to borrow more? Here κακία cannot mean moral evil but refers to the natural trouble, pain, and burdens incident to our present life; it is well translated by Luther with *Plage*, "plague." Each day has its own sufficient share of "trouble,' ἀρκετόν, neuter; yet this is not a breach in gender with regard to the feminine κακία, R. 411.

# CHAPTER VII

**Christ's Sermon on the Mount.    Part III.**
**Chapter 7**

*The Children of the Kingdom in the Righteousness
that Is theirs.*
*The Judgment is their warning, and thus they
attain the Kingdom above.*

The development by personal admonitions rests on
the background of the judgment.

1)    The note of the judgment is struck clearly and
strongly in the very first words and thus marks a new
part of the sermon.    **Do not be judging in order that
you may not be judged.**    The very fact of having a
righteousness that is far better than that of the scribes
and Pharisees might lead the disciples into the vicious
fault of the scribes and Pharisees who set themselves
up as judges over all others, gloried in their own false
holiness, and despised all others (John 7:49).    Jesus
is not contradicting John 7:24; I Cor. 5:12; I John
4:1; or the disciplinary judging of the church, 18:17,
18; John 20:23.    What he forbids is the self-righteous,
hypocritical judging which is false and calls down
God's judgment on itself.    The present imperative μὴ
κρίνετε may mean to resist a course of action or to desist
from such a course, R. 890; here it most likely has the
former force.    The punctiliar aorist κριθῆτε refers to
God's final judgment; if the judgment of men were
referred to, the durative present subjunctive would have
been used.    Both verbs are neutral, "to judge" irrespective of the verdict rendered.    Luke 6:37 adds the
parallel regarding adverse judging.    The Pharisees

acquitted each other and condemned the rest; they were wrong in both their verdicts.

2) Jesus substantiates his command by establishing its fairness and its justice. **For with what judgment you judge you shall be judged; and with what measure you measure it shall be measured to you.** First two duratives to express our practice of judging and measuring, then two punctiliars (aorists) to state God's reciprocations. Again both the verbs and their cognate objects are neutral; but neutral only with regard to the false judging and measuring whether this acquits or condemns. God would be unjust if he judged these false judges in any other way (Luke 19:22). The justice of God's application of the false standard of these judges to themselves is made clearer by the parallel statement regarding the measure with which they measure. That very measure shows their falseness; hence by that very measure God justly condemns them as being false.

3) The whole matter is now illustrated in a personal and most striking way. Jesus addresses the false judge. **Now, why dost thou see the sliver in the eye of thy brother but the beam in thine own eye thou dost not perceive? or how sayest thou to thy brother, Hold, I will take the sliver out of thine eye; and, lo, the beam in thine own eye! Hypocrite, first take the beam out of thine own eye and then shalt thou see clearly to take out the sliver out of thy brother's eye.** In real life the suppositions here used are frankly impossible. Nobody could possibly have a piece of timber such as a plank or a beam in his eye. The same is true regarding a κάρφος, which is more than a "mote" or tiny speck; it is a dried twig or a straw. Who could endure that for a moment? The supposition is intended to be ridiculous: a man with a plank in his own eye seeing a splinter in his brother's eye and attempting to draw it out. In the interpretation of

this parabolic language the eye is often overlooked.
The splinter is thought to be some small moral fault,
and the beam a fault correspondingly greater. But
why are splinter and beam placed in the eyes? why not
in other parts of the body? Jesus is not speaking of
faults or sins in general, one being tiny, the other immense, but of moral perception which is slightly wrong
in the one man, totally wrong in the other. He who is
devoid of all truly moral judgment pretends to aid
another who is slightly wrong in his judgment. The
very idea is farcical — yet men act thus.

4) Jesus first scored the pretence of the eye with
the beam in it seeing the eye with the splinter in it;
he next scores the pretence of the eye with the beam
in it aiding the eye with the splinter in it. This preposterous idea is carried to its climax. We may say
that the man with the beam in his eye will knock out
both of the eyes of the other man who has a splinter in
his eye. A grand eye specialist he would be! Ἄφες
(always singular) is a mere adjunct to the volitive subjunctive ἐκβάλω, R. 430, 931: "hold, I will take out"
(compare 3:15). "And, lo," etc., is an exclamation,
hence there is no copula.

5) In the vocative, "Hypocrite!" the Lord's indignation flares out; on the term see 5:16; 6:2, 5, 16. The
aorist ἔκβαλε is peremptory. Again the thought is not
that one should first correct his own grave faults before
he tries to correct his brother's minor faults, but that
one should clear his own eyes and judgment before he
tries to lend aid to another in making some correction
in his judgment. The scribes and Pharisees were eye
doctors who had beams in their own eyes of which they
were not even aware. What they did to the people we
can imagine. The disciples are not to trust in their
own righteousness and thereby make of it a beam for
their eye and then judge others in blind folly.

6) Those who think that chapter seven consists of "miscellaneous subjects" are relieved of finding a connection between v. 5 and 6 and also between the following paragraphs. But we do not believe that in the last third of his great sermon Jesus merely stated a number of disconnected thoughts. The command not to judge others lest we be judged has its obvious limits. This command does not extend to dogs and to swine. They are to be adjudged and treated as such, and we who are to do this judging have nothing to fear from the divine Judge. **Give not the holy thing to the dogs, nor throw your pearls in front of the swine lest, perhaps, they trample them under their feet and, having turned, rend you.** To the Jew dogs and hogs represent the height of uncleanness. In the Orient the dogs acted as scavengers, and no Jew was allowed to possess swine. The parallelism of the statement shows that one type of men is referred to, not two. These cannot be the Gentiles as such although the Jews called them dogs. Nor can this giving to the dogs refer to the preaching of the gospel to the Gentiles or to publicans and sinners; for this Jesus himself did and commands his disciples to do. Dogs and swine are those who, after the gospel has been duly preached to them, retain their vicious, filthy nature. All such the disciples are, indeed, to judge and account as what they are.

"The holy thing" and "your pearls" are also identical, being first viewed as a unit and then as made up of different parts. Jesus has in mind the holy truth of the gospel and the pure and precious doctrines of which this gospel is composed. "To give" and "to throw before" means to expose the gospel and its precious truths to the vicious and vile treatment of such men. The μήποτε clause refers only to the action of the swine which would trample the pure and precious **pearls** in the mud and then in rage might even **turn**

upon the disciples to rend them for offering nothing
that suits swinish taste.  The best commentary is found
in Paul's action in Acts 13:45, 46; 18:6; and in the
statements in Jude 10-13; I Pet. 4:4; Rom. 16:17, 18;
Phil. 3:18, 19; I Tim. 6:5.

7) Read superficially, this section regarding
prayer seems to belong after 6:15.  Others conclude
that its true place and connection are found in Luke
11:9-13.  But why should Matthew patch together het-
erogeneous sections from various discourses of Jesus
and present them as one of the great parts of the Sermon on the Mount?  Those who feel that these words
regarding prayer belong in this place in the sermon
often do not state the reason for their view.  Others
think that we are to pray for wisdom to carry out the
command given in v. 6, or for strength to live righteously in general, or that we are at least to pray for
dogs and for swine.  These verses are to be connected
with v. 1-5, where, in bidding us not to judge others,
Jesus bids us to judge ourselves (the beam in thine own
eye).  As not to judge others refers only to the splinter
and the beam not to the dogs and the swine, so the implied admonition to judge ourselves entails no false
self-criticism, no doubt or mistrust of our true relation
to God.  While we must, indeed, realize that we are evil
because of our sinful nature, God has, nevertheless,
made us his children and by his grace is ready to bestow
upon us all that our poor souls need.  Such is his judgment of us now, and such it ever will be.

**Ask, and it shall be given to you; seek, and you
shall find; knock, and it shall be opened unto you.**
The imperatives are present tenses, hence iterative:
"go on again and again asking, seeking, knocking."
The use of three verbs indicates intensity; and to seek
is more fervent than just to ask, and to knock is still
more fervent.  We ask for what we need; we seek what
we earnestly desire; we knock when our desire becomes

importunity. Each of these injunctions carries with it
a direct and an unequivocal promise which shows how
God regards us. Faulty though we are, he is eager to
bestow his "good gifts" upon us (v. 11), and this we
are never to forget when judging ourselves. The verb
αἰτεῖν is used with reference to humble asking, with reference to petition on the part of an inferior when
speaking to a superior, and is thus used only with reference to us and never with reference to Christ. "It
shall be given" matches "to ask," and this giving always
implies grace. "To seek" means to seek from God, and
"you shall find" means that you shall never seek in vain
but shall obtain the good gift you desire. "To knock"
means to seek entrance into the heavenly house of God;
and Jesus assures us of admittance.

8) So necessary does Jesus deem these promises
that he not only repeats but also individualizes them.
**For everyone asking receives; and the one seeking
finds; and to the one knocking it shall be opened.**
God makes no exceptions whatever; "everyone" is a
strong incentive. The promises of both verses are
general and must be so although Jesus here applies
them to our spiritual needs.

9) The individualization in v. 8 leads over into an
illustration, which then leads to the application Jesus
has in mind. **Or,** if this seems to you to be saying
too much, **what man is there of you whom his son
asks for bread, will he hand over a stone to him?
Or he asks also a fish, will he hand over a snake to
him?** Ἄρτον is "bread," A. V., not "loaf," R. V.
The bread was baked in flat cakes, a piece of which
might well resemble a flat stone. No human father
would treat his son so, handing over a useless stone as
though it were bread. The interrogative particle μή
expects a negative answer: "he will certainly not hand
over a stone to him." Even among men sonship and
fatherhood preclude such a thing.

10) The second "or" merely repeats the first; and καί indicates that the son may ask for something to be eaten along with the bread, which in the neighborhood of the Sea of Galilee would most likely be a fish (John 6:9). "He asks also a fish" is an independent statement and not an anacoluthon (R. 1023). The question that follows is also independent, μή again expecting a negative answer. "A snake" may resemble a fish but is unfit to eat. The idea of harmfulness is not implied, for the snake would not be alive, and if it were it would strike the father's hand even before it struck the son's. The point of this double illustration is the deception practiced by the father, reducing his fatherhood and thus the sonship of his child to an illusion.

11) **If, therefore, you, although you are wicked, know to give good gifts to your children, how much more will your Father in the heavens give good things to those asking him?** This argument from the less to the greater is unanswerable. As earthly fathers prove themselves fathers by giving "good gifts" to their children, so "your Father" proves to you that he is, indeed, your Father, and you are, indeed, his children, by giving to you, in answer to your asking, "good things," ἀγαθά, those that are beneficial to you as children. When Jesus used this illustration in another connection (Luke 11:13) he named the sum and the source of all "good" in the apodosis, namely "the Holy Spirit." With the concessive πονηροὶ ὄντες Jesus humbles the disciples. This is the judgment they must learn to pronounce upon themselves. It will keep them from self-righteously judging others. But when judging themselves thus, their need of the Holy Spirit and of his good gifts, and the assured promises of their Father in filling this need, should keep them in the consciousness of their childhood. By every good, spiritual gift the Father acknowledges them as his dear children (τέκνα), born anew by his grace.

12) **All things, therefore, whatever you would that men do to you, thus you also do to them; for this is the Law and the Prophets.** We cannot see the difficulties which are found in οὖν, "therefore," or "accordingly." Some would refer this connective to all the commands concerning righteousness given in the sermon; some go back to the commands about judging. We are told that there is no connection with the statement about prayer. Cancellation is advocated. But why not let οὖν make the Golden Rule rest on this true judgment that we, although by nature wicked, are yet by grace God's children, acknowledged as such by our Father who bids us ask the good things we need and grants them to us without fail? The consequence (οὖν) of this must be that, instead of judging others falsely, we shall do to them what we would that they should do to us. We must guard against inserting a limitation into πάντα κτλ.; ὅσα is qualitative with regard to the kind of things, R. 732, and the ἵνα clause is the object of θέλητε, while "men" is entirely general.

Rabbi Hillel's dictum is no more than the voice of selfishness: "What is hateful to thyself do not to thy neighbor; for this is the whole law, and all else is its exposition"; this is the egoism which withholds injury lest it suffer injury in return. Jesus turns this about: "what we would like to have men to do to us, whether they do that to us or not, we are to keep doing (ποιεῖτε, durative) to them." And we must note that Jesus addresses this injunction to his disciples whom he has just enjoined to realize that they are the Father's children, receiving his fatherly gifts in answer to childlike prayer. The οὖν is, therefore, highly necessary: first, to be children, proving it by faith and prayer; then, to act as such children in contact with men generally. This, of course, is the second table of the law (love to man); yet we have no reason to ask why Jesus does not also add the first table. He has already added it by all that he has said about "your Father" and about prayer.

That is why he can add: "This is the Law and the Prophets," οὗτος, masculine, assimilated in gender to the predicate ὁ νόμος, R. 704. "The Law and the Prophets" (see 5:17) = the teaching of the Old Testament which Jesus merely restates. Those who separate the Golden Rule from the first table and from our relation to God as our Father by faith in Christ Jesus ignore the Law and the Prophets when they claim that love to our neighbor is enough to admit us to heaven. Only as the second table, resting on the first, is it true of the second that "this is the Law and the Prophets." Read I John 3:14-22. Among the good gifts for which the Father's children pray daily is the power to overcome the promptings of their flesh so that by grace for Christ's sake they may love their neighbor (ἀγαπᾶν) with a truly spiritual love and thus heap upon him all the kindness they themselves would like to receive. Christ's Golden Rule has appealed to many, yet only true believers have understood it and have found the power to translate it into life in an ever-increasing degree.

13) This section (v. 13-23) is not a part of the conclusion but a further and more fundamental elaboration of the judgment that is applied to us and that we must apply to ourselves. First, two negatives show who we are (we will not judge, etc., yet will also not give what is holy to dogs, etc.); next, two positives (we will ask with trust and will do unto others, etc.); and now we have a positive plus a negative (we will enter the narrow portal and will keep away from false guides). **Enter in through the narrow portal, because wide is the portal and broad the passage that leads to the destruction, and many are those entering in through it. How narrow the portal and straitened the passage that leads unto the life, and few are**

**those finding it!** Let us judge ourselves according
to the gate and the way we enter it. We have a choice
between only two. A πύλη is an entrance portal, and
the ὁδός is the passageway to which it admits. Both
belong to a building and lead to the court from which
the rooms are reached. As he did in v. 1, 6, 7, Jesus
again begins with an imperative, this time, as in v. 6,
an aorist because of the nature of the act; to step into
a portal takes but a moment. The emphasis, however,
is not on the verb, for the contrast is not between entering or remaining outside. All enter one or the other
portal. The emphasis is on "the narrow portal." And
thus, although Jesus addresses the disciples, he may
still use the aorist. To his call, "Enter in!" their response will be, "Lord, we did!" Moreover, the imagery
is not that of a multitude still standing before two
portals but that of two classes, both of which have
entered the one or the other portal.

Jesus does not say what makes the one portal narrow and the other wide. Of course, both passageways
are like their portals. He states only to what they
lead and leaves it to us to deduce why the one is necessarily narrow, and the other most naturally broad.
Contrition, faith, and a Christian life are like a narrow
portal and passage. We cannot ride into it with our
sins, self-righteousness, false notions, vices, and follies.
We could not even get them through the portal. The
broad portal and the spacious passage are different.
There we may cart in anything we please. More than
abundant room invites us to do so. But this portal
and this passage "lead to the destruction," εἰς τὴν ἀπώ-
λειαν, "to utter, final ruination." In the New Testament this negative term refers to the state after death
and the complete loss of the true, heavenly life (ζωή),
C.-K. 789. The term never means annihilation, neither
does any synonymous term nor any description of what
it represents.

Ὅτι states that the reason why we should enter in through the narrow portal is that the other portal and passage are so broad and inviting, they that lead to destruction. And the sad thing is that so many look only at the broad, easy entrance, the spacious passage, and not to what they lead to. And thus they enter. The singular δι'αὐτῆς refers to ἡ πύλη as οἱ εἰσερχόμενοι plainly indicates; hence we need not cancel ἡ πύλη as some texts do.

14) Most of the uncials and many other texts read τί not ὅτι. The latter would add a second reason for entering the narrow portal. The former converts this verse into an exclamation: "How narrow the portal," etc. The thought is that, no matter how narrow and straitened, this is the portal and the passage that lead "unto the ζωή or life." As the opposite of "destruction" "the life" here means the blessed existence in heaven. Of course, this "life" begins here in regeneration, but in the present imagery Jesus contemplates the final destinations at which men arrive by means of two portals and two passageways.

Again we have a statement that is loosely attached with καί: "and few are they finding it," αὐτήν, this portal. The voice is sad that speaks these words. Its very sadness increases the warning. The wide portal need not be found. It stands wide open in the sight of all men and is easily drifted into. The narrow portal, however, is found. It is like making an astonishing discovery. The fact that such a portal exists men would never even dream, to say nothing of their discovering where this portal opens. But suddenly, here it is before their eyes. This finding is not accomplished by any search of ours; it is wholly by the grace of him who places this portal before us. Our finding it is like the double finding mentioned in 13:44-46; also like the finding recorded in John 1:41-45. The participle οἱ εὑρίσκοντες includes a perception of what is thus found, namely that this portal leads to the life. Those who find thus enter. God's grace draws them (John 6:44) by its attracting power. The title page of Calvin's *Institutes*, published in 1561, bears a picture of the two portals: one narrow with a thornbush in the entrance and a crown over the top; the other broad with a flower in the entrance and flames flaring over the top.

15) A natural transition leads from the portals to the false guides who propose to direct us. The call to enter the narrow portal is at once a warning against entering the wide portal. This warning is expanded, when Jesus now adds: **Beware of false prophets, such as come to you in garments of sheep, but within they are rapacious wolves.** We have the present imperative προσέχετε (supply τὸν νοῦν, R. 477) with ἀπό which means literally: "keep holding your mind from," i. e., "beware of," "watch out for." The ψευδοπροφῆται, "pseudo-prophets," are sham prophets who pretend to be true prophets of God but are not. The term is formed like "pseudo-Christs," 24:24; "pseudo-apostles," II Cor. 11:13; "pseudo-teachers," II Pet. 2:1. Some make a difference between these "pseudo-prophets" and others who are "pseudo-teachers." But the only difference is that prophets announce the divine will while teachers expound and apply it. Moreover, in the New Testament we find mention of two kinds of prophets: such as received direct revelations from God, Agabus, Acts 11:28; 21:10, Philip's daughters, Acts 21:9, and especially all the apostles; and all those Christians who acquired and possessed the general gift of prophecy of which Paul speaks at length in I Cor. 14 (see the author's commentary). False prophets of both types are here referred to, but, of course, the latter would appear in far greater numbers. All announce, "This is what God says!" the former add falsely, "He himself told us!" the latter, "The Scriptures say so!"

Let us also note that prophesying in the latter sense
always accompanies teaching, i. e., explaining the details of the Word.

In οἵτινες the causal idea is combined with the relative: "Beware of false prophets *since* they are *such
as*," etc. To be sure, when wolves pretend to be sheep,
we ought to beware. These prophets "come to you,"
make it their special business to do so, but they only
*come*, they are never *sent* by God. Much has been
written on the phrase "in garments of sheep" but this
seems to be the sense: these false prophets, who in
reality are fierce wolves, pretend to be gentle, harmless
sheep. The supposition that the old Jewish prophets
wore sheep pelts as garments (Heb. 11:37) cannot be
substantiated, nor that as a rule shepherds wore such
pelts. The Baptist had a burnoose made of camel's
hair. The view that "sheep" refers to Christ's flock is
without support in the context. The ἐνδύματα προβάτων
are not pelts (these would be μηλωταί) but all that sheep
have on and thus *the appearance* of sheep. For the
phrase is in contrast with the *reality*: "but within
(ἔσωθεν, R. 548) they are rapacious wolves," ἅρπαγες
emphatically at the end. "Within" refers to their real
nature which gives the lie to their appearance. They
are "wolves" that are akin to the wolf mentioned in
John 10:12, brothers to the grievous wolves of Acts
20:29, described and warned against in Rom. 16:18;
Eph. 5:6; Col. 2:4; etc. Some think that Jesus had
especially the scribes and Pharisees in mind and regard
that as the historical interpretation; but note what
Jesus himself adds in v. 21, etc. He is evidently thinking of the future and of all the false prophets that will
try to mislead the disciples.

To say regarding any matter, "Thus saith the
Lord!" when he did not say thus; or to say, "God did
*not* say so!" when he did, is to utter false prophecy.
Some prophets are completely false, others are false in

part only, but, alas, false. The innocent appearance of
all false prophets is a necessity for them; if they
revealed what they really were, all true disciples would
flee from them. The innocent appearance of their persons and their prophecy induces many to receive what
they offer; but the real nature of what they are in their
prophesying always becomes evident sooner or later.
Thus the clothing of sheep used by these wolves is conduct and preachment that are ostensibly in harmony
with God and with his Word but in reality in conflict
with both. This deviation from the divine Word makes
all false prophets wolves whose nature it is to rend, tear,
and kill, ἅρπαξ, from ἁρπάζω, to seize, snatch at, i. e., in
this case with cruel fangs. Drastically Jesus pictures
the destructive effect of all false preaching: it rends
and tears the spiritual life like the fangs of a wolf. In
spite of this drastic language men persist in considering deviations from the true prophecy (the Word of
God as it really is) as being quite harmless.

16) **From their fruits you shall recognize them.
Do people gather ripe grapes from briars, or figs
from thistles?** Note both the positive future tense
and the compound verb ἐπιγνώσεσθε, "you shall recognize
them" as what they actually are. R. 576 calls ἀπό the
source, which agrees with ἐκ in Luke 6:44. Commentators are divided in their opinions as to what Jesus
means by "the fruits" of the false prophets. Some say,
their doctrines; others, their works; still others, doctrines and works combined. The answer is found in
Isa. 8:20; I John 4:1; Heb. 13:9; II John 9, 11; Matt.
15:9; Titus 1:9-12: the fruits of the prophet are undoubtedly the doctrines he teaches. The fact that his
own personal works are not the criterion by which we
can without fail judge him is established by 24:24
("great signs and wonders"); Deut. 13:1-3 (to the
same effect); Matt. 23:1-3 (we are to observe what
the scribes and Pharisees bid us do, not what they

themselves do). True prophets often manifest sins
and faults in their lives; false prophets often have the
appearance of holiness as a part of their sheep's clothing.   God alone is able to judge men's hearts and to
distinguish hypocritical from genuine works. A prophet's sincerity is indecisive, many are self-deceived; but
their doctrines are just as pernicious as those of conscious deceivers.   The argument that the thing to be
judged (doctrine) cannot be the criterion by which it
is judged (again doctrine) is untenable. Every prophet
appeals to the Word, the Scriptures.   That is what
makes him a prophet.   Those who reject the Word are
outside of the church.   Thus even the rankest heresies
appeal to us to regard them as being the Word.   Every
prophet, therefore, is judged as to his doctrines by the
Word to which he himself is constrained to appeal.
To object that common Christians are too ignorant to
apply this criterion is unwarranted; for the gift to
discern the spirits is ample in the church and takes care
of babes and all immature Christians.

The figure found in "fruits" is extended by the double question after the intensifying interrogative particle μήτι.   The subject of the plural συλλέγουσιν is indefinite: "Certainly, people do not gather," etc.   A touch
of humor lights up the imagery: people going out to a
briar patch to gather grapes (σταφυλή, the ripe grapes
that make up a cluster; βότρυς is the cluster itself), or to
a thistle patch to gather figs!   Grapes and figs picture
true spiritual food which grows on the Word alone not
on the briars and the thistle stalks of man's own wisdom.   Every man who presents false doctrines is to
that extent a briar and a thistle.

17) **Thus every good tree produces excellent
fruits, but every worthless tree produces wicked
fruits.   A good tree cannot produce wicked fruits,
nor a worthless tree produce excellent fruits.**   The
figure now deals with trees only and first presents the

undeniable fact and then the undeniable impossibility. Moreover, the double statement is entirely general, being applicable to all men who are either good trees or worthless trees. Of course, in the present connection Jesus has in mind the false prophets. They, however, are judged, not according to some exceptional rule pertaining to them only, but according to the universal rule which applies to all. Thus also, without expressly saying so, all who follow false prophets and their false doctrines may include themselves.

The stress is on the four adjectives, and these are of such a nature as to make the figure of the trees and their fruits entirely transparent. This is especially true regarding the second kind of tree. It, too, produces fruit, perhaps in great abundance (v. 22). Hence in this connection σαπρόν does not mean "rotten" or "diseased." B.-P. rightly asks: "Do rotten (*faule*) fish enter a net? do rotten trees bear fruit at all?" The contrast is not drawn between conditions but between kinds; not between sound and healthy trees and others rotting and decayed, but between trees of excellent variety and trees of worthless variety. Both kinds may look grand and fine merely as trees, but the fruit they produce (ποιεῖν, make) invariably reveals what they are worth. When Jesus describes the fruit as being either καλός or πονηρός he really touches the realities which underlie the figure, for these are the adjectives which are used regarding man's works when they come into judgment before God.

18) It is actually impossible for a tree to bear fruit that is contrary to its constitution and nature. Jesus adds this in order to assure us the more in regard to our ability to judge men in general and false prophets in particular.

19) Moreover, the kind of tree which its fruit proves it to be is vital for the fate of the tree. **Every tree not producing excellent fruit is cut down and is**

**thrown into the fire.** That is what men do, and God
does the same: the tree that produces excellent fruit is
kept, the one that has no excellent fruit is consigned to
the fire. Here we see that Jesus views all that he says
about false prophets, including also their followers (as
indicated in the general statements about trees) in the
light of the final judgment. "Not producing excellent
fruit" defines "wicked fruits"; but in doing so it does
more: it states positively that only one kind of fruit
avails in the judgment. Hence we now also have the
collective singular καρπόν instead of the distributive
plural. The fate that awaits the false prophets makes
effective the warning against them lest by following
them and their doctrine we, too, invite such a fate upon
ourselves. Jesus describes only the two opposites and
says nothing about the prophet whose doctrine is
vicious only in part. What must be said about his fate
is found in I Cor. 3:12-15.

20) **Therefore, from their fruits you shall recognize them.** What is stated only as a fact in v. 16
is here restated as the conclusion to be drawn from the
explanations that were added, ἄραγε being illative (R.
1190), and γε adding emphasis. This restatement emphasizes the fact that we are, indeed, to recognize all
false prophets as just what they are. As we are able
to tell whether a tree is good and worth keeping or bad
and fit only for firewood, so we are able to detect every
false prophet and to keep away from him.

21) The reference to the judgment is now fully
expanded. **Not everyone saying to me, Lord, Lord!
shall go into the kingdom of the heavens but the one
doing the will of my Father in the heavens.** The
figure of the trees and their fruits is now elucidated by
the reality. Therefore also the statement is general,
applying to all who would enter the kingdom, taking
up v. 17-19. "Not everyone saying to me, 'Lord, Lord!'"
(R. 752) means that some who address Jesus thus will,

indeed, enter the kingdom, some but not all. Mere
prodigality in the use of such an address is not a ticket
of admission. The two durative present participles
λέγων and ποιῶν describe customary actions. "Saying,
'Lord, Lord!' " means to claim the relation to Jesus that
is expressed in the title "Lord." The duplication is for
the purpose of urgency in prayer and in worship. The
title Κύριος may, of course, contain more or less according to the conception of the one who uses it. Like the
English word "lord," it is often little more than our
"sir," a title of respect. But we need not reduce the
force of the word in the present connection. These
people who so ostentatiously call Jesus "Lord" may
mean "divine Lord" and not merely a great human lord.
The point is not merely the content of this word as used
by them but their claim of a connection which does not
exist except in their imagination.

This is evident from the opposite: "doing the will,"
etc. This "doing" proves that a real connection with
Jesus exists, one which he himself here acknowledges.
For "the will of my Father" includes, first of all, repentance and faith (5:6, 25, etc., 48; 6:12, 33; 7:3-11),
not the perfection of sinlessness but the righteousness
of the remission of sins and thus the power to do works
that truly please God. On this gracious, saving will
see John 6:29, 39, 40; I John 3:23. Therefore Jesus
also says, "the will of *my* Father," here, for the first
time, using this pronoun which pronounces him the Son
of the Father. He thus says more than merely "the
Father," i. e., yours; or "God," which also is general.
With "my Father" he so combines himself with the
Father that whoever does this Father's will is in true
and saving relation with him as the Son. With a separate article "in heaven" is joined to "my Father," emphatically pointing to his heavenly greatness, R. 776.
On "the kingdom," etc., see 3:2; 5:3.

The statement is misunderstood when it is regarded as placing deeds over against words; or when "doing" is restricted to good works.    Why would "saying, 'Lord, Lord!'" not also be a good work?    Look also at the great works mentioned in v. 22.    A similar misapplication results when saying, "Lord, Lord," is regarded as a reference to orthodoxy, whether dead or not, over against doing the Father's will by good works. Nor is the contrast drawn between hypocrisy and sincere religion.

22)    This is evident when Jesus now particularizes with regard to the false prophets.    **Many will say to me in that day, Lord, Lord, did we not prophesy in thy name and in thy name throw out devils and in thy name perform many works of power?**    Taking the false prophets by themselves, we see how they and all their followers kept saying, "Lord, Lord!" during their life here on earth (v. 21).    They made the Lord most prominent not merely by what they said but equally also by all that they did.    Jesus says that they will continue this and say, "Lord, Lord!" even "in that day," which needs no further specification since all know that the final day of judgment is referred to. They will then remind the Lord that they prophesied "in *thy* name," the adjective σῷ being more emphatic than the pronoun.    Three times they will repeat this significant phrase.    Here, too, (6:9) ὄνομα means "revelation," that by which the Lord is known and makes himself known to us.    On prophesying see v. 15.    The sheep's clothing of all false prophets is this use of the name and revelation of the Lord.    Whether they are sincere or not, all their prophesying and their other works are connected with the name and Word of the Lord.    All their false doctrines are set forth as being the Lord's true doctrines.    In all they say and do they will claim to represent him and his Word far more

genuinely than the true prophets and disciples of Christ.

Nor do they lack works of all kinds, they even point to great miracles, 24:24, but compare II Thess. 2:9-12: "lying wonders." Many are willing to grant that false prophets are able to drive out devils from persons actually possessed, quoting Mark 9:38-40, and Luke 9:49, etc., where, however, Jesus' own word shuts out this conclusion. "He that is not against us is for us." As these are false or lying prophets, however much they use the Lord's name and revelation, their miracles are lying wonders. The term δύναμις is used with reference to "a work of power," here including all works that seem to require supernatural power. In 24:24 these are described as being so astonishing that they would deceive, if it were possible, the very elect. But already Deut. 13:1-3 furnishes us the proper safeguard: not the apparent miracle but the Word decides who is a true prophet. When Jesus points to his works in John 10:36, etc., he does so only as these corroborate his word.

23) **And then will I confess to them** (*ihnen unumwunden erklaeren*, B.-P.), **Not at any time did I acknowledge you. Be withdrawing from me, you that work the lawlessness.** "Confess," ὁμολογεῖν, is here a frank and full statement. The consternation it will produce is left to the imagination. Ὅτι is *recitativum* although some regard it as meaning "because," yet ἀποχωρεῖτε is certainly direct discourse, and it is difficult to assume that we here have a mixture of indirect and direct discourse. The verb γινώσκειν is here used in an intensive sense, *noscere cum affectu et effectu*, "to know as one's own," hence "to acknowledge." The Lord knew all about these false prophets and their doings but he never knew that they bore any relation to him. Now that they would enter his kingdom of glory

he orders them away from himself, whose name and Word they have so long abused. The nominative of the participle is used as a vocative: "you that work the lawlessness." This command and this address are evidently appropriated from Ps. 6:8. The abstract ἀνομία matches its opposite δικαιοσύνη (5:6, 21); the latter harmonizes with the divine norm of right (δίκη), the former clashes with it. The present participle ἐργαζόμενοι indicates constant character: "they who always work," etc. In the public judgment at the last day works are decisive as being the open evidence of the inner relation of the heart. The greatest and most fatal work of lawlessness is to pervert the Lord's Word in the Lord's own name and to foist this perversion upon others. That is why the Antichrist is called ὁ ἄνθρωπος τῆς ἀνομίας, "the man of lawlessness," II Thess. 2:3. The result of this central perversion is that all works radiating from this center are likewise perverted. The ἀνομία does not imply that the law is set aside; it is anomistic and antinomistic to follow the law outwardly without the true spirit of faith and love, I Cor. 13:1-3.

In verses 21-23 Jesus does an astonishing thing: he speaks of himself as the Judge and Lord before whom even the false prophets and their followers must appear at the last day. So spoke neither Moses nor any of the prophets including the Baptist. From his lips will come the fateful words ·ᶠof v. 23, which are announced in this sermon in advance. In the expression *"my* Father" Jesus proclaims his divine Sonship. These final words of the third part of the sermon cast their glorious light over every word that precedes. Read as the utterances of God's Son and our Judge at the last day, every sentence grows clearer, every command more impressive. No wonder the effect was that which Matthew records in v. 28, 29.

24) The next verses constitute a well-marked and most beautiful conclusion. The imperatives (v. 1, 6, 7, 13, 15) are no longer used; now follows what has been called *eine prachtvolle Schlussparabel.* **Everyone, therefore, whoever hears these my words and does them shall be likened to a sensible man who built his house on the rock; and the rain descended, and the torrents came, and the winds blew, and they fell upon that house, and it did not fall; for it had been founded on the rock.** Οὖν connects the conclusion with all that precedes even as Jesus also refers back to "these my words." Yet the imagery used in the conclusion fits well what Jesus has just said regarding the judgment in the preceding verses. The two ὅστις are indefinite relatives (R. 727) : everyone, "whoever" he may be, that hears, etc., is like a sensible man, "whoever" he may be, that builds his house on the rock. The emphasis rests on "these my words," λόγοι, the substance of what Jesus has said. Both here and in v. 26 the hearing and the doing are clearly distinguished, and since the difference lies in the doing and the not doing, these two become emphatic. The Word comes to us and thus brings it about that we hear it. Then everything depends on whether we will do that Word, i. e., what it tells us. But this never means that after hearing the Word we step in with our own natural powers and do that Word. That is the case with regard to human words that please us; with our own powers we react to them. But in regard to all truly spiritual requirements we are dead and lifeless, unable to respond. The words of Christ meet this situation; they are spirit and life, carry their own power with and in them, and thus move and enable us to do what they say. This is their normal effect.

"To do these my words" in and by the power which they themselves bestow is not mere outward compliance with certain requirements. This would only repeat the folly of the scribes and Pharisees, the old error of work-righteousness. To do the words is to let them bring us into the condition described in 5:3-6, which 3:2 expresses by the command μετανοεῖτε, "repent," and Mark 1:15: μετανοεῖτε καὶ πιστεύετε ἐν τῷ εὐαγγελίῳ, "repent and believe in the gospel." The essential doing is faith, v. 21 (which see: "doing the Father's will"), John 6:29, 39, 40; I John 3:23. Then will follow the true evidence of repentance and faith indicated in the other beatitudes, 5:7-12, and in the body of the sermon. This doing of the words of Christ is the whole life of faith, including contrition, the confidence of the heart (conversion, regeneration), and the new obedience, all as one grand whole and all in the power of the grace coming to us in the Word as the divine means of grace.

Such a man "shall be likened" really means "shall be made like" the man now described, shall be put in the same class with him. The future tense is often misunderstood and even changed into a virtual present. This is due to the fact that the believer's present doing and his future fate are separated. Jesus combines the two. There is no special wisdom in building on the rock if it were not for the final outcome when the building withstands the great tempest. The fact that this builder is "sensible" appears in the future, hence the future tense is in place. We need not set up a definition of wisdom to fit the man here described, for Jesus himself states how and why he is accounted to be φρόνιμος, "sensible." Whoever (ὅστις) he is otherwise, "he built his building on the rock" ('ῳκοδόμησε τὴν οἰκίαν αὐτοῦ, the verb with a cognate object). "The rock," πέτρα, is the great body of rock formation in a cliff, ridge, or mountain and thus distinct from πέτρος, a piece of rock or a boulder. The sensibleness of this builder lies in choosing the rock for his foundation.

25) The description that follows is highly dramatic and at the same time extremely simple, καί following καί. The rain came down, the torrents arrived, the winds beat upon the house: *pluvia, in tecto; flumina, in imo; venti, ad latera,* roof, foundation, sides, all were tested. Note the paronomasia in προσέπεσαν and οὐκ ἔπεσεν; the winds *fell* against the house, but it *fell* not. The brevity is full of power. "It fell not" is an effective litotes for "it stood solidly." Since this conclusion is a masterly appeal to the hearers and is aimed at their will to become "sensible" like this builder, Jesus once more adds the point in which he showed himself "sensible": "for it had been founded on the rock" (the augment is absent in the past perfect). But note that "the rock" saves the house; it receives all the credit. The sensible act of the builder is that he saw, when he built, what the rock would do for his house.

It is natural to seek the counterparts for the figurative terms of the simile. The house is best understood as being the man's life; he built or founded his house means that he grounded and founded his life on the words of Jesus. These words are the rock (note the article already in v. 24). The rock is objective, hence we do not take it to refer to "doing the words," for "doing" is subjective. This doing is what is meant by "sensible," the adjective exactly fitting the act of choosing the right foundation. The nature of the rock is indicated in 5:18, it will never pass away. In λόγοι the substance forms the rock. Hence we may say that the rock is God himself in his Word and his grace, Deut. 32:15, 18; Ps. 18:2; Isa. 17:10; or Christ himself, Isa. 28:16; Rom. 9:33; I Pet. 2:6; I Cor. 3:11. The tempest is best taken

to refer to the supreme ordeal of death and not merely
to the indecisive trials of this life.   While one of these
may wreck a life that is not built on the rock, it again
may not.   Death alone is all-decisive.

26)   Only a slight change, and the outcome is the
very opposite.   **And everyone hearing these my
words and not doing them shall be likened to a
foolish man who built his house upon the sand; and
the rain descended, and the torrents came, and the
winds smote upon that house, and it fell; and great
was its fall.**   These words of mine and the hearing
of them is the same, but the doing failed to follow.
The two participles have the same sense as the relative
clauses of v. 24.   This man shall be placed in the same
class with the ἀνὴρ μωρός, who is dull, ignorant, and
thus foolish, no matter how sensible he may be in the
other affairs of his life: business, family, politics,
friendships, etc.   For after hearing the words of
Jesus, after being told all about the rock and the sand,
he built his house, his whole life with all its supreme
and eternal interests on nothing but "the sand."   Of
course, it was the easier way; the rock was higher
up and more difficult to reach than the smooth sand
bottom in the valley; and many others also chose the
easier site.   But to think of building one's whole life
on sand!   It is inexcusable even from the standpoint of common sense; it is no less than criminal
folly.

"The sand" is as definite as "the rock."   A simple
definition is: all teachings and doctrines that are *not*
"these words of mine."   "*All other* ground is sinking
sand."   Some of these attractive sandy sites, sold
constantly by the real estate agents mentioned in v. 15,
are extremely popular: merely hearing the Word by
church attendance; treating the righteousness that
God requires as civil righteousness, work-righteousness, a moral life according to common moral rules;

omitting true contrition and relying on historical faith; modernistic faith which alters vital doctrines of the gospel; etc. Sometimes these sandy sites are quite near the rock, the houses built on them may also be very pretentious. All is well while the sun shines. Some of the preliminary floods of adversity and the moderate winds of trouble may be safely endured, adding to the false feeling of security. Of course, sometimes already these lighter tempests cause sad wrecks among the houses on the sand. That is a good thing if it serves to expose the folly and drives men to seek the rock.

27) But the supreme test is the final tempest of death which is described with only one verbal change προσκόπτειν instead of προσπίπτειν. The former is the weaker verb, "to stumble against," "to strike the foot against," while the latter means "to fall upon suddenly," "to strike." The idea suggested is that the house on the rock withstood all the pounding of the winds and the waters while the house on the sand gave way as soon as the tempest stumbled against its foundation. Καὶ ἔπεσεν, "and it fell," is the height of tragedy. The simple aorist records the fact — the direct opposite of the one mentioned in v. 25.

Jesus could not add: "for it had been founded on the sand," for who can *found* anything on the sand? He does use a word to impress the full meaning of what he says on his hearers: "and great was its fall," like a reverberating crash, utter wreck and ruin, swept away by the swirling torrent, the sand on which the structure stood going down in the swollen tide. With this word Jesus closed his sermon. Did a hush fall on the audience? Did they expect Jesus to say something more, to close, perhaps, as he had begun, with the word "blessed"? As the silence deepened, and all understood that the last word had been spoken, and that this mighty warning was the last word, the effect must have been exactly what Matthew records.

28) **And it came to pass when Jesus did finish these words, the multitudes were amazed at his doctrine; for he was teaching them as having authority and not as their scribes.** The way in which Matthew appends this statement regarding the effect of the sermon by inserting the clause: "When Jesus finished these words," proves that the sermon was delivered as it is here recorded and that it is not in any part of it a compilation made by Matthew or by someone else. The fact that Luke has portions of it and other similar statements in other connections is not explained by the hypothesis of a compilation on Matthew's part; for this hypothesis clashes with the fact here set down by Matthew at the end.

"And it came to pass," καὶ ἐγένετο, is a Hebrew way of ushering in an important occurrence with a dignified formality. See the discussion in R. 1042. The descriptive imperfect ἐξεπλήσσοντο pictures the scene when Jesus ceased speaking. Matthew's psychology is correct: as long as Jesus spoke, every eye and every ear were fixed on him in rapt attention, dreading to miss a single word. But when the voice that held them spellbound became silent, the tension was relaxed, and amazement swept over the multitude. The verb is very strong, "to be dumbfounded," *ausser sich gebracht sein.* It was the διδαχή, "the doctrine," of this διδάσκαλος which wrought the amazement, the λόγοι or statements he made, the substance of what he spoke.

29) Matthew becomes even more specific. What shook the minds and the hearts of all these people was the ἐξουσία, "the authority," "the authoritative power," of this doctrine. But this is made personal: "he was teaching them as having authority," as himself being filled with authoritative power. The deity of Jesus

revealed itself in all that he said, whether he spoke directly regarding himself or not. It came out in overwhelming force in this instance; yet the periphrastic imperfect ἦν διδάσκων conveys the thought that the present instance was by no means an exception: this was the way in which he kept teaching right along.

The contrast with the teaching of "their scribes" was glaring: "at once erudite and foolish, at once contemptuous and mean; never passing a hair's breadth beyond the carefully watched boundary line of commentary and precedent; full of balanced inference, and orthodox hesitancy, and impossible literalism; intricate with legal pettiness and labyrinthine system; elevating mere memory above genius, and repetitions above originality; concerned only about priests and Pharisees, in Temple and synagogue, or school, or Sanhedrin, and mostly occupied with things infinitely little. It was not, indeed, wholly devoid of moral significance, nor is it impossible to find here and there among the debris of it a noble thought; but it was occupied a thousand fold more with Levitical minutiæ about mint, and anise, and cummin, and the length of fringes, and the breadth of phylacteries, and the washing of cups, and platters, and the particular quarter of a second when the new moons and Sabbaths began." Farrar. To this day it is hard to understand the arid dreariness of the old teaching of the scribes. The "talks" given in some of the pulpits of today, based on other subjects than the διδαχή and λόγοι of Jesus, with little meat for the soul, are the continuation of the deliverances of the Jewish scribes.

# CHAPTER VIII

## VI

### Christ Works Many Miracles, Chapters 8 and 9

In accord with 4:23 Matthew presents the teaching of Jesus, using for this the great Sermon on the Mount, and then the miracles of Jesus, choosing the ones that followed the sermon. As the sermon is not a compilation of utterances made at various times but a discourse spoken at one time, so the miracles recorded in chapters 8 and 9 are not a collection taken from various periods of the Lord's ministry but a series of mighty acts that followed each other in the order given after the Sermon on the Mount had been delivered. The first group, 8:1-17, fills out the remainder of the Sabbath on which the sermon was preached (see below on v. 14). Then Matthew selects another day on which Jesus crossed the Lake in the evening and returned the next morning (8:18-9:8).

Then follows a third day (9:10-34) which is distinguished by great miracles. The ἐξουσία, "authoritative power," at which the multitudes were amazed in regard to the preaching of Jesus (7:29) is thus exhibited in a new way, namely in the most wonderful and blessed deeds of power.

Incidentally we also see how Jesus constantly moved about. Even in Capernaum he does not remain in one place although this city was his home. He crosses and recrosses the Lake, thus reaching out from this center. This illustrates the remark made in 4:23 that Jesus "went about in all Galilee." At the end of

(316)

chapter 9, in v. 35-38, the summary statement of 4:23
is repeated. We thus see that chapters 5-9 form a
unit of two halves, the preaching of Jesus (5-7) and
the miracles (8 and 9). When recounting the latter,
Matthew wants us to keep in mind the other activity
of Jesus. The first three miracles follow the Sermon
on the Mount (8:1-17). The day next described
opens with the account of two men who would attach
themselves to Jesus (v. 18-22), after which follow
more miracles. Then comes the call of Matthew and,
most likely on the day following, the scene in Matthew's house and the great answer regarding fasting,
once more followed by miracles. Then in 9:35 Matthew concludes as he began in 4:23, telling us that
this is the manner in which Jesus preached and
wrought "in all the cities and villages," adding the
great motive of compassion that moved him in all
of it (9:36, etc.).

1) **And there followed him, after he came down
from the mountain, great multitudes.** The attested
reading is αὐτῷ with the dative participle and not a
genitive absolute. Both readings have been termed
awkward but without reason. The fact that the multitudes who heard the Sermon on the Mount followed
Jesus when he came down does not need to be stated;
they naturally came down, too. Luke 7:1, informs
us that Jesus traveled to Capernaum from the mount,
and Luke 5:12 adds the fact that the healing of the
leper took place "in a certain city" on the road to
Capernaum. Then, after entering Capernaum, the
second miracle occurred, and after reaching Peter's
house in Capernaum the third. Thus these first three
miracles are connected, all following the Sermon on
the Mount and all being performed on that very day.
Matthew does not say οἱ ὄχλοι, "*the* multitudes," who
heard the Sermon but only "great multitudes." What
he intends to say is only that a great mass of people

witnessed the healing of the leper. Whether these
people were the same as those who heard the sermon
is not indicated. Perhaps some of them accompanied
Jesus until he reached the town where he met the
leper. Other people may have joined the crowd along
the way. The publicity of this first miracle recorded
by Matthew is an important point in the narrative.
This healing was witnessed by "great multitudes."

2) **And lo, a leper, having come forward, was
prostrating himself before him saying, Lord, if thou
wilt thou canst cleanse me.** The fact that a leper
should do such a thing as this is truly astonishing;
hence the exclamation "lo." Luke 5:12 records that
when he saw Jesus he fell upon his face, and Matthew
adds that he came to Jesus and prostrated himself.
The question is raised whether this act of prostration and the address, Κύριε, "Lord," denote more than
reverence before a great human helper. Orientals
were very free with prostrations, and κύριε often
means little more than our "sir." Here, however, the
leper's petition reveals his true attitude toward Jesus.
It is less *what* he asks that reveals his thought; it is
more *the way* in which he asks. He fully believes in
the power of Jesus to heal his leprosy with a single
word: "thou canst cleanse me." When he adds, "if
thou shalt will," he is not voicing doubt in regard
to the will of Jesus but his own humble submission
to Jesus, regarding whom he has no doubt that Jesus
will, indeed, heal him if in his counsel and will that
is best. This humble submission, placing his own sad
case completely into the hands of Jesus just as a
true child of God must always place himself into God's
hands, marks this leper's faith in Jesus as being of
the highest type. A petition such as this can properly be addressed only to a divine helper, to one
whose will is the very will of the all-loving and all-
wise God.

This leper is willing, if Jesus shall so will, to remain in his living death. Submissive faith can go no
farther. This leper distinguishes divine temporal
from divine spiritual and eternal gifts. He knows
that he is asking only for the former which God's wisdom and love may and often does withhold from
us; but gifts such as pardon, peace, spiritual consolation and strength are always freely granted since it
is without question God's will that we have them.
How this leper came to such faith we are unable to
say; but his case is one that shows clearly how the
teaching of Jesus produced the most blessed spiritual
effects.

On leprosy see the Bible Dictionaries and Trench,
*Miracles*. Luke states that the man was "full of
leprosy"; the disease had progressed very far. The
leper was accounted as one dead and thus as unclean. It was a bold act on the part of this leper
to work his way through the crowd to the feet of
Jesus.

3) **And having stretched out the hand, he
touched him, saying, I will; be thou clean!**
Mark 1:41 adds the remark that Jesus "was filled
with compassion." The middle of ἅπτω means "to take
hold of" and hence "to touch." As a rule, Jesus
touched those whom he healed (Luke 4:40). The act,
when used, and the omnipotent word accompanying
it form a unit, both expressing the will of Jesus. The
miracle is always wrought by the volition of the will.
The view that here the touch was intended to
strengthen the leper's faith, combined with the further
idea that his healing depended on his faith, is untenable. All the miracles depended on the will of Jesus
alone. They intended to create and then to encourage
faith in the witnesses as well as in the beneficiary.
In a number of cases faith did not precede the miracle.
**Did the centurion's servant believe (v. 5, etc)? Did**

the possessed believe (v. 28, etc.) ? Did Jairus' daughter believe (9:18, etc.), or the widow's son at Nain?

Two words, majestic and almighty, suffice. This is the only case in which Jesus says θέλω, "I will," revealing the fact that his own will and power do the deed and not a power that has been delegated to him. Others work miracles in the name of and by the power of Jesus; Jesus, God's own Son, has this power in himself. In all miracles his deity shines out through the veil of his flesh, John 1:14.

**And immediately his leprosy was cleansed.** Full of leprosy the man lay. prostrate, free of leprosy he arose. The remarkable thing is the brevity with which the writer records the tremendous fact; this is the case throughout the Gospel records of the miracles. This is one of the plain evidences of Inspiration. No ordinary writer of any age would be satisfied with such brevity. God guided the minds and the hands of the Gospel writers.

The flesh that had been eaten away, the fingers and the toes that had dropped off, the raw sores that were spreading over the body were instantly restored to perfect soundness. All modern "healing" fades into nothing in comparison with this omnipotent deed of Jesus.

**4) And Jesus says to him, See to it, tell no one! but go, show thyself to the priest and offer the gift which Moses ordered, for a testimony unto them.** As Mark 1:41 notes the emotion of pity aroused in Jesus when he saw the wretched leper, so v. 43 notes the sternness with which Jesus ordered the healed leper to keep his mouth shut. And, indeed, the order is peremptory, using the aorist subjunctive on this account (the command being negative): "Do not tell a single person!" To give this fact still further emphasis ὅρα, "see to it!" is added asyndetically, "almost like a particle," R. 854. The reason that Jesus wants the man's lips to remain sealed can be gathered only from what follows. Mark again helps us: Jesus "immediately rushed him off" with the order to go and to show himself to the priest, etc. We may not introduce the man's moral condition as the reason that Jesus tried to seal his lips. The miracle had been performed in the presence of great crowds and was thus public in the highest degree. The haste and the stern orders with which Jesus sends the man away have only one explanation: the news of how this man was healed is not to reach the priests in Jerusalem until in all due legal form they have pronounced him clean of leprosy. The priest to whom he will present himself is not to know the man's story until afterward.

It cannot be proven that a healed leper might anywhere present himself to a priest for examination, in this case at Nazareth where a colony of priests is thought to have resided at this time. The procedure as described in Lev. 14:1, etc., required that the examining priest receive the man's offerings, which consumed an entire week. What a priest in Nazareth might determine as to the man's physical condition would not be recognized by the priest officiating in the Temple at Jerusalem. "Show thyself to the priest!" means in Jerusalem.

The first act of the priest on the day the man presents himself consists of the physical examination plus the offering of two live birds, etc., and the ceremonies connected with them, Lev. 14:2-8. The second act follows on the seventh and the eighth days when two lambs, etc., or in case of poverty one was offered, plus the ceremonies stated in v. 9-32. The first act restored the healed leper to the people, the second to his religious prerogatives in the Temple worship. The word δῶρον, "and offer the *gift*," etc., does not refer to a *thank* offering, for the offerings prescribed in Lev. 14 are first symbolic of physical cleansing (the birds, etc.), and secondly sacrificial for the purpose of spiritual cleansing (the lambs, etc.) as a trespass and sin offering.

Jesus thus orders this man in all due form to carry out the ceremonial requirements "which Moses ordered" and thus to have himself officially reinstated as being clean of leprosy. Jesus has not come to destroy but to fulfill the Law and the Prophets (5:17), and by his order to the leper he had healed fulfills what the Law of Moses required in the present case. This helps to explain that final phrase, "for a testimony unto them." The final αὐτοῖς must be construed *ad sensum*, R. 683. It cannot refer to the multitude who witnessed the miracle, for they are mentioned as far back as v. 1. The antecedent cannot be found in "no one," for this is negative and means nobody at all. It must be found in "the priest", who represents the class in the capital city that is hostile to Jesus. To them Jesus sends this healed leper as a living testimony. Jesus, who has been away from Jerusalem for a long time, sends them this man, who for eight days is to be a silent preacher to them, a living witness of his gracious will and power and of his reverence for the Law of Moses while it is still in force. When they finally learn this man's story after they themselves have officially pronounced him clean they will have another testimony regarding the Messiah whom they reject, a testimony backed by their own finding.

Mark reports that despite the stringency of the Lord's command this leper failed to keep silent and even caused his divine Helper great inconvenience. Instead of hurrying off to Jerusalem, he lingered in the vicinity where he was healed and advertised the miracle far and wide, so that Jesus had to keep away from the cities. Mistaken thanks are not thanks.

Let us hope that the man did better when he got to Jerusalem.

5) Luke 7:2, etc., but not John 4:46, etc., records the miracle Matthew now reports. **And having entered into Capernaum, a centurion came to him, beseeching him and saying, Lord, my servant is lying in the house a paralytic, terribly tormented.** After stopping at a town on his return from the mountain where the sermon had been preached, Jesus came to his own city Capernaum. Here he received this message from the centurion who, according to v. 10-12, was a Gentile. In times of peace the Romans had no troops in Capernaum. The officer was in the pay of Herod Antipas, whose troops were foreigners (Josephus, *Antiquities*, 17, 8, 3) of various nationalities. From Luke we learn that the centurion did not come to Jesus in person but sent his message through several of the Jewish elders. He lets these prominent Jews intercede for him, who as a Gentile felt that he had no claim upon the great Jewish Master. Matthew's omission of this detail is not a disagreement with Luke but only an abbreviation since, after all, Jesus dealt with the centurion whose spokesmen in Luke, too, are merely incidental. This holds true also regarding the friends who brought the second word from the centurion.

As in v. 2, the degree of faith expressed in the address "Lord" must be gathered from the following context, and in this case that faith is, indeed, great (v. 10). The addition of παρακαλῶν brings out the thought that the simple statement of the trouble in the centurion's home is intended as a request for help. Luke adds δοῦλος to παῖς, even as the latter is also regularly used in the sense of "servant." It is like the German *Bursche* and the English "boy," but in this case δοῦλος marks him as being a slave. The perfect middle βέβληται == "has been and thus is lying."

The adjective παραλυτικός is here used as a **predica-**tive noun, "a paralytic." The addition "terribly tormented," suffering excessive pain, shows that this was not a case of palsy (our versions) which is pain-less but of paralysis which was possibly induced by acute indigestion, rendering him absolutely help-less and causing the severest pain. That, too, is why the man could not, like other paralytics, be brought to Jesus. Luke adds that he was "at the point of death," and that the request to Jesus meant "to save" the man's life. He also adds the personal touch that this servant was "dear" to the centurion.

It is a remarkable fact that all of the centurions mentioned in the New Testament act in an honorable manner. This man must have been a proselyte of the gate (Luke 7:4, 5). Beside the unclean leper Mat-thew places the unclean Gentile, for although he was a proselyte, his home would still be accounted unfit for a Jew to enter. This explains Matthew's version of the request. The centurion merely lays his grave trouble before Jesus and refrains from indicating what Jesus is to do. He says that the servant is lying "in the house" and because of his pain cannot be moved, letting us feel the difficulty that, as a strict Jew, Jesus would deem it improper to enter a Gen-tile's house. When Luke writes, "that he would come and save his servant," this is only the general import of the request; for presently Luke, too, lets the centu-rion say, "I am not worthy that thou shouldest come under my roof." Army officers are always proud of their position, yet this commander bows humbly be-fore Jesus. He drops not only every presumption of his military rank but likewise every presumption of personal merit — he having built no less than a syna-gogue for the Jews at Capernaum.

7) **And he says unto him, I, having gone myself, will cure him.** Some fail to note the emphatic force

of ἐγώ. It does not mean, "The sick man need not be brought to me, I will go to him"; for this takes into account only the condition of the patient and not the centurion's difficulty, the Levitical uncleanness of his house. To meet this situation the reply of Jesus is regarded as a question: "Am I, a Jew, who is already being accused of violating the law, to go into this Gentile's unclean house?" Then the elders of the Jews are regarded as urging the centurion's personal worthiness for having built the Jews their synagogue, Luke 7:4, 5, thus persuading Jesus to go. But the Jewish elders urged this point in the centurion's favor in the very first place. Luke 7:6 indicates this when after the urging of the elders Jesus is on his way to the centurion's house. He thus must have expressed his willingness to go just before he started on his way.

8) So Jesus is in person going to this Gentile's house. Luke 7:6 informs us that he was already near the house when the centurion sent some of his friends with a second word to Jesus. **And the centurion responding said, Lord, I am not sufficient that thou shouldst enter under my roof; but only say a word, and my servant shall be healed.** The situation is misunderstood when it is stated that this expression of the centurion's modesty is superfluous and out of place since Jesus had consented to come to the house. Quite the contrary. The centurion had only placed his trouble before Jesus and had left it to Jesus as to how he would extend his help. Now someone reports to him that Jesus is coming in person and is already quite near his house. This the centurion had not expected. He knew that a Gentile's house was not fit for a Jew to enter, especially not such a great and holy Jew as Jesus was. The elders he had sent had been told to beg Jesus to come, but only to come near enough to extend his help. How Jesus was to

do this, if he would, indeed, help a Gentile, the centurion had left to Jesus' judgment. That Jesus would actually enter under his roof he had thought quite impossible. What he had thought we now see, namely that Jesus would just say a word and thus heal his servant. This he would not think of telling Jesus through the elders; it would have appeared as though he were dictating to Jesus. But now that Jesus is coming to his house, the thought flashes into the centurion's mind that perhaps the elders urged Jesus to come, or that in some way Jesus is under a misapprehension in regard to the kind of house he is about to enter. So the centurion hurries a few of his friends out to halt Jesus.

Note that ἀποκριθείς is quite generally used with reference to statements which respond to a situation and not merely with reference to replies to questions. Here the centurion sees Jesus' approach, and to this he makes response by rushing his friends out to Jesus. "I am not sufficient," etc., means: "I am nothing but a Gentile." The ἵνα clause takes the place of an infinitive, R. 992, 1076; and "for you to enter under my roof" refers to the Levitical uncleanness of the house sheltered by that roof. But what, then, did this officer mean by his appeal to Jesus? What he would not have said when sending the appeal he feels he must say now when to his astonishment Jesus is coming actually to enter his house. According to Luke 7:7 he adds the statement that because of his Gentile unworthiness he had not himself come to Jesus but had sent the worthy Jewish elders. And this is what he had thought Jesus might do in his unworthy case, just say a word and thus heal the dying servant. And now that in some unaccountable way Jesus is about to enter his house, he feels forced in all humility to reveal this to Jesus. Even for him to trouble to come seems like too much, Luke 7:6.

9) Lest the suggestion that Jesus merely say a word seem like presuming too much, the centurion adds an explanation as to how he comes to this idea regarding Jesus. **For I myself, too, am a man under authority, having soldiers under myself. And I say to this one, Go! and he goes; and to another, Come! and he comes; and to my slave, Do this! and he does it.** In the king's service he is under the king's authority, probably as the ranking officer in Capernaum, and as a matter of course has soldiers under him to whom he needs to say but a word in order to secure instant execution of his order, the same thing applying to his slave. The thought is: "If I, a subaltern, am able to have my will done by a mere word spoken by me, how much more thou, Jesus, who art the ruler himself." The καί should not be stressed to mean that Jesus, too, is "a man under authority." It brings out the argument from the less to the greater. If even a man under authority, in service to the king, and thus with soldiers under him is able to have his mere command executed at will, how much more Jesus in whom all authority resides, who has all powers and agencies at his command! The illustration is not a double one, namely that the centurion knows about obedience both by himself obeying the authority over him and by having his own authority obeyed by those under him. If that were the sense, he would illustrate his own obedience in the way in which he illustrates the obedience of his soldiers and of his slave. "A man under authority" humbly stresses the inferior position of the centurion over against the eminence of Jesus.

The request to save the servant from death and to do that by merely uttering a word implies divine omnipotence on the part of Jesus. The centurion thus reveals his conception of Jesus and of any word of command that may come from his lips. This answers the question as to the agencies which would execute the divine will of Jesus. A number of suggestions have been offered. Yet a man who thinks as this centurion does regarding Jesus, a man who is so devoted to Judaism as to build a synagogue for the Jews at Capernaum, could have in mind only the angels of God. And this the more since the Old Testament represents them as an army, II Kings 6:17; Ps. 103:20; 68:17; 34:7; compare Matt. 26:53.

10) **Now when Jesus heard this he was astonished and said to those following, Amen, I say to you, Not even in Israel so great faith did I find.** We see that Matthew has in mind the friends whom the centurion sent to Jesus with his message (Luke 7:6): for the centurion is not present, and Jesus turns to those following him when he praises the man's faith. The importance of what Jesus says is evidenced by the preamble: "Amen, I say to you," on which see 5:18. The implication is that Jesus had again and again found great faith "in Israel," among the Jews who had been prepared for his coming by their Old Testament religion. But this Gentile's faith was greater still; εὗρον, "did find," whereas we should use the perfect "have found," R. 844.

The greatness of the centurion's faith is evident in its *humility*. The man, although he is a high military officer and a great benefactor of the Jews, deems himself utterly unworthy. In the second place this man's faith centers in *the word* of Jesus, the very experience Jesus had so much difficulty in attaining among the Jews. On his own accord, merely from what this man had heard about Jesus, without further experience and teaching he shows absolute trust in Jesus' word; compare the court officer mentioned in John 4:50 for an example of a man who slowly arrives at faith in Jesus' word. A word is sufficient, Jesus does not need to come in person. Thirdly, and as the basis of this humble confidence in the mere word, the centurion has a proper conception of *the exalted person* of Jesus. His word, spoken at a distance, works with omnipotence to save from death. It is an ill comment on Jesus' estimate of the centurion's faith to suggest that he had some pagan conception as to how the power of Jesus would work the healing, yet that this did not affect the nature and the value of his faith. Any pagan conception would vastly reduce, if it did not make void, this Gentile's faith. The remarkable feature of the man's faith was that it accorded so fully with the truest Israelite teaching and was wholly free from pagan conceptions.

11) This Gentile's wonderful faith leads Jesus to utter a prophecy concerning the hosts of future Gentile believers who will come to his kingdom. **Moreover, I say to you, that many shall come from the eastern and the western parts and shall recline in company with Abraham and Isaac and Jacob in the kingdom of the heavens; but the children of the kingdom shall be thrown out into the outer darkness. There shall be the weeping and the gnashing of the teeth.** With δέ Jesus adds this further statement. The parts of the rising and of the setting sun include the entire world, looking in the two opposite directions from where Jesus stands. The "many" are, therefore, a vast host of Gentile believers. Two thousand years of history have verified this great prophecy in a tremendous way. The blessedness of the kingdom is frequently pictured as an Oriental feast, the guests reclining in Oriental fashion, Ps. 32:5; Prov. 9:1, etc.; Isa. 25:6; Luke 14:15, etc.; Matt. 22:1, etc.; Rev. 19:9, 17. Because Abraham, etc., are mentioned as the most prominent guests, some conclude that the kingdom is here pictured in its eschatological consummation and not in its progress of grace. But this reason is insufficient; for all except the last two passages just

referred to have in mind the church on earth. Jesus
views "the kingdom of the heavens" (on which see
3:2) as being one. Every believer at once becomes
"a son of Abraham" (Luke 19:9; 13:16) and is thus
united with the patriarchs in the enjoyment of
blessedness.

Especially Abraham is "the father of all them that
believe," Rom. 4:11, 16, and as such he is mentioned
here. The three patriarchs are mentioned together
because the covenant in Christ was made with them.
For this reason the believers of all ages assemble with
these patriarchs. Jesus' Jewish hearers at once
understand this. The point emphasized, however, is
that this host of believers will include vast numbers
outside of Judaism. This the prophets had plainly
foretold, in fact, when the covenant was originally
made with Abraham it was one that promised blessedness for all nations. The Jewish followers of Jesus
needed this reminder for they had lost this Old Testament vision of the kingdom. It is a kindly touch when
Jesus does not use τὰ ἔθνη, "the Gentiles," a term that
was tinged with contempt in Jewish minds, but the
inoffensive equivalent, "many from the eastern and the
western parts."

12) "The sons of the kingdom" and the verb
"shall be thrown out" do not necessarily imply that
these persons were actually in the kingdom. One may
be "thrown out" when he attempts to enter a place
without ever getting into it. And that is the situation here. For these are "the sons of the kingdom"
who imagined that they had the fullest right to the
kingdom. For υἱοί, "sons," as distinct from τέκνα,
"children," conveys the idea of legal standing. As the
physical descendants of Abraham the Jews were, indeed, the first heirs of the Messianic covenant and
kingdom. The only trouble was that they failed to
inherit. John 8:37-41 states why. Although they

were beyond question "the sons of the kingdom" because they were "Abraham's seed" and thus the poten-
tial heirs, they forfeited their inheritance of the kingdom by unbelief; they disavowed their father Abraham, annulled their birthright, and lost their place
in the kingdom. When, in spite of all this, they
proudly demanded entrance they compelled God "to
throw them out." The Gentiles were never thrown
out because they never presumed to have the right
to come in.

The image of the kingdom is that of a vast hall
for feasting and joy, all blazing with light. The opposite of this picture is "the darkness, that farthest out."
The adjective, being added by a separate article, has
the same emphasis as the noun, in fact, is an appositional climax, R. 776. Moreover, ἐξώτερος, comparative
in form, is used as a superlative, B.-P. *aeusserst;*
B.-D. 62, "only superlative." At least two darknesses
are indicated. The one would be the spiritual darkness which is simply ἔξω, "outside" of the kingdom
in the ignorant, deluded, lying world. From this
darkness men can be saved. The other is the darkness that is "utterly outside," from which none can
escape. But the expression is not eschatological, for
each unbelieving Jew is thrown into this darkness
when, at death, he would enter heaven. Note that
"darkness," σκότος, σκοτία, denotes not merely the absence of light, life, and joy but also the dread power
that drags men away from the light and holds them
forever in its grasp.

This "outer darkness" is conceived as a place, ἐκεῖ,
"there," even as heaven is also pictured as a place.
Already τὸ σκότος is very definite, just as is ἡ βασιλεία.
The awfulness and the terror of the utter darkness
produce "the weeping and the gnashing of the teeth,"
the definite articles pointing to the specific effects that
accompany this specific darkness. There is no other

weeping, etc., that is like this weeping. All are agreed
that the weeping is the effect of the complete loss of
happiness. But many think of rage or of helpless
despair as causing "the gnashing of the teeth." We
prefer to think of the excruciating torment of the
outer darkness. Compare 13:42, 50: "the furnace
of fire: there shall be the wailing and the gnashing
of the teeth." These two passages, together with
22:13; 24:51; 25:30; Luke 13:28, make the words
a standard description of the place of torment. The
damned shall not be annihilated. To the Jews who
were following Jesus his words served as a terrible
warning against unbelief. When the kingdom invited
them to take their place as "the sons of the kingdom,"
would they choose the outer darkness? When
Luke 13:28-30 reports that Jesus used what Matthew here records in a different connection and also
changed the order of the sentences, it is obvious that
Jesus repeated this mighty warning, which certainly
also deserved repetition. Neither Matthew nor Luke
makes a combination of his own, nor can one be played
against the other.

13) **And Jesus said to the centurion, Go thy
way. As thou didst believe be it unto thee. And
the servant was healed in that very hour.** From the
Jews who were following him and whom he had
addressed in v. 10-12, Jesus turns to the centurion as
represented, according to Luke, by the friends he had
sent. Throughout his narrative Matthew wants us to
understand that Jesus is dealing with the centurion
as such irrespective of his representatives. "As thou
didst believe" must be understood in the light of v. 8:
without coming to the house, by merely uttering a
word in the place where Jesus was. The centurion's
trust was in perfect accord with the realities inherent
in Jesus, and that is the reason that Jesus met that
trust as he did. Any trust that rests on imagina-

tions regarding Jesus is not met by him. The royal officer mentioned in John 4:46, etc., who thought Jesus could save his son only by coming to that son, found that Jesus would not come.

We should not generalize this word of Jesus so as to make it mean: whatever we believe he will grant us he will grant, or that the degree of our faith insures the gift we desire. A wrong faith may be ever so strong in expecting a wrong gift; Jesus will not meet that faith and expectation, he will first correct it. And often he will do wondrous things where there is no faith present in order to produce faith. The word ὥρα does not always mean sixty minutes or the specific hour of the day but quite often "time," whether a moment or a longer period is referred to. So here the servant was perfectly restored the instant Jesus spoke the mighty word.

14) **And Jesus, having come into the house of Peter, saw his mother-in-law lying down and suffering with fever. And he took hold of her hand, and the fever left her. And she arose and went to ministering to him.** The connecting participles: v. 1, "having come down from the mount"; v. 5, "having entered into Capernaum"; and now v. 14, "having come into the house of Peter," bind these miracles together and make them successive. Even the style indicates this: a dative, a genitive absolute, a simple nominative participle. And in v. 18 the participles are no longer employed. Taking Mark 1:21-34 and Luke 4:31-41 in connection with Matthew, we arrive at the following succession: the Sermon on the Mount on the morning of the Sabbath; the leper healed on the return from the mount; the centurion's servant healed when entering Capernaum; Jesus preaching in the synagogue in the afternoon with the same ἐξουσία as on the mount and again not "as the scribes" (Mark 1:22; Luke 4:32); also freeing a demoniac in

the synagogue; toward the close of this Sabbath going to Peter's house and healing his mother-in-law; after the Sabbath is over all the additional miracles reported in Matthew 8:16; Mark 1:32-34; Luke 4:40, 41.

The objection that Jesus would not walk so far on the Sabbath does not hold, for a Sabbath day's journey was 2,000 paces from the city wall, ample for the distance here indicated. The view that the Sermon on the Mount was preached at the height of Jesus' ministry (which is correct) while the healing of Peter's mother-in-law took place at the beginning of Jesus' ministry, is untenable. For Mark 1:21 and the following, and Luke 4:31 and the following reveal that Jesus was at the full tide of his preaching and his miracles.

We do not have the impression that Jesus was asked to come to Peter's house in order to heal the mother-in-law's fever — not after v. 8. Since Jesus himself had a home in Capernaum, it is more likely that he was asked to dine at the home of Peter and Andrew. Mark adds the detail that James and John were also present, from which we may conclude that these two and Jesus were to be the guests. Matthew states only that when Jesus reached the house "he saw" the patient, but Mark adds that they told him of her, and Luke that they besought him for her. Perhaps, when Jesus did not see the woman he asked where she was and then heard about her ailment with an added request. We here learn that Peter was married, and that his mother-in-law lived at his home. From I Cor. 9:5 it is certain that Peter's wife was living at this time, afterward accompanying him on his journeys. Her mother, who would gladly have helped with the meal was prostrate with "a great fever" (Luke 4:38), an unfortunate situation when guests were to be served.

15)   Luke's narrative is the most graphic of the
three: "he stood over her and rebuked the fever."
Mark adds that Jesus "raised her up by grasping her
hand." Matthew is content with "he took hold of her
hand." Immediately "the fever left her." Nor did
any weakness remain as is always the case when a
fever subsides; for she not only "arose" but with her
daughter "went to ministering to him," διηκόνει, the
durative imperfect. This verb suggests that Jesus had
been invited to the house to dine there.

16)   Great and wonderful as the three miracles are
which have been described with some detail, these are
really only a part of the great story. **Moreover,
when evening was come, they brought to him many
demoniacs, and he expelled the spirits with a word;
and he healed all that were ill.** All three synoptists
mention the coming of the evening and the sunset, because then the Sabbath ended, and the sick could be
carried to Jesus. Matthew here repeats and abbreviates 4:24, in connection with which the demoniacs
were fully discussed, also κακῶς ἔχων. Both Mark and
Luke describe the healing of a demoniac in the synagogue just before Jesus went to Peter's house. Their
accounts make plain just what possession is, for the
evil spirit in the sufferer utters things which the sufferer himself could not utter, and Jesus clearly distinguishes the demon from the man. So here Matthew:
Jesus expelled τὰ πνεύματα, the devils that held the
sufferers in possession. This he did λόγῳ, "by a
word," as in Mark 1:26, and in Luke 4:35. The
other sufferers are summarized in the expression "all
that were ill." Not a single case of the great number
that were brought during those evening hours was
left without being instantaneously and perfectly
restored.

The three aorists intend only to add these many
miracles to the three reported in detail. Hence it is

not advisable to make a major division at v. 17. In 9:35 Matthew indicates that he is closing the account begun with 4:23-25. This appears from the imperfect περιῆγεν followed by two durative present participles; Jesus "continued to go about busy with preaching and healing" as described in chapters 5 to 9.

17) In all this work of healing Jesus was fulfilling the prophecies recorded regarding him as the Messiah: **in order that it might be fulfilled what was spoken through Isaiah, the prophet** (see 1:22), **saying, He himself took our infirmities and bore our diseases.** Disregarding the LXX, Matthew himself translates Isa. 53:4 with exactness: Jesus "took" (*nasa'*, λαμβάνειν) and "bore" (*sabal*, βαστάζειν, carried as a load) all the ailments that came upon men as the result of sin. The thought is not merely that he took hold of these ailments and rid the sufferers of them. Isa. 53:4-7 describes the Messiah as our substitute. Loaded down with our terrible burden, he appears as the suffering and dying Messiah. From this grand prophetic portrait Matthew quotes one line, which, however, he regards as a part of the whole. He sees Jesus in his entire ministry as our substitute, as the burden-bearer who loaded on himself all our sins and all their penalties. At the close of that ministry, by the atoning death, the whole load would be borne away. But throughout the course of that ministry Jesus took up and treated as his own burden men's sins and the terrible ravages of these sins. By means of all his preaching and teaching he was freeing men from the grip of their sins, and by means of his constant healings he was freeing them also from the disease and the pains brought on them through sin.

Like the prophet, Matthew does not separate the two. For only he who would die for our sin on the

cross and work an eternal redemption from sin could
work a ministry of healing from disease. It is an
untenable, mechanical view to think of a transfer of
these diseases to the body of Jesus. The old Jewish
view even imagined that the Messiah would be a leper.
Just as the sins Jesus expiated did not become sins
that he had himself committed, for he was and had
to be holy and sinless in order to be our expiation,
so the diseases did not become the diseases of his own
body, which was and had to be untainted by any results
of sin in order to be fit for his vicarious work. Any
difficulty in this regard is thus wholly without cause.
"He himself took and bore" implies a vicarious, ethical
assumption of this burden. It was vastly more than
typical, i. e., by what he did with the diseases portray-
ing what he would do with the sin by which they were
caused. "He himself took and bore" was actual removal,
and this as a part of his removal of the entire sin burden that was destroying us. It was done by his "word"
(λόγῳ) just as he forgave sins by his word (9:5:
"whether is easier to say," etc.) But both the pardon-
ings and the healings rested on his atoning death (Isa.
53:11). And his word was always an expression of
his will, that wondrous will of mighty grace which
stooped to the whole vast burden in a ministry that
worked our relief.

"He himself took and bore" cannot refer only to
the drain put upon the heart of Jesus because of the
sympathy he spent upon sufferers; nor to the mental
and the physical strain of healing so many, for the
first ones to be healed would not tire Jesus. All his
compassion and all his strain of prolonged labor were
only incidental to this part of the burden and not at
all comparable to the final ordeal of the *passio magna.*
Matthew introduces Isa. 53:4 at this point, not as
closing the section on the miracles, but as applying
to the healings just recorded. The next miracle

(v. 23-27) is of a different nature, as is also another recorded in 9:23-25.

18) It is now the evening of another day at another time (Mark 4:35), hence the transitional δέ. **Now when Jesus saw great multitudes about him he gave orders to go to the other side.** It was evening, the Lord was tired (v. 25, sleeping), and now wished to be relieved of the crowds by sailing across the lake to its eastern side.

19) **And a scribe, having come forward, said to him, Teacher, I will follow thee wherever thou wilt go away.** On εἶς as a substitute for the indefinite article, like the German *ein* and the French *un*, see R. 282 and 674, etc. As "a scribe" this man would himself be a "teacher," one who had graduated in the law and had been qualified to teach by the Jewish authorities. Moreover, the scribes as a class joined with the Pharisees in opposing Jesus. Yet here is one scribe whose association with Jesus has brought him to the point of offering himself as a permanent pupil to Jesus as his permanent "Teacher" or Master. What better offer could Jesus wish? It is without *if* or *but*, "wherever thou wilt go away" (R. 969, the futuristic subjunctive), whatever the destination, whatever the length, difficulty, or hardship of the way, "I will follow thee." This scribe cannot be identified.

From the reply of Jesus we see that this man is too ready, his offer too complete. It is like that of Peter, John 13:36, 37; Luke 22:33. He is like the seed on stony ground which grew quickly but lacked root to withstand the hot sun. He is an idealist, enthusiastic, of sanguine temperament. He is superficial and does not count the cost. He sees the soldiers on parade, the fine uniforms and the glittering arms, and is eager to join, forgetting the exhausting marches, the bloody battles, the graves, perhaps un-

marked. It is less cruel to disillusion such a man
than to let him rush in and go down to disappointment.

20) **And Jesus says to him, The foxes have dens,
and the birds of the heaven abodes; but the Son of
man has not where to lay his head.** Jesus neither
accepts nor declines the offer. His reply strikes the
heart of the matter: the man must see, not in idealism,
but in sober, sane realism, what his offer involves.
Jesus illuminates the way upon which he leads his disciples, and this way is not bordered with roses.
Though he is not merely a man, a human being, but
the great Son of man who is both man and yet more
than man he actually has less of creature comforts
than the wild animals and the wild birds ("birds of
the heaven," not confined). The foxes, for instance,
using a specific example, have their dens; the birds,
taking another class, have shelters. But Jesus, constantly on the move, has no fixed home where he can
lie down and take his rest (v. 23, asleep in the boat).
Even when he was in his home city, we do not read
that he rested at his mother's house; the ministrations
recorded in Luke 8:2, 3 were called out by the hardships he endured. Yet Jesus was no pauper; he did
not live in the squalor of poverty; he was no mendicant
monk, no ragged and emaciated beggar. His company had a purse and a treasurer who handled enough
money to give to the poor at times, enough for Judas
to steal from. What Jesus impresses upon this scribe
is the fact that his whole calling and work are engaged
in not for mere earthly interests but for the kingdom
and for that alone.

It would be too narrow a view to think that Jesus
wanted this scribe merely to forsake his easy life for
a hard one. Jesus refers to his homelessness merely
as an illustration of the path his followers must walk,
choosing the spiritual instead of the carnal, the life

with eternal purposes instead of the temporal, heavenly treasures instead of earthly. That does not imply that one must become a monk or a nun, although it may imply that one must lead a life such as the apostles, Paul for instance, led and it always means placing the kingdom first, last, and all the time, letting God attend to the rest (6:33). It is well to build the tower but first to count the cost. Did this scribe follow Jesus? We are not told, for Matthew's real interest is concerned with Jesus. If *you* had been in that scribe's position, what would *you* have done?

Many monographs have been written on "the Son of man" without unanimity as to the meaning and the derivation of this title which was used exclusively by Jesus, save in John 12:34, and in Acts 7:56 which reflects Matt. 26:64. It is clear that the title was coined by Jesus himself, was unknown before his time, and was not used in the church until at a later date. Jesus always used it as a subject or as an object, always in the third person, never as a predicate. He speaks in the full consciousness that he is "the Son of man" yet he never says, "I am the Son of man." The title is always ὁ υἱὸς τοῦ ἀνθρώπου, with two Greek articles, which is quite distinct from "*a* son of man," i. e., a human being. There is a mystery in the title which is still felt as we read the record of its use by Jesus and is clearly evident also in the questions which Jesus asks in 16:13, etc.

"Of man," never the plural, "of men," is generic; not descended from some man but having the nature of man, a son of mankind. The fact that the human nature of Christ is thus indicated is beyond question. But "*the Son* of man" lifts this one man out from among all men as being one who has this human nature in a way in which no other man has it, who, while he is, indeed, true man is more than man, is also ὁ υἱὸς τοῦ Θεοῦ τοῦ ζῶντος, "the Son of the living God." This, too, is very clear from the mighty acts attributed to "the Son of man," acts that are infinitely greater than any that are possible to man. Hence "the Son of man" is not merely "the ideal man," *homo* κατ' ἐξοχήν, the flower of our race, toward whom all creation tended; but "the Word made flesh," the Son ἄσαρκος who became ἔνσαρκος, who joined our human nature to his divine nature, the Son of God who assumed our human flesh and blood. In the use Jesus makes of this title two lines of thought converge: the one is lowliness, suffering, etc.; the other greatness, power, exaltation beyond men. We see at once how eminently the title fits Jesus during his earthly sojourn (used first when speaking to Nathanael, John 1:51). To give it an exclusively eschatological sense because it is used also in connection with the consummation is to generalize from a fraction of the facts instead of from all of them.

Whence does Jesus derive this title? The answer is from Dan 7:13, 14 (which read). Efforts are made by von Hofmann, C.-K., Zahn, and others to regard "one like the Son of man" in Daniel as a symbolical figure (like the "beasts" in the preceding verses), picturing Israel. But the words of Daniel do not support this sense. The Hebrew *ki*, ὡς, "like," is taken to mean that this image resembled a man but *was not* a man. But in Rev. 1:13; 14:14, this "like" is carefully retained when this passage is utilized. Again, in Matthew 24:30 and 26:64 the Son of man comes in the clouds exactly as in Daniel's description. God alone uses the clouds as his vehicle, hence "one like the Son of man" is divine. Yet when Daniel sees him "like the Son of man," this, without saying in so many words that "he is man," clearly intimates that the grand person described is also man. See the thorough exegesis of Keil in *Bibl. Com. ueber d. Propheten Daniel*, 197, etc., 288, etc. Unsatisfactory is the explanation that Jesus drew the title from the general reference of the Old

Testament to the *bene adam,* or *ben adam,* Aramaic *bar enasch,* "children of men," "child of man," and that only in this general sense are Dan. 7:13 and Ps. 8:5 a source. But from such terms which denote men as men a title could not be derived which denotes the one unique man who is the very Son of God. A late view goes back to Iran and the Persian sources and the eschatological view that the first man, deified, will return at the end and bring the divine kingdom. But a pagan legend could not have been the source whence Jesus derived this term.

Dan. 7:13, 14 pictures the Messiah. Yet the Jews had derived no title for the Messiah from this passage. This Jesus himself did. Hence, when he kept using this title, it seemed strange, and he was asked, "Who is this Son of man?" John 12:34. Hence also no political ideas could be attached to this title. That was the trouble with the title "Messiah" which Jesus avoided for this very reason, using it only in John 4:26.

In Daniel's description the idea of universality is prominent: he who is like the Son of man rules all people, nations, etc., in an everlasting kingdom and judges all the world. By this new title Jesus denationalized his Messiahship and his Kingship and lifted it above all narrow Jewish conceptions — he was the Redeemer of all men. In Daniel the term is eschatological; Jesus uses it in the same way in 24:30 and in 26:64, and this is done also in the Revelation passages. But this Judge at the time of the great consummation cannot be the judge only then, his work must reach back through the entire process of redemption, the consummation of which is the final judgment. Very properly Jesus thus expands the title and uses it with reference to his person during the days of his humiliation.

What Aramaic expression Jesus used for "the Son of man" no one can determine. The references in the book of Enoch, even if the sections concerned are gen-

uine, are inadequate. The suggestion that, since Jesus
also spoke Greek, as for instance, to Pilate, he may have
himself employed the Greek expression ὁ υἱὸς τοῦ ἀνθρώπου, may be correct although the Gospels, Revelation,
and Acts are wholly sufficient.

21) **Now another of the disciples said to him,
Lord, permit me first to go away and to bury my
father.** Like the scribe, this man is already a disciple of Jesus. The Lord is now leaving this vicinity
(v. 18), and so in the case of both men the question
arises whether they should follow him. In v. 23 he
leaves in a boat, and Mark 4:36 informs us that other
boats went along with him. The scribe is overready
and needs to be cautioned, this man would later join
Jesus. For he has just received word about his
father's death. The Jews generally buried without
delay; if there was time enough, on the same day, otherwise at least on the next day. Both natural affection
and the obligation enjoined toward parents by God
prompt the man's desire to hurry home for the last
service he could render his father. Yet he is a disciple
of Jesus, one who has made the Master's word the law
of his life. He, therefore, asks the Lord for permission
to hasten to the funeral. The idea is not that he has
any doubt as to whether he should go or not, and far
less that he has a bad conscience in regard to leaving.
"Permit me *first* to go away" also does not mean "to
take care of my father until he dies," a thought that is
foreign to the situation.

22) The answer of Jesus is direct and decisive.
**But Jesus says to him, Keep following me, and let
the dead bury their dead.** Here ἄφες is followed
by the accusative with the infinitive. The sentimentality connected with dead relatives is still so strong
today that this word of Jesus sounds harsh to our ears.
What Jesus says is that the man is to let the spiritually
dead bury their own physically dead. When one who

is spiritually dead, though he be a close relative, reaches
his end, the matter of putting his body into the grave
is something that need not exercise us unduly. Jesus
does not imply that the disciples are forbidden to attend
funerals of this kind. But they are really only secular
affairs which people whose lives are wholly devoted to
such affairs can attend to without our presence when
supreme spiritual affairs claim our attention; compare
12:48, etc. Christless associations make it one of their
objects "to bury their own dead," and they might thus
fittingly take this word of Jesus as their motto. Our
great concern is with the heavenly life and with him
who bestows it. Where there is no opportunity to
work in the interest of this higher life, our spiritual
obligation ends. The soul of this man's father was
beyond his son's reach; let him attend to his own soul
by following Jesus. Luke adds to the word of Jesus,
"but go and publish abroad the kingdom of God." A
double spiritual duty beckons this man, one regarding
his own soul, and the other regarding the souls of others
whom he could reach by the call Jesus would soon
extend to him, to go out with other disciples to proclaim
the kingdom.

The harshness of this word is removed except in the
case of the sentimentality of the worldly-minded who
pay a good deal of attention to fragrant flowers and
flowery tributes to the dead while they blink at the harsh
reality of death itself and of that which is worse, spiritual death and eternal damnation. The manly, brac-
ing words of Jesus are better. The best balm for this
son was to follow Jesus and to prepare for the work
Jesus would assign to him. Did he remain with Jesus?
The answer is withheld for the same reason that was
stated in connection with the other case. Luke 9:61, 62
records still another case which Matthew omits.

23) Now Jesus embarks. **And when he had
entered a boat, there followed him his disciples.**

Luke 8:22 combines Matt. 8:18 and 23. Mark 4:36
adds the detail that the multitude was sent away, and
that the disciples took Jesus "as he was," tired by his
labors of the day. The questions regarding the chronology that enter here are treated at length in the
author's comments on Mark 4:35. The verb ἀκολουθεῖν
repeats v. 19 and 22; "his disciples" includes others
besides the future apostles, and these used the other
boats, Mark 4:36. The storm on the lake brought all
these boats into distress.

24) **And lo, a great tempest arose in the sea,
so that the boat was covered by the waves; he, however, was sleeping.** The exclamation refers to the
entire situation: the sudden tempest, the swamped boat,
and the Lord sleeping peacefully.

A comparison of the narratives of the three synoptists is highly interesting for showing the independence
of each account. Matthew alone has σεισμός, the word
for earthquake, here used with reference to the tossing
water; the other accounts speak of the storm of wind.
The result is described by ὥστε with the infinitive: "so
that the boat was covered by the waves," "filling" as
the others state it, Luke adding the jeopardy. Matthew is especially dramatic. The reader wonders about
Jesus. Luke tells us that he went to sleep before he
records the coming of the storm; Mark, after he tells
about the storm but he adds the details: "in the stern,"
and "on the cushion" which was provided for such a
purpose. Matthew states it all with three Greek
words: "he, however, was sleeping," αὐτός emphatic:
"he" over against the others, ἐκάθευδε, the descriptive
imperfect, R. 679. The roaring winds and the waves,
the commotion of the disciples trying to save the boat
and themselves never disturbed Jesus in the least — he
continued sleeping. Astounding indeed!

The lake lies between high hills and is thus subject
to sudden tempests which develop excessive fury as

they roar through the great trough in which the lake
lies. Some commentators think that more than natural causes were involved in this storm. We see no
necessity for making the devil or the presence of Judas
in the boat responsible for this storm, and we cannot
accept the allegories which some commentators propose,
such as that where Jesus is present upheavals must
occur. We likewise consider out of place the discussion
about the two natures of Jesus and such questions as:
did his deity sleep? did he foreknow the coming of the
storm? and similar questions. The storm was brought
about in the providence of God in whose hand are all
the forces of nature. The peaceful sleep of Jesus is
due to the total absence of fear in his heart and to his
absolute trust in his Father's care.

25) **And having come to him, they aroused him,
saying, Lord, save!  We are perishing!**  Matthew is
still the most dramatic‚ evangelist, only Luke approaches him in this respect. The fact that these disciples should come to Jesus for help is astounding. A
number of them were expert sailors who knew all about
handling a boat and who had been in many a violent
storm on this lake. They appeal to Jesus who had
never handled boats but had worked as a carpenter
with his father in Nazareth. How could a former carpenter help these expert sailors when all their skill was
at an end, and death in the roaring waves was their certain fate? In the providence of God this storm brought
to view such faith as they really had. Completely at
the end of their own resources in which they had always had great pride and confidence, they now cast
themselves upon Jesus as their only hope. They forget that he had never sailed a boat; they think not of
human but of divine ability in him. They abandon all
human help, the best of which they possessed in their
own skill; they cast themselves completely into the
divine hands of Jesus.

That was faith. But their terror, their resort to Jesus only in their extremity, their fear of death in the waves are not faith but littleness of faith, which is in glaring contrast with the calmness of Jesus. This littleness of faith God's providence also revealed. They aroused Jesus, broke in on his sleep. Their cries are differently reported, for one man cried this, another that. Matthew records two of their cries; that recorded by Mark is poignant to a degree, voicing, as it does, a question. Κύριε matches σῶσον, the omnipotent "Lord" alone could "rescue." The strong aorist which expresses one mighty act of deliverance is the more effective because it has no object, thus placing all the emphasis on the act as such. Then note the present tense ἀπολλύμεθα, just the one word, "we are perishing," admitting the disciples' abject helplessness, the imminent catastrophe. The picture could not be more dramatic.

26) **And he says to them, How frightened you are, men of little faith! Then, having arisen, he rebuked the winds and the sea, and there came a great calm.** Not a trace of fear or even of startled surprise because of the terrible danger! The absolute serenity of Jesus is astounding. Matthew records the rebuke to the disciples before the stilling of the tempest; but Mark and Luke seem to have the true order of these acts. Jesus stills both the storm in the hearts and the storm in nature. The observation is correct that τί δειλοί belong together, that τί is not "why," introducing a question, but "how," marking an exclamation (compare the explanation of the correct reading τί in 7:14): "How frightened you are!" If Jesus were asking *why* they are frightened, this question would be superfluous because he himself indicates why, namely because their faith is so small. What he does is to express surprise *that* they are so terribly frightened, *that* they reveal themselves as "men of little faith."

The rebuke lies in this exclamation which implies that Jesus felt that he had the right to expect more of them.

Two points, however, deserve attention. There is nothing in the text which would indicate that, because Jesus was in the boat, the disciples had no right to be afraid. They had no right to be afraid even if Jesus had not been in the boat. As disciples of Jesus they were ever in their Father's care like Jesus himself, and that was the case whether Jesus was physically present with them or not. The fact that Jesus is now always invisibly present with us (28:20), and that we are thus in his keeping and care just as we are in our Father's care should not confuse us in regard to the necessity for his physical presence.

The other point is that the disciples had no right to fear even if they perished in the waves. We have no promise that danger shall never plunge us into death just because we are Christ's own. In the counsel of God it may be his will that we die; then we should die with the mighty assurance that God's will sends us what is best. We should die in confidence, without fear. The reason these points are sometimes overlooked is that this historical narrative is often allegorized, and even when the effort is made to avoid allegory, allegorical ideas often are in the preacher's mind.

Jesus rose to his feet as the waves splashed into the boat and with two mighty words of rebuke (Mark 4:39, literally: "Be silent! Put the muzzle on and keep it on!" perfect tense, R. 908) stilled the tempest. Both Mark and Luke mention the wind and the raging water. All three synoptists record the great calm. They use the significant aorist ἐγένετο, "there came," i. e., at once, in obedience to the double command. The brevity of Matthew is even more effective than the fuller wording of Mark and of Luke. It was God's will when letting this tempest occur at this time that Jesus should reveal his omnipotent power over the vast forces of nature

by calming wind and waters with a word.   Why should
disciples be terrified by the threatening violence of natural forces when the hand of omnipotent power is over
them?   Mark and Luke transpose the order of the
rebuke to the tempest and that to the disciples.   The
rationalistic efforts to eliminate the miracle from the
narrative are unconvincing.

27) **Now the men marvelled, saying, What kind
of person is this that even the winds and the sea
obey him?**   All commentators note that Matthew
writes οἱ ἄνθρωποι, *die Menschen,* whereas Mark and
Luke continue their accounts with verbs that refer to
the disciples.   As far as the facts are concerned, these
two evangelists certify that the disciples marvelled and
exclaimed thus.   It is also quite correct that generally
"the men" is used in distinction from "the disciples."
But the conclusion would be hasty, that Matthew here
refers to people who heard about the miracle after the
disciples landed and spread the report.   Mark 4:36
says that "other boats" were with that of Jesus.   Matthew uses οἱ ἄνθρωποι to designate all the men in all the
boats.   At once, on witnessing the miracle, they asked
each other this question of astonishment.   "The men,"
however, is not in contrast to οὗτος as one might conclude from our versions, for "this" merely indicates the
person of Jesus.   All that we can say is that οἱ ἄνθρωποι
connotes human limitations and weakness which cause
men to exclaim when they note the works of Jesus.

All the synoptists have the significant οὗτος, "this
person," but Matthew alone has ποταπός, "what kind
of."   The point of asking thus lies in the consecutive
ὅτι (R. 1001) : "seeing that," or simply "that."   The
great single occurrence is generalized: "even the winds
and the sea obey him," present tense, ὑπακούουσιν, do
so as a matter of course.   These men recognized that
the winds and the sea were wholly and always subject
to the will and the command of Jesus.   Their expe-

rience was too tremendous to permit any rationalizing explanation, such as men sitting at their desks have offered.    All the evangelists stop with the great question and append none of the answers that were given. When, however, we are told that the thought is in no way indicated that by stilling the tempest Jesus revealed himself as God, we at once disagree.    Who save God can make the raging winds and the sea obey at a word?

28)    **And when he had come to the other side, into the country of the Gadarenes, there met him two demoniacs coming forth out of the tombs, very fierce, so that no one was able to pass along through that road.**    The maps and the comments usually place the locality where Jesus landed too far north; it was on the lower eastern shore of the lake, named "the country of the Gadarenes" after the main city of that territory, Gadara, lying a little south of the Yarmuk, a confluent of the Jordan.    Josephus calls this country "the Gadaritis"; it was a section of the Decapolis.    On demoniacs see the discussion in 4:24, also Trench, *Miracles*, 160, etc.    The cases here described are the most interesting of all.    We need lose no time on an explanation of Matthew's mention of two demoniacs whereas Mark and Luke speak of only one.    The latter do not say that there was *only* one, hence contradiction is shut out.    Evidently, one of the two was the leader and spokesman, the other only his companion.

Matthew's description is brief; Mark 5:2-6 is much fuller, yet he leaves out Luke's remark that the men were naked.    The tombs were chambers hewn into the rock walls of the cliffs and were some little distance from the lake and from the road that ran back from the shore.    Some of these old tombs may have been abandoned and thus afforded dens in which these demoniacs established themselves.    Among the unclean places of the dead these men, possessed by unclean spirits, made their habitation. Their ferocity was so great that they rendered the road along this way unsafe by rushing out with wild cries and horrible threats upon any who tried to pass that way.

29) **And lo, they yelled, saying, What have we to do with thee, Son of God? Didst thou come ahead of time to torment us?** The question τί ἡμῖν καὶ σοί; is idiomatic, literally translated, "What is there for us and for thee?" Here it has the sense, "Do thou leave us alone!" The plural identifies this spirit with others of his kind, and he speaks for all of them. In John 2:4 this formula is used for putting off an implied request while here it is used to ward off hostile action, B.-P., 335, under ἐγώ. The astounding thing is that the demoniacs, here as elsewhere, recognize and address Jesus as "Son of God." And with this is combined the supernatural knowledge of his coming to oust them from dominion.

Those who deny that evil spirits actually took possession of human beings resort to rather arbitrary and radical means to deny these facts. In the present case the words yelled at Jesus are not the words of these two men but of the vicious spirits that had possessed them. Jesus had come to deliver not to torment these men. In Mark 5:7, etc., the conversation of the demons with Jesus is fully detailed and it cannot be attributed to the men.

From Mark and from Luke we gather that the yell of the devils was preceded by the command of Jesus to come out of the men. The reply of the devils is a complaint that they are to leave their human victims "ahead of time," καιρός, an appointed or fixed season. To be ousted thus implies torment for them, i. e., to be sent back into the fiery abyss, Luke 8:31 (Rev. 20:10). The implication is that the devils know that they are doomed to torment in the abyss of hell. Satan's temptation of Jesus (4:1-11) was not an effort to escape the abyss but rather an attempt, by drawing Jesus into sin, to drag him, too, into the abyss. The καιρός is best referred to the final judgment when all the destructive powers of Satan and of the devils shall end; others think of the time of the death and the resurrection of Jesus when Satan was bound, Rev. 20:1.

30) **Now there was far from them a herd of many swine, feeding,** Mark 5:13: "about two thousand." We need not assume that the country was altogether Gentile, and that, therefore, the owners of these hogs were pagan. The eastern shore of the lake belonged to the tetrarchy of Philip and was part of the Jewish land; for Jesus, who confined himself to his own people, travelled as far north as Cæsarea Philippi in this tetrarchy. He was thus on Jewish territory. And, indeed, it would have been strange if the Jews, who at this time spread themselves over all the Roman empire, should not have migrated into Philip's tetrarchy, especially to the shore of the lake opposite the populous Jewish cities.

31) **And the demons were beseeching him, saying, If thou throwest us out, send us away into the swine.** The imperfect παρεκάλουν is descriptive and holds our attention until the aorist εἶπεν brings the answer of Jesus. Note how the demons speak about themselves. Beyond the fact that swine were unclean according to God's law as given to the Jews and thus in affinity with the unclean spirits, we have no further explanation for this strange request of the demons. They are already under orders to quit their present abode as they themselves indicate by the condition of reality, "if thou throwest us out."

32) **And he said to them, Be going! And when they had come out they went off into the swine. And lo, all the herd rushed down the bank into the sea and died in the water.** The present imperative ὑπάγετε, "be off," "away with you," can be understood

only as granting permission to the demons to enter the herd of swine. Mark and Luke tell us this in so many words; and from them we learn that a host of demons had taken possession of these two sufferers. This, too, is beyond our comprehension although we know that seven devils had taken possession of Mary Magdalene (Mark 16:9). It was illegal for Jews to possess swine; their destruction was, therefore, the execution of God's law. The fact that devils were used for this purpose is the constant practice of God who uses the devil to punish the wicked and sin and crime to execute judgment upon sinners. The fact that these devils destroyed the swine is only in harmony with their nature; nor can we think that they would be content to make their abode in mere brutes.

If these swine were owned by Gentiles, we should be left without a real explanation for their destruction. To say that the devils were ordered merely to leave the men, and that their entering the swine was their own act, contradicts their request to Jesus and the plain statements of Mark and of Luke that Jesus gave them permission. Equally untenable is the idea that when the swine felt the touch of the demons they reacted by rushing into the sea of their own volition. The demons drove them down the bank and into the water. We may agree that Jesus desired this action on the part of the demons and this fate of the swine as affording an ocular demonstration of the deliverance of the two men and at the same time a further exhibition of his divine power. The view that the demons went out of the men in a violent paroxysm is not indicated in the records.

33) **Now those feeding them fled and, having come into the city, reported everything, also the things concerning the demoniacs.** The reason for the flight of the swineherds is their fright at seeing the swine rush into the sea. To speak of terror because of the magic power of Jesus is unwarranted. Jesus never

acted like a sorcerer, and no man ever thought him to
be a magician.   These swineherds were responsible for
the swine, and this fact lent added speed to their feet.
The city here referred to is a small place that was only
a short distance from the lake.   While we may take it
that the swineherds ran to make report to the owners
of the swine, what they did was to tell everybody
"everything," καί adding especially "the things concerning the demoniacs," how Jesus had driven the devils out of them.

34)   **And lo, all the city came out to meet Jesus;
and, having seen him, they besought him that he
would depart from their borders.**   Everybody in the
small place (and neighborhood, Mark and Luke)
started out to the place where Jesus was with the
disciples who had come in the boats and with the two
men he had delivered.   There they saw Jesus (and the
two men, Mark and Luke) and heard the account of
all that had happened.   Matthew records only the main
points.   After they had been fully informed they ask
Jesus to leave their neighborhood.   Mark and Luke
name their motive, which was fear.   The aorist
παρεκάλεσαν implies that Jesus did as he was asked.
These people feared, not the sorcerer Jesus, but further
loss to themselves.   They cared nothing for the wonderful deliverance of the two demoniacs but only for
their swine.   Any further deliverance of poor human
sufferers at such a cost of material values, even though
these were owned in contravention of the divine law,
seemed to require too great a price for them to pay.
So Jesus departed, yet, as Mark and Luke report, he
ordered the men he had healed to remain behind and to
tell what the Lord had done for them.   This they did
faithfully in all the country (Mark 5:20), and not
without good results.   To some men hogs are more
valuable than men.

# CHAPTER IX

1) **And having entered into a boat, he crossed over and came into his own city.** This must have taken place on the same day, in the morning of which he healed the two demoniacs on the lake shore of Gadaritis (see 8:28) and then was asked by the inhabitants to leave their region. He left promptly. "A boat" is indefinite, yet we take it to be the one in which he had arrived, not one of the others that had accompanied him (Mark 4:36). Jesus returned to Capernaum which is here called "his own city" in contrast with the place he was leaving, where the people refused him the right to stay. Mark 2:1 bridges a gap, and Luke 5:17 offers only a loose connection as to time and place.

2) **And lo, they bring to him a paralytic lying on a bed. And having seen their faith, he said to the paralytic, Cheer up, child, dismissed are thy sins!** Matthew is acquainted with all the details recorded by Mark and by Luke but concentrates on the vital points of the story. The exclamation "lo" hints at the fact that this was not an ordinary case of bringing a sick man to Jesus. He was lowered through the roof by four of his friends because the throng in and around the home of Jesus was too dense to admit penetration. On the disease of paralysis compare 8:6. The faith that Jesus saw manifested itself plainly enough. It was more than the ordinary faith which sought help of Jesus; it was a faith strong, persistent, inventive enough to discover the most unusual way of placing the sick man before Jesus. Why *"their* faith" should exclude the faith of the paralytic, as some assert, is hard to see. Surely, his friends did not bring him against his will,

and surely, he must have consented to be lowered through the roof. It is true that Jesus healed some who had no faith at the moment and waited for faith to follow the healing; but no man's sins are forgiven without faith being present in his heart. Instead of ruling out the faith of the paralytic, we must credit him with stronger faith than that of his friends. They may have had faith only in the power of Jesus to heal miraculously. This paralytic felt that he suffered from a greater ailment than paralysis, and thus he came to Jesus with his burden.

Not a word is uttered by either the paralytic or his friends. More eloquent than words is the prostrate form lowered through the ceiling to the feet of Jesus, interrupting his teaching in the packed house. As a true καρδιογνώστης Jesus sees all that is involved in this sufferer's case and also all that it will mean for the present assembly and for all future time. First the soul, then the body. With the greatest tenderness Jesus absolves this sufferer's soul. Men saw only his bodily affliction, Jesus saw the guilt and the contrition in the man's heart. "Cheer up," the present imperative θάρσει, takes away the gloom and the discouragement from the man's heart and puts courage and happiness in its place. The address τέκνον, "child," is far more tender and gentle than "son"; it is like a mother's loving embrace. Jesus actually enters into this man's heart and condition with the master-touch of his love.

Now the mighty word of release, "dismissed are thy sins." The readings vary between the passive present ἀφίενται (or ἀφίονται) and the Doric yet common passive perfect ἀφέωνται (R. 315), the latter having its strong present implication. For both forms imply that the sins are dismissed the instant Jesus speaks this word. This is the great ἄφεσις, "dismissal" or "remission," of which the Scriptures speak so constantly. The sins are sent away from the sinner so completely that they

shall never be found again, to the depth of the sea, and
so far that no one can possibly bring them back, as far
as the east is from the west (Ps. 103). Only God is
able to send our sins away in this manner. The claim
that the agent back of this passive verb is God and not
Jesus is untenable. The entire narrative that follows
rests on the contrary. This case of healing furnishes
the clearest evidence for the deity of Jesus: as God he
forgives sins and proves it by healing the paralytic.

It is not necessary to conclude that this man's ailment was the direct product of his sinful life. In John
5:14 we have a case of this kind; but in John 9:3 an
entirely different case. As regards the paralytic, it is
sufficient to assume that his paralysis brought all his
sinfulness to mind just as every sickness and misfortune tells us that we are, indeed, nothing but sinners.
To assume more in this case would require a plain
intimation in the text. The Christian rule of charity
holds good also in the case of exegesis, namely, that we
should not make any man worse than he may be. To
this day hundreds of people suffer from paralysis without having lived a vicious life.

3) **And lo, certain of the scribes said within
themselves, He is blaspheming.** Luke adds that also
Pharisees were present. These men had come from
Jerusalem and Judea as well as from Galilee to keep
track of Jesus and to gather such evidence as they could
against him. Now they thought that they had a clear
case against him. Mark 2:7 and Luke 5:21 indicate
wherein they found the blasphemy. God alone, they
thought (and rightly), can forgive sins; in their estimation Jesus was not God but a mere man, hence when
he arrogated to himself the right to forgive sins he was
pretending to be God — the very worst type of
blasphemy.

4) All was silence — the only word uttered was
the absolution pronounced by Jesus. **And when**

**Jesus saw their thoughts he said, Why are you thinking wicked things in your hearts? For which is easier? to say, Dismissed are thy sins? or to say, Rise and be walking?** We retain the reading ἰδών as in v. 2, this being more unusual than εἰδώς, "knowing"; Jesus "saw" what these his enemies were thinking and he did this not merely by observing the look on their faces but by direct vision into their hearts, John 2:24, 25. This power he exercised whenever it was necessary for his ministry and to the extent to which it might be necessary. With stunning directness Jesus confronts these scribes with their own thoughts. He does not ask on what ground (διὰ τί) but for what purpose (ἱνατί, or ἵνα τί), they are thinking as they do; R. 739. That is why Jesus says "wicked things" and not faulty, incorrect things. Their hatred and their hostility to Jesus produced in their hearts corresponding reflections on what Jesus was doing and saying. These were "wicked" because they were prompted by the motive to injure and to destroy Jesus. Look well to the purpose of your reasonings for the secret motive is the vicious factor not the simple facts themselves.

5) That was the case here. We must regard γάρ as being merely explanatory, R. 1190. Jesus sets the right thoughts over against the vicious ones of the scribes. This is what they should ask: "Which is easier," requiring less exertion, "to say (εἰπεῖν, aorist: say effectively), Dismissed are thy sins! or to say (again the effective aorist), Rise and be walking!" Evidently, both require the identical power of God. As he alone can dismiss sins, so he alone can restore a paralytic on the instant. Note the aorist imperative ἔγειρε to denote the momentary act of rising up and the present imperative to indicate the continuous act of walking away.

6) In the same breath Jesus continues: **But in order that you may know that the Son of man has authority to dismiss sins on the earth (then says he to the paralytic), Having risen, take up thy bed and leave for thy house.** Jesus has performed the one act, forgiven the paralytic's sins. The effect of this act is invisible: no one saw the sins piled up on the man's soul, and no man saw that mass of sin vanish from his soul. Now Jesus follows this with the second act, he heals the paralytic. The effect is visible to all: they see the man rise, pick up his couch, and walk away not only freed of paralysis but restored to perfect health and strength, all this having been done in an instant. The act which the eyes are able to see verifies the other act which no eyes can see. As the one is wrought by the ἐξουσία, "the right and might" of him who is God, so is the other. For both are done by Jesus, not in and by the name of another, but in his own person, by the ἐξουσία that resides in himself. On "the Son of man" see 8:20. The fact that the title signifies one who, while he is truly man, is at the same time God, is evident from the demonstration which Jesus here gives. The title is especially in place over against the scribes who regarded Jesus as being only a man. Remitting sins "on the earth" is in harmony with the title "the Son of man" which Jesus gave himself during his stay on earth. He still forgives sins, but now he does so in his glorious heavenly state.

The ἵνα clause is not construed with a main clause, for dramatically Jesus turns to the paralytic and completes what he intends to say by the command which heals him. All that the insertion introduced with τότε intends is to tell the reader that in the middle of his words Jesus turns to the paralytic. This makes the insertion a parenthesis (R. 434) rather than an anacoluthon (R. 463). The Greek marks the man's rising up as being secondary to the main action and thus uses only a participle. The momentary acts of rising up and of taking up the couch are naturally expressed by means of aorists, while the longer act of walking home is expressed by means of a present imperative. Four men brought him on his pallet, he himself walks away carrying that pallet. The command to the paralytic (identical in all three records) is quite full, telling the man all he is to do, so that these hostile scribes may hear and then see it all.

7) **And having risen, he went to his house.** Mark adds "before them all; Luke, "before them," but appends, "glorifying God." Whereas the scribes charged Jesus with blasphemy, this man utters nothing but praise.

8) **But when the multitudes saw it, they were afraid and glorified God who gave such authority to men.** The effect upon the crowds inside and outside of the house was that "they were afraid," which implies more than astonishment or holy reverence. They felt themselves in the very presence of God as this was made manifest by this double act of Jesus. Peter had the same feeling in Luke 5:8. Matthew tells about the crowds only here at the end of his account, but we see that, while he abbreviates his account, he is acquainted with the story exactly as it happened. We cannot agree that some of the people were afraid while others praised God. We do not agree that the fear and the praise could not be attributed to the same people as Matthew records. The fear was the reaction of hearts that felt their sinfulness in this almost tangible presence of God; and the words of glorifying praise were uttered because of the wondrous benefactions this mighty presence had bestowed.

The aorist participle τὸν δόντα refers to one act of giving, and τοῖς ἀνθρώποις is an ordinary plural. R. 409 is right when he calls our attention to the double sense

of the participle, the giving to the man Jesus being
quite different from the giving to men. By sending
Jesus with the divine ἐξουσία men in general had it in
and through Jesus who was one of them, had it in the
actual wondrous gifts it bestowed. Note how the multitude borrows the word ἐξουσία from the lips of Jesus,
v. 6. Here the uneducated people saw more clearly
than the educated scribes. They saw God back of
Jesus, the divine right and might exercised by Jesus,
and this as a divine gift to men as a mass or whole.
In their praise to God the people generalize from what
they saw in the case of the paralytic, but this was easy
for them, for they had seen many other miracles and
now through this latest one understood all of them
more correctly. What the hateful scribes said and
did is passed by in significant silence.

9) **And as Jesus was passing by from thence he
saw a man sitting at his tax office, called Matthew,
and says to him, Be following me. And having risen,
he did follow him.** Jesus had left his own house
(ἐκεῖθεν) where he had healed the paralytic; he was
returning from the shore of the lake (Mark 2:13, 14)
and so came by Matthew's τελώνιον or tax office, where
he sat, busy with his work of collecting taxes. It seems
that the office had been located at the entrance to Capernaum, most likely on the great caravan route that came
in from Damascus and the East.

The Roman taxes were bought up by the *publicani,*
men of wealth and credit, in later times by Roman
knights, who paid a fixed sum into the state treasury
(*in publicum*). Under them were "chiefs of publicans" who were in charge of an entire taxing district
(like Zacchæus), and under these again common collectors who took in the taxes. "A man called Matthew"
most probably belonged to the latter class, and he collected the duty on goods that moved into and through
Capernaum. He was a custom officer, and in order to

hold that position had to know Greek and to be well educated. These collectors were hated and despised by the Jews, both because they served the Roman oppressors and thus lacked all patriotism, and because of their greedy exactions, for they usually demanded all they could get in order to enrich themselves. Naturally, only men of lower types of character took positions of this kind. We must note the humility with which Matthew designates himself, omitting his Jewish name Levi and that of his father Alphæus. All he does is to identify himself as the one chosen in 10:3 as one of the Twelve.

Although his call meant everything to him personally, he records only the simple facts. Jesus saw him and said only the one word, "Be following me!" He responded immediately; Luke 5:27 adds, "he forsook all." He got right up (ἀναστάς) and "did follow him," the aorist indicating that he did this permanently. It is plain that he must have had decisive personal contact with Jesus prior to this call, but nothing is said about it either in his own record or in that of the other evangelists. The call to attach himself to Jesus permanently involved financial loss, yet it replaced that loss with infinite spiritual gain. Perhaps Matthew was the last of the Twelve to be called. The fact that one of them should come from the despised class of the publicans is highly significant. How he came to have the name "Matthew" or Theodore is nowhere stated.

10) **And it came to pass while he was reclining at table in the house that, lo, many publicans and sinners, having come, were reclining at table together with Jesus and his disciples.** Luke 5:29 records that Levi made a great feast in his house for Jesus. The exact time is not indicated; compare v. 18. This feast has the appearance of being a celebration in honor of Jesus who had deigned to call Matthew, a

publican, to be a permanent follower of his. The Hebraistic turn καὶ ἐγένετο καί followed by a finite verb is common in the Gospels. We translate the second καί "that," since it introduces the thing that came to pass. The whole expression is circumstantial and introduces an occurrence of importance. On the grammar see R. 1042. Some are inclined to think that the first αὐτοῦ refers to Jesus, and that ἐν τῇ οἰκίᾳ with its article refers to the house of Jesus to which Matthew and these publicans and sinners were invited (ἐλθόντες) by Jesus. But why should Matthew and Luke differ on a little point such as this? If the first αὐτοῦ has the force; "he (Jesus) reclining at table in *the* house (that of Jesus)," Matthew could not withhold the name "Jesus" until toward the end of the sentence; he would have to write: "And it came to pass while *Jesus* was reclining . . . reclined *with him* (αὐτῷ) and his disciples." It is because αὐτοῦ refers to Matthew that toward the end we have no pronoun but the name τῷ Ἰησοῦ.

The present participle in the genitive absolute and then the imperfect tense of the main verb are beautifully descriptive. As the host Matthew takes his place on the couch, and it is understood that Jesus and his disciples do the same. The invited publicans and sinners who had come (ἐλθόντες) do likewise, and we thus see them as they "were reclining" in this intimate association with (σύν in the verb) no less a person than Jesus himself. The sentence is perfect in construction.

The fact that the publicans were "sinners" in the popular estimation, i. e., disreputable persons, does not need to be stated. The ἁμαρτωλοί are other men (no women would be present) of this general type who were classed as being outside of the Jewish pale (John 9:24, etc.), who, indeed, were living lives contrary to the divine law. But we dare not stop at this point and conclude that Christians in general and Christian pastors in particular may thus freely associate with men of the type here indicated. These publicans and sinners knew why they were invited, namely in order that Jesus might free them from their sins. It was he who had control of the entire situation and kept control of it, doing his necessary and blessed work upon them. This is an entirely different thing from being drawn into questionable company where we stoop to the low level of those present and allow them to use us for their purposes.

**11) And when the Pharisees had seen it they said to his disciples, On what ground is your teacher eating in company with the publicans and sinners?** We need not ask how the Pharisees saw what took place. They were always on the track of Jesus and thus noted the company that assembled at the house of this publican Matthew. They themselves would not enter and contaminate themselves by entering. They hovered about on the outside until the guests departed and then assailed the disciples; for despite their hostility to Jesus they never show any real courage in facing him on the issues they feel constrained to raise. With διατί they ask for the ground or reason of this practice on the part of Jesus (ἐσθίε, durative present), his eating with this class of people (one article combining publicans and sinners) ; compare the different ἱνατί in v. 4, which inquires after the purpose. The Pharisees shunned such people as outcasts and expected that Jesus would do no less. When he acted quite otherwise, they held this against him, Luke 15:1, 2. How could the disciples follow a διδάσκαλος whose practice was of this kind?

**12) But when Jesus heard it he said, The healthy have no need of a physician, but they that are ill. But go and learn what this means, Mercy I want and not sacrifice; for I did not come to call righteous men but sinners.** Perhaps Jesus saw the Pharisees questioning his disciples and thus heard about their objection to his conduct. Promptly he himself answers these men. His reply is an *argumentum ad hominem* which answers them on the basis of their own premises. They imagined that they were οἱ ἰσχύοντες, "those that are strong," sound, and healthy; and certainly they looked upon the publicans and sinners as "those that are ill," οἱ κακῶς ἔχοντες, the verb ἔχω with an adverb always meaning "to be." According to their own finding Jesus' course is justified. A physician is for the sick not for the healthy. It would be ridiculous and wrong for a doctor to remain away from his patients. It is his very business to deal with the sick in order to cure them, though without contaminating himself. Jesus does not associate with men of questionable lives in the ordinary way as "birds of a feather flock together." His great mission is to seek and to save the lost. He is the divine ἰατρός or Physician: "I am the Lord that healeth thee," Exod. 15:26. We know his power and his remedies. These Pharisees, however, refuse his healing ministrations and delude themselves that all is well with them. Yet in their heartlessness they would let those whom they themselves call sick perish. Their guilt is double, their disease twofold.

13) Jesus can do nothing but dismiss these self-deluded Pharisees. Yet in doing so, physician that he is, he gives them the remedy that they need, hoping that they may take it and return to him for complete healing. Jesus tells them to go and learn what the Lord said in Hos. 6:6: "Mercy I want and not sacrifice," i. e., merely sacrifice. "Mercy," ἔλεος, is pity and sympathy with the suffering. God's great mercy embraces us, and so he wants to fill us, too, with the quality of mercy. "Be ye therefore merciful as your Father is also merciful," Luke 6:36. "Sacrifice," θυσία, the offering itself as well as the act of bringing it, is here placed in opposition to "mercy," hence the latter must

mean human mercy. Here it is the merciful feeling that would bring the true Physician and his help to those that are sick. This the Pharisees not only lacked but even failed to understand. To their blind eyes the Scriptures were dark on this vital point as on so many others. They made their boast and their reliance the outward act of sacrifice and omitted what alone could make this act acceptable unto God, divinely-wrought mercy and love in their hearts, the reflection of God's mercy in themselves. They simply scorned and expelled publicans and sinners and made no effort to reach and to help them. Hence the command to go and learn what this is, μάθετε, the aorist imperative to indicate actual learning.

"For" indicates that, when the Pharisees have learned the sense of this divine word, they will understand the purpose and the work of Jesus, that he did not come in his great mission "to call righteous men but sinners." For the figurative language of v. 12 Jesus now substitutes the literal. He thus still continues the *argumentum ad hominem*. He takes these Pharisees' own estimate that they are, indeed, "righteous men." Then, of course, they do not need him. His business has to do only with "sinners," the unrighteous, to give them the true righteousness. But the very way in which the argument is stated shatters the supposition of these Pharisees that they are really δίκαιοι, able to stand before God's judgment bar. They had to feel that their claim to be righteous shut their own mouths when they complained about the help Jesus was offering to unrighteous sinners whom they only despised. And thus the hollowness of their own claim became apparent. Could they really be righteous when they knew no mercy for the sinners, were blind to the prophet's word demanding that they have mercy, and railed at the merciful Physician who labored among those who, according to these Pharisees themselves, so sorely needed his help? We thus see how the reply of Jesus to these Pharisees was a masterful effort to reach their hearts; for they were even worse sinners than those whom they despised.

In the Gospels the verb καλεῖν has the sense of "to invite," namely with the power of grace which kindles faith and attaches to Jesus. As thus used, many are called, yet not all are won. In the epistles καλεῖν and the cognate terms have a narrower sense, "to invite effectively" so that acceptance is included.

14) **Then there come to him the disciples of John, saying, What is the reason that we and the Pharisees fast many times while thy disciples do not fast?** Jesus and his disciples had just come from the feast in Matthew's house; and this seems to have occurred on a day when the disciples of John and the Pharisees likewise thought they had to fast (Mark 2:18). Here they were fasting, and the disciples of Jesus were feasting! The Baptist himself was in prison, 4:12; 11:2. Such of his disciples as were still attached to him were left to themselves. We here see them in touch with Jesus, and again two of them in 11:2. With διατί (compare v. 11) they ask the reason for this difference, in other words, who is right in this matter of fasting? Their question is not prompted by hostility but by perplexity. They want to know the reason for this great difference in regard to fasting.

The only fasting demanded by the law was that on the Day of Atonement (Lev. 23:27, etc.) The Pharisees voluntarily fasted twice in the week in their pretense to holiness; see 6:16; Luke 18:12. They are mentioned here only in a general way as people being given to regular fasting. The Baptist's stern call to repentance would naturally go together with fasting although none of the evangelists has preserved to us the exact teaching of the Baptist on this point. All that we can gather is that he had allowed his disciples to continue the practice of fasting.   By not asking his disciples to fast Jesus in no way contradicted the law. We see in 6:17 that he was by no means opposed to fasting as such when it was done for the proper purpose and in the proper way.   Note that these disciples of John come to Jesus himself with their perplexity and do not, as the Pharisees, take their accusation to the disciples of Jesus, v. 11.   They want enlightenment, the Pharisees want to discredit Jesus.

15)   **And Jesus said to them, Certainly, the sons of the bridal hall cannot mourn as long as the bridegroom is in their company?   But there will come days when the bridegroom shall be taken from them, and then they shall fast.**   The interrogative particle μή assumes that a negative answer will be given.   In a very simple way Jesus describes the present condition of his disciples to the followers of John.   They are like men at a wedding, even "the sons of the bridal hall," *die Hochzeitsgesellen,* the bridegroom's friends who have charge of all the wedding arrangements; see Edersheim, *The Life and Times of Jesus the Messiah,* I, 354, etc.; 663, etc.   How could they possibly be in sorrow and mourning when the bridegroom is in their midst?   We must stop with the relation here sketched and not bring in the bride or other essentials of a wedding.   But πενθεῖν, "to be mourning," should be noted. Fasting accompanies mourning and is not to be a mechanical arrangement that is followed merely on fixed days.   When the heart is bowed down, fasting is a proper expression of its feelings.   Who cares to eat at all, or more than a little, when he is greatly depressed?

Jesus predicts the coming of very sad days for the disciples who are now so happy with him, "when the bridegroom shall be taken from them," the days when Jesus shall lie dead in the tomb.   Then, indeed, they shall fast, and no one will need to tell them to do so.

16) More must be said. The question in regard to fasting is only a small part of a far greater subject. Hence to understand fully why the disciples of Jesus are not fasting at present, also how they will come to fast in a way that is totally different from that of the Jews, Jesus explains that what he brings cannot be fastened to an outworn garment as a mere patch, nor be confined in old, dried wineskins, like new wine. **Moreover, no one fastens a patch of new goods on an old garment; for its filling tears something away from the garment, and the rent becomes worse.** The new consideration is indicated by δέ. Jesus is not like a foolish woman who patches an old outer robe that begins to give way with a patch (ἐπίβλημα) taken from a piece of goods (ῥάκος) that is fresh from the loom (ἄγναφος). The reason is that the piece used to fill in (τὸ πλήρωμα αὐτοῦ) tears or carries away something from the old garment (ἀπὸ τοῦ ἱματίου, partitive: a portion from the robe) and leaves the rent worse than it was before. To preserve the old by attaching a little of the new is worse than useless. Discard the old entirely and accept the new completely. Not a new patch but a new robe.

Jesus is uttering a principle, one on which he acts and is training his disciples to act. John's disciples were perplexed when they saw him and his disciples acting on this principle, for they did not understand either what that principle was, or how true and genuine it was. The old robe is the Judaism of that period, namely, what the scribes and the Pharisees had made of it with their doctrine and their practice, all the old formalism, outward observance, and false righteousness (5:20). It was useless to try to patch this with a bit of the teaching or the practice of Jesus. The new would only tear the old more than ever. The doctrine of grace and faith and the life that springs from it cannot possibly be combined, even in small part,

with Pharisaic Judaism either in its ancient or its modernistic forms.    Discard the old, rotten robe, take in
its place the robe of Christ's righteousness!

17)    **Nor do people put new wine into old wineskins; else the skins burst, and the wine is spilled,
and the skins are destroyed.    But they put new wine
into fresh skins, and both are preserved.**    This illustration advances the thought.    The old cannot be
kept by adding *a little* of the new, nor by combining
*all* of the new with it.    In this respect there is a parallelism of thought.    But again both illustrations speak
of conserving: the first, the old robe; the second, the
new wine.    The old robe cannot be conserved by adding
the new patch; the new wine cannot be conserved by
pouring it into old wineskins.    In this respect the illustrations are opposites.    The second, however, ends in
a climax: both the new wine and the old wineskins are
lost.    A wineskin was a goatskin that was removed
from the animal without slitting it; the openings at the
feet and the tail were bound up, leaving the neck as
the mouth of the wineskin.    In Palestine we saw these
skins still being used by watercarriers.    When it is
new, the skin stretches to a certain degree; but when it
is old, it becomes stiff and splits under pressure.    People, therefore, never put new wine into old and dried-
out skins.    The result would be disastrous, for the
skins would burst, and both skins and wine would be
lost.    In εἰ δὲ μήγε we have a protasis that has been condensed to a mere formula; νέος is "new" as not having
existed before, while καινός is "new" over against "old"
or παλαιός.    Jesus is not a foolish person who tries to
combine the old Pharisaic ways with the glorious new
doctrine of grace and faith, by this folly ruining both,
with a result that is even worse than if he combined the
old ways with a scrap of the new doctrine.    Nor does
Jesus want others to attempt this folly.    Cast aside

all the old Pharisaism with all its ways; take only the new ways of life that fit the new doctrine.

The illustrations here used have often been misapplied. Because Christ's teaching is now old, modernistic thinkers have compared it to old, dried-out wineskins and state that it is no longer to be combined with the new religious ideas now current. They call for new moral codes and standards, new "categories of thought," new conceptions of sin and righteousness, new visions of God, etc. But their new ideas are ancient and the teaching of Christ is still as new, true, and glorious as it was in the days when he walked on earth. The ancient Pharisaism has changed only its name and its applications; the verities which Jesus taught are still verities and will be nothing less until the end of time. Away completely with the former; let us keep only the latter, even as Jesus still tells us to do!

18) **While he was saying these things to them, lo, a certain ruler, having come, worships him, saying, My daughter just died; but, after coming, place thy hand upon her, and she shall live.** Compare Mark 5:21 and Luke 8:40. Matthew furnishes the exact sequence of events. In the morning Jesus returned to Capernaum from the country of the Gadarenes and went to his own house. There a crowd gathered, and he healed the paralytic. Then Jesus dined at Matthew's house, probably in the late afternoon, and following the meal he answered the Pharisees and the disciples of John. Matthew's office and house, we assume, was located at the landing place on the road beside the lake. Thus "he was now by the sea," Mark 5:21. As he was still speaking to John's disciples, Jairus appeared, one of the rulers of the synagogue whom Matthew designates only as ἄρχων εἷς (the latter word being used like the indefinite τὶς), "a certain ruler." On this indefinite use of the numeral compare

12:11; 18:5; 21:19. The ruler prostrates himself before Jesus in the Oriental fashion of utmost humility
and utters his petition. Mark writes ἐσχάτως ἔχει, "she
is at the last," i. e., at the point of death; Luke, αὕτη
ἀπέθνῃσκεν, "she was dying," i. e., when the father left.
Matthew, however, writes ἄρτι ἐτελεύτησεν, "she just died."
Matthew narrates the entire story in a single paragraph while Mark and Luke devote much more space
to it. So Matthew omits mention of the coming of the
messengers who tell Jairus that death had just set in.
Instead of adding these details, Matthew at once lets us
learn the essential fact from Jairus, namely, that his
daughter was actually dead. The explanation that in
his perturbation Jairus overstated the case and called
the girl dead when she was only at the point of death
affords no solution but merely inverts the matter.

When Jairus asks that Jesus shall come and lay his
hand upon his daughter he is thinking of other cases in
which Jesus touched the person when working the
miracle and assumes that Jesus will do so in this
case. To be sure, this is less faith than that of the
centurion (8:8), yet when Jairus says, ζήσεται, "she
shall live," he shows that his faith is by no means
insignificant.

19) **And having started, Jesus followed him,
also his disciples.** The participle ἐγερθείς, like ἀναστάς,
by no means compels us to assume that Jesus was
sitting and thus arose, or that he was still reclining
at table in Matthew's house and arose to go with
Jairus. This participle is used to mark the beginning
of an action in the sense of "having started"; we may
translate, "And Jesus up and followed him." Matthew indicates that he is acquainted with all the
details of the story although he omits them from his
record; for he mentions the fact that also the disciples went along. From Mark's and from Luke's
accounts we know that Jesus took three of them,

Peter, John, and James, into the room where he brought the child back to life.

20) **And lo, a woman, suffering hemorrhage for twelve years, having come up behind, touched the tassel of his robe; for she was saying within herself, If only I may touch his robe I will be restored.** Eusebius calls her Veronica, a heathen from Paneas; the Acts of Pilate call her Bernice. We credit neither story, least of all that she was a heathen. The nature of her ailment is not determined by the mere participle, and guesses are gratuitous. From Mark's and from Luke's accounts we gather that the drain on her strength was constant, for it ceased the moment the woman touched the tassel. She was ashamed to expose her case; moreover, her ailment rendered her Levitically unclean. Matthew omits mention of the fact that for twelve years (accusative of extent of time) she had vainly spent her money in seeking a cure, and that thus at this time her case was beyond human help. Matthew says nothing about the crowds that accompanied Jairus and Jesus. He states only that, working her way up behind him, she reached out and touched the tassel of his robe. Like all true Jews, Jesus wore the *shimla,* a square cloth that was used as an outer robe and had tassels (*tsitsith,* κράσπεδον) at the four corners according to the requirement laid down in Deut. 22:12. The tassels were attached to blue cords. The Pharisees loved to make the tassels large and prominent in order to display their compliance with the law. Two of the corners of the *shimla* were thrown back over the shoulders so that two of the tassels hung down the back. One of these the woman managed to touch.

21) This she did with the inner conviction that the touch would bring her healing; σωθήσομαι, "I shall be saved," i. e., from my ailment.

22) **But Jesus, having turned and seen her,
said, Cheer up, daughter, thy faith has restored
thee! And the woman was restored from that very
hour.** Matthew is again very brief as compared
with Mark and with Luke; he notes only the mere
essentials. Jesus does not let the woman slip away
as she desired to do. And does this first because of
his concern for her and secondly because of the others
present. They, too, are to know what has been done
for her. She is to know just how she has come to
be healed. According to Mark and to Luke, Jesus
makes her declare herself, which she does with fear
and trembling, thinking that Jesus may be angry
with her. But his purpose is to impress upon her
the fact that she was healed by his knowledge and his
will. Many in that throng touched Jesus and nothing
resulted. Only to this woman's touch of faith did
Jesus respond with his power. With the bidding,
θάρσει, θύγατερ! Jesus dispels all her fear and reveals
his tender concern and love.

Those who refer to superstition on the woman's
part which manifested itself in her merely touching
the tassel, or to magnetism on Jesus' part as producing the healing, misunderstand this miracle; for superstition obtains no instantaneous or any other cures,
and magnetism, electric current, etc., bestow no instantaneous, miraculous cures. Why not accept the
word of the Savior who tells this women, "Thy faith
has restored thee"? Certainly, her faith not as the
*causa efficiens* which was the will and the power of
Jesus, but as the ὄργανον ληπτικόν, the hand that received
the gift. The idea that this woman's faith rested only
on touching his garment and not on Jesus' Word, is
also untenable. Luther has a better idea: she believes that divine, omnipotent power resides in Jesus;
that he can answer the secret, unspoken trust of her
heart; that all she needs is the Word and the preach-

ing by which he has made himself known, and she uses the touch of his garment only in some way to come into contact with him. Who has seen such wonderful people: this Jairus who trusts that the hand of Jesus touching his dead child can bring back her life, and this woman who trusts that her touch of his garment will bring her restoration? No wonder that Jesus rewarded such faith. The perfect σέσωκε reaches back to the instant in which Jesus restored her and includes her continued restoration; the same effect is produced by the aorist ἐσώθη followed by ἀπό.

23) **And when Jesus had come to the house of the ruler and had seen the flute players and the crowd making a din, he was saying: Be leaving, for the girl did not die but is sleeping. And they were laughing him to scorn.** Matthew at once takes us to the house where the Jewish mourning is in full blast. Judging from the indications of time in this chapter, it must have been toward dusk, and the child would be buried the next morning. Matthew alone mentions the hired "flute players"; beside them would be found the hired wailing women with hair streaming, beating their breasts and filling the air with loud moans and bursts of sobs. The prominence of the family would call for a goodly number of these hired mourners. Besides there would be present many friends of this important family. The whole house was thus full of noise. Paid mourners were professionals at the business, and the custom of having them in houses of mourning and at funerals dates far back, even beyond the times of Jeremiah (9:17), and is found among Jews and pagans alike. Naturally, Jesus would order these people out and hush them; a deed such as he was about to do called for the decency and the dignity of silence.

24) The word with which Jesus put out the noisy crowd has sometimes been misunderstood as though it implied that the girl had merely lapsed into a coma and appeared to be dead while still holding to life. "Did not die" is taken to deny the death, and "sleepeth" is understood to refer to sleep. But the people who were ordered out of the room knew better; from their loud wailing they turned to scornful laughter at this word of Jesus, *sie lachten ihn aus.* According to Mark 5:35 Jairus is informed: ἀπέθανεν, "she did die"; Luke 8:49 has τέθνηκεν, "she has died" and thus is dead, and adds the statement that the people "knew that she died." The explanation that Jesus spoke as he did because he wanted to veil his miracle, is unacceptable; he does not equivocate or deceive. "Did not die but is sleeping" is spoken in view of the omnipotent power and will of him who can bring life back with a word. The word is true because of him who makes it true. What is gained by the rationalistic assumption of a coma? Can human power abolish a coma with a grasp and a word? Note the two imperfect tenses ἔλεγεν and κατεγέλων; they picture the scene in its progress and hold us in suspense as to the outcome.

25) **Now when the crowd was put out, having gone in, he grasped her hand, and the girl rose up.** Here we again have marked abbreviation. Nothing is said about the five witnesses who were admitted to the death chamber, the word spoken to the girl, the resulting amazement, and other details found in Mark and in Luke. The latter adds: ἐπέστρεψεν τὸ πνεῦμα αὐτῆς, "her spirit did return," leaving not even the shadow of a doubt that the girl had been dead and was brought back to life. With a record of this restoration of the dead unto life Matthew is content — all the details are entirely minor. Note that after the two imperfects in

v. 24 two aorists report the outcome and thus conclude the action.

26) **And this report went out into that entire
land.** The parents may have followed the command
to tell no one what had been done (Luke 8:56), but
the miracle itself could not be kept quiet: it stood
out above the other miracles, forming a climax to all
of them.

27) **And as Jesus was passing along from there,
two blind men followed him, yelling and saying,
Show us mercy, Son of David!** It was the evening
of this memorable day. Jesus is on his way home
after having performed the miracle at the house of
Jairus. Here two blind men, led by somebody, follow Jesus with the loud yell that he have mercy on
them, ἐλεέω is transitive. The exceptional feature is
that they address him as "Son of David," a Jewish
designation for the Messiah, bearing with it the conception of kingship and royal dominion. Jesus walks
along the street and pays no attention to these peti-
tioners. "Son of David," like "Messiah," bore a
political significance to the Jews, one that Jesus did
not want to foster in the minds of the people who
would thus be moved to the attempt to make him
a political king. That seems to be the real reason
why Jesus disregards these blind men on the public
street.

28) **Now when he was come into the house, the
blind men came to him. And Jesus says to them,
Do you believe that I am able to do this? They say
to him, Yes, Lord.** Already the aorist ἠκολούθησαν
indicates that the blind men were successful in their
following Jesus. The article with οἰκίαν points to the
particular house in which Jesus made his home in
Capernaum. We see that the blind men persist in
their request for help. The question of Jesus in re-

gard to their faith in his power to heal them does not
imply, as has been supposed, that their calling him
"Son of David" is insufficient evidence of faith in
his power; for their cry for mercy proves that very
faith. Nor does this question imply that it is always
necessary to have faith before Jesus can work a
miracle of healing or of help. This generalization is
voided by the cases in which the miracles precede faith
and in which faith is expected to follow, compare the
healing of the two demoniacs in 8:28, etc. The purpose of Jesus' question is to turn the thoughts of
these blind men way from any political Messianic
ideas regarding Jesus and to direct them to the divine
power and grace found in him. The emphasis is not
merely on "do you believe" but equally on the object
clause, "that I am able to do this." One who is able
to restore sight by means of a touch and a word is
far greater than any national king, however grand
his reign may be.

29) **Then he touched their eyes, saying, According to your faith be it unto you!** Jesus now heals
them at once. Since they were blind, the touch of
Jesus had a special significance. This did not imply
that he conveyed his power through the physical
touch but that he let them feel that his power and his
will were dealing with their blind eyes. "According
to your faith" mentions faith, not as being the *causa
efficiens*, in fact, not as being the cause in any sense
(contra R. 609), but as being the norm. The
measure of their expectant trust is matched by the
measure of help extended by the word and the will of
Jesus. Their trust in his divine power is justified by
what this divine power works in them. Note the punctiliar force of the aorist γενηθήτω: "let it be on the
instant!"

30) **And their eyes were opened,** i. e., to perfect sight. The aorist states the astounding fact.

So brief the record, so tremendous the fact it reports. **And Jesus sternly charged them, See to it, let no one know!** The verb ἐμβριάομαι is very strong, "to snort at one," *anherrschen*, here to demand in the sternest way. The reason for this sternness lies in the manner in which these men called Jesus the Son of David. The claim that Jesus did not wish to be known as a worker of miracles is not tenable, for he constantly worked miracles in the most public way before great multitudes, and the report of his miracles penetrated even to the countries round about. These commands to keep silent have each their specific purpose. In this instance the aim cannot be that no one is to find out that Jesus healed these blind men, for all their relatives and their friends would see their restored eyes and thus know what had happened. The object must be that Jesus is not to be proclaimed as the Son of David. Yet he could not specify this point and the reasons for not allowing himself to be broadcast as the great heir to David's throne; for such explanations could not be made clear to these men, mere beginners in faith that they were.

**31)** **They, however, having gone out, advertised him in that entire land.** Let us hope that they kept still about anything that suggested a political tinge to Jewish minds. It seems to be poor gratitude thus to do, in a way at least, what their great benefactor ordered them not to do. But they probably intended it as real gratitude to him.

**32)** Jesus has not yet completed his labor for the day. **Now while they were going out, lo, they brought to him a dumb demoniac.** The connection of time is plainly marked: those coming in passed those going out. To the more remarkable miracles which have already been related in this chapter these last two which are less remarkable are added because they occurred on the same day. By giving us this list of

miracles in chapters 8 and 9 Matthew takes us through
a few days of the full tide of Jesus' ministry. Friends
or relatives brought in this poor sufferer. The demon
that possessed him inhibited his power of speech.
Comparing this man with the two described in 8:28,
we see how differently demoniacal possession affected
its victims. The supposition that this man's loss of
speech was due to natural causes is not tenable. For
the words and the deeds of Jesus regard him as one
who was actually possessed.

33) **And when the demon was expelled, the
dumb man spoke.** Merely the two facts, the historical aorist participle indicating the one, and the
historical principal verb the other, λαλεῖν meaning "to
utter," the opposite of being silent. **And the multitudes were filled with wonder, saying, Never was
it seen thus in Israel. But the Pharisees were saying, In conjunction with the ruler of the demons does
he expel the demons.** When closing his two chapters on the miracles of Jesus, Matthew summarizes
the general effect produced upon the people. The
statement about the wonder of "the multitudes" cannot be restricted to this last miracle, for no multitude was present when this was performed, this
miracle, also, being less impressive than others
recorded in this section. The people are speaking of
all that they have witnessed and heard from other
witnesses. In the entire history of Israel nothing
has ever appeared that is comparable to all that Jesus
has just done. The second passive aorist ἐφάνη is impersonal: "it did appear," hence, "it was seen."

34) The remark regarding the Pharisees and
what they kept saying (ἔλεγον, imperfect) is questioned
by some who say that it does not belong in this place
since a similar remark occurs in 12:24. But the two
remarks are not identical. There is no reason to
think that the Pharisees did not repeat this vicious

explanation and finally adopt it as a fixed reply to
Jesus. The fact that they have an answer only to
the miracles wrought upon demoniacs indicates that
they had no reply for all the other miracles. Matthew
thus informs us that in his miracles Jesus met this
opposition and that it centered only on this one type
of miracle. We take ἐν in its ordinary meaning:
"in connection with," "in union with." The Pharisees
charged that Jesus was in league with Satan whom
they call "the ruler of the demons." Satan obliges
Jesus by withdrawing the demons from their victims
when Jesus wants this done. In due time Jesus exploded this charge. It is typical of all the "explanations" which unbelief has given regarding the
miracles.

We may here glance at some of the efforts to explain the miracles of Christ. The miracles are divided
into the following clases: exorcisms, cures of diseases,
nature miracles. The last-named are the most difficult
to explain, and the modernist sometimes finds that "it
is necessary to question the literal accuracy of the
narrative." But we ask, if "the literal accuracy,"
or as it is also stated, "the historicity of these narratives," is "questioned," which means *denied,* what
have we left? Only what the questioner may offer
us. What the inspired writer recorded is taken from
us, what the "modern mind" thinks is substituted.

Why apply this process of reasoning only to the
nature miracles? Scientific consistency ought to apply
it to all the miracles, and not to the miracles alone but
to Scripture in general. This would give us a Bible
made by the "modern mind" according to its own ideas,
subject also to any future changes this "mind" may
find desirable. The following is a sample which
removes the literalness and the historicity of the
text: "The miracle of the stilling of the storm
may have been a complete change in the minds of

the disciples, rather than in the actual state of the weather." To the "modern mind" exorcism "can easily be explained on psychological principles, which are gradually being understood." The curing of diseases — advanced leprosy, paralysis, and we may add congenital blindness and deformity of limbs — is explained as being due to "the intense convictions" and "the unique personal force" of Jesus, and "thus need cause no serious difficulty." But such hazy remarks are unsatisfactory and do not do justice to the facts in the case.

35) **And Jesus continued to go about all the cities and the villages, engaged in teaching in their synagogues and in proclaiming the good news of the kingdom and in healing every disease and every sickness.** This repeats 4:23 with only minor verbal changes. The program outlined in 4:23 is thus completed, yet we now learn that Jesus continued it. What Matthew has in chapters 5-9 shown us of the preaching, teaching, and miracles is only a grand sample of Christ's constant ministry. On the details of this verse compare 4:23.

36) **But when he saw the multitudes he was filled with compassion for them because they were distressed and prostrate like sheep not having a shepherd.** From the work of Jesus, Matthew takes us to the motive that lay back of all this work, the Lord's great compassion. The aorist tense is historical and refers to a specific time, when, standing, perhaps, on a height with the Twelve, he saw the multitudes coming toward him from various directions. The verb σπλαγχνίζομαι means to have the viscera moved, lungs, heart, and liver, which are considered to be the seat of the feelings, such as love, pity, etc. We may say, "his heart was stirred." Of the three words translated "being compassionate" this is the strongest, for it indicates not only a pained feeling at sight of

suffering, but in addition a strong desire to relieve
and to remove the sufferings; συμπάσχειν stops with the
sympathy which feels the other's suffering, and ἐλεεῖν
means to show mildness or kindness. On Christ's
compassion compare 14:14; 15:32; Mark 1:41; 6:34;
Luke 7:13. "These instances in which the compassion of Jesus is expressly recorded are so much
evidence, proving that his heart was ever filled with
merciful kindness and feelings of pity for the distressed of every description. Whenever and wherever
suffering and sorrow of body or soul met his eyes, his
heart was moved with compassion. The compassion
of Jesus is one of the deepest, richest, most comforting
of all his Savior qualities." The author's *His Footsteps*, 245.

The casual observer of the multitudes would never
have seen what Jesus saw. This required a heart
such as the Savior's. The two perfect participles
are regarded as adjectives; their tense describes a
present condition as resulting from a past act.
Ἐσκυλμένοι means, "having been flayed," or milder,
"having the skin torn," as this happens to sheep
wandering among brambles and sharp rocks.
Ἐρριμμένοι (variously spelled, from ῥήγνυμι) means,
"thrown down prone and helpless" like exhausted,
spent sheep; this verb is used with reference to corpses
lying prostrate on the ground. Both participles are
made vivid by the comparison: "like sheep not having
a shepherd." Soon they look abject, torn and exhausted, a sight to rend the heart.

What follows shows that Jesus is thinking of the
spiritual condition of the people. Such shepherds as
they had were no shepherds, were often worse than
none. Their souls received no wholesome spiritual
food and care, for, as far as that was concerned, they
were left to shift for themselves. Material and
physical destitution moves our humanitarian age

deeply, but who cares for or even sees spiritual distress? Matthew's description of the compassion of Jesus is so striking that in all probability he derived it from an expression uttered by Jesus himself.

**37) Then he says to his disciples, The harvest abundant, the workers few. Ask, therefore, of the Lord of the harvest that he throw out workers into his harvest.** Here Matthew makes the transition to the new section, the commissioning of the apostles. We also see how the compassion of Jesus at once manifests itself in action. First, Jesus points to the two great facts: "the harvest abundant — the workers few." The beautiful balance of μέν and δέ cannot be reproduced in English; the "truly" and "but" of our versions is too coarse. Jesus does not say, "the *field* is large," i. e., to till and to sow. He views only the harvest. We must remain with the *tertium comparationis* and not speak of sowing, cultivating, and producing the harvest. The harvest has already been produced — Jesus sees it.

"The harvest" is sometimes misunderstood. Some think that it refers to the multitudes that Jesus saw coming to him; but some of these people would not be gathered into the heavenly garner. The great missionary authority G. Warneck looks at the harvest through synergistic eyes; he thinks of it as representing the seekers after God, supposing that even among the heathen there is a "better" class of men. Yet all are equally lost, and by nature none seek after God. He is found by them that sought him not, Isa. 65:1; Rom. 10:20; compare John 6:44. Others think of the gathering of a new congregation from the scattered old congregation, namely its receptive members. The harvest are the sheep which the Lord knows, including also "the other sheep," John 10:14, etc. "The Lord knoweth them that are his," II Tim. 2:19. By "the harvest" Jesus means all those in whom the work of God's grace succeeds. And this harvest is πολύς, "much" or "abundant." The number of those that will be saved is large. Like a great, ripe field of grain they stand before the eyes of Jesus, needing only to be gathered in.

That is why he speaks of "the workers." Up to this point Jesus alone was working at bringing in the harvest, training the Twelve at the same time, so that they were now ready to help him. How small this number, considering Palestine alone! The remarkable thing is that Jesus asks the disciples to be concerned about this paucity of workers, and that in a significant way: "they are to ask the Lord of the harvest to throw workers into the harvest." According to 3:12 Jesus himself might be considered the owner of the harvest, but in 3:12 we have a different imagery. Here God is "the Lord of the harvest," its Κύριος, not only the owner, but the one who controls the entire management of the harvest. God has put this harvest and its ingathering into Jesus' hands. It is his great mission to bring in this harvest. That explains all he has already done and all he will yet do, including his atoning death and resurrection. Without him the harvest could not at all be brought in. In the compassion of Jesus for the lost sheep and in his word to the Twelve we see his own deep, personal concern for the harvest. He has, however, now trained the Twelve sufficiently so that they can join him in this concern. And that to the extent that they not only themselves lay hands to the work of ingathering but also see the need of more workers and are moved to pray for them.

38) Verbs of praying are construed with ὅπως, which ἵνα has not crowded out, B.-D. 392, 1; R. 995. We cannot argue that the Lord of the harvest, owning it as he does, will naturally see to it that it is brought in. We may be sure that he will do so even with-

out our    prayer (as Luther remarks in connection
with the Second Petition of the Lord's Prayer).    Our
prayers do not save the harvest or even a part of it.
Our prayers unite in God's concern for the harvest,
make us of one mind, heart, and will with him, partners of Jesus himself.    The matter goes much deeper
than rationalizing thoughts are able to penetrate.
Jesus does not tell the disciples to go out and to get
workers.    This mistake has often been made, and
workers are brought in that God has not called.    The
harvest is God's, and he must provide the workers,
ἐκβάλλειν εἰς, "throw them out into the harvest," i. e.,
hurry them out.    All that we are to do is "to ask"
this of God, and we know that this is his will, and
that he will hear our request.    He is the one who
in his own way will find and send out the workers.
The wonder will always remain that God, the primal
cause, uses us and our prayers, the secondary causes,
and does not discard them.    The secret of this conjunction lies in the infinite grace of the divine will
which unites him and us through Jesus.    When
one note is struck, the other responds, keyed as
they are to the one tone.    What a blessed relation
between the workers in the harvest and the Lord of
the harvest!

# CHAPTER X

## VII

### Christ Appoints his Apostles, Chapter 10

1) Although 9:36-38 prepares for chapter 10, the contents of this chapter form an independent section. Compare Mark 3:13, etc.; Luke 9:1, etc. When Jesus sent out the Seventy a little later, he again spoke the word about the plenteous harvest and the few laborers (Luke 10:1-3; Matt. 9:37). Nor need it cause surprise that some of the directions given to the Twelve in our present chapter were likewise given to the Seventy, Luke 10:4, etc. The exact time of the commissioning of the Twelve is not indicated; for 9:35 places us into the midst of the travels of Jesus in Galilee where Jesus saw the multitudes in their deplorable condition. **And having called unto him his twelve disciples, he gave them authority over unclean spirits, to expel them, also to heal every disease and every sickness.** This reads as though it at once followed upon 9:36-38. Matthew repeatedly uses προσκαλεσάμενος in the ordinary sense of calling someone unto himself to face him. Here the Twelve are asked to stand before Jesus in order to receive their commission. We see that Matthew emphasizes the number "twelve," repeating it in verses 2 and 5. The Twelve, as here introduced, appear as already being a fixed group of whom Matthew's readers know without his needing to state how these twelve men came to be such a group. The word "disciples" is broader. It may refer to some or all of the Twelve together with others

who followed Jesus as believers, according as the context requires.

Only the fact is stated that the Twelve were given
the mighty ἐξουσία over unclean spirits (an objective
genitive, R. 500), the term denoting both the power
and the right to use that power. With what words
this "authority" was given we are not told. "So as to
expel them," ὥστε with the infinitive, is scarcely pure
purpose (R. 990) but contemplated result (R. 1089-
1090). The second infinitive, "and to heal," etc., cannot depend on ὥστε but must be construed with ἐξουσία:
"authority also to heal." The notion that *all* disease
and sickness is due to evil spirits is not supported in the
Scriptures and cannot in this instance be based on a
grammatical construction alone. The demons, of whom
we have heard before, are here called "unclean πνεύματα,"
spirit beings, evil angels, denominated "unclean" or
impure to describe their defiled and defiling character;
they are the very opposite of God and of his holy angels.
Sin is always vile. "Authority over unclean spirits" is
defined by the ὥστε clause. Jesus grants the Twelve
the very same power which he possesses, to free men
from demoniacal possession and to heal them from all
kinds of ailments. The bestowal of this "authority"
upon the Twelve and then upon the Seventy (Luke
10:17-20) reveals his deity.

2) **Now the names of the twelve apostles
are these: the first, Simon, called Peter, and Andrew,
his brother; James, the son of Zebedee, and
John, his brother; Philip and Bartholomew;
Thomas and Matthew, the publican; James the son
of Alphæus, and Thaddeus; Simon, the Cananæan,
and Judas Iscariot, the one that did also betray him.**
Ἀπόστολος, derived from ἀποστέλλειν, "to commission," the
verb which Jesus often uses to define his own mission
from the Father, denotes much more than a servant
sent to deliver a message; it denotes a duly empowered

representative, an ambassador or legate who acts for his lord or king. While this word is at times used in a broad sense so as to include the helpers of the Twelve and Paul, here "the twelve apostles" include only this definite number. They have an immediate call from Jesus, and this is issued because of their future fundamental work (Eph. 2:20) in the church; their inspired records constitute the doctrinal foundation of the church. Jesus now made the Twelve such "apostles," hence the list of names. "Twelve" is repeated (in v. 5, and in 11:1), matching the twelve patriarchs and the twelve tribes of Israel.

The list is grouped in pairs — they at first went out two by two. Peter is always named first, Iscariot always last, and (making three groups with four in each group) the same names are always found in each group only the order being changed here and there. Matthew mentions only Judas and Peter in the rest of his Gospel. Πρῶτος, "the first," does not place the others under Peter as being the pope but names him as *primus inter pares.* He was not even the first to come to Jesus (John 1:41, 42). Writing for Jews, Matthew calls him "Simon" and adds the other name by which he was distinguished from other Simons and by which the Lord prophetically honored him. His brother Andrew is naturally associated with him. James and John, a second pair of brothers, are listed according to age, and James is distinguished from others who bore this name by the modifier "(son) of Zebedee" (he was martyred, cf. Acts 12:2).

3) Bartholomew is a patronymic: son of Tolmai (Ptolomy), the Nathanel of John 1:45, etc. Matthew places his own name after that of Thomas and also humbly adds "the publican," a designation which none of the other three lists contains. The second James is also identified according to his parentage. It seems that Thaddeus had two other names: Lebbeus and

Judas (John 14:22). This latter name would naturally
be dropped after the betrayal on the part of Judas
Iscariot. See the critics in regard to the reading.

4) The second Simon is distinguished as "the
Cananæan," which term has nothing to do with Canaan
but is a transcription of the Aramaic term which means
ὁ Ζηλωτής. Simon was a former adherent of the Jewish
party of "the Zealots" (Acts 5:37; Josephus, *Ant.*, 18,
1, 1 and 6; *Wars*, 2, 8, 1). Judas is identified as "Iscariot," "the man of Kerioth," being thus named from
his home town in Judea. In John 6:70 his father.
Simon bears this appellation. In the Gospels he is designated as the traitor, ὁ παραδούς, the aorist participle
being used as an apposition and denoting the historical
fact: "did betray," i. e., hand over to the Jews.

5) **These twelve Jesus commissioned, having
charged them, saying, etc.** This group of men and
their number are again stressed. The chief act is expressed by the finite aorist ἀπέστειλεν, to which the secondary act is added by means of the aorist participle
παραγγείλας. Mark 6:7-13 reports how the Twelve were
sent out, the charge to them being abbreviated, and
the work they did on their first mission is briefly
sketched. Luke 9:1-6 is similar. In Mark 6:30, etc.,
and in Luke 9:10 we hear about the return of the
Twelve and the quiet conference Jesus had with them.
Matthew says nothing about the mission of the Seventy
and the charge with which they were sent out (Luke
10:1, etc.). The fact that this would be similar to the
charge given the Twelve need not be stated. This
leaves Matt. 10:16-42 as a unit, which is sometimes
regarded as incorporating or containing instructions
that were issued much later (such as Mark 13:9-13;
Luke 21:12-19). This conclusion may be questioned.
Matthew, himself one of the Twelve, records the complete charge as it was given by Jesus when the Twelve
were first sent out. He is telling us, not, like **Mark**

and Luke, only of the mission to Galilee during the next
days or weeks, but of the complete apostolic mission of
the Twelve, now into Galilee and then at last into all
the world. This explains v. 16-42. A view of their
entire mission would be valuable at the very start; and
the fact that portions of this charge with natural verbal
changes should later be repeated is due to their importance.

First, the instructions for their preliminary mission
in Galilee. **Do not go off on a Gentile road and do
not go into a Samaritan town.** The genitives are
possessive: a road belonging to Gentiles, a town belonging to Samaritans. Gentiles and Samaritans are
classed together since the latter were a mixed race that
was hostile to the Jews and had a false religion (John
4:22). The time for world-wide evangelization had
not yet come. What Jesus had done on one occasion
in Samaria (John 4:3-42) and on certain occasions for
individual Gentiles (as in 8:5, etc.) and what he had
hitherto said about salvation for all men (5:13, 14;
8:11) was prophetic; was not intended for the present
but for the great days of the future.

6) **But keep going rather to the lost sheep of
Israel's house.** Compare Jer. 50:6; Ezek. 34:2, etc.
The imperatives used in v. 5 are properly aorists: not at
all are the Twelve to go to Gentiles and to Samaritans.
But now the imperative is a durative present: continually are they to go to the Jews. There is a strong
motive in the expression "lost sheep of Israel's house"
which is repeated by Jesus in 15:24. The perfect participle ἀπολωλότα describes a present condition (R. 881),
which is due to a past act. These are the sheep that
ought to be with the flock but are far from their Shepherd. Surely, therefore, all effort should be made to
restore them to the flock. But this participle denotes
more than the thought that the sheep have strayed
away. Its opposite is σωθῆναι, "to be saved and thus to

be safe." These sheep are in a perishing condition;
having entered it, they are still in it. For their own
sake they should be helped, restored. Compare 9:36.
They are "the sheep of Israel's house," precious on that
account. "Israel's house" is an Old Testament expression for the chosen nation as descended from its ancestor Israel whom God called "Israel," one who rules
with God. These perishing sheep of Israel ought to be
sought first of all.

7) Here is stated what the Twelve are to do.
**Now as you go keep proclaiming, saying, The king-
dom of the heavens has come near.** They are to
make this their chief work, to announce this good news
as heralds (κηρύσσειν, "to make a public proclamation").
They are thus to continue the work the Baptist began
(3:2) and Jesus continued (4:17). On "the kingdom," etc., see 3:2. Only the theme or substance of
the proclamation is given; this naturally required elaboration. The kingdom is the rule of grace, power, etc.,
*die Koenigsherrschaft,* which is now at hand and in
progress in Jesus, the King.

8) **Sick heal; dead raise; lepers cleanse;
demons expel; freely you received, freely give.** Note
the beauty and the power of the form — each clause
having only two terms. The power to work miracles
had already been bestowed upon the Twelve (v. 1);
here they are merely told to exercise this power. After
healing the sick they are to turn their attention to the
dead; and the lepers who were regarded as unclean are
placed next to the unclean demons. We have no record
that any of the Twelve raised a dead person on this
evangelistic tour. The power to do so was in the possession of each. For that matter, most of the Twelve
never raised the dead, and on this tour each of the
Twelve did not work the different kinds of miracles
here enumerated. Note the durative present imperatives, all save the last, δότε, which is a constative

or comprehensive aorist. No objects are attached to the last two verbs, which means that none are to be supplied, all the stress being on the two adverbs "freely" and on their verbs. The great gifts to be bestowed ("give") are to be offered gratis, without charge or pay of any kind. This applies to the entire mission of the Twelve throughout the future. That is why raising the dead is mentioned here at the start, for Jesus looks farther than this brief tour.

9) Here is what the Twelve are *not* to take along. **Do not provide gold or silver or brass money for your girdles,** in which money was usually carried. They were to take no money, not even a few coins made of the baser metal.

10) **Nor a pouch for the road, nor two tunics, nor sandals, nor a staff; for worthy is the worker of his nourishment.** They are not to provide a pouch in which to carry food or clothing; the addition of εἰς ὁδόν, "for the road," as well as the fact that "a pouch" is mentioned after the money and *not* after "freely give," is conclusive evidence against Deissmann's view (*Light,* etc., 108) that here πήρα is "a beggar's bag" for collecting alms. Just as the Twelve are not to carry anything for the journey in their girdles, so they are to carry nothing in any other receptacle, hence are to have no pouch at all.

"Nor two tunics" implies that the one they are wearing is enough. Travellers often had two or even more, not only in order to make a change, but also to wear both together against cold. "Nor sandals, nor a staff," compared with Mark 6:8, "except a staff only," is best taken to mean that the Twelve are not to provide new sandals and a new staff in view of the tour but are to go with the sandals and the staff they have. In other words, the Twelve are not to outfit themselves for the tour.

This does not indicate that they are to endure special hardships but that they are to dismiss all care for their bodily needs.   He who sends them out will provide for them in all respects.   Their first experience is to teach them complete trust, Luke 22:35.   "For worthy is the worker of his nourishment" is, of course, not intended as an academic or abstract proposition. *Jesus* is sending out these workers, and as their Lord *he* says that they are worthy of their sustenance.   In other words, he himself gives them assurance on this point.   Therefore they must act without the least worry.   In ἄξιος we have the idea of equal weight between the worker and his living or support, τροφή, in Luke 10:7 and in I Tim. 5:18, μισθός, with little difference in force.   Other employers may rob their workers, Jesus never does so.   He may seem to have nothing, but everything is at his command.   This truth the faith of the Twelve is to realize by their own experience.

11)   Just how the Twelve are to proceed is now stated in detail, δέ being quite in order.   **Now into whatever town or village you enter search out who in it is worthy and there remain until you leave.** Note that in these verses Matthew is more specific than either Mark or Luke.   Here, too, "worthy" has the idea of equal weight: the apostles (i. e., two always going together, Mark 6:7) as the representatives of Jesus on the one hand, and the man who is of a type and character to be willing to lodge them, on the other.   It would not be a difficult matter to determine who is such a man.   The two apostles would make their public proclamation in the place (v. 7: κηρύσσετε), the people would hear and see who had come into their midst, and so in most cases it would prove an easy matter to find the proper person with whom to lodge.   The idea is not that the apostles would inquire about a fit place to stay *before* they had begun to preach; or that their inquiry was made in order to avoid lodging in a dis-

reputable house; or that Jesus expected them to work only privately in the homes and not publicly before the people in the town or the village. "There remain" means: while you are in the place. The apostles are not to shift to another host who, perhaps, may offer better lodging and fare. The hospitality first offered is to be honored.

12) **And on going into the house** (thus selected) **salute it; and if the house is worthy, let your peace be upon it; but if it is not worthy, your peace — let it return to you.** The greeting or salutation would, of course, be, "Peace to you!" (John 20:19, 26). But this would never be a mere conventional phrase but the full reality; *shalom*, spiritual well-being with all that this connotes would come to and upon that house, i. e., the family it shelters. By their presence and their work the apostles would in reality bestow this gift. Of course, this involved that the gift would be received. "Worthy" implies that there was a balance between the offer and the reception of the gift, and not between the value of the gift and the merit of the owner of the house. Those that hunger and thirst after righteousness are the only ones that shall be filled, 5:6. The imperative ἐλθάτω expresses the will of Jesus: "let it come upon it!" and the aorist implies: fully and completely, once for all. Here we again see that the apostles are only the agents of Jesus.

13) But the apostles may make a mistake. The house (family) may, after all, turn out to be "not worthy." After extending a warm welcome, the owner, on learning more about Jesus and the kingdom, may show his dislike for both. Cases like this still occur in mission work. The offer of peace is made, but the response to it ceases; the two are out of balance, "not worthy." Then the will of Jesus is that the peace return to the apostles who brought it as a gift. This cannot mean that at least the apostles will have this

peace as a blessing when it returns to them, getting something for themselves out of the disappointing transaction. When men refuse God's gifts, these are never wasted or lost; the bearers will find other men who are happy to receive these very gifts. Where one door closes, another is opened.

14) **And whoever does not receive you, nor hear your words — on going out of the house or of that city shake off the dust of your feet.** The relative clause beginning with ὅς is left suspended in the construction (R. 437); more than this, the relative refers *ad sensum* not merely to the owner of one house but equally to the inhabitants of an entire town: "out of the house or of that city." We again see that Jesus is not thinking of the first entrance into a house or a town and of a leaving immediately after the first salutation. For both μὴ δέξηται and μηδὲ ἀκούσῃ are aorists and refer to definite receiving and effectual hearing. Jesus here warns the disciples that, when it comes to definitely receiving them as the heralds of Jesus and of the kingdom, they may be disappointed; after their true character and purpose become known, they may find themselves altogether unwelcome. In fact, they may come to a town where, after their preaching has been heard, nobody may have a welcome and hospitality for them. What then? Leave, of course, the house for another, the town for another. But "on leaving (ἐξερχό-μενοι) shake off the dust of your feet." This symbolic act signifies that the feet of the heralds of the kingdom have actually been in the house or the town and that they leave this their dust in witness to the fact that they were there but were forced to leave because they were unwelcome. This act was not a sign of contempt; nor was the dust of the place defiling, nor does it indicate that the apostles will have absolutely nothing to do with the place; nor was this act equal to exclusion from the kingdom.

15) **Amen, I say to you, more endurable will it be for the land of Sodom and Gomorrah in the day of judgment than for that city!** To this extent Jesus backs up his representatives. On "amen," the seal of verity, and on, "I say to you," the seal of authority, see 5:18. Ἀνεκτότερον (from ἀνέχομαι, "to hold up" or "to endure") refers to the lesser penalty to be inflicted at the final judgment at the end of the world (11:22, 24). Sodom and Gomorrah (in the Greek two neuter plurals) are types of extreme wickedness and at the same time preliminary examples of the final judgment itself. Great as their guilt was, the guilt of those who reject Christ's apostles and refuse to hear their words of peace is greater, and the final punishment will thus be harder to bear. "Land" and "city" are common figures for their inhabitants. To lie in sin and thus to perish is bad; to lie in sin and in addition to reject grace and thus to perish, is worse. The fact that this saying of Jesus involves the resurrection of the wicked should not be questioned. Hell has degrees of suffering. To say that the fate of the damned is yet to be definitely determined is to overlook the fact that Jesus has here already determined it. "In the judgment day" what has now been settled in the Word will be rendered as the verdict publicly, before the universe, by Jesus, the Judge himself. "More endurable" does not suggest probation after death; the implication is the very reverse.

16) We decline to attribute to Matthew what belongs to Jesus: the conception of this commissioning address. Matthew did not conceive the idea of it and then compile it from words of Jesus spoken at various times; Jesus conceived and spoke this address as it stands. Jesus feels, and rightly, that with this preliminary tour he is really sending the apostles out on their great mission in life. It is thus that he gives them a survey of what they may expect. The great

pronoun ἐγώ, "I," runs through the address (verses 16, 22, "because of my name," 24, 25, 27, 32, 33, 34-38, 40, 42). The theme of the address is the statement: **Lo, I myself am commissioning you as sheep among wolves!** This means first, that you shall fare accordingly (v. 16-23) ; secondly, just like your Teacher (v. 24-33) ; thirdly, because I came to divide (v. 34-39) ; fourthly, you will be received (v. 40-42).

The interjection "lo" indicates the surprising nature of what Jesus tells the Twelve. Who would think of sending sheep among wolves? How long would they last? But this is what *I* am doing, Jesus says. Therefore, go and dismiss all fear and keep *me* in mind! Ἐν μέσῳ is a compound preposition (R. 648) and is often regarded as one word: "among." The idea is not: "into the midst of wolves," but: "as already among wolves." "As sheep" characterizes the apostles. They have lost all the viciousness that is due to sin and wickedness. "Wolves" characterizes the world of men as being viciously wicked because it is filled with and animated by sin. The combination of the two comparisons produces the idea of the helplessness of the apostles among wicked men. As sheep they have no defense against wolves. But this only shows what lies in ἐγώ — Jesus is their protector. The verb ἀποστέλλω, from which "apostle" is derived (see v. 5), is more significant than πέμπω, "to send"; it means to send as a representative, "to commission." The verb implies that Jesus cannot abandon them, and that all they do is the act of Jesus done through them.

The statement regarding what their whole commission is like is at once followed by another which tells them what their whole conduct should be like. They are sheep among wolves; **therefore be keen as the serpents and guileless as the doves.** The verb γίνεσθε (present imperative to indicate continuous conduct) takes the place of the corresponding form of εἰμί,

B.-P. 250. Since the incident recorded in Gen. 3 the
serpent was regarded as a type of a keen mind, the
German *Klugheit.* "Wise" is too lofty a word, "pru-
dent" has a different connotation, "smart" is also off-
color; perhaps "keen" best conveys the thought. As in
Luke 16:8, the good feature suggested in keenness is
referred to. Hence the qualifying addition, "guileless," etc., ἀκέραιοι, without admixture, i. e., of base
motives such as falseness, cunning, and the like, the
type of this good quality being the doves who hurt no
one. Luther: φρόνιμοι, "that they may have no just
cause against you"; ἀκέραιοι, "heartfelt goodness toward
all men." The outstanding examples of such conduct
are David under Saul's persecution and Paul in his
whole ministry.

17) **And beware** (προσέχω with ἀπό) **of men; for
they will deliver you up to councils, and in their
synagogues they will scourge you; and before governors, moreover, and kings shall you be brought on
account of me for a testimony to them and to the
Gentiles.** We regard δέ as copulative, "and," adding
something that is somewhat different. In order to
comply with the command of v. 16 the apostles must
always be on their guard (present imperative) against
men who may show hostility, by nature being wolves
toward these sheep. The reason for this attitude of
carefulness is introduced by the explanatory γάρ. The
idea is not that the apostles will escape all harm by
being keen and on their guard, for they shall suffer
nevertheless; it is rather that they shall understand
the temper of men and thus avoid all thoughtless acts
which might needlessly inflame that temper. The
συνέδρια (σύν plus ἕδρα or "seat") are the minor, local
Jewish courts, in which a number (twenty-three) of
judges sit together to try cases. To be haled before
such a council was an indignity. These councils could
decree scourging with rods as a penalty, the penalty

being at once carried out in the synagogue where the council sat (Acts 22:19; 26:11; II Cor. 11:24).

18) From Jewish tribunals Jesus turns to the pagan courts which were presided over by "governors" or procurators and even by kings. The Herodian rulers were popularly styled kings although in reality they were only tetrarchs (over a fourth); Archelaus was called an ethnarch. The implication is that severer penalties, even death itself awaited the apostles in these courts. A terrible prospect, indeed! But Jesus never concealed or softened it (5:10-12). He places the emphasis on the final phrase, "on account of me." Whatever they suffer is suffered for *him*. He sends them; him they represent, him and his royal rule in the kingdom they proclaim. A second phrase interprets the first: "for a testimony to them (the Jews who will be the prime movers in these persecutions) and to the Gentiles" (the governors, the kings with all their officers and men). This will be a grand testimony, indeed, greater even than ordinary preaching. For it will compel these high authorities to investigate judicially the whole cause of the gospel, noting all that it contains and all that it does for men. Whether this testimony makes a salutary impression or not, its mere rendering is the will of Jesus (Acts 1:8, "witnesses unto me"): and its saving effect will always be successful in the case of some.

19) For these severe trials Jesus has special instructions that are full of the greatest comfort. **Now, whenever they deliver you up, do not be distracted, how and what you shall utter; for it shall be given to you in that hour what you shall utter; for you are not the ones making utterance but the Spirit of your Father, the one making utterance in you.** To be arrested and haled before judges low or high is enough to upset anyone. In addition to the shame, the fear, and other conflicting emotions the trial

itself and the matter of their defense would cause the apostles terrible anxiety. They would, however, not merely be concerned that they might defend themselves and escape the infliction of penalties, their anxiety would be chiefly concerned with the honor of Christ and the gospel, and they would fear that because of their mental confusion, mistakes, weakness, ignorance, or other handicaps they might injure the Lord's cause. After a sleepless night or more in a foul cell, with no advocate at their side, in what condition would they be to do justice to the gospel? "Do not be distracted!" contemplates and meets these situations. In negative commands in the aorist the subjunctive not the imperative is used. The aorist is peremptory, "Drop all worry completely!"

You are not to have even a thought as to "how or what you shall utter." Note the use of λαλεῖν (not λέγειν) throughout, "to make utterance," as opposed to keeping silent. The direct questions: "How, what, shall we speak?" would have the deliberative subjunctive in the Greek; this is retained in the indirect form. A fine psychological touch puts "how" and "what" together with "how" being mentioned first. In his uncertainties the poor prisoner would imagine the trial as taking, perhaps, this turn or that turn, and then he would think as to *how* he would respond. Despite all his thinking the trial, after all, might take a turn he never thought of.

From these thoughts the prisoner would revert to just *what* he would say, the real substance of his defense, whatever turn the proceeding might take. The command not even to give the matter a thought is astonishing. Even the powers, abilities, faculties, talents, wisdom, faith, courage, etc., which God gave the apostles and which he wants them to use, are to be entirely disregarded in these ordeals.

The mystery is explained by the γάρ clause: "it shall be given to you," etc. This is an unqalified promise. The passive verb suggests God as the agent. In the verb "give" lies the strong idea of grace. When God gives, the gift corresponds to him. The τί clause is like the preceding one; R. 738 makes it relative. When God gives a man what he shall utter, the proper name for this is Inspiration. In fact, verses 19, 20 are an exact description of this divine act. Without previous thinking, planning, imagining, at the time of their trials in court the apostles will receive directly from God just what to utter. It will come into their minds just as it is needed, and thus they will utter it aloud. That, in fact, is their entire role: λαλεῖν, "to utter."

20) What is involved in the fact that they shall be given what they shall utter is made fully clear by γάρ: the one who really makes the utterance is "the Spirit of your Father" That this Spirit is a person, namely the Third Person of the Godhead, is beyond question. Note that λαλεῖν continues. The apostles, indeed, make utterance, and yet they do not, for their act is due to the Holy Spirit, so that most properly he is the one who does this uttering. Everything that is mechanical, magical, unpsychological is shut out by ἐν ὑμῖν. The apostles will not be like the demoniacs, their organs of speech and their very wills being violated by a demon. Absolutely the contrary: mind, heart, will operate freely, consciously, in joyful, trustful dependence on the Spirit's giving, who enables them to find just what to say and how to say it down to the last word, with no mistake or even a wrong word due to faulty memory or disturbed emotions occurring.

This, of course, is Inspiration, Verbal Inspiration (λαλεῖν throughout), than which none other exists. It is here promised to the apostles for specific occasions, but that does not change *what* is promised. The argument is quite invincible that, if God's Spirit inspired

the apostles when they were subjected to court trials,
he was able to inspire them in the same manner at other
times, for interests that were far greater (the Word
for all ages and nations), according to Christ's promise, John 14:26. That he did so is attested in II Tim.
3:16; II Pet. 1:19-21; by the long list of διά phrases,
Isa. 59:21; Hos. 12:11; Ezek. 3:27, and, beginning with
Matt. 1:22, throughout the New Testament. It is most
tremendously attested by the result, the Bible itself, its
every page, which is a product beyond human ability.

What Jesus here promises the apostles was not mere
"presence of mind" at the time of the court trials;
what Jesus promises is vastly different. The view that
inerrancy is not promised here is untenable. We cannot suppose that, when "the Spirit of your Father"
makes utterance, he is liable to utter falsities, mistakes,
errors. The fact that Jesus could extend what he here
promises the Twelve to others also no one should doubt.

The main point remains: what Jesus here promises
makes the Spirit the *causa efficiens*, men the *causae
instrumentales*, as the old dogmaticians stated it. God
moves men to speak (or to write), furnishes the
thought and the words (*suggestio rerum et verborum*),
so that the utterance is also properly called his. These
are not "two factors," hitched up, like two horses, in a
synergistic partnership between which theologians can
draw the line. There is only a Giver from whom emanates the whole gift; beneath him only the recipients
who receive the whole gift. The thing is a fact not a
"theory"; although it is incomprehensible to us it is yet
real, actual. Our dogmaticians illustrate it: a man dictates to his amanuensis, a blower plays a flute, the plec-
trum strikes the lyre. The first of these illustrations has
been misapplied by calling it "the dictation theory."
But why not also "the flute theory," "the lyre theory"?
An illustration should not be mistaken for a theory.
If these illustrations are inadequate, then, please, bring

on better ones.  It is not very "scientific" to center on
an *illustration* and deny the fact or the doctrine which
it would illustrate because the illustration seems to be
inadequate.

21)  To what extremes hatred of Christ will go
is graphically described.  **And brother will deliver
up brother unto death, and father, child; and children will rise up against parents and bring them to
death.**  These are frightful cases of denunciation
before pagan courts, some of which happened during
the ten great persecutions.  Besser writes that two
things are stronger than natural love, the one born of
hell, the other born of heaven.  The verb ἐπανίστημι is
regularly used to designate rebellious uprising.

22)  **And you shall be hated by all on account
of my name; but he that did endure to the end, he
shall be saved.**  The periphrastic future, ἔσεσθε with
the present participle, brings out prominently the continuing nature of this hatred, R. 357, 889.  "By all" is
the popular way of expressing general hatred.  The
reason for it is the ὄνομα of Christ which here, too, signifies more than merely the personal names "Jesus,"
"Christ," etc.; it includes all by which he is known.
Hence in phrases such as this, "name" is equivalent to
"revelation."  In dislike and opposition men will turn
against everything that really reveals Christ and makes
him known.  The implication is that the apostles and
those who succeed them will always proclaim this name
or revelation (v. 7), and thus this hatred will be
aroused.  In the Acts the persecutors even avoid pronouncing the name Jesus wherever this is possible; the
same phenomenon is observed in the rituals of certain
secret orders.

The aorist participle ὁ ὑπομείνας, "he that did endure," is in relation to the future verb "shall be saved."
The enduring all completely is followed by the deliverance and the condition of safety (σώζειν always includ-

ing the two). "To the end" must refer to death; for "bring to death" immediately precedes. The phrase cannot refer to the Parousia and the Judgment Day. Οὗτος emphatically repeats the subject in the sense that *he*, he alone, shall be saved and not he that fails to endure; the tense "shall be saved" is the effective future, R. 871.

23) **Moreover, when they are persecuting you in this city, start to flee into the next,** τὴν ἑτέραν, R. 748. Despite all their courage the messengers of Christ are to use prudence. They are not to throw away their lives. Thus Jesus himself acted; Peter also did so, Acts 12:17, as did Paul on various occasions. The present imperative is conative: "start to flee," or permissive: "you may go and flee."

With γάρ an explanation is added. **For, amen, I say to you, you shall by no means finish the cities of Israel until the Son of man shall come.** On the formula for verity ("amen") and authority ("I say to you") see 5:18. To finish the cities of Israel means to get to all of them, but not, as some think, reaching them as places of refuge, but reaching them in order to do their work in them. The verb τελεῖν does not have the connotation of flight and seeking refuge; it means "to complete" the cities, reach all of them with the gospel.

In this section (v. 16-23), as in the following, Jesus reaches out into the future, far beyond the lifetime of the Twelve, and yet he reverts also to the Twelve and to what shall occur during their lives. He now does the latter. According to Acts 1:8 the Twelve are to begin with the Jewish land. And now Jesus tells them that before they finish this territory, the Son of man shall come (the title is explained in 8:20). He again speaks about this coming in 16:28; 24:34; 26:64; and interprets it for us in 22:7; 23:38, 39. The coming here referred to is the terrible judgment which came upon the Jews in the war of the year 66, ending with

the total destruction of Jerusalem, making 90,000 Jews
slaves, and permanently depriving the nation of its
land.  Because Jesus speaks of the judgment visited on
the Jews he uses the title "the Son of man," for as such
he exercises judgment.

Spiritualizing interpretations of this coming are
out of place.  Those who find in the words of Jesus a
reference to the Parousia at the end of the world think
that Jesus says that this will take place before the
Twelve cover the cities of Israel in their work.  But
this view cannot be harmonized with 24:36, for the
Parousia is still to come.  The very fact that Jesus
says "the cities of Israel" makes the coming of Jesus
refer to these and not to the world in general.  Incidentally, we may accept the deduction that the way in
which Matthew here reports this statement of Jesus
indicates a date for the writing of his Gospel prior to
the year 66.

24) Considering the world of men into which
Jesus sends the Twelve, it is only natural that they
should find themselves treated as sheep among wolves
(v. 16-23) ; considering also their relation to their
Teacher, the same treatment is to be expected
(v. 24-33).  **A disciple is not above his teacher,
nor a slave above his lord.**  This double statement
is axiomatic, so self-evident as to need no proof.  On
μαθητής see 5:1; he is an individual who has imbibed
the spirit of his teacher.  But as one who is a disciple
he remains under his teacher, for the thing that makes
him what he is he has obtained from his teacher.

This relation is even more evident in the case of a
slave and his lord.  The lord actually owns the slave,
who can thus never be above his lord.  Yet two sides
of this relation are indicated.  Disciple and slave are
intimately joined to teacher and lord, we may say identified with them, the disciple of his own volition, he
choosing the teacher, the slave by the lord's volition, he

buying the slave. While the statements are entirely
general, they are also quite evidently intended to indicate the relation obtaining between the Twelve and
Jesus. Moreover, we cannot stop with the Twelve but
must include all who to this day are truly μαθηταί and
δοῦλοι of Jesus.

25) The thought is carried a step farther. **Enough
for the disciple that he be as his teacher; and the
slave as his lord.** If either actually reaches this
height (γένηται, aorist), this is sufficient. He may not
have advanced that far, but this would be his goal.
Jesus, of course, is not thinking of incompetent teachers
or tyrannical lords. He is also thinking of permanent
disciples who do not leave their teacher, just as the
slaves remain their lord's own. "As" their teacher or
lord (ὡς) does not, of course, refer to equality, which
the very terms shut out, but to what is characteristic
of the teacher or the lord. One who knows the disciple
or the slave will be able to notice to whom they belong.
In the second clause ὁ δοῦλος is a nominative which is
construed without reference to ἀρκετόν which requires
the dative. The ἵνα clause does not express purpose but
is a nominative clause in apposition with ἀρκετόν, R. 992.
The reference to our relation to Jesus is again transparent, Phil. 2:5; Matt. 11:29; John 13:15; I Pet. 2:21;
I John 2:6. He is "the head over all things to the
church," Eph. 1:22; ye are to "grow up into him in all
things, which is the head, even Christ," Eph. 4:15; Col.
1:18; in fact, "we are members of his body," Eph. 5:30;
Col. 3:11.

After the principle has been laid down and elucidated, Jesus makes the application. **If they called
the Houselord Beelzebul, how much more those of
the house?** The condition is one of reality: they
have actually gone that far. If they did this to Jesus,
would they not much more readily do it to the disciples?
So these experiences are only to be expected. When

Jesus refers to himself as "the Houselord" he takes up the idea of "lord" and "slave" found in the preceding, hence also the disciples are the οἰκιακοί, "those of the house." The most vicious slander the Pharisees directed against Jeus is that they called him "Beelzebul," referring to instances such as are recorded in 9:34; 12:24 (John 8:48), where he was virtually called this, or to others not recorded, where the epithet was directly applied. The derivation of "Beelzebul" has not as yet been cleared up, the term not being found in the old Jewish literature. It is thought to mean "Lord of the dwelling" and was used as a designation for Satan. Beelzebub was the name for the Philistine god Baal, to whom Ahaziah applied to cast out his disease. In some manner, at which linguists thus far only guess, the Jews adopted it as a vile term for Satan. Some think they corrupted it to "Beelzebul," "Baal of flies" and thus "Baal of dung"; but this is not certain, being, perhaps, due only to pronunciation. That Jesus intends to indicate a correspondence in meaning between "Houselord" and "Lord of the dwelling" has not as yet been convincingly established. The Jews called Jesus a devil's name because he drove out devils; and Jesus says that they will treat his disciples in the same way and with less hesitation.

**26) Therefore, do not be afraid of them; for nothing is covered that shall not be revealed; and secret that shall not be known.** With οὖν Jesus draws the conclusion from what he has just said about himself and their relation to him, and that conclusion is that the disciples are not to fear. Only because they are "those of his house" will they be mistreated, only because they share his higher lot. If anyone is to fear, it would be Jesus. Because the matter is entirely in his hands who knows no fear, they, too, are not to begin to be afraid; this is the force of the negative aorist imperative, R. 852.

While οὖν reaches back, γάρ looks forward: everything will be absolutely exposed. Note the parallelism and the rhythmic repetition in the two clauses. There is a similar parallelism in v. 24. The perfect passive participle κεκαλυμμένον, "has been and thus is now covered," has exactly the same sense as the adjective κρυπτόν, which is the predicate after the copula. Whether it is actually covered up and kept so or profoundly secret in the first place, whatever it may be, it will be revealed and uncovered, will become known everywhere. The statement is general and here refers both to the enemies of Christ and all their secrets and to the disciples and the blessed gospel secret. Everything shall come to light, so do not have the least fear either that you shall fail, or that they shall succeed.

27) In regard to the secret of the gospel Jesus adds: **What I say to you in the darkness, say in the light; and what you hear in the ear, proclaim on the housetops.** What is told in the darkness is the same as what is covered; and what is whispered into the ear is, of course, secret. Much of Christ's instruction was given in private. He often took his disciples aside, and they asked him many things in private. Some things he asked them to keep to themselves for the time being because they could not yet fully understand and were thus not yet fit to tell them. In due time they would be called on to make them public. Nor will the hostile efforts of men be able to prevent their publication. The gospel cannot be suppressed. The disciples are to understand this thoroughly from the very start and are thus to speak out fearlessly, holding nothing back. The flat Oriental housetops were ideal pulpits from which to shout out news to the crowds standing in the street beneath; κηρύσσειν = "to proclaim as a κῆρυξ or herald." The two imperatives are peremptory aorists.

28) "Do this," Jesus says, **And do not be afraid of those that kill the body but are not able to kill the soul; but be afraid rather of him who is able to destroy both soul and body in Gehenna.** The command not to be afraid is repeated, the reason for fearlessness being woven into the object of the verb. First, be not afraid, the gospel will not be suppressed; secondly, be not afraid, men can kill only the body. Here φοβέομαι is used with ἀπό, indicating a fear that causes one to flee from what is feared; but see R. 577. Jesus minces no words when he calls the foes of the disciples "them that kill the body," nor should we underrate what this means. Think of Stephen, the first martyr. Bodily death has caused many to fear and to deny Christ and the gopel. Yet this is the limit of the power of hostile men: they can murder the body but they cannot touch the soul. To lose the body is to lose little, to lose the soul is to lose all. Here ψυχή is in contrast with σῶμα and hence does not mean merely "life" but what the English calls "soul," the seat and bearer of the spiritual life; and thus in substance it is the same as the πνεῦμα.

Jesus knows that it is not enough for so many who are of little faith (8:26) to point to the causelessness of fear; he must apply stronger medicine and *by the fear of God* drive out *the fear of men.* "He who is able to destroy both soul and body in Gehenna" is not the devil who is merely one of the foes not to be feared but to be resisted, when also he will flee from us, I Pet. 5:9. It is God who is referred to. God in his omnipotent power and his absolute justice. Some texts have the present imperative φοβεῖσθε, "keep fearing," instead of the aorist which may be regarded as constative. Beyond question this verb has the same meaning throughout these repetitions: "to be afraid" or thoroughly scared. This is not childlike fear, the motive of filial obedience, but the terrifying fear of God's holy, burning wrath which would have to strike us if we yielded to the fear of men and denied his Word and his will, Ps. 90:11; Matt. 3:7. This is the fear which really belongs to the enemies of God and of Christ, the fear from which they try to hide by their self-deceptions, which yet will at last overwhelm them. It is really not to touch the disciple's heart save as a last extremity when nothing else will keep him true. What Jesus says is this: "If the disciple is going to yield to the low motive of fear, then let him be scared, not of the minor danger, but of the supreme danger." The sound sense and the logic of this word are beyond question. On Gehenna as a designation for hell, the place of the damned, see 5:22. "Soul and body in Gehenna" implies the bodily resurrection of the damned.

29) God's special providence regarding Christ's disciples is the third reason why they should be without fear. **Are not two sparrows sold for an as? And one of them shall not fall on the ground without your Father.** Of course, it takes two little sparrows to bring in one little assarion or as (the two words are really diminutive), the tenth part of a drachma, about one cent. So cheap they are when they are sold for meat; ἀσσαρίου is the genitive of price. Beside this fact Jesus places the other (καί) that not a single one of them (partitive ἐκ, R. 515) shall fall on the ground, i. e., lose its life by being shot or caught, except by the will and the permission of "your Father." So vast is his providence and care, and such little creatures it includes. "Your Father" hints at the far higher and more intimate relation of the disciples, for they are this Father's children in Christ.

30) From smallness outside of us Jesus advances to smallness connected with us, and at the same time he makes the smallness minute. **But even your hairs of the head have all been numbered.** On the

average the human head has about 140,000 hairs.
Jesus says that each hair is not only counted as one
but has its own number and is thus individually known
and distinguished. So if any one hair is removed,
God knows precisely which one it is (Luke 21:18;
Acts 27:34). These illustrations exemplify the infinite extent of God's provident care. The smaller these
objects are in our eyes, and the less in value, the
greater is the force of the argument when God's own
children are now mentioned.

31) **Therefore, do not be afraid. You excel
many sparrows** (the genitive is due to the idea of
comparison). If the present imperative is used instead of the aorist, this would have the force of, "quit
being afraid," R. 853. Note the emphasis on ἡμεῖς,
which emphasis is increased by its position. Will
God who watches every little sparrow for one moment
neglect *you* who, to use an understatement, excel in
value to him any number of sparrows? How simple
the facts here put together, and how convincing and
satisfying the conclusion that results! Here absolutely every trace of fear should vanish.

32) We have still more. From the entire preceding elaboration "therefore," οὖν, draws the most
blessed conclusion in the form of a glorious promise.
**Everyone, therefore, whoever shall confess me in
front of men, I myself also will confess him in front
of my Father in the heavens.** The idea of fear is
exchanged for the act which fear is likely to prevent
or to modify, namely our confession of Christ in front
of men. This is the cardinal act in the life of every
disciple and believer, and Jesus has it in mind from
the start. The ἐν used with ὁμολογεῖν is due to the
Aramaic *be* with *'odi*, R. 108, 475. The verb really
means "to say the same thing" as another, to voice
agreement with him, and thus to acknowledge and
to confess him. "In front of men" emphasizes the

public character of this confession; and ἐν ἐμοί should not be reduced in any way, since it includes Christ in the fullest sense of the term, him with all that pertains to his person, his work, and the teaching or doctrine that presents both (7:22). The fact that this confession will cost the confessor something, in some instances as much as life itself, has already been fully brought out. "In front of men" again touches upon this point.

Whoever (ὅστις) thus confesses and identifies himself with Christ, with him Christ will identify himself, him Christ will confess. The future tense refers especially to the last great day. Significantly Jesus says, not "your Father," but "my Father," from whom Jesus came, whose mission he is executing, to whom he will return, through whom alone we are accepted by the Father. Note the contrast: "in front of men" — "in front of my Father in the heavens." Nothing but men who are on earth for a little while — the eternal Father in the glorious, heavenly world (Luke 12:8). Who would exchange the latter's approval for that of the former? See how Jesus sets forth the actual realities so simply and so clearly that every sane mind must draw the right conclusion. What a prospect to hear Jesus calling my name and confessing me as his very own before the Father, the hosts of angels, and men! Shall any persecution by men during these brief days make me forget that prospect?

33) Yet the reverse must be added although it is implied in the positive statement. **But whoever shall deny me in front of men, I myself also shall deny him in front of my Father in the heavens.** In substance ὅστις with the future indicative (v. 32) is the same as ὅστις ἄν with the subjunctive; but its aorist tense sums up the life's course of the one who denies, and ἄν adds the note of expectancy that such

disciples will be found.   For Jesus is here not referring to men who will ever spurn him, but to disciples
who, because of men, fail to confess him.   Peter denied
Jesus because of fear.   During the ten great persecutions many denied by sacrificing to idols or to Caesar
because they feared the threats of the authorities.
Many fear to lose the favor of men and the profit and
the advantages men offer them.   In thousands of cases
self-deception veils the secret motive, for the heart is
deceitful above all things.

The consequences are terrible beyond all description.   In 7:23 we have the very words with which
Jesus in turn will deny those who denied him.   Confusion, dismay, consternation, eternal misery will overwhelm them.   Would to God that the warning might
strike home in all disciples and doubly in the pastors
who are to lead others!

34)   Jesus now advances to the real cause which
produces all this hostility of men and necessitates all
these admonitions not to be afraid of them.   This the
Twelve must thoroughly understand in order that proper intelligence may fortify their fearless courage and
their trust.   **Do not imagine that I came to throw
peace upon the earth; I came not to throw peace but
a sword.**   Do not for a moment imagine this!   The
implication in the tense of the imperative is that the
Twelve might conceive this to be the purpose of
Christ's coming.   Was he not the Prince of peace, his
church the haven of peace, his greeting "Peace to
you!" and his apostles the bearers of peace (v. 12, 13)?
All this was true, indeed.   But "upon the earth" takes
in the world of men, and the effect of Christ's coming
which, of course, means his mission is the opposite
of "peace," namely war as symbolized by "a sword."
By this contrast, in this connection εἰρήνη is peace in
the sense of harmony, an undisturbed condition.   Compare Luke 12:51, where "division" expounds "a

sword." The idea is this: if Christ had not come, the
earth would have gone on undisturbed in its sin and
its guilt until the day of its doom. Now Christ
came to take away that sin and that guilt. At once
war resulted, for in their perversion men clung to
their sin, fought Christ and the gospel, and thus produced two hostile camps. Christ foresaw this effect
and willed it. Emphatically he declared that he came
to throw a sword on the earth. Better the war and
the division, saving as many as possible, than to let
all perish in their sin.

35) With γάρ Jesus elucidates. **For I came to
set a man at variance against his father, and a
daughter against her mother, and a daughter-in-law
agaist her mother-in-law; and a man's foes those of
his own house.** Concretely Jesus describes the
worst feature of what "sword" or "division" (Luke
12:51) means: the rending of intimate family ties.
Compare Luke 12:52, 53, where the number of persons
is mentioned as being "five." The family instanced
consists of father and mother, a married son and
his wife, and an unmarried daughter. According to
Oriental custom the son would bring his wife to live
in his father's home. The daughter is still unmarried
and at home, for after marrying, she would live with
her husband's people and no longer be at home. The
verb, διχάζω, from δίχα, "intwo," means, "to cleave
asunder" (R. 581), and κατά adds the idea of opposition,
"down on" and thus "against" (R. 607). The division is one of opposition, v. 21. Luke 12:53 does not
define the sides, but in Matthew "a man down on
his father," etc., seems to indicate that the son is down
on his father for embracing Christ, the daughter down
on her mother for the same reason, and also that the
daughter-in-law takes sides. Of course, this is only
a sample; another division may also be possible.

36)　For the real point of the example is the fact that the members of one's own family (οἰκιακοί, as in v. 25) will become his ἐχθροί, his personal enemies.　In v. 35, 36 Jesus appropriates Micah 7:6, using a free rendering into Greek although retaining the relationships expressed by the prophet.　Jesus does not quote, he only appropriates for his own purpose, which is different from that of the prophet.

37)　The great danger lying in these family strains is that natural affection will triumph. Hence the warning: **He that has affection for father or mother more than for me is not worthy of me; and he that has affection for son or daughter more than for me is not worthy of me.** The two statements are exactly parallel.　No matter to whom the conflict comes, child or parent, the issue is the same.　The proper verb is φιλεῖν which denotes natural affection as distinct from ἀγαπᾶν, the love of intelligence and purpose (see 6:44).　We are to have both types of attachment to Jesus (John 21:15-17; 15:14, 15, φίλοι).　Since natural affection is involved in the case of close relatives, and not ἀγάπη as distinct from that, it is retained in this comparison which involves Christ.　The idea, then, is: if one does not have enough of even the lower form of love for Jesus to outweigh his attachment to his family, he is not worthy to be counted as a disciple.　On the use of ὑπέρ with the accusative with the idea of comparison in the sense of "above," "beyond," and thus "more than," see R. 633.　Ἄξιος (v. 11, 12) refers to equality of weight or value.　To be "worthy" of Jesus is to balance the scales with him.　Yet our affection for him does not give us such moral value; quite the contrary. When we would rather forsake all our relatives than him we declare that he is more to us than they are.　In other words, our need of him exceeds all our other

needs. When our realized emptiness balances his fulness we are "worthy."

38) First, the one influence that would draw us
away from Christ; then, the other that would repel us
from Christ. **And he who does not receive his
cross and follow behind me is not worthy of me.**
So precious is Christ to be to us that no suffering or
shame should ever be able to repel us from him. The
figurative language is taken from the established
custom that the condemned had to bear their own
cross out to the place of execution. The fact that
receiving the cross is to be understood figuratively
appears from the added verb "follow behind me," both
verbs being construed with the one οὐ, and the second
being the regular verb to express permanent attachment to Jesus. What is referred to is faithful adherence to Christ in spite of any, even the worst persecution. In view of what we know about the actual death
of Jesus we may say that on this account he chose
this figure of the Roman mode of execution, although
there is no intimation in the wording itself that this
is his thought. If "follow behind me" is added to the
figure, we should have only the extension: go to crucifixion in company with me. Yet the whole would
remain figurative, for as far as the Twelve are concerned, we know that only Peter was actually crucified,
and that John died a natural death. Ἄξιος has the
same meaning it had in v. 37. Fear of suffering and
shame would prove us unworthy by revealing that
our need of Christ does not balance the value of
Christ.

Also the critics admit that Jesus used the illustration of taking up the cross, together with finding
and losing one's soul, more than once; compare
16:24, 25; Mark 8:34, 35, and Luke 9:23, 24,
where all the people are present. It is, therefore,

unwarranted to say that the reference to the cross was not spoken by Jesus when he commissioned the Twelve but was introduced into this discourse by Matthew on the basis of a later saying of Jesus.

39) A striking, highly paradoxical, literal statement makes plain the matter of the cross and of our worthiness. **He who finds his life shall lose it; and he who loses his life on my account shall find it.** All translations are inadequate. In the first place, the two substantivized aorist participles do not express time as do the relative clauses of the translation. Note in the R. V. and the margin the wavering between "findeth" and "found," "loseth" and "lost." The participles express only actuality, the fact of the actions; thus, "the finder of his life," "the loser of his life." R. 1111, etc. The main verbs which are in the future tense tell what follows the moment the life is found or is lost.

In the second place, ψυχή is neither exactly the English "life" or "soul" although we must choose the one or the other when translating (R. V. and margin, again wavering). We get little help from the observation that in the Semitic *nephesh* is used for the reflexive "himself" and yet is translated ψυχή in the Greek: "he that finds (loses) himself." Nobody knows whether Jesus here used *nephesh* or whether he used it in this sense. We can be sure only in the case of certain quotations from the Hebrew. Now ψυχή, as in the present connection, faces in two directions: it animates the body (in fact, it always refers to the body) and yet contains the ἐγώ and the πνεῦμα and is like the English "soul" and may be controlled by the spirit. Thus the two statements of Jesus become plain.

The finder of his ψυχή is the one who, frightened at the prospect of bodily suffering and death (the

cross, v. 38), succeeds in warding off the latter by
denying Christ. The loser of his ψυχή succeeds in
doing the very opposite. In both cases the ψυχή is
at stake but only as it is related to the body, bodily
suffering, loss, death: in the one instance, to preserve the ψυχή from these, in the other, to yield the
ψυχή to them. And now the paradox: although it is
found in one way, sheltered, and kept from suffering,
the ψυχή will be lost in another much more terrible
way, ἀπολέσει, lost so as to perish forever. By following the physical, fleshly promptings it gains nothing
higher than what these aspire to. The reverse is
likewise true: although it is actually lost by being
abandoned to suffering, perhaps even to death for
Christ's sake (or the gospel's, Mark 8:35), by placing him above every temporal interest the ψυχή will
be found in a vastly higher way. By disregarding
the fleshly promptings, by responding to those of
Christ, by losing what the former offer, all that the
latter assure are gained. The two future tenses of
the verbs need not be dated on the judgment day.
"Shall lose," "shall find" after he finds, after he loses.
Compare Delitzsch, *Biblische Psychologie*, 160, etc.
Thus the division Christ came to bring on the earth
(v. 34) is fully elucidated.

40) While the prospect the Twelve must face in
their mission through life is dark, it is by no means
entirely so. The inaugural address ends with the note
of success. **He who receives you, me he receives;
and he who receives me, receives him that commissioned me.** The two substantivized present participles are durative though timeless. They picture,
not a single act, but a course of action, a receiving
that goes on and on. The aorist τὸν ἀποστείλαντά με
indicates the single act by which the Father sent Jesus
into the world. Jesus constantly called his Father his
Commissioner or his Sender. Note how Jesus com-

bines himself with the Twelve: he was commissioned, they are commissioned (hence "apostles"), John 17:18; 20:21. This is the basis for what he now says. Some to whom the Twelve come will, indeed, "receive" them, i. e., hear their words (v. 14) in true faith and therefore make them welcome in every way. By so doing they will receive Jesus himself as well as the Father himself. For Jesus, commissioned by the Father, represents him, and the apostles, commissioned by Jesus, represent him. To receive Jesus and the Father means to take them into the heart and the life, to find the ψυχή with a finding that is eternal blessedness. The opposite of this statement is here left unexpressed.

41) This matter of receiving the Twelve (ὑμᾶς) in the way in which they ought to be received rests on a general principle, one which refers to all prophets and, in fact, to all who are righteous. **He who receives a prophet in a prophet's name, a prophet's reward shall receive; and he who receives a righteous one in a righteous one's name, a righteous one's reward shall receive.** In the case of Jesus and his Father this is the general principle. Its statement brings out what receiving me and what receiving my Commissioner means (v. 40). When, by receiving the apostles, a man receives (welcomes, entertains, etc.) Jesus and the Father, this means that by his act he will share in whatever reward the apostles shall receive. Nor need it be a prophet, one who is immediately and especially commissioned, that is thus received. It may be only a true believer, an ordinary disciple (v. 42), one of the followers of Jesus who is here called δίκαιος in relation to προφήτης. The task of all the Old Testament prophets was to make Israel "righteous." This is now the work of Jesus, of his apostles and of all ministers. But this must be a better righteousness than that of the scribes and Phari-

sees (5:20), one that obtains God's verdict in its favor
at his judgment bar.

Thus to the prophet is added a follower of the
prophet. What is true of him who brings God's Word
is true of him who believes and accepts God's Word
that is thus brought. Each has his μισθός, "pay,"
"reward." God's blessing rests upon him. We may
take any of the Old Testament prophets as an example.
God always acknowledged them as his own, was ever
with them in their work, and showed this in a thousand ways. The same is true of the righteous, whose
blessings are sung throughout the Old Testament. We
may think of Zacharias and Elizabeth, of Simeon and
of Anna. This μισθός was always one of pure grace,
beyond any merit of their own, as generous as the
great Lord God whom they served. Compare especially 19:28, 29; also in the parables Luke 19:17, 19;
Matt. 25:21, 23.

These righteous should not be referred to as *die
grossen Heiligen,* nor should it be said of those who
receive them that they tried to realize this ideal in
themselves. No legalistic taint should he introduced
into the term. Theirs is the gospel righteousness of
true faith in the Messiah not the righteousness of
works after which the scribes and Pharisees (ancient
and modern) strove. We have beautiful examples of
receiving "one righteous" in the history of the early
church. Wherever believers travelled they received
open hospitality in the homes of believers. This was
true of the reception of the apostles in their travels
and of their assistants likewise. It extended also to
others (Acts 28:2, 7-10).

The point of the reception of which Jesus speaks
lies in the phrases, "in a prophet's name," "in a righteous one's name." Here εἰς is quite the same as ἐν
would be, R. 593, and all that the newer grammars
present on this point. The preposition is merely

locative, R. 525, and ὄνομα "brings out the notion that one has the name or character of prophet, righteous man, disciple," R. 649. The effort of B.-P. 910, second column, to regard εἰς as distinct from ἐν by referring to the rabbinic *leshem* and translating *in Ruecksicht auf den Namen,* is due to the older conceptions which will not accept the idea that in the Koine εἰς has heavily invaded the territory of ἐν. The phrase means, "in the name." The reception takes place in the sphere marked by the name (prophet, one righteous). The prophet comes as a prophet, the righteous one (disciple, v. 42) also comes as such; and each is so received. This reception, as it were, joins together the person receiving and the person received, and thus the great blessing of the latter flows over also to the former. No, the Twelve and all believers are not beggars. What they carry with them and what flows out from them is of wondrous value. They give more than they receive and do this in accordance with v. 8 (last clause).

42) **And whoever shall cause one of these little ones to drink only a cup of cold water in a disciple's name, amen, I say to you** (see 5:18), **in no way shall he lose his reward.** The seal of truth and of authority marks this assurance as a climax. This least act of kindness is thus combined with only a single disciple (ἕνα) from among the least important of them all. On these services compare Heb. 6:10; I Tim. 5:10. The verb ποτίζω is causative and hence has two accusative objects, R. 484: "cause one to drink a cup"; with ψυχροῦ supply ὕδατος. The fact that Jesus is speaking of the disciples, which, of course, includes the apostles, the emphatic phrase, "in a disciple's name," shows. The genitive "of these little ones" is not spoken with reference to the world's judgment, nor with reference to the great Old Testament prophets, but as in 25:40: "one of the least of

these my brethren." In 25:40 we also see why even a cool drink (25:37) is rated so highly by Jesus: "Ye have done it unto me." Some of the disciples will not be prominent, even as far as faith and works of faith are concerned. Yet they are disciples, and whoever renders them the least service in connection with their discipleship, recognizing that they are believers in Jesus although among the very least, shall have his reward. The οὐ μή with the subjunctive or the future indicative is the strongest type of negation: "by no means shall he lose his reward." The fact that this μισθός is the same as that mentioned in v. 41 is evident. The εἰς phrase has the same force. It is not the magnitude of the service that determines the size or the reward but the motive and its appreciation by the Lord. Into the sphere of this humble disciple the act of service places him who performs it "in a disciple's name"; hence the blessing includes also him.

# CHAPTER XI

## VIII

### Christ's Answer to the Baptist.  His Further Words of Judgment and of Grace, Chapter 11

1) **And it came to pass when Jesus finished giving orders to his twelve disciples he departed thence in order to be teaching and preaching in their cities.** The two aorists report the facts.  Matthew does not report how the Twelve fared on their first tour, or when they came back.  Jesus himself, for the time being without the Twelve, went from one place to another as he had done before this time.  The Twelve were not replacing but were only aiding him.  His great purpose is expressed by τοῦ with two present infinitives.  Since these infinitives are construed with the one article, preaching and teaching express one great activty.  The final αὐτῶν is construed *ad sensum*, R. 683.

2) **Now when John heard in his prison the works of the Christ, having sent by his disciples, he said to him, Thou, art thou the One Coming, or shall we be expecting someone else?**  We know about John's imprisonment from 4:12, and shall learn still more in 14:3.  In his prison John heard all about the activity (τὰ ἔργα) of Jesus, whom Matthew here calls "the Christ" in order at once to state what these "works" actually revealed about Jesus, namely that he was "the Christ," the Messiah.  The supposition that ὁ Χριστός is here a personal name is answered when we read a few chapters and see how Matthew designates the Lord's person.  We may be sure that in his confine-

(424)

ment the Baptist longed the more for news of Jesus.
That confinement in the fortress Machærus (Josephus,
*Ant.* 18, 5, 2) permitted free intercourse with the
friends of the Baptist. After his execution they were
allowed to bury the body of their master. The fact
that the Baptist should continue to have disciples of his
own implies no more than that he continued his work
of preparing the way for Jesus, and the simplest way
to do this would be to win devoted followers to whom
he could convey all that God had revealed to him.

The reading διά is preferable to δύο. The question
asked is John's, and the disciples he sends are only his
medium (διά is regularly used to indicate the medium)
for communicating with Jesus; Luke 7:19 informs us
that two were sent. Πέμψας, like the aorist εἶπεν, indicates that they executed their mission.

3) John's question and the unindicated reason
for sending a commission to get an anwer to it have
perplexed many interpreters. The discussion centers
about the question as to whether John doubted, and if
he did so, in what way and to what degree he doubted.
In attempting to answer this question we should not
separate the two parts of the question and lay undue
emphasis on the first part. Ὁ Ἐρχόμενος, "the One Coming," undoubtedly signifies the Messiah and is used in
that specific sense especially also by the Baptist, 3:11;
Mark 1:7; Luke 3:16, etc.; John 1:27. This designation was derived from Ps. 118:26 and Ps. 40:7, which
is evident from the acclaim of the multitude on Palm
Sunday, 21:9 (23:39), and from the use of Ps. 40:7 in
Heb. 10:5-9. We may take it that "the Coming One"
was both understood and used by the Jews. The second part of the question with its verb "shall we be
expecting" matches this designation, for men expect
one who is coming. The present participle is timeless,
and its substantivization indicates that coming characterizes this person. "Thou (emphatic σύ), art thou

the One Coming?" has its complement in the addition, "or shall we be expecting someone else?" ἕτερον, for which word Luke 7:19 substitutes ἄλλον. The former may imply one that is different; the latter, one that is like thee, although we must remember that both were often used without this distinction. "Like thee," after all, implies "somewhat different from thee" and not an exact duplicate.

The fact that John sends to Jesus for an answer proves John's faith in Jesus. This answers those who think that John had lost confidence in Jesus and doubted as some moderns doubt — in disbelief. In that case John would not have directed his question to Jesus, nor would Jesus have sent an answer, and least of all the answer he did send. John's question was prompted by a difficulty that his faith encountered. God had pointed out to him that Jesus was the Messiah, John 1:33, 34. Jesus, then, was to do all the great Messianic works, both those of grace (3:11) and those of judgment (3:12) ; compare Luke 3:3-6 regarding the grace, and v. 9 regarding the judgment. Thus John believed, preached, expected. But as Jesus carried on his work, it seemed to be nothing but grace without one single act of judgment. This is what perplexed the Baptist "when he heard in the prison *the works* of the Christ." Where were the works of judgment, the swinging of the fan, the crashing blows of the ax? They were not being done. How, then, was this to be explained? Would another One follow, another who would perform these works of judgment? For we must remember that throughout the prophecies, just as in the Baptist's proclamation concerning Jesus, one feature is not revealed by God: the interval of time between the first coming with grace and mercy and the second coming with judgment. The prophetic picture is without perspective as to time; grace and judgment are simply predicated, and the point of time when they will occur is left with God (Acts 1:7). The form προσδοκῶμεν may be either an indicative used in an ordinary question for information: "Are we expecting another?" or a subjunctive used in a question of deliberation as when people ask themselves or others what they should do: "Shall (or should) we be expecting someone else?" (R. 934). Either is in place here. The latter seems preferable psychologically.

4) **And Jesus answered and said to them, When you are gone, report to John what you are hearing and seeing: blind are seeing, and lame are walking; lepers are cleansed, and deaf are hearing; and dead are being raised, and poor are receiving the gospel preaching. And blessed is whoever is not trapped in connection with me.** The addition of ἀποκριθείς, a circumstantial participle, helps to mark the importance of the answer. This answer is typical of Jesus: strongly suggestive yet reticent, decisive in substance yet not direct as far as the form of the question is concerned. "Report to John," says Jesus. This answers the view that John had no doubts and perplexities, that these existed only in the minds of his disciples; that not on his own account but on their account John sent them to Jesus. This view casts reflection on the integrity of John as though he were asking a question when in reality it was being asked by his disciples. It also reflects on the integrity of Jesus who says, "Report *to John*," and thus continues the pretence as though John wanted to know, whereas only John's disciples were in doubt. In trying to save the honor of John as being one who was wholly free of doubt, the honor of both John and Jesus is sacrificed. I Pet. 1:10, 11 states plainly that the prophets themselves searched their own prophecies, especially in regard to the time of the sufferings and of the glory of Christ. John was now doing that and he went to the right source.

5) The mastery of the answer is the fact that it takes John back into the very Old Testament prophecies concerning the Messiah which had caused his perplexity. The reference to the blind, deaf, and lame is adapted from Isa. 35:5, 6. To the unfortunates mentioned in this passage Jesus adds the lepers and the dead and presents works of grace that were even greater than those promised by the prophet. Then, as the climax of all, Jesus cites from Isa. 61:1, the preaching of the gospel to the poor (meek) whom we have already met in 5:3, those who have come to realize that spiritually they are wholly empty and destitute. While the gospel is preached to all, only those who realize their need of it receive it. The verb εὐαγγελίζεσθαι, which is generally used in the active sense, is here and in Heb. 4:2, 6 regarded as a passive: the poor "are being evangelized." All the other works receive their value from this last work. We have no reason to allegorize the blind, etc., for "what you hear and see" cannot apply to spiritual recovery of sight, etc. Jesus is speaking of his miracles of grace, and Luke 7:21 brings out the fact that just at the time when John's disciples came to Jesus with their question Jesus was especially busy working miracles; he had also just raised the son of the widow at Nain. In his answer Jesus says nothing about the "vengeance" (Isa. 35:4) and the judgment. This omission is significant. John is to leave that in the hands of him who is so gloriously fulfilling the prophecies regarding the Messianic works of grace.

6) That is why a gentle touch of warning is added at the end. Its gentleness lies in its form; it is a beatitude, "Blessed is," etc. Jesus does not want John to lose the treasures and the joy that make up this blessedness; on μακάριος see 5:3. Hence the negative description of the blessed man: "whoever is not trapped in connection with me." The figure in σκανδαλίζω is that of a trap with a crooked stick to which the bait is

affixed and which, when touched, springs the trap and
catches and kills the victim. The point of this verb
is that the trap is fatal, the victim is killed. The verb
does not refer to stumbling; for one may stumble and
even fall and yet not be killed. As regards the meta-
phorical "to offend," this would have to be offense that
destroys faith. Compare M.-M. 576. The danger to
which Jesus points John is mortal — blessed he who
escapes it. He is not to let the absence of certain
works blind him to the glorious presence of the works
now in full progress. Let him be satisfied with these
and trust that in due time the others will follow just
as these are now being done.

Except for the order to report to John the answer
of Jesus is couched in general terms. Jesus states only
what occurs to the blind, etc., and leaves it to John's
disciples to add that Jesus is bringing this about. This
omission of his own name and person marks his humility. The verbs are present tenses to express things
that happen continuously. The final statement is also
general: "anyone, and thus also John, is blessed, whoever," etc. John's disciples are to apply this word to
themselves, as also are all others who heard it.

7) **Now when these were going, Jesus began to
say to the multitudes concerning John: What did
you go out into the wilderness to behold? A reed
swayed by wind? Well, what did you go out to
see? A man enrobed in soft clothing? Lo, those
wearing the soft clothing are in the houses of the
kings. Well, what did you go out to see? A
prophet? Yea, I say to you, and far beyond a
prophet!** In the three questions the infinitives belong to these questions and τί then means "what"; or
the three infinitives belong to the three secondary questions, and then τί means "why." The R. V. translates
τί "what" in verses 7, 8, and "wherefore" in v. 9; and
construes two infinitives with the questions introduced

by τί and places the third into the secondary question. But such a distinction is scarcely to be recommended. When the infinitives are placed forward in the secondary questions they have entirely too much emphasis.

At once, after John's disciples have left, Jesus addresses the multitudes concerning John. The implication is that the crowds knew what had transpired. Lest any persons present draw wrong conclusions concerning John, Jesus makes John his topic, and Matthew's formula "began to say" indicates the importance of the discourse that follows. Jesus gives his great estimate of John; and the fact that he was now in prison and was perplexed regarding the works of Jesus in no way reduces the estimate. This is a comforting thought for us who today may have perplexity in understanding the Scriptures. But Jesus aims his remarks at the hearts of the multitude (note v. 15), and what he says "concerning John" thus becomes an indictment of these people who were satisfied with neither John nor Jesus (v. 16-19).

When John was active "in the wilderness," the uninhabited western banks of the Jordan, thousands also from Galilee flocked out to see him. Jesus now asks them, "What did you go out to see?" They are to answer that question. Three times Jesus repeats his question, which makes it the more impressive. He probes for the answer. Each of these questions is followed by another. These form a climax and at last state what the crowds really went out to see. Then Jesus confirms this as the reason for their going.

To behold "a reed as swayed by wind?" It has been well observed that Jesus could not have changed "reed" to tree, water, fish, or other objects that were found out in the Jordan wilderness. "A reed swayed by wind" is symbolic of a man who yields to popular opinion, veers with it, and has no solid convictions of his own. Some interpreters think that John now

seems to be manifesting himself as a reed, by having
asked the question that he did; and that Jesus is saving
his reputation among the people. But this is evidently
a misconception. Jesus is not worried about the impression that John's question may make either in regard
to himself or in regard to John. He is thinking and
speaking only of the past (ἐξήλθετε three times) and of
what the people saw at that time. It would be strange,
indeed, for Jesus to refer to the question just asked by
John as a swaying reed, and then by reference to the
soft clothing to revert to something entirely different.
No; all the questions form a grand whole. All of them
show what John *was* in the wilderness and most certainly imply that he has never been or is anything else.
All that is said about John is not said in John's interest,
as though his reputation needed shielding, but in order
to stir up and to rebuke these callous people who, having had John and now having Jesus himself, found fault
with both and gained nothing from either (v. 18, 19).

We see no reason for stressing θεάσασθαι over against
the two ἰδεῖν. There is a touch of irony in the idea of
going miles out into the wilderness to behold a reed
swaying hither and thither in the wind as though this
were a great phenomenon. The verb θεάσασθαι fits this
ironical implication. The shores of the Lake of Galilee
had plenty of reeds like that. Why run down to the
lower reaches of the Jordan for such a view? The fact
that Jesus is referring to John is evident. What drew
the people out to him was the fact that he was the very
opposite of such a reed. The entire Jewish land was
filled with men who were unstable, were like reeds
swaying with the wind of the opinions of the day. But
here in the wilderness there was a man of a different
type. At this very moment he was in prison because
he would not compromise regarding one of God's commandments. Herod's sin was passed by in silence by
all the Jewish authorities and the whole Jewish nation

but never for a moment by John.   He arose against it
as a rock.   Well, that merited that men should go out
into the distant wilderness to see him.   "But was that
really the reason why you went out to him?" Jesus asks
these people.   He leaves the answer to them.

8)    The German commentators give ἀλλά the force
of *sondern* (B.-P. 59; B.-D. 448, 4), which is slightly
better than the translation "but" in our versions.   But
this particle only turns to a new point, the previous one
having been finished.   Its force is:  "Well now, if that
is not what you went out to see, for what, then, did
you go out?"   The suggestion that, perhaps, they went
out to see "a man enrobed in soft clothing" (the perfect
participle ἠμφιεσμένον with a present implication: having
been and thus now being enrobed, cf. 6:30), carries the
thought of the swaying reed a step farther.   A man
who yields to popular opinion, who bends to the will
and the word of the influential and the mighty, will be
rewarded by them, will be given a high place and the
finest kind of garments.   With μαλακοῖς supply ἱματίοις.
The adjective "soft" (i. e., to the touch) conveys the
idea of the finest and the most costly material.   The
word is exactly the right one.   It brings out the sharp
contrast between such clothing and the rough, harsh,
cheapest kind of material that was used in the coat of
camel's hair worn by John.   The idea in this reference
to clothing is that, if John had sought to please and to
gain favor, he could have worn a courtier's rich robes
and could have basked in royal favor.

The exclamation "lo" in connection with the statement that people who wear such soft clothing are "in
the houses of the kings" marks this as being far more
than an ordinary piece of information.   Soft and rich
garments are worn also outside of royal courts.   The
people of Galilee could see finely robed courtiers in
Herod's palace in Tiberias without going to the lower
Jordan.   But this peculiar specification that softly

robed gentlemen are "in the houses of the kings," here used when speaking of John, undoubtedly intends to convey the thought that John was now in the royal house of Herod, the fortress of Machærus facing the Dead Sea, but not as a handsomely dressed courtier but as a wretched prisoner who still wore his rough coat of camel's hair. So the question implies: "When you went out did you intend to see a man who knew how to secure royal favor and rewards? To do that you would not have had to go very far. But no; you went out to see a man who dared to rebuke even a king, who could be bought by no royal favors, who showed absolute fidelity to God and to his Word." Yet Jesus asks, "Did you really go out to see such a man?" Again he leaves the answer to them.

"To see" does not mean merely "to look at"; for ἰδεῖν, the aorist, is used in an intensive sense as in John 3:3; Acts 2:27; consult the word in Young's *Concordance*. Some have the idea that here ἰδεῖν means less than the preceding θεάσασθαι, but it means more.

9) Once more the question for what they went out. And now the addition: to see "a prophet?" The intensive force of ἰδεῖν is plain here. Jesus does not mean "merely to look at a prophet" but "to see him so as to get into personal touch with him," i. e., to hear him and his proclamation with their own ears, to let him move them to repentance and to the baptism for the remission of sins. Did they really go out for that purpose? All three infinitives denote purpose, and all three are construed alike.

While Jesus puts this final question, as he did the others, so that the people may give their own answer — did they really intend to regard John as a prophet of God? — he at once and most emphatically gives his own answer. "Yea, I say to you, and far beyond a prophet!" "Yea" affirms that John is a prophet, and καί adds to this an estimate that goes beyond that. We may regard the comparative περισσότερον as a neuter: "something beyond a prophet," or as a masculine: "one beyond a prophet."

10) Jesus at once establishes this estimate of John. **This is he of whom it has been written, Lo, I myself commission my messenger before thy face, who shall make ready thy way in front of thee.** John is the one prophet who himself was prophesied. This made him more than a prophet. And John was the ἄγγελος or messenger who, not only, like the other prophets, announced Christ's coming, but actually prepared the way for him and was immediately followed by Christ. This, too, made him more than a prophet. Mal. 3:1 is introduced as a direct quotation with the usual perfect γέγραπται with present force: "has been written" and thus now stands so.

Jesus refers to the original Hebrew not to the LXX. The translation is usually called "free," but it is not at all "free"; it does vastly more than to give the general sense of the original. The translation is interpretative, and the interpretation is most exact as it is preserved in Mark 1:2; Luke 7:27. Jehovah addresses the Israelites who are expecting "the Lord" (*Ha'adon*), "the Messenger of the Covenant" (*Mal°ach Habb°rith*), i. e., the Messiah. Even Malachi distinguishes between Jehovah and this Lord and Messenger, as does Ezek. 34:11, etc., compared with 34:23, 24. This is what Jesus makes plain by the use of the pronouns ἐγώ and μου (Jehovah) and the three σου (the Messiah). Jehovah himself will come to his people, but he will do so in the person of the Messiah. And John is Jehovah's "messenger" who is to prepare the way of the divine Messiah, "in front of thee," as the Messiah's immediate forerunner; the relative ὅς with the future tense of the verb denotes purpose, R. 960. The sense of Mal. 3:1 is thus made plain by showing that in John and in Jesus this prophecy was fulfilled; and thus the greatness of John is alo revealed.

11) To this prophetic word concerning John, Jesus adds his own declaration: **Amen, I say to you** (verity and authority, 5:18), **there has not arisen among women-born a greater than John the Baptist!** The verb "has arisen" refers to John's office and his career. Hence also Jesus uses not merely his personal name but with it the title that distinguished John from all other men, "the Baptist." "Born of women" evidently goes back to Job 14:1; 15:14; 25:4; plus Ps. 51:5, and thus strongly emphasizes the sinfulness and the mortality of men. John is one of these men, but in his career and his work he is so great that, taking all his fellow-mortals into consideration, there is none greater than he. Jesus speaks of John as being one whose great work is done; soon his life will be ended. Did these people realize who and what John was when they went into the wilderness?

It is the height of paradox when in the same breath Jesus now adds: **Yet he that is less in the kingdom of the heavens is greater than he.** We disregard the interpretation that John's doubt was of such a nature as, in spite of his high office, to place him beneath a common believer in Jesus. John asked Jesus to solve a perplexity, and such an action, which itself showed complete confidence in Jesus, could not and did not reduce the estimate Jesus had of John.

Some think that Jesus here compares himself with John. Since he had submitted to John's baptism, it is thought that Jesus calls himself the one who is now less than John but who shall presently appear far greater than John, namely as the King of the kingdom. This view contradicts 3:11, 12; John 1:26-34; 3:28-36; and when Jesus was baptized, it was John who yielded to

Jesus as being the greater.    Although the Greek places
no emphasis on the phrase "in the kingdom of the heavens," some would make everything turn on this phrase,
and they understand it in the sense of "the Messianic
kingdom" over against "the old theocracy."    The sense
would then be: all those in the new covenant are greater
than even the greatest in the old covenant.    Thus the
vast superiority of the former would be graphically
presented.    Yet "the kingdom of the heavens" (see
5:3) or "of God" is never restricted to the new covenant but goes back to eternity.    To say, "it comes,"
always means that it existed long before this time. John
was in the kingdom, for faith admitted him into it as it
did all other believers.    The view that John belonged to
the old covenant is contradicted by Jesus himself who
describes him as being an object of Old Testament
prophecy which ended with Malachi.    Jesus thus combines John with himself as inaugurating the promised
new covenant.

He that is less than John in the kingdom is one
who either has no office or has one that is less than
John's.    He can be called greater than John in the
kingdom for one reason only.    This is not personal
faith, to which the context makes no reference, nor does
Jesus ever present John as a weak believer.    The greatness of those who are officially less than John consists
in the great treasures of revelation given to them by
God.    Read 13:16, 17.    Jesus is speaking of the time
now in progress.    In spite of his great office John could
not in prison see the great miracles Jesus was working.
Soon he would give up his life, and, therefore, could not
see the consummation of Jesus' work (death, resurrection, etc.).    All believers who witnessed these things
thereby had an advantage over John.    Note how Jesus
here again turns from John to his hearers.    They
neither prized John as they should nor understood what
Jesus was now offering them.    Yet by receiving all

that he was presenting to them they could be greater
than John who would soon be dead.

12) With δέ Jesus adds a necessary statement, one
which stresses the glorious time in which the hearers
of Jesus were privileged to live. **Now from the
days of John the Baptist until now the kingdom of
the heavens presses forward forcefully, and forceful people snatch it.** We consider it of little import
whether βιάζεται is the passive (C.-K. 219 at length) or
the middle used in an active sense (Zahn and others,
giving examples). The passive, however, cannot
mean "suffers violence," but means, "is brought with
force," namely by John and by Jesus. "Suffers violence" assumes that the βιασταί are the agents, and that
both clauses mean the same thing, which is scarcely
probable. In substance it is quite the same whether we
say, the kingdom itself "comes forward powerfully" or
"is brought forward powerfully" by John and by Jesus.
This statement obviously characterizes the years "from
the days of John the Baptist until now," from the day
when John began to baptize until now when Jesus was
in the full swing of his work. Of course, "until now"
does not imply that this urging of the kingdom on men
ceases at this moment; the matter goes on. We have
no reason to make the enemies of the kingdom the
agents of βιάζεται (when it is regarded as a passive)
and to refer the verb to their violence against it, letting
the second clause express the same thought. The trend
of the entire discourse deals, not with violence against
the kingdom, but with the indifference and the dissatisfaction that hinder men from entering it with zest.

The absence of the article shows that βιασταί does
not refer to a special class of men but only to the quality which those who appropriate the kingdom manifest.
The translation "men of violence" might pass if hostility were referred to; the idea of violence is too strong
an idea in the present connection. This word is not

found in the secular Greek which uses βιατός in the sense
of strong, courageous.    The correspondence between
βιάζεται and βιασταί is obvious, being a play on words.
The energy and the force with which the kingdom
comes (or is brought) instills a similar energy and
force in those whom the kingdom wins for itself.    They
are not "forceful" by nature and thus better than
others; but the kingdom itself with all its gifts, treasures, and blessings puts power and courage into them
"to snatch," let us say "to grab" it all.    For the opposite action see v. 16-19; Rev. 3:15.

13)    Jesus adds further explanations in regard to
this time.    **For all the prophets and the law did
prophesy until John.    And if you are willing to
accept it, he is Elijah, the one about to come.**    Why
did Jesus say "from the days of John the Baptist," etc.?
Because John introduces the grand new era.    For 430
years, since the last prophet, Malachi, spoke and wrote,
the completed Old Testament Scriptures ("all the
prophets and the law") gave forth their utterance.
"Until John" does not mean that they then ceased, but
that the fulfillment came in John.    Then "the days of
John the Baptist," etc., set in when the kingdom
pressed forward as it had never done before.

14)    Then Mal. 4:5, the very last word spoken by
that prophet, was fulfilled.    John is the "Elijah"
whom Jehovah promised to send, hence ὁ μέλλων ἔρχεσθαι,
"the one about to come," whose work on the hearts
of the people the prophet describes briefly.    Since
John's work was a stern call to repentance, he resembled Elijah, cf. Luke 1:17, "in the spirit and
power of Elias."    The Jews thought that Elijah himself would appear, cf. John 1:21, which, of course, even
John had to contradict; compare Matt. 17:10, etc.

Jesus does not affirm that John is the promised
Elijah but states the matter conditionally: "if you

are willing to accept it." This implies that they may
not be willing to consider John that great promised
Elijah. It is also not a matter of the understanding,
as though the meaning of the prophecy were doubtful, but a matter of the will. Jesus often points to
the will as the source of unbelief (23:37, "ye would
not"; John 5:40). This was the case with John. All
that the Jews were willing to do was to rejoice in
his light for a season (John 5:35), to exult in the feeling of again having a prophet in their midst. But to
treat him seriously as the Elijah to come, to wake up
to the great era that began with John — that was
another matter (v. 18). This heart condition Jesus
touches with his "if."

We note that Jesus does not reckon John with
the Old Testament prophets, does not regard him as
the last of them who completes their work. Their
work was completed by Malachi. John is himself the
object of prophecy, with him begin the new days of
the kingdom, his place is in the New Testament.

15) The "if" of v. 14 is justification for the call:
**He that has ears to hear, let him hear!** This is not
a concluding formula as 13:43 and Mark 4:23 show,
for Jesus continues to speak. In other connections
the call to use the ears may end a discourse. We
retain ἀκούειν because it is found in the decisive texts.
The thing that is to be heard properly so as to affect
the hearer's heart is this fulfilled prophecy, the fact
that John is Elijah as Jesus presents this in his discourse on John. In "he that has ears" lies the implication of wilful guilt when those ears that were made
to hear (and understand) are not used for this purpose, 13:14, 15.

16) Without a pause Jesus now turns his attention to the deplorable conduct of his hearers. How
miserably they had used their ears is shown by a
telling illustration. **Now to what shall I liken this**

**generation?** namely the one already indicated by
the period of time mentioned in v. 12: "from the
days of John the Baptist until now." The verb is
the deliberative aorist subjunctive, and the question
does not imply that Jesus is casting about for an
illustration, but that his hearers are now to see just
what they are like. **It is like to children sitting in
the market places who, calling to their companions,
say, We piped to you, and you did not dance; we
wailed, and you did not beat your breasts.** The
parable is plain and simple if we leave it thus instead
of inverting it or ignoring the *tertium comparationis*
by making this generation like two sets of children.
The large, open market places were convenient play-
grounds for the children of the neighborhood when
the market was not in progress. Jesus has in mind
a group of such children, such as he had occasionally
watched. This group tried to direct the play first
to one game, then to another, as their mood and fancy
dictated. They expected all the other children to
accept their suggestion; and when these did not
comply, they pettishly cried out and blamed the
others.

17) At one time they insisted on playing wedding.
So they copied what they had seen their elders doing:
they piped or fluted, imitating the flutes used in wedding processions, by either blowing little whistles they
had made or merely whistling with their lips. They
were determined that all the other children should
forthwith join them by hopping and skipping in a
procession as did those who followed the pipers at a
wedding. But the other children did not want to play
this game, they refused to skip after the whistlers.
So these complained and blamed them: "We piped
to you, and you did not dance!" *They* wanted to have
it their way and acted in an ugly fashion when they
could not. Jesus purposely chooses a joyful game.

Then he selects the opposite: a sad game. All at once these children want to play funeral. So they again copy their elders. They started the loud wailing of the professional wailing women that were hired for funerals (9:23; Eccles. 12:5; Amos 5:16). And they wanted all the other children to act as the bereaved always acted: beat their breasts, head, hips, etc. But these other children refused to join in, and then the group that was determined to lead complained: "We wailed, and you did not beat your breasts, ἐκόψασθε, strike yourselves." This sad game is purposely chosen as being the opposite of the glad one. The point lies in the fact that one group of children assumed the leadership in the games and veered, as the notion struck them, from one game to its opposite and then made loud complaint when they could not have their way. "This generation," Jesus says, "is exactly like this group of children."

18) **For John came, neither eating nor drinking, and they say, He has a demon! The Son of man came, eating and drinking, and they say, Lo, a glutton of a man and a winebibber and friend of publicans and of sinners. And justified was wisdom from her works.** "For" gives the reason that the parable of the willful children describes this generation so aptly. But this "for" has led some into letting the piping and the mourning children represent Jesus and John (the one eating, etc., the other not), and the other children who refused to dance and to beat themselves represent the unresponsive Jewish people. But the parable has this pointed heading: "To what shall I liken *this generation?*" and not, "myself and John." Then the parable continues: "It is like," etc. Nor does Jesus present himself and John as veering from one extreme to another and then complaining that people are not ready to veer with them. Moreover, the piping is mentioned first in the

parable, the wailing second; but the stern Baptist
came first and is also named first by Jesus, and he
himself is named in the second place. This shuts
out the interpretation that Jesus and John did the
piping and the wailing. The reverse is true: John
and Jesus would not accomodate themselves to the
fickle multitudes with their moods and notions. The
parable is not trying to explain the small success of
John and of Jesus but pictures the silly, childish way
in which this generation, which had both John and
Jesus before their eyes, passed judgment on both. The
two opposite games, wedding and funeral, do refer
to Jesus and to John, but the arrangement in the
parable and in the  application is not parallel like
this === but chiastic like this X: piping and Jesus
eating and drinking first and last and in between
wailing and John not eating.

These Jews were like silly children. When God
sent them the Baptist, they wanted to pipe and have
everyone dance with them. When the Baptist refused
to join them in such a game, they called him morose,
intolerable, and turned from him aggrieved and disappointed. These people likewise failed to understand the golden days of Jesus, which God sent them.
Then they insisted on the game of funeral, on fasting
(9:14), on rigorous traditional Sabbath observance,
etc. "Not eating nor drinking," i. e., in the way
men freely did, describes John's asceticism, who lived
as a Nazarite. His whole appearance was a rebuke
to his generation. Instead of heeding that rebuke,
many said: "Something is surely wrong with a
man who lives like this; a demon must have upset his
mind!"

When Jesus came "eating and drinking" (the
wording making him the very opposite of John), the
Jews were again dissatisfied. Jesus moved freely
among men, ate and drank with them on all manner

of occasions, yet always observed every propriety and
the divine ceremonial law, and was open and friendly
with all. Instead of understanding the purpose of
this difference between the messenger of repentance,
sent in the spirit of Elijah (v. 14, 15), and the Messiah as "the Son of man" (see 8:20), made in the
likeness of men and found in fashion as a man
(Phil. 2:7, 8), the Jews abused him, too. What they
demanded of John they condemned in Jesus; what
they condemned in John they demanded of Jesus. In
reality, by both actions they condemned themselves.
With the same slanderous tongue that attributed a
demon to John they viciously called Jesus ἄνθρωπος
φάγος, "a glutton of a man," the two nouns being used
like one term, and "a winebibber," one who ate and
drank to excess. Wine was the common drink at
meals and was used at the Passover and in connection with sacrifices. The climax is reached in the
addition, "a friend of publicans and of sinners"
(9:10, etc.; Luke 15:1, etc.). The viciousness of the
charges, both against John and against Jesus, is
apparent. Jesus scorns to enter into any sort of
defense.

All he does is to add the pithy statement, "And
justified was wisdom from her works." In Matthew's
account the texts support the reading ἔργων, in
Luke 7:35, the reading τέκνων, to which πάντων is added.
The difference may be due to the Aramaic term which,
when written without the vowel points and even when
pronounced, might mean either "works" or "children."
But ἀπό does not mean "by" as though the works or
the children of wisdom pronounced the verdict of
acquittal. The preposition indicates the source from
which the acquittal is drawn: *von ihren Werken her.*
Materially there is no difference, for the works of
wisdom are always done by the children of wisdom.
In this instance these are the works of John and of

Jesus who were exponents of the divine wisdom which sent the Jews exactly what they needed in the actions of both John and Jesus. The verb has the full emphasis: "nothing less than fully justified was" wisdom. The aorist is in place, since the works were performed in the past. John's career is at an end, and the actions of Jesus which the Jews slandered were also performed in the past. The agent back of the passive is most likely "this generation." To slander wisdom in such a childish fashion, one slander contradicting the other, is to pronounce her innocent. The verb is forensic in the fullest degree as it is wherever it is used (review the exhaustive treatment by C.-K. 317, etc.). The statement is not ironical: "This is the silly way in which this wise generation was justified by the treatment it gave John and Jesus!" By closing with the ἔργα Jesus returns to the ἔργα (v. 2) which prompted the entire discourse.

20) Luke 10:13-15 incorporates the "woes" in the address with which Jesus sent out the Seventy. Matthew writes only "then" and adds no special circumstances. **Then he began to upbraid the cities in which the most of his works of power were done because they did not repent.** On the circumstantial "began" compare v. 7; it marks the importance of what follows. The terrible words that follow, which are well characterized by the severe verb "to upbraid," reveal the gentle Jesus as being also the mighty and the terrible Jesus. The whole divine power that is behind the sweet Beatitudes is equally behind the judgment woes on all who spurn those blessings. The cities here named formed the populous center from which Christ's Galilean ministry radiated. Jesus says nothing about his Word and his preaching and calls his miracles δυνάμεις, "power-deeds," and not σημεία, "signs." The latter term is usually combined with his person and his Word as being productive of faith. Here Jesus

remains on the lowest level and deals only with the
first and natural impression which his works of *might*
ought to produce in men's hearts.  These works ought
at least to‚ check men in their careless course of sin
as the men of Nineveh halted in their wickedness
when Jonah announced the destruction of their city
and brought them nothing but the condemnation of
the law without a word of the gospel.  But these
Jewish cities remained obdurate.  The aorist "they
did not repent" marks the awful fact.  This verb is
here used in the narrow sense, denoting the act of
contrition.  The entire passage is obscured when repentance is here taken in the wider sense of contrition plus faith.  Works of might cannot produce faith,
but they ought to produce contrition and terror at the
thought of Almighty God.  Naturally, where this first
effect is absent, all other effects, those caused by the
Word, will also be absent.

21) **Woe to thee, Chorazin!  Woe to thee,
Bethsaida! because, if in Tyre and Sidon had been
done the works of power done in you, long ago
would they have repented in sackcloth and ashes.
But I say to you, for Tyre and Sidon it shall be more
endurable in the day of judgment than for you.**
Chorazin is mentioned only here, and Bethsaida only
a few times.  Because both were so near Capernaum
they witnessed, according to Jesus' own statement,
many of his mighty works.  "Woe" is an interjection
and is here construed with the dative.  It really states
a judgment on the part of him who utters it upon
those with reference to whom it is uttered; and ὅτι
introduces the reason for this woe, "because."  By
a conditional sentence of past unreality (εἰ with the
aorist and the aorist with ἄν) the two pagan cities
on the Mediterranean coast, Tyre and Sidon, are compared with the two cities on the shore of the Lake of
Galilee, Chorazin and Bethsaida.  Both pagan cities

on the Mediterranean had the reputation of being
wicked, and the former was to be left as "a place to
spread nets," it was to be completely obliterated.
Sidon was located twenty miles above Tyre.

The remarkable thing is that Jesus says that these
cities would have repented if the same works had
been done in them that were done in the two Jewish
cities.   God's omniscience includes all possible actions.
Since the possible lies between the absolutely necessary
(God himself) and things that are free (such as actual
human actions), the knowledge of the possible is called
*scientia media:* under certain conditions certain possible things would become actual which, however, for
lack of the conditions do not become actual; yet God
knows all about them.   In the second place, Jesus is
here speaking of repentance in the sense of outward
desistance from gross sins and crimes, the so-called
*peccata clamantia* for which Tyre and Sidon were
famous, not of the repentance which consists of spiritual conversion.   The case of Tyre and Sidon thus
lies in the realm of divine providence not in that of
saving grace.   This answers the question as to why
such mighty works were not done in Tyre and Sidon.
This is only the general question why any number
of possibilities (and they are countless) did not and
do not become actualities. They belong to the
mysteries of providence which lie beyond mortal
comprehension.

Yet all these possibilities, although they never become actualities, are taken into account by the divine
Mind, especially also in the final judgment which shall
be meted out with absolute justice to every man.   If
Tyre and Sidon would have put on sacking, a dark,
rough stuff worn next to the skin as the symbol of
remorse and deepest humiliation, and would have sat
in ashes or covered head and shoulders with ashes
(Job 2:8) as a second sign of utmost sorrow and

mourning, without question this possibility will not be forgotten in God's reckoning.

22) On πλήν as an adversative see B.-D. 449; R. 1187. In "I say to you" speaks the voice of authority which shall pronounce the sentence "in judgment day." On the lighter sentence for Tyre and Sidon see the comment on 10:15. Also the wicked dead shall arise, and eternal punishment has degrees.

23) **And thou, Capernaum, shalt thou be exalted to the heavens? To hades shalt thou go down! Because, if in Sodom had been done the works of power done in thee, it would have remained until this day. But I say to you, that for the land of Sodom it shall be more endurable in the day of judgment than for thee.** Capernaum, the worst of all, forms the climax. Here Jesus made his home, and here more numerous works of power were wrought — yet here, too, in vain. The interrogative particle μή implies a negative reply on the part of the speaker: "Thou surely dost not expect to be so exalted because thou hast been mine own city and so highly favored by me?" Yet the speaker hints that the negative reply may not be forthcoming. With terrific force the hesitation is ended: "To hades shalt thou go down!" — whatever thou mayest expect. Note the clashing contrast between the phrases ἕως τοῦ οὐρανοῦ and ἕως ᾅδου. This contrast is intensified by the terms "up" and "down" in the compound verbs.

The English hades and hell should not be written with a capital letter; neither should heaven or the heavens be written in this manner. Here "hades," the unseen place (*a privativum* plus ἰδεῖν) is beyond question the opposite of "heaven" and thus must mean hell. Here "hades" is not a translation of *sheol*, for Jesus is not quoting although he may have used *sheol* in the Aramaic. Note that Jesus does not postpone Capernaum's descent into hades until the judgment day. Sodom had already been destroyed, Tyre and Sidon would experience a similar fate as would also Chorazin, Bethsaida, and the worst of them all, Capernaum. "Hades" cannot mean *das Totenreich,* the realm of the dead, into which all the dead descend as some think. If a place that was different from heaven and hades, a receptacle for all dead men, existed, it would really be pointless for Jesus to declare that obdurate Capernaum shall descend thither. Where else would dead men go? Matthew has written "hades" only once more, in 16:18, and there, too, it has the sense of hell, the place of the damned, cf. Smith, *Dictionary of the Bible,* ed. by Hackett, the discussion by Bartlett under "Hell," II, 1039; Philippi, *Glaubenslehre,* VI, 57. Compare Gehenna in 5:22, 29; 10:28. Speculative thought makes hades a condition instead of a place, but such a view clashes with the words here uttered by Jesus.

The cause for Capernaum's descent to hell is the same as the one mentioned in v. 21, and is expressed by the same type of conditional sentence. But now Sodom (see 10:15) is used as a signal example of God's wrath and judgment. Instead of "it would have repented" we now have "it would have remained to this day." The sense is the same. Sodom would have repented in so far as to desist from its abnormal and horrible sins. Like other godless cities, God would then have let it remain.

24) The fate of Sodom in the final public judgment before the universe of men and of angels shall be according. See v. 22 and 10:15.

25) **At that season Jesus answered and said, I openly confess to thy honor, Father, Lord of the heaven and of the earth, that thou didst conceal these things from wise and intellectual men and didst reveal them unto infants. Yea, Father, because**

**thus it was well-pleasing before thee.** Matthew
connects this incident with the preceding only by the
phrase "at that season," καιρός, the time marked and
distinguished by what he has just reported.
Luke 10:21 adds more· the Seventy had returned,
and *"in that hour* Jesus rejoiced in the Spirit and
said" what is now reported. We must assume that
also the Twelve returned. The participle ἀποκριθείς
is often used in a wider sense, not as indicating a
response to some question but a response to some
situation. So here the καιρός calls forth the words
now spoken.

The verb ἐξομολογεῖσθαι with the dative means more
than "to thank" or even "to praise." The intensification by means of ἐκ adds to the idea of acknowledging or confessing the notion of greatness or of open-
ness: "I openly confess (or acknowledge) to thy
honor"; and ὅτι states what is thus acknowledged.
As the Son in the essential sense Jesus uses the unqualified address "Father" and repeats this in the
next verse. He is speaking to the Father but in the
presence of the assembled disciples (Luke 10:23) so
they all may hear him. But another relation is here
to be noted, one which reveals the supreme majesty
of this Father of Jesus: "Lord of the heaven and
of the earth," i. e., as the Creator and the Ruler of
the universe. This majesty stands out in overwhelming contrast to the "wise and intellectual men" who
close their foolish hearts against his revelations and
in another contrast to the "infants" who are blessed
with these revelations. What a marvel that the
eternal Father of the eternal Son, to whom all heaven
and earth bow in submission, should condescend to
people who are nothing but infants and helpless babes!
Yet in the very word νήπιοι, "infants," lies the hint
of the reason for thus blessing them. As the Father

of the Son and through this Son they are his dear little ones to whom, therefore, "these things" may be, yea, must be revealed.

The act on account of which Jesus exalts his Father is a double one: concealing certain things from wise and intellectual men and revealing them to men who, compared with these, are nothing but babes. The absence of the articles before σόφοι and συνετοί keeps the stress on the qualities here indicated. The two terms refer to one general class, and the verbal συνετός is one of the few used in the New Testament in an active sense, R. 1097. While the scribes and the Pharisees are the type here referred to, all those are included who are filled with the sufficiency of their own intellectual and educational acquirements in matters of religion. Being wise and intellectual like the rabbis with their false theology and its equally false application to life, nothing of the true revelation and theology of God can be conveyed to them. Hence Jesus says: the Father "did conceal these things from them." The ταῦτα refers to all that formed the substance of Christ's teaching and preaching, i. e., the gospel of the kingdom with its great principle of salvation by grace through faith in Christ.

The aorists are important: ἀπέκρυψας, ἀπεκάλυψας, and ἐγένετο. This proceeding on the part of God is something that has been settled from the very start, is a fixed and unalterable thing that has been determined by him from the beginning and is never to be changed. Only the great fact is stated by these aorists, a reason for this great act of God is not added. Yet in the designations "wise and intelligent men," on the one hand, and "infants," on the other, the reason for God's act is suggested. The wise and intelligent are filled with their own wise and learned ideas, and thus God, finding them filled and satisfied with what they have, can give them nothing. The infants, however, are those who lack everything and realize their emptiness. They are the poor that mourn and are meek and hunger and thirst, 5:3-6; 18:3; Phil. 3:8. Having nothing, God can fill them with everything.

The Father's action, therefore, comports with his whole plan of universal grace. He arranged it so that nothing should be required of us, that all should come from him. If high intellectual attainments on our part were required, this would automatically shut out all who have no such attainments. If we had to bring something, grace would be only partial and not complete on God's part. Moreover, the fact is that no man can bring anything and if he thinks he can, he deceives himself  The Father had to proceed as he did.

We must add, however, that no man is a νήπιος by nature, be his education ever so primitive. I Cor. 1:26 makes it plain that the sense of Christ's word is not that the gospel is intended only for the ignorant and not for the educated. The terms wise, intelligent, as well as infants, are here used, not to describe men in their state before the gospel comes to them, but as subsequent to its work upon them. Every man, even the most ignorant, has some pet wisdom of his own with which he at first reacts against the gospel of grace. By its power this gospel removes that pet wisdom and makes men infants so that they receive everything from God. This work succeeds in the case of some of the most learned and highly educated. But some cling to their foolish wisdom in spite of all efforts of grace. Such were not only the scribes and the Pharisees but the unlearned Jews as well who allowed these men to influence them (v. 15-24). So today some of the worst opponents of the gospel are those who follow the scientists and advanced religious thinkers of our time.   All these are the wise and intelligent referred to by Jesus.

26)   With "yea" Jesus emphatically affirms what he has just said.   The Father's action has the fullest approval of Jesus.   The article may be used with the vocative as the Hebrew and the Aramaic regularly use it, and the nominative form may be used as a vocative: ὁ πατήρ.   Does ὅτι here mean "because" ("for," our versions), or is it   a repetition of the ὅτι used in v. 25, with the meaning "that"?   Have we the reason why the Father concealed and revealed as he did or simply a repetition of what he did in other words?   Grammar cannot decide the issue.   Most commentators prefer "that" and supply ἐξομολογοῦμαι from v. 25.   Observe that in the A. V. both ὅτι are regarded as being causal.   The simple fact is that in the case of verbs of this kind it makes no practical difference whether we state why we praise or what we praise: the thing we praise is the reason for the praise.

Yet why the Father did what he did calls for an explanation.   One explanation we have noted, the one that speaks of the persons concerned.   But this takes us only halfway.   The profoundest reason lies in the Father himself.   And this Jesus gives us by saying that it was his εὐδοκία.   The objection that the incomprehensible acts of God are not made comprehensible by being traced back to his equally incomprehensible will, misunderstands the εὐδοκία, a standard term in the New Testament.   This is not an arbitrary, incomprehensible will or decree but the "good pleasure" or "good thought" of God, his gracious purpose and will of salvation, as the following clear passages show: Eph. 1:5, 9; Phil. 2:13; II Thess. 1:11; Luke 12:32; II Pet. 1:17.   "In Christ he saves us out of pure mercy, without any merit or good works of ours, according to the purpose of his will," *Concordia Triglotta*, 1092-3.

The ultimate source of our salvation is this great εὐδοκία. When God's acts (concealing, revealing) are traced back to this source, the ultimate point is reached. If man was to be saved, God had to save him by his "good thought" or εὐδοκία, by devising means and ways that were in harmony with him who devised them. Since οὕτως refers to the acts of concealing and revealing, we understand ὅτι as giving the reason for these acts: "Yea, so thou didst do, Father, because thus it was *eudokia* in thy sight." And who in all the universe could suggest a better plan and method than this that found God's approval? In ἔμπροσθέν σου, "in front of thee" the majesty, indicated in "Lord," etc., (v. 25), is again evident.

27) With the same elevated feeling and in the same exalted tone Jesus now turns from the Father to the disciples and continues to speak of his Father. **All things were given to me by my Father. And no one really knows the Son except the Father; nor does anyone really know the Father except the Son and he to whom the Son may will to reveal him.** Here Matthew records some of the deep things about which John delights to write. In view of 28:18; John 3:35; 13:3; 17:2, "all things" cannot be restricted. Those who attempt a restriction such as "all things connected with the *eudokia*, or the kingdom, or the work of salvation," must reckon with Eph. 1:10, 22. Since the establishment of the kingdom involves power over all hostile forces in earth and in hell, there is nothing that might be exempted from πάντα. "All things: earth, heaven, and hell; men, angels, and devils; time, death, and eternity; all things: salvation and damnation; grace and judgment; life and death; all things: truth, righteousness, glory, peace, and joy, consolation and refreshing, rest and hope, deliverance from sin, victory in temptation, overcoming the world, communion with God, the love of God, the life in God — all things have

been delivered unto him.   He is the almighty Lord, the
Giver of divine gifts of grace, the Executor of all divine
works, the Prince of life, and therefore the Captain of
our salvation."   Petri.

The passive παρεδόθη has the agent added in the
regular manner by ὑπό: "were handed over by my
Father."   "By this he indicates that he is true man,
who has received them from the Father.   For neither
would God deliver all things to one who was only man,
nor would one who was only God receive them from
another.   For neither is it possible for one who is only
man to be over all things, nor for one who is only God
to be beneath God.   Thus in this one person true God
and true man are joined together."   Luther.   The
aorist cannot refer to the exaltation of Christ's human
nature but goes back to the Incarnation.   Then "was
given" to him all divine power and majesty which, however, during the days of his humiliation, he used only
as needed in his ministry (as in performing the miracles), and upon the absolute use of which he did not
enter until he arose from the dead in the exaltation of
his human nature.   As the Son he was equal to the
Father, but as man he was beneath the Father and
received "all things" from him.   *Conc. Trigl.* 1033, 55.

Καί coordinates; it is not the equivalent of γάρ.
Jesus is laying the foundation for the great invitation
of v. 28, etc.   The first buttress is the fact that all
things were given over to him as a man.   The second
is the fact that only the Father knows him, and he the
Father; to which is added the third, and he to whom
the Son reveals the Father.   First we had the human
nature, regarding which we must know that all things
were given to it when it was joined to the divine nature.
Now we hear about the divine nature as joined to the
human.   Between the Son and the Father there exists
a peculiar relation: these two alone "really know" each
**other.**   All others are excluded.

'Επιγινώσκει is γινώσκω strengthened by ἐπί and means a knowing that really penetrates. This is heightened when the two subjects and the objects are noted: the Son and the Father, and their divine relation to each other. While the mutual knowledge of these persons is ineffable because of its divinity, Luther rightly points out that this knowledge is here mentioned with reference to us and our saving knowledge of the Son and of the Father. He calls it *theological* and not at all philosophical and by this term has in mind what especially concerns us, namely that the Father and the Son know each other's will, mind, and thought as these pertain to us.

The third statement follows: "and he to whom," etc. Luther writes that here there is no reluctance on the part of the Son to reveal the Father but the vast condescension of the Son of this Lord of heaven and earth (v. 25). He to whom all things have been given speaks here. "He to whom," etc., has reference to the "infants" mentioned in v. 25. In βούληται we have the εὐδοκία; the Father's good pleasure and the Son's will are one. This is not an arbitrary selection of persons who are admitted to this knowledge but the pure grace which fills all whom it can induce to discard their own empty and haughty wisdom. The strong verb ἐπιγινώσ-κειν applies also to these persons. They shall know with real experimental heart knowledge as children know their Father on the basis of all the manifestations of his fatherhood and his love. This is supreme spiritual blessedness but a closed book to the wise and intelligent of this world. Only by the Son's revelation can any man really know the Father and by no wisdom of his own. "Here the bottom falls out of all merit, all powers and abilities of reason, or the free will men dream of, and it all counts nothing before God; Christ must do and must give everything." Luther. Jesus wills to reveal the Father only through his own person, work, and Word, John 14:6; 9-11; for in no other way can a poor sinner ever come to know God.

28) On the tremendous basis thus laid down rests the call that now follows: **Hither to me, all those laboring and having been loaded down! and I myself will give you rest. Take my yoke upon you and learn from me, that I am gentle and lowly in heart, and you will find rest for your souls. For my yoke is pleasant, and my load is light.** Here the good pleasure of the Father's and the Son's will is most delightfully voiced. Here the babes receive the revelation which, because it is distasteful to the wise, is lost and hidden from them because of this very folly. The adverb δεῦτε has the force of an imperative, "Hither to me!" The gospel has a double power: one that is efficacious; the other, collative. In every gospel word a power comes to us that is strong to make us heed, accept, yield to that word; and at the same time in every gospel word a power comes to us that is full of heavenly gifts that are designed to place these into our hearts. "Hither to me!" draws and moves and at the same time holds out to us all that Jesus has. "I believe that I cannot by my own reason or strength believe in Jesus Christ, my Lord, or come to him," Luther. His Word and his call enable me. "Unto me" contains all that Jesus has said about himself in the foregoing; and "unto me" means "to me alone" and not to another. Note this pronoun: unto *me* — and *I* will give — *my* yoke — learn of *me* — *I* am gentle — *my* yoke — *my* load. Does this make plain why he so fully revealed his relation to the Father?

"All those laboring" (present active participle) are all those who are trying to work out their own salvation, and the more serious they are, the more they will toil. "All those having been loaded down" (perfect passive participle with present implication) are all those who have let others load them down with what the latter think will secure salvation. These terms really apply to all men, for none have true rest save those who come to Christ. All the vain, fruitless striving after peace, contentment, happiness, rest, and joy, which is found the world over, is this constant laboring; and those who come with their deceptions and their proffers of help only load men down the more. Then the suffering, unrest, trouble, fear, grief, pain, an evil conscience, against which men rebel so vainly, adds to the labor and the load. In endless variety, sometimes mixed with tragedy, sometimes tragically trying to laugh it all away, this wretchedness meets us in our race. Yet a difference appears the moment Christ and his call are met. Some cry out as did David in Ps. 38:4; others revile as did the Pharisees and the scribes, v. 18, 19, or turn disdainfully away. Normally and according to the divine intention all, actually all, ought to be drawn to Jesus. It is the height of abnormality and irrationality to spurn the divine help when it is so absolutely needed.

The emphasis is on the strong ἐγώ, "I, I myself, will give you pause or rest." The verb is a volitive future, expressing Christ's will, not a futuristic future (R. 924). In this "I" lies all the majesty of the previous verses and the implication that he alone can give, yes, most assuredly will give this rest. The verb ἀναπαύσω, "I will rest you, make you recover," fits the case perfectly: the laboring shall end forever, and in place of it there shall be relief. Christ is the end of the law to those who believe. He removes the sin and the guilt, he does the saving. All we need to do is to commit ourselves to him. "Thou, God, hast created us unto thyself; hence our heart is restless until it rests in thee." Augustine.

29) Laboring and being loaded down are the opposites of rest, yet Jesus points out a similarity between them when he bids us, "Take my yoke upon

you!" This sounds like exchanging one load for another, for a yoke is placed on an ox that by means of it he may be harnessed to a load. Indeed, the gospel and the doctrine of faith are a yoke in that they are full of commands, all of them gospel commands, however, commands to take, to trust, to feast, to inherit, and the like. The rest and the yoke are two pictures of the same blessing; by taking this yoke upon us we shall find rest for our souls. Indeed, this is a yoke that rests its bearer. The aorist ἄρατε expresses one definite act. *We* take this yoke when *he* gives us rest.

"And learn from me that I am gentle and lowly in heart" intends to encourage us to take Christ's yoke. The aorist μάθετε means, "learn once for all." Note that this makes a true μαθητής, disciple, i. e., one who has learned. Learn "from me," ἀπ᾽ ἐμοῦ, means from contact with me, and ὅτι cannot be causal, leaving us to surmise *what* we are to learn, telling us only *why* we are to learn something that has not been told us. Once for all we are to learn that Christ is not another Moses, is not like the scribes and the Pharisees who heartlessly pile on burdens (23:4). He is πραΰς, "gentle" and mild and at the same time ταπεινὸς τῇ καρδίᾳ, "humble or lowly regarding the heart." R. 523 calls this a locative dative, but it is, perhaps, better to call it a dative of relation. The heart of Christ is not haughty and overbearing but humble, stooping down to us. First, his majesty and his omnipotence as the Son, and these attributes bestowed also on his human nature in the unity of his person — this in order to guarantee all his mighty promises. Then, his gentle and humble heart — this to attract us to come to him and to take his restful yoke upon us. The idea that we are to follow his example in gentleness and lowliness is quite foreign to the connection. Nor is the yoke the cross, suffering, etc., for his sake, under which we are meekly and

humbly to bow. These ideas lose the chief thought, the
rest and the relief which Jesus offers us.

To this he reverts: "and you shall find rest for your
souls." This gift is the burden of his promise. He
gives us rest, and thus we find the rest; hence ἀναπαύσω
and ἀνάπαυσις. We find it as though it were a blessed
discovery, yet the finding is caused by his giving. "For
your ψυχαί" shows the nature of this rest. The souls
that animate our bodies shall find themselves free from
every strain and burden, with no worry, no fears, and
no distress. Think of the happiness that results!

30) But how about the yoke? Is not the Christian profession a hard life, much harder than the other
type of life? Here is the answer: "For my yoke is
pleasant (χρηστός), and my load is light (ἐλαφρόν)."
"What can be lighter than a burden which unburdens
us and a yoke which bears its bearer?" Bernhard.
"Christ's burden does not oppress but makes light and
itself bears rather than is borne." Luther. The burden and the yoke are one, the former defining the latter,
and φορτίον is chosen to match πεφορτισμένοι in v. 28. We
take on a new Master, and he lays on us a new load —
but what a difference! Since, however, we are bound
to think of the cross, affliction, persecution, and hard
trials entailed in coming to Christ, let us say that all
these are more than counterbalanced by the power,
help, strength, and consolation supplied by him. On
the other hand, those who spurn Christ's yoke have
only dismay and despair when the judgments of God
begin to strike them.

# CHAPTER XII

## IX

### Christ's Clash With the Pharisees, Chapter 12

The fact that Jesus opposed the scribes and the Pharisees Matthew has indicated in 5:20. He now presents a number of instances in which the Pharisees come out boldly against Jesus. Matthew's connections of time are of such a nature as to warrant the conclusion that all these incidents occurred in the order in which he records them and all within a few days.

1) **At that season** (cf. 11:25) **Jesus went on the Sabbath through the grain. Now his disciples were hungry and began to pluck ears and to eat.** Judging from the ripeness of the grain, it must have been April, near the time of the Passover, a year before Jesus' death. The hunger of the disciples is mentioned only in order to explain their action. Yes, Jesus and the disciples were hungry at times. Note τοῖς σάββασι (a plural) for "on the Sabbath," and ἐν σαββάτῳ in v. 2 (a singular); the plural is used with reference to one Sabbath as well as to several. Deut. 23:25 permitted plucking a few ears in a neighbor's grainfield.

2) **But when the Pharisees saw it they said to him, Lo, thy disciples are doing what it is not lawful to do on a Sabbath.** The antagonism of the Pharisees (see 3:7) has already been noted in 9:11, 34, that of the scribes in 9:3. They kept constant watch on Jesus and were now thus engaged. Matthew makes the remark that they saw what the disciples were doing, and Luke says that they assailed the disciples, the attack, however, was directed against Jesus. The

(460)

exclamation "lo" brings out the thought that these
Pharisees pretended to be horrified while they were
in reality glad that they had a clear case against Jesus.
The charge is "doing what it is not lawful to do on a
Sabbath," οὐκ ἔξεστι. It was a flagrant breaking of the
law, namely of Exod. 20:10, as illustrated by Exod.
16:22, etc., but as interpreted according to the *Patres
Traditionum*: He who reaps on the Sabbath is chargeable; and to pluck ears is a species of reaping. And
whoever breaks off anything from its stalk is chargeable under the specification of reaping. The deeds
which make a man chargeable with stoning and death
if he does them presumptuously, or with a sacrifice if
he sins ignorantly, are either generic or derivative.
Thirty-nine kinds of the generic are enumerated: to
plow, to sow, to reap, to bind sheaves, to thresh, to
winnow, to grind, to pound, to powder, etc., to shear
sheep, to dye wool, etc.; and the derivatives are of the
same class and likeness: furrowing = plowing; cutting up vegetables = grinding; plucking ears = reaping.

Jesus assumes full responsibility for what his disciples are here doing although he himself plucked no
ears. In the case of the other charges regarding the
Sabbath the same was true: with his own hands Jesus
did nothing on which the Jews could pounce. This
gave Jesus the tactical advantage of defending others,
not himself, and of compelling the Pharisees to raise
the question about the real principle at issue: "Is it,
or is it not, lawful?" instead of passionately assailing
his person. The law itself was the issue, and what
men did were only illustrations for or against it. This
was wisdom and mastery.

3) **But he said to them, Did you not read what
David did when he was hungry and those with him?
how he entered into the house of God and ate the
showbread, which it was not lawful for him to eat**

**nor for those with him but only for the priests?**
Jesus lays his finger on the real trouble: too much
reading of rabbinical law and not enough of divine law.
Of course, the Pharisees had read I Sam. 21, but not
as interpreting Exod. 20:10. The ἄρτοι τῆς προθέσεως,
"the bread-loaves of the setting forth," were twelve
loaves, each made of about 6¼ pounds of flour, set
forth in two rows on a gold-covered table in the Holy
Place every Sabbath day, and, when removed, to be
eaten only by the priests, Lev. 24:5-9. Jesus assumes
that the Pharisees agree with him that David, whom
they esteemed so highly, did the right thing in the
instance to which reference is made.

4) David did not enter the Holy Place and take
the loaves there set forth. "House of God" includes
the courts of the Tabernacle, as in Ps. 122. The bread
which Ahimelech gave David was that which had been
removed from the Holy Place yet was considered "most
holy," Lev. 24:9. The point is that David *ate* of this
bread, and this act was οὐκ ἐξόν (present neuter participle), *"unlawful"*; it was made so, not by a rabbinical
finding, but by the divine ceremonial law itself. Jesus
overtops the charge of the Pharisees. He proves by
David's own example that even the ceremonial law was
not absolute in its application. The rabbinical refine-
ments are ignored as being unworthy of notice. We
must not misunderstand the hunger of David and his
companions: they were not starving to death but were
only badly in need of food. Already this sufficed to
set the ceremonial law aside. God cares far more
for the proper spiritual condition of the heart than
for the outward observance of his own ceremonial
regulations.

The argument is overwhelming. David's hunger
'sets aside even a divine regulation; shall not the
hunger of the disciples set aside mere rabbinical
notions?

5)  Jesus does not stop with the first argument, which from the one case of David by inference limited all ceremonial laws, including the sabbatical law, in their application.  To the generic he adds the specific. **Or did you not read in the law that on the Sabbath the priests in the Temple profane the Sabbath and are guiltless?  But I say to you that something greater than the Temple is here.**  Of course, the Pharisees had read the very matter to which Jesus here refers.  He words it in a staggering manner: one reads in the law (the Old Testament) itself that on the very Sabbath the divinely appointed priests in the very most holy Temple profane the Sabbath, βεβηλοῦσιν, make it common or unholy.  The climaxes are piled high.  The law breaks the law — in the very Temple — by its own priests — and yet these lawbreaking priests are ἀναίτιοι, no indictment under any law (this is the sense of the term) standing against them.  If the other example was not directly concerned with the Sabbath, this one makes up for it.  What the law itself (for instance, Num. 28:9, etc.) commanded the priests to do in the Temple was to break the Sabbath law right on the Sabbath by all this butchering of sacrificial animals and a large amount of other work.  And the Pharisees had never perceived this in the law!

So the law itself shows that its ceremonial requirements are not absolute and he who makes them so contradicts that law itself.  The ceremonial law is itself subservient to a higher law and principle.  It, indeed, required certain outward restrictions on labor in the old covenant, but it also required certain laborious ministrations in the Jewish Temple.  Both were required, *yet not on their own account but only for the spiritual need of the people.*  By the satisfying of *this* need a good and gracious God was honored and not by a lot of outward regulations and forms.  These latter were the shell and no more.  In the new cove-

nant all of them were abolished, even the Sabbath itself
and all the Temple sacrifices and the priests of the
Temple into the bargain.

6) With the voice of authority, "But I say to you,"
Jesus now makes the striking application to what his
disciples were doing by plucking ears on the Sabbath
to appease their hunger. We prefer the neuter μεῖζον,
"something greater than the Temple is here," to the
masculine μείζων, "One greater." In order to understand this neuter note that all three cases refer to the
Temple: David went to "the house of God" — the
priests serve in the Temple — and here in the case of
the disciples is something greater than the Temple. The
neuter μεῖζον is due to this parallel with οἶκος and with
ἱερόν, with which a direct personal designation would
not be so fitting. The gradation thus is: 1) the Tabernacle (David), 2) the Temple, 3) something greater,
i. e., the presence of the God-man himself, of whom
both Tabernacle and Temple were a symbol or a type.
In the case of all three something occurs that is contrary to the Pharisaic conception but perfectly in harmony with the divine thought which gave to Israel
Tabernacle, Temple, and the presence: David eats the
showbread; the priests butcher sacrifices; the disciples
pluck ears. And the last act is not even a breach of
the ceremonial law but is only thought to be such by
the Pharisees. The argument is: if God's Word sanc-
tions the acts of David and of the priests, it cannot
condemn the act of the disciples.

In v. 3 the argument is from the major (the holy
showbread) to the minor (ears of grain). In v. 5
the argument is from the minor (the Temple) to the
major (something greater than the Temple). Both
are equally unanswerable. In v. 6, moreover, the full
divine authority of Jesus meets presumptuous Pharisees. He who is greater than Tabernacle and Temple
is here, he who alone has authority to judge what con-

stitutes a violation of the Sabbath which is served by
Tabernacle and Temple. Against these arrogant
Pharisees who never read the law aright and yet arrogate this judgment to themselves Jesus protects his
disciples by asserting the full might of this authority.
Those were little ears of grain, but they were the occasion for pointing the Pharisees to the presence that is
greater than the Temple. What must these fanatics
have thought when Jesus thus pointed to himself? As
he stood there amid the waving grain on that beautiful
April day, his majestic presence and words must have
overawed and at least for the time being silenced them.

7) The argument now reaches its climax, revealing both the inwardness of the law under which the
Jews then lived and of which they knew nothing, and
the inwardness of the Son of man who, while he was
at that time a servant of the law for our sakes, was
at the same time "Lord of the law." **But if you had
known what this means, Mercy I want and not sacrifice, you would not have condemned the guiltless.
For Lord of the Sabbath is the Son of man.** R. 904
makes the past perfect ἐγνώκειτε a virtual imperfect.
Then the condition would be one of present unreality:
"if you knew," and the conclusion one of past unreality: "you would not have condemned." But B.-D.
347, 3 points out that the past perfect is more or less
aoristic, and this can well be applied in this case, allowing the condition, too, to be one of past unreality: "if
you had known." Perhaps the past perfect intends to
add the idea of duration in the past. "If you had
known" is a climax to the two questions, "Did you not
read?" Jesus quotes Hos. 6:6 (as in 9:13). "Mercy,"
ἔλεος, is pity and sympathy for anyone in distress (5:7;
Luke 6:36) ; θυσία is a sacrifice sent up in smoke, also
the act of bringing sacrifice. As between the two, God
wants the former. While he himself has ordered sacrifice, sacrifice alone could never satisfy him. God

wanted the sacrifice of a true heart, one full of mercy, for instance, toward hungry fellow men, and corresponding acts for God's sake.

Jesus is not speaking of mere humanitarian pity, nor of merciful actions inspired by the law. The mercy that Hosea refers to comes from the gospel, which fills also the Old Testament. It is born of the new life kindled by this gospel. And so this mercy is known by the inner experience of having it and of putting it to delightful practice. When the Pharisees condemned the disciples, who were utterly guiltless, having transgressed not even a ceremonial law, they revealed that Hos. 6:6 (and every other gospel word similar to that) was foreign territory to them. Men's actions reveal what affinity they have for God's Word and how they meet or fail to meet what God really wants.

8) The γάρ is usually regarded as substantiating τοὺς ἀναιτίους: "I, as Lord of the Sabbath, find them guiltless." But this γάρ includes much more. The entire exposition regarding the Sabbath is given by Jesus as the Lord who has instituted the Sabbath, who *thus* knows what the Sabbath law involves. The emphasis is on κύριος, but this does not imply that as Lord of the Sabbath Jesus can disregard the Sabbath, set it aside, do what he may please with it. As Lord of the Sabbath, who instituted it, he upholds it, he will tolerate no Pharisaical interference with its true purpose. It is thus that Jesus protects his disciples against the charge (αἰτία) that they are violating the Sabbath. As Lord of the Sabbath he would be the first to condemn every violation. As Lord of the Sabbath he is now condemning the Pharisees' perversion of the Sabbath. "Lord of the Sabbath" has the same meaning as "something greater than the Temple." Sabbath and Temple go together, Jesus maintains both and rids both of Jewish perversion.

As "the Son of man" (see 8:20) Jesus is Lord of the Sabbath, and his presence is something greater than the Temple. The entire ceremonial law, all Jewish worship, in particular Sabbath and Temple, were arranged, not by God as Elohim, but as Yahweh, as part of the plan of salvation, and were thus under the Messiah as being κύριος of it all. Hence not as the essential Son but as the God-man Jesus was Lord of the Sabbath, and, we may add, of the Temple, "my Father's house." He who thus was above all these institutions was now here to fulfill all that they implied (5:17). He who had instituted the Sabbath law was fulfilling the Sabbath law, and he would be the last to let his own disciples become guilty of any violation. But in the Son of man and in his fulfillment the whole ceremonial law would accomplish its purpose and would thus become ineffective as no longer being needed. This would come about through the death and the resurrection of the Son of man. The new covenant without ceremonies would supersede the old with its ceremonies. Thus the Temple and the Sabbath and all the sacrifices would disappear.

It is a mistake to think that Jesus was already abolishing the Sabbath, Temple, etc. The Christian Sunday still lay in the future. Jesus was still under the law, redeeming them that were under the law, Gal. 4:4, 5. After Pentecost, led by the Spirit, the apostles and the church would in perfect Christian liberty choose a day for divine public worship; but this would not be another law and Sabbath but only a free expression of their desire to use the Word in public and unitedly and in proper order to worship the Lord. Col. 2:16, 17; *Concordia Triglotta*, 91, §§ 57-60.

9) The second clash is also one regarding the Sabbath; but this one was incited by the action of Jesus himself. Matthew reports far more regarding

this case than Mark 3:1-6, and Luke 6:6-11. **And after departing thence he went into their synagogue,** i. e., that of the Pharisees just mentioned. But Luke shows that this was done on another Sabbath.

10) **And, lo, a man having a withered hand! And they inquired of him, saying, If it is lawful to heal on the Sabbath** (let us know)? **in order that they might accuse him.** Dramatically attention is drawn to the man and to his infirmity. A hand that is withered and shriveled is beyond human help. Mark and Luke state only that the Pharisees watched Jesus to see whether he would heal him, so that they might accuse him; Luke adds that Jesus knew their thoughts. From Matthew we learn that these thoughts did not remain unspoken. Jesus, knowing them, compelled the Pharisees to speak. They, of course, hide their evil intention in order to secure a legal charge against him. They say that all they want to know is whether it is lawful to heal on the Sabbath (the dative is plural and is used interchangeably with the singular to designate a Sabbath, v. 1, 2). On the use of εἰ before direct questions see R. 916; B.-D. 440, 3; it is probably elliptical as far as the Greek is concerned: "Tell us, or we would know, if," etc. We see how little impression Christ's word regarding mercy has made on them, v. 7. They still ask only ἔξεστι, "is it lawful," and not, "is it merciful?"

11) **But he said to them, What man shall there be of you who shall have one sheep, and if this shall fall into a pit on the Sabbath, will he not lay hold of it and lift it out? By how much, then, does a man excel a sheep? Wherefore it is lawful to do good on the Sabbath.** From Mark and from Luke we learn that Jesus made the man with the withered hand stand forth before the whole assembly in the synagogue. The scene was dramatic. Matthew alone

records the example of the sheep. The argument is
*ex concesso*: no man present would let even the one
sheep lie in the pit; whatever exertion and work its
rescue entailed he would perform on the Sabbath and
would not think that he had broken the law. "One"
sheep is sometimes understood to mean: therefore it
was the more valuable. But the reverse seems to be
correct: for a whole flock one might do a great deal,
but one lone sheep amounts to nothing. The argument
is from the minor to the major, and thus the idea is
to make the value of the sheep as low as possible.

12) This is brought out in so many words. A
man, a human being, certainly excels a lone sheep,
διαφέρει differs vastly from it in value. The two questions regarding the sheep answer themselves. No man
present would dare to risk giving contrary answers.
And now Jesus draws the conclusion. In Mark and in
Luke this is done by means of a question which presents
the alternatives involved. These evangelists also remark regarding the silence of the Pharisees. Because
of this silence Matthew makes only the brief assertion
the conclusion of his account. "Wherefore it is (indeed) lawful to do good on the Sabbath." Here we
have one of those cases when the question had to be
corrected before an answer could be given. The Pharisees had posited the alternative: "to do or not to do?"
And they answered, "No doing at all on the Sabbath."
The moment the question is rightly put: "to do good
or to do harm; to save a life or to kill" (Mark 3:4;
Luke 6:9) ; or, as Matthew has it: καλῶς ποιεῖν, to perform actions that have moral qualities, the question
answers itself. Deeds that are morally excellent
would grace only the old Jewish legal Sabbath. Such
a deed was the restoration of the shriveled hand. A
blessing such as this certainly harmonized well with
the Sabbath which was intended as a blessing to man.
To leave the man unhealed would be κακῶς ποιεῖν, to act

with moral baseness, the greatest desecration of the old Sabbath.

The second alternative which Jesus states: "to save life or to kill, i. e., destroy life," carries the question to its ultimate extreme. It would be the highest moral excellence actually to save life, and it would be the basest deed to destroy life, by either killing outright, or by killing indirectly, by refusing to rescue from mortal danger. The ultimate always includes the less that is of the same nature. Thus in Matt. 5:21, etc., murder includes the lesser sins that Jesus names; and in v. 27, etc., adultery does the same. Here in the synagogue Jesus answers the whole question at issue, of which the healing of a withered hand on the Sabbath is only a part. But could not Jesus wait and do his healing on a weekday? To have waited would have left the impression on all concerned that it was, indeed, unlawful to heal on the Sabbath, the very error Jesus was determined to eradicate.

13) **Then he says to the man,** who was standing before the assembly, **Stretch forth thy hand! And he stretched it forth, and it was restored sound like the other.** Instantaneously and before the very eyes of all the withered hand (Luke, the right one) became as sound and as well as the other. Thus omnipotence works. Let modern healing cults equal it. Matthew states only the facts. They are so tremendous that embroidering them with words would only detract from their significance. But Jesus makes the case hard for the Pharisees. He does not so much as touch the hand, he does not even command that it be healed; he only asks the man to raise his hand, that is all. Was this "work" in the Pharisaic sense of the word? Even their perverted minds would have a hard task trying to prove this.

14) **But after they had gone out the Pharisees took counsel against him that they destroy him.**

The enormity of this reaction speaks for itself. Luke remarks about their rage, and Mark that they joined efforts with the Herodians. The ὅπως clause is like the infinitive (cf., B.-P. on the word) and states what was actually resolved (ἔλαβον, aorist), namely to destroy Jesus. R. 994 makes it an indirect deliberative question. To heal on the Sabbath — a mortal crime; but to plot murder — a perfectly lawful act!

15) **Now when Jesus realized it he withdrew thence; and many followed him, and he healed them all and charged them that they should not make him public.** Until the time for his death came, Jesus used all prudence and withdrew from violence, the last resort of vanquished opponents. "Them all" is used *ad sensum* with reference to the sick — not one was left without help. In addition to retiring from the plotting Pharisees Jesus strongly urged that (ἵνα in an object clause) his miracles be not used to make him φανερός, thus exciting still more opposition.

17) All this activity of Jesus, plus the manner of it, is fulfillment of prophecy: **in order that it might be fulfilled what was spoken through Isaiah, the prophet, saying, etc.** On this formula of quotation see the exposition of 1:22. Yahweh is the agent of ῥηθέν, and διά marks the human instrument. This is Verbal Inspiration. In the written Isaiah we have what God spoke, and Isaiah 40-60 is composed by Isaiah and not by someone else. Isa. 42:1-4 reads:

> **Lo, my Servant, whom I did select,**
> **My Beloved, in whom my soul is well-pleased.**
> **I will place my Spirit upon him,**
> **And he shall announce right to the Gentiles.**
> **He will not wrangle, nor will he shout;**
> **Nor shall anyone hear his voice in the streets.**
> **A reed that has been bruised he will not**
> **break in pieces,**

**And a flax smoking he will not quench**
**Until he puts forth to victory the right.**
**And in his name Gentiles shall hope.**

Matthew follows the Hebrew and not the LXX, save
in the last line, v. 21, where for *lethoratho*, "for his
law," he has, like the LXX, "in his name." Matthew
omits the first line of Isa. 42:4: "He shall not fail,"
etc. These and a few minor points are no warrant for
the conclusion that Matthew followed some Targum
instead of the Hebrew, or had peculiar readings in his
Hebrew original. The purpose of the quotation is not
literal reproduction of the original but application of
the ancient prophecy to the great beginnings of its
fulfillment. The best commentary on the Hebrew text
is Aug. Pieper's *Jesaias II.*, 116, etc.

Matthew contradicts the Jewish-rabbinical and the
naturalistic-modernistic exegesis which states that this
Servant (παῖς) and this Beloved of Yahweh is the people of Israel and not the Messiah, Christ. This exegesis finds support in the LXX, which has "*Jacob, my
servant*," and "*Israel, my chosen.*" This support van-
ishes when, with Pieper, we note that the great concept
"Servant of Jehovah" like "Seed of Abraham" resembles a pyramid: its broad base is the whole nation; on
this rests the believing part of the nation; and on this
rests the apex, Christ. Or, in the broad circle of
humanity the center is Christ, the second Adam; in the
narrower circle of the Jewish nation the center is
Christ, the other David; in the silll narrower circle of
believers the center is Christ, the Seed (one, Gal. 3:16).
The interpretative translation of the LXX thus does not
lend support to naturalistic conceptions.

Dramatically this great person is introduced: "Lo,"
here he is! "My Servant," "my Beloved" = Jehovah's
own. Both titles should be considered in connection
with the added relative clauses which express his great

mission. Jehovah took him with great firmness ('*ethmak-bo*), ἡρέτισα, "chose him," to perform the great Messianic task; and he is the one in whom Jehovah's soul delights, thus ὁ ἀγαπητός μου (3:17); there is nothing in him that could displease Jehovah.

After this description of Christ's relation to his Sender we learn about his equipment and his task. "My Spirit" is his equipment, 3:16; this is sent down on him to enable his human nature to do its great part. Here the entire Trinity appears in working out our redemption. "My Spirit" and not outward, mere earthly power and glory. For it is his mission "to announce right to the Gentiles," Hebrew, "to bring it out to them." The idea is that from the chosen people, among whom this "right" has its home, Jehovah's Servant shall carry it out to all the world, which, of course, will be done by means of the Word. *Mishpat,* κρίσις is not "religion" but "right" as established forensically at the judgment bar of Jehovah. Christ brings it with gentleness (v. 19) not with force; it neither bruises nor breaks (v. 20); in it the Gentiles hope (v. 21). This "right" is not the Sinaitic law but the gospel verdict which conveys "righteousness," δικαιοσύνη, the acquittal of pardon through God's grace. Back of it lies redemption.

This description of Christ's mission takes in its ultimate object, the bringing of the gospel of grace, redemption, and justification from Israel, where it was prepared, to the whole Gentile world. This is what Matthew saw occurring at this time. How Christ's present work was already reaching out to the Gentiles we see in Mark 3:8: Idumea, Tyre, and Sidon.

19) "He will not wrangle," etc., describes the manner in which he will make his announcement of the divine verdict; we see the fulfillment in v. 15. His method is the opposite of violence; he will not even cry

down his opponents.   He is no turbulent agitator.   He wins by meekness.

20)   Beautiful are the figures which picture what Jehovah's Servant will actually do for men.   The soul about to perish is "a reed that has been bruised" and is now in that condition, "a flax (wick) smoking," the flame being almost out, as the smoke indicates.   Why bother with them?   But to all such souls the love of Christ goes out.   The negatives "he will not break in pieces" by treading down, "he will not quench" form a litotes, negation where the corresponding affirmation is intended: he will make that reed whole again, will make that flaxen wick burn brightly.   Those who are destroyed by sin he will save.   This is fitting when it is applied to Christ, but great difficulty is encountered when the Jewish nation is regarded as the Servant.

Some interpreters devote a good deal of discussion to Matthew's substitution of εἰς νῖκος, "unto victory," for Isaiah's *le'emeth* (LXX εἰς ἀλήθειαν), "unto truth." But the Hebrew means only "in reality and truth," cf., I John 3:18, i. e., with actual success.   Hence v. 21 (and the entire fourth verse of Isaiah), which, according to the prophet's frequent usage, verifies this success.   Actually to bring the gospel "right" or righteousness to success is to put it forth "to victory."   Matthew translates the thought and is not hampered by mechanical literalism.

21)   Matthew omits the first two lines of Isa. 42:4. We need not speculate about the reason for this abbreviation.   It lies in the phrase "to victory," which has already expressed the thought of the omitted lines, namely, that Christ shall not fail.   So Matthew closes with the final line:   "And in his name Gentiles shall hope," reproducing:   "And the isles shall wait for his law."   The rendering is plainly interpretative.   The inhabitants of the islands were Gentiles.   To wait for is to hope.   And Torah ("law") is his Name.   Here

we have one of the many instances in which the ὄνομα denotes "the revelation" which makes Christ (or God) known to men, only part of which is expressed in the special terms used as personal names. This waiting and hoping is misunderstood when in Pelagian fashion it is regarded as an unconscious religious desire for Christ and the gospel on the part of the so-called better class of pagans. I Cor. 1:23 teaches the opposite. This waiting and hoping expresses the great need of Christ on the part of the pagan world. In the whole world the heathen find nothing that can save them; their only hope is Christ. This objective fact is put into fervent subjective form by the poetic prophet (Isa. 40-66 is one grand poem, the greatest ever penned by human hands).

22) **Then was brought to him a demoniac, blind and dumb; and he healed him so that the dumb was speaking and seeing.** "Then" means at this season (v. 1). Matthew selects another notable clash with the Pharisees that occurred at this time. The miracle that furnished the occasion is, therefore, only briefly sketched: the sufferer was brought, blind and dumb, and healed so that he spoke and saw.

23) **And amazed were all the multitudes and kept saying, Can this be the Son of David?** The aorist recites only the fact of the amazement, while the imperfect pictures how this question circulated and continued to be raised. The interrogative μήτι has a negative implication: "We can hardly think so." At the same time it conveys the idea that this negation is quite doubtful: "It seems as though he is after all." R. 917. Their unbelief is breaking before the astounding miracle. The English can render this μήτι only imperfectly; the German is more flexible: *Doch nicht etwa ist dieser der Sohn Davids?* Οὗτος is purely deictic, R. 697, and "the Son of David" is the Messiah (1:1).

24) The Pharisees were not present. **When the Pharisees heard it they said, This fellow does not expel the demons except in connection with Beelzebul, ruler of the demons.** When they discovered what was passing from mouth to mouth the Pharisees tried to check the growing conviction. Their οὗτος is highly derogatory: "this fellow." So also their explanation is negative: "does not . . . except," etc. They intend to say that he himself is unable by his own power to expel demons; the only way in which he does it is by some connection with Satan. These demons leave their victims only at Satan's behest, by obeying their ruler with whom Jesus is in league. Ἐν is usually called "instrumental": "by" or "through," which, however, changes the thought. R. 590 makes it locative, which is hard to visualize. The preposition simply means "in connection or in union with Beelzebul." On this name for Satan see 10:25. The absence of the article before ἄρχοντι does not make Beelzebul only one of the rulers any more than "Herod, king of Galilee," ·is made one of the kings of Galilee by the absence of "the" before "king."

Some would cancel 9:34, on the plea that this verse inserts what happened later. Likewise it is said that 10:24-33 was spoken at a later time because of v. 25 and Beelzebul. In reality this blasphemy began early in the ministry of Jesus, just as Matthew indicates in 9:34, and was finally advanced with great boldness, as we now see. Therefore Jesus now crushes this vicious blasphemy.

25) Jesus called the Pharisees to him (Mark 3:23) and made his full reply to them. **But knowing their thoughts, he said to them, Every kingdom divided against itself becomes waste; and every city or house divided against itself will not stand.** The Pharisees said nothing in Jesus' presence, but he knew their

thoughts about himself, i. e., the vicious, blind hatred from which their blasphemy had sprung. In his reply to them he meets also these their thoughts. The two observations with which Jesus begins sum up the universal experience which no sane man contradicts. A kingdom, city, or house, once divided against itself (μερισθεῖσα, aorist passive participle), one part fighting the other, is devastated and as a result will not stand, i. e., goes down in ruin. This is the major premise.

26) Now the minor, introduced by "if," since it embodies the assertion of the Pharisees: "If it were true as you boldly claim." **And if Satan expels Satan, he was divided against himself.** And now the conclusion (οὖν) in the form of a question, showing the utter absurdity of the Pharisaic claim: **How, then, shall his kingdom stand?** How strong the absurdity is the idea of Satan expelling Satan makes plain. This is not one Satan expelling another Satan, as some would suppose, for only one Satan exists. But he acts through his demons, and thus, if he did the expelling through Jesus, in a very real sense he would, indeed, be expelling himself. For the sake of the argument the present indicative ἐκβάλλει after εἰ assumes that the untrue assertion of the Pharisees is true. R. 1008. The aorist ἐμερίσθη may be gnomic and thus timeless, or it may intend to imply that even before Satan expelled himself he *was* already divided. The conclusion: "Therefore his kingdom will not stand," is made a question with "how," thus forcing upon the Pharisees the giving of an answer which neither they nor anyone else can give.

Opposition to Jesus upsets men's logic. They may put forth as being convincingly sound what is absurdly unsound. The view that as a ruse and to gain other evil purposes Satan might allow Jesus to expel a demon is refuted by the fact that Jesus expelled all the demons he found in possession of men; and no other purpose of Satan has ever been pointed out for his allowing Jesus to expel these demons.

27) **And if I in connection with Beelzebul expel the demons, your sons — in connection with whom do they expel them? For this they shall be your judges.** This second proof rests on the first. The emphasis is on the subjects: "I — your sons." The latter are not physical sons or pupils of the Pharisees but, as is suggested by the similar expression "sons of the prophets," *Genossen eurer Zunft,* experts of your own guild of whom you approve and are proud, because they are able to expel demons. The fact that Satan neither could nor would lend himself to such expulsions, v. 25, 26 have put beyond question. Whoever drives out devils can do so only by being in the necessary connection with God. What a desperate self-contradiction, therefore, to claim that when Jesus drives them out, this is done in connection with *Satan;* but when their own experts drive them out, this is done in connection with *God!* Something is viciously wrong with men who ascribe the identical effect to absolutely opposite causes. "Because of this," i. e., the thing Jesus here exposes, "they," their own associates, "shall be their judges" before God's judgment bar. God will let these Pharisaic exorcists pronounce sentence on these blaspheming Pharisees. What their verdict will be need not be stated.

The argument of Jesus has been considered apart from v. 25, 26, and has been inverted. And this is done on the basis of Josephus' *Wars* 7, 6, 3; *Ant.* 8, 2, 5, the story of the drawing of a demon through the nose by means of a mythical root, called Baaras, which is secured in a truly magical manner. Acts 19:13, etc., is quoted. But the reason for this is not apparent. The conclusion is drawn that in their exorcism these Pharisaic exorcists used witchcraft and charms which

contained the names of demons. The argument of
Jesus is said to be this: your sons drive out devils by
means of devils; how, then, can you object to me for
driving out devils by the help of the chief devil? your
own sons will convict you of injustice. But if this were
the argument, Jesus would not deny but rather admit
and defend his connection with Beelzebul and would
prove only that the Pharisees were the last persons who
had a right to blame him for such a connection. We
cannot assume that the sons of Sceva mentioned in Acts
19:13 substituted the name of Jesus for the name of
some demon they had before used because they regarded the former as being more potent. The way
in which they tried to use the name of Jesus indicates
that hitherto they had used some sacred not some
demon formula. The Son of God cannot admit even
for the sake of argument that he uses the power of
Beelzebul.

28) **But if I in connection with God's Spirit
expel the demons, then the kingdom of God did
already reach to you.** This is the proper conclusion
to be drawn from the fact that Jesus is expelling the
demons as the Pharisees constantly see him doing.
Back of this conclusion lies the logical dilemma: either
a connection with God or one with Satan; *tertium non
datur*. The connection with Satan has already been
exploded as being absurd and impossible, v. 25-27.
Hence the connection with God alone is left. The Spirit
of God is mentioned because in Christ's work all three
divine persons are active (3:11, 16; 12:18), and it is
the Third Person whose special task it is to build the
kingdom on earth. Jesus expelled the demons by his
word alone, and every word of his is the product of
the Spirit.

Thus every demon expulsion effected by Jesus is so
much evidence of the Spirit's presence and work, in
other words, so much blessed proof that "the kingdom

of God did already reach to you," φθάνειν, "to overtake," "to reach or arrive," thus used especially in the New Testament.  The tense is interesting: the demon expulsions show that the kingdom is not merely on the way but "did already reach to you" (we should say "has reached," R. 842), is in your very midst.  Here Jesus uses the expression "the kingdom of God" to correspond with "God's Spirit," whereas he otherwise employs the expression the kingdom of the heavens.  The sense is quite the same.  On this βασιλεία see 3:2, *die Koenigsherrschaft,* the rule of God as the King.  This royal divine rule has reached to you, is present as having arrived for you, and you can see it in the abject defeat of Satan and his demons in every demoniac's deliverance.  Only devilish minds could deny what was so evident.  In all of the Gospels the Spirit is mentioned as the Third Person of the Trinity without the slightest objection on the part of any Pharisee.

29) The whole matter is made clear by an illustration which Luke 11:21, 22 reports with a little more detail.  **Or,** if this matter of God's Messianic kingdom for which you have been looking and hoping seems strange to you, answer this simple question: **how can one enter the house of the strong and plunder his goods unless he first binds the strong?  Then he shall plunder his goods.**  Isa. 49:25 seems to have suggested this question to Jesus.  The *tertium* in the illustration is the fact that complete defeat must precede the act of plundering: God's kingdom must have come before demoniacs could be liberated as Jesus was liberating them.  "The strong" is Satan although in the case of this singular the article is generic, R. 757.

Satan is like a powerful brigand or robber.  His οἰκία or "house" is his lair or dwelling, here the kingdom of Satan, in which he is ἄρχων or ruler (v. 24).  Luke adds the details about his being armed and guarding his goods.  For τὰ σκεύη αὐτοῦ Luke has τὰ ὑπάρχοντα αὐτοῦ;

his "goods" are his "possessions," such as the demoniacs whom Satan has in his power. Now, how can
anyone do what Jesus is doing right along: go in and
"plunder" the strong man's goods, take them away,
snatch demoniacs out of Satan's power without first
actually "binding" (δήσῃ) this strong bandit? This
binding was the victory recorded in 4:1-11. The
objection that the latter was moral while the power
over the demoniacs was physical, is irrelevant, since
Satan gained his physical power to hurt by his moral
victory in tempting man into sin. Hence the victory
of Jesus reversed this moral victory by vanquishing
Satan in another temptation.

It was thus that the kingdom did already reach to
you (v. 28), *quod erat demonstrandum*, as Zahn puts it.
"And then he will plunder his house," i. e., at will, just
as Jesus is taking the demoniacs from Satan at will.
This statement clinches the point. All that Jesus here
says would be senseless if Satan were not the personal
being he is represented to be in the Scriptures from
Gen. 3 onward, and if demoniacal possession, like the
demons themselves, were an ordinary mental ailment.

30) Up to this point Jesus' reply to the Pharisees
is strictly objective, dealing with Satan and Jesus, correcting the wrong thoughts of the Pharisees (v. 25,
"knowing," etc.). Now the discourse becomes subjective and, although for the greater part it retains
the third person it reaches its climax in the second,
in v. 34 and 37. The general personal principle is first
laid down: **He that is not with me is against me;
and he that does not gather with me scatters.** This
is regarded as self-evident. In the case of Jesus neutrality is impossible. In μετά we have personal association and attachment, and in κατά, "down on me," hostility. But we cannot agree that at this time the Pharisees were trying to assume a neutral position, and that
v. 24 is only an expression of embarrassment on their

part, that they were at a loss for a better explanation; the very next verses refute this view. The Pharisees were against Jesus; from the very moment when they decided not to be "with him" they had swung to the other side. In the battle against Satan every man who does not side with Jesus is against him and for Satan. Luke 9:50 and Mark 9:40 agree with this view; for to do a miracle or a kind deed "in Jesus' name" is neither neutral nor hostile to Jesus.

Both attitudes have their immediate effect on others: the one gathers, the other scatters. Since no objects are mentioned, of the three suggested: sheep, grain, and fish, we choose the first (9:36; 10:6; John 10:12, where σκορπίζει is also used in connection with sheep). The great work of Jesus was to gather the lost sheep; the wolf, Satan, scattered them.

31) **For this reason I say to you, every sin and blasphemy will be remitted to men, but the blasphemy against the Spirit will not be remitted.** "For this reason" means: because neutrality in regard to Jesus is impossible, since he who is not with him is thereby already against him. This makes it necessary for Jesus to tell the Pharisees and for them to know about the possibilities in regard to finding remission. This is, indeed, great, including every sin no matter what it may be, even blasphemy, mocking and vicious utterances directly against God or holy things connected with God. But the one exception is the blasphemy against the Spirit. Here the possibility of remission comes to an end.

The verb ἀφίημι means "to send away," to remove the sin from the sinner so that he is free of it, and so that the sin can never be found and charged against him before the judgment bar of God. This verb as well as its noun ἄφεσις, "sending away," "remission," are the most blessed terms in the Scriptures. The agent in the passives is God; he alone remits. The futures are predictive; see R. 873 which discusses their expression by "shall" or "will."

32) The matter is so important that Jesus restates and amplifies. **And whoever shall say a word against the Son of man, it will be remitted to him; but whoever will say it against the Holy Spirit, it will not be remitted to him neither in this eon nor in the one to come.** Blasphemy is now defined; it means "to say a word against the Son of man" or "against the Holy Spirit." The parallel shows that, like the former, the latter is also a person. It is now evident that the genitive τοῦ Πνεύματος in v. 31 is objective (R. 494, 500), for it is restated by κατά, "against" ("down on," R. 607). The blasphemy that may be pardoned is now specified; it is that "against the Son of man" (see 8:20), the divine Savior and Son of God in human form. "To say a word" means to utter a statement such as the one uttered by the Pharisees in v. 24. But when it is directed against the Holy Spirit, such blasphemy is absolutely unpardonable. "The Spirit, the Holy One," puts emphasis on both terms and makes the adjective a sort of climax in apposition with the noun, R. 776, last paragraph. "This eon" is the vast period of time as marked by the form and the condition of things that now fill it. "In this world" will do as a translation as long as time is kept in mind and not merely place. "The eon to come" is the world age that shall follow in the consummation at the last day when heaven and earth are joined. The temporal term αἰών is still retained although eternity is the opposite of time, namely, timelessness; this retention is due to our mental inability to think of anything apart from time.

Jesus is warning the Pharisees who had never believed in him. Hence the sin against the Holy Ghost may be committed, not only by former believers (Heb. 6:4-6; 10:26-31; I John 5:16), but also by men who have never believed. Zahn's effort to make all sins in which men persist impenitently to the end the sin against the Holy Ghost is contradicted by the entire teaching of Scripture on the subject of sin. The distinctive mark of this one sin is blasphemy, and this the blasphemy against God's Spirit. The fact that a large number of other sins fails of pardon and brings damnation, and that in varying degrees, is shown, for instance, in 11:21, 24.

It is rationalizing to assert that the expressions "in this eon" and "in the one to come" imply that one may die without pardon and yet at the end of the world obtain pardon. This view assumes that the phrases are in opposition to each other. But οὔτε — οὔτε does not involve an opposition. The second phrase is added to reinforce the first: "neither in time nor in eternity," i. e., absolutely never. The sense is that the man who blasphemes the Spirit thereby and at that moment places himself at a point where God's pardon cannot possibly reach him. He is then in the same hopeless position as the devils. Jesus' words already now pronounce upon him the verdict of damnation. "In the one to come" teaches no purgatory and no probation after death as though for other sins that are less fatal remission may be had in the hereafter. The only judgment in the world to come is that pronounced at the last day, and in its verdict this is identical with the judgment pronounced on every man at the time of his death.

Jesus does not state in so many words what gives such an exceptional quality to blasphemy against the Spirit. Yet this quality is indicated. The Pharisees were evidently on the verge of forever placing themselves beyond pardon. Jesus points this out in v. 28: he is expelling demons "in connection with God's Spirit." By blaspheming Jesus (v. 24) the Pharisees came very near to blaspheming God's Spirit.

All other sins and other blasphemies are, of course, never pardoned unless repentance (3:2; 4:17), i. e., contrition and faith, are in evidence. Thus the blasphemy against the Spirit is unpardoned forever because it forever lacks repentance; Heb. 6:4-6, "impossible to renew them again unto repentance"; there is no sacrifice for sins, only a frightful looking forward to judgment and fiery indignation. This explains why other blasphemies may be pardoned: they do not render repentance "impossible." It is the specific work of the Spirit to produce repentance; hence to blaspheme him produces a state which forever bars out him and his work.

Because of his divine power Jesus was able to see how close to this state the Pharisees were. With our limited human powers we are never able to judge so accurately. Hence we can never say of any man, however blasphemous he may be, that he has committed this sin; that verdict belongs to God alone. The words of Jesus and those of Hebrews we are able to use only as a warning, which is enough. Yet we may say that whoever fears that he has committed the unpardonable sin thereby furnishes evidence that he has not done so. Nor can any man commit it inadvertently or unconsciously. Its commission is possible only when the Spirit through the Word has come upon a man and has been clearly recognized as God's Spirit with his divine power and grace to save. When a man deliberately answers him with blasphemy he forever nullifies even the Spirit's power to change him. His is already then the unalterable condition of the devils and of the damned in hell. It constitutes his *character indelebilis*.

33) **Either make the tree excellent and its fruit excellent, or make the tree worthless and its fruit worthless; for by the fruit the tree is known.** It seems impossible to let "the tree" represent the Pharisees. How can Jesus order them either to make themselves morally excellent (καλός) or morally worthless (σαπρός) when they already were so vicious that he had

just warned them against committing the sin against the Spirit? Nor can we think that Jesus here explains only the λόγον in v. 32 as being the fruit which betrays the nature of the tree; for this "word" is blasphemy, fruit that only too plainly reveals the tree. Both imperatives, too, would be out of place, for no man can make himself a good tree, and every man is already by nature a worthless tree. On σαπρός see 7:17. A "rotten," "corrupt," diseased tree cannot be referred to but a "worthless" variety of tree, the fruit of which is not good for eating.

The tree is Jesus himself, and ποιεῖν refers to mental action (much like John 5:18; 8:53; 10:33) in good Greek fashion: "In your thinking and judging you will have to make the tree and its fruit the same, either excellent or worthless; for it is certainly beyond question that a tree is known by (ἐκ) the fruit it bears." The argument is to the same effect as that employed in v. 25, 26. The evident good deeds of Jesus performed by freeing demoniacs cannot come from a person connected with Beelzebul; to have such a person, his deeds would have to be of the same type. Compare the same argument in John 10:25; 37, 38. The absolute irrationality of the blasphemy of the Pharisees exposes its devilish animus.

34) This explains the address which Jesus hurls into the faces of these Pharisees just as the Baptist did in 3:7; see the exposition there given. **Offsprings of vipers, how can you utter beneficial things when you are wicked? for out of the abundance of the heart the mouth makes utterance.** Being men filled with deadly hypocrisy, base treachery, and fatal self-deceit, moral offspring of like progenitors whose ancestor is the old Serpent himself (John 8:44), how can they, being πονηροί, actively, viciously "wicked" as they are, allow anything ἀγαθά, wholesome and beneficial, to come out of their mouths (λαλεῖν)? Jesus lays

bare what is really in the hearts of these Pharisees.
When they claimed that his expelling the demons
proved his connection with Satan they revealed only
with what their wicked hearts were overflowing (i. e.,
were more than full), real devil's thoughts.  The heart
is like a reservoir: it holds much, but when it gets too
full, the mouth carries the περίσσευμα, the overplus, off in
speech.  The heart overflowing in speech through the
mouth is about the same as the tree with its native
fruit.  The overflow shows what is in the reservoir.

35) Hence the further figure concerning the
heart.  **The good man** (representative singular,
R. 408) **out of his good treasure puts out good
things; and the wicked man out of his wicked
treasure puts out wicked things.**  The "treasure" is
both the receptacle and its contents.  Each man stores
up what he thinks is valuable in thoughts, judgments,
convictions, and the like.  As occasion arises, he
draws on these treasures of his.  They are exactly
like the man who has stored them away.  Ἀγαθός =
"good" in the sense of "beneficial," of such quality as
to bring advantage to its possessor as well as to others.
And the opposite, πονηρός, depraved and depraving, of
such quality as to tender both its possessor as well
as others "wicked."  Each man has only his own fund
on which to draw.  Men are divided into only two
classes, for here the case of a good man (a believer)
who is still afflicted with sin need not to be brought
in.  To which class the Pharisees belong is evident
from the sample of their treasure (v. 24) which they
have exhibited.

36) **Moreover, I say to you that every idle utterance which men may utter, they shall render due
account concerning it on judgment day.  For in
accord with thy words wilt thou be acquitted, and
in accord with thy words wilt thou be condemned.**
Δέ turns to another slightly different point.  Jesus

cuts off the excuse that one may give voice to an utterance (ῥῆμα, matching λαλήσωσιν) that is merely ἀργόν, "idle," not carefully considered, just popping out of his mouth. But even such an utterance betrays the state of the heart. Hence men "shall render due account" (this is the meaning of ἀποδίδωμι λόγον) concerning it "on judgment day." This applies to the wicked alone, for all the sins of the godly will have been dismissed and thus will have utterly disappeared at that day. The construction is usually called an anacoluthon, being broken by taking up πᾶν ῥῆμα by περὶ αὐτοῦ (R. 718); but the subject (or object) "every utterance" may also be called a pendant nominative (or accusative) which is left hanging in the sentence structure, R. 436, 439, 459.

37) The reason for this accountability is that ἐκ τῶν λόγων σου thou shalt be either acquitted at the final judgment or condemned. Note the forensic sense of both passive verbs which have God as their agent. B.-P. 366 lets ἐκ mean *nach, gemaess, entsprechend,* according to the rule that lies at the bottom of these acts. This accords with Luke 19:22: "Out of thine own mouth I shall judge thee." Here the two phrases have λόγοι, "words" as conveying thought, and not ῥήματα, "utterances" as opposed to silence. The reason for using λόγοι here is the fact that even the ῥήματα shall be weighed in the judgment according to what they reveal concerning the man who uttered them. By what we say from day to day, including every idle utterance as well as every sentiment, we are writing our own verdict for deliverance to us "on judgment day." For our mouths reveal what our hearts are and contain; they do it even in the case of hypocrites and liars. Let not the Pharisees say that "Beelzebul" (v. 24) only slipped out of their mouth and was not intended seriously. Even as an idle ῥῆμα it betrays the speakers.

38) The fourth clash with the Pharisees is connected with the third, as Luke 11:15, 16 shows, as well as Matthew's ἀπεκρίθησαν. **Then answered him certain of the scribes and Pharisees saying, Teacher, we want from thee a sign to see.** On the verb "answered" see 4:15. It is quite broad: any response to any situation. One response to the healing of the demoniac recorded in v. 22 is the charge of satanic help made in v. 24; the other is the demand for a visible sign. This demand came from "certain of the scribes and Pharisees," one Greek article making them a single small group. The Pharisees made the charge voiced in v. 24, and then some of them who were also scribes made the further demand for a sign. These were the *sopherim,* lawyers who had passed due examination and shown the necessary learning. At thirty years of age they were formally admitted to the chair of the scribe by the laying on of hands and by receiving tablets on which to write the sayings of the wise and "the key of knowledge" wherewith to open or shut the treasures of wisdom. They were the authorized expert expounders of the law. Coming from them, the demand for "a sign to see" means that as they understood the law such a sign would have to be furnished by the Messiah to receive Jewish acknowledgment.

Luke 11:15, 16 thus reveals two attitudes: the ordinary Pharisees see in the healing of the demoniac nothing but satanic help, while the learned experts among them would add a decisive test, "tempting him" (Luke 11:16). They feel certain that Jesus will be unable to furnish this sign. If he tries it he will fail, and this will prove that he is operating only with Satan's help. The respectful address, "Teacher," is one of hypocrisy. For while they acknowledge that Jesus is one who, like themselves, is learned in the law, they were in reality seeking utterly to ruin his

standing with the people. We paraphrase their
request: "What we really want from thee (θέλομεν)
is a genuine sign that we can see." The indicative
is abrupt (R. 923) and not like the "we would see"
of our versions; it does not intimate that they are,
perhaps, asking too much but that they are letting
Jesus feel that they will be satisfied with nothing
less.

"A sign to see" is an objection to the signs Jesus
had thus far wrought. What these scribes and Pharisees could "see" in them was to them not nearly
enough. For all these signs, shining with grace,
mercy, and help to poor sinners and sufferers, were
aimed at a seeing with the spiritual eyes of faith, at
recognizing Jesus as the divine Deliverer from sin and
Satan's power, John 10:38. In the spiritually blind
eyes of these men such signs amounted to nothing.
They demanded something that required no faith but
just ἰδεῖν, sight. Shall we say that they asked that
the heavens be moved, the clouds made to gyrate, sun,
moon, and stars to perform antics, visions to be
painted in the sky with unearthly colors, angel hosts
to parade down the milky way?

Suppose for a moment that Jesus had met this
demand. Such prodigies and portents meet no spiritual need, point to no deliverance from sin, have
no affinity with saving faith. Moreover, they respond
only to the morbid side of our nature, stimulate the
unhealthy craving that, when fed, only demands more,
and when more and more is not forthcoming, reverts
to the old dissatisfaction, doubt, and denial. The faith
these men promise Jesus for just one such sign is
a spurious faith. Their demand and Christ's steady
refusal show only how far they were inwardly removed
from him.

39) **But he answering said to them, A generation wicked and adulterous is out after a sign; and**

**a sign shall not be given to it save the sign of Jonah, the prophet.** For just as Jonah was in the belly of the sea monster for three days and three nights, so shall the Son of man be in the heart of the earth for three days and three nights. The circumstantial ἀποκριθείς marks the importance of the answer. The reply is lofty, masterful, and authoritative to a degree. Men are dictating to the Messiah what he should do. These are not his friends, who, despite all good intentions may ask for something that is amiss, but men with hostile intent, set on a course that is opposed to the Messiah. They must be answered as Jesus here answers them.

Note the superior objective tone in "a generation wicked and adulterous." Jesus here characterizes the entire Jewish nation of his day. As a generation they were "wicked and adulterous," the second adjective defining the first. Πονηρός is always used in the active sense. The wicked actions Jesus has in mind are "adulterous," breaches of the covenant relation with God which is conceived as a marriage bond, Hos. 1:2-2:15; Jer. 3:6-13; Ezek. 16. This spiritual adultery includes all unfaithfulness to God, not only the old idolatry practiced during the history of the Jews, but turning from him in hypocrisy (Jer. 3:10), inward hostility to him (Hos. 7:13-16), friendship of the world (James 4:4, etc.). In this instance this adulterous character appears in the scorning of the signs of love and grace, in rejecting Jesus' saving ways. By their illegitimate demand they revealed their inner divorce from God. Their covenant and marriage tie no longer held them. They were out after (ἐπιζητεῖ, with ἐπί being directive) something else.

When it is applied to our own generation, "adulterous" can be applied only to those who outwardly belong to the church and claim connection with God through Christ and yet violate this connection by perverting his Word, disobeying its gospel commands, and by uniting with others of this type. This word was never applied to the Gentiles and should not be applied to men who are outside of the church.

The kind of sign these Jews demand "shall not be given" to them. The passive verb leaves the Giver veiled and states only the cold fact. It is morally impossible for either God or Christ to grant such a sign. The motive back of this demand which rejects God's signs and prescribes a sign of its own is divorced from God. The scribes and Pharisees are correct: Jesus is unable to meet the demand they make. But let them not smile and say, "I told you so!" God has a sign, a very special sign, for just such people as they are. Do they act aggrieved because the sign they want is denied them? The most significant of signs is waiting for them, one in which their own guilt will culminate (crucifying Christ) and their own judgment will be indicated (Christ's resurrection and glorification). It is "the sign of Jonah, the prophet." By means of the article this sign is marked as one that is well known to all who are acquainted with the book of this prophet.

40) With γάρ Jesus explains just what this sign is. "The sign of Jonah" means that what happened to Jonah pictures and typifies what the same divine power will do with Jesus who is here again called "the Son of man," his human nature by which he will die and rise being joined to the divine nature. Let us give due attention to the fact that Jesus himself states that Jonah was in the belly (κοιλία, abdominal cavity) of the sea monster "for three days and three nights" (quoted from Jonah 1:17) exactly as the book of Jonah records. Jesus puts his own seal upon this historical fact. Whoever rejects the miracle must settle with Jesus. The issue centers on the very point that is so objectionable to modern skeptics. Nor does

Jesus regard it as a side issue but as a type of the very climax of his own work, his death and his resurrection and the effect that followed these. And Jesus does this; v. 40 is not an explanation inserted by Matthew.

The word κῆτος = "sea monster," the *dag gadol* of Jonah 2:1. The "whale" of our versions is only an effort at translation. "The great fish" is not described as to genus or species. Delitzsch thinks of either *canis carcharias* or *squalus carcharias L.,* a shark, and adds accredited accounts regarding what they are able to swallow. The miracle, however, is not the fact that Jonah was swallowed by such a fish but that, after being swallowed, he was preserved alive, ejected on the third day, and escaped to execute his mission. It is exactly like all other miracles recorded in the Scriptures, a work of the omnipotent power of God.

How can Jesus say that his stay in the grave would be "for three days and three nights" when he actually spent only two nights in the grave? The difficulty disappears when in Tobit 3:12 we read, "Ate not nor drank for three days and three nights," and yet in the very next verse, "Then on the third day," the fast being ended. Similarly Esther 4:16 compared with 5:1. "Three days and three nights" is, therefore, not proverbial for "a brief time," nor can we say that Jesus is concerned only to obtain a parallel experience to that of Jonah as far as the number of days is concerned. The manner of numbering nights with the days is an idiomatic Jewish usage. As Jonah escaped on the third day, so Jesus arose on the third day. And since the Jewish day begins with the night (or evening), it is the night that forms part of the first day which seems to us to be overcounted, not the one that forms part of the third day — the Sunday of the resurrection began at dusk on Saturday.

"In the heart of the earth" must refer to the tomb in Joseph's garden and not to hades, hell, or the mythical "realm of the dead," the intermediate state between heaven and hell. Jesus is not speaking of his descent into hell (I Pet. 3:19). This took place after his vivification in the tomb. It was a timeless act, for which no duration in terms of time is or ever can be given. The fish had swallowed Jonah bodily, and his bodily stay in the fish typifies the stay of Jesus' body in the tomb. We know of no place where that body might have been during those three days except in Joseph's tomb; that tomb was not empty during those three days. The unusual expression "in the heart of the earth" is due to the prophetic and hence veiled nature of the statement. It signifies "inside the earth" as "in the belly" signifies "inside the fish." The idea that a great depth must be referred to is thus excluded.

The location of either hell or the fabled intermediate "realm of the dead" in the core of our physical globe is an idea that is foreign to Scripture, just as heaven is not located in the physical sky. The typical feature is simply this: when Jonah disappeared in the maw of the monster, his career seemed to have been ended — it was not; he returned alive and preached with wonderful success in Nineveh. So when the Jews saw Christ laid in the tomb, they thought that his career was ended — it, too, was not; he returned alive, and his mighty work went on according to the divine will. The parallel is emphasized and placed beyond question by the three days. The antitype thus fits the type exactly according to the divine design which arranged both.

In order to avoid acceptance of the miracle in connection with Jonah some interpreters find "the sign of Jonah" in the latter's preaching. But this is no more a sign than is the preaching of any other prophet.

Jonah did not preach in the belly of the fish, nor Jesus in the tomb. This also settles the question in regard to the historical reliability of the miracle. If it were a myth, a parable, a poetical or symbolical invention, something that transpired only in Jonah's mind, it could not be a sign. Only an objective reality can serve as a sign. The myth destroys the sign, and the sign the myth. Compare Delitzsch on the book of Jonah.

41) Jesus now states what this sign of his own death and resurrection will reveal to this wicked and adulterous generation — their condemnation. **Ninevite men will stand up in the judgment together with this generation and will condemn it, because they did repent at the proclamation of Jonah and, lo, something more than Jonah is here.** With an adjective denoting locality or race ἀνήρ and ἄνδρες are customary. The absence of the article leaves the stress on their being from Nineveh. Jesus sees them at the final judgment, standing up together with (μετά), side by side with this generation of the Jews. And then not these Jews will condemn those Gentiles, but those Gentiles these Jews. When both appear before God's judgment bar, and their cases are laid before the Judge, the case of the Ninevites will in the eyes of the Judge serve as a condemnation of the case of the Jews. And, of course, the Judge will so recognize and pronounce.

Why? Because the Ninevites repented when they had nothing but Jonah and his preaching, while "lo," just look, "here is more than Jonah," the neuter πλεῖον including everything the Jews had in Christ. The case is doubly bad: the Ninevites had so little and repented; the Jews have so much and refuse to heed it. In general the idea is the same as that expressed in 10:15; 11:21, 24, but now we have Gentiles that actually repented. The character of this repentance

is discussed in 11:21. The points to be noted are
these: wicked Gentiles to whom a strange prophet from
a foreign land is sent, one who had by God's own hand
been miraculously rescued from a terrible death,
who brought nothing but the threatenings of the law,
yet these Gentiles believe that prophet, repent by fasting in sackcloth and ashes, desist from sin and amend
their ways. On the other hand, these Jews, who, in
addition to all their other prophets, now have the
Messiah himself, whom God would glorify by the
resurrection from the dead, who came with the gospel
and its consummation in his own resurrection, and
these Jews spurned it all. What God will do with the
Ninevites because of their measure of repentance Jesus
does not indicate. On that day we shall witness the
mercy as  well as the justice of God in his dealings
with the Gentiles.

A sign such as the Jews demanded would not be
given them but they had "the sign of Jonah" which signified Christ's resurrection. When God would be ready
for this, the typical Jonah would receive his antitype,
Christ. The Ninevites who heeded Jonah and this
generation of Jews who spurned Christ would thus be
thrown into terrible contrast, the Gentiles by *their*
very action condemning the Jews for *theirs*. In this
contrast the Jewish guilt for crucifying Jesus is
omitted; Jonah typifies only the resurrection. The
promised sign is thus one of crowning grace. Yet
even this these Jews will reject even as they are now
rejecting him and thus will seal their fate.

42) A second comparison has the same purpose.
**A queen of the south will arise in the judgment
together with this generation and will condemn it,
because she came from the ends of the earth to hear
the wisdom of Solomon and, lo, something more than
Solomon is here.** Although "a queen" is indefinite,

it refers to the queen of Sheba mentioned in I Kings 10:1-13, who came a thousand miles from what were then literally the ends of the earth. Danger, hardships, time, and expense were as nothing to her compared with the wisdom of Solomon which she desired to hear. The aorist ἀκοῦσαι indicates that she heard and appropriated Solomon's wisdom. Nothing is said about the religious character of Solomon's wisdom, but that is certainly included, for she found far more than had been reported to her. Here again we have these points: a benighted Gentile and a woman at that in a far distant land who had only more or less uncertain reports to inform her undertakes a journey of such proportions to hear the wisdom of one who again is a type, though only a type, of Christ. And once more the exclamation because of the telling contrast: "and, lo, something more is here," the same neuter πλεῖον for all that is embodied in Christ. People of the covenant here in their own land with Wisdom itself come to dwell among them, and yet they will not hear. We may parallel this comparison with the preceding one, including the resurrection and its apostolic preaching, for Jesus speaks of the total unbelief of "this generation." So this queen, too, shall rise up (the future passive is used in the middle sense) and in the same way condemn these Jews. She might have had an excuse for not obtaining the wisdom of Solomon, but the Jews had none for scorning the heavenly wisdom of salvation in Christ. This reference to wisdom is especially pertinent to the scribes whose very profession it was to seek and to dispense the true wisdom of God.

43) With δέ Jesus introduces an illustration which pictures the condition of "this generation" of Jews. He describes the case of a demoniac, one that at times happened. **Now when the unclean spirit is gone out from the man he goes through waterless places**

**seeking rest and does not find it.**   In some way the demoniac is delivered from the demon that had taken possession of him; the details of the deliverance are not necessary for the illustration.  The Greek articles with "spirit" and "man" indicate only that a specific case is being presented, not that what is here said is repeated in the case of every healed demoniac.  The expelled spirit, now without fixed abode, wanders from place to place seeking ἀνάπαυσις, "pause," i. e., some place where he may satisfy his unclean or morally vile desires.  Why he flits about "through waterless places," which must refer to arid and desert localities and cannot be figurative (heretics, unbaptized people), has often been asked but never really answered.  We are referred to Tobit 8:3; Baruch 4:35 (both apocryphal) ; and to Isa. 34:14; Rev. 18:2, with the remark that desert places were thought to be the abode of demons.  But Jesus is not voicing opinions that were current in his time, he is stating a fact.

Nor is it likely that the expelled demon is seeking healing for his wounds.  Would they heal more quickly in "waterless" places?  Or that he hates the sight of men who remind him that he has been driven out.  Why, then, does he go back to the man from whom he was expelled?  Jesus knows the ways of demons; we do not.  He went into the wilderness to be tempted of the devil and now tells us about demons passing througth waterless regions.  As in the case of other facts for which we have no explanation, we accept this as a fact.

44) **Then he says, I will return to my house whence I went out!  And having come, he finds it standing vacant, having been swept and having been set in order.**   The context indicates nothing regarding the demon's having recovered from his defeat and his wounds.  The only implication is that the demon, **weary** of drifting about and unable to find pause

elsewhere, bethinks himself of his former house and determines to return to it. Even after the vain attempt against Jesus, Satan departed from him only "for a season" (Luke 4:13). The fact that one has been freed from the devil does not grant perpetual immunity from the devil's assaults. The figure of the "the house" is transparent and is carried through the second statement. After εὑρίσκει the participles are indirect discourse. The demon finds the house "standing empty," the present participle σχολάζοντα merely describing its condition. It is literally "at leisure," nobody is occupying it. This is most significant. The Holy Spirit is not occupying the man and his heart. Why he is not is easily guessed. No true spiritual change has been wrought in him. The man was merely in some way freed from demoniacal possession, he had not become a child of God.

The two perfect participles are not merely thrown in for good measure. "Having been swept and having been set in order" belong together and picture this house as having been made ready for a tenant. And now the old tenant has arrived, anxious to move in again. Since this house is now untenanted, these participles cannot denote sanctification and spiritual gifts, for then God's Spirit would be dwelling there. All we may say is that this man who was once the victim of the demon's violence with everything in him unclean and disordered through the demon's presence is now living an outwardly reformed life but apart from God.

45) **Then he goes and takes with himself seven other spirits more wicked than himself and, having entered in, dwells there.** This demon is not breaking into this house. Hence he does not get seven more spirits to help him break into it. Nor are they called "stronger than he." Quite the contrary, the house is now so inviting that this demon can have the

company he wants. He sees that there is room enough
for eight and so he goes and gets the seven. Why he
secures just seven is another question that remains
without an answer. Since there are eight, this cannot be an imitation of the sacred number seven.
Whereas at one time one demon played havoc with this
man, eight now violate him.

**And the last conditions of that man are worse
than the first.** Why? Eight demons instead of one,
and seven of them "more wicked" and thus more vicious than the one. The two neuter plurals say nothing about the comparative difficulty of freeing the
man; they compare only his two conditions, the last
being worse than the first.

And now the application of this illustrative ex--
ample is made. **Thus will it be also with this wicked
generation.** Note that "this wicked generation"
repeats v. 39 and reveals the unity of this discourse.
By adding πονηρᾳ with a second article it is made
emphatic, R. 776. "Thus" = the last conditions of
this wicked generation will be worse than the first.
Which are the conditions here compared? "This generation" forbids our going back to times of the Old
Testament, or going forward into the later history
of the Jews. Jesus is speaking of the generation that
was helped by the Baptist, and we may include the
work Jesus did in support of the Baptist's (John 4:1,
2). It helped only for a time. Even now the spiritual
condition of the Jews was worse, as witness this
entire chapter and its culmination in the blasphemy
of v. 24 and in the warning against the unpardonable sin, v. 31, 32. This would go on until judgment
would descend in the destruction of Jerusalem and
the deportation of the people. One striking feature
in Christ's revelation is the fact that Jesus answers
the charge of being connected with Satan (v. 24, etc.)
by pointing out that the Jews themselves were like a

man who was repossessed by eight demons instead of
by one. Yet all these terrible revelations were uttered
as warnings in order to save those who could yet be
saved: "Save yourselves from this untoward generation!" Acts 2:40.

46) This probably is the reason that Matthew
ends this section on the clash with the Pharisees by
adding the incident in which Jesus calls his disciples
his brothers, sisters, and mother. However hopeless
this generation as such may be, some are won for
Christ even among such people. **While he was still
speaking to the multitudes, lo, his mother and his
brothers were standing outside seeking to speak to
him.** The genitive absolute, "he still speaking to
the multitudes," makes it certain that Matthew gives
us the true connection of events. The strange nature
of the incident is marked by the interjection. It is
certainly strange to find the mother of Jesus participating in this affair. Although she is mentioned
first because she is the nearest relative of Jesus, we
cannot think that she was the instigator but prefer
to believe that she permitted herself to be drawn into
this affair by the fears and the urgings of the others.
Even so, here we have a picture of Mary that is far
different from the legendary image of "the Mother
of God" found in medieval and in Romish tradition.
She is carried along by a mistaken movement. On the
other hand, we refuse to charge Mary with unbelief
(John 7:5) and opposition to her son; she grew in
faith as others did.

Who "his brothers" are, in the writer's opinion has
not been determined. Modern commentators answer:
the sons of Joseph and Mary who were born later than
Jesus. But here and elsewhere they act as though
they were older than he. Others think of sons of
Joseph by a former marriage. In Mark 6:3 Jesus is
called "the son of Mary" in a marked way (compare

John 19:26) and is kept distinct from the brothers and
the sisters. In Acts 1:14 Luke writes: "Mary, the
mother of Jesus, and *his* brothers" — not *"her* sons."
Still others, for instance, the Latin Church since
Jerome and older Protestant theologians and some
interpreters of our day, think of the sons of Clopas,
a brother or a brother-in-law of Joseph. Thus these
brothers would be first cousins of Jesus. This little
company was standing (the past perfect εἱστήκεισαν
is always used as an imperfect) outside, ἔξω, i. e., of
the packed crowd. Jesus probably sat on a raised
place where all could see and hear him, and the crowd
sat around him cross-legged in Oriental fashion so
densely packed that no one could pass through.
Luke 8:19 has διὰ τὸν ὄχλον, and no house is mentioned; the house mentioned in Mark 3:20 has no
connection with the present incident.

What Mary and his brothers wanted to speak to
him about is indicated in Mark 3:21. They thought
that Jesus was "beside himself," was using himself up
in his excessive labors, was like one who is no longer
in his rational mind. Their object was to lay hold of
him and to take him away to a place where he could
be quiet. We may take it that their intentions were
the best, the dictates of solicitous affection. It is difficult to decide whether the charge of the Pharisees
that Jesus was possessed by Beelzebul precipitated
this move on the part of his relatives, they assuming that the charge had so much truth back of it, that
Jesus was showing an unbalanced mind, was consuming himself with his labors.

This created a delicate and a trying situation for
Jesus, yet he meets it with perfect mastery. He shows
no impatience with his relatives — his mother should
have known better. He is absolutely truthful and
resorts to no equivocation either before the people or
before his relatives. He utilizes the untimely and ill-

advised interruption for defining and for impressing a
most momentous truth upon them.

47) **Now one said to him, Lo, thy mother and
thy brothers are standing outside seeking to speak
to thee.** If this verse, which is omitted in some
codices, is not genuine, it might as well be, for Mary
and the brothers did not push through the crowd, someone must have shouted to Jesus, not in order to interrupt
his severe censures (v. 38-45), but to do Jesus and
his relatives a service. The perfect ἑστήκασι always has
a present meaning. The reason for speaking with
Jesus is still unrevealed. The suggestion that it was
about some domestic affair overlooks Mark 3:21.

48) Instead of turning to his relatives, Jesus turns
to the man who told him about them. **And he answered and said to him that told him, Who is my
mother? and who are my brothers?** The circumstantial participle added to the verb marks the reply
as being important (3:15). Yet why put more than is
necessary into it by saying that Jesus was lifted above
family and human life, was the Son of God and no
longer a son of Nazareth or of Mary or of Israel, that
his Messianic feeling was wrestling with his filial feeling? This question intends to fix this man's attention
and that of all those present on the thing Jesus asks.
They are to pause and to think and to ask just who is
Jesus' mother and who are his brothers. And the
dramatic question, thus put, automatically lends a
deeper significance to "my mother" and "my brothers."
And while men's minds are still searching, and before
they can center on a wrong answer, Jesus himself gives
the terse, striking, perfect answer which, because of the
way in which it is introduced, will the more remain
fixed in the memory.

49) **And having stretched out his hand toward
his disciples, he said, Lo, my mother and my
brothers! For whoever shall do the will of my**

**Father in the heavens, he is my brother and sister and mother.** First, the illuminating gesture, the extended hand pointing to the μαθηταί and differentiating them from the ὄχλοι, the crowds. A μαθητής is one who has learned from his master and thus has imbibed his spirit; see 5:1. This gesture is like the action of Jesus on the last day when the same hand shall separate the disciples (believers) from all others, whoever they may be. But does Jesus here exclude his own mother from his spiritual family? Nothing in this action or in his words says this. The dramatic gesture is matched by the dramatic word which reduces the answer to the fewest words: "Lo, my mother and my brothers!" All of the disciples were men. When Jesus calls them "my mother and my brothers," this grouping together of mother and brothers helps to show that Jesus is speaking of something that is higher than blood ties.

50) Just what he has in mind he explains by γάρ. Christ here confesses his disciples before men as he will confess them at that day before his Father and the holy angels. But he does it in a way that opens the blessed relationship to all who may want to enter it. Whoever — he; ὅστις — αὐτός; universal — yet particular; open to all and excluding none ("whoever") — yet embracing only those who become truly his ("he," i. e., "he alone"). What really makes us one with Christ is stated most exactly: ὅστις ἄν, an indefinite relative clause with the futuristic subjunctive. The aorist ποιήσῃ is complexive, summing up into one point the person's life of doing the Father' will. "The will (θέλημα) of my Father in the heavens" is *what* this supreme and exalted Father wills. "My Father," Jesus says, not "your Father," because he must connect himself and his entire mission with this Father of his, this Father's will that we are to do. Jesus reveals this will, invites, draws, enables us to perform it. This θέλημα is the Father's gracious gospel will, the will which, unlike the

will revealed in the law, furnishes us the power whereby we may truly do it. The Scriptures are full of
statements declaring this will. Read John 6:29, 40,
47; II Pet. 3:9; I Tim. 2:4. The Baptist proclaimed it
in 3:2; Jesus repeated the proclamation in 4:17; the
Twelve were to do the same in 10:7, and did it in Acts
2:38, etc. The Father's will is that by his grace we
repent and believe, turn from our sins, and by faith
receive his pardon in Christ Jesus. His will is our
regeneration, James 1:18; John 3:3, 5; Eph. 2:1-5;
our restoration to childhood and heirship, Gal. 3:26-29.
We do this will when we let Christ work all this in us
and bestow all this upon us.

The gravest perversion of this θέλημα and this ποιῆσαι
is that of Pelagianism and of synergism as well as that
of all Pharisaism or work-righteousness, which call on
us and our natural powers to do the works of the law
and thus to earn heaven, or by our own natural powers
to believe in Christ and to obey him, or at least to aid
in our repentance and conversion. Ποιεῖν is indeed an
activity, but it is one wrought in us wholly by grace,
Phil. 2:13.

Αὐτός is emphatic: "he and he alone." He is "my
brother and sister and mother" welds all three into
one concept, that of the most intimate spiritual relationship. As Jesus came to do his Father's will, the
will that involved our salvation, so we are one with
him when we do his Father's will, that same will regarding our salvation. Yet this does not imply that
we are to do over again what Jesus did, but that we are
to let him bestow on us all that he did for us. While
in v. 49 mother was placed emphatically first, it is now,
equally emphatically, placed last; and in the middle
Jesus adds "my sister" (Matt. 13:56), thus the more
wiping out any distinction and bringing out the thought
that the one true relationship of spiritual connection is
in the mind of Jesus. "Sister" and "mother" no more

refer to women disciples than "brother" refers only to men, cf. Gal. 3:28. All believers are of the household of God (Eph. 2:19), of the household of faith (Gal. 6:10). All others are "strangers and foreigners" who, indeed, may possibly become disciples and relatives but who, if they remain as they are, will be sundered forever from the divine family of believers.

To Jesus this tie is supreme. Alas, the earthly ties have often been placed above the heavenly, men have loved wife, child, father, mother more than Christ, 10:37. Did Mary and Jesus' brothers get to speak with him as they desired? The evangelists have no interest in giving us this detail. In his Messianic work Jesus allowed no dictation or interference even on the part of his mother (John 2:4). Yet 13:1 would indicate that Jesus finally went home with his relatives, on this very day once more to go out to preach and to teach.

# CHAPTER XIII

## X

### Christ Speaks Many Parables, Chapter 13

1) **On that day Jesus, having gone out from his home, was sitting by the sea.** **And there were gathered together unto him great multitudes so that, after entering a boat, he was sitting down.** **And all the multitude was standing along the beach.** The two imperfects ἐκάθητο and εἱστήκει (a past perfect always used as an imperfect), together with the present infinitive καθῆσθαι, paint the scene before our eyes. It was the same day on which his relatives had tried to reach him (12:46). ᾿Απὸ τῆς οἰκίας is sometimes connected with ἔξω in 12:46: Jesus left the house in which he had been when his relatives came. But then the phrase "on that day" would seem to be superfluous. We take it that Jesus went home with his mother and his brothers and after a while, yet on the same day, walked to the seaside and sat down there.

2) Soon the crowds gathered, facing him (πρὸς αὐτόν). They were so great (πολλοί) that Jesus stepped into a boat and took his seat there, the crowd standing along the beach. The Teacher, seated in Oriental manner, has his audience before him.

3) **And he spoke to them many things in parables saying, Lo, there went out the sower in order to sow.** These parables Matthew now narrates. The best definition and the most thorough discussion of the parable are found in the introductory sections of Trench's *Notes on the Parables of our Lord*. As far

as we know, the first typical parable of all those uttered by Jesus is the one about the Sower. The exclamation "lo" calls our attention to the man now introduced and to his action. The article with ὁ σπείρων gives the participle a generic or representative sense, R. 764: "the one whose business is sowing." "He went out" at once places him in the field, but the present infinitive with τοῦ tells us that his purpose is to carry on the work of sowing; it says nothing about the completion of this work.

**4)  And in his sowing some fell along the path; and the birds came and ate it up. And other fell on the rocky soil where it had not much earth; and immediately it sprang up on account of not having depth of earth, yet when the sun was risen, it was scorched, and on account of not having root it was dried up** (ξηραίνω). **And other fell upon the thorns; and the thorns came up and choked it off** (ἀποπνίγω). The entire description is typically Palestinian. The wheat or barley is sown by hand. The patch to be sown is not extensive and is unfenced. Along its side runs a path which, perhaps, divides it from a similar patch, and in the sowing some of the seed may fall at the side (παρά) of this path, escape being covered up, and thus be eagerly eaten up by the birds. The neuter plurals ἃ μέν, αὐτά, ἄλλα need no formal antecedents, these being understood. Christ's parables are gems; the language is filed down to the exclusion of every unnecessary word.

**5, 6)**  So much of Palestine consists of rocky elevations that any tilled spaces may contain spots where the underlying rock comes close to the surface and has only a thin covering of soil. These are τὰ πετρώδη, which lack sufficient earth, where the seed, indeed, sprouts quickly because of the underlying rock and the warmth it causes in the film of soil (διὰ τὸ μὴ ἔχειν βάθος γῆς), but where the hot sun burns the seed and dries it up before it has attained sufficient rootage.   Luke 8:6: "it had no moisture," could not root properly.

7) Other spots in the patch are infested with thorns, ἄκανθαι.   Their roots escape the plow, but after the sowing they shoot up new growth amid which the grain is soon choked, being unable to maintain itself.

8) **And other fell on the excellent earth and went on to yield fruit, the one a hundred, the other sixty, the other thirty.   He that has ears, let him be hearing.**   While in three places there is no yield and only in one a harvest, the proportion is not three to one.   All that is pictured is the different type of soil and the resultant effect on the seed.   Τὴν καλήν means "excellent for its purpose," and the repetition of the article makes the adjective an emphatic apposition to the noun (R. 776).   The imperfect ἐδίδου is intentionally used after the aorist ἔπεσεν (R. 838, 883).   The parable limits itself to the time of sowing, and the imperfect, starting from that time, pictures the development of the fruit.   In ὃ μέν, etc., we have individual grains of seed (σπέρμα), corresponding to the neuter plural ἃ μέν in v. 4, etc.   One grain proceeds to produce a hundred, etc.   This increase merely states the maximum, the medium, and the minimum, the figures being without symbolical significance.

9) The parable closes with a call to the hearers to use their ears.   The implication is that this simple narrative about the seed has a hidden meaning, and that if one applies his ears aright he will grasp this meaning, but if one has no ears, i. e., if his ears refuse to function aright, he will only be mystified.   Mark 4:3 begins the parable with the call ἀκούετε, "be hearing" or "pay attention," thus helping to bring out the thought that the real subject of the parable is the hearing of the Word.   Jesus' call to be hearing is interpretative of the parable, for it pictures the different kinds of hearers which the Word finds.

10)   We must imagine that a pause and an interval of time occurred between the different parables; note how this is indicated in v. 24, 31, 33; and in Mark 4:21, 26, 30.   These parables were not given to the hearers in one mass, but were spoken in spaced succession, so that all might be enabled to get the full effect of each.   This helps to explain v. 10-23. **And having drawn near, the disciples said to him, For what reason doest thou speak in parables to them?**   From Mark 4:10 we learn that the Twelve, in company with other disciples, asked about the parables but that they did this when Jesus was alone. Both Matthew and Mark have the question deal with parables (plural) although they have as yet narrated only one.   The disciples even ask for the reason (διατί; not the purpose or aim, which would be ἱνατί) that Jesus is using parables.   All this indicates that Matthew, like Mark, inserts after the first parable what happened afterward when Jesus was alone in his home (v. 36). Then they "drew near" and asked.   The question was really a double one.   They wanted to know why Jesus was using parables and what this first parable meant (Luke 8:9), likewise the second.   Since the answer of Jesus contains a full and detailed exposition of the first parable, the standard for the interpretation of all parables, both Matthew and Mark insert this reply of Jesus here instead of at the end of the parable-sermon.

11)   **And he answered** (see 3:15) **and said to them** (recitative ὅτι), **To you it has been given to know the mysteries of the kingdom of the heavens** (see 3:2), **but to them it has not been given.   For whoever has, to him shall be given and he shall be made to abound; but whoever has not, even what he has shall be carried away from him.   For this reason I am speaking to them in parables, because, seeing, they do not see and, hearing, they do not hear nor understand.**   The mysteries of the kingdom are

all the blessed realities contained in the divine rule of
grace and of glory. These are "mysteries" because
men by nature and by their own abilities are unable to
discover and to know them. It must "be given" to a
man "to know" them. This divine giving is done by
means of revelation, through the preaching and the
teaching of the gospel of the kingdom. In the verb
"has been given" lies the idea of pure grace, and the
agent back of the passive is God. On the kingdom
of the heavens see 3:2.

When Jesus now tells the disciples that to them the
great grace has been given "to know the mysteries"
while to the others, the Pharisees and the multitudes,
this privilege "to know the mysteries" (the aorist
γνῶναι to indicate actual inner grasp and appropriation)
has not been given, he is speaking of the present condition of the disciples and of the others. Due to something that transpired in the past, the one group now
has this gift to know, the other has it not. What had
occurred in the past that caused this present difference?
The Scriptures answer: no unwillingness on God's part
to give (I Tim. 2:4; II Pet. 3:9; John 3:16; Matt.
28:19, 20) but only the unwillingness of so many to
receive his grace and gift (23:37; Acts 7:51; Hos.
13:9). Persistently declining the grace and gift
when it first came to them, these people remained without it. Thus they are now without the necessary
requisites for receiving the knowledge of the blessed
mysteries of the kingdom. To know these "has not
been given to them" because they nullified every effort
of God and of Christ to bestow this gift on them.

12) With γάρ Jesus does not explain the past. All
had nothing to begin with. This γάρ explains the present, it states why the disciples can and do receive more
while the others now even lose what they may have.
"Whoever has" by accepting what God first gave, "to
him shall be given," as being one who is willing and

able to receive more, and so "he shall be made to abound" or "to superabound." He shall roll in spiritual wealth. All that the kingdom has in the way of blessed realities shall be open to him. Both verbs are passive with God as the agent. He shall continue the stream of his giving, he shall fill their hearts with knowledge in superabundance even as he is doing now and in v. 18, etc., through Christ's teaching.

But he who "has not" because he declined what the others accepted, because he thought he was rich and sufficient in himself, he shall not merely remain as he is, without all the riches that flow to the others, he shall lose even "what he has." In our relation to Christ we either go forward or go backward; we do not stand still. "What he has" means whatever he may possess of moral endowments from God. The scribes and Pharisees and the foolish people who followed them instead of Jesus lost steadily as their contact with Jesus progressed (11:16-24; 12:38-45). They lost even the natural sense of fairness, right, and justice. Behind the healing of the demoniacs they thought they saw Beelzebul (12:24), and in spite of the noblest and greatest deeds of mercy they took counsel to destroy Jesus (12:14). The passive "shall be carried away from him," i. e., by God (passive from $αἴρω$) refers to.the divine judgment which works itself out in a man of this kind.

13) $Διὰ$ $τοῦτο$ may mean, "for the reason just stated," or, which is preferable, "for the reason now stated," since ($ὅτι$) they neither see nor hear so as to understand. Thus the question, "for what reason?" is answered directly. The work of Jesus has progressed so far that many have definitely rejected him and the kingdom and rule of grace he is establishing. What they have all along spurned is now being withdrawn from them. The parables begin to hide it from them. God's judgment is beginning: what they would not

know they eventually shall not know. God's grace has
its limits. He will not always strive with men. It is
absolutely useless, "because, seeing, they do not see"
what Jesus shows them; "and hearing, they do not
hear," which is defined by adding, "nor do they understand" by inwardly appropriating (11:25, 26); συνιοῦσι
from συνίημι.

14) The quotation from Isa. 6:9, 10, which follows the LXX without attention to verbal exactness
and yet reproducing its thought adequately, is not an
insertion by Matthew but was spoken by Jesus and
follows naturally after the ὅτι clause in v. 13 which
already recalls Isaiah. **And there is filled up for
them the prophecy of Isaiah which says:**

> **By hearing you shall hear and in no wise
> understand;**
> **And seeing you shall see and in no wise
> perceive.**
> **For the heart of this people was made dull,**
> **And with their ears they did hear with dif-
> ficulty,**
> **And their eyes they did shut**
> **Lest ever they might perceive with their eyes**
> **And hear with their ears**
> **And understand with their heart**
> **And turn around again,**
> **And I should heal them.**

Since Jesus quotes and not Matthew, why expect the
standard formula used by the latter (as seen in 1:22)?
Nor is Jesus merely quoting, for he says that "the
prophecy of Isaiah is being filled up" like a vessel that
is almost full, into which enough is being poured to fill
it completely. God was sending the nation to its doom.
This doom was now fast approaching completion. The
wrath of judgment would overflow forty years later at
the time of the destruction of Jerusalem. That seems

to be the reason why Jesus prefers the LXX to the Hebrew. For the future tenses "you shall hear" and "you shall see" have the same imperative force as the Hebrew verbs; while the historical aorists of the LXX in v. 15, "was made dull," "they did hear," "they did shut," express just what Jesus wants to point out, namely, what this λαός has done until this very time which now leaves only a little to be added to make the measure completely full.

The dative ἀκοῇ has the same force as the participle βλέποντες, which reproduces the Hebrew infinitive absolute (R. 94). When unbelief has progressed far enough, all its hearing and all its seeing will not only produce nothing but it is also God's will (the *voluntas consequens*, not by any means the *voluntas antecedens*) that it shall be so. In other words, God casts off such people and in his judgment lets the very Word become for them a savor of death unto death. See the discussion on John 12:39, 40, *Interpretation of St. John's Gospel.*

15) What is said of the eyes and the ears, of course, pertains to the heart. The passive of παχύνω means that by casting off God these unbelievers made their heart fat, gross, utterly irresponsive, and thus they heard βαρέως, i. e., became "hard of hearing," could not hear at all, and even deliberately shut their eyes. The description is true in every detail of the great representative part of the Jews at the time of Christ.

Μήποτε, "lest ever," expresses the divine judicial purpose of the *voluntas consequens*, which, however, is the very purpose of this people. They are determined not to perceive, hear aright, and understand; therefore, too, God intends that they shall not. They are set on not turning around, ἐπιστρέφειν denoting conversion in the gospel sense: "to convert" (intransitive; more usually in our idiom "to be converted," A. V.). Note the aorist subjunctives, all of which express actuality: "actually perceive," etc. These are now followed by the future indicative ἰάσομαι, which is still dependent on μήποτε and is a quite regular construction in the Koine, R. 988, especially in the case of the last verb in a series of verbs: "lest I should heal them" spiritually and thus save them. The Jews acted as though for them the greatest calamity would be to turn so that God might heal them. They needed to have no such fears: God intends to force no man into heaven.

16) **But blessed your eyes because they see, and your ears because they hear.** For amen, I say **to you, that many prophets and righteous desired to perceive what you are seeing and did not perceive it, and to hear what you are hearing and did not hear it.** Μακάριοι has exactly the same force that it has in the Beatitudes, see 5:3. The emphasis is on ὑμῶν which is placed prominently forward. The great contrast is drawn between the others who lose all blessedness by the way in which they see and hear and the disciples who have all this blessedness by the way in which they see and hear. But note that here the means are mentioned, the eyes and the ears being adjudged "blessed," not the source of the blessedness which has been mentioned already in v. 11, the divine Giver and his giving. The source and the means should never be dissociated. God uses the ordinary eyes and ears of the disciples when bestowing his blessedness and when increasing this to the highest degree (v. 12). That is why only the ordinary functions of the eyes and the ears are mentioned, βλέπειν and ἀκούειν. As far as the disciples are concerned, they do no more than the unbelieving Jews did, they just see and hear. The fact that through *their* eyes and *their* ears (the two ὑμῶν being placed chiastically, both being in the emphatic posi-

tions) they obtain the great blessedness is due solely to the divine giving of grace which the others might likewise obtain but lose because of their wilful and persistent unbelief.

17)     With γάρ Jesus explains how great the blessedness of the disciples really is.   He adds the impressive formula for the verity and the authority of his statement: "amen," etc., which is explained in 5:18.   The greatness of the disciples' blessedness becomes evident when it is compared with that of "the prophets and the righteous" of all past times.   The prophets were certainly highly blessed by receiving immediately and directly the revelations God made to them.   They saw and heard the Messianic promises.   The righteous, who are declared such by the divine· Judge, are the true believers that lived in the days of the old covenant, who accepted the revelations brought to them by the prophets.   Greater than the unquestioned blessedness of all these (and their number throughout the centuries was "many") is that of the disciples at present.   The former had only the promises, shadows, types, etc., on which to rest their faith and with which to delight their souls.   Naturally, the higher they prized these, the more they longed for the fulfillment so that they might enjoy also this.   But they died before it arrived.

This fulfillment, which is now in progress, the disciples see and hear (βλέπετε, ἀκούετε, durative presents). When stating what the ancient saints desired Jesus uses ἰδεῖν and οὐκ εἶδον, which was intensified in v. 14, 15 by being contrasted with the mere βλέπειν.   What the saints of old desired to see were not merely the outward features of the fulfillment now in progress but to see all with inner perception.   That is why both in v. 14, 15, and now in v. 17 the tense of ἰδεῖν is the effective aorist, denoting actual perceiving.   In v. 14, 15 mere hearing (ἀκούειν) is in the same way matched with hearing that really understands (συνίειν, B.-P. under συνίημι, 1266), the subjunctives are properly the aorist tense. But when speaking of the saints of old, Jesus could not say that, although they desired to hear (ἀκοῦσαι, constative aorist) what the disciples are now hearing, they "did not understand," as he had immediately before this said that they "did not perceive." This would have been wrong. For they saw and heard with true understanding what revelation they had. Jesus says only, "They did not hear it," οὐκ ἤκουσαν. Yet this aorist is to be understood in the same sense as the preceding οὐκ εἶδον, they did not get to hear all that Jesus was now teaching with the added knowledge this hearing would have brought to them just as it was brought to the disciples by their hearing.

18) Mark 4:10 tells us that the question of the disciples was comprehensive: "they asked of him the parable," compare also v. 13. So Jesus expounds the first parable. **Do you, therefore, hear the parable of the sower!** Both the emphatic ὑμεῖς and the οὖν rest on v. 11, 12: "you, therefore," to whom it has been given to know, you who have and to whom far more shall be given by divine grace. The aorist imperative ἀκούσατε is used with exactly the same force as the preceding aorist indicative ἤκουσαν: "hear with all the knowledge the hearing is intended to convey." Jesus now makes this hearing possible.

19) **When anyone** (no matter who, R. 744) **hears the word of the kingdom and does not understand, the wicked one comes and snatches away what has been sown in his heart. This is the one seeded along the path.** We prefer (R. 1105) to regard παντός with the two genitive participles as a genitive absolute, the present tenses describing the hearing without understanding as being in progress. Satan does not wait until the hearing is completed, just as the birds do not wait until the sowing is done. He snatches the Word away while the man is still hearing it. Others

regard the construction as an anacoluthon with a pendant genitive: "anyone hearing and not understanding." The genitive participles are then resumed by the
genitive αὐτοῦ. This justification of the genitive is unsatisfactory. The parable presents *persons,* each being
described according to what happens to the Word he
hears. Matthew mentions one of each kind (οὗτος)
although he indicates that each represents a class
(παντός, "anyone") ; Mark and Luke use plurals.

Matthew uses the expression "the word of the kingdom," which latter is best regarded as a subjective genitive: the word spoken by the kingdom, by which the
kingdom comes to a man's heart. The kingdom is the
Messianic rule of grace and salvation; see the exposition in 3:2. Luke calls this word the seed; it is sown
every time a man hears it. The sower is not interpreted. Yet "kingdom" suggests Christ; for ἐξῆλθεν
in v. 3 exactly describes his activity. The entire sowing is his, all that, too, which he does through others.
The parable deals only with the preaching and the
teaching of the true Word; we must not introduce perversions of the Word.

Now here is an individual who hears this precious
Word and does not understand it. It is the identical
Word that brings the richest fruit in another hearer.
The fault of not being understood, therefore, lies, not
in the Word, but in the hearer. What happens is this:
"comes the wicked one and snatches away what has
been sown in his heart." Through his ears the Word
was sown into this person's heart. It does not stay
there. Moved by his inordinate wickedness and opposition to God, the devil snatches away from the man
whatever has been sown. We need not regard the
birds as devils (plural), they represent Satan in his
different methods of snatching the Word away from a
heart. At one time he tells a man that the Word which
disturbs the conscience is mere exaggeration and only

unbalances the mind; again, that it is uncertain, that
there is no solid fact in it, that no up-to-date man believes it; then, that the preachers themselves do not
believe it, that they preach it only to make an easy living and are really hypocrites as their own actions show.
Endless are these birds through which Satan operates.

The passive masculine ὁ σπαρείς is the man on whom
the seed was sown "along the path." Ὁ σπαρείς is the
counterpart to ὁ σπείρων (v. 3). The latter does the
seeding, the former receives the seeding, hence "was
seeded," *der Besaete.* Zahn's objections that this
aorist passive participle is found only in the poets is
met by the fact that it here occurs four times in succession and in exactly this sense. The objection that
the style forbids this sense, that it refers to a man
immediately after another passive τὸ ἐσπαρμένον had
referred to the seed, is not tenable, because the genders
are so marked, and the ideas so clear and striking. Of
course, the gender of the predicate participle is not
attracted from the neuter τὸ σπαρέν to the masculine of
the subject οὗτος, so that we should read, "he is *what*
was sown" — which would be senseless. Σπαρείς denotes
the person. The interpretation which asks us to believe that in ὁ σπαρείς the man and the seed are identified,
asks the impossible, asks it four times, without being
able to point to another similar usage in all literature.

Now we know *whom* Jesus has in mind when he
speaks of seed falling along a path where the birds
quickly pick it up: the man from whose heart Satan
at once snatches away the Word he happens to hear.

20) **Now he that was seeded on the rocky soil
(see v. 5), this is the one hearing the Word and immediately receiving it with joy; yet he does not have
root in himself but is transient and, tribulation or
persecution having arisen, immediately is caught.**
We have ὁ σπαρείς with a phrase exactly as in v. 19: "he
that was seeded," was sprinkled with seed on the soil

underlaid with rock.  This is the one who hears the
Word and at once receives it with joy, leading you to
expect great things of him.

21)   But something is wrong from the start: this
man "has no root in himself."   Let us not say that the
man and the seed are identified in this expression, for
"in himself" means in himself as the kind of soil he
is.   He received the seed but had no root for the seed.
The seed was not at fault, it was entirely the soil.
Hence this man is πρόσκαιρος, "for a season," "transient."   How transient is at once stated.   "Tribulation," θλῖψις, when pressure is exerted upon us, and
"persecution," when we are made to suffer on account
of the Word, arise, and then the trouble begins for this
man who is without good, healthy roots in the soil of
his heart.

The remarkable feature of this figure is the fact that
the shining sun is here used to represent tribulation
and persecution.   The seed that is sown in the good
soil must have the sun in order to grow as it should.
That is what makes it bear fruit.   Just as little as
grain grows without the sun, so little the Word thrives
in us without our suffering "because of the Word."   But
where the soil is shallow, the ugly rock, the hidden
hardness in the man's heart are found, he "is caught."
The figure in σκανδαλίζεται is that of a trap which is
sprung by a crooked stick to which the bait is attached.
But this figurative sense is largely lost, as the present
tense used here also shows.   This tense is durative,
hence it does not express the instantaneous act of being
caught by the springing of the trap but the condition of
lying caught in the trap: he is scandalized, offended by
what is happening to him in this tribulation, etc.   "He
stumbles" (R. V.) changes the figure of the verb; "he
is offended" (A. V.) is much better.

22)   **Now, he that was seeded into the thorns,
this is the one hearing the Word, and the worry of**

**the times and the deceitfulness of riches smother the
Word, and it becomes fruitless.** "Into" is correct.
The man received the seed into a heart in which the
sprouting runners of thorny growths were hidden.
These shoot up thick and strong, far faster and higher
than the grasslike wheat or barley, and quickly
"smother the Word." We have no reason to make anything but ὁ λόγος the subject of γίνεται; the Word is prevented from producing fruit. Αἰών, a peculiar Greek
term, always denotes an age or eon marked and distinguished by what transpires in it. And τοῦ αἰῶνος is
definite, equivalent to "this eon." B.-P. 42 furnishes
the best rendering: *die Sorge der Gegenwart,* "the
worry connected with the times," those into which one's
life is cast. The idea is that every age has its own
types of worry, and whoever lets these fill his heart will
surely smother the Word of the kingdom which deals
with higher interests. Beside the broader expression
is placed one that is more specific: "the deceitfulness
of wealth" (in the Greek abstract nouns may have the
article), I Tim. 6:6-10. The two genitives may be
subjective: the times worry the man, wealth deceives
him; or simply possessive: worry belongs to the times,
deceit to riches. Wealth as such, whether one has it
or not, deceives. It promises a satisfaction which it
can and does not bring, deceiving him who has it and
who longs for it (19:23).

23) **Now he that is seeded on the good earth,
this is the one hearing and understanding the Word,
who, indeed, bears fruit and makes the one a hundred, the other sixty, the other thirty.** Matthew
says that this man understands the Word; Mark, that
he accepts it; Luke, that he holds it fast. All three
have the same thing in mind, but Matthew's συνιών
repeats this verb from v. 13-15, where it occurs three
times in a marked way. The second article before
καλήν gives the adjective the emphasis (R. 776).

"Who is just the man who" is a translation of δή (R. 1149), the German *eben*. R. 695 is right: we must have the reading ὃ μέν, ὃ δέ, neuters, but these are accusatives, not nominatives. The reading that has the masculines ὁ μέν, ὁ δέ, would give the sense that the one *man* produces a hundred, the other *man* sixty, etc. But ὅς is already singular and cannot be divided; and this reading would leave "a hundred," etc., undetermined — a hundred what? Jesus says that this man, in whose case the seed has been sown on the good earth, makes one seed a hundred, another seed sixty, another seed thirty seeds. Why should one object that one seed (one portion of the Word) produces (ποιεῖ) a hundred seeds (or portions of the Word) when the business of every believer of the Word is to testify to the Word and thus to spread the Word? The Word as such is, indeed, a fixed entity which is neither to be increased or decreased; its multiplication lies in its spread in one heart and from one heart to other hearts.   This is how the Word bears fruit.

The question regarding the difference in yield when the hearer with a good heart makes one seed of the Word bear a hundred seeds, another only sixty, and another only thirty, is part of the greater question as to why the Word fares so differently in different hearers.   In one it does not get beyond the surface; in another it gets only just beneath the surface; in a third its top is smothered; but in the fourth it flourishes, some of its parts producing from thirty to a hundred.   The accepted view is that neither the parable nor its interpretation by Jesus offer any explanation of the differences described.   Those who, nevertheless, attempt an explanation, restrict the parable to *the very first* contact of the Word with the human heart.   Then even a man like Trench, who intends to hold most firmly to the unquestioned doctrine that all hearts are by nature wholly depraved, and none are made better save by the Word alone, gets into plain contradictions of this doctrine by calling some hearts *"fitter* for receiving the seed of everlasting life than others," *"latent* sons of peace," containing tinder which the Word may set afire, while others have no tinder; or containing "particles of true metal" which the magnet of the Word draws to itself, while other hearts have no such particles. Such an explanation leads to Pelagian views.

What the parable and its exposition describe is *the final fate* of the Word in the hearts of men. When life is done, some show a harvest, grains running from 30 to 100; all the rest show none. Some never let the Word in, some never let it root, some smothered its growth. But this *final* fate of the Word is shown us *now*, so that we may examine ourselves as to how we are treating the Word *now*, before life is done. And this is done because, though no man can change himself, God has means to change us all (trodden path, rocky places, briar patches) into good soil for his Word. This means of God is the Word itself as exhibited in this very parable. Like all the Scriptural revelations of man's sinful state, this one, too, aims at the conscience and repentance, thus opening the soul for the gospel. And the more it is opened, the more fruit will there be in the end.

24) **Another parable he placed before them saying, The kingdom of the heavens has become like a man that sowed excellent seed in his field; but while men were sleeping, his enemy came and resowed darnel among the grain and went away.** The formula with which Matthew introduces this second parable is used also for the third and the fourth. It seems to indicate that there was an intermission between the parables which permitted the hearers to absorb each parable by itself. Παρέθηκεν αὐτοῖς is used only in the case of these parables, each of which was

presented to the hearers as being a thing by itself. The progress of thought in these parables, as well as the advance step by step in the imagery employed, are such as to shut out the view that these parables were compiled by Matthew from scattered discourses of Jesus. They hang together and thus also could be easily remembered by those who first heard them presented in this order.

The idea of the kingdom was in the previous parable introduced only in connection with its interpretation (v. 19: "the word of the kingdom"), but from now on "the kingdom of the heavens" (explained in 3:2), some one side or feature of it, is made the subject of each parable. The heavenly rule of the Messiah-King with his grace here on earth among men resembles this, that, and the other. But we must remember that none of these resemblances is merely accidental, the invention of a versatile mind; also and especially that it is not the heavenly that is patterned after the earthly, but the reverse (Trench, *Parables*, "On Teaching by Parables"). The aorist passive ὡμοιώθη is like ὁμοία ἐστίν, used in the presentation of the following parables. R. 835 explains that the stress is on the end of the action and thus calls such aorists "effective," the opposite of "ingressive." The passive is used in the sense of the middle as no agent is implied, and the English prefers the perfect to the Greek aorist. So we translate, "has become like."

All this has an important bearing on the parable thus introduced, for the kingdom "became like" what is here narrated only after Satan did what is here stated. This aorist, therefore, is not timeless but historical. The sowing which Jesus had made was actually followed by the devil's sowing. Since the parable presents the kingdom, the likeness here used centers in the King, the man who sows (see v. 19:

the Sower is Christ), "the Son of man," v. 37, and all that happens to his sowing.

The historical idea contained in ὡμοιώθη is retained throughout: we are told what has happened. Hence we have the aorist participle σπείραντι, "a man who sowed." He put "good," "excellent" seed into his field.

25) But "while men were sleeping," i. e., at night when no one was about to see his nefarious work, "there came his enemy and resowed" the field, ἐπί in the verb denoting that he sowed over the other seed. The compound preposition ἀνὰ μέσον adds the thought that the new seed was sown "between" the good grain. The ζιζάνια are "darnel," most probably *lolium temulentum*, which has grasslike foliage resembling that of wheat and of barley. "And went away" adds a touch that emphasizes the criminal character of the act. In some of the parables acts are presented that never occur in ordinary life (21:37, for instance) but, although it is exceptional as being the act of the most vicious and cowardly hatred, the act here described has occurred. Trench reports that Roman law made such conduct a crime; he also reports cases that occurred in India and even in Ireland. The noxious weeds thus secretly sown were usually of such a nature as to come up before the good grain, crowd it out, ripen before the grain, and were most difficult to eradicate.

26) **Now when the blade sprouted and made fruit, then appeared also the darnel.** The field showed nothing exceptional until growth was well advanced; ὁ χόρτος, the grasslike foliage of both the wheat and the darnel. Its sprouting up and making heads causes the darnel to appear, for this now begins to stand out from the wheat.

27) Now follows the second part of the action. **And the slaves (δοῦλοι, B.-P.) of the houselord, hav-**

**ing come forward, said to him, Lord, didst thou not
sow excellent seed in thy field?    Whence then has it
darnel?    And he said to them, An enemy did this.**
Δοῦλοι and οἰκοδεσπότης correspond and indicate a wealthy
landowner who had many slaves on his estate.    The
subordinate action is expressed by the participle.
They are surprised to see the grain full of darnel.    It
is an uncalled for remark to say that even the dullest
farmhand would know how the darnel got into the
grain.    Dastardly acts such as that of the ἐχθρὸς
ἄνθρωπος, "an inimical fellow," were not so common,
and someone might have tampered with the good seed.
The question and the answer bring out the flagrant
nature of this enemy and of his act.

28)    **And the slaves say to him, Wilt thou, then,
that we go and gather them up?    But he said: No;
lest by gathering up the darnel you root up together
with it the grain.    Let both grow together until the
harvest, and at the season of the harvest I will say
to the harvesters, Gather up first the darnel and
bind it in bundles for burning it up.    But the grain
gather up into my storeroom.**    Θέλεις is not a substitute for the future, "shall we gather up," but
inquires after the owner's will, R. 878, and is joined
to the deliberative subjunctive συλλέξωμεν without a
connective, R. 924, 935.    These slaves are entirely subject to their lord yet show their personal interest in his
property.

29)    When οὔ is used in the sense of "no" it receives an accent, R. 1154; and only here is ἅμα used
as a preposition.    So concerned is the landowner
about the wheat that he will not risk having any of
it uprooted when the darnel is removed.

30)    The darnel does not worry him, he will take
care of it in due time.    We have ἄφετε combined with
the infinitive, here an aorist, "do you let both finish
growing."    In τοῦ θερισμοῦ and τοῖς θερισταῖς we have

a case of natural wordplay; also in δήσατε εἰς δέσμας
(some texts omit εἰς, "bind bundles"). We must,
however, recall the Oriental fashion of reaping either
by means of sickles only, or by pulling up the grain
with the hands roots and all — in 1925 the writer saw
such grain with its roots pulled by hand in Palestine.
In either way of reaping it would be easy to cull out
the darnel. And that is what πρῶτον means: "first
the darnel." The idea is not that the wheat but that
the darnel would be culled out. And while binding
into bundles suggests the presence of much darnel,
the picking out the darnel first suggests even more
wheat. The aorists in the command to the harvesters
are effective (R. 835), they look to the end of the
action: gathered and tied up to the last bundle. Πρὸς
τό with the infinitive is one way of expressing purpose:
"to burn them up." The interpretation of the parable
follows in v. 36, etc.

31) **Another parable he placed before them
saying** (see v. 24), **Like is the kingdom of the
heavens to a mustard kernel which a man, having
taken, sowed in his field. It, indeed, is smaller than
all the seeds yet, when it has finished growing, is
greater than the vegetables and becomes a tree, so
that the birds of the heavens come and go tenting in
its branches.** Again a seed is used as an illustration, not, however, one of wheat or of barley but of
the mustard plant, *Sinapis nigra,* the garden variety,
since it is compared with garden vegetables, and not
*Salvadora persica,* the mustard tree. The kingdom
(see 3:2) is like a mustard kernel because, like it,
the rule of Christ's grace among men has a phenomenal
growth from the tiniest beginning. Instead of the
ὡμοιώθη used in v. 24, Jesus from now on uses the form
ὁμοία ἐστίν. The parable is very evident once it is
stated: yet who of us would have detected the resemblance without having our attention called to it?

The comparison becomes the more striking when we see that this mustard kernel is Christ himself, for the entire kingdom grows from him as the King. Some think that the mustard seed was chosen for this parable, not only because of its size, but also because of its pungent taste. "Its heat, its fiery vigor, the fact that only through being bruised it gives out its best virtue, and all this under so insignificant an appearance and in so small a compass," Trench thinks, may have prompted the choice. In the parable, however, the point of comparison is *the growth* of this small seed.

If the mustard kernel is Christ, then the man who planted the kernel cannot again be Christ, as has been thought in view of John 12:24. This man is surely the Father who *gave* his only-begotten Son and *sent* him that the world might be saved, John 3:16, 17. The field (Luke has "garden") is the world, which is God's because he made it although sin has filled it with weeds, briars, and stones. Luke seems to have a more specific sense in mind. Christ was planted in the *world* by being planted in the *garden* of Israel; salvation for the world is "of the Jews," John 4:22. By special cultivation God made Israel his garden. The circumstantial participle λαβών is not without meaning. The kernel did not come from the field, nor was it dropped accidentally, compare λαβοῦσα in v. 33.

32) The neuter ὅ may refer to the masculine antecedent and disregard its gender. Jesus is speaking of the seeds that were ordinarily planted in ancient gardens, hence the remark that botanists know about many seeds that are still smaller is pointless. Μικρότερον is the comparative "smaller" not the superlative "least" (R. V.).

Think of the little Babe in Bethlehem, of Christ's small following when his work seemed to have come

to an end by his death. In this despised corner of
the world, from a carpenter's home, came a teacher
who gathered a handful of unlettered, ordinary disciples, then fell into the hands of his enemies and
died a wretched malefactor's death. This was no
tower of Babel, nothing big in the eyes of the
world. Yet this was the kingdom that was to
encircle the world and is to shine in glory forever.
I Cor. 1:27, 28.

The passive aorist subjunctive αὐξηθῇ is to be understood in the middle sense, and the aorist points to
the end of the growing: "when it has finished growing" (the English prefers the perfect). The clause
is prophetic of the vast extent of the coming growth.
"Greater (not 'the greatest,' A. V.) than the vegetables" compares the kingdom with all other religious
growths, none of which equals this kingdom. Read
the fine description in Ezek. 17:22-24. This little
kernel actually "becomes a tree," and one of such
size that the wild birds (called "birds of the heavens")
come (aorist to indicate the arrival) and go tenting
in its branches (present tense to picture their sheltered stay). Only their stay is mentioned and not
their eating of the seeds of this mustard tree. Since
the mustard tree itself is the kingdom, all who belong to the kingdom are part of this tree. The wild
birds who also go tenting in it are not members of
the kingdom but men in general who find the church
beneficial and enjoy its beneficent influence in the
world. The infinitives with ὥστε are here used to
express actual, and not merely intended, result,
R. 1000.

This parable shows the kingdom in its *visible*
growth. A number of thoughts are directly involved
or necessarily implied. The power of this kingdom
is *divine*. It is *a living organism,* and its life and its
power are *undying* — all other growths of earth have

the germs of decay and death in them. The growth
continues *throughout time* (24:14). As long as God's
kingdom was present in God's Old Testament believers, it was confined to them; this parable describes
*the kingdom in the New Testament* where it is uncon-
fined and spreads over the whole world. *Vital growth*
is described and not outward organization which
boasts great numbers (the ideal of Rome and of not
a few Protestants). The kingdom, being Christ's rule
of grace, is always *spiritual*. This spirituality, however, is itself power, and, although it is invisible,
it makes its presence manifest in many outward
and visible ways. This parable stimulates *faith*,
encourages us in our *work*, and fills us with *hope
and joy*.

33) **Another parable he uttered for them, Like
is the kingdom of the heavens to leaven which a
woman, having taken, hid in three measures of flour
until they were completely leavened.** This and the
preceding parable evidently form a pair. Matthew's
introductory formula is slightly varied. Leaven or
yeast (ζύμη, from ζέω, to ferment) is used extensively
in an evil sense to portray something that corrupts.
Jesus uses it thus in Luke 12:1, and St. Paul in
I Cor. 5:7, 8; Gal. 5:9. It is impossible to use leaven
in this sense when picturing the kingdom. This time
leaven pictures the good power of Christ's rule of
grace which secretly yet effectively produces its beneficent results. "Lion" is thus used in an evil sense
(I Pet. 5:8), again in a noble one (Rev. 5:5);
"serpent," likewise (Rev. 20:2, compared with 3:14);
"dove" (silly, in Hos. 7:11; harmless, in Matt. 10:16).
The world has many ferments, all of which are decom-
posing and destructive; Christ and his gospel (or in his
gospel) alone penetrate with beneficent power.

Just as in the parable recorded in Luke 15:8, "a
woman" cannot be the same as "a man" in v. 31. The

latter is the Father, the former is the church, to whom the gospel of the kingdom is committed, to do with it what is here described. The idea that the woman pictures the divine Wisdom of Prov. 9:1-3, or the Holy Ghost is unsatisfactory. It would be lacking good taste to picture the Spirit as a woman.

The participle λαβοῦσα, like its counterpart in v. 31, is more than "picturesque vernacular" (R. 1110). It indicates that this leaven came from elsewhere, not from this earth, and that the act of mixing it with the flour was deliberate and done with specific intention. It was not a mere impulse that led this woman to put the yeast into the flour. The church preaches the gospel with most intelligent purpose. The verb ἐνέκρυψεν εἰς (the preposition is static and merely means "in") says more than that the yeast was mixed with the flour. The yeast disappeared completely, it worked *secretly, invisibly,* like a power that is wholly hidden from view. In his gospel Christ works mysteriously, gradually, spreading silently. We have the history of the gospel's permeating the ancient Roman world until even the emperor became a Christian. Its greater work, however, were the unseen inner changes, the removing of superstition, social evils, vice, and the lifting of all it touched to a higher plane. The church just applies the gospel, and through it the leavening takes place. This does not mean that the church is to enter the fields of politics, sociology, or public reform. When this is attempted, she loses her power. The yeast does not work in that way. To many this process seems too slow and so they "take" something to hasten the working of the leaven along, thereby only hindering its silent, steady progress of fermentation.

A *saton,* Hebrew *se'ah,* the third part of an *epha,* is about $1\frac{1}{2}$ peck, and three *sata* was the quantity used by Sarah in Gen. 18:6. Many fancies have been associated with the number three: the three sons of

Noah; the three parts of the world as then known;
Greeks, Jews, Samaritans; spirit, soul, and body; or
simply the usual quantity of flour used for an ordinary
baking — although the woman must have had a large
family to require a baking of over a bushel of flour!
It seems best to follow Gen. 18:6; Judg. 6:19;
I Sam. 1:24, all of which mention the same quantity,
and to combine with this flour what lies in ὅλον:
although the baking used up no less than an
entire *epha* of flour, the whole of it was completely leavened.

The aorist "was leavened" is prophecy. What shall
come to pass Jesus states as already having been
accomplished. Yet the verb must not be stressed to
mean that all men in the whole world will eventually
be converted and saved. This would confuse the
woman and the flour. Chiliasm finds no support in
this parable. It describes the silent, beneficent influence of the gospel in the world. We may instance
many points: the overthrow of slavery, the improved
status of woman, the appreciation of the child, the
abolition of many barbarous practices, etc. Any land
in which the gospel has an opportunity to exert its
influence is raised to a higher level.

Here again ye see *divine* power; again it is wholly
*spiritual*, and, while it operates altogether *invisibly*,
produces any number of tangible effects, every one of
them being *wholesome*. The gospel cannot but *succeed*, and the one work of the church is to preach,
teach, and spread it in the world. The parable teaches
faith, patience, hope, and joy. A perfect progression
of thought runs through the four parables, showing
that their order cannot be changed. First, the kingdom in its *breadth*, for the Sower casts his seed to
the ends of the earth; next, the kingdom in its *length*,
all grows until the final harvest; third, the kingdom
in its *height*, the mustard seed becomes a tree that

is higher than all else in the field or the garden; finally,
the kingdom in its *depth,* penetrating all lands and all
nations (Besser).

34) **These things all Jesus uttered in parables
to the multitudes, and without parables he was
uttering nothing to them in order that it might
be fulfilled what was spoken through the prophet
saying,**

> **I will open my mouth in parables;**
> **I will speak out what has been hidden from
> the world's foundation.**

The doubling of the statement is for the sake of
emphasis: nothing was spoken to the crowds at this
time except in parables. But ταῦτα πάντα, which is not
the same as πάντα or πάντα ταῦτα (R. 705), informs us that
"the mysteries of the kingdom of the heavens" (v. 11),
these, though, indeed, all of them, were uttered in parables. Why Jesus used parables he himself explains
in v. 10-17; here Matthew adds the detail that this mode
of utterance was in accord with prophecy. The aorist
ἐλάλησεν states the fact as such; the imperfect ἐλάλει lets
it unroll before our eyes like a moving picture.

35) On Matthew's formula of quotation see 1:22.
The attempt of Zahn to substantiate the reading:
"through the prophet *Isaiah,*" which would permit
Matthew or some ancient copyist to say that Ps. 78:2
was spoken by one who did not speak it, is frustrated
by the weight of textual authority and much else.
"Isaiah" was introduced from 3:3; 4:14; 8:17; 12:17.
Jerome's substitution of "Asaph" for "Isaiah," does not
establish what Matthew originally wrote; nor does the
scoffing remark of Porphyrius. The fact that Asaph is
called "a prophet" (*hachozeh,* "seer," LXX, προφήτης),
as is actually done in II Chron. 29:30, just as Acts 2:30
calls David a prophet, does not make him the writer "of
a prophetical book," as Zahn contends; and therefore

to quote from him without naming him is certainly not proof that Matthew wrote "Isaiah" by mistake. Aside from Inspiration, the honest assumption would be that Matthew made no mistake such as this; and another equally strong assumption would be that, if he had, those about him would have detected and at once corrected it.

Asaph's second line reads, "I will utter dark sayings (*chidoth,* riddles) of old," which Matthew renders in his own way. Asaph defines *mashal* by *chidah,* "a pointed, pithy saying," "a riddle." His psalm shows that he drew these from Israel's history, and they all had a meaning for the people for whom he composed this psalm. The parable is both a *mashal* and a *chidah,* a form of presentation long known to the Jews.

Asaph was a type of Jesus, and in this sense his word is a prophecy. This does not imply that Asaph said that the Messiah would do what he was doing, but the implication is that what Asaph was doing would be repeated and far more perfectly done by Jesus. Divinely intended correspondences, such as this, antitype crowning type, are classed as prophecy and fulfillment in the Scriptures (see 3:17, 18). Asaph says *'abbi'ah,* "I will bubble forth" riddles; Matthew has ἐρεύξομαι, "I will spit or spue out," a rough word, but one that like σκύλλω, τρώγω, χορτάζω, was greatly softened by use: "I will utter aloud," and thus it is contrasted with κεκρυμμένα, "things hidden," that one would pass on only in secret. But even then, unless one had the key (v. 11, 12), these things would be and remain only riddles to him. This brings out the two features of parables: they are unsolved riddles to some (unbelievers) but are highly illuminating illustrations for those having or receiving the solutions (believers).

The kingdom began "of old." Asaph refers to things that were taken from Israel's history only. So

Matthew writes "from the world's foundation." This is not a free translation, as it is usually termed. It is a frank statement of what the type means regarding the antitype. Asaph's "dark sayings of old" were for Jesus "things hidden from the world's foundation." They were in God's mind and plan so early, at the time of the very birth of creation and of the kingdom, but were kept hidden until they were now uttered aloud by Jesus, and even then they are still hidden from the unworthy but are seen and received by the disciples.

36) **Then, dismissing the multitudes, he went into the house; and his disciples came to him, saying, Make clear to us the parable of the darnel of the field.** Jesus returned to his own home, whence he had come (v. 1). Here, in private, he expounded everything to his disciples, Mark 4:34. Verse 10, etc., was spoken in this house. The disciples asked especially to have the parable of the darnel made clear to them.

37) **And he answered** (see 4:15) **and said, The one sowing the excellent seed is the Son of man; and the field is the world; and the excellent seed, these are the sons of the kingdom.** The exposition states with all clearness just what the imagery of the parable means. Fault has been found with the exposition because it does not stop with this but goes on into a description of the judgment (v. 40-43). Critics call these verses additions made by Matthew, the very language being like that of Matthew, etc. But the climax of the parable is, indeed, the final judgment. There is no law that would prevent a teacher from elaborating on any point, to say nothing of the main point. The language Matthew uses is the language he learned from Jesus. The *ethical* object of this parable should be kept in mind, just as the ethical purpose of the first parable was in the foreground of Jesus' thinking. Jesus wants *you* to ask *yourself*, "What kind

of soil *am I?*" So here, "Am *I* a son of the kingdom
or a son of wickedness?" and, "How will *I* fare at the
final harvest?" We may also remember that Judas
was one of the Twelve. All the teaching of Jesus, however, clear and lucid as it is intellectually, has an
ethical or spiritual aim, i. e., it seeks to save.

That the sower should here be "the Son of man"
(see at length on 8:20) is what we expect. This title
also fittingly describes his work: he who is man and
yet infinitely more than man fills the world with believers.

38) Of supreme importance is the statement that
the field is ὁ κόσμος, "the world," and, therefore, not "the
church." This is so vital because it excludes two
serious errors: the one, that the sons of wickedness
may remain undisturbed in the congregation (no
church discipline, no expulsion) ; the other, that the
sons of wickedness may be removed from the world
(the use of the sword against heretics, either by the
church herself or by her use of secular power). When
Jesus forbids his *douloi* to go out into the field to pull
up the darnel he does not forbid church discipline
(18:17-19; I Cor. 5:3-5) ; what he forbids is that these
*douloi* do what is reserved for the angels and the final
judgment. The remarkable thing is that "the excellent
seed are the sons of the kingdom," not the Word or
the gospel but persons, true believers. They are placed
into the world by the King who rules this domain. The
parable itself does not deal with regeneration and the
origin and birth of these sons; that is not illustrated.

Jesus does not call them members or subjects of
the kingdom, for these terms do not fit the idea of his
kingdom and substitute for it the ideas we connect with
mere earthly kingdoms. He does not even use τέκνα,
"children," but υἱοί, "sons," which term always involves
a legal right, the right of inheritance. As sons we are
princes of the kingdom not subjects; the kingdom is

ours by inheritance. We ourselves are kings and rule in this kingdom (I Pet. 2:9; Rev. 1:6; 5:10; see the author's *Kings and Priests*). Christ's rule of grace here on earth places such kings into the earth or world at this time.

**But the darnel are the sons of the wickedness.** We might translate, "of the wicked one" (our versions), but "of the kingdom" is abstract and not personal "of the King," so we make also the other statement abstract. And the wicked one is not so named in the next verse but is called "the devil." Here νἱοί has the same idea of legal right and inheritance. These people are not merely the unregenerate in the world, sinners as they are by nature. Then the entire parable would be difficult to interpret. All men are such sinners at the start, even those who afterward are made sons of the kingdom. The parable deals with two opposite sowings: the one establishes sons of the kingdom everywhere; the other, the direct opposite of these, men who reject the kingdom. They have met the kingdom, have been touched by its powers of grace, and have turned from it, preferring wickedness instead (John 3:17-21).

It required a special sowing on the devil's part to scatter the sons of wickedness among the sons of the kingdom. Not until after Christ had sown did the devil do this sowing. And that explains why the two kinds of sons are always found side by side. Satan never sows his sons off in a corner of the world by themselves. While both genitives are, of course, possessive: *belonging* to the kingdom — to the wickedness, they are at the same time qualitative: *characterized* by Christ's rule — by the influence of the wickedness.

39) **And the enemy that sowed it is the devil. And the harvest is the consummation of the world-age** (αἰών, see v. 22). **And the reapers are angels.** On Judas, as sowed by Satan, compare John 6:70, 71;

13:27; Luke 22:3; on Ananias, Acts 5:3. It is the harvest as such, the final judgment, which forms the συντέλεια, "the completion," when all things shall reach their goal and end. When saying that "angels" are the reapers, Jesus cannot intend to assert that they will be competent to distinguish the wheat from the darnel, for the slaves were quite able to do this when they reported to their lord. The point is that the separation is to be delayed until the end of the world and is not to take place before that time. At the last day the *douloi* will be part of the wheat over against the darnel. Thus the angels, who are throughout the Scriptures represented as the ministers of the judgment, shall do both: tie up the darnel for the burning and carry the wheat into the storeroom.

40) Jesus dwells on the fate of the darnel, thereby impressing it on the disciples so that everyone might search his own heart for secret unbelief. **Just as, therefore, the darnel is gathered up and burnt up with fire, so will it be in the consummation of the world-age.** There will be just such a gathering up of darnel and just such a burning up with fire. In v. 30 only the verb is used, here in the interpretation the noun "fire" is added, and even more is said in v. 42.

41) Let no disciple be uneasy. Jesus tells him how he will attend to the sons of wickedness when the time comes. **The Son of man will commission his angels, and they shall gather up out of his kingdom all the offenses and those that work lawlessness and shall throw them into the furnace of fire. There shall be the wailing and the gnashing of the teeth.** Here "the Son of man," to whom the final judgment is committed (John 5:22, 27), appears in all his divine power and majesty, commanding the angels that are "his" to cleanse the kingdom that is also "his." This King and Judge tells the disciples in advance just what he will have done; ἀποστελεῖ is voluntative not merely

futuristic. "Out of his kingdom" refers to the kingdom as it now exists in the world where it is like gold
mixed with dross. The preposition ἐκ does not imply
that the darnel, cheat, and cockle, are part of the wheat,
R. 598.

There is a tendency to read the neuter πάντα τὰ
σκάνδαλα as a reference to persons because "those that
work lawlessness" are persons. This is correct in so far
as the offenses are part of the lawlessness perpetrated
by these persons. What Jesus says is that their entrapments as well as they themselves shall be finally
and completely gathered up out of the kingdom they
have helped to distress. The remarks on σκανδαλίζεται in
v. 21 apply to the noun as well. The plural "all the
things that entrap," i.e., are liable to catch and destroy
the godly, is summed up in a unit by ἡ ἀνομία. The
plural speaks of what these actions are with reference
to the godly, to which the singular adds what they are
in regard to God, the contradiction of his law, which is
the expression of his holy will.

42) These men, with all the works that make them
what they are, the mighty angels of the Son of man
"shall throw into the furnace of the fire," the two articles leaving nothing indefinite as to what furnace or
what fire are here referred to. "Whatever 'the furnace of fire' may mean here, or 'the lake of fire' (Rev.
19:20; 21:8), 'the fire that is not quenched' (Mark
9:44), 'the everlasting fire' (Matt. 25:41; Luke 16:24;
Mal. 4:1), elsewhere, this at all events is certain, that
they point to some doom so intolerable that the Son of
God came down from heaven and tasted all the bitterness of death that he might deliver us from ever knowing the secrets of anguish, which, unless God be mocking men with empty threats, are shut up in these terrible words: 'there shall be wailing and gnashing of
teeth' (22:13)." Trench. Those who in some way —
no matter how — eliminate from the Scriptures the

terrors here described, plus all that they say concerning
Satan and the demon kingdom, destroy the entire structure of the Scripture and with hell and the devil
eliminate the very Savior who delivers from both.   On
weeping and gnashing of teeth see 8:12, and note
22:13; 24:51; 25:30; Luke 13:28.   The statement is
stereotyped, and the anguish described includes the
bodies of the damned, hence implies their bodily resurrection.   The descriptions of hell are necessarily figurative to a large extent (note "the furnace"), as are
also the descriptions of heaven, because the realities
transcend all human experience.   Like the parable of
the Sower, this about the Tares is heavy with warning.

43) But the end is bright with hope and joy.
**Then the righteous shall shine forth as the sun in
the kingdom of their Father.   He that has ears, let
him be hearing!**   "Then" means: when the final
separation takes place.   "The righteous" are "the
wheat" of v. 30.   The term δίκαιοι, which is always forensic, denotes those who possess the quality of righteousness by virtue of having the divine verdict in their
favor, that verdict pronouncing their acquittal.   See
5:20 on this righteousness.   Note ἐκ in the verb: from
within the righteous a wonderful light shall shine
"out."   The glory that became theirs when they were
declared righteous shall at last break forth as did the
glory of Jesus at the time of his Transfiguration
(17:2).   The expression is modeled after Dan. 12:3,
"sun" being substituted for "brightness of the firma-
ment."   Read I John 3:2.   The Scriptures constantly
connect fire with darkness, the devil, and hell, and light
and its shining with God, Christ, and heaven.   "Like
the sun" brings in a simile that is taken from an earthly
phenomenon to portray what is beyond our experience.
Yet we think of the sun's brilliance and splendor!   The
kingdom a moment ago called that of the Son of man,
is now called that "of their Father," making all the

righteous princes and inheritors of this kingdom ("sons," v. 38). When that glorious day arrives, then shall be fulfilled Isa. 52:1; 60:21; Rev. 22:14, 15, and many other promises.

As he did in v. 9, but now at the end of the exposition of this parable, Jesus calls on him who has ears to use them. Both parable and exposition need open and receptive ears, different from those mentioned in v. 13. The divine instruction and illumination calls upon all our faculties, plus the will that directs their use. The durative present imperative calls for no mere single act but for a constant attitude, and every word Jesus utters operates to produce and to justify that attitude.

44) How Jesus came to add these three parables we see from v. 51, 52. **Like is the kingdom of the heavens to a treasure having been hidden in a field, which a man, having found, hid, and for the joy of it he goes and sells all whatever he has and buys that field.** Ὁμοία ἐστίν indicates a parable, and the likeness is always found in the whole action then described. The four preceding parables show how the kingdom is bestowed (sowing seed) and how it operates (growing, permeating). Now Jesus shows how it is acquired. On the kingdom see 3:2, and note that this and the following parable describe how one becomes an *owner* of this kingdom; on "sons of the kingdom" see v. 38.

The points of the parable are: treasure — hidden — field — finding — securing ownership. The practice of hiding great treasure, such as gold and jewels, was far more frequent in ancient days, especially in the East, due to war, changes of rulers, and the like. Trench reports that men of wealth often divided their wealth into three parts: one for doing business, another part converted into precious stones with which to flee, if necessary, a third part to be buried in a safe place. Thus it could happen that someone died, and with that all trace of the buried hoard was lost until by accident another stumbled upon it.    That is the situation in this parable.

The perfect participle has its usual present implication: "having been hidden" and thus being still hidden. The likeness does not lie merely in the tremendously valuable treasure as such but in this treasure being hidden away where no one would supect it to be, buried in an open field.    The term "treasure" is comprehensive, so that we may think of all the precious things in the kingdom: righteousness, pardon, peace, etc., all that is spiritually priceless.    The *tertium comparationis* stops with the hiding and does not extend back to the owner.    He hid it for himself in a place where he alone could find it, and he is now long dead and gone, nor is his connection with the hidden treasure any longer known.

God's treasure, hidden, indeed, is to be found by us (11:25; Col. 4:3, 4; Luke 19:42) ; his connection with the treasure remains and is obvious the moment it is uncovered. "In the field" thus serves two purposes. As part of the imagery it fits the man who buried the treasure, for it is most unlikely that others would hunt for his treasure there.    As regards the reality the field brings out the thought that God did not hide his treasure far off in the heavens where no human being could even come near it but in a common, lowly place, where it could, indeed, be found, but certainly not by the earthly wise, proud, and self-sufficient.    I Cor. 1:27-29, also v. 22-25.    B.-D. 255, 1 calls the article in the phrase "in the field" incorrect; but we may certainly regard it as the generic article.    In this case, however, the article does not refer to some field; Jesus has a very specific field in mind just as did the human owner who selected just this and no other field.

The field is undoubtedly the Scriptures, John 5:39. The fact that the field is bought is not an objection, for **buying denotes the real, true appropriation of the**

Scriptures once a man knows the treasure they contain.
Since the church has the Scriptures, we may add her
preaching and her teaching when interpreting the field.
How plain, common, ordinary is this Scripture field!
Many walk over it again and again in their reading or
in their hearing and find precious little in it. But the
great treasure is there. And lo, "a man," ἄνθρωπος,
found it. He was just "a man," one of the "whosoever" so often named in the Scriptures. These terms
are really blank spaces in which you are to write your
name. Follow the word "find" in John 1:41, etc. You
will see that this finding excludes all human merit and
effort. Its divine counterpart is giving. It seems
accidental, this finding. Was the man merely walking
across the field, or was he hired to work in it? No
matter — he found. God placed the treasure, led the
man to it (John 6:44, 65), and so he found it.

The man's actions are dramatically described: he
hid the treasure, and for the joy of it goes and sells all
he has and buys that field. Just why the aorist ἔκρυψεν
should be gnomic (B.-D. 333; R. 837) is difficult to see;
this is certainly not due to the fact that it is followed
by vivid present tenses. This aorist is just as little
gnomic as is its attendant participle εὑρών. This aorist
tells us what the man did in this case (historical aorist)
not what happens in every case of this kind (gnomic).
His whole action is directed toward securing the treasure and doing that in a legitimate way, because the
kingdom can be secured in no other way. He covers
the treasure instead of carrying it off surreptitiously.
Then, his heart being filled with joy because of his tremendous find, he goes and buys the field, making the
treasure legally and rightfully his. The moral obliquity that some find in this action and in its employ-
ment by Jesus does not exist, because the whole presentation intends to describe the very opposite. Since
the owner of the treasure is dead and forgotten, who

according to law or to morals has a claim to the treasure except this happy finder?

The field was not so high in price but what the man, selling all that he had (see this repeated in v. 46), could buy it. Purposely Jesus says that he sold "all whatever he has." See Phil. 3:7, 8. The Scriptures know of two extraordinary ways of buying: one is, without money or price, Isa. 55:1; Rev. 21:6; the other is to give up for the sake of the eternal treasures of God all that would prevent our possessing them. Both are the same, for both imply the acceptance of God's gift, the latter adding only the thought that the vessel must be empty so that God's grace and gift may fill it. The field, not the treasure, is bought. Both the value of the treasure and its being without an owner that might be reached, precludes its being bought. Christ and the treasures of salvation shut out any and all payment and purchase on our part. But by giving up every self-made, human doctrine and philosophy, however deep these may seem to be, we may make the Word our own and in and with it all the treasures of salvation.

45) Because the preceding parable could not bring out all the points concerned in acquiring the kingdom, Jesus adds a companion parable in order to cover especially these points. **Again, like is the kingdom of the heavens to a merchantman seeking excellent pearls; and having found one pearl of great price, he went away, has sold whatever he had, and bought it.** "Again" introduces this as a second comparison. "Like to a treasure" and "like to a merchantman" are only formal differences because the likeness consists in the actions: what is done by the man regarding the treasure, and what the merchant does regarding the pearl. An ἔμπορος is a wholesale merchant, one who travels (ἐν plus πόρος) and imports, and ἄνθρωπος is pleonastic, like our "merchantman"; the opposite is κάπηλος, a retailer or a peddler. This wealthy merchant is

out to acquire "excellent pearls," it being his business
to deal in them.   In order to appreciate this point one
must know the esteem in which pearls were held by the
ancients, sums almost incredible being paid for a single
pearl when it was a perfect specimen of its kind.  Great
skill was required to gauge the value of a pearl, noting
its defects in shape, tint, smoothness, etc.

There was evidently a difference between "a man"
mentioned in v. 44, a mere ordinary peasant or laborer,
of whom the world has a large number, and this rich
merchant, whose profession it was to inspect and to
buy pearls in foreign cities, a man such as the world
has but few.   The "excellent pearls" he seeks represent
all the higher things of this earthly life which are
prized accordingly by men: philanthropy, humanitarian
work, peace, moral living, justice, better social conditions, science, art, and the like.   These pearls this merchantman knew, sought, and bought.

**46)**   But herein he is like the other man: he knew
absolutely nothing of "the pearl of great price," and
the way in which he came upon it is again the same: he
*found* it.   Where, when, and how makes no difference;
it all seems accidental and yet is not.   God lets even
those who seek high things in the world just "find"
Christ.   Alas, most of this class (I Cor. 1:26), poets,
philosophers, literati, scientists, artists, etc., fail to
recognize the priceless pearl when they do stumble upon
it; yet not all.

In the expressions "excellent pearls" and "one pearl
of great price or value" the thought is that Christ and
his salvation are to be ranked with the very highest and
best in this world, they are a pearl among pearls; but
also that this pearl absolutely outranks all other pearls
the world has ever seen.   It is "one" ($\tilde{\epsilon}\nu\alpha$, the numeral) ; there is and can be no second.   Note that here
the unity is stressed, whereas in treasure the multi-
plicity of spiritual values is indicated.   Each idea is

a necessary complement of the other. This pearl is really beyond all price, beyond any possible equivalent. In the parable this is reduced to a very great price, otherwise the likeness would be destroyed.

The sequence of the verb forms found in this verse is highly interesting although it is impossible to reproduce it in English, which in a wooden way eliminates all the psychological play of the imagination in the shading of the Greek forms and reduces everything to drab past tenses (R. 847). The momentary act of finding, subordinate to what follows, is the aorist participle εὑρών, likewise the act of hurrying away ἀπελθών. Then the vivid dramatic historical perfect πέπρακεν (R. 900): "he has already sold," not one of the common pearls is now left; εἶχε, the imperfect to denote the long while he was in possession of them. And finally the final, decisive aorist to expres the great fact: ἠγόρασεν, "he bought" — completing everything and bringing it all to rest. The selling has the same force that it had in the other parable (Isa. 55:1; Matt. 25:9, 10; Rev. 3:18; Prov. 23:23). Only an empty vessel can God fill. "Sold" means that his whole heart was transferred from other noble interests to the one supreme interest, Christ. The idea is not that we cannot devote time and attention to great and good earthly interest and at the same time own Christ, but that for good and all these interests leave the soul wholly free for Christ.

We are to understand the imagery properly and must stop where it stops and not go beyond. Thus the buying of the pearl does not deprive another man of its use; for though the pearl is but "one," every one of us is to buy it and to own it irrespective of others. There is nothing in this parable which corresponds to the field in the other, the Word being sufficiently illustrated there.

47) The last one of the seven parables is not the last link in this chain only but reaches back through

all the previous parables and in one comprehensive
sweep presents the kingdom (see 3:2) from its beginning to its end. **Again, like is the kingdom of
the heavens to a seine that was thrown into the
sea and collected of every kind; which, when it was
filled, having hauled up on the beach and having
sat down, they gathered together the excellent into
vessels while the worthless they threw outside.** The
σαγήνη, "seine" or "dragnet," is the largest kind of net,
weighted below with corks on top, sweeping perhaps a
half mile of water, the opposite of the small ἀμφίβληστρον,
or casting net, mentioned in 4:18. The two aorist participles, like the temporal clause in v. 48, describe the
net after its work has been accomplished: "it was
thrown out and it did collect" all kinds of fish. This
net is the gospel. The sea is the world, and "of every
kind" means: some (partitive ἐκ) of every kind, race,
type, social and intellectual grade of men. Being the
gospel, the net belongs to God or Christ and, of course,
is handled by all who promulgate the gospel, i. e., the
church. But the parable omits mention of these, as
not belonging in the picture at this time. To bring
them in, nevertheless, spoils the whole comparison, for
all the members and the pastors of the church are also
the fish caught in the net.

What the first three parables picture as sowing, the
fourth as leavening, is here pictured as catching in a
net, and this catching takes in the entire work of the
gospel — the whole of it is one great sweep of the net
through the waters of the sea. The picture is not that
of repeated casting.

48) Note the success of this grand sweep of the
net: "it was filled." The gospel does its work. What
now follows is an ordinary scene of the activities of
fishermen: the net hauled to the beach, the fishermen
sitting down and picking out all the edible and salable
fish, throwing them into vessels and throwing all the

worthless fish "outside," on the ground. The subject is again left indefinite because the comparison lies not in the persons who do all this but in the acts alone. The net is hauled up on the beach; the gospel era and work are done. When we note the natural limitations of every comparison, we shall not think of dragging the net through every ocean, lake, and river of the world in order to secure the universality of gospel grace.

The "vessels" (ἀγγεῖα) are the counterpart of the "storeroom" in v. 30, the "many mansions" (John 14:2), the everlasting habitations (Luke 16:9). As the opposite of καλός, σαπρός cannot mean "rotten." We have seen this when trees and their fruit were the subjects in 7:17, 18, and here the same word is used with regard to fish. The word means "worthless," and what it implies Jesus himself explains.

49) **Thus shall it be in the consummation of the world-age** (see v. 40) : **the angels shall go out and shall separate the wicked from the righteous and shall throw them into the furnace of the fire; there shall be the wailing and the gnashing of the teeth.** The Lord's exposition deals with what shall happen at the consummation, for all that precedes this has already been made plain. The net and its great catch are brought in as being necessary to understand what happens at the end. When they are fishing, the fishermen handle the net and pick out the good fish. But the gospel is preached by the church, and the separation of the godly from the wicked is made by the angels. The fact that the latter belongs to the angels is the constant teaching of the Scriptures (25:32, 33). The all-sufficient reason is that the entire church is a part of those who are to be separated.

Τὰ σαπρά, "the worthless (fish)," are οἱ πονηροί, "the wicked"; and τὰ καλά, "the excellent (fish)," are οἱ δίκαιοι, "the righteous." In what sense the former are wicked the second term shows: they lack the righteousness that avails before God. The parable deals with all those who are caught by the great gospel net. All kinds and conditions of men are swept into its meshes, but these are of two classes. Here on earth both are mixed together in the outward body of the church. They all confess and profess faith, but not all are *vere credentes* and thus pronounced "righteous" by the divine Judge. Some are hypocrites, sham Christians, mere adherents of the church, etc. Church discipline cannot eliminate them, for we cannot judge men's hearts. The demands of Donatistic minds are failures of the worst kinds. The other extreme is the liberalism which discards the Scriptural church discipline. Therefore in two of these first seven parables (v. 24, etc.) Jesus points us to the consummation with its divine separation of the false Christians from the true. In ἀφοριοῦσι note the preposition ἀπό which is followed by the compound preposition ἐκ μέσου; the separation is "from" in the sense of taking the wicked "out of the midst" of the righteous (R. 578, 648). These wicked are the ones that shall be done away with as being "worthless." In v. 30 the darnel is "first" collected and tied in bundles. The imagery used requires this dealing first with the wicked; yet it agrees with 25:32, 33.

50) The fate of only the wicked is here described, and this is done by repeating v. 42 (which see). This means that, in addition to the instruction which it conveys, the parable is intended chiefly as a mighty warning. All you who are in contact with the gospel, what kind of fish are you? How will the judgment day find you? What if you should be thrown into that furnace? How some are found to be "excellent" and others "worthless" is not detailed in the imagery, but it is indicated in the exposition. Every proclamation of "the kingdom of the heavens" is a call to repent (3:2; 4:17) and to accept the righteousness by faith in Christ (5:20) and thus to become "righteous." The

wickedness of "the wicked" lies in this very point; outwardly they accept the gospel but inwardly they refuse to repent and to rest their faith on Christ. They are like the hard path, the rocky soil, the briar patch in v. 4, etc. See v. 23, also the last paragraph.

51) This group of parables had reached its end. The fact that there are seven seems to be intentional, this sacred number symbolizing the kingdom (three to present God in his rule of grace plus four to show the world of men to whom this rule comes). The idea that they represent seven periods of history is a fancy. They picture the great work of the gospel-rule of Christ from start to finish, its success and the reason why it fails in some men. Hiding much from the unspiritual, these parables are full of the clearest light for true disciples.

Jesus now asks: **Did you understand these things all?** with the final πάντα (R. 705) inviting any question that might yet be asked; συνήκατε, first aorist, R. 310, 1216. **They answer him, Yes.**

52) **And he said to them, For this reason every scribe, trained as a disciple of the kingdom of the heavens, is like to a houselord who brings forth out of his treasure things new and old.** With διὰ τοῦτο Jesus refers to what he has accomplished in his disciples, having brought them to the understanding they have just acknowledged. In effect Jesus says, "This is what makes each of you like a houselord who," etc. But he states it in the third person and thus objectively — perhaps he was thinking of Judas. The title "scribe," used to designate rabbis who were educated in the law in the peculiar Jewish fashion, is here used in a broad sense to designate anyone who is versed in the Word. This is made evident by the specification "trained as a disciple of the kingdom," etc. The passive μαθητεύομαι with the dative means to become someone's disciple, and the aorist participle one who **has**

graduated as such a disciple (B.-P. 763), gone through the school of the kingdom and imbibed its full spirit. Variant readings with ἐν or εἰς should not lead us to think the dative is locative, as R. 521 supposes. To be "discipled to the kingdom" makes the kingdom the teacher, which is not strange when we know that the kingdom centers in the King.

And now another little parable which is no more than a simile follows. Such a real disciple himself becomes a teacher, the very thing for which Jesus was training the Twelve. He is thus "like a houselord" (ἄνθρωπος being added pleonastically as in v. 45), and ὅστις κτλ., shows in what respect he is like such a man: as these are needed by those of his household, he brings forth out of his treasury things new and old. So the well-trained disciple has acquired a rich fund of all kinds of spiritual knowledge from the kingdom and its King, and puts it forth for use as it is needed. "Things new and old" are by no means only new and old comparisons from nature and the life of man but truths, some new, not known and taught before, others old, long known and often taught, yet the former resting on the latter, hence the two are mentioned in this order.

53) **And it came to pass when Jesus finished these parables he departed thence,** i. e., left Capernaum. Mark 6:1 agrees with this and shows that Luke 4:16, etc., occurred when Jesus was at the height of his ministry as also v. 14, 15 indicate. The first words are the same as those found in 7:28, and in 11:1.

54) **And having come into his native town, he was teaching them in their synagogue, so that they were amazed and said, Whence to this man this wisdom and the works of power?** The πατρίς of Jesus is Nazareth where he had been brought up, Luke 4:16. Here, on a Sabbath (Mark and Luke) he engaged in teaching (ἐδίδασκεν, imperfect) "them," his

old town people. The effect (ὥστε with the infinitive to express actual effect, R. 1091) was utter amazement and the question whence he had this astounding wisdom. When he had left them, they had noted nothing wonderful about him. Luke indicates that Matthew's σοφία refers to the substance as well as to the form of teaching, in particular to what Jesus said concerning himself. They add "the works of power," the miracles (see 11:20-23), of which, at least for the greater part, they had only heard; some may have seen a few miracles wrought in other places.

55) **Is not this the carpenter's son? Is not his mother called Miriam, and his brothers James and Joseph and Simon and Juda? and his sisters, are they not all with us? Whence, then, to him these things all?** A τέκτων, *faber*, is one who makes things out of hard material, but even in the papyri (M.-M. 628) this word always means a carpenter, yet only one who makes furniture, utensils, and house fittings, for in Palestine all houses were constructed of stone. The view that Joseph was a stonemason lacks support. According to Luke he was also mentioned although he had been dead this long time. Mark 6:3: "Is not this the carpenter?" adds only the detail that some knew that Jesus himself had worked at his father's trade. Note the derogatory tone in both τούτῳ (v. 54) and οὗτος, meaning, "How does this fellow set himself up to be so much?"

Matthew writes Μαριάμ, (B.-D. 53, 3) Aramaic *Miryam,* namely Mary. Note that Mark 6:3 unites "son" only with "Mary" and does not connect Joseph with Mary, thus joining Jesus and his mother in a special way. On the ἀδελφοί and the ἀδελφαί see 12:46, the names of the latter are not known. Not long before this time the brothers and Jesus and Mary had moved to Capernaum.

56) The sisters remained πρὸς ἡμᾶς, being married and having settled in their husbands' homes in Nazareth; πᾶσαι reads as though there were at least three. After thus detailing their familiarity with the whole family, these people of Nazareth recur to the question: "Whence, then (considering all these facts), *to this man these things all?*" abutting τούτῳ ταῦτα and adding πάντα (see R. 705).

57) What all these questions and their implied answers involve is stated: **and they were caught in connection with him,** ἐσκανδαλίζοντο ἐν αὐτῷ, as in a trap which is sprung by a crooked stick holding the bait; see v. 21. In a modified sense this verb means that they took offense in connection with Jesus. Knowing him as they did, they could not bring themselves to think that his widom and his works of power were of divine origin, they were sure there was something wrong. The imperfect states that they continued in this offended and hostile attitude.

**But Jesus said to them, A prophet is not honorless except in his native town and his own house or family.** This sounds like a proverbial saying, except for the addition "and his own house." Familiarity breeds contempt. The fact that Jesus here classes himself as a prophet is perfectly in order, for the contempt arose during his teaching. Mark 6:6 adds that he marvelled at their unbelief.˙ The right answer to their question "whence" lay so near the surface that they were wholly without excuse for rejecting it.

58) **And he did not do many works of power there because of their unbelief.** He was ready to do many, as he had done elsewhere, but could do only a few. Note, however, that he did some. It has become traditional to assume that faith precedes every miracle although this tradition is disregarded every time a miracle is wrought where faith is plainly not present (as for instance in 8:28, etc.) How unbelief

prevented the performance of many miracles is shown
in Luke 4:28-38.   The people of Nazareth rose up,
thrust Jesus out of the city, and tried to kill him.

This incident closes the chapter on the parables,
revealing in a glaring way the opposition that had
developed which had also caused him to resort to parables, v. 10, etc.   The whole idea of this chapter is thus
rounded out.   In Nazareth even the sisters of Jesus
and their families refused him faith.

# CHAPTER XIV

## XI

### Christ Hears of the Baptist's Execution and Begins to Withdraw.   Chapter 14

1) **At that season Herod, the tetrarch, heard the report of Jesus and said to his servants: This is John the Baptist; he arose from the dead, and for this reason these works of power are operating in him.** The "season" referred to is the one marked by the growing hostility indicated in the two preceding chapters.   Josephus regularly calls this Herod "Antipas."   His tetrarchy consisted of Galilee and Perea, the two territories that were separated by the Decapolis. Only by courtesy was he styled "king."   Where and how "the report of Jesus" (objective genitive) came to him is of no moment, only his opinion of Jesus is worthy of notice.   On Luke 9:7-9 see the commentaries on Mark and on Luke.

2) This he uttered "to his servants," παῖς being regularly used in this sense also with reference to Jesus as the great servant of Jehovah.   Here Herod's courtiers are evidently referred to.   Superstition and an evil conscience are combined in making this cowardly criminal jump to the conclusion that Jesus, who is now for the first time brought to his attention, is John the Baptist returned from the dead, ἠγέρθη used in the middle sense, and the aorist indicating only the fact as such. That, Herod asserts, explains the miracles reported regarding Jesus; δυνάμεις has its ordinary meaning, "works of power," being followed, as it is, by ἐνεργοῦσιν ἐν αὐτῷ, and αἱ is nearly demonstrative: "these powers," R. 694.

3)    It is now, after the brief reference to John's being in prison (11:2), that Matthew recounts the entire tragic story, appending it to Herod's word about John's resurrection.    **For Herod, having taken John into his power, bound him and placed him in prison because of Herodias, the wife of Philip, his brother.** The aorists report only the facts, and we know no more. John was snatched out of his ministry by Herod's order to some of his minions who carried John away bound as a criminal and lodged him in prison in the fortress Machærus (Josephus, *Ant.* 18, 5, 2), on the southern border of Perea, on the height near the Dead Sea. "Herodias" is a feminine patronymic from "Herod" (Herod the Great), her grandfather. She was the, daughter of Aristobulus, one of the sons of Herod the Great and Mariamne. She first married her uncle, Herod, called Philip, a brother of Aristobulus. This Philip was disinherited through the treachery of his mother and lived privately in Rome with Herodias and their daughter Salome. Herod Antipas was a son of Herod the Great and the Samaritan Malthake and thus a half-uncle of Herodias, and was married to the daughter of Aretas, King of Arabia Petrea. While he was on a visit to Rome, Antipas and Herodias eloped, and the wife of Antipas, not waiting to be divorced, returned to her father, and a war followed between Aretas and Herod Antipas.

An effort has been made to remove "of Philip" from the text, and its presence in Mark 6:17 is called "a historical error" on the assumption that Herod the Great had only one son by the name of Philip. But he had two: one (the husband of Herodias) the son of Mariamne, the high priest Simon's daughter; and the other (the tetrarch) the son of Cleopatra. Salome, the daughter of Herodias, married the tetrarch Philip, her half-uncle. Two of the sons of Herod the Great were also called Antipas. The fact that two half-

brothers were called Philip does not prove the presence
of an error in the text.

4) **For John was saying to him, It is not lawful
for thee to have her.** We should like to know what
lies back of this imperfect and this dative; ἔλεγεν αὐτῷ.
It seems to be improbable that Herod met John, who
spent all his time in the uninhabited wilds. There is
no hint that Herod ever summoned John into his presence; ἔλεγε implies that John said what he did more than
once. Even the personal "for thee" does not necessarily imply that Herod stood or sat before John. It is
probably best to assume that the flagrant sin of Herod
was castigated by John in the course of his preaching
and thus came to the ears of Herod and to those of his
illegal second wife. And it evidently was Herodias
who instigated John's arrest. Mark 6:17 reports that
Herod commissioned his men to go and to capture John.

Herod's crime was a public outrage. The woman
Herodias had first married her own father's brother
and then had run away and lived with the half-brother
of her husband, who thus was also her half-uncle and
who already had a wife. Two marriages were disrupted, and the new union was not a marriage. It was
plain adultery and within the forbidden degrees of con-
sanguinity. Josephus charges Herodias with the intention of confounding her country's institutions. No
wonder John raised his voice although Herod was his
ruler. "To have her" = to have as a wife.

5) **And though ready** (θέλων) **to kill him, he
feared the multitude because they considered him
as a prophet.** Mark 6:19 explains this readiness
as being due to the strong influence of Herodias who
was set on John's death. Herod would have killed John
to satisfy her. Mark also adds a detail to Herod's fear
of the people who considered John a prophet, namely
that Herod himself knew John to be a righteous and a
holy man. Thus Herod was swayed by mixed motives.

Ἔχειν τινά with a predicate, here προφήτην with or without ὡς (R. 481), means "to consider someone something," ὡς here adding, "something in the nature of a prophet" (see also 21:26, 46).

**6)  Now when a birthday celebration of Herod's took place, the daughter of Herodias danced in the midst** (of the company) **and pleased Herod.** The neuter plural γενέσια is used to designate a festive birthday celebration. We expect the genitive absolute, but Matthew has what appears to be a dative absolute. This construction is passed by in R.; B.-D. 200, 3 conjectures that it is a mixture of the genitive absolute with the temporal dative, which is somehow due to copying τοῖς γενεσίοις from Mark 6:21; but this is rather improbable, since Mark wrote *after* Matthew, and no copyist would add the participle, and such a conjectured mixture of constructions is untenable. Zahn thinks the dative tries to reproduce the Latin ablative absolute, which, however, is improbable in the case of a man like Matthew. We simply have the locative dative of time, and the participle is added in order to emphasize the arrival of the time which precipitated the catastrophe. The Jews abhorred the keeping of birthdays as being a pagan custom, but the Herods even outdid the Romans in these celebrations, so that "Herod's birthday' (*Herodis dies*) came to be a proverbial expression for excessive festival display. Mark 6:21 remarks regarding the grand feast.

The climax of the entertainment was the spectacular dancing of Salome, the daughter of Herodias; ἐν τῷ μέσῳ means "in the midst," before the company of guests. The exhibition was thoroughly pagan and had been learned while the girl and her mother lived at Rome with Philip.

**7)**  Herod's delight in the performance carried him completely away: **wherefore he promised with an oath to give her what she might ask.** In ὅθεν we

have the source "whence" the action flowed, here
Herod's pleasure in Salome's dancing. Heated with
wine and excited by the company, the man lost his reason. We must add his desire to make a grandiose
display in the most magnificent royal style. Mark
records the words of the oath. The verb ὡμολόγησεν is
to be construed with the oath: "he made acknowledgment accompanied by (μετά) an oath." First he made
the promise and then acknowledged or sealed it with
an oath, thus making it absolutely irrevocable. A blank
promise as such, no matter how it is to be fulfilled, is
sinful and silly at the same time. An oath added to
such a promise is directly forbidden in Lev. 5:4, etc.
No promise or oath of this kind is binding; when it is
made, it must be confessed as sin (v. 5) and retracted,
and pardon must be sought.

8) **And she, instigated by her mother, says,
Give me here on a platter the head of John the
Baptist.** The present participle may be rendered,
"while under instigation," and it describes tersely what
Mark 6:24 spreads out in detail: the girl running to
her mother, getting the instigation from her, and then
coming quickly to make her request. She never hesitated because of the crime involved and because of the
gruesomeness of such a gory gift. The force of ὧδε,
"right here," is significant; here where all the company
may see in the delivery of the gift that Herod kept his
promise and oath. The same viciousness is manifested
in the request for "the head." Herodias wants the
head, the absolute evidence of John's death, and no mere
promise of John's death at some future day. A πίναξ is
really a "board," and thus any flat dish.

9) **And the king was grieved, yet because of
his oaths and those reclining together at table he
ordered it to be given.** Since he was called "king"
only by courtesy, Matthew's use of the title here has a
touch of irony: a king made the tool of a woman. In

the king's grief we have no conflict with v. 5, as some suppose; for the grief was due to the very considerations which had hitherto kept Herod from killing John. The plural "his oaths" indicates only that the king had emphasized his promise by repeating his oath. Instead of letting the outcome of his rashness open his eyes to the enormity of his folly, thus inducing him to declare that a gift involving a horrible crime was beyond his granting, this morally helpless fool imagined that his oaths really bound him. Coupled with this moral impotence was his pride. His sworn promise was intended to impress his guests, in fact, had been made for their sake not for that of the girl. To deny her request appeared like a disgrace in the eyes of those reclining with him at the feast. Thus Herod perpetrated his greatest crime, filling the cup of his iniquities. The fact that Matthew has not mentioned the guests before this need not be explained and is no point against his record. All that he has said makes it clear to any intelligent reader that a feast at which many notables were present is in progress. Why ask for common prolixity where conciseness is more forcible?

10) This is also true regarding the tragic brevity of the next sentence. **And having sent, he beheaded John in the prison.** Though it was done by the hand of an underling (πέμψας), Matthew makes the deed entirely that of Herod.

11) **And his head was brought on a platter and was given to the girl, and she brought it to her mother.** The three cold aorists record nothing but the awful facts. The term κοράσιον does not necessarily support the view that the girl was only twelve years of age. In arriving at her age we should not think only of her first going to her mother for advice but also of Herod's promise to her. Such a promise would not be made to a mere child, and even an older girl would, after such a promise had been given her,

consult a mother who was as dominating as Herodias. To what indignities John's head was subjected we are left to imagine.

12) **And his disciples, having come forward, took up the corpse and buried him; and, having come, made report to Jesus.** From 11:2, etc., we see that John's disciples had access to him in his prison, and thus they were permitted to give the headless body decent burial in a tomb (πτῶμα, "a fallen body"). The fact that John's disciples report the tragedy to Jesus shows that they automatically turned to him. The answer Jesus had sent to John (11:4) must thus have satisfied John. From the Acts we know that some of John's disciples sought to continue by themselves (Acts 18:25; 19:3), but most of them now probably followed Jesus.

While this account of John's death explains the remark of Herod to his courtiers in v. 2, it evidently has a deeper significance. It reveals the entire attitude of the ruler of Galilee as regards both John and Jesus and thus offers one of the reasons why Jesus began to withdraw himself more and more. The time of John's death was about a year before Jesus' own death. Jesus died at the Passover, and John's death occurred just prior to the preceding Passover, John 6:4; for the feeding of the 5,000 and Jesus' walking on the sea occurred at this time, John 6:5-21, the same as Matt. 14:15-33. John's bloody death pointed forward to that of Jesus.

13) **Now when Jesus heard it he withdrew thence in a boat to a desert place in private.** The motive for this withdrawal is the news of John's murder. With this, however, went another motive. The Twelve had returned from their tour of evangelization (10:5), and Jesus wanted to get away from the crowds in order to confer with them in private (Mark 6:30, 31). Matthew does not mention this additional motive,

yet, as Zahn points out, by the use of ἀκούσας he by no
means excludes it, for the participle may be regarded
as being merely temporal. Matthew does not report
about the return of the Twelve.

That fear of Herod moved Jesus to this action is
an unworthy surmise. Matthew does not say, as some
suppose, that Jesus left Herod's domain, for he permits
his readers to find out only incidentally that Jesus
crossed the lake from the west to the east; and it is
unfair to say that Matthew forgot that Jesus presently
returns to Capernaum. What we are told about is
more than an ordinary change of locality. This withdrawal of Jesus with the Twelve is the beginning of a
new course on his part. In 4:12, when the news of
John's imprisonment was brought to Jesus, Matthew
uses the same words as here in 14:13, and tells us that
Jesus withdrew to Galilee in order to prosecute his
ministry with the greatest vigor and publicity. This
period was now ended, and even the Twelve had completed their part in it. The great hostility had arisen.
John's murder thus marks a new turn for Jesus. He
begins his withdrawal. While he still meets multitudes
and heals the sick, etc., we no longer see him seeking
publicity; he often moves to distant parts and gradually
prepares the Twelve for the end.

**And when the multitudes heard it they followed
him on foot from the towns,** taking the longer route
by land around the upper part of the lake. The crowds
swelled as they passed from town to town along the
populous west shore.

14) **And having come forth, he saw a great
multitude and had compassion on them and healed
their sick,** ἀρρώστους, those without strength. Jesus
landed on the eastern shore hours ahead of the arrival
of the crowds. He chose a spot near Bethsaida (Luke
9:10, which must be distinguished from the Bethsaida
on the west shore) and found a retired place up in the

mountain where he spent some time with the Twelve
(John 6:3). It was from this retired spot that he came
forth and saw the multitude that had gradually assembled near the shore. Mark's (6:33) προῆλθον αὐτούς is
textually questionable (see the data in Souter) and is
without parallel in the sense of "outwent them" (our
versions), i. e., arrived there first, which would be
ἔφθασαν αὐτούς. The arrival on the eastern shore, plus
the finding of a private place in the uninhabited locality, are contained already in v. 13 with its aorist ἀνεχώ-
ρησεν and must not be overlooked. Hence ἐξελθών cannot
mean: "when Jesus landed and stepped out of the boat."
Both in Matthew and in Mark (who has the same participle) mention of the boat lies too far back. Jesus
"came forth" from the private place (κατ' ἰδίαν) which,
according to the aorist in v. 13, he had actually reached.
John 6:3 places this beyond doubt. Then he saw the
"great multitude." We have no reason to suppose that
the boat of Jesus loitered long enough to let the great
crowd arrive, which would entail hours; and we have
no right to reduce "a great multitude" to a few fast
runners who arrived ahead of the rest of the crowd.

The heart of Jesus goes out in compassion to the
great crowd which Jesus sees assembled on the lower
levels. The verb σπλαγχνίζομαι seems to be "a coinage of
the Jewish Dispersion," "to be moved as to the
σπλάγχνα," the nobler viscera, heart, lungs, and liver,
here conceived in the Hebraic sense as the seat of the
affections (cf. M.-M. 584 on verb and noun). It means
much that, in spite of all the unbelief that Jesus encountered and in spite of his intention to withdraw
from his great public activity, his heart should thus
be moved at the sight of this crowd that had followed
him. Matthew reports that in this compassion of his
"he healed their sick." The very word indicates that
these "strengthless ones" could only with great difficulty have been transported to this distant, uninhabited

place, which fact makes it still more certain that Jesus
spent some hours alone before the crowd came.  Mark
and Luke add the detail that Jesus also taught, but the
healings must have preceded, for Jesus would certainly
not let the sick suffer while he taught.

15)  **Now evening having come, his disciples
came to him, saying:  Desert is the place, and the
hour has already gone by; dismiss the multitudes
in order that, having gone away into the villages,
they may buy themselves food.**  At this point
John 6:5-7 must be inserted.   When Jesus first stepped
out of his retirement on the mountainside he put the
question to Philip about buying bread for all these
people, and this Jesus did to test out one of his disciples.
Already then Jesus knew what he would do when evening would come.  But the only reply that Jesus
received from Philip was that it would take more money
than they had in their treasury to provide even a very
little for so many people — not an inkling that Philip
remembered Cana or thought of miraculous help on
the part of Jesus in any way.  Disappointed in Philip,
Jesus descends to the multitude, heals the sick, and
teaches about the kingdom until evening has actually
come — entirely unconcerned about the needs of the
people and the passing of the time.  Jesus evidently
intended that Philip was to report the question to the
other apostles, and thus all of them were to think about
it as the hours wore on.  They did that but arrived at
nothing definite.

So evening came at last, γενομένης, an aorist to express the simple fact.   The disciples can stand the pressure no longer.   Despite all that Jesus had said to Philip
a thought such as Jesus desired had not occurred to
them.  In a body they come to him, and one, as their
spokesman, reminds Jesus of what he seems to have
entirely forgotten.  He is now not in a city but out
here in a desert place.  And it is beyond the hour (R.

613, παρά in the verb) ; hence it is reasonable for this
crowd to scatter and to try to find something to eat
by buying what they can in the villages along their
way back.   The implication is that it is already past the
time for this, and that probably only some will succeed
in buying something, and, if Jesus waits any longer,
none will be able to do so.   "Buy themselves food"
(βρώματα *Speisen,* bread and fish) shows that Jesus' conversation with Philip about buying had been talked
over by the Twelve.

16) **But Jesus said to them: They have no need
to go away.   Do you give them to eat!**   Astonishing
reply to these dull-witted men and yet wholly transparent!   If *they* are to give food to this tremendous
host with no food in *their* possession, and if there is
no need for any to go away in search of food, Jesus
must mean that *they,* the Twelve, have a source of
supply they have thus far entirely overlooked.   But
even now they fail to understand.   Mark and Luke
report that the disciples ask whether Jesus has in mind
that *they,* at this late hour, are to go out and buy up
food.   What a hopeless proposition!   This would require at least 200 denarii (more than they had) ; and
how could they, twelve men, gather and carry food for
so many?

17)   Vainly Jesus tried to call out the faith of the
Twelve.   He now proceeds with the miracle.   It is he
who tells the disciples to go and to see what bread is
available (Mark 6:38).   John informs us about the
lad who had this tiny supply and about Andrew speaking for the rest in reporting to Jesus.   **And they say
to him, We haven't here but fives breads and two
fishes.**   They put it negatively: nothing but so small
a bit.   The ἄρτοι are round, flat cakes of bread, literally "breads," and not loaves in our sense.   In this lake
country the common addition (*Zukost,* ὀψάριον) to bread
was fish.

18)  **And he said** without the least explanation,
**Be bringing them here to me!**  Matthew alone reports this order, which means, of course, that the food
should be bought from the lad.  The disciples, who
heard this peculiar order, and those who went to hunt
up the lad must have wondered at Jesus' intention.  The
bread and the fish are brought.

19)  All the minor actions are expressed by aorist
participles, and all these actions precede those of the
main verbs (R. 1136) ; in English this distinction
between minor and main actions is usually not made.
**And having ordered the multitudes to recline on
the grass, and having taken the five breads and the
two fishes, and having looked up to the heaven, he
spoke a blessing and, having broken, gave the breads
to the disciples, and the disciples to the multitudes.**
Comment is scarcely needed, for all is graphic and clear.
The Greek uses the plural when speaking of grass. Near
the Passover season (John 6:4) the open spaces would
be covered with grass, which afforded an ideal place
for dining out.  The guests reclined as if on couches.
The five flat cakes and the two small fish were easily
held in the hand while the blessing was being pronounced.  This must have been the usual grace before
a meal, for nothing unusual is reported concerning it
by any of the evangelists.  Looking up to heaven was
a common attitude in prayer while one was standing.
The idea that Jesus first had to have God's consent
and help and here asked for it before he could work
the miracle, misconceives not only this but all the miracles, all of which were wrought by the omnipotence
which belongs equally to the three Persons.  The breaking, which is in no way symbolical, is merely done for
the sake of distribution.  The cakes which were about
one-half inch thick were never cut for the purpose of
eating them.

As Jesus broke the bread and the fish, both multiplied in his hands. Instead of indicating this by an imperfect tense, Matthew has the constative aorist ἔδωκε, the whole extended action being regarded as a unit: "he gave." This weighty verb stands alone; what the disciples did with the food handed to them is not stated by means of a verb. They were merely the waiters who were to serve the guests at this feast. Yet as such they could and did carry out v. 16.

20) **And they did eat all and were filled; and they took up what was superfluous of the broken pieces, twelve baskets full.** More was left than had been at hand in the beginning. "They did eat all," by the order of the words emphasizes both the verb and the subject. There was not one who did not eat. How much? As much as each could eat. The verb is really coarse, it is borrowed from animals who are fed to capacity for fattening by using grass (χόρτος) or fodder. All, having had little or nothing to eat all day, were certainly hungry. No stinting here as when Philip thought of each having a little.

Moreover, broken pieces of both bread and fish were left. Some people always take too much. So here some took pieces from the disciples of which they could not take even a bite, being so filled. Jesus intends that none of his gifts are to be wasted. This miraculous food was not to be thrown away. It filled exactly twelve of the little wicker baskets that were used by travellers to carry food and necessaries and were here probably used by the disciples when serving as waiters. Twelve — one for each of the Twelve, none for Jesus, which means that he who had created all this bounty created an opportunity for the Twelve to share their abundance with him. From all that he gives to you you are privileged to give a little back to him. What were the feelings of the Twelve when, as the dusk approached, they finally sat down around Jesus with twelve baskets full of food before them?

21) **Now those eating were about five thousand men without women and little children.** This parenthetical addition shows exactly what the more indefinite "multitude" and "multitudes" spoken of in the previous verses implies. Mark 6:39, 40 helps us to see just how the count was made. Since the women and the little ones were not counted, we must place the actual figure of those who were fed considerably above 5,000. The present participle οἱ ἐσθίοντες (as in 2:20) describes the people according to the progress of the act: "the eaters"; it is not like the aorist which indicates completion (as our versions do).

22) **And immediately he compelled the disciples to enter into the boat and to be going on ahead of him to the other side while he dismissed the multitudes. And having dismissed the multitudes, he went up into the mountain privately to pray; and when it was evening, he was there alone.** It is John (6:15) who informs us regarding the reason for this hasty compulsion. The multitudes were so affected by this miracle that they were scheming to kidnap Jesus and in triumph to carry him as king to Jerusalem at the time of the Passover now close at hand (John 6:4). The Twelve would have delighted in such a scheme. Therefore Jesus separates them from the multitude and sends them away by themselves, in order soon to give them a new revelation of the kind of King he really is. The aorist ἐμβῆναι is punctiliar to express the one act of embarking, it is followed by the durative present προάγειν to indicate the journey across the lake. R. 857 regards the former infinitive as constative. "To go ahead of him to the other side" implies that later on Jesus would join the disciples. Mark has, "to the other side towards (πρός) Bethsaida"; while John writes that "they were going to (εἰς) Caper-

naum," and that the next day the multitude also went
to Capernaum. Bethsaida was merely a suburb of
Capernaum, and thus either could be named as the
destination.

A one-sided emphasis on the clause introduced by
ἕως οὗ has this imply that Jesus would join the Twelve
*immediately* after dismissing the multitude, and some
even charge Jesus with breaking his word by not doing
so, or Matthew with writing as though this were the
case. But this is answered by the implications made
already in the main clause. The Twelve were to go by
boat and to the other side and thus ahead of Jesus.
That means that he would join them, not at once after
being rid of the multitude, but "on the other side,"
hence after they would arrive there. How this was
done John 6:21 indicates. The ἕως οὗ clause (here
meaning not "until" but "while," Zahn) states only
what prevented Jesus from going along with the disciples in the boat; he must dismiss the multitudes.

23) The serious turn which was now taking place
in the affairs of Jesus explains his dismissal of the multitude and his ascent into some lonely spot to spend
hours in prayer. On the very next day so many turned
away from him that he asked even the Twelve whether
they would also go away, John 6:66, etc.; and his reference to Judas being a devil shows that his mind was
facing the coming betrayal and crucifixion. The reading φεύγει instead of ἀνεχώρησε, in John 6:15, expresses
the fact: he actually fled up into the mountain, alone,
by himself. When at last he was where none could find
him in the dark he prayed, and the aorist προσεύξασθαι
merely states the fact without intimating continuous-
ness. Note that the dismissal of the multitude is mentioned a second time and following it, as in vital connection with it, comes the hurrying away to prayer.

That multitude wanting to make him king was one
of Satan's temptations to Jesus, and the sending these

crowds away shows the temptation overcome. And thus the prayer in the dark that stormy night may well have been an outpouring of his heart to the Father for the renewed victory, glorifying the Father by his obe- dience in facing the cross and interceding for the Twelve and all his disciples that they might not be led away by these false Messianic conceptions. We thus catch just a glimpse of the deep inner life of Jesus. His praying was perfect, pure, and exalted communion with his Father. The genitive absolute, "evening having come," is the same as in v. 15, but there it marked the beginning of the evening while here we have its end; that "evening" was also divided into a first, "when the day began to decline" (Luke 9:12), and a second, when the shadows began to fall just before darkness.

24) **Now the boat was already in the midst of the sea, distressed by the waves, for the wind was contrary.** When the disciples started before dark, all was fair and beautiful and, experienced sailors as most of them were, they hoisted sail and expected a pleasant voyage to their destination. But this soon changed. One of those sudden storms, for which this lake is noted, lying, as it does, between high ridges, descended and swept over the water, lashing the waves furiously. The adverb ἤδη looks back to the time Jesus spent in prayer and hence means "already." The sail had been hurriedly furled, the men took to the oars and held the boat straight against the wind to keep it from being swamped. Matthew says, "the boat was dis- tressed," literally, "was being put to the test by tor- ture"; Mark, that the disciples "were distressed in row- ing." Both are graphic. The variant reading: the boat "was many stadia distant from the land," dis- tressed, etc., may be original. John 6:19 gives the distance as being 25 or 30 stadia, 3⅛ to 3¾ miles, a stadium being one-eighth of a Roman and English mile.

But this must not be understood as being a great distance. Only thus far had they come, out into the middle of the lake, and still far from their port. The necessity of holding the boat against the strong wind prevented them from making any appreciable progress.

25) The miracle is told in the briefest and the most restrained manner. **And in the fourth watch of the night he came to them, walking on the sea.** Matthew and Mark mention the time, to which John, who constantly supplements, adds the distance covered. The first watch is from 6 to 9, the second from 9 to 12, the third from 12 to 3, and thus the fourth from 3 to 6. So many hours the disciples had labored; they must have been at the point of exhaustion. But now, when strength and hope were nearly gone, "he came to them." One might inquire whether he had walked all the way out from the shore through the storm in the dark, or had suddenly transported himself to the spot where the disciples saw him. Curious questions deserve no answer, and in Holy Writ receive none. The present participle pictures Jesus' progress: "walking on the sea." The wind howled, the waves dashed but affected him not at all. He was not pitched about or tossed up and down; he was not soaked with waves or spray striking him. Before him as he moved his feet a smooth, apparently solid path lay on which he walked as on ordinary ground. He did not move or float in the air as a specter is supposed to do; no unearthly light played around him as painters generally imagine. It was simply Jesus just as they had seen and left him the evening before — but now walking on the storm-tossed sea.

And "he came to them," πρός, towards. Had they not wished for his presence most ardently during those long hours? Well, here he was! "Toward them" when they were in such danger and distress could mean only one thing: help, deliverance, safety at last. Walking as he did could mean only that he was coming with omnipotent power, one that made the water bear his weight and prevented wind and water from in the least disturbing him.  With such power he was now so near.

26) **And the disciples, having seen him walking on the sea, were upset, saying, It is a ghost! and they shrieked from fear.**  It was the walking on the sea, this incredible thing, that caused the fright.  Mark adds the fact that "all" saw him, not merely one or two who were, perhaps, inclined to see things and might have been quieted by the rest.  They think they see a φάντασμα, an unearthly form, a specter, or ghost.  The darkness, the hour of night, the storm and the danger still in full force, the physical exhaustion, all combine to make the disciples give way to the superstitions still lurking in their minds.  What would some who now smile at superstition have felt if they had held an oar in that boat?  They are shaken because they think that this unearthly form walking toward them is a sure sign that they are all doomed men.  So they shriek aloud, giving expression to their terror (ἀπό).

27) **Immediately Jesus spoke to them, saying: Cheer up!  It is I!  Stop being afraid!**  The reason they saw Jesus, though it was dark, was because he was only a short distance away.  At once he checks their terror.  With θαρσεῖτε he calls to them to take courage and to be filled with cheer.  "It is I!" furnishes the reason:  "I" — not a specter!  Away with your superstition!  I, your own Lord and Master, whose voice you know so well!  The present imperative in prohibitions often, as here, means to stop what one is already doing, i. e., to end it permanently: "stop fearing!" there is no cause for it (R. 851, etc.).  The first imperative is positive and is matched by the second, a negative: fear out, cheer and courage in!

28) The word of Jesus had its effect.  The astounding reality that it was their own Lord and

Master standing out there on the water by the exercise of his divine power penetrated their minds. **And Peter answered him and said, Lord, if it is thou, order me to come to thee upon the waters. And he said, Come! And having stepped down from the boat, he walked on the waters to come to Jesus.** From superstitious terror Peter leaps to the opposite extreme, the daring of faith. It is characteristic of him to act thus quickly. Convinced that Jesus actually walked on the water, the thought suddenly flashed into his mind that with Jesus' consent he, too, could do so.

It is a mistake to read doubt into the conditional clause "if it is thou," for this is a condition of reality, meaning, "if it is, as indeed it is." It is added by Peter because a moment ago he and the disciples had other thoughts. The English subjunctive, "if it *be thou,*" subtracts from the reality. Moreover, Peter wants to express his faith to Jesus, namely that he really believes Jesus is standing out there on the water. He intends to say that he believes this so completely that Jesus can make him, too, walk out to the place where Jesus is on the water. This was true boldness of faith on Peter's part, that strength of faith which knows and trusts that even natural impossibilities yield before the will, word, and power of Jesus. For note that Peter asks Jesus to command him to come, for only such a command will enable him to do so. And that command implies, when it is acted on by Peter, full faith that trusts that command.

29) Only under those circumstances could Jesus say, "Come!" The faith which Peter manifests Jesus accepts and justifies. If it had not been true faith, or if wrong and foolish motives had prompted Peter, Jesus would never have given his command. Those who criticize Peter ought to see that their criticism really strikes Jesus who consents to Peter's proposal. Peter is ready to make up for the cowardice of the supersti-

tious fear he had had a moment ago by the courage of
faith which now trusts Jesus' power enough to walk
out to him at his command. We cannot agree that
Peter intends to outdo and to outdare the other disciples, to show off his faith before them before the Lord
as being greater than theirs as he afterward did when
he said, "Although all shall be offended, yet will not I"
(26:23). Peter makes no comparison between himself and the rest. If he had done so even silently, the
Lord would never have replied, "Come!" but would
have warned and corrected him exactly as he did on the
later occasion. The Lord's "Come!" is the bidding
Peter asks, and it is uncalled for to qualify it as Trench
does: "Come, if thou wilt; make the experiment, if thou
desirest!" This reads something into the simple command that it does not contain.

So Peter went over the side of the boat and walked,
actually walked, on the waters in order to go to Jesus.
In Jesus' eyes it was good for the others to see Peter's
faith and its full justification on the part of Jesus. But
we must not suppose that the boat still pitched in dire
distress and that Peter climbed out onto raging waves.
The boat must have lain in the path that extended
before Jesus as he had walked and now stood on the
water, which was a stretch of calm amid the surrounding tumult. As one of the good sailors among the
Twelve, Peter otherwise also could not have forsaken
his oar which was necessary in holding the boat on its
course.

30) **But in looking at the wind he became
frightened; and having begun to sink, he yelled, saying, Lord, save me! And immediately Jesus, having stretched out his hand, took hold of him and
says, Man of little faith, why didst thou doubt?**
For a little while Peter regarded the terrific force of
the wind, piling up the waves about him far above his
head. It is difficult to imagine this if Jesus and Peter

were tossed up and down by these waves, their waters
dashing over them. Before their feet the waters must
have been smooth enough for walking. Peter was not
in danger, but fright struck him when he looked at
what was threatening all about him, and the thought
that he was now away from the boat and that these
waves were liable to swallow him at any moment. In
that moment of fright Peter's faith gave way. He
looked at the terrifying wind and forgot Jesus who was
only a few paces away. And then he began to sink.
The solid water was again becoming fluid under his
feet. It is uncalled for to refer to Peter's ability to
swim. The thought of swimming never came to Peter.
When he felt himself sinking, he was afraid that the
wind and the waves stirred up by it would engulf him.
But this very fear that was due to what his eyes saw
and his heart forgot made him instantly remember and
turn to Jesus with the cry, "Save me!"

Peter had not overestimated his faith, nor had he
wanted to show it off; nor did Jesus want to teach him
a lesson by properly humbling him. Jesus never humbles faith but always encourages it. He encouraged
that of Peter mightily when he told him to come. The
trouble was that, instead of holding to his faith, Peter
let go of it. This often happens even to men of strong
faith. The things that faith has to overcome are such
as, when they are looked at by themselves, are bound
to create dismay and depress faith. The will of Jesus
made the water solid only for Peter's faith and only in
response to that faith. Thus, when doubt took the
place of faith, the water began to return to its natural
state.

31) The Lord merely stretched out his hand and
took hold of Peter; the genitive αὐτοῦ means that he
grasped some part of Peter. With a few quick steps
Jesus was at Peter's side. Not with both hands did he
grasp Peter's body in order to hold him up by main

force; only with one hand, only taking hold of him, not lifting his entire weight. The saving for which Peter cried was a physical deliverance out of the engulfing water. The saving Jesus granted him was more, namely this physical deliverance by the spiritual restoration of his faith. At the touch of Jesus' hand Peter again stood upon the water which held him up as it had done before. To be thus helped by having faith created, restored, increased in us is the most essential and perfect help, even apart from physical succor.

Jesus' word to Peter is usually regarded as a rebuke. In reality it in a gentle way points out to Peter just what caused his trouble: too little faith when he looked at the wind, and doubt crowding out faith at the thought of danger. "Man of little faith" is intended, as is the plural in 8:26, again to increase that faith. And εἰς τί refers not to cause but to purpose (R. 739). The cause of Peter's doubting was apparent, but what purpose could he have in doubting (the aorist to indicate the momentary doubt that assailed him) when he knew that Jesus' call to him to come was intended only for faith and that his ability to walk over the water was wholly dependent on faith? Jesus' question must ever remain without an answer, for no rational or sensible answer can be given. No believer can ever find the least purpose for doubting, for doubting can have but one result, namely disaster. Every believer's purpose should be connected solely with his faith, for faith alone and always results in deliverance, safety, and praise of the Lord.

32) **And when they had gone up into the boat, the wind stopped,** κοπάζειν, to grow tired, to abate. Peter walked to the boat with Jesus and climbed into it. It lay in the calm water that surrounded Jesus. We cannot conceive the boat as pitching up and down and being distressed by the waves. The force of the genitive absolute is temporal: at that moment the wind

**ceased**; not causal: the entering the boat made the wind **cease.** Yet this sudden stopping of the wind at that moment was evidently not a singular coincidence. The wind stopped through the will of Jesus. More than that. John 6:21, supplementing Matthew and Mark, adds the detail that immediately the boat was also at its destination — there in the dawning light lay the docks of Capernaum. Now we see why the distance the boat had travelled was mentioned, and why we were told so particularly that it was still in the midst of the sea. He who walked on the sea and enabled Peter to do so caused the storm to cease in an instant and caused the boat to be transferred to its destination. The fact that Matthew and Mark omit the latter detail is the plainest evidence that they are not intent on magnifying the miracles or their miraculous features. They never overstate but, as in this case, often understate the facts.

33) **But those in the boat worshipped him, saying, Thou art truly God's Son!** The Twelve were overwhelmed by the manifestation of the omnipotence of Jesus. They bow before him in the boat by an involuntary act of worship, confessing him as God's Son. The adverb ἀληθῶς is to be construed with the copula, but its force is that the disciples have for a long time recognized Jesus' Sonship and now find it confirmed in the strongest manner. The absence of the articles with Θεοῦ υἱός does not make this predicate indefinite: "*a* Son of God," as though there were other such Sons. With proper names and again with nouns that denote only the one of this kind that exists articles are not needed. The disciples have in mind the one and only one who can be called "God's Son." By this title they declare both who and what Jesus is. It is grammatically untenable to bar out the who and to retain only the what. The absence of the articles stresses the quality, but it does this equally for both nouns. Hence

just as Θεοῦ does not mean "of *a* God," so υἱός does not
mean merely "*a* Son." As there is only the *one* God,
so there is only the *one* Son. More than this, the genitive as such, as is the case where a genitive is added to
a noun, makes the noun thus modified definite. "Son"
might mean one of a number, but "God's Son" cannot
have this meaning. The context also implies that this
divine title is intended to be the direct opposite of mere
men or of one who is only a man.

The claim that "God's Son" is not the same as
"Messiah," and that the miracle here wrought has nothing to do with Christ's Messiahship, is specious. Who
would the true Messiah be but the Son of God? Are
not all his miracles a revelation of his omnipotent
power over the forces of nature? Furthermore, this
miracle was to give the Twelve a true conception of the
divine power and majesty of Jesus over against the
unworthy conceptions of the multitude that was planning to make him a mere earthly king (John 6:15)
even against his will.

Among the other criticisms of Matthew's narrative
we note the claim that Matthew must have had a special
collection of stories regarding Peter which he worked
into his Gospel. Well, Matthew was in the very boat
out of which and into which Peter climbed, and Matthew was not blind.

Again we are told that "God's Son" was not uttered
here in the boat; "the historicity of the words at this
point in the life of Jesus" is to be doubted; they voice
a much later faith which Matthew "has read back into
the story." But Matthew himself was one of those
who prostrated themselves before Jesus and called him
God's Son. And later on this very day Peter, speaking
for all the disciples, once more made the same confession, only in ampler form, John 6:68, 69.

34) **And having crossed over, they came to the
land of Gennesaret.** John's record (6:21 and the

following discourse on the Bread of Life) makes it certain that after the storm Jesus and the Twelve landed at Capernaum where the multitude that had been fed so miraculously found him later in the day and heard his discourse and then turned from him. And the argument that this was the Sabbath, since Jesus was in a synagogue, and that this Sabbath must then have been a later day, since on a Sabbath the crowds would not travel the distance from the east side to the west side of the lake, cannot be maintained. The Jews assembled in their synagogues also on Monday and on Thursday. The facts are that Jesus landed at Capernaum and on that day spoke on the Bread of Life and some days later visited Gennesaret. The aorist participle "having crossed over" is quite general and only means that, when Jesus was through in Capernaum, he visited Gennesaret. This is a triangular plain that lies south of Capernaum and north of Tiberias, which is made by the recession of the mountains. It was praised by Josephus for its fertility. The lake is called the Sea of Gennesaret after it.

35) **And when the men of that place recognized him they sent into that entire neighborhood and brought up to him all those that were ill; and they kept beseeching him that they might only touch the tassel of his robe. And as many as did touch it were made well.** Why οἱ ἄνδρες, only the men? Evidently, because some of them had been to Capernaum and perhaps elsewhere and had seen Jesus, which could not be said of the women and the children. The conclusion is correct that this was new territory for Jesus; he had not been here before. This, then, is also a sample of how Jesus withdrew from the center of his great activity and sought out retired and even distant localities. As soon as he is recognized (R. 827), these people realize their opportunity for healing, send messengers, and from their

small territory (about three miles along the lake and two back from the shore) bring up to him all their sick; κακῶς ἔχειν is entirely idiomatic (R. 546), for which we use "to be" with an adjective. They collected everyone who had any ailment whatever.

36) They are also so trustful as to the healing power of Jesus that they do not ask him to touch the sick but only to let the sick touch him, namely the κράσπεδον of his robe (explained in 9:20). The ἵνα clause is the object of the verb, it is exactly like an infinitive (R. 993). Mark adds that in every town, village, and even in the country they had the sick ready for him. Jesus consented to this procedure and honored this faith — every touch brought perfect restoration to health. Nothing is said about teaching, for Matthew and Mark intend to record only what was exceptional on this brief tour of Jesus to this little region.

**Christ Again Clashes with the Pharisees and
Withdraws and Warns the Pharisees and
the Sadducees and His Disciples,
Chapter 15-16:12**

1)  **Then there come unto Jesus from Jerusalem
Pharisees and scribes, saying: Why are thy disciples
transgressing the tradition of the elders? for they
are not washing their hands when they eat bread.**
The adverb "then" marks the time only in a general
way and thus furnishes no warrant for the assumption
that Jesus was still in the country of Gennesaret.  Matthew, as well as Mark, consider the place of no importance.   The clash recorded in chapter 12 seems to have
been one with the local Pharisees in Galilee.   Now,
however, a delegation of Pharisees and scribes (see 2:4
and 3:7) has arrived from the capital, both to spy upon
Jesus and to help in discrediting him in the eyes of
the people.   We see that the violent opposition that had
arisen in Jerusalem was joining hands with that manifesting itself in Galilee.   Since these men came up from
the capital they had more prestige than the local members of their party.   Jesus also handles them with more
severity.

2)  With διατί they ask why the disciples of Jesus
are setting aside (note παρά in the verb) "the tradition
of the elders," the entire body of rules of conduct
handed down orally by the πρεσβύτεροι, the old, venerable,
learned rabbis.   Part of "the tradition," which was
afterward compiled in the Talmud and the Midrashim,

consisted of the *haggada,* expositions and legendary
expansions of the historical and the prophetical books
of the Old Testament, and of the *halacha,* rules which
in casuistic fashion regulated conduct down to the
smallest details.   Here the *halacha* is referred to, "the
fence" erected around the law, rules that were in part
derived from Moses personally, in part were based on
his writings, 613 of them, to which seven additional
duties were added with a debate as to whether they
were to be rated as inferior, equal, or superior to the
written canon.   In practice "the tradition" was placed
above the canon, a plain example of which Jesus gives
in v. 3-6.   The seriousness of the charge implied in the
question is that Jesus *teaches* this transgression of the
tradition.   That is why Jesus personally did not need
to be mentioned as himself transgressing these traditional rules.   What the disciples were doing they were
doing as disciples of Jesus, thus involving him in the
most serious way.   These Pharisees might disregard
some individual transgression, but to teach transgression as a matter of principle was a different thing.

The implied charge is broad: the setting aside of
the entire *halacha.*   The γάρ clause illustrates by introducing one plain example: the disciples of Jesus do
not wash themselves (νίπτονται, middle) as to their
hands whenever they dine (the present subjunctive
to indicate repetition, R. 972).   "To eat bread" means
to partake of a meal.   The neglect of this formality
could be easily verified, yet its observance was considered as essential, not for sanitary reasons or for the
sake of ordinary cleanliness, but for fear that the hands
had brushed against a Gentile or against something
belonging to a Gentile.   Mark 7:3, etc., written for
Gentiles, explains in more detail. The divine Levitical
law required no such washing.   Jesus and his disciples
observed the Levitical law but disregarded the rabbinical tradition.   Yet they did so, not because human

customs as such are to be disregarded, but because
the Pharisees considered the tradition as binding the
conscience by divine authority, binding it even more
severely than the written law of God.

3) **But he, answering, said to them: Why are
even you yourselves transgressing the commandment
of God for the sake of your tradition?   For God
said, Honor thy father and thy mother; and, He that
reviles father or mother, let him die the death.   But
you on your part say: Whoever shall say to his
father or to his mother, A gift! whatever from me
thou mightest be benefited by, he shall not honor
his father.   And you revoked the Word of God for
the sake of your tradition.**   The answer of Jesus is
not an argument *ad hominem,* which simply silences the
Pharisees by pointing out that they are doing an equal,
yea, a greater wrong.   Such an argument would be an
admission of guilt on Jesus' part.   Note that the question asked by Jesus is the exact counterpart of the one
put to him by the Pharisees.   But in his question he
nullifies and wipes out their appeal to "the tradition
of the elders" by facing them with "the commandment
of God" which is set aside "for the sake of your tradition."   In this simple way Jesus annihilates their tradition.   It violates God's own law and commandment.
This is the reason that Jesus teaches his disciples and
must teach them to observe none of this tradition.

The καί before the emphatic ὑμεῖς is not "also" and
does not place these Pharisees alongside of Jesus' disciples; it signifies "even you yourselves," the very ones
who are truly guilty of trangression while they pretend
to find transgression in others.   And διατί, as in v. 2,
asks for the cause.   This cause is that God's commandment means nothing to them when it comes to their
self-invented tradition.   Note that Jesus does not refer
to the tradition "of the elders," behind whose skirts
these Pharisees crawl; but says "your" tradition, mak-

584     *The Interpretation of Matthew*

ing these Pharisees personally responsible for the tradition they accept and promulgate.

4)  Jesus, too, follows with a γάρ and furnishes a
striking example of the transgression which he charges
against the Pharisees.  He quotes what "God said,"
the Fourth Commandment.  This is not a deduction
of the rabbis but the plainest example of God's own
commandment.  He even reinforces this (Exod. 20:12)
by another thing that "God said" (Exod. 21:17), which
shows how highly God wants parents esteemed.  In the
civil law of the Jews he placed the death penalty on the
mere reviling of a father or a mother (κακολογεῖν, not
necessarily "to curse" although it would include cursing).  The Hebrew *moth yumath* the LXX reproduces
by θανάτῳ τελευτάτω, and this is retained by Matthew:
"let him die the death."

5)  All this, though it is absolutely divine, counts
for nothing with the Pharisees when it comes to their
self-invented tradition.  Over against what "God said"
Jesus now puts what "you on your part (emphatic ὑμεῖς)
say," the present tense λέγετε to indicate their constant
and established teaching.  Jesus quotes their own teaching, a piece of their "tradition" regarding a son's obligation to his father or his mother.  It is a specimen
from their chapter on vows, which they had extended
beyond all reason.  Any man might withhold help and
support from a needy parent simply by declaring that
what would be required for such need was vowed to
God or to the Temple as a sacred gift.  Such a vow,
Pharisaic tradition held, came ahead of every other
obligation involving the money or the goods vowed.
Δῶρον is simply an exclamation: "A gift!" and means
that the thing is a gift which by this exclamation is
dedicated to God or to the Temple and is therefore not
to be used in any other way.  How soon the man ex-
claiming: Δῶρον! when his father or his mother asked
him for something would turn over this "gift" to the

priests, was another matter — sometimes he failed to do so although Jesus is not citing such a case.

The clause with ὃ ἐάν describes what is thus vowed away, and the accusative is the ordinary case with the passive, here the aorist from ὠφελεῖν: "whatever thou mightest be benefited by from me," i. e., it is a gift vowed away whatever otherwise might bring you help and benefit. The relative clause ὃ ἐάν modifies the exclamatory δῶρον, which makes the construction entirely regular (there is no καί before οὐ μή). B.-D. 360, 1 would change ἐάν to ἄν in order to produce unreality: "thou wouldest have been benefited," i. e., if it were not δῶρον, "a gift"; but this is too great a change. The matter of vowing away things was greatly abused. Thus, when a creditor came to collect, and the debtor was reluctant to pay, the creditor cried: "A gift," and thus compelled the debtor to pay the priests.

6) "He shall not honor his father" is the future tense used in legal commands, here the finding pronounced by the Pharisees in their tradition; of course, it is volitive (R. 875), and οὐ μή is the strong negation often used with the future indicative or the subjunctive. The remark that the Pharisees would scarcely have contradicted the Fourth Commandment so flatly does honor to Christian feeling but fails to understand the Pharisees. Jesus could never have charged them to their faces with saying this if they were not actually saying it.

The charge is thus complete. Jesus sums it up: "And you revoked the Word of God (some texts have "the law of God") for the sake of your tradition." The aorist ἠκυρώσατε states the past fact, and the present λέγετε states what is still being done. The verb (a plus κῦρος) means to leave without a lord, hence to deprive of all authority. And the διά phrase is the answer to διατί in v. 3: "for what cause?" — "for the cause of your tradition."

7) And now Jesus turns upon these men and sub-jects them to the very Word of God they so brazenly annul and demand that Jesus must also annul. **Hypocrites, excellently did Isaiah prophesy concerning you, saying:**

> **This people honors me with their lips,**
> **But their heart keeps far away from me.**
> **By teaching as teachings precepts of men.**

One word characterizes these Pharisees and scribes: "Hypocrite!" and ὑπό in the term (R. 633) adds the idea of an actor behind a mask. C.-K. 638: "The hypocrite tries to appear before men as he ought to be before God and yet is not." The term, found only in the Gospels, always has this religious sense. The worst form of hypocrisy is that which carries its self-deception to the point where it thinks that it really is what it only pretends to be. Such were the Pharisees. The more their hypocrisy came in contact with the holy integrity of Jesus, the more it appeared as what it actually was. The most vicious enemies of Jesus were these hypocrites. Instead of here himself branding them, Jesus lets Isaiah do this. The very Word they pervert is made their judge.

8) What Isaiah told his own generation as the utterance of Jehovah concerning them was thereby said also concerning the Pharisees and the scribes of Jesus' time, for they fully repeated the hypocrisy of that former generation. In this sense Isaiah "did prophesy concerning you." Isa. 29:13 is not quoted mechanically but with purpose. Out of the much longer sentence Jesus selects only those four lines that establish that purpose, namely, to present Jehovah's picture of the hypocrites. Since only these four lines are used, they are very properly taken out of the subordinate construction of Isaiah's long, complex sentence and are made ordinary simple statements by the

omission of "forasmuch." Jesus omits "this people
draws near me with their mouth" and uses only the
coordinate line regarding the lips. The *textus re-
ceptus*, and thus the A. V., have added the omitted line.

The two great marks of fully developed hypocrites
are presented in Jehovah's characterization: honor that
is mere pretense (with the lips not with the heart);
teachings that are likewise empty pretense (presented
as being divine when they are framed only by men).
The two are always found together, for the moment
the heart keeps far from God it leaves also his Word.
The very first requirement of his Word which is also
fundamental for all true worship of God is genuine sincerity toward him and his Word.

9) The Hebrew line: "and their fear toward me
is taught by the precept of men," is rendered by the
LXX: "moreover, in vain do they worship me, teaching precepts and teachings of men." The sense is the
same, for the reverent fear of God is expressed by the
worship of him, and every bit of such reverent worship
rests on God's Word and is shaped and controlled by
that Word. The moment mere human precepts are
substituted for that Word the entire fear of God and
its expression in worship are vitiated, become μάταιος,
"useless," in the sense that they lead to no good results,
are μάτην, "in vain." The verb σέβομαι means "to render divine worship," while προσκυνεῖν denotes only the act
of humble prostration. The latter may be practiced
before a human superior as well as before God. There
is the worst kind of contradiction between divine worship (fear of God) and precepts of men (in place of
the Word). To be blind to this contradiction is the
very essence of hypocrisy. It is bad enough when it is
practiced by an individual; it becomes far worse when
it is taught as the true way to fear and to worship
God and thus builds up a national system of hypocritical worship.

The teaching is emphasized; it substitutes that of man for that of God and makes the former appear as if it were the latter. The Hebrew collective "the precept of men" the LXX expands into "precepts and teachings of men" (two terms for one idea), which Jesus combines more closely: "as teachings precepts of men," making the first noun predicative to the second. The thought is the same throughout. "Of men" is subjective; they invented these precepts. The ἐντάλματα are all the practical regulations of the religious life, but all of them as the outgrowth of underlying facts and principles.

One of the specious errors of today is the separation of so-called doctrines from practice. Every religious practice, whether it is only a single minor act or a set church policy, goes back to the corresponding doctrine which is nothing but an expression of what is conceived as really being God's will and Word. The false practices of the Pharisees sprang from utterly false conceptions of that will and Word; hence Jesus clashed so violently with them when he insisted on the true conception of what God actually willed and said in his Word. The same conflict continues to this day.

**10) And having called the multitude to himself, he said to them: Pay attention and understand: not what enters into the mouth defiles the man, but what proceeds out of the mouth defiles the man.** The Pharisees are dismissed; they have their verdict "hypocrites," sealed by the Lord's word quoted from Isaiah. When they presented their question and their charge (v. 1), the multitude of common people respectfully drew back and, after Jesus had answered them, watched them depart. Now Jesus calls the people to him. They are the ones who are being misled by these Pharisees and scribes whom they revere and follow, and with loving concern he tries to set them right. "Pay attention (literally: be hearing) and under-

stand!" makes impressive what Jesus has to tell them.
He puts it all into the simplest and clearest kind of a
statement, one that is self-evident, axiomatic, and needs
only to be heard to have its truth comprehended.

When Jesus says that nothing that is outside of a
man can, by entering into him, defile him (see Mark
7:15) he refers to eating with unwashed hands. The
Pharisees claimed that such hands defiled the food they
touched and thus defiled the man who ate that food.
Jesus says that the principle is wrong on which this
specific case is based; in fact, it turns the entire principle upside down. For not what enters into but what
comes out of the mouth defiles the man. Defilement is
not physical but moral and spiritual. It never comes
into the mouth but is in the heart, so that the mouth lets
it come out. But did not God in the Levitical law forbid certain kinds of food to the Jews, and would not
putting such food into the mouth and eating it defile
the man? The answer that Jesus is here abrogating
the Levitical law is untenable; as a Jew he himself
fulfilled every requirement of it and he kept that law
in force for his disciples until Pentecost (Acts 11:1,
etc.). The answer is that it was not the food as food
entering the mouth that made unclean but the man's
disregard of the Levitical law given him by God, the
disobedience he would voice by asking for such food
and by justifying his eating thereof. So, indeed, it is
exactly as Jesus says. Yet it calls for a little thought,
consideration, and understanding to get rid of our
untrue ideas and to see the full, lucid truth of what
Jesus says. With this pithy word, the net result of his
clash with the Pharisees, the multitude is dismissed.

12) **Then the disciples, having come forward,
said to him, Dost thou know that when the Pharisees
heard that word they were offended?** Mark 7:12
has Jesus in a house, away from the multitude; perhaps εἰς οἶκον may mean that Jesus went "home," which

would locate this scene during a brief return to Capernaum.  By τὸν λόγον the disciples refer to the word just
uttered to the multitude. Others regard it as a reference
to v. 3-9, and then think that the disciples considered
this reply unnecessarily sharp.  But this does not satisfy the deictic article *"this* word or saying," and we
never read that the disciples criticized Jesus' treatment
of the Pharisees as hypocrites.  The word spoken to
the people forms the climax to the previous episode, and
what was so intolerable to these self-appointed leaders
of the people was the fact that Jesus took this leadership from them and here taught the people the direct
opposite of what they had taught.

13)  **And Jesus, answering, said: Every plant-
ing which my heavenly Father did not plant shall be
uprooted.  Let them go on; as guides they are
blind; and if the blind guides the blind, both shall
fall into a pit.**  The abstract φυτεία is used for the
concrete φύτευμα, "plant."  There is a debate as to
whether the figure deals with the persons (here the
Pharisees) or with the false doctrine or with both.
The analogy of 13:29 favors a reference to persons;
moreover, doctrine can never be separated from those
that teach it, for that is what makes them the persons
they are.  The figure is that of a garden or a park, and,
in the fashion of Biblical allegory, it is woven together
with the interpretation when the owner and planter of
this garden or grove is called "my heavenly Father."
The plants which he plants are the true believers who
hold to his Word, and the rest, not planted by him, are
all who lack faith and hold to the doctrines of men.
The uprooting refers to the divine judgment that shall
overtake them in due time.

14)  "Let them go on," ἄφετε αὐτούς, *lass sie gewaehren,* has its analogy in 13:30.  After the general
statement made in v. 13 Jesus now turns to the Pharisees in particular.  Since their judgment awaits them,

the disciples are to let them go on.  Nothing is so terrible as when Jesus abandons a man.  In v. 13 their lack of connection with the Father is stated, to which is now added their own spiritual condition.  Their blindness is brought forward because the entire connection deals with the Word of God and its opposite, "the precepts of men" (v. 9).  Nor is this blindness a mere misfortune or only the natural blindness of men that is due to their inherited sinful state.  Theirs is that self-willed and obdurate blindness which consists in a fixed and final opposition to the light.  They deliberately choose the darkness rather than the light (John 3:19) and proudly call their blindness sight (John 10:40, 41), desiring to be designated as οἱ βλέποντες. Hence they also set themselves up as ὁδηγοί or "guides" of others.  With what result, Jesus states in a proverbial expression in which τυφλός and τυφλόν are made emphatic by being placed before ἐάν.  Seeing eyes would avoid a pit, but when neither guide nor guided have such eyes, both will plunge down and break their necks; and βόθυνον may well intend to symbolize hell.

15) **Now Peter, answering, said to him, Explain to us the parable,** i. e., the *mashal,* which Jesus spoke to the people (v. 11) when he summed up the whole contention with the Pharisees.

16) **And he said: Even yet are you, too, without understanding?  Do you not comprehend that everything that goes into the mouth passes into the belly and is then expelled into a privy; but the things that go out of the mouth come out of the heart, and those are the ones that defile the man.  For out of the heart come wicked considerations, murders, adulteries, fornications, thefts, false testimonies, blasphemies.  These things are what defile the man; but to eat with unwashed hands does not defile the man.**  The rebuke that "up to this point," ἀκμήν (adverbial accusative, R. 488), the disciples are

still without understanding of truths as plain as the
ones in question, is surely deserved.  Yet the idea that
in themselves certain foods produced defilement merely
by being eaten, apart from the condition of the heart
(whether it intended to disobey God or not), still confused Peter and the others for whom he spoke.

17)    The rebuke continues with the question, "Do
you not comprehend?" meaning that this is so easy to
grasp.  In Mark 7:18, 19 two points are added, namely
that food is something outside of the man and does not
go into his heart but only into the κοιλία, the abdominal
cavity containing the stomach and the intestines.  Defilement is impossible unless the heart is involved. Mark
says that this made all meats clean as far as they themselves are concerned.  This, however, was no abroga-
tion of the Levitical laws concerning meats.  For here
the heart would necessarily be involved: forbidden
meats could be eaten only by a Jew who was set on
disobeying God's Levitical law.  An ἀφεδρών is not a
"draught" or a "drain" but a place to which one retires
(ἀπό) and sits down (ἕδρα, seat).  Food merely passes
through the body in the common process of nature.

18)    Matters stand entirely different with what
comes out of the mouth.  That, as Mark 7:21 states it,
is "from within," ἔσωθεν, originating inside of the man,
namely in his heart, the seat of all thought, emotion,
and volition in the Biblical and the Greek conceptions.
Here is where the defilement is to be sought.  This does
not, however, imply that the defilement ensues only
when the contents of the heart are uttered through the
mouth; they are what they are before they ever begin
to be expressed.

19)    "For" explains the defilement by stating what
comes out of the heart and hence what is in the heart.
This is an actual cesspool filled with wicked "consideration," πονηροί, "actively and viciously wicked."  In the
New Testament διαλογισμοί is always used in an evil

sense even when no modifier is added, C.-K. 683.   The
appositions give us a list of these thoughts, six in Matthew but twelve in Mark 7:21, 22.   The fact that some
of these sins are deeds and not merely words makes no
difference when we recall Jesus' exposition of the Commandments in 5:21, etc.

20)   These sins that arise from the heart defile the
man, and the disregard of the man-made precept of
washing does nothing of the kind, no matter what the
Pharisees teach.

21)   **And having gone out from thence, Jesus
withdrew to the parts of Tyre and Sidon.**   He thus
continues his course (14:13) of withdrawing from
the populous centers into retired places and thus
avoiding his enemies.   This is not flight but well-con-
sidered prudence.   Since εἰς may mean "to" as well
as "into," it leaves uncertain whether Jesus crossed or
only approached the border.   "The parts of Tyre and
Sidon," however, refer to sections of Syrophoenicia
and not merely to the border sections of Galilee.

22)   **And lo, a Canaanite woman, having come
out from those borders, cried out, saying: Show me
mercy, Lord, son of David!   My daughter is badly
demon-possessed.**   "Lo" pictures the case as being
remarkable.   Even here in this distant section Jesus
and his miraculous power are known (4:24).   Writing for readers of Jewish descent, Matthew uses
"Canaanite," recalling the Old Testament account that
the   Jews   had   not   completely   exterminated   the
Canaanites as God had commanded.   This woman was
a descendant of that old pagan race.   Mark (7:26),
writing for Gentile Christians, calls her a Greek in the
sense of a Gentile, to mark her religion; and a Syrophoenician by race, using the more modern term for
her nationality.   Before Jesus could enter her country,
she "came out from those borders" to find Jesus at
the edge of Galilee.   Mark 7:31 makes it certain

that Jesus afterward went through Sidon, but this
woman took no chances — he might turn back from
the border and so get beyond her reach.    Jesus wanted
no man to know of his presence, but word got out,
nevertheless.    When Mark tells us that he was in a
house, this means only that he was in retirement and
doing no work among the people.    It does not place
the following scene in the house, for v. 23 transpires
in the open.

Jesus and his disciples had probably just dined
in the house, which would make the reference to "the
children's bread" in v. 26 the more suggestive.    As
he leaves the house to go on, the woman is there,
having, perhaps, anxiously waited for him.    With the
aorist imperative she begs for an act of mercy, and
ἔλεος always means pity for the suffering, for the sad
and painful consequences resulting from sin and our
sinful state; while χάρις always refers to the guilt of
sin.    She begs the act of mercy for herself, but her
sad state is due to the terrible state of her little daughter who is demon-possessed.    The mere verb is enough
— there is no need to add the particular havoc the
demon wrought.    On the actuality of demoniacal possession see the notes on 4:24.

When the woman combines "Lord" with "son of
David," she understands "Lord" in the higher sense
as being in fact the Messianic title.    She plainly reveals that she has knowledge of the Messianic hopes
of Israel and had heard that they were being connected with Jesus as the promised great descendant
of King David.    It is not necessary to regard her as
a Jewish proselyte, and it is quite enough to believe
that knowledge had come to her from the reports
that had been carried into her heathen land.    She
surely had tried the remedies offered in her neighborhood for her daughter's recovery, all of which had
proved ineffective.    Then she heard of Jesus and how

he with a mere word had expelled demons from poor sufferers like her daughter. These reports found fertile soil in her heart. How she had longed to reach this mighty Helper! Now he had come to this far corner of Galilee, and here she finds him with her fervent prayer.

23) **But he did not answer her a word.** This apparently strange silence on the part of Jesus must not be separated from what follows. **And his disciples, having come forward, kept requesting him, saying, Dismiss her, for she is yelling from behind us.** The picture presents Jesus walking on in silence, the woman following him with her frantic cries. The imperfect ἠρώτων is descriptive, and the verb denotes respectful asking. One after another of the disciples comes up to Jesus and joins in this request. The verb "dismiss her" is neutral in force and leaves to the discretion of Jesus whether he will dismiss her by granting or by denying her request. Yet the disciples had never seen Jesus deny anyone pleading for help, although at times he had delayed a little while (John 4:47, etc.; Matt. 8:5, etc.), namely whenever some question had first to be settled. It is fair, therefore, to conclude that the disciples think of a dismissal by granting the woman's prayer. They indicate, however, that they are not moved entirely by pity for her distress. Jesus did not want his presence to become known, but the outcries of this woman were bound to attract public attention. It was quite a scene for thirteen men to walk along with a woman shouting ὄπισθεν, not "behind them," but with the greater precision of the Greek, "from behind them," R. 645. The thing may also have appeared unseemly to the disciples.

24) The motives that prompt the action of Jesus are by far more profound. **He, however, answering said, I was not commissioned save to the sheep**

**that have been lost of Israel's house.** Since Jesus
is about to cross the boundary of the Holy Land and
to go into Gentile territory for a brief time, all those
present must know that this in no way implies a
transfer of his ministry from the Jews to the Gentiles
or even an inclusion of the Gentiles into his Messianic
ministry. The working of this miracle was not to be
understood as ushering in the performance of a great
number of additional miracles among the Gentiles of
this territory. The divine plan, according to which
Jesus "was commissioned," was to work out redemption in the Jewish nation and not elsewhere; as soon
as it had been worked out, it would be carried to all
the world. Moreover, this would begin in less than
a year, following the next Passover. With this divine
plan Jesus was in fullest accord, and his great work
was already hastening to its climax. These mighty
facts must be thoroughly understood. That is why
Jesus delays and explains them in advance in the most
impressive way and does not postpone the explanation until after the woman has gone.

We must, therefore, give up the explanation, so
offensive to moral feeling, that Jesus pretended to be
hard and tortured the woman with uncertainty for the
purpose of testing her faith in order then to praise
her. Jesus never plays the actor, and any edification
secured from such a view has doubtful value. Akin
to this view is the other that Jesus puts off the woman
in order that she may overcome his refusal by the
strength of her faith or until Jesus was led to change
his mind. Confusion is also introduced by referring
to other Gentiles whom Jesus had helped, for instance,
the centurion mentioned in 8:5, etc. But why overlook the many Gentile sick mentioned in 4:24, and the
demoniacs in 8:28, etc.? Jesus never hesitated to
heal Gentiles as long as no wrong deductions could
be drawn from these acts. Here the case was far

different. While Jesus granted this woman's request, although he went through Sidon (Mark 7:31), we hear of no further teaching or healing in this pagan land. And Jesus acted thus, not because this would have obviated his acceptability as a Messiah by the Jews — his nation had already rejected him! — but because of the divine plan of redemption.

When he calls the Jews "sheep," all his love and kindness toward his nation is revealed. He thus also denominates himself as their true Shepherd. The perfect participle, added emphatically by a second article (R. 776), "that have been lost," has its present implication, "and are thus now in this condition." "House of Israel" is not a mixing of figures, since it is a stereotyped title of high honor for the chosen nation.

25) **But she, having come, was worshipping him, saying, Lord, be helping me!** While Jesus was answering the disciples, the woman found her way to the feet of Jesus, prostrated herself in utter humility and deepest appeal, and begged for his help. The imperfect pictures the scene in its progress: we see her bending her head to the dust. Whereas she at first used the aorist ἐλέησον to indicate the one gift of mercy, she now uses the present βοήθει to express the enduring help she desires. Whatever divine directions Jesus follows and must follow in his divine office this woman is sure will not conflict with helping her in her distress.

26) **But he, answering, said, It is not an excellent thing to take the bread of the children and to throw it to the little pet dogs.** Even now Jesus does not directly address the woman; an αὐτῇ, "to her," is not found in the text. Like the previous statement, this, too, is a general proposition and is even phrased in proverbial form. Yet Jesus does not say: οὐκ ἔξεστιν, "it is not right," but: οὐκ ἔστι καλόν, "it is not

a fine thing" to do.  He does not say "dogs," as our versions translate the diminutive κυνάρια, but "little dogs," such as are kept in the house as pets.  This difference is vital.  In the Orient dogs have no owners but run wild and act as scavengers for all garbage and offal.  Such "dogs," the Jews called all Gentiles — ownerless, unclean in every way, always to be avoided.  Jesus offers an entirely different thought when he speaks of "the little pet dogs" when referring to the Gentiles.  These have owners who keep them even in the house and feed them by throwing them bits from the table.  No Oriental dogs of the street were ever allowed in a house, to say nothing of a dining-room.

The thought expressed is thus identical in substance with v. 24, adding only one point.  The bread is the ministry of Jesus and the blessings he dispenses.  This is for the children, the chosen nation.  They recline at table while Jesus dispenses his blessings to them.  Any little pet dog in the house is not allowed to lie on one of the couches as though it, too, were a child; this certainly would not be καλόν, "a fine thing" to allow.  A pet dog is given his food in a different way: he is allowed to pick up anything the children may drop while they are eating at table.  God has not altogether excluded the Gentiles from the ministry of Jesus.  Let us note that "the little pet dogs" does not refer to all the Gentiles in the world but only to such as lived among the Jews or came into contact with them and could thus in a way obtain some of their blessings.

The word of Jesus is thus not nearly as "hard" as interpreters have made it.  This word is not a "temptation" which this woman is asked to overcome.  Such ideas miss the real point.  In both v. 24 and 26 Jesus simply asks the disciples and the woman to accept the divine plan that Jesus must work out his mission among the Jews alone, and that thus the blessings dispensed during his ministry by that mission shall be set before the Jews alone. Any share of Gentile individuals in any of these blessings can be only incidental during Jesus' ministry in Israel. Jesus was now about to pass into Syrophoenician territory, it was vital that this be understood, especially right here and now when a Gentile woman was begging for Messianic help (note her cry, "son of David").

27) **But she said, Yea, Lord; for the little pet dogs, too, eat some of the little crumbs that keep falling from the table of their lords.** The woman's answer is wonderful in every way. Wholeheartedly she accepts what Jesus says about the divine arrangement of his Messianic mission as being confined to the chosen nation. Her consent to it is far more than formal or superficial: she *understands* and consents, and she submits without question or thought of objection. She does not even ask why God acted as he did. The keen ears of her faith catch also the full implication as regards the children and their little pet dogs. In Homer they are called τραπεζῆες κύνες, "dogs fed from their master's table" (Liddell and Scott). The present ἐσθίει means: "they usually eat," and ἀπό is to be taken in the partitive sense: "some of the little crumbs"; all of them would require the accusative, R. 519 and 577. The present participle τῶν πιπτόντων is durative: "that keep falling" from their lords' table. She even calls the children "the lords" of these little pet dogs. She keeps entirely to the figurative language of Jesus and by means of it expresses her faith in all its humbleness and submissiveness, begging, as one of those little pet dogs, a few tiny crumbs which the children, in eating, inadvertantly keep dropping on the floor. Here is faith in all its lowly beauty.

28) **Then, answering (3:15), Jesus said to her, O woman, great is thy faith! Let it be to thee as thou wilt. And healed was her daughter from that very hour.** Now Jesus grants her prayer. It is unwarranted to think that Jesus kept her on tenterhooks for the purpose of making her faith stretch itself to the utmost; his action was not like holding a morsel higher and higher to make a dog jump to the limit of his ability before rewarding him. The greatness of this woman's faith, here openly praised by Jesus, lies not in its strength and its intensity which overcome obstacles set up by Jesus and grow greater as these obstacles were increased. The greatness lay in submissively accepting and in rightly understanding what Jesus said about his Messianic mission. Her great distress did not dull her ears or darken her mind to Jesus' word. The view that she overcame the reluctance of Jesus to help her attributes to Jesus what was foreign to him and gives a wrong turn to the narrative.

This is the second Gentile whose faith Jesus praised (8:10). In both cases a faith was manifested that truly understands and wholly accepts the Lord's Word. Note the necessity of this understanding and perceiving as expressed in 13:13-15, 51; 16:9; also in Eph. 1:17, 18. Every misconception on which one relies is false faith, no matter how strong the reliance may be. All right knowledge of the actual facts revealed by Christ forms the eternal basis of faith (5:18), and faith is great according to the measure of the confidence ($\pi i \sigma \tau \iota s$) it places in this basis, neither questioning nor rationalizing about all the facts involved nor about the divine will revealed in them.

The Greek ὦ is used sparingly with vocatives, so that, when it is used, it carries with it both emotion and solemnity, R. 463, etc. "Be it unto thee," as in 9:29; "as thou wilt," as in 7:12; "healed is thy daughter," as in 8:13; "from that very hour," as in 9:22. No further miracles and no teaching are reported during this visit of Jesus' to the parts of Tyre and Sidon.

29) **And having departed thence, Jesus came alongside the Sea of Galilee ($\pi\alpha\rho\acute{\alpha}$, R. 615) ; and having gone up into a mountain, he was sitting there.** From the far northwest Jesus travelled in a wide sweep to the far southeast into Decapolis, the country of the Ten Cities. How he crossed to the far side of the lake is not indicated; we are told only that afterward he took a boat on the eastern shore and crossed to Magadan, v. 39.

30) **And there came to him numerous multitudes having with them lame, blind, dumb, cripples, and numerous others; and they flung them at his feet. And he healed them, so that the multitude wondered, seeing the dumb speaking, the cripples sound, the lame walking around, and the blind seeing; and they glorified the God of Israel.** For three days this went on (v. 32) somewhat as in the territory of Gennesaret (14:34, etc.). The sufferers were simply deposited at Jesus' feet who healed them all — a tremendous statement!

31) The effect was astonishment, the constative aorist registering the fact, $\ddot{\omega}\sigma\tau\epsilon$ with the infinitive here expressing the actual (and not the contemplated) result. Significant is the statement that they glorified "the God of Israel." This shows that the majority of the people were Gentiles. We know, too, that this section was predominantly Gentile although it was a part of the tetrarchy of Herod Antipas. Since it, together with Galilee, was regarded as a Jewish domain, Jesus had no need to emphasize his being sent only to Israel, for this territory belonged to his people. It differed in this regard from Syrophoenicia (v. 24,

26). The many Gentiles healed are thus in the same class with those mentioned in 8:5, etc.; 8:25, etc.; 4:24, 25. The latter passage shows that at a previous time some had come from Decapolis to Galilee and had found healing at his hands; but not until this time has Jesus visited this section, except for the brief landing reported in 8:28, etc. While nothing is said about teaching, we cannot agree that Jesus spent three days with these multitudes without teaching them about "the God of Israel" and his kingdom of salvation.

**32) Now Jesus, having called forward his disciples, said: I have compassion on the multitude because three days already they remain near me and have not what they may eat. And I am not willing to dismiss them fasting lest, perhaps, they grow faint on the road.** Some modern interpreters regard the accounts of the two feedings of multitudes as in reality referring to the same incident. But there are differences in time, place, number fed, number of loaves, of fishes and of baskets full left over. Matthew was present at both miracles and is a safe authority. The inner difference is not discussed by these interpreters. The feeding of the 5,000 intends to reveal Jesus as the Bread of Life as John 6:26-65 shows *in extenso;* while the feeding of the 4,000 does not go beyond the care of Jesus for our bodily needs.

In the case of the 5,000 Jesus broached the question of feeding them to Philip alone as soon as Jesus saw the crowd assembling; see verses 14 and 15 and the author's commentary on John (6:5-7). Here three days elapse before Jesus speaks. In the other miracle the disciples become worried regarding the multitude and toward evening come to Jesus and urge him to send it away. Here the disciples remain unworried for three days, and it is Jesus who finally

speaks to them about feeding the crowds before he
sends them away and himself leaves the locality.

On σπλαγχνίζομαι see 14:14; even the unsatisfied
hunger of men awakens the compassion of Jesus.   This is all the more the case since these
people have for three days remained near (πρός in
the verb, R. 623) Jesus; ἡμέραι τρεῖς is a parenthetic
nominative of time, R. 460. After this long stay
near Jesus, during which they forgot everything else
except what they saw and heard from him, and after
all supplies they had brought along had been consumed, he cannot simply dismiss them by telling them
to go home since he is himself leaving.   The fact
that he is thinking of their physical needs becomes
evident in the final clause: "lest, perhaps, they grow
faint on the road," ἐκλυθῶσιν, aorist, literally, "be completely unloosed" as a bowstring is unstrung.   In
τί with the subjunctive φάγωσι we have an indirect
question, one of deliberation used in place of a relative object clause, R. 737, etc.

33) **And the disciples say to him, Whence have
we in a desert place so much bread as to fill so much
of a multitude?**   The emphasis is on ἡμῖν together
with ἐν ἐρημίᾳ (supply χώρᾳ), with the copula εἰσί being
omitted: "Whence *to us in a desert place* (are) so
many breads (flat cakes of bread)?"   Mark 8:4 asks,
"Whence shall *one* be able to fill these men?" meaning
"one of us."   The disciples declare that it is *beyond
them* to furnish the required quantity of bread from
any source here in the desert.   They imply that it is
*Jesus alone* who could do that.   The τίς in Mark cannot include Jesus but must be modified by the ἡμῖν
in Matthew.   Note, too, that the disciples do not
speak of a minimum: "that everyone may take a
little," as they did in connection with the other miracle
(John 6:7) ; but of a maximum: "so as to fill so much
of a multitude," the aorist χορτάσαι to indicate complete

filling. This is the very verb used in 14:20 to state
that the 5,000 were actually filled.

The disciples remember that other miracle. They
are not again worried. They have learned that Jesus
does not have in mind that they are to find a supply
somewhere. Yet they do not tell Jesus what he should
do; they have learned to  leave everything in his
hands. To say that the reply of the disciples gives
no evidence of the knowledge of a previous miraculous
feeding and betrays nothing but complete perplexity,
is to misread not only this reply but also all that
precedes this reply. We regard ὥστε with the infinitive
as expressing contemplated result: "so as," and not
"so that," R. 1089.

34) **And Jesus says to them, How many breads
have you?    And they said, Seven, and a few small
fishes.** The compassion of Jesus intends to delay no
longer. As far as the multitude is concerned, the
record emphasizes only this compassion in the performance of the miracle. We read of no astonishment on the part of the people, or of any movement
to proclaim him king.

The seven flat cakes of bread and the few small
fishes (evidently more than just two) are what is
left of the supplies of the disciples themselves and
are not secured from anyone in the multitude. No
one now speaks as Andrew did (John 6:9): "What
are they among so many?" The disciples answer with
alacrity; they feel quite certain as to what Jesus
intends to do. That other miracle has taught them a
valuable lesson.

It is unfair to them to speak of their forgetfulness
and their obtuseness and to say that Jesus might have
rebuked them and yet refrained from doing so but
with a sigh asked only what amount of food the disciples had. Nothing of this appears in the record;
on the contrary, just about the opposite is indicated.

We note only that Jesus deals in particular with his
disciples. They are to know about his motive of compassion; they are to see that he is repeating what he
has already done; they are to realize that this repetition implies that Jesus is able always to provide bread
and to supply earthly needs. We are in that period
of Christ's ministry when the intensive training of the
Twelve is his great concern, for there are only a few
more months before the final Passover shall arrive.

**35) And having passed an order to the multi-
tude to recline on the ground, he took the seven
loaves and the fishes; and having given thanks, he
broke them and kept giving to the disciples, and
the disciples to the multitudes.** The procedure followed in this miracle is identical with that recorded
in 14:19. Apparently, the people were again divided
into groups of 50 and 100 as in Mark 6:39, 40. But
now they must lie down on the bare ground (ἐπὶ τὴν γῆν)
for the season has advanced to summer, and the grass
has been dried up.

36) Mark's account reads as though Jesus performed two acts: one with regard to the bread, the
other with regard to the fish. "To give thanks" is,
of course, quite the same as "to bless" in 14:19; both
mean that Jesus pronounced the prayer usually spoken
at a meal. If anything of special significance had distinguished this prayer in either miracle, at least one
of the evangelists would have given us the exceptional
words. The miracle was thus not wrought by the
words of thanksgiving but simply by the silent will
of Jesus when he broke the bread and the fishes and
passed out the pieces. The aorist ἔκλασε reports only
the summary fact that Jesus "broke" the food; but
the iterative imperfect ἐδίδου, "he kept giving" to the
disciples, describes the multiplication of the food in
Jesus' hands. He again and again loaded each disciple's basket with pieces to be distributed to the peo-

ple. Always there was more to hand out. Only after
all had been supplied with all that they reached out
for were the seven loaves and the few fishes entirely
used up. The waiters at this miracle-meal were the
Twelve.

37) Exactly as in 14:20, the tremendous fact is
now reported in the very briefest form. **And they
did eat all and were filled; and they took up what
was superfluous of the broken pieces, seven baskets
full.** On ἐχορτάσθησαν see 14:20. It seems that this
time the fragments that were left over — some people
being afraid that they will not get enough — were
gathered up by the disciples without a further order
from Jesus (John 6:12), although we cannot be sure
of this since both Matthew and Mark omit this order
in their records of the first miracle. But now they
use σπυρίδες for "baskets," whereas before they wrote
κόφινοι. Both were woven of wicker, but the former
seem to have been larger as is indicated by Acts 9:25
and by examples given by M.-M. 618, one σφυρίς
holding fifty loaves of bread. It is, therefore, not
safe to say that, while this time only 4,000 were
fed, the food left over was but little more than half
the amount that had remained over at the former
feeding. The seven *spurides* may have held even more
than the twelve *kophinoi*. The distinction between
the types of baskets is retained in a marked way in
16:9, 10 and in Mark 8:19, 20, where, if they had
been practically identical, only one of the terms
would have sufficed.

38) **Now those eating were four thousand men
apart from women and little children.** Again a
great host was fed, and again only the men were
counted; and οἱ ἐσθίοντες, the present participle,
characterizes them according to the continuous act
of eating: "the eaters." The numbers mentioned
in connection with both miracles are merely historical,

and all efforts to give them an allegorical meaning have proved unsatisfactory.

39) **And having dismissed the multitudes, he went into the boat and came into the borders of Magadan.** This dismissal implies that Jesus himself was leaving. A sojourn of only three days did he grant this neighborhood. The dismissal is made without a word being said about the miracle which crowned all the many that had been wrought during those three days. We read of no excitement such as that which occurred after the other feeding. It is due to the great reticence of the inspired writers that nothing is added about the effect upon the people, which, surely, must have been profound. Nothing was said about a boat in v. 29, but the article in the phrase εἰς τὸ πλοῖον indicates that Jesus left in the same boat in which he had arrived. "The borders of Magadan" (not "Magdala," from Mary Magdalene), for which Mark 8:10 has, "the parts of Dalmanutha," have not been located. It is usually supposed that this locality adjoins the lake on its western shore. Since both names are so unknown, the conclusion that the place was very small seems to be warranted.

# CHAPTER XVI

1)   **And the Pharisees and Sadducees, having come forward tempting, asked him to show a sign from the heaven to them.**   It is overdrawing the picture to think that these opponents were watching for the boat of Jesus to arrive and then pounced upon him with their demand. They came forward when the news of his arrival had spread. They may have been waiting at Capernaum and, on getting word, hurried to Magadan. The fact that the Sadducees were joining the Pharisees in their hostility to Jesus plainly marks the rapid progress of this hostility. And Matthew keeps repeating and thus emphasizing this conjunction, v. 6, 11, 12. This prepares the reader for the revelation recorded in v. 21.

On the Pharisees and the Sadducees, here classed together by one Greek article, see 3:7. The former stood for stern holiness and by virtue of their numbers carried the common people with them; the Sadducees, skeptics and high livers, represented the aristocracy of the land, having at their head the high priest and his connection as a kind of priestly-political nobility that was at once rich and powerful. One of the wives of Herod the Great was Mariamne, the daughter of Simon, the high priest. The Sadducees must thus be classed as Herodians (Mark 3:6; 8:15) who naturally sought the favor and the support of the Herodian family. Local Pharisees of Galilee (9:3, 11; 12:2, 14, 24, 38), followed later by a delegation of Pharisees from the capital (15:1), had clashed sharply with Jesus; and now even a delegation of Sadducees unites with the Pharisees.

They put on a pleasing mien and pretend that they would be willing to accept Jesus if he would only present the necessary credentials. They imply that the signs he has hitherto wrought are insufficient, being only earthly, and they must require of him (ἐπηρώτησαν) something more adequate and convincing, namely "a sign out of heaven," some visible heavenly display (ἐπιδεῖξαι). This repeats the demand recorded 12:38. And Matthew now adds the remark that it was renewed with an evil intent, "tempting him." They felt sure that Jesus would not be able to furnish this kind of a sign and that they would thus be able completely to discredit him with the people. They hid their wicked purpose under a fair outward approach. These men made themselves the devil's tools by suggesting to Jesus that he perform a deed for which his Father had not commissioned him, that he make himself a Messiah after the fashion of men, so as to gain their favor and their support by self-chosen means. We need not add that Jesus at once saw through the temptation and most vigorously repelled the cunning suggestion.

On the sign here again demanded see 12:38. A σημεῖον, whether it be a miracle or some other deed, always signifies something, points beyond itself by making a revelation, not by means of a word, but by means of a deed. Here the sign is to prove that Jesus is the Messiah. The unbelief of these Pharisees and these Sadducees declares that only a sign "out of heaven" could suffice. There had been such signs: when Joshua made the sun and the moon stand still, when Elijah caused fire to fall from heaven, and when upon Samuel's prayer thunder discomfited the Philistines (I Sam. 7:9, etc.). The reasoning seems to be that, since the Messiah will be greater than all the prophets and greater even than Moses, he will prove this by doing at least one sign which in outward

grandeur will exceed all other signs that have ever
been wrought. But this conception is wrong, as
wrong as the unbelief from which it springs. The
value of a sign does not lie in the display it makes,
nor in what may make it a τέρας, prodigy, or wonder,
but in what it signifies: grace, mercy, deliverance, and
salvation. In 15:32, etc., as in 14:15, etc., there was
no display; the same was true with regard to a large
number of Christ's miracles, but, oh, how blessed is
what they signify!

As far as unbelief is concerned, even the signs that
Moses wrought did not affect Pharaoh's obdurate
heart. Though one arose from the dead and warned
the five brothers of Dives, they would not believe.
Voltaire casts off the mask when he declares: "Even
if a miracle should be wrought in the open market
place before a thousand sober witnesses, I would rather
mistrust my senses than admit a miracle."

Unbelief always finds a way to refuse to accept
the truth, no matter with what credentials it is presented. As was the case here, another credential can
always be demanded and those already furnished be
discredited. What would prevent the Pharisees from
attributing any "sign out of heaven" to the aid of
Beelzebul? This applies to all modern unbelief which
rejects the testimony of the divine records regarding
the reality and even the possibility of miracles and the
signs as well as all that they signify. Where the Word
plus the signs awaken no faith, all that is left is what
Jesus points out to his opponents.

2) **But he, answering, said to them: When
evening has come, you say, Fair weather! for the
heaven is fiery; and at morning, Storm today! for
the lowering heaven is fiery. The expression of the
heaven you know how to discern but the signs of
the seasons you cannot.** The decision regarding the
question as to whether this part of Christ's reply be-

longs in the text or not we leave to textual criticism. The external textual evidence is against the genuineness of these words. It is certain that they have not been introduced from Luke 12:54-56, where showers and great heat are indicated by weather signs in the west and in the south, whereas here west and east, fair and foul weather, are contrasted. The internal testimony, as Zahn points out, is in favor of the genuineness of the words. As regards the use of γινώσκειν where Zahn thinks Matthew would have used εἰδέναι, see below. The omission of these verses from so many texts may be due to an effort to bring Matthew's record of the present incident into conformity with that of Mark (8:11-13).

The phenomena mentioned are those that occur in Palestine. When the sky is fiery red in the evening, the wind has driven the clouds and the vapors to the west, over the Mediterranean Sea; and this naturally indicates that the following day will be fair, as in that country rain and clouds come from the west where the sea is. With ὀψίας supply ὥρας in the genitive absolute: "a late hour having come"; and εὐδία is a nominative that needs no verb: "Fair weather!"

3) The reverse is true when the fiery redness is seen in the morning, when the sun rises above the eastern horizon. Then the prediction is foul weather because during the night the wind has carried the vapors from the sea over the land. What applies to Palestine, does not, of course, apply to other lands where land and sea have other relative positions. Yet everywhere we have expert weather prophets who know all the signs even though they fail at times. "Storm," χειμών, is again the nominative without a verb, and στυγνάζων, "lowering," threatening and ugly, is the descriptive present participle.

The Jews had asked for "a sign out of the heaven"; for that reason Jesus uses this illustration about "the heaven" and its signs of weather. "Speaking about signs from heaven," he says, "the only signs from heaven you can at all read are the signs regarding the weather." There is a sad touch of irony in his words. The verb γινώσκετε seems to be in place here since it conveys something more than εἴδετε, namely: "you have sense enough to comprehend." The use of this verb thus strengthens and does not weaken the internal evidence for the genuineness of this part of Jesus' answer. On πρόσωπον Bengel remarks: "The *expression* of the heaven, not the *face*; the expression of a man alters, not his face." "To discern" is to distinguish or discriminate, here between one and the same phenomenon: the fiery red glow of the heaven as it appears in the west at evening or in the east in the morning.

When Jesus adds: "but the signs of the seasons you cannot" (discern), he indicates that his illustration involves a metaphor. These Jews see only the physical and not the spiritual heaven (the kingdom of the heavens that has now come). Here is this other heaven that is just full of "the signs of the times," and these men do not have sense enough (γινώσκειν) to read these infinitely more important signs. Καιρός is qualitative over against the quantitative χρόνος; it always signifies a section of time (a "season") that is marked by what it contains. Here were these wonderful days that were marked by the most significant events, all kinds of "signs" and not merely miracles, for the term is wider. These days were marked by the coming and the message of the Baptist, by the fulfillment of the Old Testament prophecies, by the appearance and the work of Jesus, and by all the effects these produced upon the people. All these were signs that were like the red sunset; they brought εὐδία, "fair weather," grace and every Messianic blessing. But these Jews saw nothing.

There were also signs that were like the redness in the morning sky, that heralded σήμερον χειμών, "storm today." For here were the blindness and the obduracy of the Jewish leaders and the unresponsiveness of the nation as such; here were the rankest hypocrisy and the most wilful resistance to every proffer of grace. It was the same sun, but it was shining from the other side, and it was the same redness, but it was "lowering," threatening. For these signs of the times presaged the storm of the divine judgment about to descend.

We are expert in meteorology and weather forecasting, and the business outlook and the political changes are most carefully weighed. But what about the spiritual signs of the times? Thousands do not know that there are such signs, or they look at them and then see no meaning in them: the spread of the gospel over the world; the Bible being translated into language after language and being ready to every man's hand; the renewal of true faith in unexpected quarters; the testimony of martyrs being repeated from time to time; the works of mercy and of Christian devotion. On the other hand, the rise of the infernal powers on the horizon: the increase of lawlessness; the spread of Christless altars; the open attacks on the Bible, on Christ, and on the gospel; the rise of antichrists; the defection of the churches under modernism, etc. Have men not sense enough to read these signs?

4) With words that are quite identical with those found in 12:39 Jesus proceeds. **A generation wicked and adulterous is out after a sign** (i. e., is set on seeking one) ; **and a sign shall not be given to it save the sign of Jonah.** Here we have a clear case where Jesus used the same words a second time on a different occasion; he did this repeatedly, and it is to no purpose to assume that he did not. See the exposition of 12:39. The sign of Jonah is the resur-

rection of Christ, the climax of the signs of grace for
believers, but at the same time given also to these
Pharisees and Sadducees and to all unbelievers as the
final, fateful sign of their judgment and destruction.
For the Christ whom his enemies crucified and recru-
cify will come as the risen Christ to be their judge and
to send them to their doom (26:64). Scorning to
waste another word on these men, Matthew writes:
**and having left them, he went away.** This, too, was
a sign; for when Jesus leaves a man, this means that
grace leaves him to judgment.

5) **And the disciples, having come to the other
side, forgot to take bread.** Because the disciples
are not mentioned in 15:39, and Jesus is not mentioned
in 16:5, the claim is made that in 15:39, Jesus sailed
to the west shore alone and that the disciples now
follow him (16:5) to that shore; and those who make
this claim find these statements in contradiction with
Mark 8:13. But a careful reading will show that
Jesus alone is mentioned in 15:39, etc., because something pertaining especially to him is to be recorded;
and in the same way the disciples are mentioned in
16:5, because something especially referring to them is
to be told. Besides, it would be rather ridiculous for the
disciples to forget bread when going to the western
shore where the population was numerous and any
amount of bread desired could be quickly obtained.
Going to the eastern shore was a different matter.
So Jesus and his disciples first cross to Magadan on
the west, and he and they now cross again to the east
or the northeast. The two aorists express simultaneous action: ἐλθόντες and ἀπελάθοντο, both recording facts
merely as such. When the disciples arrive at the other
side, the discovery is made that they forgot ἄρτους, cakes
of bread, having only a single cake in the boat (Mark
8:14).

6) **Now Jesus said to them, See to it and beware of the leaven of the Pharisees and Sadducees!
But they considered within themselves, saying, We
did not take bread.** The reaction due to the
encounter recorded in v. 1, etc., continues. Again
the Pharisees and the Sadducees are mentioned by
name and as constituting one class. In Mark 8:15 the
mention of Herod refers to the Sadducees as being the
supporters of Herod (see above on v. 1).

7) The disciples fail completely to understand
what Jesus has in mind when he mentions this leaven.
They think it over in their minds and while they are
doing so quietly say, "We did not take bread" — that
is what he has in mind.

8) **Now, when Jesus knew it, he said: Why are
you considering within yourselves, men of little
faith, that you do not have bread? Do you not yet
comprehend nor remember the five loaves of the five
thousand and how many baskets you took; nor the
seven loaves of the four thousand and how many
baskets you took? How do you not comprehend
that I spoke to you not concerning bread? But you
beware of the leaven of the Pharisees and Sadducees!**

Jesus knew by using his divine means of knowing.
Both the question why they are thinking of nothing
but bread and the address, "men of little faith," indicate that Jesus is disappointed in his disciples and
that he is moved to let them feel how much more he had
expected from them.

9) The next questions reveal just "why" they are
thinking as they do, and just what makes them "men
of little faith." Even yet, at this advanced stage of
their training, they do not comprehend, i. e., do not
apply their νοῦς or mind to what Jesus has taught
and shown them. One of the great weaknesses of

faith is this slowness, dullness, ignorance of the mind. It tries the patience of Jesus and makes him speak with sharpness. As far as worry about forgetting to take bread along on this trip is concerned, do these disciples fail to remember the bread Jesus provided for the 5,000, with twelve baskets full for the disciples? Do they suppose for a moment that Jesus will now starve them?

10) Likewise, how he fed the 4,000, with seven baskets full left over for the disciples? Jesus himself retains the distinction between κόφινοι and σπυρίδες, from which fact we conclude that they were not identical; see 15:37.

11) These two miracles should have made it impossible for the disciples to think that Jesus was speaking about bread. The unmodified νοεῖτε of v. 9 now receives its object in the ὅτι clause, and the question introduced with πῶς brings out the denseness of the minds of these disciples and shames them for not using their minds.

The next statement is independent; it does not depend on the preceding ὅτι. Jesus merely repeats the warning given in v. 6, but now "leaven" is in contrast with "bread" (plural "breads"). Jesus declines to give a further explanation of what he means by this "leaven," thereby he demands that now at last the disciples are to use their minds. He insists that we use our mind when he speaks to us.

12) **Then they understood that he did not say to beware of the leaven of the bread but of the teaching of the Pharisee and Sadducees.** Mark 8:18, etc., brings out still more the sharpness with which Jesus rebuked the disciples. Finally it dawned on them what Jesus had in mind by the figure of the leaven, συνῆκαν from συνίημι, first aorist, reporting the fact that they finally understood. What contamina-

tion could the disciples receive from bread that was bought from bazars or bakeries belonging to Pharisees or Sadducees? Such ideas should have been impossible to them. Their failure to take bread along (save only one, Mark 8:14) had led them to think that Jesus intended to warn them never to buy bread from these opponents.

Now they saw that he was warning them against the διδαχή, "teaching" or doctrine of the Pharisees and the Sadducees. It is unwarranted to claim that here Matthew is mistaken, because in Luke 12:1, leaven is used with reference to hypocrisy. Luke speaks only of the leaven of the Pharisees and makes no reference to Sadducees. Again and again Jesus called the Pharisees hypocrites, and Luke 12:3, etc., follows that tone. There is no law that Jesus must always and in every connection use a figurative term in the same sense. Moreover, conduct and doctrine never lie far apart, for doctrine produces conduct and often is formulated so as to justify certain conduct. But here Jesus combines the distinctive teaching of both Pharisees and Sadducees and warns against it as being so much dangerous yeast, for these are the leaders of their people and promulgate their teaching among them.

Although they are diverse, the Pharisees teaching spurious legalism and formalism, whereas the Sadducees advocate skepticism and liberalism, both teachings have an appeal to the unwary and to all who are not grounded in the truth, including even the Twelve who, as we see, are still so slow to comprehend. The Pharisaic teaching appeals to the religious sense and leads men into a mere show of holiness (as legalism invariably does) ; that of the Sadducees appeals to the natural reason and leads men into empty rationalism and disbelief and thus into loose living. Both act like leaven which silently penetrates heart and mind when it is not recognized and expelled and thus antagonize the divine truth and ruin the soul.

## XIII

### Christ at Caesarea Philippi; Preparing the Disciples for His Death, Chapter 16:13-17:23

13) **Now Jesus, having come into the parts of Caesarea of Philip, was requesting his disciples, saying, Who do men say that the Son of man is? And they said: Some, John the Baptist; and others, Elijah; and still others, Jeremiah or one of the prophets.** We are advancing to the critical point of the Galilean ministry. John 6:66 marks the great turning point in the case of the people of Galilee, and since the twelfth chapter Matthew has been sketching the opposition of the ruling classes in its growing intensity. The murder of the Baptist caused Jesus to withdraw to distant places, now to this, then to that corner of the land, and so now after sailing from Magadan (15:39) to the north shore of the lake where the Jordan enters it, he takes the Twelve up to the neighborhood of the Caesarea that Herod's son Philip (who ruled this country as the tetrarch) had enlarged and beautified and had named after both Caesar and himself, "Caesarea of Philip," built by Philip in honor of Caesar. Mark adds the detail (8:27) that Jesus was in the outlying villages and asked his questions while he and the disciples were walking along the road.

The verb ἐρωτᾶν is dignified and marks the solemnity of the questions. The imperfect tense is descriptive and holds our attention to see what the answer will be. The first question is plainly preliminary. Jesus is not asking for information for his own sake, for he knows the different opinions of men. What he desires

is to have the disciples state the wrong opinions of men
in order to set over against them their own right conviction. These foolish opinions he does not care even
to discuss; the disciples themselves will brush them
aside. On "the Son of man," so appropriate in this
connection, see 8:20. The με in front of this title
should be cancelled in the codices that have it, for
Jesus always uses the title itself instead of the pronoun, and the addition of the pronoun to the title
would lend a peculiar and inappropriate sense to
the question, namely, "I, in so far as I am the Son
of man."

14) Perhaps the answer the disciples gave was
divided between several of them. The superstitious
idea of Herod has been discussed in 14:1; being that
of a king, it, no doubt, was seconded by others. Some
referred to Mal. 4:5, and considered Jesus to be Elijah,
the prophet returned to life and acting as a herald of
the Messiah (but see 11:14). Others made this forerunner the prophet Jeremiah, most probably basing
their idea on Jewish legends concerning Jeremiah. Or
they made Jesus at least one of the old prophets
(Luke 9:19). From Luke's record we also learn that
even the last of these opinions involved a resurrection
from the dead. Judaism was so conversant with the
resurrection that it made the Sadducees stand out as
an unbelieving sect when they denied the possibility
of the resurrection.

15) **He says to them, But you, who do you say
I am? And Simon Peter, answering, said, Thou art
the Christ, the Son of God the living.** The emphasis
is on ὑμεῖς over against οἱ ἄνθρωποι in v. 13. Jesus is
asking for a confession on the part of his disciples.
With λέγετε Jesus asks for a confession of the lips
but, of course, only as a true expression of their
heart's conviction. Any other confession is a falsehood. Jesus could see the heart, we cannot and must

thus accept the confession of the lips. Our only aid
is the conduct, the acts of the individual, the practice
of a congregation or of a church body. This, too, is
a confession and should harmonize fully with the confession of the lips. When it clashes with that, the
confession by deeds is the real confession by which we
must then judge. Deeds and practice always speak
louder and are more weighty than words.

16) It is natural for Peter, because of his readiness for action, to speak for the Twelve who undoubtedly indicated or voiced their assent. When
Jesus said "you," he had in mind the Twelve as a body,
for presently he speaks of "my church." Matthew
uses the full name "Simon Peter" as though to mark
the solemnity of the occasion: *he* is the one who spoke
for all of them. In σὺ εἶ ὁ Χριστός, the pronoun "thou"
has the emphasis, and this emphasis "passes on to
the remainder of the sentence and contributes point
and force to the whole," R. 678. Since the predicate
has the article, it is identical and interchangeable with
the subject, R. 768. Just as "thou" denotes one person and only one, so "the Christ" is one and only one,
and "thou" and "the Christ" are identical, and either
may be used as the subject or as the predicate. These
linguistic points are quite essential.

Ὁ Χριστός is appellative; the substantivized verbal
adjective from the verb χρίω, which denotes ceremonial or sacred anointing, is made a title: the Messiah,
the One Anointed, i. e., by God (3:16) for the great
office for which God commissioned Jesus. The conviction that Jesus was the Messiah promised in all the
Old Testament revelations (see 1:1) first drew the disciples to him, beginning with the Baptist's testimony
in John 1:32-34, and with the faith of the first disciples who attached themselves to Jesus in John
1:41, 45, 49. Over two years of constant intercourse

with Jesus had deepened and fully established this
conviction.

All those mentioned in v. 14, however highly they
were willing to rate Jesus, refused to see in him the
Christ, and it is over against this refusal that Peter
sets his confession that he *is* the Christ. This confession is thus most emphatic, without qualification,
brief, and decisive. Yet we cannot assume that only
the Twelve believed in Jesus as the Christ. Others
agreed with them. In v. 14 these are not introduced
for the simple reason that a right confession can be
listed together with several wrong confessions only
in an abstract way. Among οἱ ἄνθρωποι who deny the
Messiahship of Jesus any who accept it have no place.
They would belong in another class, namely in that of
the Twelve. They are not mentioned now because
Jesus is in a special manner  dealing only with the
Twelve; yet in v. 18 we see that Jesus has them in
mind: "my church."

Already Peter's first designation is sufficient, but
he places his meaning beyond all doubt when he adds
the apposition, "the Son of God the living." In 14:33,
where the article is omitted (but see the comment),
some may argue about the meaning of the expression,
but certainly there is no room for argument here; compare what the disciples had learned from the Baptist
in John 1:34, and what one of them confessed in
John 1:49. Other believers may have thought of
Jesus as a mere human Messiah when they gave him
that great title; but Peter confesses Jesus to be the
very Son of God. All that the disciples saw in the
life, words, and deeds of Jesus revealed to them the
Second Person of the Godhead in the man Jesus.
Peter is not stating mere intellectual reflections and
deductions but the conviction of his soul, which was
wrought by the revelation under which his soul had

lived. Nor is it fair to modify Peter's confession by prying into his mind and by asking what conception he may have had of the Son of God as being present in Jesus. The fact stands that Jesus accepted his confession as being entirely adequate; and to this day the mystery of the Incarnation, with the exception of the tremendous fact of it, is beyond human comprehension.

When Peter adds τοῦ ζῶντος, the article with the participle (as with an adjective) makes the modifier prominent (R. 776). As "the living," who has life and power in himself, God is the opposite of all other gods who are dead, lifeless, powerless idols. But here "the living" means more: he sent his Son and thus attests himself as living, and through his Son he is the one source and fountain of life (ζωή) for sinful man. The Son of God is "the living" like the Father whose mission he is performing.

Peter uses no extravagant language. He uses very few words, all of which are simple and direct and true in every respect. All believers of all future ages have joined him in his confession and have understood it in the same sense that he gave to it. We know that he did not always live up to his confession, but his inconsistency in this respect is only like our own and changes nothing of the substance or the truth he here confessed.

**17) And Jesus, answering, said to him: Blessed art thou, Simon, son of John, because flesh and blood did not reveal it to thee but my Father in the heavens.** Here, as so often, the participle ἀποκριθείς simply means that this is the response of Jesus. He acknowledges Peter's confession, accepts it, and stamps it with his approval; he is, indeed, "the Christ, the Son of God the living." The Unitarian and the rationalistic claim that Jesus never called himself the Son of God is squarely denied here as it is throughout the

Gospels. Jesus speaks of what this confession means to Peter: "Blessed art thou," μακάριος (exactly as in 5:3, etc., which see), filled with the divine spiritual blessing, the possession of the essential soul treasure which produces eternal happiness and joy. Truly to know, believe, and confess that Jesus is the Christ, the Son of God the living, makes a man "blessed" as Jesus understands that word. It ought not to be necessary to explain that this attribute in no special sense applies to Peter alone but equally to all of the Twelve for all of whom Peter speaks and to all others who join in Peter's confession.

The name "Simon, son of John," (*Bar-Jonah*, the Aramaic patronymic) significantly points to what Peter was by nature. Over against his natural powers and abilities Jesus intends to place his new spiritual gifts. The contrasting of the two names in v. 17, 18 is too marked to be viewed as being accidental and without import. Yet there is nothing to indicate that this is a play on the etymology of either "Simon" or "son of John." In his natural state this disciple, like the others, would be inclined to follow only natural reason, "flesh and blood." By the grace of God he was led to avoid this — hence his blessedness.

Jesus himself justifies the judgment he expresses by calling Simon "blessed": "because (ὅτι), etc." Peter's confession is in no way the product of his own reason, his superior intellect, or of any meritorious quality or effort on his part. All of that is already shut out by his old name Simon, etc. The faith and the knowledge which uttered Peter's confession were not in any way the product of "flesh and blood," i. e., of fallible and mortal man. The Hebrew expression *basar wadam* is frequently found in Jewish literature and describes man in his mortal state of weakness and fallibility. Here Jesus has in mind Peter's own flesh and blood. What is true of the inability of Peter's flesh and blood is equally true of the inability of the flesh and the blood or the natural powers of all men. To make a confession such as that which Peter made requires far more. In the verb "did reveal" Jesus declares the contents of Peter's confession to be an impenetrable mystery as far as the powers of mere flesh and blood are concerned. Actually to realize in the man Jesus the presence of the Christ and Son of God requires more than sinful flesh and blood is able to muster. It remains so to this day.

This realization is produced by a revelation, one that is wrought by "my Father in the heavens," who is thus infinitely exalted above "flesh and blood." It lies on the surface that the revelation here referred to goes beyond mere intellectual knowledge and extends to spiritual conviction and apprehension. But we must not suppose that the Father exercised either an arbitrary or an irresistible will in regard to Peter. This revelation was not made to him without means. The Father revealed Jesus to Peter through Jesus himself, and he endeavors to do this in the case of all men by bringing Jesus into contact with them. Verses 13, 14 show how in that day men refused to receive the Father's revelation and preferred their own foolish estimates of Jesus. This word of Jesus is proof for our own confession: "I believe that I cannot by my own reason or strength believe in Jesus Christ, my Lord, or come to him." Only those know Jesus whose souls have come into living touch with him through faith that is wrought by the Father's revelation; others, even when they call him God's Son, do not know what they are saying.

18) **Moreover, I, too, say to thee that thou art Peter, and upon this rock will I build my church, and hades' gates shall not prevail against it.** The copulative δέ adds something that is slightly different. Peter has made a mighty statement, Jesus now makes

another that is allied to it but goes much farther. This
is the force of καί with ἐγώ: "I, too, say to thee." Peter
has confessed Jesus, Jesus confesses Peter. All the
pronouns are emphatic: "*I*, too, say to *thee* that *thou*
art Peter," etc. What Jesus here does regarding Peter
he promises to do for all who confess him as Peter did,
10:32. In John 1:42 Jesus promised Simon, "Thou
shalt be called Cephas," i. e., Peter, the rockman. Here
Jesus now states that by his confession Simon has qualified for that name. It is essential to note that the
masculine πέτρος denotes a detached rock or boulder, and
that the feminine πέτρα signifies a rocky cliff. Liddell
and Scott define the latter: "A ledge or shelf of rock, a
rocky peak or ridge," and add the statement: "There
is no example in good authors of πέτρα being used in the
sense of πέτρος, a stone, for even in Homer πέτραι are not
loose stones but masses of living rock torn up and
hurled by giants." The distinction is beyond question
although M.-M. sidestep the matter; and it is enhanced
by the demonstrative "this rock," ἐπὶ ταύτῃ τῇ πέτρᾳ.

Both the plain distinction and the evident correla-
tion between these two terms should be noted. Πέτρος,
the person of Peter, and αὕτη ἡ πέτρα, "this rock," are not
identical; the latter does not signify the Apostle Peter.
This linguistic fact is supported by other considerations. If by "this rock" Jesus had Peter himself in
mind, he could easily have said, ἐπί σου, "on thee" will
I build my church; or, "on thee, Peter," adding his
name. But Jesus is already through with Peter, both
as regards his old nature (Simon, son of John,) and as
regards his new nature (Peter). In neither instance
does he receive credit, for all belongs to the Father's
revelation. Eph. 2:20 makes all the apostles the
"foundation" of the church (not, indeed, their persons
or their faith but their inspired preaching and writing)
and knows nothing of a prerogative in the case of Peter.
In Matt. 18:1, 4, and in Luke 22:24, the Twelve debate

as to who is the greatest among them and evidently do not think that Jesus has assigned this position to Peter. Matt. 18:18; John 20:23 has no intimation of a supremacy of Peter. He is only one among the rest; sometimes, not always, however, *primus inter pares*. The highest authority bestowed upon his followers by Jesus is given to all alike and not to Peter alone, either in his capacity as the human head of the church or as the *princeps apostolorum*.

Yet Πέτρος and αὕτη ἡ πέτρα are an *annominatio* which has reference to the sense of the words and does not play merely with the similarity in sound, R. 1201. The feminine term indicates what made Peter a rock. That was, of course, not his confession but the divine revelation from which that confession sprang and to which Jesus refers so significantly in v. 17. But this revelation was not intended for Peter alone; all the disciples shared it, and, due to this revelation, all of them confessed Peter's confession. To bar out the rest is unwarranted even when Peter's confession is made the rock on which Jesus erects the church. Luther is right: "All Christians are Peters on account of the confession which Peter here makes, which is the rock on which Peter and all Peters are built" — understanding Luther to refer to the truth held and confessed by Peter and these Peters.

We decline to make "this rock" signify the rock nature of Peter. The church does not rest on a quality found in Peter and in others like him. The foundation of the church is not subjective but objective, namely God's revelation. Nor does "this rock" signify Peter's confession. The church is not built on the confession her members make, which would change the effect into the cause. By her confession the church shows on what she is built. She rests on the reality which Peter confessed, namely on Jesus, "the Christ, the Son of God the living." Some think of Peter's

(subjective) faith and tell us that he was the first to
voice this faith — forgetting John 1:49-51. His faith
is then called "the first foundation stone." We also
challenge the reference to the Aramaic in order to wipe
out the distinction between πέτρος and πέτρα. We know
too little about the Aramaic to assert that when Jesus
spoke these words he used the same Aramaic term in
both statements. We should like to know more about
the Aramaic as it was spoken at the time of Jesus.
Therefore this appeal to the Aramaic substitutes something unknown and hypothetical for what is fully
known and insured as true on the basis of the inspired
Greek of the holy writers themselves.

On the rock named in Peter's confession Jesus says,
"I will build my church," the future tense being volitive,
R. 889. We may take it that he refers to the day of
Pentecost, or, if we wish to speak more exactly, that
this building process has already begun and would continue in the future. Since Jesus speaks of himself as
the builder, he does not call himself the foundation but
makes the foundation "this rock" which Peter had just
named. As the Lord of the church he says, "my
church." Only here and in 18:17 does Matthew employ ἐκκλησία, which really means the "assembly" called
out to meet as a body. We do not think that the etymology of the term is altogether lost in New Testament
usage (contra R. 174). To be sure, the ἐκκλησία is not
always an assembled body called out for a meeting, but
it certainly is the body of those who have by faith heard
and accepted the gospel κλῆσις (καλεῖν), whether they are
gathered together in a meeting or not. The ἐκκλησία
consists of κλητοί who are called out of the world into
the kingdom as Christ's own. Both by virtue of this
effective call and as a building built on a foundation
the church forms a unit body, the great *Una Sancta*
of the Apostles' Creed, stone laid against stone, fitly
framed together, a living temple of souls joined to

Christ, the Son of God. No Peter could bear this structure, nor could any personal faith or confession emanating from him.

When he speaks of the foundation on which he will build his church, Jesus is thinking of her mighty enemies. Although the articles are missing from πύλαι ἅδου, both nouns are definite. On "hades" see 11:23. "The unseen place" is here viewed as a mighty fortress, the opposite of the sacred Temple of Christ; and the πύλαι, or portals of hades, are a figure for the mighty warring hosts that issue from these portals. "Hades" does not mean "the realm of the dead," the hypothetical place to which the souls of all dead men descend until the judgment day. How could "the gates" of such a place war against the church on earth? Here "hades" must mean hell, the abode of the devils, whose one object it is to destroy the church. The future tense οὐ κατισχύσουσιν must be futuristic: "shall not prevail against," be strong and mighty against, and not volitive as R. 875 suggests. This is the prophetic future. The object is put into the genitive because this is a verb of ruling, R. 510. The implication is that hell's gates shall pour out her hosts to assault the church of Christ, but the church shall not be overthrown (Rev. 20:8, 9). What makes her impregnable is her mighty foundation, Christ, the Son of the living God (I Cor. 15:24 b). As a curiosity in exegesis we mention the view that at the end of time the church will batter down the gates of the lower world in order to release the dead that are held there. This adds to Christ's descent into hell a descent of the church of believers to the same place.

19) **And I will give thee the keys of the kingdom of the heavens. And whatever thou shalt bind on the earth shall be as having been bound in the heavens; and whatever thou shalt loose on the earth shall be as having been loosed in the heavens.** These words become clear when we note that "the keys"

belong to "the kingdom of the heavens," and that this
kingdom is not identical with "my church" in v. 18.
The *Ecclesia* represents only the earthly side of the
kingdom, while "the kingdom of the heavens" includes
both the earthly and the heavenly sides. It thus includes the great King himself and all who reign with
him. But we must not think of an organization as
earthly kingdoms are arranged; for the divine kingdom is not patterned after any earthly realm but is
superior to all of them. This kingdom of the heavens
is the entire domain in which Christ exercises his saving grace. Here on earth he does it by means of the
gospel so that wherever that is preached his kingdom
is present and operative; in heaven he exercises his
grace by the bestowal of the heavenly glories so that
also there his kingdom is in full sway. Compare 3:2.

The future tense "I will give" is important. The
apostles were not at present ready for the gift; in v. 20
Jesus still has to restrain them from proclaiming him
as the Messiah. Nor was Jesus himself quite ready to
have them undertake this proclamation; for his redemptive work had not as yet been accomplished. The figure in the word "keys" suggests the ideas of binding
and loosing. While the number of the keys is not
specified, the two verbs used lead us to think of only
two. It ought not to be difficult for us, as it certainly
was not for Peter and for the Twelve, to understand
that a key which binds is simply the power to shut out
from the kingdom of the heavens, and a key that looses
is the authority to admit to this kingdom. Here is the
place to follow the old hermeneutical rule: *Scriptura
ex Scriptura explicanda est.* In 18:18 we find the same
two verbs, but there they are applied to all the disciples
and are to be understood in the very same sense, giving
us Jesus' own commentary on the keys: "What things
soever ye shall bind on earth shall be bound in heaven;
and what things ye shall loose on earth shall be loosed

in heaven." To this add John 20:23: "Whose soever sins ye remit, they are remitted unto them; and whose soever sins ye retain, they are retained." The fact that the order is reversed in this passage is certainly no reason to say that here Jesus does not refer to the keys.

The Scriptures themselves thus explain the neuter "whatever" (ὅ) as "what things soever" (ὅσα) in 18:18, and as "sins" in John 20:23. This neuter, then, does not refer to *persons* but to the *acts* of persons, and thus it accords with the universal principle of the Scriptures that all public judgment, even that of Christ at the last day, rests on a man's works. By means of his omniscience God, of course, sees the heart with its faith or its lack of faith. Yet, wherever God's judgment or that of his agents is to be justified in public before men and before angels, the works are invariably brought forward. So in binding and in loosing we are especially bound to deal only with the works of men, with what they confess by word and by deed, and dare never arrogate to ourselves the function of judging the heart as to whether faith be present there or not. Whatever our moral convictions may be regarding a man's faith or lack of faith, this is not our business; we deal with his works alone. The key that binds is the power and authority to retain sins; the key that looses is the power and authority to remit sins. The one shuts out of the kingdom, the other admits. The tense of δώσω thus refers to the time when Peter and the rest were sent out to preach the gospel to the world.

How the keys are to be used is shown with great clearness in 18:18. Always the power in them is Christ's own for us to use only in accord with his will. Only repentant sinners are to be freed of their sins, only the impenitent are to be sent away unforgiven. The keys are stronger than we; they never work according to any man's perverted will. Each fits its own lock, nor can you work the loosing key where the binding key alone fits, or vice versa. All true administration of the gospel is the exercise of the keys whether this occurs in public preaching, in church discipline, in the divine service of confession, or in other instances where single souls are dealt with.

All those who think that the keys were given to Peter alone foster the error of the papacy with its tyranny of souls. "Tell it unto *the church*" (18:18) is decisive on this point. The apostles and after them the pastors are only the ministers of the church. Through them the church speaks and acts. And when she does this in accord with Christ's command, whatever is bound on earth "shall be as having been bound in the heavens"; and whatever is loosed on earth "shall be as having been loosed in the heavens," i. e., both as having been done by Christ himself, he being the agent back of both the perfect passive participles. We prefer to regard the two ἐσται as copulas and the two participles as predicates; R. 361 and 907 makes these forms the periphrastic future perfect passive, "shall have been bound or loosed." The difference is merely formal.

Lightfoot, who is followed by others, lets "bind" and "loose" mean forbid and allow, but this can be done only on the authority of the Talmud which uses *'asar* and *hittir* (Aramaic *'asar* and *sheʳah*) in this peculiar manner. Peter is thus made the οἰκονόμος of the house of the church, the supreme rabbi who decides what the members of the household may do or not do, what is forbidden, and what is allowed. With this idea goes the statement that 18:18 and John 20:23 have no connection with our passage; they would upset this Talmudic usage. But this is not interpreting Scripture by means of Scripture but by means of a late Jewish usage of terms. It leads to the conclusion that what this supreme rabbi Peter forbids as morally wrong and allows as morally right here on earth shall be equally forbidden or allowed *in the heavens*. The labored efforts of Zahn and of others to secure this sense of the words, that bind and loose mean forbid and allow, reveal how futile it is to bring in the Talmud and to disregard 18:18 and John 20:23.

Moreover, where did Peter exercise the function thus ascribed to him? In the Acts and in the Epistles we see the keys employed. In Acts 15, not Peter, but James is the chairman; and not Peter, but James formulates the decision which is then adopted by "the apostles and elders *with the whole church.*" The case of incest mentioned in I Cor. 5:11, 13 (II Cor. 2:6-8) is another instance. Here Paul formulates the binding resolution which the Corinthian congregation was to adopt (see the author's commentary on the passage) and also did adopt, and not until that time was the man expelled. Throughout we see that *the church* administers the keys and that the apostles and the elders (pastors) as the proper ministrants of the church lead in the work. Luther and the Reformation have gone so thoroughly into this portion of the Scriptures and have established once for all from the Scriptures themselves what the power of the keys is, in what sense Peter had it, and in what sense the church has it, that no Talmudic references can affect this true finding.

20) **Then he charged the disciples to say to no one that he was the Christ.** The future tenses used in v. 18, 19 explain this charge to the disciples. Their great confession was not as yet to be made publicly, but in due course, after only a few months, the time would be propitious. The best authority reads διεστείλατο, other texts have ἐπετίμησεν, "he gave strict orders." Either verb is strong, for Jesus intended to seal the lips of the disciples for the present; ἵνα is subfinal and is equal to an infinitive. The emphasis on αὐτός is due to v. 13, 14 and the notions of the people that, whoever Jesus might be, it was certain that *he* was not the

Christ. Over against this stands the assertion "that *he* is the Christ" nevertheless; and the Greek retains the ἐστίν of the direct discourse which the English translates "was" after the past tense of a verb of saying.

The great reason why Jesus throughout his ministry did not proclaim himself as "the Christ" or Messiah was that the Jews connected the most extravagant political ideas with this title. That explains why they could not see "the Christ" in Jesus. He had nothing of that which they imagined "the Christ" should have. Thus they made him a lesser person. The course Jesus followed was simply to be "the Christ," to do the work of the Messiah, and to let this produce the conviction, as it did in his disciples, that *he*, indeed, was "the Christ," not the political and secular figure which filled the Jewish imagination but the Christ of God, promised in the Scriptures, the very Son of the living God, sent to redeem and save the souls of men. After his work had been completed on earth, the world was to ring with the confession that this Jesus was "the Christ," Acts 3:13-26; 4:10-12; 5:30-32; etc.

21) **From then on Jesus began to show to his disciples that he must go away to Jerusalem and suffer many things from the elders and high priests and scribes and be killed and on the third day be raised up.** One great task had been accomplished: the disciples had been brought to the full realization of *the divine person* of Jesus as Peter voiced this conviction for the Twelve in his great confession (v. 16). Another task had to be finished: the disciples had to be made to understand *the redemptive work* Jesus was about to complete. Often enough he had in a veiled way spoken of this work; now he speaks of it in the plainest terms. Over two years ago, behind the temptation after the forty days of fasting, Jesus saw the shadow of the cross. When he cleansed the Temple the first time he spoke of the temple of his body which the Jews would

destroy and he would raise up.   To Nicodemus he said,
"The Son of man must be lifted up."   But now the time
had come for plainer language.   "From then on" marks
the time and intimates that Jesus continued to speak
of his Passion as he had not done heretofore.   The
aorist ἤρξατο indicates the point of beginning, and the
present infinitive δεικνύειν what now followed.   Jesus
"shows" these things "to his disciples."   They are to
draw no false conclusion from his divinity such as they
were too much inclined to draw because of the vain
Jewish hopes still lurking in their hearts.   Although
Jesus is God's Son and the Messiah, no golden, glorious,
refulgent earthly kingdom and grandeur lie ahead but
the very opposite.

Matthew gives us a simple summary of what Jesus
revealed to his disciples during these last few months.
The ὅτι clause very likely reports just what Jesus said
right after his reply to Peter's confession.   Later he
repeated this statement with additions.   All that awaits
Jesus is a necessity; and while δεῖ is used to express all
types of necessity, here it evidently expresses the gracious will and counsel of God in the mission of Jesus.
These things "must" take place, and Jesus himself wills
that they shall, for without them he could not redeem
the world.

We have seen how Jesus withdrew himself from the
populous center west of the lake, spending his time in
distant parts, now near Tyre and Sidon, then in Decapolis, finally in the neighborhood of Cæsarea Philippi.
Even in Galilee the opposition had grown so keen that
Pharisees and Sadducees from Jerusalem had come up
to interfere with him.   But now Jesus tells the disciples that presently he himself will again go away to
Jerusalem, to the very capital itself, where the real
center of hostility against him had been formed.   The
Jews would not need to follow him, to arrest him in
some distant locality, he himself would place himself

into their hands.   Jerusalem would be the place of his
sacrifice, Luke 13:33.  Here he is "to suffer many
things," πολλά still leaving the veil over the details.
Jesus knew what these "many things" were.  The
prophets had foretold them in all their terribleness, and
Jesus knew even more fully just what they included.
Despite their number their severity would in no way
be softened.  In the many things Jesus was to suffer
we may well see the reflection of the many sins he bore,
which in his great Passion hymn on the thorn-crowned
head of Christ Paul Gerhardt likens to the grains of
sand upon the seashore.

Jesus states positively who shall inflict the many
things upon him, namely the Sanhedrin, the full designation for which is here used (in 2:3 we have an abbreviation).   This was the highest judicial body of the
Jewish nation, more representative than the high priest
alone.  "The elders" were the old, experienced men of
the nation who had served as judges in the local courts
and, due to their prominence, had risen to membership
in the highest court. "The high priests and the scribes"
are described in connection with 2:3.  All three classes
are combined into a unit by means of the one article.
The naming of the Sanhedrin as the agent of Jesus'
suffering points to a trial and a formal condemnation;
ἀπό, "at the hands of," points to the source and thus to
the agency, R. 579.   The disciples also well knew that
the chief enemies of their Master were the Sanhedrists
who had already planned and plotted to destroy him.
Thus far Jesus had frustrated their schemes but now he
tells the disciples that the Sanhedrin will succeed.  Not
only will he suffer many things but he shall actually "be
killed."  Jesus omits the mockery, the scourging, the
delivery into the hands of Pilate, for the disciples cannot now bear these details.  Also the method of the
killing is withheld and is not revealed until 20:19.  But
the fact of the killing is positively stated.  The preced-

ing mention of the Sanhedrin points to a judicial killing, but ἀποκτανθῆναι simply means "to be killed" in the
sense of to be put out of the way, murdered, robbed of
life.  It suggests no thought of justice on the part of
the Jewish tribunal but, in connection with the foregoing παθεῖν, the gravest kind of injustice: judicial
murder.

Jesus is brief in this first formal announcement.  He
is like one who is breaking a piece of terrible news to
his dearest friends.  The shock cannot be avoided but
is softened as much as possible.  The very thought of
seeing their beloved Master, whom they had just confessed as the Christ and Son of God, a bleeding, murdered victim of the Sanhedrin at Jerusalem must have
overwhelmed the hearts of the disciples — and not only
because of their love, attachment, and high hopes, but
also because of their conception of the Messiah which
included the very opposite of suffering and being killed,
namely earthly grandeur and triumph.

Yet glory and triumph, though of a far higher kind,
are included, namely his resurrection on the third day
after being killed.  This, too, "must" occur; it is in
accord with the same necessity that applies to what
precedes.  "On the third day" is so important because
it foretells the exact time.  Jesus would be raised up,
not at some indefinite future time, but already on the
third day.  Jesus sees the future with a direct vision;
for none of the prophets had foretold this third day;
all that the Old Testament contains is the analogy of
Jonah's stay in the belly of the great fish (12:39, 40;
16:4).  Jesus uses only the one word, ἐγερθῆναι, "shall
be raised up," and gives no further intimation concerning the glorification connected with this resurrection.
A real conception of this stupendous act was at this
time beyond the comprehension of the disciples.  It
was enough for them to hear that Jesus would not

remain in death but be brought back to life as the Messiah. Back of the passive verb stands God as the agent; in Mark 9:31 and in Luke 18:33 the active is used. Both are true: the Son of man was raised up, and the Son of God arose, for the *opera ad extra sunt indivisa aut communa.*

Beyond relating Peter's attempt to dissuade Jesus from his passion, Matthew tells us nothing about the effect of this startling announcement upon the disciples. Peter's attempt proves that the disciples certainly understood what Jesus intended to tell them. And yet we see that Peter thinks only of the suffering and the being killed and thus reveals that in the minds of the disciples the climax of the Messiah's career is entirely beclouded. This explains Mark 9:31 and Luke 18:34.

To this day unbelieving criticism denies both the prophecy Jesus here utters and the fulfillment recorded by all the evangelists and preached by all the apostles. These critics regard the death as historic but deny the glorious resurrection. Equally untenable is the supposition of other less radical interpreters who assume that Jesus did not speak as plainly as Matthew here records his statement, but that the evangelist wrote as he did on the basis of his later knowledge; this applies especially to the prophecy that Jesus would be raised from the dead. Only in this way, they think, the reluctance of the disciples to believe the news of the resurrection can be explained. But Peter's act shows conclusively that the disciples centered on the suffering and the death of their Master and failed to heed what he added concerning his resurrection. The last discourses of Jesus, recorded by John *in extenso,* make this still plainer. It is one thing to sit in a cool study and to rationalize regarding the actions of the disciples, and quite another thing to pass through the terrible experience of the disciples when their Master was cru-

cified and then buried in the tomb. All the preceding
assurances that he would rise again on the third day
were lost in the night of the calamity that engulfed them.

22) Peter again shows his impetuosity. **And
taking him to himself** (the middle participle with
πρός), **Peter began to rebuke him, saying, Mercy on
thee, Lord! In no way shall this be to thee! But
he, having turned, said to Peter: Get behind me,
Satan! A trap art thou of mine; because thou hast
not in mind the things of God but the things of men.**
"And" sounds as though Peter's action at once followed.
Undoubtedly, he thought that he was again doing the
right thing and was doing it for the Twelve. The act
of taking Jesus aside so that Peter has him by himself,
was intended to make Jesus listen more readily to
Peter's expostulation. Inadvertently, however, this
reproduced the situation that obtained when Satan
tempted Jesus in the wilderness. Peter "began" to
rebuke him just as a moment ago Jesus "began" to
announce his passion and his glorification, but what
Peter began was immediately squelched as one crushes
a serpent that raises its ugly head. The verb ἐπιτιμᾶν
is full of vehemence. It suggests a person who comes
powerfully at another to show him that he is wrong.
The elliptical ἵλεώς σοι includes God as the subject and
the optative of wish εἴη as the copula: "Merciful (be
God) to thee!" And the sense is that in his mercy
God may ward off this calamity, B.-P. 585, etc.

The negative future οὐ μὴ ἔσται σοι τοῦτο is, of course,
volitive (R. 875), but it is the future of command as
used in legal enactments, and οὐ μή is the strongest form
of negation with the future (as it is with subjunctives,
all of which are also future): "Nevermore shall this
happen to thee!" We at once see that Peter had caught
only what Jesus said about his suffering and his death
and did not grasp the word about his resurrection and
properly combine the two.

The psychology here revealed is so true that we can substantiate it by a large number of examples in our own lives. But these experiences of ours are usually of lesser importance as when present pain or loss prove too much for us and blot out any joy or gain that may be achieved through them. Here in Jesus' case the most terrible loss of life itself was involved, and to Peter this was a calamity so frightful as entirely to blot out anything glorious that might follow it. The mystery of the Baptist's "Lamb of God" with its implication of bloody sacrifice was still hidden from Peter. What lay in the little word δεῖ, "must," namely the necessity of the atoning, cleansing blood of the Messiah, Peter did not at all grasp. His mind brushed that aside and thought of the Messiah as God's Son who needed only to stretch out the hand of his power in order to achieve his great rule and kingdom among men.

To this day, all who fail to see the damning power of sin are blind to the true necessity of the cross. They see in Christ crucified (since he was, indeed, crucified) nothing but a noble martyrdom, a sacrifice only in this sense and reject "the blood theology" of the gospel, the sacrifice which involves substitution, redemption by the blood of God's Son, and the cleansing of the soul from guilt by faith in this sacrificial blood. Thus they need no essential Son in their theology, and his resurrection may be regarded as a myth. Like Peter, they would have a kingship without the Messianic priesthood. But the very thing for which Peter started to rebuke Jesus afterward became the kernel, yea, the Alpha and the Omega, of his apostolic preaching.

23) Peter began but never finished. Jesus never paused for an instant to ask his urgent disciple, "Why?" or, "What makes thee think so?" Peter is not allowed to add that it would not behoove the Son of God to allow himself to be killed, or that he should not go to Jerusalem to place himself into the hands of

the Sanhedrin.  Jesus does not for one moment enter-
tain the tempting thought or turn it over in his mind.
Here is an example for us who frequently dally with
the serpent and then find his poisonous fangs lodged
in us.

Some think that Jesus "turned" his back on Peter
in disgust because of his words; others, that he turned
away from Peter and faced the other disciples.  But
to turn and to speak to a person — note that the two
actions go together — means that Jesus faced Peter
squarely.  If Jesus had turned his back on Peter he
would himself have placed Peter "behind" him, whereas
he tells Peter, *"Get thee* behind me!"    Compare Luke
9:55, where no commentator lets στραφείς mean, "having
turned his back."

So also, "get thee behind me," means, "Get out of
my sight!"    With a Peter who speaks as he does Jesus
will have nothing whatever to do.  This peremptory
word with the address, "Satan," is identical with the
one with which Jesus ordered the devil out of his sight
after the third temptation (4:10).  For this reason
here, too, "Satan" is the archfiend.  Unwittingly and
though moved by the best intentions Peter had made
himself an agent of Satan.  What a warning to watch
our love, our good intentions, our best acts, lest, perhaps
after all, they agree with Satan and not with Christ.

Romanists are concerned to remove the name
"Satan" from Peter and let it mean only "adversary,"
or call it an address, not to Peter, but only to the devil.
Others follow with the claim that in the East "Satan"
is commonly used to designate any bold, powerful
enemy.  But there is no evidence for such common
usage.  What is decisive for us is the fact that we here
have an exact repetition of 4:10, both commands come
from Jesus' lips, and both were spoken during temptations, yea, in the same kind of temptation.  In both

"Satan" has the same force, but in the second case the fiend is connected with Peter.

The contention that immediately after praising Peter as the *rock* Jesus could not have called him *Satan* or an agent of Satan overlooks the fact that Peter had the flesh as well as the spirit, ignorance as well as faith, weakness as well as strength. And we may ask, how Jesus could call him a rock when he knew that Peter would most shamefully deny him. The name pointed to what the grace of Christ would eventually make of Peter; as yet the work had only begun. The fact that the Scriptures tell us the faults of the apostles so openly and so truthfully proves their absolute reliability. These faults comfort us, not as excuses for our faults, but as assurances that Christ will not reject us on their account but will correct our faults as he did those of Peter.

On σκάνδαλον and the verb σκανδαλίζειν see 5:29. The word always means the crooked stick to which the bait in a trap is affixed. R. 174 has the correct explanation but he is mistaken when he adds the thought of "impediment" which leads to "stumbling block" (R. V.). Here it is important to retain the original meaning. One may *fall* over a stumbling block and yet may rise again. But this is not the case with a *skandalon,* for merely to touch the bait affixed to it would spring the trap, and Jesus would be *caught* in its death grip. Thus we translate the word "trap," which conveys the idea of an enticement that, if it be entertained, means destruction. No wonder Jesus turned so sharply against Peter; he saw the satanic trap set for him in Peter's words.

Jesus states why Peter's effort is a trap for him (ὅτι) : "because thou hast in mind," etc. "The things of God" and "the things of men" are opposites; the former are the great, blessed, saving purposes, plans, and acts of God; the latter, the blind, erring, sinful purposes and ways of men. Peter had in mind only the

latter, his thinking and his desires were set on these
not on the former. "To the world the cross was offensive, to Christ whatever opposed the cross." Bengel.

Peter must have been shocked at Jesus' reply to his
well-meant urging. At that time he could hardly
have understood that by his attempt to dissuade Jesus
from the cross he was placing arrows on the bow of
Satan to be shot at his beloved Savior. The more reason why he should be instantly stopped. One thing,
however, must have penetrated his mind, namely that
all this regarding Jesus' passion, death, and resurrection was divine, "of God," and therefore holy, blessed,
saving; and that every contradictory thought and suggestion was evil, dangerous, satanic. Thus the very
temptation Peter brought upon Jesus was by Jesus used
to help him from the things of men to those of God.
We are not told that the other disciples heard what was
said, but the following indicates that this was most
likely the case.

24) **Then Jesus said to his disciples, If anyone
wills to come after me, let him deny himself and
take up his cross and be following me.** "Then"
means immediately after Peter's attempt, and this
leads us to think that all the disciples witnessed this
incident. They must also be set right, not Peter alone.
But Jesus says nothing further regarding his own
future course. This is fixed once for all. He speaks
about the course of those who would be his disciples.
His words involve all that precedes concerning himself,
that he is the Christ, the Son of God the living, and
must be killed and raised up again. Whoever would
belong to this Messiah must do what Jesus here says.
In εἰ θέλει we have the condition of reality, and θέλει
points to the will as being engaged in a continuous
volition, R. 878 ("would" in the R. V. is inadequate).
"To come after or behind me" means, of course, to
attach oneself to Jesus as a disciple; but here this idea

is deepened: to follow this Son of God who is going into death and the following resurrection. "Christ does not pull his sheep by a rope; in his army there are none but volunteers." E. Frommel. Jesus knows of no irresistible grace but only of the grace which draws the will and wins it for himself. And this grace excludes no one — τίς is like a blank space into which you are invited to write your name, no matter who you may be.

Whoever wills to come after Christ, "let him deny himself," ἀπό plus ἀρνέομαι, which means to turn someone off, to refuse association and companionship with him, to disown him. The one to be denied is here ἑαυτός, SELF, self altogether and not merely some portion, some fault, some special habit or desire, some outward practice. The natural, sinful self is referred to as it centers in the things of men and has no desire for the things of God. As Peter later denied Jesus saying, "I know not the man!" so must you say regarding yourself, "I disown myself completely." This is not self-denial in the current sense of the word but true conversion, the very first essential of the Christian life. The heart sees all the sin of self and the damnation and the death bound up in this sin and turns away from it in utter dismay, seeking rescue in Christ alone. Self is thus cast out, and Christ enters in; henceforth you live, not unto yourself, but unto Christ who died for you. Moreover, you can deny only one whom you know, a friend, for instance, by breaking off relations with him. So here you are to deny your own old self and to enter into a new relation with Christ.

This will mean that "he take up his cross," αἴρειν in the sense of λαμβάνειν in 10:38. On "his cross" see this passage. Jesus undoubtedly chose this figure because he himself was to be crucified. Although this was a Roman mode of execution, it was universally known. Jesus will bear *his* cross, one which he alone could bear.

In regard to his disciples he says that each is to bear *his* cross, i. e., the particular one allotted to him. This word has grown too familiar because of constant use. It is a mistake to call all our suffering a cross. The wicked have many sorrows (Ps. 32:10) but no crosses. The cross is that suffering which results from our faithful connection with Christ. And Jesus here intimates that each disciple will have his share of such suffering.

The thought is overwhelming: Christ, carrying his cross, leads, and all his disciples, each bearing his cross, follow in one immense procession like men being led away to be crucified. Paul carries the figure farther: they that are Christ's have crucified the flesh (Gal. 5:24); and Paul himself is crucified with Christ (Gal. 2:20). The earthly prospects of a disciple are not alluring. However heavy your cross may be, he helps you to bear it after him.

So Jesus says, "let him be following me." He uses the word that is usually employed to express the attachment of faith and faithfulness, it has quite the same meaning as to come after Jesus. Let no one think of changing the course of Jesus which leads to the cross but only of following him with our cross. Godet says that when travelling three things are necessary; first, to say farewell (to self); secondly, to carry our baggage (the cross); thirdly, to proceed with the journey (follow me). The only question concerns our will to make this journey. The first two imperatives are properly aorists, for to deny self and to shoulder the cross are momentary acts; but the third is present, for to follow is a long and continuous course of action. This means that the first two acts are the preparation for the third. We need not add that all three are impossible to us, for no human power is able to bring about conversion and the new life. Christ's Word and grace alone bring about both.

25) **For whoever wills to save his life shall lose it; but whoever shall lose his life on my account shall find it.** Here we have the reason for the previous gospel commands. It sounds like a warning, and its highly paradoxical form is sure to embed it in the memory. Once before, but in a different connection, Jesus used this paradox with only verbal changes. In 10:39 the two subjects are substantivized aorist participles: "the finder — the loser of his life"; now the subjects are relative clauses with a somewhat fuller meaning. See 10:39 for the meaning of ψυχή. "Whoever wills to save his life" again stresses the will (as in v. 24), for the decision is always made in this center of our personality. The verb σώζειν means not only to save by rescuing but in addition to preserve in a safe state. This is the terrible folly of the man who would save his life, namely by not denying himself, taking up his cross, and following Jesus: by this very volition of his he shall lose his life. Though he enjoys every earthly delight, his ψυχή has really perished, for it is doomed.

On the other hand, Jesus does not again say, "Whoever *wills* to lose his life," for this willing is understood. So he at once advances to the fact that this man "shall lose" his life, thinking of a case where the loss becomes actual (aorist subjunctive). This man may even become a martyr, losing not merely many earthly treasures and advantages but earthly existence itself. Does his case seem sad and deplorable? Far from it! In and by the very loss he shall find his ψυχή, i. e., safe and blessed with Christ and with God. But note the significant phrase "on my account," which explains "his cross" in v. 24. Compare 5:10, 11; 10:18; Mark 8:35; 10:29: "for my sake and the gospel's." On the one hand the gain is only temporal and a delusion, while the loss is irreparable; on the other hand the loss is only minor while the gain is immense and eternal. We cannot have both; only one of the alternatives can be ours.  Hence the urging in v. 24 to choose the right one.

26) A second γάρ elucidates the reason given for Jesus' command.  **For what shall a man be benefited if he shall gain the whole world yet forfeit his life; or what shall a man give as exchange for his life?**  Here we see what underlies the paradox of v. 25.  To save the ψυχή means to secure for it as much as this world affords; and thus to lose the ψυχή means to forego what the world affords.  Jesus now supposes the absolute limit, that a man secure for himself "the whole world" — all the world's wealth, power, pleasure, glory, the beauty of all the fair things that ever graced the world, the sweetness of all the delicacies that it ever offered, the grandeur of all the high things that ever towered aloft on it, all sensations, all enjoyments, all achievements, all satisfactions.  Of course, such a thing is frankly impossible to any human being, and that is understood.  But granting the impossible and for the moment accepting it as actual, what is this man benefited if, though he have the whole world, he forfeit his ψυχή?  The question answers itself.  But again compare 10:39 on ψυχή, and note Luke 9:25 where ἑαυτός is made its equivalent, "his own self."  A man need not at once die to forfeit his ψυχή, for he forfeits or loses it when he fails to secure salvation.

The Jews are keen in regard to finance — well, here is the whole matter reduced to a simple question of profit and loss.  Write on the credit side of the ledger "the whole world" and then on the debit side "the life," the man himself, and the profit is nothing, yea, infinitely worse than nothing.  Yet Satan needs no such price to buy men's souls; all he needs is a little piece of this world.

Make the reckoning in another way.  "What shall a man give as exchange for his life?"  What equivalent in value or price could he offer, supposing even that he possessed the whole world, in order to release his life from forfeit and to place it into the safety of eternal salvation? No equivalent can be named; no man will even try to name one. The genitive used with ἀντάλ-λαγμα is objective: "exchange for his soul," R. 501; like many passives, ζημιωθῇ has the accusative. Only in one way can any man make his life safe and thus find it for time and for eternity, namely by following the directions given in v. 24. Christ is our only hope. The entire presentation is as clear as crystal and in most perfect accord with the psychological norms of the human will, so that only the height of unreason and wilful self-deceit is able to resist following the right course. Even the interrogative form employed in v. 26 is masterly, for it makes the hearer himself utter the inevitable answers.

27) How vital all this is regarding the ψυχή is now stated prophetically. **For the Son of man is about to come in the glory of his Father in company with his angels, and then shall he duly give to each one according to his doing. Amen, I say to you, there are some of those standing here who shall in no wise taste of death until they shall see the Son of man coming in his kingdom.** Divine judgment awaits every man, hence everything depends on whether we follow Christ irrespective of what we lose in the world, or disregard him and seek as much as possible of the world for our life. On "the Son of man" see 8:20. As the one who is man and yet more than man he will appear as the Judge. Our Redeemer will be our Judge. Μέλλει with the present infinitive is a circumscription of the future tense and here states that Jesus' coming to judgment is impending. He will come "in the glory of his Father," in the full display of all the divine attributes. This refers to the human nature of Jesus, that nature according to which he would undergo suffering and death (v. 21), which, however, possessed the divine

attributes by virtue of its union with the divine nature
and person of the Son, and which would be rendered
glorious and refulgent in his exaltation and heavenly
enthronement. God's "glory" is always the sum of his
attributes or any number of them shining forth so that
his creatures may see. Jesus shall appear in "his
Father's" glory, as possessing that glory equally with
the Father. The angels of the Son of man (both αὐτοῦ
refer to him) shall accompany him as his servants in
the work of the great judgment.

When that day arrives, "then" Jesus shall "duly
give (this the force of ἀπό in the verb) to each one
according to his doing" πρᾶξις, the sum of his actions in
this life. Κατά states the norm. The final, public judgment shall be regarded as a just one by the entire universe; hence the Judge will pronounce sentence according to the works, namely those mentioned in v. 24,
whether they are present in a man and characterize
him or not. The entire dealing of Jesus with his disciples mentioned in v. 13-28 (the people were also present from v. 24 onward, as Mark 8:34 states) must have
affected them most profoundly. One tremendous revelation follows another.

28) The final statement is ushered in by the solemn formula of verity and authority which has been
explained in 5:18. It assures those standing before
Jesus that some of them shall live to see the beginning
of this return of Jesus to judgment. The perfect of
ἵστημι, here the participle ἑστηκότων, is always used in the
present sense: those standing here. The relative clause
introduced by οἵτινες has the futuristic subjunctive, R.
955. The expression "to taste of death" refers to its
bitterness which remains even for the disciples because
they are still sinners.

The promise here given refers to the destruction
of Jerusalem with its definite transfer of the offer of
the gospel from the obdurate Jews to the receptive Gen-

tiles. The Parousia of Christ is here viewed in the wider sense and thus includes the divine judgment on the Jewish nation. The decisive points have been mentioned in connection with 10:23. Jesus does not say that the end of the world will come before some of his hearers have died; for 24:36 assures us that the time of the end is not known even to Jesus. Because v. 27 speaks of the judgment on the last day we are not compelled to make v. 28 do the same. It is an addition. And it will have this effect: those who live to see the destruction of Jerusalem will have in this fulfillment of Jesus' prophecy the proof that his prophecy concerning the final judgment shall also be fulfilled. They shall see him coming "in his kingdom." On the βασιλεία see 3:2. "The kingdom" is never a place but always the royal rule of the Messiah. This is the rule of his grace in the hearts of all his believers and the rule of his power in the world protecting his believers and bringing judgment upon the wicked. Ordinarily both are invisible; but in the judgment on the Jews this royal rule of Jesus would become visible. In this calamity some of the hearers were actually to "see" the Son of man coming in his βασιλεία, i. e., clothed with royal majesty as the King that he is.

"Jesus thus used the word concerning his coming once and again (10:23; 16:28) so as to combine the preparatory beginnings of the end (24:8, 32, etc.; Luke 21:28, 31), after the manner of prophetic speech, with the supreme point of the final events, his Parousia . . To say that Jesus erred in this and prophesied falsely appears, in view of the more detailed prophecies separating more sharply the individual features of the picture of the future, to be just as foolish as if someone would call the Baptist a false prophet because the kingdom whose nearness he preached was not realized at once as completely as he pictured and described its coming." Zahn, *Evangelium des Matthaeus*, 673.

# CHAPTER XVII

1)   **And after six days Jesus takes with himself Peter and James and John, his brother, and brings them up into a high mountain in private.**   This is one of the narratives which answers the hypothesis of those who make Matthew dependent on Mark, for Matthew adds points that are not found in Mark.   The complete independence of Matthew is the more assured when we note that Matthew was not one of the three disciples who were with Jesus but that Peter was, from whom Mark obtained his information.   Evidence for the complete independence of Matthew such as this is found in many parts of his Gospel.   This in passing.

The exact interval of time is stated, "after six days," in order to connect the new occurrence with what is recorded in 16:13-28.   Jesus is preparing his apostles for the close of his earthly life and work.   So after the great confession of his divinity in 16:16, the announcement of his passion, etc., in 16:21, and the words regarding the coming judgment in 16:27, 28, Jesus reveals his divine glory.   Luke gives only the approximate interval, "about eight days," meaning "about a week."

The verb παραλαμβάνω is to be understood in the same sense as in 1:24 and 2:14, 21, "to take to oneself." Jesus asks these three disciples to go with him and takes them up into a high mountain, away from everybody else, including their own companions, κατ' ἰδίαν, "in private," where they will be by themselves.   Peter, James, and John constitute the inner circle among the Twelve.   They were selected by Jesus himself as special witnesses in Mark 5:37, here, and again in Matt.

(650)

26:37. Only these three were to see and to hear what was now to be revealed, for the testimony of two or three witnesses is sufficient. Peter, speaking for all of them, had called Jesus the Son of God. They are now to see Jesus in the glory of the Son of God. To him that hath shall be given. In addition to all the evidence of his divine Sonship which the disciples had already received Jesus will now reveal himself to them in actual heavenly glory. In II Pet. 1:16-18 Peter himself stresses the great revelation thus vouchsafed to him. The attempts to identify the "high mountain" are quite futile. Not until v. 24 are we told that Jesus went back to Capernaum, which makes it quite certain that he had not already gone as far south as the old traditional site of the transfiguration, Mt. Tabor. Others think of one of the slopes of the great Mt. Hermon, which, however, seems entirely too far north. It is sufficient to think of one of the high ridges in the mountainous region not far from Caesarea Philippi where we know that Jesus was at this time (16:13).

2) **And he was transformed before them. And his countenance shone like the sun; moreover, his garments became white like the light.** Luke adds the detail that this happened while Jesus was praying, and we may note that many of the great moments in the life of Jesus are marked by prayer. The transfiguration was a transaction between the Father and his beloved Son incarnate, who always received everything from that Father. Jesus did not ask to be transfigured just as he did not ask to have the Spirit descend upon him as a dove. But, knowing the Father's intention, Jesus ascended the mountain and brought the needed witnesses with him. The passive aorist μετεμορφώθη simply records the fact and involves the Father as the agent. Moreover, the noun μορφή, from which the verb is derived, always denotes the essential form, not a mask or a transient appearance

but the form that expresses the very nature. So here the actual μορφή of Jesus was changed; he underwent a metamorphosis.

This God did to him "before them," in the actual presence of the disciples. Luke 9:29-31 records the facts of the transfiguration and in v. 32 states that the disciples were heavy with sleep yet carefully adds that, having been aroused and being wide-awake, they saw his glory and Moses and Elijah standing with him. Perhaps the communing of Jesus with the Father in prayer continued awhile, so that the three disciples sat down and began to doze, entirely unconscious of what was about to transpire. Then suddenly, as with sleepy eyes they looked up at Jesus standing a short distance from them, they beheld the change.

This was astounding. The body and the human nature of Jesus were glorified. Mark says nothing about the countenance, and Luke only that it came to be other (ἐγένετο ἕτερον). It is Matthew who reports that "it shone like the sun." This is often passed over lightly by the commentators. The aorists μετεμορφώθη, ἔλαμψε, and the following ἐγένετο with reference to the garments report objective facts, actual changes in Jesus himself, and not something subjective only that appeared to the eyes and the minds of the three disciples. The explanations of rationalists, that the rays of the sun lighted up the face and the clothes of Jesus while he was standing on a higher elevation than the disciples, are efforts to evade the acceptance of another miracle. When the disciples looked at the countenance of Jesus they looked at a refulgence that was as brilliant as the sun itself. This extended to Jesus' entire form, for his very garments had the translucent whiteness of pure light. Instead of thinking of the radiance that shone on the face of Moses (Exod. 34:29; II Cor. 3:13), we have far more reason to think of John's vision of Jesus in Rev. 1:13-15.

The philosophizings regarding this transfiguration
are of little value. As one such we mention the misleading alternative as to whether the transfigured
body was a *donum superadditum* or a *donum naturale,*
which introduces a dogmatical distinction that applies
to the image of God in the creation of man but does
not apply to the transfiguration. Peter writes
(II Pet. 1:16): "We were eyewitnesses of his
majesty" (μεγαλειότης). John 1:14 adds: "We beheld his glory, glory as of the Only-begotten from the
Father." It was the same body and human nature
that the Virgin bore but joined by that birth to the
nature and the person of the Second Person of the Godhead. By virtue of this union the human nature
shared in the divine attributes but, during the days
of the humiliation, used these attributes only on exceptional occasions, for instance, in the performance of
the miracles. One of these occasions was the transfiguration when for a brief time the whole body of
Jesus was permitted to shine with the light and the
refulgence of its heavenly divinity. So Jesus now
shines in heaven forever. Of the holy city (heaven)
it is said: "The Lamb is the light thereof," Rev.
21:23. The remarkable thing is that the earthly
clothes Jesus wore were transfigured in the same manner as his countenance.

It may sound learned and impressive to speak of
a process operating from the spirit of Jesus upon his
body, a process that was now so far advanced as to
permit his divine spirit (he had only a human spirit!)
to shine out through his body. Of such speculation
the Scriptures know nothing. The disappearance of
the glory after the transfiguration weakens this theory
of a process and does so in spite of the explanation that this disappearance was only an element in
the process and in the final result of permanent
glorification to be achieved. Jesus came to his final

glorification through no process between his spirit and his body, or between his divine and his human nature. From his conception onward he was the very Son of God, and here on the mount his divine glory was permitted to shine out through his body for a little while.

3) **And lo, there appeared to them Moses and Elijah in company with him, speaking together.** The verb ὄπτομαι is used with reference to the appearance of angels (Luke 1:11; Acts 7:35), to God (Acts 7:2, 30), to Jesus to Paul (Acts 9:17), and to other manifestations; Young, *Concordance*, lists all the passages. The passive with the dative means: "was seen by them." Also these two appeared (were seen) "in glory" (Luke 9:30). The effort to make this appearance merely subjective is as ineffectual as was the same effort regarding the glorious appearance of Jesus. Moses and Elijah stood beside Jesus, talked with him, and were seen by the three witnesses just as they saw Jesus himself. They were sent from heaven by God and thus "in glory," as the saints appear in heaven. As regards all three, Jesus, Moses, and Elijah, their glorious appearance was made in a form that was sufficiently subdued so the earthly eyes of the disciples could behold it without being blinded. Here again a spiritual process is introduced by some commentators: the three disciples advanced sufficiently in this process to see this vision, i. e., this inward picture not realities. This opens the door to all manner of religious hallucination on the part of those who deem themselves sufficiently advanced in holiness.

The question is inevitable, "Why just these two, Moses and Elijah?" The best answer seems to be, "Moses was the great representative of the law, Elijah the great representative of prophecy." Both are outstanding figures of the Old Testament, and both represent prophecy as well as law. Moses stands at the head of Israel's history, Elijah appears when Israel had declined so that only 7,000 were left who had not bowed to idolatry. The days of Elijah were like those which Jesus found when all the rulers and the great mass of the people had lost the true faith and had departed far from God. The observation that the appearance of these two with Jesus (μετ' αὐτοῦ) intended to assure the disciples that the death of Jesus (16:21) was in perfect accord with the Old Testament prophecies concerning the Messiah, may be accepted as correct; the disciples had other ideas and found the death of Jesus a great σκάνδαλον.

How did these three disciples recognize Moses and Elijah? Certainly not by the correspondence of their features and their dress to ideas the disciples and the Jews had formed concerning their appearance. Nor do we hear that the disciples had to wait until Jesus told them who these two glorified men were. A far better answer is that the saints in heaven need not be introduced and named to us but are at once known through heavenly intuition. If anything is needed beyond this, it is the fact that, when God makes a revelation, he makes it fully by conveying to the beholder all that he is to know. Elijah ascended to heaven bodily and thus undoubtedly appeared in his own glorified body. There is much speculation in regard to Moses. According to Deut. 34:5, 6 he died, and his body was buried in an unknown place by God himself. We read of no transfer of his body to heaven. Only the soul of Moses has entered heaven.

Here we must brush aside all the speculative assertions that prior to the final resurrection the souls of the saints in heaven are clothed temporarily with some kind of heavenly body; II Cor. 5:1, etc., furnishes no support for this view, for note v. 8, "absent from the body." Like the angels, the saints in heaven have no bodies of any kind, yet, when an angel is sent to men on earth, he is seen and heard (28:2-5)

and performs other acts. In the same way God sent
Moses who was both seen and heard and then departed
with Elijah.

Μετ' αὐτοῦ combines Jesus with Moses and Elijah
and makes συλλαλοῦντες mean that the three were speaking together. Mark writes, "Together they were
speaking with Jesus." Luke adds the subject of their
conversation: "the ἔξοδος (outgoing or final outcome)
which he was about to fulfill (πληροῦν) in Jerusalem,"
which is usually understood to mean "the decease" or
death, yet the word includes all that Jesus indicated
in 16:21, including also the resurrection, as his death
and resurrection also always go together. We fail
to see why some think that the disciples only saw
Moses and Elijah talking with Jesus but did not hear
what was said but later learned this from Jesus.
There is nothing in the three records that would indicate this. It was God's intention that these three
disciples should be witnesses of this transfiguration
and, as all that precedes (16:13-28) and the following (v. 9) show, this transfiguration was intended to
cast light on the death and the resurrection of Jesus.
Why, then, should the conversation have been withheld from the disciples?

4) **Now Peter, responding, said to Jesus: Lord,
it is excellent that we are here. If thou art willing,
I will make three booths here, for thee one, for
Moses one, for Elijah one.** Here we have one of the
plain instances in which ἀποκριθείς is used in the wide
sense. No one has spoken to Peter, all three disciples merely watch with great intentness; then Peter
speaks. He merely responds to the situation; what
he says indicates his reaction to his great experience.
He addresses only Jesus, his beloved and now so glorious Master. Mark indicates that Peter's words are
rather foolish; he does not know what he is talking
about. Mark had no doubt received this information

from Peter himself, as also the additional fact that
that he and his companions were under the spell of
great fear or awe, as certainly they had reason to
be. Naturally also Peter receives no answer; perhaps Jesus does not even look at him; other more
important things are now transpiring. It is, of course,
like Peter to speak when he should have kept still.

What he says is valuable in one respect. He feels
it καλόν to be here, and the simple positive "excellent"
is more expressive than the comparative or superlative would be, R. 661. Peter felt as though he
and his fellow-disciples were very near to heaven.
Though they were filled with deep awe they felt themselves in the presence of heavenly glory, with Jesus
being glorified so unspeakably in divine majesty
(II Pet. 1:16), and two dwellers of heaven also appear-
ing in glory (Luke 9:31). Peter's one desire is to
prolong this experience; hence his foolish suggestion
that, if it please Jesus, he will erect three booths, one
for each of the three glorious persons. The foolishness lies in the idea that beings who are in such an
exalted state would need shelter for the night like
men in the ordinary state of human existence. He
says nothing of a shelter for the disciples; perhaps
he felt so humble that he and the other two disciples
would lie out in the open. The idea that Peter is
here placing Moses and Elijah on the same level with
Jesus and is thus introducing saint worship could
hardly have entered his foolish head.

Peter's words are misunderstood when ἡμᾶς is made
emphatic: "It is a good thing that *we* (disciples) are
here" — *we* can build booths for you. Since καλόν is
impersonal, the subject εἶναι must be written. Peter
addresses Jesus, and that fact makes "we" include
him and not merely the disciples. Finally, Matthew
undoubtedly has the exact wording in ποιήσω, which
indicates that Peter alone desires the task of building

the three booths; therefore he also adds εἰ θέλεις, "if thou art willing." Mark and Luke combine this in the volitive subjunctive ποιήσωμεν, "let us make three booths" (R. 931), which tacitly asks the consent of Jesus but thus includes Jesus in the "us" of the verb form.

5) **He still speaking, lo, a bright cloud overshadowed them; and lo, a voice out of the cloud, saying: This is my Son, the Beloved, in whom I was well pleased! Be hearing him!** The cloud did not come slowly but suddenly, before Peter's words were out of his mouth, which fact explains Matthew's exclamation "lo!" Matthew is here more exact than Mark, and his ἔτι is better even than Luke's statement. So also Matthew alone remarks about the brightness of the cloud, which symbolizes the beneficent (and not the threatening) presence of the Father. He it is, as his words show, who speaks from this bright cloud. The words uttered are the identical attestation given Jesus after his baptism 3:17, where they have been explained in detail. We need to note only that Luke has ὁ ἐκλελεγμένος in place of ὁ ἀγαπητός; and in our discussion of 3:17 these terms are shown to be identical in sense. The addition with a second article makes an apposition of the verbal adjective (or of the perfect passive participle in Luke) and thus lends the term great emphasis, R. 776.

The aorist εὐδόκησα is historical not gnomic nor timeless and thus equal to the present tense. The only alternative to the historical aorist, both in 3:17 and here, is the Greek idiom of using an aorist to express something that has recently happened, the English equivalent of which is the perfect: "in whom I have been well pleased," R. 842. But in the present instance, where Luke can render ἀγαπητός as ἐκλελεγμένος, "the one I have chosen, who is such now," εὐδόκησα is undoubtedly the simple historical aorist.

All three synoptists have the durative command, "Him do you hear!" i. e., always, and αὐτοῦ is the genitive of the person; an accusative would indicate the thing that is to be heard. On this command, as already transmitted through Moses, compare Deut. 18:15, last clause, and especially v. 18, 19 with their threat against those who fail or refuse to hear Christ. "Him be hearing!" is in effect to this day. This is God's own confirmation of Peter's great confession 16:16, and God's own seal upon the deity of the Son who is to die and to rise again. As far as Jesus and God were concerned, they certainly left nothing undone to prepare the disciples for what was impending.

6) **And when the disciples heard they fell on their countenance and were exceedingly afraid. And Jesus, having come, touched them and said, Arise and stop being afraid! And having lifted up their eyes, they saw no one except Jesus alone.** The question is asked why, when the voice is heard in 3:17, no one falls upon his face in great fear, while here, when the same voice is heard, this occurs. The situations are very different. Here Jesus is transfigured, his countenance is shining like the sun, etc., Moses and Elijah are present in glory, then comes the sudden shining cloud and the voice of God out of that cloud — all this proved too much for mortal, sinful man. It is Matthew who reports this prostration of the disciples.

7) Matthew also states that Jesus went to them and touched them, bidding them to rise and to stop being afraid. The former is an aorist imperative to indicate the single art of rising, the passive being used like the middle in the active sense; the latter, a present imperative, as so often in prohibitions, forbids what has already begun, R. 851, etc.

8) Now the three disciples raise their eyes and see that Moses and Elijah have departed, the bright, super-earthly cloud likewise, and that Jesus alone is with them, and in his natural state. All that Luke adds is that Jesus was alone when the voice spoke out of the cloud. So we need not ask as to who is referred to by αὐτούς: "the bright cloud overshadowed *them.*" It overshadowed all that were present, nor did it envelop Moses and Elijah and thus allow them to disappear. These were taken away in the same manner as they had suddenly appeared, by the power of God.

9) Luke reports only the silence of the three apostles regarding what they had seen. Matthew and Mark tell us that this silence was ordered by Jesus. **And while they were coming down out of the mountain, Jesus ordered them, saying, Tell to no one the vision until the Son of man is risen from the dead.** We cannot agree that they were allowed to tell the rest of the Twelve; for why, then, had the latter not also been allowed to be present? We now see why Jesus took only these three — the rest were not to know as yet. The reason for this restricting of the witnesses of the transfiguration is not far to be sought. Even the disciples had wrong expectations concerning the Messiah. These wrong, fleshly expectations, if the news of the transfiguration had been spread abroad, would have been fanned into flames and would have caused a great deal of harm. The lips of the chosen witnesses were sealed regarding this revelation for the very same reason that Jesus so constantly avoided the use of the title "Messiah" because it had become connected with fanciful and extravagant political ideas of earthly grandeur. Yet the transfiguration and what accompanied it took place as a part of the great foundation of faith. It is one of the major acts of our salvation. It established the fact that Jesus was the Son of God and did this, not by word alone, nor

by an inference from deeds (miracles), but by withdrawing the veil from his divine glory. He who would die and rise again for our redemption, who thus walked in lowliness in the fashion of man, for a little while let the divine majesty (II Pet. 1:16) and glory which belonged to his person and through it also to his human nature and body, shine forth to be seen by these witnesses. Heaven sent its great saints to confer familiarly with him. The Father came and sealed the scene with his personal attestation.

The time to tell it all was fast approaching. Peter has made his record in II Pet. 1:16, 17. Jesus calls what had been seen τὸ ὅρομα, "the vision." But this term does not warrant reducing this event to a mere subjective experience. For Mark calls this vision ἃ εἶδον, "what they saw," and Luke τὰ ἑώρακα, "the things they have seen." This "vision" is like that which Moses had (cf. Acts 7:31; Exod. 3:2). The open and waking eyes beheld the actual realities. This alone agrees with the narratives of the three Gospels. Note that Jesus here calls himself "the Son of man" (see 8:20). His resurrection, when it finally occurred, made this vision and many other things plain. Until that time the lips of the three disciples were to remain sealed.

The phrase ἐκ νεκρῶν denotes separation and nothing more, R. 598. The absence of the article points to the *quality* of being dead not to so many individuals left behind in death; and the sense of the phrase is "from death." In the interest of the doctrine of a double resurrection the effort is made to obtain the meaning: "out from among the dead." Linguistically and doctrinally this is untenable. When this is applied to the unique resurrection of Jesus, it is at once apparent, the idea being, not 'that he left the other dead behind, but that he passed "from death" to a glorious life. No wonder ἐκ νεκρῶν is never used with reference to the ungodly.   The misinterpretation of this phrase is like the Jewish misunderstanding of the phrase "in three days."   This phrase is used 35 times with reference to Christ, a few times figuratively with reference to other persons, and twice with reference to the resurrection of many, Luke 20:35; Mark 12:25.   In 16:21 Jesus uses the passive: "to be raised up," ἐγερθῆναι; now he uses the active "is risen," ἀναστῇ.` For both are true, he rises and he is raised, the *opera ad extra* being *indivisa aut communa.*

10)   **And his disciples inquired of him, saying, Why, then, do the scribes say that Elijah must first come?**   In regard to the rising from the dead Mark reports that the disciples questioned only among themselves.   We see that this point was by no means clear to them.   But what engaged them to the extent that they made inquiry of Jesus was the matter concerning Elijah.   For a brief moment this great prophet had appeared and then disappeared.   Was this the fulfillment of Mal. 4:5, 6?   Was this what the scribes taught in the synagogues?   It did not seem to be sufficient — and yet, Elijah had appeared to them in his own person and had talked to Jesus.   What adds to their perplexity is the fact that they are to say nothing about what they had seen, nothing about Elijah.   It is to this that οὖν refers, namely to the command of silence.   If the appearance of Elijah, which the disciples had just witnessed, was the one expected by Israel according to prophecy, it would seem that it should be publicly proclaimed instead of being concealed in silence.   With τί they thus inquire whether there is real reason or not for the teaching of the scribes, the men who were skilled in the interpretation of the Torah or Old Testament Scriptures, that Elijah must first come, πρῶτον, before the Messiah.   It was the popular expectation that Elijah would first teach the Jews, settle all their disputed questions,

again give them the pot of manna and Aaron's rod
which blossomed, etc.

11) That this is the meaning of the inquiry is
evident in the answer which Jesus gives. **But he,
answering, said: Elijah is coming and will restore
everything. But I say to you that Elijah did already
come, and they did not recognize him but did in his
case whatever they willed. Thus also the Son of
man is about to suffer at their hands. Then the
disciples understood that he spoke to them concerning John the Baptist.** In his answer Jesus, first of
all, adopts the doctrinal formula of the scribes regarding the coming of Elijah as being quite correct. This
explains the prophetic present tense (R. 870) : Elijah
"is coming." Jesus also adopts the second statement
of the scribes, which has the prophetic future: "and
will restore everything." The scribes, of course,
understood this in their own way, as indicated above,
Jesus referred it to the work of the Baptist, which
brought about a spiritual restoration and returned
the hearts of the people to God in true repentance and
faith. "Everything" is mended and restored when
this spiritual renewal is wrought. Without it all outward reforms and restorations are in vain.

12) The scribes were right, and yet they were
sadly wrong. With the voice of authority, "But I say
to you," Jesus states the facts concerning Elijah's coming: He "did already come," using the aorist ἦλθε,
whereas we prefer the perfect: "he has already come."
From 11:10-14 the disciples knew whom Jesus had in
mind. Then Jesus adds how this "Elijah" fared.
The plural subject of the verbs is purposely left indefinite because the disciples knew only too well who
was referred to. "They did not recognize him." The
nation as such and especially as represented in its
leadership, the Sanhedrin, the whole party of the
Pharisees, including the scribes mentioned in v. 10,

together with Herod and his court never as much as realized that the Baptist was the promised Elijah, the Messiah's forerunner.

Accordingly "they did in his case," ἐν αὐτῷ (R. 484), which is almost like an indirect object (R. 588), "whatever they willed," paying no attention to the God who had sent them this Elijah. The expression is purposely veiled and thus quite broad so as to include 3:7, etc., and John 1:19, etc., the treatment accorded him by the Sanhedrin and by the Pharisees in particular, as well as 14:3, etc., the wilful murder by Herod. The fact that the latter is included is evident from the addition: "thus also," etc. The Baptist's bloody fate is only the preliminary to the fate of "the Son of man" (see 8:20). He, too, unrecognized as the person that he is, shall in the same way suffer "at their hands," ὑπ᾽ αὐτῶν, "by them," regarding πάσχειν as though it were a passive, which it is in sense. Thus once more Jesus speaks of his passion and his death as impending (μέλλει).

13) Jesus has more than answered the inquiry addressed to him. He has cleared up the entire question regarding Mal. 4:5, 6 and the coming of Elijah. The prophecy, already fulfilled, is now being carried out with regard to Jesus himself. Matthew adds that the disciples understood what had been told them about the Baptist. The restriction, however, intimates that as yet they did not understand and grasp what Jesus had added about himself.

14) All three synoptists follow the account of the transfiguration with that of the healing of the epileptic demoniac boy. The miracle itself is evidently not the chief point of the narrative but the unbelief of the disciples which prevented them from curing the boy. Note the contrast: Jesus transfigured in his divine glory; the nine disciples still hampered by unbelief. Poignant is the complaint of Jesus, which permits us

to see under what discouragement he had to approach
his passion. This burden, too, he had to bear. Jesus
heals the boy and then speaks the mighty word regarding faith, the full realization of which would come to
pass after his resurrection. His sadness of the
moment is relieved by the prospect of the future now
near at hand.

**And when they came to the multitude, a man
approached him, kneeling to him and saying: Lord,
show mercy to my son since he is epileptic and is in
a bad state; for often he falls into the fire, and often
into the water. And I brought him to thy disciples,
and they were not able to heal him.** It is the day
after the transfiguration (Luke). Matthew's narrative concentrates and yet presents all the essentials;
Mark is more descriptive. Yet Matthew writes in-
dependently and has features of his own.

A crowd of people is gathered about the nine
disciples, also some of the scribes, all are disputing
(Mark). Thus Jesus gets to hear from the father
of the afflicted boy what the disturbance is about. The
man kneels before Jesus and presents his earnest petition to him.

15) The address, "Lord," must always be gauged
according to the person who uses it; here it expresses
deep reverence and high honor but is not intended
in the sense of divine Lord or God's Son. The aorist
imperative begs for an act of mercy for the man's
son, namely that Jesus heal him. Since the appeal
is made to the mercy of Jesus, the pitiful state of
the child is described. Luke adds the detail that it
is the man's only child, and Mark puts the demoniacal
possession forward and adds that it renders the child
dumb. But the worst feature of the affliction is the
epilepsy brought about by the demon. This puts the
child into a bad state, the texts varying between πάσχει
and ἔχει with κακῶς. Both amount to the same thing

and indicate an exceedingly bad condition: "he is
badly afflicted" (B.-P. 1013), or "he is in a bad condition." The fits to which the boy is subject are then
described. He often falls into the fire or into the
water. These symptoms are still to be found in such
cases. Mark adds the foaming at the mouth, the
gritting of the teeth, and the pining away, all of which
accompany severe epilepsy.

16) While Jesus was on the mountain, the father
brought his boy to the nine disciples who had remained
behind. He then tells Jesus that they had been unable to heal him. This is one of the chief features
of the narrative which is unlike anything that had
happened before.

17) **And Jesus, answering** (i. e., responding to
the situation thus presented to him), **said: O generation unbelieving and having been perverted, how
long shall I be with you? how long shall I bear with
you? Bring him here to me!** This is one of the
instances in which the deep feeling of Jesus is permitted to express itself. Pain and disappointment
wring these words from his lips. It is true enough
that γενεά means "generation" and thus applies to
the people of Jesus' time. As a generation they
deserved the characterization ἄπιστος, "faithless," and
διεστραμμένη (perfect participle of διαστρέφω, having been
twisted and still being thus), "perverse," their hearts
always being turned in the wrong direction. Ὦ is
seldom used with vocatives, and when it is used it
expresses a certain solemnity (R. 463) and deep
emotion (R. 464). Note that γενεά has the same form
in both the vocative and the nominative, ἄπιστος also
remains unchanged (R. 464),

But the point is the failure of the *nine disciples* to
drive out the evil spirit. Nowhere does the narrative
stress the unbelief of the multitude. It is unfair to
charge the boy's father with unbelief, for he brought

his boy to the disciples and then to Jesus with an appeal for mercy. From Mark 9:24 we see that there was some faith in his heart. The disciples are rebuked by Jesus. They are the ones "with whom" Jesus has been so long in a special way, and with whom he has borne for nearly three years. Yet here the old unbelief (see v. 20) which marked their entire generation again cropped out, so that because of it they had failed to heal this child. From his own disciples Jesus had a right to expect something better.

The pained lament, so fully justified, is followed by the prompt action of Jesus: "Be bringing him here to me!" The command is already a promise. The plural φέρετε is not addressed to the father but, it seems, to the nine disciples who had tried to heal the boy. At this point Mark adds to the narrative, but Matthew omits these minor details and confines himself to the main issue as is his constant practice.

18) **And Jesus rebuked him, and the demon went out from him, and the boy was healed from that very hour.** Mark records the words Jesus spoke, also the facts that the boy was thrown into a paroxysm by the demon and that Jesus raised him from the ground. On the subject of possession see 4:24. But the man point is that the lad was perfectly healed by Jesus after the disciples had failed so completely. The multitude, mentioned before, is a side issue; only Luke records that the people "were all astonished at the majesty of God" manifested in this deed of Jesus'.

19) **Then, the disciples having come to Jesus in private, said, For what reason** (διατί, "because of what") **were we not able to throw it out? And he says to them: Because of your unbelief. For, amen, I say to you, if you shall have faith as a mustard kernel you will say to this mountain, Remove from here to there, and it will remove; and**

ʍothing shall be impossible for you. The fact that
the disciples failed to expel the demon (αὐτό, neuter
since δαιμόνιον is referred to) is in the foreground,
hence this sequel to the miracle deals with this point
alone. The matter is on the minds of the nine disciples, and so they ask Jesus, when at last he and
they are by themselves, just why they had failed.
The objection that they would not have asked thus
if in v. 17 they had been referred to by the "generation unbelieving," etc., does not hold good. For this
pained lament is expressed in a broad way and combines the disciples with their generation. So their
question, "for what reason," is quite natural.

20) The answer is straight to the point: "Because of your unbelief!" The reading ἀπιστίαν seems
to have been supplanted by the milder term ὀλιγοπιστίαν
since "unbelief" seems to be too strong a term to apply
to these nine disciples, and "littleness of faith" seems
more fitting. That, too, is one reason why in v. 17
"generation unbelieving" is often regarded as leaving
out the disciples. But v. 20 implies that when the
nine disciples dealt with this possessed boy they lacked
the faith that was equal to a mustard kernel. So the
reading ἀπιστίαν must be preferred.

We may puzzle about this unbelief in view of the
command given in 10:8, but the heart is deceitful
above all things (Jer. 17:9) and proved itself so in
this instance. But this "unbelief" must not be understood as the complete loss of the faith confessed for
all the disciples by Peter in 16:17, i. e., faith in Jesus
in general. It is the lack of faith in the promise given
in 10:8: "Cast out demons!" From 7:22 and I Cor.
13:2 (also 12:9) we see that Jesus had in mind charismatic faith, which one may have even without having
saving faith and may lose or be without though saving
faith remains. In the case of the disciples even this
type of unbelief was a serious fault, for Jesus was send-

ing them out with this very power, to work miracles and thus also to cast out demons.

But while Jesus minces no words when pointing out the grave cause of the disciples' failure, he at the same time stimulates the faith of the disciples, including their charismatic faith in particular. In 10:8 he had simply given them his commands with the implication that, if they acted on them, the miracles would follow. Now he adds a mighty assurance and promise that, if only they believe him, the impossible itself will become possible to them. The γάρ makes plain that their failure was due to their unbelief and not to a lack in Jesus or in his empowering of them. The formula "amen," etc., see 5:18, seals the statement with the seal of verity and of authority. It is truly so because Jesus says so. The regular conditional sentence of expectancy does not present an impossible case but one whose repeated occurrence Jesus expects. The language is figurative: telling this mountain to remove from its place to another and instantly having it do so — a supreme example of what is impossible to a human being; yet, let it not be overlooked, the easiest thing for God.

Jesus himself interprets this figurative language: "And nothing shall be impossible for you." He means, of course, for his disciples and in their calling as disciples. Infidelic literalism may challenge a disciple to transfer a mountain or two and laugh at him when he is unable to do so; blind fanatics may tempt the Lord to keep his Word, to do what that Word never promised, and may even persuade themselves that their folly has come to pass. But neither of these aberrations affects the promise as it stands. God does no silly things, no useless things, and it is his power (19:26) that he places behind Jesus' disciples when they are charged to do the things he commands them to do.

The vital thing is this "faith as a mustard kernel."
The reason this and not some other seed is here named
appears already from the parable recorded in 13:31,
etc.   First, the tiny size of this mustard seed; then,
its ability to shoot up into a towering plant.   This
is the *tertium comparationis*.   Even a little faith in
the divine promise, when it is genuine in quality, will
at the critical moment shoot up into a mighty power
and accomplish wonders.   Such was the faith of
Gideon, such that of the apostles after Pentecost, and
such that of a large number of God's saints.   As far
as the miracle to be performed upon the boy is concerned, this depended entirely on the faith or lack
of faith of the nine disciples.   It was not dependent
on the faith of the boy, of his father, or of the multitude.   Here we must remember that *not* all miracles
are alike.   In some instances Jesus seeks to instil
faith prior to the miracle, while in other cases he is
content to have faith follow the miracle (8:28, etc.;
John 5:5, etc.; 9:1, etc.; and others).

21)   Textual criticism cancels this verse on the
ground that it was interpolated from Mark 9:29.
This leaves it as a part of the story of the healing
that shows how faith must be stimulated by fasting and prayer, but removes it from Matthew's
narrative.

22)   Jesus returned to Galilee from the extreme
northern territory of Caesarea.   **While moving
about in Galilee, Jesus said to them:   The Son of
man is about to be delivered into the hands of men,
and they will kill him, and on the third day he will
be raised up.   And they were grieved exceedingly.**
The correct reading in the genitive absolute is
ἀναστρεφομένων, "wandering about," and not συστρεφο-
μένων, "gathering themselves together," which seems
rather out of place.   At some unnamed place before

he reached Capernaum (v. 24) Jesus repeats the announcement made in 16:21. It is in substance the same. This time he calls himself "the Son of man" (see 8:20) and says that "he is about to be delivered into the hands of men," those already named in 16:21, the Sanhedrin. A new point is found in the verb which is passive and hints at some agent (Judas) who will hand Jesus over to the supreme Jewish authorities. In this way the strange thing will happen that he who is "the Son of man," true man and yet more than man, namely God's very Son, shall be placed into the murderous power of mere "men." And even God will not intervene (δεῖ in 16:21).

23) The rest of the announcement is the same. These men will execute their will upon Jesus and "will kill him," yet, again naming the exact time, "on the third day he will be raised up," i. e., by God, who will more than nullify this bloody deed of men (Acts 4:10; 5:30, where the contrast is powerfully brought out: *you* killed him, but *God* raised him up). Although Jesus no doubt journeyed about in Galilee for a considerable time before he returned to Capernaum, Matthew has recorded only this incident of the extended tour. We see that Jesus is intent on preparing his disciples for the coming events. This announcement again plunged the disciples into great sorrow. Mark adds that they really did not understand and were afraid even to inquire further; and Luke is still more emphatic. Jesus could not spare the disciples this sorrow; it would have been cruel to be silent and to give them no warning. We are too familiar with the crucifixion and the resurrection of Christ properly to place ourselves into the position of the disciples when he foretold these things. His words concerning his resurrection seemed as strange and as incredible to them as those regarding his death. To

the last their minds struggled against the plain meaning of what was dinned into their ears, and thus what
they did not want to know they actually did not understand.

## XIV

### Christ at Capernaum, Instructing His Disciples, Chapter 17:24-18:35

24) The visit to Capernaum is brief, indeed. It
is the last time that Jesus visits his own city. Nothing of a public nature takes place. Jesus deals with
his disciples alone, and the time spent with them is
less than one day. The subject matter of this section
makes it stand apart: offenses are to be avoided, and
after they occur are to be removed in the right way.

**Now when they came to Capernaum, they that
collect the double drachmas came forward to Peter
and said, Does not your Teacher pay the double
drachmas?** While Jesus is absent, Peter is accosted
on the street by the collectors of the Temple tax. Since
the return from the exile every Israelite, after reaching the age of twenty, was required (Exod. 30:13, 14;
II Chron. 24:6; Neh. 10:32; II Kings 12:4) to pay
half a shekel toward the support of the Temple; in
Greek coin this was a δίδραχμον or double drachma,
which amounted to about 40 cents. The very term
δίδραχμα, plural, came to mean Temple tax in the expression "to pay the didrachma." The effort to make
didrachma a secular tax that was levied in Galilee by
Herod has failed and is contradicted by what follows.

The collection of this tax began outside of Jerusalem on the fifteenth of Adar, our March, and the collection in the capital followed ten days later and thus
occurred a short time before the Passover. The fact
that Jesus at once paid the tax leads to the conclusion
that it was being collected at this time. Yet the plural

in the question: "Does not your Teacher pay the double drachmas?" refers to the payment of this Temple tax in general (Jesus also speaks of it in this way) and not merely to the tax that was due during the present year. Moreover, οὐ is not an interrogative particle and does not imply an affirmative answer; it is simply construed with the verb, and the question merely asks whether Jesus is accustomed to pay this tax.

The motive for the question seems to be simply the desire for information. It was not a demand for the payment of this year's tax, for then the singular δίδραχμον would have been used. The local collectors, residents of Capernaum where Jesus had his home, knew that in many matters he acted in a manner that to them seemed contrary to the Jewish law. They were also conversant with his superior claims and thus inquired about his attitude regarding the tax. It seems also that the priests were exempted from payment although the rabbis differed regarding that question, some contending that the priests were to be exempted, others that they were at least to be allowed to pay The collectors probably thought that for some reason or other Jesus, too, might consider himself exempt. The idea of forcing payment as our government and law does with regard to the secular taxes, is not involved in the question addressed to Peter

**25) He says, Yes. And when he came into the house, Jesus spoke first to him, saying: How does it seem to thee, Simon? The kings of the earth, from whom do they collect custom or poll tax? from their own sons or from the outsiders? And he having said, From the outsiders, Jesus said to him, Then the sons are free.** Peter knew that Jesus always paid the Temple taxes and answers accordingly As regards this year's tax, the time for its payment had evidently not yet expired. Peter was accosted on the street, most likely while he was on his way to Jesus' home in Capernaum. When he comes to the house and before he is able to say a word, Jesus speaks to him and reveals that he knows all about the conversation with the tax collectors. To deny that this indicates supernatural knowledge is unwarranted. The claim that, if such knowledge were implied, the fact should have been stated is met by the verb προέφ-θασεν: Jesus "spoke first." This power Jesus exercised, not absolutely or always, but, like all his other powers, when and to the degree that his work required. Peter must have been surprised to learn that Jesus knew about the conversation on the street.

Jesus asks Peter for his opinion on a question that is quite easily answered. The address, "Simon," has no special significance in this connection; it seems to have been the ordinary name used regarding him in the circle of the Twelve (note, for instance, Luke 24:34). To be sure, earthly kings do not make their own sons, the princes of the royal house, pay taxes, for the entire royal family is supported in regal state by taxing the people. Kings collect taxes only "from outsiders," i. e., the ἀλλότριοι, other than their own immediate families, i. e., the people of their nation. Τέλη are "customs," taxes on wares or goods, while κῆνσος is a tax on the person, a "poll tax."

26) The genitive absolute εἰπόντος (the noun being understood) makes Simon's correct answer a minor part of the narrative. The main point is the deduction made from Simon's answer (ἄραγε), which Jesus emphasizes: "Then the sons are free," i. e., from any taxation. The entire conversation with Peter is in the nature of a parable or at least furnishes an analogous illustration. The whole is so lucid that no explanation is added by Jesus. It is beyond question that he and the disciples are sons of "the great King" (5:35) for whose Temple the tax is collected; Jesus

is the essential Son, and through him his disciples are sons by adoption. This they are irrespective of their national connection and not merely as Jews for whom the Temple was built. The sonship of Jesus and his disciples in no way emanates from or depends on the Temple at Jerusalem. John 4:20-24. Thus, like the sons of earthly kings, these spiritual sons of "the great King" are, therefore, "free," and no one can with divine right levy any Temple tax upon them. Since Jesus, nevertheless, intends to pay this tax as he has always done, he wants it thoroughly understood that by doing so he is not placing himself and his disciples on a common level with the Jews.

27) The reason that he submits to this tax is quite another **Nevertheless, lest we entrap them, having gone to the sea, throw a hook and take up the first fish that comes up; and having opened the mouth of it, thou shalt find a stater. Having taken this, give it to them for me and thee.** The principle which Jesus follows in consenting to pay the tax is the one enunciated in 3:15; 5:17, and indicated in 8:4. It is the consideration for others as imposed by their great mutual calling that prompts Jesus also in this matter. They must not "entrap them." On the verb σκανδαλίζειν see 16:23. It goes beyond the idea of causing one to stumble, for such a person may rise again, but to catch one in a trap is always fatal. The two ideas are by no means identical though they are often so regarded.

If Jesus and his disciples refused to pay the Temple tax, the people, unable to understand the true reason, would conclude falsely that Jesus and the disciples despised the Temple and its worship and would thus reject them and their gospel message. The refusal to pay this tax would be equal to baiting the crooked stick in a trap by which it is sprung; simple-minded people would bite at that bait and be hopelessly caught in the trap thus set for them. With hypocrites, who make traps for themselves of the words and the acts of Jesus, he has no patience (15:12, etc), but he is always considerate of ordinary and sincere souls.

The way in which Jesus orders the tax to be paid by miraculously providing the money again gives evidence of his divine Sonship as well as of the connection of Peter and the disciples with him as the Son who makes sons also of them. Peter is the one who is to catch this fish with the stater in its mouth, Peter at the order of Jesus and thus connected with him. Since he is to catch only one fish he needs only "a hook" not a net. How this fish would come to have a stater in his mouth is left unsaid, also how it would come to be the first fish Peter would catch (πρῶτον is to be construed with ἰχθύν, R. 657), because these are both miraculous. "Thou shalt find" is futuristic. The finding is assured by Jesus' word.

A stater is the equal of four drachmas, hence is also called *tetradrachmon* and would be sufficient to pay the tax for two persons. Peter is to hand this stater over "to them," the collectors, "for me and thee," the Greek preferring this order of the persons. The ἀντί does not suggest the idea of substitution; the entire context deals with the ordinary annual Temple tax and does not say anything about an expiatory sin offering. R. 573 finds a compression of statement in "for me and thee," the stater strictly corresponding to the tax that is due to be paid by Jesus and by Peter rather than money that is due to the persons of Jesus and of Peter. Since Peter is to catch the fish, the amount of the coin will pay the tax also for him. The other disciples, Jesus indicates, are to pay their tax from their own resources, which shuts out the idea that they are never to pay out their own money for such a tax.

How one can read this narrative, in particular also the order to pay the stater as a tax, and then say that

Peter never caught this fish, that Jesus never paid this tax, is rather beyond comprehension. One may call the whole story "a sea tale" (why not "a fish story"?), and dismiss it as fable; but what Matthew writes is plain beyond question. Peter caught the fish and paid the tax as directed. Matthew does not need to elaborate, he has a right to assume some intelligence on the part of his readers. Moreover, throughout his Gospel he is content to bring out the essentials, and here the essentials are the words of Jesus regarding the Temple tax. His followers are to pay that tax as long as the Temple shall stand. The conclusion is warranted that Matthew wrote his Gospel before the destruction of the Temple in the war of the years 66-70.

Modernism treats this narrative in a rather derogatory fashion. We are reminded of the ring of Polycrates and of other stories of fish that were caught with some valuable object in them. Matthew's account is classed with these. Yet, even then, his record is misunderstood; for Jesus would then say: "Your only chance for paying this for us would be to find the coin in the mouth of a fish — you know what the probabilities are. If you could do that, it would be a sign that, after all, we were really liable for the tax."

Some think that Peter sold the fish. Blass arrives at this meaning by changing εὑρήσεις, "thou shalt find," to εὑρήσει, the fish "will bring" when it is sold. But this involves an unwarranted change of the text.

# CHAPTER XVIII

1) **In that hour the disciples came to Jesus, saying, Who then is greater in the kingdom of the heavens?** Jesus had just returned to Capernaum (17:24) and had just attended to the payment of the Temple tax. "In that hour" means that almost immediately Jesus attended to the dispute among his disciples regarding greatness. All that is recorded from 17:24 to 18:35 took place on one day, which appears to be the time spent on this final visit to Capernaum. Mark tells us that Jesus was "in the house," which cannot be Peter's house, as some think, but must be the home of Jesus himself who at the beginning of his ministry had transferred his home to Capernaum. The definite article points to "the house" as being one that was well known, one where Jesus stayed regularly while he was in his home city.

When Matthew writes that "the disciples came to Jesus" he intends merely to say that now the whole company was assembled in Jesus' home. We must not assume that the disciples came to Jesus in order to have him answer this question about greatness. Mark tells us that Jesus broached the subject by inquiring about what they had discussed among themselves on the road to Capernaum. They "held their peace" because of a guilty feeling, and only Mark leads us to conclude that some of them at last told Jesus. Matthew states directly that they wanted to know who was "greater in the kingdom of the heavens." Yet ἄρα in the question, "Who, then, is greater?" hints at what Mark states about the previous hesitation. The Greek uses μείζων, the comparative "greater," which is more exact. The implication is that all of the Twelve would be great, yet that some would be greater than the rest.

(678)

The singular does not refer to one only but is to be understood in a general sense as a reference to any one over against others, so that for various reasons several might be ranked above others. The present tense is modified by the future idea lying in the phrase "in the kingdom of the heaven" (see 3:2), here referring to the great Messianic kingdom which the disciples thought Jesus was about to establish with wondrous earthly grandeur.

Jesus himself had furnished an occasion for this question concerning the relative position of the disciples in his approaching kingdom. He had given some distinction to three of the Twelve on two notable occasions (Mark 5:37; Matt. 17:1). Often enough Peter had been allowed to take the lead and to speak for the rest; and even on this day he had been ordered to catch the fish with the stater in its mouth and to pay the tax for Jesus and for himself. So on the road the Twelve had had their dispute, and Jesus had delayed until this time in order most thoroughly to settle this question that was so fraught with danger because of envy, jealousy, pride, and hatred. There was a possibility that it might disrupt this little band of twelve.

2) Mark describes Jesus as sitting down and then calling the Twelve to himself and making an opening statement before he called the little child to himself. So, after the disciples had confessed their dispute, we must imagine that Jesus formally seated himself, his manner indicating that he intended once for all to clear up this question of precedence and greatness in his kingdom. We may take it that when the Twelve were called to him at this moment they sat about Jesus in the usual Oriental fashion. **And having called forward a little child, he stood it in their midst and said: Amen, I say to you, unless you turn and become as the little children you shall in no wise**

**enter into the kingdom of the heavens.** It is most natural to assume that this παιδίον (the diminutive is always neuter) belonged to someone who lived with Mary in Jesus' house, and that the child thus knew Jesus and readily came at his call. We have no reason to assume that there was anything marvelous or extraordinary about this child. This little one ran up to Jesus who then, seated as he was, told it to stand in the midst of the disciples facing the half-circle of seated men. In this way the attention of all was drawn to the child. But Mark adds the beautiful action that Jesus also took the child in his arms, lifting it to his breast as he sat before his disciples. As readily and as willingly as the child had come at Jesus' call, so it now came to his arms and laid its head on his bosom or his shoulder. Here was a *demonstratio ad oculos,* one that would impress itself indelibly upon the minds of the disciples.

3) With the child held thus, Jesus speaks, sealing his statement by the solemn formula of verity and of authority: "Amen, I say to you" (5:18). From the high places in the kingdom after which the disciples were striving Jesus takes them back to the very portals of that kingdom. They are told on what conditions alone they are admitted, and, of course, these vital conditions apply also to continuance in the kingdom. There is a hidden warning in these words: by contending about the higher places in the kingdom the disciples were losing their childlikeness and were thus endangering their very continuance in the kingdom.

"Unless you turn and become as little children" is one and the same act. By thus turning they will become as little children, and becoming such means to turn. The second aorist passive is used reflexively, στραφῆτε, "turn yourselves," it is like the participle στραφείς used in 16:23. Here an action of the heart is referred to, one that is possible only through the

power of grace (Jer. 31:18). This turning should
not be reduced to a mere change of conduct: "unless
you turn from your rivalry and seeking after outward
greatness." The conclusion speaks of entrance into
the kingdom, and the requisite for this is something
far more vital than forsaking a few of our faults.
Jesus has in mind the turning which is usually called
conversion, it is equivalent to the regeneration he required of Nicodemus in John 3:3.

To turn thus is to "become as little children," to
become like the one that was being held in Jesus' arms.
Besser writes: "It came at the call of Jesus' kindly
voice just because it was a child, without any conscious
gratification because of its own tractableness. Just
because it was a child, it in all simplicity allowed this
kind man to do with it what he pleased without thinking: What an excellent child I am that I am thus set
before these men! It allowed Jesus to take it into his
arms and to caress it, feeling itself, indeed, a beloved
child but knowing nothing of its loveliness. Well, this
child in the arms of Jesus is for the disciples an illustration of what excellence in the kingdom of God is."
Then the childlikeness to be manifested in conversion
is sketched: "To permit oneself to be called, led,
loved, without pride and without doubt, in simple trust,
that is childlikeness even as this is the nature of children who possess nothing but need everything; who
are able to do nothing but receive everything; to earn
nothing but receive everything as a gift — thus must
all who desire to enter the kingdom of heaven become
by conversion." Humble trustfulness is a good summary of what Jesus has in mind, this translated into
the spiritual realm, into our relation to Jesus. A
king's child plays with a beggar's child, and neither
feels above the other or beneath the other. We bring
our children up, God brings his children down. Many
have thought that children must first grow to man-

hood before they can enter the kingdom; Jesus reverses this: these twelve men must go back and become
little children.

The two verbs στραφῆτε and γένησθε are rightly aorists,
for they describe a momentary act; and οὐ μή is the
strongest form of negation with either a future indicative or a subjunctive: "in no wise." The subjunctive εἰσέλθητε is volitional, cf. R. 933 on 5:20. Jesus
closes the kingdom against all who refuse to become
as little children.

4) Now Jesus is ready to speak regarding greatness in the kingdom.    The fundamental requirement
for entering the kingdom continues in effect throughout the kingdom and thus decides our position in it,
whether this is to be low or high. **Whoever,
therefore, shall humble himself like this little child,
this is the greater one in the kingdom of the heavens.
And whoever receives one such little child on my
name, receives me.  But whoever shall entrap one
of these little ones that believe in me, it is fortunate
for him that an ass's millstone be hanged about his
neck, and that he be sunk in the high sea.**  Luther
writes:  "Oh, do not think to be great but to be little.
Becoming great will come of itself if you have become
little."  The connective οὖν, "therefore," bases all
greatness in the kingdom on the original condition
required for entrance.   The sentence that has ὅστις with
the future indicative (some texts have the aorist subjunctive) and those having ὃς ἐάν with the subjunctive
(v. 5, 6), have practically the same force.   The respect
in which one is to become like a little child is now
plainly stated: "humble himself" (we prefer the reading with the future indicative to that with the punctiliar aorist subjunctive).   First the turning that gives
us entrance; then, as the natural continuance of that
act of turning, this growing humbleness of mind which
makes us greater and greater in the kingdom after we

have entered. This ταπείνωσις makes no claims, insists on no rights, comes with no demands, but bows lowly and humbly under the Lord's will and Word, yields completely to him, and is happy and content in doing that. With "this child" Jesus again uses it as an illustration.

The child in Jesus' arms looked up to him, depended on him, was content with what he did. This was its humility or lowliness. It claimed nothing, pointed to no merits, was proud of no achievements. This was the natural state of this child; Jesus uses this to illustrate what the spiritual state of greatness in the kingdom is. Yet we must be warned. Pope Gregory the Great called himself *servus servorum*. He did it in order to be the greatest, did it in a mechanical fashion, by a shrewd kind of calculation, putting on humbleness in order to secure greatness. Any proceeding of this kind defeats itself. True humility does not hanker after greatness, does not even think of it. Its very delight lies in being nothing. Its own character is its greatness. In v. 1 μείζων may be regarded as a comparative, but here ὁ μείζων seems to be used for the superlative "the greatest." See R. 281 and 667 regarding the replacement of the superlative by the comparative in the Koine.

This is greatness as God estimates it, thus is genuine and not spurious and sham as is that which men set up and prize. The paradox is striking: the least is the greatest. He who thinks of making no claims shall have all that others claim and by claiming cannot obtain. But the paradox is easily solved. Only an empty vessel can God fill with his gifts. And the emptier we are of anything that is due to ourselves, the more can God pour into these vessels his eternal riches, honors, and glories. It is hard for our minds, trained, as they are, to worldly ways of thinking about greatness, to grasp this thought of Jesus', and harder still to make it the motivating principle of our lives; but God's grace in us will not be in vain.

5) When Jesus adds the word about receiving "one such little child," we find it unwarranted, in spite of what some commentators say, to have this exclude children. Since Jesus had a child in his arms and used it as a living illustration and then said, "one such little child," this word can scarcely be understood metaphorically. Nor should one speak about a "physical" child. For Jesus says, "Receive one such little child on my name," which plainly makes the entire act spiritual. The more usual phrase is *"in* my name," i. e., in connection with it; *"on* (ἐπί) my name" merely modifies the idea: on the basis of my name. These phrases do not mean "on my authority." When we study the connection of all these ὄνομα phrases, it will become clear that "name" is that by which Jesus (or God) is known, hence his revelation (6:9; 7:22; 10:22, 41,42; 12:21; and elswhere in this and the other Gospels).

To receive such a little child ἐπὶ τῷ ὀνόματί μου means to do this "on the basis of the revelation of Jesus that one has received." The whole act rests on this and on no other considerations. Of course, this means that a person will treat the child thus received as the revelation and the teaching of Jesus require, which include especially tender spiritual care. The point of this act is the fact that it is only one such little child that is thus received. In the eyes of the world a reception for such spiritual reasons has no value. Even today, when the world has come to value children more highly, it values them thus only for natural and secular reasons (providing for their physical and their educational needs). But Jesus regards it as an act of greatness when we receive such a child on the ground of his revelation. This act is not great in the sight of men, is not praised and applauded by the world, is not understood by the multitude; but the trusting humility of the one who performs this lowly act makes for spiritual greatness in the kingdom.

For Jesus declares, "Me he receives," with emphasis on ἐμέ. This does not mean that Jesus identifies himself with the child as a child. This "me" refers to the way in which the child is received, to the ὄνομα of Jesus on which the act rests. And here all its spiritual greatness appears. The act is as great as Jesus himself who is the King of the kingdom. If it could be made a visible deed that the glorious Son of God and Savior of the world was being tendered a grand reception, the headlines of all the daily papers would appear in the heaviest type; but since it is invisible, it is covered with the humble mantle of faith, and its greatness will not appear until the judgment day (25:40, "unto me").

Those who admit that Jesus here has in mind an actual child often claim that this is all he has in mind. But he has just used an actual child in his own arms as an illustration of the true and humbly trustful members of his kingdom; all these are exactly like little children. We also see that in the next statement, which is the opposite of this one, he uses as the equivalent of "one such little child" the interpretative term, "one of these little ones who believe in me." In 25:40 this is made still plainer: "One of these my brethren, even the least." This makes it certain that Jesus has in mind not only an actual child but also any disciple of his who has spiritually become like a child. To receive such a childlike believer "on the name of Jesus" is most surely receiving no one less than Jesus himself. It would be arbitrary and illogical in the highest degree for Jesus to make all his disciples children in spirit and then to make their greatness depend only on receiving aright an actual child and not a believer who has become like a child.

Now the point of this reception, both of a child and of a believer who has become a child, lies in the words that their reception is equal to the reception of Jesus himself. Humble as they are, it will be impossible for us to treat them with disdain, because in them we would mistreat Jesus himself. They may be the very least of his brethren, without any outward prominence, and in their childlike spirit wholly unassertive and altogether lowly (thank God, the church has always had many of these "little ones"!), yet we who know the greatness of this littleness and have it in our hearts will treat them as we should treat Jesus himself. In this way Jesus spreads his protecting hand over them; as we receive them, we receive Jesus himself. James 2:2-9.

6) The opposite of receiving a child or a childlike believer on the name of Jesus is to "entrap" one of them. On σκανδαλίζειν and σκάνδαλόν see 16:23, and again note that the terms go beyond the idea of stumbling (from which one may rise) and always denote spiritual destruction. The figure is that of an animal caught by touching the bait affixed to the crooked stick in a dead-fall trap. The sense is: whoever destroys a child or a childlike believer spiritually incurs the greatest wrath of Christ. Jesus thus describes the extreme mistreatment, for nothing worse could be done. This he often does on the correct principle that the extreme includes all lesser wrongs. In 5:21, etc., Jesus makes murder include anger, etc.; in 5:27 adultery, lustful looks. Moreover, the extreme must be mentioned lest its omission lead to wrong conclusions. By forbidding the entrapment which kills spiritually all lesser spiritual harm to others is equally forbidden.

Let no one deceive himself by saying that only a child is thus destroyed or hurt or one of the insignificant believers. Jesus has indicated how precious these are in his sight, for what is done to them is as though it were done to Jesus himself. This is a word that should awaken all of us, parents, pastors, teachers, and all who hold positions of influence. What if only one humble soul should he lost through our teaching and our conduct!

We see that Jesus again uses the numeral "one." He knows every single one of his own. But now he uses the broader term "one of these little ones that believe in me." Those who hold that v. 5 does not include children take the same view in regard to this verse. Often this is done because of τῶν πιστευόντων εἰς ἐμέ. They are unwilling to admit that little children can believe. Their exegesis thus becomes dogmatic. But the whole context so manifestly refers to children that some penetration of the thought is required to find in it a reference to childlike adult believers.

To believe means to trust. Even in adults the inner essential of their faith, let it be filled with ever so much discursive thought, intelligent knowledge, introspective consciousness, is childlike trust. In the matter of this trust the child is the model for the man, not the man for the child. Jesus uses the natural traits of a child to illustrate what he desires his disciples to become. As capable as a little child is of natural trust toward mother, father, etc., so capable it is of having spiritual trust in its heart. Not the discursive features make faith what it is but this essential quality of trust. As faith remains in a state of sleep, coma, insanity, senility, so it can also be active in earliest infancy (Luke 1:41, 44). Delitzsch, *Biblische Psychologie*, 353.

It is true enough that the impersonal συμφέρει does not express a comparative idea such as, "it is better for him," but means only, "it is beneficial or fortunate for him," the subfinal ἵνα clause indicating what is so considered R. 992. Yet, as in 5:29; John 11:50; 18:14,

a comparative thought is suggested by the two ideas
that are linked with συμφέρει. We must note that ὃς ἄν
with the subjunctive does not really describe an actual
case but only supposes one in a vivid way. When a
deed such as this is supposed with regard to a man,
when one thinks of him as ruining a little one spiritually, it would, indeed, profit him, i. e., be preferable,
if the most awful death at once removed him, i. e., before he is able to carry out this deed. The thought is
that such a fate συμφέρει αὐτῷ, "is profitable," when one
considers the guilt and the penalty his deed, if it be-
somes a reality, would surely bring upon him. That
is why Jesus here speaks of this unheard-of manner of
death, a plunging a man into the sea with a millstone
around his neck. No human judge or court ever decreed such a penalty. This answers the view that such
a penalty is here thought of as one that alone befits
the crime of destroying one of these little ones.

The adjective ὀνικός means "pertaining to an ass"
and describes the μύλος, here millstone, that was
operated by an ass. This was much heavier than the
parts of a hand mill. Πέλαγος means "the high sea"
or the depth of the open sea and with τῆς θαλάσσης may
be translated, "the depth of the high sea," the genitive
helping to emphasize the concept. We must not lose
the intent of Jesus when he places these two side by
side: a man who is drowned as indicated, and a man
who ruins a little one spiritually, making the former
preferable. The enormity of the crime thus indicated
could hardly be expressed more strikingly.

7) The subject of entrapments is now broadened
so as to include all of them, and in v. 10 Jesus returns
to "the little ones." **Woe to the world because of
the entrapments! For it is necessary that the
entrapments come; nevertheless, woe to that man
through whom the entrapment comes!** Jesus sees
all the σκάνδαλα that await his disciples in the world.

The world will be full of deathtraps (not merely "occasions of stumbling," R. V.) for them. The exclamation "woe" is, of course, not an accusation, but likewise not a mere expression of sorrow. Like μακάριος, "blessed," (for instance, in 5:3, etc.) all the "woes" of Jesus are verdicts. Here the world, all the men in it who remain outside of the kingdom, are sentenced to "woe," and this sentence will be duly carried out. Here ἀπό has the idea of cause, R. 580; for "from" the entrapments that are wickedly designed against believers by the world will come this woe for the world itself.

The reason for this exclamation on the part of Jesus is brought by γάρ; he so exclaims because he sees the ἀνάγκη or "necessity" that brings about "the entrapments." Since the world is what it is, it cannot let the believers (τῶν πιστευόντων, v. 6) alone. The world will always set deathtraps for them and bait them in all sorts of ways, and some believers will be caught. Because Jesus knows the nature of the world and the dangers to which his believers are exposed he pronounces this woe. Πλήν is used as an adversative conjunction, R. 646, 1187, and is rare in the New Testament. "Nevertheless" expresses the thought that the necessity just indicated is not an excuse for the world. Since saving grace is so great and rich, the world should not remain as it is; when believers are multiplied, the world should, like them, turn to Christ. But now the collective "the world" is resolved into its individual members, those who make it their special business to set these traps: "woe to that man through whom (διά, as a willing medium) the entrapment (any specific deadly act of this kind) comes." In the world each man shall receive his woe according to the spiritual damage he does or tries to do.

8) But entrapments may come to us, not only through other disciples or through the world, but even

from within our own selves because of the sin that
still remains in us. **Moreover, if thy hand or thy
foot entrap thee, cut it off and throw it from thee;
it is excellent for thee to enter into the life maimed
or lame than, having two hands and two feet, to be
thrown into the everlasting fire. And if thine eye
entrap thee, pluck it out and throw it from thee; it
is excellent for thee to enter into the life one-eyed
than, having two eyes, to be thrown into the Gehenna of the fire.** In 5:29, 30 these two statements
appear in reverse order, and while they are identical
in substance, the wording varies. Instead of "it
profits thee" (συμφέρει, is better for thee) we have the
equivalent, "it is excellent (καλόν) for thee." More important is the change from, "that one of thy members
perish, and not thy entire body be thrown into Gehenna," to, "for thee to enter into, the life maimed or
lame than, having two hands and two feet, to be thrown
into the everlasting fire." The positive "to enter into
the life" explains the previous negative "not to be
thrown into the Gehenna." In both verses "the life,"
ζωή, is the true life of heaven, the opposite of eternal
death in hell. In 5:29, 30, "thy whole body" means
the body as joined to the person, hence, when the
thought is repeated, the person as such is indicated.
We also see that "Gehenna" means "the fire, the everlasting." The addition of the adjective by means of
a second article makes it emphatic; it is like an apposition and a climax, R. 776. This fire can be only hell.

9) There are less changes regarding the right eye,
etc. Jesus now says simply, "thine eye," which may
refer to either eye. The rest conforms to v. 8, except
that the final phrase "into the Gehenna of the fire"
(each noun being definite and having its own article)
even combines the Gehenna and the fire and thus most
emphatically indicates what place is referred to by
either "Gehenna" (5:29, 30) or "the fire, the everlast-

ing" (v. 8). The genitive in "the Gehenna of the fire" is descriptive, R. 496; and the positive καλόν is stronger than the comparative, it is more like a superlative: "it is best," although the context suggests a comparison.

For the substance of the thought expressed in these two verses turn to 5:29, 30.

10) With the little child most likely still in his arms as he sat in Oriental fashion, Jesus reverts to v. 5, etc., and amplifies what he has already said. There he warned against the extreme mistreatment, any entrapment of his little ones. As was the case in 5:21, etc., he now adds that by forbidding the extreme he includes all minor wrongs. **See lest you despise one of these little ones! For I say to you that their angels in heaven always see the countenance of my Father in heaven.** Here Jesus touches the bottom of all wrong conduct toward any "one of these little ones," children or beginners in the faith or any in the church that seem unimportant. The term is retained from v. 6 and thus shows that the subject is still the same. "To despise," καταφρονεῖν, is really "to think down on" as though these little ones could be disregarded, as though they amounted to little or nothing. This is the attitude that runs roughshod over the little ones, that neglects their spiritual needs and works them harm in all sorts of ways. The numeral "one" should not be overlooked, for every little one is precious in his sight, he will not have one of them looked down upon. The imperative ὁρᾶτε, "see to it," is both emphatic and durative as though Jesus foresaw how often his little ones and especially the children would be neglected in the church.

"I say to you" means "with all my authority," and γάρ furnishes the reason that none of us dare despise one of these little ones. They are so precious that God delegates his angels to watch over them. The idea of guardian angels, one being assigned to each little one,

can scarcely be supported by the mere genitive pronoun
"their" angels. Tobit 5 is apocryphal and even then
does not support the idea assumed; and other Jewish
literature has no more value. God uses his angels as
ministering spirits and often assigns individual angels
for special duties. That thought suffices also here.
Acts 12:15: "It is his (Peter's) angel" does not state a
Scriptural doctrine but only the superstitious ideas of
those who were alarmed by Rhoda's report. What is
to impress the disciples and to keep them from despising even one of these little ones is the fact that "their
angels in heaven always see the countenance of my
Father, of him in heaven" (ἐν οὐρανοῖς here used twice
without the article). We cannot make a division and
think of some angels that see the Father's countenance
in the angelic *visio Dei*, and of some who do not. While
angels are of different ranks (each having his own
principality, power, might, dominion, and name or title
to correspond, Eph. 1:21), all of them stand in the
presence of God. Jesus is thus not speaking of the
"throne angels," or of the highest angels; nor does
seeing the Father's countenance recall Ps. 123:2
(which has "hand" and not face) in the sense of being
on the alert for his orders. It is enough to understand
that the greatness of the angels is here impressed upon
the disciples.

Here Jesus mentions two classes of ministrants for
each of these little ones: the disciples who are still on
earth, and these heavenly angels; the disciples who
have not yet attained perfection and the *visio Dei*, and
the angels who always see the countenance of the
Father. God appoints both classes of ministrants to
carry out his gracious will (v. 14) regarding each of
these little ones. Let the disciples always remember
with whom they are associated in this blessed task. If
these angels delight in it (Heb. 1:14), shall they not?

If the angels never think of despising one of these little ones, dare the disciples ever think of such a thing?

With the possessive "my" Father Jesus puts himself in the fullest accord with that Father in this matter. By adding the phrase "in heaven" by means of a second article he indicates the greatness of God even more emphatically (R. 776) than when he adds this phrase to the angels without such an article. We know too little about the dwellers in the heavenly world to explain how these angels always (διὰ παντός) see the Father's face even while they execute their mission in behalf of these little ones. The human term πρόσωπον, here used with reference to the Father who has no body of any kind, can have in mind only his glory and his glorious presence — at least, we are able to say no more.

11) The textual evidence against this verse is so strong that we must cancel it from Matthew's account. It was probably inserted from Luke 19:10.

12) An illustration resembling the parable of Luke 15:3-7, though it is much briefer, advances the thought to the spiritual help that the disciples ought to offer any of these little ones who may be endangered by going astray. As 5:29, 30 is repeated in 18:8, 9, so it need cause no comment that Jesus should use the beautiful parable of recovering the lost sheep twice in different and yet entirely suitable connections. **How does it seem to you? If a hundred sheep belong to some man, and one of them strays away, having left the ninety-nine on the mountains and having gone, does he not seek the straying one? And if he comes to find it, amen, I say to you, that he rejoices over it more than over the ninety-nine that have not strayed away.** The introductory question puts the matter before the disciples; and there is

no doubt as to what they will think.    Bengel writes: *suavis communicatio*.    Here is a man who owns a hundred sheep, yet, though he owns so many, when but a single one happens to stray away and get lost, the moment he detects its absence, does he not leave the ninety-nine out there on the mountains and go and seek that one lost sheep?    The interrogative particle οὐχί expects an unhesitating affirmative answer.

Here γένηται with the dative is like εἶναι and denotes possession, the aorist stating this as a fact: if a hundred sheep "shall actually become" to the man, i. e., be his.    So the aorist passive πλανηθῇ means, "shall actually have strayed away."    This verb and its present passive participle at the end of v. 12 seem significant, for πλανᾶν means "to deceive," and its passive "to be deceived."    This is exactly what has happened to the lost sheep: in some way it was deceived and thus strayed away.    This is precisely what may happen to an inexperienced child or some other believer: deceit causes them to stray away.    The subordinate actions are expressed by participles, ἀφείς and πορευθείς, to mark them as such although some texts have the future indicative for the former.    In those texts the apodosis has both a future and a present tense: "will he not leave and does he not seek?"    This is not unusual.    R. 1019 remarks that the condition (ἐάν with the two subjunctives) is future in conception, while the conclusion (the present ζητεῖ) is present in reality: "he does seek." The phrase "on the mountains" modifies the preceding participle: he leaves the other sheep there; and not the following participle: "he goes on the mountains," for in the Greek the forward position of the phrase would lend it a disproportionate emphasis.    The fact that he goes on the mountains and not elsewhere is self-evident, for that is where he is pasturing his flock.    This also accords with the topography of Galilee, the greater part of which is mountainous.

13) The clause with ἐάν and the aorist subjunctive
expects the man to find the strayed sheep although it
leaves open the possibility that he may not succeed in
this. The infinitive εὑρεῖν is the subject of γένηται, R.
1043, 1058. Now Jesus turns from the question he
asked in v. 12 to the strongest kind of assertion and
even seals it with the formula of verity and authority:
"amen, I say to you" (5:18). The thought never comes
to this man that he has the ninety-nine sheep, and that
the one that has strayed away, being only one, amounts
to very little in comparison. His feeling is quite the
contrary. When he succeeds in finding the stray sheep
"he rejoices over it more than over the ninety-nine that
have not strayed away." He rejoices over them, too,
though they have caused him no special trouble but,
strange to say, and yet not strange at all, the one that
caused him all the trouble gives him the greater joy.
Jesus is simply stating what we constantly experience:
a sheep, a jewel, a child, any treasure take on greater
dearness when they are lost and then found or when
they are endangered and then brought to safety.

14) When making his application from this
illustration Jesus states his Father's will only in
negative form. **Thus** (namely as here illustrated)
**it is not a thing willed before your Father in heaven**
**that one of these little ones perish.** Just as the man
in the illustration cannot suffer his strayed sheep to
perish, so the great Father in heaven ("yours," the
more important text; "mine," the less important) could
never will this thing that (subfinal ἵνα stating the contents of this θέλημα) one of his little ones perish. We
should understand θέλημα objectively, "a thing willed,"
even as this is then stated. Abbott-Smith calls ἔμπροσθεν
a targumic formula; yet this seems to be the case only
when it is used with εὐδοκία as in 11:26 (Zahn on the
passage). The idea in "before your Father" seems to

be that such "a will" could never be expressed "before him" and in his presence as a decree of his.

The reading ἕν (neuter) is to be preferred to εἷς (masculine). On the hypothesis that Matthew's Greek Gospel is a translation by a late, unknown person, this neuter has been called a bit of faulty translation. Others think that this neuter is due to the continuance of the idea of a πρόβατον (the neuter noun for sheep). But this is untenable when the illustration is to be applied. No; the expression, "one of these little ones," intends to take us back to v. 6 where it was first used; and then to v. 10 where it was repeated. Thus this neuter ἕν again takes up the diminutive neuter παιδίον, "a little child" (v. 2), "this little child" (v. 4), and "one such little child" (v. 5).

This makes it certain that Jesus is still speaking of children. Whoever else may belong to his "little ones," children certainly do. Even if εἷς were the correct reading, the expression would include children in v. 14. The entire section from v. 1 onward turns on "the little child" and others who have become like this child. It is quite probable that Jesus held the child in his arms throughout this address. The view that "the little ones" Jesus had in mind are all his believers alike misunderstands the passage. By means of true child-likeness we become great in the kingdom (v. 4) and cease to be "little ones." And it is thus that Jesus teaches us to make our will agree with the Father's will by never hurting and by always helping all his little ones, undeveloped children and weak adult believers.

It is certainly true that v. 14 excludes the idea of reprobation. If any "little one," babe or adult, is lost, this thing was not the Father's will but contrary to his will. In this very place he forbids causing hurt and harm to these little ones and commands that all support and help be given them, and makes it plain that this is his good and gracious will. The negative "not to perish" includes its corresponding positive "but to be saved" (John 3:16). Our passage is especially valuable for little children, since they are here so clearly included, and God's will regarding them is so positively stated. He does not want them to perish, and that is why Jesus instituted a sacrament that can be applied to children and can give them the grace that saves (Tit. 3:5; Acts 2:39, "and to your children").

But what about babes that die before they are baptized, can this be applied to them? The answer of the church rests on this divine θέλημα, on the fact that it is not his will that one of these little ones perish. He has bound us to baptize them and thus on our part to execute his gracious, saving will; he has straightly charged us not to despise one of these little ones. While he has thus bound us he has not bound himself to specific means. He has made no definite revelation concerning babes that die in an unbaptized state. But in the expression of his will regarding them as here stated the church is justified in seeing *the hope* that in some way and by some means not revealed to us he will carry out his gracious will nevertheless, for his arm is not shortened, and he can save to the uttermost. We have only this *hope* and no more. The inexcusable neglect of those who presume upon this hope, leave their little ones unbaptized and untaught, and yet demand that God save them when they die, God will judge (v. 6).

15) The disciples wanted to be great (v. 1), and Jesus told them how to become great and then showed them how the great must receive and not destroy the little ones (5, etc.), must never despise but always help them in distress (v. 10, etc.). The progress of thought is clear. Only one additional step is needed. From the straying away, like a sheep, on a sinful course Jesus advances to the final possibility that one brother sins against another brother. What then? By such a sin the erring one shows that he is "a little one" in a

lamentable sense. By a wrong treatment of him the wronged brother would only share the other's fault. Jesus tells what this brother is to do. We note that Jesus speaks about his church and the coming conditions to be found in it with perfect foreknowledge. This fact deserves more attention than it often receives.

**If thy brother commits a sin against thee, go, convict him between thee and him alone; if he hears thee, thou didst gain thy brother.** Here for the first time in this chapter Jesus uses "thy brother" in the sense of thy fellow-believer and thus thy fellow-church member. And, as the sequel shows, a case arises in which the continuance of this relation is jeopardized. Yet until the clear denial of brotherhood is established, I must treat the offender as a brother in Christ and in no other way. With ἐάν and the subjunctive Jesus treats an expected case; and his expectation has certainly been fulfilled. In ἁμαρτάνω we have the regular verb for "to sin," literally, "to miss the mark," the one set by the divine law, and the aorist indicates a specific act of sinning.

"Against thee" is textually very strongly assured. The phrase indicates what sins are here considered; those of a general nature are treated in v. 10-14, here the sin is specified as being committed against a brother. It is necessary, however, to note that only a real sin is referred to, one that is apparent as such when one or two other brethren are called in on the case and when the whole congregation considers the matter. This excludes what a sensitive brother may deem a sin without due warrant that it is such. The context furthermore supplies the directive that the sin is of such a nature that it cannot be permitted to pass as a weakness and fault such as we all commit, sometimes daily. These do not endanger the fraternal bond. They call for a word of rebuke and are then allowed to pass. This occurs often enough, especially where these lesser faults are mutual, one brother perhaps provoking another to act faultily. Brotherly patience and forbearance heal the scar.

Jesus has in mind graver sins such as all brethren would be compelled to consider too serious and too dangerous to allow them to pass without plain evidence of repentance. Sins of this kind often involve more than the offense against one brother; they may wrong several brethren, all of them seeing and knowing about the deed. Or the sin may be altogether public, at once involving the entire congregation, such as some open scandal or some crime. Jesus takes up the least serious case, leaving it to us from it to draw the proper procedure to be followed in the graver ones. If one brother who is sinned against must take action as Jesus directs, then likewise must several if the sin be committed against a larger number, and the church as such if the sin be public from the start.

"Go, convict him" (the first imperative is a mere auxiliary, hence there is no connective), means: show him his sin so that he will see it as a sin and feel guilty accordingly. The aorist implies that this really be done, not bungled or merely attempted. Of course, in the case of a real sin this will not be difficult. Note that while ἐπιτιμῶ means simply "to rebuke," ἐλέγχω means "to rebuke so as to bring conviction."

"Between thee and him alone," *unter vier Augen,* enjoins strict privacy and forbids blurting out the matter in public, or spreading it in secret by telling one or the other, or at once lodging complaint before the church authorities. This direction intends to shield the sinning brother and is prompted by love. It also makes it as easy as possible to confess the sin and to ask for pardon. Compare 7:3. Let both brethren respond to the Lord's kindly intent. "If he hears thee" is again a condition of expectancy; Jesus looks for such an outcome. "Hear" is to be understood in the pregnant sense: hear so as to yield the conviction and thus to confess and in sorrow to ask pardon. The person heard is construed with the genitive. The aorist expresses conclusive hearing that requires no further rebuke.

Here we have a case in which the condition looks to the future while the conclusion turns to the past, which R. 1020 attributes to the swift leap of thought. But this past is a past only to that future: "thou didst gain" if thy brother "shall hear." Moreover, the Greek uses the aorist to express this past, whereas the English would prefer the perfect "hast gained"; yet we do not regard this as a gnomic aorist (R. 842). The thought to be expressed by these tenses is perfectly normal. To gain or win the brother is the original purpose of the procedure. Sorrow and disappointment are to fill the wronged brother when this purpose fails. The motive Jesus desires to find operative in his heart is love toward the sinning brother, the true, spiritual love that desires to assert no rights of its own but only to gain the brother by freeing him from his sin. To gain him thus is to help to save him and is much like gaining a new member for Christ and for the church.

16) But the case may turn out differently. **But if he does not hear, take along with thee one or two more in order that everything may stand on the mouth of two witnesses or three.** The going alone is usually called the first step. The idea is, of course, not to go only once, but until there is no further hope of gaining the brother. This first step is automatically omitted when the sin is one that has been committed against more than one person. The aorist "does not hear" is definite refusal to hear and to be convicted. Every time a brother really sins against another, this is a test as to whether he really intends to stay with Christ and with the church by repentance and amendment of heart, or to let the devil succeed in plunging

him into impenitence. But the battle is not lost in the
first engagement even when this turns out adversely.
"Take along with thee one or two more (ἔτι)." The
Lord leaves the number to the brother concerned. The
object is still the same, and the supposition is that the
offending brother will yield when one or two additional
brethren appeal to him. These ought, of course, to be
most carefully chosen if the task is to be successful.
Jesus does not need to repeat that if the brother heeds
he is won; that is a matter of course. If he is now
won, the matter is settled, and the lips of the brethren
are to be sealed accordingly.

One purpose in taking along a second or a third
brother is the proviso stated in Deut. 19:15 (John
8:17; II Cor. 13:1; I Tim. 5:19) and quoted freely
from the LXX, "that everything may stand (the passive aorist intransitive, B.-P. 596) on the mouth (word
or testimony, Hebraic) of two witnesses or of three."
In case the matter is ever inquired into, and any dispute or uncertainty arises, the case can be properly
settled as to the facts by the two or the three witnesses.
Or if the sinning brother still remains unconvicted, and
the case must be brought before the church, decisive
testimony can be produced. Πᾶν ῥῆμα is not "every
word (utterance)," but "every thing," *die ganze An-
gelegenheit*, the whole matter.

17) Now the worst contingency, the third and
final step. **But if he fails to hear them, tell it to
the church. But if he fails to hear also the church,
let him be to thee even as the Gentile and the
publican.** After the one or the two or the three
fail, the entire ἐκκλησία is to use its united endeavors to
gain the brother. See ἐκκλησία in 16:18. Here, still
more than in 16:18, the original idea of "a called
assembly" is retained, for the body of believers must
hold at least one duly called meeting. We may thus
also translate, "Tell it to the congregation!" for evi-

dently the local gathering of believers is referred to.
Yet the idea of ἐκκλησία is not that of an assembly called
for an outward meeting but one called to be a spiritual
body in Christ by the effective κλῆσις of grace, all its
members being κλητοί as having both received and accepted this call although in the meeting pretended
believers (hypocrites) may also be present. The
ἐκκλησία is not only the clergy, priests, presbyters, or
other heads of church bodies as distinct from the membership. As far as the outward organization of the
local *ecclesia* is concerned, this Jesus has nowhere prescribed, hence it is left to the believers themselves and
to their best spiritual judgment. Once more then, if
the brother that sinned against another now at last
hears at least the congregation, the congregation has
gained him by accepting his repentance and assuring
him of pardon.

But he may refuse to hear even the church, either
refusing to face the church, or facing it and the testimony of the witnesses with an impenitent heart. For
we must note throughout that the sinful act, which
calls for all this action, is in truth sinful and can be
convincingly shown to be such. If all the brotherly
effort of the church fail, then the church must consider
the sinner self-expelled and must take due note of the
fact and act accordingly. This is the so-called ban or
excommunication — the man's membership ceases.

"Let him be unto thee" mentions only the brother
originally sinned against, but certainly what applies to
him applies to all the rest, even as they finally act
jointly, and the brother acts only in accordance with
the verdict of his other brethren. The sinner is now
(not until now) to be regarded and treated as "the
Gentile or the publican," the articles with these singulars making them representative of their respective
class. Every Gentile as such was outside of the commonwealth of Israel, none of its spiritual blessings

belonged to him; and every publican (9:10) was expelled from that commonwealth and thus was in the same category, as one who had separated himself from Israel. By his sin the sinner thus makes himself "one who is not a sheep, nor wants to be sought, but intends to be completely lost," Luther using the imagery of v. 12, 13. Yet even the very severity of this action of the church is intended to bring the offender to his senses, if this be still possible. This action of the church must lead him to see the gravity of his own impenitence. Thus expulsion is the last warning to strike the obdurate conscience. He who laughs at this, laughs at his own doom.

The church (congregation) is thus the final court of appeal. Those who would place above it a still higher authority: the pope, a bishop, some church board, a house of bishops, or a synod composed of clerics, or these combined with lay delegates, go beyond the word of Christ and the teachings of the apostles. In a difficult case the local congregation may seek counsel or advice, but the final jurisdiction in regard to a sinning member belongs to the congregation alone, and no one ought either by direct or indirect means to nullify that jurisdiction. Zahn voices the old Christian exegesis: *Die Gemeinde also ist die hoechste richterliche Instanz auf Erden.* False greatness and authority have often been arrogated to themselves by high officials in the church who have robbed the congregations of their divine authority; and congregations have often been remiss in exercising the Lord's will; but that will stands as it is.

18) **Amen, I say to you, whatever things you bind on the earth shall be as having been bound in the heaven; and whatever things you shall loose on the earth shall be as having been loosed in the heaven.** With the double seal of divine verity and of divine authority (on which see 5:18) Jesus confirms

the power he has here ordered the church to exercise.
To avoid repetition read the exegesis of 16:19, where
the identical power is conferred on Peter.  We add the
following.  The effort to make the second person plural
"you shall bind," "you shall loose" refer, not to the congregation, but only to the Twelve, i. e., the apostles,
overlooks the fact that Jesus here addresses them, not
in an official capacity, but as members of his church.
If this is denied, then what about the person first
addressed: "If *thy* brother sins against *thee*," etc.?
Does this apply only to the relation of the apostles
among themselves: "If thy brother-apostle sins against
thee, an apostle"?  No; this power (the keys) belongs
to the church which, indeed, uses the called ministers
to administer discipline, but the power put forth is that
of Christ which has been entrusted to no special order
of men but to the entire church.

The fact that the binding and the loosing denote
judicial functions and not legislative authority (see
16:19) is plain in the present connection.  "If thy
brother *sins* against thee," shuts out the views that
apostles are to legislate and to make the laws which
determine what is and what is not sin.  This God has
long ago done through Moses, and the verb "to sin" here
used operates with that well-known law.  But Jesus appoints the members of the church and the congregation
to guard that law, to bring sinning members to repentance, or to rid themselves of them as members.

Here again the neuter is used; but now we have ὅσα,
the plural.  The church judges, not the hearts, but the
words and the deeds, see 16:19.  The two perfect participles (here plurals) seem to be the predicates of the
two ἔσται although the grammars regard them as periphrastic future perfect tenses.  The question is one of
grammar.  So fully has Jesus bestowed the power of
the keys upon his church that, when first one brother
spoke to the offender and then afterward two or three

spoke to him, they could bind the impenitent by reporting to the church for final action, or could loose, ab-
solve, and forgive the penitent, thereby closing the
matter forever.

19) The greater the power that Jesus bestows
upon the church, the more necessary is it that we
not only follow his instructions but also look in prayer
to him for guidance and rely on his presence in our
midst. **Again I say to you** (with my divine authority) **that if two of you agree on the earth concerning
any matter that they may ask, it shall be done to
them from my Father in heaven. For where two
or three are, having been gathered together in my
name, there am I in their midst.** "Again" is like
"furthermore." It adds something that is necessary
as a separate point. "I say to you" is only a little less
strong than the fuller formula used in v. 18; Jesus
speaks with his full authority as the head of the church.
He cites the smallest number, namely "two" that may
unite on a matter, and we rightly think of the two
witnesses mentioned in v. 16 and their special duty as
one of the matters on which they will ask help from their
Lord. "On earth" recalls the same phrase used in v. 18.
It reminds us of our earthly state in which we have so
many needs and also have to help each other to shake
off the bonds of sin. The verb συμφωνεῖν means "to agree
by talking a thing over," the two persons thus weighing
it well before they formulate their prayer. They will
inquire as to what Christ's will is in the matter and will
thus "ask" of him what he will be sure to give and will
not ask amiss. The verb αἰτεῖν is used also with reference
to petitions directed to men but quite frequently with
reference to some gift that is desired of the Lord. The
relative οὗ is attracted from the accusative to the genitive of the antecedent.

Jesus solemnly promises, "It shall be to them," etc.
This is a specific promise given to joint and congrega-

tional prayer.   Yet it is not given in the sense that our
mere agreement assures the granting of the request,
for even this prayer will end, "Let the will of the Lord
be done!" and will leave the answer to the wisdom of
God and to his own good time.   Thus this promise does
not go beyond Christ's other promises but only as far
as they go, because they already go to the limit.   "Combined prayer is precious," writes Luther, "and the most
effective, for which reason we also come together, and
from which also the church is called the house of
prayer.   Oh, if God would that any gathering might
pray in this manner, so that a common cry of the heart
on the part of all the people might rise to God, what
immeasurable virtue and help would follow such
prayer!   What more terrible thing could happen to all
the spirits of evil?   What greater work could occur on
the earth? by which so many godly people would be
preserved, so many sinners converted.   For truly the
church on earth has no greater power or work than
such united prayer against everything that may strike
against her.   This the evil spirit well knows, wherefore also he does all that he can to prevent this prayer.
It surely does not depend on places and buildings in
which we come together, even though it be under a
thatched roof, but on this invincible prayer, that we
may practice this properly and make it come before
God."

20)   With γάρ Jesus states the reason for the effectiveness of united prayer.   It is his own unseen presence wherever even only two or three are gathered in
his name.   This again reminds us of the two or the
three witnesses and their special task, but, of course,
extends beyond them to believers who are concerned
with any matter (v. 19).   Εἰς is to be taken in the static
sense, R. 593, as it is used extensively for ἐν in the
Koine.   "In my name" = in connection with my revelation, ὄνομα, as in v. 5 and in all these phrases.   The

phrase, of course, implies true faith in this revelation
and thus in him who is revealed.

"There am I in their midst" must be understood
with reference to the special and gracious presence of
Christ and must not be confused with his universal
presence with all creatures alike. This is the presence
of the whole Christ in his two inseparably united natures by both of which he is the Christ; and the distinctive feature of this presence is his grace which is
effective to guide, direct, keep, and bless those to whom
it is vouchsafed. Although it is invisible, it is no less
real than it was when he stood visibly in the midst of
his disciples after his resurrection. Since he is thus in
the assembly of the church or present when two or
three are convicting a brother of sin, it is he himself
who acts with his church and its members when they
carry out his Word by invoking also his presence and
his help.

In all that Jesus here tells his disciples he implies
that soon his visible presence will be removed from
them. The tone is that found in John, chapters 14-16,
and is just as great, mighty, and blessed, with assurance and joy for all his true followers.

21) **Then Peter, having come forward, said to
him: Lord, how often shall my brother sin against
me, and I remit it to him? Up to seven times?**
Matthew gives only the connection of time, "then," and
lets his readers judge as to the material connection, as
to why Peter came to Jesus with this question. The
participle προσελθών intimates that there was a brief
interval during which Jesus probably dismissed the little child that he had been holding while speaking (Mark
9:36). In Luke 17:4 the connection is no clearer than
it is in Matthew. The idea that Peter's question is
intended to raise an objection against the practicability
of the proceeding just outlined by Jesus, is evidently
not in accord with the facts. Neither is the supposi-

tion that Matthew has abbreviated and thus has lost
the connection, which is then sought in a version of the
Gospel to the Hebrews; but this version only repeats
what Matthew writes and does that in a decidedly
inferior manner.   It is best to give credit to Peter who
here again feels free to speak.   He seems to have
caught the Lord's meaning expressed in v. 15: the
brother against whom another has sinned and who is to
go and to rebuke the sinning brother will be able to do
this properly only when he at once, before he goes, forgives the wrong that has been done to him.   It seems as
though Peter sees that fact and thus raises the question about the number of times he should extend such
forgiveness.

The two interrogatives are deliberative, R. 934;
and ἀφήσω αὐτῷ is the significant verb used for forgiving,
here being construed only with the dative of the person,
the accusative of the sin being understood; "remit it to
him," i. e., send it away as far as he is concerned.   This
remission on the part of the wronged brother is an
entirely separate thing and is not to be confused with
the remission God may grant.   We must at once forgive every wrong, whether the wrongdoer repents and
makes acknowledgment to us or not.   That clears us.
We hold nothing against the man who has wronged us.
But he has his sin to settle with God.   It is to help him
settle it aright with God, so that God, too, will remit
and dismiss his sin, that Jesus orders the procedure
outlined in v. 15, etc.

We must also give credit to Peter for extending
such personal remissions of personal wrongs "up to
seven times."   For the old Jewish teaching was that
three times was enough: *Homini in alterum peccanti
semel remittunt, secundo remittunt, tertio remittunt,
quarto non remittunt*, R. Weiss, from *Babyl. Joma*, f.
86, 2, basing this on Amos 1:3; 2:6; and Job 33:29, 30.

Peter more than doubles this limit and thus reveals that he has progressed under his Master's teaching.

22) **Jesus says to him, Not, I say to thee, up to seven times, but up to seventy times seven.** Not for one moment does Jesus say that such a case as seven repetitions of wrongdoing could scarcely occur, and that thus seven repeated remissions would suffice; instead he takes Peter's breath away by calling for no less than 70 x 7 remissions, a number that is so great that keeping such a count would be almost impossible. His meaning evidently is that we are to forgive all wrongs done to us, no matter how many they are.

Jesus arrives at this figure through Peter's "seven times," which he multiplies by another seven raised to the tenth degree (70). There is no symbolism in these figures. Thus also an allusion to Gen. 4:24 is excluded. In this passage the figure is stated as "seventy and sevenfold"; moreover, the reference is to the very opposite of forgiveness, namely to vengeance. In addition, if, nevertheless, an allusion to Gen. 4:24 is assumed, the point would have to be that Jesus makes the times of forgiveness (70 x 7) exceed by far the times of the vengeance (77). The 70 x 7 of Jesus should not be reduced to 77 because of Gen. 4:24. The LXX translates the Hebrew *shib'im w⁰shib'ah* with the same words that Matthew has: ἑβδομηκοντάκις ἑπτά and leaves out the "and" of the Hebrew. The LXX evidently mistranslated and regarded the Hebrew "seventy *and* sevenfold" as equivalent to "seventy times seven." Yet such authorities as J. H. Moulton (*Prol.*, 98; *Einl.*, 158), B.-P., 330, B.-D., 248, 2, R. V. margin, Abbott-Smith, and apparently also R. 673, etc., ask us to regard the mistranslation of the LXX as equivalent to "77 times," like the Hebrew Gen. 4:24, and then state that Matthew's words likewise mean only "77 times."

23) Because it seemed almost unbelievable to Peter that Jesus should demand 490 remissions, Jesus

makes the whole matter clear by means of one of his
finest parables.   Since he is speaking only to disciples,
only the first purpose stated in 13:11, etc., is here
attained: it is given them to know; and since  they
have, more is given to them.   Since it is the parable
that clears up the subject better than any direct explanation could, we must say that parables, too, have the
force of Scripture proof.   **On this account the kingdom of the heavens has become like a certain king
who resolved to settle up with his retainers.**   It is
not Matthew who has added the phrase "on this account" but Jesus: because Peter is to forgive so often,
this is the reason that the kingdom has been made to
be what it is.   Every time Peter has any doubts regarding the number of times he is to forgive, let him
think of this parable and the king it pictures, and all
his doubts and his hesitation will disappear.

On "the kingdom of the heavens" see 3:2; it is the
rule of God's grace on earth through Christ.   Wherever God exercises his grace through Christ, there this
heavenly kingdom is found in all its blessed power.   In
13:24, R. 835 regards ὡμοιώθη as the effective aorist, but
in this passage R. 837 regards this same aorist as
gnomic and thus timeless.   We prefer the former view;
see the remarks on 13:24.   In 13:31, 33, 44, 47 the
present ὁμοία ἐστίν is used, but the effective aorist "became," or as the English prefers, "has become," also
brings the comparison up to the present.   The addition
ἄνθρωπος to βασιλεύς uses this word pleonastically in a
colorless way like τίς, B.-P. 107, as in 11:19; 14:45, and
elsewhere.   Hence we translate "a certain king."   We
see no reason for stressing ἄνθρωπος, either by regarding
it as being in contrast to Θεός, or as denoting "a king
of flesh and blood," an expression that is found in certain Jewish parables.   The fact that the parable presents a human king is as self-evident here as in 22:2,

for unless such a king is referred to we should have no
parable.

The real point is that this king came to the decision
(ἠθέλησε, aorist) "to settle up" (συνᾶραι λόγον, also aorist
and effective) with his retainers. The verb συναίρω
means "to take up together," and λόγον is often added
as a part of the concept, M.-M. 601. We do not
refer δοῦλοι to ordinary slaves belonging to this
king's household. The idea that slaves were often
entrusted with large sums of money with which to do
business for their master (25:14, 15; Luke 19:13)
seems too weak here where the sum involved is so immense. These *douloi* were the king's satraps who had
been appointed by him to rule great parts of his domain
and to turn into his treasuries the grand revenues of
their provinces. Under an Oriental king, great lords
though they were in their own right, they would be
subject to his absolute authority and would thus be
nothing but the king's δοῦλοι.

24) **Now, he having begun to settle up, there
was brought to him one, a debtor of ten thousand
talents.** The very first man who appears owes this
great sum. The fact that he was summoned first
because he owed so much is nowhere indicated. Others
may have owed similar sums. This reckoning of the
king does not picture the final judgment but (like Luke
16:2) a reckoning that is made during this life. It is
like to that of the sinner who is brought face to face
with all his sins by the awakening of his conscience.
In the providence of God such hours of judgment come
to us and often shake us to our inmost souls. Just as
little as "a hundred denarii" in v. 28 is a definite figure
to indicate an indefinite sum, "a little sum," so little is
"ten thousand talents" a definite figure to indicate "a
great sum" or "many talents."

A talent was a weight of silver or of gold coin, and
these weights varied in different nations and also at

different eras. The Attic talent is $1,200; the great Roman, $500, and the small, $375; while the Hebrew, Assyrian, and Babylonian ran from $1,550 to $2,000. Many are inclined to think of the Attic talent in this instance, thus $12,000,000; others, of the Hebrew, $15,500,000 to $20,000,000. An Attic talent amounts to 6,000 denarii, and 10,000 of these talents to 60 million denarii, that is 600,000 times as much as was due this debtor by his fellow-*doulos*. And one denarius was a laborer's daily wages (20:2).

For the purpose of comparison note that Archelaus drew an annual revenue of 600 talents from Judea and Samaria, and Herod Antipas one of 200 from Galilee and Perea. Trench refers to the great sums mentioned in the Old Testament. The figure 10,000 used in the parable seems symbolical since the law contains Ten Commandments. Boos makes the practical reckoning and lets the righteous man sin seven times a day, 2,555 times a year, and thus in a number of years — how many times! This estimate is far too low.

Sins are often considered debts, as in 6:12. This great debtor "was brought" to the king in the sense of being summoned and conducted into the royal presence, there to render an account of the revenues due the king. Of his own accord the sinner never comes to face his reckoning with God. In false security he loves to go on piling up his debts. But it is a blessed thing for him to be brought to account before it is too late.

25) **But he not having in order to pay, his lord ordered him to be sold and wife and the children and all whatever he had, and payment to be made.** The man is unable to make payment for the enormous sum he owes. How he incurred so vast a debt is immaterial for the purpose of the parable, but the fact that he owed it and could not pay it is essential. While Jewish debtors were also often sold into bondage (Lev. 25:39, 47; Exod. 22:3; II Kings 4:1; Neh. 5:5; Isa.

50:1; Amos 2:6; 8:6), the imagery of our parable seems to be drawn from the courts of the great eastern kings with their vast wealth and their grand dependencies; for this king also uses βασανισταί (v. 34), "torturers." The fact that the members of the debtor's family were also to be sold into bondage need not surprise us, for they were considered the man's property, and this was the case even according to Roman law. Some texts have ἔχει instead of εἶχε, the present referring to what the debtor "has" at the time. In the statement, "and payment to be made," the same verb is used that was employed with reference to the great debt, but this does not imply that the proceeds of the sale of the debtor and his belongings will equal the amount of the debt but merely that the proceeds will be paid into the king's treasury. In both infinitives ἀπό adds the idea of paying what is due.

The total inability to pay the vast debt pictures man's spiritual bankruptcy before God. His sins are the debt, and they are so great in number that he has literally nothing to pay. While here the number of the sins is stressed, every single sin is beyond human payment. This king is not represented as a tyrant; he acts according to strict justice. He has been lenient by not demanding a reckoning much sooner, and in a moment we see his royal grace. So his act pictures the divine justice regarding the sinner and his sins. The guilty sinner is cast out from the presence of God and through his own guilt lands in the bondage of the devil. Divine justice is not popular in the world and in certain types of preaching; but aside from the Scriptures the moral sense of men and their frequent experience bring home to them the fact that God is just and visits the iniquities of the sinner upon his head. We also see daily that one sinner draws others into his guilt and his punishment. None of us lives to himself or dies to himself.

26) **The retainer, therefore, having fallen down, worships him, saying, Lord, extend longsuffering to me, and I will pay thee all!** When the verdict goes against him (οὖν), the man breaks down completely. He does not deny his debt but admits it. He is overcome and crushed when he realizes its enormity. He throws himself at the feet of the king and pleads for a postponement of the sentence. These are good effects produced in him, not by himself, but by the king and the king's just reckoning. Luther writes well: "Before the king drew him to account, he had no conscience, does not feel the debt, and would have gone right along, made more debt, and cared nothing about it. But now that the king reckons with him, he begins to feel the debt. So it is with us. The greater part does not concern itself about sin, goes on securely, fears not the wrath of God. Such people cannot come to the forgiveness of sin, for they do not come to realize that they have sins. They say, indeed, with the mouth that they have sin; but if they were serious about it they would speak far otherwise. This servant, too, says, before the king reckons with him, so much I owe to my lord, namely ten thousand talents; but he goes ahead and laughs. But now that the reckoning is held, and his lord orders him, his wife, his children, and everything to be sold, now he feels it. So, too, we feel in earnest when our sins are revealed in the heart, when the record of our debts is held before us, then the laughter stops. Then we exclaim: I am the most miserable man, there is none as unfortunate as I on the earth! Such knowledge makes a real humble man, works contrition, so that one can come to the forgiveness of sins."

It is correct psychology when Jesus lets this debtor beg for time and promise to pay this vast debt. This is the first thought that comes to the sinner. He does not at once realize the enormity of his guilt and, as

Luther says, cannot think that God will actually forgive
it all but imagines he must pay it off and in his fright
promises to do it. The law does not at once produce
its full effect. The verb μακροθυμεῖν means "to be longsuffering," i. e., a long holding out of the mind before it
gives room to action or passion, Trench, *Synonyms*, II,
12; who finely distinguishes it from ὑπομένειν. The latter is never attributed to God, the former refers to
persons, the latter to things (bravely enduring them),
hence this latter is inapplicable to God.

27) **But, moved to compassion, the lord of that
retainer released him and remitted the loan to him.**
God is just and must confront us with our sins; but
he is equally compassionate and full of grace and ready
to remit our sins. Now the moment the sinner realizes
his sin, confesses it, and turns to God, God pardons the
guilt. On σπλαγχνίζομαι see 9:36 (also 14:14; 15:32):
the pained feeling at sight of the sinner's plight, coupled with the strong desire to help him. Compassion is
the inner motive of God, from which pardon flows. And
this pardon is at once complete. The king "released"
this debtor and cancelled the order to his officers to sell
the debtor and all he had. And in the same instant "he
remitted the loan to him." It is called τὸ δάνειον, "the
loan," because it was tribute that was long due to the
king. But the verb ἀφῆκεν is most significant: "he remitted" the debt, literally, "dismissed and sent it
away." This is the verb we usually translate "to forgive," and the Greek word means: "As far as the east
is from the west, so far hath he removed our transgressions from us" (Ps. 103:12): "and thou wilt cast all
their sins into the depths of the sea" (Micah 7:19).
The noun is ἄφεσις, "the sending away."

Here is vast comfort: God does not wait until the
sinner perfects his contrition. He does not keep him
on the anxious bench (Luke 15:20). He remits the sin
the instant it is possible for him to remit it. And the

entire debt is remitted, not only a part, even though it be the greater part, while some part is still to be paid by the debtor himself. The debtor pays nothing; in full truth *can* pay nothing. The only change that takes place in the man is contrition, and this is wrought in him by God through the law. The king's word of release and remission is forensic; God on his throne declares the sinner free from guilt, as free as though he had never incurred that guilt. This is Biblical justification, the central doctrine of the Christian faith: God declares the sinner free from guilt and righteous in his sight.

Luther writes: "All jurists, the wise and learned, say: righteousness must be in the man's heart and soul. But this Gospel teaches us that the Christian righteousness is not in all respects in the man's heart and soul, but we are to learn that we are righteous and redeemed from sins through the forgiveness of sins. Therefore is this a high preaching and heavenly wisdom that we believe, our righteousness, salvation, and comfort is outside of us, namely that before God we are righteous, acceptable, holy, and wise, and yet in us there is nothing but sin, unrighteousness, and folly . . . I myself must confess, that it is sour and hard for me to believe this article. For by nature I am thus minded as also I was accustomed in the papacy, that I would gladly do good works to pay for my sins."

The debtor is pardoned. His debt is as though it had never existed. This state has come about through pure compassion and grace. He has not yet fully realized it all, but he is to enter into this realization, his contrition is to deepen when he thinks of what he has escaped, and his faith and joy will increase when he thinks what has been granted to him.

Rationalists use this parable to support their rejection of the atonement of Christ. They play one part of Scripture *against* the other instead of combining one part *with* the other. But a parable presents only one side of the matter and no one expects it to present all sides of a subject, let alone one that is as great as the heart of the Bible.

28) **Now that retainer, having gone out, found one of his fellow-retainers who was owing him a hundred denarii and, having laid hold on him, he choked him, saying, Pay, if thou owest anything!** It is the evident intention of Jesus *to reverse* the position of this retainer; over against this fellow-retainer he is now where the king was a moment ago in regard to him. This explains the relative positions of these two δοῦλοι, the one stood high in the realm and could owe the king 10,000 talents; the other occupied some humble position at the court, where he somehow came to owe this lofty man the trifling sum of 100 denarii, each of which amounted to 17 cents or the day's wages of a laborer.

But it is Jesus' intention *to reverse* still more, in fact, to present this retainer's action as morally outrageous. He comes from the presence of the king who remitted his enormous debt of 10,000 talents. That astounding experience which snatched him and his family from their doom produces no glow of gratitude and generosity in his soul; it leaves him cold. His own debt to the king was so enormous that the king had to summon him and to make a grand reckoning to determine the amount; this fellow-retainer's debt is so trifling that the other who deals in grand sums would have forgotten it had he not accidentally happened upon and "found" the humble debtor.

The reversal goes farther. The violence used is in glaring contrast to the refined royal dignity and brings out the meanness of this fellow's soul. Although holding a grand position in the realm, he descends to grabbing, choking, and the rudest, hardest demand. The aorist ἀπόδος, "pay up!" is violent. The reading εἴ τι

must stand over against ὅ τι ("what thou owest").    "If
thou owest" is not a bit of Greek politeness that is used
even in a case of harshness, although ironically; nor
does it indicate uncertainty as though the retainer were
not quite sure about his claim and yet used violence,
for the clause, "who was owing him," settles that.    The
condition of reality, "if thou dost owe," implies, "as
thou dost and knowest only too well."    The point is
that this retainer intends to make no reckoning such as
the king made in his case.    "If thou dost owe" is
shouted in a challenging tone and dares the poor fellow
to deny that he owes this sum.    "What thou owest"
would leave open a chance for reckoning; the other
form completely cuts it off.

The application lies on the surface.    Compared
with our sins against God, our sins against each other
are mere trifles; the one sum is absolutely unpayable,
the other is easily payable.    The action is made extreme in the parable, not because it is always extreme
in reality, but this extreme is intended to include all
lesser cases just as in 5:21, etc., murder includes all
lesser sins against the Fifth Commandment; and in
5:27, etc., adultery does likewise.    Here we have the
opposite of 6:12, that we be forgiven as we forgive.
The debt of 100 denarii is real, as real as that of the
10,000 talents; our sins against each other are real.
But here the moral enormity is brought out that one of
us should take remission of a guilt so vast and yet
refuse remission of a guilt so small.    If grace is denied
for the latter, then by as much as 10,000 talents exceed
the miserable 100 denarii grace must be denied also
for the former.    The moral sense still left in sinful
men's hearts is bound to approve such action.

29)    **Having, therefore, fallen down, his fellow-
retainer entreats him, saying, Extend longsuffering
to me, and I will pay thee!**    The scene of v. 26 is
repeated.    How could it help but remind this harsh

creditor of his own prostration and prayer a little while ago? The few slight differences are significant. The worship is omitted, and the address "lord"; both befit the king but not a mere retainer. Yet παρεκάλει is substituted; one of us may "entreat" or beseech another. And "all" is left out, the sum is too small. The entreaty which is so nearly the same must surely reach the other's heart.

30) **But he was not willing; on the contrary, having gone away, he threw him into prison until he should pay what was owing.** While the king "was filled with compassion" and thus remitted the debt, this man is filled with unwillingness. The contrast is glaring. It lies in the will, the center of the personality. "The negative imperfect commonly denotes resistance to pressure or disappointment" (R. 885), and this is true of ἤθελεν. All moral obliquity is blind; by not willing what it should will it wills its own undoing. Here the aorist ἔβαλε at once states what the outcome of the unwillingness was. He went away and threw him into prison is usually taken to mean that he haled the poor fellow to prison. Here we have a case of imprisonment for debt which persisted until Christian influence produced a more humane law regarding debtors. We take it that imprisonment was all that could be inflicted in this case because of the small amount of the debt; if it had been large enough, this man would have sold the poor debtor into slavery. This also brings out the difference between our sins against God and our sins against each other. Comparing the full measure of both (10,000 talents over against 100 denarii, the multiples of 10 denoting completeness), the penalties correspond (selling into bondage, imprisonment).

"Until he should pay," etc. (ἀποδῷ, subjunctive) intimates nothing regarding the eventual outcome as to whether payment would or would not be made. The point is only this: the creditor refused to remit, he held the debt against the other. The fact that this is no figment thousands of cases in the church have shown.

**31) Accordingly, his fellow-retainers, having seen what occurred, were grieved exceedingly; and having gone, explained to their lord all that occurred.** These men are attached to the king of the parable in a special way, and none of them is called a mere citizen; this implies that Jesus is speaking of the members of his church. The article in οἱ σύνδουλοι points to the fact that the one who would not forgive is an exception among Christians; the others see the great wrong of such action. The effect upon them is that "they were grieved exceedingly." A detail to the effect that they admonished the offender is omitted in order not to extend the parable. To them great grief is attributed, to the king anger. Trench is right when he attributes the difference to the consciousness of our own sins when we see another sinning, while in God holiness and the abhorrence of sin is perfect. Thus God's reaction is his holy and righteous wrath, but ours great grief.

It is true that God is omniscient and knows before any man explains to him; and yet he waits for our prayers, waits for us to explain to him our needs and our helplessness. Unable to do anything themselves, these retainers go and lay "all that occurred" before him (διασαφεῖν as in 13:36). As far as the two readings ἑαυτῶν and αὐτῶν are concerned, the difference in meaning should not be stressed since the simple possessive often equals the reflexive. In the church we often reach the end of our resources and must turn "what has occurred" over to the Lord who still rules in his church and knows how to proceed with the wrongs occurring in its midst.

**32) Then, having called him to him, his lord says to him: Wicked retainer! all that debt I remitted to thee when thou didst entreat me. Was**

there no need for thee also to show mercy to thy
fellow-retainer even as I on my part showed thee
mercy? And, angered, his lord delivered him over
to the torturers until he should pay all that is owing.
Not only did this man forfeit his own remission, his
penalty is made vastly worse. In the parable it happens
at once, in actuality it happens as certainly as though
it happened at once. No man is able to resist the
divine summons. The verdict here pronounced is already in effect in the case of every unforgiving church
member who still flatters himself that he still has God's
forgiveness. The adjective "wicked" contains the verdict (Luke 19:22; Matt. 7:23; 25:41). The man's
whole person and his true nature are described by this
one word. The evidence for the verdict is at once
added. First, what the king had done for him, using
the historical aorists. "All that debt" recalls its excessive greatness, and "when thou didst entreat me"
the readiness and the wondrous grace which asked no
more.

33) The impersonal δεῖ expresses all manner of
necessity, and here the imperfect, ἔδει, the moral necessity resting continually upon this man over against all
companions of his. He should have extended an act of
mercy as an act of mercy had been extended to him;
hence the two aorists ἐλεῆσαι and ἠλέησα. And ἐγώ, abutted
to σε, is decidedly emphatic and places the two into
contrast. The interrogative form brings out the absolute justice of the king's verdict. The affirmative
answer implied by the interrogative particle οὐκ appeals
to the moral sense of even this wicked man. He does
not dare to answer "no" or to equivocate in any way.

The translation into reality is wholly obvious. It
would be a moral monstrosity for one of us to receive
God's remission of all our sins and yet refuse remission
of the little wrongs done against us. If any one of us
is still blind to that fact, his blindness will turn to ter-

rified sight when he faces God in his heavenly court.
God's unspeakable mercy and compassion always come
first, and they melt our hearts to mercy and compassion
toward others.   Where this result is not effected the
divine mercy and remission are forfeited, and that with
the most terrible results.

34)   The anger or wrath of God is the reaction of
his holiness, righteousness, and justice against all sin
and above all against obdurate and unyielding sin.
The anthropopathic terms used in the Scripture in no
way lower God by making his holy wrath like that of
men which is at best tainted by passion.   This supposition reveals that God's own revelation of himself has
not been accepted.   The action prompted by the king's
wrath is absolutely just.   The man has brought his fate
down upon himself.   In the three penalties: jailing for
debt, selling into bondage for debt, delivering to the
torturers for what is worse than such debts, Jesus evidently pictures three types of penalty: one inflicted by
one man upon another (vengeance), two inflicted by
God (these differing as the few and the many stripes
mentioned in Luke 12:48).

In v. 25 the verdict is not carried out because pardon takes its place; in v. 34 the parable ends, and thus
nothing is said about the execution of the verdict.   We
must not expect too much of a parable; it cannot illustrate every detail of the reality, it illustrates only certain points.   The parable thus should not be used to
alter the realities but must be interpreted according
to them.   That is also true in this case.   Our many
sins deserve hell and, when these include the sins committed against the divine grace, they deserve the worst
penalties of hell.   This is what the parable presents.
The verdict rendered in v. 25 did not cut off the possibility of grace, for the sinner actually received grace
although he presently forfeited it.   The silence after
v. 34 is, to say the least, ominous.   Did the sinner re-

turn to contrition, or did he remain obdurate? The
silence of Jesus intensifies the warning which is evidently intended for us. But that warning implies that
the possibility of heeding it is not cut off. In other
words, one who is unforgiving today may, if he heeds
this warning, turn again and find pardon.

But if the heart remains hard, the βασανισταί will go
into action. The opinion that the term means jailors
is unwarranted; it means "torturers." They may at
the same time be jailors, but they are more than that.
Among the tortures anciently applied also to imprisoned debtors were: dragging about heavy chains, near-
starving, excessive labor, and *carnificia* or bodily tortures proper, Trench. The gravity of the imagery is
that the wrath of the king orders these penalties. It
is spiritualizing to regard these "torturers" as the
pangs of conscience and self-accusation. Hell will be
full of these, to be sure. But it will also be full of
hideous devils whose one occupation it will be to plague
and to torture the damned.

Catholic exegesis finds a proof for purgatory in the
last clause: "until he should pay all that is owing."
The conjunction ἕως οὗ is regarded as implying that the
point of this "until" can and will be reached. As far
as the force of the conjunction is concerned, this is
possible. Sometimes "until" contemplates what follows this terminus although it sometimes does not.
Chrysostom saw that here the context shuts out a limit:
"That is, perpetually; for neither will he pay ever."
The "until" clause thus really becomes the strongest
proof against the idea of purgatory and for the eternal
duration of punishment. Saying "until an impossible
thing takes place," simply says "never." "When the
Phocians, abandoning their city, swore that they
would not return until the mass of iron which they
plunged into the sea once more appeared upon the surface, this was the most emphatic way they could devise

of declaring that they would *never* return." Trench.
The self-contradictory thing in regard to purgatory is
the view that God remits the severer penalties, the
*poenas aeternas,* while the lighter ones which the
church must exact, the *poenas temporales,* it does not
remit if they remain unpaid, but transfers to purgatory — making God more merciful than the church
(she being the unforgiving creditor!)

Once the sinner dies he passes into the power of the
tormentors. The parable, however, stops short of this
as we have pointed out. And this means that the
"until" clause is not to be dated as beginning with
death but as beginning in the hour of the divine verdict during the sinner's life. In other words, if this
merciless man allows the warning to crush him in true
repentance before death shuts out that possibility, he
shall, indeed, be able to pay all that he owes — through
the merits and atonement of Christ. As long as life
lasts, all sins (save that against the Holy Spirit) are
pardonable. During life also all verdicts, whether it
be that of pardon or of condemnation (Jonah 3:4;
4:11), are conditional; the pardon may be lost by impenitence, the condemnation escaped by repentance.

35) The parable itself is clear, so Jesus makes
only this summary application: **Thus also will my
heavenly Father do to you if you do not remit each
one to his brother from your hearts.** The parable
is intended as a mighty warning; Peter is never to
refuse a brother forgiveness. "Thus" means as the
king finally did. "My" Father seems more in place
here than "your" Father, for those who lose the remission cannot call him their Father. As the parable pictures a king acting with supreme authority, so the
supreme greatness of the Father is indicated by ἐπου-
ράνιος (used only here with reference to the Father),
which is added with a second article and thus makes
the adjective emphatic. The future tense ποιήσει is

volitive, "will do to you," not merely futuristic, "shall do." And ἐάν with the subjunctive expresses expectancy. The plural "if you do not remit" is individualized by the partitive apposition (R. 746) "each one"; and we now see that the Twelve were present. Here the remission is that granted the fellow-disciples; "to his brother," while in 6:15 it is extended to men generally. The former naturally broadens out so as to include the latter. Jesus does not fail to add that this remission must be genuine, "from your heart," and not a remission spoken by the lips alone. God sees the heart, he himself remits from the heart, and he can be satisfied with no pretense on our part.

"On the declaration itself we may observe that the Christian stands in a middle point, between a mercy received, and a mercy which he yet needs to receive. Sometimes the first is urged upon him as an argument for showing mercy: 'forgiving one another, as Christ forgave you' (Col. 3:13; Eph. 4:32); sometimes the last: 'Blessed are the merciful, for they shall obtain mercy' (Matt. 5:7); 'With the merciful thou wilt show thyself merciful' (Ps. 18:25); 'Forgive, and ye shall be forgiven' (Luke 6:37; James 5:9); and so the Son of Sirach (28:3, 4), 'One man beareth hatred against another, and doth he seek pardon from the Lord? He showeth no mercy to a man who is like himself, and doth he ask forgiveness of his own sins?' and thus, while he must ever look back on a mercy received as the source and motive of the mercy which he shows, he looks forward as well to the mercy which he yet needs, and which he is assured that the merciful, according to what Bengel beautifully calls the *benigna talio* of the kingdom of God, shall obtain as a new provocation to its abundant exercise." Trench.

# CHAPTER XIX

## XV

### Christ Beyond Jordan.    Chapter 19:1-20:16

1)    All that Matthew reports in the preceding section took place in Capernaum in less than one day.
Jesus made only a brief visit to this city and then left
it never to return.    Now his destination is Jerusalem,
but he proceeds slowly, spending some time on the way.
**And it came to pass when Jesus finished these say-
ings he departed from Galilee and went to the boundaries of Judea, beyond the Jordan.    And great
multitudes followed him, and he healed them there.**
The formula regarding the finishing of his sayings is
used repeatedly when transition is made to a new section (7:28; 11:1; 13:53; 26:1).    Jesus left Galilee,
and his destination is Judea.    The phrase introduced
with πέραν does not modify "Judea" but the verb ἦλθεν
and states that Jesus took this road "beyond the Jordan" in order to reach the boundaries of Judea instead
of following the road through Samaria.    At no time
did the borders of Judea extend eastward beyond the
Jordan; our versions read as though they did and
should be corrected.    Matthew writes for former Jews
who knew the geography of their land and also knew
that the Jews of Galilee preferred the road "beyond
the Jordan" when going to Judea and Jerusalem because it avoided Samaria with its hostile population,
which was especially hostile to Jews who were going to
the festivals at Jerusalem.

Perea was new territory for Jesus, and so he travelled slowly.    Matthew does not intend to record the

details, so he summarizes: crowds followed Jesus, **and he healed many of their sick** ἐκεῖ, there "beyond the Jordan." What Matthew does record has scarcely any reference to the inhabitants of Perea but centers chiefly in the instruction of the Twelve.

3) This is true with regard to the question of the Twelve (v. 10). **And there came to him the Pharisees, tempting him and saying, If it is lawful to release one's wife for every charge,** (let us know). The Pharisees found in Perea (we retain οἱ) were of the same temper and type as those residing in Galilee and in Jerusalem. They were entirely hostile to Jesus and bent on ruining him. So here their object is to tempt Jesus to make a pronouncement that will discredit him.

The question raised was one on which the schools of Shammai and of Hillel differed. Shammai interpreted Deut. 24:1 as follow: "The man is not to release his wife unless he have found something indecent in her." He reverses the two Hebrew nouns *'erwath dabar* and their grammatical relation and thus himself needs interpretation. The LXX translate: ὅτι εὕρηκεν ἐν αὐτῇ ἄσχημον πρᾶγμα. Hillel allowed as a charge the fact that in cooking the wife had burnt her husband's food; and Rabbi Akiba, referring especially to the expression, "that she find no favor in his eyes," permitted her release when the husband found a better-looking woman. Shammai was stricter, Hillel utterly lax.

The Pharisees lay Hillel's teaching before Jesus with the phrase "for every αἰτία," i. e., accusation that in some way charges guilt; κατά contains the idea of cause, R. 609. Since it is easier to be lax than to be strict, to go down hill than to go up, Hillel's views were followed by the Jews; and Josephus, *Antiquities*, 4, 8, 23 writes: "He that desires to be divorced from his wife *for any cause whatsoever* — and many such

causes happen among men — let him in writing give
assurance that he never will use her as his wife any
more, for by these means she may be at liberty to
marry another husband, although before this bill of
deliverance be given she is not to be permitted to
do so."

So the question before Jesus is, whether he agrees
with Hillel's exposition of Deut. 24:1. "Tempting
him" means that they tried to make him compromise
himself in some way.   If, for instance, he should agree
with Hillel and the common Jewish practice, the Pharisees could side with Shammai and charge Jesus with
moral laxity.   If he sided with Shammai who held
that only actual shameful conduct could be a cause for
divorce, Jesus could be reproached for his own friendly
treatment of sinners.   The choice of either view would
involve Jesus in the Jewish party disputes.   If, however, as the Pharisees most likely expected, Jesus
should reject both Hillel and Shammai and declare
himself against all divorce, they could charge him with
contradicting even the law stated in Deut. 24:1.   The
Pharisees felt quite certain that they had asked a
question which Jesus could not answer without great
harm to himself.   See 12:10 on $\epsilon i$ in a direct question,
and R. 916; B.-D. 440, 3.

4) **But he, answering, said:   Did you not read
that he who made them from the beginning made
them male and female and said, On this account
shall a man leave his father and his mother and be
glued to his wife, and the two shall be one flesh?
Wherefore they are no longer two but one flesh.
What, therefore, God yoked together, let man not
divide apart.**

The way in which the Pharisees propounded their
question by asking, "Is it lawful ($\check{\epsilon}\xi\epsilon\sigma\tau\iota\nu$)?" revealed
that they considered marriage and its dissolution a
matter of legislation.   They expected Jesus to enter

into a discussion of Deut. 24:1. Marriage is bound up
with the very creation of man. It is not a product
of some progress or development that came about later.
Therefore Jesus starts with a rebuke to these Pharisees who would raise a tricky discussion of Deuteronomy. He brushes aside their cunning temptation by
asking them whether they have never read Gen.1:27,
"He, who made them from the beginning made them
male and female," using the two adjectives as nouns.
The object of ὁ ποιήσας is understood, and the best texts
have this participle and not ὁ κτίσας. Although Eve
was created after Adam, the latter was at once created
male, and thus, by that creative act, marriage was
instituted by God. It was a one-sided reading of the
Scriptures when the Pharisees wrangled about Deut.
24:1, and overlooked Gen. 1:27.

5) On top of that God stated what marriage
really is. Because he created them male and female,
*"on this account* shall a man leave his father and his
mother (the articles have the force of possessives) and
shall be glued (passive, R. 819) to his wife." Nor is
the verb προσκολλᾶν too strong, for the marital union
is closer than one's connection with father or mother;
"and the two shall be one flesh." Jesus quotes Gen.
2:24, using the LXX which reproduces the Hebrew
exactly save that οἱ δύο, "the two," is added in order
to bring out the sense of the original, an addition that
is retained whenever the New Testament quotes this
passage. Although Adam spoke Gen. 2:24, he voiced
only God's thought regarding what marriage really
is; hence Jesus and the New Testament regard this
as a word of God. On the use of εἰς after the
copula instead of a predicate nominative see R. 458
and 595.

6) In order still more to impress the point regarding what God made of marriage at the time of creation
Jesus adds: "Wherefore they are no longer two (like

father and son, mother and son) but one flesh." The
physical sexual union consummated in marriage actually makes "one flesh" of the two. And it ought to be
self-evident that, therefore, this union is to be permanent. But since this is vital for the question brought up
by the Pharisees, Jesus states this deduction (οὖν) in so
many words: "What, therefore, God yoked together,
let man not divide apart." When persons are involved, a neuter such as ὅ makes the reference abstract and general and thus stronger: "anything"
joined together by God. The aorist is generally considered timeless, yet here it marks time antecedent
to the main verb and is thus in place for this reason.
In connections such as this the English prefers the perfect, "has yoked together." The implication is that
any man who divides what God has thus by his own
creation united into one, flies into the face of God
and his will — a serious opposition, indeed. How in-
dissoluble marriage is according to God's own creation
is thus made clear. Did these Pharisees never read
these words of Scripture and think on what they obviously declare?

7) Without attempting to contradict Jesus these
men cling to their view of Deut. 24:1 and the dissolution of marriage which it seems to permit. **They
say to him, Why, then, did Moses command to give
her a divorce certificate and to release her?** The
whole question rests on a false supposition. They
present it as though Moses "did command" this in
an absolute way, and as though dissolution of marriage for sufficient cause was originally contemplated
in the will of God concerning marriage. These Pharisees could and should have seen their shallow error.
It was an easy matter to see why Moses gave the command mentioned. Even its substance dealt only with
the legal procedure followed in the release of a wife:
a divorce certificate had to be given. It is immaterial

whether βιβλίον is added to ἀποστάσιον or is omitted as
in 5:31.

8) Jesus corrects this false supposition. **He
says to them, Moses, for your hardness of heart, permitted you to release your wives; but from the beginning it has not been thus.** We regard ὅτι as recitative and not as matching the τί of the question:
"why . . . because," for Jesus does not state the
cause alone, which would be only, "Because of the
hardness of your hearts." This brief reply would not
be enough. What Jesus says is that the command
of Moses was only a permission and nothing more.
Something had intervened since God, by creating man
as he did, created marriage, namely sin, which
wrought havoc also in the marriage relation. It produced the hardness of the heart which at times made
marriage a bond that people wanted to dissolve; πρός
states the cause, R. 626. The regulation of Moses was
nothing more than a concession to this evil condition
and never went beyond this. It thus consisted of
nothing but a legal form for dissolving marriage. It
thus also bore testimony only to the hardness of so
many hearts, and no man in his senses could conclude
that by this Mosaic regulation God had altered his
original intention concerning the permanency of marriage. Any man who wanted to know God's will concerning marriage would not, therefore, examine only
Deut. 24:1; he would go back to Gen. 1:27 and 2:24.
as Jesus had just done. He would have to see how it
"has been in the beginning."

Note also "your" hardness of heart, and again, permitted "to you," both pronouns referring only to the
Jews and the Pharisees. Godly Jews themselves made
no use of the Mosaic permission but kept their marriages inviolate as God had intended. These pronouns
read as though Jesus disavows the permission of Moses
as far as his disciples are concerned. As true fol-

lowers of Jesus no hardness of heart will develop in them that requires such a humiliating concession.

9) **And I say to you, that he who releases his wife, excepts for fornication, and marries another, is made adulterous.** The main variant readings, as also the addition of a second sentence are textual insertions from 5:32; and thus nothing is gained by repeating them. From Mark 10:10, 11 one might conclude that Jesus spoke this word only to the disciples after they and Jesus had gone into the house; but this is not necessary. We may assume that Jesus concluded his answer to the Pharisees with this final statement and then repeated it in the house during the discussion with the disciples, of whom Matthew also speaks in v. 10.

"And I say to you," here without the emphatic ἐγώ, does not intend to contradict what Moses wrote in Deut. 24:1; Jesus has already explained how this Mosaic regulation had been arranged because of the hardness of heart of the Jews. With "I say to you" Jesus contradicts the Pharisaic perversion of Deut. 24:1, and goes back to Gen. 1:27 and 2:24 by which he has made the correction. The statement itself differs only slightly from 5:32. There Jesus brings out the thought that the man who rids himself of his wife (save for fornication) commits a grave sin against her and thus also against any man who may later on marry her. In 5:32 it is enough to say, "Every man releasing his wife," for already that, without his marrying another, constitutes the terrible wrong against her. In Mark 10:11 this wronging of the wife is retained in the phrase ἐπ' αὐτήν, "in regard to her." Matthew's simple μοιχᾶται without this phrase in no way says that the wife is not wronged, for it is self-evident that she is; the unmodified verb stresses the wrong act committed by the man.

In 5:32, ὁ ἀπολύων characterizes the man by means of the substantivized present participle: he is one who, by the very act of releasing his wife by a writ, inflicts the grave wrong on her. But now Jesus uses a relative clause (with the ἄν of expectancy) and the aorist of the completed act. Moreover, two verbs are used: "he that releases his wife and marries another." We cannot agree that Jesus says nothing here about a man who releases his wife and then does not marry another. The real sin is beyond question the disruption of the marriage, which is caused by sending away the wife. The man's marrying another is only the aggravating circumstance. It is here added on this account and because the Jews rid themselves of their wives for the very purpose of marrying another. As in 5:32, μοιχᾶται is passive but with a decided difference. In 5:32 we have two passives μοιχευθῆναι and μοιχᾶται, and the agent with these passives is the wicked husband who does all the damage to the innocent victims by sending away his wife and disrupting her marriage. Hence the translation of these passives offered in 5:32. Here the passive μοιχᾶται stands alone, and not only its agent but its very subject is the wicked husband, and this passive deals only with this wicked husband's action as affecting himself. This makes the transaction easier: "He is made adulterous" by his own act. We could even admit that this is a middle (which is impossible in 5:32): "he becomes adulterous" or "makes himself so." This would not alter the sense, the effect of this man's act upon others being left out of consideration.

"Except for fornication" is explained in 5:32. The wording is different, but the sense is quite the same. The claim that nothing can be determined from these words regarding the man who releases his fornicatious wife and then marries another, is unwarranted. The

implication is too plain that if he marries again he is
not rendered adulterous. Jesus spoke to Jews whose
law gave the right of divorce only to the husband and
not to the wife. When Mark in 10:11, 12, writes for
former Gentiles he places husband and wife on the
same level; for the sense of Jesus is that neither is to
get rid of the other. Since fornication, by itself disrupting the marriage, forms the exception, this, like
any exception, may or may not be added when the
principle is stated; thus in 5:32 and in 19:9 it is added,
while in Mark 10:11, 12 it is not.

In all his utterances Jesus treats only the immorality involved in the disruption of marriage, whether
this immorality emanates from the husband or from
the wife, and not the legal actions of a court of law.
Even when he refers to Deut. 24:1 and what was considered legal among the Jews (among whom, however,
no court action took place in dissolving a husband's
marriage) Jesus treats only the moral side, namely the
hardness of the heart and the consequent defection
from God's original intention. It leads only to confusion when we speak of "divorce," and think of a
court action and apply the utterances of Jesus to that.
The sin of destroying a marriage is in the heart and
the action of the husband or of the wife (possibly in
both); this is what destroys the marriage. Going to
the court for a legal edict is only a subsequent result
and not the main point. A disrupted marriage is a
disrupted marriage and thus a vicious sin against the
will, Word, and command of God, whether some court
action is added, as in our day, or is not needed, as in
Jesus' day.

In the case of a disruption by fornication only the
Roman Catholic Church and a few others deny remarriage to the innocent party. In the case of a disruption from other causes many more deny remarriage
to the innocent. This denial cannot be based on 5:32

and its insertion into 19:9, by the translation: "causeth her to commit adultery" (i. e., by her marrying again). The A. V. makes also the man she marries "commit adultery," the R. V. has about the same meaning. The point of the utterances of Jesus is his condemnation of *the disruption* no matter what the cause may have been. The point should not be shifted to the cause of the disruption, whether this be grave or light. Whatever the cause, a disrupted marriage is a disrupted marriage. So Paul treats the class of disruptions that came within his experience, I Cor. 7:15, and permits the innocent to remarry. As regards the guilty one who causes the disruption, the way of repentance is surely open also for such a sinner as it is for any other who has caused an irreparable wrong to another.

10) **The disciples say to him, If the charge of the man in association with** (μετά) **the wife is thus, it is not expedient to marry.** The disciples are now alone with Jesus (Mark 10:10 "in the house"). What they say to Jesus is this: "If the only charge a man can bring against his wife is that of fornication in order to get rid of her after he is once married to her, it would be better not to have married at all." The difficulty regarding αἰτία disappears when we note that τοῦ ἀνθρώπου is the subjective genitive: "the charge which the man raises against his wife," and not objective: "the charge that lies against him when he sends away his wife for any reason except fornication." Αἰτία is to be understood in the same sense as in v. 3, "an indictment." It never means "relation" or *Verhaeltnis* or *causa* in the sense of *res*. As far as μετά is concerned, this modifies "the man"; the man who is still with his wife raises the charge and, according to Jesus, this is the only charge he can bring. By drawing the conclusion that it would then not be expedient for a man to marry, the disciples reveal that they are still under

the influence of Jewish ideals.   To be so tied to a wife
that only her fornication — a remote contingency that
was also freighted with severe penalty — would ever
release the husband from her and thus to be compelled
to put up with her faults for a whole lifetime seemed
an intolerable yoke, to which remaining unmarried
would be preferable.

11)   The disciples show, not that they are in favor
of the asceticism of celibacy, but are reluctant to give
up the Jewish ease of getting rid of a wife.   As Peter
advanced from three to seven in 18:21, they would be
willing to reduce the number of the charges for releasing wives but feel that Jesus goes too far in this reduction.   **But he said to them:   Not all have room for
this saying, only those to whom it has been given.
For there are eunuchs, such as were born thus from
their mother's womb; and there are eunuchs, such as
were made eunuchs by men; and there are eunuchs,
such as made themselves eunuchs on account of the
kingdom of the heavens.   He that is able to have
room, let him have room.**

The verb χωρεῖν means "to have room or space for
something" as a vessel holds a certain quantity; thus
metaphorically it means to embrace in the mind or
heart.   Here the word goes beyond mere intellectual
apprehension and evidently includes the moral will
that leads to the corresponding action.

The main question is, "What is understood by 'this
word' or 'saying'?"   Furthermore, are the two classes
here indicated by οὐ πάντες the unbelievers (like the
Pharisees in v. 3) and the believers or two types of
the latter, one not having and the other having the
gift of celibacy?   In regard to the latter question some
are misled by an apparent correspondence with I Cor.
7:7, against which I Cor. 6:12 and especially I Cor.
7:29-31 should guard them.   Since an explanatory γάρ
(R. 1190) introduces v. 12, "this saying" does not refer

to the contents of v. 12. But some think that "this saying" refers to v. 10. This is untenable, for v. 10 is
an objection to what Jesus has just said and one that
voices ideas similar to those expressed by the Pharisees concerning marriage. The fact is rather obvious
that by nature all men have only too much room in
their hearts for lax ideas regarding the permanency
of the marriage relation. How, then, could Jesus say
that "only those to whom it has been given" of God
have room for this word of the disciples? Since this,
too, is rather obvious, v. 10 is divided, and only its
last half, "it is not expedient to marry," is referred to
"this saying" of which Jesus says that not all have
room for it. But an apodosis is not true when it is
cut off from its protasis; without the condition the
conclusion has no validity. This saying of the disciples was *all* that they said and not only a part of it.
Moreover, Jesus most emphatically declared that marriage was a creation of God in the very beginning,
created in man who was made male and female. If
Jesus should now say that "it is not expedient to
marry" he would contradict himself and cast reproach
upon God's creative act of making man as he did.
This exegesis is the result of the secret influence of
Roman Catholicism which finds a higher sanctity in
celibacy than in marriage. Moreover, this exegesis
affords modernism an opportunity for charging Matthew with introducing into the mouth of Jesus "the
opinion of the early church  . . . .  as the epitome
of what they believed his will to be."

"This saying" is Jesus' own word spoken in v. 4-9.
The fact that "not all" have room for it the Pharisees
amply demonstrate. In v. 10 even the Twelve show
that they do not yet have room in their hearts to submit to this saying and to carry it out in their lives.
But this had been their trouble before this time (15:16;
16:8, 23; 17:17-20). That is why Jesus elucidates

what he has said and admonishes the Twelve (v. 12, last sentence) to make room for what he tells them. To men such as the Pharisees it was not given to know the things of the kingdom, but it certainly was given to the disciples (13:11) ; hence Jesus expects them to measure up to this gift; δέδοται with a present implied, "has been given so that they now have."

12) When this verse is thought to say that it is expedient not to marry at all but to make oneself a eunuch for the sake of the kingdom of God, it would regard Jesus as contradicting all that he has said concerning the divine creation of marriage. In order to avoid this contradiction a limitation is introduced into the phrase "on account of the kingdom of the heavens." This is taken to mean: "on account of *their special calling in* the kingdom." But in the discussion from v. 3 onward nothing is said about special calling, work, or position in the kingdom. Even the last word of the disciples concerns "*the man* (τοῦ ἀνθρώπου) in association with the wife" and not an apostle or a pastor in the church. Regarding the latter I Tim. 3:2, "husband of one wife," and Titus 1:6 are plain. Jesus is not speaking of a charism which only a few receive from God. In the consideration of a charism the idea of expediency (συμφέρειν) would be out of place; the charisms are not matters of expediency. "On account of the kingdom," etc., applies to *all* believers and to their relation to the kingdom. Only in the papacy could celibacy be called a charism; the Scriptures speak of it otherwise, I Tim. 4:3.

Jesus is speaking of the believer's ἐγκράτεια, his self-mastery, self-control as far as sexual desires are concerned. Some men, he says, are born eunuchs, are physically so constituted that they are free from sexual appetite. Others have been made eunuchs by men (τῶν is the generic article), have been castrated; in ancient Oriental lands they constituted a special class (see the Concordance on eunuchs in the Old Testament, also Deut. 23:1). These two classes are the exceptions. Since they are devoid of sexual desires, Jesus says nothing about the moral side of their condition. He mentions them only in order to cast light on another class, because he intends to call also this class "eunuchs," namely in a spiritual sense. These last are the believers, and "they made themselves eunuchs on account of the kingdom of the heavens." As they have done with regard to other natural desires, so they have put also the desire of sex under complete subjection because of their spiritual life in the kingdom. They deal with their physical nature as they do with father and mother, with life itself (10:37-39), with the whole world, if they had it (16:25,26), with any property or possession (13:44-46; 19:21). They will not let anything earthly stand in the way of their life in the kingdom. How some fail in regard to this vital matter we see in Luke 14:18-20; Matt. 22:5; II Tim. 4:10 (Demas); and in admonitions such as I John 2:15, etc. One should not overlook these analogous cases and view the sex life apart from them. Paul combines matters in the right way, including sex, in I Cor. 7:29-31.

The chief feature of this self-mastery is inward, is found in the heart itself. As far as the outward action is concerned, we may have cases such as those of the Twelve, 19:27-30, who left home, property, and all; such as that of Paul who accepted no support and had no wife that the churches needed to support (I Cor. 9:4, etc.). The married believers are to practice sexual self-control be refraining "with consent for a time" in order to practice fasting and prayer (I Cor. 7:5). Each in his place, as his connection with the kingdom may require, is to keep himself free from anything worldly that would hurt his spiritual life. Thus fornication will be abhorrent to the believers because it disrupts even marriage itself (v. 9). The permanency and the sanctity of marriage will be beyond question for him as Jesus has taught so thoroughly (v. 4-6). In marriage the believer will remain master of his sexual life, submitting this, too, completely to the Lord and to the kingdom. In οἵτινες we have equality, R. 727. The final admonition is addressed to all believers and not to a separate, superior class selected by God. This command is similar to all other commands concerning earthly matters that play a part in the believer's life.

It is well known that young Origen castrated himself. He sought to follow this word of Jesus' in a mechanical and literal way. Others did likewise, and writings were issued to promote such practice. Priestly celibacy is demanded by the Roman Catholic Church today, and the celibate state for monks and for nuns is regarded as being more holy than the married state of the rank and file of the church. Thus it is also thought that celibacy acquires merit with God; yet Jesus knows only about the gift of grace ("to whom it has been given"), and this gift is not celibacy but self-control for spiritual ends.

13) **Then there were brought to him little children in order that he might put his hands upon them and might pray; and the disciples rebuked them.** First marriage, then children, a sequence that is eminently fitting. The Pharisees mentioned in v. 3 are absent, have been since v. 10. This scene is often placed out-of-doors, but Mark 10:10 places it in a house, which fact also explains how the disciples could rebuke those bringing the children. They did this outside of the house, not in Jesus' presence, and thus, as Mark says, he finally saw it. Matthew has the historical aorist passive "there were brought," which

states only the fact; likewise the active aorist: the disciples "rebuked." Mark (10:13) has two imperfects which picture the actions in progress: certain persons "were bringing," and the disciples "were rebuking," and both tenses hold our attention to see what would eventuate. It seems as though these persons started to bring their children of their own accord. Somebody conceived the thought, and others followed in a little procession. The masculine αὐτοῖς would be used although most of the persons bringing children were mothers, sisters, or nurses. Most of them were evidently parents, fathers and mothers. The disciples started to interfere and probably succeeded until Jesus, looking out, saw what they were doing and stopped them. All three evangelists use the strong verb ἐπιτιμᾶν, "to rebuke," "to threaten."

The scene loses a good deal of its beauty when it is supposed that superstition prompted these parents to bring their children, and that they supposed that the touch of Jesus' hands had magical power. We may be sure that, if this had been the case, Jesus would himself have rebuked these people and would not have touched a single child. To place the hand upon someone in connection with prayer is a symbolical act, it is an invoking of the divine blessing upon the person touched. We still use this act in this sense. Matthew writes παιδία, "little children," for which Luke 18:15 has τὰ βρέφη, "their babes" or sucklings, the word that is used in I Pet. 2:2; it is used to designate even an unborn babe in Luke 1:44. Because they were so tiny, it was, of course, impossible for them to understand what Jesus was doing for them. The only intimation we have regarding the reason that the disciples stopped these babes from being brought to Jesus is found in the word of Jesus, other reasons may also have been present, such as that the disciples did not want Jesus to be troubled by having all these babes brought to him,

that they considered his time too valuable to be wasted
on infants, and that they desired his time for themselves and for further discussions.

14) **But Jesus said, Suffer the little children
and stop restraining them from coming to me; for of
such is the kingdom of the heavens. And having
put his hands on them, he went from there.**    Mark
contributes the detail that, when Jesus saw what the
disciples were doing, he was indignant, and Luke adds
that he called the babes to him (into the house).    Here
Jesus appears as the great Advocate of babes by opening his mouth for the dumb, out of whose mouth, by
his grace, he perfects praise.    It has been well said
that without these words of Jesus and the attitude
here expressed toward infants the Christian Church
would have been far different from what it is.

With shamed faces the disciples stood before their
Master.    The two imperatives ἄφετε and κωλύετε are
present and thus durative; the second is negative and
thus means to stop something already begun (R. 851,
etc.).    The first is well rendered, "suffer the little children," *lasset sie gewaehren*; and Mark and Luke have the
accusative with the infinitive, "suffer them to come to
me."    This positive command is enhanced by the negative; the disciples are to stop restraining them; and here
Matthew has the accusative with the infinitive just mentioned, "from coming to me."    But Matthew has the
effective aorist infinitive ἐλθεῖν, which means coming
and actually getting to Jesus; while Mark and Luke
have the present infinitive which describes only the
action of coming.

The implication is that children, and this includes
babes (βρέφη), are ready to come to Jesus and need
only that men let them do so.    And this coming has
the same purpose as the coming to Jesus of any adult,
namely to receive of him the Messianic salvation.
Their affinity for Jesus lies in their need of him which

is due to their inborn sin. Pank writes: "As the
flower in the garden stretches toward the light of the
sun, so there is in the child a mysterious inclination
toward the eternal light. Have you never noticed this
mysterious thing that, when you tell the smallest child
about God, it never asks with strangeness and wonder,
'What or who is God? I have never seen him!' — but
listens with shining face to the words as though they
were soft, loving sounds from the land of home? or
when you teach a child to fold its little hands in prayer,
that it does this as though it were a matter of course,
as though there were opening for it that world of
which it had been dreaming with longing and anticipa-
tion? or tell them, these little ones, the stories of the
Savior, show them the pictures with scenes and per-
sonages of the Bible — how their pure eyes shine, how
their little hearts beat!"

The coming of these babes is not accomplished without means, for v. 13 has already stated that it was
done by their being brought. Not to come means not
to be brought. These were Jewish children who were
already in the old covenant of grace; yet Jesus lays no
stress on this but speaks of children in general, even
as the church has applied his words to all children.
Indeed, if Jewish children who were already in the
covenant and the kingdom needed to be brought to
Jesus in order to be blessed by him as the Messiah, how
much more is this the case with regard to all other
children to whom no grace has been applied. Jesus
once for all forbids every obstacle which our blind
reasoning about babes may raise against their coming to him.

This double command itself would be enough, but
Jesus goes much farther, he adds his reason for this
command: "for of such is the kingdom of the heavens."
He does not say τούτων, "of these," the ones now being
brought to him, but τῶν τοιούτων, "of such," which says

far more, namely the great class of beings to which babes as such belong. Bengel says that if the kingdom is "of such," then with a special right the children must be included. They are the model examples of the whole class. If we want to know the character of the class we must study the children (18:3). It is their receptivity to which Jesus refers. In them sin has not yet developed so as to produce conscious resistance to the power of divine grace, which necessitates the convicting power of the law. What children are in their condition of infancy, ready and willing to accept the gift of grace, adults must become by the operation of the Spirit and the Word. The moment this receptiveness is produced in us, regeneration and justification follow, and we, too, are saved.

On "the kingdom of the heavens" see 3:2; it is where Jesus, the King, is found with the rule and the work of his grace. To be "of" this kingdom is to have his grace operative in us. If Jesus had intended to say that all children, merely as children, had already experienced this operation, were already saved, then children would not need to come to him, they would be already his. But Jesus says nothing of the kind. What is born of the flesh is flesh, John 3:6 (Gen. 5:3; Ps. 51:5). It is in vain to deny original or inborn sin, the total depravity of our race, and to call babes "innocent and pure" in the sense of "sinless." Every babe that dies contradicts this claim.

It is also no more than an assumption that at birth (or already at the time of conception) all children are made partakers of Christ's atonement *without any means whatever*; the Scriptures contain no word to this effect. Because men have been misled by such thoughts the little ones have been left outside of the kingdom until receptiveness for grace has passed away and their salvation became jeopardized. Baptism, in particular, was denied them, and this sacrament itself was considered a symbol that did not give or convey anything but only pictured something. Baptism was regarded as an act of obedience (a law) that was possible only to an adult and not longer an act of the Triune God by which he adopted us as his children, deeded to us a place in heaven, gave us the new birth of the Spirit. Who can estimate the wrong thus done to helpless babes, even in the name of Christ, by denying them the one divine means by which they can be brought (v. 13) and can come to their glorified Lord?

15) Mark and Luke add another statement here that recalls 18:3. The fact that Matthew aims to be quite terse we see also from the way in which he concludes his account of this incident. Whereas Mark tells us that Jesus took the children up into his arms, blessed them, and laid his hands upon them, Matthew records only the latter, "and having put his hands on them." The fact that this was done in connection with a prayer (and thus with a blessing) v. 13 shows. These are the essentials; taking the babes into his own arms is a beautiful addition. The conclusion is justified that, like the other synoptists, Matthew records this incident as the answer to the question whether infants are to receive baptism. The use which Tertullian (born about 160) makes of this account as a substantiation of infant baptism is evidence that long prior to his time the church so understood the words and the actions of Jesus. "He went from thence" means that Jesus left not merely the house but the place itself.

16) We must place v. 3-15 somewhere in Perea. What is now described, occurred later "while he was going forth on the way" (Mark 10:17, i. e., on the road to the next village or town). First marriage, then children, now earthly possessions — the inner connection seems evident. **And lo, one, having come to**

**him, said, Teacher, what good thing shall I do in order to have life eternal?** The interjection "lo" points to the man's action as being remarkable; and, indeed, he was a ruler (Luke), and he came running and then kneeling (Mark). Here is a young man of prominence, eager in regard to the highest question, and full of the expectation of obtaining the true answer from Jesus. Matthew records only the word "teacher" as the address to Jesus; he omits "good" because he intends to omit also that part of the reply of Jesus which deals with this adjective as applied to himself. The attitude of the young man and the great question he asks of Jesus indicate that he regarded Jesus as a teacher and expected the great answer he had hitherto failed to secure. By saying, "Teacher," he puts himself into the position of a pupil.

The question this man asks is not *how* he may obtain life eternal as though he were entirely at a loss as to the way and the means to obtain it. On the contrary, he thinks he knows quite well how to obtain this life, namely by doing some "good thing," ἀγαθόν, "good" in the sense of bringing him "life eternal," *heilbringend*, C.-K. 5. He is not thinking of something that is merely "morally good," for he knows that obedience to the divine commandments is morally good, and yet in spite of all this obedience on his part he still lacks this life and knows it. He asks Jesus this question because he thinks that Jesus has managed to discover this "good thing" and by it has acquired life eternal. This man would like to do the same thing. In this sense he calls Jesus "good Teacher" (Mark and Luke). His conception of Jesus is thus much like that of the modernists. Jesus is a man who has discovered this good thing and by it won eternal life. His essential Sonship as also his atonement are set aside. The only question is: "Lord, how didst thou do it? tell us so that we may do likewise."

In the question, "What shall I do?" lies, of course, the assumption that the questioner has the necessary ability and may easily reach the goal Jesus has reached. He feels that all he needs to know is the thing that is to be done. This is Pelagianism in its worst form. The ποιήσω, "shall I do," suggests the willingness to do what may be required. He is not thinking of a divine command; he does not ask what he "must" do, δεῖ ποιεῖν (ποιῆσαι). The best feature about this wrong and twisted question is the fact that the man wants "life eternal."

John uses ζωή thirty-four times, and the word always means the life principle itself which makes us spiritually alive. The reception of this "life" is the regeneration of which Jesus spoke to Nicodemus at length. This life is αἰώνιος, "eternal," going on through the eons unaffected by temporal death which only transfers this life into the heavenly world. It may be lost and cease in us when we wickedly and wilfully cut ourselves off from its divine source, Christ, the Life. Just what conception the man had of this life which he so much desired we are able to guess only from the way in which he imagined it could be acquired: by himself doing something *heilbringend* he supposed it would be given him. For "have" life eternal Mark and Luke write "inherit." Often the latter is stressed as though it made the ruler's question self-contradictory: *doing* in order to *inherit*. Yet Matthew's "have" interprets the others' "inherit"; κληρονομεῖν is often used in the sense of to obtain or to have a portion in something. Moreover, inheriting often rests on merit as many last wills and testaments show, when a larger portion is bequeathed to a more faithful child, or when a friend, a benefactor, or a person who has rendered some valuable service is remembered. Jesus, too, says nothing and intimates nothing regarding a contradiction in the question.

The picture thus drawn of the young ruler is really pathetic: so eager to do the good thing, so desirous of life eternal (whereas so many young men are carried away by the world), so strongly attracted to Jesus — and yet so far from the right road to eternal life!

**17) And he said to him: Why inquirest thou of me concerning the good thing? One is The Good. If thou hast the will to enter into the life, guard his biddings.** The entire answer must be considered together in order to understand its three parts. Jesus refers this man to God and to God's Word. Not for one moment will Jesus allow this man to speak as though God had failed to reveal what "good" he must do if by doing he would have life eternal. Does this man presume to ask Jesus and thus to ignore God? Does he think that Jesus has certain secret information that has not been revealed by God? Is this why he calls Jesus "good" (Mark and Luke, "good Teacher"), a man who has done that thing and thus gained life for himself, found and done it apart from God's Word? With one stroke Jesus corrects all these wrong ideas: "One is The Good," *der Gute*, the very embodiment and source of all that is *heilbringend* and "good" in this sense; and Mark and Luke add that this is "God." If this man has the will to enter into life (and by the condition of reality Jesus implies that the man has) by way of his own doing, then what good thing he must do has long been set down in God's Word, let him guard and keep inviolate his biddings (the article has the force of the possessive), τὰς ἐντολάς, what he has told and ordered men to do. On that point Jesus has no more to say.

The phrase περὶ τοῦ ἀγαθοῦ is not masculine, to be explained by the following ὁ ἀγαθός; it is neuter and takes up the preceding τί ἀγαθόν. He who is himself "The Good" must be asked what is to be done by us that he would consider "good." And ὁ ἀγαθός with its

article makes this predicate identical with and interchangeable with the subject, R. 768. Moreover, here
is a case where the positive "good" and "The Good"
are more absolute than the comparative or the superlative, R. 661. This is "good" in the absolute sense.

Rationalism and Unitarianism regard Mark and
Luke as saying that Jesus does not claim goodness for
himself but attributes perfect moral goodness only to
God. Their object is to reduce Jesus to a man who
at most was only relatively good morally. This is
to think and to speak of Jesus as the young ruler did
who regarded Jesus as a mere man, as one who had
acquired life by doing this unknown good thing and
might likewise show others how to do it. No wonder
Jesus declines to be called "good" in this sense! The
question (Mark and Luke): "Why callest thou me
good?" is not a pronouncement of any kind in regard
to Jesus' moral quality. Nor does ἀγαθός mean "kind"
when it is used in the address to Jesus and something
else in the three following instances. Jesus uses
"good" in the sense indicated above. Let the man
stop and think. Jesus is not a Teacher who instructs
men as to how to obtain salvation by their own efforts.
If that is what this man wants, God has already told
him what to do.

18) After Jesus said, "Just guard his biddings!"
**he says to him, Which? And Jesus said: Thou
shalt not murder (5:21); Thou shalt not commit
adultery; Thou shalt not steal; Thou shalt not testify
falsely; Honor thy father and thy mother; and, Thou
shalt love thy neighbor as thyself.** Mark and Luke
abbreviate by omitting the last, and Mark inserts,
"Thou shalt not defraud." The neuter article τό before these commandments merely marks the quotation,
R. 766. The future tense is commonly used in laws
and is thus imperative, R. 874. The intent of Jesus
seems to be to pile one commandment upon another.

Matthew has the regular order from the fifth to the eighth, to which Mark adds the ninth and the tenth in the form: "Thou shalt not defraud."

19) Then comes the fourth, and after that the sum of the entire second table of the law. By placing the fourth thus Jesus shows that he does not feel bound by the order found in the decalog. By using only the second table which demands that we love our neighbor as we do ourselves Jesus takes this ruler to a place where he felt surest of himself; for these are the commandments which most men imagine they are able to obey with little effort — but see 5:21, etc.

20) And sure enough, this ruler, too, is convinced that he has fulfilled them. **The young man says to him: All these I did watch. As to what am I yet behind?** He says this without blinking an eye. The divine law has no terrors for him; he has kept it all. The verbs τηρεῖν and φυλάσσειν are synonyms, like *bewahren* and *bewachen,* to guard and keep inviolate and to watch over and keep safe. Here is a sample of Pharisaic training which nullifies the very effect God intends the law to produce, namely contrite knowledge of sin and the *terrores conscientiae.* This young man, νεανίσκος (between the ages of 24 and 40), is altogether self-righteous in the face of the law. Perhaps he was disappointed in hearing Jesus recite nothing but the old commandments that he had kept "from his youth up" (Mark and Luke). Is this all "the good" this "good" Teacher could hold up to him?

He *had* lived an outwardly exemplary life, he had shunned grave outward transgressions, being aided and protected, no doubt, by both his training and his environment. Many would today be only too well satisfied with themselves if they were like him, and others would praise and perhaps envy him if they saw him in modern form. Picture him: an exemplary young man in early manhood, fine and clean morally,

as the phrase now goes, the son of wealthy parents
but not spoiled by wealth, with a strong religious bent,
an esteemed member of the church, in fact, one of its
pillars, a ruler of the local synagogue who was more
important than a member of the church council in
our present congregations is. Where are the parents
that would not be proud of such a son? Where the
church that would not give him a prominent place?
Where the maid that would not be attracted by his
position and his personal excellence? Yet all this is
worthless in the eyes of Jesus. In fact, the man himself is not satisfied. If Jesus thought that he had
trouble in regard to the old commandments, this, he
assures Jesus, is not the case. Somehow he has come
to feel that he lacks something. What can it be?
He puts the question to Jesus; he thinks that Jesus
must now be able to tell him in what he still falls
behind.

21) Mark inserts the remark that Jesus looked
earnestly upon the rich young ruler and loved him:
this man who is dissatisfied with his Pharisaic self-
righteousness, is groping in the dark and unable to get
beyond it, and now appeals to Jesus. **Jesus spoke to
him** (ἔφη is a mere variation of εἶπε): **If thou hast
the will to be perfect, go sell thy possessions and give
to the poor and thou shalt have treasure in heaven;
and hither, be following me!** Jesus agrees that he
still lacks one thing (Mark and Luke). Because of
his love for him he tells him what this really is. The
answer is surprising, and this surprise has lasted these
1900 years. The condition is one of reality, which
implies that Jesus assumes that the young man has
the will. With εἶναι we have the nominative as the
predicate; and τέλειος is explained in 5:48. It does
not mean perfect or sinless morally but complete as
having reached the τέλος or goal. Here it is easy to
understand this word; it means possessing the one thing

he yet lacked, needing nothing more. We must regard all that Jesus says as "one thing," but not as one that is to be ranged alongside of others but as one that is totally different from all others. Thus far the man has attained only an outward obedience to the law and has not even discovered that this is utterly useless for salvation. The thing he lacks begins with this discovery and thus with the realization that what he needs is *a complete inward change.*

This change Jesus describes to him in detail. The present imperative ὕπαγε is used without a connecting word when it occurs with other imperatives: ὕπαγε πώλησον καὶ δός. When he tells this man to go and sell his possessions and to give them to the poor Jesus is laying his finger on the chief sin in this man's heart, the love of his earthly possessions. Jesus is demanding no mere outward act which would be as valueless as the other acts of this man have been. The outward act is to be merely the evidence of the inner change. This change is to be, first of all, *the true sorrow of contrition.* Heretofore he has clung to his earthly wealth with his heart. What a sin against God's law! By selling and giving away everything this inward sin is to be swept out by true contrition, μετάνοια.

Abandoning what was hitherto his heart's treasure is only the negative side; the positive side is that now he has "treasure in heaven" with his whole heart fixed on that. The future "shall have" means from that moment onward when his heart is separated from his earthly treasure. It is a serious misunderstanding of this word of Jesus when it is thought to mean that by selling and giving away his earthly wealth this man would receive this treasure in heaven as a reward. This treasure is the unmerited grace and pardon of God. For the other side of the one thing this man yet lacked is *the true and saving faith in Christ.* Δεῦρο, "hither," is used with or without an imperative. It is apparently always a singular, as δεῦτε is the plural; and the present imperative ἀκολούθει denotes continuous following. To follow Jesus thus is the evidence of true faith in him.

When Jesus demands true repentance and faith he does not always ask us to give up our earthly possessions. This passage cannot be referred to as proof for the abolition of personal ownership of wealth. Zacchaeus was not required to give all his possession to the poor; Joseph of Arimathaea was a disciple and rich; Ananias was free to do with his own what he would as long as he did not practice hypocrisy or tried to deceive the Holy Ghost; St. James warns the rich only against trusting in riches instead of trusting in God. Luther is, therefore, right when he draws attention to the domestic state and its requirement of certain possessions such as house and home, food, clothing, etc., for wife and children. The case of this young man is a special one and comes under the statements made in 18:8, 9. We are not certain either that this young man was asked to assume voluntary poverty in order to follow Jesus and to take part in the work of the gospel. This is often assumed, but we have no intimation as to how Jesus intended to use this new follower. Others besides the Twelve were in his following for their own persons only and certainly did not divest themselves of their possessions.

Roman Catholicism considers voluntary poverty a work that merits salvation; it calls this command to give all to the poor a *consilium evangelicum* that goes beyond the decalog, and the observance of such counsel an *opus supererogativum*. The rationalistic view is that the one thing the young ruler lacked was moral power, the energy of the moral will. Others think of the ability to sacrifice all for the sake of reaching the highest moral goal; or of the ability really to fulfill the second table, the law of loving one's neighbor as one-

self, by which eternal life would be gained. But such
views are legalistic and not evangelical.

22) **But the young man, having heard the word,
went away, being aggrieved; for he had much property.** The result shows that Jesus had struck home,
had bared the man's most vulnerable spot, the love
of his great wealth. First, such enthusiasm; now,
such sorrowful going away! Mark says that the man's
face grew "lowering"; it is the same word that was
used regarding the dark weather mentioned in 16:3.
He, indeed, left Jesus, but Jesus' words went with him.
The fact that he was not changed on the instant need
not cause surprise. It would cost him a struggle, perhaps one that was severe and prolonged. The synoptists do not record the outcome, for their interest lies,
not in this case, but in the words of Jesus which go
far beyond one case.

23) **And Jesus said to his disciples: Amen, I
say to you, that with difficulty a rich man shall enter
into the kingdom of the heavens. And again I say
to you, easier it is that a camel go through a needle's
eye than that a rich man go into the kingdom of the
heavens. And when the disciples heard it they were
shocked exceedingly, saying, Who, then, is able to be
saved? But, having looked at them, Jesus said to
them, With men this is impossible, yet with God all
things are possible.**

These utterances of Jesus are not to be separated
from the preceding narrative. Both treat of the way
to salvation, and both deal with one great obstacle to
salvation, the love of riches. What appears in the
narrative is more fully elucidated in the words
addressed to the disciples. God's grace alone is able
to save the rich man. A comparison with Mark shows
that Matthew mentions the emotions displayed at the
end of his narrative, Luke omits them altogether.
Matthew preserves the solemn formula of verity and

authority (see 5:18) ; on the kingdom compare 3:2.
The emphasis is on the adverb δυσκόλως; only "with
difficulty" will a rich man ever enter into the kingdom,
i. e., receive the gifts and the blessings that are bestowed by the rule of the King's grace. The fact that
Jesus has in mind a man who *trusts* in riches is
emphasized by Mark. He may or may not have wealth;
its deceptive power is always present.

24) How great the difficulty is, is illustrated by a
remarkable comparison, that of the impossibility of a
camel passing through an orifice as tiny as a needle's
eye. The Talmud uses the elephant in the same illustration; elephants were not known in Palestine. The
Koran has the same illustration that Jesus employs.
Not until the fifth century was κάμελος, "camel," changed
to κάμιλος, the heavy "rope" or cable attached to the
anchor of a ship (R. 192). This change was no gain for
a cable cannot be threaded through a needle's eye.

In the fifteenth century the opposite was tried, the
needle's eye was enlarged by reference to a small portal that was used by footpassengers when entering
a walled city, through which a camel might pass
on its knees after its load had been removed. This
changed the impossible into the possible and became
attractive because it suggested that, as the camel had
to leave its load and crawl on its knees, so the rich
man had to shed his riches or his love for them and
humble himself on his knees. But as in 23:24 Jesus
had an actual gnat and an actual camel in mind, so
here camel and needle's eye are actual. The impossibility thus illustrated is without a single exception.
Abraham, David, Zacchaeus, Joseph of Arimathaea are
not exceptions in any sense; for how the impossible becomes possible Jesus explains in v. 26.

25) At this point Matthew, too, notes the emotion
of the disciples. The disciples were shocked "exceedingly," ἐξεπλήσσοντο, the imperfect picturing their con-

dition, and the verb itself, plus its adverb, are very strong: "were utterly dumbfounded." Their question reveals what so upset them: "Who, then, is able to be saved?" meaning that, if these statements of Jesus are true, no man can be saved. Their emotion is not concerned with the few who are rich and thus seem to be utterly shut out but with themselves, including all men generally. For τίς cannot be restricted. All men have a secret longing for riches. The question is thus a confession of sin on the part of the disciples. This is excellent. It is well that they do not try to shield themselves by a reference to what Jesus once said about "the poor," 5:3.

But another thing is not so excellent, namely the confession that the disciples believed that a man can and should do something on his part toward being saved. They really say: "If the illustration of the camel is true regarding a rich man's entering the kingdom, then the rich man can do nothing toward being saved, nor can we who, like the rich, are afflicted with the desire for riches." In the verb σώζειν lies the idea of rescue from mortal danger and of a condition of safety produced by the rescue. The passive σωθῆναι leaves God as the agent, but δύναται betrays the synergistic suggestion in the disciples' minds.

26) The fact that Jesus, too, speaks with feeling is betrayed by his earnestly looking at the disciples. He has elicited from the disciples the very thought he wishes to correct once for all. The illustration of the camel is abolutely true: "With men this (to be saved) is impossible." The last door of hope on that side is shut and sealed forever. Here perishes all Pelagianism, moralism, synergism; man himself can do absolutely nothing toward his salvation by natural powers of his own. The *Concordia Triglotta*, 785, etc., and 881, etc., is most certainly right. But the more all hope of our own activity dies, whether we are rich or poor,

the more our hope in God and his grace rises like the morning sun with healing in his wings: "yet with God all things are possible," even the saving of the rich. Who will measure the ability of his grace? Who will describe the miracles it is able to work?

We might here think of God's omnipotence as it is revealed in the physical creation by applying our abstract mode of reasoning; but Jesus is here speaking of the kingdom of the heavens which is not of this world, and of the great work of saving men, including the rich, which is entirely a spiritual work. We are here not in the First Article of the Creed but in the Second and the Third. Christ "is able to save them to the uttermost," Heb. 7:25.

27) From one extreme the apostles go to the other. First they fear that on the basis of what Jesus said none of them can be saved; now, with their fears allayed in that direction, they want assurance that they will not only be saved but will be rewarded according to the sacrifices they have hade. **Then Peter spoke up and said to him: Lo, we on our part did forsake all things and followed thee. What, then, shall be ours?** Ἀποκριθείς is often used in a wider sense; it is so here. It occurs to Peter that he and the Twelve had done exactly what Jesus required of the rich young ruler and so he speaks up and says so. It strikes Peter that they have done this, hence the interjection "lo." The emphasis is on ἡμεῖς, which contrasts the Twelve with the ruler who went away aggrieved. Peter, too, does not forget to add that the Twelve followed Jesus even as Jesus had just bidden the ruler to follow him. The aorists are here to the point, they present the two undeniable facts: we *did* this.

But already this preamble has a suspicious ring with its emphasis on what "we on our part" have done. It does not intend to proceed, "and we have found more than satisfaction in thee"; for that first "we" would not harmonize with that thought. To express this acknowledgment Peter should have begun, *"Thou thyself* hast drawn us to forsake all and to follow thee." What Peter's ear had caught was the word to the ruler, "and thou shalt have treasure in heaven." But he had not caught Jesus' meaning that this would be a treasure of pure grace and not a merited reward earned by the ruler in giving away his possessions and then following Jesus. He regards the word as a reference to a profitable trade to which the ruler was invited. And thus Peter asks, "What, then, shall be ours" ("to us") ? i. e., "What are we going to get?" Here the old spirit of work-righteousness, of human claims and merit crops out. The more *we* do, the more *we* earn, and the more *God* owes us.

28) **And Jesus said to them: Amen I say to you** (see 5:18), **that you that did follow me, in the regeneration when the Son of man** (see 8:20) **shall seat himself on his throne of glory, you, too, shall seat yourselves on twelve thrones, judging the twelve tribes of Israel.** What Jesus said was intended for the Twelve, all of whom had heard Peter's statement and question. First, a great promise; then, in v. 30 and the following parable, a necessary warning, both being sealed with the solemn formula of verity and authority. The generosity and the magnanimity of God are so great that he accepts nothing from us without rewarding it beyond all computation (25:21, 23; Luke 19:17, 19). The vast disproportion existing between our work and God's reward of it already displays his boundless grace, to say nothing of the gift of salvation which is made before we have even begun to do any work. The first part of Jesus' promise is intended for the apostles alone but only in a pre-eminent way (Dan. 7:22; I Cor. 6:2, 3; Rev. 2:26; 3:21; 20:4). Hence also they are called only "you that did follow me," which indicates that also others follow him.

The ἐν phrase states when the promise here made shall be fulfilled; hence it is modified by the temporal ὅταν clause. "In the regeneration" or "rebirth" is thus dated at the time "when the Son of man shall seat himself on his throne of glory," namely visibly before the whole world, which he will do on the great day of judgment. This "rebirth" thus refers to the rebirth of the world (Isa. 65:17; II Pet. 3:13; Rev. 21:1, 5). The term παλινγενεσία is abstract, but, like many abstracts, is used for the concrete and denotes, not the act of rebirth, but the reborn world. In Titus 3:5 it is used to designate the rebirth wrought in the individual by baptism. The use of this word as a technical term by the mystery cults and among the Pythagoreans and the Stoics has been extensively investigated and has produced much of interest but nothing that is of value for the interpretation of the New Testament. Philo and Josephus also use the word in their way.

The great act that distinguishes the time indicated is that the Son of man "shall seat himself on his throne of glory." The two forms of καθίζειν are middle: "seat himself," "seat yourselves," B.-P. 608, and should not be translated "sit." This seating is done for the performance of a judicial act and does not refer to an indefinite enthronement; compare 25:31. The omission of the articles in the expression ἐπὶ θρόνου δόξης αὐτοῦ is scarcely a case of imitating the Hebrew *status constructus*, for the addition of the articles would refer to the specific throne in heaven, while all that is had in mind here is a glorious throne for judgment.

On that great day the apostles shall also seat themselves on twelve thrones and for the same purpose, to judge the twelve tribes of Israel. The place of Judas is thus to be filled. We see the correspondence between Israel's twelve tribes and Jesus' twelve apostles. But there is no indication that each apostle is to judge one tribe, nor that Peter's throne will be higher than those

of the rest.   The present participle κρίνοντες presents the
action in its progress; the aorist would be constative
and would present the act in its completeness.

The opinion that the rebirth is to be dated after the
ascension of Jesus involves the idea that the apostles
would judge only mediately through their preached
word, would spiritualize their twelve thrones as the
pulpits they occupied, and would expand the twelve
tribes of Israel so as to include all men or at least Christians in general.   The latter would be the case if κρίνειν
is thought to mean "rule" and not "judge."   The verb
always has the latter meaning.   It has this meaning
also in Luke 22:30, where the promise is repeated, and
where the sense of κρίνοντες must be the same as it is in
Matthew.   Weiss writes:  "As they were the nearest
to Jesus in his earthly activity, so they will have the
closest portion in the dignity of the exalted Messiah;
and as they proclaimed salvation to the twelve tribes
(10:5, 6), so they will also pronounce the verdict upon
all and not only on the unbelieving Israel, according as
they accepted or declined this offer of salvation."   This
judgment, however, will not be restricted to the generation of the Jews that actually heard the apostles but
will take in the entire nation from the days of the
patriarchs down to the last day, the lost ten tribes of
the past era as well as all Israelites of future ages.
From the way in which Jesus here speaks it is possible
to conclude that the Jews will be the first to receive
their judgment at the last day.

29)   Now Jesus adds the promise he gives  to all
believers, individualizing where a moment ago he combined.   **And everyone that left houses, or brothers,
or sisters, or father, or mother, or wife, or children,
or fields, for the sake of my name, a hundredfold
shall he receive, and life eternal shall he inherit.**
Not one will miss his due reward.   "Or wife" has the
superior textual support and should not be dropped,

being genuine also in Luke 18:29. This list has no exceptions. In 10:37, "loveth more than me," and in Luke 14:26, "hate," help to explain the meaning of "leaving" which Jesus has in mind. It may include outward separation, but often the inward act of the soul is enough. "For the sake of my name" is explained by "for the sake of the gospel" in Mark 10:29, and by "for the sake of the kingdom of God" in Luke 18:29. Here ὄνομα again means "name" in the sense of "my revelation," "gospel" and "the kingdom."

"A hundredfold" has been called hyperbolical. In order to avoid this hyperbole some transfer the entire reward into the other world by resorting to allegory. But in Mark νῦν ἐν τῷ καιρῷ τούτῳ states that this reward is given here in time and is distinguished from the life eternal ἐν τῷ αἰῶνι τῷ ἐρχομένῳ, "in the eon to come"; so also Luke 18:30. "A hundredfold," the neuter plural, is like the same proportion in 13:8, and raises the replacement to the highest degree. On the new spiritual relationships compare 12:48-50; Rom. 16:13 (John 19:27); I Tim. 1:2; 5:2; II Tim. 2:1; Philemon 10; I Pet. 5:3, and other passages; on other possessions Ps. 37:16; Prov. 15:16; 16:8; I Tim. 6:6. The new riches are the divine blessings which substitute thankfulness for worldly anxiety (6:25, etc.) and delight in imperishable treasures (6:19, etc.). Mark 10:30 has the significant addition "with persecutions," as though this were the butter on the bread. Persecutions are, indeed, a constant assurance that we truly belong to the Lord, more than the asurance that lies in other blessings.

"And life eternal (see v. 16) shall he inherit" has both a markedly different verb and an object so great that it cannot be classed with any blessing bestowed in this life. This alone is enough to indicate that life eternal is not a reward for forsaking relatives, property, or for enduring other afflictions for Christ's sake.

In fact, before we are able to perform a single good work, namely the moment faith is kindled in the heart, the inheritance is ours, and that out of pure grace for Christ's sake alone. The analogy of the entire Scripture is solid on this point. Mark 10:30, as well as Luke 18:30, make it certain that the inheriting here referred to is the reception of our heritage in the other world; but this changes nothing in regard to the way in which the inheritance first becomes ours. Here the entrance into the heavenly life is mentioned to impress upon the disciples what an infinite blessing awaits those who are here called upon to forsake this or that temporality. What is any loss compared with this gain? While inheriting does not always exclude merit on the part of an heir (see v. 16), inheriting eternal life most certainly does. For no sinner can by his own will or strength produce any merit that would in the least move God to make him an heir of life eternal.

30) At this point the warning begins. The fact that it was needed even for the Twelve the case of Judas shows, thief that he was, traitor that he became. **Nevertheless, many first shall be last, and last first.** In 20:16 Jesus repeats this warning, but there he does it by means of οὕτως, "thus," which indicates that the intervening parable reveals just how it comes about that so many that are first in the end are last, and others who are last finally become first. In view of 20:31, 32 and Luke 13:24-30, "last" cannot mean "last in the kingdom." "Last" means outside of the kingdom; and hence "first" means inside the kingdom. Jesus is not saying that many who for a time were in the front ranks in the kingdom shall eventually find themselves in the rear ranks, and vice versa. What he says is that many who at first were in the kingdom will finally be out of it; while many who at first were out of it will at last be in it. But the wording "first — last" and "last — first" is so general that it includes

also all cases where men think themselves "first" or in the kingdom and then, too late, find that they are "last," not in it at all.

The proper understanding of this pointed saying is of vital importance for the correct interpretation of the parable that follows. Its very purpose is to show how so many first will be last, and last first. If the "last" are conceived as still being in the kingdom, the parable will not be properly interpreted.

# CHAPTER XX

1) The connection with 19:30, or rather with 19:27-30, is made by γάρ, "for," in the sense of, "in order to elucidate." And v. 16 seals this connection by repeating 19:30. **For like is the kingdom of the heavens (3:2) to a houselord who went out at once at early morn to hire laborers for his vineyard.** "Is like" means in one respect, the one stated in 19:30; and "the kingdom" is the rule and operation of God's grace. The resemblance runs through the entire story that is told as a parable. Moreover, the story is purposely molded so as to reflect what occurs in God's rule of grace. The addition of ἀνθρώπῳ to οἰκοδεσπότῃ is pleonastic (R. 120) and may be omitted in translation, as was done in 13:52. In 10:25 οἰκοδεσπότης is used with reference to Jesus, and in 13:27 it is used in a parable. "Houselord" is a property owner, one who is the possessor of a homestead, here one whose holdings include also an extensive vineyard to which he devotes especial care. This "houselord" pictures God in his grace, and his lordship appears throughout the story. "His vineyard" is his visible church on earth where the work of his grace appears.

The figure of the vineyard is Old Testament imagery. When the question is asked as to why the vineyard is thus used, no one point furnishes the answer, such as that it is symbolic of peace, of hard labor, of drawing wine out of the earth. The image is used in a variety of ways. Here the point is the dealing of the owner with his laborers. Thus nothing is said concerning the vines or the harvest of grapes.

The owner is represented as being grand and wealthy; he has an ἐπίτροπος or "steward" and hires a large number of laborers and does none of the work himself. So the whole work of the church is turned over to Christ (note the meaning of ἐπιτρέπειν), and the actual tending of the vineyard or church is done by means of men, the Christians, who are called and appointed to this work. The middle μισθώσασθαι is causative: "to let out for wages" and thus "to hire," R. 809. The owner is such a man, ὅστις, one of this type, R. 728, thus picturing God. Although he has his steward he hires the laborers himself and has so great a personal interest in his vineyard that he goes out "at once" (ἅμα) "at early morn" (πρωΐ) to hire laborers. We need not object that Christ or the Spirit calls men into the work of the church, for all the *opera ad extra sunt indivisa aut communa* and are thus ascribed to any one of the Persons. But right here at the start we must note that Jesus is speaking of our *work* ("laborers") in the church and of our *wages* for that work ("hire"). On this feature of the kingdom we are to be enlightened, for in 19:27 Peter betrayed his ignorance regarding this point.

2) **And having agreed with the laborers on a denarius for the day, he sent them into his vineyard.** "With the laborers" refers to the ones hired so early. The denarius is equal to seventeen cents but at that time constituted the regular wage of a day laborer, also the day's pay of a Roman soldier; and ἐκ has the idea of cause which is here modified to price, R. 599. Extent of time is expressed by the accusative τὴν ἡμέραν, R. 470. But the chief point is that these laborers insist on a definite wage, so much per day; and not until this agreement is reached do they go to work. Such a contract was not demanded by the other laborers who went to work later. These first laborers thus manifest a mercenary spirit. We hear the voice of Peter in 19:27, "What, then, shall be ours?"

Since this is a parable which was composed in order to teach certain facts about the kingdom, the entire first group of laborers is pictured as being mercenary. This is done, not only to show how in the end some first shall find themselves last, but also to accord these laborers the highest justification, such as it is, for their mercenary expectation that they ought to receive more pay than the rest (v. 12). Jesus lets this group alone work the entire day.

The moment we ask what is meant by the denarius we must consider a variety of interpretations. The interpretation of this detail necessarily involves the entire parable and centers in the main thing Jesus intends to teach. Thus, if the denarius is Christ himself as our sacrifice, the parable merely says that in the end all workers will be alike, no matter whether some were mercenary and murmured when they received their pay. We have the same result when the denarius is thought to mean the image of God, or as many still think, eternal life. This view leads those who interpret thus to dissociate the words about the first and the last spoken in 19:30 and 20:16 from the parable, or they interpret these words so that the first become last only by receiving a rebuke, and the last first by receiving no rebuke. Then Jesus should have said, "Thus there will be neither first nor last, but all will be alike." It should not be difficult to see that these interpretations are unacceptable. How can anyone who has Christ, the divine image, or eternal life, murmur in the end? What can any man expect to receive more (v. 10) than these treasures? If this "more" is to be an especial degree of glory in heaven, the parable itself in no way mentions this glory. Then, too, these interpretations teach that by our labor we earn Christ, the image, or life eternal, a doctrine that is contrary to the teaching of Christ and of the Scriptures.

In the face of this Luther gives up the effort to interpret the denarius: *Man muss nicht achten, was Pfennig oder Groschen sei.* Few have cared to follow him. Melanchthon, Luther's associate, found the solution. The denarius stands for the temporal blessings, the *bona temporalia,* of the work in the church; and the goodness ("because I am good," v. 15) is life eternal and grants the *bona spiritualia.* The laborers who regard themselves first receive only the former and thus become last; the rest, who are considered last, receive both *bona* and are thus made first. No man who enters the visible church and accepts the call to work in this church shall be left without his due pay. The Lord will not have it said that any man worked for him without pay. The blessings of even an outward connection with the church are many. All her associations and her influences are highly beneficial. They shield us against evils that ravage the world and cause endless harm; they surround us with the highest morality and with all that is best for mind and for heart in this life. And often the church offers social, business, and other advantages of no mean value. They are all included in the denarius of the parable. But eternal life is not one of these.

"He sent them into his vineyard," and this made them κλητοί, placed them among the called. In the epistles the called are always those who truly believe, but in the Gospels those who are invited to believe, who thus, after all, may not believe. These laborers are the members of the church who join her ranks and aid in her work, who thus have every opportunity to become true believers but who also may remain only lip Christians, mere outward adherents. These first laborers picture members of the latter type. They worked beside the other laborers as though they, too, were believers, but what they really were the end of the parable reveals.

3) **And having gone out around the third hour, he saw others standing in the market place idle, and to those he said, Do you, too, go into the vineyard, and whatever is right I will give you. ·And they went on. Again having gone out around the sixth and the ninth hour, he did likewise. Now around the eleventh, having gone out, he found others standing, and he says to them, Why are you standing the whole day idle? And they say to him, Because no one did hire us. He says to them, Go you, too, into the vineyard.**

All these laborers who were hired from the third to the eleventh hour form one class, for in the end none of these murmur. In the evening there are only two groups: one that murmurs, and one that does not. This brings up the question regarding the hours, on which again we find a most serious difference of views which interlock with the various interpretations of the denarius and affect the gist of the entire parable and greatly multiply the interpretations. The hours have been referred to the eras of the kingdom beginning with Adam and extending to the apostles, or to the conversion of the Gentiles. Luther calls this *Geschwaetz* with which to kill time. Often the hours are regarded as the different periods in an individual's life, childhood being the early morning, and so on. But many die in childhood and in youth and never get to bear the burden and the heat of the day. The parable certainly also applies to the apostles and to them as "first" and thus as the laborers who were hired in the early morning. But they were of different ages and many far younger persons had been led to follow Jesus. So this interpretation breaks down.

The parable speaks of only a single day, and the hours are viewed in relation to the evening. Into this brief day with its daylight of twelve hours all the workers in all the ages of the Christian Church are

placed. The one or more hours they work do not refer
to time but to accomplishment. The hours thus measure the amount of each man's labor. Nor does this
indicate mere quantity over against quality. Some do
more that is of value in a single day of their lives than
others do in a whole year. A person who suffers martyrdom as a child endures more of the burden and the
heat of the day than a church member who lives long,
quiet years entirely undisturbed. The ἀγορά is necessarily the world, for what is not in the kingdom is
outside of it.

4) The second group of laborers is sent to the
vineyard as was the first; the call of God is always the
same. But in the parable the stress is laid on the work
which this call involves. A point worth noting, however, is the fact that beginning with this second group
of laborers, no contract is made regarding wages. This
belongs to the chief point of the parable, namely that
even the first shall be last if they work in the kingdom
with the spirit voiced by Peter, "What shall we get for
what we do?" Without themselves mentioning wages,
the owner promises to give them what is δίκαιον, "right"
when judged by the proper standard. Even in connections such as this δίκαιος is always forensic. Without
saying another word these men go to work.

5) This action is repeated at the time of the sixth
and the ninth hours. God keeps calling laborers into
his vineyard of the church. But he has his fixed hours
for this. The owner does not stay in the market place
all day. We are called when *God* is ready not when *we*
decide to be called.

6) Even at the eleventh hour, when only one short
hour of the workday is left, the owner goes out and for
the last time finds laborers "standing," i. e., idle and
not yet employed in his vineyard. As in v. 3, the perfect participle ἑστῶτας has its present sense. Since this
is a parable, a story arranged solely for the purpose of

illustrating something, it allows such improbabilities as that laborers should be hired for only part of a day, down to a part as short as one hour. Whenever such improbable points appear in parables (and they certainly appear often) they serve to turn the mind the more to what the parable seeks to convey and to keep before us the fact that the parable is only a parable that has been composed for no other purpose.

In the case of these laborers the hiring is accompanied by a rebuke: "Why are you standing the whole day idle?" Eleven hours out of twelve wasted. Through a fault of theirs they will be able to do so little for the kingdom. Here especially we must remember that the hours refer to the measure of accomplishment. The figure of the hours will lead into insuperable difficulties when this is not done. The rebuke is pronounced only on these laborers who are the worst idlers. This is another feature of parables that should be noted. The rebuke administered to the last laborers is intended also for the others who idled, but not for so long a time. The parable would be overloaded with detail, and its main point would thus be obscured if every minor point were actually illustrated. So some points are left to inference. None of us are justified in decreasing our accomplishment by as much as one hour's idleness would picture.

The owner at last "found" these idlers. *He* found them, which means that all the credit for even the little work they did belongs to him and not to them. If *he* had not gone out at this late hour when no ordinary employer goes out to hire workmen, these laborers would never have accomplished anything. Grace is so wonderful that any human illustration must be strained in its portrayal.

7) The question asked by the owner of the vineyard really has no answer. Yet these idlers offer a reply. They present an excuse where no real excuse

can be made. They shift the blame from themselves to the owner of the vineyard. In the parable he is the only employer and not one among several. "No one hired us" means, "neither thou nor any of thy agents." The reason this statement receives no answer is due to the fact that it has already been most thoroughly answered by this owner's going out to his laborers in the early morning and then at three additional times. The fault, then, for not finding these idlers sooner is evidently not his.

Here the parable stops. It does not say where these idlers had spent the eleven hours, so that they were not "found" before this time. We have no right to extend the story beyond the limits set by Jesus as is done when some say that the owner passed these laborers at three different times and that they refused his call to work until the eleventh hour. We cannot regard the reply of these laborers as being quite in place. This view assumes that the hours picture the time of our present lives, which has already been shown to be untenable. We are pointed to the heathen who can enter the vineyard only after the gospel reaches them, which is, perhaps, late in their lives. What are we to say about Christian lands where the gospel is constantly preached? What is the situation concerning the children in heathen lands who were, perhaps, brought into the church in infancy? Even by making the hours picture various periods in an individual's life it is quite impossible to defend the excuse of these laborers and to say it really exonerates them. In all the parables the excuses made never excuse but do the reverse.

Just as this owner hires the laborers who insist on making a verbal contract for their wages, so he hires those who offer an empty excuse for their long idleness. This pictures God's grace, who takes us into the work of his church despite many a fault. The idea is not that we may continue our faulty ideas and ways, but that the actual contact with him and his blessed church and work will remove such initial faults. The best texts omit the clause, "and whatever is right you shall receive." So we have this gradation: a fixed contract (v. 2), a general promise of what is right (v. 4), the mere order to go to work. We shall see that already the latter is more than sufficient, and that insistence on the first is a serious mistake.

8) **Now, evening having come, the Lord of the vineyard says to his steward, Call the laborers and duly give them the pay, beginning from the last to the first.** Now the climax of the parable begins. The evening is a natural accompaniment of the hours and thus is neither the last judgment nor the end of each individual's life. The fact that the hours plus the evening do not refer to time becomes evident when payment is made. The denarius paid at evening constitutes the temporal blessings connected with our Christian profession and work, and these blessings are made ours already during the entire time that we work. That is why the parable condenses everything into a single day. The hours that end at evening represent what each of us does in the work of the church, and certainly our accomplishment varies greatly (irrespective of the actual time spent in our efforts). But what does God do? Every one of us gets his denarius; every one enjoys the same temporal benefits that are connected with life in the church. They come to the new convert exactly as they do to the old, to the preacher as well as to the layman, to the child as well as to the octogenarian.

All interpreters recognize that Christ is the ἐπίτροπος. All God's blessings come to us through this one and only Mediator. Throughout the Scriptures he is presented as the Judge of our work, hence also here. Those who think that the denarius is eternal life, of course, regard the evening as the final judgment or the hour of death.

Even in this verse this cannot be the sense, for eternal
life is never earned by any man's work. The combination of ἀπό with δός (δίδωμι) means, "give what is due."
Eternal life is never due anyone either at the time of its
first bestowal in conversion or at the time of its full
enjoyment when the believer enters heaven. "Duly
give" seems to apply only to the first group of laborers
with whom an explicit contract was made; but it really
applies to all the rest, too, because the owner of the
vineyard (now called its "lord" because he decides
everything) bound himself to do what was "right."
And he is not a haggler as is the first group of laborers;
he is "good," generous and magnanimous, and pays
accordingly when men trust his goodness. The commentary on ἀπόδος is found in v. 13-15.

On the aorist ἀρξάμενος see R. 1126; it is punctiliar,
and its action precedes the paying, each group is first
called forward and then paid the money. The order
followed when the hiring was done is reversed in the
paying off. The parable has in view that the laborers
who were hired first shall see how the lord of the vineyard deals with the others. If they had been paid off
first they would have gone their way and never found
out what the other men received. Because in life we
always compare ourselves and our merits with others
and thus only too often feel that by comparison the
Lord is treating us unjustly, this feature was necessary
in the parable. Matters are so arranged that the first
laborers have the opportunity to compare their wage
with that received by the rest.

9) **And when those about the eleventh hour
came they received a denarius each. And when the
first came they supposed that they would receive
more; and they, too, received a denarius each.** The
fact that the other three groups also came in due order
does not need to be stated. The laborers are now
divided into two opposite groups: those who are satis-

fied, and those who are not. Those who were hired
first beheld how the others were paid off. They were
surprised to see each of the eleventh hour men get a
denarius, a full day's wage for a single hour's work;
ἀνά is used in the distributive sense. These men had
neither a contract nor a promise of any kind. By paying them as he did the lord of the vineyard certainly
showed his generous character.

10) Those hired first make their comparison with
those hired last. It was not necessary to bring in the
other three groups. In a case such as this the most
obvious is chosen. Having worked three hours longer
than the second group, the first, if they were so inclined, could, by comparing themselves with them, still
imagine that they would receive more. In the Greek
the ὅτι clause of indirect discourse retains the original
tense of the thought, "We shall receive more," after a
past tense; the English has a conformation of tenses,
"thought that they would receive more." The force of
the parable is weakened when the supposition is introduced that the first group loafed at its work and actually accomplished no more than the last group because
these late-comers worked most strenuously. The very
opposite is the case; the hours of work state the measure of accomplishment.

11) **Now when they received it they started to**
**murmur against the houselord, saying, These last**
**worked only one hour, and thou didst make them**
**equal to us who bore the burden of the day and its**
**heat.** The aorist λαβόντες cannot mean that these
men did not actually receive the money but only had it
offered to them and refused to take it. The two preceding aorists, ἔλαβον, shut out this view. These men
took their money and then started to complain, ἐγόγγυζον,
an inchoative imperfect, which pictures their action
and intimates that something followed and ended it.
Here, it ought to be plain, the possibility of making the

denarius equal eternal life is removed. The thought
that a saint in heaven may murmur against God is
appalling.

12) So important is this complaint that its very
words are introduced. It charges the houselord with
rank injustice and voices open envy of the other workers. The effort to soften this complaint by taking the
sin out of it is misdirected. This is not an expression
of surprise and of admiration of the way in which the
last group of laborers is treated. It does not help this
view to make the denarius equal the degree of glory in
heaven, for these degrees differ and are *not* equal. Quite
often οὗτοι is derogatory: "These" who amount to next
to nothing. But ἐποίησαν cannot mean that they worked
and really accomplished nothing; nor is it necessary to
reduce their labors to nil. They worked, but "only one
hour," the idea of "only" lying in the expression. The
owner's injustice lies in the fact that he made "them
equal to us" (ἡμῖν αὐτούς, abutted for emphasis). The
contrast between us and them is made stronger than it
would be by setting the twelve hours over against the
one. We hear what they bore: "the burden of the
(whole) day," this entire load of the day; and on top
of that "its heat," its burning, καύσων, which is not the
sirocco, *Glutwind,* but the scorching sun during the
middle of the day. The eleventh-hour men felt no
burden at all by working only one lone hour, and they
scarcely sweat, for this hour came in the cool of the
evening.

The parable makes this charge against God as
strong as it can be made in the minds of those who do
not unlearn Peter's question (19:27). Peter is here
shown the end of the road to which his question would
lead. Judas, too, thought that he ought to get more
out of Jesus and he got it, stolen money, and then the
thirty pieces of silver. This charge must be put into
words in the parable because it must be refuted to the

last letter. So jealous is God for his absolute justice that in several parables this justice is vindicated beyond all question.

**13) But he answered and said to one of them: Fellow, I am not treating thee unjustly. Didst thou not agree with me on a denarius? Take up thine own and be gone! But it is my will to give to this last just as to thee! Is it not lawful for me to do what I will with my own? or is thy eye wicked because I on my part am good?**

The answer is made individual in order that each one may ask, "Lord, is it I?" See the same individualization in 22:11. We do not understand how some commentators can regard this reply as a mild rebuke or a *freundliche Zurechtweisung*. These words are like the crushing blows of a hammer. They are fired like a volley. Each brief sentence snaps like a whiplash. When the address ἑταῖρε is compared with φίλε, the force of this word is not understood. Trench is on the right track when he calls this a word of evil omen and points to 22:12 and to 26:50. It is not the word itself that determines its force but the tone of the connection in which it is used. Perhaps our English "fellow" will do. A flat denial repudiates the charge of injustice: "I do thee no injustice!" While οὐκ ἀδικῶ is a durative present it has almost the force of a perfect, R. 881. The very terseness of the expression shows indignation.

Instead of using a mild γάρ with an explanation as to why no injustice is being done, this lord of the vineyard utters a dramatic, self-answering question which is again terse and crushing: "Didst thou not agree with me on a denarius?" the genitive of price, δηναρίου, R. 510. This fellow was one of those who insisted that the wages be fixed and sealed before they would go to work. That showed his true character. If he now got in full exactly what he had so carefully bargained for, what right had he to cry, "injustice"? It was kindness on the part of the lord that he was at all employed. Did he not know how long a workday was, and how warmly the sun would shine? He insisted that the denarius be specified in a regular verbal contract — had it not been paid him in full? During his work in the vineyard he could have learned something about its lord. He failed to do so; but he will now learn.

14) The declaration and the question are followed by an equally effective command: "Take up thine own and be gone!" This lord is done with him. And this is the climax of the parable. This ὕπαγε cannot mean, "Go and be content with thy wages!" It is exactly like the imperative found in 4:10, and always means to leave, cf., 8:13; 19:21. Luther gives the sense with his *von dannen traben*, "trot along." This is a man who works in the church for what he can get out of the church. He has what he worked for — and nothing more. He is treated exactly as the hypocrites are who are mentioned in 6:2, 5: "Verily, I say unto you, They have received their reward!" i. e., are paid in full (we have the same ἀπό in ἀπέχουσι that we had in ἀπόδος in verse 8). Those who will learn nothing about divine grace even when they are working in the church will finally be left without this grace; those who are set on justice and refuse to go beyond it shall finally have justice.

Then this lord deals with this fellow's envy. He could not see why another should receive a whole denarius for only one hour's work when he himself worked a whole day of twelve hours for the same sum. But this envy really assails the lord of the vineyard and would forbid him to exercise grace when bestowing his bounty. Such a thing as grace, which gives what is not earned, dare not be shown. To be sure, men who are set on justice have no understanding of grace — which seems to them to be injustice. Since they spurn

grace and condemn it when they see it exercised in
regard to others, grace cannot be bestowed upon them.
Here again the parable makes it plain that eternal life,
which is given out of pure grace, cannot and will not be
given to those who condemn grace.   In v. 10 the supposition that they would receive more than the denarius
the others received means more according to justice, as
having earned it; and not more by grace and unearned.

But if this lord vindicates his untarnished justice
he defends his grace even more.   The grace of God is
his fairest, noblest attribute, if we should be permitted
to state it in this way.   He always vindicates its exercise.   Any grace, that means any unearned favor, is
absolutely within the will and the power of him who
grants this favor.   No man dare dictate to him regarding what he must or must not do in any case of bestowal
of this favor.   Grace is truly sovereign.   Anyone who
appreciates grace as what it really is can only praise
and glorify whenever he sees it granted.   And every
man who charges such grace with injustice when with
evil, envious eyes he sees it bestowed on others, only
insults the Giver of that grace and makes any bestowal
of it upon himself impossible.   So here his lord declares the sovereignty of his grace:   "But it is my will
($\theta\acute{\epsilon}\lambda\omega$) to give to this last man just as to thee," i. e., the
same amount though he never earned it.   The un-
earned eleven twelfths are grace.   And the same was
true in the case of the other laborers; each unearned
fraction was a pure gift, and that means grace.   Any
grace is subject wholly and solely to the giver's will.
Let evil-minded men rebel as much as they will, this
glorious fact remains.

15)   Now we have the refutation of the charge that
grace is ever unjust.   The absence of connectives marks
the sharpness of all these terse sentences.   "Is it not
lawful to do what I will with mine own," i. e., freely to
give it where I decide?   The question answers itself.

There is no law, no principle of right in heaven or on earth to forbid this sovereign exercise of grace.  There is only one alternative, the very opposite of law and right, that could ever interfere with the free exercise of grace, and that alternative is rank wickedness, the selfish wickedness of greedy envy: "or is thy eye wicked (πονηρός) because I on my part am good (ἀγαθός)" by freely granting gifts that are unearned?  This question, too, carries with it its own self-evident answer. While the first question vindicates the right of grace, the second question pronounces the verdict upon him who accuses this grace.  This sword is two-edged.  The charge of injustice against this lord recoils upon the accuser's head.

The application of all this to God and to the exercise of his grace needs no elaboration.  Even in the temporal good which our connection with the church brings to us great portions of grace appear, which we have not earned.  Those who rejoice in these gifts of grace learn the joy of receiving the greatest grace of all, namely the gift of eternal life.  Those who object to grace, who stipulate that so much work will be done for so much pay, shall end as they have stipulated, shall, indeed, get their stipulated pay in full, and shall then be told to go.  The pearls of grace are never thrown before the wicked, self-righteous swine.  To accuse and to condemn grace is the surest way to lose grace.

16) The parable is finished.  All that remains is to repeat the thesis of which it forms the exposition, the repetition making it certain that the main thought and the warning shall not be overlooked.  **Thus shall the last be first, and the first last.**  "Thus," as the parable has shown.  The order is the reverse of that found in 19:30, and the word "many" is omitted.  These seem to be only formal differences; compare also Luke 13:30.  Perhaps Jesus wanted ἔσχατοι with its tone of warning to be the last word in the sentence.  The in-

terpretation is, of course, the same as that given in
19:30. One view calls for some attention: when the
last becomes first, and the first last, all difference will
be wiped out, for then all will be alike; doing much in
the church brings no advantage, and doing little loses
no advantage. But we cannot believe that Jesus would
teach such indifference.

The question as to whether the sentence, "for many
are called ones, but few are chosen ones," was uttered
by Jesus at this point or was transferred from 22:14
by some copyist, must be left to the text critics. The
textual evidence in favor of retaining these words is by
no means insignificant; the only question is whether it
is sufficient. One thing is certain, the words are fitting in this place, and no one has as yet explained how
they could have been inserted from 22:14.

The first who become last are only κλητοί, which, in
the Gospels, means the *invitati* who enter the visible
church and no more. They are not among the ἐκλεκτοί,
those who finally enter heaven. These "elect ones" are
plainly the last who become first; while the "called
ones" are the first who become last. Κλητοί and ἐκλεκτοί
are passive verbals and much like past passive participles. The agent back of both verbals is God. Some
note only that certain persons are thus designated: "the
called," "the elected"; others see that the call itself and
the election itself are predicated by these terms, that
in κλητοί lie κλῆσις and καλεῖν, and in ἐκλεκτοί lie ἐκλογή and
ἐκλέγεσθαι. Thus all that the Scriptures say regarding
both acts of God belongs into these terms, for both acts
terminate in persons.

The parable itself is objective, and its summary as
stated in 19:30 and 20:16 is likewise expressed in an
entirely objective form. The question, "To which of
these two classes do I belong?" I am to answer by examining this parable. By means of this parable Jesus
makes it easy for me to find the answer. The form of

the parable, together with its preamble and its conclusion points a warning: See to it that thou art not
among those that end as last, as only called, but among
those that end as first and thus elect. The called and
the elect thus constitute opposites; the first end in hell,
the second in heaven. Why this difference? Because
the called rejected grace and resisted it to the end
although this grace was all about them. God did not
exclude them from the elect, they shut themselves out.
The call takes place in time, the divine election took
place in eternity. This should not confuse us. God is
not bound, as we are, to time and its succession. He
sees all of time already before time, in eternity. "The
foundation of God standeth sure, having this seal, The
Lord knoweth them that are his," II Tim. 2:19. This
knowledge is absolute and eternal. It is the knowledge
*cum affectu et effectu,* he knows the elect as his own
and cannot and could not know the others thus. The
warning presented in the parable suggests our responsibility. If we close eye and heart against grace, no
matter how high we stand in the church or how much
we work, we shall lose life eternal.


## XVI

### Christ on His Way to Jerusalem, Chapter 20:17-34

17) Note how plainly Matthew marks the sections
by references to places: 16:13, the coming to Caesarea
Philippi; 17:24, the coming to Capernaum; 19:1, leaving for Judea; now 20:17, going to Jerusalem; then
21:1, entering Jerusalem. **And, while going up to
Jerusalem, Jesus took to himself** (the same verb as
in 1:24 and in 2:21) **the twelve disciples in private
and on the road said to them: Lo, we are going
up to Jerusalem, and the Son of man shall be delivered to the high priests and scribes, and they**

**shall condemn him to death and shall deliver him to the Gentiles to mock and to scourge and to crucify; and on the third day he shall be raised up.**

The journey through Perea on the east side of the Jordan is finished, the river had been crossed near Jericho, and now the road led directly toward Jerusalem. Mark 10:32 describes the emotions of the little band that thus, with Jesus leading the way, moved toward the evil city. Instead of allaying their fear and amazement, Jesus takes the Twelve to himself in private somewhere along the road, away from other disciples (Salome, cf., v. 20; and other women with her, Luke 8:2, 3; and most likely a number of men); and now he tells them far more plainly than before (16:21; 17:22, 23) what shall occur. This announcement warrants the exclamation "lo"; going up to Jerusalem for all these things is astonishing indeed.

18) In 16:21 Jesus points to the necessity of these things ($\delta\epsilon\hat{\iota}$); in 17:22 he says that they are impending ($\mu\acute{\epsilon}\lambda\lambda\epsilon\iota$); now he states that they are on the very way into them: "we are going up," i.e., right now, and Jerusalem is now quite near. The Twelve are going with him, and this means that they shall be there when all these things happen, they shall witness them. The fact that they shall be immensely affected by it all goes without saying. As he did in 17:22, Jesus calls himself "the Son of man" (see 8:20), man and yet far above man. God's incarnate Son. The main verbs are future tenses and state what shall occur, occur without fail. In 17:22 the deliverance is made "into the hands of men." This is now specified first as a deliverance to the Sanhedrin of the Jews and following that a deliverance by the Sanhedrin to the Gentiles (v. 19). The part the Sanhedrin shall play is thus advanced beyond the statement made in 16:21. Only two terms are here used to describe the Sanhedrin, on which see 16:21 and 2:4. A new point is the fact that

the Sanhedrin shall subject Jesus to a trial and thus "condemn him to death."

19) Since the Sanhedrin has lost the power to inflict the death penalty, Jesus reveals that this Jewish court "shall deliver him up to the Gentiles," which can mean only the Roman governor Pilate and the men under his authority. The result is stated by εἰς τό and aorist infinitives. While εἰς τό is regularly used to express purpose and intention, it at times broadens so as to include contemplated or even actual result. "To mock," etc., thus means that the deliverance to the Gentiles will result in Jesus' being actually mocked, etc. Whereas Mark 10:34 adds the spitting upon and mentions only the killing, Matthew includes the spitting upon in the mockery and states the actual mode of this killing by using the terrible verb σταυρῶσαι, "to crucify." Matthew is the only evangelist who has preserved this word in Jesus' predictions of his death. While scourging often preceded crucifixion, it was more often a separate penalty (10:17; II Cor. 11:25; Heb. 11:36). Luke 18:32, 33 increases the specifications that ended in killing and shows how explicitly Jesus revealed his passion. Again, in words unchanged, Jesus sets over against this black background the glorious assurance: "and on the third day he shall be raised up," see 16:21; 17:23. Matthew confines himself to the facts of the announcement. The manner in which it was received is a minor matter to him.

20) **Then went to him the mother of Zebedee's sons together with her sons, doing obeisance and asking something from him. And he said to her, What dost thou wish? She says to him, Say that these my two sons shall sit, one on thy right, and one on thy left in thy kingdom.** Mark 10:35 mentions only the sons James and John; but from Matthew's account we see that their mother was the prime mover and that her sons supported her request. This

was Salome, called "the mother of Zebedee's sons,"
most likely because Zebedee, the father, was dead, at
least we hear nothing more about him in the Gospels.
The view that Salome was a sister of the Virgin Mary
is an interesting surmise, yet the evidence on which
it rests is not complete.

James and John belonged to the inner circle of three
apostles who were distinguished by Jesus himself
(Mark 5:37; Matt. 17:1; 26:37). Perhaps it was for
this reason that their mother conceived the idea of
having her two sons placed above the rest. So she and
they together, on finding an opportunity to speak to
Jesus alone, make the attempt to secure this supreme
honor. Salome does the speaking. In Oriental fashion she makes obeisance as one does who is preferring
a request before a great king. It is only a part of this
attitude toward Jesus as such a king that the request
is at first indefinite: "something from him," as Mark
states it, "Do for us whatsoever we shall ask of thee."
We must not read τί as "a certain thing" (our versions); it is indefinite. The surmise that Salome
wanted to bind Jesus in advance by promising her the
favor before he knew what it would be, is untenable.
So also is the deduction that Salome felt that Jesus
might have some hesitation or objection if he knew the
nature of the request in advance. The situation is that
Salome regards Jesus as a potentate who is able to
grant any request without needing to know what it
might be. Great kings and emperors had done things
such as that; we have such an offer made by Herod
in 14:7.

21) But Jesus declines to assume this royal role.
Salome betrays only what blinded her eyes and those
of all the disciples to Jesus' words concerning his passion and his resurrection. Even in Acts 1:6 they still
think that Jesus will establish an outward earthly Messianic kingdom. When this kingdom becomes reality.

Salome wants her sons to have the highest places in it. So Jesus asks her what she wants. He certainly avoids binding himself in advance. To promise something without a clear statement as to what this is to be, is morally wrong. Even when we are solemnly assured that the thing will not be wrong against God or our conscience, this would put our conscience into the keeping of another. If the promise is one that we may rightly make, then every reason why it should not be stated openly disappears. This is the case still more when we are to seal the promise with an oath. The example of Jesus points the right course.

But Jesus knew what Salome intended to ask (John 2:24, 25). This makes his example of first desiring to know what Salome wanted him to promise only the more emphatic. But it also involves something else. He wants her to state her desire because of the explanation he must make to her and to her sons in regard to their desire. With all readiness Salome responds. Matthew's εἰπέ and Mark's δός are substantially the same: to say or declare (aorist, once for all) is the same as to give or grant. Yet εἰπέ is what Salome most likely said. Like a great king Jesus is to make this decree (i. e., grant). She assumes that in his coming kingdom Jesus can do whatever he may please. Usually the disciples expected too little of Jesus, they showing themselves as men of little faith. Here is a woman of such faith that she actually expects too much of Jesus.

Salome and her sons regard Jesus as some royal personage who is about to step out of the obscurity in which he has thus far lived and is presently to ascend his glorious throne. With far-reaching foresight Salome wants to pre-empt for her two sons the very highest honors which shall then be forthcoming. Since they were the first to see the near approach of the glorious future, the first to honor Jesus by acknowledging

it, and the first to ask for positions in the kingdom
that shall be, all three confidently expect that, like the
king they make him, Jesus will grant this early and
honorable request.  This request is that Salome's sons
may sit "one on thy right, and one on thy left in the
kingdom" (Mark, "in thy glory").  Salome sees the
great throneroom with the king sitting in state and all
the royal court assembled to do him honor, and on his
right hand and on his left the chief ministers of the
king who are next to him in glory and reflect the light
shed upon them from the throne.  So Solomon honored his mother Bathsheba, I Kings 2:19; compare Ps.
45:9.  So Micaiah saw the heavenly court, the Lord
on his throne, the host of heaven at right and left,
I Kings 22:19; II Chron. 18:18.  In Neh. 8:4 Ezra
stands in the pulpit with his assistants to right and to
left.  Compare also Zech. 4:3, 11-14.  Whereas in a
case of division and judgment the right signifies honor
and acceptance and the left shame and rejection, in a
royal court both sides are places of honor, the left being
only slightly less glorious than the right.

The Greek idiom in the ἐκ seems strange to us.  It
means literally "from" thy right and "from" thy left
and designates the sides "from" the person's hands,
whereas the English looks to those sides and speaks of
what is "at" or "on" them.  Which of the sons is to
have the respective position is apparently left to the
decision of Jesus.

It is most remarkable that Salome asks nothing for
herself; her glory will be the fact that she is the mother
of such sons.  This request has some foundation in
19:28, but there all the thrones are equal.

Despite all its fault, Salome's request contains
something worth noting.  All about us men seek the
world's honor and high places, here are three persons
who put the βασιλεία and the δόξα of Christ above everything else.  The wish of Salome, duly purified, has been

seconded by many a mother who prayed for her son
that he might serve Christ in some high work in his
church.

22) **But Jesus answered and said: You do not
know what you are asking. Are you able to drink
the cup which I myself am about to drink? They
say to him, We are able.** Luther says that Jesus
treated the presumptuous pride of the Pharisees with
severity, but the ambition of these disciples he treats
with gentleness; for it springs from faith and needs
only to be purified. We see that he is addressing the
two disciples, which explains the fact that Mark leaves
out their mother. They do not know what they are
asking because they are ignorant as to what their request involves in the real kingdom he is establishing.
"They sought the exaltation but did not see the step."
Augustine. The idea is not that, if they knew, they
would not seek those high places, but that then they
would not make a request which plainly reveals their
mistaken idea of the kingdom and of the manner in
which its high places are bestowed. On the distinction
between the active αἰτεῖν and the middle αἰτεῖσθαι see R.
805. In v. 20 αἰτοῦσα is active, Salome asks devoutly as
one asks of God; Jesus uses the middle αἰτεῖσθε, for this
asking was really in the nature of a business transaction (B.-D. 316, 2).

So Jesus proceeds to enlighten them. He asks
whether they are able to drink (πιεῖν, aorist: drink completely, empty) the cup he himself (emphatic ἐγώ) is
about to drink (πίνειν, present tense: about to set to his
lips and proceed to empty). By this cup Jesus refers
to suffering (John 18:11: Matt. 26:39, 42), and to
drink means to accept and to endure the suffering.
Matthew is content to record the one question, Mark
10:38 adds a second that employs a different figure but
has the same meaning. With this question Jesus points
out to James and to John that the way to greatness in

his kingdom is not, as they think, by means of a mere decree on the part of Jesus but by way of the deepest humiliation (Luke 14:11) ; and this is due to the spiritual nature of his kingdom. Do these two realize that? Their ready, all too ready reply, "We are able," reveals that they do not.

23) Patiently Jesus continues: **He says to them: My cup you shall drink; but to sit on my right and on my left is not mine own to give but for whom it is prepared by my Father.** The two disciples spoke in ignorance when they said that they were able. They did not realize what that cup and its drinking involved. Here, as in the Lord's Supper, the cup is the common grammatical (not rhetorical) figure of common usage which mentions the vessel instead of its contents. These disciples shall, indeed, advance to the spiritual ability of drinking Christ's cup. So Jesus declares that they shall drink his cup. Here Jesus identifies the sufferings of all his disciples which are endured for his sake and the gospel's with his own sufferings, including his entire passion. I Pet. 4:13: "Rejoice, inasmuch as ye are partakers of Christ's sufferings"; II Cor. 4:10: "Always bearing about in the body the dying of the Lord Jesus"; Gal. 6:17: "I bear in my body the marks of the Lord Jesus." John 15:20; Matt. 10:24, 25. The cup thus denotes only the suffering as such and does not include the distinction that the suffering of Jesus was exceptional because it was expiatory and atoning while the suffering of the disciples is only confessional. In the case of the disciples this suffering does not necessarily involve death by martyrdom. It did in the case of James (Acts 12:2) but not in the case of John who was simply "our brother and companion in tribulation, and in the kingdom and patience of Jesus Christ." Rev. 1:9, who was imprisoned (Acts 4:3, 21; 5:18), scourged (Acts 5:40), had his life endangered (Acts 5:33), in exile (Rev.

1:9). In regard to such severe suffering Paul exceeded the rest (II Cor. 11:23-33), he also died a martyr's death.

In μέν and δέ we have a good example of the use of these particles for balancing two clauses. The way to greatness in the kingdom lies along the path of suffering. But many besides James and John will walk this path. Who, then, shall attain the highest places remains a question. James and John are not shut out. But this is certain, and they must know it, the seats in glory at Jesus' right and left — and such seats will, indeed, be found there — are not bestowed after the fashion of earthly monarchs, as grants to favorites by the mere whim or will of the grantor. They are "not mine own to give," i. e., merely to grant. The according of these glory seats is a far higher matter. To sit thus is "for whom it is prepared by my Father," the present tense being used timelessly. The relative οἷς contains its own antecedent τούτοις (not τούτων, R. 721), for the dative as well as the genitive may be used with ἐστίν to denote possession.

The eternal counsel of the Father, which fixed all things in regard to the kingdom, included also the disposition of these glory seats. With this counsel and disposition Jesus is in full accord. Jesus is now carrying out the Father's counsel of grace and thus says regarding these glory seats that they are not at this late date his own to dispose of in some way of his own apart from the Father. Their very preparation God has attended to long ago. Who will occupy these seats Jesus does not intimate; perhaps this knowledge was withheld from Jesus during his state of humiliation. Hence we cannot be certain whether only two will occupy those seats; perhaps more will be seated there.

Was Salome disappointed; her sons, too? Even Mark is silent, and we know that Matthew is still less inclined to record emotions.

**24)** **And having heard it, the ten were indignant concerning the two brothers. But Jesus, having called them forward, said: You know that the rulers of the Gentiles lord it over them, and the great exercise authority over them. Not thus shall it be among you; but he who wills to be great among you shall be your servant, and he who wills to be first shall be your slave; even as the Son of man did not come to be served but to serve and to give his life as a ransom in place of many.** Here we see how Jesus turned the incident regarding Salome and her sons to good account for all his disciples. How the ten heard of it is not indicated. Did James and John tell them on the supposition that the places would after all be theirs? Mark says that the ten "began" to be indignant and that Jesus at once intervened. The ten prove themselves no better than the two. Many feel wronged by the success of others when similar success on their part appears quite without wrong to them.

**25)** With all calmness Jesus gives the explanation which the Twelve needed. All of them were misconceiving his kingdom and following a wrong principle in regard to greatness in this kingdom. They were degrading it to the level of heathen kingdoms. So Jesus points out the vast difference. He points to what we all know: that heathen rulers of all kinds oppress their subjects and thus maintain their rulership; come down on them with authority and thus maintain their greatness. In both verbs κατά means that from their high places these rulers and great men come "down" with power and authority on those beneath them, *herrschen hoch her, ueben hoch her Gewalt,* Lange. Jesus states only the well-known fact and does not say that these actions are wrong. At least Rom. 13:1 is clear regarding the institution of government; anarchy and rebellion are not countenanced by the Scriptures. Jesus purposely instances the Gentile governors and rulers not the theocracy of the Jews which was of a different order; he confines his comparison to secular states. The Jews were at this time themselves under Gentile rulers; in fact, Jesus himself was, and we know that he bade the Jews give to Cæsar what was Cæsar's. So by his present description of Gentile rulers he does not intend to remove his disciples from such governmental authority.

26) But while he thus allows it to obtain in its own secular sphere, he confines it to that. In fact, "not thus shall it be among you," demands the very opposite. How it shall be is then stated with two clauses that match the two regarding the Gentiles. But whereas Jesus began with "the rulers" and advanced to "the great" (the plurals indicating classes), he now begins with the one who wills to be "great" and then rises to the very pinnacle by speaking of the one who wills to be "first" (the singulars individualizing). Moreover, to be great, to be first, is open to all: ὃς ἐάν with the subjunctive, "he who wills (shall will)," no matter who he may be; Jesus is vividly thinking of such cases. Now the Gentile idea of greatness is inverted, turned upside down, the pyramid resting on its apex, the great man not sitting atop the lesser men, but the great man bearing the lesser men on his back. "Let him be your διάκονος, your ready servant." The word is nobler than δοῦλος used in v. 27. Note the two in 22:2-14. In John 2:5 we have only *diakonoi*. Compare Trench, *Synonyms*, I, 55. A *diakonos* is one who is intent on the service he is rendering to others. Thus greatness in the kingdom is measured by the readiness and the amount of blessed service rendered to Christ's people. It makes no difference whether they reward and exalt us for this service or not.

27) This idea is carried to its climax. One wills with a holy will to be "first," above even those who are "great" in the kingdom. The way in which to attain

this height is to be "your slave," δοῦλος, the humblest and lowest of all servants who actually slaves for others in the kingdom and who, despite all his slaving, is ready to remain without praise or honor.

Because this true spirit of the kingdom is absent, the Gentile spirit has often entered, and we have the Roman papacy with its lordship and authority and among Protestants little popes who dictate instead of serving or slaving. Yet, strange and paradoxical as this principle of Jesus seems, it is literally true. Greatness is measured by service and not by the power and the authority arrogated and assumed.

28) A flood of light is cast on what Jesus says about his own example, ὥσπερ, "even as." On "the Son of man" see 8:20: he who was man and yet far more than man, God's incarnate Son. Although he was infinitely great in himself, omnipotent to lord it over all, he came (in his incarnation) on a mission that was the very opposite. He could have compelled all men to be his *diakonoi*, yea, his *douloi*, but he came not "to be served," "on the contrary (ἀλλά) to serve." In both verbs we have διάκονος (διακονία) and not δοῦλος because of the divine dignity of this great Servant, a dignity which remained during his service, and because of the exalted service which he rendered. Some humble ministrations offered by his friends he accepted (Luke 8:2, 3; John 12:2, 3), but the purpose of his life was to give not to receive or to take.

Καί is epexegetical, "namely to give his life as a ransom for many." The act is voluntary, he gives of his own accord. The aorist indicates actuality. We think of the death on Calvary, and rightly so; yet in the act of giving we must include all that lies between ἦλθε and δοῦναι. Here ψυχή means life (John 10:17, 18), that which animates the σῶμα or body and is separated from it by death. Only in this specific sense can it be said to be equivalent to the reflexive pronoun "myself."

This "life" is the τιμή or "price" with which we are
bought, I Cor. 6:20. The real point lies in the object
predicate "a ransom for many," and we must combine
into one "to give his life a ransom for many." The
phrase ἀντὶ πολλῶν depends on λύτρον, C.-K. 704. The
idea is not that *Jesus* paid what the *many* should but
could not pay; for we have no ἐγώ to indicate such a
contrast.

The λύτρον (or its plural λύτρα, LXX) is the price
paid to effect the release (λύειν, the loosing) of one who
is held in some kind of bondage. This meaning is
extended to the payment for release from guilt and
penalty. The ransom becomes a payment by expiation.
Jesus uses the singular because the ransom he lays
down is his life; he could not have used the plural to
designate the kind of λύτρον he made. Whether λύτρον
is a price paid in money or an act of expiation, an expiatory sacrifice, is decided by the context. Here the
ransom is the life, i. e., the life of Jesus given into
death; the ransom is effected by the sacrifice of this
life, the shedding of Jesus' blood (26:28; Mark 14:24;
Luke 22:20; I Cor. 11:24, etc.).

The death of Jesus thus effects the ἀπολύτρωσις, "ran-
soming" of many. It is true, when men deal with each
other they may haggle about the amount of the ransom
and may end in some kind of compromise. But it is
unwarranted to transfer this to the ransom of Jesus
as though what he paid was merely accepted although
it was in reality not the full price. The justice and
the righteousness of God are never described as striking a bargain. The blood of the Lamb of God, God's
own Son, exceeds computation in the figures of a price.
The ransom he laid down by the sacrifice of himself
was so completely an equivalent for the divine claims
against the many that one must say, if he says anything, that it exceeded these claims.

Christ's ransom was paid for our sin and our guilt. John 1:29. Our sin and our guilt made us liable to the penalties due them at the hands of God; and but for the intervention of Christ's bringing his sacrificial ransom (λύτρον), release (λύειν) for us was impossible (5:26; 6:12; 9:2; 18:23-35). The ransom was offered to God, against whom we have sinned and who alone has power to inflict the penalty (10:28), and not, as Origen dreamed, to the devil; so also Jesus laid his spirit, not into Satan's, but into God's hands (Luke 23:46). "In whom we have redemption (τὴν ἀπολύτρωσιν, redemption by the payment of a ransom) through his blood (sacrifice)," Eph. 1:7; Heb. 10:5-10. Luther has stated it perfectly: "purchased and won me from all sin, from death, and from the power of the devil, not with silver or gold but with his holy, precious blood and with his innocent suffering and death."

On the root idea of ἀντί: "face to face," see R. 572, etc., who writes: "The idea of 'in the place of' or 'instead' comes where two substantives placed opposite to each other are equivalent and so may be exchanged" — thus the ransom is exchanged for the many. Here follow examples and then: "In λύτρον ἀντὶ πολλῶν (Matt. 20:28; Mark 10:45) the parallel is more exact" (i. e., than in the last example offered by R.). "These important doctrinal passages teach the substitutionary conception of Christ's death, not because ἀντί of itself means 'instead,' which is not true, but because the context renders any other resultant idea out of the question."

The efforts to overthrow these findings are to a great extent not exegetical but dogmatical — reasonings that Jesus could not have said or did not say what his words evidently do say. A. Deissmann, *Light from the Ancient East*, 332, scores "the modern dogmatic exegesis" for obscuring the ancient popular metaphors. He has in mind the orthodox exegesis. In the recently

discovered papyri Deissmann found many references
to the manumission of slaves who were freed to serve
some pagan god, and this colored his view of the atonement. It is not in accord with fact that Paul expanded
and adapted Jesus' λύτρον to the Greek world, nor that
this "ransom" was at a later time regarded as Christ's
blood. In arriving at a conclusion we must first of all
go back to the Old Testament and note its conception
of this "ransom" and then examine Christ's own words
(all of them) in regard to this term. And after obtaining these solid results we turn to see what the
papyri may have to offer, which in reality amounts to
little enough, compare C.-K. 703. To speak of "a fine
for sin" is to show a lack of good taste. To call "ransom" nothing but "rescue," and Christ's sufferings only
"something of priceless value," is to equivocate. To
take out of the Old Testament only what seems to suit
such views, is to use only a part of the evidence.

The redeemed who are bought by the ransom of
Christ's sacrifice on the cross are called "many" in
comparison with the one Son of man. Since we have
no indication in the text that Jesus has in mind especially those who accept his redemptive price by faith,
it is scarcely correct to say that "many" refers to these.
The price is paid for all men, I Tim. 2:6; compare Rom.
3:25; Eph. 1:7; I Pet. 1:18, 19; I Cor. 6:20; 7:23; Gal.
3:13; Titus 2:14; Acts 20:28. He who gave his life
a ransom for all men by that act also became our model
in the highest sense: "And walk in love, as Christ also
hath loved us, and hath given himself for us, an offering and a sacrifice to God for a sweet-smelling savor,"
Eph. 5:2. Those who follow his example will shed all
worldly ambition, will partake somewhat of the greatness of the Son of man, will be that much nearer to
him, and will share in his glory accordingly. "His
life a ransom for many" — thus Jesus led his disciples
to Jerusalem and to Calvary.

29) **And as they were going out from Jericho there followed him a great multitude.** So Jesus had crossed the Jordan and was following the usual route to Jerusalem, which led through Jericho near the Jordan. At first glance there seems to be a decided discrepancy between Matthew's account: "they going out from Jericho," and Luke's statement: "in his drawing near to Jericho." One says that these blind men were healed when Jesus left Jericho, the other says that they were cured when Jesus entered Jericho. In order to remove this supposed contradiction different efforts have been made, even to postulating three different healings. But the matter is quite simple. Jesus passed through Jericho (Luke 19:1) and, though it was late in the day, no one offered him a night's lodging. On the other side of the town Zacchæus awaits Jesus, who calls him down from the tree and then retraces his steps, goes back into Jericho and spends the night at the publican's home. It was on this return that the blind men were healed. Luke separates the two events because he wants to give a continuous account of Zacchæus without inserting into it the healing of the blind men. Matthew and Mark omit the story of Zacchæus. Thus all three evangelists are correct. The apparent contradiction fades away the moment we note *all* the facts.

30) **And lo, two blind men, sitting beside the road, when they heard that Jesus is passing by, yelled, saying, Lord, show us mercy, Son of David! The multitude, however, rebuked them to be silent; but they yelled the more, saying, Lord, show us mercy, Son of David!** After we have heard about the many miracles of Jesus, the healing of two additional men does not warrant the exclamation "lo." This interjection points to the exceptional feature of this healing, namely the fact that Jesus is addressed by the Messianic title "Son of David," that he accepts this

title before the multitude and performs the miracle as
the Son of David. The period of comparative retirement to the borders of the land, as much as possible
away from the crowds, and the reluctance to accept
Messianic titles that might stir up political and nationalistic feelings, are now past. Let the whole nation
know that he goes up to Jerusalem as the Son of David
— to die. There is now no danger of a political up-
heaval. The episode with regard to these blind men
is only the prelude to the entry into Jerusalem, at which
time Jesus again accepts the acclamation "Son of
David," shouted by thousands and expanded to its full
Messianic length, 21:9.

Mark's account offers more details; the excellency
of Matthew's record lies in the fact that here again he
keeps our eyes entirely on the main point and purpose
of this narrative. Twice in his short record "Son of
David" rings out. The nominative is regularly used
with appositions to vocatives. The fact that these
were beggars is not stated since it was only a detail;
nor is the name of one of these beggars, which Mark
preserves, stated. Luke 18:36, 37 adds the detail that
the beggars learned that the crowds on the road indicated that Jesus was passing by. Yet Matthew alone
informs us that two men were involved. The mention
of only the one by Mark and by Luke is, of course, not
intended to imply that there was only one.

A favorite hypothesis is that Matthew's Gospel is
largely drawn from Mark's, and those who hold this
view think that here Matthew misread Mark. But
Matthew was present in person on the road near Jericho and thus writes on the basis of personal and complete knowledge. It is rather easy to explain the fact
that the other evangelists pass over the second blind
man. Mark even names Bartimæus, the son of Tim-
æus. He was evidently the leader of the two and made
the most frantic efforts to attract the attention of

Jesus? The blind men could not see where Jesus was, and the noise of the crowds prevented their judging by the sound. Yet this was their one chance, and if it slipped by, they would remain blind the rest of their days. So Bartimæus got his name into the divine record because of the excessive demonstration he staged.

The aorist imperative ἐλέησον calls for an act of mercy and compassion as in 9:27; 15:22; 17:15. In the first two of these instances (9:27; 15:22) Jesus is also addressed as the Son of David, but the two blind men mentioned in 9:27 are severely forbidden to tell about their healing, and the Syrophœnician woman lives in a pagan neighborhood where the use of this title was politically harmless.

31) We learn only the fact that the crowd tried to silence the beggars and not the reason for this attempt. Of the variety of reasons which commentators suggest scarcely one commends itself. The ἵνα is like the one used in v. 33, it is elliptical and imperative, R. 994; also 933. The beggars only yell the more. Their one chance of healing shall not slip by. All three synoptists repeat their cry with its significant address, "Son of David." Mark and Luke have "Jesus" in the first cry but not in the second. Matthew has "Lord" in both cries, but this is only a general title of honor; the emphasis is on "Son of David."

33) **And Jesus, having stood still, called them and said, What do you wish that I shall do for you? They say to him, Lord, that our eyes be opened. And Jesus, filled with compassion, touched their eyes; and immediately they saw again, and they followed him.** Matthew presents only the kernel, but even then we notice his independence from the other narrators. He alone states that Jesus was filled with compassion, and he alone remarks that Jesus touched their eyes. The cries of the beggars halted Jesus — his ears are ever open to our cries. He called the

beggars by having them brought to him (Mark and Luke). He makes them state what they want. On ἵνα see R. 933; it is like an expletive, and the subjunctive is volitive (cf., Mark 10:51 and R. 994), it is elliptical with imperative force: "to have our eyes opened."

34) On σπλαγχνίζομαι see 9:36; his heart was stirred by the pitiful sight of these blind beggars; his deepest motive is compassion. With a touch he heals them, at the same time he uttered the words preserved by Mark and by Luke. Verbs of touch are followed by the genitive. Jesus used both avenues: words for the ears and a touch for the feeling of these sightless men. The miraculous effect was instantaneous. Luke adds the detail regarding the praise of the people, and all three evangelists tell us that these beggars now followed Jesus. The Son of David had again proved himself.

# CHAPTER XXI

## XVII

### Christ Enters Jerusalem, His Last Teaching Ending with the Woes upon the Pharisees, Chapters 21-23

1) This section of the Gospel is well marked, Jesus enters the city and the Temple, does his last public work there, and then departs (24:1, beginning the next section). From Jericho (20:29) we are without further remark transferred to the Mount of Olives to witness the royal entry into Jerusalem. **And when they drew near to Jerusalem and came to Bethphage to the Mount of Olives, then Jesus sent two disciples, saying to them: Go into the village over against you and immediately you shall find an ass tied and a colt with her. Having loosed them, bring them to me. And if anyone shall say anything to you, you shall say, The Lord has need of them; and immediately he will send them.** John materially supplements the accounts of the synoptists which he assumes are well known to his readers. From him we learn that the day is the Sunday before Jesus' death. While Jesus makes ready to ride into Jerusalem, the multitude of festival pilgrims, having heard of his coming, starts out to meet and to receive him (John 12:12). In v. 9 two multitudes are referred to: one that was with Jesus, and another that went out to meet him. John makes this point clear. From him we also learn that the enthusiasm grew so high because of the raising of Lazarus and that, after spending the

Sabbath in Bethany, Jesus started from this village for his entry into the city.

Judging from the way in which Mark and Luke combine Bethphage and Bethany, the two were close together, the former lying in the direction toward Jerusalem. All trace of Bethphage has disappeared, but Bethany is still known; it lies a little over the ridge and on the far side of Mount Olivet. Here Jesus paused.

2) This time he will not walk but will ride into Jerusalem. No one knows which two of the disciples were sent to secure the necessary animal. They receive the most explicit orders. Bethphage is visible, right before them. All they need to do is to go in, and at once, without effort, they will find an ass tied (δεδε-μένην, the perfect with its present implication: "having been and thus still being tied") and a colt with her, also tied (Mark and Luke, who add that the colt had never been ridden). These animals the disciples are to untie and to bring to Jesus Mark tells us just where the animals were found.

3) The disciples are further told just what to answer in case anyone says anything to them about their taking the animals. One word will be enough: "The Lord has need of them." There will be no difficulty whatever. Mark and Luke add that this also happened, and that the owners at once let them have the use of the animals. We draw the obvious conclusion that these owners were very good friends of Jesus and of his disciples. Matthew alone tells us about the two asses, the dam and her colt. Here again he shows his independence. Both animals are brought together, for neither would be content if they had been separated. Jesus rode the colt, the dam trotting by its side. The orders of Jesus to the disciples reveal his divine knowledge of which, as of his other divine powers, he makes such use as his work requires. Here especially, when fulfilling one of the remarkable prophecies concerning

the Messiah, it was eminently fitting that his divine personality should reveal itself.

4) **Now this has occurred in order that it might be fulfilled what was spoken through the prophet saying:**

> **Say you to the daughter of Zion,**
> **Lo, thy King comes to thee,**
> **Meek and riding upon an ass**
> **And upon a colt, a son of a burden-beast.**

The point to be noted is the fact that already here, when Jesus gives this order to the two disciples, Matthew makes the statement that the prophecy was fulfilled; he does not wait and say that it was fulfilled after v. 7, after Jesus mounted the colt and rode forward. This can have only one meaning, namely that Jesus himself knows and by his order proceeds to fulfill this prophecy. He did not fulfill it unconsciously in the way in which the Jews ignorantly fulfilled so many prophecies concerning him. Matthew employs the same formula that he used in 1:22 and repeated in 2:15, 17, 23; 8:17; 12:17, which see. The passive τὸ ῥηθέν points to God as the speaker, and διά makes the prophet his medium or mouthpiece. This is the Biblical doctrine of Inspiration — a fact, not a "theory."

5) The prophecy is quoted from Zech. 9:9. This begins with a jubilant tone: "Rejoice greatly, O daughter of Zion; shout, O daughter of Jerusalem!" For this jubilant call Matthew substitutes the more sober line: "Say you to the daughter of Zion," which is taken from Isa. 62:11. The idea underlying the substitution seems to be the fact that, when the daughter of Zion is told who is coming, she will rejoice greatly. She certainly ought to rejoice. But it is necessary that she be told who this is that comes, for she does not recognize him as what he is nor the joy he brings to her. The substitution is interpretative. The Biblical

**writers** refuse to quote mechanically, in slavish fashion. We shall see this a second time in what follows.

The great news is intended for "the daughter of Zion." Matthew omits the synonymous term "daughter of Jerusalem"; the former alone answers his purpose. "Zion" seems to have been the name of the locality where Jerusalem was built and was then restricted to the highest eminence in the city. The Temple, however, was not erected on this high point but on the lower hill called Moriah. "The daughter of Zion" thus names the people according to the most prominent eminence which distinguished its capital. By a legitimate transfer this poetic title is now applied to the New Testament Israel, the Christian Church. "Lo" dramatically points to the figure of the Peace-King who is now most literally "coming to her." Zion is to awake out of its indifference and its unbelief, and is to welcome this King. The great moment has at last come.

"Thy King" is more than "the King destined for thee": by his very birth as the Son of David he belongs to Zion (II Sam. 7:12, etc.; Ps. 110:1, 2; Rom. 1:3). He is a King indeed, none is like him; he has a kingdom that is not of this world and lasts forever. "He comes," ἔρχεται recalls one of his Messianic titles; ὁ ἐρχόμενος, "the One Coming." In this verb "he comes" lies the thought of all that he brings. Hence "to thee" has the sense of "for thy benefit, for thy salvation." The subjects of other kings humbly come to them, this King comes to his subjects. Other kings draw all that they have from their people, this King gives all that he has to his people. Luther writes: "He is a peculiar King: thou dost not seek him, he seeks thee; thou dost not find him; he finds thee; for the preachers come from him not from thee; their preaching comes from him not from thee; thy faith comes from him not from thee, and all that thy faith works in thee comes from him not from thee."

Matthew omits Zechariah's next line, but he scarcely does this because of its faulty translation in the LXX, which has crept into our A. V.; for Matthew could have given an independent translation of the Hebrew. This line is not: "He is righteous and having salvation," but: "He is righteous (i. e., has God's verdict in his favor) and experiences God's rescue"; not σώζων, saving others, but σωζόμενος, himself saved or rescued (Isa. 53:8 a; Phil. 2:9). In Acts 3:14, 15 Peter calls Jesus "the Just or Righteous One" (Acts 7:52; 22:14), just as Zechariah had done, and points to God's act of raising him from the dead, which is the rescue Jesus experienced. The Hebrew niphal *nosha'* is passive and not active like the hiphil. All this explains why Matthew omits this line. It does not pertain to the royal entry into Jerusalem, it describes the resurrection and the exaltation of Jesus. The prophet saw all this together with the humble entry as one picture.

Here we see that the evangelists never quote mechanically and are not misled by wrong translations in the LXX; they quote with full use of intelligence. This line describes the Messiah's relation to God, and Matthew is stressing his relation to Zion. God's verdict in favor of Jesus which is declared by raising him from the dead as "One Rescued," belongs after the royal entry and is not a part of this entry.

The same insight leads Matthew to retain the LXX translation πραΰς, "meek," for the Hebrew *'ani*, "one who cannot resist" (C.-K. 964); he does not change it to πτωχός or ταπεινός. "The Messianic King appears in an unexpected form and conducts himself contrary to all expectation, not as one armed and exercising force, not panoplied and on a steed." C.-K. 965. The claim that the Hebrew word for "meek," *sanftmuetig*, is not *'ani,* but *'anaw,* is settled by Ed. Koenig, *Heb. Woerter-buch,* who accepts *sanftmuetig* as the proper rendering of Zech. 9:9 and of other passages, and regards it as closely synonymous with *'anaw;* and C.-K. defines the first as "one who cannot resist" (with force), and the second as "one who does not resist." The very mission on which Jesus came excluded his use of force as he told Pilate in John 19:36, 37, and as he proved throughout his passion. He came to win men's hearts with the truth not to coerce them with force.

This is symbolized by his riding into Jerusalem astride an ass. This animal is nothing but the common ass of the Orient, of which it has been well said: "The ass, the camel, and the woman are the burdenbearers." All efforts to make the ass on which Jesus rode a very superior beast (Smith, *Bible Dictionary,* and others), one that has nothing to do with the meekness of Jesus, are unsatisfactory. Since the times of Solomon no king bestrode an ass. The Hebrew has "an ass and a colt of asses," such as asses have. The LXX translates this: "on a burden-beast, a new colt," and Matthew: "on a colt, son of a burden-beast." Whatever other asses of superior type and breeding existed, the animal that Jesus used was entirely ordinary; nor would Beth-phage have a man who owned very superior stock. Nor is the ass more peaceful than the horse, it is only far inferior. The idea of peace may, however, be added to this King's meekness because asses were employed for the humble tasks that go with times of peace, horses especially in wartimes.

In his meekness the great Prince of Peace enters his capital riding only an ass. To call the colt "untamed" and thus to see in its use by Jesus a symbol of his power over nature, is fancy. The colt was gentle enough. When Luke 19:30 says that it had never been ridden he indicates that it was fitting for this King to use because it was not an old animal, on which others had ridden but one that was entirely new. The assertion that Zechariah had in mind only one animal: "an ass, namely a colt," etc., but that Matthew understood him to have two asses in mind: the colt plus the dam, is unwarranted, as Matthew's own words show. The fact that Jesus rode only the colt is beyond question.

The fact is worth noting that the Jews referred Zechariah's prophecy to the Messiah. All the evangelists report its *literal* fulfillment; Matthew and John quote the prophecy. This fulfillment would not have been so striking if Jesus had usually ridden about the country (like the good Samaritan, Luke 10:34) but he always went on foot until this time when, by his own orders, this beast was found for him. Yet, although it was so striking, the fulfillment of the prophecy was not at the time perceived even by the disciples (John 12:16), to say nothing of the Jews generally or of their rulers.

**6) And the disciples, having gone and done just as Jesus appointed them, brought the ass and the colt and put on them their robes, and he sat thereon.** The two aorist participles report what the two disciples did in Bethphage according to Jesus' orders. Mark records more details.

**7)** Matthew writes "the disciples," referring, of course, to the two sent to Bethphage. They are the ones that brought the animals. Because of the brevity of his account Matthew does not extend the subject when he says that "they put on him their ἱμάτια," their long, loose outer robes. That he does not intend to restrict this action to the two disciples we see in the last clause ἐπάνω αὐτῶν, referring to the robes not to the two asses, even considered successively. Several of these thin, long robes were thrown over the back of the colt, and on these Jesus sat. Robes were thrown also **over the** dam, for the disciples did not at once know

which of the two animals Jesus would use. They
did not ask. We may imagine that because of the
crowd that came from Bethany with Jesus (John 12:9,
17) it was not convenient to ask. This act was spon-
taneous on the part of the disciples.

8) **And most of the multitude spread their own
robes on the road, and others were cutting branches
from the trees and were spreading them on the road.
And the multitudes, those going before him and
those following, kept shouting, saying: Hosanna, to
the Son of David, blessed the One Coming in the
Lord's name! Hosanna in the highest!** As Jesus
starts to ride toward the city, the multitude, actuated
by the same feeling that moved the disciples, make a
carpet of their *himatia* and place them on the dusty
road so that he may ride over them (cf., II Kings 9:13).
This act is one of submission combined with the bestowal of the highest honor. Collectives such as ὄχλος
may have a plural verb. In fact, the multitude outdoes
itself and exhausts its resources in its efforts to honor
Jesus as its Messiah-King. The people cut branches
from the trees and strew them on the road. But here
Matthew turns to imperfects and drops the aorists; R.
838 says that the aorist lifts the curtain, and then the
imperfects continue the play. They describe the scene
as it progresses, they are like a moving picture.

John alone tells us that these were palm trees and
palm branches. Palms have long ago disappeared
from Olivet; in fact, the country has long ago been
denuded of forests and of trees generally. All that the
evangelists report is that the crowds made a path that
was carpeted with their clothes and with palm
branches. The fact that they also waved branches is
possible although it is not stated. There is no need to
refer to the custom of carrying a "lulab" or festive
spray as was done at the time of the Feast of Taber-

nacles. On the character of palms see the author's commentary on John 12:13.

9) Matthew plainly distinguishes two sections of the crowds and even uses the plural ὄχλοι: one that preceded, and one that followed. We might suppose that this was just one multitude that was spread out along the road before and behind Jesus; but John gives us the information that there were two crowds: one had assembled in Bethany to see Jesus and Lazarus risen from the dead and had started to Jerusalem with him; the other came out from Jerusalem to meet him when it got word that he was coming. The crowd that met him was the one in front of him. But both crowds joined in the acclaim, "Hosanna," etc. The words are from Ps. 118:25, 26, to which interpretative additions are made, some shouting one, some another expression (compare the different evangelists). Psalms 113-118 constituted the *Hallel* which was sung at the Passover when the festive procession was received by the priests; it was also sung in sections before and after the Passover meal (Mark 14:26).

The most distinctive part of the chant was "Hosanna," three of the evangelists recording a transliteration of the Hebrew *Hoshi'ah-nna', schaffe Heil,* "grant salvation" ("save now," A. V.), reminding us of the *nosha'* used in v. 5. It is scarcely safe to assume that the people did not understand the real meaning of this expression although they seem to use it less like a prayer and more like a joyful acclamation, like our: "All hail!" The significant addition made by the multitude is the ethical dative: "to the Son of David" (see 20:30, 31). This title is both royal and Messianic. Some said, "the coming kingdom of our father David" (Mark); others, "the King coming," etc. (Luke), or, "The King of Israel" (John). Here at last Jesus enters the great capital as the divinely prophesied Messiah-King and accepts the jubilant applause of the nation as it is rep-

resented in these great crowds of pilgrims who have
come from all parts of the Jewish land.  But the character of his kingship and royal rule is not made secular or political by any feature of this royal entry.

The words: "Blessed the One Coming in the Lord's
(Yahweh's) name!" constitute a welcome.  The perfect participle εὐλογημένος, "having been blessed," has its
usual present force, "having been and thus now still
being blessed."  Ὁ ἐρχόμενος here, too, has its Messianic
meaning, "the One Coming," the promised Messiah.
This is re-enforced by the phrase "in the Lord's name."
The enthusiastic multitudes thus acclaim Jesus as being
blessed by Jehovah, not merely with a verbal benediction, but, as Jehovah always blesses, with the gifts and
the treasures implied in the benedictory words; and
they acclaim him as coming and bringing all these
blessings to them and to their capital and their nation.
John shows what these crowds had in mind when he
pictures how their enthusiasm was fired by the latest
miracle of Jesus, that performed upon Lazarus, which
was a climax to all his other deeds.  "In the Lord's
name" does not mean "by the Lord's authority"; for
the ὄνομα is the divine revelation by which the Lord
makes himself known (see 6:9).

"Hosannah" is repeated in the shouting with the
added phrase "in the highest," a neuter plural, ἐν τοῖς
ὑψίστοις, which signifies the abode of God (R. 670) and
resembles "out of the house of the Lord" which is found
in the Psalm.  The grammarians prefer to regard this
ἐν as a locative (R. 525), the hosanna is to sound in
heaven itself; but in its first and fundamental meaning
ἐν signifies "in connection with," hence here, "in connection with God's abode."  It is just like the previous
phrase, "in connection with Jehovah's revelation."

The full import of all that was done in connection
with this entry of Jesus even the disciples did not realize until later as John 12:16 confesses.  But this in no

way reduces the action and the acclaim of the multitudes. It is fruitless to speculate on just what they had in mind when they used the words of the Psalm as they did. Whatever of wrong earthly expectation still clouded the vision of the "disciples" (Luke) and of the multitudes of pilgrims, this is certain, a holy enthusiasm caught their hearts on this Sunday, a wave of real spiritual feeling and joy, the direct product of "all the mighty works they had seen" (Luke), which moved them when thus welcoming Jesus to "praise God" (Luke). This helps us to understand why Jesus accepted this welcome and by his every act lent himself to this enthusiasm as he rode into the city as the King of Israel that he was.

10) **And when he came into Jerusalem, the whole city was stirred up** (σείειν), **saying, Who is this? But the multitudes kept saying, This is the prophet, Jesus, he from Nazareth of Galilee.** His coming into the city in the remarkable manner just described caused this universal stir. The news spread far and wide, and those who had not witnessed the entry, wanted to know who this man was (οὗτος, a good example of the purely deictic use without a derogatory tone, R. 697).

11) The ὄχλοι, the pilgrim multitudes that had accompanied Jesus (v. 9, this same plural), offer the correct information. They keep telling all questioners that the man whom they hailed as the Messiah-King is the well-known prophet (hence the article ὁ προφήτης) whose personal name is Jesus and who hails from Nazareth of Galilee. This reply sounds as though it was made by festival pilgrims from Galilee. We may note the tone of pride with which they name his home town. Most of the ministry of Jesus had, indeed, been devoted to Galilee, and these pilgrims from Galilee sum it up in the title "the prophet." Perhaps

they told of his wonderful teaching and of his astounding miracles.

12) We take it that the entry took place in the late afternoon of Sunday, and that Jesus proceeded to the Temple but on this afternoon did nothing more than to look around "upon all things" going on in the Temple, presently retiring to Bethany with the Twelve, Mark 11:11. The next morning the incident with regard to the fig tree occurred, as Mark reports, and on Tuesday morning, when the tree was found dead, Jesus gave his explanation. In other words, Mark 11:13-26 reports the actual sequence of events. The cleansing of the Temple thus occurred on Monday morning after the cursing of the fig tree. Matthew's account is *sachlich* (factual) instead of chronological. He thus combines into one paragraph all that pertains to the fig tree (v. 18-22) although this includes two mornings as the readers also will note. In a similar way he places the royal entry and the authoritative cleansing of the Temple side by side since in both of these Jesus displays his Messianic greatness. Throughout his Gospel we meet this trait of Matthew's that minor details are made subordinate or are even left out, and attention is focused on the main issues and subjects. Yet the supposition that therefore his chronology is loose as compared with that of the other evangelists, is unwarranted. We have seldom found that his attention to the subject matter makes him neglect the sequence of time; in fact, the other evangelists write more loosely in this regard than does Matthew. Yet here we have a case where the chronology is disregarded for an object that seems more important to the writer.

**And Jesus entered into the Temple of God and threw out all those buying and selling in the Temple, and the tables of the money-changers he upset, and**

**the seats of those selling the doves, and he says to
them:  It has been written, My house shall be called
a House of Prayer; but you on your part are making
it a robbers' den.**  The cleansing of the Temple reported by John 2:13, etc., is not the same as the one
reported by the synoptists.  It is, therefore, unwarranted to assert that what John placed at the very beginning of Jesus' ministry the synoptists placed at
its very end, or that John put into the beginning what
the others put at the end.  The thesis that John corrects the synoptists is not acceptable.  To be sure, the
effect of the first cleansing  was not lasting.  Is anything needed to explain that fact beyond the hostility
of the Sanhedrin toward Jesus?  So Jesus cleanses the
Temple a second time.   Both are Temple cleansings
and thus resemble each other.   But we should not
overlook the differences, especially the greater ones.
In connection with the first cleansing Jesus is at once
confronted by the authorities, and his reply is made
to them; in connection with the second cleansing no
one dares to confront him and to challenge his act,
and the word he utters is addressed only to the mob
that he throws out.  In connection with the first his
word is first a rebuke and secondly a challenge; in
connection with the second his word is a most scathing
rebuke; in connection with the first Jesus uses words
of his own, in connection with the second he quotes
Scripture (even "robbers' den" is a quotation).  In
connection with the first the disciples recall Ps. 69:9;
in connection with the second they recall nothing.

On Monday morning Jesus returned to "the Temple
of God."   Although τὸ ἱερόν is frequently mentioned in
the New Testament, we never find τὸ ἱερόν τοῦ Θεοῦ, but
here this unusual genitive is so appropriate for indicating the sacredness of the Temple that one is
inclined to consider this genitive textually genuine
in spite of the fact that important texts omit it.   The

ἱερόν refers to the Temple courts as distinguished from
the ναός or Sanctuary proper into which only the officiating priests entered.  Facing the Sanctuary and the
court of the priests was first the court of the men and
behind it the court of the women, and then came a
large area, the court of the Gentiles, into which alone
Gentiles were allowed to enter.  In this extensive court
of the Gentiles the present scene is enacted.

Cattle and doves were a necessity for the prescribed
sacrifices but a poor excuse for making this great court
of the Temple a stockyard.  Places to change money
were also needed; for a tax was collected from every
Israelite who was twenty years old, Exod. 30:11-16.
This was due during the month preceding the Passover
(17:24, etc.) and was either sent in by those who lived
at a distance or paid in person by those who attended
the festival, who then, however, had to have Jewish
coin, which fact compelled those who came from
foreign parts to have their money exchanged.  For
this exchange a small fee was charged.  But this
necessity was no excuse for making the Temple a mart
of petty bankers who were intent on business and rates
of exchange.  Moreover, the Temple authorities themselves controlled this volume of trade and in typical
Jewish fashion operated what amounted to a grand
lucrative monopoly.  If one bought his animals
here, had his money exchanged here, these would be accepted; otherwise he might have trouble on that score.

What all this did to the great Temple court may be
imagined (cf. Farrar, *The Life of Christ*, 455, etc.,
quoted in the author's commentary on John 12:14).
Matthew, disregarding details, simply says that Jesus
threw out all the sellers and the buyers — the latter
as well as the former; and that added phrase, buyers
and sellers "in the Temple," points to their violation
of its sacredness.  The fact that the verb ἐξέβαλε is
**without a trace of gentleness is seen from Jesus' up-**

setting of the little stool-like tables of the money-
changers behind which they sat on the ground cross-
legged. In a like manner he upset the benches of
the sellers of doves. He most likely kicked these over.
Whether he again made a scourge no one knows.
The κολλυβιστής is named from the κόλλυβος or small
coin which he takes for making an exchange of coins.
The picture of Jesus here presented does not please the
tender souls who think only of "the gentle Jesus" without the holy, fiery indignation that makes him act as he
here does. But read Mal. 3:3.

In connection with this second cleansing we note
as little resistance as we observed in connection with
the first. Yet at the time of the first cleansing Jesus
came as one who was unknown, now he comes as the
great Messiah-King who was acclaimed by the multitudes of festival pilgrims. The explanation of moral
cowardice on the part of these transgressors is
not satisfactory. Sin is often arrogant, especially
when money is at stake. Were these sellers not within their legal rights, having duly paid for their con-
cessions and doing business under the highest author-
ization? In regard to this second cleansing as in regard to the first only one explanation suffices: the Son
of man wielded his *divine* authority.

But, it is asked, what good was this outward
cleansing as long as the hearts were not cleansed? Let
us at once say that, if the object of Jesus was only
to stop this outward abuse, he would sink to the level
of our modern reformers who try to mend the leaking
ship by repairing the rigging. The question regarding this point may be misleading. Against flagrant
abuse the law and the light and the knowledge men
have must be applied. Nor is there a difference between the first and the second cleansings. Both are
filled with the dire threat of the divine law. Already
at the time of the first cleansing Jesus tells the Sanhe-

drists that they will end by destroying their own
Temple; and we need not ask how long God will
tolerate a Temple that is called his House and yet is
turned into a robbers' den. What good is the law and
its vindication on the part of God? It always vindicates
God himself, his holiness, and his justice.

13) No Temple police, no Sanhedrists hurry up
to question the authority of Jesus as was done three
years before. Did they know his authority by this
time? With one word Jesus brands this desecration
of the Temple: "It has been written (and thus stands
forever, Isa. 56:7), My House shall be called a House
of Prayer"; and to this he adds, "but you on your
part (emphatic ὑμεῖς) are making it a robbers' den,"
the latter designation being quoted from Jer. 7:11.
Here is the law "written" in their own Scriptures that
tells them what Yahweh's House was to be, what name
it should bear; and here was the verdict on their
crime, Jesus, their Judge, pronouncing it on these
transgressors. This was to be God's House where
he might dwell among his people with his grace, and
where they might enter into communion with him by
means of prayer, προσευχή, often, as here, used in
the wider sense of worship since prayer in some
form is at the bottom of all true worship of the
true God.

Matthew writes for former Jews and thus does
not add the final phrase found in Isaiah; Mark, who
writes for Gentile Christians, naturally adds it: a
House of Prayer "for all nations." That is why it
contained this court of the Gentiles; and what a sight
met the eyes of any visiting Gentile right here in this
court? What must he think of a House whose greatest
court was thus desecrated and of the God to whom such
a House belonged?

When Jeremiah used the expression "robbers' den"
in the threat Yahweh commanded him to pronounce,

he did not intend to say that the Jews robbed in the
Temple.   A robbers' den is not used for robbing but
as a refuge for robbers.   Jer. 7:10 states that, after
perpetrating the worst kind of wickedness, the Jews
went to the Temple, thinking and saying, "We are
delivered to do all these abominations," i. e., we can
go on in them as long as we have the Temple.   Compare also v. 4.   It was thus that they made the Temple
a regular robbers' den and refuge.   That is exactly
what the Jews are now repeating.   No matter what
they do even by violating the sanctity of their Temple,
they imagine that their adherence to this Temple will
protect and shield them from any penalty.   But no,
God will not let his Temple serve as a refuge for robbers.   The Temple will not protect the wicked who
show right in the Temple how they regard the God
of the Temple.

The church is no refuge for sinners who go on
in their sin and think that they are safe when they
go to the church; and certainly not for the sinners
who support the church by desecrating the church
and justify their desecration by crying, "It is for
the church!"   Jer. 7:12-15 declares what God would
do with this Temple: he would destroy it even as he
destroyed Shiloh for the same reason.   So here the
word of Jesus prepares us for 23:38 and 24:2, the same
threat appears also in John 2:19.

14)    But the hour of doom had not yet struck; the
work of grace continued to the very end; escape was
possible even in the eleventh hour.   Some at least
might be led to escape.   **And there came to him
blind and lame in the Temple** (note the recurrence
of this significant phrase), **and he healed them.**
Matthew alone informs us regarding the miracles that
were performed during the last days Jesus spent in the
Temple.   In the House of Prayer these sufferers prayed

to Jesus, the Son in his Father's House, and none of
them prayed in vain.

15) **But when the high priests and the scribes
saw the marvels which he did and the boys shouting
in the Temple** (again this phrase) **and saying,
Hosanna to the Son of David! they were indignant
and said to him, Dost thou hear what these are saying?** Not until this time did the Sanhedrists interfere with Jesus although they were determined to kill
him. The high priests were members of the Sadducean family and connection of the ruling high priest
Caiaphas, and the scribes were rabbis who were learned
in the law and members of the Pharisaic party. "High
priests and scribes" is a designation for the Sanhedrin, see 2:4. The "marvels" are the miracles Jesus
performed and are called θαυμάσια only here, for that
is the way they appeared to these Sanhedrists. These
authorities saw the marvels and the effect these marvels had especially on the boys (παῖδες and not παιδία
which means "children") in the Temple courts. These
were the lads who were twelve years old and over,
who had come to Jerusalem as the boy Jesus had done
at that age, for their first obligatory attendance at
the Passover. As boys are apt to do, they imitated
what they had seen their elders do on the preceding
day. In his famous picture of this scene the French
painter Tissot depicts them as marching up and down
the Temple courts in rows, with locked arms, shouting
in unison what they had heard their elders shout the
day before, "Hosanna to the Son of David!" They
were voicing the praise of Jesus for the miracles he
was performing here in the Temple.

16) This was intolerable to the Sanhedrists, but
their hands were tied. They dared not call out the
Temple police to break up the demonstration the boys
were making, and still less did they dare to assault

Jesus. They knew what the multitudes of pilgrims filling the Temple courts would do. So they come to Jesus and ask him to stop this disorder of the boys, which he had caused by his wonderful deeds. We must catch the irony in this action as Matthew presents it. The most awful disorder of the buyers and the sellers, the stench of cattle, the bawling and the bleating, the haggling and the dickering, were quite acceptable to these priests and these scribes — there was money in it for them, but these innocent lads who were voicing the praise of Jesus and giving him the title which his great deeds demonstrated was his due, were intolerable to these men. Yet they venture to remonstrate only by implication · "Dost thou hear what these are saying?" Dost thou not see that this is improper here in the Temple?

But Jesus says to them: **Certainly! Did you never read, Out of the mouth of babes and sucklings thou didst perfect praise?** With his decisive *ναί*, "yes" or "certainly," Jesus answers the accusing implication that these boys were doing something improper and that he were abetting them in the wrong. He places his fullest approval upon their shouting and their marching. He had come as the Son of David, the Messiah-King, and all who acclaimed him were doing exactly what he desired. And then Jesus seals his own approval by quoting that of God himself as stated in Ps. 8:2. He answers question with question; but whereas he could begin with a mighty "yes," they cannot begin at all. With disconcerting force he asks, "Did you never read" Ps. 8:2? You certainly act as though you had never even read this utterance of David's.

God perfects praise (brings forth perfect praise) "out of the mouth of babes and sucklings." This matches what Jesus said during his royal entry the day before when the Pharisees objected to the Hosanna shouting, Luke 19:40, that if the people would be silent, the stones would cry out. God will have the praise due him even if inanimate stones, inarticulate babes must offer it to the shame of men. We cannot agree with Delitzsch who says that *'olel* mean babes who are old enough to play, and *yoneq* sucklings of a similar age, since Hebrew mothers suckled their babes for about three years. The latter word would include not only babes who were nearing the end of their suckling age but equally those who had just been born. And the point which this interpretation makes is that all such babes — take them from birth until they are three years old, if you will — are as yet incapable of praising God. Others say that this praise comes from these babes and sucklings when they grow up to be like these boys in the Temple court, and then they obtain what seems an attractive thought to them: in these children Jesus sees the new Israel that leaves the unbelieving ways of its fathers and praises the Messiah in true faith.

These efforts seek to figure out *how* praise *can* be gotten out of the mouth of these babes. Delitzsch makes them old enough to lisp praise, the others go farther and say the praise is voiced when the babes have grown up. But neither the Psalm nor the use Jesus makes of it is concerned about this *how*, just as little as Jesus was concerned about *how* stones could be made to shout. All that Jesus says is that God will perfect praise for himself (note the middle), *no matter how*, if grown and intelligent men will not respond. The Sanhedrists considered these shouting boys as being too young to know what they were saying and doing. Jesus stuns these wise fellows by holding the passage from the Psalm before them which speaks of praise coming out of the mouth of babes and sucklings. When they are through with the Psalm let them talk about these boys and not until then.

The fact that this Psalm, as well as the rest of
Scripture, makes room for infants in the kingdom,
ought to be plain.   They are intended for God who
made them.   The cooing of a babe glorifies its Maker
as do the heaven and the earth, the moon and the stars
and all the works of his fingers.   What a blessed sight,
then, when young boys, such as these in the Temple
praise their God and Savior!   It is all a lovely harmony   But the eyes of these Sanhedrists are blind,
and their ears are deaf to it all.

The Hebrew has '*oz*, "founded strength," which
the LXX rendered, "perfected praise," and which Jesus
retained.   Ed. Koenig calls this an abstract for a
concrete and regards '*oz* in the Psalm as meaning
*maechtiger Chor*.   Hence the rendering of Matthew
and of the LXX are not a mistranslation but one that
is interpretative of the Psalmist's meaning.   The
mighty chorus of these babes and sucklings rises like
a bulwark before which the roarings of the Lord's
enemies sink to silence.   Let men rave in their enmity,
the very babes in their cradles reveal the Lord's greatness and his glory

**17) And having left them behind, he went on
outside of the city to Bethany and passed the night**
(αὐλίζομαι) **there.**   Jesus turned his back upon these
Sanhedrists.   Let them puzzle over these words
(13:11, 12)   One thing was plain even to them:
Jesus used Ps. 8:2 as a reference to himself as God
and as the God-Messiah, David's Son, who was rightly
being praised by the boys as well as by the multitudes
on the day before.

Jesus spent the night "outside of the city" lest
these Sanhedrists seek to effect his arrest.   While
he was sure that, until God sent his hour, no man
could lay hands on him, he, nevertheless, never acted
in a foolhardy fashion but always used proper caution.
Jesus spent Sunday night in Bethany (Mark 11:11),

also the succeeding night and many think that he spent these nights in the home of Lazarus. Where he spent the nights of Tuesday and of Wednesday no one knows. While the verb used often means to camp out in the open, it is also used for spending the night, which may then be done in some house.

18) **Now in the morning, returning to the city, he was hungry.** This was not some indefinite morning of this week. Mark 11:11-13 does not permit the acceptance of such a view. It was Monday morning (see v. 12). The point we cannot explain from the records is the fact that Jesus was permitted to leave Bethany without having eaten breakfast. The supposition that he rose before daylight and slipped away for prayer is not acceptable. Even Mark who loves to add details states only the facts of his hunger.

19) **And having seen a fig tree by the road, he went to it and found nothing on it save leaves only; and he said to it, No more shall there be fruit from thee forever. And forthwith the fig tree withered.** It should be noted that "by the road" (ἐπί is used in this sense, R. 603) indicates that this tree was ownerless; Jesus did not blast another man's property. Some commentators think that εἰς means a "lone" tree (R. V. margin "single") whereas this is only a substitute for the indefinite article; it is like our "a tree," R. 674. But did Jesus not know that this tree had no fruit? Sometimes all supernatural knowledge is denied to Jesus, but again he is expected to have and to apply such knowledge. Some say that he learns everything in the ordinary way, others that he ought to have extraordinary knowledge. We have already has occasion to note that Jesus used his divine power to know, just as he used his divine power to do, only when and where it was needed for his great mission.

The explanation of Trench that the act of Jesus by looking for fruit where he knew none was to be found, by leading men to think that he really expected fruit when he did not, was like telling a parable which is not an actual fact and yet is true in a higher sense because of the lesson it conveys, is not acceptable to all. A man's acts are not parables, and Jesus never acted out parables. And here the parable (if one is pleased to use the term) is found not in this act of Jesus' seeking fruit, but in the tree that has leaves but no fruit.

The fact that led Jesus rightfully to expect fruit was the full foliage of the tree, for Mark 11:13 writes: "Seeing a fig tree having leaves, he came, if haply he might find anything thereon." If it had been without leaves, Jesus would not have gone to this tree; for the other fig trees were just sending out leaves, since, as Mark adds, "it was not the season of figs," i. e., so early. Here, then, was an exceptional fig tree that grew in so favored a spot that it already had full foliage and was far ahead of the other fig trees. Since in the spring the fig tree puts out its fruit first and lets its leaves gradually follow, the full foliage of this tree gave promise of fruit. Three crops of figs follow each other. the early ones come in June, the second in August, and the third in December, these latter ones sometimes hang on the tree until spring. See the discussion on Mark in Smith's *Bible Dictionary.*

Jesus was thoroughly disappointed, "he found nothing on it save leaves only," not even green, unripe fruit, for this is what "leaves only" means. Jesus would not have blasted this tree if it had had even a little immature fruit. But here this tree with its grand foliage was nothing but empty pretense, and whereas it led one to expect that it might have at least a few figs that were fit to eat, it had absolutely nothing "save leaves only!" This lying tree did not make Jesus angry, nor did he curse it in his anger. The character of Jesus need not be defended against such a charge. His own words tell us why he cursed this tree. The subjunctive γένηται is volitive, R. 943; Jesus utters his will, and that will is done.

The tree withered παραχρῆμα, "forthwith." This adverb does not mean: "right before the eyes of the disciples while they stood there and watched." The tree dried up "from the roots," and the disciples saw this fact the next morning, Mark 11:20, 21. Matthew indicates the interval of time only slightly and follows his constant practice of stressing the great essentials without weaving in a great deal of detail.

20) **And when the disciples saw it they marvelled, saying, How did the fig tree wither forthwith?** This happened the next morning when Jesus again passed this tree on his way from Bethany, Mark 11:20. That is why we have the aorist ἰδόντες; if the tree had withered before the eyes of the disciples, the present participle would have been used. It was dark when Jesus and the disciples returned to Bethany on Monday night, so the condition of the tree was not noticed until Tuesday morning. What astonished the disciples was the fact that the tree had been struck dead by the word of Jesus and had died so suddenly. For all he had said was that it should never bear fruit anymore. It was now dead and *thus* would never bear fruit. Hence their question is, not *why,* but *how* this happened. The answer is formulated accordingly.

21) **And Jesus answered and said to them: Amen, I say to you, If you have faith and do not doubt you shall do not only this of the fig tree but also, if to this mountain you shall say, Be thou taken up and cast into the sea, it shall be done. And all things whatsoever you shall ask in the prayer, believing, you shall receive.** This explains *how* the tree was blasted so as not to bear fruit forever, it especially casts light on the phrase Jesus had

used: εἰς τὸν αἰῶνα, "for the eon," in which the idea of
death is suggested. The only thing that does not
match the question exactly is the fact that Jesus speaks,
not of what he has done, but, using what he has done
as a basis, of what the disciples themselves shall most
assuredly do although not of themselves but by the
power they will receive from God through prayer.
The weight of this answer is marked by the solemn
introductory formula explained in 5:18.

The word about removing mountains has been explained in 17:20. Here only a few additional points
need to be noticed. "Have faith" is made clearer by
the negative, "and do not doubt." The first verb is
a present subjunctive, for to have faith is a continuous
activity, the second verb is an aorist subjunctive, for
the doubt deals with the single act regarding which
hesitation occurs. For the moment the doubt blocks
the faith and prevents the act faith should accomplish.
The middle of διακρίνειν has the passive form in the
aorist and really means "to be in conflict with oneself," to hesitate and to waver, one thought pulling
us in one direction, the other thought in the opposite
direction: the act *can* be done (faith), it *cannot* be
done (lack of faith). The blasting of the tree is made
a small thing over against which a far greater impossibility is placed, the removal of a mountain, the
sea swallowing it up completely. This word becomes
more impressive when one has stood on this Mount of
Olives. From its ridges one is able to look right down
into the Dead Sea 1,292 feet below sea level. "The
mountain" would disappear entirely in that deep depression. In the plain words of 17:20, "And nothing
shall be impossible for you."

22) It should be noted that in v. 21 both ἄρθητι
and βλήθητι are passives. "be thou taken up," "be thou
thrown." The agent back of these passives is God.

The disciples use only God's power when they blast with judgment (the fig tree), and when they do the humanly impossible (19:26). For this reason Jesus adds the promise given to prayer, in which αἰτεῖν is merely "to beg" something (used with reference to God or with reference to men), and προσευχή is the sacred word for prayer to God alone. The article points to the particular prayer involved in these special cases. On God's part all is certain, but on our part this certainty must produce trust, πιστεύοντες, true reliance on that certainty. If doubt breaks this connection, insults God, instead of honoring him and his divine power, nothing will result.

But this is only the preliminary answer to the disciples. It shows only one part of what this miracle implies. The other part becomes evident in the following discourses, 21:23-22:14 and beyond. For it was at once obvious that a tree has no moral responsibility, and that Jesus used this tree merely for a higher end. It was similar to other illustrations in which trees were involved, cf., 7:17-20; 12:33; Luke 13:6-9; Joel 1:7; Ezek. 17:24; Ps. 1:3; Hos. 14:8; Num. 17:8. This fig tree made only a pretense at bearing fruit (leaves) and a great pretense at that. Men remove fruitless fruit trees.

This tree pictured unbelieving Judaism. Its withering because of the word of Jesus pictured the divine judgment that blasted this nation — Judaism stands blasted from the roots to this day. Read the agonized prayer for Israel in Isa. 63:7-64:12, and then the Lord's answer of judgment on Israel in 65:3-7, and compare the author's *Old Testament Eisenach Selections*, 118, etc. Jesus used a tree only for this one miracle of his which revealed the dreadful, deadly, and irrevocable divine judgment. As far as men were concerned, he had not come to judge them now (John

3:17), that would follow in due time (John 5:27, also the Baptist's word with its imagery of the ax lying at the foot of the trees, Matt. 3:10)

23) **And when he came into the Temple there came to him, while teaching, the high priests and the elders of the people, saying, By what authority art thou doing these things, and who gave thee this authority?** This occurred on Tuesday   On the high priests see 2:4; on the elders 16:21   Mark and Luke add also the scribes.   These two, however, would not be more exact than Matthew; for he seems to mention only the high priests and the elders because in this case the action was executive not legislative and thus not requiring the special function of the scribes although these, too, were present.   Jesus was in the midst of his teaching, this is the force of the present participle.   Luke makes this still stronger   From Mark we learn that this important representation of the Sanhedrin did not interrupt Jesus in his teaching and preaching the gospel (Luke) but waited for a pause during which Jesus was walking around   Then they came to him with all formality, but only to question him regarding his authority not to arrest him, not even to stop him in his work.   When they had received their crushing answer they retired and attempted nothing further   The fact that they waited until Tuesday before challenging Jesus shows how these rulers feared the pilgrims who overflowed the city during these days (v. 26 and 46).

The form of their challenge is mild because it is a question.   The two questions are really only one question, for "what" authority is made plain when the giver of this authority is named.   The ἐξουσία is both the right and the power that goes with this right.   "These things" implies more than the teaching, for any rabbi had the right to teach in the Temple or elsewhere. "These things" refer to the royal entry, the cleansing of the Temple, the whole bearing of Jesus, and his miracles. The challengers had always known that Jesus claimed authority from God, his Father. These men expect Jesus once more to assert that authority and are set on demanding the fullest proof from him that such, indeed, was his authority and are ready on their part to deny the validity of any proof Jesus might venture to offer. They had undoubtedly discussed the entire matter and had planned their procedure. Yet we see that in three years they had not advanced a single step beyond the first challenge they made in John 2:18. Unbelief is really non-progressive.

24) **And Jesus answered and said to them, I, too, will inquire of you just one thing, which, if you tell me, I, too, will tell you by what authority I am doing these things. The baptism of John, whence was it? From heaven? or from men?** The Sanhedrists knew the authority on which Jesus acted, but their one purpose was to deny him this authority, for to admit it was to accept Jesus as the Messiah, against which everything in them rebelled. But even under these conditions Jesus does not really refuse to declare to these Sanhedrists what he had declared and even proved all along. His counterquestion is not an evasion. Jesus merely returns the question of the Sanhedrists to them by substituting John for himself. "Whence" and the two ἐκ denote origin, but origin is here authority: if "from heaven," then John had divine authority; if "from men," then his authority amounted to nothing. The authority of John and that of Jesus are identical. So Jesus says, "If you will answer me, I will answer you." The right answer to the question about John was the right answer to the question about Jesus. A subtile irony is involved: these men ask of Jesus what they ought to know already from John's activity. Hence the dignified verb ἐρωτᾶν. Jesus proceeds "to inquire"; see Trench, *Synonyms*, I, 195. He

is not asking for something that he needs to know, he is inquiring about something that he himself well knows. The idea of λόγον ἕνα is "just one matter" and no more.

25) "The baptism" sums up the essentials of John's ministry, for which reason he is also called "the Baptist." Here Jesus uses a deadly dilemma, a form of logic which caught the Sanhedrists on its two horns. The baptism of John was either from heaven or it was from men; it was either divine or not divine (only human) *Tertium non datur* A third possibility was excluded. The Sanhedrists are compelled to choose one of the two horns and thus to impale themselves. **And they were reasoning with themselves, saying: If we say, From heaven! he will say to us, Why, then, did you not believe him? But if we say, From men! we are afraid of the multitude; for all hold John as a prophet.** It was the unbelief of these Sanhedrists which caught them in this dilemma, unbelief and the type of immorality that goes with its defense. They were not concerned about the truth regarding John, what was decisive for them were the consequences involved in the two possible answers they could give. They find themselves impaled by either answer Διατί asks for the reason, and they would certainly have none whatever to offer and would be self-condemned.

26) On the other hand, the host of pilgrims attending the festival would condemn these Sanhedrists; for to assert that John's baptism was from men openly denied that he was a prophet, and such a denial would inflame these pilgrims. To them John was a prophet, no matter how untrue they had been to his message and his baptism.

27) **They answered and said to Jesus, We do not know.** They dared not take either horn of the dilemma. Their answer is the most pitiful and dis-

graceful surrender. They dodge the issue which no
Jew dared to dodge. As Sanhedrists it was their
supreme duty to know, and here they dare to say that
they do not know. **And to them said he, too,
Neither do I say to you by what authority I am doing these things.** The reply of Jesus implies that
these Sanhedrists have refused to answer his question,
deliberately refused as arrant cowards. Since the true
answer to Jesus' question is the true answer also to the
question of the Sanhedrists, by refusing to give the one
they refuse to receive the other; and so Jesus is compelled to refuse to offer it to them.

28) While the Sanhedrists stand before Jesus
with their defeat rankling in their wicked hearts, Jesus
utters a simple, lucid parable that ends in a question
that could be answered in only one way. He elicits
this answer; and then by means of this answer exposes
the wickedness of the unbelief of these Sanhedrists.
It is done with perfect mastery, psychological and
otherwise. **And how does it seem to you? A man
had two children. And having gone to the first, he
said, Child, go work today in the vineyard. But he,
answering, said, I will not! Yet afterwards, having
regretted it, he went. And having gone to the
second, he said likewise. And he, answering, said,
I will, Lord! and he did not go. Which of the two
did the will of his father?**

The parable makes the whole scene objective and
thus enables even these Sanhedrists to give an answer
that is wholly objective, which they then also do without hesitation. The subjective application is entirely
hidden; it will be made presently with tremendous
effect. This was a perfect manner of penetrating
through the unbelief and the hostility of these men, and
it was so effective because it made them themselves
state how wrong their own conduct was. Jesus is
going to leave the whole matter to them, "And how does

it seem to you?" or, "What do you think of it?"  Compare 17:25; 18:12.

Here is a man who has two "children," and he addresses each as "child."  This intends to bring out the idea that because they were born to their father, he held them dear, and, because they were his children, they should hold him dear.  Fatherly and filial love is the bond between them, and this involves the most tender obligation on their part.  This relation between the children and their father is the basis of what is here presented.  The word υἱός, "son," is far less tender, for it points more to the legal relation involved, while τέκνον points to affection as is so evident in I John 2:18; 3:7, 18; 4:4.  We are "sons" by adoption, legally, but "children" by birth (I John 5:4).  The father goes to the one child with the kindly address, "child," and bids this child, "Go, be working today in the vineyard," the article meaning "my" vineyard.  No connective is needed between ὕπαγε and the next imperative.  Work and vineyard is similarly connected in 20:1, etc.

God's vineyard is an image that is frequently found in the Scriptures, and pictures his church on earth.  That is why it is so fitting in this parable although no special use is made of the vineyard in this instance.  The application which Jesus makes of the parable shows that "work" should here not be restricted to good works as distinct from faith. The father means, "Child, go show thyself as a child today by helping in my vineyard!"  In the application Jesus speaks of those who "go into the kingdom," and of those who "believed" John.  So we must combine faith (John 6:40) and good works (John 15:8).  This helps to explain "today."  Whenever it is called upon, a child of God should show its relation to God by its works of faith.

29) The reply of this first child comes as a shock; it is blunt, rude, without a trace of respect: "I will

not!" "He has dismissed even the hypocrisies with which others cloak their sins; cares not to say, like those invited guests, 'I pray thee have me excused'; but flatly refuses to go." Trench. Οὐ θέλω — the *will* is wrong. In 23:37, "I willed," ἠθέλησα, but "you willed not," οὐκ ἠθελήσατε. But what happened? Later on this wicked child "regretted" his refusal, and while μεταμέλομαι is not as strong as μετανοεῖν, the sense is much the same. This is certainly not strange. Everything he knew about his "father," about his own relation as a "child" of his father, and about his obligation toward that father, and about his unnatural and wicked action in treating his father as he had done, led him to regret his shameful course. The same power of grace is today effective in all who know anything about their heavenly Father. So, a changed man, this child "went away" to the vineyard; now he was indeed a true child.

30) The father speaks to the second child exactly as he had done to the first. He wanted *both* to work in his vineyard. The kingdom has room for all of us. One takes another's place only when the former *will* not take his own place. *Aequitas vocationis*, Bengel. The call is no stronger in the case of the one than in the case of the other, so that neither may excuse himself by saying, "I would have come if the Father had asked me as he asked my brother." The response is again astonishing: Ἐγώ κύριε! an emphatic "I" with the implication, "to be sure" and the very respectful address, "lord." The reply sounds as though this son at once turned and ran for the door, caught up spade and pruning hook from the wall, and rushed for the vineyard. His readiness takes away our breath. That is, indeed, how we all ought to respond and never cease responding. Jesus does not add a third child, one that said "yes" and then worked as it should. He leaves it to us to supply this third child. But alas, the second

child "went not." His promise was false, his character is plain.

31) When Jesus now asks, 'Which of the two did his father's will?" only one sane answer is possible. He says "did," ἐποίησεν, and thus wants the answer to disregard what each child *said*. **They say, The first. Jesus says to them:  Amen, I say to you, that the publicans and the harlots are going into the kingdom of God ahead of you.**  **For John came to you in the way of righteousness, and you did not believe him, but the publicans and the harlots did believe him; moreover, having seen it, you did not regret later on so that you believed him.**  By their answer the Sanhedrists condemn themselves. So will every man who refuses to do the Father's gracious will utter his own damning verdict.  David did it before Nathan.  The case against every transgressor, when it is viewed in the clear light of reality, will be so overwhelmingly simple and strong that he himself will do either what the Sanhedrists did here: damn himself with his own words, or what the foolish fellow did in another parable (22:12)  remain dumb and thus damn himself.

All that Jesus needs to do is to draw the curtain aside and to show these Sanhedrists what their answer says concerning themselves.  He begins with the solemn formula of verity and authority (see 5:18).  With this he, first of all, seals the undeniable fact that the publicans (see 9:9) and the harlots, the two most despised classes of open sinners, are actually going into the kingdom ahead of the Sanhedrists, the highest men among the Jews, to whom he is talking.  The last sentence of v. 32 makes it plain that προάγουσιν implies that the Sanhedrists are not going in at all.  To them, as to the second child, the Father had also said, "go in," but, though they said they would, they did not go in.  So this, Jesus tells these men, is exactly what your answer

means. You are right in commending that first child;
these publicans and harlots who at first openly refuse
the obedience of faith and yet later on regret their
wickedness and go, believe and obey.  You are again
right in not commending the second child who said
"yes" but went not — but this child pictures you yourselves with your refusal of faith and its obedience.
They go in, you stay out of God's kingdom (see 3:2).
On the latter see 23:3: "they say, and do not"; Exod.
19:8, "we will do," and they did not; and Isa. 29:13.

All those who today confess with their lips but deny
by their lives are like these Jewish rulers.  But mark
that the parable represents the publicans and the harlots and these Sanhedrists and Jewish dignitaries as
*brothers*.  All the self-righteous, haughty, and proud
are today *brothers* of the outcast and the criminals.
Rom. 3:22.  Romans 2 and 3 put Jew and Gentile on
the same basis as brothers.  See Rom. 12:32.  Among
these *brothers* in disobedience and sin the publicans
and harlots "go in before."

32) The present tense, "go before into the kingdom," makes the statement uttered in v. 31 general,
really without any particular reference to time.  But
the explanation now added with γάρ advances to the
specific facts and therefore has the historical aorists.
Here are the things that actually occurred. "John came
to you in the way of righteousness."  The term ὁδός,
"way or road," like the Hebrew *derek*, is often used
in an ethical sense to represent a course of life that is
controlled by a certain doctrine or principle and then
also to designate that doctrine or principle itself.  Thus
faith in Christ is pre-eminently THE WAY.  The genitive is qualitative: the way marked by righteousness,
by the approving verdict of God which declares righteous.  John's teaching, baptism, and life were marked
by righteousness, and his coming or mission brought
this righteousness to "you," the Sanhedrists.  John

labored to have you, too, walk this way. "He preached
the baptism of repentance for the remission of sins,"
Luke 3:3. In the language of the parable, the father
bade you, too, to go and to work in the vineyard as he
did his other child. But you Jewish rulers who professed to be God's dearest children, the most diligent
observers of his will and Word, when the test came
through the activity of John, "you did not believe him."
"The Pharisees and lawyers rejected the counsel of God
against themselves, being not baptized of him," Luke
7:30. "They went not" into the vineyard, into the kingdom. These facts are beyond dispute. By not commending the second child the Sanhedrists did right.
Their verdict stands: they condemn themselves.

But the publicans and the harlots "did believe him."
Note the direct opposite. This fact, too, cannot be disputed. Though they were flagrantly wicked at first,
they regretted it (repented) and changed. "Believed"
records this change. The fact of the change was visible,
for Jesus can say to the Sanhedrists, "you saw it." See
Luke 7:29. Yet even this did not affect the Sanhedrists.
Even when they saw others believe and beheld the power
of righteousness from the change wrought in them, these
rulers "did not repent" later on and also become like the
father's first child, "so that you believed him" (John).
The infinitive with τοῦ denotes result, B.-D. 400, 5. The
Sanhedrists actually had a double reason for believing
John (and thus also Jesus), namely not only the saving
truth of righteousness preached by John but also its
saving effect in the case of great sinners. But the very
richness of the grace thus vouchsafed to them made
them the more stubborn and vicious in their unbelief.

33) The preceding parable presents the past
(John, not believed — then believed). The one now
related advances to the present and the future. The
first deals with the Sanhedrists as men; the second
deals with them as the rulers of their people, in their

official capacity. Guilt and punishment are according: in the first, remaining outside of the kingdom; in the second, the vineyard taken away and these miserable men destroyed. The second parable is the complement of the first.

Another point of difference between the two parables is the fact that the first presents likely imagery, the second imagery that never did and never will happen. A man may have two sons that act like the two presented in the parable; but no owner of a vineyard who had had a servant killed would then send other servants also to be killed and on top of that his own son, only to have him killed also. He would immediately bring the police down upon these men and at once end their career in the vineyard. The reason for this astounding imagery is that in his longsuffering God does act, in fact, did act in the way here depicted. There is no imagery within the experience of men that can picture the amazing grace and patience of God. The hearers might well exclaim: "Why, we never heard of an owner doing such a thing, not stopping until his own son was killed!" Of course, they had not. But this is the very point Jesus wants to make. With this unheard of imagery Jesus pictures the unheard of wickedness of these Jewish leaders who murdered not only the prophets sent for their salvation but were now about to murder God's own Son.

**Hear another parable.** This sounds as though the Sanhedrists tried to leave and that Jesus detained them while a crowd of pilgrims gathered close around him. **There was a houselord, such as planted a vineyard and set a fence around it and dug a winevat in it and built a watchtower and leased it to vinegrowers and went abroad.** A few simple strokes, and the entire picture is before us in vivid, plastic form. It matches the striking parable recorded in Isa. 5:1, etc., but the action is entirely dif-

ferent.    Isaiah makes Israel as such guilty; Jesus, the
rulers of Israel.    The apposition ἄνθρωπος is merely
pleonastic and is dropped in the translation (R. 399).
This great and wealthy houselord establishes a grand
vineyard on his estate and leaves out nothing that a
complete vineyard ought to have.    "The vineyard of
the Lord of hosts is the house of Israel, and the men
of Judah his pleasant plant," Isa. 5:7.    The details
show all it took to make Israel such a vineyard.    The
vines had to be "planted."    "A fence" had to be built
all around to protect the place.    In this we may see the
law which acted as "a middle wall of partition," which
protected Israel from the Gentiles, all its regulations
and ceremonies keeping even the minds of the Jews
from Gentile ways.    The law was aided by the geo-
graphical location of Israel.    It was tucked away in a
safe corner of the world by itself, having the high Leb-
anon mountains on the north, lakes and the Jordan
gorge on the east, desert to the south, the Great Sea
on the west.

The winevat is dug out of the rock floor, like a figure
eight, the upper half being a basin for treading out the
grapes, the lower half (or lower part of it) being a
deeper basin into which the juice flows and from which
it is dipped out.    The author saw such a "winepress"
on the grounds of the Garden Tomb (the real tomb in
which Jesus may well have been buried).    "The two
vats were usually hewn in the solid rock, the upper
broad and shallow, the lower smaller and deeper."
Fausset, *Bible Encyclopedia*.    The tower was built for
watchmen and at the same time as a storehouse.    The
vineyard lacked nothing.

So Israel had everything for its religious needs,
from the Temple on down.    "What could have been
done more to my vineyard, that I have not done in it?"
Isa. 5:4.    And now, after all was completed, the owner
"leased it ("gave it out," ἐξέδοτο, some texts have ἐξέδετο,

R. 308) to vinegrowers," his rental being a part of the grape harvest as the following shows (not cash, as some suppose). He did this because he "went abroad," literally, "far away from home." We have this same feature in other parables, 25:14, 15; Luke 19:12; Mark 13:34. This going abroad pictures the great trust God imposed on the leaders of Israel — the precious vineyard of God's people was completely in their care. Yes, God brought Israel from Egypt into Canaan, planted, fenced it, equipped it there, and placed it under these spiritual rulers, whose office was continuous — the prophets appear elsewhere in the picture, they were sent for a special purpose at special times.

34) **And when the season of fruit drew nigh, he sent his slaves to the vinegrowers to receive his fruit. And the vinegrowers, having taken his slaves, hided the one, killed another, stoned another.** A vineyard is naturally planted for the sake of the fruit it will yield. But this parable does not center our attention on the productivity or unproductivity of the vineyard or of its vines, as does the parable recorded in Isa. 5, but on the vicious actions of these vinegrowers to whom the vineyard had been leased and who now had to meet the terms of that lease. In what condition the vineyard was under their management, whether it was full or empty of fruit, is not the point to be brought out. Our eyes are focused altogether on these outrageous vinegrowers who were in possession of the precious vineyard when the great owner now at the proper season sends for the fruit that is due him according to the lease. The δοῦλοι are thus clearly distinguished from the γεωργοί. The slaves are *sent* at this particular time, the vinegrowers are in permanent charge. As the latter are the permanent religious rulers of Israel, so the former are the prophets who were sent at particular times. In the imagery these times are naturally compressed into one time although even in Matthew and

still more in Mark and in Luke intervals are indicated. These slaves are sent "to receive his fruits," αὐτοῦ referring to the owner not merely to the vineyard. When the prophets were sent to Israel, God expected the fruits of contrition, faith, and obedience. It is a mistake to think only of the law and of fruits which the law might work, namely "the need of a redemption." Vineyard means law and gospel, the full riches of divine grace with fruits according, the chief of these being faith.

35) The *tertium comparationis* is not these fruits, it is the vinegrowers and their unheard of atrocity: they hided the first slave (literally "flayed" him, beat him bloody) ; they killed the next (just murdered him) ; and stoned the third (as though he were a criminal). We note the climax. For the reality see 23:34; Acts 7:52; Heb. 11:37, 38. Jesus is past mincing words. He makes the stark, bloody, devilish reality stand out in all its horror. It is without a single mitigating circumstance. More than this, Jesus is looking these very vinegrowers who murdered the owner's representatives squarely in the eye — and they knew that Jesus referred to them, v. 45. Let us not overlook this supreme dramatic feature.

The fact that no ordinary lessor of a vineyard ever did a thing such as that depicted here only brings out the more the enormity of what is illustrated. Nor would any owner of a vineyard send a second and a third slave as this owner did. The patience of God toward Israel's rulers is without parallel in all human history. An illustration must be invented to picture it, and the illustration must be unreal.

36) **Again he sent other slaves, more than the first ones; and they did to them likewise. And finally he sent to them his son, saying, They will respect my son.** The unheard of action continues on both sides: more and more slaves, and all being

treated in the same way.   The reality required that the
parable should be carried to such a length.

37)   Now comes the climax: the owner actually
sends his own son to these murderers.   At this point
the parable becomes prophetic: Jesus is speaking of
himself.   Where is the earthly father who would send
his son as God actually sent his?   But the parable had
to say also this about the son.   The son, too, is "sent."
In this respect God's Son resembles the prophets, and
yet they were only δοῦλοι, he is and remains ὁ υἱός μου.
The prophets were God's slave-servants as a result of
being sent; Jesus is sent as a result of being the Son.
In the one case the mission makes the man, in the other
the Man makes the mission.

The second future passive of ἐντρέπω, "to regard
someone," is used without the passive idea (R. 819), it
is like the transitive aorist; yet this future is scarcely
prophetic (R. 873) since it merely expresses expectation.   "They will respect my son" is similar to the previous imagery, the sending of other slaves after the
first ones.   The problem of the foreknowledge of God
does not belong here.   As regards God, this entire
imagery goes far deeper.   On the one hand is the
incomprehensible love and patience God exhibited in all
these sendings; yet on the other hand is the justice of
God which lets the Jewish leaders fill the measure of
guilt to the very top, yea, to overflowing, by killing
even his Son.

38)   **But the vinegrowers, when they saw the
son, said among themselves: This is the heir.   Come
let us kill him, and let us have his inheritance!   And
having taken him, they threw him out of the vineyard and killed him.**   Jesus here tells his murderers
exactly what they are even now on the point of doing.
What they as yet kept under cover he tells them openly
to their faces before the assembled crowds (21:26).
Note that each generation of Jewish leaders sanctioned

the deeds of their fathers by repeating them. They made all the previous murders their own by adding to them; and the climax was reached by the last generation of these leaders when it killed Jesus. The lessons in killing taught them by all former persecutors of the prophets they put into final practice by killing God's own Son.

At this point the parable is exceedingly exact. "They said among themselves, This is the heir" does not refer only to the secret thoughts of the Sanhedrists; John 11:47-53 reports that this is the very thing they said. They killed Jesus because they feared to lose their own positions. Their blind unbelief hid the spiritual nature of the kingdom from them, and thus the fact that they could never hold the outward rule while its inwardness was foreign to them, remained hidden from them. "Let us have" means "possess" the inheritance; and the aorist definite possession. They wanted to possess the branch on which they sat by sawing it off from the tree which bore that branch.

39) Jesus does not say merely that they took and killed him; no, they first threw him out of the vineyard. This agrees too closely with the place where Jesus was put to death, John 19:17, and Heb. 13:12, 13, "without the gate," "without the camp," to be a meaningless feature of the parable; compare I Kings 2:13, Acts 7:58. Jesus was taken to Calvary which was outside of Jerusalem. This indicates that this parable referred especially to Jerusalem, the seat of the Sanhedrin. "Cut off in the intention of those who put him to death from the people of God, and from all share in their blessings." Trench.

40) And now, as in the previous parable (v. 31), Jesus asks the same kind of a question. **When, therefore, the lord of the vineyard comes, what will he do to these vinegrowers? They say to him: As wretches wretchedly will he destroy them, and his**

vineyard will he lease to other vinegrowers, such as
will duly give him the fruits in their season.  The
hearers are to complete the parable.  Note that Isa.
5:3, 4 makes a similar appeal.  It is simply taken for
granted that something will happen to these vinegrowers; likewise, that now "the lord of the vineyard" will
come.  This is the same noble designation that was
used in the parable recorded in 20:8.  The greatness of
this "lord" intimates similar greatness for his son. This
lord's coming in person pictures God's coming on Jerusalem in judgment.

41)  Jesus must have told the story so dramatically
that his hearers at once gave him the answer.  These,
however, must have been the pilgrims not the Sanhedrists (v. 45).  We have the same λέγουσι in v. 31, both
leave the subject to be supplied; yet in v. 31 the context: αὐτοῖς in v. 27, and ὑμῖν, twice, in v. 28, leads us to
think of the Sanhedrists in v. 31.  There is no such
connection in v. 41.  This answer is so correct because
these pilgrims have their minds only on the objective
facts stated in the parable and do not realize who these
vinegrowers really were.  They thus follow their own
sense of justice, that justice which will vindicate God's
judgments on all unbelievers.  The answer thus keeps
to the imagery of the parable.  Κακούς is the predicate
apposition to αὐτούς, and κακοὺς κακῶς forms a striking
paronomasia, R. 1201, which we have sought to imitate
in our translation.  We regard the future tenses in
both the question and the answer as volitive and not as
predictive (R. 873).  Who these "other vinegrowers"
would be Pentecost began to reveal.

42)  **Jesus says to them:  Did you never read in
the Scriptures:**

> **A stone which those building rejected,**
> **This became corner head.**
> **From the Lord came this,**
> **And it is marvelous in our eyes?**

**For this reason I say to you:   The kingdom of God shall be taken away from you and shall be given to a nation producing its fruits.   And the one fallen on this stone shall be crushed together; but on whom it falls, it shall pulverize him.** The parable is dropped, its possibilities being exhausted since its imagery could not picture the resurrection of Jesus. From their own people the Sanhedrists present have heard their terrible verdict. It is, of course, the verdict of Jesus himself as Luke 20:16 also presents it. According to Luke some of the hearers must have perceived what this verdict really involved and thus cried out, "God forbid!" The true verdict is now endorsed by the Messianic word quoted from Ps. 118:22, 23 (the very psalm from which shortly before this the Hosanna cries were taken!) and then restated by Jesus himself in the plainest possible literal words.

"Did you never read?" raises this question in order to make all these people think and try to understand what, of course, they had read. This psalm was, most likely, composed to express the joy of the people after their return from the Babylonian Captivity, either at the time of the laying of the cornerstone of their new Temple, or at the time of the dedication of the completed structure. It contained the prophetic lines which Jesus now quotes. More will happen than the rejection of the Sanhedrists and their replacement by better leaders. An entirely new structure will be raised. The old covenant shall yield to a new covenant of which Jesus, rejected by the Jews, will be the mighty cornerstone.

The climax of the parable, the death of the son himself, is repeated in the first line of the psalm: "A stone which those building rejected" (λίθος is attracted into the accusative by its relative, R. 718). The killing == the rejection, and ἀποδοκιμάζειν means "to discard after testing." Those building are the Jewish leaders, the

Sanhedrin, the vinegrowers of the parable. But what happened? That very stone "became corner head" (the absence of the articles stressing the quality of each noun). Jesus is the "son" that was killed, the "stone" that was thus rejected as being entirely unfit for the building. But his death and his rejection did not eliminate him. The very contrary is true: this made him what the new structure needed: "corner head," cornerstone. The dead Jesus arose from the grave. The cornerstone does not mean "bearer and support" of the building. This would be the whole foundation. Jesus may, indeed, be called the foundation ($\theta\epsilon\mu\epsilon\lambda\iota\sigma$) as he is in I Cor. 3:11; but in Eph. 2:20 he is distinguished from the foundation, he is the cornerstone. As such he is set at the chief corner and thus governs every angle of both the foundation and the building itself. This Jesus does in the great spiritual temple of God, the new covenant.

"From the Lord came this" in the execution of his wonderful plan. The Greek places the emphasis on both ends of the sentence by putting the phrase first and the subject last. The feminine $\alpha\ddot{\upsilon}\tau\dot{\eta}$ (for $\tau\sigma\ddot{\upsilon}\tau\sigma$) and, following it, the feminine $\theta\alpha\upsilon\mu\alpha\sigma\tau\dot{\eta}$ is probably due to the Hebrew which uses the feminine instead of the neuter for abstract ideas; or it may be due to the feminine $\kappa\epsilon\phi\alpha\lambda\dot{\eta}$ which precedes, R. 655. The $\epsilon\dot{\iota}s$ is also frequently found in predicate nominatives: *zum Eckstein.* Rightly the psalmist adds: "And it is marvelous in our eyes," $\dot{\epsilon}\nu$ is like the Latin *coram*, R. 587. It causes all the godly who see this deed of Yahweh's to wonder and to praise.

43) Now all figurative language is dropped, and the tenses become literal futures instead of prophetic aorists. "For this reason" means: because the son who was killed by the vinegrowers, the stone rejected by the builders, did not remain killed and rejected, but — speaking of the stone alone — was made the corner

head by God himself. "The kingdom of God," namely his power and his grace in all that he works through Christ (see 3:2), "shall be taken away from you" by God. We find little distinction between "the kingdom of God" and "the kingdom of the heavens," both of which Matthew uses. The one names the ruler, the other his throne. Why the former should cover the rule of grace in both covenants, and the latter his rule only in the new, is difficult to see. Hitherto the kingdom had been confined to the Jews. This was true even with regard to the ministry of Jesus; but now this would be changed. "From you" includes both rulers and people. The Jewish nation as such no longer has what it so shamefully abused. This is evident from the contrast: "from you" — "to a nation." But here ἔθνος does not refer to an individual nation such as the Jewish nation. This would imply merely substituting one nation for the other. Nor is this singular the equivalent of τὰ ἔθνη, the Gentiles. This would substitute them for the Jews. This new "nation" is defined as one that produces the fruits of the kingdom. It is the new spiritual Israel of true believers, composed of men of all nationalities including also Jewish believers, but because of this very fact distinct from both the mass of hostile Jews and the masses of Gentile unbelievers, a "nation" with the God of grace ruling in their hearts through Christ. The term "fruits" recalls the parable but only in such a way as to describe the "nation" referred to. These fruits are, of course, contrition, faith, and works of faith.

44) The textual evidence for the genuineness of this verse is far too strong to justify its elimination. Jesus might have stopped with the judgment on Jerusalem and the Jews ("the kingdom shall be taken from you") and with the continuation of the work of grace ("given to a nation," etc.) ; but he makes his prophecy complete by announcing the judgment that shall come

upon all, whoever they may be, who set themselves
against the Christ of God. He does this by using the
figure of the stone in a new way, one that is independent of the idea of a building. In a striking way Jesus
presents the two possibilities: one may fall on this
stone by opposing Christ; and the stone may fall on
such an opponent, Christ may strike him with his judgment. The singulars speak of the individual persons,
for the guilt of unbelief and hostility is always personal. In both Isa. 8:14 and Luke 2:34 Christ is presented as a stone of stumbling and a rock of offense.
A fall on this stone never hurts the stone but only dam-
ages the one who falls (ὁ πεσών, the aorist, to denote the
one act) : "he shall be crushed together," keeping the
figure. Trench thinks that this need not be fatal in
every instance; and the imagery is such that the possibility of recovery may be admitted. But when this
stone itself falls on an unbeliever, "it shall pulverize
him," λικμήσει, as the dust is winnowed out of grain, the
verb after a fashion suggesting Ps. 1:4 and Matt. 3:12.
The chaff, reduced to fine particles, shall fly like dust.
Judgment can be pictured with no greater severity.

45) **And when the high priests and the Pharisees** (see 3:7) **heard his parables, they realized that
he was speaking concerning them; and, though seeking to lay hold of him, they feared the multitudes
since they continued to hold him a prophet.** The
elders mentioned in v. 23 are now termed Pharisees.
The two articles designate two classes, for the high
priests belonged to the Sadducees. While they were
united against Jesus, Matthew here conveys the thought
that each group was affected by the parables in its own
way. Both groups realized at least that these parables
dealt with them, λέγει is retained from the direct discourse: "he is speaking about us." The fact that this
stirred their anger instead of giving them pause, need
not be stated.

46)    The present participle, ζητοῦντες, does not imply that these rulers now resolved to get hold of Jesus, for they had resolved this long ago.   But now, having this determination in their hearts although Jesus here condemned them to their very faces, they dared not stir a finger.   Why did they not arrest Jesus then and there? They were afraid of the hosts of festive pilgrims who were thronging all parts of the Temple courts.   These people, speaking generally, considered Jesus to be at least a prophet — to be no more definite about it. John's Gospel offers us more details.   Εἰς has the same force as the one used in v. 42 (R. 481).   With the jubilation of these crowds (v. 8, etc.) fresh in mind, and the courts filled with the easily excited throngs, it certainly behooved the Sanhedrists to take no radical measures with regard to Jesus.

# CHAPTER XXII

1) **And Jesus answered and spoke again in parables to them, saying: The kingdom of the heavens has become like a king, who made a wedding for his son and sent his slaves to call those that had been called to the wedding; and they were not willing to come.** The closing verses of the preceding chapter mark a pause. Then Jesus continued to speak (πάλιν εἶπεν) to the same persons (αὐτοῖς), Sanhedrists and the pilgrims, but now making response (ἀποκριθείς) to what was in the hearts of his hearers when they perceived whom he had in mind when he spoke his previous parables. The plural "in parables" may be regarded a plural of category or a reference to the many parabolic features found in this extended parable. The situation is thus carefully sketched, and from this opening sentence to the very end of the parable the differences between this parable and the one recorded in Luke 14:16-24 are so great and so numerous that they must be regarded as two separate and independent parables.

2) All that was said in regard to ὡμοιώθη in 13:24 applies here as well. In the course of its history the kingdom of the heavens (see 3:2) became like this picture through the unbelief of sinful men, some of whom were open and even violent unbelievers from the very start, others of whom were secret unbelievers or believers only for a time and who were then at last unmasked. But the historical aorist "did become like" is spoken from the standpoint of the end of the world when the earthly history of the kingdom will be complete as here portrayed. What happened throughout the whole New Testament era is compressed into this

brief story of the King's Son's Wedding Feast.  The
addition of ἀνθρώπῳ to βασιλεῖ is pleonastic and need not
be translated, cf., 21:33 and other parables; hence "a
*certain* king" (our versions) is incorrect.  The royal
features must be noted throughout.  This king is God,
and his son is Christ.

The unity of the parable is at once expressed: "a
king who made a wedding for his son."  We are told
what happened in connection with this wedding, namely
how the king and his son were treated by the various
persons who had been invited to the wedding.  For this
reason nothing is said about the bride of the king's son.
The moment we perceive the force of the opening statement and note that it governs everything that is introduced into the parable, its grand unity will be apparent,
and we shall not agree with those who speak of two
parables pasted together (v. 3-10, and v. 11-14) or of a
parable consisting of two parts.  The perfect unity of
the whole is again stated at the conclusion in v. 14.
The word γάμος or its plural may mean either "a wedding" or "a wedding feast"; in v. 2-9 we have the
plural, but in v. 8 and in 10-12 the singular.  This wedding and the invitations to attend it picture the grace
of God that provides salvation for the world of sinful
men in connection with Christ.  It includes redemption, the means of grace, and the efficacy of the Holy
Spirit, as these apply equally to all men.

3)    The τοὺς κεκλημένους are the Jews.  They are the
ones who had received advance invitations through the
Old Testament and its many prophets and promises.
When in and through Christ the wedding was ready,
the king sent them his δοῦλοι "to call them," to ask that
they should now come.  These "slaves" of the king are
not John the Baptist and Jesus, for the wedding was
not as yet ready.  These "slaves" are the apostles and
their gospel call after the death and the glorification of
Jesus.  This interpretation relieves us of making Jesus

one of the "slaves," who is nothing less than the king's son, and of then laboring to make the fact of his being one of these slaves plausible. We are also relieved of bringing in the brief preaching tour of the Twelve (10:5, 6) and that of the seventy (Luke 10:1, 17), which may well be combined with the advance invitations of the prophets. These first "slaves" were the apostles and their ringing call on Pentecost and throughout the years following.

"And they were not willing," with its negative "brings out sharply the element of will." And the imperfect, as so often, leaves in the balance what the outcome of this unwillingness will be; this will be stated presently. "Were not willing" casts its light on all the preliminary and advance invitations the Jews had received. They had meant nothing to the Jews. God's wonderful plans of grace had never captivated their hearts. The king had treated these men as nobles of his realm, but now we see how they regarded him.

4) Now we learn what the imperfect tense led us to expect. Yet what the king now does fills us with surprise. An ordinary king would resent and punish the insult offered by such a treatment of his gracious and grand invitation. But not so this king who pictures the astounding grace and patience of God in Christ. **Again he sent other slaves, saying: Tell those that have been called, Lo, I have prepared my breakfast, my steers having been slaughtered and all things prepared. Come to the wedding. But those that made light of it went away, the one to his own farm, the other upon his business; while the rest, having laid hold on his slaves, maltreated and killed them. But this king grew angry and, having sent his armies, destroyed those murderers and set fire to their city.**

So this king actually repeats his invitation after it has been turned down — a true picture of God's re-

peated calls of grace.   And the sincerity and the earnest desire of his invitation are brought out by giving
us its actual wording.   Note that the invited are again
designated as "they that have been called."   Are all
those advance and now these final calls to be in vain?
The new delegation of slaves is to tell these men the
great news ("lo") that the king has made everything
ready (perfect tense, ἡτοίμακα) and thus is now waiting
to begin the round of feasting and celebration.   That
is why we have ἄριστον, "breakfast," the first meal of the
day that was eaten about nine o'clock.   Common Jewish weddings were celebrated for seven days.   This
royal wedding would go far beyond that.   The magnitude of the feast is indicated by the information that
the steers have been slaughtered — so many guests
were to be fed.   No specific interpretation of this detail
has ever been suggested that could be regarded as
acceptable.   "All things prepared" adds the thought
that the vast amount of other viands and drink are likewise waiting to be consumed.   Nothing further needs
to be provided or prepared.

The call is renewed, "Hither to the wedding!"   This
new delegation of slaves is not identical with the first
delegation.   If the first delegation pictures the apostles, this second pictures their successors throughout
Judaism.   Again and again the men of Israel were
made to hear the gospel call.   Rom. 10:21.

5) Two classes of these unwilling guests are
named: οἱ δὲ ἀμελήσαντες, and οἱ δὲ λοιποί (v. 6).   The first
class treated the invitation with disdain; they had far
greater counterattractions than this wedding of their
crown prince.   What could these be?   Two are mentioned as samples.   One man went away to his own
land instead of to the king's palace; the other to his
business affairs.   Both must be thought of as lords;
one who had landed estates, the other who had his great
merchant enterprises.   Each found more satisfaction

in these possessions than in accepting the king's grace
and favor offered at this son's wedding.  This class is
found among the Jews as well as among men of all
ages.  They prefer the earthly to the heavenly, the
transient to the eternal.  They always treat the divine
call with indifference; they always "go away."  Because
they are so numerous Jesus spoke a special parable
about them, Luke 14:16-24.

6)  Another class, here called "the rest," is more
vicious.  They laid hold of the king's messengers, maltreated and even killed them.  These are the Jewish
persecutors, a part of whose vicious acts are preserved
for us in the Acts.  These, too, have had successors
beyond the confines of Judaism.

7)  This king's grace and his patience have their
limits.  God's love will not be insulted forever.  The
fact that ἄνθρωπος is now omitted before βασιλεύς has no
special significance; it would not be in place after the
article.  To say he is now altogether "king" and not
"man," is to misunderstand the Greek — he is now just
what he was from the start.  The fact that God should
grow angry (ingressive aorist, R. 834) has always met
objection on the part of rationalists who cannot appreciate the conception of a holiness and righteousness
that must finally settle with sin and the obdurate sinner.  Yet God's anger is never a human passion.  The
Scriptures present a far different picture.

The fact that the king sends out his armies against
the murderers of his ambassadors is regarded as a
departure from the parable and an introduction of the
reality instead, since no king would start war in the
middle of preparations for a wedding.  But this seems
strained.  A word spoken by the king would set his soldiers in motion.  The grandness of this king grows.
We note the immensity of his wedding preparations,
the many slaves that rush about at his bidding, the
captains and the armies that are ready for war on the

instant. The picture of God shines through this imagery; we are led to think of "his angels that excel in strength, that do his commandments, hearkening unto the voice of his·word," Ps. 103:20.

We surely know that his destruction of those murderers and his burning their city was just about literally fulfilled in the terrible destruction of Jerusalem, 23:38. We need not ask where the king had his palace and prepared the wedding. It was not in the city of those murderers. They were his high officials (the Sanhedrin), peers of his realm, in charge of the king's people and his possessions. They were destroyed in the bloody ruins. The king dwelt in his glory, for this king pictures God, his palace is the church, his armies the angels, his loyal subjects all true believers in Christ — and these alone can partake of the wedding he prepares. Since so great matters are to be pictured in one human illustration, let us not expect too much from the illustration. Those citizens that merely disdained to accept the invitation lost their possessions when the city went up in flames. The destruction of Jerusalem is one of the outstanding examples of the divine judgment which in some way and in due time overtakes all who obdurately reject the Son and his wedding.

8) **Then he says to the slaves: The wedding is prepared, but they that have been called were not worthy. Be going, therefore, to the outlets of the roads, and as many as you shall find call to the wedding. And those slaves, having gone out into the roads, brought together all, as many as they found, both wicked and good; and the wedding was filled with those reclining at table.** The deplorable fact, so significant for the Jewish hearers of Jesus, is stated by the king himself: the wedding ready — those called (here named thus for the last time) not worthy. The word ἄξιος is here used as in Acts 13:46: the unworthi-

ness lies not in the lack of some merit, but in the wicked rejection of the king's gracious invitations.

9) "Be going" is a durative present tense and implies that the slaves are to keep on going until the wedding was provided with guests. The διέξοδοι τῶν ὁδῶν are usually thought to be crossroads, yet this leaves the genitive unexplained. The first noun in this combination is used to designate the outcome of a trial and, when it is applied to roads, refers to their terminals, where all the traffic that passes along the roads is bound to arrive. This seems to be the sense of this noun and its genitive in the present connection. Yet these are not the roads that come to an end in the open country but the roads as they come in from the outlying districts to the various cities of the king's great realm. The greatness of the king and of his domain thus becomes more impressive. At the points thus indicated all the inhabitants of the king's realm will be reached. Thus the outlets or terminals of the roads express the universality of the gospel call which is also indicated in the addition: "and as many as you shall find call to the wedding."

10) The slaves do this very thing. The addition of ἐκεῖνοι is important. The very slaves who were sent to those who refused to come (the Jews) were now sent to invite whomever they found (also the Gentiles), as Paul expresses it in Acts 13:46. Yet the emphatic "*all*, as many as they found," includes Jews and not only Gentiles. Jerusalem was destroyed, the Jewish leaders had perished, but Jews were scattered everywhere, and these together with the Gentiles were bidden to come. The fact that many of those called would not come is omitted from the parable in order not to overload it. Besides, if any still repeated the rejection of the call, their fate has already been sufficiently indicated by what befell those who were first called. The point now stressed is the fact that the wedding was

completely "filled with those reclining at table" in order to dine in Oriental fashion, by being stretched out on broad couches. The wedding was celebrated by prolonged feasts (v. 4).

Those actually brought in are described as "both wicked and good," and by bringing in both indiscriminately the slaves made no mistake. No one class of men is excluded from the gospel call. As far as "the wicked" are concerned, we have 21:31, 32. This helps us to understand "the good"; for these are such as had not practiced open sin such as the publicans and harlots were guilty of. Take the malefactor as a sample of "the wicked," and Nicodemus and Joseph of Arimathaea as samples of "the good." Before God all men are equally guilty, and the gospel call finds them in this condition. A distinction between wicked and good *before* men are called necessarily refers only to the common judgment of men who call those wicked who descend to vice and crime and those good who cultivate the *justitia civilis*, an outwardly decent and respectable life. The thought is not that the latter accept the gospel call more readily than the former. It is the call alone with the divine grace that is operative in it that brings men into the kingdom irrespective of their former condition, whether they were despised or admired by the world. Parables sometimes turn from the figure to the reality, for at some point figures fall short of the reality. This is scarcely the case here where "wicked as well as good" helps to bring out the universality of the call for all types of sinners.

11) The story is not completed at this point as those suppose who think that the rest is a little parable by itself or only a sort of appendix to the parable proper. If the parable stopped at verse 10, it would be incomplete and its climax would be missing. We should have "wicked and good" at the wedding without a solution of this duality. We should have men trans-

planted into the kingdom just as they are in the world.
Nor should we know what a real acceptance of the
gospel call is in distinction from a sham acceptance.
The parable would stop with the entrance of the Gentiles, which occurred in the very middle of the gospel
work, whereas it ought to go on to the very end of the
work, even as it was designed to do this from the very
start. So Jesus takes us to the point where the gospel
call is complete and no further slaves are sent out to
invite guests to the wedding.

**And the king, having gone in to view those re-
clining at table, saw there a man not having been
garmented with a wedding garment. And he says
to him, Fellow, how didst thou come here not having a wedding garment? And he was struck speechless. Then the king said to the ministrants: Having bound his feet and hands, throw him out into the
outer darkness. There shall be the weeping and the
gnashing of the teeth.**

The supreme moment when the king steps in to see
the guests ranged on magnificent couches at the endless
tables, is the climax of the entire parable. All else
led up to this moment, and what follows is the result
of this moment. The infinitive θεάσασθαι, "to view," "to
behold," the aorist to indicate one complete act of viewing, suggests nothing of a judicial nature. He came in,
not as a judge with critical eyes, perhaps to find something wrong, but as the glorious king he was to feast
his eyes on the entire scene and on all the guests at the
royal tables of his royal son's wedding.

The fact that when the king thus comes in he is met
by an insulting sight does not alter the sense of θεάσασθαι.
No one would have thought it possible that among these
many, many guests, so graciously invited, one would
have dared to come in with his own old clothes on and
not clad in a wedding garment like all the rest. The
king's eyes light upon such a man. It is well, when

in preaching we apply this parable and say with Luther
and others that this was only one of many such men.
But this is a parable, and this one man is introduced
into the parable as is the one mentioned in 18:24 and
again the one spoken of in v. 28, to make each of us
search himself and ask, "Lord, is it I?"

The perfect participle ἐνδεδυμένον is passive, R. 485,
"not having been garmented" by the attendants, those
who had garmented all the rest. The perfect participle, of course, has its present force: he was now without the necessary garment. This is the only case
in Matthew's Gospel where οὐ instead of μή negates a
participle, and this οὐ is used to make the negation the
more clear-cut and decisive (R. 1138) and thereby to
stress *the fact*. In the very next verse we have μὴ
ἔχων ἔνδυμα γάμου to express the very same thought,
and there μή lays stress on *the argument* expressed in
the king's question. So this is the outrageous *thing*
the king saw: a man minus the wedding robe.

There is a difference of view among the commentators as to what this wedding garment is. Is it the
righteousness of life or that of faith; a garment the
guest provides for himself or one the king provides for
his guests; good works or Christ's merits? It is surprising to note that so many favor the former. The
parable shuts this out. If this man was unable to furnish a fine garment for himself, he would have had a
sound reply ready when the king asked him why he had
no proper garment; but the man is struck dumb by the
question. In all that precedes those who were invited
from the roads are not represented as first going to
their distant homes to get their wedding garments. The
very idea is precluded. How could such people have
garments that were grand enough for a royal wedding?
The king also at once notes this man's garment which
is a glaring blotch among the garments the others
wore. The king did not ask whether each man's gar-

ment was fine enough and then found one that was
below par with the man wearing it saying that it was
the best he had. No; all the rest have wedding garments, this man has no wedding garment; all the rest
had the garments that were provided by the king himself which were grand beyond anything they could
afford and hence were at once recognized by the king,
but this man had no such garment, he was garbed in his
own clothes.

The evidence that in the Orient and even among the
Greeks garments were provided for honored guests, not
one but several to be worn in turn, thus relieving the
guests of undue expenditure on their part, and adding
to the magnificence of the grand host, is quite sufficient,
and we may point to Gen. 45:22; Judges 14:12, 19; II
Kings 5:22, notably also 10:22 and Esther 6:8; 8:15;
Rev. 19:8, 9. Moreover, the Analogy of Faith completely excludes the thought that our own works and moral
fitness ever enable us to become acceptable to God.
Works do not admit into the kingdom. When we have
done all we are unprofitable servants, "we have done
that which was our duty to do," Luke 17:10. The wedding garment is the *justitia Christi,* the imputed righteousness which is ours by faith. If faith is the garment (Luther), it is the faith that, like a cup, holds
this free gift of righteousness; no other saving faith
exists. "He hath clothed me with the garments of salvation, he hath covered me with the robes of righteousness," and these are bridal as Isa. 61:10 shows.
In Rev. 19:8, we have the same bridal scene, the white
bridal linen is provided for the bride by the bridegroom, and this is "the righteousness of saints."

12) On the king's address to this man, ἑταῖρε, compare 20:13. This is not a gentle word such as "friend";
it is rather like our "fellow," even etymologically. It
is the opposite of an address the king would use when
speaking to the other guests. It indicates this fellow's

fate. When he is asked *how* he came in without the wedding garment, the μή used with ἔχων (unlike οὐ with the participle in v. 11) indicating that the king is considering this insult to his grace, we already hear the king's verdict: this man insults the king, his son, the wedding, and the guests. How did he dare to reject the wedding garment offered him and yet force himself into this wedding? How did he dare to regard his own garments as being good enough when here everything was royal? No reasonable answer is possible. Note that ἐφιμώθη is passive; it does not mean, "he was speechless," but, "he was made speechless," i. e., by the question. In the parables this speechlessness or, when an answer is attempted, the very answer condemns. The righteousness and the justice of God are thus made to stand out. Woe to him who rejects Christ and then faces God speechless or attempting some folly of speech!

13) This man was not one of the guests, he only pretended to be one. By rejecting the wedding garment he excluded himself from the blessed number of the guests. His pretense endures only for a moment, concerns only himself and not the king. No man ever deceived God. Hence the terrible order for his immediate expulsion. He is to share the fate of those mentioned in v. 7. Like a criminal the man is bound hand and foot and thrown out. This is still an Oriental figure. But at this point the figurative language of the parable is frankly abandoned because it is unable to picture the reality, and the reality itself is brought forward: "into the outer darkness," etc., see the exposition of the sa words in 8:12. He is cast into hell. Whatever name may be given to this outer darkness, its description as here repeated is more than sufficient to identify it and to make us recoil from its horrors.

14) At the conclusion of the parable Jesus sums it up in brief: **For many are called ones, but few**

**elected ones.** Both κλητοί and ἐκλεκτοί are verbals and
are equal to passive participles, the agent back of the
passive idea being God: "called by God," "elected by
God." Moreover, in both verbals the entire action is
included, that of God's calling and that of God's elect-
ing. This, too, is plain, that here the calling (καλεῖν)
signifies the invitation of grace which may be accepted
by means of the grace it contains, or which, in spite of
that grace, may be rejected by man's vicious perversity.
Hence "many" are called ones, and far fewer are elected
ones. As so often, the absence of the articles intends
to stress the quality of the nouns. To be sure, the
parable shows us *who* the elect are, namely those who
accept the call and the garment of Christ's righteousness; and thus also *who* the non-elect are, all those who
obdurately reject the call either in violence, or by indifference, or by spurning Christ's righteousness. The
first are those who never believed, the last those who
pretended to believe. Among the latter those who
secretly fall from faith, often also called *the Zeitglaeu-
bigen,* are included. Therefore it is unwarranted to
assert that this parable shows us *only who* the elect are.
In the very word ἐκλεκτοί we have the whole divine act
of election, even as we cannot have elect without their
election. The parable reveals this great act of election.
It shows us *how* some are chosen, *how* the rest could
not be chosen. This is the reason why this parable
constitutes one of the supreme *sedes doctrinae* for the
doctrine of election (*Concordia Triglotta* 1069, 14) together with Rom. 8:29, etc.; and Eph. 1:4, etc., and
why in the statement of what constitutes election (paragraphs 15-22) most of the items are drawn from this
parable, just as Chemnitz also chose this parable as the
text for his notable sermon on election.

The divine act of election occurred in eternity. Since
human minds cannot think in terms of eternity, Jesus
uses the terms of time, but in such a way as to show

us with entire clearness what God did in eternity. God
is not hampered by time. All that would occur in time
was absolutely present to him before time began: his
whole plan of grace with all its operations and effects,
exactly as these are sketched in the parable. We thus
see *why* the elect are so few in number — so many eliminate themselves in one way (v. 3-7) or in another
(v. 11-13). We see how in eternity there came to be
an ἐκλογή and an act of ἐκλέγεσθαι with these ἐκλεκτοί as the
result. Jesus enables us to see just what God's election
is. The one great act of God he spreads out in its component parts in the parable. Election is all that this
parable presents from beginning to end, from the redemption of the whole human race to the glorification
of those who enter heaven. Because of our limited
understanding we are like children for whom Jesus
must take it all apart when showing it to us, whereas
to God it is all one whole. For God the end is already
in the beginning. That is why the whole is truly God's
election. It is the sum of God's eternal grace which
produces and thereby accepts saints that are clothed in
Christ's righteousness as his own forever in eternal
glory.

The essential point in this comprehensive act is the
one pictured in v. 11: the king's looking for the wedding garment, Christ's righteousness embraced by
faith. The whole act culminates in this point. Noting
this culmination, we may also say that the divine election is that specific part of God's eternal grace which
accepts the saints whom he has succeeded in clothing
in Christ's righteousness as his own forever in eternal
glory.

The identical grace is present in both views. The
former looks from the cause of God's election (the
grace) to its effect (the elect) ; the latter looks at the
effect (the elect) as produced by the cause (the grace).

Neither cause and effect nor effect and cause can be separated, for the attempt to separate them would lead to a misunderstanding of both.

15) Sanhedrists, high priests and elders, confronted Jesus in 21:23, and in 21:45 we see that these elders were Pharisees. The Sadducees and Pharisees from the Sanhedrin had fared ill at the hands of Jesus (21:23-22:14). From now on the two groups operate separately (here, and in v. 23, 34, 41). **Then the Pharisees went and took counsel how to ensnare him in a statement.** It is still Tuesday; see 21:12, and compare 26:1. The Pharisees retire in a separate group and concoct a cunning scheme to ensnare Jesus (this verb is found only here in the New Testament) like a bird in a hidden noose of thread. It is to be done "in a statement" that he is to be led to make, not realizing its fatal consequences for him until it is too late.

16) Their scheme is carried out. **They send to him their disciples in company with the Herodians, saying: Teacher, we know that thou art truthful and teachest the way of God in truth and carest for no one, for thou dost not look on men's countenance. Tell us, therefore, how does it seem to thee? Is it lawful to pay poll tax to Caesar or not?** Luke 20:20 calls these emissaries of the Pharisees "spies who feigned themselves to be righteous," and adds that their plot was to deliver Jesus into the hands of the governor. These disciples were men whom Jesus had not met before, who thus could pose as honest inquirers. The Pharisees arranged matters so that their disciples were accompanied by the Herodians. The latter were to act as witnesses, and their word would be more effective with the Roman governor than that of mere disciples of the Pharisees. The preposition μετά precludes the idea that these disciples and the Herodians should act as though they were disputing with each other about

the tax and were now appealing to Jesus to settle their dispute. The Herodians, likewise strangers to Jesus, would not be recognized as Herodians by him.

We meet "Herodians" only incidentally in the Gospels. They appear as a minor political, non-religious party among the Jews and were supporters of the alien Herodian dynasty which ruled under Cæsar, an arrangement which was far preferable to the Jewish nation than Cæsar's direct rule through Roman procurators. The Herodians thus favored the Roman tax because of the dependence of the house of Herod on Rome. In all such matters the Pharisees opposed them and ever demanded complete independence from Rome and autonomy for the Jews. To them any Roman tax was thus "unlawful" in the sight of God. Yet as the Pharisees joined hands with their opponents, the Sadducees, in their attack on Jesus, so here they ally themselves with their other opponents, the Herodians, in this attempt to destroy Jesus. In a few days Herod and Pilate became friends in the same manner.

This delegation comes with an astounding acknowledgment of the teaching and the character of Jesus as though they themselves were about to become Jesus' most ardent disciples. With honeyed words of flattery, a great *captatio benevolentiae,* they seek to throw Jesus off his guard. Their masters have coached them well, for they have put into their disciples' mouth an acknowledgment of Jesus which every Jew should have most sincerely made. In their lying fashion they ape the truth quite perfectly. Jesus was indeed ἀληθής, absolutely "truthful." He taught "the way of God" (see 21:32) marked out by God for every Israelite to follow "in truth," most perfectly. He "cared for no one" and in anything he said was never swayed by any man's fear or favor. This elaborate preamble will certainly lead Jesus to live up to the estimate thus made of him: he will consider no man, not even Cæsar in

Rome when giving his answer. To men who think of him so highly he will speak without the least reserve. He is thus assured in advance that, whatever men like the Sanhedrists would do, these men who are now speaking to Jesus will accept and prize his answer and will thank him for it from the bottom of their hearts.

Jesus certainly lived up to this estimate of him: he saw their hypocrisy (Mark) and craftiness (Luke) with his eyes of truth (John 2:24, 25). The way in which they tried to lure him into their snare was rather silly. Even a lesser mind than that of Jesus could have detected the false tone in their flattering words.

17) Now their question. Jesus is to tell them just what he thinks, "Is it lawful to pay personal tax to Cæsar or not?" Mark adds, "Shall we pay it or shall we not pay it?" Mark 12:15, we who above all want to walk in "the way of God." The answer was almost laid upon the tongue of Jesus. He whom no man's fear or favor could possibly sway would not even stop to think but would say frankly, "In God's eyes it is not lawful." The κῆνσος is the poll tax which was exacted from every individual and was thus considered as a special badge of servitude to the Roman power by the Jews; hence the disputes among the rabbis about paying especially this tax. Compare 17:25 and note that the τέλη (plural) are levies on goods and wares at harbors, piers, and city gates which were less galling to the Jews.

18) **But having perceived their wickedness, Jesus said: Why are you tempting me, hypocrites? Show me the poll tax coin. And they brought him a denarius. And he says to them, Whose this image and the superscription? They say to him, Caesar's. Then he says to them, Duly give, therefore, the things of Caesar to Caesar and the things of God to**

**God.  And having heard, they marvelled and, having left him, went away.**  Matthew calls the motive behind the flattery and the question downright "wickedness," πονηρία, the active, vicious evil in the hearts of these disciples of the Pharisees.  That is how *their* teachers had trained them.  Jesus addresses them as "hypocrites," ὑπό in the word conveying the idea of show actors wearing a mask as the ancient actors did (R. 633).  Their fair speech distils only poison. "Why are you tempting me?" exposes their secret, vicious intention in a flash.  And these liars have no defense. Yes, Jesus told them the truth, and without fear or favor!

19) Yet, although they are unworthy of an answer, Jesus gives an answer to their question and does so in his own impressive way.  He demands to be shown the coin with which this poll tax was always paid, and promptly one of his questioners hands him a denarius, see 20:2, in purchasing value the price of a day's labor and the wage of a Roman soldier, 17 cents in our money.  The Roman senate had the right to mint only copper coins; the right to mint gold and silver coins was reserved for the emperor.  The denarius was a small silver coin which was usually stamped with the emperor's head (occasionally with that of a member of his household) and invariably with the name and the title of the reigning emperor.  Jesus asks, "Whose this image and superscription?"

20) "Jesus begins in a childish and foolish way as though he did not know the image and the inscription and could not read, so that they quickly thought, surely, here we have him, he is afraid and intends to dissimulate about the emperor and dares not speak against him.  But he takes the word right out of their mouth, making them surrender with their confession. They dare not be silent, for just as they bade him answer, so he now bids them answer.  If they were silent, he would say, 'If you will not give answer to my

question, neither will I answer your question (21: 27).'" Luther.

21) Besides, the question seems so innocent and so harmless that they see no reason to pause and thus reply without hesitation, "Cæsar's." Digging a pit for Jesus, they have now tumbled into it themselves. Unwittingly they have answered their own question. All that Jesus does is to point this out to them.

Trench, *Synonyms*, 1, 78, points out the exact meaning of εἰκών, "image," which always implies a prototype which it does not merely resemble but from which it is drawn. It is the German *Abbild*, which presupposes a *Vorbild*. The emperor's face is depicted on the coin; so the sun shines in the water, the statue presents the man, the child is the image of its parent. But ὁμοίωμα or ὁμοίωσις, "likeness," means only resemblance and does not include derivation: two men may look alike; one egg resembles another.

In ἀπόδοτε the ἀπό should not be overlooked for it gives the verb the force "to give what is due," what our obligation requires us to give. The admirable nature of Jesus' answer was fully recognized already by his hostile questioners the moment they heard it, and few have ever found fault with it, although some have failed to see all that these brief words convey. The answer is so perfect because it is so complete. The Jews considered the poll tax by itself; the only way to consider it properly was to place it among all "the things of Cæsar" and then to look at these in connection with (καί) all "the things of God." Then all difficulties, those of the poll tax and a thousand others, at once disappear. The trouble with regard to so many casual questions is that we look at only the one question and fail to rise to the comprehensive view which takes in the whole domain of which the one question is only a trivial part. Jesus always saw the whole, and Paul rises to the same height, notably in solving the intricate problems that had arisen in Corinth. The wisdom that can do this is from above.

Jesus asked for an actual coin that might be taken out of the wallet of one of his questioners. All of them carried such money. He makes them say that this is the emperor's coinage. They have accepted it, and it is their money, the money accepted by their entire nation. This implies that their nation belongs to the empire. This coinage was one of the advantages they enjoyed under the emperor's rule, a sample of other similar advantages. The emperor was their ruler — this coin that bore his image, taken from their own pockets, is the incontestable evidence. In the providence of God the Jews are this emperor's subjects. That suffices. That settled their obligations toward the emperor, the matter of paying him the poll tax now in force and all other duties toward him. This is the force of οὖν, "therefore," with which Jesus connects his reply with the coin and its image. "Duly give, therefore, to Cæsar the things that are Cæsar's" includes *all* their obligations to "the higher powers ordained of God," Rom. 13:1-7. "The things that are Cæsar's" include, not only tribute, but likewise fear and honor. Whether a government makes this easy or hard for us makes no difference. Our duty is plain. Let the rulers look well to theirs and recognize that also they are answerable to God who likewise rules over them.

This is only a part of the answer. The question, "Is it lawful or not?" referred to God and implied, "Is the payment of this tax in harmony or in dissonance with our obligations to him?" Therefore Jesus answers by adding, "and the things of God to God." This "and" places the two obligations side by side. There is to be no clash between them but quite the contrary. Neither obligation interferes with the other. "The things of God" are all that our relation to him involves: contrition, faith, love, worship, obedience, submission to his providential guidance, even to his correction and chiding. We misunderstand Jesus when we think that he says that the obligation to God has nothing to do with the obligation to our government. The "and" of Jesus intends to cancel the "or" of his questioners (v. 17). These are no alternatives, they harmonize, yea, more; by giving to God what is God's we for his sake give to the ruler what is his. For our obligation to God includes everything in our life, its citizenship as well as our religion. This "and" connects a small field with the whole field. And only by seeing both in their true relation do we see either aright. From Cæsar Jesus rises to God; he does not make them parallel.

The emperor's image was on the coins that were in the pockets of the Jews, and Jesus pointed to that image when he said, "Duly give to Cæsar the things that are Cæsar's." He connected the obligation with the image. When he now adds in identical words, "and the things of God to God," are we not led to think of a corresponding connection of this obligation with an image, namely the image of God in which he created us and which his Son now restores in us? To say the least, the thought is captivating. And in fact, only as we truly attain God's image in us shall we truly render to him what is his due.

Jesus acknowledges the state as a divine institu tion that is willed by God. His own conduct before Pilate exemplifies this fact, in particular his word recorded in John 19:11. His word about Cæsar regards the state and our relation to it as a separate domain, and the doctrine of the separation of church and state is thus the only legitimate conclusion to be drawn from what he says. Yet church and state are not mere parallels and equals. Our obligations to God are the whole of life, those to the state one part of this whole. While church and state are separate in the way indicated, there is no gulf between them. They are not like two watertight compartments. The church will always put conscience, namely as governed by God, into our relation to the state (Rom. 13:5). This the church constantly contributes to the state. What the state normally contributes and always ought to contribute to the church Rom. 13:3, 4 make plain. Thus each aids the other, but the second aids in the higher way. When either seeks to control the other, usurps the functions of the other, havoc results for both as history bears witness.

22) Well might all who heard the answer of Jesus "marvel"; the pity is that they did no more. All they did was to leave him and to go away. No man ever spoke like this man (John 7:46); why then did they leave him?

23) **On that day there came to him Sadducees, claiming there is no resurrection, and inquired of him, saying: Teacher, Moses said, if one shall die, not having children, his brother shall espouse his wife and shall raise up seed for his brother.** Lest we put too much into v. 22 and think that the departure of the Pharisees and the Herodians implies that Jesus was through for the day, Matthew writes that the new interrogation took place on the same day (Tuesday). This time a group of Sadducees (freethinkers, morally loose, see 2:7) confront Jesus. No outstanding persons among them are named, and thus we may think of a group of these men who represented the opposition of their entire party to Jesus and had conceived a way to trip Jesus and at the same time to maintain their skeptic views against the orthodox Pharisees. "Claiming there is no resurrection" summarizes their position on the point at issue, hence no article is needed with the participle; εἶναι is the tense of the direct discourse (ἐστίν). We still use the present tense in general and in doctrinal propositions. "They inquired," the verb implying, "with all due dignity."

24) Behind their formality they hide their **real** purpose, hence they use no flattery such as **the** other delegation employed. Feeling their lofty superiority as Sadducees, they were also naturally disinclined to exalt Jesus even in hypocrisy. Josephus comments on their coarse manners, a sample of which appears in John 11:49. While they formally address Jesus as "Teacher" they really intend to show what a wretched teacher he is. They summarize the Mosaic law regarding levirate marriage (Deut. 25:5, etc.). The verb ἐπιγαμβρεύειν means "to marry as a brother-in-law" or levir, *beschwaegern*. The idea behind this law was, not to let the dead, childless brother's line die out; the first son of the new marriage (none of the other children) would be regarded as the dead man's child.

25) All this is preamble. Now comes the real question. **Now there were with us seven brothers; and the first, having married, ended and, not having seed, left his wife to his brother; likewise also the second, and the third, until the seven. And last of all the woman died. In the resurrection, therefore, whose wife of the seven shall she be; for all had her?** The logic of the case presented is a *reductio ad absurdum* against the defenders of the resurrection. This is done by means of a supposed dilemma, either horn of which offers an impossible, untenable, really ludicrous situation. The fallacy of the logic lies in the falsity of the assumption that in this Sadducean dilemma *tertium non datur*. These men thought that they were wielding a two-edged sword, either edge of which would be fatal to Jesus, and they never dreamed that he would strike the flat side of their blade and snap it off at the very handle. They are a sample of how some men study the Scriptures by means of their own logic.

These deniers of the resurrection still have many followers. The view that Judaism developed the doctrine of the resurrection at a late date (say at Solomon's time) and that it was little known even after that period is untenable.   Abraham believed that God could raise his son from the dead (Heb. 11:19).   Only the skeptic Sadducees disbelieved the resurrection, and their objection shows how extensively this doctrine was held.   Between these two terminals there is extensive Scriptural evidence, and even Abraham speaks of the resurrection as something that was long and fully known.

26)   The Sadducees cite the case of the seven brothers as a real case, and Jesus does not contradict them in regard to the reality.   It is wrong to call even Sadducees liars without proper evidence.   While they use this case of seven brothers because they had it, for the sake of their argument two brothers would suffice, and such cases were certainly numerous among the Jews.

27)   The death of the woman is necessary for the argument in order to transfer all the persons concerned into the other world and thus to show actually, and not merely hypothetically, how absurd the resurrection appears when it is considered in the light of Deut. 25:5, etc.   The playing of one word of Scripture (one that seems to suit error) against some great Scripture doctrine and to buttress this by a number of Scripture passages, was practiced already in the days of the Sadducees.

28)   Thus the conundrum is propounded to Jesus. Supposing for the sake of argument that there is a resurrection and that these dead bodies of ours rise again from their graves, what then about this woman?   All seven brothers were equally her husbands.   In the resurrection will all seven be her husbands?   The very idea is monstrous already in this life and how much more so in the life to come!   Or which one of the seven

will be her husband, and why the one, and why not
some other one of the seven, she having had a child by
none? With seven holding equal rights, why set six
aside? Again an impossible situation. The Sadducees thus are certain that there is no resurrection, and
that Moses himself proves it in Deuteronomy, and that
no man can overthrow this solid proof. We may well
suppose that they had tried this proof against many a
Pharisee and made a laughingstock of every opponent.
Jesus was to be their next victim.

29) **But Jesus answered and said to them: You
are deceiving yourselves, not having known the
Scriptures nor the power of God. For in the resurrection neither do they marry, nor are they given in
marriage, on the contrary, they are as angels in
heaven.** The bubble blown by the folly of the Sadducees is punctured. We must regard πλανᾶσθε as a
middle, "you are deceiving yourselves," namely by
drawing a false conclusion from the word of Moses, one
that does not lie in his words about the levirate marriage. How the Sadducees come to do this the participial clause explains, "not having known the Scriptures," μὴ εἰδότες, the aorist to express prior action. A
genuine previous knowledge of the Scriptures would
have made it impossible for the Sadducees to misuse
that word of Moses as they did. This is guilty and by
no means unavoidable and thus excusable ignorance on
the part of the Sadducees. Their Old Testament plainly teaches the resurrection of the dead, and in spite of
it, and though they have had these Scriptures constantly before their eyes, they "have not known," what
they teach. In this way they came to abuse Moses'
word. The Sadducees introduce a false premise, one
that is absolutely foreign to Moses, namely that in the
other world the same conditions prevail that obtain in
this world. Where does the Old Testament teach anything of this sort?

"Nor the power of God" have they known, i. e., from the Scriptures. This is not God's power to raise the dead but his power in regard to the dead bodies as he raises them, as though the only possible way in which he could raise them would be to make them exactly as they were in this earthly life. What a pitiful conception the Sadducees had of the power of God in the world to come! That conception was the product of their blindness not of the revelation God had placed into their hands. But that is the way in which many make use of the Scriptures to this day, and they do so especially in regard to the revelation concerning the resurrection of the dead. Jesus declares that the Old Testament reveals the resurrection, even the power of God in the way in which he will raise the dead; but many modern theologians deny what Jesus asserts regarding the Old Testament.

30) The γάρ clause points out where the error lies. With one stroke it sweeps away the seven men that the Sadducees refer to in their self-deception. The horns of the dilemma on which Jesus is to impale himself crumple up and fade into nothing. "For in the resurrection neither do they marry (namely men), nor are they given in marriage (namely women)," R. 392. Luke 20:35, 36 expands this statement by emphasizing the fact that Jesus speaks of the resurrection of the blessed and of their condition in heaven. The entire arrangement of sex, marriage, reproduction, and childbirth, and all laws pertaining to these is intended for the earthly life only and not for the life to come. The Sadducees should have known this from the Scriptures. But this difference between our present life and that to come does not imply that our bodies will be discarded. Jesus expressly says that the change will take place "in the resurrection," in the divine act which will bring forth *our* bodies from their graves.

"But (they shall be) as angels in heaven," says
Jesus who came from heaven. He does more than
merely to refute his opponents, he instructs them and
us besides. Not "angels" but "*as* angels" in regard to
sex and marriage. "Just as the children of the resurrection no longer die (in heaven), so also they no longer
need marriage to replenish the race." Besser. "Where
there is no dying, there is also no succession of children." Augustine. As the number of the angels is
complete and fixed, so will be that of the children of
God in the resurrection. Already this is enough to
establish the likeness existing between the angels and
the saints. But we may add that our bodies will be
lifted above the narrow limitations of matter as it is
at present; they will be made perfect instruments of
the spirits and accord in all things with the glorious
conditions obtaining in the world to come.

The idea that the angels, too, possess corporeity is
without a basis in Scripture. This idea assumes that
the angels have an etherial, firelike body; and when it
is consistently held, attributes a body of some indefin-
able form also to God. But the Scriptures know the
angels only as πνεύματα, spirits, and in many connections
use this term as the opposite of all that is bodily or
material. See the fuller discussion in Philippi, *Glaubenslehre*, II, 296, etc. When angels appear to men on
earth they are given a form in order to become visible,
just as Jehovah assumed a form in the theophanies.

31) **But concerning the resurrection of the
dead, did you not read that spoken by God, saying,
I am the God of Abraham, and the God of Isaac, and
the God of Jacob? He is not the God of dead men
but of living men.** The Sadducees had falsely appealed to the Scriptures (as Satan did in 4:6) ; Jesus
crushes this appeal by himself truly appealing to the
Scriptures (as he did in 4:7). The Scriptures *are*

the true court of appeal. Jesus unmasks one of the hidden batteries of Scripture and delivers a volley that is the more annihilating because it comes from an unexpected quarter. But why does he use Exod. 3:6 or its parallels instead of obvious passages such as Dan. 12:2? Some answer, because the Sadducees accepted only the Pentateuch and rejected the prophetic books; but the proof for this view seems to be rather slender. Jesus probably used Exodus because this passage involves a deduction as a proof for the resurrection. The Sadducees had made a false deduction from Deuteronomy; Jesus shows them how to make a correct deduction from Scripture, one that clearly lies in the words of Scripture themselves and does not go one inch beyond them.

Once more the point at issue is stressed: "concerning the resurrection of the dead." And here the genitive τῶν νεκρῶν is added in order to shut out every misconception regarding the word "resurrection." "The dead" are the dead bodies in the graves; these bodies shall experience the resurrection by being made alive again and being glorified at the last day. Modernistic exegesis says to us, "Positive proof of the resurrection — or rather of the life after death." "He thought of the life after death as non-material." But the whole question at issue is concerned about the dead bodies in the graves — shall they be raised up and live again or not? Regarding this question Jesus asks (as he did in 21:42) with a tone of surprise, "Did you not read that spoken by God?" Of course they had read this word — but how? Just as so many read God's words today. Jesus cites a word that was uttered by God in person and was recorded as having been uttered by him, and not merely a regulation communicated through Moses for the period of the old covenant only: the arrangement of levirate marriages.

32) This word is the covenant name which God
gave to himself, "I am the God of Abraham," etc., and
it is not necessary to say how the Jews gloried in this
name and title. Through the patriarchs it connected
the Jews with God as his children; it placed them into
the covenant through which this connection was made;
and it made that covenant the seal by which all the
promises it contained were divinely guaranteed. Among
those promises was "the resurrection of the dead." And
now the asyndeton lifts the cover and reveals what lies
underneath: "He is not the God of dead men but of
living men," both νεκρῶν and ζώντων are masculine. Moreover, ὁ Θεός is the predicate, the article making it identical and interchangeable with the subject which is contained in οὐκ ἔστιν, R. 768. Since Θεός is used as a proper
name, the sense is the same whether the article is added
or omitted; this is likewise true of terms that denote
persons or objects only one of which exists. Exegetically the textual question whether the article is genuine or not does not alter the interpretation. Our versions make ὁ Θεός the subject. This is probably done
on account of the article; the predicate is then to be
implied. But the Greek would naturally connect the
genitives with ὁ Θεός as their natural governing noun,
which thus must be the predicate in the sentence. And
the emphasis is on these genitives: not the God "of dead
men" but "of living men."

"Dead men" are men whose *bodies* are lifeless, who
are lying as such in their graves. If there is no resurrection, then the bodies of Abraham, Isaac, and Jacob
would remain dead forever, and that would make God
"the God of dead men" — an impossible thought. That
would mean that death was not conquered; that death
was holding its prey and was stronger than God; that
redemption had failed, leaving death still triumphant.
But no; the resurrection proves that God is "the God
of living men." Death has suffered its deathblow.

Redemption has not failed.  It has changed the death of God's saints into a mere sleep.  The proof is the resurrection by which God wakes these dead bodies from their slumber.  The precious dust of God's saints may, indeed, appear to our eyes as other dust, *dead dust;* in reality God, Christ, heavenly power is over and in that dust, it is living dust, we shall see it live in glory forever.  Thus the very name and title which God gave himself in the Old Testament as early as Exodus proves the resurrection.

The untenable interpretation is offered that the souls of the patriarchs are in *sheol,* the fabled "realm of the dead," and that Christ had in mind a release of their souls from *sheol,* and that this would be their resurrection and prove God to be "the God of the living." But such an interpretation makes Jesus' refutation of the Sadducees a farce.  They denied the resurrection of *the dead bodies,* and the substitution of a statement regarding *only their souls,* would be a deception, which, if detected, would seriously reflect on the entire character of Jesus.  It is an evasion of the real issue to say that the patriarchs were "not absolutely dead men, non-existent men," but "living" because they were enjoying eternal life in heaven.  Then the Sadducees (ancient and modern) would be right in asserting that no resurrection of *the dead bodies* will take place. Jesus himself would be a Sadducee.  He would be pretending to assert something "concerning the resurrection of the dead," namely its reality, when in fact he says nothing at all about it and thus by his silence abolishes its reality.

33) **And when the multitudes heard they were amazed at his teaching.**  Matthew purposely uses the plural οἱ ὄχλοι, for not all these "multitudes" were present when Jesus answered the Sadducees.  Many could not hear the voice of Jesus.  They "heard" the report spread far and wide among the pilgrims who

had assembled in vast numbers for the Passover. All
who heard the story continued in a state of amazement
(the verb is the durative imperfect) "at this teaching"
which so thoroughly refuted the Sadducees on the basis
of the Scriptures themselves and filled the very covenant name of God with the glorious truth of "the resurrection of the dead." That name now shone in new
splendor for them.

34) **Now the Pharisees, when they heard that
he muzzled the Sadducees, where gathered together
at one place; and one of them, learned in law, inquired, Teacher, what kind of commandment is great
in the law?** In 21:23 we see "high priests and
elders" confronting Jesus; these were Sadducees and
Pharisees in their official position, all of them Sanhedrists. In 22:16 only disciples of the Pharisees are
put forward. Now we have a general assembly of the
Pharisees, a gathering of all their forces in one place
(ἐπὶ τὸ αὐτό is common in this sense). While συνήχθησαν
is passive in form, "were brought together," i. e., by
being summoned, it may here be used in the middle
sense, "they assembled themselves." What caused
them to gather was the news that Jesus had muzzled
or silenced the Sadducees after their denial of the resurrection. This pleased the Pharisees exceedingly because they believed in the resurrection (Acts 23:8).
That is what induced them to propound another question to Jesus which they hoped would likewise lead
Jesus to utter a pronouncement against the Sadducees.
To make the motive of the Pharisees the desire to en-
tangle Jesus, as had been done in the previous attacks
on him, is rather unsatisfactory. The outcome of the
present questioning is entirely too friendly for that
(Mark 12:34). The one place where all the Pharisees
assembled was in the vicinity of Jesus in the Temple
court; a very few texts read ἐπ᾽ αὐτόν, "unto him," which
is substantially correct.

35)    One of their number, a νομικός, who was versed
in the law or Torah, whom Mark calls "a scribe," acts
as their spokesman, apparently by general agreement.
Mark tells the story as it pertains to this man alone,
Matthew as it involves the whole crowd of Pharisees,
none of whom, however, opens his mouth.    This one
man had heard the Sadducees reasoning together
(Mark 12:28) after their defeat and had perceived how
well Jesus had answered them.    Now he has a question
to ask Jesus, one that is of special interest to all the
Pharisees.    They all agreed that he shall proceed to
ask it, and they all go along to see what Jesus will answer.    "Tempting him" thus means, "trying Jesus out"
to see how he would solve the new conundrum.

36)    We should translate, "What kind of commandment is great in the law?"    Since often ποῖος has
lost its qualitative sense, we must decide whether it has
lost it here, so that the question might be, "Which *specific* commandment must be considered great?"    We
at once see that then the word used in the question should
be the superlative: "greatest in the law."    But sometimes the positive is used in this way: "great" — all
other commandments being regarded as less (R. 660).
So this is not decisive, and R. 740 wavers.    What is
decisive here is the answer of Jesus which makes two
commandments great and at the same time indicates
what makes them so great.    The qualitative ποία in the
question is matched by the qualitative force of the
answer.

To understand both the question and the great answer we must recall that the rabbis had no less than
613 commandments, 248 positive, 365 negative.    In
order to obtain so large a number they used gematria, a
cabalistic method of interpretation by which the rabbis
interchanged Hebrew words whose letters have the
same numerical value when they are added.    Among so
many commandments some, of course, would be less

important than others, and in a conflict of duties the
more important would have precedence. To what this
casuistry led we see in 15:4-6. Now, how was the
greatness of a commandment to be determined? Of
what kind (ποία) must it be? One method was to judge
by the severity of the penalty attached. Thus some
magnified the commandments regarding the sacrifices,
others the Sabbath laws, and still others the law and
regulations regarding circumcision. What would Jesus
say? But the chief point to these Pharisees was the
fact that the Sadducees rejected all the Pharisaic commandments that were not plainly written in the law, all
those that were only the tradition of the fathers. This
was one form of their skepticism. Josephus, *Antiquities,* 13, 10, 6; 18, 1, 4. Would Jesus side with the
Sadducees?

37) **But Jesus said to him: Thou wilt love the
Lord thy God with thy whole heart and with thy
whole soul and with thy whole mind. This is the
great and first commandment. And a second, like
it, this, Thou wilt love thy neighbor as thyself. In
these two commandments the whole law hangs and
the prophets.** This is an answer without a preamble
of rebuke, cf., v. 18 or v. 29. We note also that it is
directed only to the questioner (αὐτῷ) and disregards,
as it were, the assembled crowd of Pharisees who are
conspicuous as such because of their phylacteries and
their tasseled robes (23:5). Jesus offers nothing but a
simple and a direct answer; and Mark adds the remark
that the lawyer who asked the question fully appreciated and even repeated the answer as being one that
truly answered the question, and that thus he received
the commendation of Jesus. The answer first quotes
Deuteronomy 6:5, but not exactly according to either
the Hebrew or the LXX; for in the last phrase these
latter have "might," whereas Jesus has "mind." Mark
records the three phrases that Matthew mentions, but

adds a fourth that has "might" ("strength") and is like the third in the Hebrew and the LXX. There is no difference in substance. Mark, however, adds the introductory statement, "Hear, O Israel," etc.

On ἀγαπᾶν as expressing the love of intelligence and purpose, thus differeng from φιλεῖν which is the love of mere liking or affection, compare 5:44. In this instance it would be impossible to substitute φιλεῖν for ἀγαπᾶν. The latter implies that we know the true God in all his greatness and grace and that we turn to him with all our being. It would be impossible to apply to φιλεῖν the deep phrases, "with all thy heart," etc.; but ἀγαπᾶν really involves these phrases. The future tense ἀγαπήσεις is used in legal phraseology as a substitute for the imperative (R. 330), and the future is volitive (R. 943) and expresses the lawgiver's will. The three phrases are not condensed into "with thy whole heart, soul, and mind," but spread out so as to place equal emphasis on each one. Yet the heart is mentioned first, the soul properly next, and the mind last. To understand the psychological necessity of this order, study Delitzsch, *Biblische Psychologie*, 248, etc. In the Biblical conception the *leb*, καρδία, "heart," is the very center of our personality; here also dwells the ψυχή, "the life" or "soul"; and here functions the διάνοια, "the mind" or power to think. The *nephesh* or ψυχή is the life that animates the body, the consciousness of which is in the "heart"; and the διάνοια is the reason together with all its functions, namely its thoughts, ideas, convictions, according to which the heart or personality acts. Since this is God's own commandment, uttered by his own mouth, we here have a psychology of man as it is conceived by man's own Creator who certainly knows man better than man can possibly know himself.

The word "whole" in the three phrases receives great emphasis because of its very repetition. God will have no mere part, allow no division or subtraction.

Not even the smallest corner is to be closed against God.
The whole heart, the seat of our personality; the whole
soul, our sentient being itself; and the whole mind, the
entire activity of this our being is to turn to God in
love; Josh. 22:5, "to cleave unto him." And this is to
be done because he is the covenant God: *Yahweh*, "I
am that I am," the unchanging Lord who drew us into
covenant relation with him; and *'Eloheka*, the God of
power and might, and, as the possessive shows, he who
employs his power in our behalf. This great name
is the epitome of the gospel. Both titles, and especially when they are combined, denote divine love and
grace toward us. By that name God proclaims the
gospel to us as the supreme motive for us to return his
love. Believing in such a God, how can we help but
love him and render him the obedience of love? Luther
was correct when, in his explanation of the Ten Commandments, he begins the explanation of each commandment with fear and love.

Moreover, this divine name proclaims the oneness
of God. By so doing it in no way conflicts with his
trinity, since this is the oneness of being not of person.
This one God has revealed himself in three persons.
As regards other gods, each one of these is, of course,
also one. To call Israel's God one would thus mean
nothing at all, might even bear the false implication
that he was the one and special god for the Jewish
nation as other nations had this or that god. The oneness expressed in *Yahweh 'Eloheka* is the fact that he
is the *only* God who is able to make and to keep a covenant; all other gods are nonentities, dead figures, non-
living, empty idols. In New Testament phraseology:
as our Father in Christ Jesus loves us with the divine
love of fatherhood, so we are in turn to love him as his
devoted children in Christ Jesus.

38) Because of the quality of this commandment
which reaches up to the covenant of God and extends

down through all our being, Jesus rightly says, "This
is the great and first commandment," by its very quality outranking all others that may be added.  Once
this is stated in all simplicity as Jesus states it here,
how could any man even attempt a contradiction?  By
this commandment, therefore, all the other commandments and the many regulations given to the Jews
through Moses are to be weighed and gauged.  We
have the illustrations given by Jesus himself in v. 21,
and again in v. 32, where twice God's name is made
decisive in regard to legal questions ("Is it lawful,"
v. 17; the law of levirate marriage, v. 24).

39) But where supreme quality is the issue, a
second commandment must be mentioned, namely the
one in which the long list given in Lev. 19 culminates,
the eighteenth verse: "Thou wilt love thy neighbor as
thyself."  In quality it is "like" the one regarding God.
Here again we have "love," and here again we have
the full extent of this love which includes every contact
with our neighbor or our fellow-man.  Some manuscripts have the dative: "like to this," i. e., to the previous commandment.  Compare 5:44, and again note
that φιλεῖν would be out of place here, whereas the love
of understanding and corresponding purpose is exactly
what God does and must demand of us toward our
neighbor even if that neighbor be a stranger to us
(Luke 10:37) or a man who is filled with enmity toward us.  The point in quoting this commandment in
addition to the other is in this instance not the fact that
love to God includes love to our neighbor, which is true
enough; but that the quality and the high character of
both commandments are "alike."  This, of course,
leaves them in their natural order, the one concerning
God remains "first," and the other concerning man
"second," for God is infinitely above man.

40) Because of their nature and their quality as
indicated "in these two commandments the whole law

(Torah, Pentateuch) hangs and the prophets" (all the
other books of the Old Testament). These two are the
nail from which all else written in the Old Testament
hangs suspended. Take away this nail, and everything
else would fall in a heap. It would lose its true meaning, significance, and purpose. Here again we have
the emphatic ὅλος, "the *whole* law." We cannot reduce
"the law and the prophets" to the *legal* contents of the
Old Testament books and say that the prophets explain
and elucidate the many laws and regulations of Moses.
This would obscure the gospel contents of the Old Testament. But the fact that this is included in the First
Commandment we have shown by pointing to the covenant name of God. See how Mark 12:29, 30 makes
this gospel name prominent. No; the gospel, too,
"hangs in these two commandments." Only those who
have and hold the gospel can to any degree fulfill these
commandments, even as they are intended peculiarly
for God's own children. And these two commandments, as do no others, show the true need of the gospel; for, however well they may outwardly perform
deeds of the law, by nature men lack the love demanded
by these commandments, are thus altogether guilty
before God, and can be saved and restored only by
means of the gospel.

The answer of Jesus to the lawyer is so complete,
so rich and satisfying, so illuminating in every way,
that the lawyer himself said so in his own way (Mark
12:32, 33). When he said that this twofold love "is
much more than all whole burnt offerings and sacrifices," he indicated the kind of commandments he had
hitherto considered of prime rank. But he yielded to
Jesus and thus receives a significant commendation.
This incident, however, stopped all further questioning
of Jesus.

41) After submitting to the various questionings
recorded in 21:23-22:40, Jesus, in turn, propounds a

question in all sincerity in order to lead his hearers to the truth. **Now since the Pharisees had gathered together, Jesus inquired of them, saying: How does it seem to you concerning the Christ? Whose son is he? They say to him, David's.** Jesus has before him the same assemblage of Pharisees that was mentioned in v. 34. The perfect participle συνηγμένων plainly recalls συνήχθησαν of that verse, and its form implies that they were still thus assembled. Together with them there was present a throng of festival pilgrims, οἱ ὄχλοι, to whom Jesus turns after he has concluded his address to the Pharisees (23:1). In all dignity, as the verb implies, Jesus makes his inquiry.

42) A variety of explanations has been offered as to why Jesus asks this question about the Messiah. Already the ancient fathers saw that Jesus here renews the supreme question he had a few weeks ago addressed to his own band of disciples, 16:13-16. Peter had given the true answer; the Pharisees refuse to give that answer. Until Palm Sunday Jesus had avoided use of the name "Messiah" because of its political and nationalistic implications. Now the time has arrived to disregard all such implications. On Palm Sunday Jesus had entered Jerusalem and the Temple as David's son, Israel's King, the Messiah. The pilgrim multitudes had shouted his great titles, the boys marching in the Temple courts had echoed those shouts. As the Messiah Jesus now asks the Pharisees this question, and they know that it is not an academic or a theoretical inquiry but the supreme question concerning his own person. It is put objectively, in the third person: "What do you think about the Messiah? Whose son is he?" It is thereby made easier to answer; but it pertains to Jesus himself nontheless.

Luther finds a natural connection between the question concerning what makes a commandment great in the law (v. 36) and the answer Jesus gave (v. 37-40)

and this great question which Jesus now asks and
answers from Ps. 110. This connection has been
denied, and yet it is only too obvious. Why would the
covenant God of Israel, *Yahweh Eloheka,* ask his people
to love him as he did if that love could never be realized
in their hearts because of their sin and their doom
under sin? His very covenant name points to the covenant promise of the Messiah in and through whose
grace Israel would, indeed, come to love the Lord their
God with the whole heart, soul, and mind (Jer. 31:33,
34). "The great and first commandment" (v. 38) and
the Messiah, David's son and David's Lord, will ever
belong together.

Jesus has one and only one object in asking this
question: to add to the other revelations of his deity
that Jesus had made this revelation which is quoted
from David's Psalm, which is so clear and complete
that every Jew who believed the Scriptures must at
once see and accept it. The purpose of Jesus is to win
even these Pharisees to faith — remember the one that
was not far from the kingdom (Mark 12:34)? The
motive that prompts Jesus is the pure and mighty love
of the two great commandments which are repeated by
his own lips.

The Pharisees answer with great readiness, "David's." In fact, every Jewish child would have at once
given the same answer. That is what all their scribes
taught them on the basis of the Scriptures, Mark 12:35.
When modernists reduce this to the subjective "normal
belief of his (Jesus') day" and admit only that the
Messiah *"might* be descended from David," and intimate that he might also have been descended from some
other ancestor, they ignore all that both Testaments
declare about the human ancestry of the promised
Messiah. As far as Jesus is concerned, his *legal* sonship in David's line is established by Matthew's genealogical table in chapter one; and his *natural* sonship

from David's line is equally established by Luke's table, 3:23, etc. His whole family connection was fully known (13:55, 56; 12:47). No more deadly weapon against the Messiahship of Jesus could have been found than the proof that he was not of David's line; but his bitterest enemies never ventured to cast even the least doubt upon his human descent from David.

43) The answer of the Pharisees was perfectly correct as far as it went. But it had to go much farther. For David had a large number of descendants. How was the one to be distinguished who would. be the Messiah? If God had revealed no more concerning the Messiah than the fact that he would be a son of David he would have left his people altogether in the dark. Davidic descent was only one mark. What was the other, the one that would make *one* of David's sons stand out far above all the others, far above even a Solomon and a Hezekiah, would beyond a doubt make him the promised Messiah? Surely, the Scriptures would answer that question. In order to help these Jews and other bystanders to find this answer in the Scriptures, Jesus continues his question. **He says to them: How, then, does David in Spirit call him Lord, saying, The Lord said to my Lord, Be sitting at my right until I put thine enemies beneath thy feet? If, therefore, David calls him Lord, how is he his son?**

These questions assume that it is self-evident that the Messiah would be David's son and, in fact, rest on this assumption as an unquestionable fact. Moreover, these questions, together with their plainly implied answer, would be senseless unless two further things are true: first, that David wrote Psalm 110 and no one else; and secondly, that *Yahweh* actually did call this one son of David nothing less than David's *'Adonai*. The Jews have consistently interpreted this psalm as a Messianic psalm in spite of the New Testament and the

Christian application to Jesus whom the synagogues reject as the Messiah.

Against the critics who on subjective grounds deny that this Psalm was composed by David we put the word of Jesus in this passage; that of Luke and of Peter in Acts 2:34, 35; that of Paul in I Cor. 15:25, plus that of Hebrews 1:13; 10:13. David wrote this Psalm ἐν Πνεύματι (ἐν τῷ Πνεύματι τῷ Ἁγίῳ, Mark 12:36), "in connection with the Spirit," under the Holy Spirit's influence, which, if it means anything, means by divine inspiration.

If this is denied, the result is more than disastrous. If David did not write this psalm, if David did not call this one son of his "my Lord," if the Pharisees and all Judaism were mistaken regarding this point, and if Jesus, as a child of his times, was equally mistaken: then we have the sad picture of the great Jesus by a mistake proving to Jews caught in the same mistake what the mistakes of both disprove instead of prove. But if only the Pharisees were mistaken regarding the authorship of this psalm, if Jesus knew better, then Jesus used the ignorance of the Pharisees for his purpose and sinks to the level of a tricky modern lawyer who capitalizes on the ignorance of his opponent at court. In either case Jesus proves his deity by a false proof, according to one view ignorantly, according to the other consciously. In other words, he proves his deity by really disproving it. A mistaken Jesus, or a tricky Jesus, is not the model for us which the critics would make him.

44) But even when the authorship of this psalm is attributed to David, we are not through. For in this psalm he most clearly distinguishes between himself and the far greater person of the Messiah, his future son and yet his almighty Lord. We are told that in no other psalm David thus distinguishes the type from the antitype. The answer is that in this psalm David

does not operate with type (himself) and antitype (the Messiah). Even if this were his conception and if here alone he distinguishes clearly between the two, there is no law of God or man that a thing must be done more than once before it can be done at all. We are born only once, die only once, and no man denies either because they cannot point to repetitions. But the thesis that only in this psalm David clearly distinguishes between himself and the Messiah is untenable; he does so in II Sam. 23:1-7; again in Ps. 2:7, 12; and in Ps. 22 he goes so far beyond anything that he experienced that here, too, the Messiah stands out distinctly from David.

"The Lord said" is more expressive in the Hebrew: *n*ᵉ*'um Yahweh*, "communication of Jehovah," *Eingerauntes*, something secretly whispered into the ear, the communication of a mystery. The expression is at times placed into the middle of a divine communication, like the Latin *inquit*, sometimes at the end, but repeatedly also at the head as is the case in this psalm. At times the recipient of the communication is added as here: "to my Lord," *'Adonai*. The fact that this is David's future son is understood by all concerned, is placed beyond question by Jesus himself, and is accepted by both Jewish and Christian exegesis. Yet this his own son David, who as the king had only *Yahweh* above him, calls "my Lord," and the kind of *'Adon* or "Lord" he has in mind is brought out by the description of him given in this psalm: he is one who sits at *Yahweh's* right hand, one whose enemies are made his footstool, one who has the rod of strength out of Zion; and so on through the psalm. No wonder David called this son of his "my Lord." This is the Messiah, the God-man, and thus even King David's "Lord." Note that *Yahweh* is here distinct from *'Adon;* a clear revelation in the Old Testament of the persons of the Godhead. Here one divine person speaks to the other. All

three persons appear clearly in the Old Testament. No
wonder the Baptist could freely mention all three, and
no Jew ever objected when he heard mention of the
Father, the Son of God, and the Spirit of God. The
Jews' sole objection was due to the fact that Jesus, the
lowly man of Nazareth, called himself the Son, and that
men received him as such. David was a prophet who
by the illumination and the inspiration "in Spirit"
wrote as he did.

Here divine exaltation is predicated of David's son,
the Messiah: "Be sitting (present imperative, durative) at my right (ἐκ, in the Greek idiom the right, the
left, too, are always designated "from" the person,
20:21)." The Hebrew imperative *sheb limini* has actually become a Messianic title, "Sheblimini." *Yahweh's* right hand is his divine power and majesty,
therefore also it is called "the right hand of power."
Compare the parallel passages on God's right hand.
To be sitting at God's right is to exercise this power
and this majesty to the fullest extent. This invitation
to sit is thus the divine exaltation of Christ's human
nature. For as the Son, begotten from eternity, he is
coequal with the Father and together with the Father
and the Spirit exercises all power and majesty. When
the Son assumed our human nature he communicated
all his divine attributes to that nature. Just as a king
who marries a humble maiden by virtue of that marriage makes her a queen so that she shares in all his
royal prerogatives, so the Son did when he wedded our
human nature. But in order to accomplish his redemptive work it was necessary that the human nature pass
through a state of humiliation while it was here on
earth. So the human nature had the divine attributes
bestowed upon it, but ordinarily, except when working
miracles, did not use these attributes, Phil. 2:6, etc.
Then at last followed the glorious exaltation: Christ in
his human nature sat at his Father's right hand.

Now comes the astounding clause "until I put thine enemies beneath thy feet." *Yahweh* himself declares that he will put the exalted Messiah's enemies under his feet (the variant reading, "put . . . as thy footstool," follows the LXX and the Hebrew). These are ἐχθροί, personal enemies, who, unlike David, will not have this man to reign over them. Jesus faces some of these very enemies as he utters these mighty assurances of *Yahweh* concerning himself. These words must have burned into the souls of these Pharisees, but *Yahweh's* terrible threat as it came from the lips of the despised Jesus only enraged them.

But the object of Jesus did not lie in this threat but in the revelation of the divine nature of his person whom David himself called "my Lord" and exalted as very God in this psalm. We need scarcely trouble about the interpretation which makes the Father and not the Son active. We have known for a long time that the *opera ad extra sunt indivisa;* all the persons of the Godhead share in all of them, and the Father works in and through the Son and the Spirit. In Ps. 2:9 the Messiah-King smites with a rod of iron, dashes in pieces like a potter's vessel. That shows the Son at the Father's right. God laughs at the raging of kings on the earth and at the violent hosts of men and of devils who assail his Son's kingdom.

These expressions, such as making a footstool of enemies, Josh. 10:24 are anthropomorphitic. Conquering kings gave evidence of their triumph by placing a foot upon the neck of some conquered king. But here the figure is vastly magnified: all the Messiah's enemies shall be his footstool. "Footstool" (Hebrew) matches the figure of the exalted Messiah's "sitting" on the throne with the Father. "Temporal history shall end with the triumph of good over evil but not with the annihilation of evil but with its subjugation. To this point it will come when absolute omnipotence

for and through the exalted Christ shows its effectiveness." Delitzsch. On '*ad*, ἕως, "until," see the author's
commentary on I Cor. 15:28.

45) Here follows the question that is so deadly for
these unbelieving Pharisees yet so illuminating and
blessed for all believers: "If, therefore, David calls
him Lord, how is he his son?" With οὖν Jesus makes
his question a deduction from the statement of the
psalm, just as in v. 43 οὖν deduces the question there
asked from the answer of the Pharisees. The condition
is one of reality: all must admit that in the psalm
David calls the Messiah "his Lord." The condition of
reality challenges any denial of David's own word
recorded in Holy Writ.

The remarkable fact is that Jesus does not turn
the question around and ask: "Since he is David's
son, as we all know, how can he at the same time be
David's Lord?" But no, Jesus puts it the other way:
"How is he his son?" Nor dare we generalize: a
man's son is his lord. We must limit ourselves to
David, Israel's mightiest king, who lived and died having no man above him — and yet this great David
makes *his own son* his Lord. The question of Jesus,
put in the form he used, throws the Pharisees against
this stone wall: the Messiah *is* David's son!

The terrible error of the Pharisees is here exposed.
Their conception of the Messiah was that he was
David's son and only David's son, a mere human Messiah, however great and mighty he might be in his
human glory and power. His deity was a closed book
to their blind reading of Scripture. They dared not
say that he was *not* to be David's son; they knew that
he would be. They dared not deny David's inspired
word that the Messiah would at the same time be
David's Lord and thus very God. Yet the Pharisees
would not admit the Messiah's deity.

46) **And no one was able to answer a word. Nor did anyone dare from that day on to inquire of him any further.** The Pharisees remain dumb and silent. They had no answer since they were obdurate and refused to give the right answer. Although convicted, they will not yield. This was Tuesday. None of the evangelists reports what Jesus did on Wednesday or during the day on Thursday. It seems that after he left the Temple courts on Tuesday he never returned to teach there.

# CHAPTER XXIII

1) **Then Jesus spoke to the multitude and to his disciples, saying: On the seat of Moses sat down the scribes and the Pharisees.** All things, therefore, whatever they say to you, do and keep guarding; but according to their works stop doing, for they say and do not do. Besides, they tie together loads heavy and hard to carry and put them upon the shoulders of men; yet they themselves are not willing even with their finger to stir them.** Since 21:23 we must imagine the presence of the ὄχλοι or crowds of festival pilgrims as listening to what went on. The Pharisees, whose assembling has been mentioned in both 22:34 and 22:41, are still present. Right before them Jesus warns the pilgrims against them; and, having done that, he turns and hurls his fearful woes into their faces (v. 13-39). We write all this quite calmly, but the scene was charged with a dramatic tenseness that is hard for us to imagine. Together with the pilgrims Jesus warns his own disciples.

2) The very first words show that Jesus is speaking *of* the scribes and the Pharisees not *to* them. The two articles distinguish two classes (R. 758). The scribes were, indeed, also Pharisees, but they were the professional students of the Old Testament and thus a distinct class; the rest of the Pharisees accepted the teaching of their scribes and made a strenuous profession of translating it into life, holding the common people to follow their example. In this way "they sat down on the seat of Moses." The aorist ἐκάθισαν is historical; R. 866 makes it gnomic and thus timeless, seemingly in an effort to justify the English translation "sit." With ἐκάθισαν Jesus states merely the fact, which

does not in any way admit the right of these men to
Moses' seat. They were not called to this seat as Moses
had been. He assumed that seat reluctantly, but these
false followers of his assumed his seat of their own
accord and were determined to have and to hold it.
They were self-appointed usurpers and acted as though
their dicta were as binding as the revelations God made
to Moses, 15:3-9.

3) The οὖν should not be regarded as admitting the
right of these usurpers to Moses' seat; in John 10:1,
etc., Jesus calls them thieves and robbers. "Therefore" means: under the circumstances thus described.
In the Orient teachers ordinarily sit, perhaps on a platform, with their legs folded underneath them. In Constantinople and in Damascus the author saw prominent
Mohammedan teachers sitting thus on platforms while
their hearers sat cross-legged on the floor of the
mosque. What course are the people now to follow?
They are to recognize the falsity of these self-appointed
successors of Moses and are to avoid their falsity.

"All things whatever they say to you" does not refer
to all their misinterpretations, all the false traditions
they may hand out. *Concordia Triglotta*, 449, 21.
Seated in Moses' seat, these teachers read the word of
Moses and of the prophets, and these are the words,
whatever they may be, that Jesus bids the people "do
and keep guarding." The first verb is an effective
aorist imperative: ποιήσατε, do, perform, so as to finish
the thing. The second is a durative present imperative: τηρεῖτε, always keep guarding, so that no one may
mislead you, and you may keep these divine words.

Jesus does not say that the people are to perform
and to cherish what the scribes and the Pharisees
"teach" (16:12, 13) but only what they "say" ("bid"
in our versions is misleading). When these false
teachers *say* the divine words, the people are not to disregard them because they come from teachers of this

kind. The blessed power of these words is not derived
from those who speak them truly, nor lost when false
men do the speaking; it is due to the words themselves
because they come from God. *Concordia Triglotta,* 47
(VIII).

The warning, "but according to their works stop
doing," has μὴ ποιεῖτε, the present imperative in a prohibition, which so often denotes that an action already
begun is to stop and to remain stopped (R. 851, etc.).
The scribes and the Pharisees were greatly revered by
the common people, and thus their example was constantly followed. Jesus tells the people to stop this.
Γάρ states the chief reason: "for they say and do not."
These present tenses are not gnomic nor timeless but
durative: "they keep saying, and they keep not doing."
They read the Scriptures even in public and yet do not
what the Scriptures say.

This is the first specification of the hypocrisy of
these religious leaders, and in a moment (v. 13, etc.)
Jesus will call down woe upon them as arrant hypocrites. But this doing should not be restricted to the
legal commandments and regulations of Moses and of
the prophets. The Old Testament is full of the gospel
which requires and works faith in God and in his Messiah (22:41-45). This grand part of the Word the
scribes and the Pharisees never saw. So they failed
altogether "to do" this part, to believe. And this naturally ruined also the other part, the law in the Word.
They missed its supreme purpose: the knowledge of
sin and true contrition; they abused the law by their
rank work-righteousness. How often had Jesus held
up the true sense of the Torah before them, but, even
when they had to admit the validity of this sense, they
barred their hearts against its saving effect.

4) With δέ, "besides," Jesus turns to something
else. The "heavy burdens" are often regarded as all
the Pharisaic traditions; but the Pharisees did try to

carry these. After telling the people to heed the words of Moses although they may be brought to them by false teachers and to do and to treasure up these words by faith in the Messiah and by a new life according to his will, Jesus describes what these false teachers actually do with Moses' words. They omitted, not from the reading indeed, but from their teaching, all the gospel promises. They turned everything they read from the Old Testament into law only. They take those blessed words and "tie them together as loads heavy and hard to carry," like heavy sheaves or bundles of faggots. These loads "they put upon the shoulders of men," and make them slaves. Blind to the gospel in the Scripture, they knew nothing but law, and this law they perverted for self-righteous purposes.

The δέ is plainly adversative: "yet they themselves are not willing even with their finger to stir them." "The finger" is placed in opposition to other men's shoulders, and "to stir" the loads with a finger, an exceedingly slight action, is put in opposition to piling these loads on others. The commentary is given in v. 23: while omitting all the weightier matters of the law such as judgment, mercy, and faith, they were keen on tithing little things such as mint and cummin. They piled nothing but law, law upon others, but themselves did not make the slightest effort even to stir the real law of God by honest obedience, to say nothing of assuming its full burden.

5) **Moreover, all their works they do in order to be beheld by men; for they broaden their phylacteries and enlarge the tassels; moreover, they like the chief reclining place at the dinners and the chief seats in the synagogues and the salutations in the markets and to be called by men Rabbi.** Whatever works the Pharisees do, they do only to be viewed by men, for men to see, admire, praise, and honor; they forget God who seeth in secret (6:1, etc.). This is

again rank hypocrisy. With γάρ the specifications are
introduced. They make their phylacteries real broad,
thus as prominent as possible, so that everybody may
at once see them. The phylacteries, *totaphoth* or
*tephillim*, were capsules with bands passed through
them in order to tie them, the one on the forehead, the
other on the left wrist. These capsules contained a
little strip of parchment that had Exod. 13:3-16; Deut.
6:5-9; 11:13-21 inscribed upon it. Thus in the most
mechanical, superficially literal fashion they made the
law "for a sign upon thine hand, and for a memorial
between thine eyes." While they were originally to be
worn only during the *sh<sup>e</sup>ma* prayer in the morning (the
words of Deut. 6:4, 5, which are repeated in Mark
12:29, 30), many Pharisees wore them constantly, even
during the night. Various regulations governed their
construction, the way to tie and to knot the bands, etc.,
all in true Pharisaic fashion.

They likewise "enlarge the tassels," namely of the
*shimla* or large square cloth that was worn as an outward robe, at each of the four corners of which a
κράσπεδον, *tsitsith*, was fastened according to Deut.
22:12. These tassels were attached with blue cords,
and the Pharisees made the tassels long so that especially the two that were at the corners thrown over the
shoulders should be as prominent as possible (9:20).
This show before men was naturally combined with the
desire to impress men and to have these prove it by
greatly honoring such holy men. So they like to occupy "the chief reclining place at the dinners," δεῖπνα,
the evening meal which would be made a feast by the
invitation of guests. Here φιλεῖν is sufficient, and ἀγαπᾶν
would say much more (5:44). When they were thus
invited, the scribes and the Pharisees dearly liked to
have the foremost place on each divan or couch. This
was the place at the extreme left of the couch, and was
considered the foremost because the person occupying

it could overlook the entire table without throwing back his head or turning around. Each couch had its head place, and these hypocrites wanted these badly. So also they loved the prominent seats in the synagogues beside the rulers of the synagogue, where everybody could see their prominence; they also counted on being called upon during the services to offer their wisdom.

7) "The salutations in the markets" are the greetings they liked so well to receive in such public places. Jesus mentions one of these: "to be called by men Rabbi," to receive this coveted title, which was like our D. D., from men. Their hypocrisy was shown by their liking and their selfish desire for such human honors. Their falsity lay not only in utterly perverting the Word of God but in adding thereto the most despicable religious vanity and pride.

8) At this point Jesus turns especially to his disciples. **But you for your part be not called Rabbi! For one is your Teacher while all you are brethren. And father of yours do not call anyone on the earth. For one is your Father, the heavenly One. Nor be called leaders, for one is your Leader, the Christ. And the greater of you shall be your ministrant. Moreover, whoever exalts himself shall be humbled; and whoever shall humble himself shall be exalted.** All this applies directly to the disciples, hence the emphatic ὑμεῖς, "you on your part," which also runs through most of this section. The words are also intended for the rest of the hearers; they are to apply them to themselves.

Two things are to be kept in mind; first, what Jesus has just said concerning the prideful desire for honors and titles on the part of the scribes and the Pharisees and, secondly, the conclusion stated in v. 11, 12 as this explains what precedes in v. 8-10. The use of the name "Rabbi," "my teacher" is not forbidden by Jesus; for it is evident that he himself gives his church teach-

ers and leaders who have various offices which also
have their distinctive titles, Eph. 4:11; I Cor. 12:28.
The subordination of one brother to another which is
expressed by the term "Rabbi" is not contrary to the
Lord's will, for he himself speaks of "the greater of
you," v. 11. What Jesus forbids is that any disciple
of his should arrogate to himself an authority as the
scribes and the Pharisees did who usurped the seat of
Moses and despised the common people as knowing
nothing and as thus being accursed for following Jesus,
John 7:49; an authority which would set aside our true
Rabbi or Teacher, Jesus, and would destroy the equality
which puts us all on the same level as "brethren."

Therefore the prohibition is illuminated by the explanation that One only is our "Teacher" and that
under this One all of us are "brethren." It should be
noted that Jesus does not say, "All of you are disciples
or pupils," for he does not want to bring out our relation to himself but our relation to each other. We all
are equally God's children, and his saving truth belongs
equally to all of us, none is thus dependent upon another, all religious autocracy is abolished. Any title
that is contrary to this equality of brethren in Christ
Jesus, even the desire for such a title and honor, is
arrogation as far as the brethren are concerned and
wicked usurpation as far as our one real Teacher is
concerned. We all sit at his feet, although what one
has learned from him he may teach his brother either
as a brother or as a duly called pastor.

9) As no one shall lift up himself unduly, so also
no one is to be lifted up unduly. No one is to be called
"father" by us in a religious sense. The Greek can
separate $\pi\alpha\tau\acute{\epsilon}\rho\alpha$ and $\acute{\nu}\mu\tilde{\omega}\nu$ and thus lend emphasis to both
words. The title "father" was accorded only to the
most prominent and revered teachers; the question
would thus be one less of wanting to be so honored as of
disciples bestowing such an honor. Now spiritual

fathers are rightly called "father"; in I Cor. 4:15 Paul
calls himself the father of the Corinthians, and in I Tim.
1:1, Timothy's father, compare Gal. 4:19 and John's
Epistles.  Here again the explanatory γάρ helps us by
pointing to our one and only Father, the heavenly one.
We are to obey no man, however great he may be or may
have been in the church, so as to set aside the one and
only real authority in force for us, that of our heavenly
Father whose children alone we are in the proper sense
of the word.  Paul may call Timothy his son and may,
like a mother, travail again till Christ be formed in the
Galatians; we may call the great old teachers "Church
Fathers," the Reformer, "Father Luther," the old and
revered men in the church "fathers" — all such loving
terms are bestowed on the basis of our common brotherhood in Christ only, on the basis of our common childhood through faith only.  The moment one of these old
teachers errs from our Father's Word, we would not
accept such an error.  No man in the church today has
authority to make us do anything that is out of harmony with the Word of our heavenly Father.  In the
last analysis there is only *one* Father over us all.

We thus challenge the claims of the Roman Catholic
catechism:  *"Quamobrem omnium fidelium et episco-
porum . . . pater ac moderator universalis ecclesiae
ut Petri successor Christique verus et legitimus, vi-
carius in terris praesidet."*  We reject the false authority of "the holy father," "the vicegerent of Christ."
And in the same way we reject all others who come
with a similar authority, whether it be in doctrine, in
church practice, or in matters of Christian living.
Even the state has no authority in these matters.

10)    With the word καθηγητής, "leader," Jesus does
not merely repeat "rabbi" and "father," whether the
Hebrew equivalent is *rabbon* (Mark 10:51) or *rabboni,*
"my leader," John 20:16.  This καθηγητής is a leader
who assumes full responsibility for those led and who

thus commands and is obeyed. No one can claim a leadership of this kind in the church that is in conflict with our one Leader, the Christ. He, indeed, bears all responsibility and does that with unquestioned and unquestionable results. This does not imply that men may not also lead us, and that great assemblies of the church may also pass resolutions both as regards doctrine and practice. But all these human leaders must ever and only follow Christ's leadership. And all of us have the fullest right to test out all their decisions by the standard of Christ's own decisions and summarily to reject what is contrary to his Word and to accept only what his Word approves. No man may ever curtail this right of ours on the plea that he will assume the responsibility for keeping in agreement with Christ. Since the time of the Reformation and of Luther we know this as the Right of Private Judgment. "One is your Leader, the Christ" means that he is such forever. His leadership is being exercised at this very moment, namely by his living Word. Rebels and traitors are all those who leave that Word and lead God's people otherwise. That Word condemns them from the great Antichrist down to the little antichrists and all other spurious and false teachers, including those who may lead wrong in only one doctrine or one church practice. "The Christ" is appellative, "the Messiah"; but while this word is strongly objective, Jesus plainly refers to himself.

11) Once more, clearly and distinctly, Jesus states what makes great in his kingdom (20:26, 27). So some shall, indeed, be greater than others; they have greater faith, knowledge, gifts, and results, such as the Twelve, such as Paul, such as brethren of lesser note possessed. We may designate them as we deem best, but all of them are greater than others only as "your ministrant," διάκονος, one who is eager to render service for the benefit it brings others. Over against Christ

we are all δοῦλοι, "slaves," such as render unquestioning obedience; but over against each other we are διάκονοι, who gladly minister wherever we can. Such "ministrants" are all true teachers, fathers, and leaders in the church, and in the spirit of such ministry they bear the titles accorded them. Their greatness is in proportion to their ministration, the good they do, and the lowliness with which they do that good.

12) All that has thus far been stated has been phrased in the second person and is applicatory because of this form. Now Jesus becomes objective and by use of the third person announces the great principle upon which all the peremptory aorist imperatives since v. 8 rest. Self-exaltation is a mortal offense in the Christian Church. It has produced the great pope, a large number of little popes, and men and women "bosses" in congregations. But all self-exalted men "shall be humbled." There is no question about it. The agent of the passive is Christ. When such humbling occurs in this life, however bitter it may be, it may lead to true self-humiliation. The reverse is equally true: true self-humiliation "shall be exalted" by Christ. Self-exaltation is wholly a product of the flesh; Christian self-humiliation is wholly a product of the Spirit and of his grace working in us. "God is above all. Thou exaltest thyself and dost not reach up to him; thou humblest thyself, and he stoops down to thee." Augustine. "Thus Christian brotherhood does not exclude the thought that because of his office and his gifts one brother may be above another. Not disorderly equality of all does Christ teach, he rather commands that the brethren who are greater than others may in heartfelt humiliation place themselves at the service of the rest and hold themselves in humility." John Gerhard.

13) Without the least warning Jesus turns from the pilgrim crowds and his own disciples and pours out the most terrific denunciation upon the scribes and

the Pharisees. These seven woes are the most awful
words that the lips of Jesus ever uttered. They were
spoken with all the power of Jesus' divine personality,
without angry passion, without the heat of excitement,
with deadly calmness, with absolute truth, with crushing power. Through every οὐαί there rings a tone of
sadness, which breaks out in full strength in v. 37: "I
would, but you would not." **But woe to you, scribes
and Pharisees, hypocrites, because you are locking
the kingdom of the heavens in front of men; for you
yourselves are not going in, neither are you permitting those going in to go in.**

Every one of the seven "woes" is an exclamation
like the "blessed" in the Beatitudes. It does not state
a wish but a fact. It is not a curse that calls down
calamity but a calm, true judgment and verdict rendered by the supreme Judge himself. Hence six of
these judgments have the evidence attached by means
of a causal ὅτι clause which furnishes the full reason for
the verdict "woe"; and in the remaining judgment (v.
16) the varied form of expression does the same by
means of an apposition. On "scribes" see 2:4; on
Pharisees 3:7. The word ὑποκριταί has the sense of
show actor, ὑπό suggesting the mask under which he hid
his true identity on the stage, for the ancient actors
appeared with masks.

The sin because of which the verdict "woe" is pronounced is the fact that by their teaching and their
hypocritical practices these Jewish leaders "are locking
the kingdom of the heavens in front of men," yet this
does not imply that they have the keys of this kingdom
(the true gospel), but that the falsity of their teaching
and their life deceives those who follow them, so that
the kingdom (see on 3:2) with its heavenly rule of
grace is kept from them. They lock it by barring men
out of it by their false teaching. They are guilty of
double sin. They themselves (emphatic ὑμεῖς) are not

going in, which already means "woe" for them; nor are they letting those go in who, if they were not hindered thus, would go in. R. 892 makes the present participle εἰσερχομένους inchoative: "on the point of going in"; but it may be futuristic (R. 891) like the present indicative that indicates expected action: "I am going to town," i. e., I expect to go soon. To bar others out of the kingdom is truly the devil's work.

14) The slight textual evidence for this verse rules it out; its substance is found in Mark 12:40, and in Luke 20:47 in the same general connection, but there it is not one of the woes but a part of the warning against the Pharisees spoken to the people. Both Mark and Luke abbreviate. The supposition that Matthew himself compiled the seven woes from various discourses of Jesus, has the historical situation against it.

15) **Woe to you, scribes and Pharisees, hypocrites, because you run around on the sea and the dry land to make one proselyte, and when he became one, you go on making him a son of Gehenna twice more than yourself.** The fateful repetition of the verdict plus the address sound like the tolling of the bells of doom. These men are great missionaries who try to spread their religion among the pagans. In this they are tireless, scouring sea and land to make one pagan a proselyte. Jesus is not speaking of a proselyte of the gate, one of a large class of pagan converts to Judaism who accepted the faith in the true God, worshipped in the synagogues, but were not circumcised and not incorporated into Judaism; their name is derived from Exod. 20:10. The scribes and the Pharisees were not content with such proselytes but sought to make proselytes of righteousness, converts that accepted all their rules and practices, circumcision, and the entire Levitical and traditional system, becoming complete Jews in every way. They succeeded in the case of only a few. But, almost as a rule, these

converts became more bigoted and fanatic than the
scribes and the Pharisees themselves. To this Jesus
refers when he says that the moment a man became
such a proselyte (γένηται, the aorist to indicate preceding action) the scribes and the Pharisees start a process (ποιεῖτε, durative) which makes that man "a son of
Gehanna" (see 5:22; the genitive indicates quality)
whose whole character and actions mark him as truly
belonging to hell. By adding "twice more than yourselves" Jesus implies that the scribes and the Pharisees
are also "sons of Gehenna." The comparative speaks
of degrees of hellishness; and opposition to the divine
saving truth has many degrees of both intensity and
of extent.

16) **Woe to you, blind guides, who say: Whoever swears by the Sanctuary, it means nothing;
but whoever swears by the gold of the Sanctuary,
he is morally obligated. Fools and blind! For
which is greater, the gold or the Sanctuary which
did sanctify the gold?** The blindness (ignorance)
here charged is wilful; hence these men are morally
guilty. Jesus illustrates this by a reference to the casuistic teaching concerning oaths. The Pharisees delighted in taking the binding power out of some oaths.
One could swear such oaths with all solemnity, yet
according to Pharisaic casuistry they meant οὐδέν, not
a thing. Those who were not acquainted with this,
when they heard a Pharisee swear "by the Sanctuary,"
that is, the Temple building containing the Holy and
the Holy of Holies, imagined that a binding oath had
certainly been sworn. For what was there that was
more sacred than this "Sanctuary"? But no; unless
the Pharisee swore "by the *gold* of the Sanctuary" he
was under no moral obligation.

17) These men were not merely blind (ignorant),
they were worse: μωροί, plain senseless "fools." No
more than the most ordinary common sense is needed

to see that the gold is not greater than the Sanctuary, but that the Sanctuary is vastly greater, for it sanctifies the gold used in its ornamentation.

18) Another sample of equally senseless swearing. **And whoever swears by the altar, it means nothing; but whoever swears by the gift upon it, he is morally obligated. Blind! For which is greater: the gift, or the altar that sanctifies the gift?** We must note that the Scriptures maintain a fine distinction when they throughout use θυσιαστήριον as a designation for the altar of the true God and never for that of an idol, and never use the word βωμός with reference to God's altar but only with reference to the altars of idols. The guidance which lies back of such marked distinctions is more than human, it is divine, a part of what we know as inspiration. Here we have the same folly that was evident in the preceding case.

19) The altar sanctifies the gift placed on it. Any child can see that. To disregard the altar and to place the binding power only in the gift, is to act silly. Another neat distinction is noted in the use of the aorist participle ἁγιάσας in v. 17, and the present participle ἁγιάζον in v. 19. The gold received its sanctification long ago (historical aorist), having long ago become a part of the Sanctuary; but when a gift is placed on the altar, its sanctification is brought about by the act of the priest when he makes the offering.

20) But more must be said. **He, therefore, that swears by the altar swears by it and by everything upon it. And he that swears by the Sanctuary swears by it and by him that dwells in it. And he that swears by the heaven swears by the throne of God and by him that sits upon it.** We may follow R. 859 and his authorities and regard the aorist participles used in these verses as timeless: ὁ ὀμόσας, "the swearer." Yet we are not entirely certain in view of the aorists used after ὃς ἄν in v. 16 and in v. 18. It may

after all be possible that ὁ ὀμόσας refers to an oath made
in the past and is definite and punctiliar for that very
reason; and the main verb, the present ὀμνύει, like the
present verbs in v. 16 and 18, refers to the present
enduring effect of that past oath. With οὖν Jesus draws
the evident conclusion from the Sanctuary's sanctifying its gold and the altar's sanctifying the sacrifice
upon it that, when swearing, no person can separate
gold and Sanctuary, altar and sacrifice, as the scribes
and the Pharisees attempted to do. Jesus reverses the
order and speaks first of the altar. He also broadens
the statement by referring to the altar and *everything*
upon it.

21) In the case of the Sanctuary he goes still
farther by omitting the gold and everything in its construction and by making the Sanctuary one with God
who dwells in it. In v. 20 the oneness is outward, here
it is inward. Yet we see that both the altar and its
gift are one because they belong to God. The outward
connection of altar and gift is already enough for any
man who is not blind and a fool, to say nothing of the
inward connection.

22) The same is true with regard to an oath such
as "by the heaven." The heaven is God's throne, and
to swear "by heaven" is to swear by the God who sits
on this throne of heaven. It is ridiculous to try to dissociate any sacred object from the God who lends it
sacredness, or by mere indirectness to escape contact
with God.

23) **Woe to you, scribes and Pharisees, hypocrites, because you go on tithing the mint and the
dill and the cumin and did dismiss the heavier
parts of the law, the judgment and the mercy and
the faith. Yet these it was necessary to do, and
those not to dismiss. Blind guides, who filter out
the gnat yet swallow down the camel!** The scribes
and the Pharisees were rigorists when it came to the

easy features of the Jewish regulations. They demand
that tithes be paid of even the small flavoring herbs
of which a family might grow a few such as mint, dill,
and cumin (obsolete: cummin), the latter being like
anise seed but larger and used to a greater extent. But
they dismiss, as needing no attention at all, the real
moral, spiritual parts of the law; and here Jesus again
mentions three points.

The κρίσις is the act of judging righteously, a κρίνειν
that ever defends those who are wronged (Prov. 31:8,
9) and thus is synonymous with δικαιοῦν and parallel
with σώζειν, C.-K. 629. Its companion is thus τὸν ἔλεον
(ἔλεος, R. 261), the act of showing mercy (Col. 3:12,
13). The trio is completed by ἡ πίστις, which is understood, not in the active sense of trusting a person, but
in the passive sense of ourselves being trustworthy,
*Treue, Zuverlaessigkeit,* C.-K. 885. All three refer to
our relation to our fellow-men. All three are both
virtues of the heart and acts that grow out of these virtues. All three are achieved by our covenant relation
to *Yahweh Eloheka* (22:37) who by means of his covenant grace plants the law into our inward parts (Jer.
31:33). These parts of the law are weightier, essential, even as they are valid for all men and for the
church of all times, compared with the Levitical regulation of tithing which was intended for the Jews alone,
especially the tithing of mere flavoring herbs.

One of the outstanding facts is that the Gospels
mention tithing only three times, in three condemna-
tions of the Pharisees, all three being scathing in their
severity. The three other references are found in
Hebrews 7:5-9, and are merely historical. Although
all of the apostles were originally Jews, reared in tithing, with not one word did any one of them even intimate that in the new covenant the Christians might find
tithing a helpful method of making their contributions
to the work of the church. This strong negative is

immensely re-enforced by the totally different method
suggested by Paul when he called on the churches for a
great offering, I Cor. 16:1, etc.; II Cor. 8:4, etc. Exegetically and thus dogmatically and ethically the New
Testament is against tithing as a regulation in the new
covenant. Desire for more money also for more money
in the church and for the church must not blind our
eyes to the ways employed for getting more money.
The present tense ἀποδεκατοῦτε and the aorist ἀφήκατε (a κ
aorist, R. 347) are used to express a contrast: demanding the tenth goes strenuously on (durative), the real
parts of the old Jewish law were dismissed long ago, so
long ago that nobody now thinks of them.

Jesus does not want to be misunderstood. The new
covenant has not yet been inaugurated, he as well as all
his hearers are still under the old covenant, and for
that God himself had appointed tithing (Lev. 27:30,
etc.; Num. 18:21; Deut. 12:6; 12:22-27). If that
tithing be done conscientiously, even in little things,
Jesus would not forbid it to a Jew. Jesus safeguards
against perversions when he adds: "These it was necessary to do (ποιῆσαι, effective: do completely) and those
not to dismiss (ἀφεῖναι, also the effective aorist)." Some
texts omit ἔδει which makes the infinitives imperatives
(R. 1092), an idiom that we also have in English:
"these to do" = "these do." But when ἔδει is retained,
this is neither like the present nor the ordinary imperfect but denotes past necessity, merely that, although in
fact the necessity may still continue to exist (R. 919).

24) "Blind guides!" is double-edged: blind men
who yet pretend to show others the way; and others
who consent to be guided by blind men. And their
ridiculous, almost unbelievable blindness is described:
"who filter out the gnat" by most carefully straining
all drink lest some little insect be swallowed and defile
the drinker (Levitically, not hygienically), "yet swallow down the camel," the biggest, Levitically unclean

beast known in Jewish lands (19:29), and this without blinking an eye. Could blindness go any farther? To fail to pay the full tenth of tiny garden herbs — a mortal crime! to disregard the heavenly virtues themselves — not a qualm, not even a thought.

25) **Woe to you, scribes and Pharisees, hypocrites, because you are cleaning the outside of the cup and the dish, but inside they are filled with result of robbery and incontinence. Blind Pharisee, clean first the inside of the cup and the dish so that also the outside of it is clean.** The παροψίς was the dish on which dainties were served. The verb γέμειν is followed by the genitive, but here ἐξ with its genitive points, not to *what* fills the vessels, but *from what* they are filled: "with results of robbery and incontinence." Thus cup and dish make the indictment concrete; they refer as well to clothes, houses, all possessions, in fact, to the entire life. These hypocrites were keen for external, physical cleanliness, but moral cleanliness meant nothing to them. They saw to it that the cup from which they drank their costly wine was clean and that the dish from which they had their dainties served was clean, but they altogether disregarded the manner in which they secured the wealth from which they feasted and the extent to which they carried their self-indulgence.

"The outside" refers to the surface of the vessels as vessels, "the inside" to their contents, both as to their origin ("robbery" and all dishonesty) and as to their actual use ("incontinence," *Schlemmerei,* ἀκρασία, absence of moral restraint). These two abstract terms plainly indicate that Jesus had in mind the whole Pharisaic mode of living as this was defiled by these and their allied immoralities. Here clean does not mean Levitically, ritually clean, and, of course, does not refer to our modern sanitary cleanness but to the ordinary cleanness to which elegant aristocrats and even com-

mon, decent people are accustomed. This indictment
of Jesus' applies to this day to all who secure their living and their luxury in questionable ways and in their
living practice excess and extravagance.

26) The dramatic singular makes the indictment
personal. With the peremptory aorist Jesus calls for
the moral cleanness of what is served inside cup and
dish. That is the supreme thing. It will affect also
the outside of the cup (now he uses τὸ ἐκτός in the same
sense as the previous τὸ ἐξωθέν). For ἵνα may here be
considered consecutive: "so that also the outside of it
is clean," namely as a result of this cleanness of the
contents (read R. 997-999). Jesus wants a better outward cleanness than mere physical polish. These vessels as mere vessels are to be morally clean not purchased with questionable gain, not used for *Schlemmerei*. They cannot have such cleanness unless the
drink and the food they serve are morally clean.

27) **Woe to you, scribes and Pharisees, hypocrites, because you resemble tombs that have been
whitewashed, such as outside appear beautiful but
inside are filled with bones of dead men and with
all uncleanness. Thus you also appear to men as
righteous but inside you are full of hypocrisy and
lawlessness.** As a basis for this woe Jesus uses
a simple but terrible παροιμία (see the word in John
10:6; 16:25, 29), but here he employs the verb. On
the 15th of Adar, before the Passover, it was a Jewish
custom to whitewash all graves and tombs with lime.
We are told that this was done in order to mark them,
so that no Jew would touch one unawares and become
Levitically defiled. Whatever the reason for this may
have been, the point Jesus wishes to make is that the
outside of these tombs was thus made beautiful: they
looked white, pure, clean. The inside was unchanged,
was full of bones of dead men, full of all uncleanness,
rotting flesh and putrid stench. Here and in v. 28 we

have two samples of μέν and δέ balancing two contrasting clauses. With abstract nouns πᾶς without an article following need not be stressed to mean "every," since in connection with such nouns "all" and "every" become quite indistinguishable in thought.

28) When bringing out the likeness Jesus says, "You appear unto men as righteous," implying, "Of course not unto God." Men judge by appearance, God never does so. In δίκαιοι, "righteous," the forensic idea should not be lost sight of: *Die in der Furcht Gottes wandeln, auf ihn hoffen und seines Heils warten und als solche vor dem Urteil Gottes bestehen, unter dem Gesichtspunkt des Urteils Gottes als δίκαιοι bezeichnet werden.* C.-K. 309. Jesus says that to men, who judged only the appearance, the Pharisees, by their whitewash of legal observances, appear as people who surely had the verdict of the heavenly Judge in their favor. But what was the fact as this divine Judge — and it is he himself who here speaks — saw it? Inside they were literally filled full of hypocrisy (ὑπό in the compound, R. 633; see v. 13) and with ἀνομία, "lawlessness," opposition to the genuine contents of the divine law. Among all the sins that Jesus found among men none aroused his fiery indignation more than hypocrisy with its sham of righteousness and holiness. Against no class of men did he hurl invectives that were as severe as those directed against the scribes and the Pharisees: *"hypocrites."*

29) **Woe unto you, scribes and Pharisees, hypocrites, because you build the tombs of the prophets and decorate the grave memorials of the just and say, If we had been in the days of our fathers we would not have been their partners in the blood of the prophets! Wherefore you bear witness to yourselves that you are sons of them that murdered the prophets. Even you — go fill up the measure of your fathers!** The final woe naturally rings out as

a crushing climax. The scribes and the Pharisees were great in building mausoleums over the bones of the ancient prophets and on decorating these memorials (μνημεῖα, from the verb "to remember") "of the righteous" (so designating the dead prophets), the term is again used in the forensic sense (see v. 28). They took great pride in and credit for thus treating the dead prophets.

30) They even carried their hypocrisy so far as to declare that, if they had lived in the ancient days when their fathers heard and murdered these prophets, they would never have been their partners in those murderous deeds. They were ever so much better than their fathers, they with their punctilious observance of even the smallest regulations of the law as compared with their fathers who always inclined toward idolatry. To be sure, the prophets would have been pleased with them and would have had a delightful time in their midst! They never dreamed of taking a warning from their fathers; they were blind to the fact that they were following the word of the prophets just as little as their fathers did. The condition εἰ ἤμεθα οὐκ ἂν ἤμεθα, though it has imperfects, is one of past (not present) unreality, R. 922.

31) But their boast is shattered, "Wherefore." By the very declaration they thus continue to make, by not showing a single evidence of humble repentance but nothing but impenitent pride they keep bearing witness to themselves and needing no others to testify that they are sons of those that did murder the prophets. The verb φονεύειν is the exact word for "to murder," and φονεύς is the noun for murderer. "Kill," so generally used, is not as correct and may denote far less guilt.

32) Because καὶ ὑμεῖς precedes an imperative it causes some difficulty in translation. Our versions

translate καί "then": "Fill ye up then." A modern
commentator alters the imperative to, "And you will
fill up." A prominent scholar wants to join καὶ ὑμεῖς
to v. 31: "you are sons, etc., even you." This
is the ascensive use of καί (R. 1181), it is a kind of
climax, the tone rising like the crescendo in music.
All we need in English is to mark the verb as a strong
imperative: "Even you — go fill up the measure of
your fathers!" The command is one of irony (R.
948), of high scorn (R. 1198). The thing that these
men are determined to do, from which no moral power
can restrain them, they are told to go and do. We
have this kind of command in John 2:19. It is the
dreadful voice of judgment, "Do it and take the consequences!"

Judgment is like a measure into which guilt is
poured. One wicked Jewish generation after another
has already poured in all its black guilt, making the
nation's measure almost full. When these late sons
of those murderous Jews now pour in their bloody
guilt by murdering not only God's own Son but also
the messengers he will send them after his murder,
the vessel will not contain it all, the guilt will overflow, the judgment will descend. Jesus is speaking of
one peculiar guilt, the most fatal of all, the bloody rejection of grace, of the Messiah, and of the gospel,
not of the guilt of incidental sins. Jesus is speaking
of the total and final rejection of the Jewish nation in
the judgment of God. It is in effect to this day and
is a type of the judgment at the last day. The Jewish
people (no longer a nation but an outcast from the
kingdom) still second the deeds of their forefathers
by still rejecting Jesus, the divine Messiah, his gospel,
and his kingdom of grace. Nothing can stay the continuance of their judgment. Only those escape its
doom who turn to Christ in repentance and faith, and
they are not many.

33)   **Serpents, offsprings of vipers, how are you
going to escape from the judgment of Gehenna?
On this account, lo, I myself am sending to you
prophets and wise men and scribes.   Some of them
you will kill and crucify, and some of them you will
scourge in your synagogues and persecute from
city to city, in order that there may come upon you
all righteous blood poured out on the earth from
the blood of Abel, the righteous, to the blood of
Zachariah, son of Barachiah, whom you murdered between the Sanctuary and the altar.   Amen,
I say to you, there shall come these things all on this
generation!**

The burning intensity rises to its highest pitch.
The flow of thought is uninterrupted to the end.  Jesus
tells the scribes and the Pharisees to fill up their
fathers' measure of guilt — that will seal their doom.
Just how they fill it up is told them with stunning,
literal plainness, and with the same cold plainness the
guilt and the doom that will thus overwhelm them are
stressed.  The dramatic intensity of it all is terrific.
Criticism has busied itself with this passage.  It points
to the scene that occurred in connection with the meal
in the Pharisee's house (in Luke 11:37, etc.) in Galilee
at a much earlier time and there finds some of the same
indictments that were uttered on this last Tuesday in
the Temple court.  Criticism then claims that both
denunciations could not have occurred as they are
recorded by the two evangelists — pray, why not?  It
contends that a document was in existence from which
both writers drew, each shaping his material accordingly.  To bolster up this hypothesis the further hypothesis is added that in this document the Twelve are
not mentioned.  But all these indictments spoken by
Jesus would be inexplicable if they had never been
voiced before in all the clashes with the Pharisees and
were hurled against them only here at the very end.

The Twelve were present in the Pharisee's house as they are now with Jesus in the Temple.

On the characterization "offsprings of vipers" see the exposition of 3:7 (12:34) and note how the end harks back to the beginning. The addition "serpents" is merely more general and recalls more directly than the other designation did the original ancestor of these offsprings, the old Serpent, Satan, Rev. 20:2. The poisonous, deadly hypocrisy thus described must meet its doom. Hence the question of deliberation with the aorist subjunctive, its aorist indicating successful fleeing, namely escape. Jesus naturally uses the second person, but this deliberative question (R. 934) is one the Pharisees would themselves ask: "How can we arrange to escape?" No way is open to them. And that is what Jesus has in mind. "From the judgment of Gehenna" has the objective genitive, "from the verdict that consigns to hell," see Gehenna in 5:22. Their doom is sealed.

34) It is "on this account" that Jesus himself (strong ἐγώ) will do the startling thing ("lo") he now announces, and that they will do the outrageous things that Jesus foretells regarding them. Jesus will send his messengers as sheep among wolves (10:16); and they will persecute and slay them. Διὰ τοῦτο applies to the entire sentence (v. 34, 35). An untenable view is advocated when this phrase is interpreted to mean that "God must have some valid excuse" for destroying the Pharisees and that he secures it by the sending of these messengers concerning whom he knows beforehand that the Pharisees will kill them. This is thought to be Old Testament theology. Jesus, however, never said such a thing. It is introduced from "a work otherwise unknown, *The Wisdom of God.*" In Luke 11:49 ἡ σοφία τοῦ Θεοῦ is not a book but the divine wisdom and foreknowledge. This wisdom has made its prophetic utterances regarding the fate of all the un-

godly, most particularly regarding the obdurate Jews
who were called to be the chosen nation.

"On this account" means: because the judgment
of Gehenna is already yours without hope of escape,
therefore Jesus, their Judge, here and now dictates
how it shall descend upon them. He himself will so
arrange the final work of grace upon the Jewish nation
that these sons of their murderous fathers will rush
to their great opportunity with all possible speed to
fill the cup of their fathers and to plunge their criminal
heads into judgment. This is part of the real Old
and also the New Testament teaching regarding judgment. Up to a certain time the Lord's hand restrains
with warnings ever more intense; then the restraint
ceases, the doom has begun, the gates are thrown
open, the sinner is speeded to destruction. The
word goes forth, "That thou doest, do quickly!"
John 13:27.

"*I* will send or commission," says the great Messiah-
King himself. He first of all calls his apostles and ministers "prophets," men who are exactly like those mentioned in the Old Testament upon whom the bloody
fathers of these sons of Gehenna (v. 15) laid their
hands. Then he calls them "wise men" who are filled
with "the wisdom of God" (Luke 11:49) and promulgate that wisdom far and wide. Finally he calls them
γραμματεῖς, "scribes,' but they are the very antithesis of
the Pharisaic scribes, they are writers and expounders
of the new covenant gospel. Each title is full of peculiar significance. The Jewish nation shall once more
ring with the calls of grace far beyond anything that
occurred in Old Testament days. The volitive "I will
send" is now followed by a series of similar volitive
future tenses. Over against the final will of grace is
set the equally final will of wicked unbelief.

Jesus distinguishes two classes, each with partitive
ἐκ (R. 599), the one will lose their lives: "some you will

kill or crucify"; the other will nearly lose them: "some
you will scourge in your synagogues and persecute from
city to city." When Jesus says "crucify" he refers to
executions that will be carried out by the Roman authorities but not also to his own crucifixion. Some of
the deaths recorded in Acts 22:4 may have been
brought about by means of crucifixion. That of Peter
in Rome and that of Simeon in Jerusalem in the year
107 (Eusebius 3, 32) may also be mentioned. The
non-mention of more specific, known cases is due
solely to the lack of records; even of the killings that
were directly inflicted by Jewish hands only a few are
known such as that of Stephen who was stoned by
the Jews.

Paul received five scourgings from the Jews who
always used rods instead of the Roman whips, II Cor.
11:24. Minor Jewish tribunals met in synagogues,
hence scourgings were administered there (10:17; Acts
22:19; 26:11). In the latter passage Paul himself
confesses that he also persecuted many unto strange
cities. The point of all these Jewish crimes is not their
resemblance to those of their ancient fathers but the
fact that these were the final answer of the Jews to the
Lord's final offer of grace.

35) Ὅπως with the subjunctive expresses the divine purpose. When all God's grace is spurned, his
judgment must follow. Moreover, guilt and penalty
are also cumulative. While each individual and also
each generation receives the due reward of its deeds,
when one generation after another duplicates the wickedness, the pent-up wrath of outraged justice breaks
forth like a volcano. Divine justice is not as superficial as ours; it demands more than a reckoning for
individual and separate crimes. Each crime, when it
is re-enacted, involves a guilt that reaches back to the
beginning. The last acts "allow" or sanction all the
former that were of the same type, and so the last acts

involve guiltiness for all. In this way there came upon the last generation of the Jews "all the righteous blood poured out on the earth from the blood of Abel, the righteous, to the blood of Zachariah," etc. "Blood, blood, blood," three times in one verse, "being poured out," present tense, as though to make us see one red stream poured out after another. "Righteous blood," "righteous Abel," righteous in the forensic sense with God's verdict in their favor, Heb. 11:4. And this points to the crime involved in shedding such blood: it has God's verdict against it.

The first righteous man that had his blood poured out innocently was Abel. The last notable representative of righteousness who suffered such a fate was Zachariah who is mentioned in the last book of the Hebrew Bible, II Chron. 24:20-22. Between the two, what red streams of equally righteous blood flow! Zachariah's martyrdom is a murder that was so terrible, his blood being shed between the Sanctuary (Holy and Holy of Holies) and the altar of burnt sacrifice, thus in the very presence of God, that even the Talmud deplores it as one of the most heinous of Jewish crimes against God's servants. When Zachariah died he exclaimed, "The Lord look upon it and require it!" This dying call for just retribution makes Jesus' reference to Zachariah the more effective. Historically the martyrdom of Urijah (Jer. 26:23) occurs 200 years later, but that of Zachariah stands last on the Old Testament pages and thus is used as a terminal by Jesus.

The apposition "son of Barachiah" has proved troublesome to interpreters. Some regard it as a lapse of memory on the part of Matthew. Others say that Matthew confused two men of the same name, namely the son of Jehoiada (II Chron. 24:20) and "the son of Berechiah" (Zech. 1:1). Matthew can scarcely be charged with lapse of memory, for he adds this apposition for the express purpose of identifying this Zachariah.

Luther has offered a satisfactory solution: "Jehoiada with the added name Barachiah." The giving of new or additional names was a common practice among the Jews. The son of Joash is called both Jerubbaal and Gideon (Judges 8:29, 32; compare 6:32 and 7:1). Another solution is that Jehoiada was really the grandfather and Barachiah the father. This is possible when we remember the great age of Jehoiada, 130 years, and when we recall his great deeds, making it highly creditable to be called his son. So in Chronicles Zachariah would be named after his illustrious grandfather but in Matthew after his father, the name of the father having been preserved by Jewish tradition or in genealogical records. The Jews also frequently called a man a son of a mighty grandsire, especially while the latter was still living. Both explanations cannot be correct; perhaps someone will discover which must be dropped. Both, however, keep to the canons of exegesis.

36) With the seal of verity and of authority (see 5:18) Jesus assures his hearers that "these things" (ταῦτα) and "all" (πάντα) of them shall come "on this generation." All these deeds of blood will descend like an avalanche on "this generation," the one now living. Many who were standing before Jesus would see it all. In only a few years Jerusalem would be in ruins, the Jewish nation would be destroyed.

37) The entire chapter has been one of stern denunciation — calm, measured, irresistible, fortified with absolute proof at every step, final. Now at last the note of tenderness breaks into that stern judgment, and the hope that still continues to the last moment sends forth its ray of light to penetrate the midnight gloom. **Jerusalem, Jerusalem, that art killing the prophets and stoning those having been**

**sent to her, how often did I will to gather thy chil-
dren together the way a bird gathers together her
own young birds under her wings, and you did not
will. Lo, there is left to you your house desert!
For I say to you: in no way shall you see me from
now on until you say, Blessed the One Coming in the
Lord's name!**

These words are filled with tenderness; they come
from a breaking heart. The Jews are without feeling,
cold and hard as stone; Jesus is surcharged with emotion because of their obduracy and their consequent
inevitable judgment. There is no "reverberating thunder" in the repetition "Jerusalem, Jerusalem!" These
repetitions of address are found elsewhere in the Scriptures, cf. II Sam. 18:33, "O my son Absalom, my son,
my son Absalom!" and again, "O Absalom, my son, my
son!" Luke 10:41, "Martha, Martha!" Acts 9:4,
"Saul, Saul!" These repetitions are the voice of tender love. Here, as in II Sam. 18, the deepest pathos of
grief is added. "Jerusalem" stands for the nation
whose capital and religious citadel this city was. The
view that "Jerusalem" refers to the rulers and "thy
children" to the common people is untenable, for the
very ones whom Jesus willed to gather refused to be
gathered: rulers and people alike.

"Jerusalem" means "city of peace"; but what a city
of peace: "killing the prophets and stoning those having been sent (commissioned) to her" by God (the
agent in the passive) to bring her his peace. Here all
her guilt is summed up. Recall "prophets" used in v.
29-31 and in v. 34: "those having been sent" is wider:
the prophets and all other messengers of grace and
peace. The present participles "killing," "stoning"
mark conduct that is characteristic and constant and
thus include more than aorists would, which would denote only past acts as such. "Unto her" instead of
"unto thee" matches the participles which present the

subject they modify as the third person. "How often"
— not just once but with utmost persistence did Jesus
seek to save his nation until it actually stilled his voice
by death. John describes Jesus' ministry in the capital at length, but all of Jesus' ministry to the Jews
is here included: "thy children," the nation. One of
the inexplicable features of divine love is the fact that,
in spite of the infallible foreknowledge that all will be
in vain, its call and its effort to save never cease until
the very end. Judas is another example. Such knowledge would either stop us at once or make our efforts a
mere pretense. So far is God above us in this respect
that our minds cannot follow his ways.

The verb ἠθέλησα denotes the gracious, saving will of
Jesus. It is the so-called antecedent will which takes
into account only our lost condition from which it works
to deliver us and not our reaction to this will. The will
which deals with this reaction is always the subsequent
will, and for the obdurate this will is judgment. Deter-
minism and other confusions result when this distinction is ignored. The gracious antecedent will and its
call to grace is equal for all. To make it serious and
real only in the case of one class of men and only a
pretense in the case of another class, is to attribute
duplicity to God, against which all Scripture cries out,
Rom. 11:32. The preaching of the Word is no *Spiegel-
fechten* (fencing only before a mirror, hence no real
contest), *Concordia Triglotta,* 1072. Who dares to
say that Jesus willed to save even the Sanhedrists less
than he willed to save the Twelve; or Judas less than
Peter?

The figure of the bird and her brood is not only
beautiful in itself but is especially so for Jews whose
rabbis spoke of the *Shekinah* as the gathering place of
the proselytes. See the expressions in Deut. 32:11;
Ps. 17:8; 61:4; Isa. 31:5. Ὄρνις is any bird and not
only "hen." The idea of the hen has led to the intro-

duction of the swooping hawk. The idea is rather that the brood, τὰ νοσσία, "the young birds," belongs to the mother bird and that thus she gathers them together under her wings; note ἑαυτῆς, the reflexive, which is far stronger than αὐτῆς, the possessive. So this nation belonged to Jesus, and as his very own he willed to gather it together. This gathering together is itself the essential thing: all these children of Jerusalem are to be attached to Jesus as his very own, wherefore also we have the aorist infinitive: to gather thus once for all. In the simile the present "gathers" is proper, for the customary action of the bird is used as an illustration of the one great act of Jesus.

Nothing is more tragic than the outcome of this gracious will of Jesus: "and you did not will." As so often, the adversative idea is added with a telling copulative καί. It brings out all the abnormality, the utter unnaturalness, the absolute unreasonableness of the negative. The sentence ought to close: *"and* you willed"; but now it closed: *"and* you willed NOT!" Only this, nothing more, is said. No qualification, no modifiers, no explanations, no additions. The one fatal thing is: "you did not will."

Despite its brevity this expression includes many facts. Grace is not irresistible; every case of resistance proves this, notably this glaring case of the Jews. Damnation results from man's own will which becomes permanent, obdurate, unaccountable resistance against God's will of grace. The more God draws the will with the power of grace, the more this will rejects God until grace can do no more. To introduce the omnipotence of God is to confound his attributes and to darken all saving Scripture. *Concordia Triglotta,* 1077, quoting Matt. 22:3, etc.

Why do some wills resist thus? This asks for a reasonable explanation for an unreasonable act — no such explanation exists. To say that this is due to

inborn sin is not an explanation, for men who have
the same inborn sin are won, and their wills assent
under grace. Moreover, this obdurate resistance is produced only when grace operates with its power. The
spring is poisonous and throws out a poisonous stream.
The *gratia sufficiens* is applied to spring and stream
with power *sufficiens* to unpoison both. Behold, *now*
the spring and the stream are a hundred times more
poisonous than before. Explain that! All we know is
that the mystery of this resistance lies in the will itself
and in no way in God. How could Satan fall? How
could Adam sin? How can man resist grace and salvation? How can a believer whose will is changed
turn to unbelief and be damned? It is all one and the
same question.

"A master of music has put all the power which
his art gave him into this lament of the Messiah, and
he into whose ears has once been sung 'And ye would
not!' will never forget this heart-penetrating music.
What? shall the art of music do more than the voice
of eternal love speaking from heaven? No; let it
penetrate our hearts when Jesus calls to us: 'How often
would I have gathered you even as a hen her nestlings
under her wings — and ye would not!' Then we shall
will what he wills, our salvation, and shall flee from the
judgment of Jerusalem which scorned the wings of
the hen and fell into the talons of the eagle (24:28)."
Besser.

38) An exclamation may well introduce the verdict of the subsequent will which Jesus now states:
"Lo, there is left to you your house desert!" Some
think "your house" is the Temple, but the context is
not so specific and points rather to Jerusalem which
naturally includes the Temple. Today Jerusalem is
not a Jewish city, to say no more. All that ἔρημος (the
reading that has this term is textually certain) includes
the history of Jerusalem tells all too plainly, and back

of this history lies the answer of God's will to the obdurate will of this nation. According to Luther, "desert" means without Word and Sacrament. "Their soul no one cultivates, and no God dwells among them." Referring to Isa. 5:5, 6 he adds: "What is this that the clouds shall not rain upon them but that they shall not hear the gospel? They are not to be pruned and digged — what is this but that no one shall rebuke their error and heal their infirmities? Hence their vineyard bears only briars and thorns, that is, workholy people who are without faith, bear no fruit of the Spirit, and grow only to be cast into eternal fire."

39) "For I say to you" is the voice of divine authority; and γάρ introduces the reason that the "house" shall be left "desert": Christ will leave, and the Jews shall not see him. Compare John 7:33, 34; 8:21. "In no way shall you see me from now on" (referring to his death) with its strong οὐ μή and the futuristic subjunctive announces Jesus' complete withdrawal from the Jews. The last clause, "until you say (or: shall say), Blessed the One Coming in the Lord's name!" has ἕως ἄν with the subjunctive and thus the thought of expectancy. In whose case this expectation will be fulfilled we see from Isa. 65:8-10: "that I may not destroy them all" — "a seed," "an inheritor," "mine elect" — "that have sought me." Read the whole of Isa. 63:7-65:10. Paul answers: "a remnant"; read Rom. 10:18-11:5. A remnant of the Jewish nation that shall be made up of all those Jews who, beginning with the days of the apostles and continuing through the many years of history, turn to repentance and faith and greet Jesus with the Palm Sunday cry of Ps. 118: 26, "Blessed the Coming One," etc.

Εὐλογημένος is the perfect participle with present connotation, "has been and now is blessed"; ὁ ἐρχόμενος, "the Coming One," is a standard designation of the promised Messiah; note also the verb "he comes," used with reference to the Messiah. "In the Lord's (*Yahweh's*) name" means, "in connection with the revelation Jehovah has made"; in all such phrases "name" is the equivalent of revelation (compare 21:9). Both the Psalm and the acclamation on Palm Sunday exclude the idea that these words could be applied in a double sense, namely that would be spoken willingly by believers and unwillingly by the obdurate (at the second coming of Christ). Ps. 118:26 adds as the other half of the greeting, "We have blessed you out of the house of the Lord!"

While the words of Jesus do not directly declare that any, or many, or all Jews at any particular time or era of the future will greet him as the Messiah, they do express the expectation that some will do so. And Jesus says that whenever any, few or many, do so, namely by faith, they shall see him, not indeed with eyes of the flesh — for no Christian sees him in this manner although he is always with us, and we are therefore by no means desolate — but in this world with the eyes of the spirit and in heaven by actual sight.

All chiliasts and a few others refer v. 39 to the final conversion of the Jews as a nation. They also add their elaboration: the Jewish nation will stand at the head of all nations, will constitute the cream of Christendom, will have Jerusalem as the center of the millennial kingdom, the metropolis of the whole earth, and from Jerusalem the heathen living during the millennium (!) will be converted by Jewish missionaries, etc.

But ὑμῖν, ὑμῶν, ὑμῖν in v. 38, 39, together with the second person plural of the verbs, are addressed to the Jewish hearers before Jesus: *their* house is left desert, and those among *them* who acclaim Jesus as the blessed Messiah shall see him. By implication this can naturally be extended to any Jews of future times who likewise accept Jesus.

# CHAPTER XXIV

## XVIII

### Christ's Discourse on the Destruction of Jerusalem and on His Parousia, Chapters 24 and 25

1) It is still Tuesday but near the end of this momentous day. **And in leaving, Jesus was going from the Temple. And his disciples came to him to point out to him the buildings of the Temple. But he, answering, said to them: Do you not see all these things? Amen, I say to you, In no way shall there be left here stone upon stone which shall not be thrown down.** The imperfect ἐπορεύετο describes Jesus in the act of leaving the Temple courts; the preceding aorist participle ἐξελθών does not indicate antecedent action but punctiliar simultaneous action, R. 1112, etc. Jesus is definitely leaving (aorist participle) and when so doing is walking through the courts (imperfect indicative). Why the disciples come to think of showing or pointing out to Jesus some of the great structures, on the new and grander erection of which fifty years had already been spent, we see from 23:38, "your house desert." The thought of the disciples is: "Look at all these grand structures — and they are all to be completely deserted?"

2) Read Farrar's impressive description of the Temple of this time and then the response of Jesus that not only shall all these buildings and courts be deserted but they shall also be turned into absolute ruin, not one stone shall be left upon another that is not thrown down, literally "destroyed." On "amen," etc., see 5:18; on the force of κατά with λύω, R. 828; the form ἀφεθῇ is the aorist passive subjunctive (futuristic)

with the strongest form of negation οὐ μή to express future action. That is all that Jesus said as he left the Temple courts for the last time. This word is the height of tragedy.

3) **Now, while sitting on the Mount of Olives, there came to him the disciples in private, saying: Tell us when these things shall be and what the sign of thine own Parousia and of the complete finish of the eon.** The writer stood on the lower slopes of Olivet toward evening and looked across the valley to the Temple hill where now stands the Mohammedan Dome of the Rock (sometimes called the Mosque of Omar), its great dome of dull gold magnificently lighted up by the rays of the sinking sun, the city on Zion hill behind it rising to a higher elevation. So Jesus is now sitting with Herod's great Temple and the brilliant Sanctuary (Holy and Holy of Holies) sparkling with its golden roof in the dying sun. When Jesus was leaving the Temple, crowds surrounded him; now he is alone, κατ' ἰδίαν, with the Twelve. Four disciples (Mark 13:3) speak to Jesus and ask him to tell them more; all, of course, wanted to know. By ταῦτα they refer to the destruction of the Temple (v. 2) — when will that be? They ask for "the sign of thine own Parousia" by which his own Coming and Presence at the end shall be indicated — they already know about this Parousia (the possessive adjective is stronger than the genitive pronoun) — as well as the sign of "the complete finish (συντέλεια) of the eon," of the world-age, αἰών, which does not refer to time only but to the great era marked by what transpired in it.

The πότε does not ask for a date, Jesus never gives a date (Acts 1:7), and Jesus has no date to give (v. 36; Mark 13:32). This "when" should be considered together with "the sign" as indicating the nearness of Jesus' return to judgment and of the winding up of all the affairs of the world-age. Those texts which

have only one article with Parousia and finish of the
eon combine the two nouns into one concept; yet even
when two articles are used, the two nouns are regarded
as belonging together and are thus put together into
this second question.  It is rather fruitless to speculate as to just how the Twelve conceived their questions, what wrong or what right ideas they had in
their minds.  Far more fruitful is the proper understanding of the long reply of Jesus by which he intended to enlighten the Twelve in regard to all they
had asked; he went even beyond their question.  Matthew and the synoptists show us only how Jesus was
prompted to deliver this discourse.

4) **And Jesus answered and said to them:  See
to it lest anyone deceive you!  For many shall come
in my name, saying, I myself am the Christ, and they
shall deceive many.**  The way in which Jesus begins
shows that his heart is full of concern for the disciples.
The introduction to the great discourse is a mighty
warning.  They are to "see to it," to keep their eyes
open, "lest anyone deceive you" (πλανᾶν, trick you into
believing what is not true).  There is only too good
reason for the warning: many shall try this deception,
they shall even boldly say, "I myself (emphatic ἐγώ)
am the Christ."  Their statement is, of course, a summary.  Their coming "in my name" means that they
will arrogate to themselves this name "Christ."  Others
may not seek to thrust Jesus aside but to elevate
themselves by means of him.

The procession of such deceivers from Simon Magus
and Barcochba onward, in the great Antichrist and in
the little antichrists, goes on to the end of time.  Some
are petty and have some little sect of fanatics following
them, some sit on thrones like the popes in their long
succession; some are out for the hard cash, some are
viciously lascivious.  The sad thing is that they shall
actually succeed in deceiving many; for all men have an

affinity for religious error, and many yield to it with avidity and develop the strongest fanaticism. They are limitless in perverting to their own ends what the Scriptures say about the kingdom.

The introduction to this discourse is misconceived when it is regarded as a rebuke to the Twelve for thinking of the glory of the end instead of thinking of the coming passion of Jesus. It is not a rebuke, and the last discourses of Jesus as recorded by John most certainly comfort the disciples by pointing to his spiritual and also to his glorious coming.

6)    The first section of the discourse deals with the signs of the end of the world (v. 6-14). The fact that these signs include also those connected with the end of the Jewish Jerusalem is self-evident although Jesus will speak of the latter by themselves. **Now you shall be about to hear of wars and of rumors of wars. See to it, be not disturbed! For it must be. But not yet is the end. For nation shall rise up against nation, and kingdom against kingdom; and there shall be famines and earthquakes from place to place. But all these things are a beginning of birthpains.**

The circumscribed future, the future of μέλλω with the present infinitive, reveals that the disciples are soon to hear of wars, namely right at hand, and of rumors of wars in places that are more distant. These, indeed, are signs of the end, for they signal the rotten condition of the world. But the end will not come immediately. Hence the two imperatives stated asyndetically: "See to it, be not troubled!" both being durative. These noises of war are not to upset the equanimity of the disciples. Why? "For it must be," δεῖ, impersonal, used to express any type of necessity; here it is a necessity that is due to the condition of the world and to God's judgment upon that condition. The aorist infinitive γενέσθαι is naturally constative; "be" includes all

these wars and these rumors. "The end is not yet,"
τὸ τέλος, the goal which God has set. These are only a
part of the birthpains.

7) The fact that wars result when nation rises
against nation, a body of people that is held together
by the same customs, and kingdom rises against kingdom, a body of people that is under one king or government, is rather self-evident. But these clashes are
always the height of abnormality. We may translate
ἐγερθήσεται as a passive, "shall be raised up," or as a middle, "shall raise itself up" and thus "rise." The passions that cause such uprisings need not be mentioned.
Since famines and earthquakes are mentioned together,
and the latter are not produced by wars, famines are
here likewise independent of wars. The distributive
κατά means, "from place to place." The world of nature
is affected by sin in the same way as the world of men,
and thus these disturbing manifestations are a sign of
the end. But they are not a sign after which the end
is at once due. O no; more of these manifestations
will occur, not always consecutively but often concur-
rently and simultaneously.

8) These are only a prelude, "a beginning of birthpains." Much severer pains and writhings must be
added before the new heavenly eon comes to full birth.
Jesus adopts the term which was used by the rabbis
to designate the sufferings and woes which they
thought were to precede the Messiah's coming: *cheblē
hammashiach, dolores Messiae.* All these tribulations
would bring forth the new era. Jesus shows here that
these "birthpains" pertain only to his second coming
and the judgment.

9) **Then they shall deliver you up to tribulation, and they shall kill you, and you shall go on
being hated by all the nations because of my name.
And then many shall be trapped and shall deliver up
each other and shall hate each other. And many**

**false prophets shall rise up and shall deceive many. And because of the multiplying of the lawlessness the love of many shall grow cold.** From the conditions which point toward the end in the world of men generally Jesus turns to sketch the conditions that shall appear in the church. There the sign is persecution, defection, and deception. The adverb "then," used here and in v. 10, is not "thereafter," but then, at the time the first birthpangs appear. "You," of course, is not all of you but those of the believers who will be affected as here described. "To deliver up" refers to tribunals, courts, police, but may include mobs as in Paul's case. No subject is needed to indicate the enemies of Jesus who will act thus. The word θλῖψις is highly expressive: *Bedrueckung,* suffering that is due to pressure. The climax will be: "they shall kill you." This began soon in the cases of Stephen (Acts 7:60) and of James (Acts 12:2) and also included Paul and Peter.

In order to make the future durative it is circumscribed: ἔσεσθε μισούμενοι: "you shall go on being hated by all the nations," not one of them will offer you refuge. This hatred motivates all the persecutions and causes it to manifest itself in violent action every now and then. The reference to "all the nations" hints at 28:19, and is an implied prophecy of how far the gospel will penetrate. The interpretation which would restrict this paragraph to the Twelve is thus not acceptable. The story of persecution did not stop with the Twelve. God alone knows when the last persecution will come.

"Because of my name" reveals the inner cause of all this hatred. The ὄνομα is really the person of Jesus himself and all that he stands for but as known, revealed, and made manifest to men, i. e., in his gospel. When the great body of men among the nations comes in contact with Christ as he is revealed in the gospel,

they will not have this man to rule over them. Like
Festus and Agrippa they spurn his grace, like the
Jewish rulers they rage against it. Again and again
as we press Christ upon men today this hatred of his
name comes to view and vents itself upon those who
make this name their hope of salvation.

10) In these outbreaks of persecution many "shall
be trapped," σκανδαλισθήσονται, be caught so as to have
their faith killed, like an animal that springs a trap
(see 5:29) ; not "shall stumble" (our versions), for
one may quickly recover after stumbling. These are
the wormy fruit which falls when the wind blows.
Even when some worldly connection is to be broken,
some sinful and dangerous practice to be given up, how
many fail to prove true! But let money, goods, position, honor, liberty, or blood be the price of faithfulness, how many will then deny the Name!

These perverts who have turned traitor to the
Name will, like Judas, use their knowledge and their
former connection to help to destroy the faithful by
denouncing and by delivering them up. Could there
be a worse spectacle? 10:35, 36.

11) To upset and to try the believers still more
many pseudo-prophets shall arise (the verb is used as
it was in v. 7). These differ from the false Christs
by teaching what is false and drawing believers away
to follow them (sects) and to antagonize the truth of
Christ. We have discussed these prophets in 7:15,
which see. Regarding the damnableness of even a
single false teaching that is held in opposition to
Christ's word nothing further need be said here. To
state that pseudo-prophets are only such as subvert the
whole teaching of faith is to excuse the lesser errorists
and to make their errors the more innocent.

12) Doctrinal defection and laxity automatically
entail moral defection and laxity. When one plays
fast and loose with a doctrinal statement of the Scrip-

ture and does not permit it to bind his conscience, how can he play firm and fast with a moral requirement and let that bind his conscience? Thus "the lawlessness" will be multiplied; the hold of the law which directs the Christian in avoiding sin and in doing good works will be broken. So all manner of lawlessness will multiply: the license practiced by the one will infect others; and on this account ἀγάπη, the love that flows from faith and evidences its presence and strength, "shall grow cold" as though it had been struck by an icy blast. Its fervor and its strength depart. And that means that its root, faith, has withered and is dying or is dead. One of the pitiful sights in the life of the church is the effort to galvanize back into warm activity the love that has been chilled to death.

Such is Jesus' picture of the sign which marks his Parousia and the end of the world. It is dark, and the darkness increases steadily. Does this picture suggest a wonderful golden age that will rise in triumph in the world prior to the end? No, in his description of the future Jesus says not one word about a millennium.

13) **But he that endured to the end, he shall be saved. And there shall be preached this gospel of the kingdom in the whole inhabited world as a testimony to all the nations; and then shall come the end.** This is the bright aspect of the prophecy: in spite of every opposition the church of true believers will endure. Jesus uses the singular, "he that endured," because he wants each disciple to think of himself. When the verb is intransitive as it is here it means "to remain under," to stand one's ground. The substantivized participle is naturally an aorist, for the endurance is complete.

In the phrase εἰς τέλος we have but the simple idea of endurance to life's end here on earth, Rev. 2:7.

Τέλος has no article as it has in v. 6 and in v. 14,
which means that this is not "the end," namely of
the world, although, unfortunately, we must use an
article when we translate εἰς τέλος into English. The
three τέλος used in this chapter cannot refer to the
end of the world and imply that this end is to come
when Jerusalem is destroyed, and that he who holds
out so long shall be saved. Why should one say anything about Jerusalem when the whole world comes to
an end at the same time? Why make Jesus a false
prophet? Why talk as though no Christian would die
before the year 70? To endure means to bear whatever a true confession of Christ brings upon us. Jesus
himself says that in the case of some this will mean
*death*. The aorist ὁ ὑπομείνας marks the point where
the future σωθήσεται shall set in. Back of the passive
is Christ, the Savior; he will at that moment bestow
the heavenly salvation. The positive "shall be saved"
is a mighty and a glorious promise.

14) Another glorious promise follows. It is combined with the clearest statement found in the Gospels
concerning the time of the end of the world. First,
the gospel "shall be heralded" in the whole οἰκουμένη
(supply γῇ) or inhabited world (28:19; Acts 1:8).
Nothing shall stop its spread. It is called εὐαγγέλιον,
a word that was originally used to designate the reward handed to a messenger of good news, then it
came to mean the good news itself. "The gospel" is
an old English term. "This gospel" refers to it as
Jesus was now proclaiming it. Its contents was "the
kingdom" (see 3:2), the rule of the Messiah over men's
hearts and lives which includes both his rule of grace
and of glory as the context indicates. What a promise!
Imagine Jesus sitting with the Twelve on the slopes
of Olivet and speaking of this world-wide penetration
of his gospel! Yet this is exactly what has come
to pass.

"For a testimony to all the nations," μαρτύριον, one
that is intended, as all testimony naturally is, to arouse
faith and, when in spite of its absolute truth it is rejected, to testify and to witness against those who
refuse to believe.   The latter must be included because
of what Jesus has just said in v. 9.   "To all the
nations" specifies what "in the whole world" really
means.   Every nation will eventually face this gospel
testimony and together with that testimony the question of faith or unbelief.   To reject that testimony
is to stand self-condemned.   The truth *must* be accepted as truth; when it is turned down as being
a lie, the man who turns it down pronounces his own
verdict.

"Then," meaning, "not until then" "shall come the
end," subject and predicate are reversed in order to
give each more emphasis.   In v. 6 and here τὸ τέλος
evidently has the same meaning: "the goal or end" of
the world.   In the face of so many chiliastic dreams
of false prophets it is highly important to grasp exactly what Jesus says: we are to expect the rising
hostility against his true followers; many who at first
believe shall again be carried away; the gospel preaching, however, will go on steadily until it penetrates to
all nations — then the end!   No other and different
world era shall intervene.   "He which testifieth these
things saith, Yea: I come quickly!   Amen: come, Lord
Jesus!"   Rev. 22:20.

15) From the events which constitute "the sign"
of the end of the world Jesus turns to directions and
warnings that pertain to the destruction of Jerusalem.
The change in subject is obvious.   As far as treating
both with clear distinction in the same discourse is
concerned, who can object when the destruction of
Jerusalem, like the Flood and like the destruction of
Sodom and Gomorrah, is made a type of the end of
the world?   **When, therefore, you see the abomina-**

tion of desolation, that spoken of through **Daniel,
the prophet, standing in the holy place (he that
reads let him understand!), then those in Judea —
let them flee upon the mountains.** He upon the
**housetop — let him not go down to remove the
things out of his house; and he in the field — let
him not return back to remove his robe. But woe
to them that are with child and to them suckling in
those days. Pray, however, that your flight may
not occur during winter nor on a Sabbath; for there
shall then be great tribulation such as has not been
from the world's beginning until now, neither at any
time shall be.** The connective *οὖν* is most naturally
regarded as presenting, on the basis of the survey of
the world-age until its end, the instructions the Twelve
need in particular regarding the coming destruction
of Jerusalem.

First of all Jesus tells them when to flee out of the
country, namely when they see the abomination of desolation standing in the holy place, the Temple itself.
"Abomination" is the main term, something that is
utterly abominable in God's sight, and this will occur
right in the Temple that is consecrated to God. The
genitive "of desolation" characterizes the abomination
according to the effect it must produce, namely desolate the desecrated Temple, leave it empty of worshippers. The moment the believers see this (and it
is something unmistakable and easy to see) they are
to flee the country posthaste. This is the same abomination that was "spoken of" (passive, by God)
through Daniel, the prophet, in 11:31 and 12:11
(scarcely in 9:27) when he prophesied what is recorded
in I Maccabees 1:20-68, note v. 57. Antiochus Epi-
phanes erected a pagan altar on top of the great altar
of burnt sacrifice before the Sanctuary (Holy and
Holy of Holies). Jesus does not say that Daniel
prophesied the event that would usher in the destruc-

tion of Jerusalem. He says only that the same kind of an abomination with the same kind of an effect would appear in the Temple.

Commentators have wrestled with this word of Jesus, and many interpretations have been offered. Those are excluded which make "the holy place" the Jewish land, or which think that the abomination occurred during or after the siege of Jerusalem by the Romans. The latter views are shut out by the fact that it would then be impossible to flee the land. All those views are likewise shut out which regard the abomination as a person, Antiochus *redivivus*, an impersonation of the antichrist, for the abomination to which Jesus refers is neuter as τὸ ῥηθέν shows.

The abomination of desolation occurred in the Temple prior to the siege under Titus. It took place when the Zealots, who held the Temple under arms, admitted the Idumeans and as a result the Temple was deluged with the blood of 8,500 victims. Read Josephus, *Wars*, 4, 5, 1-2; also 4, 6, 3 the last sentences: "These men, therefore, trampled upon all the laws of men and laughed at the laws of God; and for the oracles of the prophets, they ridiculed them as the tricks of jugglers. . . . For there was a certain oracle of those men that the city should then be taken and the Sanctuary burnt by right of war when a sedition should invade the Jews, and their own hands should pollute the Temple of God." Whatever may be said of this "oracle" to which Josephus refers, the pollution of the Temple which he describes tallies with the abomination to which Jesus refers. Because the Jews themselves, in conjunction with the Idumeans, made their Temple an abomination, the application of Daniel's prophecy calls for special insight, and thus Jesus adds parenthetically, "he that reads let him understand," namely reads the words of Daniel.

16) "Those in Judea" are all the Christians, including, of course, those in Jerusalem. They are to flee "to the mountains," but not to those of Judea itself where they would never be safe during the war; these mountains lay outside of Judea, beyond the Jordan, in Perea. The Christians followed Jesus' bidding. Eusebius, 3, 5, reports that the congregation in Jerusalem, following a revelation received by reliable men before the war, migrated to Pella in Perea. As far as one can judge, this must have been done at the very time when bloody factions in the city were making an abomination of the Temple.

17) Jesus named the latest moment for flight, hence the haste that must be employed when one waits that long. This haste, however, is due not only to the brief time left, but likewise to the mounting dangers. A man is to get himself away and is not to stop to remove things out of his house. He may be stopped, robbed, turned back, and fail to escape.

18) A man who is out in the field, working only in a tunic, is to speed away and not to go to the city to get his clothes, not even his large outer robe, τὸ ἱμάτιον. Life is worth more than many robes.

19) Jesus' heart melts at the thought of the hardships that such flight from the doomed city and country will bring upon pregnant and suckling women, the former being burdened with unborn babes, the latter with babes in arms. "Woe" to them amid all the hurry and the dangers of the road!

20) He thinks of other things: the cold and the wet of the Palestinian winter and the possibility that the time of "your flight" may occur at that season. Or it may occur on "the Sabbath" when the country is filled with fanatical Jews, who would become furious at a supposed desecration of the Sabbath. The view that at this time the Christians would still be observ-

ing the Jewish regulations, including those regarding the Sabbath, is without warrant. Jesus bids the Christians "to keep praying" (present, durative imperative) that these possibilities may not come to pass; for everything is in God's hands. He can both speed or delay the day of judgment upon the Jewish nation. In "keep praying" there lies the veiled promise that God will hear.

21) The reason for all these biddings is the terrible state of the nation when the Roman war will begin. The word of Jesus about the "great tribulation," θλῖψις, *Bedraengnis*, that will then ensue, the like of which has not been witnessed since the world's beginning and will never again occur, is literally true — read the detailed account of Josephus in his *Wars*. No nation had ever piled up a guilt such as that of the Jews who were chosen of God, infinitely blessed, and yet crucified God's Son and trampled upon all his further grace. No judgment had ever and can ever be so severe. In the history of the world no judgment can be compared with this that wiped out the Jews as a nation.

22) **And unless those days had been shortened, no flesh would have been saved; but because of the elect those days shall be shortened.** The intensity and severity of the θλῖψις will be so great that a prolongation of them would claim the lives of everybody in the nation. The conditional sentence is one of past unreality; it is perfectly regular also in using μή as the negative in the protasis and οὐ in the apodosis. The Greek idiom construes the negative with the verb and has "all flesh" as the subject; in English we reverse this so that οὐ . . . πᾶσα becomes "no flesh." We see the force of the two passive verbs in the word κολοβός which means "docked." "Those days" (v. 19) are the days of the fanatical rebellion which eventuated in war. It was a period of about four or

five years, from 66 to beyond the year 70. And still
these days were "docked," and the history of this brief
period furnishes the strongest evidence that, if the
Jewish fanatical craze of this time had continued, it
would have ended in Jewish self-annihilation. The
agent back of the two passive verbs is, of course, God
in whose hand is the entire course of every judgment.
Here the verb ἐσώθη means "saved" from physical death.
This shortening was, of course, not due to the wicked
Jews whose day of reckoning had come. In them God
could see nothing that would cause him to withdraw
his hand before extinction had been accomplished.

He looked at "the elect," at their interests, and for
their sakes docked those days. This act of God's is
misunderstood when it is restricted to the elect who
were then living. It is then conceived as enabling
them to live through those days without losing their
faith. But the elect did not pass through the horrors
that occurred prior to the siege and during the siege.
Those that were in Jerusalem escaped betimes. Moreover, at that time many elect were scattered about
elsewhere in the Roman empire, far from the horrors
going on in Judea. The very first clause states that
the shortening enabled some of the Jews to remain
alive. This shows that "because of the elect" refers
not only to the elect in general but also to their
spiritual interest. By the power of God the Jews were
at that time kept from extinction and they are still
being kept as a strange phenomenon in the world. They
never amalgamated with other nations and races, and
thus they are a sign for the elect of all ages. The
Jews of today are scattered over all the world, without a land, a government, or any other tie such as
other nations have, are outcasts from their own country, and thus are miraculously marked for all time
for all the elect, whose enlightened eyes cannot but
see what God has thus placed before them.

23)    Jesus repeats the warning given in v. 5 and
in v. 11 but now restricts it to the period marked by
the disintegration of the Jewish nation. **Then, if
anyone shall say to you, Lo, here the Christ! or
there! do not believe.   For there shall arise** (passive
as in v. 11) **false Christs and false prophets and shall
furnish signs and wonders so as to deceive, if possible, even the elect.   Lo, I have told you beforehand.   If, therefore, they shall say to you, Lo, he is
in the desert! do not go out; Lo, in the inner rooms!
do not believe.   For even as the lightning comes out
of the eastern parts** (see 2:1) **and shines to the
western parts, thus shall be the Parousia of the Son
of man.   Wherever the carrion is, there the eagles
shall be gathered together.**

"Then" makes it plain that Jesus is speaking of
this particular time when Jerusalem was heading for
destruction; ὑμῖν agrees with this.   The condition of
expectancy, ἐάν with the subjunctive, indicates that
such cries would, indeed, reach the Christians.   As
former Jews who are now believers in Jesus as the
Christ they would be especially susceptible to the
deception involved; for had not Jesus promised them
his glorious return, and might he not be returning
at this very time?   The old love for their nation would
also have its effect, for it believed that Jesus would
deliver the Jews and make them conquerors of the
world.   "Lo here or there!" reveals an uncertainty.
But the peremptory aorist subjunctive (always the
subjunctive and not the imperative in prohibitions
that have the aorist) stops any trust in these cries
about "the Christ."   When men are in dire need they
often enough long for "the Christ," for one who fits
their notion of deliverance.

24)    The clause introduced by γάρ still refers to
"then" used in v. 23, and the supposition that Jesus
is now speaking more generally about the great world

era is untenable. During this very period of Jewish calamity false Christs and false prophets shall arise and shall furnish even signs and prodigies (τέρατα, astounding things) to deceive the people. The assertion is made that the history of the destruction of Jerusalem furnishes no evidence for the fulfillment of this prophecy. But the accounts of Josephus are quite to the contrary although even he could scarcely have collected all the cases that occurred. Read *Wars*, 2, 13, 4: "These were such men as deceived and deluded the people under pretense of *divine inspiration*, . . . and these prevailed with the multitude to act like madmen and went before them *into the wilderness*, pretending that God would there show the signals (signs) of liberty." The next paragraph (5) tells of the Egyptian who "pretended to be a prophet also" and started "from the wilderness" with 30,000 men and ended in miserable *defeat on the Mount of Olives*. *Wars*, 6, 5, 2: "A false prophet was the occasion of these people's destruction, who had made a public proclamation in the city that very day that 'God commanded them to get up upon the Temple, and that there they should receive miraculous signs for their deliverance.' Now there was then a great number of false prophets who had been suborned by the tyrants to impose on the people, who announced this to them, that they should wait for deliverance from God." It is true, Josephus mentions no false Christ, but the line of demarcation between a prophet and a Christ fluctuated in the minds of the Jews, and at a critical time such as this, if ever, the hope of a Messiah to deliver them must have flared up in connection with all these prophets.

In ὥστε with the aorist infinitive we here most likely have only purpose; contemplated result is the view of B.-D. 391, 3, and R. 990. Then this statement would mean that these Christs and these prophets intended

The Interpretation of Matthew

to deceive "even the elect," which, however, was impossible. The πλανῆσαι is effective, actually to deceive so that the elect would really regard these false Christs and false prophets (some one of the former) as true Christs and true prophets and thus believe their purported revelations. "If possible" denies the possibility objectively. However many others the great signs and prodigies offered (δώσουσι) by these deceivers to substantiate their claims may deceive, they will fail in the case of the elect.

We have no intimation that these signs and wonders are actual miracles that were wrought by diabolic powers; those who think that they were overlook II Thess. 2:9, where even the great Antichrist is credited only with "all power and signs and *lying* wonders," false, pseudo, sham miracles. Almighty God alone works true miracles. Satan's whole purpose is attained when, by means of a "lying" wonder, he makes men think that they see a genuine miracle. There is a tendency to ascribe too much power to Satan and his demons which is liable to do much harm. If the elect could be actually and permanently deceived, they, of course, would not be the elect. Yet what prevents their fatal deception is not a mysterious decree of God protecting them alone but the effective power of his grace, the effectiveness of which in their case is foreknown by God. This also explains the title given them in Scripture, οἱ ἐκλεκτοί, those whom God chose as his own from all eternity, those who already then were present to God as being saved effectively and forever by his grace which is bestowed in Word and Sacrament.

25) We see this grace operating right here; Jesus even calls especial attention to it by the exclamation "lo." The perfect, "I have told you beforehand," views matters from the standpoint of the event when these deceptions begin to operate. Then the be-

lievers are to tell themselves, "He has told us in advance," and already the fact that he truly prophesied and forewarned them is to keep them undeceived and safe.

26) What "lo, here!" and "lo, there!" means in v. 23 is now restated more plainly, "lo, in the desert" (recall Josephus': "in the wilderness") ; "lo, in the inner rooms," ταμεῖα. No Christian is to pay any attention to such cries and is neither to go out to see for himself nor to believe without going to see. The deception is too palpable and gross.

27) The Parousia of the Son of man (see 8:20), his Return and Presence when he returns as he has promised, will be absolutely different. He will not be hidden away in the wilderness nor in some guarded and secret inner room in a building. His coming and his presence will be like a flash of lightning which illuminates the sky from the east or sunrise (see 2:1) to the west or sunset. The whole world will see him in the brilliance of his heavenly glory. No man will then cry : "Lo, come and see!" or, "Lo, I know where he is, believe me!" Sham Christs have always been poor shams. The glory of the real Christ is beyond imitation. But men's ignorance of the Son of man is still stupendous.

28) Christ's sentence about the carrion drawing the eagles has perplexed the commentators and has thus produced even nauseating interpretations: Christ is the carrion, believers are the vultures; or believers are the carrion, and Christ is the vultures! "The eagles" are then turned into vultures. The introduction of a non-textual γάρ (A. V.) which makes this statement an explanation of the Parousia is misleading. Nor is this a universal statement: wherever, no matter where, the carrion is to be found, there the eagles will invariably gather. The statement is, indeed, general, but even in Luke 17:37 it re-

fers, proverbial as it is, to a specific case. The view that it must have the same application in Luke that it has here is another misleading idea that helps to darken the present connection. Some compare the judgment angels with vultures who swoop down on carrion and point to 13:41. Eagles, as well as vultures, gorge themselves with carrion. That is here the point of comparison, and that dispenses with the angels.

In every comparison the *tertium comparationis* must be discovered or we may go astray. Who acts like eagles that pounce on carrion to fatten upon the reeking flesh? Why these false Christs and these false prophets. They seek to get an advantage from the dead and decaying body of their nation. So Jesus says to his disciples: "When you hear these cries to come here or there in connection with false Christs and false prophets, remember that Christ comes in a glory that is instant and visible to the whole world, and that you have in those raucous cries only another case of eagles going to feast on carrion." With πτῶμα Jesus indicates the hopeless state of the Jewish nation; carrion is death gone into putrefaction. It is fit only for vultures. When the Jewish nation is so far gone, it is fit for nothing but false Christs and false prophets who are to finish the horrible job of removing that nation from existence.

29) We see how exactly Jesus answers the questions addressed to him in v. 3; first, about the destruction of the Temple and, then, about the end of the world and his Parousia. The first sketch (v. 4-14) presents a world survey which brings us to τὸ τέλος, "the end." The second sketch (v. 15-28) presents the overthrow of the Jewish nation and brings us a reference to the true παρουσία which will be like a mighty flash of lightning and will *not* occur in connection with the Jewish calamity. Now Jesus tells just what "the end" and the Parousia will be, for the two will

occur together. **Now immediately after the tribulation of those days the sun shall be made dark, and
the moon shall not give her brightness, and the stars
shall fall from the heaven, and the powers of
the heavens shall be shaken. And then shall
appear the sign of the Son of man in the heaven;
and then all the tribes of the earth shall beat the
breast and shall see the Son of man coming on
the clouds of the heaven with power and much
glory.**

Much effort has been spent on εὐθέως (which some
make equivalent to "suddenly") and on the μετά phrase.
Why not take into consideration the whole paragraph
v. 29-31? This presents the actual Parousia as it shall
occur. Why look only at the θλῖψις occurring in Jerusalem, v. 21, and disregard the one mentioned in v. 9;
the former is very limited, but think of the latter.
When seeking to determine what "those days" and
their "tribulation" are, why overlook v. 14, the gospel
extending to all nations (which must take place after
the end of the Jewish nation), and the end of the world
not occurring until then? The discourse is entirely
plain. When the last day arrives, when the tribulation of all the preceding days is concluded, "immediately" all that is now stated shall, occur. No
intervals shall lengthen this time. All shall happen at once.

The whole siderial world shall collapse. All these
καί present what happens at once. This is made plain
by the last, "the powers of the heavens shall be
shaken" or dislocated. All that holds the heavenly
bodies in their orbits and enables sun and moon to
light the earth will give way. Thus the sun's light
will be extinguished, the moon's radiance will disappear in the same instant, and the stars will fall from
their places. Let no man try to imagine this cataclysm! It is utterly beyond human conception.

30) "And then," here and again in the next sentence, merely denotes succession and one that is instantaneous. "The powers of the heavens" by which God held the universe of the skies in place are broken and removed; God's omnipotent hand reaches down to wind up the affairs of earth and of man. Some effort is made to find a distinction between "the sign of the Son of man" and its appearance and "the Son of man himself coming on the clouds," etc. But why seek for a distinction? In v. 3 "the sign of thy Parousia and of the complete finish of the eon," as the two genitives indicate, refers to the comprehensive signs that foretell that Parousia and the end. In "the sign of the Son of man" the genitive is subjective: the sign by which he shows his presence; not objective: the sign which points to him as being about to come. The stress is on the verbs, all of them are placed forward for this reason: φανήσεται — κόψονται — ὄψονται. And the first and the last are correlative: "there shall appear," and, of course, at once all the tribes of earth "shall see these." No sign, say a glowing, dazzling light shall hang over the earth for a shorter or a longer period after which sign the Son shall arrive. All will be one grand act: the Son's manifestation in glory will be what the tribes see. On "Son of man" see 8:20; on the second passive future φανήσεται as being without passive force cf. R. 334, and on the fact that it is punctiliar and not durative cf. R. 871; yet κόψονται and ὄψονται are durative.

The effect of the appearance is that "all the tribes of the earth shall beat their breasts," the Oriental expression for grief, fear, or despair that overwhelms the heart. Luke 21:25, 26 tells us that the consternation of men will begin with the appearance of the first cataclysmic signs. The αἱ φυλαί, clans or tribes, are the different aggregations of men, each group being marked by its own characteristics and thus

being bound together by common ties. "Tribes" are
more numerous than nations. The question is asked
whether one of these tribes includes the Christians
who are alive at the end. That would be a strange
name for them. They are called "the elect" in v. 31,
and Jesus has particular instructions for them in order
to remove any fears they might have. The consternation of the tribes is due to the judgment that now
overwhelms them. This Son of man they despised,
his promised Parousia they thought a dream, the
world cataclysm they ruled out by their science
(II Pet. 3:3, 4).

Now they see him "coming on the clouds of the
heaven" (Dan. 7:13) as was promised in Acts 1:9, 11.
The clouds are God's chariot, Ps. 104:3; Isa. 19:1, the
symbol of his heavenly majesty. In μετά (as also in
v. 29) we have the idea of accompaniment: "in company with power and much glory." This "power" is
Christ's omnipotence which was manifested in the
heavenly bodies (v. 29); and his "glory" is the sum
of all his divine attributes as displayed before men
(Tit. 2:13; I Cor. 1:4, revelation; II Thess. 1:7;
I Pet. 1:7; 4:13). At one time the Son of man
appeared on earth in lowliness and allowed himself to
be crucified; but at the end his omnipotence and his
great glory will be fully displayed.

31) **And he will send his angels with a great
trumpet, and they shall gather up together his elect
from the four winds, from heavens' ends to their
ends.** Compare 25:31-33. The trumpet shall sound
with a mighty tone to call the dead back to life
(I Thess. 4:14-17). The angels shall then gather all
the elect, whose souls are now united with their glorified bodies, together (σύν), up to one place (ἐπί), namely Christ's right hand (25:33). Nothing is said in
regard to the rest except what was stated in v. 30
about their beating their breasts. The Biblical concep-

tion of the earth is that it is made up of four quarters, the four directions from which the winds blow. This conception is still common: north, south, east and west. The apposition "from heavens' ends to their ends," Mark's (13:27) "from earth's end to heaven's end," only emphasizes the preceding phrase by pointing to every remote part under the heavens.

Some call these phrases poetical, and that is due to the fact that the ideas here expressed remain and must remain beyond adequate human conception. We prefer the idea of a globe, the one hemisphere being opposite to and hidden from the other hemisphere. And so we might ask how both hemispheres shall at the same time see the Son of man in the clouds, hear the angel trumpet, and yield up the dead. Or with our ideas of space we might wonder how all the millions that have lived on earth shall find room to stand, and with our conceptions of time we might ask how long it will take until the last person has been judged. The answer to all these questions is that after the events mentioned in v. 29 none of these present limitations of ours will exist.

32) **Now from the fig tree learn the parable. When now her branch becomes tender and makes the leaves grow out, you realize that the summer is near. So also you, when you see all these things, realize that it is near, at the doors. Amen, I say to you: In no wise shall this generation pass away until all these things shall occur. The heaven and the earth shall pass away, but my words shall in no wise pass away.** We now enter the admonitory section of the Lord's address. While his prophecy has unrolled a picture of dread, it is, nevertheless, bright with hope for the elect. So Jesus bids the disciples learn from the fig tree "the" in the sense of "this" parable: when its branch becomes soft with swelling sap and starts to grow leaves, the disciples realize that

summer, beautiful summer, is at hand, and that makes
them glad. The aorist γένηται is punctiliar, the softness
is attained; but ἐκφύῃ is durative (present active subjunctive), the branch is in the process of growing
leaves. The incorrect ἐκφυῇ would be the second aorist
passive subjunctive, R. 232.

33) In the explanation of the parable καὶ ὑμεῖς is
emphatic. The budding of the fig tree is observed by
all men, but in order to understand its significance as
presented by Jesus even the disciples need to be told,
"Realize" what all these things mean! When the πάντα
ταῦτα is unduly stressed, strange views may be the
result. We may follow ταῦτα back to the question of
the disciples in v. 3, and we find it with πάντα in v. 8.
Jesus thus speaks of occurrences that, like the beginning of birthpains, presage the end and his own Parousia. Thus also all that pertains to the destruction
of the Jewish nation is included. Yet it is unwarranted to stress "all" so that it implies that the disciples could not come to the realization of what the
signs signify until they had actually seen all of them
occurring repeatedly through the centuries. They
need to see false Christs, false prophets, wars, and
persecutions only once in order to see them "all" and
thus to be impressed by what these things really
signify. It also ought to be plain that v. 29 is not
included, because these events themselves are the end.

In ἐγγύς ἐστιν ἐπὶ θύραις the subject is omitted. It
seems best to suppy no subject, at least not "he" (the
Son of man) as is done in the R. V., on the ground
that "at the doors" refers to a person who is about
to enter a building. The general context is sufficient.
The Greek needs to supply nothing, but the English
would need "it" (A. V.) in the general sense of the
end. The meaning of Jesus is that every sign adver-
tises the end as being "near." From the days of the
disciples to our own time these advertisements are to

the same effect. Just when the end will come no man knows. We are to be ready at all times for its coming, since all the signs have already occurred again and again.

34) With profound solemnity, using his well-known seal for verity and authority (see 5:18), Jesus declares that "this generation shall not pass away until all these things shall occur." The view that γενεά and especially ἡ γενεὰ αὕτη, refers to the contemporary generation, those living at the time when Jesus spoke, is untenable . A look at the use of *dor* in the Old Testament and at its regular translation by γενεά in the LXX reveals that *a kind* of men is referred to, the evil kind that reproduces and succeeds itself in many physical generations. Compare Ps. 12:7: "Thou shalt preserve them from this generation *forever*"; 78:8, the fathers (many physical generations of them); 14:5, "the generation of the righteous"; 24:6; 73:15; 112:2; Deut. 32:5, 20; Prov. 30:11-14; Isaiah often; Jer. 7:29; etc. From these passages turn to the New Testament and in addition to the Gospels note Acts 2:40; Phil. 2:15; Heb. 3:10. Sometimes the evil manifested by the kind of men referred to is indicated by modifiers, as in Matt. 16:4; 17:17; Mark 8:38, but often the context does this. In the present connection the meaning of "generation" is plain, for already in v. 14 we were referred to "the end," and in v. 29-31 the end itself is described. The contention that πάντα ταῦτα must have the same meaning that these words have in v. 33 claims too much because it overlooks the verbs. In v. 33 the disciples shall see "all these things," evidently not all of them throughout the ages to the very end; but in v. 34 "all these things shall occur" before this generation passes away — the succession of signs through the ages while this kind of men continues and their tribe has not ceased.

Accordingly, "this generation" does not mean the human race, nor does it refer to Christians, nor are all the wicked included in "this generation." Why such a solemn assurance with "amen, I say to you," for a thing so obvious as that a race of wicked unbelievers and persecutors shall persist through the ages? Does Jesus not in v. 30 show them beating their breasts in dismay at the time of his Parousia?

"This generation" consists of the type of Jews whom Jesus contended with during this Tuesday, 21:23-23:39. He foretells the destruction of their nation (24:15-28); and one might easily conclude that this would end the generation of Jews such as these Sadducees and these Pharisees. But no; solemnly we are assured (and this assurance is in place) that this type of Jew will continue to the very Parousia. It has continued to this very day. The voice of Jewish rejection of Christ is as loud and as vicious as ever: he is not the Messiah, not the Son of God! Here, therefore, is Jesus' own answer to those who expect a final national conversion of the Jews either with or without a millennium.

35) The statement that "the heaven and the earth shall pass away, but my words shall in no wise pass away" loses much of its force when it is regarded as an assurance of the fact that the contemporaneous generation of Jews will not have disappeared before all things foretold by Jesus shall have reached an end. The statement gains in force when the prophecy of v. 34 is properly understood. This verse is only one of Jesus' words. Jesus does not restrict his statement to his present discourse and to the many statements it includes. He does not say, "These my words," but all-inclusively, "my words shall in no wise pass away," οὐ μή, the strongest negation with either the indicative or a subjunctive as here and in v. 34. Despite their apparent durability the physical heaven and earth

"shall pass away." The question as to whether this
means annihilation, reduction to nothingness, or trans-
formation to a different form of existence cannot be
answered by a consideration of παρελεύσεται in this
passage or the indeterminate wording of many other
passages. The most decisive passage is Rom. 8:19-23,
together with I Cor. 7:31 (only the fashion, σχῆμα, of
the world shall pass away), and Rev. 21:1-5 (the
divine heaven and the earth shall be united). So the
physical heaven and the physical earth will change
completely; when they are changed at the Parousia,
we shall not recognize them. But the words of Jesus
will never undergo even the slightest change either in
meaning or in form.

36) **Now concerning that day and hour no one
knows, neither the angels of the heavens, nor the
Son, save the Father only. And just like the days
of Noah, so shall be the Parousia of the Son of
man. For just like they were in those days before
the deluge, eating and drinking, marrying and
giving in marriage until the day Noah went into the
ark, and they did not realize until the deluge came
and took them all away; thus will be the Parousia
of the Son of man. Then two men shall be in the
field — one is taken, and one is left; two women
grinding at the mill — one is taken, and one is left.
Watch, therefore, because you do not know what
day your Lord comes.** In a manner Jesus has told
the disciples when the end and his Parousia would
come, namely by pointing them to the signs. But,
after all, this is not specific. Jesus tells them that
the Father alone knows the precise date. The ἡμέρα
is here "the day" in the narrower sense, and the ὥρα
in the wider, the general period of time. We must not
refer the latter to the hour of a specific day.

The fact that the angels, although they are in
heaven, do not know the date does not especially sur-

prise us, but the fact that "the Son" should not know the day and hour does cause surprise. The term "the Son" is here placed alongside of "the Father." But while it names this person according to his divine nature, it predicates something concerning his human nature. Compare similar expressions in Acts 3:15, and I Cor. 2:8. In their essential oneness the three persons know all things, but in his state of humiliation the Second Person did not use his divine attributes save as he needed them in his mediatorial work. So his divine omniscience was used by Jesus in only this restricted way. That is why here on Mt. Olivet he does not know the date of the end. How the incarnate Son could thus restrict the use of his divine attributes is one of the mysteries of his person; the fact is beyond dispute.

37) The Parousia will be like the days of Noah, i. e., its coming as far as men's knowledge is concerned.

38) In the days preceding the deluge men were wholly unconcerned (ἦσαν with an indefinite subject). They spent the 120 years which God had fixed as the limit of his grace "eating (τρώγειν, 'to munch,' audible eating, used in John 6:54-58) and drinking, marrying and giving in marriage" as though no judgment were impending. These are neutral actions that are not sinful in themselves; but they obtain a sinister significance when the total disregard of God's warnings is observed which underlies this conduct. These men should have repented in sackcloth and in ashes. The participles are predicates of ἦσαν. And this was done until the very day that Noah, at God's command, entered the ark. The relative is drawn into the clause: ἄχρι ἧς ἡμέρας instead of ἄχρι τῆς ἡμέρας ᾗ, etc., R. 717. "Ark" is κιβωτός. This suggests the word used in Heb. 9:4 for the ark of the covenant, and in Rev. 11:19 for the ark of the heavenly sanctuary; the word itself means a wooden chest.

39) They never "realized" anything until the final, fatal moment. The fact that an ark was being built on dry land, that Noah told them why he built it, seemed a great joke to them "until the flood came (κατακλυσμός, from κατακλύζειν, to overflow with utter destruction — note the English derivative cataclysm) and took away all." Exactly so shall be the Parousia: warnings enough and more than enough, but ears deaf, hearts obdurate, every sign being explained away "naturally," "reasonably," even "scientifically" until the fatal day arrives. It is not the wickedness of immorality that Jesus stresses but this ungodly, guilty, and damnable blindness.

40, 41) So it will happen that two men will be in the field, working there side by side, and two women "grinding at the mill," ἀλήθουσαι, present feminine participle, and μύλος is a handmill for preparing the meal for the day. One is taken, received, the other is left, abandoned. The agent hidden in the passives is the Son of man. Why the one is graciously received by Christ while the other is left (see v. 31) does not need to be explained. The one was like Noah, the other like those caught by the deluge.

42) Jesus draws the proper conclusion for his disciples (οὖν): "Be watching, therefore," durative, "constantly keep your eyes open," namely to see the signs that presage the Parousia, to remember the promised final day, and ever, ever to be ready for it. Returning to v. 36, Jesus states the great reason: "because you do not know what day your Lord comes," ποίᾳ is nonqualitative, R. 740. For despite all our watching no one will ever figure out the day. In fact, when we ourselves think that on *this* day he will not come, *that* may be the very day that he comes.

43) **Moreover, that realize, that, if the house-lord had known in what watch the thief comes, he would have watched and would not have permitted**

**his house to be broken through. For this reason be
you also ready; because in what hour you do not
think, the Son of man comes.** The illustration is
drawn from the contrary: a houseowner had failed to
watch because he did not know in which of the four
watches of the night the thief would appear, of whose
coming he had a general warning. The result was
that he slept, and that the thief broke through door or
window and stole what he wanted. Jesus puts this
into a condition of past unreality, "If he had known he
would have watched and would not have left," etc. In
the protasis the second past perfect ᾔδει is regularly
used for the imperfect, and this leads some to think
that the condition is mixed, "If he knew (present unreality) he would have watched," etc. (past unreality).
But this would be a strange mixture; the imperfect is
also found in conditions of past unreality, and that is
plainly the case where (as in the case of the present
verb) the aorist is not in use. In the Greek the direct
discourse, "in what watch the thief comes," is retained.

44) "On this account" or "for this reason," namely because this houselord acted so foolishly, do "you,
too," not repeat his mistake but "be ready," γίνεσθε,
durative present, "be ever ready!" And the reason
for this only sane and safe course is the fact that in the
very hour (period) when you feel sure that he is not
coming, in that very hour he will come. That is the
astonishing feature about the uncertainty regarding
the time. Even those who are constantly on the watch
will be completely surprised. For they will feel quite
sure that at this or that time he will not come, and one
such time will be chosen for his coming. The present
ἔρχεται matches the present δοκεῖτε.

45) **Who, then, is the trustworthy and sensible
slave whom the lord did set over his household to**

**be giving them the food in due season? Blessed that slave whom his lord, having come, shall find doing thus! Amen, I say to you, that over all his possessions he shall set him.** But if that base slave shall say in his heart, My lord delays, and shall begin to beat his fellow-slaves, moreover shall also eat and drink with the drunken, the lord of that slave shall come in a day in which he does not expect and in an hour in which he does not realize and shall cut him in two, and his portion he shall place together with the hypocrites; there shall be the weeping and the gnashing of the teeth.

This is the first of three parables in which Jesus describes and emphasizes the fact that we should be ready for his coming. The connective ἄρα indicates correspondence with v. 44, "according to" the unexpectedness of the coming of the Son of man. Who is the slave that is πιστός, faithful, and φρόνιμος, sensible in view of the undated coming of his lord? The predicate has the article and is thus identical with the subject (R. 768), and καί carries the force of the article forward to the second adjective (R. 777). But this is not an ordinary slave, his lord did set him over (R. 845, the English prefers the perfect: "has set") his οἰκετεία, household of other slaves; and he did this that he might "be giving them (τοῦ with the present infinitive expresses purpose; the present, continuous action) their food in due season" (ἐν καιρῷ). Jesus is speaking of the ministers and pastors of his church whose obligation is double and includes that of the household committed to them. It is a great distinction to be taken from the ranks of the common slaves and to be made the headslave over all the rest. The trust thus imposed ought to act as a strong incentive to be πιστός, trustworthy, in return, and φρόνιμος, sensible and capable of living up to the trust received.

46) Instead of saying anything further about this slave, Jesus exclaims because of his blessedness: μακάριος (see 5:3), a verdict, the blessedness consisting of the possessions of the kingdom and of the happiness that goes with them (v. 47). "That slave" is the one Jesus has in mind, whom he describes in the relative clause, "whom, on having come, his lord shall find doing thus." The emphasis is on the aorist participle ἐλθών. Until his lord comes he faithfully does exactly what his lord told him, and his lord finds him so engaged (ποιοῦντα οὕτως). He does not sit idly outside of the house looking for his lord and speculating about his return; he is inside, steadily doing his lord's bidding.

47) So important is this conduct that Jesus announces with the seal of verity and of authority (see 5:18) just what this slave's blessedness shall be, "over all his possession he shall set him"; the phrase is placed forward for the sake of emphasis. The lord will make that slave the head steward of his estate and keep him as such. The reality here pictured is far greater than the picture but beyond our adequate conception; compare 25:21, 23; Luke 19:17, 19.

48) With a condition of expectancy Jesus turns to "that base slave," κακός, *nichtswuerdig,* whom he has in mind; this is the force of ἐκεῖνος. "To say in the heart" is to think without betraying oneself, and this false slave's thought is, "Delay doth my lord," the emphasis being on the verb. He accepted his lord's trust, he promised faithful and competent service, and now see what his secret thought reveals! He is a base hypocrite (v. 51).

49) Since his lord is gone he casts off restraint and reveals the inner baseness of his nature which has only been hidden hitherto. Instead of attending to the other slaves, he now lords it over them as the tyrant that he is. He is a sample of those ministers

in the church who act like popes. Instead of doing
the work graciously entrusted to him, he gives rein to
the lower passions which he has had to hide while his
lord was present. He now carouses, eats, and drinks
in company with base fellows like himself. Now he
is a sample of the ministers who are self-seekers, who
also indulge their flesh, even its basest side, when they
think they can do so with safety.

50) What will happen? He will be caught in his
own folly. His lord will come in a day in which he
does not expect; and Jesus emphasizes this by adding
in an hour (wider sense of hour) in which he does
not realize. In the Greek the verbs do not require objects, these being understood. Many have thought
themselves shrewd enough to indulge their wickedness
and have imagined that they could call a halt in time
and thus escape. But every yielding to indulgence
blinds the moral sense and only helps to make a greater
fool. His end will be his execution, he will be cut
in two (II Sam. 12:31; I Chron. 20:3) with a horrible saw and thus receive the just reward of his faith-
lessness.

51) At this point Jesus breaks off the parabolic
language and speaks literally, "and his portion he shall
place together with the hypocrites" ("unbelievers,"
Luke 12:46). What this μέρος or lot is the Lord plainly
declares: "There shall be the weeping and gnashing
of the teeth," namely in hell. On this clause see 8:12;
13:42, 50; 22:13; 25:30.

This parable was also used on an earlier occasion
when Jesus had occasion to speak of our being ready
for his second coming, Luke 12:35-48; note v. 42-46.
The repetition helps to impress his words the more
deeply.

# CHAPTER XXV

The three parables recorded in 24:45-25:30 belong together and should be studied together. The observation is correct that the first deals with both faithfulness and wisdom, the second with wisdom alone, and the third with faithfulness alone. The first is intended especially for the ministers of the church, the second and the third for all her members: the second dealing with the spiritual life, the third with spiritual gifts and good works. In the first the hypocrites are exposed; in the second, the formal Christians; in the third, the slothful Christians. But this very inner coherence of the parables and their close connection with the great discourse that precedes shuts out the hypothesis that Matthew combined these pieces and made them read like a collected whole whereas Jesus did not utter them in the sequence here given. Was Matthew not present when Jesus spoke this discourse on Mt. Olivet?

**1) Then the kingdom of the heavens shall be made like to ten virgins who, having taken their lamps, went out to meet the bridegroom. But five of them were foolish, and five sensible. For the foolish, having taken their own lamps, did not take with themselves oil; but the sensible took oil in their vessels together with their lamps.** "Then" places us prior to the Lord's Parousia sketched in 24:4-44. We may at once say that the parable applies to all of us during this entire time. This does not imply that we shall live to witness the Parousia, for only a few will be alive at the last day. At the Parousia each of us will meet the Lord in the very condition in which we were when death removed us from this world. Foolish or wise, with or without oil, we shall appear when Jesus returns. On the kingdom of the heavens see 3:2; it is God's heavenly rule of grace through Jesus Christ and in this case God's rule as it turns from grace to glory.

The imagery employed is that of a grand Jewish wedding. Groom and bride have been betrothed by the parents. This has made them man and wife. This arrangement was unlike our engagements today in which two persons only promise to enter marriage, to become man and wife, at some future day. After the Jewish betrothal a certain time, usually not a very long time, was allowed to elapse, and then on a certain evening the groom, accompanied by his friends, proceeded in a festive procession from his own or his father's house to the home of his bride to bring her and her maiden companions to the groom's home for the consummation of the marriage with its days of wedding festivities. This homebringing was not connected with a marriage ceremony. The husband merely took his wife unto himself. This was the common procedure, and we have no reason for thinking that another procedure was followed when the wedding feast was held at the bride's home. In the Parousia the heavenly Bridegroom takes his bride, the true church, to his heavenly home, and the feast is held there although heaven and earth shall then be united, Rev. 21:1-5.

This explains the action of the ten virgins who took their lamps and went forth to meet the bridegroom. These were friends of the bride who went out from their homes with the necessary lamps, not to the bride's home, but to a place that was conveniently near. When the groom brought the bride out of her home, these virgins came forward and joined the procession with their lighted lamps and had their part in the feasting and the joy of the wedding in the groom's house. These λαμπάδες were vessels that contained oil. There was a

place for a round wick at one end of the vessel.   They
were somewhat like a torch.   In the parable the bride
and her special attendants and the companions of the
bridegroom are not mentioned because the *tertium
comparationis* deals only with the bridegroom and with
the action of these virgins.

The number ten is not accidental but symbolical.
It denotes completeness.   Thus we have Ten Commandments, ten talents (25:28), ten pieces of silver (Luke
15:8), ten servants, ten pounds, ten cities (Luke 19:13-
17), an instrument of ten strings (Ps. 33:2), at least
ten families needed to establish a synagogue, and ten
persons for a funeral procession.   These ten virgins
represent all the followers of Christ during all the ages.
All of them "shall be made like to" these ten virgins
when the Parousia of Christ occurs.

In 13:24 we have the passive aorist "was made like
to" because there is a reference to the past; here it is
the passive future, the agent being God.   The effort to
find a mystical meaning in παρθένοι, "virgins," as though
this indicated the purity of the Christians, is fanciful;
we have "virgins" because this parable deals with a
fine Jewish wedding.

2)   The *tertium comparationis* is now summarily
stated: five virgins were foolish, μωραί, stupid, and five
were φρονιμοί, wise or sensible (the same term that was
used in 24:45).   The actions of both groups will prove
it, but the decisive point is stated at the very start.
Some were senseless, and some were sensible before
either did a thing, and already that, or really that,
decided the fate of each group. We have two fives, each
a broken ten.   These figures have no further symbolical significance.   We have no right to say that as many
Christians will be foolish as will be wise.   But this
division of the number ten intimates that quite a host
of Christians will be found without sense at the Lord's
coming.

3) It was necessary for the great purpose of the parable to set out first of all and apart from the following action this basic fact: some foolish — others wise. For this is really what decides all that follows, and this is the heart of the warning for us. We are also shown without delay the plain evidence for the senselessness of the one group and for the sensibleness of the other. The foolish took their lamps along but took no oil! Can you imagine anything more foolish? Of course, no Jewish maidens would do such a thing as that; but this is a parable. Jesus has to picture such maidens in order to make us see how silly we are when, in our preparation for meeting the heavenly Bridegroom, we do exactly this silly thing in a spiritual way. Lamps, perhaps with a few drops of oil left in them from a former burning — and no oil!

4) The others took both their lamps and oil in separate vessels in order to be fully supplied. Sensible, indeed! But we must not let our own imagination spoil the parable: the foolish brought no oil at all — that was their folly; the wise brought what they needed, fully enough, but not a bit too much. The interpretation of this, the main, point in the parable is not difficult when we clearly see what is to be interpreted: on the one hand, lamps without oil; on the other, lamps with oil. The fact that the oil is kept in convenient vessels is a matter of course.

Lamps without oil are the forms of Christian life that are without the substance of this life; lamps together with oil are the forms that are vitalized by the true Christian life. Compare 5:14. We may call this oil spiritual life, faith with its works, even the Holy Ghost as some do. We prefer to think of faith and its works as being the flame of the lamp, the grace and the power of Christ in his Word as the oil, and the outward forms of Christianity as the lamps. We have the exposition in II Tim. 3:5: "Having the form of godliness

but denying the power thereof." We must have both.
Hundreds of people attach themselves to the church but
are never reborn and renewed. They may even do
great deeds in and for the church yet inwardly remain
strangers to Christ, 7:22, 23. Their folly is revealed
in the end.

5) **Now, the bridegroom delaying, they all
nodded and were sleeping.** This is the delay mentioned in 24:48. Jesus clearly intimates that he will
delay his Parousia. He does not, however, indicate
how long he will delay. The uncertainty regarding the
extent of this delay is the reason that we should never
speak as did the slave in 24:48, but keep in mind 24:44.
"All nodded and were sleeping" (descriptive imperfect, R. 838) means just what it says: the wise as well
as the foolish virgins nodded. If the wise had kept
awake, they would have been guilty had they not
aroused the foolish. It should be noted that the point
of the parable does not turn on this sleeping.

The fathers interpreted the sleep as death, which is
unavoidable because of the Lord's delay. This is far
better than the interpretation that even the godly become negligent and careless while looking for the
Lord's coming. Such an interpretation would allow
Jesus to condone a certain degree of carelessness in
true believers; but this is contrary to all his instructions and warnings which call on us *never* to be unprepared. The true preparation and the absence of such
preparation lie farther back, in the fact that the one
group has oil and the other disregards the oil.

This nodding and this sleeping merely match the
bridegroom's unexpected delay. Both groups of virgins had done all that they considered necessary for
meeting the bridegroom. If he had come at once, or
if he had delayed even longer than he did, the preparation which the two groups had made would have
been the same: some would have had oil and others

would have been without oil. Even if all had kept
wide-awake, they would not have been more ready than
they were when they slept. When the call came, "Lo,
the bridegroom!" the wise virgins were perfectly ready.
So this sleeping pictures the security and the assurance
with which the virgins awaited the bridegroom's coming; they felt that they were perfectly ready, that they
could add nothing more to their preparation. In the
case of the wise virgins this security was justified:
they had lamps and oil; but in the case of the foolish
virgins this security was unjustified: they had only
lamps and by sleeping securely they allowed the precious time to elapse during which they might have
remedied their mistake. When in v. 13 Jesus says
"watch" he means: see that you have the oil. All the
waking in the world and not going after oil avails the
foolish no more than their long sleep while they have
no oil.

An unwarranted turn is given the parable when
it is thought that the virgins kept their lamps burning
during the entire time that they were waiting for the
groom, the foolish merely running out of oil at the
critical moment at midnight. No; the lamps were not
lighted until the bridegroom came. If they had burned
from the start, the lamps of some of the foolish would
have gone out quite soon, and their lack of oil would
have been discovered. No, v. 3 settles this point: the
foolish never had oil, *that* was their folly.

6) **Now at midnight a cry has come: Lo, the
bridegroom! Be going out to meet him! Then all
those virgins arose and arranged their lamps. But
the foolish said to the sensible, Give us some of your
oil, because our lamps are going out. But the
sensible answered, saying: Nevermore! In no wise
will it suffice for us and for you. Be going rather
to those that sell and buy for yourselves. And while
they were going away to buy, the bridegroom came;**

**and those ready went in with him to the wedding, and the door was shut.** R. 775 calls μέσης νυκτός the old partitive construction; it seems to express time within (genitive) "during the middle of the night." Jesus uses the dramatical historical present perfect γέγονεν which brings out the suddenness of the cry (R. 897) : "a cry has come" and is now ringing in the ears. "Lo, the bridegroom!" is the joyful announcement. This cry is directed to the waiting virgins, "Be going out to meet him!"

In the parable the people who see the lights of the bridegroom's procession raise the cry. Since the bridegroom's arrival is the Parousia of Christ, we may say that the signs mentioned in 24:29, 30 raise this cry. The whole world will ring with it. The great moment for all who are ready to meet Christ has come.

7) Now all the virgins arise in great haste. **All** of them think they are ready. We need not locate them in the bride's house or in its courtyard nor along the open country road (some: in a ditch!) Why could they not have been in a house close by where the bridegroom could not pass without their seeing him? The verb ἐκόσμησαν means *sie schmueckten*, they made beautiful their lamps by lighting them so that they would burn with a clear, bright flame. Jesus does not need to say what trouble the foolish virgins had with their lamps.

8) We hear this from these virgins themselves. They are without oil. They beg oil from the wise "because our lamps are going out." They earnestly tried to light them, but the dry wicks caught only for a moment and then went out, σβέννυνται, descriptive present tense (R. 879), the form being middle (R. 318). Too late the foolish maidens see what they lack: oil for their lamps. Do not ask why they had so completely disregarded the oil until this critical moment. A foolish action has no sensible explanation. That is the

trouble with all folly, spiritual folly, too; it cannot explain itself.

9) The answer the wise give to the foolish virgins is parabolic language for the fact that it is now *too late*. We regard μήποτε as an independent expression, as the direct answer to the δότε of v. 8: "Nevermore!" We regard οὐ μή with its aorist subjunctive ἀρκέσῃ as the ordinary form of denial of something future, this double negative being used with either the future indicative or the subjunctive (usually the aorist). R. wavers between other possible constructions, see his reference. "In no wise will it suffice for us and for you" is the exact truth. Every believer has no more of spiritual grace and power than he needs for himself. It is impossible to divide this grace. Romanists interpret the oil as being good works but then get into difficulty because of this passage, for it declares that no person has enough good works to turn some of them over to others as works of supererogation. Thus the foolish virgins are caught by this impossibility. When it is *too late*, we resort to impossible appeals in vain.

The wise virgins have only the suggestion that the foolish go and buy the oil. The implication is that the wise bought their oil thus though they did it betimes. This has been called irony, but irony is improper for the wise virgins; nor do the foolish treat the suggestion as irony, for they act on it. The only way to get oil is to buy it (Rev. 3:18; Isa. 55:1). Those that sell are Moses and the prophets in the Scriptures, the only source of saving grace and power (Luke 16:29). This advice to go and to buy is sound and good, but it is *too late* to act on it now when the bridegroom is actually coming. This is the point of the parable and what it portrays regarding Christians who let their days of grace pass without securing grace for faith and a new life.

10) The parable shows how true this is. The foolish virgins make a frantic effort to buy after it is too late. We are not told even by intimation that at midnight they still found a bazaar open and bought oil; the implication is the opposite. While they are gone, the bridegroom came, and the other virgins were ready and went with him to the wedding. Here we have γάμοι the plural (the singular and the plural are used in the same sense in 22:1-14).

Some think that the wedding was held at the bride's home because of the correspondence of ἦλθεν and εἰσῆλθον. But this would make the wedding exceptional, and the parable has no reason for picturing such an exceptional feature and to do that by an implication that lies in two verbs. "With him to the wedding" is the main point; the verb in the middle of the sentence is without emphasis. The coming of the groom has only the one purpose, namely to take his bride "to the wedding" which has been prepared by him in his own home.

After the wedding procession had entered the house, "the door was shut." Subject and predicate are reversed in order to make both emphatic, "shut was the door" (Luke 13:25). This situation is the reverse of Rev. 3:20. The day is past for 7:7. Grace is vast in its extent but it has its limits. "Was shut" means never again to be opened. "No one's penitence, no one's prayer, no one's groaning shall anymore be admitted. That door is shut which received Aaron after his idolatry; which admitted David after his adultery, after his homicide; which not only did not repel Peter after his threefold denial but delivered its keys to be guarded by him (16:19)." Trench.

11) **Now, afterward the rest of the virgins come, saying, Lord, lord, open for us! But he, answering, said, Amen, I say to you, I do not know you!** In these two verses parable and reality meet. It is

still parable when the foolish virgins, after vainly seeking oil, come and try to enter the marriage feast. They simply carry their original folly to its ultimate limit. Their cry κύριε, κύριε, recalls 7:21, 23, and the duplication is as poignant as in 24:37. These foolish virgins disregard the oil to the last. They are the people who have despised grace and have thought that they could enter glory without grace. Even when they ran after grace too late they had no appreciation of grace. "Open to us!" to us who come without the grace that admitted the others! They add even the folly of an impossible demand. The wise who came by grace did not shout and demand. That was due to the fact that they came by grace.

12) Here the reality begins. Jesus speaks as the great Bridegroom, "Amen, I say to you," verity and authority, see 5:18. He has again pictured his Parousia. It will take place as here described. Many carelessly let the day of grace pass by until it is too late. In ὑμῖν and ὑμᾶς the parabolic language is still retained. But while these pronouns refer to the foolish virgins they are now quite transparent because Jesus introduces himself into the parable. "I do not know you," like, "I never knew you" in 7:23, completely disowns. Here the verb is οἶδα, in 7:23 it was ἔγνω, but the sense is the same, but the former says more; not only, "I have no relation to you," but, "You have no relation to me." C.-K. 388.

13) The final word is not a summary of the parable, it is a repetition of 24:42. **Be watching, therefore, because you do not know the day or the hour.** The admonition to be constantly watching should not mislead us to lay the final stress on v. 5 and to make that nodding and sleeping the fatal thing against which Jesus warns. The pivotal words of the parable are "foolish" and "sensible," and these two center in the "oil" (grace). This verse is really an epilog.

It emphasizes our utter ignorance of the day and of the hour of Christ's final coming (24:36). This is why we must constantly be watching. Our watching means that we must constantly look to ourselves, to be ever ready, to be ever rich in grace so that, when the day and the hour arrive, there may be no question as to our being received.

14) To the wisdom which relies on grace over against the folly which disregards grace Jesus adds another parable regarding the faithfulness which makes full use of this grace by producing good works. The connective γάρ makes this parable an exposition of v. 13. It indicates the scope of the parable: our watching for our Lord's coming by faithfully using his talents in his service. Thus grace which kindles faith and a new life that entitle us to enter the heavenly marriage is for this very reason to be followed by the fruits of grace and faith and a new life in good works. The order of the two parables cannot be changed. "Especially in these last times it is no less needful to admonish men to Christian discipline and good works and remind them how necessary it is that they exercise themselves in good works as a declaration of their faith and gratitude to God, than that the works be not mingled in the article of justification; because men may be damned by an Epicurean delusion concerning faith, as well as by papistic and Pharisaic confidence in their own works and merits." *Concordia Triglotta,* 801, 18.

This parable and that recorded in Luke 19:11-27 are not the same parable. Gerhard answered the efforts of Moldonatus and others to make one parable out of the two. Some take out of Luke's parable what pertains to the rebellious citizens, make this a parable by itself, and then combine what remains with Matthew's parable. But the scope and the persons addressed are different in the parable of the Pounds and that of the Talents. The parable of the Pounds was

spoken when Jesus drew nigh to Jerusalem, that of the
Talents on Mt. Olivet on Tuesday evening after Palm
Sunday.   The parable of the Pounds includes Christ's
enemies and was spoken to the disciples and to the multitude; that of the Talents deals only with the disciples.
That is why the second parable is simpler than the first.
In the parable of the Pounds the lord gives the same
amount to each servant (the gift of Word and Sacrament) ; in that of the Talents he bestows greater and
lesser gifts (different measures of spiritual gifts, abilities, opportunities, and the like).   The parable of the
Pounds shows that, as we differ in fidelity to the Word,
so shall our eventual rewards of grace be; that of the
Talents shows that, according as we have been favored,
so shall it be required of us.

**For just as a man going abroad called his own
slaves and gave over to them his possession.   And
to one he gave five talents, to one two, and to one
one, to each according to his own ability, and he
went abroad.**   The first sentence is abbreviated (R.
1203) ; ὥσπερ has no οὕτως following.   The sense is quite
plain.   Jesus is still speaking of "the kingdom of the
heavens" (v. 1) and is adding another resemblance.
This is one concerning a man who goes away from
home into another country, ἀποδημῶν, and remains away
for a considerable time.   Unlike the man mentioned in
Luke 19, he is not a nobleman or a ruler.   He is a
wealthy man who has ὑπάρχοντα and these consist chiefly
of money.   This παρέδωκεν, "he duly gives," to his own
slaves.   The implication is not that they are entitled
to such a gift, but that his plans necessitate this procedure.   This man and his going abroad are a picture
of Jesus who is about to leave his disciples to enter the
glory of heaven, to be gone a long while, and then at
last to return.   The aorists in this and in the next
verse state the facts.

He called his own slaves (δοῦλοι) who belonged to him and whose personal interests were identical with his own. He called them in order to inform them of his plans and of the great and honorable way in which he intended to employ them during his stay abroad. To turn all this wealth over to men who were nothing but his slaves implied that he was honoring them with a great trust. This appealed to the noblest motive in their hearts to show themselves worthy of such a trust. It involved a corresponding responsibility on their part and a resolve that they would measure up to this responsibility.

15) But the money is entrusted to them with all due wisdom on the man's part: to one slave five talents, to another two, to a third only one. Why the difference? To each according to his particular personal (ἰδία) ability. Only three slaves are mentioned. For the purpose of the parable that is enough to show diversity. In the parable of the Pounds we have ten slaves and ten pounds, to each slave one pound. The one pound given to each slave is the Word and the Sacraments which belong alike to each of us and can never be divided. In the present parable the number of the slaves is not important. The point stressed here is the diversity, one getting more, another fewer talents. This very diversity helps us to explain the talents. They are our abilities and gifts, of which each of us has his personal and different share. We may think of the spiritual gifts, but we must include the natural (sanctified as they ought to be by grace) faculties of mind and of body, position, influence, money, education, and every earthly advantage and blessing. They come to us from the same Lord as a sacred trust to be employed in his service.

We at once see that the parable of the Pounds was properly spoken first, that of the Talents a few days later. It is most remarkable, however, that when the

Lord pictures his priceless Word and Sacraments he makes these a pound, in Hebrew silver amounting to only about $32 (heavy standard), or half that sum (light standard) ; but when he pictures our personal gifts, he makes these talents, each amounting to nearly $1,940 in silver (heavy), or half that amount (light). Thus the first slave received about $9,700, or half of this; and even the slave that received one talent had a tidy sum. This parabolic use of the pound or *mina* and of the talent or hundredweight appears to be a bit of sacred irony. That is the way in which men might evaluate the Word and their personal gifts. Yet, however valuable our gifts may seem to us, they aid the Lord's work in only a very subordinate way.

The inequality: five, three, one, shows the height of wisdom and of love. We are not alike even by nature. Both in the world and in the church there is endless variety. In both life is complex and calls for a variety of service and of corresponding gifts. Read Paul's presentation of this in I Cor. 12:12, etc. So the Lord apportions the gifts. He alone has the wisdom, the complete view, and the corresponding power. Each has his place to fill, his ability (δύναμις) for that place, and receives his talent or his talents accordingly. What a calamity it is when a man who has ability to handle only one talent is burdened with five and makes a wreck of matters! Why give only one talent to him who can well handle two? Men do this to the detriment of their business, but the Lord does not. After all his business funds have been duly entrusted to his own slaves, this man goes abroad.

16) **Proceeding immediately, he that received five talents worked with them and made another five talents. Likewise he** (that received) **the two** (worked) **with them and acquired another two. But he that received the one, having gone, dug up the earth and hid away the silver of his lord.** Here

is a picture of Christ's followers as they deal with his gifts to the present day. Some are faithful, and the results are according; some unfaithful, with the result corresponding. Already the fact that the first slave went immediately is a sign of his faithfulness. He does not put his work off and think that there is no need for hurry. The two aorists "he worked and made another five talents" are constative and sum up all that he did. He succeeded in doubling the amount, he made a hundred per cent profit.

17) The second slave did the same thing, ὡσαύτως. The Greek is able to abbreviate, but the English cannot do so. He, too, "acquired" or gained a hundred per cent. In regard to the percentage of the gain these two are alike, the one is as faithful as the other. The gains represent what the Lord requires of us, namely that we shall return unto the Lord according to what we have received. The talents gained are the graces and the gifts found in others whom we win for the church and whom we help forward in their Christian life. There is a constant extension and multiplication of gifts in the church, talent producing talent. But the point of the parable is the faithfulness of the slaves. One has a higher office in the church, wider opportunities for service, and a greater measure of knowledge, etc. Equal faithfulness will thus produce unequal results; five or only two talents. The question of degrees of faithfulness is not treated in this parable; it belongs to that of the Pounds. Of course, we may think of it here, too. A man who has received five talents may waste time, be careless, and end with only one or two additional talents. But the Lord omitted this variation; he limits himself to one point only.

18) Over against the faithful slaves Jesus places one who is unfaithful; only one, like the one mentioned in 22:11, and in 19:20, intending that each of us shall ask, "Lord, is it I?" To illustrate unfaithfulness Jesus

uses the slave who had received only one talent. This, of course, is not to teach that only those who have the fewest gifts prove unfaithful. Jesus takes the one whose responsibilities were the lightest; he had no more than he could easily handle. If he had been burdened with more talents he would have had an excuse; but as it is he has none. Nor could he claim that, if he had received five talents, he would have proved faithful; his unfaithfulness would have been only greater. Since only three slaves are used in the parable, each stands for a complete type that includes lesser variations. So this slave who was burdened with only one talent since his ability was no greater, had no more required of him than was required of any of the others, no more than he could and should easily have done.

In Oriental fashion (13:44) this slave dug a secret hole in the earth and "hid away the silver of his lord." Since it was ἀργύριον, we think of silver and not of gold talents. The wrong feature of his action is indicated by the genitive: this is how he treated the gift "of his lord." But Jesus sketches the lightest type of guilt; the money was only buried and left to lie idle and unproductive, whereas it is the very nature of our gifts that they should be productive. The man might have squandered the money, and that would have been worse. By revealing the grave guilt of the less glaring forms of unfaithfulness the still graver guilt of all other forms is established. This slave regarded the gift as something he did not desire; it aroused no response in his heart. Since he had it he kept it, indeed, but only because he could not avoid this. He kept it in a manner which revealed his real attitude toward the gift and the Giver: he buried it. He thus was like one who had no gift at all; but it was he himself who made himself thus. In this he is a picture of all those in the church who for any reason refuse to use the gifts of Christ in his service. By such non-use the gifts are

buried, and those who have them put themselves into
the same state with those who are without them. Moreover, this slave's complete unfaithfulness includes all
degrees of partial unfaithfulness. Does anyone among
us want to be like this slave? To do in part what he
did seconds his act at least to that extent.

19) **Now after a long time  the lord of those
slaves comes and settles accounts with them. And
he that received the five talents, having come forth,
brought forth another five talents, saying, Lord, five
talents thou didst give me; see, another five talents I
acquired! His lord said to him:  Well! slave good
and faithful! Over few things wast thou faithful,
over many will I station thee. Enter into the joy
of thy lord!  Now he also having come forth who
(received) the two talents, said, Lord, two talents
thou didst give me; see, another two talents I
acquired! His lord said to him:  Well! slave good
and faithful! Over few things wast thou faithful,
over many will I station thee. Enter into the joy of
thy lord!**

The great moment has come, hence the vivid touch
in the present tenses "comes and settles account."
"After a long time" seems almost like a hint to the
Twelve that the Parousia would not come as soon as
they might expect. Yet the parable deals only with the
lives of the men it presents, and the phrase is after all
indefinite. But this long time surely implies two
things: the delay thoroughly tests out the faithful, and
at the same time it gives the unfaithful a long period
to repent and to amend. Many start well but do not
hold out; some begin ill but come to better thoughts.
Deissmann, *Light from the Ancient East*, 118, etc.,
reports that Moulton found συναίρω λόγον in two papyri
in the sense, "I make a reckoning, I compare accounts."
The point is this reckoning at the end. It comes eventually. It is the judgment that accompanies the Parousia.

20) The French painter Burnand has the two
faithful servants standing side by side when reporting
to their lord. We see how Jesus pictures them as being
exactly alike save for the difference in the number of
the talents. See how they show "boldness in the day
of judgment," as does Paul: "What is our hope, or joy,
or crown of rejoicing? Are not even ye in the presence
of our Lord Jesus Christ at his coming?" I Thess.
2:19. But behind all such joy in faithful accomplishment for Christ there appears the sure confidence of
faith in Christ's accomplishment for us; this also motivates our faithfulness. First, the clear and significant
and we may add grateful acknowledgment: "Lord,
five talents thou didst give me." The credit is his;
without this gift the slave could have accomplished
nothing. In the Greek, "See, another five talents I
acquired," we have no ἐγώ but only the inflection of the
verb. This is not a boast of what *I, I* have done. The
stress is on the great amount acquired, "See, five talents!" as though it were spoken in surprise. Jesus
purposely varies his parables. In Luke 19:16, 18 it is:
"Thy pound produced ten (five) pounds," προσειργάσατο
and ἐποίησε, Word and Sacrament produce. But here
he twice has ἐκέρδησα, both effective aorists (R. 835), "I
acquired" or gained. Our gifts are ours in a different
sense than the Word is, and Jesus gladly accords us the
feeling that our efforts have not been in vain, I Cor.
15:58.

21) The slave is rewarded beyond all deserts.
Being his master's slave, he and all his labor and skill
belonged to that master, thus also all the profits the
slave might acquire. But this master is to be a picture of Christ with all his heavenly generosity. The
single adverb, "Well!" i. e., "it is well," is complete in
itself, a judgment or a verdict. We might translate,
"Fine!" or, "Excellent!" The same is true in regard
to δοῦλε ἀγαθὲ καὶ πιστέ, which is an exclamation that is

complete in itself. The adverb εὖ is a verdict on the work, the vocative a verdict on the worker, "Slave excellent and reliable!" and thus furnishing his master great satisfaction. No higher commendation can come to any believer from the lips of Jesus. This significant praise outranks all the flattery and the honor the world may bestow. Jesus holds up this commendation to us in advance in order that we may ever keep it before our eyes and allow it to make us always faithful.

This slave's master might have stopped with this praise, many masters would; or he might have added something tangible, a small sum taken from the profit gained by the five talents. Not so this master who is to be a picture of Jesus: "Over few things wast thou faithful, over many will I station thee." So all these talents are only "few things," just enough to try us out to see what kind of slaves we are. What, then, will the "many things" be? They are here veiled by their multitude and their richness, partly because the imagery of the parable is so restricted, and partly also because our poor earthly minds cannot reach up to these coming heavenly glories. But here all the Lord's goodness and his grace appear: his one thought is our elevation and our joy. He places us first over few things, then over many things, and both of these phrases are placed forward for the sake of emphasis. Note ἐπί in the sense of "over" (R. 604). The future, "I will station thee," is volitive; it voices the power and the authority of this master. Think of what these words that are addressed to us by Christ imply!

If we have reached the limit of the imagery in the preceding word, we are now taken beyond that limit: "Enter into the joy of thy lord!" It is not strange that in several parables the imagery is too weak to present the full reality that Jesus wishes to convey. So here "the joy of thy lord" is the reality itself, the heavenly joy of Christ himself. "It is but little we can receive here, some drops of joy that enter into us; but there we shall enter into joy as vessels put into a sea of happiness." Leighton. Gerhard had the same thought: *Homo intrat in illud incomprehensibile gaudium.*

22) The report of the second servant is exactly like that of the first. He has been equally faithful with his two talents.

23) He hears exactly the same commendation and receives the very same reward of grace. Thus not the measure of the gifts we have in this life decides our station above but the measure of our faithfulness in using whatever gifts we have. Some who have had but few gifts but were altogether faithful in the use of those few will outshine others who were favored with many gifts, but were not fully faithful in administering the many gifts.

24) **Now he also having come forth that received the one talent said: Lord, I knew thee, that thou art a hard man, reaping where thou didst not sow and gathering from where thou didst not scatter; and afraid, having gone, I hid thy talent in the earth. See, thou hast thine own!** Yes, he also came. He was compelled to come. Every unfaithful servant will be compelled to come. The καί has a peculiar shading of thought: "Now he *also*," etc.; it adds him to the rest with whom he ought to belong but with whom he in reality does not belong. In a parable the characters are made to act and to speak frankly. We see exactly who and what they are. This will be especially true at the time of the judgment when every secret motive will be bared. So this slave says brazenly, "Lord, I knew," etc. The whole parable flatly contradicts this slave's alleged knowledge of his lord. This fellow imagines his great and generous lord to be as envious and as self-seeking as he himself is. He calls his lord "a hard man," σκληρός, one who is like a

dried stick that will no longer bend, he is hard in a moral sense, is set absolutely on obtaining his own advantage. As proof of the hardness he mentions the fact that this lord is "reaping where thou didst not sow, and gathering from where thou didst not scatter." The two present participles express usual and thus characteristic actions. The sense is: "Thou makest thy slaves sow in order that thou mayest get a fine harvest through their labor; and thou makest thy slaves thresh in order that thou mayest fill thy barns with the grain they have cleaned." "To scatter" refers not to sowing grain but to letting the wind scatter the chaff after the grain is threshed.

What this slave says is true in a manner: we do all the work for the Lord. Did not the first two slaves bring their entire gain to the master? The trouble is that half a truth may be the very worst kind of a lie; so it is here. We are the slaves of Jesus Christ, and that may sound as though he profited by our labor; but think what it cost him to elevate us to the position of being his slaves: the price of his own blood! If we labored for him a million years we could never repay him. Secondly, all our gifts are his, freely, generously bestowed upon us; and these were given us in order that with joy we may serve and honor our rightful Master — or shall we serve the tyrant Satan? Finally, this blind slave saw only the gain that was turned over to the lord; he never saw what that lord had in mind concerning these talents and his beloved slaves. The thing is, indeed, one-sided, but not in the Lord's favor; it is all in our favor. The perfect participle εἰληφώς is used in the description of this base slave whereas the simple aorist λαβών is used in the case of the faithful servant mentioned in v. 20. This perfect participle preserves this idea of this tense (R. 909). Whereas λαβών simply notes the reception of the talents, εἰληφώς adds the thought that this base slave had had his talent during this long time. Ὅθεν is only a compact way of saying ἐκεῖθεν ὅπου or οὗ, R. 718, 548.

25) This slave now claims that he was impelled by dread of such an evil master (φοβηθείς) when he went and buried the talent in a secret safe place until he could return it intact on the day of reckoning. He feared that he might lose his talent or a part of it if he tried to trade with it. Alas, he points his fears in the wrong direction. He is not afraid to call his good master hard names and to bring back the talent without having put forth the least effort to make it produce at least something. No; he did not fear to insult his kind and generous master. "See, thou hast thine own!" ἴδε is probably just an interjection as it is in v. 20 and in v. 22. Hitherto Matthew has used the middle ἰδού (1:23, etc.) with the accent of an interjection.

Here at last, perhaps unconsciously, this slave speaks a true word, *"thine* own" — the talent had never been *his* own in any true sense of the word. It is asked how any unfaithful slave of Christ can return to him the gift he has received. That, however, is not the point of the picture. The point is what such a man thinks. And remember, he is one of the better class who has not spent and squandered his talent in riotous living as the prodigal son did, he had simply done nothing, and thus expected to escape blame. He was not guilty of the world's abuse of God's gifts; he remains in the outward church but remains idle as a drone. He has his faculties, his life, his health, his abilities and his influence, but that is all. No fruit gained by these was returned to the Lord. Faith without works is dead. And thus shall be his judgment.

26) **But his lord answering, said to him: Wicked slave and slothful, thou knewest that I reap where I did not sow and garner whence I did not scatter! Therefore it was necessary for thee to**

**deposit my silver with the bankers, and, having
come, I would have received back my own with interest.** The very way in which he is addressed is
a judgment and a verdict upon this slave. The chief
emphasis is on πονηρέ which even precedes the noun.
"Wicked," namely in the active, vicious sense, is this
slave. And that "wicked" attitude prompted his action
in seeing to it that this lord should obtain no gain;
ὀκνηρός is timid, hesitant, but in this context it has the
evil turn "slothful."

Instead of defending himself against this treacher-
ous slave's slanders his master turns the tables on him
and convicts him out of his own mouth and shows him
that he is basely lying and is pronouncing his own condemnation. In 22:12 the man is dumb and by his inability to furnish a real answer damns himself. The
parables use both: dumbness and self-condemnatory
answers. In either way the guilty reveal their own
guilt, and sentence is pronounced accordingly. So this
slave was afraid of losing the talent and knew what a
harsh man his master was? These are the premises.
But see the lying conclusion: he buries the talent! That
is exactly what does *not* follow from those premises.
Wickedness always argues like a fool when it dares to
open its mouth. The open falseness here displays the
slave's whole inner character and attitude. It completely blighted his soul.

27) With οὖν his master draws the correct conclusion from this liar's premises. And the master states
what is the very least that truly follows from the premises. More activity on the slave's part might have followed if he really thought his master hard and grasping
and was afraid of losing the talent; but at least this
should have followed: the slave should have felt compelled to deposit the silver talent with the bankers and
should have allowed it to earn a bit of interest for the
master. This would have involved no risk whatever

but even less labor than digging and hiding it in a
secret place. But (and this is the main point) the
talent given this slave in order to produce something
for his master would have produced it, a small sum at
least. The A. V. has "usury." The older English
version employed the word in the good sense like our
"interest." The least we can do with Christ's gifts is to
let others, who do business for the Lord on an extensive
scale such as bankers do, use us and our small gifts in the
Lord's work. Our gifts will then earn at least something.

The imperfect ἔδει is a simple statement regarding
the past. It may speak only of the past as it does here,
but it may also reach into the present, R. 919.   "Verbs
of propriety, possibility, obligation, or necessity are
also used in the imperfect when the obligation, etc.,
has not been lived up to, has not been met. The Greeks
(and the Latins) start from the past and state the real
possibility or obligation, and the reader, by comparing
that with facts, notes that the obligation was not met.
The English and the Germans start from the present
and find trouble with this past statement of a present
duty (an unfulfilled duty)." R. 886.   We are compelled
to think a little in the Greek idiom — that is all.   Thus
the clause with ἔδει is not the protasis of a conditional
sentence but an independent statement; and ἐκομισάμην ἄν
is an apodosis of past unreality without a protasis
except by implication, "if thou wouldst have done that,
I would have received," etc.

28) With this as the truth of the matter the
slave's sentence is pronounced. **Take away, therefore, the talent from him and give it to him having
the ten talents.   For to him that has shall be given,
and he shall be made to superabound; but from him
that has not, even what he has shall be taken away
from him.   And the useless slave proceed to throw
out into the outer darkness; there shall be the weeping and the gnashing of the teeth.**   The slave had

never made the talent his own in any true sense of the word. We feel the justice of his now being deprived of its nominal possession. But the command to give this talent to the man who already has ten comes as a surprise. Yet which one of the three slaves was best able to take on an additional burden? Evidently, the first. Also this fact is made plain: none of the Lord's gifts shall be lost. He takes care of them, for they are valuable to him both here below and in the higher world. He who neglects his gifts only enriches others and doubly defeats himself.

29) But the Lord himself explains (γάρ). The divine law of the kingdom is that he who has (by using his gifts aright and thus getting more and more) shall be given, namely by his Lord's hand of grace; and the effect shall be that this man shall be made to superabound (passive, by his Lord's grace). And exactly the reverse is true according to this divine law: from him that has not (by his wicked refusal to employ the gifts bestowed upon him), from him shall be taken away even what he hath (namely, in an outward and a merely nominal way).

While this is the law of the kingdom it appears also in the ordinary affairs of men. The wealthy miser who keeps his money locked up is really a poor man. The mentally gifted man who neglects his gifts is like a man that does not have such gifts. And thus a nominal Christian who knows the gospel and confesses it but never appropriates it inwardly and makes it a part of his life is like a non-Christian. The very opportunity which one neglects to his loss is given to another for his gain; the crown which one lets go bedecks another's brow. Here in time we may recover a loss, it will be too late to escape the operation of this law when the long day of grace ends.

30) The negative part of the verdict is followed by the positive. Note how the object is placed forward

for the sake of emphasis, "the useless (or unprofitable) slave," and the imperative is the descriptive present, "proceed to throw out," etc. Here we learn that none who are ἀχρεῖος, useless to the Lord, can remain in his kingdom. That is why he takes us into his trust, fits us out with great gifts, and tries us out to see whether we really have faith in him and love for him. To whom is this command addressed? The Analogy of Scripture prevents us from answering, "To the other two slaves"; for the Lord's assistants in the final judgment are the angels. Moreover, the imagery of the parable is here dropped for the sake of the reality, exactly as was done in 22:13; and in 24:50. On the reason for this as well as on the outer darkness, etc., see 8:32.

31) Jesus sketched the entire course of the world until the end (24:4-14) ; he followed this with a sketch of the destruction of Jerusalem and of the Jewish nation (24:15-28) ; and to this he added the account of his actual Parousia (24:29-31). Then came the admonitory sections that were marked especially by three parables (24:32-25:30). Jesus needed yet to add the description of the final judgment itself (25:31-46). Beyond question this entire series forms one of the grandest and the most important of Jesus' discourses.

**When, however, the Son of man shall come in his glory, and all the angels with him, then shall he sit on his throne of glory; and there shall be brought before him all the nations, and he shall divide them from each other just as a shepherd divides the sheep from the goats; and he shall stand the sheep on his right, but the goats on the left.** On "the Son of man" see 8:20. Of his coming in the Parousia for the judgment Jesus has already spoken most definitely in 24:30, 31, where also "his glory" is mentioned and the activity of his angels. It ought to be clear that

Jesus is connecting this scene with 24:30, 31, and is now bringing the whole subject to completion.

"The Son of man" who is more than man, the incarnate Second Person of the Godhead, shall come as such; but not in his humiliation as he once came for our redemption but "in his glory," in the sum of the divine attributes (δόξα), in their unrestricted exercise, use, and display also by his human nature. In 24:31 "his angels" are introduced only incidentally, and we hear of them only as they receive his order. Now we learn that "*all* the angels" shall be "with him," accompanying him (μετά) at his coming. What a grandiose coming that will be! Here we see who this "Son of man" really is.

32) The formalities of a court are fully observed. After the Judge, decked with all his authority, arrives he "shall sit on his glory throne," αὐτοῦ making the throne definite, the absence of the articles emphasizing both "throne" and "glory," but almost as though the two were a compound, "glory-throne." The word "throne" conveys the thought that this is a King come to judgment (18:23), and like every other feature in this prophecy reveals the infinite greatness of the scene. In the passive "there shall be brought before him" the angels are undoubtedly the agents as is clear already from 24:31. Always the angels are the heavenly ministrants of the Judge.

Strange ideas have been associated with πάντα τὰ ἔθνη and with the separation of "all the nations" into two groups, sheep on the right hand, goats on the left hand. It is stated (without warrant, however) that τὰ ἔθνη always refers to Gentiles, pagan people, and that Jesus here makes two groups of these, and besides these there is a third group, his elect. A part of the Gentiles, non-Christians, unwittingly (v. 37) showed kindness to the elect or Christ's brethren and are thus sent into heaven;

while the other non-Christians who offered no such
kindness are sent into hell.  This would, indeed, be a
new way of salvation, and one that would contradict
everything else that is said in the Bible in regard to it.

Πάντα τὰ ἔθνη denotes universality as does πᾶν ἔθνος
ἀνθρώπων in Acts 17:26.  Jesus chose this expression in
order to match 24:14, εἰς μαρτύριον πᾶσι τοῖς ἔθνησιν ("to all
nations").  The Parousia will not come until the gospel has been proclaimed as a testimony to all nations;
see πάντα τὰ ἔθνη in 28:19.  The whole human race will
be assembled for the final judgment.  Through the
agency of the angels the whole human race will be
divided into two groups, one being placed on the right
and the other on the left of the heavenly Judge.  This
division and this placing are already a judgment and a
verdict.  What follows only justifies this act.  No
human court can thus determine pardon or guilt in
advance.  During all these centuries sheep and goats
(wheat and tares) have been intermingled, and no man
could really separate them; but now at last the separation is made and shall stand forever.

The Greek idiom uses the neuter plural to indicate
the right and the left hand (omitting "hand").  It
thinks of these two places as being composed of parts,
while to us each is a unit.  On the idiom ἐκ, "on the
right (left)" see 20:21.  The ὥσπερ clause is only a
comparison, "just as a shepherd," etc.  In Palestine
the sheep and the goats are often pastured together and
then divided into separate folds at night.

33)  Jesus places more into "sheep" and "goats"
for he uses these terms figuratively as designations of
the elect and the non-elect (24:31; 22:14).  We note
this regarding the sheep in John 10:2, etc.; especially
in v. 14-16; also in John 21:15, etc.  It is thus by contrast easy to determine who is referred to by the goats,
and we may well refer to Ezek. 34:7-24, in particular
v. 18, 19.  The sheep are here those who do the works

of faith which Jesus will recognize as having been done
unto him; the goats are those who fail to produce the
works of faith, whose works, whatever they are, Jesus
cannot recognize as having been done unto him.   Needless difficulties are encountered by playing one set of
passages such as John 3:18; 5:24, which exempt the
believers from judgment, against another set of passages such as John 5:29; Rom. 14:10; I Cor. 3:13;
II Cor. 5:10, which declare that the believers, too, shall
be judged.   Jesus makes the whole matter plain: not a
single sin of the believers is mentioned in the judgment, examined, probed, and judged, only the good
works of believers are named; so they are, indeed, not
brought into judgment, and yet they are judged.   All
the sins of the unbelievers are brought forward, and on
the basis of these sins they are damned forever.

34) **Then shall the King say to those on his**
**right:   Hither, you that have been blessed by my**
**Father, inherit the kingdom that has been made**
**ready for you from the world's foundation.**   What
the term "throne" in v. 32 led us to expect is clearly
stated by "the King" in the present verse.   Here is
judgment, indeed, but the royal judgment of our heavenly King, which is, on the one hand, a dispensing of
royal grace and favor, and on the other hand, a dispensing of justice.   The adverb δεῦτε which is used with
plurals must be combined with the imperative κληρονομήσατε and has no independent meaning.   The comment
that, as the King turns toward those on his right, they
shrink back from him and must be encouraged to come
forward again, is based on a misconception of the adverb.   The address, "you that have been blessed by my
Father," is highly significant.   We regard the genitive
τοῦ πατρός μου as stating the agent who blessed them;
their blessed state is due, not to themselves, but to the
Father.   The King names the ultimate source of their
blessing, "my Father,". and the possessive "my" im-

plies that the Father has blessed them through the Son. We know, too, that the Father used also the Holy Spirit. All the *opera ad extra* involve the Three Persons of the Godhead.

The substantivized perfect participle οἱ εὐλογημένοι has its usual meaning, an act of blessing that occurred in the past, whose effects continue to the present. When God blesses he does more than to pronounce words of blessing and praise, as we poor creatures do when we bless him; he bestows his grace with all its gifts upon us and thus makes us persons that were and still are blessed. This perfect participle refers to all that God's grace wrought upon these people during their earthly lives. They died in this grace, and thus after they have been raised from the dead (or suddenly transformed), they are "those that have been blessed."

The aorist imperative κληρονομήσατε bids them forthwith to enter upon their inheritance. They have thus far been, as it were, minor heirs, the inheritance was held for them, but they did not assume its possession and its enjoyment. And their inheritance is "the kingdom." They have thus far been crown princes, they are now to be actual, reigning kings. "The kingdom" is evidently what we call the kingdom of glory, namely heaven and its rule of glory and blessedness as distinguished from the kingdom of grace here on earth, by which we are first made heirs through grace. This word is sometimes thought to mean that the blessed are to be subjects of Christ, the King, in heaven. But none of us shall be subjects in heaven, all of us shall be actual, reigning kings, reigning conjointly with Christ in heaven. Heaven will be a kingdom that is composed entirely of kings, a kingdom raised to the n*th* degree. And thus Christ shall be the King of kings (us) and the Lord of lords (us). Compare our heavenly rule and kingship, Luke 19:17, 19; and passages like Rev. 20:4; Rev. 3:21; Paul awaiting his crown, II Tim. 4:8 (only kings have crowns) ; James 1:12.

The King adds the statement that this kingdom "has been made ready for you from the world's foundation." In his eternal and infallible foreknowledge God beheld all of us before we were born, and beheld us as all that his grace would succeed in making of us. Far, far in advance he prepared the kingdom in which we should rule as the coheirs of Christ (Rom. 8:17). The perfect participle "has been prepared" has the same force as the preceding perfect participle. So this heavenly rule and kingdom is already awaiting us; it is not something that is yet to be prepared. Sometimes, as here, we have *"from* the world's foundation," whereas in Eph. 1:4 we have *"before* the world's foundation." This is only a formal difference. All God's saving plans go back into the timelessness of eternity.

35) The King's judgment and his astounding award are now fully established as being just. **For I did hunger, and you did give me to eat; I did thirst, and you did give me drink; a stranger I was, and you did take me in; naked, and you clothed me; I was sick, and you did look in upon me; in prison was I, and you did come to me.** The dispute as to whether γάρ is illative or merely elucidative is really unnecessary. Some of the fathers were afraid that, if γάρ offered the actual ground for the award, works would be meritorious as the Catholics claim. This γάρ is illative, it states the grounds on which the judgment and the award rest, and these grounds are beyond question our good works. Moreover, this is the universal teaching of Scripture, Rom. 2:6, etc.; II Cor. 5:10; Matt. 16:27. But these works are decisive in the final judgment, not because of an inherent meritorious quality, but because of their evidential quality. As in any proper court of law the evidence and the evidence alone decides in harmony with the law, so in this most

supreme court at the end of the world this same procedure is followed.

This King's judgment is one that is rendered in public, before the whole universe of angels and of men. This is different from the secret judgment that is pronounced upon each man at the moment of death. Hence in the public judgment faith cannot be used as a criterion of judgment, for this the King alone is able to see directly and without fail. The evidence of faith is used, namely the works which faith alone is able to produce. These all angels and all men are able to see when they are brought to perfect view in the light of the last day, when every sham and every deception fall away forever. Sometimes these works are called works of love, and their love is stressed without regard to faith, but that view perverts and Romanizes. They are, indeed, works of love but of that love which is the product only of faith. So love, properly understood, brings us back to the ultimate source of these works which is faith.

The significant point in the six works here named is that all six refer to the King himself: "I did hunger," "I did thirst," etc. Each work is thus made personal as having been done to and for the King. That makes plain most clearly the inner motive that prompted these works, love for this King, the love that springs from faith in this King. Having received his saving grace by faith, our gratitude responds by works that are intended for him.

The next significant point is the fact that all the works mentioned are of the humblest and the lowliest kind. Not one grand work is listed; this is in glaring contrast with the claims made in 7:22. All these are works which even the smallest faith can easily produce. For even the smallest faith saves. In connection with giving drink note Mark 9:41. In συνηγάγετε the σύν con-

veys the idea of taking the stranger into the family and
there giving him lodging.

36) The verb περιβάλλειν is used to designate the
putting on of any kind of clothing, and γυμνός refers to
insufficient covering, it does not necessarily mean absolute nakedness. The verb ἐπισκέπτομαι, "to look upon,"
has the sense of "to visit with help." The last work,
going to those in prison, helps to cast a light on all
these works. They recall what Jesus said about the
persecutions his believers would have to suffer. Any
comfort and any help, ever so slight, offered to believers
in these circumstances would really be a confession of
Christ and thus in the highest sense a work of faith.
What is commonly called "charity," namely works done
from humanitarian impulses, are thus ruled out. The
works of faith are far more than such charity, they are
confessional.

37-39) **Then the righteous shall answer him,
saying: Lord, when did we see thee hungering and
did feed thee** (aorist from τρέφειν)**? or thirsting and
did give thee drink? And when did we see thee a
stranger and did take thee in? or naked and did
clothe thee? And when did we see thee sick and
in prison and did come to thee?** Here we are told
who these people are: οἱ δίκαιοι, "the righteous." This
adjective and all its cognate terms are always used in a
forensic sense as a study of C.-K. will show in a most
convincing manner. The righteous are those who have
God's verdict in their favor. The great Judge pronounces them free from guilt and righteous; and as a
righteous Judge he must do so, namely on the strength
of the righteousness of Christ which all the righteous
have as their own by faith. The entire doctrine of
justification by faith through the atoning merits of
Christ is contained in οἱ δίκαιοι. We now see that the
six works (some have counted seven) are merely three
double works, the sacred number three, which refers

to Christ, being emphasized by each work being doubled by means of another that is quite similar to it.

The astonished questions of the righteous are the best evidence as to how far their thoughts are from any idea of merit on their part. They have, indeed, learned from the gospel to serve Christ, their King, in even the lowliest of his brethren. But when they now note infinite glory as their inheritance in the heavenly Kingdom, the award of this inheritance on the ground of such little works seems impossible to them. They kept no record of their works, they trusted solely in grace and forgot all their works. This is the truth that Christ brings out by means of these questions. It is further evidence to show how just and righteous the award he makes is.

40) **And the King, answering, shall say to them: Amen, I say to you** (on this formula see 5:18), **In so far as you did it to one of these the least of my brethren, to me you did it.** This declaration is worthy of the seal of verity and of authority which the King adds to it. These least of works, doubly least because they are often done to the least of Christ's brethren, the humblest of his followers who had nothing whatever to distinguish them save that they were believers in Christ, are great in the King's eyes. Since they were done for his sake, he rightly regards them as having been done to him. Here we see what the verbs of the first person in v. 35, 36, "I did hunger," etc., really mean. And not only does this King, seated on his glorious judgment throne, call these humblest believers "my brethren," he practically identifies himself with these brethren. So close is the union between true believers and Christ, but its glorious nature will not appear until the King declares this his identification with his brethren before the whole universe.

The least of the brethren (the addition of the adjective by means of a separate article making "least" emphatic, R. 776) are mentioned merely because kindness done to them would not be highly rated among men. Of course, all the good done to the greatest of his brethren such as the apostles, the great confessors, and the martyrs, the King will also regard as having been done unto him. But if he had mentioned these great brethren, we might have thought their greatness made our deeds precious. By naming the least of the brethren the King really includes all brethren. Usually the greatest is regarded as including the less, but here we have a clear case where the very least include even the very greatest.

The view that these least of the brethren cannot be a part of "the righteous" is untenable. How about the brethren that are not the least; are such brethren not included? Are they, too, not addressed by Jesus? This view in regard to the least is akin to the other that was discussed above by Jesus, namely that all these righteous are pagans who unwittingly treated these least of the brethren with kindness and for that kindness are now to inherit the kingdom. The righteous are all the believers, and as such they are all the brethren of Christ, the King, from the least to the greatest (5:19; 11:11; 18:4) ; and what the King says is that what they have done to each other for his sake he regards as having been done unto him; ἐφ' ὅσον is scarcely causal (R. 963) but denotes degree, "in so far."

**41) Then shall he say to those on the left: Be going from me, such as have been cursed, into the fire, the eternal, the one that has been made ready for the devil and his angels!** Verses 41-45 are the direct opposite of v. 34-40. Is it accidental that αὐτοῦ is twice added in v. 32:33: "on his right"; but is omitted in both v. 32 and v. 41: "on the left"? We now see

who those on the left are: κατηραμένοι (from καταράομαι),
"having become the subjects of a curse," R. 1096. Note
that this is a perfect participle like εὐλογημένοι in v. 34,
but does not have the article. We have, "*the ones* that
have been blessed," but only, "*such as* have been
cursed." The righteous and elect are one body that
has been fixed in the counsel of God from all eternity;
the damned are only a conglomerate mass made up of
all types and kinds. The perfect participle is passive,
these people have incurred God's curse, B.-P. 652. In
v. 34 the imperative is the strong aorist but here it is
the descriptive present, "be going," as though it were
marking the brief delay granted them until the final
words that justify this terrible verdict have been
spoken.

The best commentary regarding "the fire" is found
in the previous references, 3:10, 12; 5:22; 7:19; 13:40,
42, 50; 18:8, 9. Some ask about the nature of this fire.
One answer is that it is here described as one that has
long ago been prepared for the devil and his angels. It
is a fire that tortures both spirits and men that have
bodies. We need to know nothing more than its terrible nature. Note that each modifier of "the fire" is
added by a separate article: "the fire, the eternal, the
one made ready," etc. These articles make each modifier a kind of apposition and thus form a climax, R. 776.
The effect of this should be carefully noted when we
think about this fire. "The fire" is terrible, indeed,
but "the eternal one" increases its terribleness, and
"the one made ready for the devil," etc., raises its terrible nature to the ultimate degree.

Regarding αἰώνιος as meaning "eternal" little needs
to be said. Those who would reduce the fire of hell to
a shorter or a longer period of time must then similarly
reduce the joys of heaven. But αἰώνιος was spoken by
the King after time has already ceased, and after all
angels and men have entered on their final fixed and

unchanged fate and, therefore, cannot be understood in this limited sense. And if this Greek adjective does not mean "eternal," which Greek adjective does have that meaning? Or did the Greek world, including the Jewish (Jesus spoke Aramaic), world have no words for eternity or eternal?

The remarkable thing is that hell fire was originally prepared for the devil and his angels as the fit punishment for their irremediable apostasy from God; and not for men. It is a fair deduction that men are consigned to this devil's fire for the simple reason that they have turned from God to the devil and have become incurably apostate even as he is. The devil and his angels whose promptings these men followed on earth will be their constant companions in the eternal fire. Bengel brings out the following parallelism:

> *Hic: venite:*
> *benedicti patris mei:*
> *hereditate regnum:*
> *paratum vobis:*
> *a fundamenti mundi.*

> *Illic: abite a me:*
> *maledicti:*
> *in ignem:*
> *paratum diabolo, etc.*
> *aeternum.*

42, 43) The proof for the absolute justice and righteousness of this damning verdict is couched in exactly the same words that were used to establish the blessed verdict (v. 35, 36), so that we need not translate v. 42, 43, but add only the negatives: "did *not* give me to eat — did *not* give me drink — did *not* take me in"; etc. All these *ού*, piled up one on the other, produce a terrible indictment, indeed. Not in one instance did these accursed people do even the slightest little deed for Christ, the King. Not in a single case was there a motive that the King could recognize as an intention really to trust and to accept him.

The sins charged against them are negative, they are omissions not commissions. And this is another case where the lesser and the least include everything up to the greatest. The comment that sins of omission are here named because we are to be warned especially against these sins, is unacceptable. Jesus is speaking as a prophet and is prophetically revealing how the verdict pronounced on the damned will be established as a righteous verdict in the sight of the whole universe. It will be done by means of these simple but unanswerable negatives. Each one of them and all of them definitely, positively, unalterably thrust Christ, the King, away. Why mention positive sins, crimes, outrages, horrors? This *no — no — no* with which Jesus was met tells the tale so that we really understand the King's verdict. In the last analysis it is not sins as such that damn, whether they be great or small, many or few, commissions or omissions. For all sins can be pardoned and wiped out forever by grace. In the final analysis it is unbelief that damns, the unbelief that ever says "no" to grace, continues to say this "no" even in hell (Luke 16:30), and thus retains also the guilt and the damnation of all its other sins. This "no" was first spoken by Satan in Eden, Gen. 3:4, and by means of his man-murdering lies he instills it into all his children, John 8:44.

44) **Then shall answer also they saying: Lord, when did we see thee hungering, or thirsting, or a stranger, or naked, or sick, or in prison, and did not minister unto thee?** This question only continues the "no" of these people, for its sense is, "We never saw thee in a condition in which we might have been able to minister unto thee." The contrast with the reply of the righteous in v. 37-39 is also significant.

The righteous repeat the words of Jesus in full, the accursed abbreviate them. It has been said that this is only a formal difference in order not to tire the reader by a complete repetition. But why, then, not abbreviation in v. 37-39, and why the complete repetition, even for the third time, by the King himself in v. 42, 43? Even in the final judgment the accursed care so little for the King's words that they abbreviate them. To be sure, in the King's glorious presence they dare not falsify them. All they can do is to raise their false denial. But this very final "no" seals their everlasting doom. They, too, address the King as Κύριε. What else would they dare to call him in the majesty of his glory?

45) **Then shall he answer them, saying: Amen, I say to you, in so far as you did it not to one of these the least, neither to me did you do it.** Here we have another repetition, but one that has two fatal negatives and omits "my brethren." This omission is certainly not intended to reduce their guilt. The significance of the omission lies in the fact that the accursed are addressed. The righteous aided each other for Christ's sake, as brethren of Christ; the damned denied both Christ and his brethren and acknowledged neither. While they were in this life here on earth they saw in the righteous only a set of people whom they despised, "these least," whom they either ignored or antagonized.

The King takes the damned at their own word. They declare that they never saw Jesus hungry, etc. They challenge Jesus to point out to them one time when they saw him thus and did not minister unto him. They imply that, if they had seen him under such circumstances, they would have ministered unto him. That claim falls to pieces before the facts. The gospel was heralded over the entire inhabited world, it was a testimony to all the nations, 24:14. The accursed met preachers and teachers of the gospel and came into

contact with the believers in this gospel. They regarded them as fools. They never saw Christ, the
eternal King himself, in them; they did not realize
that their treatment of all these believers and confessors was really the treatment they were according the
eternal King himself. This was not ordinary ignorance but the obdurate and vincible blindness of unbelief. Even now they cling to their blind unbelief with
damnable persistence (v. 44; Luke 16:30). Thus they
never ministered unto "these least," and by that very
fact never did a thing for Christ; ἐμοί is the emphatic
form of the pronoun as in v. 40. They disowned Christ,
they repudiated his grace and his salvation. The evidence for this are these negative acts of theirs which
even they themselves admit as facts though for a false
and a lying purpose. The long day of grace is past,
now the hour of judgment has struck. The evidence
is clear to the universe, the sentence of hell-fire is the
only sentence the eternal Judge can pronounce if he
himself is to remain absolutely righteous and just.

46) There is no indication that even a slight
interval occurred between the pronouncement of the
verdicts thus substantiated by the universally admitted
evidence and the execution of these verdicts. **And
these shall go away into punishment eternal, but
the righteous into life eternal.** So brief the words,
so tremendous the realities they state. Some think
that the righteous stand by while the damned leave and
then also depart. But the words make the impression
that both the righteous and the damned (let us say
under the guidance of the angels) go to their eternal
abodes. Here we have a plain commentary on "the
fire, the eternal" of v. 41, namely "punishment eternal."
Who would want either? The opposite is ζωὴ αἰώνιος,
"life eternal." The punishment is the absence of this
ζωή, the removal from the enjoyment of God and of the
saints and the angels in the new heavenly world. In-

stead of God, the devil; instead of the saints and the angels, the company of the other damned and of the devil's angels. Instead of heavenly joy, hellish torture that will exactly match the moral condition of the damned. Here αἰώνιος plainly refers to both punishment and life, so that it is impossible to give the word two different meanings. This settles the question: hell is as eternal as is heaven; heaven no more so than hell.

The question is sometimes asked: "Can God damn to hell forever?" Those who argue away the existence of hell and of the devil are not "the righteous" but those who contradict the King and are in danger of arriving in hell. God seeks to keep all of us out of hell; but many nullify all his grace. They contradict God and Christ even on the judgment day. They have reached a devilish state which God himself cannot change. They exclude themselves and also must be excluded from God and all holiness, and that means hell. On the day of judgment no arguments will avail but only the facts, whether we accept them or rebel against them. All that the writer desires is that he may be among the righteous on that last day when they go away into life eternal.

# CHAPTER XXVI

## XIX

### Christ's Passion, Chapters 26 and 27

1) **And it came about, when Jesus ended all these words, he said to his disciples, You know that after two days comes the Passover, and the Son of man is handed over to be crucified.** The unnecessary ἐγένετο that introduces the sentence is due simply to the strong Greek tendency to begin a sentence with a verb rather than with a modifier of time (here the ὅτε clause) and generally this ἐγένετο does not influence the construction, B.-D. 442, 5; 472, 3. Here εἶπε follows as though no finite verb preceded. Matthew has repeatedly used this formula about Jesus finishing his words (7:28; 11:1; 13:53; 19:1), but this time he adds "all these words," as though he intended to imply that no further "words" or discourses such as these would be reported in the remainder of his Gospel.

2) The statement that Jesus himself makes fixes its time, "after two days comes the Passover." So it was still that great Tuesday that was filled so full of conflict and instruction (Matthew's account of this day extends from 21:23 to our present chapter, 26:5). For there is no question that here τὸ πάσχα does not refer to the entire Passover week but to the actual Passover Feast, the eating of the Passover lamb on the fourteenth of Nisan (Thursday). Two days before would be the twelfth of Nisan (Tuesday).

With a simple καί Jesus adds what shall then happen, "the Son of man (see 8:20) shall be handed over (delivered up, betrayed) to be crucified." The present

tense παραδίδοται is not merely a prophetic present but
also expresses the certainty of what is about to occur,
R. 870. As the Passover "comes," so Jesus "is delivered up to crucifixion" (εἰς τό to indicate purpose that
shall be effected). This is not an announcement of the
Passion; Jesus has already attended to that. It is an
announcement of *the exact time* of the Passion, which,
indeed, began with the betrayal of Judas in Gethsemane
on Thursday night. It is *Jesus* who here two days in
advance fixes the time. The point is not that Jesus
merely indicates that he *knows* the time — this is not
an impressive display of supernatural knowledge. By
an infallible prophecy Jesus authoritatively *fixes* the
time: it shall be Thursday night, then, and at no other
time.

3) We see what Matthew has in mind when he reports that on Tuesday evening Jesus so exactly fixed the
time of his Passion. **Then were assembled the high
priests and the elders of the people in the hall of the
high priest who is called Caiaphas, and they resolved
to arrest Jesus with craft and to kill him. But they
went on to say, Not at the festival, lest there be an
uproar among the people.** The point is the last
statement: arrest and kill but *not* at the festival, not
until the seven days of the celebration are over, and the
festival pilgrims have gone, not until *we* say so, when
we think it safe. On the very same evening (τότε),
perhaps at the very same hour and moment, Jesus says,
"It will start Thursday night"; and the Sanhedrin says,
"It shall start a week later." God rules even in the
midst of his enemies. That Jesus should die, how,
where, and just *when*, is entirely God's decision and
not at all the decision of Christ's deadly foes. When,
where, and how God opens the gates, the flood of their
damnable hate shall rush in and never otherwise,
against God's will. The thought is tremendous in
every way. It is Matthew alone who brings these two

decisions into vital connection; Mark 14: 1, 2 and Luke 22:1, 2 refer only in a general way to the decision of the Sanhedrin.

"The high priests and the elders of the people" is a designation of the Sanhedrin which uses only two of the three terms that are often employed; see 2:4, "high priests," and 16:21, "elders," and in both passages note the designation by naming only two groups. The αὐλή is either the palace of the high priest or the hall in the palace. This was a secret meeting and thus was not held in the usual place, namely in the Chanujoth (*tabernae, mansiones*), on the south side of the great Temple court. Any public meeting would have drawn attention to itself, and its object would have provoked inquiry. Some think that the αὐλή was the unroofed inner court of the quadrangle of the palace, but this would be exposed to the passing of servants and attendants, and thus also too public for taking secret steps to kill a man. The high priest, τοῦ λεγομένου introducing his name as Caiaphas, was the head of the Sanhedrin and presided at its meetings. Josephus calls him Joseph, but this name is never used in the New Testament. His character stands out clearly in the Gospels. He is domineering, unscrupulous, criminal.

4) The aorist συνεβουλεύσαντο, followed by subfinal ἵνα, means that the assembly passed a joint resolution, ἵνα stating what the resolution was. The resolution passed is "to arrest Jesus with craft and to kill him," hence the subjunctives are properly aorists. That a body such as this could pass such a resolution casts a flood of light on the moral and the spiritual condition of the nation and of these its leaders. "With craft" may refer to the offer Judas had made to betray Jesus at an opportune moment.

5) With the descriptive imperfect Matthew paints the scene: one after another went on to say, "Not at the festival," not during the seven days when Jerú-

salem would be filled with pilgrims from far and near. Matthew wants us to dwell on this word because it clashes so directly with Jesus' word in v. 2. The reason for this delay is obvious enough. Because the people had been so enthusiastic in their welcome of Jesus, the Sanhedrin had every reason to fear an uproar among them if they should arrest and kill Jesus during the feast. This was human calculation. Jesus was killed on Friday, and no uproar of any kind arose.

6) The two companion pieces, v. 1-2 and v. 3-5, connected with τότε, are now followed by two more that are likewise joined with τότε, v. 6-13 and v. 14-16.

**Now when Jesus was in Bethany in Simon's, the leper's, house, there came to him a woman having an alabaster vial of perfume, very costly, and she poured it out upon his head while reclining at table.** The first part of Matthew's account is greatly condensed; the same is true of Mark's. We are thankful to John 12:1, etc., for having added so much to those two brief records. Neither Matthew's genitive absolute, "when Jesus was in Bethany," nor Mark's similar phrase (14:3) give the date of the anointing, and all efforts to find a date in these expressions lead to unsatisfactory conclusions. John gives us the exact date. Jesus arrived in Bethany "six days before the Passover," on the eighth of Nisan, the Friday before Palm Sunday. It was too late to make a supper at that time, for the Sabbath began at dusk. Jesus rested during the Sabbath, and then, when at dusk of this day the Sabbath was over, the feast in honor of Jesus was served; see the complete details in the author's commentary on John.

We know nothing further in regard to "Simon, the leper"; but it is fair to conclude that he offered his house, was himself present, and was called "the leper" as a result of the great miracle by which Jesus had healed him.

7) Matthew does not devote space to a description of the occasion when this woman came to anoint Jesus, namely a grand supper that was served in honor of Jesus, Lazarus being present among the guests (some 15 in all), and Martha and Mary helping to serve. But his omission of the woman's name, especially when we consider v. 13, can scarcely be due to mere brevity of writing. Matthew saw her perform her great deed with his own eyes and must here withhold her name because, when Matthew wrote, she was still alive, and to publish her name might entail evil consequences for her on the part of the Jewish haters of Jesus.

Matthew mentions the container, ἀλάβαστρον, "a thing of alabaster," i. e., a vessel or a vial that was made of this semitransparent stone, which was so constructed and sealed that the neck of the vial had to be broken in order to get at the contents, and the entire contents (a pound, John 12:3) had to be used after the vessel had been broken. The contents Matthew calls only μύρον, a general term for this volatile "perfume." The translation "ointment" conveys a wrong impression, and "oil" does likewise. This μύρον left no oily stain but evaporated rapidly like our finest perfumes; John states that the whole house was filled with the delightful odor.

All the three evangelists remark about the great value of the perfume; Matthew calls it βαρύτιμον, "very costly." Matthew and Mark mention only the fact that the head of Jesus was anointed; John supplements this by stating that Mary, the sister of Martha and of Lazarus, anointed Jesus' feet and dried them with her hair. Matthew's only reference to.the fact that this occurred at a feast is the participle ἀνακειμένου, "while reclining at table"; it is John who tells us about this feast.

8) **Now when the disciples saw it they were indignant, saying: To what purpose this waste? For**

**this could be sold for much and be given to poor people.** John aids in making the scene clear. Judas, who carried the funds and stole from them, inaugurated this indignation and carried some of the other disciples with him, these not taking time to think. Judas uncorks the vial of his poison, and the vile odor begins to spread. In the basest of moves a man may often have supporters and abettors, especially if he is able to hide his motive and his intent under some plausible plea.

Judas might have found various objections to Mary's act and to Jesus' acceptance of it: it ill became a man of simple manners; anointing the feet as well as the head was a piece of extravagance and of effeminacy that was offensive to Jewish custom; such luxury did not comport with the life of a prophet; had not Jesus himself said that they that wear soft clothing are in kings' houses? they might use costly perfumes but not a man who was practically without a home. It is characteristic of him that Judas attacks the financial side of this transaction; he sees only the ἀπώλεια, the terrible waste, all this valuable perfume now gone. At the same time Judas takes credit for speaking out as he does right here in public, right before Jesus himself in whose honor this feast had been made, at once and not long after. What a brave, high-principled man he was! No wonder some followed his lead!

9) The imperfect ἐδύνατο, like the ἔδει in 25:27, is difficult for the English and the German mind. In verbs of propriety, obligation, possibility, or necessity the Greek starts from the past and states the real possibility or obligation, and the reader, by comparing that with the facts, notes that the possibility (this is the type of verb here used) is not met, R. 886. Once the possibility of selling "this" was in existence (imperfect tense), now it no longer exists. Matthew writes only πολλοῦ, "for much," the genitive of price; John lets Judas state the exact amount: 300 denarii, $48.

"And given to the poor" hides the thieving motive of Judas behind the assumed motive of charity toward the poor. Think of it, Judas speaks up for the poor! But note that he condemns. not only Mary but Jesus himself. Judas implies that Jesus is robbing the poor; that he is lavishing upon himself what rightfully belongs to charity; that for his own glorification he allows a waste that is utterly wrong; that his example is harmful to others; and that Judas is the man who knows what is right, proper, charitable, and is not afraid to mention it! This is the traitorous touch in the action of Judas. Those of the other disciples who supported him most likely wanted to criticize only Mary and thought how good helping the poor would be.

10) **But when Jesus perceived it he said to them: Why are you distressing the woman? For an excellent work she did work on me. For always you have the poor with you, me, however, me you have not always. For this one, in casting this perfume upon my body, did it for my entombment. Amen, I say to you, Wherever this gospel shall be proclaimed in the whole world, there shall be uttered also what this one did as a memorial of her.**

We need not stress γνούς unduly; Mark has "some expressing indignation toward themselves," starting to object at the place where Judas reclined, and where Jesus did not at once perceive what was going on. Soon he realized it and interfered. It is remarkable that Jesus completely ignores the covert attacks made against himself for allowing such waste in his own honor. He first defends Mary. He rebukes her critics, "Why are you distressing the woman?" furnishing burdens (κόπους παρέχειν) for her? The τί suggests that these critics can in no respect justify themselves. As proof the positive fact and the verdict of Jesus are adduced: "an excellent work she did work on me," καλόν,

excellent in every way.  The idea of work lies in both
the verb and the object.  Jesus thoroughly understood
that it took a mighty resolution on Mary's part to do
a deed such as this, which, as a mere anointing, might
meet the sharpest objection, but which, as an anointing
of Jesus' body for his burial, would be utterly beyond
the minds of these men and would invite the more
intense criticism.  With ἔργον καλόν Jesus accepts her
whole work, and any attack on it must reckon with him
and not with the woman.

11) Matthew abbreviates the word regarding the
poor and writes only that the disciples always have the
poor with them.  His readers may note what is added
in Mark, namely, that they can do them good at any
time, whenever they feel like doing so.  But the real
point Matthew brings out clear and sharp: "always the
poor — me not always" (chiasm).  The latter is really
an understatement, especially when it is considered in
connection with Mary's act.  The disciples would have
Jesus with them only for a few more days, during
which time they might honor him; but this very evening was the only possible time to show him the honor
Mary had in mind.

12) Jesus states directly and in so many plain
words just why αὕτη, "this one" (i. e., woman) lavished
(βαλοῦσα) all this perfume upon Jesus.  He says, "upon
my body," for Mary had in mind the entire sacred body
when she anointed its head and its feet so lavishly.
"For my entombment she did it"; πρὸς τό with the infinitive denotes aim, intent, purpose: "she did it that I be
entombed" (aorist: laid away in a tomb).  The words
mean exactly what they say.  Nor does ἐνταφιάζειν mean
"to prepare for burial" (R. V.) but simply "to entomb."
But did Mary actually and consciously anoint Jesus for
his burial?

Some think of only a general providence and say
that Mary unconsciously fulfilled God's purpose. Others

say that Jesus "lent" this significance to Mary's act. Still others think of a foreboding and an indistinct premonition on which Mary acted by a sort of instinct. But the three texts say, "she did it for my entombment"; Mark, "she did anoint my body aforehand (προέλαβε with the infinitive μυρίσαι) for the entombment"; John, "she kept it for the day of my entombment." Again and again Jesus had spoken of his death by violence, by crucifixion at the hand of the Gentiles. What if the disciples failed to grasp what this implied? Why should not one heart realize that Jesus meant exactly what he said? The character of this woman is such that it ought not to surprise us so much to note that, whereas dull-witted men failed, she saw that Jesus was now going straight to his death by crucifixion as he had said. Thus her mind leaped to the conclusion that, when the tragedy became reality, it would be utterly impossible to reach Jesus and to anoint his dead body for its burial. That is why she acted now and unhesitatingly embraced the opportunity which she had hoped would come and for which she was prepared. We may add that only on the supposition that Mary knew that she was now anointing the body of Jesus for its burial is the tremendous praise accorded her act by Jesus himself justified.

13) To this praise is affixed the seal of verity and of authority (see 5:18). It refers to the world-wide spread of the gospel proclamation (24:14), and the prophetic future passive λαληθήσεται most positively assures us, "There shall be uttered also what this one (αὕτη, namely, woman) did," and this utterance, this telling of what she did this night at Bethany, shall be "for her memorial," shall ever keep her memory alive, αὐτῆς being the objective genitive. This prophecy of Jesus has been literally fulfilled.

14) **Then one of the Twelve, called Judas Iscariot, having gone to the high priests, said, What**

are you willing to give, and I myself will deliver him to you? But they weighed to him thirty silver pieces. And from then on he was seeking an opportunity to deliver him. As in v. 3 the τότε in point of time connects the two incidents related in v. 1-5, so now τότε connects the anointing in Bethany and the dastardly act of Judas in point of time. "Then," after the rebuke in connection with the anointing; "then," when already his attack on Mary and on Jesus showed how traitorous was his heart, Judas went ahead with his damnable deed.

Whenever he is introduced as such (Mark 14:10; Luke 6:16; John 6:71), the naming of the traitor is always tragic, "one of the Twelve," one of this sacred number, one who was raised so high by Christ, one who was destined for one of the twelve apostolic thrones in heaven, and one who now not only lost this grace and this glory but transformed it into the absolute opposite: a tool of Satan (Luke 22:3), one who was sold for thirty pieces of silver to the whole world's execration, the one traitor beyond whom none in the whole world can go. His full name is also added: "Judas Iscariot" = *Ish-Kerioth*, "man of Kerioth," a town in Judea (Josh. 15:25). He is thus distinguished from the other Judas among the Twelve as well as from all the others of the Twelve, he alone hailing from Judea while the rest hailed from Galilee. But the place of his origin has nothing to do with his crime.

No one can say precisely when he went to the high priests. Did he slink away late on that Saturday night? It would be possible. To no less known persons does he go than to the "high priests" themselves, to Caiaphas and to his relatives in the Sanhedrin.

15) Matthew does not state that these leaders of the Sanhedrin were overjoyed. Whereas they feared that the whole nation was being carried away by Jesus,

one of his most intimate followers is ready to sell him
for a price.   Here was an opportunity that was almost
too good to be true, one no man would have dared to
predict.   Matthew presents only the essentials.   After
having been admitted to the great men's presence,
Judas is almost brutally direct, "What are you willing
to give me, and I myself (emphatic ἐγώ) will deliver
him to you?"   That is all: "How much?   If the price
is right, I myself, one of his own Twelve, will do the
job for you."   Matthew alone reports these words of
Judas.   We find no trace of haggling about the price.
The bargain is very promptly struck.   And again it is
Matthew alone who states that the price was thirty
pieces of silver (compare Zech. 11:12, 13), 30 shekels,
or 60 drachmas or denarii, about $10.

It is Matthew who informs us that the pieces of silver were weighed out to Judas right then and there. For
ἔστησαν αὐτῷ, just as the Hebrew of Zech. 11:12, means,
"they weighed" the money, literally "stood it" on the
scales, by this common test giving him 30 pieces of full
weight and not worn pieces that had depreciated in
value.   See the up-to-date dictionaries on ἵστημι when
it is used in connection with coins, also the R. V., which
corrects the "covenanted" of the A. V.   Mark's "promised" leaves the payment in doubt.   The promise and
the agreement were carried out then and there.   Judas
would do nothing unless he had the money paid down.
"What are you willing to give me?" means give me
right here and now.   Judas intended to run no risk in
regard to getting his money later on.   The priests ran
no risks, because they had the power to arrest this man
at any time.   So Judas left with the blood money
weighing heavily in his bag.   He carried the funds of
Jesus and of his band, and during this season the little
treasury must have been flushed.   After Jesus was in
the hands of the high priests, Judas would retain also
this money for himself.

The amount has been called too small a sum, being
only the price paid as a penalty for accidentally killing
a slave (Exod. 21:32), and hence the amount has been
questioned. But amounts of money are always relative in men's mind; to some men a small sum takes on
great proportions. The fact that our criminals demand large sums is no reason for questioning the
amount Judas took. But think of these high priests
and of what this criminality implied in regard to their
moral character! Yet often, the higher and the holier
a man has been regarded, the baser was his real moral
character. Too many authorities have paid Judas'
money as these high priests did.

16) Judas went back to Jesus with the price for
his Lord and Master already in his greedy hands. But
from then on he had only one thing in mind: the εὐκαιρίαν, the favorable time or opportunity to carry out his
part of the bargain, "to deliver him," the ἵνα clause
being subfinal and in apposition with εὐκαιρίαν. So the
divine and the human plans for Christ's death are laid.

17) There is no record of anything that Jesus
said or did on Wednesday. It is certain that he did
not go to the city; the probability (we have no more)
is that he remained in Bethany. From Tuesday (v. 1,
2) Matthew now takes us to Thursday. **Now on the
first day of the Festival of the Unleavened Bread
the disciples came to Jesus, saying, Where wilt thou
that we make ready for thee to eat the Passover.
And he said: Go into the city to so and so and
say to him, The Teacher says, My special time
is near. With thee I am keeping the Passover
in company with my disciples. And the disciples
did as Jesus ordered them and made ready the
Passover.**

Matthew purposely abbreviates his account, for he
leaves out all that Mark and Luke report about finding
this unknown host. But Matthew records independent

details of an intimate nature in the message addressed to the unnamed host.

There is no need of an elaborate discussion of τὸ πάσχα and ἡ πρώτη τῶν ἀζύμων. The former originally designated the celebration that occurred on the afternoon and the evening of the fourteenth of Nisan (the eating of the Paschal lamb) and naturally led to the inclusion of the entire seven-day week of the unleavened bread; similarly "the days of the unleavened bread" soon included also the day on which the Paschal lamb was slain, the fourteenth of Nisan, thus making eight days of unleavened bread. "The first day of the unleavened bread" is thus beyond question the fourteenth of Nisan. At this time it was a Thursday.

Matthew, like Mark, makes it plain that all of the disciples were concerned about the place where Jesus would celebrate the Passover that night. Note the force of σοί, "we make ready for thee"; they do not say, "for us." The disciples have no suggestions of their own, they simply inquire in regard to Jesus' will. "The Passover" means all that belongs to the Passover meal (φαγεῖν).

18) Matthew's account is quite lucid although it is brief. All the arrangements were made, apparently in Bethany, early on Thursday in the presence of the Twelve. Any reader of Jewish origin would understand that twelve men were not needed for this task. Mark tells us that Jesus delegated two, and Luke names these as Peter and John, and Jewish sources tell us that no more than two were allowed in the Temple court when the lamb was killed in the afternoon. So ὑπάγετε εἰς τὴν πόλιν is quite clear.

In all three synoptic accounts Jesus withholds the name of the man in whose house he intends to celebrate the Passover, and, of course, this means that Peter and John alone will know who the man is and where his house is located, and that they will know this only after they have found the man's house in accordance with the directions given by Jesus (Mark and Luke). In all probability Peter and John did not return to Bethany where Jesus and the ten remained until toward evening when Jesus took them to the place which he alone in addition to Peter and John knew. We have only one answer to the question as to why Jesus (it is not Matthew) kept the man's name and thus the location of his house secret: the traitor is not to know, is not even to be able to find out. Jesus keeps the traitor hopelessly guessing as to where this place may be found. Jesus will celebrate this Passover in perfect security, right in the city itself, and that at night, whereas ever since his entry into the city on Sunday he had left the city every night.

There is no warrant for thinking that Jesus had talked matters over with this unnamed man of Jerusalem; that Jesus quietly told Peter and John the man's name; that the Twelve knew who was being referred to without needing to be told; that the reason for calling him ὁ δεῖνα was only to keep his name secret at the time of the writing of this Gospel, just as Matthew had not mentioned Mary's name in v. 6-13, lest Jewish haters single out this man for persecution. Incidentally, the grammarians state that this is the only place in the New Testament where ὁ δεῖνα, "Mr. So and So," R. 744, is found. It is quite fruitless to speculate regarding his identity and to refer to Joseph of Arimathæa, Nicodemus, or Mark's own home in the city.

The message that Peter and John are to deliver indicates not only that this unnamed man is a disciple of Jesus but also that he is one who has advanced in his faith. He will at once know who ὁ διδάσκαλος is when Peter and John speak to him. And the mysterious expression, "My special time (καιρός) is near," will be intelligible to him and will at once move him to action. Note the possessive "my καιρός" and the fact that this

noun always designates a short time that is in a
decided way marked by what occurs within its narrow limits. "My special time is near" must refer to
the special time that is marked by Jesus' passion. And
here is a disciple in Jerusalem who knows that this is
what Jesus has in mind when he sends this message.
Never again will Jesus celebrate the Passover; his end
is close at hand. No wonder that Jesus kept this man's
name and his residence a secret; he would not this night
have it raided by the Jewish authorities who would follow the traitor's directions.

All the synoptists present Jesus as taking it for
granted that he will celebrate the Passover at this
friend's house. Matthew reports the message as follows: "With thee (emphatically forward) am I keeping
the Passover together with my disciples." Mark and
Luke agree with this when they word the message of
Jesus so that it asks where the room is which is to be
reserved for Jesus. Jesus is certain of all this in
advance, as he was in 21:2, etc. But now everything
has a sinister background, for 26:14-16 has occurred.
The expression ποιῶ τὸ πάσχα is common in the LXX as a
translation of "to celebrate the Passover."

19) Matthew states that the directions of Jesus
were duly carried out and the Passover made ready.

20) **Now when evening was come, he was reclining at table together with the twelve disciples.
And while they are eating he said, Amen, I say to
you (see 5:18), that one of you shall betray me.
And being exceedingly grieved, they began to say
to him each one, Surely it is not I, Lord? But he,
answering, said: He that dipped his hand with me
in the bowl, he shall betray me. The Son of
man (see 8:20) goes away even as it has been
written concerning him; but woe unto that man
through whom the Son of man is being betrayed.**

**Excellent were it for him if that man had never been born.**

It is Thursday evening. But this is the beginning of the Jewish Friday, for with the appearance of the first star in the sky the new day began. Matthew at once transfers us to the beautiful and secluded upper room where the Passover is now in full progress with Jesus and the Twelve participating.

21) Matthew records none of the conversation, he intends to relate only how the traitor exposed himself. "While they are eating" refers to a special part of the Passover. This followed a fixed order: 1) the first cup with its blessing; 2) the bitter herbs to recall the bitter life in Egypt; 3) the unleavened bread, the *chasoret*, the roasted lamb, and the *chagiga* (other sacrificial meat); 4) the housefather dips the bitter herbs into the *chasoret* with a benediction, then eats, and the others follow; 5) the second cup is mixed (wine with water), a son asks, and the father explains the feast; 6) the first part of the *hallel* is sung, Ps. 113 and 114, and with a prayer of praise the second cup is drunk; 7) the father washes his hands, takes two cakes of bread, breaks one and lays it on the unbroken one, blesses the bread out of the earth, wraps a broken piece with herbs, dips it into the *chasoret*, eats it and a piece of the *chagiga*, and a piece of the lamb; 8) then all join in the eating, and it is to this point of the feast that Matthew refers with "while they are eating." At no previous point could the exposure of Judas have been made without spoiling the ceremonial. 9) The close came when the father ate the last morsel of the lamb, after which no one ate. Then came the third cup; 10) the second part of the *hallel*, Ps. 115-118; the fourth cup, sometimes a fifth; the conclusion of the *hallel*, Ps. 120-137. This is the rabbinical description.

The emotion of this scene Matthew allows us to feel from the dialog; but note John 13:21. The entire pro-

ceeding of Jesus is marvelous: he does not expose Judas
but reveals the act of Judas and its effect upon Judas
himself, so as to bring the most powerful pressure to
bear upon Judas in order to lead him to repudiate his
act even now, to fall at Jesus' feet in repentance and to
receive pardon. In fact, Jesus proceeds in this way
until the last scene in Gethsemane. Under the pressure of such treatment Judas proceeds boldly to expose
himself. So all that Jesus at first does is to assert most
solemnly, "One of you shall betray me!" This statement must have exploded like a bombshell among the
disciples. It merely asserted a fact, but with the indefinite "one of you" (ἐξ, partitive) it put every man
present in the shadow of guilt. And this was the intention of Jesus.

22) The word was intended to shock the guilty
soul of Judas out of its guilt, and Jesus thus used the
effect produced upon the eleven guiltless disciples by that
word as an added force to reach the will of Judas. Judas had to tell himself that Jesus must know all about
his traitorous act. Judas had to feel that, when all the
others asked, "Is it I?" they were sure that Jesus knew
which one it was. Judas heard the voice of innocence,
filled with dismay, ask, "Is it I?" and that must have
struck his heart that was black with guilt, for *he* could
not ask thus in honesty and in innocence.

"Being grieved exceedingly" is the first reaction
and, prompted by it, the question of εἷς ἕκαστος, "each
one," in quick succession, Μήτι ἐγώ εἰμι, Κύριε; The interrogative particle μήτι implies a negative answer on the
part of the questioner, which we are able to reproduce
only in a cumbersome way: "Surely, it is not I, Lord?"
A degree of uncertainty is nevertheless mixed with
each man's assurance. Each man knows of no act so
terrible in himself; but each man knows that what
Jesus says must be fact; and each man knows how
weak he is and how, ignorantly or in some other way,

he *might* do something to hurt Jesus. Note that the
eleven say, Κύριε, which at this advanced stage meant to
them, "divine Lord"; Judas says only, "rabbi."

23) Jesus does not answer these anxious and excited questions. Judas had not joined in the chorus.
His attention had certainly been aroused. He was
thinking rapidly. What did Jesus really know? Was
he working only on suspicion? What was Jesus after?
So Jesus not only continues, he increases the tension by
answering with a significant description of the traitor:
"He that dipped his hand with me into the bowl, *he*
(οὗτος, emphatic) shall betray me." This, of course,
does not furnish a mark of identification. Both ὁ
ἐμβάψας in Matthew's account, and ὁ ἐμβαπτόμενος in
Mark's, the one an aorist participle, the other a present,
are timeless. Nor should we think that Matthew is
here reproducing John 13:23-26. The verses recorded
by John follow what Matthew relates: John supplements by telling how he and Peter were shown that the
traitor was Judas.

The real point of the designation "he that dipped
his hand together with me in the bowl!" is the same
one as that made in John 13:18, and as that noted in the
mode chosen to inform John and Peter (John 13:26):
it characterizes Judas as a second Ahitophel, the man
who turned traitor to David and ended by hanging
himself. He is the prototype of the traitor Judas; and
it ought to be noted that this is the only reference in the
Old Testament regarding Judas; we lack even a single
prophecy. II Sam. 16:15-17, 23; Ps. 41:9 (John
13:18); Ps. 55:12-14. Jesus says, "in the bowl," and
μετ' ἐμοῦ, "in company with me"; we put too little into
these expressions when we fail to see that this was the
Passover of Jesus (σοι in v. 17), that the Twelve were
here at his invitation, not he at theirs, that this was
Jesus' bowl, and that to be allowed to dip into it with
Jesus supreme honor, indeed. Thus Jesus makes plain

how despicable, how utterly low-down Judas' act is. All this, spoken before the whole company, had to strike the conscience of Judas with double force. He who could resist impacts such as this was beyond hope.

24) But let no man think that Jesus is at the mercy of some vile wretch; no, "the Son of man (i. e., the incarnate Son of God, God's great Messiah) goes away even as it has been written concerning him." His course, even to this tragic end, was recorded in Scripture and is now on record there; (this is the force of the perfect). It has been divinely planned and will surely be carried out just as Jesus now declares ("shall betray me"). Jesus is not appealing for sympathy with himself, the sympathy and the commiseration should go to the traitor. Jesus is indicating to the Twelve, including Judas, why he does not interfere and make this dastardly betrayal impossible. Jesus is in absolute harmony with what "has been written." In order to have all that perfectly fulfilled he became "the Son of man."

He turns the thought from himself in whose case all is going as it has been written to the awful condition and fate of the traitor. He cries "woe" upon "that man" and designates him as one who is distant from himself. This is not a woe of indignation such as the woes uttered in 23:13, etc., but a woe of deepest grief and pain. And yet this woe, like all others, and like its opposite "blessed," is the verdict upon the traitor. All that causes wretchedness and agony in time and in eternity is his portion. When Jesus says, "is being betrayed," he lets Judas know that he knows just how far Judas has already gone.

Although no γάρ is written, we must say that we now have an explanation of the "woe" if not the actual reason for it, "excellent were it for him if that man had not been born." The thought is: "If he had had no life at all rather than a life that is marked by such a

deed." It thus really makes no difference whether we
translate οὐ ἐγεννήθη, "not to have been conceived," or,
"not to have been born" after having been conceived.
The sense remains: non-existence is preferable to this
betrayal. R. 886 regards καλὸν ἦν αὐτῷ as another Greek
idiom that indicates that the past is not met by the
present (like 23:23; 25:27; 26:9). But here we probably have a mixed condition of unreality: the protasis
is one of past unreality: "if he had not been born," and
the apodosis one of present unreality: "it would have
been excellent." The fact that the negative οὐ appears
in such a protasis is quite exceptional, and neither R.
1161 nor B.-D. 428, 2, have more to say. The fact that
ἄν is missing is of no moment (R. 1014), yet its absence
would harmonize with the decisive force of οὐ. At this
point insert John 13:23-26.

25) Now Judas betrays the full devilishness of
his character. **And Judas, who was betraying him,
answering, said, Surely, it is not I, rabbi? And he
said to him, Thou didst say it.** Here Judas betrays
what effect the treatment of Jesus has had on him.
Although he was at first startled, he has recovered and
come to the conclusion that this rabbi is only guessing,
only groping around to see whether he may discover
something. He thus meets the situation with the bra-
zen face of hypocrisy. Prompted instantly by personal
distress, voice after voice had promptly asked, "Surely,
it is not I?" No such distress was evident in Judas,
and hence no such prompt inquiry came from him. But
the thought comes to him that Jesus or some of the
others may have noticed that he did not join in the
questioning. Moreover, he notes that Jesus had really
said neither "yes" nor "no" to all these questions but
had just prolonged the uncertainty. So this hypocrite
puts on a bold front with his lying question, "Surely,
it is not I, rabbi?" He challenges Jesus to divulge
whatever information he may have. And the address,

"rabbi," whereas the rest used, "Lord," inadvertently betrays his real estimate of Jesus. Judas is resolved to carry his betrayal through.

Straight as a shot the answer of Jesus smites through Judas' lying pretense. *Him* Jesus gives an immediate and direct answer, "Thou thyself didst say it!" This is the common Jewish way of affirming something by using the very statement made by the questioner himself. Hence the emphatic σύ, "thou thyself," and then either the present λέγεις, "art in the act of saying it," or the aorist, "didst already say it."

Some think that this interchange of words was not heard by any of the eleven, but this view is untenable. Since these thirteen persons were reclining on couches, it is difficult to see how Judas could ask and be answered in secret unless he arose from his place and spoke to Jesus at close range. We must not forget that this occurred "while they were eating," v. 21, during the eighth part of the ceremonial. Nor would anything be gained by secrecy, for, according to John 13:23-26, John and Peter already knew, and that implied that the rest would be told quietly by these two. Besides, Jesus is through with Judas. As soon as the traitor has compelled Jesus to expose him, Jesus orders him to go and to do quickly what he is engaged in doing, John 13:27-30. Matthew does not say that Judas left. He certainly does not need to; for after Judas had been exposed as a traitor he would no longer remain in the company of the "rabbi" he was betraying and in the company of his loyal disciples. Thus the question as to whether Judas received the Lord's Supper or not is answered in the negative.

26) Matthew at once adds the account of the Lord's Supper. **And while they were eating, Jesus, having taken bread and having blessed it, broke it; and, having given it to the disciples, said, Take, eat! This is my body. And having taken a cup**

**and having given thanks, he gave it to them, saying: Drink of it, all!  For this is my blood, that of the covenant, that in the act of being poured out for many unto remission of sins.**  First note the repetition ἐσθιόντων αὐτῶν, "while they were engaged in eating," cf. v. 21.  Both genitive absolutes refer to the same eighth part of the ceremonial which was described in detail in connection with v. 21.  We see that this must have been the case, for the ninth part took but a moment, it merely stopped further eating; and the tenth part was the singing and the drinking of the last cup.  We shall be safe in assuming that the institution of the Lord's Supper came at the close of the somewhat ample period of freely eating the Passover food.  No one was to be stinted.  So about the time the housefather would have gone over to number nine, the eating of the last morsel of the lamb, thus stopping all further eating, Jesus proceeded to do something that was entirely new.  The new act is also an eating and a drinking, but one that consisted of bread and wine and was engaged in only by the disciples.  It has its thanksgivings, but these and the added words refer directly to Christ's sacrificial body and his blood and to their saving effect.  From the first word onward the disciples understood.

First, Jesus "took bread."  The participle indicates that this is only a preliminary act.  Note that this participle is an aorist, and that throughout all participles (except λέγων) and all main verbs that refer to the acts of Jesus are aorists, all being historical and stating so many facts.  The entire account is so simple and so lucid in its wording that even a grammar the size of Robertson's finds only one very minor point to be noted.  The ἄρτος was not a "loaf."  No "loaves" in our sense of the word could be baked of unleavened dough.  This ἄρτος was a thin sheet of unleavened bread, pieces of which were broken off for the purpose of eating. The author saw these thin sheets of bread baked on a hot plate in Syria; the woman stacked these up and gave us one that was still hot, which we broke and ate in the ancient way. How else could we have eaten it properly?

The second act is still preliminary, hence we again have an aorist participle, εὐλογήσας, "having blessed." Luke and Paul have εὐχαριστήσας, "having given thanks." But we at once see that the two words have the same sense, for Matthew and Mark use the second when they come to speak of the cup. None of the four accounts of the Supper has preserved for us the words of blessing and thanksgiving that were spoken over the bread and the wine by Jesus. We shall not go astray when we say that these words referred to the bread (and then to the wine) that were in Jesus' hands and to the heavenly gift which the respective element was to convey. Thus this blessing enlightened the disciples and prepared them for the proper reception of the bread and of what it conveyed (of the wine likewise); for they were to receive both intelligently and were not to wonder what Jesus was trying to convey to them. All we can say about these words is that, after they were once spoken by Jesus, they remain efficacious for all time wherever the sacrament is really celebrated. Because of their very nature they could not again be efficaciously repeated, and that seems the reason that the power that guided the holy writers led them to omit these words from their records.

The acts of breaking and of giving go together in the sense of distributing. No symbolism is involved in the breaking, for "a bone of him shall not be broken," John 19:36. The bread was broken merely so that it could be more readily eaten. "Bread is an inanimate thing: how can breaking it be like the putting of a human being to death? Breaking bread is the very symbol of quietness and peace, who would

dream of it as an appropriate symbol of the most cruel
and ignominious death? Bread is the representative
food, and, used in metaphor, is the symbol of spiritual
and supernatural food. The breaking of bread is the
means of giving it as food and as a symbol, the symbol
of giving and taking a higher food. No one would
dream of the breaking of bread as the symbol of killing a human body; and if so extraordinary and symbolic use of it were made, it would require the most
explicit statement on the part of the person so using
it, that such was his intent; and when he had made it,
the world would be amazed at so lame a figure."
Krauth, *Conservative Reformation*, p. 723. In regard
to the wine we have no counterpart to the breaking of
the bread, which shows that the breaking was only
incidental to the distribution.

Just how Jesus "gave to them" no man can say.
Nor is the point vital. When we now adopt a mode
of distribution we cannot say that *any* mode will
do; for various modes that are used at present indicate wrong views of the nature of the Sacrament. Our
mode must in every way harmonize with the essentials
of the sacrament and also with the spirit of its original
institution. As Jesus gave he said, λάβετε, φάγετε, two
aorist imperatives to indicate two brief actions. And
now the disciples hear what Jesus really gives them,
τοῦτό ἐστι τὸ σῶμά μου, "this is my body." Luke adds
to body the modifier, "being given for you," i. e., in
sacrifice on the cross; and Paul adds to body the modifier, "which is for you," i. e., in sacrifice.

We must note that τοῦτο is neuter and hence cannot, grammatically or in thought, refer to ἄρτος which
is masculine. The English "this" and "bread" obscures this distinction in gender, yet we dare not
ignore it. "This" means, "This bread which I have
now consecrated by blessing and thanksgiving"; or
more tersely, "This that I now give to you"; *hoc quod*

*vos sumere jubeo.* "It is no longer mere bread of the oven but bread of flesh, or bread of body, that is, bread which is sacramentally one with Christ's body." Luther.

Much has been written on ἐστί which is merely the copula connecting the subject and the predicate. Jesus spoke in Aramaic and used no copula in that language, for none was needed; but this does not remove or in the least alter the inspired ἐστί found in the Greek records. It cannot mean "represents" as Zwingli contended. The characters $1,000, written on a piece of paper, "represent" one thousand dollars, but no man can say that this "is" a thousand dollars.

"My body" means exactly what the words say, "in truth and reality my body." The modifiers added by Luke and by Paul strongly substantiate this view. Luke's ὑπὲρ ὑμῶν διδόμενον must refer to the real body, for no symbol of the body, no bread, was this day being given for our redemption on the cross. It is only the rationalizing question, "*How* could the Lord give his disciples his true and real body by means of bread?" that has caused the trouble in regard to these exceedingly simple words. Some think of a transubstantiation of the bread into the body, so that Jesus does not give bread but only body. Others deny that he gives his body. They say that this is impossible and that, therefore, he gives only bread as the symbol of his body.

We refuse to answer the question in regard to the *how* because the Lord has withheld the answer. We probably could not understand the answer because the giving of Christ's body in the sacrament is a divine act of omnipotence and of grace that is beyond all mortal comprehension. The Lord declares *the fact*: "This is my body," and we take him at his word. He knows the mystery of this giving; we do not. The rationalizing objection that this involves a gross, car-

nal, Capernaitic eating of the raw flesh, is unwarranted.  The first disciples, who had the body of Christ
before their very eyes when Christ's bodily hand in
a supernatural way gave them the gift of his sacrificial
body, never dreamed of such an eating.  "My body"
does not mean "a piece of my body."

Matthew and Mark are quite brief in their reports
of the institution.  Both omit what Luke and Paul add,
namely, that the sacrament is to be repeated again and
again by the disciples.  But it would be unwarranted
to play the other accounts against Matthew and Mark
on this point or to assume that these two evangelists
intended to cancel this command of Christ's.  The four
records are four historical testimonies, and any point
in any record that is not found in the rest is only so
much valuable addition.  Matthew and Mark sense
that permanency is indicated by the very nature of
the sacrament; for not the Twelve alone but all disciples were to be partakers of Christ's body and blood
for the assurance of their salvation.

27) Matthew and Mark relate the consecration
of the cup exactly as they related the consecration of
the bread while Luke and Paul abbreviate by writing
"likewise." We prefer the reading ποτήριον without
the article which a number of good texts and also Luke
and Paul have.  Whether a different cup was used for
each  of the four or five times of drinking in connection with the Passover, or whether only one cup was
used and this was refilled as needed is not certain and
quite immaterial.  The point is that Jesus instituted
the sacrament with the use of one cup and that he
bade all the disciples to drink out of this one cup.
Any change in what Jesus here did, which has back
of it the idea that he would not for sanitary or similar
reasons do the same today, casts a rather serious reflection upon Jesus.

"Cup" may refer to the empty vessel, the filled vessel, or only to the contents of the vessel as the context decides. "Having taken the cup" means the vessel with its contents; "having given thanks" refers only to the contents of the vessel. "He gave it to them" means the vessel with its contents. The order to drink ἐξ αὐτοῦ means to drink the contents of the vessel. But τοῦτο refers to the consecrated contents alone.

The cup contained wine mingled with water, on which all are agreed save those who for special reasons believe that wine was not used. When Matthew 26:29 writes, "of *this* fruit of the vine," i. e., that which the Passover cup contained, he shuts out any and all other products of the vine save actual wine and thwarts all modern efforts that speak of unfermented grape juice, raisin tea, or diluted grape syrup. The expression "fruit of the vine" is derived from the Hebrew *pheri hagiphen,* a choice liturgical formula for wine. The matter is of utmost importance and lies beyond our powers to alter. To alter a testament is to invalidate that document. Hence the use of any other liquid than actual wine that is made from grapes — this alone was "wine" in Christ's day, this alone was used in the Passover — renders the sacrament invalid so that it ceases to be the sacrament. Christ's testament is valid only in the form in which he made it and not as men today may alter it.

We note that Jesus adds πάντες to the command to drink, "all" of the eleven are to drink; and Mark adds that "all" did drink. This "all" indicates the necessity that all who ate must also drink in order properly to receive the sacrament. The contents of the cup are thus to be drunk so that all will receive a portion and none be left without such a portion. The fact that the πάντες in Matthew and in Mark plainly contradicts the Roman Catholic practice is obvious. But Rome makes an asset of this πάντες: it claims that this word is not used in connection with the bread because this bread is intended for all Christians; but "all" is added to the cup, and this has reference only to all those present, the apostles and then their successors in the priestly office, "all the clergy alone." In other words, "all" means "not all but only some" — the opposite of what Jesus actually says.

28) Here the explanatory γάρ is inserted; in substance it is present also in the statement regarding the bread. We have τοῦτο exactly as in v. 26: "this," the consecrated wine; "this," that I bid you drink. So also ἐστί is the copula and nothing more. And τὸ αἷμά μον matches exactly τὸ σῶμά μου, and all that indicates the reality of the latter likewise indicates the reality of the former. "Body" and "blood" are given separately, for in the sacrifice the blood flows out and is separated from the body.

By means of a separate article, and thus as a kind of emphatic apposition, Jesus adds: τὸ τῆς διαθήκης, and then also τὸ περὶ πολλῶν ἐκχυννόμενον κτλ. On the force of these articulated additions see R. 776; and on the force of the article with the predicate τὸ σῶμά μου and τὸ αἷμά μου, cf. R. 768. These grammatical points are valuable exegetically in order to perceive just what Jesus says. Monographs have been written on the term διαθήκη, "testament," in connection with the Hebrew bᵉrith, "covenant." We see how the translators of our versions waver, the A. V. using "testament" in our passage, the R. V. "covenant" with "testament" in the margin. Compare on the subject C.-K. 1062. We offer the sum of the matter. The Old Testament dealt with the promises God gave to his chosen people. God placed himself in "covenant" relation to Israel. The heart of this relation, like the promises and the gifts of God to Israel, is wholly onesided. In is always God's covenant not Israel's; and it is never a mutual agreement. This covenant, indeed, obligates Israel, and Israel assumes these obligations, but the covenant itself emanates wholly from God. The LXX translated *b*e*rith,* "covenant," διαθήκη, "testament," since this term has the strongest one-sided connotation. A will and testament emanates only from the testator. Christ, however, brought the fulfillment of the Old Testament promises. The result of this was that now God's people have the inheritance and are God's heirs, joint-heirs of Christ, Rom. 8:17. It is thus that in the New Testament *b*e*rith* becomes διαθήκη, "will and testament," by which God bequeathes to us the blessings Christ has brought.

Both the old *b*e*rith* or covenant and the testament of Christ's fulfillment were connected with blood. The former could be sealed with the blood of animal sacrifice: "Behold the blood of the covenant, which the Lord hath made with you concerning all these words," Exod. 24:4-8. This blood typified and promised the blood of Christ, God's own Son, to seal "the new testament" by which we inherit all that this blood has purchased and won for us. The old covenant could be written in animal blood because it consisted of promise; the new testament could be written only in the blood of the Son of God because it conveys the complete fulfillment of the promise, the actual purchase of our redemption.

The word "blood" is not merely a reference to "death," because a specific death, namely a sacrificial death, is involved. No other type of death could establish the "testament." Hence the crowning modifier with another τό, "that in the act of being poured out for many." Jesus means that now this pouring out of his sacrificial blood has begun. And, indeed, he has truly entered upon his sacrifice. So "body" and "blood" appear separately in the sacrament; nevertheless, the two always appear together. No sacrificial

body without sacrificial blood and vice versa. The
Scriptures never speak of the *glorified* body or the
*glorified* blood. The miracle of the sacrament is not
that Christ makes us partakers of his *glorified* body
and blood but of the body *given* and of the blood *shed*
for us on the cross. The sacrament draws on Calvary
not on heaven.

The phrase περὶ πολλῶν means, "concerning or in regard to many," and conveys the general idea that the
pouring out of the blood took place for their benefit;
and the next phrase completes the thought, "unto remission of sins." Thus περί indicates the persons involved
and εἰς the purpose or contemplated effect upon these
persons. The absence of the articles stresses the nouns:
"remission," sending away and complete removal, "of
sins," whereby we miss the mark. These πολλοί are all
men, for all of whom the blood was shed "for remission
of sins," and not merely the believers in whom this
remission was realized. They are "many," and thus
extend far, far beyond the eleven. Mark combines this
by using ὑπὲρ πολλῶν, "in behalf of many" in the sense of
"in place of many," ὑπέρ having the idea of substitution.
See Robertson, *The Minister and his Greek New
Testament*, the entire chapter on ὑπέρ. Matthew's
wording conveys the same idea.

**29)** **Moreover, I say to you, that in no wise will
I drink from now on of this fruit of the vine until
that day when I shall be drinking it with you new
in the kingdom of my Father.** The sacrament has
been instituted. The sacrament was also made the
conclusion of the Passover, save for the singing of
the hymn (v. 30), the second part of the *hallel*. The
importance of the statement is evidenced by the
formula, "I say to you," and Mark shows that Jesus
even used "amen" as the first word. With verity and
with authority Jesus declares that he will die that very
day (Friday), for he will not taste another cup of

wine.  But to this sad announcement he adds one that is most glorious, that the day is coming when he will be drinking wine that is wonderful and new with his disciples in the kingdom.  The negative οὐ μή is the strongest form of negating a subjunctive or a future indicative; and πίω is the aorist subjunctive, punctiliar to express a single act: not once will Jesus drink.  He had offered the cup of the blood of his testament to the disciples; but for Jesus there remained only the cup of his suffering.  But the following πίνω is the durative present subjunctive; in the kingdom the drinking will be repeated.

Because οἶνος does not appear in this account, the use of wine is at least gravely questioned, which means practically denied.  The fact that Matthew writes not merely "fruit of the vine," *pheri hagiphen*, the lovely liturgical term for wine used in the Passover ritual, but most definitely "*this* fruit of the vine," the one regularly used in the Passover and thus used by the Lord also for his Supper, is not appreciated by those who will not use wine in the celebration of the Lord's Supper, for they think that grape juice fits this phrase better than wine although in April such a thing as grape juice was an impossibility in the Holy Land of Christ's time.  It could be had only when grapes were freshly pressed out, before the juice started to ferment.

Jesus not only dies on this day, but by his dying all the Jewish Passovers have served their purpose and have really come to an end.  That is why Jesus instituted the sacrament of the New Testament; this is to be used by his disciples "until that day" when Jesus will drink the fruit of the vine "new" in the heavenly, glorious kingdom of his Father.  On this heavenly feast compare 8:11; Luke 22:30; Rev. 19:9. Note the present subjunctive πίνω, "be drinking," for that feast shall never end; also καινόν, "new," as com-

pared with what is old, not νέον, "new," as never having
existed before. All descriptions of heaven are necessarily figurative, so also this one regarding the drinking of wine at the heavenly feast. Yet from Luke
22:16 we gather that the heavenly feast will be a
heavenly fulfillment of the Passover plus the Lord's
Supper. All that is promised in the latter regarding
our union and communion with Christ will then be
brought to its eternal climax.

"In the kingdom" has been used to find chiliasm
in this statement of Jesus', and this affords opportunity to revive the chiliastic dream of Papias concerning "this fruit of the vine" in heaven which grows
endlessly in enormous clusters on the most astounding
vine that ever was imagined. When the floodgates of
imagination are opened, the strangest romances
appear.

30) **And having sung the hymn,** the second
part of the *hallel*, Ps. 115-118, perhaps also the last
part, Ps. 120-137, with which the Passover was usually
concluded, **they went out to the Mount of Olives,**
namely to the Garden of Gethsemane.

31) **Then Jesus says to them: All you shall be
trapped in connection with me in this night. For
it has been written, I will smite the shepherd, and
scattered wide shall be the sheep of the flock. But
after I am raised up I will go before you into Galilee.**
On the way to Gethsemane, Jesus makes this dis-
closure. We see that all he needs to know concerning
the details of his passion is most clearly known to
him. All of the eleven, not one excepted, σκανδαλισθήσεσθε,
shall be caught as in a trap, ἐν ἐμοί, in connection with
Jesus. The idea of the verb is that of a crooked stick
to which the bait is affixed and by which the trap is
sprung. So this night the trap will catch all the disciples. They will be trapped by what will happen to
Jesus; it will completely upset them. On retaining

the native meaning of the verb see M.-M. 576. The translations, "ye shall be offended because of me," and, "in me," are both incorrect and misleading. The disciples took no offense because of Jesus, of anything that he was or did this night. They took no offense at all. They were simply caught (trapped) and overwhelmed by what happened to Jesus, namely his sudden arrest and trial. And this that caught them was ἐν ἐμοί, "in connection with Jesus," and not "in (within) me" or "because of me."

"For" intends to explain by pointing to what "has been written" and thus is still on record, the prophecy of Zech. 13:7. Jesus uses only two statements of the prophecy and himself translates these from the Hebrew. Whatever other fulfillment Zechariah's prophecy may have, Jesus here uses it with reference to his own death and its effect upon the disciples. "I will smite the shepherd," etc., means that *Yahweh* will give Jesus into death. And this ordeal the disciples cannot be spared. We now see what being caught in a trap means: the disciples will be so upset that they will leave Jesus and like a shepherdless flock will flee in all directions. But though this sad and terrible thing is now about to happen, it means much that Jesus himself informs the disciples of it in advance. This advance warning contemplates bringing these scattered sheep together again.

32) And that is exactly what Jesus promises. The accusative with the infinitive ἐγερθῆναί με is converted into a substantive by means of the article τό and is then made the object of μετά. Jesus will be raised from the dead by *Yahweh* who gave him over to death. Repeatedly Jesus had announced his resurrection to his disciples and had stated definitely that it would occur on the third day after his death. Now in consolation and blessed assurance Jesus adds that, after he has risen from the dead and is glorified, he

will precede the disciples into Galilee. In other words, as the great Shepherd that leads his flock he will appear to them in Galilee where he had gathered most of that flock. That this was to be a signal and an exceptional meeting we see from the constant references to this gathering in Galilee, 28:7, 10, 16. The only direct mention we have of it is found in I Cor. 15:6, to which must be added Matt. 28:16, etc.

33) **And Peter, answering, said to him, If all shall be trapped in connection with thee, I at least will never be trapped.** Jesus warned Peter twice: first, in the upper room, John 13:36, etc., and Luke 22:31, etc.; secondly, on the way to Gethsemane, Matthew and Mark. On this question see the author's commentary on John 13:36. Peter is not checked by the warning received in the upper room. On the contrary, he is more sure of himself than ever. Openly he contradicts Jesus: not all will be trapped, Peter will be the exception. Openly Peter compares himself with the other disciples to his own great advantage; note the emphatic ἐγώ, "I at least." Instead of the simple negative οὐ he also uses the universal οὐδέποτε, "never." He will now get a second positive warning, but he will disregard this as he did the first.

34) **Jesus said to him, Amen, I say to you, that in this night, before a cock crows, three times wilt thou deny me.** This time Jesus adds the seal of verity and of authority (see 5:18). He no longer combines Peter with the others but singles out Peter and tells him the outrageous acts he alone will perform. Peter will give his own grand words the lie by doing exactly the opposite of what he says. He will even deny Jesus, utterly disown him, and that no less than on three separate occasions this very night. He will do this, not by implication, but with the same loud voice he is now using and in public before even more witnesses than hear him now. The verb ἀπαρνέομαι means,

"to say no," and thus to deny and to disown. The aorist subjunctive is volitive, "wilt (not shalt) deny me."

The crowing of a cock is not some casual crowing of some individual cock. Two crowings were distinguished: one, sometime after midnight; the other, just before dawn. They divided the night into the midnight or the silent period, the period before dawn, and the period after dawn. Pliny calls the fourth watch *secundum gallicinium*. The second warning to Peter (Mark 14:30) refers to both crowings, "before the cock crow twice," i. e., before the day dawns. Luke and John refer to the crowing that took place before dawn. The phrase is not a mere expression of time but refers to the actual crowing of the cocks on that night.

This word is spoken with a special purpose. It does more than merely to foretell how soon Peter will sin, it prepares the help to raise Peter from his fall into sin. Peter will actually hear the crowing when it begins; that will bring Jesus' word to his mind; and this, together with a look from Jesus' eyes (Luke 22:61), will cause the tears of repentance to flow. The effort to discredit the reliability of the evangelists by stating that in a city such as Jerusalem no chickens were kept, and that thus no cocks crowed within range of Peter's ears, has been met by ample evidence to the contrary.

35) **Peter says to him, Even if I must die with thee, in no wise will I deny thee. Likewise also all the disciples said.** In the upper room Peter had already declared his willingness to die with Jesus. Of course, he can now do no less. He now uses the condition of expectancy which pictures the situation vividly and combines Jesus' death and Peter's dying with him (σύν, accompaniment, R. 628). And now he again flatly contradicts Jesus' "three times wilt thou deny

me" by stating, "In no wise will I deny thee" (the future is volitive, R. 875). Carried away by Peter's mighty assertions and promises, the rest of the disciples spoke in the same way. Jesus is silent, for his object is already attained; he had paved the way for Peter's repentance.

36) **Then Jesus comes with them to a place called Gethsemane, and he says to his disciples. Sit here until, having gone yonder, I pray. And having taken Peter and the two sons of Zebedee, he began to be sad and worried. Then he says to them : Exceedingly sad is my soul unto death. Remain here and be watching with me.** There are various opinions in regard to Gethsemane, the Hebrew words most likely meaning "Oilpress." Some call it a *Meierei,* a regular farm, and think that there were buildings on the place. They base this view on χωρίον and on the strange young man mentioned in Mark 14:51, but this is rather slender evidence. The statements made in the Gospels lead us to believe only that it was a large grove of olive trees, a secluded place that had nothing further on it than what was needed to take care of the olives, which were probably a building for tools and an oilpress. Jesus used this place because it was so quiet and secluded.

The place now shown to tourists lies too near the road and is too close to the bottom of Olivet. Titus cut down all the trees, and although olive trees become very old, the present trees shown to tourists are of later growth and are located on the wrong site. A stone wall most likely encircled Gethsemane. The whole country is full of stone.

A short distance inside the entrance Jesus tells his disciples to sit down while he proceeds "yonder" (he probably pointed to the place) to pray, προσεύξωμαι, aorist subjunctive, "to make a definite prayer and to complete it," not merely "to engage in prayer."

37) But Jesus does a strange thing; he takes three
of his disciples that on other occasions had served as
special witnesses again to serve as such, "Peter and
the two sons of Zebedee," James and John (Mark 5:37;
Matt. 17:1). As he walks with them beyond earshot
of the others, his agitation becomes visible to them even
before he speaks. It was so great that Matthew, like
Mark, uses two strong verbs, "he began to be sad and
worried." The ἤρξατο indicates that this condition sets
in, and the two present infinitives picture its duration.
Instead of λυπεῖσθαι, "to be sad, grieved, distressed with
sorrow," Mark has ἐκθαμβεῖσαι, "to be completely upset
by distress." As the second verb both Matthew and
Mark have ἀδημονεῖν, "to be away from one's δῆμος or
home," *mir ist unheimlich,* to be filled with uneasiness
and dread. In this pitiful condition these three disciples see Jesus as they walk on with him. All his
power seems to be gone; he is crushed and beaten down
and has only one recourse: prayer to his Father.

38) Now the Lord utters his distress in words.
The predicate περίλυπος, "exceedingly sad," is placed
forward, περί intensifying the preceding verb λυπεῖσθαι.
Jesus tells how sad he is, "until death," and we shall
soon see that this phrase conveyed the actuality: Jesus
was now on the very verge of death. It is his ψυχή
which animates his body that is in such deep distress;
just as distress takes hold also of our "soul." But
the rapid approach of phyical suffering and death did
not bring about this agony in Jesus' soul.

Jesus now orders the three disciples to stay where
they are (μείνατε, aorist, punctiliar) and to keep watching (γρηγορεῖτε, present, durative) with him. Their
nearness and their watching are to be a slight comfort
to Jesus in his distress of soul. Alas, this comfort was
denied him, for the three disciples slept. But the battle that Jesus fights in this hour he must necessarily
fight alone. He alone must now will "to lay down his

life" (John 10:17, 18), "to give his life as a ransom for many" (Matt. 20:28), to be made sin and a curse for us (II Cor. 5:21; Gal. 3:13). The imagination faints before the images thus rising up before it. Who can imagine all this abominable sin, all this damnable curse! And the holy Son of God is *now* to plunge into it — the great and awful moment is almost here. Shall Jesus go on, or since his pure and holy nature recoils from the unspeakable ordeal, is there yet a way out?

**39) And having gone forward a little, he fell on his countenance, praying and saying: My Father, if it is possible, let this cup pass away from me! Nevertheless, not as I will, but as thou. And he comes to the disciples and finds them sleeping and says to Peter: So — you had not the strength to finish watching one hour with me? Be watching and praying lest you come into temptation. The spirit is eager, but the flesh weak.**

The agony of Jesus is revealed by his attitude. Having gone forward "a little," he kneeled down, but Matthew and Mark say that he fell on his countenance, that he lay on the ground like a worm (Ps. 22:6). From the kneeling position he must have sunk prone upon the ground. Never had these three disciples seen him thus. Otherwise, when Jesus prayed, he said merely, "Father," but under the pressure of his soul he cries, "*my* Father," reaching up as closely as possible to his Father's heart. From Heb. 5:7 we learn that these words of prayer in Gethsemane were uttered with "strong crying ($\kappa\rho\alpha\nu\gamma\tilde{\eta}\varsigma$ $\iota\sigma\chi\nu\rho\tilde{\alpha}\varsigma$) and tears" and were certainly heard by the three disciples.

We must note that from the first word of the prayer to the last Jesus submits to his Father's will. Even a mere supposition of not doing so is foreign to his soul. The true humanity of Jesus is revealed by these prayers; it had to be thus revealed because his entire passion was undergone by way of his human nature. The word "cup" is here used figuratively and does not refer only to contents but to bitter, burning, deadly contents. "If it is possible" leaves the decision in regard to that to the Father. The condition is one of reality and assumes that, if such a possibility existed, the Father would avail himself of it. Back of the brief condition lies the thought, "if it is possible to redeem the world without drinking this horrible cup of death and wrath" then relieve me of this cup. "Let it pass from me" means, "Do not put it to my lips."

With πλήν, "nevertheless," Jesus implies, "whatever may be involved in this possibility." Although in his agony Jesus has mentioned the possibility, he really intends to yield everything to his Father's will and to put aside his own will. It is the human will of Jesus that speaks here. The agony suffered in Gethsemane will always bear an element of mystery for us because of the mystery involved in the union of Christ's two natures. For one thing, we have no conception of what sin, curse, wrath, death meant for the holy human nature of Jesus. Because he was sinless, he should not die; and yet, because he was sinless and holy, he willed to die for our sin. The death of Jesus was far different from that of the courageous martyrs; they died after Jesus' death had removed their sin and guilt, the sting had been removed from their death through Christ's death, but Jesus died under sin and its curse, the sting of death tortured him with all its damnable power. The world's sin had, indeed, been assumed by Jesus during his whole life, but here in Gethsemane the final moment of that assumption had come: with the coming of Judas and his band Jesus now actually stepped into the death that would expiate the world's sin.

40) Intense were the prayer and the agony, but the words were few. Jesus returns to the three disciples whom he had bidden to keep awake with him. Any comfort he might derive from a word or two with

them is denied him. Their nearness is no support whatever, for they are nodding in sleep. Jesus addresses Peter, but the words apply to all three disciples. This brave, mighty Peter had promised to die with Jesus and now he cannot even stay awake at his Master's bidding! The word plainly shows the disappointment of Jesus: "So — you had not the strength to finish watching one hour with me?" The aorist infinitive γρηγορῆσαι means, "to finish watching," and "one hour" in the sense of "only one hour" indicates how long Jesus wanted the three disciples to watch with him.

41) Jesus rouses them out of sleep with a renewed call to watch, to be awake, to be ready, to be on their guard, and to pray. And now he does not say, "watch *with me*," but he combines watching and praying both of which are to be *for themselves*, "lest you come into temptation," i. e., come into it in an unready state and be caught accordingly. To watch is to be ready in advance, and to pray is to receive from God the help needed in the critical hour. The remarkable thing is that the rebuke of Jesus is so gentle, and that even in his agony and distress Jesus can think of the needs of these sleepers. The πειρασμός is a trial or test and a "temptation" in that sense. With μέν and δέ the two members of the next sentence are neatly balanced, but the English cannot reproduce this delicate balance. "The spirit is eager, but the flesh is weak," reveals the situation exactly. All true disciples are no longer simple but altogether complex personalities. Regeneration has produced "the spirit" in them, the new divine life, we may call it faith. This spirit is open to God and to Christ and thus ready to respond to their promises and their directions. Every Christian constantly has this experience.

On the other hand, he still has in himself ἡ σάρξ, "the flesh," which, when it is thus placed in opposition to τὸ πνεῦμα, refers not to the body or σῶμα, or to the substance of which it is composed, but the old sinful nature that still clings to our being after conversion. This flesh opposes the spirit (Gal. 5:17), in fact, would like again to get complete control of the personality. When Jesus says the flesh is ἀσθενής, "weak," "sick," he speaks of it from the standpoint of the spirit. The spirit is eager enough to endure and to overcome the temptation, but the flesh in us is "weak," utterly helpless in temptation, a drag and a terrible handicap to the spirit in us. By calling on the disciples to watch and to pray Jesus seeks to rouse their spirit into full activity. By sleeping and giving way to sleep-producing sorrow of heart they were yielding to the flesh. So the word of Jesus warns them in regard to this flesh; and the test of their trial is almost at hand.

The idea that this statement regarding spirit and flesh applies also to Jesus himself in his agony, is unwarranted. No duality such as spirit and flesh ever existed in Jesus; no trace of sin ever appeared in him. His agony was not due to sinful flesh as were the sleeping and the lack of prayer in the disciples. It was the pure and holy sinless human nature that shrank from the ordeal, not of death as death, but of death as a curse for the world's sin. Jesus stood on a higher level than Peter and his companions.

42) **Again, having gone away a second time, he did pray, saying, My Father, if this cannot pass away unless I drink it, let thy will be done. And having gone back, he found them sleeping, for their eyes had been made heavy.** A second time Jesus turns to his Father as the only source of help. The second prayer is identical with the first save in the wording. It has the same reference to possibility, "if it is possible." The Greek is more obvious, εἰ δυνατόν, "if it can"; εἰ οὐ δύναται, "if it cannot." A positive thought is changed only in form by being expressed negatively. Here again is the same absolute submission to the

Father's will, "let thy will be done," i. e., the will of the
Father regarding the redemption of the world, that will
which Jesus had come into the world to do, that will
which is now attaining its climax in the redemptive
passion and death of the incarnate Son. To match "let
this cup pass away from me," we have in the second
prayer the corresponding positive thought, "unless I
drink it," πίω, aorist subjunctive to indicate the one act
of emptying the bitter cup.

It is unwarranted to say that "if it can be" in v. 39
means that Jesus thinks that it actually can be and that
he prays accordingly; and that now in v. 42, "if it cannot be," indicates a change to the conviction that after
all it cannot be and that he now prays differently. This
overlooks the two equally strong expressions of absolute submission to the Father's will. Both conditions,
the positive as well as the negative, are realizations
that the escape from drinking the cup and yet redeeming the world are impossible. Note the strong negative οὐ in the condition of reality with εἰ, R. 1160; B.-D.
428, 1; it is not found often in the classics but is more
frequent in the Koine.

**43)** Torn hither and thither in his agony, Jesus
comes back to his three disciples. He finds that his
admonition has produced no result whatever. The
disciples are asleep, in fact, their eyes are weighed
down with heavy sleep, they cannot keep them open
even now when Jesus returns to them. He is compelled
to fight his dreadful battle without even a word of
comfort from his own dearest friends.

It has been claimed that under these circumstances
this sleeping is a psychological impossibility. But this
view cannot be sustained on psychological grounds; for
great and continued sorrow of soul brings on an inner
dulness of mind and thus the physical reaction of profound sleep when the soul yields to its burden and no
longer rails against it as Jesus urged the disciples to do

by watching and by prayer. From Mark we learn that
Jesus spoke to the disciples, but that they did not know
what they answered him, their replies were unintelli-
gent; and so he again left them.

44) **And having left them, again having gone
away, he prayed for the third time, saying the same
words again. Then he comes to the disciples and
says to them: Go on sleeping for the rest and take
your ease! Lo, the hour has arrived, and the Son of
man is being betrayed into sinners' hands. Be rising, let us be going, lo, he has arrived that is betraying me!** The three prayers are throughout
couched in the same words, i. e., the same in substance
(τὸν αὐτὸν λόγον) certainly not also the same verbatim.
As a rule, the commentators do not discuss the question
as to how Luke 22:43, 44 are to be combined with Matthew and with Mark. In connection with which of the
three prayers did Jesus sweat blood and have an angel
strengthen his body that was already so near to dissolution? We are satisfied with John Bugenhagen's
*Passion History* which places the supreme agony and
the angel's strengthening last. Then the agony ceased,
and Jesus now speaks to his disciples in a different tone.

45) He now tells these sleepers to go sleep and
take their rest. In τὸ λοιπόν we have an adverb (R.
487), which, like others when the adjectival idea en-
croaches, retains the article (R. 294). On account of
this adverb we cannot regard the words as an exclama-
tian, "You are still (τὸ λοιπόν does not mean still) sleeping!" or as a question, "Are you still sleeping?" Both
imperatives are permissive (R. 948) and, of course,
durative (R. 890), "Go ahead and sleep for the rest of
the time and take your ease!" Sentimental reasons
deny a touch of irony to these words. We are told that
the solemnity of the occasion forbids the use of irony.
But the deepest sorrow of heart, when it is coupled
with full mental clearness, is not averse to the use of

irony. The view that irony is not proper for Jesus misunderstands him. Here the situation is such that all interpreters almost automatically feel the touch of irony, and then some seek to remove it in some fashion. O these dreadful sleepers! They slept throughout their Lord's agony! Well, let them go ahead and sleep on for the few moments that are left!

The idea is not that Jesus now leaves them undisturbed so they may sleep some more. No; he makes two mighty announcements that ought to drive every trace of sleep from any disciple's eyes. First: "Lo, the hour has come" and thus is now here, perfect tense, ἤγγικεν. After we have previously been told that his hour has *not* yet come, namely the hour to endure suffering and death at his enemies' hands; now the cry suddenly rings from the Savior's lips: "Lo, the hour is here!" ("your hour and the power of darkness," Luke 22:53). Secondly, the hour that is referred to is placed beyond question, "and the Son of man (see 8:20) is being betrayed into sinners' hands" (the absence of the articles stressing the quality of the nouns), into the power (hands) of sinners who have their wills set against God. What this traitorous act means to the Son of man need not be said.

46) It is not necessary to think that an interval occurred between the call to sleep on and the announcement of the hour. So there was not an interval between the announcement of the betrayal and the call to go to meet the traitor. We need think only of sufficient time to permit the disciples to awake from their sleep and to utter some words to the strong, courageous, victorious Jesus now standing before them. Here are bold commands without a connective, "Be rising (present imperative), let us be going" (present subjunctive, hortative) ; it is like our, "Up, let us be off!" When R. 430 says that this combination of verbs is paratactic in origin and hypotactic in logical sequence

and thus lends life and movement (R. 428) to the language he intends to say that from the start verbs such as this were used side by side, and yet the first verb is only subordinate to the second, ἄγωμεν, "let us be going!" expressing the main thought. These two verbs and the following "lo" reveal the excitement of the tragic moment. Even these heavy-lidded sleepers could now begin to see the distant lights and hear the noise and surmise that something fearful was about to happen. "Has arrived," perfect tense, has the same connotation it had in v. 45, "and is now here," namely, "he that is engaged in betraying me," substantivized present participle.

47) **And while he was still speaking, lo, Judas, one of the Twelve, came, and with him a great multitude with swords and clubs from the high priests and elders of the people.** The eleven must have stared in wide-eyed fashion at the crowd that was assembled before the entrance of Gethsemane. The multitude was indeed great. The only hint Matthew gives as to its composition is the mention of the weapons, μάχαιραι, "short-swords" that were carried only by the Roman legionaries, and ξύλα, "clubs," the regular weapons of the ὑπηρέται, "underlings," or Temple police. John adds the detail that they carried also torches and lanterns. He also adds the details concerning the heavy detachment sent out with Judas. The Levitical police were under their στρατηγός or "general," the Roman cohort, not the entire 600 stationed at Antonia but about 200, were under their chiliarch or chief commander. The Sanhedrin had sent this entire force. Their own men had failed them on a previous occasion (John 7:45, etc.), and so they now took no chances. Because of the danger (Jerusalem being full of pilgrims) the Sanhedrists had no trouble in persuading the chiliarch to accompany the expedition and to take with him a force of legionaries that would be able to

cope with any eventualities that might arise when Jesus
was brought to the city as a prisoner.   Yet we nowhere
have an intimation that Pilate's cooperation was
sought.   See the author's comments on John 18:1, etc.
All four evangelists make Judas the guide of this
multitude, and the synoptists call him "one of the
Twelve" in this connection.   The fact that this intends
to agree with the information given in v. 14 is obvious.
There is no canon in literature which would forbid a
writer to express his horror more than once.   If "one
of the Twelve" is tragic in v. 14, it has a right to be
even more so in v. 47, for now the traitor's act is actually being carried out.   "The high priests and the
elders of the people" is a designation for the Sanhedrin;
see 2:4 and 16:21.

48)   **Now the one betraying him gave them a
sign, saying: Whomever I shall kiss, he it is.   Arrest
him.   And immediately, having gone to Jesus, he
said, Greetings, rabbi! and he kissed him thoroughly.**
About 200 Roman soldiers and certainly at least as
many Temple police and besides that a nondescript rabble that ran along to see the excitement block the entrance to Gethsemane.   Jesus meets this crowd, his
disciples are ranged behind him.   He is perfect master
of the situation, and all that occurs does so only with
his consent.   Things seem to be playing into Judas'
hands, but this only seems so.   The traitor gave the
men a sign by which they could without fail know
whom to seize and to arrest.   "Whom I shall kiss ($\phi\iota\lambda\epsilon\hat{\iota}\nu$
is used in this intensive sense), he it is."   Judas is the
inventor of this "sign."   A devilish refinement distinguishes it.   The symbol of most intimate affection and
love, the kiss, is made the signal for marking this trait-
or's victim for the army of his captors.

49)   Judas at once steps forward and gives this
sign.   The verb $\chi\alpha\iota\rho\epsilon\iota\nu$ is used to indicate all kinds of
friendly greeting and always expresses the wish of

happiness and well-being. So Judas acts overjoyed
when he meets Jesus and exclaims so that all the soldiers and the police may hear, "Greetings, rabbi!"
Without waiting for a response, κατεφίλησεν αὐτόν, he
threw his arms about Jesus and kissed him not once, as
the simplex of the verb denotes (v. 48), but showered
him with kisses, the addition of κατά thus intensifying
the verb: *er kuesste ihn ab.* This intensive act was
evidently for the sake of the captors, it was prolonged
in order not to leave anyone in doubt. "This," Judas
intended to say, "see, this is the man you want!" With
his excessive kissing Judas at the same time acts the
black hypocrite toward Jesus, he pretends that his
heart is breaking because of what is now to happen to
Jesus. He acts like one that is overcome, even now
he thinks that he is still deceiving Jesus. Another
motive for all this kissing is suggested; he intended to
close the mouth of Jesus as long as possible and thus to
disarm him at this critical moment. Jesus is not to
display his strange power before this mob and thus to
prevent his arrest.

Jesus does not hurl the traitor from him nor use
his omnipotent power to blast him. Jesus submits to
this traitorous kissing; it is his Father's and his own
will to accept all the indignities, shame, suffering, agonies men will heap upon him even unto death. Again
Judas (see v. 25) addresses Jesus only as "rabbi," and
perhaps unconsciously reveals his real estimate of
Jesus. Here, too, is a hint as to how the traitor's mind
must have worked when he thought that he was really
deceiving Jesus until this moment. This is possible in
the case of evil minds, for their very hypocrisy and
falseness lead them to reason fallaciously, especially
when it comes to judging the character and the actions
of the holy Jesus.

50) **But Jesus said to him, Fellow, for this thou
art here?!** **Then, having come forward, they laid**

**the hands on Jesus and arrested him.** For the last
time Jesus strikes at Judas' conscience. It is just one
brief, penetrating word. The conscience was seared;
no repentance followed. On the address ἑταῖρε see
20:13, and 22:12. It is anything but our mild, gentle
"friend," the Greek φίλε. In all three places in which
it occurs it is like our "fellow," and this word thrusts
a man away. No other disciple of his did Jesus ever
address as ἑταῖρε.

There is uncertainty in regard to the brief, striking
word of Jesus: ἐφ᾽ ὅ πάρει. R. 725 admits that a direct
question may be possible; on the other hand (696), he
finds that ὅ may be demonstrative. The old grammatical dictum is that ὅς can never appear in questions, but
this is not so certain in the usage of the Koine. We
pass by the surmises of B.-D. 300, 2. Also the idea of
an ellipsis such as that of the R. V., "Friend, do that
for which thou hast come!" and other ellipses. Judas
*had* done that for which he has come (the betrayal),
why should Jesus tell him to do it? The word is half a
question, half an exclamation: "for this thou art
here?!" — think of it, "for this"! Ὅ is simply demonstrative. And πάρει is derived from παρεῖναι, "thou art
here." It is interesting to note that Deissmann defends the question (A. V.), "wherefore art thou come?"
*Licht vom Osten,* 100, etc.; E T XXXIII, 1922, p. 941-
945, on the basis of an inscription found on a Syrian
cup that dates from the time of the Gospels. The
grammars will have to reckon with that.

Before a move is made to arrest Jesus what John
18:4-9 records takes place: Jesus delivers himself into
the hands of this multitude. The betrayal of Judas
was worth nothing. Jesus points himself out, prevents
any molestation of the eleven, and actually gives himself up. His passion was wholly voluntary. It is thus
that the *chiliarch* and possibly also the *strategos* order
men to step forward in order to take Jesus prisoner.

John says they bound him.  Yet they never touched a more willing prisoner.

51) Now comes Peter's rashness that, but for Jesus' immediate intervention, might have caused a calamity.  **And lo, one of those with Jesus, having stretched out his hand, drew his short sword and, having struck the slave of the high priest, slashed off his ear.**  Luke 22:38 tells us that there were two μάχαιραι, Roman short-swords in the upper room at the celebration of the Passover, and we are not surprised to learn that Peter has one of them.  The moment a move is made to take Jesus captive, out flashes Peter's sword.  Luke 22:49 tells us that about the same moment the other disciples asked whether they should smite with a sword.  Peter delivers his blow at the first man that is near him, the slave of the high priest, intending to split his head open; but the man evidently sought to avoid the blow, and the sword sheared off his right ear, being stopped by the heavy armor on the shoulder.  We must reckon with the excitement of the moment.  The falling back of the entire armed force at the one word of Jesus may have led the disciples and Peter to feel that, although they were armed with only one sword, they might rout this opposing army.  Had not Peter protested his readiness to lay down his life for Jesus?  Had not the others, stimulated by Peter, done the same?  So Peter here redeems his word.  Jesus is to see that he was in earnest.  But the disciples and Peter act as though Jesus were not laying down his life by a deliberate act and at the same time commanding his captors to let the disciples go free.  Was this not a command also to them to go their way and to let Jesus submit to arrest?  Peter acts as though Jesus meant none of the things he said.  His love does not listen and obey, it assumes to dictate and to rule.

The remarkable fact that none of the synoptists mentions Peter's name in connection with this incident might
be due to consideration for Peter, the Sanhedrin being
still in power when the synoptists wrote; but this is
doubtful. A similar case is that of Mary, v. 7. The article
τὸν δοῦλον puts this man in a class by himself. He is not one
of the "underlings," ὑπηρέται, or police force; he belongs to
the high priest himself personally. He must have been a
trusted and an important member of the high priest's
own household who had been sent with this expedition
as the high priest's personal representative. That explains why he is out in front within reach of Peter's
sword. That, too, is why John, who was so well
acquainted in the high priest's family, mentions his
name (Malchus) and refers even to his relative.

52) **Then says Jesus to him: Return thy sword
into its place! For all that take a sword by a sword
perish. Or dost thou think that I am not able to
appeal to my Father, and he shall present me on the
instant more than twelve legions of angels? How,
then, shall the Scriptures be fulfilled that thus it
must be?** Jesus takes instant control of the situation
and we hear about no untoward results of Peter's rashness. Peremptorily he orders Peter to return his
sword to its place and by this order completely disavows Peter's act, and he does that before all concerned.
John 18:11 likewise reports that Peter was summarily
rebuked. This is a threefold rebuke. In "all that take
the sword," λαβόντες is timeless, "take it" at any time
(R. 859); and the aorist participle is effective, "all who
resort to the sword as their final effort." This statement does not include those to whom God delegates the
sword (government and legal authorities) but those
who, like Peter, arrogate the sword to themselves, i. e.,
the sword that represents violence and bloodshed.
This sword shall strike back at them with just retri-

bution. It is the old law of Gen. 9:6, the basis of all
Jewish criminology, which is reiterated in Rev. 13:10.
Jesus holds it up to Peter in warning, and it is futile
to quote him and the Scriptures against capital punishment. Peter had started on a wrong course; Jesus
points out what its end would be. The use of ἐν is
equivalent to the instrumental case, R. 534.

53) Does Peter think that Jesus is dependent on
him for help, if he, indeed, sought help at this late
moment? Peter interferes with God who forbids us
to resort to the sword and at the same time with Jesus
who knows what help he could most surely get. One
word of appeal ("beseech" is misleading as a translation of παρακαλέσαι) and for every apostle (including
Judas) the Father of Jesus "shall present," have ready
right there, ἄρτι, "now," this moment, "on the instant"
(the idea of verb and the adverb being, without a second's delay), not only twelve legions of angels but more
than that number. A legion had 6,000 foot soldiers
and a body of horsemen. This is the consciousness
with which Jesus goes into his death: at any moment,
at his simple word, the sky could blaze forth with a tremendous host of mighty angels, whose swords could
annihilate all these or any other enemies of his. That
is the real help Jesus can call. How silly for Peter to
flash his little human sword!

We must note ἄρτι, "now," at this moment. It
points back to the prayers in Gethsemane, to the subjection of Jesus' will to that of his Father, to the perfect voluntariness of his suffering and his death. But
here the true nature of this submission and this voluntariness comes clearly to view: it is combined with the
ability (δύναμαι) at any moment (ἄρτι) to avoid this suffering and this death and to do this with absolute moral
perfection. As in the Father, so in the incarnate Son,
the will to redeem us by that Son's blood and death was
his and his alone with absolutely nothing outside to

coërce that will. From the beginning to the end of the passion this was true. It is again evident in John 19:11.

54) Since these tremendous possibilities are ever open to him in his passion, Jesus rejects the blind, pitiful help Peter here tries to offer him. But all these things have long been decided by the divine will, hence this οὖν, which bases the statement regarding the Scriptures on the one regarding the possibility of receiving instant help from heaven. The subjunctive is an effective aorist (R. 851) in a question of deliberation, which is here rhetorical (R. 934) and does not expect or need an answer. Does Peter intend to thwart the fulfillment of the Scriptures, αἱ γραφαί, plural, in their divine statements "that thus it must be," δεῖ in the divine redemptive will of incomprehensible love? This δεῖ or necessity lies in God alone, that is, in the eternal, free volition he has exercised to save us through his Son. And as such it is recorded in the Scriptures. The basic assumption is that it is absolutely certain that the Scriptures are to be fulfilled. But how shall they be fulfilled if Peter follows his idea of smiting with the sword? There is no answer to such an assumption; the only answer would be that Peter would instantly be brushed aside.

This answer is given only to Peter, but it reveals the divine background of the voluntariness of Jesus' passion. We catch a brief glimpse of the depths that lie beneath what Jesus here does by giving himself up without a struggle. Only Luke informs us that Jesus healed the severed ear of Malchus; that he performs a miracle of healing for the benefit of one of his own captors. In that healed ear this man to his dying day bore the mark of Jesus' omnipotence and grace. This is one of those plain miracles which show that faith on the part of the person healed is not necessary. Did Malchus have faith?

55) **In that hour Jesus said to the multitudes: As against a robber did you come out with short-swords and clubs to capture me? Day by day I was sitting in the Temple teaching, and you did not arrest me. But this all has come to pass in order that the Scriptures of the prophets should be fulfilled. Then the disciples all, having left him, fled.** All the synoptists record the protest of Jesus against his arrest and against the manner in which it was made. Mark writes that he "answered" his captors, Matthew that he spoke to them "in that hour," right there at the time and not later on. Luke adds that high priests, commanders of the Temple, and elders were present. The priests and the elders followed, we may assume, because they were too excited to stay in the city, too anxious to find out whether the effort would succeed. The words of the captive, whose hands are bound with a rope, who is apparently helpless, are calm and measured without a trace of excitement; but they are keen and cutting to these leaders who now gloat over their capture.

Jesus asks them just what they have done. They have come as though they were going out to meet a robber from whom the most violent resistance might be expected; they went out with a great expedition that was armed "with short-swords and clubs" as though they expected a regular battle — and all this, Jesus asks, "to capture me?" The whole thing is actually ridiculous. Why, "from day to day (κατά is distributive) I made a practice of sitting (iterative imperfect, R. 884) in the Temple engaged in teaching (durative participle), and you did not arrest me." And now all this violent demonstration, this army of legionaries and Temple police! Jesus, the harmless teacher, is not responsible for this arrest and such an arrest; they, these blind, fear-filled leaders, have perpetrated this. If there were any cause for arresting Jesus, why had they failed to act day after day in the Temple? Jesus had not hidden from them. He had no cause to hide. He had none now, nor had he hidden; on the contrary, he had handed himself over to them when they said they wanted him. A man, whom they permitted to sit and to teach publicly and frequently in the Temple, they now come to arrest with an army? Of course, the protest is useless; and yet no proper protest is useless although men disregard it, for it registers the truth, and truth stands forever.

56) Nor are these men to think that with their superior cunning in hiring a traitor and with their crush of arms they have really captured Jesus. Not a bit of it. They could and would have captured nothing. This whole thing (τοῦτο ὅλον) has occurred for one reason and for one alone: "in order that the Scriptures of the prophets (subjective genitive: written by the prophets) should be fulfilled." Here are the real forces at work in what is taking place this night: God is carrying out his prophetic plans, Jesus is thus voluntarily putting himself into his captors' hands. That and that alone is why this army is scoring such a huge victory against a single humble man! But let these victors think of the part they are playing in God's plan as recorded in the Scriptures.

Now v. 36 was fulfilled. As Jesus is led away, all the disciples fled, Matthew, too, and Peter, the hero. But Matthew uses the participle ἀφέντες which expresses an action that is subordinate to that of ἔφυγον and yet conveys a sadder touch. They all had "to leave him," think of it, "leave him" in order to flee! So entirely alone he was led away to his death.

57) **Now they that arrested Jesus led him away to Caiaphas, the high priest, where the scribes and the elders were gathered together.** Matthew omits an account of the preliminary judicial examination before Annas, John 18:19, and at once takes us to the

Sanhedrin and the main trial. On Caiaphas see v. 3.
When news came that they were really bringing Jesus
as a prisoner, the leaders knew that delay was not
advisable. Messengers hastened through the dark
streets of the city to summon at least a legal quorum
for a session of the Sanhedrin. This body was ready
for action after Annas had detained Jesus for awhile.
The session must have been held in the same hall that
was mentioned in v. 3; and by comparing v. 69 we see
that this could not have been the open inner court of
the palace but was a hall in the building proper. Since
the high priest has been mentioned, Matthew is content
to name only the scribes and the elders; in v. 59 we
have the term "Sanhedrin."

The legal restrictions that forbade trials at night
were summarily set aside in the case of Jesus. Modern
Jews make every possible effort to discredit the evidence of the evangelists regarding this vital point and
declare outright that this night trial never took place.
Aside from the motive back of these efforts, the evidence of the four Gospels is a bulwark that modern
Jewish tactics and bold assertion cannot overthrow.
The leaders who deliberately plotted the murder of
Jesus were not men to balk at a technicality of legal
procedure when they finally had their victim' in their
grasp.

58) **But Peter was following him from afar up
to the court of the high priest and, having gone inside, he was sitting with the underlings to see the
outcome.** This is really a parenthetical statement
that is inserted here in preparation for v. 69-75. All
the disciples fled when Jesus was made a prisoner in
Gethsemane. But two, Peter and John, recovered sufficiently to follow Jesus from a distance by keeping
themselves out of sight. Love drew them, fear held
them at a distance. The imperfects ἠκολούθει and ἐκάθητο
are descriptive of the actions. To the very court of the

high priest's palace Peter manages to follow. The entrance, it seems, was a passageway that had a door-
keeper at the street end. This passageway led to the
open inner court. Jesus was led in. The Roman
soldiers marched off to their fortress barracks. A sufficient number of the Temple police went into the court.
John, too, had no trouble in entering. But at first
Peter got only "up to the court," i. e., its entrance, and
feared to go farther.

"Having gone inside" simply states the fact that
Peter got inside; John 18:16 shows how this was managed, how John himself abetted Peter's disobedience to
Jesus and thus helped Peter on to his denials. So on
the inside Peter was sitting together with the underlings, the ὑπηρέται, the Temple police, hypocritically pretending to be one of their number. The other evangelists mention the fire around which the men warmed
themselves. The reason Peter gave himself for ven-
turing in here was that he wished to see τὸ τέλος, "the
end" or "outcome" of the affair, as though Jesus had
not told him exactly what this would be. We always
invent good reasons for doing what we ought not to do.
The two imperfect verbs, however, intimate that something final is to follow

59) Now Matthew reports the essentials of the
night trial of Jesus before the Sanhedrin. **Now the
high priests and the whole Sanhedrin were seeking
false witness against Jesus in order to put him to
death; and they did not find it although many false
witnesses came forward.** "The high priests" are the
leaders of this supreme Jewish court: Caiaphas as its
president, Annas, and others of his family; and τὸ συνέ-
δριον (from ἕδρα, "seat") are the rest of the members of
this court. As they were seated on a raised platform
in a semicircle, the prisoner, under guard, faced them
from the floor. Matthew presents the center of the
whole illegal action of this court when he pictures it

as "seeking false witness against Jesus in order to put him to death." The Jewish law required an indictment first of all and then on the strength of that indictment the arrest. The trial would begin with that indictment and with the testimony on which it had originally been issued. But here was a prisoner against whom no indictment had been found and no witnesses had been heard in order to arrive at an indictment. In an illegal and a most high-handed way he had been arrested, and no crime had as yet been charged against him. Thus, unindicted, illegally arrested he stands before the Sanhedrin at this illegal hour.

The situation was legally frightful. A large number of the judges should have risen up and protested against such outrageous proceedings. It casts a black moral pall on all Judaism of this time that such a session of the Sanhedrin should have been possible. But remember v. 3-5. The Sanhedrin had drawn far more than an indictment, it had already without witness, indictment, or anything else decreed its victim's death. That death is to be secured, no matter how. Those who could decree that death would certainly now not be squeamish about the means to be employed to attain their end. It is an old observation that the most villanous judges still cling to a show of legal formalities. So here this Sanhedrin seeks for some accusation, however irregularly it may be obtained, on which they can with at least some show of right pass the verdict of death. Only one way is open to them to stage this legal farce: they must seek false witness against Jesus, lying, perjured testimony, to bring him to death.

60) This they proceed to do. But to their dismay they do not find what they thought would be so easy. A whole array of witnesses offers itself, man after man is brought in and testifies falsely, but no two witnesses agree, to say nothing of three or more, so as to charge

something fatal against Jesus. He lived and taught
openly, thousands saw and heard him, and now nothing
of a criminal nature can be proved against him even
by lying witnesses. Many of the ὑπηρέται probably vol-
unteered testimony in order to curry favor with these
leaders or on promise of good pay — remember the
money given to Judas. But it is all in vain.

61) **And finally two, having come forward,
said: This fellow said, I am able to destroy the
Sanctuary of God and after three days to build it.**
We may well imagine a collusion between these two.
They, of course, testified singly, one stepping into the
hall after the other. Matthew gives us their testimony; Mark's version of it is more detailed. They
claim to quote what Jesus had said about three years
ago when he cleansed the Temple the first time, John
2:19. A glance shows that Jesus never said what these
witnesses allege, that they garbled his words and put
a malicious meaning into them. He never said, "I am
able to destroy the Sanctuary of God," or, "I will destroy this Sanctuary." He spoke of the Jews destroying their own Sanctuary; see the author on John 2:19.
Matthew does not need to say that also this malicious
effort failed; but Mark reports that even then their testimony was not ἴση, "equal," the version of the one witness failed to agree with that of the other. In what
respect they disagreed we are not told. When two
testify that they heard the accused say a certain thing
they dare not differ on any vital point in regard to what
they claim to have heard. Even after a collusion it
was a difficult matter to get two witnesses such as this
to testify in such a way that their witness would be
acceptable.

The ναός is the central building of the Temple area
which contains the Holy of Holies and the Holy; the
ἱερόν is the entire Temple complex with its courts as
well as its structures. The phrase with διά denotes **an**

interval of time: "through three days," i. e., there being
that many days between.  So we must translate, "after
three days" although διά does not mean "after," R. 581.
Of course, οὗτος is derogatory, "this fellow," R. 697.

62)    Here was the great Sanhedrin that finally had
Jesus in its power, and all its efforts to fasten something of a criminal nature upon him had proved
abortive.  The situation had grown desperate.  Resolved that Jesus must die and die quickly, it now
appeared as though, for lack of indictment and testimony, the case would have to be adjourned.  It is
Caiaphas who then saves the situation.  **And the
high priest, having risen, said to him:  Dost thou
answer nothing?  What are these witnessing against
thee?  And Jesus remained silent.**  Sitting gravely
on the platform, the Sanhedrists watched the futile
proceedings.  Caiaphas, as chairman, now arises, as
Mark adds, "in their midst," thus confronting Jesus,
and puts on his actor's stunt.  He is so outraged and
indignant because of what the two witnesses have just
testified that he cannot wait for a finding on the compe-
tency of this testimony.  He acts as though it were a
closed matter.  Regular legal procedure has led to
nothing, he will try something else.

He turns on Jesus, and his display of passion is of
such a nature that the grammarians are undecided as
to whether τί introduces a direct and thus separate
question or an indirect question that is still a part of
the first question (R. 738).  "Dost thou answer nothing?  What are these witnessing against thee?"  Such
incriminating testimony, and not a word in reply from
thee?  The object of Caiaphas is transparent: He aims
to hasten Jesus into some explanation that may be dis-
torted into a corroboration of the perverted testimony
of the last two witnesses.  He thus snatches the right
to pass on the legitimacy of that testimony from the
Sanhedrin.  His dramatics direct all eyes toward Jesus.

63)  Calmly undisturbed, Jesus looks at Caiaphas with unflinching eyes. The silence grows more and more intense. Jesus utters never a word. Ἐσιώπα, "he continued silent," a dramatic, descriptive imperfect. And gradually it dawns on the Sanhedrin that this significant silence is the actual answer to the hollow questions of the excited high priest, an answer that is more meaningful and more crushing than any words could have been. That answer went home. Even Caiaphas dares not regard it as a silent admission of guilt on the part of Jesus. He would lose out completely before the Sanhedrists if he did.

What did this silence say?  Opinions differ as men visualize this scene. These points are certain:  The Sanhedrin had not yet admitted the false and conflicting testimony as competent. Until that time a reply on the part of Jesus would have been as disorderly as was the show-acting of Caiaphas himself. To testimony of this kind, however Caiaphas might try to play it up, the only competent reply of Jesus was — absolute silence. Innocence and dignity could make no other reply. Then this was a loud silence that literally spoke volumes. As it grew and grew in the ears of all present it fairly shouted that the whole proceeding, plus this last act of Caiaphas', was absolutely illegal, and no more upsetting conviction of this travesty of a just court could be borne in upon the minds of this court. We need add no more.

That this was, indeed, the significance of Jesus' silence is shown by the sudden abandonment of the testimony of the last two witnesses and by the new turn of Caiaphas. **And the high priest said to him, I adjure thee by the living God that thou tell us, whether thou art the Christ, the Son of God!** Caiaphas, feeling the full force of Jesus' silence, intends to counteract that silence. And he acts with instant quickness. The one and real matter on account of

which the Sanhedrists wanted Jesus out of the way
was not some individual act of his or some one word
that caused offense but his great claim that he was the
promised Messiah, the Son of God. Caiaphas sees how
flimsy the testimony of the many witnesses was, how
futile even the last two bits of testimony. So he boldly
and in the most dramatic way presents the main issue
fully and squarely.

We do not agree with those who think that Caiaphas still tries to retain the testimony of the last two
witnesses and makes the deduction that, if Jesus claims
that he will replace the Sanctuary, he must claim to be
the Messiah and God's omnipotent Son. But Caiaphas
does not propound his oath and his question because
he reasoned in such a roundabout way. Unscrupulous
type of man that he is, he leaps directly to the main
issue. He acted in the very same manner in John
11:49, 50. The testimony of the two witnesses, Caiaphas saw, could at best lead only to a charge of blasphemy — and what would that avail before Pilate? So
Caiaphas makes the bold strike to obtain more.

As the head of the court he puts Jesus under oath:
ἐξορκίζω σε, "I put thee under oath," "I adjure thee."
This was the regular Jewish way of placing a man
under oath and implied that anything he would say
would be regarded as a sworn statement. On whom or
what the oath was made κατά indicated, here, "by the
living God." The idea of this preposition "down" is
that of swearing by placing the hand down on the thing
by which the oath is taken, R. 607. The participle "the
living One," refers to the God who, as living, hears
what is sworn by him and will without fail punish any
falsehood that is uttered in his name. The ἵνα clause
is subfinal (R. 993) and states the substance of the
oath: "that thou tell us (the legal authority of Israel)
whether (εἰ in indirect questions, R. 1045) thou art the
Christ, the Son of God." Regarding this supreme

point Jesus is to make a sworn statement: yea or nay. Jesus is to say under oath who he is officially and essentially.

We at once see what Caiaphas has in mind: the Baptist's word, "This is the Son of God," John 1:34; Nathanael's word, "Thou art the Son of God," John 1:49; the Jewish realization that Jesus said, "God was his Father, making himself equal with God," John 5:18; "I and my Father are one," and the effort to stone Jesus "because that thou, being a man, makest thyself God," John 10:30, 33. Throughout his teaching Jesus had spoken of his Father and his Sender in the most unmistakable way, cf., John 5:19-47; 8:16-19, 53, 58. The supreme objection to Jesus on the part of all the Jewish leaders was the claim of Jesus to be "the Son of God." With this was combined his claim that he was the Messiah. But the two were a unit in the case of Jesus; he, the Son of God, was the Messiah. No less a person could be the Messiah. All his miracles (John 10:37-39) attested his Sonship and his Messiahship.

The claim that the question of Caiaphas did not imply that Jesus was "the Son of God" metaphysically in the sense of deity is refuted by the story of the Gospels, in which this is the very point on which the issue between Jesus and the Jewish leaders turns (John 5:18; 10:30, 33; and other passages). If Jesus had claimed a sonship in any other sense, this would not have been regarded as a criminal claim by the Jews, for they all claimed such sonship. Nor can we agree to the thesis that "the Son of God" was equivalent to "Messiah" in the Jewish mind. Modernism claims that "the Son of God" was but a current "Jewish category of thought" for "the Messiah." The term did not involve deity. This was a sense that was later given to it. In this way modernists would eliminate the deity of Jesus from the sacred pages. But the sim-

ple Gospel facts are a decisive answer to it. Caiaphas
himself calls Jesus' claim blasphemy when Jesus declares himself to be the Messiah in the sense of the Son
of God. If Son of God had been equivalent to Messiah,
blasphemy would have been out of the question; Caiaphas could have called Jesus only a fanatic or a lying
pretender.

64) **Jesus says to him: Thou didst say. Nevertheless, I say to you, from now on you shall see the
Son of man sitting at the right hand of the power and
coming on the clouds of the heaven.** Jesus breaks
his silence. Since the truth is demanded of him regarding his office and his person, silence would be a
wrong answer, and so Jesus speaks. By his affirmation Jesus swears that he is, indeed, just what the
adjuration asks, "the Messiah, the Son of God." The
reply of Caiaphas puts the sense of the answer of Jesus
beyond question. The assertion is sometimes made
that Jesus never called himself "the Son of God." Here
he *swears* that he is no less.

As regards πλήν, R. 1187; B.-D. 449, 1 settle the
point that, when it is used as a conjunction, the sense
is always adversative, it is like "nevertheless." Here
the statement thus introduced is not adverse to the one
just made ("Thou hast said") but to this statement
as it was received by Caiaphas and the Sanhedrin.
They consider it blasphemy when Jesus says, σὺ εἶπας;
"nevertheless" they themselves shall see with their own
eyes that what Jesus here swears to is true. Some
think that Jesus here speaks of his Parousia, and that
then, at the end of the world, these Sanhedrists, too,
shall see him enthroned in glory. But ἀπ' ἄρτι, "from
now on," obviates that view. The phrase must modify
ὄψεσθε; it would be rather meaningless as a modifier of
λέγω. "From now on," namely from the time of the
death of Jesus onward, which death the Sanhedrin is
bound to effect and which will usher Jesus into glory,

they, too, shall see his glorification. In the miracles
occurring at the time of his death they shall begin to
see, in his resurrection likewise, and thus onward in
every manifestation of his power, including especially
the destruction of Jerusalem and of the Jewish nation.
But ὄψεσθε does not refer to physical or spiritual seeing
but to experimental perception. It is like the seeing
mentioned in John 1:51, but is without the faith there
indicated.

Jesus calls himself "the Son of man" (see 8:20)
because his glorious enthronement refers to his human
nature joined to the divine. This is, indeed, his great
self-chosen Messianic title which always points to both
of his natures. "The right hand of the power" names
the power instead of the omnipotent God himself; yet
the genitive is not possessive, "the right hand that
belongs to the power"; but appositional, "the right
hand that is the power." To sit at the right hand of
God is to exercise the power of this hand; and this
invariably refers to the human nature of Jesus. This
is the nature that was glorified at the time of the resurrection and ascended visibly to heaven. In deepest
humiliation that nature appeared before the Sanhedrin,
and this body of men could not conceive the thought
that in a little while all this lowliness would give way
to divine glory. Without indicating it, Jesus is using
Ps. 110, the very psalm with which he had silenced the
Pharisees on Tuesday, 22:41, etc. Some displays of
divine power the humble Jesus had made during his
ministry (the last, John 18:4-6; Luke 22:51) ; but these
would be as nothing compared to the everlasting operation of his power through his human nature in glory.

"And coming on the clouds of heaven," together
with "the Son of man," is a reference to Dan. 7:13,
whence also this title is derived by Jesus. "The clouds"
cannot here refer only to the majesty and the greatness
of Jesus; as in the original passage in Daniel, and then

also in Matt. 24:30 and in Rev. 1:7, the clouds symbolize the divine judgment. These Sanhedrists shall soon have their obdurate shell pierced, they shall see Jesus ruling in divine majesty and power and coming to judgment in divine glory. Event after event shall drive this conviction home to their wicked hearts, no matter how they may resist it.

This helps to answer the question that is often asked as to why Jesus added this word regarding his rule and his judgment. He is not threatening these human judges of his with his divine judgment (I Pet. 2:23). On the other hand, this is not a declaration of grace and forgiveness. Jesus adds this statement in order to bring his judges to a realization of just whom they are about to condemn to death. He is defining for them who "the Messiah, the Son of God" is: he whom they themselves will see in his divine power, rule, and majesty. At this supreme moment and before this supreme court of his nation Jesus, put under oath, must make a full and a complete and not merely an abbreviated statement of the full realities concerning his office and his person.

Incidentally we see that Jesus unhesitatingly swears an oath before the constituted governmental authority of his nation. This settles the interpretation of 5:34, and at the same time bars out all oaths that are demanded by self-constituted authorities, whoever these may be. Jesus swears to his own harm. Truth must be uttered though it be turned to our own damage by wicked men.

65) **Then the high priest rent his robes, saying: He blasphemed! What further need have we of witnesses? See, now you heard the blasphemy! What do you think? And they, answering, said, Guilty is he of death!** Caiaphas has exactly what he wants and he makes the most of it. His dramatics are hypocritical and histrionical and are intended to

sweep the whole Sanhedrin along with him over all legal requirements to the one goal on which he knows all are set: the condemning of Jesus to death. Some think that Caiaphas was sincere or at least partly sincere when he seemed shocked by what he regarded as blasphemy. But this Sadducee who deliberately plotted the judicial murder of Jesus was past shock in regard to God or the manner in which men spoke of God. So, instead of submitting the sworn statement of Jesus to the court for its judicial decision as the law required, Caiaphas himself makes that decision. In great excitement he shouts as one who can scarcely believe his own ears, "He blasphemed!" the aorist whereas we prefer the perfect to indicate what has just happened, R. 842. Suiting the action to the word, "he rent his ἱμάτια," Mark says, "his χιτῶνας," in the Jewish fashion to symbolize his outraged feeling. The inner or the outer garments, sometimes both, as seems to have been the case here, were gripped at the neck by both hands and with a jerk a rent about the width of a man's palm was torn down the front and exposed the chest, so that all could see that something terrible had happened.

The assertion that the high priest dared not rend his garment is untenable; Lev. 10:6 and 21:10 forbid this only in connection with the dead; in I Macc. 11:71 we see a high priest rending his clothes. This custom was followed by Greeks, Romans, and barbarians, as well as by Jews. And all Jews were expected to rend their garments upon hearing blasphemy, all except the witnesses. We should not think that the high priest wore his official robes and rent these; these robes the Romans kept locked up and passed out only at the time of the three great festivals, and the high priest wore these robes only on those three occasions. Painters have disregarded this when depicting the passion scenes. To Caiaphas the blasphemy is beyond question, and it is just the thing he wants for his purpose, for the penalty of death had been decreed for this crime, Lev. 24:16, and death was what Caiaphas wanted for Jesus, summary death.

With one sweep he brushes aside the long proceedings that tried to secure false witness: "What need have we of witnesses? See, now you heard the blasphemy!" With this quick turn Caiaphas gets rid of all the ineffectual testimony and inadvertently reveals the hollowness of his previous demand that Jesus make a reply to these witnesses. As far as Caiaphas was concerned, the case is settled right here and now.

66) So he demands a verdict from the Sanhedrin on the instant: "What do you think?" Now according to Jewish legal procedure in capital cases the verdict could be passed only at a second session of the court that was to be held on another day and never on the same day. And this verdict was arrived at in a fixed, formal way: two scribes recorded the votes which had to be written, the one scribe tabulating the votes for acquittal, the other those reading guilty. All these legal safeguards that had been established in the interest of justice are here summarily overthrown. Yet not a single voice is raised in question, to say nothing of protest. The hatred of Jesus that was focused in the passionate demand of Caiaphas animates every judge present. To Matthew's "they, answering, said," Mark adds *"all";* the *viva voce* vote was unanimous. No reflection, no careful consideration was needed. All of that had been attended to when the plot for the judicial murder of Jesus had been definitely planned. Matthew records the verdict itself: "Guilty is he of death!" Mark describes: "They all condemned him to be guilty of death." The criminal deed had been put across.

67) What follows is an outrage that is so beastly and brutal as to seem almost incredible. **Then they did spit into his countenance and they hit him**

**with fists. Some slapped him, saying, Prophesy to us, Christ, who is it that slapped thee?** The San-hedrists, the supreme judges of the nation, in whom all the dignity and the grandness of the nation should be vested, here show their real inner nature: they are rowdies of the lowest kind. The proud Sadducees, the aristocrats of the Sanhedrin and the nation, here re-veal what they really are: low-down rabble of the coars-est type. Once they have shouted their illegal verdict, definitely repudiating all reverence for God and for his laws, they lose even common human decency. They leap to their feet and crowd around the lone, bound prisoner. We now get to see what is in the hearts of these men who pretended to try Jesus.

Matthew reports only their main acts. "They spat into his countenance," any number of them. This is the climax of personal insult. By this they show what they think of "the Son of God" about to sit at the right hand of power and to come on the clouds of heaven. They cannot act vile enough toward him. And now comes the most cowardly brutality: "they strike him with their fists." A man who is wholly unable to de-fend himself — upon him they vent this viciousness just to hurt him as much as possible. They act like savages. Here we combine Mark and Luke with Mat-thew: somebody conceived the idea of mocking the prophetic claims of Jesus. He threw a cloth over Jesus' face so that Jesus could not see; and then slap after slap rained upon Jesus' face, blows of the fist, too, according to Mark.

68) Then they cried derisively, "Prophesy to us, Christ, who is it that did slap thee?" Ribald laughter, no doubt, accompanied this supposed joke regarding this Christ and regarding the idea of his being a pro-phet. But this was not all. The Sanhedrists tired of their abuse of Jesus, and the high priest turned him over to the ὑπηρέται, "the underlings," or police guard,

and Mark reports that they received him with fisticuffs, following the noble pattern of their superiors. How long this went on who will say? The condition of Jesus at the end of this experience can more easily be imagined than described. Here Isa. 50:6, and Jesus' own prophecy, Mark 10:34 and Luke 18:32, in regard to being spitted upon, were fulfilled literally.

69) **Now Peter was sitting outside in the courtyard. And there came to him a certain maid, saying, Thou, too, wast with Jesus of Galilee!** This carries forward the story of Peter begun in v. 58, where Peter was sitting in the courtyard, among the ὑπηρέται or Temple police. He imagined that he could succeed in carrying out his plan, and that no one would pay attention to him. But he was sadly mistaken. From John we learn that it was the very maid who had admitted Peter that exposed him. From the synoptists we supply the details that she left her post at the entry, came over to Peter, fixed her eyes upon him, and then made her startling assertion. This must have happened some time after she had admitted Peter.

But what made her do this? Was she afraid that she had let the wrong man in and did she take this means of making herself safe? If so, then what about John whom she knew much better? The καί in the assertion shows that this maid arrived at the conclusion that Peter must have been a disciple of Jesus ("with Jesus" means this) from the way in which John intervened to have Peter admitted. Yet she makes no issue of John. Was she merely teasing Peter, trying to make him uncomfortable when she saw that he was trying to hide his identity? Her words do not sound like banter. She most likely wanted to make herself important. She wanted these men to know that she knew something they did not know. Here they were talking about Jesus and about what had just taken place and yet did not know that right in their

own midst sat one of Jesus' own disciples. No doubt,
all cocked their ears when she made her assertion.

**70) But he denied in front of them all, saying,
I do not know what thou art saying.** The suddenness of his exposure, its publicity before the crowd
about the fire, the feeling that he was in danger at
once upset Peter and filled him with panic. He saw
no way out except to lie out. The devil loves to pounce
upon the foolhardy and to sweep boasters off their feet.
The words of the denial were scarcely as brief as any
one of the four evangelists records them. Matthew
writes, "I do not know what thou art saying!" to which
Mark adds a second verb; but Luke has, "I know him
not," for which John writes simply, "I am not," i. e.,
one of his disciples.

It took only a menial maid to fell the chief of the
Twelve. Gone were all his high and heroic protesta-
tions to Jesus; gone was the spurious courage from his
heart and from the hand that had snatched out the
sword in Gethsemane. Here stands the arrant coward,
unable to confess his heavenly Lord, cringing with
lying denial. Some think that Peter was frightened
without real cause, that he misjudged the situation and
really should have confessed. But whether it is with
or without cause, fright operates, nevertheless. Peter
was undoubtedly in danger. Surely he would have
been arrested forthwith, taken before Annas, and held
at least for a time; and if his slashing off the ear of
Malchus should have become known, serious punishment might have been the result.

**71) Now another maid saw him after he went
into the entryway and says to those there, This fellow also was with Jesus of Nazareth!** Peter waited
long enough to have attention safely withdrawn from
him and then quietly approached the πυλών, the long
entryway that led out from the courtyard to the street
through the front side of the building. Mark calls it

the προαύλιον, "the vestibule" (M.-M. 537) ; it was not another courtyard in front of the palace.   It is his evident intention to get away unobserved.

The second αὐτόν is the object, to which the accusative participle and another αὐτόν are added.   But this very move precipitates the second and severer denial. Matthew says that "another" (feminine, hence "maid") saw him.   Mark says, "The maid, having seen him, began again to say," etc., which must refer to the maid who exposed Peter in the first place.   Luke writes that after a little ἕτερος, masculine, "another man," saw him. This appears to be a contradiction, but it harmonizes most naturally when we keep the situation in mind. Peter had been exposed, and the matter was being talked about.   On a night like this more than one maid would be on duty at the entry.   Peter meets two maids and a man, all three of whom are certain that he is a disciple of Jesus.   There are also others in the entrance since a large crowd is present.   So Peter is again recognized, and that by three persons, and his case now seems more desperate than it was before.

While these were one after the other addressing, not Peter, but each other and the others that were there, and were saying that "this fellow" (derogatory οὗτος) had been "with Jesus of Nazareth" (the most ordinary way of naming Jesus), Mark says the cock crowed. That marks the time of night as being beyond midnight; for Mark notes this crowing as being a fulfillment of the prophecy of Jesus, Mark 14:30, "before the cock crow twice."   This was the first crowing.   In his excitement Peter never heard it.   This first crowing, too, is not as loud and as continuous as the second.

72) **And again he denied with an oath, I do not know the man!**   Matthew alone mentions the oath with which Peter tried to secure credence for this denial.   He recognized that he would have to offer something stronger than he had offered at the time of

the first denial. He swears that he does not even know Jesus and acts as though he really does not know Jesus' name. Yet these lips had uttered 16:16; John 6:68, 69!

73) Peter promptly gave up the idea of trying to get out through the entryway. Twice he had been positively recognized, and we can imagine the uneasiness and the fear with which he now tried to efface himself in the crowded courtyard. **Now after a little those standing by came forward and said to Peter: Of a truth, thou, too, art one of them! For even thy dialect makes thee evident.** Luke makes the interval "about an hour." The most decisive effort is now made to identify Peter as a disciple of Jesus. Matthew and Mark mention only the fact that some of the men who were standing by and had evidently been discussing Peter came up and again confronted him. Luke makes one of the men the spokesman, and John is able to supply the detail that this was a relative of the Malchus whose ear Peter had cut off. Here, then, was danger indeed.

With great positiveness they say, "Of a truth," i. e., in spite of thy previous denials, "thou art one of them!" So Peter had not succeeded in allaying suspicion regarding himself, he had only strengthened it. And this time the λαλία, "utterance," namely the Galilean brogue with which Peter spoke was brought forward as evidence (γάρ) that Peter was "one of them," for all of them save Judas hailed from Galilee. But John tells us that the relative of Malchus was able to add more to this personal connection and this circumstantial evidence: he is almost certain that he saw Peter in Gethsemane.

74) **Then he began to curse and to swear, I do not know the man. And immediately a cock crowed.** He called down all manner of evil on himself and with oaths called God to witness that he did not know him. In fact, we see that he is ready to resort to anything

to save himself from discovery. Peter was no longer a man of even ordinary manhood; he was a groveling coward who was too pitiful to look upon. Somehow even now Peter was not arrested on suspicion and held for judicial investigation. But immediately after his curses and his oaths "a cock crowed." He began his crowing just before the dense morning dark began to lighten (see v. 34).

75) Nobody paid attention to this crowing of the cock save one man. **And Peter remembered the word of Jesus who had said, Before a cock crows, thrice shalt thou deny me. And having gone out, he sobbed bitterly.** Jesus had spoken that word about the cock's crowing because he foresaw Peter's situation and intended that Peter should recall that word to his great benefit. That cock's crowing thus released the tension of fear, recalled Jesus' love and warning, and thus opened the door to genuine repentance. Luke adds the detail that at this very moment Jesus turned and looked at Peter, and that this led to his repentance. But the cock's crowing and the Lord's look move Peter to the same end. In divine providence all this had been timed so as to effect this gracious result. There is some discussion as to how Jesus could look upon Peter at this moment. The best answer is that the Temple police were leading him from the hall of trial to a place for safekeeping until he should again be wanted. With his face all contused and black and blue from the blows he had received, with spittle still defiling his countenance, Jesus looked upon poor Peter as he passed through the courtyard. No wonder that look went home.

It seems that Peter encountered no difficulty in getting out of the courtyard. Some therefore conclude that he would have had no difficulty at any time. But the maids kept the door locked, and Peter did not risk it to make a demand to be permitted to leave. But the transfer of Jesus changed this situation. The crowd of the ὑπηρέται, Temple police, that had been kept waiting in the courtyard until this time were ordered out, and so Peter could leave without difficulty.

His repentance is stated in two words: ἔκλαυσε πικρῶς, the verb denoting loud, audible weeping, "he sobbed bitterly." The adverb does not refer to the physical sobbing but to the bitterness of the contrition that was back of it. Contrition includes the realization that we have sinned and the consequent genuine sorrow for our sin. The story of Peter has two important features: first, Jesus' prophecies and their fulfillment, which were at first frantically denied; secondly, the foremost of the apostles sins most terribly and is yet restored by true repentance. For all time this calls sinners to the pardon which Jesus has ready for them.

# CHAPTER XXVII

1) Now, when it was morning, all the high priests and the elders of the people passed a resolution against Jesus to put him to death. And having bound him, they led him away and delivered him up to Pilate, the governor. We have already stated the Jewish law regarding capital crimes. It required that the verdict of death should be rendered at a second session of the Sanhedrin which was to be held after an interval of at least a day; moreover, night sessions were illegal. Now the Sanhedrin was determined to rush Jesus to death, for it feared an uprising of the people in case of a delay. So the illegality of the night session was simply disregarded. But the formality of holding a second session was found feasible even though in this case it was illegal because it would confirm an illegal night session; yet it lent a show of legality to the procedure by being a second session. Mark makes it plain that this second, early morning session was attended by the three groups that made up the Sanhedrin and even adds, "the whole Sanhedrin." This was a plenary session although the entire number of seventy-one judges was not required to be present and some probably were absent.

The expression συμβούλιον ἔλαβον does not mean "took counsel" in order to put Jesus to death. It was entirely plain how they must proceed to secure that death: Pilate had to be asked to confirm the death verdict they had pronounced upon Jesus. This case would be similar to others in which the Sanhedrin had decreed death. The Roman government had reserved the right of inflicting the death penalty; the Sanhedrin had lost

that right. It could decree but had to ask the Roman
governor to carry out the execution of the death penalty. The expression means, "to pass a resolution,"
and the resolution that had to be passed in this case
was the confirmation of the death verdict that had been
pronounced at the night session; and Burton (R.
1089) is right: the ὥστε clause states the contents of that resolution, "to put him to death." So in all due formality
the final vote on the death penalty was taken. The
next step followed as a matter of course: the Sanhedrin
had to apply to Pilate. B.-P. 1248 defines συμβούλιον
λαμβάνειν as *consilium capere, einen Beschluss fassen;*
R. 109. Luke 22:66-71 gives us some of the details; it
relates how Jesus was re-examined, how he reaffirmed
that he was the Son of God, and how this was declared
to be sufficient to condemn him.

2) After these formalities had been settled, the
Sanhedrists, with Caiaphas, of course, in the lead, led
Jesus away and in due form delivered him up to Pilate,
the Roman governor.

3) At this point Matthew introduces the account
regarding the end of Judas. **Then Judas who betrayed him, having seen that he was condemned, having repented, returned the thirty pieces of silver to
the high priests and elders, saying, I did sin by betraying innocent blood! But they said: What is
that to us? Thou wilt see to it! And having hurled
the silver into the Sanctuary, he left the place and,
having gone, hanged himself.** On returning from
Gethsemane, Judas must have remained near the high
priest's palace in order to see what would happen.
Matthew's "then" takes us to the moment when the procession formed that was to take Jesus to Pilate. "Then"
Judas saw, saw with his own eyes what had happened,
"that he was condemned," and that they were taking
him to his death. This explains the participle μεταμεληθείς, "having repented." Judas repented of the conse-

quences not of the sin itself.    Already that shows the
spurious nature of his repentance.    Many a criminal is
exceedingly sorry when the consequences of his sin
catch up with him, but the sin itself does not frighten
him.    Matthew calls Judas ὁ παραδιδοὺς αὐτόν and uses the
timeless qualitative present participle.    The betrayer
saw what his betrayal had brought about.

After his conscience had been thus awakened by
remorse, the blood money burns in Judas' hands, and
he attempts to return it.    It is not necessary to think
that this scene took place in the Temple, and that some
of the high priests and elders were busy with duties
there.    No; this scene took place before Caiaphas'
palace.    Here Judas confronts the Sanhedrin itself
and not only one or two of its representatives; for
according to Matthew's usage "the high priests and
elders" indicates the body as such.    In his state of des-
peration Judas offered the thirty pieces of silver to
them in public, and his remorse becomes evident in
the confession, "I did sin, having betrayed innocent
blood!"    His true sin Judas did not realize or confess.
To him Jesus is no more than "innocent blood," a guiltless man who is now being regarded as guilty of death.
Because Judas' betrayal was leading to this result, he is
sorry, he makes confession, and he wants as much
as possible to free himself from these bloody consequences by returning the money to the Sanhedrin.
Note that μεταμεληθείς is the ingressive, "having begun
to repent" (R. 858) ; and παραδούς is constative (R. 859)
and expresses action that is simultaneous with that of
ἥμαρτον (R. 860) and is causal (R. 1128) : "because I
betrayed," etc.

There is no evidence to assume that Judas wanted
to reverse his bargain and that he wanted to repurchase
Jesus from the Sanhedrin.    His return of the silver
was due to psychological reasons.    Since Jesus is being
led to his death, this silver becomes blood money and

thus burns his hands with blood guilt. The money that was at one time greedily grasped becomes intolerable to him. His conscience will not let him keep it; it seeks at least the easement that riddance of this money will bring. From start to finish these were the same thirty pieces of silver, and in themselves underwent no change whatever; and yet they were completely changed: once so attractive, they are now so utterly abhorrent.

4) The Sanhedrists have no desire to waste much time on Judas; besides, they were through with him the moment he had performed his part of the bargain for which he had been paid even in advance (26:15). Their brief answer does not refer to this pitiful sum of money, which they refuse to accept, but to the remorseful confession when they say: "What is that to us? Thou wilt see to it!" Cold, hard as stone are these spiritual leaders of the Jews. A soul in travail means absolutely nothing to them, in fact, not even a soul they themselves have helped to get into this desperate travail. They are busy even now in taking the victim of Judas' sin to be murdered on the cross.

What a fool Judas was to expect relief from such men! But the one who could have helped him he did not find. Oh, he was only a few paces away and could have been found easily enough. But Judas saw in him only a "rabbi" (26:25, 49) and even now only "innocent blood" and not the Messiah and Son of God; and his heart was stirred only by remorse (revulsion because of the consequences of his act) and not by repentance (grief over his sin itself). The expression τί πρὸς ἡμᾶς; has classical support, R. 626; and the future ὄψει (also written ὄψῃ) is volitive and thus equal to an imperative: "see thou to it," R. 874.

5) Remorse now drives Judas to his last desperate acts. He hurls the silver "into the ναός or Sanctuary." Some think that this was the place (they call it the

room) in the Temple where the receptacles for the receipt of money stood in the court of the women. But then ἱερόν would have been the proper word. The term ναός refers to the Sanctuary which included the Holy and the Holy of Holies. Judas went up to the top of the priestly court, took the sack of silver, and flung it into the open entrance of the Holy Place. Then he turned and "went away," to what place is not stated; and, "having gone away," he committed suicide by hanging himself. Acts 1:18 adds the further terrible details. Remorse — suicide: they often go together.

6) The priests saw what Judas had done and promptly picked up the money. Matthew concludes the account at this place, his readers will understand that this happened after Jesus' death. **But the high priests, having taken the pieces of silver, said, It is not lawful to throw them into the treasury since it is blood price. And after passing a resolution they bought with them the field of the potter for burial for strangers. Wherefore that field was called Field of Blood until this day.** The high priests alone act in this case. The silver was, no doubt, brought to them with the request that they state what should be done with it. Perhaps they made a deduction from Deut. 23:18 and declared it to be unlawful (οὐκ ἔξεστι) to deposit this silver in the κορβανᾶς (related to κορβᾶν, Mark 7:11, "gift"), the Temple treasury or treasure which was made up of all the taxes and the votive gifts of the people. The reason stated is that this silver is "blood price." So they, indeed, recognize this silver as what it really is but not as themselves having made it "blood price" by paying it, perhaps out of this very treasury, but as Judas having earned it as a "blood price" by selling Jesus' blood for this sum. Here, indeed, are the fine casuists: it would be a crime to put such money back into the Temple treasure, but it was no crime to pay it to Judas.

7) As in v. 1, συμβούλιον λαβόντες does not mean "to take counsel" but "to resolve" or "to pass a resolution," which resolution was, of course, carried out. This was to devote the money to a long-felt need, namely to provide a burial place "for strangers," certainly not for Gentiles (whom the Jews hated to see in Jerusalem) but for poor Jews who visited the festivals, etc., and happened to die while in the city, or for such as wanted to spend their latter days in the Holy City and thus wanted to die there. It may be true that the authorities had neglected this matter, and that now a way was found to meet this long-delayed need. One thing is certain in regard to the location of this field: it was Levitically pure ground otherwise it would never have been accepted for use as a cemetery. Thus it could not have been located in Tophet, the valley of Hinnom or at some similar place. The site cannot be determined at this date.

The two things that were certain are indicated by the two articles: "the (well-known) field of the (well-known) potter." Perhaps both became so well known after this piece of ground had been bought.

8) The purchase of this field by means of this money gave the place the name "Field of Blood," and Matthew says that the name continued "until today," i. e., when he wrote his Gospel. This is one of the assured indications in the Gospel itself that it was *not* written after the destruction of Jerusalem when the long siege had destroyed the identity of a large number of sites in the city itself. How long before the destruction Matthew wrote is, of course, not indicated by this phrase. In Acts 1:14 a different reason is assigned for calling this field *Chaqual Dᵉma'*, "The Field of Blood," namely the horrible end of Judas. It is difficult to understand why this should be regarded as a discrepancy since both names center in Judas, a man who was guilty of blood and who had a bloody end. It

was the bloody feature that drew and held public attention. The English would use a perfect tense instead of the aorist ἐκλήθη because of the reference to the present in the phrase "until today," R. 848.

9) **Then was fulfilled what was spoken through Jeremiah, the prophet, saying: And they took the thirty pieces of silver, the price of the one that has been priced, whom they of the sons of Israel priced, and they gave them for the field of the potter just as the Lord did appoint to me.** Matthew uses the regular formula to indicate the fulfillment of a prophecy. The fact that τὸ ῥηθὲν διά involves all the essential points of verbal inspiration has been shown in connection with 1:22; and Matthew uses this expression constantly. The fact that Matthew wrote "through Jeremiah, the prophet," has caused a great deal of discussion since not Jeremiah but Zechariah 11:12, 13, records this prophecy. The reading "Jeremiah" is textually confirmed. The exegetes are divided in their interpretations: some think that Matthew was guilty of a lapse of memory, others that this is impossible, but that a solution or explanation must be found. Some find an excuse for Matthew's faulty memory by referring to Jer. 18:2-12; 19:1-15 which speak about a potter; they think that this confused Matthew. But this view destroys the inspiration and the infallibility of the Scripture.

If "Jeremiah" cannot be explained by any information that is available to us today, the exegete should be entirely ready to confess his ignorance and to wait until the explanation has been found. But in this case it has been found by Lightfoot. One of the older ways of dividing the Scriptures was to begin with the law and to call this part "The Law." Next the section commencing with the Psalms was called "The Psalms" although it contained other writings. The third part began with Jeremiah and included all the other pro-

phets, and yet the whole was called "Jeremiah." Lightfoot cites the Baba Bathra and Rabbi David Kimchi's
Preface to the prophet Jeremiah as his authorities.
Horn, *Introduction,* 7th ed. II, 290. Thus any passage
taken from this third section of the Old Testament
would be quoted as coming from "Jeremiah." We
honor the efforts of those who have sought to find the
prophecy in Jeremiah's own book; but after all is said
and done, neither Jer. 18:2-12, nor 19:1-15, nor both
combined, will answer; we must go to Zech. 11: 12, 13.

We cannot in this case expect an exact quotation,
because the prophecy of Zechariah is a symbolic action,
and the fulfillment is ordinary history. So it becomes
Matthew's aim to present the striking correspondence
between the two as this appears in the main points.
Some have the idea that every prophecy must be a
statement that this and that will happen, and that the
fulfillment must then be recorded word for word:
and just exactly so it did happen. That is why we find
so much discussion regarding Matthew's deviation from
the wording of Zechariah. But a verbatim quotation
would not convey what had to be conveyed when this
prophecy is combined with its remarkable fulfillment.

The two points of the symbolic prophecy and its
fulfillment pertain to the thirty pieces of silver as the
price paid for Jesus and to the payment of this sum to
the potter. Delitzsch writes: "The moment we carry
the form of the prophecy back to the idea, the difference is dissolved into harmony." In Zechariah the
payment of thirty pieces of silver was made in order to
get rid of Israel's Shepherd. That same price was
paid to get rid of Jesus who is Israel's Shepherd. At
such a miserable price the Jews valued Jesus and gladly
paid it to get rid of him. All that Zechariah thus
states in regard to this price Matthew restates interpretatively in order to impress upon us this shameful
point: "the thirty pieces of silver the price of the one

that has been priced, whom they of the sons of Israel priced." The emphasis is on this miserable price, and the ἀπό phrase states the subject in the sense of οἱ ἀπό, "they from the sons of Israel," i. e., the Jewish leaders. Here Matthew gives us the substance of what Zechariah states regarding the price, but he combines it with the fulfillment which occurred with the payment of this sum to Judas.

10) The second point is that eventually this sum was paid over to the potter. In the prophecy God does this, in the fulfillment the high priests do it. But this is not a difference, for God so guided the action of the high priests that they made this astonishing disposition of the silver. Even this feature is added that the thing was done "in the house of the Lord." There the money was found, and there the high priests decided to pay it for the potter's field. This Matthew states by again combining prophecy with fulfillment, each interpreting the other: "And they took . . . and gave them for the field of the potter." This money did not lose its identity by being mixed with other money that was in the Temple fund. A special purchase was made with it, and by that purchase it was made to stand out forever by lending its name to the field purchased as "the Field of blood." The final clause, "even as the Lord did appoint unto me," repeats Zech. 11:13: "And the Lord said unto me," which states the order of the Lord regarding what was to be done with the money. It was the Lord's will that directed this disposition of the money, and that will was carried out: by being invested in that field of the potter the money was forever to stand out and apart as the blood money the leaders of Israel paid to get rid of their Messiah forever. Καθά = καθ' ἅ, "just as," "according as."

11) **Now Jesus stood before the governor. And the governor asked him, saying, Thou, art thou the King of the Jews? And Jesus said to him, Thou**

**sayest it.** With exceeding brevity Matthew mentions this incident from Pilate's examination of the prisoner that had been turned over to him for the execution of the death penalty. We must add John 18:20-37, and especially John's fuller version of Matthew's account in v. 37. In order to understand how Pilate came to ask about Jesus' being a king, we must add Luke 23:2, the series of charges against Jesus, the last of which was that he pretended to be "Christ, a King." After hearing these charges, Pilate took Jesus into the Prætorium and examined him privately by taking up the central charge in which all the rest were involved. John shows how the direct question was reached: "Thou, art thou the King of the Jews?" This question shows how little like a king Jesus appeared to Pilate; of course, he was thinking of a political king. Yet Jesus affirms that he is a king: "Thou sayest it." The difference between σὺ λέγεις and σὺ εἶπας, "thou art saying it," and, "thou didst say it" (English, "hast just said it"), is rather slight, R. 915. It is the regular way of affirming the contents of a question; compare 26:25, 64. From John we learn that Jesus told Pilate what kind of a king he was, namely a spiritual and not a political king, and that Pilate was fully convinced of the latter.

12) A second incident is briefly sketched. **And in being accused by the high priests and elders he answered nothing. Then Pilate says to him, Dost thou not hear how many things they are witnessing against thee? And he did not answer him on not even a single utterance so that the governor wondered greatly.** This is the second great silence of Jesus; the first is recorded in 26:63, the third in John 19:9. It must be placed where Matthew and Mark have it, after Pilate's examination of Jesus and his declaration to the Sanhedrin that he was guiltless. Then a flood of vicious accusations of all kinds bursts from the Sanhedrin, "the high priests and elders," one Greek

article; this is the regular title for this body. After Jesus had again been brought out of the Prætorium to face his accusers, he "answered nothing." When the shouting of angry accusations subsided, when all eyes turned on Jesus, he simply looked at the governor who was seated on the judicial seat on the platform before the Prætorium, and since every ear was straining to hear, the silence became only the more intense. Not a word came from Jesus' lips.

13) Pilate breaks the strange silence with the astonished question, "Dost thou not hear how many things they are witnessing against thee?" Yet the situation should not confuse us. It may appear to be fair and strict justice when the accused is permitted to face his accusers and to speak freely in his own defense. But Pilate has himself just pronounced Jesus guiltless after due investigation of the charges that were first preferred. Does that verdict not stand? If Pilate is uncertain after hearing all this added testimony, it is Pilate's business to examine farther into the case just as he made an examination at the beginning of the trial. The silence of Jesus speaks eloquently against Pilate. Why does Pilate by means of his question shift the responsibility upon Jesus? It is the duty of this Roman judge either to silence all these angry accusations or, if he cares to do so, to examine into one or more of them. It is because of his cowardice that he does not forthwith enforce his verdict of innocence by using his legionaries, if necessary, to disperse this Sanhedrin and its following but allows that verdict still to be questioned and turns the task of upholding it over to the prisoner Jesus. Secondly, the silence of Jesus is directed against the Jews and expresses his contempt for their accusations; they are not worthy of a word on his part.

14) Even after Pilate's urgent question had been asked the lips of Jesus remained sealed. Matthew

makes it strong by adding "on not even a single utterance," ῥῆμα, spoken word that came from Jesus' accusers. At least as far as Pilate was concerned, that silence went home. This, indeed, was no ordinary prisoner. Not for one moment did Pilate deem Jesus
guilty because he remained silent. He felt the very
opposite. The astounding patience of Jesus, his willingness to suffer unjustly, and the majesty of his person by following the course he did had made a deep
impression on Pilate. It has been well said that Pilate
was touched by something akin to what we feel when
we see in him the Lamb that opened not his mouth.

15) The vacillation of Pilate which finally brought
Jesus to the cross culminated in Pilate's scheme to
induce the Jews to choose Jesus in place of Barabbas.
**Now festival by festival the governor was accustomed
to release to the multitude one prisoner whom they
wanted. And they had then a notorious prisoner
called Barabbas. Accordingly, having been brought
together, Pilate said to them: Whom do you want
that I release to you? Barabbas? or Jesus, who is
called Christ? For he knew that because of envy
they delivered him up.**

Κατά is distributive (R. 608), hence ἑορτήν needs no
article; yet "festival by festival" refers only to the
annual Passover festival (John 18:39). The pluper-
fect εἰώθει is regularly used in the imperfect sense (R.
888) and is iterative in this case (R. 884). How far
back this custom of setting one prisoner free at the
Passover dates no one knows; yet it seems certain that
it was followed before the Romans came into power
and was continued by them as being so well established
as to be considered a necessity (Luke 23:17). The
people of the Jews were permitted to select the prisoner
they wanted freed (ὃν ἤθελον, iterative imperfect).

16) At this time an especially notorious prisoner
was being held whose name was Barabbas. The εἶχον

refers to the Jews. This was their prisoner, not in the
sense that they confined him in prison, but that he was
one of their race, a Jew. Matthew indicates his evil
character by the use of only the neutral adjective ἐπί-
σημος, "a mark (σῆμα) placed on him." The fact that
this was a most vicious mark we learn from the other
evangelists: Barabbas was a robber who had been
caught in an insurrection in which he had committed
murder. The name "Barabbas" is recorded only for
the purpose of identifying the man whom the Jews
preferred to Jesus. The evangelists do not play with
its composition: "son of Abba," with "Abba" denoting
some prominent rabbi and thus forming a sort of parallel to Jesus' title "Son of God." The textual evidence
for the view that this man was called "Jesus Barabbas"
is so inferior as to require no discussion. Yet some
would retain "Jesus" on the plea that no scribe would
have inserted "Jesus" and that, therefore, it must be
original. But the reverse seems to be true. Those
who desire to allegorize and to play with names and
with words seem to have inserted "Jesus" in order to
obtain: "Jesus, the Son of God," and "Jesus Barabbas
(the son of Abba)." We discard these fancies and the
poor evidence adduced in support of them.

17) From Mark we learn that the people were the
first to think of this custom and perhaps sent a delegation to Pilate to ask that he observe it. They did
this probably because Pilate was available to them at
this time. They certainly selected a favorable moment.
According to Luke 23:16, Pilate had just made the offer
to the Sanhedrin to chastise Jesus and to let him go.
The request of the people opened a new way to Pilate
to release Jesus with Jewish consent, and he embraced
it with avidity. He calls the Sanhedrists together and
submits his proposition. The nomination of the prisoners, one of whom would be pardoned, seems to have
rested with the governor. Whether more than two

were ever nominated seems to be unknown. On this occasion at least Pilate nominates only two in order to make the selection certain in advance. He takes the worst criminal he has in prison at this time, this Barabbas, and as the only alternative he offers "Jesus, who is called Christ," or, as Mark and John write, "the King of the Jews." He is fully certain in his mind that the Jews cannot possibly unite on the selection of Barabbas.

The proposition is announced to the Sanhedrin, but we see that not this body as such but the Sanhedrin together with the people have the right to make the choice. So Jesus is placed beside a murderer, the man whom Pilate declared innocent beside the man whose bloody guilt was beyond doubt. The flagrant injustice to Jesus is glaring: he is treated as a condemned criminal, is placed beside another of the same kind, and the people are to make a choice between the two. Strange to say, Pilate who is guilty of this injustice expects the Sanhedrin and the Jews to make a just choice. Although he is himself fearfully remiss, he expects others to be true to higher ideals.

18) Matthew, like Mark, openly states the reason that moved Pilate to resort to this method to free Jesus. He knew all along (ᾔδει, second past perfect, always used as an imperfect) that the motive of the Sanhedrists in delivering Jesus to him was nothing but pure "envy." The people were flocking to Jesus, and this made the Sanhedrists envious. But we see that Pilate rested his reliance on the people and trusted that these would vote in favor of Jesus in spite of the Sanhedrin. In this as in many other things that occurred in connection with this trial Pilate was sadly mistaken.

19) Matthew alone reports the next incident. **And while he was sitting on the judgment seat, his wife sent to him, saying: Nothing to thee and to that just one! For I did suffer many things today**

**along in a dream because of him.** At this critical
moment when Pilate was about to observe the old custom and had laid the fate of Jesus into the hands of the
Jews themselves; while he was sitting on the βῆμα, the
judge's chair on the raised platform in front of the
Prætorium, about to hear the choice of the Jews and
to make decree accordingly, a strange interruption
occurs. The governor's wife herself is in such distress
of mind that she feels constrained to send a messenger
to Pilate in the midst of his judicial affairs, yea, on
account of these very affairs, because they deal with
Jesus. Since the days of Augustus, Roman magis-
trates were permitted to take their wives along with
them to their posts in the provinces.

The message consists of a most fervent warning:
Μηδὲν σοὶ καὶ τῷ δικαίῳ ἐκείνῳ, "nothing to thee and to that
just one!" i. e., nothing common to you two, nothing
by which you interfere with him. She calls him "that
just one" because she knows that her husband is compelled to deal with Jesus as a judge, and she warns him
by calling Jesus "just." The designation "that just
one" thus explains itself and is the right term in the
right place. This designation is evidently based on her
dream. Whether the messenger reported the dream,
or whether Pilate took time to ask why his wife was
sending this message, we are unable to say. But the
main point was impressed upon him: his wife had suffered (ἔπαθον, aorist, whereas we should prefer the perfect) all kinds of agonies (πολλά) this very day, most
likely before arising from sleep, "along in a dream"
(κατά to denote extent as in 1:20) because of him. The
language is transparent: she suffered on her husband's
account. She most likely dreamed of him as having
Jesus, "that just one," before his judgment seat. In
her dream Jesus appeared wholly guiltless, and the
dream probably suggested that Pilate was on the verge
of condemning this just man. She suffered agony be-

cause she feared that Pilate might do this. Either in her dream or immediately after awakening, when the dream was still very vivid in her mind, the terrible consequences of such an act on her husband's part overwhelmed her. She felt that she must at all hazard stop him from an act such as that.

Tradition names the wife of Pilate, Procla or Claudia Procla, but this tradition has little to support it. Imagination has busied itself with this woman and her dream; but all we have are the facts that Matthew reports. We are safe in adding only so much, that Pilate and his wife knew not a little about Jesus (note v. 18) and discussed him and his position among the Jews, perhaps they had done so the day before or that very night. Tradition makes the wife favorably inclined toward Jesus, if not a kind of proselyte to Judaism; and the Greek Church canonized her. But this is again altogether uncertain. To deduce from her dream that Pilate had sent the Roman cohort to help in the arrest of Jesus is unwarranted; for under those circumstances Jesus would not have been turned over to the Jews but would have been held in the custody of Pilate himself.

The dream has been studied psychologically, but its psychological possibility under the known circumstances cannot be assailed. We may well believe that the dream and the wife's reaction to it were providential. It then becomes a part of the hindrances that God put in Pilate's way in order to deter him from the crime of judicial murder. Judas had been warned, Peter likewise, and Jesus himself warned Pilate in unmistakable language (John 18:36, etc.; 19:8, etc.)

20) **But the high priests and the elders persuaded the multitudes that they ask for Barabbas and destroy Jesus. And the governor, answering, said to them, Whom of the two is your will that I release to you? And they said Barabbas!** Because the high priests and the elders acted separately, each

circulating among the crowds, we have two articles with "high priests" and "elders." The effective aorist ἔπεισαν (R. 835) states that the Sanhedrists actually did persuade the multitudes. In the case of their own ὑπηρέται or following this was easily done. But they seem to have had no difficulty with regard to the many who had come to swell the crowd before the Prætorium. Matthew says, they "persuaded," but Mark uses a stronger term, "they stirred up" or incited the crowd. Just how this was done is not stated. It has been suggested that the Sanhedrists pointed out that Pilate was trying to protect Jesus, and the Jewish opposition to Pilate was thus associated with Jesus. These and similar arguments may have been used. The one thing that was decisive was the fact that "the high priests" and "the elders" wanted Barabbas. The crowd yielded to their authority and thus became stirred up sufficiently to make this strange choice. The ἵνα clause is subfinal (R. 993) and states what the crowds were persuaded to do. The middle of αἰτέω is used in business transactions and hence is in place, R. 805.

21) A sufficient interval must have been allowed the people to permit the assembled crowd to determine upon its choice. The participle ἀποκριθείς is frequently added when one speaks in response to a situation. The time had come to ask what choice the Jews would make. In ἀπὸ τῶν δύο the preposition is partitive. R. 577. In all confidence Pilate asks for the choice, for he thinks that he had certainly made sure the election of Jesus by associating him with Barabbas. With a shock of disillusionment he heard the unanimous shout, "Barabbas!" His scheme to free Jesus in this way had failed completely. He had underestimated the influence and the power of the Sanhedrin; he had counted on others acting with some moral consideration when he himself could not rise to even simple justice.

22) The whole pitiableness of Pilate comes to
view. Throughout he had not acted the judge, determined the case, rendered the verdict, and enforced it
through his legionaries, if necessary. No; he wants
the accusers to offer him a verdict, the very verdict
that nothing in the world could move them to pronounce. All they did was to hold out against him
firmly to the end. All that Pilate did was to yield to
them more and more until he surrendered completely.
**Pilate says to them, What, then, shall I do with Jesus
who is called Christ? They all say, Let him be crucified! But he said, Why, what evil did he do?
And they kept yelling exceedingly, Let him be crucified! Now when Pilate saw that he gained nothing, but rather that a tumult was arising, having
taken water, he washed his hands before the multitudes, saying: Innocent am I of the blood of this
just one! You yourselves shall see to it! And, answering, all the people said, His blood on us and on
our children! Then he released to them Barabbas;
but having scourged Jesus, he delivered him to be
crucified.**

The complete helplessness of Pilate is revealed by
his question to the Jews and to their leaders. Οὖν
refers to the request for Barabbas' release. This will
leave Jesus on Pilate's hands. When he calls Jesus
"Christ" he certainly does not intend to cast a reproach
on Jesus but to arouse a favorable sentiment toward
Jesus among the Jews. Here, too, Mark has "the King
of the Jews," so that we must conclude that both titles
were used. But instead of arousing a favorable feeling Pilate aroused the very opposite. He the governor,
the ruler of the whole country, asks these Jews what he
should do with Jesus! So he did not know what to do?
So he was not in the least sure of himself? Did he
want the Jews to say that he should release Jesus also?

But these Jews who obediently followed their high
priests and their elders in demanding Barabbas instead
of Jesus were the last to be moved by "Christ" and
"King of the Jews."

Pilate had asked what he should do. He certainly
got his answer, and Matthew says it came from "all":
"Let him be crucified!" Probably the Sanhedrists
were the first to shout, σταυρωθήτω, and the whole crowd
of the Jews then joined in this cry. If Pilate did not
know what to do, the Jews knew and told him. The
question has been asked as to how these Jews, whose
death penalty was stoning, came to demand crucifixion
in the case of Jesus. The fact that Barabbas was to
have been crucified, and that Jesus was now to take his
place, seems a doubtful answer. The one satisfactory
answer is that the Jews had turned Jesus over to
Pilate to be executed by him. The Romans had deprived them of the right of inflicting the death penalty,
so they held Pilate to its execution, and he could do
this only by means of crucifixion.

23) The γάρ in Pilate's next question is little more
than an intensive particle, R. 1149; it is like the German *denn* in questions, B.-D. 452, 1. Here we have
the spectacle of the supreme judge trying to convince
the accusers by means of the argument of the innocence
of the accused! For Pilate's question, "Why, what evil
did he do?" intends to tell the Sanhedrists that Jesus
has done no κακόν, "good-for-nothingness," and that they
are unable to prove anything of that kind against him.
But when the judge lowers himself to such a degree, not
he but the accusers will dictate the verdict.

Pilate received the answer he deserved: no more
shouting of accusations (v. 12) but the most frantic
yelling, ἔκραζον, imperfect, continuous: "Let him be
crucified!" The mob spirit was beginning to rise, and
it is a terrible thing in the East. The more they yelled,
the more agitated and wild the scene became. Even

now one word on the part of Pilate could have gained
control: a sharp military order to the cohort of 600
legionaries to clear the place of Jews in short order and
to protect Jesus from molestation. But such a courageous and just act was beyond Pilate's ability. His very
vacillation encouraged the Jewish insistence that he
bow to their will. In that loud yelling and the threatening tone it began to assume we see where the mastery really lies.

24) The complete surrender follows. Pilate finally
saw that he had gained nothing, but rather that a
tumult was arising; in other words, he saw that he had
lost out completely. Both ὠφελεῖ and γίνεται are present
tenses that are retained from the original thought in
the Greek: "He sees that he gains nothing," etc. After
the past verb "saw" the English requires a past tense.
Even now Pilate is not honest; he tries to shift the guilt
of his condemning an innocent man to the most horrible
death from his own soul to that of the Jews.

The symbolical act of washing the hands in water
in order to make the impression that they are clean of
blood, is scarcely of pagan origin although there are
points of contact in the few examples adduced. Among
pagans such washings were performed after the murder and would not be followed by a judge. We may go
back to Deut. 21:6 for the beginning of this act; and
then we may add Ps. 26:6; 73:13; II Sam. 3:28; the
apocryphal Susanna v. 46; also Acts 20:26. When
Pilate became supreme judge of the Jews he also became acquainted with this Jewish symbolical act; and
this their own custom he now uses with great impressiveness before these Jews. The middle ἀπενίψατο means,
"he himself washed his hands," R. 810, and ἀπέναντι
means "right in the presence of" the multitude so that
all might see and understand.

The word ἀθῷος (see v. 4) means "without penalty,"
"innocent." Here Pilate finally pronounces a judg-

ment, but alas, it is not a just judgment on Jesus but a
judgment on himself, and even then it is unjust, a verdict that cannot stand when it is compared with the evidence. No man can pronounce a verdict on himself,
for then every criminal would be acquitted on the
instant. Pilate is a judge, indeed, but he cannot pronounce judgment on himself; he is under a higher
judge, under God himself who will render the verdict
regarding his guilt.

Here Jesus is again called "this just one" (the more
assured reading over against "this one"), and the designation used by Pilate's wife in v. 19 is repeated. If
Jesus is, indeed, "just," δίκαιος, one who has God's verdict in his favor, how can Pilate or any other man
remand him to death as being unjust, yea as being a
wicked criminal, and yet hope to be regarded innocent
in the court of God?

Now Pilate refers the guilt to the Jews: "You
yourselves shall see to it!" It is the same word the
Sanhedrists had hurled at Judas (v. 4); it now comes
back to them. The future ὄφεσθε is again volitive with
an imperative tone. This time Pilate spoke the truth.
Since that day the Jews have seen to it as their present
condition very plainly shows.

25) Something demoniacal possesses these Jews.
As far as the blood with which Pilate dreads to stain
his hands is concerned — these Jews make light of it.
They offer to take it completely off the governor's hands
and to load it upon themselves. That implies that they
assume all the guilt, that they make themselves liable
for any punishment that may follow, that they will face
God's justice and will suffer his wrath. And to this
sacrilegious declaration they add even their children,
all future generations of Jews. Why did these Jews
have to challenge God's justice in so horrible a way?
Why did they not keep still and let Pilate indulge in his
little performance with the water? Was the devil rid-

ing them so completely that they cared not what damnation they called down on themselves?

This prophetic word has been confirmed. The curse the Jews so gayly and so unanimously (note πᾶς ὁ λαός) took upon themselves that morning has turned out to be a curse indeed. They are now a separate people, are scattered over the whole earth, they have no country, no government, no entity and are a disturbing element among the nations. Even this fact shows that Jesus' blood is still upon them. *Die Selbstverwuenschung traf mit dem Ratschlusse der goettlichen Vergeltung zusammen und ward zur unwillkuerlichen Prophetie.* Meyer. God is not mocked. The idea that the blood of Christ brings only pardon is true indeed, but this pardon is intended only for the penitent and not for those who trample on that blood, Heb. 10:29. If the blood of Abel cursed impenitent Cain, the blood of Christ must far more curse those who shed it and their children who still consent to that shedding by spurning Christ.

26) All the synoptists report that Pilate released Barabbas to the Jews but delivered Jesus to be crucified. Matthew and Mark insert the detail that Pilate scourged Jesus. But this compactness of writing merely summarizes, and we must remember that these statements are merely three facts which occurred in that order. We see this in connection with v. 27-31, which Matthew and Mark narrate by itself; but the mockery did not occur after Jesus had been ordered to be crucified. It would have been senseless at that time. The scourging and the mockery belong together, and it is John who furnishes the key to both. The proof that has been adduced to show that scourging preceded crucifixion is, therefore, beside the mark. Pilate's object in scourging (and in mocking) Jesus was the very opposite, he wanted to free Jesus from the cross.

When Pilate's scheme with regard to Barabbas failed, he did not give up. From Luke 23:16 we learn that at the beginning of the trial he had offered the compromise to scourge Jesus and to let him go. He now reverts to this idea and has Jesus scourged. Matthew and Mark use only the one word φραγελλώσας, "having scourged" Jesus, the Latin *flagellare;* John has the regular Greek term μαστιγοῦν. Stripped of clothes, the body was bent forward across a low pillar and the back was stretched and exposed to the blows. In order to hold the body in position the victim's hands must have been tied to rings in the floor or in front at the base of the pillar and his feet to rings behind. We cannot agree that the hands were tied behind the back, for this would place them across the small of the back where some of the blows were to fall and would shield the ribs where the whipends were to lacerate the flesh.

The Romans did not use rods as the Jews did, each rod making only one stripe and cutting only the back; they used short-handled whips, each provided with several leather lashes and ugly, acorn-shaped pieces of lead or lumps of bone that were fastened to the end of each short lash. The strokes were laid on with full force, the officer often shouting, *Adde virgas!* (Livy, 26, 16), or.*Firme!* (Suetonius, Caligula, 26), in order to get more vigor into the action. Two whips were applied, one from each side. The effect was horrible. The skin and the flesh were gashed to the very bone in every direction, and where the armed ends of the lashes struck, deep bloody holes were torn. See Josepus, *Wars,* 6, 6, 3; Eusebius 4, 15.

The scourging of Jesus must have taken place outside of the Prætorium, before the eyes of Pilate and of the assembled Jews; for both Matthew and Mark report that for the purpose of mockery, which, according to John, at once followed the scourging and really formed its completion, the soldiers took Jesus into the Prætor-

ium, into the αὐλή or courtyard where the whole cohort
found room. To the scourging we may attribute the
fact that Jesus broke down under the weight of the
cross and died long before the usual time when those
who had been crucified passed out of life. The object
Pilate had in mind in scourging (and also in mocking)
Jesus was to show these Jews what this insignificant
man really was about whom they were making such a
violent demonstration: a joke of a king; let them look
for themselves. Crucify him? act as though this harmless, helpless dreamer amounted to so much? The very
idea was ridiculous. But this attempt on the part of
Pilate to have the Jews content themselves with less
than the actual death of Jesus also failed, and Matthew
and Mark thus at once add that Pilate ordered Jesus
to be crucified.

27) Matthew and Mark narrate the mockery as a
separate event. John 19:1-16 gives us the details in
order, and shows how the scourging and the mockery
occurred simultaneously in order to make a pitiful and
a ridiculous figure of Jesus. This was Pilate's last
effort to save Jesus' life. When that failed, John tells
us, then and not until then, did Pilate order the crucifixion. **Then the soldiers of the governor, having
taken Jesus into the Praetorium, gathered together
to him the entire cohort. And having stripped him,
they threw around him a scarlet cloak. And having plaited a crown of thorns, they put it upon his
head and a reed in his right hand.** Τότε indicates
only the general time and not the sequence after the
delivery to crucifixion. This is clear from John's account. This mockery followed and completed the
scourging. This answers the question as to how an
act such as this mockery of Jesus could be staged.

This mockery did not customarily accompany the
scourging. The mockery of Jesus was so exceptional
that nothing resembling it has ever been found. Those

who suppose that Jesus was scourged as one who had already been condemned to the cross think that the mockery was staged merely to fill in the time until the cross and the other paraphernalia needed for the execution had been made ready. But even then, why fill in the time with this peculiar type of mockery? If Jesus was scourged only in preparation for crucifixion, this mockery remains unexplained. Those who note that Jesus had not as yet been condemned to the cross regard the mockery as an inspiration that came to the soldiers who guarded Jesus. It is then supposed that Pilate gave his silent consent and paid no attention to the noise going on in the Prætorium. These are unsatisfactory explanations.

"The soldiers of the governor," who were guarding Jesus under the governor's orders, "having taken Jesus into the Prætorium" implies that they took Jesus there on an order from Pilate. They could not and did not move this prisoner about on their own initiative. John 19:4 shows that Pilate himself was in the Prætorium while Jesus was being mocked, for it is he who comes out after the mockery with Jesus, who had been dressed as a mock king. This was a stage play that Pilate engaged in with regard to Jesus in order, if possible, to save his life from the cross. He argued: "Who would insist on crucifying such a pitiful travesty of a king?"

On Pilate's order the whole cohort was assembled in the courtyard. A σπεῖρα, *manipulus*, is the tenth part of a legion, 600 men, with auxiliary troops running up to 1,000, so that the commander was called a chiliarch. Such a cohort was the force that Pilate had with him at Jerusalem, it was the garrison of Antonia. The idea is not that the entire cohort was present to a man, but that as many as were not detained otherwise could and did come. The court was thus thronged with legionaries. Pilate's orders were to show the Jews what sort of a king their Jesus was.

**28)** Either reading, ἐκδύσαντες, or ἐνδύσαντες, leaves us with a problem, and the textual authority for either is almost equal. "They, having stripped him," reads as though Jesus was stripped in the Prætorium. Had he been clothed while he was outside, and were his clothes again taken off him when he was led into the Prætorium after the scourging? "Having stripped him" may refer to the stripping that took place in the court.

The other reading would seem to indicate that in the Prætorium the soldiers clothed Jesus with his own clothes, some say with only the tunic, leaving off his outer robe. But what soldier would have carried Jesus' clothes into the Prætorium? or had Jesus been ordered to carry them himself?

In order to dress Jesus as a king they bring out an old, worn soldier's cloak and throw that around Jesus' shoulders. Imagine how the rough, soiled cloth made the bloody wounds on Jesus' back shoot with pain. John calls the χλαμύς or "soldier's cloak" a ἱμάτιον, an outer garment. Matthew says that its color was scarlet, John says that it was purple; but the color could not have been very distinct, for the *sagum* or *paludamentum* was old, worn, soiled, and faded with age. This scarlet cloak was to take the place of the royal purple mantel that was worn by kings and thus was intended to enrobe Jesus as a king.

**29)** But other means are at hand to lend a royal touch to the proceedings. They plait a crown of ἄκανθαι, twigs that were full of thorns, and set that, bristling with thorns, on Jesus' head. A crown suggested itself naturally for a king. On some coins emperors were pictured with a laurel wreath. The problem as to how to improvise the right kind of a mock crown for Jesus was probably solved by the thorny bush that grew in the courtyard. What plant this was no one knows. The purpose was fully met. It made this king ridicu-

lous and did it in a cruel way. Everybody would recognize the circlet as a crown. And what a bloody
crown it was! Trickles of blood disfigured the contused face of Jesus. He did not appear in the artistic
elegance of so many of our great painters but in the
stark hideousness of brutal reality.

To the royal robe and the crown a royal scepter
lends the final touch. This was a reed that had been
found somewhere and had been thrust into Jesus' right
hand. The king is dressed for his part, now follows
the mock adoration with its further brutalities. **And
having kneeled before him, they continued to mock
him, saying, Hail, the King of the Jews!** The soldiers thus acclaimed Jesus as the King of the Jews.
On χαίρειν as used in greetings see the word spoken by
Judas in 26:48; and note the imperfect (durative)
ἐνέπαιζον. The article is frequently used with the vocative, which then sometimes has the nominative form.
The cutting sarcasm of this adoration was intended to
humiliate the soul of Jesus as much as possible. Jesus
was in reality not only the King of his nation but the
very King of kings, God's own Son! The mind stag-
gers before the scene here depicted.

30) **And having spit on him, they took the reed
and kept beating on his head. And when they
finished mocking him they took off him the cloak
and put on him his clothes and led him away to crucify him.** This spitting upon Jesus (see 26:67) is
the most disgusting insult human beings can offer anyone. It intends to show what these pagan soldiers
really thought of Jesus; he was a king fit only to be
spit upon. So with the scepter of his kingly authority
they showered blows upon the thorn-crowned head of
Jesus. The fact that the thorns were driven more
deeply into the head and that the blows themselves
inflicted torturing pain was only incidental. The real
point of this continuous striking of the king's head with

the king's own scepter was to demonstrate to this king
that his authority was less than nothing. Any man
could take this scepter and knock this king in the head
with it, and what could he do? John 19:3 adds the
detail that they also gave him blows with their hands,
slapped him soundly right and left. How long this
went on none of the evangelists intimates. Pilate
finally intervened with an order and, as John reports in
full, took Jesus out with him and presented him to the
Jewish crowd outside the Prætorium, and we know
with what result.

31) It was after this vain spectacular effort on the
part of Pilate to save Jesus from death, that he was at
last remanded to the cross. Matthew has stated this
fact already in v. 26. So he adds that, after the soldiers were through with their mockery, Jesus was led
away to be crucified. The aorist ἐνέπαιξαν stresses the
completion, "when they finished mocking him"; R. 840
shows that we should use the past perfect in such a
connection. The fact that Jesus was naked during the
mockery, save for the red cloak, appears from what is
now said: that robe was removed in front of the Prætorium, and the ἱμάτια (note the plural), the clothes of
Jesus which had been left-lying there since their removal for the scourging were again put upon Jesus for
the journey to the cross. Verbs of clothing have two
accusatives, one of the person and the other of the
clothes, R. 483.

32) **Now, while going out, they found a man, a
Cyrenean, by name Simon. Him they impressed to
bear the cross.** Immediately after the sentence had
been pronounced Jesus was led to the place of execution. There was no law that required a delay. In the
provinces no such law existed. The imperial laws on
this point applied only to Roman citizens. Matthew
summarizes a good deal with the one present participle
ἐξερχόμενοι: the procession is formed, Jesus bears his

cross and is passing through one of the gates of the walled city. All this lies in the "they going out." This must be "going out of the city," for the procession (think of the Jews in it) never went out of the Præ-torium.

Executions always took place outside of the city, this was true with regard to the Jews (Num. 15:25; Acts 7:58; Heb. 13:12) as well as the Romans. The prisoners were generally led through the most populous streets; and the place of execution would be near a highway where many people would congregate. The traditional *via dolorosa* which is now shown in Jerusalem as the street over which Jesus passed is of late construction; the city was completely destroyed several times, and even many of its levels were greatly changed; in some places the declivities were filled with debris so that some of the present streets are sixty to eighty feet above the original levels.

Matthew only implies that Jesus bore his cross and that for some reason another man had to be provided to relieve him of this burden. Mark and Luke write in the same way. We are certainly right in thinking that Jesus broke down under the load, broke down so completely that even his executioners saw that no blows and cursings of theirs could make him stagger on. The effect of all the abuse heaped on Jesus since his arrest became apparent. The cross was not a light load. Much has been written regarding its shape, as to whether it was an X or a T or had a crossbeam, †, and whether the beams were fastened together before the procession started. All the evidence points to that form of the cross which the church everywhere accepts, but it is often pictured as being entirely too high. Jesus bore this cross and not merely the crosspiece or *patibulum*, John 19:17. By literally bearing his cross Jesus lends a powerful effect to his figurative words

about our taking up our cross and bearing it after him,
10:38; 16:24.

The evangelists offer little to describe Simon. He
hailed from Cyrene but was now a resident of Jerusalem, was one of the many Cyrenians dwelling there
(Acts 2:10). Mark names his sons who, it is agreed,
later on held prominent positions in the church. From
these data the conclusion is drawn that this strange
contact with Jesus led to Simon's conversion and thus
to the prominence of his sons in the church. Mark and
Luke know that he had been out in the country that
morning and was just coming into the city at this hour.
No Jew would, of course, work in the field on this festival day and to assume this in the case of Simon is
unwarranted. The executioners of Jesus seized this
Jew and forced him to carry Jesus' cross. They pounced
on the first man that came along, perhaps caught Simon
right at the city gate, where he could not flee. No
Jew would willingly touch a cross because he regarded
it as accursed. No Roman soldier would disgrace himself by carrying a cross for a criminal. So the soldiers
caught a Jew and probably thought it a good joke on
this unsuspecting Jew that he had to carry another
Jew's cross. On the interesting Persian word ἀγγα-
ρεύω see 5:41; and ἵνα is merely a substitute for the
infinitive, R. 993.

33) **And having come to a place called Golgotha, which is to say, Skull's Place, they gave him
to drink wine having been mixed with gall. And
having tasted it, he was not willing to drink.** By
means of the participle ἐλθόντες Matthew places us on
Golgotha, which Aramaic name he translates into
Greek: Κρανίον, or Κρανίου τόπος, in English, Cranium
or Cranium Place. It was evidently so called because
the hill had the shape of a cranium, the round top
of a skull. There is some dispute in regard to the

site, but it has been certain for a long time that the
site now shown in Jerusalem in the Church of the Holy
Sepulcher is spurious. Far more acceptable is the
skull like hill outside the walls which is now a Mohammedan cemetery, a hill rising above the recently discovered "Garden Tomb" (also called "Gorden's Tomb"
after its discoverer). This place bears many marks
of being the place of both the crucifixion and the
entombment in the garden which is beneath and away
from the hill.

34) Regarding the actual crucifixion Matthew
and Mark report only the offer of doped wine which
Jesus refused. Matthew calls it wine mixed with χολή.
This was not actual gall, but the drink was so called
because of its bitter taste. Mark reports that the
drink was  wine mixed with myrrh, and this tells us
what the bitter substance was. Myrrh was added to
the wine in order to give it a stupefying effect. This
was not an evidense of mercy on the part of the executioners; it was quite the opposite, for it was intended
to make their labor of crucifying easier. A man who
had been heavily doped with this drink could be easily
handled. After one taste of this Jesus refused to
drink more of this stupefying drink, and the imperfect
ἤθελε reads as though he was repeatedly urged to drink
and as repeatedly refused. He intended to go through
the final ordeal with a perfectly clear mind; he intended
to endure all without avoiding a single agony. After
a generous drink of this wine Jesus could not have
spoken as he did and made his death what it was.

35) **And having crucified him, they apportioned
his garments by casting lot.** Among the astounding
features of the Scripture are the records of the
supreme events: one word to describe the scourging
of God's Son, one word to state his crucifixion, one
word to record his resurrection. Events so tremendous, words so restrained! Who guided these

writers to write in such an astonishing manner? This
is one of the plain marks of divine inspiration. Matthew uses only a participle, σταυρώσαντες, "having crucified him," as though this were the minor action and
the dividing of the clothes the major action. It is the
evident intention of all the evangelists *not* to describe
the awful act of crucifixion. The fact, not the details,
is to occupy the reader's mind.

From the mass of evidence that has been collected
we gather that, first of all, the cross was firmly planted
in the ground. Only by way of exception were the
crosses high. That on which Jesus was crucified
raised his feet no more than a yard above the ground,
for the short stalk of hyssop was able to reach Jesus'
mouth. A block or a heavy peg was fastened to the
beam, and on this the victim sat straddle. The victim
either climbed up himself, assisted, perhaps, by the
executioners, or he was lifted to the seat, and his body,
arms, and legs were tied with ropes. Then the great
nails (of which the ancient writers speak especially)
were driven through the hands and the feet.

A hundred years ago nearly everybody was certain that the feet of Jesus were not nailed to the cross
in spite of Luke 24:39, "Behold my hands and my
feet!" Exhaustive investigation has convinced all
who have seen the evidence that also the feet were
nailed, and each foot with a separate nail. The central seat or peg kept the body from settling to one
side after the ropes had been removed. None of the
older writers mentions a loincloth. The agony of crucifixion need not be described; we mention only the
hot sun, the raging thirst, the delay of death which
sometimes did not occur until after four days of linger-
ing torture. It was a great relief for the malefactor
to learn that he was to die on that very day.

John gives a detailed account of the division of
Jesus' garments (19:23, 24). Matthew states only

that this customary division was made, and that in this case it was done "by casting lot." How this was done is not indicated. A common way was to place lots in a helmet and to shake them until one was thrown out; another way was to reach into the helmet and to draw a lot. If the former way was used, one man would be designated, and the first lot that was thrown out would be his, the lot being marked for a certain portion of the four divisions that had been arranged; John tells us that there were four divisions. For the valuable tunic of Jesus three lots would be blank, and the other would be marked to win. The clothes of the victim were the perquisites of the executioners, the victim being regarded as one who was already dead. The soldiers were great gamblers. The fact that they gambled for the clothes of Jesus was nothing exceptional. The soldiers who crucified the two malefactors probably did the same.

The textual evidence is strongly against the addition of the reference to the fulfillment of Ps. 22:19 to Matthew's account. This seems to have been introduced from John 19:24, where it is genuine.

**36) And sitting down, they continued to guard him there.** This implies that the bloody work had been completed. All that remained to be done was to guard the cross against interference. In addition to the four executioners this guard included a detachment of Roman soldiers under a centurion that would be strong enough to cope with any situation that might arise.

**37) And they put above his head his indictment, having been written, This is Jesus, the King of the Jews. Then they crucify with him two robbers, one on the right, and one on the left.** Verse 36 shows that the work had been completed and that the soldiers were sitting and guarding Jesus. But Matthew narrates two other events that had occurred be-

fore the soldiers rested: the placing of the superscription and the crucifixion of the malefactors. John
tells us the full story of the superscription: that Pilate
wrote this title, placed it on the cross, and refused to
alter it at the bidding of the Jews. Matthew writes
that here on Golgotha the inscription was put above
the head of Jesus. This answers the view that it was
fastened to the cross when the procession left the Prætorium. "Having been written" means, of course, at
the Prætorium and by Pilate's order. It is possible
that the inscription was an afterthought of Pilate's
and that it was delivered to the centurion on Golgotha by a messenger; but it is more probable that
the inscription was at once delivered to the centurion,
not for the purpose of display on the way out to Calvary, but to be affixed to the cross at the time of the
execution.

Matthew reports only that such a superscription
was attached to the cross, but he calls it the αἰτία, the
charge or "indictment" against Jesus. The crime committed by Jesus, then, was the fact that he was "the
King of the Jews." From the start Pilate picked out
this charge as being the central one among all that
the Jews preferred. But throughout the trial before
Pilate, Jesus appears as "the King of the Jews" whom
the Jews most violently disown. They finally declare
that they have no king save Cæsar. And thus they
forced Pilate to condemn Jesus as "the King of the
Jews." To the very last the Jews had hurled at Pilate:
"King, King!" which he knew was false and which he
knew they knew was false. So Pilate has his revenge
on these Jews. They shall have Jesus on the cross,
but only as a king, only as *their* king. Let all the
world read: "The King of the Jews"! By adding
nothing further Pilate really proclaims the innocence
of Jesus even here on the cross. Pilate sets it down
as a simple fact that Jesus is, indeed, the King of

the Jews. Jesus had fully explained what kind of a king he was. So this accusation was at the same time a vindication.

38) The second act that Matthew narrates is the crucifixion of two robbers, one on Jesus' right, and the other on his left. The present tense σταυροῦνται, "they do crucify," draws our attention to this unexpected spectacle, for Matthew has hitherto said nothing about these robbers. Matthew lets us draw our own conclusions, yet he aids us when he writes, "with him," and especially when he notes, "one on the right, and one on the left." The Greek idiom ἐκ views the two sides, right and left, as projecting "out from" Jesus. Being crucified between robbers, he was certainly numbered with the transgressors, Isa. 53:12. This is Pilate's estimate of this King of the Jews. Why these two robbers were ordered to be crucified with Jesus we do not know. But we surmise that it was done in order to insult the Jews and to degrade their king even in his crucifixion. The two robbers were to cast shame on Jesus and thus on the Jews. It is not necessary to discuss the placing of one robber on each side of Jesus; this was done automatically. Since there was one important victim who was even distinguished by a superscription, the two unimportant victims would be so placed that the main criminal would occupy the central place.

39) **And those passing by kept blaspheming him, shaking their heads and saying: Thou that destroyest the Sanctuary and buildest it in three days, save thyself! If thou art God's Son, come down from the cross! In the same way also the high priests, mocking together with the scribes and elders, kept saying: Others he saved, himself he cannot save. He is King of Israel — let him come down now from the cross, and we will believe in him. He has trusted in God — let him now rescue him if**

**he wants him. For he said, I am God's Son.** We
see who "those passing by" were when we listen to
what they say. These are Jews of the city, for they
repeat the very things that were said during the night
session of the Sanhedrin. What was brought as
evidence against Jesus by the last two witnesses was
this very matter of destroying and building the Sanctuary (26:61) ; and what was used to condemn Jesus
was his own declaration that he was the Son of God
(26:63-66). People who came from a distance could
not have used these words when blaspheming Jesus;
this could be done only by people of the city who had
heard of the whys and the wherefores of Jesus' trial
and condemnation.

Matthew and Mark call the words these people
spoke to Jesus blasphemy, which means to speak
against God or anything pertaining to God in anger
or in derision. Here God was being mocked in the
person of his own Son. The shaking of their heads
has been regarded as a gesture of indignation, of
malignant joy, of derision, and of mockery, or of these
together. But this is putting a good deal into this
simple gesture. To shake the head means "no." Each
situation modifies this *no*, but the negation remains
in the gesture. So these people shake their heads in
order to express their negation and complete disapproval of the statements they attribute to Jesus, that
about destroying and building the Sanctuary, and that
about his being the Son of God.

40) Note the deductions implied in the two mocking statements. If Jesus can do so tremendous a
thing as to replace the great Sanctuary (Holy and
Holy of Holies) in three days, then he ought to be
able to save himself from his present predicament.
But it is evident that he cannot do this. So he was
the one that talked so big and is now able to do nothing for himself!

This mockery was the worse because of the grave misunderstanding of the words of Jesus on which it rested (John 2:19). What Jesus had said was that, if the Jews continued their course of rejecting the Messiah, God's true Sanctuary among his people, they would thus destroy their own Sanctuary, this symbol of the Messiah, which, of course, could not remain after the Messiah had been rejected. Then, Jesus said, he would raise up the Sanctuary, the true one, himself, from the death in the tomb, that death by which the Jews destroyed their own Sanctuary, yea, their own nation. That time was at hand now. And these mockers attended to it that what Jesus had three years ago prophesied concerning the Sanctuary should now not be forgotten at the start of its fulfillment: Articulated participles are often used in address (R. 1107) and in the Greek need no added σύ. They are almost like nouns: "the destroyer," "the builder," for the tense is quite timeless.

The same deduction is repeated: it should be as nothing for the Son of God to come down from the cross right there before everybody, not in the least hurt or harmed by what had been done to him. But, of course, Jesus could not do this. Fine Son of God he was! Those who deny the deity of Jesus point to the absence of the article before υἱός and state that this expression means no more than *ein Liebling Gottes*. But this is unwarranted. For it is the intention of these people to repeat 26:63, 64, where the article is absolutely definite. Besides, the article is not needed where only one object or person of a class exists; and the Jews knew about only one Father and consequently only one Son and, we may add, only one Spirit. The Jews of Jesus' day were not Unitarians as the Jews of today are. In their opposition to Jesus they never denied that God has a Son who is equal with himself but denied only that Jesus could be that Son.

41) In this third great mockery to which Jesus
was subjected also the Sanhedrin as such took part;
and ὁμοίως indicates that they descended to the same
low level. Matthew puts this fact beyond doubt when
he departs from his usual way of naming only two
groups and here names all three: "the high priests,
together with the scribes (so far not named in the
passion history) and elders." The implication is not
that only a few of the Sanhedrists persisted to the
end and that the rest were detained by duties at the
Temple, and the like. No; so fascinated were they
that as many as possible remained, the bulk of their
body at least. Even here in public these men throw
their dignity to the winds, forget who they are, and,
like the common herd, give way to their basest passions. What they are capable of in this respect 26:67,
68 has fully shown. They cannot now spit on him
and strike him but they can certainly wound him with
their cowardly and insulting tongues. The chief con-
tribution of these men to the mockery is, "Others he
saved, himself he cannot save!" Again a deduction
is involved. This is not a frank admission that Jesus
"did save others"; it is a denial that he actually saved
others. And this denial is based on Jesus' being unable to save himself. All his miracles in helping others
are here derided. They must be spurious since he cannot now help himself.

The evidence that this interpretation is correct we
have in the second slander. Here again we have the
direct statement: "King of Israel is he!" But again
it is said only in mockery. The opposite is intended.
This denial rests on Jesus' inability to do what his
mockers demand, namely to come down from the cross.
So they tell this pseudo-King: "Let him come down
now from the cross, and we will believe' him!" This
faith would be worthless because it would be based
on sight alone. It would also in an instant turn and

doubt what it had seen. This whole mockery reveals the mind of these Sanhedrists, their conceptions of what their Messiah-King should be, and of what is due him on their part.

All the derisions beneath the cross turn on the power of Jesus: his power to replace the Sanctuary, and his power as the Son of God to step down from the cross; again, his power to save others, and his power as Israel's King to leave the cross. That power is mocked as being nothing but sham and pretense because Jesus does not use it in his own behalf. But the mockery is silly on the basis of its own deduction. If Jesus would care to use this power of his, why should he have waited until this time to exercise it? Would he not have saved himself from the very start? These mockers think only of power that is, first of all, used in self-interest. Of grace and mercy that care only for others at the complete expense of self they know nothing. And so their mockery exposes only themselves.

43) Another deduction the Sanhedrists make from the Sonship of Jesus. If he is God's Son he naturally trusts God with a Son's trust. "Very well," the Sanhedrists shout aloud, "he has trusted on God — let him rescue him now if he wants him!" The fact that this is a reference to his Sonship is explained by the γάρ clause: "For he said, I am God's Son." So Jesus is told that God himself disowns him, God will not have him. The proof is again ocular: God does not intervene with a miracle to rescue this Son from death by crucifixion.

44) To the Jewish mockery another is added. **Moreover, the robbers that were crucified reproached him with the same thing.** The hearing about saving others and the coming down from the cross deeply affected these robbers in their excruciating pain. So they, too, shouted to Jesus to save himself and also them; and when he made no response,

they, too, mocked his inability. Οἱ λῃσταί plainly refers
to both robbers, R. 409, and a grammatical explanation
that regards this as a plural of the category is without warrant. While at first both reproached Jesus,
before so very long one of these robbers came to repentance, cf., Luke's account. Luke also informs us
that the Roman soldiers joined in reviling Jesus. The
chorus was thus rather unanimous. There is no discrepancy between Luke's account and that of the rest.
Considering all that had transpired here on Golgotha,
even psychologically a complete turn to repentance
is perfectly in line. But aside from any explanations
one may venture to give the facts as recorded by the
evangelists remain certain.

45) **Now from the sixth hour a darkness came
on all the earth until the ninth hour. And about
the ninth hour Jesus shouted with a great voice,
saying, Eli, Eli, lama sabachthani? that is: My God,
my God, for what purpose didst thou forsake me?
But some of those standing there, when they heard,
were saying, This fellow calls Elijah! And immediately one of them, having run and having taken
and filled a sponge with sour wine and having put
it around a reed, was giving him a drink. But the
rest were saying, Let us see whether Elijah comes to
save him!**

The first great sign in connection with the crucifixion of Jesus is this strange darkness that ἐγένετο,
"occurred," from the sixth Jewish hour, our noon,
until the ninth, our three o'clock. This darkness
occurred when the sun was at its zenith, shining with
strongest light, and continued for three hours into the
afternoon. All astronomical learning points to the
fact that this could not have been a natural eclipse
of the sun. This cannot take place when the moon
is about full. A search through ancient records also
produces no satisfactory results. We can arrive at

only one conclusion: this "darkness" was wholly miraculous exactly as were the following signs. God
darkened the sun's light by means of his own just as he
shook the earth and split the rocks.

The fact that this darkness covered exactly what
Matthew says, "all the earth," (γῆ cannot here mean
country) ought to be accepted. When the light of the
sun is shut off, the day half of the globe becomes dark.
Yet some contend that ἐπὶ πᾶσαν τὴν γῆν means only "over
all the Jewish land," or even over only Jerusalem and
the vicinity. Γῆ is taken in the sense of "land, region,
country." But then it seems strange that "all" should
be added. Those who translate "all the earth" sometimes weaken their correct translation by saying that
this is only "a popular way" of writing, and that, since
the darkness was rather extensive, the evangelists wrote,
"over all the earth," although they did not mean that.

Luke writes τοῦ ἡλίου ἐκλείποντος, "the sun failing,"
thus indicating that the cause of this strange darkness
lay in the sun itself and not in clouds or vapor that
interfered with the rays of the sun. When the sun
itself "fails," the entire day-side of the earth will be
in darkness. Some think that the darkness set in
gradually and then grew greater up to a certain point
and receded after that. The evangelists offer no support for this intensification. Why the darkness continued for just three hours, from high noon until three
o'clock, we are not told.

Various reasons for the darkness have been offered.
One is that nature suffered together with Jesus; another that is frequently offered is that the sun could
not endure to look upon Jesus' sufferings, yet it looked
upon the first three hours of those sufferings; and the
sun cannot be personified in the way that is here attempted. Nearer to reality is the explanation that this
darkening of the sun was a moral reaction against the
killing of Jesus. It was more. This darkness signi-

fied judgment. It was not a mere reaction of the natural sun but a sign wrought in the sun by God. Darkness and judgment go together, Joel 2:31; 3:14, 15; Isa. 5:30; 13:9, etc.; and other passages dealing with the judgment, including Matt. 24:29; Mark 13:24, etc.; Luke 21:25.

46) The judgment thus symbolized by the miraculous darkness was not one that was to be executed at some future time, perhaps at the end of the world, but one that took place during the very darkness itself, on the cross itself, in the person of the dying Savior himself. The darkness and the agonized cry of Jesus go together. Δέ is continuative, "now," or "and," indicating that what follows belongs to what precedes although it is somewhat different. "About the ninth hour" is just before the darkness ended. At the time of this climax of the sign of judgment "Jesus shouted with a great voice." It is the agony he is now enduring, has endured for these three hours, that makes his cry so loud and strong. He is very near to death; these last three hours with their darkness complete his expiatory suffering. Matthew, like Mark, has preserved the words of the cry in the original: *"Eli, Eli* (Hebrew), *lama sabachthani?"* (Aramaic). Mark has "Eloi," the Aramaic instead of the Hebrew; he disregards the Hebrew form used by Jesus. The Hebrew "Eli" or "Elei" (a variation in writing) was fully understood by the Jews although they at this time spoke Aramaic.

The words of this cry are found also in Ps. 22:1, although neither Matthew nor Mark mention the fact. The evidence that this is a prophetic psalm is stated in the author's *The Old Testament Eisenach Selections,* 428, etc. David is not speaking of himself as a type, so that Jesus would be the antitype; David is prophetically describing the suffering Messiah. Even the skeptic David Strauss saw that Ps. 22 furnished "com-

plete in advance" (prophetically) what occurred on
Golgotha. The omniscient Spirit of prophecy alone
could have placed at the head of this psalm that
supreme cry of agony on the cross. For it is not due
to the fact that David wrote this line that Christ made
it his cry on the cross, but because Christ would thus
cry out on the cross David wrote it as a prophet. The
ideas that Christ spoke aloud the entire psalm, perhaps
also the following psalms, or that he spoke aloud only
the first line and silently went through the rest, are
without support and destroy the force of Christ's cry.

The idea that either the physical agonies or the
inner mental distress of Jesus led to this cry is unsatisfactory, since men have often suffered both and
yet have felt deep inner comfort in the fact that God
was with them. Nor can the forsaking of which Jesus
complains be only an abandonment to the wicked
power of his enemies; for this would imply that Jesus
had so low an idea of God and of fellowship with him
that he felt his nearness only in fortunate days and
lost that feeling when his enemies seemed to triumph
over him. Again, this cry was not uttered only by his
human nature, as though his human nature had been
unclothed of the divine and left to stand alone in these
three hours of agony in the darkness. Such Nestor-
ianism misunderstands the agony suffered on the cross.
Jesus does not lament that the divine nature or its
divine powers have forsaken him but that another person ("thou") has left him.

Some have supposed that, when Jesus uttered this
cry, he virtually tasted of death, and that this is what
he had in mind when he spoke of being forsaken of
God. But Jesus died, actually died later and in his
actual death was not forsaken of God, for he com-
mended his soul into his Father's hands. And no
virtual dying can exceed the actual dying in intensity.
Again, it is true enough that the death of the sinless

Son of man must have been infinitely more bitter than
the death of any sinful man can possibly be. But
again we must reply that this does not explain the forsaking; for if God does not forsake the repentant sinner in the hour of death, how could he forsake his sinless Son when death came to him?

We must note the difference between Jesus' experience in Gethsemane and that on Golgotha. In the
garden Jesus has a God who hears and strengthens
him; on the cross this God has turned wholly away
from him. During those three black hours Jesus was
made sin for us (II Cor. 5:21), was made a curse for
us (Gal. 3:13), and thus God turned completely away
from him. In the garden Jesus wrestled with himself
and brought himself to do the Father's will; on the
cross he wrestles with God and simply endures. With
his dying powers he cries to God and now no longer
sees in him the Father, for a wall of .separation has
risen between the Father and the Son, namely the
world's sin and its curse as they now lie upon the Son.
Jesus thirsts for God, but God has removed himself.
It is not the Son that has left the Father, but the
Father the Son. The Son cries for God, and God
makes no reply to him.

What is involved in the fact that God forsook or
abandoned Jesus during those three awful hours no
man can really know. The nearest we can hope to come
toward penetrating this mystery is to think of Jesus as
being covered with the world's sin and curse and that,
when God saw Jesus thus, he turned away from him.
The Son of God bore our sin and its curse in his human
nature, this nature supported by the divine. That is
why Jesus cried, "my God," and not, "my Father."
But the possessive is important. Even though God
turned from him and left him, he cries to him and
clings to him as *his* God. Here the divine perfection
of Jesus appears. He is the Lamb without blemish

although he was made sin and a curse in the hour of his sacrifice.

The vocative, Θεέ μου, appears only here in the New Testament; Mark has ὁ Θεός, the nominative form with the article used as the vocative. R. 705 states that τοῦτ' ἐστι explains only the vocative whereas it introduces the Greek translation of the entire cry. The ἱνατί is distinct from διατί (διὰ τί). We are compelled to translate both with "why," but the former means, "for what purpose?" while the latter asks for the ground or the reason. So Jesus cries, "For what purpose didst thou forsake me?" The matter that is hidden from Jesus in this fearful ordeal is the object God has in forsaking Jesus. What purpose did this forsaking and this so dreadful suffering of Jesus serve as regards the redemption that was now almost completely accomplished? We need not be surprised to hear from Jesus himself that this purpose was hidden from him; for in his humiliation other things, too, were kept from him (24:36). All that we are able to say is that only thus, by actually forsaking Jesus, could the full price of our redemption be paid.

To be forsaken of God is undoubtedly to taste his wrath. Jesus endured the full penalty for our sins when God turned from him for three hours while Jesus hung on the cross. During those hours the penalty was paid to the uttermost farthing; and after that had been done, God again turned to Jesus. The forsaking is often combined with the death, yet the two are quite distinct. The forsaking had been completed before the death set in. When Jesus died he placed his soul into the hands of his Father and thus was certainly not forsaken. But while they are distinct, the forsaking and the death are closely connected. The death was the penalty for the sins of the world, and thus in connection with it this forsaking of the dying Savior was necessary. After this had been endured,

Jesus could cry, "It is finished!" and then yield his soul into his Father's hands.

47) The loud, agonizing cry of Jesus was heard for some distance. "Some of those standing there" answered it. Their answer is bald mockery. These must have been the Jews who had mocked Jesus before he spoke this word. The soldiers cannot be referred to; for what did they know about Elijah? The darkness had lasted for so long a time that its impression had gradually faded away. These wicked mockers pervert the first two words of Jesus and disregard the rest. They well knew that "Eli, Eli" meant "my God, my God," for the Hebrew for Elijah is *Elijahu* or *Elijah*, LXX, Ἡλιού or Ἡλίας. Yet the malicious minds of these Jews made a joke of this cry of Jesus' and went on to say, "This fellow is calling Elijah!" The point of this silly joke was the Jewish belief that Elijah would not only precede the Messiah and introduce him to the Jews but would also live at the side of the Messiah and attest him as the Messiah. So the mockery amounted to this "Now that this fellow is about at his end, he is frantically calling for Elijah to rescue him and to proclaim and to confirm him as the Messiah!" This was the reply men made to the Savior in that terrible hour when he drank the bitter cup of agony for the sin and the guilt of the world.

48) At this point Matthew abbreviates We must insert John 19:28, 29, the word of Jesus, "I thirst." It was the untold agony that lent such great force to the cry, "My God," etc But now the darkness gave way to the full light of the sun, and the agony of being forsaken of God had subsided. Jesus feels himself sinking and knows that his death is at hand. He does not intend slowly to sink into unconsciousness but to die with a loud shout of triumph. For this reason Jesus asks for a drink to moisten his parched lips so

as to enable him to speak his last words with a loud and a triumphant voice. Matthew reports only the fact that Jesus received the drink he asked for. The "one" that ran to answer Jesus' request must have been a soldier, for the soldiers alone had sour wine (ὄξος) for the very purpose of moistening the throats of the crucified whose tortures included the most raging thirst. We need not trouble about the question as to whether this wine helped to prolong life; for, if it did, the very object of crucifixion was such prolonged torture. The centurion very likely gave a sign of assent, and thus one of the soldiers ran for the wine.

The soldier took a reed, fixed a sponge to one end of it, dipped this into the wine, and held it up to Jesus' lips, who drank the wine from the sponge. John tells us that the reed was a stalk of the hyssop plant which has stems that are approximately eighteen inches long. This indicates the height of the cross. So short a reed was able to reach the mouth of Jesus. Like ἔλεγον in v. 47, ἐπότιζεν is imperfect, picturing the action in progress; all the auxiliary actions are indicated as such by the participles. The present instance is interesting, since there are no less than four such participles, for all or most of which the English would employ finite verbs.

49) While this was in progress, the rest kept up their mockery regarding Elijah. These must have been the Jews. Carried away by their shouting, the soldier who gave Jesus the drink joined in the same cry, Mark 15:36. Ἄφες (like the plural ἄφετε in Mark 15:36) is to be construed with the volitive subjunctive ἴδωμεν; it is much like a particle. Hence we do not translate, "Let be; let us see," etc. (our versions), as though these Jews wanted to keep the soldier from giving Jesus the drink. We translate, "Let us see," or, "We shall see," R. 430; B.-D. 364, 2; B.-P. 199.

The fact that ἄφες is singular while ἴδωμεν is plural makes no difference. The mockery of this word of the Jews lies in the intimation that, perhaps, Elijah will actually come. Thus these Jews make sport of the cry of Jesus. The future participle is rare in the New Testament, but here we have an example in σώσων. It is used to express purpose, "in order to save him." Every time these Jews speak of Jesus being saved they gloat over the fact that they now have him beyond all saving, at a point where he must certainly die. With such mockery ringing in his ears, Jesus goes to his end.

50) John alone reports the next cry, "It is finished!" and Luke alone the last, "Father, into thy hands," etc. Matthew and Mark abbreviate by at once reporting the death. **And Jesus, having cried again with a great voice, let go the spirit.** All the synoptists speak of the mighty shout of Jesus with which he died. He rallied all his powers for these last two words and spoke them as a victor whose triumph is won. Matthew indicates that he is acquainted with these final words, for he mentions "the great voice."

All the evangelists use choice words when reporting Jesus' death. None is content to say only that "he died." They also refer to the spirit or πνεῦμα, none of them only to the ψυχή although dying is also expressed by use of the latter. As a true man Jesus has both a ψυχή and a πνεῦμα. These two are one, namely the immaterial part of a human being. When they are used in their distinctive sense, ψυχή is the immaterial part as it animates the body while πνεῦμα is that same part as it contains the ἐγώ and is open to a higher world and is able to receive impressions from the Spirit of God. This distinction conveyed by the Greek terms is largely lost in the English where "soul" and "spirit" are more nearly alike. We at once see this when we note that the Greek derives its adjective ψυχικός from ψυχή. We have no corresponding English derivative from "soul" to express the fact that the immaterial part of our being is moved by the lower influences of the body.

While it is true that, when Jesus died, his ψυχή ceased to animate his body which now hung lifeless on the cross, yet it was eminently proper that the evangelists did not describe his dying by a reference to the ψυχή but only by a reference to his πνεῦμα; for the ψυχή of Jesus did not rule his person, it was always his πνεῦμα or "spirit" that exercised complete control. So it is true enough that, when Jesus died, he breathed out his ψυχή, and his body became inanimate; but much more is implied when it is stated that his πνεῦμα and all its spiritual powers left his body. Yet the exalted expressions used by the evangelists should not lead us to think that Jesus' death differed from our own. The separation of soul and spirit from the body occurred in him just as it occurs in us. Nor was the Logos separated from the human nature of Jesus when he died. Body, soul, and spirit constitute the human nature of Jesus just as they do ours, but in him the ἐγώ or personality was the Logos. The death of Jesus in no way affected the union of the Logos with his human nature. This death affected only the human nature, for it alone is able to die. God's Son died according to his human nature, and according to that alone. Compare Delitzsch, *Biblische Psychologie*, 400, etc.

The πνεῦμα of Jesus left his body, and thus he died. John 10:17, 18 does not prove that Jesus did not die from physical causes but by a mere volition of his will. That passage deals with the entire action of Jesus in giving himself into death for us. He laid down his life when, as he said in advance, he voluntarily entered his passion, the end of which would be death by crucifixion. The physical suffering killed Jesus, the Scrip-

tures assign no other cause for his death. Yet we
must conceive of his death as being one of peace and
joy and triumphant return to his Father after the hard
and bitter work of redeeming the world.

Certain older medical authorities have believed that
the death of Jesus was induced by a rupture of the
walls of his heart, so that we might satisfy our sentimental feelings by saying that Jesus "died of a broken
heart," although breaking a man's heart is not at all
physical. Our latest and best authorities inform us
that this is quite impossible. A lesion such as that
could result only from a degeneration of the heart, and
this occurs only in older persons when disease has left
its effects. This applies also to the tentative suggestion that perhaps some artery burst and thus
caused death.

Where did the πνεῦμα of Jesus go after his death?
Into his Father's hands (Luke 23:46), into Paradise
with the malefactor (Luke 23:43), into the glory the
Son had from eternity (John 17:5) ; these expressions
refer to heaven, the eternal abode of God and of his
angels and the saints.

51) **And lo, the curtain of the Sanctuary was
rent in two from above to below, and the earth
quaked, and the rocks were rent, and the tombs were
opened, and many bodies of the saints that had been
asleep were raised and, having gone out of their
tombs, after his resurrection went into the holy city
and appeared to many.** Jesus is dead, his lips are
silent; now God speaks in a language of his own. It
has been long noted that the wording of this passage
is both beautiful and highly impressive. Καί after καί
piles one great sign upon another. The interjection
ἰδού ushers them in, and they are certainly astounding.
The first is the rending of the curtain in the ναός or
Sanctuary, but this is first only in the narrative, for
all these signs occurred simultaneously the moment

Jesus bowed his head in death. Each in its way proclaimed the tremendous significance and the effect of
the Savior's death.

The καταπέτασμα τοῦ ναοῦ is the inner curtain or veil
that hung between the Holy and the Holy of Holies.
In the Herodian Sanctuary a second curtain hung in
front of the Holy. This, too, was at times called
καταπέτασμα, and the plural is used to designate both
curtains. But the regular term for this outer curtain
was κάλυμμα, and only occasionally the other term was
used. Yet this has led some to think that Matthew
referred to the outer curtain. But if Matthew had
the outer curtain in mind he would have used the
distinctive term for this curtain and not the standard
term for the inner one.

The inner curtain is described in Exod. 26:31;
36:35; II Chron. 3:14. Josephus, *Wars*, 5, 5, 4, has
the following: "This house, as it was divided into
two parts, the inner part was lower than the appearance of the outer and had golden doors of 55 cubits
altitude and 16 in breadth. But before these doors
there was a veil of equal largeness with the doors. It
was a Babylonian curtain; embroidered with blue, and
fine linen, and scarlet, and purple, and of a contexture
that was truly wonderful. Nor was this mixture of
colors without its mystical interpretation, but was a
kind of image of the universe. For by the scarlet
there seemed to be enigmatically signified fire, by the
fine flax the earth, by the blue the air, and by the
purple the sea; two of them having their colors the
foundation of this resemblance; but the fine flax and
the purple have their own origin for that foundation,
the earth producing the one, and the sea the other.
This curtain had also embroidered upon it all that was
mystical in the heavens, excepting that of the (twelve)
signs (of the zodiac) representing living creatures."

The thickness of the curtain corresponded with its great size, and its strength was according.

All at once this mighty curtain "was rent in two," and that "from above to below" as if an unseen hand severed it by starting at the top. The two pieces exposed the Holy of Holies. Consternation must have struck those who saw the sight. Jesus died at three o'clock, thus the curtain must have been rent at the time the priests were busy with the evening sacrifice. Many eyes thus saw what had happened. The sound of the rending may have attracted general attention. We have no reason to think that only one or two priests who were at the moment busy in the Holy discovered that the curtain had been rent.

This rending was miraculous. We have no intimation that it was caused by the earthquake, the curtain being stretched so tightly that, when the earth shook, it split in two. Then, indeed, it would not have split from the top to the very bottom but would have been torn in several directions. The idea that it was fastened to a great beam at the top, and that this beam broke in two, thus tearing the curtain, lacks sufficient evidence to make it acceptable.

The sign involved in this torn curtain is easily understood. Only once a year the high priest alone dared to pass inside this curtain, on the great Day of Atonement when he carried in the blood for the cleansing of the nation. In Herod's Sanctuary the Holy of Holies was empty, for the ark of the covenant that had stood there in Solomon's Temple had been destroyed. When this curtain was rent, God proclaimed that the ministration of the Jewish high priest had come to an end. What this high priest and his annual function typified had reached an end, because now the divine High Priest, Jesus, had come and had entered into the Holy of Holies of heaven itself with his own all-atoning blood. Heb. 9:3-15; Heb. 6:19, etc.; 10:19, etc.

The second sign was the earthquake and the rending of the rocks, πέτραι (not πέτροι, detached boulders), cliffs of rocky masses. These showed deep fissures and rents as a result of the earthquake. This earthquake is also a miraculous sign that was wrought directly by God in connection with his Son's death. An alternative is unacceptable, namely that this earthquake occurred accidentally just at this time and was merely coincidental with Jesus' death. Matthew alone reports this sign and the next, but this is no reason to call them myths or to deny their reality. Think of the earthquake that occurred at the time of Jesus' resurrection. We feel that God would manifest such mighty signs in connection with the death of his Son.

Nebe refers to the Old Testament for the interpretation of this earthquake. It always denotes the presence and the intervention of God among men and shows his might and his greatness as the God of the covenant (Exod. 19:19; I Kings 19:11; Ps. 68:9; 114:4, 6; Hag. 2:7; also Acts 4:31; 16:26); revealing himself as the righteous Judge in his wrath (II Sam. 22:8; Ps. 18:7; 77:18; Isa. 5:25; 13:13; 24:18; 29:6; Jer. 10:10; 49:21; Nah. 1:5; Joel 2:10; Hag. 2:6; also Rev. 6:12; 8:5; 11:13). These Old Testament passages which are corroborated by those of the New Testament explain this sign. The earthquake and the rending cliffs indicate the presence of God at the death of his Son, the presence of the covenant God in his might and his greatness for all who believe and of the Judge in his wrath for all unbelievers.

We need seek no farther. The earth is not protesting against the death of Jesus, refusing to receive his body, or to bear those who crucified him. This earthquake is not a sign that indicates a renewal of the earth. Allegory is out of place. These rent rocks do not symbolize hard hearts that are at last rent by Jesus and by the gospel

52) The third sign is most incredible to the critically minded. Not, indeed, the fact that the tombs were opened but the fact that these saints arose and appeared to persons in Jerusalem. Especially unacceptable to us is the supposition that this resurrection of the saints is connected with Christ's descent into hell. Some think that he descended there at the time of his death and released the saints in hades (realm of the dead); others say that he made this descent and effected this release at the time of his resurrection.

In the rocky country of Palestine the dead were usually not placed into graves that had been dug in the earth but into chambers that had been carved out of rocky elevations and were closed with a stone slab. Yet we are not ready to adopt the view that the quaking of the earth dislocated these slabs so that the tombs were opened and the dead within them were exposed. The opening of the tombs was a separate miracle of God's. Matthew does not intend to say that all tombs were opened, but that only the bodies of the saints were raised. When he restricts this resurrection to the saints he intends to say that only their tombs were opened. He does not say that all the saints had their tombs opened and were raised to life but only "many" of them, a certain large number that had been selected by God. This proves the presence of the hand of God and thus a miracle. Nothing is said about those that were not saints. There was no reason for raising them to life at the time of Jesus' death. Matthew leaves the impression that these tombs of the saints were opened the moment Jesus died. The immediate effect of his death was this opening of the tombs and the resurrection of the saints. This, then, is the significance of the miracle: it is a sign that

Jesus' death conquered death, these risen saints prove his great victory.  Death could no longer keep these saints in their tombs.

"They were raised," ἠγέρθη, means exactly what it says.  Their souls returned from heaven and were again united with their bodies but not in order that they might again live on this earth.  They arose with glorified bodies such as we shall have at the last day.  Their "bodies" arose, their σώματα, for the resurrection has reference only to dead bodies.  This shuts out a speculation such as that these saints arose with "spiritual bodies," i. e., other than their actual dead bodies.  They arose at once, and their now glorified bodies left the tomb.  The supposition that they were "gradually" made alive and then finally at the time of the resurrection of Jesus on Sunday made their way out of the tomb, is untenable.  The Scriptures present only an instantaneous resurrection and not one that is gradual.  Even Lazarus did not return to life gradually.  The perfect participle κεκοιμημένων, "having slept" and thus being asleep at the moment of the miracle, merely matches ἁγίων, "saints," and does not support the view that these were New Testament saints, believers who had come to faith through Jesus' words and deeds.  These were Old Testament saints.

53)  These risen saints did not at once enter heaven with their glorified bodies; they had a duty to perform here on earth before their translation to the heavenly home.  There was no interval of time between their resurrection and the leaving of their tombs.  The opening of the tombs, the return to life, and the leaving of the tombs occurred at the same moment.  This implies that the phrase "after his resurrection" be construed with the main verb εἰσῆλθον and not with the preceding participle ἐξελθόντες.  These glorified saints did not remain in their open tombs

until after Christ's resurrection. If the question is asked where they remained until Sunday, the answer is: where Jesus remained during the intervals between his appearance during the forty days after his resurrection. God had no trouble to find a place for these saints.

The reason that these saints were not allowed to leave their tombs until after Jesus' resurrection is the thought that Jesus would then no longer be "the Firstborn from the dead," these glorified and risen saints would have preceded him. But this view overlooks ἠγέρθη in v. 52: their resurrection took place on Friday afternoon. If this was the case — and Matthew's statement is very plain — then their resurrection would after all precede that of Jesus. It does not follow that of Jesus merely by having their risen bodies remain in their tombs until Sunday or until later. Jesus remains "the Firstborn from the dead" (Col. 1:18) because he alone conquered death, and even these saints arose only through the blessed power of Jesus.

The phrase μετὰ τὴν ἔγερσιν αὐτοῦ is placed before εἰσῆλθον because of its emphasis. Already the death of Jesus brought resurrection to these saints, hence the account of this occurrence is properly connected with the death of Jesus and not with his resurrection. The main point is the resurrection of these saints; secondary to this is their appearance to people in the Holy City. This occurred after the resurrection of Jesus because this appearance was a sign-testimony to the resurrection of Jesus.

Matthew does not intimate who these saints were. Speculation has named Job, the patriarchs, and others and some have thought of recently deceased believers who appeared to their relatives, Simeon and Anna, for instance. But these are guesses. Jerusalem is still called the "Holy City" although it rejected Christ.

This may well be due to the fact that the work of Christ's grace was to continue in Jerusalem until Pentecost when the Christian Church was established in this city.

As we are left without identification of the risen saints, so also the "many" to whom they appeared in the Holy City are left unnamed. Some think that these must have been believers. Yet in Acts 1:15 the believers were only 120 in number. The indefinite πολλοῖς is without restriction. Jesus did not appear to any of his enemies. May it not be possible that he sent these saints to them instead?

The great importance of this resurrection of the saints for us is the fact that the resurrection is not merely a future event; it has already begun in the case of these saints. Not only Jesus is risen from the death, an advance number of the saints has risen with him. This is an assurance that we shall also rise. What finally became of these risen saints? Some think that they ascended to heaven with Jesus; but it seems best to assume that after they had appeared to those in Jerusalem they were at once translated into heaven.

54) **Now the centurion and those with him guarding Jesus, having seen the earthquake and the things that occurred, feared exceedingly, saying, Truly, this was God's Son!** We now learn that no less an officer than a centurion was in command of the detail that crucified Jesus. We cannot determine how many soldiers were ordered out for the purpose of this execution; some think of only twelve, four for each person crucified, yet for the sake of safety an additional guard may well have been added. Matthew combines the centurion with those "with him," the soldiers "guarding Jesus." All of these heathen men are affected alike, all of them express themselves in the same way. They are upset by the earthquake in

particular and in addition by all else that occurred, τὰ γενόμενα, or that is occurring, τὰ γινόμενα (a variant reading). The latter expression includes all that happened on Golgotha. Mark lays emphasis on the way in which Jesus died: ὅτι οὕτως ἐξέπνευσεν; but this οὕτως is quite the same as that which Matthew specifies.

All these soldiers were greatly frightened. The ἐφοβήθησαν was more than reverence in this connection. The nature of this fright and the thought that inspired it are revealed by their exclamation, "Truly, this was God's Son!" Their fear was a religious fear. This centurion and his soldiers knew how Jesus was brought to the cross. The centurion had observed the conduct of Jesus throughout this ordeal. He had witnessed the mockery of the Jews in which even his soldiers had joined, and the word regarding Jesus' being God's Son had been a part of that mockery. Then came the death with the loud cry, "Father," and immediately the earthquake and the rending rocks. Considering all this together with this climax, we see how the centurion came to exclaim as he did.

This Gentile, called Longinus in tradition, comes to faith beneath the dead Savior's cross. His confession is strong because of its ἀληθῶς, "truly." This adverb is set over against the Jewish unbelief and mockery. Whatever the Jews may say, the centurion sees that the truth is the divine Sonship of Jesus. Θεοῦ υἱός is without articles, and R. 781 thinks that the context alone decides whether this means *the* or *a* Son of God." But this is not correct in regard to the articles; for even "*the* Son of God" might be read as referring to one of several Sons. Θεοῦ υἱός is like a proper name, *Gottessohn*, and hence has no articles. The centurion did not apply this name to Jesus in the sense in which it was used in his pagan mythology, namely the human offspring of some pagan god, but in the sense it had in Jewish usage. Yet he says, "This *was* God's Son," using ἦν, for this divine Son was man and was now dead. Luke reports that the centurion said, "This one was righteous," δίκαιος, thus pronouncing a verdict upon Jesus that was the opposite of the Jewish sentence. We conclude that this officer said both: "righteous and God's Son," for the two go together. Legend reports that this centurion became a believer, and there is evidence that the legionaries who were at this time stationed in Jerusalem were Gauls or Germans.

55) **Moreover, there were there many women beholding from afar, such as did follow Jesus from Galilee, ministering unto him; among whom was Mary the Magdalene, and Mary, the mother of James and Joses, and the mother of the sons of Zebedee.** All the synoptists mention these friends of Jesus who witnessed his death. In Luke 23:49 two classes are mentioned: the women and the γνωστοί or acquaintances of Jesus. From John's Gospel we learn that he was the only one of the eleven present. The women were, indeed, dear friends of Jesus, for they had ministered of their substance to him during his travels in Galilee, Luke 8:3. The hardships endured by Jesus in his arduous work had moved them to relieve him in such ways as they could. They had followed him on his last journey to Jerusalem, and now in this terrible tragedy their love conquered all fear. Here they stood with bleeding hearts watching their Lord and Master die. They stood "afar" because of necessity. The soldiers kept a space free about the crosses, and the wicked Sanhedrists crowded up as close as they dared, and a mob of people came to see the θεωρία or spectacle. It was not fear that caused these friends and these women to stand some distance from the cross but the situation in which they found themselves. During a lull in the disturbance about the cross, when the Sanhedrists had grown weary of mock-

ing, Jesus' mother and John and two other women went to the cross, unhindered by the soldiers.

56) Matthew honors three of these women especially. As Peter was the leader among the Twelve, the men, so "Mary the Magdalene," so named from her home town to distinguish her from the other Marys, was the foremost among the women. The Mary who was the mother of James and Joses was the wife of Clopas and a sister of the mother of Jesus. These two women stood beneath the cross with Jesus' mother and with John. The third woman named by Matthew is Salome (Mark 15:40), "the mother of the sons of Zebedee" (James and John). This expression indicates that Zebedee had died. Instead of giving her name, as Mark does, Matthew states her great distinction, the fact that she was the mother of two of Jesus' apostles (see also 20:20, etc.).

57) Matthew now proceeds to an account of the burial of Jesus. **And evening having come, a rich man from Arimathæa came, his name Joseph, who also was a disciple of Jesus; he, having gone to Pilate, asked for the body of Jesus. Then Pilate ordered it to be duly given up.** As wonderful as are the signs that occurred in connection with Jesus' death, so wonderful is the burial of his body. It is laid away in the most astounding manner. Its interment was a fulfillment of Isa. 53:9: "And he made his grave . . . with the rich in his death." Jesus was dead. What was to become of his body? His friends, the women, and John were utterly helpless and unprepared. It seemed as though the sacred body would be taken away by the soldiers and thrown into a pit with the bodies of the two malefactors. What else could be done? God took care of his Son's dead body.

'Οψία (supply ὥρα) is used to designate both evenings: the first from three to six o'clock, the second from six until night. Jesus died at three o'clock, and the evening Matthew has in mind is the first. Now help suddenly appeared. Joseph of Arimathæa came and took full charge of the proper disposal of Jesus' body. The form ἦλθεν does not imply that "he came" from the country and thus arrived at Golgotha, or that he had just now arrived from the city. He must have been among the spectators and now, when Jesus was dead, came forward to take charge of his body.

Joseph is named from his home town in order to distinguish him from other Josephs, and Arimathæa is the town of Rama which was originally in that part of Samaria which was transferred to Judea, thus making the town "a city of the Jews," Luke 23:51. Construe, "a man from Arimathæa," and not, "came from Arimathæa." Τοὔνομα Ἰωσήφ, "the name Joseph," is a nominative absolute that is merely inserted into the sentence. Matthew reports only two details regarding Joseph: his wealth and his discipleship. From Mark and from Luke we learn that he was a noble and a godly man, and from Luke that he was a Sanhedrist but one who had been opposed to the action of the Sanhedrin in regard to Jesus. In what manner he showed his opposition we do not know. John adds that for fear of the Jews Joseph had kept his faith in Jesus hidden until this time. The Jews had officially threatened to expel any man from the synagogue who confessed Jesus, and this meant cutting such a man off from all connection with the Jewish religion and ostracizing him from his nation.

This man, who had been fearful and cowardly thus far, does an astonishing thing. He casts all his fears to the winds and boldly takes charge after Jesus had died. Joseph is a great and an influential man, and when he "came" there on Golgotha that implied that he spoke to the centurion about his wanting the body and his going to Pilate to secure its possession. The centurion gladly consented to wait. At the request of the Jews the bones of the malefactors had already been broken and the spear thrust into Jesus' side.

58) Joseph hurries to Pilate, and προσελθών implies that he went right into the Prætorium in order to make his request of the governor. But we need not suppose that by thus entering a Gentile abode Joseph broke with the entire Jewish religion. He merely made himself liable to ceremonial pollution for that day. This the Sanhedrists had avoided when they brought Jesus to Pilate in the morning, but they did so only because they wanted to be fit to eat the *Chagiga* in the afternoon. Joseph was not concerned about eating this sacrificial meal, he intended to bury Jesus and would at any rate be ceremonially unclean because he had handled Jesus' dead body.

Pilate was surprised that Jesus was already dead, so much so that he sent for the centurion and verified the fact. Then, however, he readily granted the request and ordered the centurion "duly to give" (ἀποδίδωμι, ἀπο of obligation) the body to Joseph. But this should not be considered an exceptional favor. The Romans quite generally allowed the relatives and the friends of men who had been executed to bury their bodies if they so desired.

59) Joseph did not hurry back from Pilate to Golgotha. Mark tells us that he first bought fine linen for the body. The point is that he bought only the linen and not the spices. Matthew says nothing about Nicodemus, but John reports that he bought only the spices and not the linen. It is natural to suppose that these two men, both of whom were Sanhedrists, met early enough to confer with each other and thus to divide their purchases for the burial. So Joseph returns to Golgotha. **And having taken the body, Joseph wrapped it in clean linen cloth and placed it in his own new tomb, which he hewed in the rock cliff;**

**and having rolled a great stone to the door of the tomb, he went away.**

It is Joseph who took the body; he is active throughout this burial scene. He took full charge, and the others who helped let him lead. That, too, seems to be the reason that the synoptists say nothing about Nicodemus. Joseph must have been a masterful man. How he took the body is not indicated, but we see that he must have had help. At least three men were present counting John, besides a number of women. It is possible that at the direction of the centurion the soldiers, too, helped. Perhaps the body was lowered from the cross after the nails had been drawn out. Means to reach the crosspiece must then have been at hand, they were the same that had been used when crucifying Jesus. Perhaps the entire cross was lifted from its socket in the ground, lowered gently to the ground, and the nails then extracted. We do not know the details

All that Matthew, like Mark and Luke, tells us is that Joseph wrapped the body in σινδών, cloth of fine linen, that he had just purchased and thus was clean and fresh. This was torn into long strips that were to be wrapped around the limbs and the body. It is John who tells us that the entire body was first wrapped with linen strips, between the folds of which the aromatic spices were sprinkled; only the head was left free, for it was to be covered with a special cloth after the body had been placed into the tomb. The blood stains must have been removed before this was done; perhaps the sour wine of the soldiers was used for this purpose with the centurion's permission. No anointing of the body was possible here on Golgotha; Mary of Bethany had attended to that in advance (26:12, etc.).

60) Where could the body of Jesus be taken now that so suddenly a tomb became a vital necessity? It

is Joseph who meets this need. He himself had an
entirely new tomb that had been hewed out of the solid
rock of a cliffside. Luke and John tell us that no
one had as yet been buried in this tomb. John also
adds the detail that this tomb of Joseph's was near
Golgotha, which made it especially available when the
friends of Jesus were pressed for time, for the Sabbath
began with the setting of the sun. The body could
scarcely be carried any great distance. This fine new
tomb of his Joseph offers for the body of Jesus. There
he places the body for its sacred rest.

"A new tomb," where no decay or odor of death
had as yet entered, this was a fitting place for the
body of Jesus which no corruption or decomposition
dared to touch (Acts 2:27). Here his holy body could
have sweet rest after all its dreadful, painful work
had been done. Yet Jesus was not intended for a
tomb. He needed one only on our account and only
until the third day. Luther writes: "As he has no
grave for the reason that he will not remain in death
and the grave; so we, too, are to be raised up from
the grave at the last day through his resurrection and
are to live with him in eternity."

Quite recently in a quiet spot just outside of the
walls of the present Jerusalem, at the foot of a skull-
shaped hill (Golgotha, most likely), the so-called
"Garden Tomb" has been discovered. This corresponds in every detail with the data the Gospels
furnish in regard to Joseph's tomb. It is an ample
chamber, hewn out of the solid cliff, the face of which
is smooth and perpendicular. The floor is not sunken,
does not need to be. It is a rich man's tomb, for it
has a vestibule and in the main chamber along the
three sides only three places for bodies, the center
being left unused. It is a new tomb, for only one place
for a body has been finished, the other two are not
completed. In the place toward the cliff the floor is hewn

out a little in the shape of a human body. The three places for bodies along the sides of the three walls are cut out boxlike, the bottom of each being level with the floor. At the footend of the place finished for a body, and likewise at the headend, between this and the end of the next place for a body, the stone is left thick enough to afford a seat, so that an angel could sit, "one at the head, and the other at the feet, where the body of Jesus had lain" (John 20:12), and the angel at the feet would also be "sitting on the right side" (Mark 16:5) as one enters the vestibule. These heavier rock sections across the footend and on the left of the headend are still intact, while the thinner wall along the side of the body has mostly broken down. When the author viewed this tomb he was deeply impressed and compelled to say, "If this is not the actual tomb into which Jesus was laid it duplicates it in every respect." So many fake sites are shown in the Holy Land that to view a site like this leaves an unforgettable impression.

The great stone that was rolled before the door of the tomb was a flat, upright slab, circular like a great wheel. This moved in a groove next to the cliff and was wheeled back to the left to expose the door and forward to close it. The groove slanted upward from the door so that, when the stone was wheeled to the left, it had to be blocked in order to hold it. The bottom of the slant was just in front of the door where the stone would come to rest on a level. After the body was duly placed in the tomb, the circular slab closed the entrance as indicated.

This stone was not a "boulder." It is never called πέτρος but always λίθος, and it is difficult to imagine how a rough boulder could do anything but merely block a rectangular door. When all had been done, Joseph "went away." This simple verb reads as though we are to think of Joseph's action as being the

Lord's providence to provide the proper burial for his Son through this man's hands. No man could have guessed that one, yea, two, of the very members of the Sanhedrin would give a rich burial to Jesus whom the Sanhedrin as such brought to the cross.

**61) There was there Mary the Magdalene and the other Mary sitting in front of the burial place.** These two Marys have been mentioned in v. 56: Luke tells us that the women who had come out of Galilee with Jesus also followed to the tomb and saw how the body was laid in its place in the tomb. When Joseph left after the tomb had been closed, these women, with the exception of the two named, departed. These two lingered on, loth to leave until the shadows fell.

**62) Now on the morrow, which is after the Preparation, there were gathered together the high priests and the Pharisees unto Pilate, saying Lord, we came to remember that that deceiver said while yet alive, After three days I arise.** Matthew alone reports this incident. On its very face it is so credible, so impossible of invention, that it cannot be a myth. "The morrow" was Saturday, and in all likelihood the morning hours of this day. This designation of time would seem to be sufficient, for the ἥτις clause only repeats this thought by using other terms. Matthew adds this second designation of the day because he wants to bring out its sacredness in contrast with the desecration perpetrated by these Jews. The παρασκευή is "the Preparation," the day preceding this high Passover Sabbath, namely Friday, when everything had to be prepared in advance so that this Sabbath Saturday could be spent in perfect quiet in a most solemn manner. Matthew does not write "Sabbath," for the day after the preparation is not just an ordinary Sabbath; he wants to convey more, namely the high Passover Sabbath. Only this Sabbath had a παρασκευή.

It was not the Sanhedrin as such that went to Pilate. There was no marching in a body to the governor's residence. This would have attracted attention, both because it violated this high and holy day by their going into a Gentile's abode and because it would have made known the purpose of this visit. Matthew never designates the Sanhedrin by the terms "the high priests and the Pharisees" (compare 21:45, the only other place in which this expression is used). When two terms are used to designate the Sanhedrin, we have "the high priests and the scribes," or, "the high priests and the elders." Here, then, after a quiet agreement among, themselves the high priests and the Pharisees, all of them Sanhedrists, proceed to Pilate singly at an agreed time as though they were private persons. Yet, as far as Pilate was concerned, he might have thought that he had the official Sanhedrin before him. Now these Jews have no scruples about entering the residence of the Gentile governor, for πρὸς Πιλᾶτον naturally has this meaning. Even this high day does not deter them. On Friday, when they had a Jewish crowd about them, they pretended that they dared not enter the Gentile Prætorium. We see how they played fast and loose with their own religious regulations. Men who had stooped to murder would certainly be capable of lesser transgressions.

It is a fair conclusion that the prime movers in the present undertaking were the Pharisees. It was not that they believed that Jesus would or could rise from the dead, yet they believed in the resurrection and had taught the people to believe in it also. They were the ones, therefore, who feared that the people might come to believe that Jesus had actually risen. The high priests were Sadducees, and these scoffed at the resurrection as being an absurdity (22:23, etc.). They, therefore, would have no fears such as the Pharisees had. And yet they consented to go to Pilate with the

Pharisees. As in other instances, especially when opposition to Jesus was to be evidenced, they yielded to the Pharisees.

63) In humble fashion these Jews address the governor with Κύριε, "Lord." This, too, is done only in order to gain their end. They tell him: "We came to remember (it has just come to our minds again) that this deceiver said while yet living, After three days I arise!" It was probably true that since Jesus had died this word of his again came to their minds. Ἐμνήσθημεν is to be understood in the middle sense and most likely is an ingressive aorist. A vile epithet is used to designate Jesus, "that deceiver," which recalls the violent accusations they had made to Pilate the day before. Ἐκεῖνος is here used in a vicious, derogatory sense. "Deceiver" refers to the alleged deceptions practiced upon the people when Jesus pretended to be the Messiah and (as these Jews claimed) a political king. They scorn, as always, to use the name "Jesus."

It has been asked, "When did Jesus tell these Sanhedrists that he would rise after three days?" Passages such as 21:42; 26:61; 27:40 will scarcely give the answer; much better is 12:38. But we see no reason for excluding what Jesus told his own disciples about his death and his resurrection. These repeated and emphatic announcements could easily have found their way to members of the Sanhedrin. At least, these men sum it up most correctly, "After three days," etc.

It is certainly astonishing that these enemies of Jesus remember this word and promise of his after his death while his own disciples never grasped the word in its true meaning and now had let it pass completely from their minds. The present tense ἐγείρομαι is a futuristic present which is frequently used in predictions (R. 870) and includes the idea of the certainty of the event.

**64) Order, therefore, the burial place to be made safe until the third day; lest, perhaps, his disciples, having come, steal him and tell the people, He was raised from the dead; and the last deception will be worse than the first.** Why this request to Pilate? Why did the Sanhedrists not place a detachment of their Temple police (their ὑπηρέται) in front of the tomb about which they seem to know? The answer is that the Temple police had only the Temple area under their jurisdiction and could not be sent anywhere else. The Roman government would also allow no show of military force outside of the Temple. So these Sanhedrists go to Pilate to furnish the desired guard. When Jesus was to be arrested in Gethsemane, the real force was the Roman cohort, the Temple police only went along. "The burial place to be made safe" leaves it to Pilate as to how he will do this; the obvious way was, of course, to assign a guard.

The assumption of these Jews is that, of course, Jesus could not possibly make good his word, nor would a whole legion of Roman troops be able to prevent such a thing. But these deceivers and liars imagine that other people are like themselves. They fear that the disciples of Jesus may also recall the promise of Jesus to arise; and since Jesus would be unable to do so, they may try to play a trick by stealing the body out of the tomb and by disposing of it secretly while they fool the people by spreading the report that he was raised from the dead.

We see how evil minds work. If these Jews had known the state of the disciples, they would have seen how foolish their fears were. But providence was again at work. These Sanhedrists, the implacable enemies of Jesus who cannot be content with his death, must proceed involuntarily to aid in establishing the certainty of Jesus' resurrection. By having the tomb guarded they made certain that no deception had been perpetrated, that the body most certainly had remained in the tomb, and that, therefore, Jesus truly arose on Sunday. Both ἐγείρομαι (v. 63) and ἠγέρθη may be regarded as passives used as actives: "I rise — he rose." Because they are active in sense, both verbs exalt Jesus in the highest degree, for he himself rises by his own power.

The Jews fear that "the last deception will be worse than the first." Πλάνη is plainly intended to match πλάνος used in v. 63. "Deceiver" and "deception" go together. "Error" in our versions is wrong. By the first deception the Jews have in mind what Jesus did to the people during his life by stirring up the people, etc., as these Jews intended Pilate to believe. Thus the last deception would occur after his death. It would keep the people stirred up more than ever, for they would now be thinking that Jesus was again alive, yea had returned from the dead. The people would eagerly listen to anything that purported to come from him. Of course, these Jews spoke of rising and resurrection only in the sense of a return to this life. That they had the secret fear that Jesus might make good his word, namely in this sense, cannot be maintained.

65) **Pilate said to them, Have a guard! go make it as safe as you know how.** Curt and masterful is Pilate's reply. The matter is of little moment to the governor. He is pleased that they defer to him in so small a thing and thereby admit that he alone has authority to guard the tomb. Ἔχετε is an imperative and not an indicative (our versions), for to say that the Jews have a guard would mean that they have men of their own for the purpose of guarding. Pilate grants them a guard made up of his own soldiers. The word κουστωδία is the Latin *custodia,* a term that was used also in the Aramaic. Pilate turns the entire matter over to the Jews. Since they are so concerned, let them not trouble Pilate any further but themselves

go and make the place as safe as they know how.    We
must construe ὑπάγετε ἀσφαλίσασθε together, the first verb
is only auxiliary to the second.

66)    **And they, having gone, made the burial
place safe, sealing the stone, the guard with them.**
The Jews hasten to carry out their plan.    They even
sealed the stone, which does not mean that they
fastened the stone so that it could not be moved but
that they affixed a seal by connecting the stone with
the rock wall at the door, so that any tampering with
the stone would at once break the seal and thus reveal
what had been done.    How this sealing was done is
not indicated.    It was a simple matter that did not
require the private seal of Pilate or that of the Sanhedrin.    The circular flat stone lay close against the
wall of rock.    All that needed to be done was to make
a connection between stone and wall, one that, if it
were broken, could not be restored.    The final phrase
introduced by μετά is quite loosely attached to the sentence, and we need not try to construe it with either
σφραγίσαντες or ἠσφαλίσαντο.    It is independent and merely states that the guard was with the Jews when they
were at the tomb and made things as safe as they
knew how.

Quietly Jesus rested in his tomb.    Presently he
would arise.    In vain are all the foolish proceedings of
his enemies.

# CHAPTER XXVIII

## XX

### Christ's Resurrection, Chapter 28.

In each of the four Gospels the final section on the resurrection of Jesus constitutes the glory part. Yet this tale is told in the same sober way as is the account of the crucifixion and the death. The great facts that occurred are reported in an entirely dispassionate way. Our faith is to rest on these facts. One of the decisive tests of the Christian faith is belief in these facts which declare that Jesus rose from the dead. All who in any way alter these facts and deny his resurrection no longer deserve the Christian name.

The four accounts differ in detail, no witness reports all the facts. This fact has offered the critics an opportunity to play one witness against another in order to discredit them all together, or to discredit parts of their testimony. The Christian student has only one duty, namely properly to combine all of the testimony and thus to reconstruct the entire story.

1) **Now after the Sabbath, at the hour dawning toward the first day of the week, there came Mary the Magdalene and the other Mary to view the burial place.** It is unfortunate that the R. V. has translated ὀψὲ σαββάτων, "now late on the Sabbath day." This would say the women came to the tomb late on Saturday instead of early on Sunday. This might be the sense of the Greek words used in the classics, but in the Koine ὀψέ is used as a preposition and means "after,"

B.-P. 958; B.-D. 164, 4; Stellhorn, "long after something"; Zahn, *erst nach;* R. 517. Mark agrees, "when the Sabbath was passed." This reference to the Sabbath being passed has an implication: the women intended to do a piece of work, namely to finish the burial of the body. Hence they had to await the passing of the Sabbath during which no work could be done. In other words, they had to wait for Sunday morning. Luke tells us about their bringing spices, and Mark that they brought them.

With τῇ ἐπιφωσκούσῃ supply ὥρα; it is the dative of time. The εἰς phrase we translate, "toward the first day of the week," but this does not give σάββατα the meaning of "week." It merely puts the Jewish idiom into our own. The Jews had no names for the weekdays but designated them with reference to their Sabbath; thus μία (suppy ἡμέρα) τῶν σαββάτων, "the first (day) with reference to the Sabbath," i. e., following it. The names of the festivals are frequently plural, and thus the plural σάββατα was also used although it referred only to the one "Sabbath." Matthew agrees with Luke's "very early in the morning" (A. V.); and with John's "when it was yet dark"; and does not conflict with Mark's "at the rising of the sun." Since they started before the dawn while it was yet dark, the sun was rising about the time the women reached the tomb. Why were they on their way so early? For the best of reasons even as all the evangelists record this point. Jesus had been dead since Friday. In that climate dead bodies start to decompose very quickly, wherefore also the dead are buried on the same day, or, if it is too late for that day, on the next. Great haste was necessary in the thinking of these women, even hours counted if they wanted to find Jesus' body in such a condition that it could still be managed.

As he did in 27:61, Matthew mentions only two women, the same two that were mentioned there; he also mentioned them in 27:56 but there added a third. In all these passages those mentioned by name do not exclude the presence of others. Only the most prominent are named: Mark adds Salome, Luke, Joanna (wife of Chuza, one of Herod's stewards, Luke 8:3) and then refers to others besides who are not named. Mary Magdalene and the other Mary are described in 27:56. The former is most wrongfully identified with the unnamed prostitute in Simon's house, this being found even in the chapter heading of the A. V., Luke 7:36, etc. What is true is that Mary Magdalene was possessed of devils, and that Jesus had freed her (Mark 16:9). In prominence she was like Peter, and in her love like John. That is why she is so often mentioned first in a list of women. "The other Mary" is the Virgin's sister who is otherwise characterized by the name of her husband and by that of her sons. They went "to view the burial place" but for a very definite purpose; they intended to complete the work upon the body as Mark and Luke amplify.

2) **And lo, a great earthquake occurred; for an angel of the Lord, having come down out of heaven and having gone forward, rolled away the stone and was sitting upon it.** Matthew alone tells this feature of the story. This is one of the many incidents which show conclusively that neither Matthew nor Mark copied from each other. Mark tells of the fears of the women in regard to having the stone rolled away. The exclamation "lo" is warranted by the earthquake and by its cause. On earthquakes as indicating the divine presence of grace and of judgment see 27:51. Here we have the same sign with the same significance as in connection with the death. We might think that the jarring of the earth was caused by Jesus when he left the tomb, but γάρ attributes it to the action of the angel. When the angel appeared, Jesus had already risen.

None of the evangelists attempts to describe the resurrection itself; it had no witnesses. Jesus left the tomb silently. His dead body was suddenly quickened (I Pet. 3:18) or filled with life and in the same instant passed out through the walls of the sealed tomb. Then, after the tomb was empty, the angel came and opened the tomb to show that it was indeed empty. Those paintings which portray the glorious Savior coming out of the opened door of the tomb while the guard flees and falls in dismay at sight of him, are not in accord with the facts of the case. Silently, invisibly, wondrously, gloriously the living body passed through the rock.

This mode of existence is well described in *Concordia Triglotta*, 1004, 100: "The incomprehensible, spiritual mode, according to which he neither occupies nor vacates space but penetrates all creatures wherever he pleases; as, to make an imperfect comparison, my sight penetrates and is in air, light, or water and does not occupy or vacate space; as a sound or tone penetrates and is in air or water or board or wall and also does not occupy or vacate space; likewise, as light and heat penetrate and are in air, water, glass, crystal, and the like; and much more of the like. This mode he used when he rose from the closed sepulcher and passed through the closed door and in the bread and wine in the Holy Supper, and, as it is believed, when he was born of his mother." The latter, however, is an old belief that is no longer held. The actions of the angel are fully described, his flashing down out of heaven, his stepping forward to the stone, which, possibly at a touch, rolled from the entrance and fell flat upon the ground. On this stone see 27:20. Then the angel sat down upon the fallen stone, and ἐκάθητο (imperfect) pictures him as sitting thus, awaiting the coming of the women.

This is now a different tomb and calls for a different watchman, not for keepers of the dead but for an inhabitant from the eternal realms of light and life. First, the servant appears, presently the Master will be seen. A new era has begun, heaven and earth are now joined, for Christ our Savior is risen. The wall of separation has fallen; God is reconciled to men; the sacrifice of the Son has been accepted by the Father. This is the supreme Easter truth. The women felt the shock of the earthquake but hurried on, nevertheless, and then saw that the entrance to the tomb stood wide open. Just before the women arrived, the angel passed into the tomb.

3) Parenthetically Matthew adds: **Now his appearance was as lightning and his raiment white as snow.** This reminds us of the transfiguration of Jesus. The lightning is to picture the supernatural brilliance, and the snow the white purity of heaven.

4) **And for fear of him those guarding were made to quake and were as if dead.** The Roman soldiers who guarded the tomb saw the angel and were struck with terror; αὐτοῦ is the objective genitive, "fear of him." Compare σεισμός in v. 2 and ἐσείσθησαν (σείω) in this verse, "earthquake" and "be made to quake." Ὡσεὶ νεκροί implies that these soldiers lay unconscious for a brief time. God not only thwarted the effort of his enemies, he even turned their means for overcoming the truth into means for aiding the victory of the truth. Christ's resurrection is just as terrible for his foes as it is comforting for his friends. The Jews guarded the tomb only against molestation on the part of the disciples and their stealing the body, they forgot to guard it against Jesus himself.

5) For a description of the tomb see 27:60. Matthew does not regard it as necessary to remark that the women, who were greatly troubled to find the entrance

of the tomb open and the large, flat, circular stone lying flat on the ground, came to the entrance and went into the vestibule of the tomb; Mark writes, "and entering into the sepulcher." **And the angel, answering, said to the women: Do you stop being afraid! For I know that you are seeking Jesus, the one that has been crucified. He is not here, for he arose even as he said. Hither, see the place where the Lord lay!** The fact that the angel is now inside of the tomb does not need to be stated; it is naturally understood. Matthew and Mark speak only of "the angel." Luke and John tell us that there were two angels; the latter states that one was at the head, the other at the feet (when Mary Magdalene returned to the tomb). This is not a discrepancy between the evangelists. The two who speak of "the angel" merely intend to indicate that this one was the speaker. The participle ἀποκριθείς is used, not only when a question is asked, but also when, as here, an explanation is made. The angel "answered" the astonished thoughts and fears of the women.

Μὴ φοβεῖσθε ὑμεῖς is, indeed, a precious word, for behind it is all the grace that the risen Savior has brought us. The women who sought the body of the crucified Jesus had no cause to fear the herald at his resurrection as did the Roman soldiers. In negative commands the present imperative means to stop an action already begun, R. 851, etc.; so here, "stop being afraid," ὑμεῖς being added for the sake of emphasis. This is not an empty command, for at once a full explanation is added as to why the women have no cause for fear. In the first place, the angel informs the women that he knows all about their coming to the tomb, they are seeking the dead body of Jesus, "him who has been crucified," whom they expect to find a corpse in his tomb. Such a dead body they cannot find here.

6) Why not? "He is not here, for he arose even as he said." Here all the blessed news is at once announced. He whom they left here still and cold has departed, for "he arose," ἠγέρθη. The aorist passive may be intransitive, "he arose," and not passive in idea, "he was raised" (R. 817), although in some connections the passive idea is wholly in place. The resurrection itself is at times ascribed to God: "raised up from the dead by the glory of the Father," ἠγέρθη, Rom. 6:4; 8:11; Matt. 16:21; 17:23; 26:32; then again it is designated as an act of Jesus himself, Mark 9:31; Luke 18:33, ἀναστήσεται. Both are true even as all the *opera ad extra* are *communa*. The Greek uses the aorist to designate the past fact ("he arose"), whereas we prefer the perfect ("he has risen"), R. 845, when speaking of something that has just recently occurred.

The resurrection of Jesus was at the same time the glorification of his body; this the women were soon to know (v. 9). The angel adds, "even as he said," and thus recalls for the women all the promises Jesus made in connection with the announcement of his death. The blessed promises were now fulfilled: he had again taken up his life, John 10:18.

To assure the women still more the angel invites them to come closer and to see the place where the Lord lay; some texts omit "the Lord." But they are to see not only that the tomb is now empty; they are to see also the linen wrappings lying undisturbed although the body has gone out of them in a miraculous manner, and the headcloth laid by itself, just as Peter and John saw all this a little later; all of which was the clearest evidence for Jesus' resurrection, John 20:5, etc. Here was actual, ocular proof. Nebe is right when he says that, however much these women still lacked, they understood the resurrection better than many modern theologians who refuse to believe in the bodily resurrection in spite of the word, "he is not here," but im-

agine that only his spirit continues to bless. The
absence of Jesus' dead body and the necessity of ac-
counting for what became of it are to this day the great
stumblingblock for all who deny the resurrection of
that dead body. They can resort only to improbable
and fanciful explanations that are contrary to the
Scriptures. Δεῦτε is used with a plural imperative
without a connective.

7) If Jesus had remained dead, neither these
women nor any of the disciples would have had anything further to do after the burial had been completed in the way the women desired. But now that
Jesus is risen, the most blessed task awaits these
women, a task that is also to fill the lives of the disciples. **And having gone quickly, tell his disciples,
He rose from the dead and, lo, he goes before you to
Galilee; there you shall see him. Lo, I did tell you!**
These women are not to remain at the tomb in astonishment, they are not to give way to the fascination of
this strange sight, they are not to stay and to speculate
about this thing they had seen and heard, they must do
something that is far more important. The minor
action of quickly going is expressed by the participle;
εἴπατε is the second aorist imperative and as such is
peremptory. The angel is not making a request but is
issuing an order. Now that Jesus is risen, this news
cannot reach the poor disciples too soon. It is summed
up in the short announcement (ὅτι *recitativum*) : "He
rose from the dead" (Matthew has ἀπό, also in 27:64,
instead of the usual ἐκ). That is enough, the "many
infallible proofs" will follow presently.

It is asked why the disciples were informed through
the women; why angels did not appear to them or perhaps Jesus himself. Gerhard has listed five reasons:
God chooses the weak; because they were overwhelmed
most by the sorrow they are to be first in the joy; the
presence of the women at the tomb silences the Jewish

falsehood that the disciples stole the body; as death
came by woman, so salvation and life are to be announced by her; God wanted to reward woman's active
love. But why wander so far afield? The women
alone went out to the tomb on Sunday morning, the
women, none of the men, not even John. Thus they
were honored by being made the messengers to the
men. If the eleven had gone out, too, the story would
have been different. The love of these women receives
its fitting reward.

The fact that Jesus arose is not enough; this message must contain also the assurance that the women
as well as the eleven will see Jesus. This assurance
gives the message its fulness. Think of what expectation it aroused. Both ὑμᾶς and ὄψεσθε include the women.
But the meeting thus promised is to take place in Galilee: "He goes before you to Galilee; there you shall see
him." This mention of Galilee in no way excludes the
earlier appearances of Jesus in Jerusalem and in Em-
maus. There is to be something special about this
seeing of Jesus in Galilee. The fact is that before his
death Jesus himself had promised this meeting in Galilee, 26:32. In Galilee Jesus intended to meet all his
believers as one great body. St. Paul lists this meeting as one of the great proofs of Jesus' resurrection:
"After that he was seen of above five hundred brethren
at once; of whom the greater part remain unto this
present (are still alive), but some are fallen asleep,"
I Cor. 15:6. This answers the supposition that Jesus
had at first intended to meet the disciples only in Galilee but afterward allowed his yearning heart and the
weakness of the disciples to move him to appear to
them at once. Jesus does not plan faultily, nor does
he vacillate. All his meetings with individuals and
with small groups in Jerusalem were preparations for
that grand meeting with his entire flock in Galilee
where, far from the hostile Jews, in their own home-

land, he would bind all his believers together and give them the Great Commission, v. 16 and 18-20; Mark 16:15-18.

The heavenly messenger seals his promise with his divine authority: "Lo, I did tell you!" The aorist is used where we prefer the perfect, R. 842. This authoritative word resembles that spoken by Gabriel in Luke 1:19. It intends to remove any trace of doubt.

8) **And having gone quickly from the tomb with fear and great joy, they ran to bring his disciples word.** The second aorist feminie participle states that the women made a quick movement away from the tomb, and the main verb then states that they actually ran in order to get to the disciples as quickly as possible. Matthew gives us a glimpse into the psychology of their action: they were prompted by fear and great joy. Their fear is due chiefly to the presence of the angels. Any contact with the heavenly world must fill us sinners here on earth with fear. Their joy is due to all that the women saw and heard; and this joy predominated over the fear, for μεγάλης does not modify both nouns but only the last, the nouns have different genders. If "great" were intended to modify both "fear" and "joy," nouns of the same gender could easily have been found. Indeed, the joy was great, it must have been overwhelming considering the open tomb with the angels and their statement, and considering what the place where Jesus had lain showed.

9) But still greater joy was in store for these women. Matthew alone reports this incident. **And lo, Jesus met them, saying, Greetings! And they, having come to him, grasped him by the feet and worshipped him.** This is the first appearance of the risen Savior. The women are hurrying toward the city as fast as they can and say nothing to any person they met (Mark 16:8). All at once Jesus then meets them. We have every reason to believe that Jesus did

the same thing here that he did in his other appearances. Wherever he desired to be seen, there he was seen. So here, all at once Jesus appears on the road a little distance in front of the women and walks toward them. Thus he met them.

All that we know about his appearances shuts out ideas such as this, that Jesus walked the entire distance from the city and that, as he gradually drew nearer, the women recognized him; or that he stood waiting in some side path out of sight and then stepped in front of the women. When Matthew adds "lo," he marks the surprise of the women because they all at once see Jesus before them. We are not told how he looked after he was risen, but it is plain that the women recognized him the moment they saw him. Now all their fear left them. Here was their Lord himself, alive, and their hearts overflowed with wondrous joy.

Jesus speaks and utters a greeting: Χαίρετε! The verb χαίρειν is used to express all manner of greetings and always conveys a wish of happiness and well-being. "All hail!" in our versions is not a good rendering. Nor is this greeting a translation of the Jewish, "Peace be to you!" Whenever Jesus uses this Jewish greeting, it is translated into Greek, John 20:19. Happiness and joy in their fulness certainly came to these women when they now saw Jesus before them and heard his greeting.

A pause ensued after this word had been spoken by Jesus. The women are so overcome that they are unable to reply. But they are drawn toward him as by a magnet. "They, having come to him, grasped him by the feet." The genitive αὐτοῦ is proper because they took hold of a part of his person, and the accusative τοὺς πόδας because they grasped these entirely. The clasping of his feet implies that the women had sunk to the ground in the attitude of adoration as also προσεκύνησαν αὐτῷ, "they worshipped him," states. These acts

do not imply that the women tried to hold Jesus firmly
so as not to lose him again, but now again to have him
as they had had him before his death.    That was what
Mary Magdalene desired, and that was why Jesus
answered her as he did in John 20:16, etc.    These
women prostrate themselves before Jesus in worship.
They recognized him in his divine greatness.    We
read that various persons came and prostrated themselves in worship before Jesus, but this was only the
Oriental fashion of expressing humility on their part
and honor for Jesus.    Jesus' disciples never prostrated
themselves before their master in this manner.    Now
that he is risen from the dead, now that he appears to
them in a miraculous manner, these women truly "worship" him and by their prostration intend to give him
divine honor.    This was the proper way for these
women to meet Jesus; and he, too, accepts their worship as rightly being his due.

This act of these women was not precipitate action;
they did not rush to him but went forward deliberately
to assure themselves that this was not a phantom; their
act was more than a sign of love; it was not the result
of overpowering awe that had been produced by a superhuman appearance; it was a natural and a proper
act of worship, the first προσκύνησις in the true and full
sense of the word that was offered to Jesus.    These
women have heard the angel's word that he is risen,
they now see and feel the wonderful change that has
come over him, their hearts are deeply moved, and so
most naturally they sink at his feet and render him the
worship of their hearts.    Jesus accepts it because it
is worship and in so far is different from the act of
Mary Magdalene.    In the person of these women all
believers sink down and worship.

10) **Then Jesus says to them, Stop being afraid!
Go, take word to my brethren that they go away
into Galilee, and there they shall see me.**    On

μὴ φοβεῖσθε see v. 5. The last trace of fear, uneasiness, and lack of assurance is to leave the hearts of these women. No cause for any degree of fear exists but the very opposite, cause for full assurance and greatest joy. The angel's bidding, "Fear not!" is corroborated by Jesus; more than that, it is confirmed in a higher degree. For in the tomb only the evidences of Jesus' resurrection called out not to fear while here the risen Savior himself expels fear.

The same duty the angel had assigned the women Jesus, too, assigns them. Ὑπάγετε is regularly used without a connective. It is merely auxiliary to the main verb ἀπαγγείλατε, "to report to someone," to take a message. A remarkable feature is the designation Jesus uses for the disciples: "my brethren." They had shamefully fled from him in Gethsemane, Peter had denied him, all but John were far away when Jesus died, and yet Jesus now calls them by a name that is more intimate than any he had used during his earthly life. The most endearing name he had then used was "my friends," John 15:15. In Matt. 12:49, etc.; 25:40 the term "brethren" is indeed used, but not in addressing the Twelve. "My brethren" denotes pardon for their lack of faith. In Mark 16:7 the name of Peter is introduced into the angel's message in order to assure especially him that he was pardoned.

But "my brethren" conveys still more. With this word Jesus presses the disciples to his bosom as being most near and dear to him. It contains all his love for them, at the same time it bestows the highest honor on them. No higher honor can come to a man than to stand beside Jesus as his brother. Luther brings out one side of this spiritual relationship: "If, now, Christ is our brother, I should like to know what we still lack? Brethren in the flesh have common possessions, have together one father, one inheritance otherwise they would not be brethren; so we have common possessions with Christ and have together one Father and one inheritance which does not grow less when divided, but whoever has one part of the spiritual inheritance has it all." In "my brethren" the emphasis is on what thus becomes ours not on our work or on what we must render to our brother. All that Jesus has gained on this great day of his resurrection he has not acquired for himself only but also for all his brethren. On the strength of this word "my brethren" Zinzendorf tried to popularize the name "Brother Jesus," but the church did not follow his lead.

The same command and the same promise concerning Galilee that had been given by the angel (v. 7) are now repeated by Jesus. The exceptional nature of this meeting is thus established. Matthew gives us a brief account of it in v. 16-20. Compare the comment on v. 7.

**11)    Now while they were going, lo, some of the guard, having come into the city, reported to the high priests all that had occurred.** Matthew alone reports the bribery of the Roman guard. He makes note of this incident because he is writing for Jewish readers and thus exposes the Jewish slanders against Jesus (v. 15b). Various views have been proposed regarding the movements of the women and of the Roman guard. After the soldiers had for a brief time lain like dead men because of the shock of the appearance of the angel, they recovered and fled to the city in terror. Not until after they were safely gone did the women arrive at the tomb. Thus, by the time the women started back from the tomb, the frightened soldiers had reached the high priests and were making their report. Matthew marks this as an astonishing event by using the exclamation "lo." It was astonishing in more ways than one.

Only "some" appear in order to make a report. This does not imply that the rest remained on guard

at the tomb and were awaiting orders from the high
priests as to what they were now to do. There were no
soldiers at the tomb when the women arrived. The
most satisfactory explanation is that some came to
make a report as representatives of all. The others
waited near by to see what the result of this report
would be. If it be asked how this guard could leave
its post in such a fashion although it had been frightened almost to death, we must remember that these
soldiers had been turned over to the Jewish authorities
and were under their command. Pilate had given
them a sort of furlough because he did not care to
assume any further responsibility. Thus the soldiers
did not follow their military regulations so strictly.

In the second place, they surely knew why they had
been posted to guard this tomb, that the Jews wanted
it guarded against the disciples and because Jesus
had said he would arise from the dead on the third
day. This very thing had now happened in the
most astounding way. They had been posted out there
in vain. The disciples had not ventured near, the
guard would have made short work of them; but a
flaming, terrifying angel had appeared, the earth had
quaked, they had lain like dead for a while: all of which
could mean only one thing: Jesus had risen.

The committee of the soldiers reports only to the
high priests although also the Pharisees had had a
part in securing their services from Pilate (27:62).
The high priests were the official leaders, were at the
head of the Sanhedrin, and besides this were very likely
most easily reached. But this is the astounding thing;
these high priests receive the very first news of Jesus'
resurrection; the disciples had as yet heard nothing,
for the women were just starting back to the city.
Note also this: God sent the message of Jesus' resurrection to these high priests through their own witnesses, the soldiers they themselves had posted, the

most unimpeachable witnesses possible. Nor do the high priests dare to question this witness, they accept it as being entirely true. But what is the effect produced upon these high priests? Do they yield to this sure testimony? Does it go home to their hearts that Jesus promised to arise on the third day, and that he had now indeed arisen, and that angels from heaven had revealed the empty tomb? Not for one moment! Only one thought fills the heart of the high priests: to nullify this true testimony; and they are prepared to go to all lengths to do this. This is that same wilful resistance which these high priests have all along offered to Jesus. See John 8:45-47.

These priests cannot deny the truth of what the soldiers report. In all other affairs they are guided by the truth or the facts which they learn; but here they do the very opposite in the most unreasonable and vicious way. This is always the course followed by unbelief. To this day unbelief does the same: it makes only one attempt, namely to get rid of attested facts concerning the resurrection of Jesus. But this is a hopeless effort; the attested facts remain.

The soldiers are honest, they report "all that has occurred," they do not garble the facts or withhold any part of them. Their fright is still too great to permit them to attempt anything but an honest and a full report. The high priests have no excuse; they cannot say that they were misinformed or not fully informed. They do not even put the soldiers through a judicial examination, for, although their report contains the most astounding facts, the high priests do not for a moment attempt to question those facts. They think of only one thing: to nullify them.

12) **And when they were assembled together with the elders and, having passed a resolution, they gave much silver to the soldiers, saying, Say, His disciples, having come during the night, stole him, we**

**being asleep. And if this comes to a hearing be-
fore the governor, we will persuade him and will relieve you of worry.** The high priests are not ready
to make an independent decision as to what is to be
done. They call the Sanhedrin together, they deem
the matter so important. When Matthew speaks of
the high priests and the elders assembling, this always
refers to a session of the Sanhedrin. But συμβούλιον
λαμβάνειν means more than "to take counsel"; it includes
the discussion and the final passing of a resolution.
The expression is a Latinism, *consilium capere*, and is
repeatedly used by Matthew (12:14; 22:15; 27:1, 7),
B.-P. 1248; R. 109. Thus by a formal resolution the
ruling body of the Jewish nation determines on the
rankest lie and the most flagrant bribery. Their moral
decadence is absolute. Of course, those who perpetrated murder would not recoil from lying or other
crimes.

The resolution is at once carried out. They give
much silver (ἀργύρια, silver money) to the soldiers,
enough to serve as a strong bribe to make them lie as
to what occurred at the tomb. Judas they bought for
30 pieces of silver, a cheap price, indeed. But this
guard was very likely made up of twelve men, and this
guard was to incur personal danger by admitting that
it slept while on duty. It would take a good deal of
money, indeed, to effect their bribery. But the Sanhedrin is only too glad to pay it.

13) This money is to secure **the spreading of one
of the most wretched lies. Falsehood is stamped all
over it.** Yet it was the best the cunning minds of
these Jews could invent. Jesus was risen, the tomb
was empty although it had been guarded by Roman
soldiers. How explain that empty tomb without admitting Jesus' resurrection? That has been the dilemma of all who have tried to get rid of that resurrection.
Only falsehood can do it, and the falsehood is always

so apparent that it defeats its purpose.  The soldiers
are given most careful instruction: "Say, His disciples," etc.  Whenever they are pressed to give an
answer regarding the disappearance of the body of
Jesus, this is the answer the soldiers are to give, this
and no more; for this they are handsomely paid.

We need not ask how the soldiers could consent.
The money had its strong appeal as it always has.
These soldiers had not been posted by Pilate but had
been lent to the Jews.  Their orders came from these,
and if these, their masters, were satisfied, they, too,
could risk it.  The only real risk they ran was the admission that they had been asleep when the robbery
occurred.  But they were willing to incur this for the
money they received.

Thus the Jews plan in advance to counteract any
announcement on the part of the disciples that Jesus
was risen from the dead.  Here were disinterested
witnesses who testified even against their own interest
(admitting that they slept) that the whole story of the
resurrection was a rank fraud.  Many were bound to
believe this testimony.  But the disciples were so
crushed that none of them could even have conceived
the plan to steal the sacred body.  They were like their
Master, honest men and true, and the thing farthest
from their minds was the perpetration of a fraud.
How could they know that the soldiers would lie down
and sleep?  That must have been a sound sleep, indeed,
to enable the disciples to remove that heavy stone and
to carry away the body.  The slightest noise would
have awakened at least one or the other of the soldiers.  Did these soldiers sleep on into the dawning
day before they discovered that the tomb had been
rifled?  Only a little thought would have exploded this
shallow lie.  But so few people think.

14) The dictionaries (even C.-K.) and the grammars give unsatisfactory answers regarding ἀκουσθῇ ἐπί;

the margin of the R. V. is correct, "come to a hearing before the governor." Ἀκούειν is used in this legal sense in John 7:51, and ἐπί in Acts 25:9 (ἐπ' ἐμοῦ) and in the classics. This sense fits the connection far better than the translation of our versions, "And if this come to the governor's ears"; for if Pilate heard it at all, he certainly would institute a judicial investigation, and only at such an investigation could the Jews hope to aid the soldiers. If Pilate merely heard about the matter and did nothing about it, the aid of the Jews would not be needed. The contingency that Pilate would submit the soldiers to a hearing was quite remote. He would soon leave for Cæsarea, and it would take at least weeks before a report could reach him there. But suppose the worst should happen. In that case the Jews solemnly promise that they will come forward and "persuade" the governor and literally "make you worryless." If the soldiers knew these Jews at all, they certainly would not place much reliance on this promise. Men who even paid them to lie for them would certainly themselves lie if occasion offered. By "persuade" the Jews mean that they would express themselves as being satisfied with the service of the soldiers; and if they had no complaint, Pilate would hardly punish his own men. They could rest easy.

15) **Now they, having taken the silver, did as they were instructed. And this saying was spread abroad among Jews to this day.** So the bargain is closed, and the money paid in advance as had been done in the case of Judas. The soldiers carried out their part of the bargain, not at once, of course, for there was no need, but as soon as the apostles began to proclaim the resurrection of Jesus. A detachment of soldiers was left in the castle Antonia after the governor had left, and this small band was a part of that detachment. They would naturally be questioned since

they had been at the tomb, and then they answered as
they had been instructed. The ὁ λόγος οὗτος is this instruction of the high priests. Although it was a palpable lie, it found credence among "Jews" (no article).
Not wanting the truth, they were satisfied with a falsehood. And Matthew reports that even "to this day,"
when he wrote his Gospel, Jews believed this lie. We
may add that this continued far beyond Matthew's time.
The apocryphal and the patristic literature is acquainted with this falsehood. It appears in the twelfth
century when Judas is regarded as the thief of the
body, and again in the days of rationalism (Reimarus,
in *Wolfenbuettler Fragmente*).

Thus the Jewish leaders kept their own people from
accepting the truth. It was bad enough that they
themselves wilfully rejected the truth, but infinitely
worse that they misled their nation. Nebe adds: "Not
on historical faith but only on the faith of the heart
rests the salvation of the world as this has been shown
in an incomparable manner by the Reformers. That is
why God, in his eternal wisdom, permitted it that those
guardians of the grave who might have been able to
spread the historical faith in the world allowed themselves to be bought for this monstrous lie. The resurrection of God's Son was to be attested in this world
only by such who in their own hearts had experienced
the truth and the power thereof and by a new life
presented it in innocence and righteousness."

16) **But the eleven disciples went to Galilee to
the mountain where Jesus had appointed them.**
Matthew omits the other appearances of Jesus and
closes his Gospel with this most notable one. He speaks
only of the eleven, but we recall the angel's word to
the women in the tomb, "he goes before *you* to Galilee,"
v. 7, and rightly conclude that they, too, were present
on this occasion. In fact, we have every reason to
identify this meeting in Galilee with the one mentioned

by St. Paul in I Cor. 15:6, the Lord "appeared to above five hundred brethren at once." There is no good reason why the Lord should summon only the eleven to meet him on a distant mountain in Galilee when he had already twice met them in Jerusalem and, if they alone were concerned, might just as well have met them there once more. The appearance to the five hundred must be located in Galilee; for even after the ascension we find only 120 disciples in Jerusalem, Acts 1:15.

In I Cor. 15:5-8, St. Paul mentions only the appearances to apostles and thus cites only the main witnesses; yet he mentions this appearance to the 500, among whom the apostles must have been included. This was also a most notable occasion, for this meeting had been announced in advance no less than three times (26:32; 28:7, 10) and was devoted to the giving of the Great Commission. It is certainly proper that this meeting should have been a public meeting and should have included not merely the eleven as was the case in former private interviews. In fact, we may say that we most certainly expect that Jesus would, at least once, appear to all his believers and thus make them witnesses of his resurrection.

Galilee was the proper place for this meeting. Here all could come together and not be disturbed by foes; in fact, the homes of most of them were in this neighborhood. We take it that this appearance followed the one granted to the seven disciples at the lakeside when Peter was reinstated, John 21:1, etc. The exact day of this appearance is not indicated. Yet, judging from the tone of finality in Jesus' words (note especially v. 20b), we may safely conclude that this grand meeting took place quite near the end of the forty days; perhaps it was the last appearance before Christ's ascension. The theory of a few interpreters that "Galilee" signified a certain part of Mt. Olivet is without convincing evidence.

"To the mountain where he had appointed them" indicates a definite place on a certain mountain. The appointing must have been made at one of the previous appearances. The exact site of this mountain cannot be determined. All that we can say is that it may have been a mountain on which Jesus had preached and taught in days past. It has been well remarked that the very gathering on a mountain already marks an important event; for on a mountain Jesus preached his great sermon (chapters 5 to 7), on a mountain he chose the Twelve, on a mountain he showed himself in the glory of the transfiguration. On mountain heights heaven and earth, as it were, meet, and here the glorified Savior spoke of his power in heaven and on earth. With the vast expanse of the sky above him and the great panorama of the earth spread beneath him, Jesus stands in his exaltation and his glory — a striking vision, indeed.

17) **And having seen him, they worshipped him, but some doubted.** Suddenly he stood before them, having come to them out of the invisible world. They had come in smaller or in larger groups and had waited. Then all in an instant they saw him. The effect was powerful; προσεκύνησαν, they prostrated themselves before him in the act of worship. This worship is the recognition of his deity, the adoration of Jesus as the Son of God. Only after the resurrection did the disciples engage in this form of adoration (compare the remarks on v. 9) ; for all the Jews were averse to worshipping a creature; and so the act here reported is proof of their faith in Jesus as God exalted over all that is created.

Οἱ δέ is written although οἱ μέν does not precede. If Matthew had written both he would have divided the apostles into two classes, but that is not his intention. Only a few doubted, and this thought is brought out when οἱ δέ is used by itself. Some commentators cannot imagine that any of the eleven doubted and so conclude that some of the 500 are referred to. But Matthew speaks only of the eleven, for he is here interested in them alone; οἱ δέ must then be referred to them. But how could any of the eleven doubt? We can give only a general answer. This doubting seems to mar this occasion, but the Scriptures always tell the plain truth whether it mars the occasion and offends our ideas of what should have taken place or not. We have no reason to think that the doubt concerned the reality of Jesus' resurrection as in the case of Thomas. The context does not point to the resurrection but to the appearance and the identity of him who stood before them as causing the doubt. Was this Jesus, indeed, or was it not? While doubt thus arose in some, it did not continue, it soon vanished. All that occurred here shows that the doubt was dispelled.

Rationalism points to this doubting as a proof that the resurrection was not a reality. Yet the very fact that the disciples were not in the least credulous and quick to believe but had to have all doubts completely and thoroughly removed, is proof of the most convincing kind that Jesus did arise and that he did appear to his disciples as is recorded in the inspired record.

It is an engaging question to ask in what form Jesus appeared to his disciples. The Scriptures say nothing on this subject. Some have thought of a process of glorification which advanced to completeness in the body of Jesus during the forty days. But it is hard to believe this. More credible is the view that Jesus allowed his glory to shine forth in different degrees in the different appearances. But this, too, is only supposition. Besser attempts the following description: "So beautiful, so unfadingly beautiful was his appearance and yet so mild, so entirely human and brotherly; so almighty and powerful, the Lion of the tribe of Judah, the Conqueror of death and hell, and yet so entirely the Lamb of God with the marks of the slaughter upon him.  The dim eyes of human flesh could not at once accommodate themselves to the blessed vision of the Resurrection and the Life."

Perhaps the strangeness and the wonderful nature of the appearance were such as to perplex a few and thus to make them doubt.  But we must also reckon with the deceitfulness of the human heart, the devious windings of its thoughts, the perverse inclination to darken faith, and the peculiar satisfaction of raising doubt.  Besides, the eleven were of different dispositions.  Some were receptive, some slow to apprehend, of little faith, easily discouraged and troubled, unable to let go their old notions and to rise to the new spiritual heights.  Thus, probably, they doubted.  How they must afterward have felt ashamed as every doubter does today when the vapor of doubt has been driven away by the shining sun of truth.

18) **And Jesus, having come forward, spoke to them, saying:  Given to me was all authority in heaven and on earth.  Having gone, therefore, disciple all the nations, baptizing them in the name of the Father and of the Son and of the Holy Spirit, teaching them to guard all things whatsoever I did bid you.  And lo, I myself am with you all the days until the consummation of the eon.**  "These are the words of a Majesty which must be termed Majesty indeed."  Luther.  On one occasion the tempter took Jesus to a high mountain in order to show him the kingdoms of this world and their glory in order to induce him to avoid the cross in obtaining the kingdom.  Now Jesus himself shows his disciples the kingdoms of this world after the cross had been borne and points out the conquest his sacrifice and his love shall achieve through the gospel.  Προσελθών reads as though at first Jesus did not stand in the midst of the disciples but a little in front of them.  As they fell down to worship him, he

moved close to them and then spoke to them face to face.

The aorist ἐδόθη states a fact, "was given," and refers to the human nature of Jesus alone: for according to the divine nature all authority belonged to the Son from all eternity. It is not stated when this gift was made, see 11:27. The words πᾶσα ἐξουσία mean "all authority" (and not "every"); for with abstract nouns "all" and "every" have the same force, R. 772. Ἐξουσία denotes active power, the full ability to do as one wills. Two domains are mentioned: "in heaven and on earth." All authority in each. Nothing could be more comprehensive.

Who can fathom this brief utterance of Jesus? The kingly authority of Jesus embraces heaven, all that lives and has its being there, angels and archangels, powers, principalities, might, dominion, thrones, and the saints in glory. This authority is exercised also over the evil spirit world, whose prince is conquered and despoiled, and whose hosts lie in abject submission beneath Jesus' feet. All the powers of heaven are in his hand to do his bidding without question or pause. This the disciples are to realize as Jesus sends them forth. Never did a human army have such resources behind it. All the earth is also subject to him, its inhabitants, both friend and foe, and all the powers that are in the earth. "The means of transportation wing the passage of his ambassadors, commerce paves the way for the work of missions, the science of language furnishes new tongues for the preaching of the gospel, the spread of culture helps to break down the bulwarks of heathendom." Nebe.

"Thus there is and remains in Christ only one divine omnipotence, power, majesty, and glory, which is peculiar to the divine nature alone; but it shines, manifests, and exercises itself fully, yet voluntarily, in, with, and through the assumed, exalted human nature in

Christ.   Just as in glowing iron there are not two kinds
of power to shine and burn, but the power to shine
and to burn is a property of the fire; but since the fire
is united with the iron, it manifests and exercises this
its power to shine and to burn in, with, and through
the glowing iron, so that thence and from this union
also the glowing iron has the power to shine and to
burn without conversion of the essence and of the natural properties of fire and iron." *Concordia Triglotta,*
1039.

19) Οὖν has a peculiar force in the present connection; it draws a conclusion from the gift of all authority bestowed on Jesus.   It puts all his power and
his authority behind the commission to evangelize the
world.   This οὖν shows that what otherwise would be
absolutely impossible now becomes gloriously possible,
yea, an assured reality.

Πορευθέντες is something new.   Hitherto men were
welcomed when *they* came to Israel, God's people; now
the people of God are to go to men everywhere.   Yet
Jesus does not command, "Go!" the participle is merely
auxiliary to the main verb, "Having gone, disciple!"
To go to the nations is the self-evident and natural way
to proceed in making them disciples.   What going there
has been since Jesus spoke this word!   Who will count
the miles travelled by the messengers of Jesus?

The heart of the commission is in the one word μαθη-
τεύσατε.   This imperative, of course, means, "to turn
into disciples," and its aorist form conveys the thought
that this is actually to be done.   The verb itself does
not indicate *how* disciples are to be made, it designates
only an activity that will result in disciples.   It connotes results not methods and ways.   The translation
"teach" is, therefore, unfortunate and even misleading
to those who are not able to examine the original.
Those who draw the conclusion that we must always
teach first and use this passage as proof against infant

baptism are basing their conclusion on a mistranslation. With the participle that follows Jesus himself assigns the proper place to teaching.

The universality of the commission is made plain by τὰ ἔθνη, "all nations" of the earth. Here we have the fulfillment of all the Messianic promises concerning the coming kingdom. Τὰ ἔθνη — one wonders how this sounded to the Jewish ears of these first disciples. One thing is certain, God had to give them much additional light and leading in order to induce them to go out to "all nations." "It was not a strange world into which Christ sent his servants, but into the world the Father had laid at his feet." Besser. What diversity exists among the nations of the earth: race, color, location, climate, traits, achievements: yet they are all included in this command, for all are sinners, all have souls, all need and are capable of salvation through the grace of God. Jesus did not overshoot the mark here, the nations that have been reached by the gospel prove it today. A tremendous task: "disciple all nations!" Who would not have recoiled from it had not Jesus first declared his omnipotence in heaven and on earth ("go ye *therefore*")!

Two participles of means then state *how* all nations are to be made into disciples: by baptizing them and by teaching them. The order in which these two participles appear is not accidental. Jesus sees beyond the first missionary stage of the gospel work when adults must be taught before baptism can be administered to them; he sees his church being established among the nations and children thus entering it in infancy, and this by means of baptism.

Βαπτίζω, as all lexicographers agree, has a variety of meanings. It may mean to dip, immerse, wash, lave, sprinkle, cleanse, in fact, refer to the application of water in any form. This unquestioned fact is not altered by a reference to the original etymology, which is then limited to the meaning to immerse. The word must be understood in the sense which it had at the time Jesus spoke, and the New Testament shows conclusively that βαπτίζω was used to designate all manner of application of water.

Besides the accepted meaning of this word in Jesus' times we have the evidence of the apostolic baptisms recorded in Acts. The 3,000 who were baptized at the time of Pentecost were not immersed, because in a city like Jerusalem such an immersion was impossible. Soon other thousands were baptized there, and, of course, in the same manner as the first had been baptized. This was the first carrying out of Christ's command to baptize, and the number of those baptized ran into the thousands. This set the example for the mode to be followed in the future baptisms in the church. When it comes to historical evidence, the church fathers, etc., this Biblical historical evidence at the very beginning of the church's history must dominate and if necessary correct all that follows.

The Acts report other baptisms, but not a single one in which immersion is indicated. In almost all cases there are indications that some other mode was followed. Never do we read that the person to be baptized was led to some stream for the purpose of immersion, never that clothes were removed for the purpose of immersion, the baptism is always applied at once and without the least difficulty. Yet a striking feature evident in all these accounts is that the mode used in any instance is not described. We have not as much as a hint except that immersion could not have been the mode used under the indicated circumstances.

As regards post-Apostolic times, most valuable is *Baptism and Christian Archæology*, by Clement F. Rogers, Oxford, Clarendon Press. This layman held the common conviction that in the early church baptism was administered by immersion, but when he sought to verify this conviction, he did not find one pictorial representation of immersion, all the delineations of ancient times portrayed pouring or some other mode. Moreover, the remains of all the ancient baptistries were shallow, generally so shallow that a man could not be immersed even if he lay down in the pool flat on his back. Mr. Rogers completely reversed his opinion regarding the practice of immersion in the early church.

Εἰς τὸ ὄνομα means, "in the name," not, "into." This is the use of εἰς in the Koine, which all the newer grammars treat in full. R. 592 says without qualification: "In Matt. 28:19 βαπτίζοντες εἰς τὸ ὄνομα, and Rom. 6:3, etc., εἰς Χριστόν and εἰς τὸν θάνατον the notion of sphere is the true one." This also most probably was the case in Acts 2:38: βαπτίσθητω εἰς ἄφεσιν τῶν ἁμαρτιῶν. So completely has this point been settled that we need to say no more about it. Although this phrase is so common in the New Testament, it is rather generally misunderstood. This is probably due to the fact that all the instances of its occurrence are not studied together. It does not mean, "on the authority of." If that were its meaning in this instance, we might well ask, "Why does Jesus not say on my authority?" If only the authority for this sacrament is to be stated, why bring in the Triune God? In all these phrases the ὄνομα signifies the revelation. The sense is, "In connection with the revelation of the Father," etc. This alone also gives us a thinkable thought and frees us from the older ideas that by baptism a person is to be carried *into* the Triune God or *into* his name — something that is wholly unthinkable. We must know once for all that no preposition denotes motion.

Baptism takes place in the sphere of the revelation of the Triune God. It is the gospel revelation that is referred to, which is full of grace and truth. Baptism is thus pure gospel and by no means a legal rite. It enriches the person baptized by the gifts of the gospel, it is not a mere act of obedience to a command on the person's part. Hence again, children may be baptized as well as adults; both can be equally blessed with the contents of God's blessed revelation.

In the Scriptures the three divine persons are named singly a large number of times, often two are named together, and at times all three; yet this is the only instance in the Scriptures in which we have the Trinity named as such: "Of the Father and of the Son and of the Holy Ghost." This is God's full name; he is one God, yet exists in three persons. The mystery of his Being, of this one Essence in three persons, no human mind will ever fathom. We may say that because of its profundity and its incomprehensibleness God would not have revealed it to us, but because of the plan of salvation he had to reveal it to a certain degree; for our salvation we must know that the Father sent the Son, that the Son came for our redemption, and that the Father and the Son sent the Spirit for our sanctification. In all the confessions they have ever drawn up, beginning with the three great ecumenical confessions, all Christian churches confess the Trinity as the basic article; thus all who deny the Trinity place themselves outside the Christian Church.

Later dogmaticians have made the Trinity the *materia coelestis* in baptism to correspond to the body and the blood in the Lord's Supper. But the disparity is too great; it is also impossible to find a complete correspondence and similarity between the features of the two sacraments. "Father, Son, and Holy Spirit" designate the three divine persons in union with whose revelation we are baptized. Thus "by baptism God gives himself to us: the Father becomes our Father and adopts us as his children (Gal. 3:16-27; John 1:12, 13; I John 3:1); the Son becomes our Redeemer, for we are baptized in union with his death and cleansed by his blood to be his own (Eph. 5:26) and have put on Christ (Gal. 3:27; I Cor. 12:12, 13), so that his righteousness is our glorious dress (Matt. 22:11; Isa. 61:10), and we are members of his body (Eph. 5:30; I Cor. 12:13; John 15:4); the Holy Spirit becomes our Comforter and the earnest of our inheritance (Eph. 1:14; II Cor. 11:22), we become his temple in which together with the Father and the Son he dwells (I Cor. 3:10). In this way we assume *a new relation to God* by means of this sacrament of regeneration, our heart and our spirit being renewed and pursuing a new direction through the joint operation of the three divine persons." Rohnert, *Dogmatik*, 413, etc.

When we administer the sacrament we have every reason for using the full name of God as Jesus uttered it, and no reason can be advanced for doing anything else. While the participle βαπτίζοντες is not an imperative, it yet receives imperative force from the main verb which is imperative. Here Jesus prescribes how we are to make disciples, and what he wants us to do he states in these words which are thus called "the baptismal formula." Those who venture to alter these words and, for instance, baptize in the name of Jesus, do so at their own risk, and no man can be sure that their baptism is valid. The name as it was uttered by Jesus is much like a person's signature. This is made in a specific way, and any change renders it void. Gerhard writes: "It is safest to adhere to Christ's words and not to use a form of words different from the one he prescribed; for he certainly had his reasons for wanting the three persons explicitly mentioned in baptism, and by no means the least of these reasons was this that each and every person acts in this sacrament and dispenses his blessing. The Father receives the baptized person as his child, the Son as his brother and disciple, the Holy Spirit as his temple and habitation."

It has been denied that we have here the institution of baptism, since the Baptist administered this sacrament long before this time. It is true, indeed, that John's baptism was practically the same as that of Jesus; but John's was restricted to one nation and rested on the Messiah to come, while that of Jesus extended to all nations and rested on the Messiah who had come and whose redemptive work was complete. Yet we must say that, since John's baptism was a preparation for the Messiah, it would have come to an end. In that sense Jesus' baptism differed from that of John, it was to continue until the end of the world. So we have here, in the proper sense of the word, the institution of Christian baptism. We today baptize, not because John baptized, or because his commission to baptize extends also to us; but solely because Jesus gave us the commission to baptize.

The Great Commission was given, not to the eleven alone as apostles, but to the entire 500 as the church of Jesus. He arranged for no superior order of officials in the church. Word and sacrament were given to the entire church and belong to all. Jesus did appoint a ministry in the church, first the apostles chosen by himself and after that the pastors chosen by the church herself. To these Word and sacrament are committed for the public administration. Yet always the church is responsible to see to it that this administration is continued and that it is kept in full accordance with the Word and the will of Jesus.

20) Baptism is one means of making disciples, teaching (which includes public preaching) is another, and Jesus uses the specific word which means "teaching," διδάσκοντες, the participle being parallel with βαπτίζοντες. But we have no καί or connective. This means that either baptism or teaching is to be applied as the individual case may require. The contention that the Lord did not think of little children in this connection,

and that τὰ ἔθνη and αὐτούς (masculine, because the ante-cedent refers to persons) cannot include children, is untenable. Minor children are such a large part of every nation that the Lord, who loved children, would certainly act in a surprising manner if he intended to leave them out of his discipleship. So decidedly does he include them that he provides a simple sacrament which can be applied even to the tiniest babe, and he desires them all. So the church has the mind of Jesus when it baptizes babes and afterward teaches them, and when it first teaches adults and then administers baptism to them.

This teaching is not to be a mere intellectual pro-cess. Jesus says διδάσκοντες τηρεῖν, "teaching to guard," which means to obey and to preserve, and also to pre-serve and to keep inviolate. A living reception in the heart is had in mind, an assimilation by means of faith, one that will henceforth control and mold the entire character and life. Hence also this teaching will be so dear to the heart that no man will be allowed to take it away or in any way to alter it by false teaching. The baptizing will naturally be a single act for each person, for the effect of baptism is durative; it stamps and seals us with the holy name once for all. But the teaching goes on throughout life.

"All things whatsoever I did bid you" (ἐνετειλάμην), all of them are to be taught, for all that Jesus gave us in his gospel bidding is helpful for our salvation. Peter sums it up as "the way of righteousness," "the holy commandment delivered unto them," II Pet. 2:21; 3:2. John does the same in I John 3:23; compare John 6:29; I John 3:11. The idea that all we really need in order to be Christians is to embrace one or two central fea-tures of the gospel is here shown to be highly danger-ous. Jesus binds us to all that he has bidden us and not merely to some one or two features.

The exclamation "lo" is to rivet our fullest attention on the great promise with which Jesus closes. 'Εγώ is decidedly emphatic, "I myself." It is he whom they saw in his glorified form before their very eyes, he who held all authority in heaven and on earth. Let their eyes and their hearts remain fixed on him. Their great Lord promises to be with them all the days until the consummation of the eon. He does not send his disciples out into the world of nations alone. Invisibly he will always be at their side, assuring their success. Here he answers every fear, doubt, discouragement, weakness.

The accusative πάσας τὰς ἡμέρας denotes extent of time. And Jesus intends "all the days" to be understood literally, for he adds, "until the consummation of the eon." The αἰών is the vast era of time that is marked and distinguished by what transpires in it. Thus the world-age in which we live is one in which men go on in their earthly deeds from year to year. But this shall reach its consummation, its completion, when men shall no more live and act as they now do. The eon will have run its course and cease. This is the end of the world. Jesus here makes a promise that extends far beyond the lifetime of all who were present before him that day. It is as though he were speaking also to us. His words imply that his church will continue to the end of time. Ps. 46:5, 6: "There is a river, the streams whereof shall make glad the city of God, the holy place of the tabernacle of the Most High. God is in the midst of her; she shall not be moved: God shall help her, and that right early."

"These testimonies we do not understand as though only the divinity of Christ were present with us in the Christian Church and congregation, and such presence were to consider Christ according to his humanity in no way whatever; for in that manner Peter, Paul, and all the saints in heaven, since divinity which is everywhere present dwells in them, would also be with us on earth, which the Holy Scriptures, however, testify only of Christ, and of no other man besides. But we hold that by these words the majesty of the man Christ is declared, which Christ has received, according to his humanity, at the right hand of the majesty and power of God, namely that also according to his assumed human nature and with the same, he can be, and also is, present where he will, and especially that in his church and congregation on earth he is present as Mediator, Head, King, and High Priest, not in part, or one half of him only, but the entire person of Christ is present, to which both natures belong, the divine and the human; not only according to his divinity, but also according to, and with, his assumed human nature, according to which he has flesh and blood he will be with us, and dwell, work, and be efficacious in us." *Concordia Triglotta*, 1043, etc.

Since Matthew closes here he evidently does not intend to tell the entire story of the Lord's sudden disappearance and what the disciples did after that. He writes especially for Jewish readers, and the last message he wants to leave with them is this word of Jesus', which opens the Messianic kingdom to all the nations of the world, and does that on the same terms. Matthew could have found no grander and fitter conclusion.

**Soli Deo Gloria.**